Literature Connections
to World History, 7-12

Other Books by Lynda G. Adamson

Literature Connections to American History, K-6:
    Resources to Enhance and Entice. 1998. ISBN 1-56308-502-X

Literature Connections to American History, 7-12:
    Resources to Enhance and Entice. 1998. ISBN 1-56308-503-8

Literature Connections to World History, K-6:
    Resources to Enhance and Entice. 1998. ISBN 1-56308-504-6

Literature Connections to World History, 7-12

Resources to Enhance and Entice

Lynda G. Adamson

1998
Libraries Unlimited, Inc.
Englewood, Colorado

For Frank

LIBRARIES UNLIMITED, INC.
P.O. Box 6633
Englewood, CO 80155-6633
1-800-237-6124
www.lu.com

Production Editor: Stephen Haenel
Bibliography Copy Editor: Brooke Graves
Bibliography Proofreader: Ann Marie Damian
Layout and Design: Michael Florman

Library of Congress Cataloging-in-Publication Data

Adamson, Lynda G.
    Literature connections to world history, 7-12 : resources to enhance and entice / Lynda G. Adamson.
       xii, 511 p. 19x26 cm.
       Includes bibliographical references and indexes.
       ISBN 1-56308-505-4
       1. Literature and history--Juvenile literature--Bibliography.
2. World history--Juvenile literature--Bibliography. 3. World history--CD-ROM--Catalogs. 4. World history--Juvenile films--Catalogs. I. Title.
    Z1037.A1A27 1997
    [PN50]
    016.809'93358--dc21   97-35953
                                                                CIP

Contents

Preface

Studies show that people must respond emotionally to something in order to remember it. If readers walk with Annemarie through the dark to deliver a package that will save her Jewish friend Ellen from the Nazis in Lois Lowry's *Number the Stars* or watch the four boys in Bjarne Reuter's *The Boys of St. Petri* prepare to bomb a German supply train, they will see that tentacles of hate can spread from the country of origin into other places. Hitler's "cleansing" policies began in Germany, but these stories, both set in Denmark, show that he refused to let borders limit his pursuit. By becoming angry at the helpless situations in which Ellen and the townspeople of St. Petri find themselves, these readers remember the time and the place of the incidents. Their responses might lead them to read further in additional sources about Hitler's mistreatment of other groups such as the Gypsies and the disabled. Or they might want to know about those who escaped Hitler's net with the help of underground organizations and people who hid them in basements and attics. These vicarious experiences could even help readers empathize more readily with the difficulties of contemporary refugees from countries governed by despots.

If a reader becomes interested in a topic, a character, or a time period and asks for books or multimedia about them, the adult consulted needs timely retrieval capabilities. I have attempted to fulfill that need. This resource connects historical fiction, biography, history trade books, CD-ROMs, and videotapes for individual grade levels within specific time periods and geographic areas. The books, CD-ROMs, and videotapes included have received at least one favorable review, are well written, or fit a category for which few resources are available. Some of the books and videotapes are award winners, and I have listed awards won at the end of the annotations. Some of the books are out-of-print but are still available in many libraries. Reprints of them, especially award winners, regularly become available in paper or under the imprint of another publisher.

When I first began this project, it was to link good reads in historical fiction, biography, and history trade books. That focus has continued throughout the creation of this annotated bibliography. I did not anticipate finding as many entries as appear in this resource, but writing in both biography and history trade books has improved. For that reason, I have listed biographies about the same person by several different authors. I have not made a choice as to which is the best, because each has a different focus. Authors of biography as literature try to make their subjects come alive, and the authors here have achieved this goal. The annotations in the final section attempt to include different facts about the biographical subjects instead of always identifying a sometimes elusive nuance of difference among the authors' writing styles and themes.

History trade books differ from history textbooks because their authors rarely use passive voice, and they rely heavily on diaries, letters, documents, or other references that tell about the people who lived during the time. Thus, readers might more often respond to these books than to history textbooks that seem to be filled with dull dates and incident inventories. Some of the history trade books included have more illustrations than text, but they can be valuable for enticing slow or unwilling readers to look for other books. These information books bridge the distance between unillustrated books and videotapes.

The multimedia category covers CD-ROMs and videotapes. Because videotapes are more accessible for the classroom, or even for home use, I have omitted laser discs and filmstrips. But with computer use increasing in the home and in the schools, I have included favorably reviewed CD-ROMs or those on specific topics that will help readers find further information. Some of the more recent CD-ROMs have stunning pictures, biographical information, and other attractions that may lead a viewer to books.

Because readers become interested in a variety of topics for many different reasons, the books in the historical fiction category listed in a specific grade level may or may not contain the names of those persons in the biographies or cover the variety of time periods in the history trade titles. A specific correspondence of titles seems unnecessary. Hitler may not be named in Lowry's *Number the Stars*, but his presence permeates the book. The same reader might want more information about other people who worked under Hitler's influence. The book lists along with the annotations will reveal other resources on these subjects.

While doing the research for this reference, I realized that it should include as many good books or videotapes published since 1990 as possible and some highly regarded works from prior years. I hope that adults will find most of the recommended books on library shelves or can order them from a publisher. I have tried to include a wide range of titles so that the researcher will have choices if the first title selected from the resource is not readily available. My goal is for readers to have emotional responses to the people who have made history so that they, as future world citizens, can better understand themselves and the times in which they live.

Many publishers have made this resource easier to create by sending me recent books. Their generosity saved me many hours of searching. I would like to list their names, but I fear omitting even one of them. During this intensive period of work, two individuals have made this book possible. Elena Rodriguez at Gunston Middle School in Arlington, Virginia, allowed me to raid her library shelves for many days. Without her excellent collection, I would not have been able to easily locate many of the books that I have included. The other indispensable helper was my husband, who edited text. Additionally, Steve Haenel at Libraries Unlimited has offered advice and aid in an effort to make this resource available.

Introduction

This resource divides naturally into two main sections. The first section lists authors and book titles in the categories of historical fiction, biography, collective biography, history trade book, CD-ROM, and videotape within specific time periods according to grade levels. The second section contains annotated bibliographies of titles listed in the first part: books, CD-ROMs, and videotapes. The books, videotapes, and CD-ROMs merit inclusion because they have received favorable reviews, are well written, or are one of the few titles available on a particular subject, so the annotations are descriptive rather than evaluative.

Chapter divisions in the first section are chronological time periods or areas of the world. In each chapter, works appropriate for a particular grade level appear under that grade-level heading in their specific category of historical fiction, history trade, biography (including collective biography), and multimedia (CD-ROMs and videotapes). Books are alphabetized according to the author's last name so that the researcher can easily locate the annotation in the second section of the resource. CD-ROMs and videotapes are alphabetized in the second section according to their titles.

Some titles in the first section appear several different times. When a title about the Middle Ages is suitable for grades seven through nine, the title appears under each grade level of seven, eight, and nine in the chapter covering the medieval period, A.D. 476-1491. Other titles appear in different chapters because their settings, either fiction or fact, occur in more than one place or involve more than one nation. For example, battles fought in the Pacific during World War II have the Pacific islands as their settings, but Europeans and Americans as their participants.

I have based grade-level choices on recommended grade levels in review sources or publisher catalogs. In some cases, when the grade levels seemed unusually low or high, I have adjusted them after evaluating the text and the subject matter. In the section "Grades Eleven and Twelve," I have listed books marketed for adults that are suitable for and might be of interest to high school students. Books that might interest middle and high school students who have reading levels lower than seventh grade appear in *Literature Connections to World History, K–6: Resources to Enhance and Entice*. Many of the biographical and historical subjects in this book are the same, but the content is less complex.

Certain chapter divisions correspond as nearly as possible to major historical events in Europe and the British Isles such as the era of the Roman Empire. The chapters based on geographical areas loosely link countries within a particular part of the world—Israel with Arab countries and the Pacific Islands with Australia. Because identifying a book's country of origin in these chapters may be difficult merely by reading the title, researchers will have to rely on the annotations in the second section for more discrete information. Also, because a preponderance of English-language works on western history exists, this area of world history receives the most coverage here.

The annotations include such information as author, title, publisher, price, ISBN, paper imprint, and grade levels. The book prices are accurate at printing, based on publisher catalogs and such library buying sources as *Books in Print* and distributor Baker and Taylor. I have made a similar attempt to include sources for books and their paper imprints, if available. The range of grade levels appears at the end of each bibliographic entry.

For easiest access to this resource, researchers should find the time period or geographic area that interests them in the table of contents. Grade levels under the chapter listings will tell where to locate the book and multimedia categories. In the grade-level listings, researchers should select titles. Then they should refer to the appropriate section of the second part of the book.

Researchers unsure of the dates of a particular historical event might want to skim the listings for the seventh or eighth grade level because these grade levels have more entries with titles referring to historical events than the other levels. After finding the correct time period or geographical area, the researcher can then refer to the appropriate grade level to see if a book or multimedia source is available. If it is not, the researcher may be able to choose an appropriate title from the next highest or lowest grade-level categories. A final resource is the subject index, which lists all references to a particular subject.

Prehistory and the Ancient World to 54 B.C.

GRADE SEVEN

Historical Fiction

Brennan. *Shiva: An Adventure of the Ice Age*
Carter. *His Majesty, Queen Hatshepsut*
Coolidge. *Marathon Looks on the Sea*
Cowley. *Dar and the Spear-thrower*
Furlong. *Juniper*
Furlong. *Wise Child*
Jordan. *Wolf Woman*
Levitin. *Escape from Egypt*
Lewis. *The Ship That Flew*
Mann. *The Great Pyramid*
McGowen. *The Time of the Forest*
McGraw. *The Golden Goblet*
McGraw. *Mara, Daughter of the Nile*
Pryor. *Seth of the Lion People*
Rubalcaba. *A Place in the Sun*
Service. *The Reluctant God*
Sutcliff. *Warrior Scarlet*
Synge. *The People and the Promise*
Treece. *Men of the Hills*

Biography

Ash. *Alexander the Great*
Green. *Alexander the Great*
Green. *Tutankhamun*
King. *Pericles*
Llywelyn. *Xerxes*
Nardo. *The Trial of Socrates*
Parker. *Aristotle and Scientific Thought*
Wepman. *Alexander the Great*

Collective Biography

Baker. *Ancient Greeks*
Cohen. *Prophets of Doom*
Hazell. *Heroines: Great Women Through the Ages*
Jacobs. *Great Lives: World Religions*
Saxby. *The Great Deeds of Heroic Women*
Scheller. *Amazing Archaeologists*
Wilkinson. *Generals Who Changed the World*

History

Avi-Yonah. *Piece by Piece! Mosaics of the Ancient World*
Berrill. *Mummies, Masks, & Mourners*
Bianchi. *The Nubians*
Brierley. *Explorers of the Ancient World*
Briquebec. *The Ancient World*
Burrell. *The Greeks*
Capek. *Murals*
Chaikin. *Menorahs, Mezuzas, and Other Jewish Symbols*
Chaikin. *A Nightmare in History*
Charley. *Tombs and Treasures*
Clare. *Ancient Greece*
Clements. *An Illustrated History of the World*
Coolidge. *The Golden Days of Greece*
Cooper. *The Dead Sea Scrolls*
Corbishley. *Secret Cities*
Crosher. *Ancient Egypt*
Davies. *Transport*
Dawson. *Food and Feasts in Ancient Greece*
Dazzling! *Jewelry of the Ancient World*
Deem. *How to Make a Mummy Talk*
Descamps-Lequime. *The Ancient Greeks*
Duggleby. *Impossible Quests*
Europe at the Time of Greece and Rome
Evans. *Freedom of Speech*
Fleischman. *Dateline: Troy*
Fradin. *Medicine: Yesterday, Today, and Tomorrow*
Freeman. *The Ancient Greeks*
Getz. *Frozen Man*
Giblin. *Be Seated: A Book About Chairs*
Giblin. *The Riddle of the Rosetta Stone*
Giblin. *When Plague Strikes*
Gonen. *Charge! Weapons and Warfare in Ancient Times*
Gonen. *Fired Up: Making Pottery*
Grant. *The Egyptians*
Gravett. *Arms and Armor*
Harris. *Ancient Egypt*
Harris. *Mummies*
Hart. *Ancient Egypt*
Haslam. *Ancient Egypt*
Hernandez. *Barmi*
Hernandez. *Lebek*
Hirsch. *Taxation*
Humble. *Ships*
Hunter. *First Civilizations*

Kent. *A Slice Through a City*
Kerr. *Keeping Clean*
King. *Seven Ancient Wonders of the World*
Koenig. *The Ancient Egyptians*
Landau. *The Curse of Tutankhamen*
Loverance. *Ancient Greece*
MacDonald. *Cities*
MacDonald. *A Greek Temple*
Marshall. *Ocean Traders*
Marston. *The Ancient Egyptians*
Martell. *The Celts*
Martell. *From the Ice Age to the Roman Empire*
Martell. *What Do We Know About the Celts?*
McLaren. *Inside the Walls of Troy*
McNeill. *Ancient Egyptian People*
McNeill. *Ancient Egyptian Places*
Millard. *Pyramids*
Morley. *Clothes*
Moss. *Science in Ancient Mesopotamia*
Nardo. *The Age of Pericles*
Nardo. *Ancient Greece*
Nardo. *The Battle of Marathon*
Nardo. *The Battle of Zama*
Nardo. *Greek and Roman Theater*
Nardo. *The Punic Wars*

Newark. *Celtic Warriors*
Odijk. *The Phoenicians*
Odijk. *The Sumerians*
Oliphant. *The Earliest Civilizations*
O'Neal. *Pyramids*
Pearson. *Ancient Greece*
Platt. *Pirate*
Platt. *The Smithsonian Visual Timeline of Inventions*
Poulton. *Life in the Time of Pericles and the Ancient Greeks*
Powell. *Ancient Greece*
Powell. *The Greek News*
Prehistoric and Ancient Europe
Putnam. *Mummy*
Rogerson. *Cultural Atlas of the Bible*
Ross. *Conquerors & Explorers*
Sattler. *Hominids*
Scharfstein. *Understanding Jewish History*
Schomp. *The Ancient Greeks*
Scrawl! Writing in Ancient Times
Simon. *Explorers of the Ancient World*
Simpson. *Ancient Greece*
Singer. *Structures That Changed the Way the World Looked*
Smith. *Egypt of the Pharaohs*
Smith. *Millions and Billions of Years Ago*

Sold! The Origins of Money and Trade
Steedman. *The Egyptian News*
Steele. *The Egyptians and the Valley of the Kings*
Steele. *Kidnapping*
Steele. *Riots*
Steele. *Smuggling*
Steele. *Thermopylae*
Stones and Bones: How Archaeologists Trace Human Origins
Street Smart! Cities of the Ancient World
Tchudi. *Lock and Key*
Time-Life. *What Life Was Like on the Banks of the Nile*
Turvey. *Inventions: Inventors and Ingenious Ideas*
Ventura. *Clothing*
Ventura. *Food*
Warburton. *The Beginning of Writing*
Wetterau. *World History*
Wilkinson. *The Lands of the Bible*
Wilkinson. *The Mediterranean*
Williams. *Forts and Castles*
Wood. *Ancient Wonders*
Woods. *Science in Ancient Egypt*
Woolf. *Picture This: A First Introduction to Paintings*
Zeinert. *The Persian Empire*

Multimedia

CD-ROM

Exploring Ancient Cities
Eyewitness Encyclopedia of Science

History Through Art: Ancient Greece
Le Louvre: The Palace & Its Paintings

Religions of the World
Science Navigator
Teach Your Kids World History

Video

Ancient Egypt: The Gift of the Nile (3000 BC-30 BC)
Athenian Democracy
The Beginning Is in the End
The British Way of Life
The Byzantine Empire
Egypt: Gift of the Nile
Egypt: The Nile River Kingdom
The End Is the Beginning
Europe: Insular Region
From Mesopotamia to Iraq
The Iliad and the Trojan War

Lascaux Revisited: Exploring Cave Art
Legacies
Legacy of the Mound Builders
Life, Times and Wonders of Athens and Ancient Greece
Life, Times and Wonders of the Pyramids and the Cities of the Pharoahs
London: City of Majesty
Lost City of the Aegean
Lost Tomb of the Sons of Ramses II

Lost Treasures of Troy
Mummies and the Wonders of Ancient Egypt
The Mystery of the Cave Paintings
The Mystery of the Pyramids
On the Town
Other Voices, Other Songs: The Greeks
Safekeeping
Who Built the Pyramids?

GRADE EIGHT

Historical Fiction

Brennan. *Shiva: An Adventure of the Ice Age*
Carter. *His Majesty, Queen Hatshepsut*
Coolidge. *Marathon Looks on the Sea*
Furlong. *Juniper*
Furlong. *Wise Child*
Jordan. *Wolf Woman*
Levitin. *Escape from Egypt*
Lewis. *The Ship That Flew*
McGowen. *The Time of the Forest*
McGraw. *The Golden Goblet*
McGraw. *Mara, Daughter of the Nile*
Service. *The Reluctant God*
Sutcliff. *Warrior Scarlet*
Synge. *The People and the Promise*
Treece. *Men of the Hills*

Biography

Ash. *Alexander the Great: Ancient Empire Builder*
King. *Pericles*
Llywelyn. *Xerxes*
Nardo. *Julius Caesar*
Nardo. *The Trial of Socrates*
Parker. *Aristotle and Scientific Thought*
Stewart. *Alexander the Great*
Wepman. *Alexander the Great*

Collective Biography

Baker. *Ancient Greeks*
Cohen. *Prophets of Doom*
Hazell. *Heroines: Great Women Through the Ages*
Matthews. *Power Brokers*
Saxby. *The Great Deeds of Heroic Women*
Scheller. *Amazing Archaeologists*
Wilkinson. *Generals Who Changed the World*

History

Avi-Yonah. *Piece by Piece! Mosaics of the Ancient World*
Bianchi. *The Nubians*
Briquebec. *The Ancient World*
Capek. *Murals*
Chaikin. *Menorahs, Mezuzas, and Other Jewish Symbols*
Chaikin. *A Nightmare in History*
Clare. *Ancient Greece*
Clements. *An Illustrated History of the World*
Cooper. *The Dead Sea Scrolls*
Crosher. *Ancient Egypt*
Davies. *Transport*
Dazzling! Jewelry of the Ancient World
Deem. *How to Make a Mummy Talk*
Descamps-Lequime. *The Ancient Greeks*
Europe at the Time of Greece and Rome
Evans. *Freedom of Speech*
Fleischman. *Dateline: Troy*
Fradin. *Medicine: Yesterday, Today, and Tomorrow*
Giblin. *Be Seated: A Book About Chairs*
Giblin. *When Plague Strikes*
Gonen. *Charge! Weapons and Warfare in Ancient Times*
Gonen. *Fired Up: Making Pottery*
Harris. *Ancient Egypt*
Harris. *Mummies*
Hernandez. *Lebek*
Hernandez. *Barmi*
Hirsch. *Taxation*
Hunter. *First Civilizations*
Kent. *A Slice Through a City*
Koenig. *The Ancient Egyptians*
Loverance. *Ancient Greece*
MacDonald. *Cities*
MacDonald. *A Greek Temple*
Marshall. *Ocean Traders*
Marston. *The Ancient Egyptians*
Martell. *The Celts*
McLaren. *Inside the Walls of Troy*
McNeill. *Ancient Egyptian People*
McNeill. *Ancient Egyptian Places*
Morley. *Clothes*
Moss. *Science in Ancient Mesopotamia*
Nardo. *Ancient Greece*
Nardo. *The Age of Pericles*
Nardo. *The Battle of Marathon*
Nardo. *The Battle of Zama*
Nardo. *Greek and Roman Theater*
Nardo. *The Punic Wars*
Newark. *Celtic Warriors*
Odijk. *The Phoenicians*
O'Neal. *Pyramids*
Pearson. *Ancient Greece*
Platt. *Pirate*
Platt. *The Smithsonian Visual Timeline of Inventions*
Poulton. *Life in the Time of Pericles and the Ancient Greeks*
Powell. *Ancient Greece*
Powell. *The Greek News*
Prehistoric and Ancient Europe
Putnam. *Mummy*
Rogerson. *Cultural Atlas of the Bible*
Sattler. *Hominids*
Scharfstein. *Understanding Jewish History*
Schomp. *The Ancient Greeks*
Scrawl! Writing in Ancient Times
Simon. *Explorers of the Ancient World*
Singer. *Structures That Changed the Way the World Looked*
Smith. *Egypt of the Pharaohs*
Smith. *Millions and Billions of Years Ago*
Sold! The Origins of Money and Trade

Steedman. *The Egyptian News*
Steele. *Thermopylae*
*Stones and Bones: How
  Archaeologists Trace
  Human Origins*
*Street Smart! Cities of the
  Ancient World*
Tchudi. *Lock and Key*
Time-Life. *What Life Was Like
  on the Banks of the Nile*

Turvey. *Inventions: Inventors
  and Ingenious Ideas*
Ventura. *Clothing*
Ventura. *Food*
Warburton. *The Beginning of
  Writing*
Wetterau. *World History*
Wilkinson. *The Lands of the
  Bible*

Wilkinson. *The
  Mediterranean*
Williams. *Forts and Castles*
Woods. *Science in Ancient
  Egypt*
Woolf. *Picture This: A First
  Introduction to Paintings*
Zeinert. *The Persian Empire*

Multimedia

CD-ROM

Exploring Ancient Cities
*Eyewitness Encyclopedia of
  Science*

*History Through Art: Ancient
  Greece*
*Le Louvre: The Palace & Its
  Paintings*

Religions of the World
Science Navigator
*Teach Your Kids World
  History*

Video

*Ancient Egypt: The Gift of the
  Nile (3000 BC-30 BC)*
Athenian Democracy
The Beginning Is in the End
The British Way of Life
The Byzantine Empire
Egypt: Gift of the Nile
*Egypt: The Nile River
  Kingdom*
The End Is the Beginning
Europe: Insular Region
From Mesopotamia to Iraq
The Iliad and the Trojan War

*Lascaux Revisited: Exploring
  Cave Art*
Legacies
Legacy of the Mound Builders
*Life, Times and Wonders of
  the Pyramids and the Cities
  of the Pharoahs*
*Life, Times and Wonders of
  Athens and Ancient Greece*
London: City of Majesty
Lost City of the Aegean
*Lost Tomb of the Sons of
  Ramses II*

Lost Treasures of Troy
*Mummies and the Wonders of
  Ancient Egypt*
*The Mystery of the Cave
  Paintings*
The Mystery of the Pyramids
On the Town
*Other Voices, Other Songs:
  The Greeks*
Safekeeping
Who Built the Pyramids?

GRADE NINE

Historical Fiction

Baumann. *I Marched with
  Hannibal*
Bradshaw. *The Beacon at
  Alexandria*
Carter. *His Majesty, Queen
  Hatshepsut*

Coolidge. *Marathon Looks on
  the Sea*
Jordan. *Wolf Woman*
Levitin. *Escape From Egypt*
McGraw. *The Golden Goblet*
McGraw. *Mara, Daughter of
  the Nile*

Service. *The Reluctant God*
Sutcliff. *Warrior Scarlet*
Synge. *The People and the
  Promise*
Treece. *Men of the Hills*

Biography

Ash. *Alexander the Great:
  Ancient Empire Builder*
King. *Pericles*

Llywelyn. *Xerxes*
Nardo. *Julius Caesar*
Nardo. *The Trial of Socrates*

Stewart. *Alexander the Great*
Wepman. *Alexander the Great*

Collective Biography

Baker. *Ancient Greeks*
Cohen. *Prophets of Doom*
Mahoney. *Women in
  Espionage*

Matthews. *Power Brokers*
Saxby. *The Great Deeds of
  Heroic Women*

Scheller. *Amazing
  Archaeologists*
Wilkinson. *Generals Who
  Changed the World*

History

Avi-Yonah. *Piece by Piece! Mosaics of the Ancient World*
Capek. *Murals*
Cooper. *The Dead Sea Scrolls*
Dazzling! Jewelry of the Ancient World
Europe at the Time of Greece and Rome
Evans. *Freedom of Speech*
Fleischman. *Dateline: Troy*
Fradin. *Medicine: Yesterday, Today, and Tomorrow*
Giblin. *When Plague Strikes*
Gonen. *Charge! Weapons and Warfare in Ancient Times*
Gonen. *Fired Up: Making Pottery*
Harris. *Ancient Egypt*
Hernandez. *Barmi*
Hernandez. *Lebek*
Hirsch. *Taxation*
Hunter. *First Civilizations*
Marshall. *Ocean Traders*
McLaren. *Inside the Walls of Troy*
Nardo. *The Age of Pericles*
Nardo. *The Battle of Marathon*
Nardo. *The Battle of Zama*
Nardo. *Greek and Roman Theater*
Nardo. *The Punic Wars*

O'Neal. *Pyramids*
Pearson. *Ancient Greece*
Platt. *The Smithsonian Visual Timeline of Inventions*
Powell. *Ancient Greece*
Powell. *The Greek News*
Prehistoric and Ancient Europe
Roaf. *Cultural Atlas of Mesopotamia and the Ancient Near East*
Rogerson. *Cultural Atlas of the Bible*
Scharfstein. *Understanding Jewish History*
Scrawl! Writing in Ancient Times
Singer. *Structures That Changed the Way the World Looked*
Smith. *Egypt of the Pharaohs*
Smith. *Millions and Billions of Years Ago*
Sold! The Origins of Money and Trade
Spangenburg. *The History of Science from the Ancient Greeks to the Scientific Revolution*
Steedman. *The Egyptian News*
Stones and Bones: How Archaeologists Trace Human Origins
Tchudi. *Lock and Key*

Time-Life. *Anatolia: Cauldron of Cultures*
Time-Life. *Celts: Europe's People of Iron*
Time-Life. *Early Europe: Mysteries in Stone*
Time-Life. *Egypt: Land of the Pharaohs*
Time-Life. *Etruscans: Italy's Lovers of Life*
Time-Life. *Greece: Temples, Tombs, & Treasures*
Time-Life. *The Holy Land*
Time-Life. *Mesopotamia: The Mighty Kings*
Time-Life. *Persians: Masters of the Empire*
Time-Life. *Ramses II: Magnificence on the Nile*
Time-Life. *Sumer: Cities of Eden*
Time-Life. *What Life Was Like on the Banks of the Nile*
Time-Life. *Wondrous Realms of the Aegean*
Warburton. *The Beginning of Writing*
Wetterau. *World History*
Williams. *Forts and Castles*
Zeinert. *The Persian Empire*

Multimedia

CD-ROM

Events That Changed the World
Exploring Ancient Cities
History Through Art: Ancient Greece

Ideas That Changed the World
Le Louvre: The Palace & Its Paintings
Religions of the World
Science Navigator

Teach Your Kids World History

Video

Athenian Democracy
The Beginning Is in the End
The Byzantine Empire
First Footsteps
From Mesopotamia to Iraq
The Iliad and the Trojan War
In the Blood of Man: The Sea of the Imagination
Lascaux Revisited: Exploring Cave Art
Legacies

Life, Times and Wonders of Athens and Ancient Greece
Life, Times and Wonders of the Pyramids and the Cities of the Pharoahs
London: City of Majesty
Lost City of the Aegean
Lost Tomb of the Sons of Ramses II
Lost Treasures of Troy
Mummies and the Wonders of Ancient Egypt

The Mystery of the Pyramids
The Mystic Lands Series: Egypt: Circle of Life
The Mystic Lands Series: Greece: Isle of Revelation
Other Voices, Other Songs: The Greeks
Safekeeping
Who Built the Pyramids?
Wonders Sacred & Mysterious

GRADE TEN

Historical Fiction

Baumann. *I Marched with Hannibal*
Bradshaw. *The Beacon at Alexandria*
Coolidge. *Marathon Looks on the Sea*
Jordan. *Wolf Woman*
Levitin. *Escape from Egypt*
Robinson. *Eater of Souls*
Sutcliff. *Warrior Scarlet*
Synge. *The People and the Promise*

Biography

King. *Pericles*
Llywelyn. *Xerxes*
Nardo. *Julius Caesar*
Nardo. *The Trial of Socrates*
Stewart. *Alexander the Great*
Wepman. *Alexander the Great*

Collective Biography

Axelrod. *Dictators and Tyrants*
Baker. *Ancient Greeks*
Mahoney. *Women in Espionage*
Matthews. *Power Brokers*
Saxby. *The Great Deeds of Heroic Women*
Wilkinson. *Generals Who Changed the World*

History

Alchemy: The Art of Knowing
Anatolia: Cauldron of Cultures
Ardley. *Music: An Illustrated Encyclopedia*
Avi-Yonah. *Piece by Piece! Mosaics of the Ancient World*
Capek. *Murals*
Clare. *Ancient Greece*
Europe at the Time of Greece and Rome
Fleischman. *Dateline: Troy*
Hernandez. *Barmi*
Hernandez. *Lebek*
Marshall. *Ocean Traders*
Marx. *The Search for Sunken Treasure*
McLaren. *Inside the Walls of Troy*
Nardo. *The Age of Pericles*
Nardo. *Greek and Roman Theater*
Nardo. *The Punic Wars*
O'Neal. *Pyramids*
Pickford. *The Atlas of Shipwrecks & Treasure*
Prehistoric and Ancient Europe
Roaf. *Cultural Atlas of Mesopotamia and the Ancient Near East*
Sacks. *The Ancient Greek World*
Scharfstein. *Understanding Jewish History*
Smith. *Millions and Billions of Years Ago*
Spangenburg. *The History of Science from the Ancient Greeks to the Scientific Revolution*
Tchudi. *Lock and Key*
Time-Life. *Anatolia: Cauldron of Cultures*
Time-Life. *Celts: Europe's People of Iron*
Time-Life. *Early Europe: Mysteries in Stone*
Time-Life. *Egypt: Land of the Pharaohs*
Time-Life. *Etruscans: Italy's Lovers of Life*
Time-Life. *Greece: Temples, Tombs, & Treasures*
Time-Life. *The Holy Land*
Time-Life. *Mesopotamia: The Mighty Kings*
Time-Life. *Persians: Masters of the Empire*
Time-Life. *Ramses II: Magnificence on the Nile*
Time-Life. *Sumer: Cities of Eden*
Time-Life. *Wondrous Realms of the Aegean*
Zeinert. *The Persian Empire*

Multimedia

CD-ROM

Events That Changed the World
Exploring Ancient Cities
History Through Art: Ancient Greece
Ideas That Changed the World
Le Louvre: The Palace & Its Paintings
Religions of the World
Science Navigator
Teach Your Kids World History

Video

Athenian Democracy
The Byzantine Empire
Egypt: Gift of the Nile
First Footsteps
From Mesopotamia to Iraq
The Iliad and the Trojan War
In the Blood of Man: The Sea of the Imagination
Lascaux Revisited: Exploring Cave Art
Life, Times and Wonders of Athens and Ancient Greece
Life, Times and Wonders of the Pyramids and the Cities of the Pharoahs
Lost City of the Aegean
Lost Tomb of the Sons of Ramses II

Lost Treasures of Troy
Mummies and the Wonders of
  Ancient Egypt

The Mystic Lands Series:
  Egypt: Circle of Life

The Mystic Lands Series:
  Greece: Isle of Revelation
Wonders Sacred & Mysterious

GRADES ELEVEN AND TWELVE

Historical Fiction

Baumann. *I Marched with
  Hannibal*
Bradshaw. *The Beacon at
  Alexandria*
Gedge. *Child of the Morning*
Lambert. *Circles of Stone*
Levitin. *Escape from Egypt*
Llywelyn. *Druids*
Parotti. *Fires in the Sky*

Paxson. *Master of Earth and
  Water*
Paxson. *The Shield Between
  the Worlds*
Renault. *The Bull from the Sea*
Renault. *Fire from Heaven*
Renault. *The King Must Die*
Renault. *The Last of the Wine*
Renault. *The Mask of Apollo*
Renault. *The Persian Boy*

Robinson. *Eater of Souls*
Robinson. *Murder at the
  Feast of Rejoicing*
Rutherford. *London*
Rutherfurd. *Sarum*
Sutcliff. *Warrior Scarlet*
Thomas. *The Animal Wife*
Wolf. *Daughter of the Red
  Deer*
Wolf. *The Reindeer Hunters*

Biography

King. *Pericles*
Llywelyn. *Xerxes*

Nardo. *Julius Caesar*
Stewart. *Alexander the Great*

Collective Biography

Axelrod. *Dictators and
  Tyrants*
Baker. *Ancient Greeks*
Boorstin. *The Creators*

Mahoney. *Women in
  Espionage*
Matthews. *Power Brokers*

Saxby. *The Great Deeds of
  Heroic Women*
Wills. *Certain Trumpets*

History

Alchemy: The Art of Knowing
Anatolia: Cauldron of
  Cultures
Ardley. *Music: An Illustrated
  Encyclopedia*
Avi-Yonah. *Piece by Piece!
  Mosaics of the Ancient
  World*
Aymar. *Men in the Air*
Beckett. *The Story of Painting*
Brier. *Egyptian Mummies*
Capek. *Murals*
Castello. *The Jews and
  Europe*
Davidson. *Everyday Life
  Through the Ages*
Fleischman. *Dateline: Troy*
Hernandez. *Barmi*
Hernandez. *Lebek*
Hibbert. *Florence*
Hibbert. *Rome*
Hoffman. *Archimedes'
  Revenge*
Hughes. *Barcelona*
Keegan. *History of Warfare*

Manley. *Atlas of Prehistoric
  Britain*
Marshall. *Ocean Traders*
Marx. *The Search for Sunken
  Treasure*
McLynn. *Famous Trials*
Nardo. *Ancient Greece*
Pickford. *The Atlas of
  Shipwrecks and Treasure*
Reeves. *The Complete
  Tutankhamun*
Roaf. *Cultural Atlas of
  Mesopotamia and the
  Ancient Near East*
Sacks. *The Ancient Greek
  World*
Scharfstein. *Understanding
  Jewish History*
Schimmel. *Mystery of
  Numbers*
Smith. *Fascinating People
  and Astounding Events
  from the History of the
  Western World*
Spangenburg. *The History of
  Science from the Ancient*

Greeks to the Scientific
  Revolution
Time-Life. *Anatolia:
  Cauldron of Cultures*
Time-Life. *Celts: Europe's
  People of Iron*
Time-Life. *Early Europe:
  Mysteries in Stone*
Time-Life. *Egypt: Land of the
  Pharaohs*
Time-Life. *Etruscans: Italy's
  Lovers of Life*
Time-Life. *Greece: Temples,
  Tombs, & Treasures*
Time-Life. *The Holy Land*
Time-Life. *Mesopotamia:
  The Mighty Kings*
Time-Life. *Persians: Masters
  of the Empire*
Time-Life. *Ramses II:
  Magnificence on the Nile*
Time-Life. *Sumer: Cities of
  Eden*
Time-Life. *Wondrous Realms
  of the Aegean*

Multimedia ───────────────────────────

CD-ROM

Events That Changed the World
Exploring Ancient Cities
History Through Art: Ancient Greece

Ideas That Changed the World
Le Louvre: The Palace & Its Paintings
Religions of the World
Science Navigator

Teach Your Kids World History

Video

Alexander the Great
The Ancient Egyptians
Athenian Democracy
The Byzantine Empire
The Dawn of History
Egypt: Gift of the Nile
First Footsteps
The First World War and the Rise of Fascism
From Bronze to Iron
From Mesopotamia to Iraq

The Greek Thought
The Hellenistic Age
In the Blood of Man: The Sea of the Imagination
Lascaux Revisited: Exploring Cave Art
Lost City of the Aegean
Lost Tomb of the Sons of Ramses II
Lost Treasures of Troy
Mesopotamia

Mummies and the Wonders of Ancient Egypt
The Mystic Lands Series: Egypt: Circle of Life
The Mystic Lands Series: Greece: Isle of Revelation
The Rise of Greek Civilization
Wonders Sacred & Mysterious

Roman Empire to A.D. 476

Historical Fiction

Haugaard. *The Rider and His Horse*

Speare. *The Bronze Bow*

Sutcliff. *The Mark of the Horse Lord*

Sutcliff. *Sun Horse, Moon Horse*

Yarbro. *Four Horses for Tishtry*

Biography

Brooks. *Cleopatra: Goddess of Egypt, Enemy of Rome*

Bruns. *Julius Caesar*

Green. *Cleopatra*

Green. *Herod the Great*

Green. *Julius Caesar*

Hoobler. *Cleopatra*

Kittredge. *Marc Antony*

Nardo. *Cleopatra*

Simms. *St. Patrick: The Real Story of Patrick*

Várdy. *Attila*

Walworth. *Augustus Caesar*

Walworth. *Constantine*

Collective Biography

Hoobler. *Italian Portraits*

Jacobs. *Great Lives: World Religions*

Newark. *Medieval Warlords*

Saxby. *The Great Deeds of Heroic Women*

Wilkinson. *Generals Who Changed the World*

Wilkinson. *People Who Changed the World*

Wilkinson. *Statesmen Who Changed the World*

History

Avi-Yonah. *Piece by Piece! Mosaics of the Ancient World*

Ballard. *The Lost Wreck of the Isis*

Baxter. *Invaders and Settlers*

Baxter. *Romans*

Biel. *Pompeii*

Bisel. *The Secrets of Vesuvius*

Brierley. *Explorers of the Ancient World*

Briquebec. *The Ancient World*

Burke. *Food and Fasting*

Chaikin. *Menorahs, Mezuzas, and Other Jewish Symbols*

Charley. *Tombs and Treasures*

Clare. *Classical Rome*

Clements. *An Illustrated History of the World*

Compton. *Marriage Customs*

Connolly. *Pompeii*

Connolly. *The Roman Fort*

Connolly. *Tiberius Claudius Maximus: The Calvaryman*

Connolly. *Tiberius Claudius Maximus: The Legionary*

Corbishley. *Ancient Rome*

Corbishley. *Everyday Life in Roman Times*

Corbishley. *Rome and the Ancient World*

Corbishley. *Secret Cities*

Corbishley. *What Do We Know About the Romans?*

Corrick. *The Byzantine Empire*

Cush. *Disasters That Shook the World*

Davies. *Transport*

Dazzling! Jewelry of the Ancient World

Europe at the Time of Greece and Rome

Fradin. *Medicine: Yesterday, Today, and Tomorrow*

Giblin. *Be Seated: A Book About Chairs*

Giblin. *The Truth About Unicorns*

Gravett. *Arms and Armor*

Guittard. *The Romans*

Harris. *Science in Ancient Rome*

Haywood. *The Romans*

Hernandez. *Barmi*

Hinds. *The Ancient Romans*

Hirsch. *Taxation*

Humble. *Ships*

Kent. *A Slice Through a City*

Kerr. *Keeping Clean*

Langley. *The Roman News*

Levy. *Women in Society: Britain*

MacDonald. *Cities*

MacDonald. *A Roman Fort*

Martell. *From the Ice Age to the Roman Empire*

Morley. *Clothes*

Nardo. *The Age of Augustus*

Nardo. *Caesar's Conquest of Gaul*

Nardo. *Greek and Roman Theater*

Nardo. *Life in Ancient Rome*

9

Nardo. *The Roman Empire*
Nardo. *The Roman Republic*
Newark. *Celtic Warriors*
Newark. *Medieval Warlords*
Ochoa. *The Assassination of Julius Caesar*
Odijk. *The Romans*
Platt. *Pirate*
Platt. *The Smithsonian Visual Timeline of Inventions*
Poulton. *Life in the Time of Augustus and the Ancient Romans*
Prior. *Initiation Customs*
Prior. *Pilgrimages and Journeys*
Putnam. *Mummy*

Ridd. *Julius Caesar in Gaul and Britain*
Rushton. *Birth Customs*
Rushton. *Death Customs*
Scharfstein. *Understanding Jewish History*
Schneider. *Between the Dragon and the Eagle*
Simpson. *Ancient Rome*
Singer. *Structures That Changed the Way the World Looked*
Spencer. *Germany: Then and Now*
Steele. *Food and Feasts in Ancient Rome*
Steele. *Kidnapping*

Steele. *The Romans and Pompeii*
Turvey. *Inventions: Inventors and Ingenious Ideas*
Ventura. *Clothing*
Ventura. *Food*
Watkins. *Gladiator*
Wetterau. *World History*
Whittock. *The Roman Empire*
Wilkinson. *The Mediterranean*
Williams. *Forts and Castles*
Woolf. *Picture This: A First Introduction to Paintings*

Multimedia

CD-ROM

Le Louvre: The Palace & Its Paintings

Religions of the World

Teach Your Kids World History

Video

Ancient Rome
The British Way of Life
The Byzantine Empire
Details of Roman Life
Europe: Insular Region

France: History and Culture Legacies
London: City of Majesty
The Roman Arena
Rome: The Eternal City

Trompe L'Oeil: Paintings That Fool the Eye
Turkey: Between Europe and Asia
Ukraine: Kiev and Luov

GRADE EIGHT

Historical Fiction

Haugaard. *The Rider and His Horse*
Speare. *The Bronze Bow*

Sutcliff. *Sun Horse, Moon Horse*

Yarbro. *Four Horses for Tishtry*

Biography

Brooks. *Cleopatra: Goddess of Egypt, Enemy of Rome*
Bruns. *Julius Caesar*
Hoobler. *Cleopatra*
Kittredge. *Marc Antony*

Nardo. *Cleopatra*
Nardo. *Julius Caesar*
Powers. *Nero*
Simms. *St. Patrick: The Real Story of Patrick*

Várdy. *Attila*
Walworth. *Augustus Caesar*
Walworth. *Constantine*

Collective Biography

Hoobler. *Italian Portraits*
Newark. *Medieval Warlords*
Saxby. *The Great Deeds of Heroic Women*

Wilkinson. *Generals Who Changed the World*
Wilkinson. *People Who Changed the World*

Wilkinson. *Statesmen Who Changed the World*

History

Avi-Yonah. *Piece by Piece! Mosaics of the Ancient World*
Ballard. *The Lost Wreck of the Isis*
Baxter. *Invaders and Settlers*
Baxter. *Romans*

Biel. *Pompeii*
Briquebec. *The Ancient World*
Burke. *Food and Fasting*
Chaikin. *Menorahs, Mezuzas, and Other Jewish Symbols*
Clare. *Classical Rome*

Clements. *An Illustrated History of the World*
Compton. *Marriage Customs*
Connolly. *Pompeii*
Connolly. *The Roman Fort*
Connolly. *Tiberius Claudius Maximus: The Calvaryman*

Connolly. *Tiberius Claudius Maximus: The Legionary*
Corbishley. *Ancient Rome*
Corbishley. *Everyday Life in Roman Times*
Corrick. *The Byzantine Empire*
Cush. *Disasters That Shook the World*
Davies. *Transport*
Dazzling! Jewelry of the Ancient World
Europe at the Time of Greece and Rome
Fradin. *Medicine: Yesterday, Today, and Tomorrow*
Giblin. *Be Seated: A Book About Chairs*
Giblin. *The Truth About Unicorns*
Guittard. *The Romans*
Harris. *Science in Ancient Rome*
Hernandez. *Barmi*
Hinds. *The Ancient Romans*
Hirsch. *Taxation*
Langley. *The Roman News*

Levy. *Women in Society: Britain*
MacDonald. *Cities*
Macdonald. *A Roman Fort*
Morley. *Clothes*
Nardo. *The Age of Augustus*
Nardo. *Caesar's Conquest of Gaul*
Nardo. *Greek and Roman Theater*
Nardo. *Life in Ancient Rome*
Nardo. *The Roman Empire*
Nardo. *The Roman Republic*
Newark. *Celtic Warriors*
Newark. *Medieval Warlords*
Ochoa. *The Assassination of Julius Caesar*
Odijk. *The Romans*
Platt. *Pirate*
Platt. *The Smithsonian Visual Timeline of Inventions*
Poulton. *Life in the Time of Augustus and the Ancient Romans*
Prior. *Initiation Customs*
Prior. *Pilgrimages and Journeys*

Putnam. *Mummy*
Ridd. *Julius Caesar in Gaul and Britain*
Rushton. *Birth Customs*
Rushton. *Death Customs*
Scharfstein. *Understanding Jewish History*
Singer. *Structures That Changed the Way the World Looked*
Spencer. *Germany: Then and Now*
Steele. *Food and Feasts in Ancient Rome*
Turvey. *Inventions: Inventors and Ingenious Ideas*
Ventura. *Clothing*
Ventura. *Food*
Watkins. *Gladiator*
Wetterau. *World History*
Wilkinson. *The Mediterranean*
Williams. *Forts and Castles*
Woolf. *Picture This: A First Introduction to Paintings*

Multimedia

CD-ROM

Le Louvre: The Palace & Its Paintings

Religions of the World

Teach Your Kids World History

Video

Ancient Rome
The British Way of Life
The Byzantine Empire
Details of Roman Life
Europe: Insular Region

France: History and Culture Legacies
London: City of Majesty
The Roman Arena
Rome: The Eternal City

Trompe L'Oeil: Paintings That Fool the Eye
Turkey: Between Europe and Asia
Ukraine: Kiev and Luov

GRADE NINE

Historical Fiction

Bradley. *Forest House*
Hunter. *The Stronghold*
Napoli. *Song of the Magdalene*
Speare. *The Bronze Bow*
Sutcliff. *The Eagle of the Ninth*

Sutcliff. *Frontier Wolf*
Sutcliff. *The Lantern Bearer*
Sutcliff. *The Mark of the Horse Lord*
Sutcliff. *Outcast*
Sutcliff. *The Silver Branch*

Sutcliff. *Song for a Dark Queen*
Sutcliff. *Sun Horse, Moon Horse*
Yarbro. *Four Horses for Tishtry*

Biography

Brooks. *Cleopatra: Goddess of Egypt, Enemy of Rome*
Bruns. *Julius Caesar*
Hoobler. *Cleopatra*
Kittredge. *Marc Antony*

Nardo. *Cleopatra*
Nardo. *Julius Caesar*
Powers. *Nero*
Simms. *St. Patrick: The Real Story of Patrick*

Várdy. *Attila*
Walworth. *Augustus Caesar*
Walworth. *Constantine*

Collective Biography

Hoobler. *Italian Portraits*
Newark. *Medieval Warlords*
Saxby. *The Great Deeds of Heroic Women*

Wilkinson. *Generals Who Changed the World*
Wilkinson. *People Who Changed the World*

Wilkinson. *Statesmen Who Changed the World*

History

Adkins. *Handbook to Life in Ancient Rome*
Avi-Yonah. *Piece by Piece! Mosaics of the Ancient World*
Clare. *Classical Rome*
Connolly. *The Roman Fort*
Connolly. *Tiberius Claudius Maximus: The Calvaryman*
Connolly. *Tiberius Claudius Maximus: The Legionary*
Corrick. *The Byzantine Empire*
Cush. *Disasters That Shook the World*
Dazzling! Jewelry of the Ancient World
Europe at the Time of Greece and Rome

Fradin. *Medicine: Yesterday, Today, and Tomorrow*
Hernandez. *Barmi*
Hinds. *The Ancient Romans*
Hirsch. *Taxation*
Langley. *The Roman News*
Levy. *Women in Society: Britain*
Nardo. *Caesar's Conquest of Gaul*
Nardo. *Greek and Roman Theater*
Nardo. *Life in Ancient Rome*
Nardo. *The Roman Empire*
Nardo. *The Roman Republic*
Ochoa. *The Assassination of Julius Caesar*
Platt. *The Smithsonian Visual Timeline of Inventions*

Ridd. *Julius Caesar in Gaul and Britain*
Scharfstein. *Understanding Jewish History*
Singer. *Structures That Changed the Way the World Looked*
Spencer. *Germany: Then and Now*
Steele. *Food and Feasts in Ancient Rome*
Time-Life. *Pompeii: The Vanished City*
Time-Life. *Rome: Echoes of Imperial Glory*
Wetterau. *World History*
Williams. *Forts and Castles*

Multimedia

CD-ROM

Events That Changed the World
Ideas That Changed the World

Le Louvre: The Palace & Its Paintings
Religions of the World

Teach Your Kids World History

Video

Ancient Rome
The Byzantine Empire
Cyber Rome
D-Day
Details of Roman Life
Europe in the Middle Ages: The City of God
France: History and Culture

The History of Orthodox Christianity
Legacies
London: City of Majesty
The Roman Arena
Rome: The Eternal City
Rome Revisited: The Renewal of Splendor

Trompe L'Oeil: Paintings That Fool the Eye
Turkey: Between Europe and Asia
Wonders of Man's Creation
Wonders Sacred & Mysterious

GRADE TEN

Historical Fiction

Bradley. *Forest House*
Cross. *Pope Joan*
Haugaard. *The Rider and His Horse*
Hunter. *The Stronghold*
Napoli. *Song of the Magdalene*
Speare. *The Bronze Bow*

Sutcliff. *The Eagle of the Ninth*
Sutcliff. *Frontier Wolf*
Sutcliff. *The Lantern Bearers*
Sutcliff. *The Mark of the Horse Lord*
Sutcliff. *Outcast*
Sutcliff. *The Silver Branch*

Sutcliff. *Song for a Dark Queen*
Sutcliff. *Sun Horse, Moon Horse*
Yarbro. *Four Horses for Tishtry*

Biography

Brooks. *Cleopatra*
Bruns. *Julius Caesar*
Hoobler. *Cleopatra*
Kittredge. *Marc Antony*

Nardo. *Cleopatra*
Nardo. *Julius Caesar*
Powers. *Nero*
Várdy. *Attila*

Walworth. *Augustus Caesar*
Walworth. *Constantine*

Collective Biography

Axelrod. *Dictators and Tyrants*
Newark. *Medieval Warlords*

Saxby. *The Great Deeds of Heroic Women*
Wilkinson. *Generals Who Changed the World*

Wilkinson. *People Who Changed the World*
Wilkinson. *Statesmen Who Changed the World*

History

Adkins. *Handbook to Life in Ancient Rome*
Alchemy: The Art of Knowing
Ardley. *Music: An Illustrated Encyclopedia*
Avi-Yonah. *Piece by Piece! Mosaics of the Ancient World*
Connolly. *The Roman Fort*
Corbishley. *Ancient Rome*
Corrick. *The Byzantine Empire*
Davis. *Man-Made Catastrophes*

Europe at the Time of Greece and Rome
Fradin. *Medicine: Yesterday, Today, and Tomorrow*
Hernandez. *Barmi*
Hinds. *The Ancient Romans*
Langley. *The Roman News*
Levy. *Women in Society: Britain*
Marx. *The Search for Sunken Treasure*
Mysticism: The Experience of the Divine
Nardo. *Caesar's Conquest of Gaul*

Nardo. *Greek and Roman Theater*
Nardo. *Life in Ancient Rome*
Ochoa. *The Assassination of Julius Caesar*
Pickford. *The Atlas of Shipwrecks & Treasure*
Scharfstein. *Understanding Jewish History*
Time-Life. *Pompeii: The Vanished City*
Time-Life. *Rome: Echoes of Imperial Glory*

Multimedia

CD-ROM

Events That Changed the World
Ideas That Changed the World

Le Louvre: The Palace & Its Paintings
Religions of the World

Teach Your Kids World History

Video

Ancient Rome
The Byzantine Empire
Cyber Rome
D-Day
Details of Roman Life
Europe in the Middle Ages: The City of God

The History of Orthodox Christianity
Legacies
The Longest Hatred: The History of Anti-Semitism
The Roman Arena
Rome Art and Architecture

Rome Revisited: The Renewal of Splendor
Trompe L'Oeil: Paintings That Fool the Eye
Wonders of Man's Creation
Wonders Sacred & Mysterious

GRADES ELEVEN AND TWELVE

Historical Fiction

Bradley. *Forest House*
Bragg. *The Sword and the Miracle*
Cross. *Pope Joan*
Davis. *The Iron Hand of Mars*
Davis. *Last Act in Palmyra*
Davis. *Poseidon's Gold*
Davis. *Shadows in Bronze*
Davis. *Silver Pigs*
Davis. *Venus in Copper*

De Carvalho. *A God Strolling in the Cool of the Evening*
George. *The Memoirs of Cleopatra*
Haugaard. *The Rider and His Horse*
Hunter. *The Stronghold*
Jaro. *The Door in the Wall*
McCullough. *Caesar's Women*

McCullough. *The First Man in Rome*
McCullough. *Fortune's Favorites*
McCullough. *The Grass Crown*
Napoli. *Song of the Magdalene*
Rutherfurd. *Russka*
Saylor. *Arms of Nemesis*
Saylor. *Catilina's Riddle*

Saylor. *A Murder on the Appian Way*
Saylor. *Roman Blood*
Saylor. *The Venus Throw*
Speare. *The Bronze Bow*
Sutcliff. *The Eagle of the Ninth*

Sutcliff. *Frontier Wolf*
Sutcliff. *The Lantern Bearers*
Sutcliff. *The Mark of the Horse Lord*
Sutcliff. *Outcast*
Sutcliff. *The Silver Branch*

Sutcliff. *Song for a Dark Queen*
Sutcliff. *Sun Horse, Moon Horse*
Tarr. *Throne of Isis*

Biography

Brooks. *Cleopatra*
Bruns. *Julius Caesar*
Hoobler. *Cleopatra*
Kittredge. *Marc Antony*

Nardo. *Cleopatra*
Nardo. *Julius Caesar*
Powers. *Nero*
Várdy. *Attila*

Walworth. *Augustus Caesar*
Walworth. *Constantine*

Collective Biography

Axelrod. *Dictators and Tyrants*

Boorstin. *The Creators*
Newark. *Medieval Warlords*

Saxby. *The Great Deeds of Heroic Women*

History

Adkins. *Handbook to Life in Ancient Rome*
Alchemy: The Art of Knowing
Ardley. *Music: An Illustrated Encyclopedia*
Avi-Yonah. *Piece by Piece! Mosaics of the Ancient World*
Beckett. *The Story of Painting*
Bremness. *Herbs*
Brown. *Christianity*
Bunson. *Encyclopedia of the Roman Empire*
Castello. *The Jews and Europe*

Davidson. *Everyday Life Through the Ages*
Davis. *Man-Made Catastrophes*
Hernandez. *Barmi*
Hibbert. *Florence*
Hibbert. *Rome*
Hughes. *Barcelona*
Keegan. *History of Warfare*
Langley. *The Roman News*
Levy. *Women in Society: Britain*
Marx. *The Search for Sunken Treasure*
Mysticism: The Experience of the Divine

Nardo. *Life in Ancient Rome*
Pickford. *The Atlas of Shipwrecks & Treasure*
Porter. *London, a Social History*
Scharfstein. *Understanding Jewish History*
Smith. *Fascinating People and Astounding Events from the History of the Western World*
Time-Life. *Pompeii: The Vanished City*
Time-Life. *Rome: Echoes of Imperial Glory*

Multimedia

CD-ROM

Events That Changed the World
Ideas That Changed the World

Le Louvre: The Palace & Its Paintings
Religions of the World

Teach Your Kids World History

Video

Ancient Rome
The Byzantine Empire
Cyber Rome
D-Day
The Decline of Rome
Early Christianity
Europe in the Middle Ages: The City of God

The Fall of Rome
The History of Orthodox Christianity
The Longest Hatred: The History of Anti-Semitism
The Rise of Rome
The Rise of the Church
The Roman Empire

Rome Art and Architecture
Rome Revisited: The Renewal of Splendor
Semanta Santa in Seville
Trompe L'Oeil: Paintings That Fool the Eye
Wonders of Man's Creation
Wonders Sacred & Mysterious

Europe and the British Isles, A.D. 476-1289

Historical Fiction

Alder. *The King's Shadow*
Anderson. *The Druid's Gift*
Bradford. *There Will Be Wolves*
De Angeli. *Black Fox of Lorne*
Dickinson. *The Dancing Bear*
Goodman. *The Winter Hare*
Hendry. *Quest for a Maid*
Konigsburg. *A Proud Taste for Scarlet and Miniver*

Lewis. *The Ship That Flew*
Llywelyn. *Brian Boru: Emperor of the Irish*
McCaffrey. *Black Horses for the King*
McGraw. *The Striped Ships*
Morressy. *The Juggler*
Skurzynski. *What Happened in Hamelin*
Snyder. *Song of the Gargoyle*

Stolz. *Pangur Ban*
Sutcliff. *Blood Feud*
Sutcliff. *The Shining Company*
Sutcliff. *The Witch's Brat*
Treece. *The Road to Miklagard*
Treece. *Viking's Dawn*
Westall. *The Wind Eye*

Biography

Banfield. *Charlemagne*
Biel. *Charlemagne*
Brooks. *Queen Eleanor: Independent Spirit of the Medieval World*
Doherty. *King Arthur*

Dramer. *Kublai Khan: Mongol Emperor*
Humphrey. *Genghis Khan*
Kaplan. *Eleanor of Aquitaine*
Koslow. *El Cid*
McCaughrean. *El Cid*

O'Neal. *King Arthur: Opposing Viewpoints*
Simon. *Leif Eriksson and the Vikings*

Collective Biography

Cohen. *Real Vampires*
Hazell. *Heroines: Great Women Through the Ages*
Hoobler. *French Portraits*
Hoobler. *Italian Portraits*
Hoobler. *Russian Portraits*

Jacobs. *Great Lives: World Religions*
Newark. *Medieval Warlords*
Saxby. *The Great Deeds of Heroic Women*

Wilkinson. *Generals Who Changed the World*
Wilkinson. *People Who Changed the World*
Wilkinson. *Statesmen Who Changed the World*

History

Baxter. *Invaders and Settlers*
Biel. *The Crusades*
Burke. *Food and Fasting*
Chaikin. *Menorahs, Mezuzas, and Other Jewish Symbols*
Charley. *Tombs and Treasures*
Child. *The Crusades*
Child. *The Rise of Islam*
Clare. *Knights in Armor*
Clare. *The Vikings*
Clements. *An Illustrated History of the World*
Compton. *Marriage Customs*
Corbishley. *The Medieval World*
Corbishley. *The Middle Ages*

Cush. *Disasters That Shook the World*
Davies. *Transport*
Dawson. *Food and Feasts in the Middle Ages*
Fradin. *Medicine: Yesterday, Today, and Tomorrow*
Fradon. *Harald the Herald*
Gordon. *Islam*
Gravett. *Arms and Armor*
Gravett. *Knight*
Gregory. *The Dark Ages*
Hernandez. *Lebek*
Hinds. *The Celts of Northern Europe*
Humble. *Ships*

Husain. *What Do We Know About Islam?*
Kerr. *Keeping Clean*
Lace. *England*
Langley. *Medieval Life*
The Late Middle Ages
Macaulay. *Cathedral*
MacDonald. *Cities*
MacDonald. *A Medieval Castle*
MacDonald. *A Medieval Cathedral*
MacDonald. *The Middle Ages*
Martell. *Food and Feasts with the Vikings*

Martell. *The Vikings and Jorvik*

Martell. *What Do We Know About the Vikings?*

Mason. *Viking Times*

Morley. *Clothes*

Newark. *Celtic Warriors*

Newark. *Medieval Warlords*

Oakes. *The Middle Ages*

Pearson. *The Vikings*

Perdrizet. *The Cathedral Builders*

Pernoud. *A Day with a Medieval Troubadour*

Pernoud. *A Day with a Miller*

Pernoud. *A Day with a Noblewoman*

Pernoud. *A Day with a Stonecutter*

Platt. *Castle*

Platt. *Pirate*

Platt. *The Smithsonian Visual Timeline of Inventions*

Prior. *Initiation Customs*

Prior. *Pilgrimages and Journeys*

Pruneti. *Viking Explorers*

Rushton. *Birth Customs*

Rushton. *Death Customs*

Sauvain. *Hastings*

Scharfstein. *Understanding Jewish History*

Seymour-Jones. *Refugees*

Singer. *Structures That Changed the Way the World Looked*

Singman. *Daily Life in Chaucer's England*

Speed. *Life in the Time of Harald Hardrada and the Vikings*

Spencer. *Germany: Then and Now*

Steele. *Castles*

Steele. *Censorship*

Steele. *Kidnapping*

Steele. *Riots*

Steffens. *The Children's Crusade*

Stefoff. *The Viking Explorers*

Turvey. *Inventions: Inventors and Ingenious Ideas*

Ventura. *Clothing*

Ventura. *Food*

Wetterau. *World History*

Wilkinson. *Amazing Buildings*

Wilkinson. *The Mediterranean*

Williams. *Forts and Castles*

Woolf. *Picture This: A First Introduction to Paintings*

Multimedia

CD-ROM

Art & Music: The Medieval Era

Religions of the World

Teach Your Kids World History

Video

The British Way of Life

Budapest

Cathedrals with a Project

The Crusades

The Dark Ages: Europe After the Fall of Rome (410-1066 AD)

England's Historic Treasures

Europe: Insular Region

France: History and Culture

Hildegard: Woman of Vision

Illuminated Lives: A Brief History of Women's Work in the Middle Ages

Jewish Communities of the Middle Ages

London: City of Majesty

Medieval Times: Life in the Middle Ages (1000-1450 AD)

Medieval Women

Middle Ages School Kit

Pirates: Passion and Plunder

The Soviet Union

Turkey: Between Europe and Asia

The Vikings: Seafarers and Explorers

The Vistula

GRADE EIGHT

Historical Fiction

Alder. *The King's Shadow*

Anderson. *The Druid's Gift*

Bradford. *There Will Be Wolves*

De Angeli. *Black Fox of Lorne*

Dickinson. *The Dancing Bear*

Goodman. *The Winter Hare*

Haugaard. *A Slave's Tale*

Hendry. *Quest for a Maid*

Konigsburg. *A Proud Taste for Scarlet and Miniver*

Llywelyn. *Brian Boru: Emperor of the Irish*

McCaffrey. *Black Horses for the King*

McGraw. *The Striped Ships*

Morressy. *The Juggler*

Skurzynski. *What Happened in Hamelin*

Snyder. *Song of the Gargoyle*

Stolz. *Pangur Ban*

Sutcliff. *Blood Feud*

Sutcliff. *The Shining Company*

Sutcliff. *The Witch's Brat*

Treece. *The Road to Miklagard*

Treece. *Viking's Dawn*

Westall. *The Wind Eye*

Biography

Banfield. *Charlemagne*

Biel. *Charlemagne*

Brooks. *Queen Eleanor*

Doherty. *King Arthur*

Dramer. *Kublai Khan*

Humphrey. *Genghis Khan*

Kaplan. *Eleanor of Aquitaine*

Koslow. *El Cid*

McCaughrean. *El Cid*

O'Neal. *King Arthur*

Simon. *Leif Eriksson and the Vikings*

Collective Biography

Cohen. *Real Vampires*
Hazell. *Heroines: Great Women Through the Ages*
Hoobler. *French Portraits*
Hoobler. *Italian Portraits*
Hoobler. *Russian Portraits*

Newark. *Medieval Warlords*
Saxby. *The Great Deeds of Heroic Women*
Wilkinson. *Generals Who Changed the World*

Wilkinson. *People Who Changed the World*
Wilkinson. *Statesmen Who Changed the World*

History

Baxter. *Invaders and Settlers*
Biel. *The Crusades*
Burke. *Food and Fasting*
Chaikin. *Menorahs, Mezuzas, and Other Jewish Symbols*
Child. *The Crusades*
Child. *The Rise of Islam*
Clare. *Knights in Armor*
Clare. *The Vikings*
Clements. *An Illustrated History of the World*
Compton. *Marriage Customs*
Corbishley. *The Medieval World*
Corbishley. *The Middle Ages*
Cush. *Disasters That Shook the World*
Davies. *Transport*
Fradin. *Medicine: Yesterday, Today, and Tomorrow*
Gordon. *Islam*
Gravett. *Knight*
Hernandez. *Lebek*

Hinds. *The Celts of Northern Europe*
Lace. *England*
Langley. *Medieval Life*
The Late Middle Ages
MacDonald. *Cities*
MacDonald. *A Medieval Cathedral*
Morley. *Clothes*
Newark. *Celtic Warriors*
Newark. *Medieval Warlords*
Pearson. *The Vikings*
Perdrizet. *The Cathedral Builders*
Platt. *Castle*
Platt. *Pirate*
Platt. *The Smithsonian Visual Timeline of Inventions*
Prior. *Initiation Customs*
Prior. *Pilgrimages and Journeys*
Rushton. *Birth Customs*
Rushton. *Death Customs*
Sauvain. *Hastings*

Scharfstein. *Understanding Jewish History*
Singer. *Structures That Changed the Way the World Looked*
Singman. *Daily Life in Chaucer's England*
Speed. *Life in the Time of Harald Hardrada and the Vikings*
Spencer. *Germany: Then and Now*
Stefoff. *The Viking Explorers*
Turvey. *Inventions: Inventors and Ingenious Ideas*
Ventura. *Clothing*
Ventura. *Food*
Wetterau. *World History*
Wilkinson. *The Mediterranean*
Williams. *Forts and Castles*
Woolf. *Picture This: A First Introduction to Paintings*

Multimedia

CD-ROM

The Anglo Saxons
Art & Music: The Medieval Era

Religions of the World
Teach Your Kids World History

Video

The British Way of Life
Budapest
Cathedrals with a Project
The Crusades
The Dark Ages: Europe After the Fall of Rome (410-1066 AD)
England's Historic Treasures
France: History and Culture
Hildegard: Woman of Vision

Illuminated Lives: A Brief History of Women's Work in the Middle Ages
Jewish Communities of the Middle Ages
London: City of Majesty
Medieval Times: Life in the Middle Ages (1000-1450 AD)
Medieval Women

Middle Ages School Kit
Pirates: Passion and Plunder
The Soviet Union
Turkey: Between Europe and Asia
The Vikings: Seafarers and Explorers
The Vistula

GRADE NINE

Historical Fiction

Alder. *The King's Shadow*
Anderson. *The Druid's Gift*

Bradford. *There Will Be Wolves*
De Angeli. *Black Fox of Lorne*

Dickinson. *The Dancing Bear*
Goodman. *The Winter Hare*
Haugaard. *A Slave's Tale*

Konigsburg. *A Proud Taste
for Scarlet and Miniver*
Llywelyn. *Brian Boru:
Emperor of the Irish*
McCaffrey. *Black Horses for
the King*
McGraw. *The Striped Ships*
Morressy. *The Juggler*
O'Dell. *The Road to Damietta*

Penman. *The Queen's Man: A
Medieval Mystery*
Skurzynski. *What Happened
in Hamelin*
Stolz. *Pangur Ban*
Sutcliff. *Blood Feud*
Sutcliff. *Bonnie Dundee*
Sutcliff. *Dawn Wind*
Sutcliff. *Knight's Fee*

Sutcliff. *The Shield Ring*
Sutcliff. *The Shining
Company*
Sutcliff. *The Witch's Brat*
Treece. *The Road to
Miklagard*
Treece. *Swords from the North*
Treece. *Viking's Dawn*
Westall. *The Wind Eye*

Biography

Banfield. *Charlemagne*
Biel. *Charlemagne*
Brooks. *Queen Eleanor*
Day. *The Search for King
Arthur*

Doherty. *King Arthur*
Dramer. *Kublai Khan*
Humphrey. *Genghis Khan*
Kaplan. *Eleanor of Aquitaine*
Koslow. *El Cid*

McCaughrean. *El Cid*
O'Neal. *King Arthur*

Collective Biography

Hoobler. *French Portraits*
Hoobler. *Italian Portraits*
Hoobler. *Russian Portraits*
Lomask. *Great Lives:
Exploration*

Newark. *Medieval Warlords*
Saxby. *The Great Deeds of
Heroic Women*
Wilkinson. *Generals Who
Changed the World*

Wilkinson. *People Who
Changed the World*
Wilkinson. *Statesmen Who
Changed the World*

History

Child. *The Crusades*
Child. *The Rise of Islam*
Clare. *Knights in Armor*
Clare. *The Vikings*
Corbishley. *The Medieval
World*
Corbishley. *The Middle Ages*
Cush. *Disasters That Shook
the World*
Fradin. *Medicine: Yesterday,
Today, and Tomorrow*

Gordon. *Islam*
Hernandez. *Lebek*
Hinds. *The Celts of Northern
Europe*
Lace. *England
The Late Middle Ages*
Platt. *Castle*
Platt. *The Smithsonian Visual
Timeline of Inventions*
Scharfstein. *Understanding
Jewish History*

Singer. *Structures That
Changed the Way the
World Looked*
Singman. *Daily Life in
Chaucer's England*
Spencer. *Germany: Then and
Now*
Time-Life. *Vikings: Raiders
from the North*
Wetterau. *World History*
Williams. *Forts and Castles*

Multimedia

CD-ROM

The Anglo Saxons
*Art & Music: The Medieval
Era*

*Events That Changed the
World*
Ideas That Changed the World

Religions of the World
*Teach Your Kids World
History*

Video

Budapest
Cathedrals with a Project
The Crusades
The Crusades, 1187
*The Dark Ages: Europe After
the Fall of Rome (410-1066
AD)*
England's Historic Treasures
*Europe in the Middle Ages:
The City of God*
France: History and Culture
Gerald of Wales

Hildegard: Woman of Vision
*The History of Orthodox
Christianity*
*Illuminated Lives: A Brief
History of Women's Work
in the Middle Ages*
*Jewish Communities of the
Middle Ages*
London: City of Majesty
*Medieval Times: Life in the
Middle Ages (1000-1450
AD)*

Medieval Women
Middle Ages School Kit
The Mongol Empire, 1247
Pirates: Passion and Plunder
The Soviet Union
*Turkey: Between Europe and
Asia*
The Vikings, 1066
*The Vikings: Seafarers and
Explorers*
The Vistula
Wonders Sacred & Mysterious

GRADE TEN

Historical Fiction

Bradford. *There Will Be Wolves*
De Angeli. *Black Fox of Lorne*
Dickinson. *The Dancing Bear*
Haugaard. *A Slave's Tale*
Holland. *Jerusalem*
McCaffrey. *Black Horses for the King*

Morressy. *The Juggler*
O'Dell. *The Road to Damietta*
Penman. *The Queen's Man: A Medieval Mystery*
Stolz. *Pangur Ban*
Sutcliff. *Blood Feud*
Sutcliff. *Bonnie Dundee*
Sutcliff. *Dawn Wind*

Sutcliff. *Knight's Fee*
Sutcliff. *The Shield Ring*
Sutcliff. *The Shining Company*
Treece. *The Road to Miklagard*
Treece. *Swords from the North*
Westall. *The Wind Eye*

Biography

Banfield. *Charlemagne*
Biel. *Charlemagne*
Brooks. *Queen Eleanor*

Day. *The Search for King Arthur*
Doherty. *King Arthur*
Dramer. *Kublai Khan*

Humphrey. *Genghis Khan*
Kaplan. *Eleanor of Aquitaine*
Koslow. *El Cid*
McCaughrean. *El Cid*

Collective Biography

Axelrod. *Dictators and Tyrants*
Duffy. *Czar: Russia's Rulers*
Lomask. *Great Lives: Exploration*

Newark. *Medieval Warlords*
Saxby. *The Great Deeds of Heroic Women*
Wilkinson. *Generals Who Changed the World*

Wilkinson. *People Who Changed the World*
Wilkinson. *Statesmen Who Changed the World*

History

Alchemy: The Art of Knowing
Chivalry: The Path of Love
Fradin. *Medicine: Yesterday, Today, and Tomorrow*
Gordon. *Islam*
Graham-Campbell. *The Viking World*
Harpur. *Revelations: The Medieval World*

Hernandez. *Lebek*
Hinds. *The Celts of Northern Europe*
Lace. *England*
The Late Middle Ages
Pickford. *The Atlas of Shipwrecks & Treasure*
Platt. *Castle*
Ross. *Monarchs of Scotland*

Scharfstein. *Understanding Jewish History*
Singman. *Daily Life in Chaucer's England*
Time-Life. *Vikings: Raiders from the North*

Multimedia

CD-ROM

The Anglo Saxons
Art & Music: The Medieval Era

Events That Changed the World
Ideas That Changed the World

Religions of the World
Teach Your Kids World History

Video

Birth of an Empire
Budapest
The Crusades
The Crusades, 1187
The Dark Ages: Europe After the Fall of Rome (410-1066 AD)
England's Historic Treasures
Europe in the Middle Ages: The City of God
French Gothic Architecture: The Cathedrals

Gerald of Wales
Hildegard: Woman of Vision
The History of Orthodox Christianity
Illuminated Lives: A Brief History of Women's Work in the Middle Ages
The Italian Romanesque
Jewish Communities of the Middle Ages
The Longest Hatred: The History of Anti-Semitism

Medieval Times: Life in the Middle Ages (1000-1450 AD)
Middle Ages School Kit
The Mongol Empire, 1247
The Soviet Union
Three English Cathedrals
The Vikings, 1066
The Warrior
Wonders Sacred & Mysterious

GRADES ELEVEN AND TWELVE

Historical Fiction

Anand. *Gildenford*
Anand. *King of the Wood*
Anand. *The Proud Villeins*
Attanasio. *Kingdom of the Grail*
Bradshaw. *The Bearkeeper's Daughter*
Buechner. *Godric*
Cornwell. *Enemy of God*
Cornwell. *The Winter King: A Novel of Arthur*
Coulter. *Lord of Falcon Ridge*
Dickinson. *The Dancing Bear*
Doherty. *An Ancient Evil*
Garwood. *Saving Grace*
Garwood. *The Secret*
Haugaard. *A Slave's Tale*
Holland. *Jerusalem*
Maalouf. *Samarkand*
Marston. *The Dragons of Archenfield*
Marston. *The Lions of the North*
Marston. *The Ravens of Blackwater*
Marston. *The Wolves of Savernake*

Morressy. *The Juggler*
Newman. *Death Comes As Epiphany*
Newman. *The Devil's Door*
Newman. *Strong As Death*
O'Dell. *The Road to Damietta*
Paxson. *The Dragons of the Rhine*
Paxson. *The Wolf and the Raven*
Penman. *Here Be Dragons*
Penman. *Falls the Shadow*
Penman. *The Queen's Man: A Medieval Mystery*
Penman. *When Christ and His Saints Slept*
Peters. *The Confession of Brother Haluin*
Peters. *Dead Man's Ransom*
Peters. *The Devil's Novice*
Peters. *An Excellent Mystery*
Peters. *The Heretic's Apprentice*
Peters. *The Hermit of Eyton Forest*
Peters. *The Holy Thief*
Peters. *The Leper of St. Giles*

Peters. *Monk's Hood*
Peters. *A Morbid Taste for Bones*
Peters. *The Pilgrim of Hate*
Peters. *The Potter's Field*
Peters. *The Raven in the Foregate*
Peters. *The Rose Rent*
Peters. *St. Peter's Fair*
Peters. *The Sanctuary Sparrow*
Peters. *The Summer of the Danes*
Peters. *The Virgin in the Ice*
Stewart. *The Prince and the Pilgrim*
Stolz. *Pangur Ban*
Sutcliff. *Blood Feud*
Sutcliff. *Bonnie Dundee*
Sutcliff. *Dawn Wind*
Sutcliff. *Knight's Fee*
Sutcliff. *The Shield Ring*
Tarr. *Queen of the Swords*
Treece. *Swords from the North*

Biography

Banfield. *Charlemagne*
Biel. *Charlemagne*
Brooks. *Queen Eleanor*

Day. *The Search for King Arthur*
Doherty. *King Arthur*
Dramer. *Kublai Khan*

Humphrey. *Genghis Khan*
Kaplan. *Eleanor of Aquitaine*
Koslow. *El Cid*

Collective Biography

Axelrod. *Dictators and Tyrants*
Boorstin. *The Creators*

Duffy. *Czar: Russia's Rulers*
Lomask. *Great Lives: Exploration*

Newark. *Medieval Warlords*
Saxby. *The Great Deeds of Heroic Women*

History

Alchemy: The Art of Knowing
Beckett. *The Story of Painting*
Bremness. *Herbs*
Brown. *Christianity*
Bunson. *Encyclopedia of the Middle Ages*
Castello. *The Jews and Europe*
Chivalry: The Path of Love
Davidson. *Everyday Life Through the Ages*
Gordon. *Islam*
Graham-Campbell. *The Viking World*

Hanawalt. *Growing up in Medieval London*
Harpur. *Revelations: The Medieval World*
Hernandez. *Lebek*
Hibbert. *Florence*
Hibbert. *Rome*
Hibbert. *Venice*
Hughes. *Barcelona*
Keegan. *History of Warfare*
Lace. *England*
Pickford. *The Atlas of Shipwrecks & Treasure*

Porter. *London, a Social History*
Ross. *Monarchs of Scotland*
Scharfstein. *Understanding Jewish History*
Singman. *Daily Life in Chaucer's England*
Smith. *Fascinating People and Astounding Events from the History of the Western World*
Time-Life. *Vikings: Raiders from the North*

Multimedia

CD-ROM

The Anglo Saxons
Art & Music: The Medieval Era

Events that Changed the World
Ideas That Changed the World

Religions of the World
Teach Your Kids World History

Video

The Age of Charlemagne
Birth of an Empire
The Byzantine Empire
Cities and Cathedrals of the Middle Ages
Common Life in the Middle Ages
The Crusades
The Crusades, 1187
The Dark Ages
The Dark Ages: Europe After the Fall of Rome (410-1066 AD)

England's Historic Treasures
Europe in the Middle Ages: The City of God
The Feudal Order
French Gothic Architecture: The Cathedrals
Gerald of Wales
Hildegard: Woman of Vision
The History of Orthodox Christianity
Illuminated Lives: A Brief History of Women's Work in the Middle Ages

The Italian Romanesque
The Late Middle Ages
The Longest Hatred: The History of Anti-Semitism
Medieval Times: Life in the Middle Ages (1000-1450 AD)
The Middle Ages
The Rise of the Middle Class
Three English Cathedrals
The Vikings, 1066
The Warrior
Wonders Sacred & Mysterious

Europe and the British Isles, 1290-1491

Historical Fiction

Cushman. *Catherine Called Birdy*
Cushman. *The Midwife's Apprentice*
De Angeli. *The Door in the Wall*
Garden. *Dove and Sword*
Goodwin. *Where the Towers Pierce the Sky*

Harnett. *The Cargo of the Madalena*
Harnett. *The Sign of the Green Falcon*
Harnett. *The Writing on the Hearth*
Kelly. *The Trumpeter of Krakow*
Lewis. *The Ship That Flew*

Llorente. *The Apprentice*
McCaughrean. *A Little Lower Than the Angels*
Paton Walsh. *The Emperor's Winding Sheet*
Phillips. *The Peace Child*
Temple. *The Beduins' Gazelle*
Vining. *Adam of the Road*

Biography

Banfield. *Joan of Arc*
Bender. *Waiting for Filippo*
Burch. *Isabella of Castile*
Ceserani. *Marco Polo*

Codye. *Queen Isabella I*
Corrain. *Giotto and Medieval Art*
Dana. *Young Joan*

Hull. *The Travels of Marco Polo*
Noonan. *Marco Polo*
Simon. *Henry the Navigator*
Stanley. *Leonardo Da Vinci*

Collective Biography

Cohen. *Real Vampires*
Fritz. *Around the World in a Hundred Years*
Hazell. *Heroes: Great Men Through the Ages*
Hazell. *Heroines: Great Women Through the Ages*

Hoobler. *French Portraits*
Hoobler. *Italian Portraits*
Hoobler. *Russian Portraits*
Jacobs. *Great Lives: World Religions*
Wilkinson. *People Who Changed the World*

Wilkinson. *Scientists Who Changed the World*
Wilkinson. *Statesmen Who Changed the World*

History

Armenia
Beckett. *The Duke and the Peasant: Life in the Middle Ages*
Biel. *The Black Death*
The Birth of Modern Europe
Capek. *Artistic Trickery: Trompe L'Oeil Art*
Child. *The Rise of Islam*
Clare. *Fourteenth-Century Towns*
Clare. *Italian Renaissance*
Clements. *An Illustrated History of the World*
Corzine. *The Black Death*
Davies. *Transport*
Evans. *Freedom of Speech*
Evans. *Freedom of the Press*

Fradin. *Medicine: Yesterday, Today, and Tomorrow*
Gravett. *Arms and Armor*
Gravett. *The World of the Medieval Knight*
Hernandez. *Barmi*
Hinds. *The Celts of Northern Europe*
Kerr. *Keeping Clean*
Kort. *Russia*
Lace. *England*
Lace. *The Little Princes in the Tower*
Langley. *The Industrial Revolution*
Macaulay. *Castle*
MacDonald. *Cities*
Morley. *Clothes*

Newark. *Celtic Warriors*
Newark. *Medieval Warlords*
Nicolle. *Medieval Knights*
Osman. *The Italian Renaissance*
Paris. *The End of Days*
Platt. *Pirate*
Platt. *The Smithsonian Visual Timeline of Inventions*
Scharfstein. *Understanding Jewish History*
Spencer. *Germany: Then and Now*
Steele. *Censorship*
Steele. *Kidnapping*
Stein. *Witches: Opposing Viewpoints*

Turvey. *Inventions: Inventors and Ingenious Ideas*
Ventura. *Clothing*
Ventura. *Food*

Wetterau. *World History*
Wilkinson. *The Mediterranean*
Wood. *The Renaissance*

Woolf. *Picture This: A First Introduction to Paintings*

Multimedia

CD-ROM

Art & Music: The Renaissance
Castle Explorer
Great Artists

History Through Art: Renaissance
Le Louvre: The Palace & Its Paintings

Teach Your Kids World History

Video

The British Way of Life
Budapest
Ferdinand and Isabella
France: History and Culture
London: City of Majesty

Medieval Times: Life in the Middle Ages (1000-1450 AD)
Pirates: Passion and Plunder
Poland: A Proud Heritage

Spain: History and Culture
Turkey: Between Europe and Asia
The Vistula

GRADE EIGHT

Historical Fiction

Bosse. *Captives of Time*
Cushman. *Catherine Called Birdy*
Cushman. *The Midwife's Apprentice*
Garden. *Dove and Sword*
Goodwin. *Where the Towers Pierce the Sky*

Harnett. *The Cargo of the Madalena*
Harnett. *The Sign of the Green Falcon*
Harnett. *The Writing on the Hearth*
Kelly. *The Trumpeter of Krakow*
Llorente. *The Apprentice*

McCaughrean. *A Little Lower than the Angels*
Paton Walsh. *The Emperor's Winding Sheet*
Phillips. *The Peace Child*
Temple. *The Beduins' Gazelle*
Vining. *Adam of the Road*
Wheeler. *All Men Tall*

Biography

Brooks. *Beyond the Myth: Joan of Arc*
Burch. *Isabella of Castile*
Ceserani. *Marco Polo*

Corrain. *Giotto and Medieval Art*
Hull. *The Travels of Marco Polo*
Dana. *Young Joan*

Nardo. *The Trial of Joan of Arc*
Noonan. *Marco Polo*
Simon. *Henry the Navigator*
Wepman. *Tamerlane*

Collective Biography

Cohen. *Real Vampires*
Hazell. *Heroes: Great Men Through the Ages*
Hazell. *Heroines: Great Women Through the Ages*

Hoobler. *French Portraits*
Hoobler. *Italian Portraits*
Hoobler. *Russian Portraits*
Wilkinson. *People Who Changed the World*

Wilkinson. *Scientists Who Changed the World*
Wilkinson. *Statesmen Who Changed the World*

History

Armenia
Beckett. *The Duke and the Peasant: Life in the Middle Ages*
Biel. *The Black Death*
The Birth of Modern Europe
Capek. *Artistic Trickery: Trompe L'Oeil Art*
Child. *The Rise of Islam*
Clare. *Fourteenth-Century Towns*

Clare. *Italian Renaissance*
Clements. *An Illustrated History of the World*
Corzine. *The Black Death*
Davies. *Transport*
Evans. *Freedom of Speech*
Evans. *Freedom of the Press*
Fradin. *Medicine: Yesterday, Today, and Tomorrow*
Gravett. *The World of the Medieval Knight*

Hernandez. *Barmi*
Hinds. *The Celts of Northern Europe*
Kort. *Russia*
Lace. *England*
Lace. *The Little Princes in the Tower*
Langley. *The Industrial Revolution*
Macaulay. *Castle*
MacDonald. *Cities*

Morley. *Clothes*
Newark. *Celtic Warriors*
Newark. *Medieval Warlords*
Osman. *The Italian Renaissance*
Paris. *The End of Days*
Platt. *Pirate*
Platt. *The Smithsonian Visual Timeline of Inventions*

Scharfstein. *Understanding Jewish History*
Spencer. *Germany: Then and Now*
Stein. *Witches: Opposing Viewpoints*
Turvey. *Inventions: Inventors and Ingenious Ideas*
Ventura. *Clothing*

Ventura. *Food*
Wetterau. *World History*
Wilkinson. *The Mediterranean*
Wood. *The Renaissance*
Woolf. *Picture This: A First Introduction to Paintings*

Multimedia

CD-ROM

Art & Music: The Renaissance
Castle Explorer
Great Artists

History Through Art: Renaissance
Le Louvre: The Palace & Its Paintings

Teach Your Kids World History

Video

The British Way of Life
Budapest
Ferdinand and Isabella
France: History and Culture
London: City of Majesty

Medieval Times: Life in the Middle Ages (1000-1450 AD)
Pirates: Passion and Plunder
Poland: A Proud Heritage

Spain: History and Culture
Turkey: Between Europe and Asia
The Vistula

GRADE NINE

Historical Fiction

Baumann. *The Barque of the Brothers*
Bosse. *Captives of Time*
Cushman. *Catherine Called Birdy*
Cushman. *The Midwife's Apprentice*
Garden. *Dove and Sword*
Goodwin. *Where the Towers Pierce the Sky*

Harnett. *The Cargo of the Madalena*
Harnett. *The Sign of the Green Falcon*
Harnett. *The Writing on the Hearth*
Kelly. *The Trumpeter of Krakow*
Llorente. *The Apprentice*
McCaughrean. *A Little Lower than the Angels*

Paton Walsh. *The Emperor's Winding Sheet*
Pyle. *Men of Iron*
Skurzynski. *Manwolf*
Temple. *The Beduins' Gazelle*
Temple. *The Ramsay Scallop*
Thomson. *Morning Star of the Reformation*
Wheeler. *All Men Tall*

Biography

Banfield. *Joan of Arc*
Brooks. *Beyond the Myth: Joan of Arc*

Dana. *Young Joan*
Hull. *The Travels of Marco Polo*

Nardo. *The Trial of Joan of Arc*
Wepman. *Tamerlane*

Collective Biography

Hoobler. *French Portraits*
Hoobler. *Italian Portraits*
Hoobler. *Russian Portraits*

Wilkinson. *People Who Changed the World*
Wilkinson. *Scientists Who Changed the World*

Wilkinson. *Statesmen Who Changed the World*

History

Armenia
Beckett. *The Duke and the Peasant: Life in the Middle Ages*
The Birth of Modern Europe
Capek. *Artistic Trickery: Trompe L'Oeil Art*

Child. *The Rise of Islam*
Clare. *Fourteenth-Century Towns*
Clare. *Italian Renaissance*
Evans. *Freedom of Speech*
Evans. *Freedom of the Press*

Fradin. *Medicine: Yesterday, Today, and Tomorrow*
Gravett. *The World of the Medieval Knight*
Hernandez. *Barmi*
Kort. *Russia*
Lace. *England*

Lace. *The Little Princes in the Tower*
Osman. *The Italian Renaissance*
Paris. *The End of Days*
Platt. *The Smithsonian Visual Timeline of Inventions*

Scharfstein. *Understanding Jewish History*
Spangenburg. *The History of Science from the Ancient Greeks to the Scientific Revolution*

Spencer. *Germany: Then and Now*
Stein. *Witches: Opposing Viewpoints*
Wetterau. *World History*
Wood. *The Renaissance*

Multimedia

CD-ROM

Art & Music: The Renaissance
Castle Explorer
Events That Changed the World
Great Artists

History Through Art: Renaissance
Ideas That Changed the World
Inside the Vatican

Le Louvre: The Palace & Its Paintings
Teach Your Kids World History

Video

The Black Death, 1361
Budapest
The Fall of Byzantium, 1453
Ferdinand and Isabella
France: History and Culture

The History of Orthodox Christianity
London: City of Majesty
Medieval Times: Life in the Middle Ages (1000-1450 AD)

Ottoman Empire
Pirates: Passion and Plunder
Spain: History and Culture
Turkey: Between Europe and Asia
The Vistula

GRADE TEN

Historical Fiction

Baumann. *The Barque of the Brothers*
Bosse. *Captives of Time*
Cushman. *Catherine Called Birdy*
Garden. *Dove and Sword*

Goodwin. *Where the Towers Pierce the Sky*
Kelly. *The Trumpeter of Krakow*
Paton Walsh. *The Emperor's Winding Sheet*

Pyle. *Men of Iron*
Skurzynski. *Manwolf*
Temple. *The Ramsay Scallop*
Thomson. *Morning Star of the Reformation*
Wheeler. *All Men Tall*

Biography

Banfield. *Joan of Arc*
Brooks. *Beyond the Myth: Joan of Arc*

Hull. *The Travels of Marco Polo*
Nardo. *The Trial of Joan of Arc*

Wepman. *Tamerlane*

Collective Biography

Axelrod. *Dictators and Tyrants*
Duffy. *Czar: Russia's Rulers*

Wilkinson. *People Who Changed the World*
Wilkinson. *Scientists Who Changed the World*

Wilkinson. *Statesmen Who Changed the World*

History

Alchemy: The Art of Knowing
The Birth of Modern Europe
Capek. *Artistic Trickery: Trompe L'Oeil Art*
Davis. *Man-Made Catastrophes*
Fradin. *Medicine: Yesterday, Today, and Tomorrow*
Gravett. *The World of the Medieval Knight*
Hernandez. *Barmi*

Hinds. *The Celts of Northern Europe*
Jones. *Crusades*
Kort. *Russia*
Lace. *England*
Lace. *The Little Princes in the Tower*
Mysticism: The Experience of the Divine
Osman. *The Italian Renaissance*

Paris. *The End of Days*
Pickford. *The Atlas of Shipwrecks & Treasure*
Ross. *Monarchs of Scotland*
Scharfstein. *Understanding Jewish History*
Spangenburg. *The History of Science from the Ancient Greeks to the Scientific Revolution*

Multimedia

CD-ROM

Art & Music: The Renaissance
Castle Explorer
Events That Changed the
World
Great Artists

History Through Art:
Renaissance
Ideas That Changed the World
Inside the Vatican

Le Louvre: The Palace & Its
Paintings
Teach Your Kids World
History

Video

The Black Death, 1361
Budapest
Early Italian Renaissance:
Brunelleschi, Donatello,
Masaccio
The Fall of Byzantium, 1453
Ferdinand and Isabella

The History of Orthodox
Christianity
The Longest Hatred: The
History of Anti-Semitism
Medieval Times: Life in the
Middle Ages (1000-1450
AD)

Ottoman Empire
Spain: History and Culture
The Warrior
The World Reborn

GRADES ELEVEN AND TWELVE

Historical Fiction

Anand. *Crown of Roses*
Anand. *The Ruthless Yeomen*
Anand. *Women of Ashdon*
Baumann. *The Barque of the
Brothers*
Bosse. *Captives of Time*
Doherty. *A Tapestry of
Murders*
Doherty. *A Tournament of
Murders*
Grace. *The Eye of God*
Grace. *A Shrine of Murders*
Harding. *Red Slayer*

Holland. *The Lords of
Vaumartin*
Kelly. *The Trumpeter of
Krakow*
Lopez-Medina. *Siguiriya*
Medeiros. *Fairest of Them All*
Penman. *The Sunne in
Splendor*
Pyle. *Men of Iron*
Quick. *Mystique*
Riley. *In Pursuit of the Green
Lion*
Riley. *A Vision of Light*
Robb. *The King's Bishop*

Robb. *The Lady Chapel*
Robb. *The Riddle of St.
Leonard's*
Sedley. *Death and the
Chapman*
Sedley. *The Holy Innocents*
Sedley. *The Plymouth Cloak*
Sedley. *The Weaver's Tale*
Skurzynski. *Manwolf*
Temple. *The Ramsay Scallop*
Thomson. *Morning Star of
the Reformation*
Wheeler. *All Men Tall*

Biography

Banfield. *Joan of Arc*
Brooks. *Beyond the Myth:
Joan of Arc*

Nardo. *The Trial of Joan of Arc*
Weir. *Wars of the Roses*
Wepman. *Tamerlane*

Collective Biography

Axelrod. *Dictators and
Tyrants*

Boorstin. *The Creators*
Duffy. *Czar: Russia's Rulers*

Rabb. *Renaissance Lives*

History

Alchemy: The Art of Knowing
Beckett. *The Story of Painting*
Bremness. *Herbs*
Brown. *Christianity*
Bunson. *Encyclopedia of the
Middle Ages*
Capek. *Artistic Trickery:
Trompe L'Oeil Art*
Castello. *The Jews and
Europe*
Cole. *Perspective*
Davidson. *Everyday Life
Through the Ages*

Davis. *Man-Made
Catastrophes*
Gottlieb. *The Family in the
Western World*
Hanawalt. *Growing up in
Medieval London*
Hernandez. *Barmi*
Hibbert. *Florence*
Hibbert. *Venice*
Hughes. *Barcelona*
Jones. *Crusades*
Keegan. *History of Warfare*

Lace. *The Little Princes in the
Tower*
Mysticism: The Experience of
the Divine
Pickford. *The Atlas of
Shipwrecks & Treasure*
Porter. *London, a Social
History*
Ross. *Monarchs of Scotland*
Scharfstein. *Understanding
Jewish History*

Smith. *Fascinating People and Astounding Events from the History of the Western World*

Spangenburg. *The History of Science from the Ancient Greeks to the Scientific Revolution.*

Wroe. *Life in a Partitioned Town in Fourteenth-Century France*

Multimedia

CD-ROM

Art & Music: The Renaissance
Castle Explorer
Events That Changed the World
Great Artists

History Through Art: Renaissance
Ideas That Changed the World
Inside the Vatican

Le Louvre: The Palace & Its Paintings
Teach Your Kids World History

Video

The Black Death, 1361
The Byzantine Empire
Early Italian Renaissance: Brunelleschi, Donatello, Masaccio
The Fall of Byzantium
The Fall of Byzantium, 1453
Ferdinand and Isabella

The History of Orthodox Christianity
The Longest Hatred: The History of Anti-Semitism
Medieval Times: Life in the Middle Ages (1000-1450 AD)
The National Monarchies

Ottoman Empire
The Renaissance and the Age of Discovery
The Rise of the Middle Class
The Rise of the Trading Cities
The Warrior
The World Reborn

Europe and the British Isles, 1492-1649

GRADE SEVEN

Historical Fiction

Beatty. *Master Rosalind*
Conrad. *Pedro's Journal*
De Treviño. *I, Juán de Pareja*
Dillon. *The Seekers*
Graham. *A Boy and His Bear*
Harnett. *The Merchant's Mark*
Harnett. *Stars of Fortune*
Haugaard. *Cromwell's Boy*

Haugaard. *A Messenger for Parliament*
Hayner. *The Foundling*
Hunter. *The Spanish Letters*
Hunter. *The 13th Member*
Hunter. *You Never Knew Her As I Did!*
Kisling. *The Fool's War*
Langenus. *Mission West*

Litowinsky. *The High Voyage*
Matas. *The Burning Time*
Morrison. *Neptune's Fountain: A Young Sculptor in Renaissance Italy*
Pope. *The Perilous Gard*
Stolz. *Bartholomew Fair*
Trease. *A Flight of Angels*

Biography

Alper. *Forgotten Voyager: Amerigo Vespucci*
Ash. *Vasco Núñez de Balboa*
Bard. *Sir Francis Drake and the Struggle for an Ocean Empire*
Bernhard. *Pizarro, Orellana, and the Exploration of the Amazon*
Blassingame. *Ponce de León*
Burch. *Isabella of Castile: Queen on Horseback*
Bush. *Elizabeth I*
Chrisman. *Hernando de Soto*
Codye. *Queen Isabella I*
Dodge. *Christopher Columbus and the First Voyages*
Dolan. *Juan Ponce de León*
Dwyer. *Henry VIII*
Dyson. *Westward with Columbus*

Hitzeroth. *Galileo Galilei*
Langley. *The Voyages of Christopher Columbus*
Levinson. *Christopher Columbus*
Lilley. *Hernando Cortés*
Marrin. *The Sea King: Sir Francis Drake*
Mason. *Leonardo da Vinci: An Introduction*
Mason. *Michelangelo: An Introduction*
McLanathan. *Leonardo da Vinci*
McLanathan. *Michaelangelo*
Meltzer. *Columbus and the World Around Him*
Muhlberger. *What Makes a Bruegel a Bruegel?*
Muhlberger. *What Makes a Leonardo a Leonardo?*
Noonan. *Ferdinand Magellan*

Parker. *Galileo and the Universe*
Pelta. *Discovering Christopher Columbus*
Pescio. *Rembrandt and SeventeenthCentury Holland*
Roop. *I, Columbus: My Journal—1942-3*
Stanley. *Good Queen Bess*
Stanley. *Leonardo Da Vinci*
Sterckx. *Brueghel: A Gift for Telling Stories*
Twist. *Christopher Columbus*
Weisberg. *Coronado's Golden Quest*
West. *Christopher Columbus*
Whitman. *Hernando de Soto*
Yount. *William Harvey*
Yue. *Christopher Columbus*

Collective Biography

Anderson. *Explorers Who Found New Worlds*
Cohen. *Real Vampires*
Cush. *Artists Who Created Great Works*
Fritz. *Around the World in a Hundred Years*
Glubok. *Great Lives: Painting*
Hazell. *Heroes: Great Men Through the Ages*

Hazell. *Heroines: Great Women Through the Ages*
Hoobler. *French Portraits*
Hoobler. *Italian Portraits*
Hoobler. *Russian Portraits*
Jacobs. *Great Lives: World Religions*
Krull. *Lives of the Artists*
Krull. *Lives of the Musicians*

Krull. *Lives of the Writers*
Wilkinson. *Generals Who Changed the World*
Wilkinson. *People Who Changed the World*
Wilkinson. *Scientists Who Changed the World*
Wilkinson. *Statesmen Who Changed the World*

History

Carrion. *The Empire of the Czars*
Child. *The Rise of Islam*
Clare. *Italian Renaissance*
Clements. *An Illustrated History of the World*
Corzine. *The Black Death*
Davies. *Transport*
Evans. *Freedom of Speech*
Evans. *Freedom of the Press*
Finkelstein. *The Other 1492*
Fradin. *Medicine: Yesterday, Today, and Tomorrow*
Franck. *Around Africa and Asia by Sea*
Garfunkel. *On Wings of Joy: Ballet*
Giblin. *Be Seated: A Book About Chairs*
Hernandez. *Barmi*
Kerr. *Keeping Clean*
Kort. *Russia*
Kramer. *Exploration and Empire: Science*
Lace. *Defeat of the Spanish Armada*
Lace. *England*
Macaulay. *Ship*
MacDonald. *Cities*
MacDonald. *Exploring the World*
Marrin. *The Sea Rovers*
Marshall. *Ocean Traders*
Martell. *The Age of Discovery*
Maurer. *Airborne*
McHugh. *Western Art 1600-1800*
Morley. *Clothes*
Morley. *Exploring North America*
Osman. *The Italian Renaissance*
Perl. *Why We Dress the Way We Do*
Platt. *Pirate*
Platt. *The Smithsonian Visual Timeline of Inventions*
Ross. *Conquerors and Explorers*
Ross. *Elizabethan Life*
Ross. *Shakespeare and Macbeth*
Singman. *Daily Life in Elizabethan England*
Spencer. *Germany: Then and Now*
Steele. *Kidnapping*
Steele. *Smuggling*
Stein. *Witches: Opposing Viewpoints*
Van der Linde. *The White Stallions*
Ventura. *Clothing*
Ventura. *Food*
Ventura. *1492*
Wetterau. *World History*
Wilkinson. *Amazing Buildings*
Williams. *The Age of Discovery*
Wood. *The Renaissance*
Woolf. *Picture This: A First Introduction to Paintings*
Yancey. *Life in the Elizabethan Theater*

Multimedia

CD-ROM

Art & Music: The Baroque
Art & Music: The Eighteenth Century
Art & Music: The Renaissance
Eyewitness Encyclopedia of Science
Great Artists
History Through Art: Baroque
History Through Art: Renaissance
Le Louvre: The Palace and Its Paintings
Stowaway!
Teach Your Kids World History

Video

Art and Splendor: Michelangelo and the Sistine Chapel
Biography: William Shakespeare—Life of Drama
The British Way of Life
Budapest
Europe: Insular Region
Ferdinand and Isabella
France: History and Culture
Galileo: The Solar System
Hernán Cortés
London: City of Majesty
Martin Frobisher's Gold Mine
Martin Luther: Beginning of the Reformation
Martin Luther: Translating the Bible
Painted Princess
Pilgrims and Puritans: The Struggle for Religious Freedom in England
Pirates: Passion and Plunder
Poland: A Proud Heritage
Spain: History and Culture
This Just In . . . Columbus Has Landed
Trees Cry for Rain: A Sephardic Journey
Trompe L'Oeil: Paintings That Fool the Eye
Ukraine: Kiev and Luov
The Vistula
Zwingli & Calvin

> **GRADE EIGHT**

Historical Fiction

Beatty. *Master Rosalind*
Conrad. *Pedro's Journal*
De Treviño. *I, Juan de Pareja*
Dillon. *The Seekers*
Graham. *A Boy and His Bear*
Harnett. *The Merchant's Mark*
Harnett. *Stars of Fortune*
Haugaard. *Cromwell's Boy*
Haugaard. *A Messenger for Parliament*
Hayner. *The Foundling*
Hunter. *The Spanish Letters*

Hunter. *The 13th Member*
Hunter. *You Never Knew Her
As I Did!*

Kisling. *The Fool's War*
Langenus. *Mission West*
Litowinsky. *The High Voyage*

Matas. *The Burning Time*
Pope. *The Perilous Gard*
Stolz. *Bartholomew Fair*

Biography

Alper. *Forgotten Voyager:
Amerigo Vespucci*
Ash. *Vasco Núñez De Balboa*
Bard. *Sir Francis Drake*
Bernhard. *Pizarro, Orellana,
and the Exploration of the
Amazon*
Burch. *Isabella of Castile:
Queen on Horseback*
Bush. *Elizabeth I*
Butson. *Ivan the Terrible*
Dodge. *Christopher
Columbus and the First
Voyages*
Dolan. *Juan Ponce de León*
Dwyer. *Henry VIII*
Dwyer. *James I*
Glossop. *Cardinal Richelieu*
Goldberg. *Miguel de
Cervantes*
Haney. *Cesare Borgia*
Hargrove. *Ferdinand
Magellan*
Hitzeroth. *Galileo Galilei*
Kaplan. *Oliver Cromwell*

Langley. *The Voyages of
Christopher Columbus*
Levinson. *Christopher
Columbus*
Lilley. *Hernando Cortés*
Marrin. *The Sea King: Sir
Francis Drake*
Mason. *Leonardo Da Vinci:
An Introduction*
Mason. *Michelangelo: An
Introduction*
McLanathan. *Leonardo da
Vinci*
McLanathan. *Michaelangelo*
Meltzer. *Columbus and the
World Around Him*
Muhlberger. *What Makes a
Bruegel a Bruegel?*
Muhlberger. *What Makes a
Leonardo a Leonardo?*
Noonan. *Ferdinand Magellan*
Parker. *Galileo and the
Universe*
Pelta. *Discovering
Christopher Columbus*

Pescio. *Rembrandt and
Seventeenth-Century
Holland*
Roop. *I, Columbus: My
Journal—1942-3*
Stanley. *Good Queen Bess*
Stepanek. *Martin Luther*
Stepanek. *Mary Queen of
Scots*
Sterckx. *Brueghel: A Gift for
Telling Stories*
Stevens. *Ferdinand and
Isabella*
Twist. *Christopher Columbus*
Twist. *James Cook: Across
the Pacific to Australia*
Weisberg. *Coronado's
Golden Quest*
Wepman. *Hernán Cortéz*
West. *Christopher Columbus*
Whitman. *Hernando de Soto*
Yount. *William Harvey*
Yue. *Christopher Columbus*

Collective Biography

Anderson. *Explorers Who
Found New Worlds*
Cohen. *Real Vampires*
Cush. *Artists Who Created
Great Works*
Glubok. *Great Lives: Painting*
Hazell. *Heroes: Great Men
Through the Ages*

Hazell. *Heroines: Great
Women Through the Ages*
Hoobler. *French Portraits*
Hoobler. *Italian Portraits*
Hoobler. *Russian Portraits*
Krull. *Lives of the Artists*
Krull. *Lives of the Musicians*
Krull. *Lives of the Writers*

Wilkinson. *Generals Who
Changed the World*
Wilkinson. *People Who
Changed the World*
Wilkinson. *Scientists Who
Changed the World*
Wilkinson. *Statesmen Who
Changed the World*

History

Bachrach. *The Inquisition*
Carrion. *The Empire of the Czars*
Child. *The Rise of Islam*
Clare. *Italian Renaissance*
Clements. *An Illustrated
History of the World*
Davies. *Transport*
Evans. *Freedom of Speech*
Evans. *Freedom of the Press*
Finkelstein. *The Other 1492*
Flowers. *The Reformation*
Fradin. *Medicine: Yesterday,
Today, and Tomorrow*
Franck. *Around Africa and
Asia by Sea*
Garfunkel. *On Wings of Joy:
Ballet*
Giblin. *Be Seated: A Book
About Chairs*

Hernandez. *Barmi*
Kort. *Russia*
Kramer. *Exploration and
Empire: Science*
Kronenwetter. *Northern
Ireland*
Lace. *Defeat of the Spanish
Armada*
Lace. *England*
Levy. *Women in Society: Britain*
Levy. *Women in Society:
Ireland*
Macaulay. *Ship*
MacDonald. *Cities*
Marrin. *The Sea Rovers*
Marshall. *Ocean Traders*
Maurer. *Airborne*
McHugh. *Western Art
1600-1800*

Meltzer. *How Our Youngest
Workers Are Exploited and
Abused*
Morley. *Clothes*
Mulcahy. *Diseases: Finding
the Cure*
Osman. *The Italian Renaissance*
Perl. *Why We Dress the Way
We Do*
Platt. *Pirate*
Platt. *The Smithsonian Visual
Timeline of Inventions*
Ross. *Elizabethan Life*
Ross. *Shakespeare and
Macbeth*
Singman. *Daily Life in
Elizabethan England*
Spencer. *Germany: Then and
Now*

Stein. *Witches: Opposing Viewpoints*
Strom. *The Expulsion of the Jews*
Van der Linde. *The White Stallions*

Ventura. *Clothing*
Ventura. *Food*
Wetterau. *World History*
Williams. *The Age of Discovery*
Wood. *The Renaissance*

Woolf. *Picture This: A First Introduction to Paintings*
Yancey. *Life in the Elizabethan Theater*

Multimedia

CD-ROM

Art & Music: The Baroque
Art & Music: The Eighteenth Century
Art & Music: The Renaissance
Eyewitness Encyclopedia of Science

Great Artists
History Through Art: Baroque
History Through Art: Renaissance
Le Louvre: The Palace and Its Paintings

Stowaway!
Teach Your Kids World History

Video

Art and Splendor: Michelangelo and the Sistine Chapel
Biography: William Shakespeare—Life of Drama
The British Way of Life
Budapest
Ferdinand and Isabella
France: History and Culture
Galileo: The Solar System
Hernán Cortés

London: City of Majesty
Martin Frobisher's Gold Mine
Martin Luther: Beginning of the Reformation
Martin Luther: Translating the Bible
Painted Princess
Pilgrims and Puritans: The Struggle for Religious Freedom in England
Pirates: Passion and Plunder

Poland: A Proud Heritage
Spain: History and Culture
This Just In . . . Columbus Has Landed
Trees Cry for Rain: A Sephardic Journey
Trompe L'Oeil: Paintings That Fool the Eye
Ukraine: Kiev and Luov
The Vistula
Zwingli and Calvin

GRADE NINE

Historical Fiction

Beatty. *Master Rosalind*
Conrad. *Pedro's Journal*
De Treviño. *I, Juan de Pareja*
Dhondy. *Black Swan*
Dillon. *The Seekers*
Graham. *A Boy and His Bear*
Harnett. *The Merchant's Mark*
Haugaard. *Cromwell's Boy*

Haugaard. *A Messenger for Parliament*
Hayner. *The Foundling*
Hunter. *The 13th Member*
Hunter. *You Never Knew Her As I Did!*
Llywelyn. *The Last Prince of Ireland*
Matas. *The Burning Time*

Pope. *The Perilous Gard*
Willard. *A Cold Wind Blowing*
Willard. *The Eldest Son*
Willard. *A Flight of Swans*
Willard. *Harrow and Harvest*
Willard. *The Iron Lily*
Willard. *The Lark and the Laurel*
Willard. *The Sprig of Broom*

Biography

Bard. *Sir Francis Drake*
Bernhard. *Pizarro, Orellana, and the Exploration of the Amazon*
Bush. *Elizabeth I*
Butson. *Ivan the Terrible*
Columbus. *The Log of Christopher Columbus*
Dolan. *Juan Ponce de León*
Dwyer. *Henry VIII*
Dwyer. *James I*
Erickson. *The First Elizabeth*
Erickson. *Great Catherine*
Erickson. *Mistress Anne: Anne Boleyn*

Glossop. *Cardinal Richelieu*
Goldberg. *Miguel de Cervantes*
Haney. *Cesare Borgia*
Hargrove. *Ferdinand Magellan*
Hitzeroth. *Galileo Galilei*
Kaplan. *Oliver Cromwell*
Lilley. *Hernando Cortés*
Marrin. *The Sea King: Sir Francis Drake*
Mason. *Leonardo Da Vinci: An Introduction*
Mason. *Michelangelo: An Introduction*

McLanathan. *Leonardo da Vinci*
McLanathan. *Michaelangelo*
Meltzer. *Columbus and the World Around Him*
Muhlberger. *What Makes a Bruegel a Bruegel?*
Muhlberger. *What Makes a Leonardo a Leonardo?*
Parker. *Galileo and the Universe*
Pelta. *Discovering Christopher Columbus*

Pescio. *Rembrandt and Seventeenth Century Holland*
Reti. *The Unknown Leonardo*
Stanley. *Good Queen Bess*
Stepanek. *Martin Luther*

Stepanek. *Mary Queen of Scots*
Sterckx. *Brueghel: A Gift for Telling Stories*
Stevens. *Ferdinand and Isabella*

Weisberg. *Coronado's Golden Quest*
Wepman. *Hernán Cortéz*
West. *Christopher Columbus*
Whitman. *Hernando de Soto*
Wilford. *The Mysterious History of Columbus*

Collective Biography

Anderson. *Explorers Who Found New Worlds*
Burton. *Journeys of the Great Explorers*
Cush. *Artists Who Created Great Works*
Glubok. *Great Lives: Painting*

Hoobler. *French Portraits*
Hoobler. *Italian Portraits*
Hoobler. *Russian Portraits*
Lomask. *Great Lives: Exploration*
Wilkinson. *People Who Changed the World*

Wilkinson. *Generals Who Changed the World*
Wilkinson. *Scientists Who Changed the World*
Wilkinson. *Statesmen Who Changed the World*

History

Bachrach. *The Inquisition*
Child. *The Rise of Islam*
Clare. *Italian Renaissance*
Evans. *Freedom of Speech*
Evans. *Freedom of the Press*
Finkelstein. *The Other 1492*
Flowers. *The Reformation*
Fradin. *Medicine: Yesterday, Today, and Tomorrow*
Franck. *Around Africa and Asia by Sea*
Garfunkel. *On Wings of Joy: Ballet*
Hernandez. *Barmi*
Kort. *Russia*
Kronenwetter. *Northern Ireland*
Lace. *Defeat of the Spanish Armada*
Lace. *England*

Levy. *Women in Society: Britain*
Levy. *Women In Society: Ireland*
Macaulay. *Ship*
Marshall. *Ocean Traders*
McHugh. *Western Art 1600-1800*
Meltzer. *How Our Youngest Workers Are Exploited and Abused*
Mulcahy. *Diseases: Finding the Cure*
Osman. *The Italian Renaissance*
Perl. *Why We Dress the Way We Do*
Platt. *The Smithsonian Visual Timeline of Inventions*
Ross. *Elizabethan Life*

Ross. *Shakespeare and Macbeth*
Singman. *Daily Life in Elizabethan England*
Spangenburg. *The History of Science from the Ancient Greeks to the Scientific Revolution*
Spencer. *Germany: Then and Now*
Stein. *Witches: Opposing Viewpoints*
Strom. *The Expulsion of the Jews*
Wetterau. *World History*
Wood. *The Renaissance*
Yancey. *Life in the Elizabethan Theater*

Multimedia

CD-ROM

Art & Music: The Renaissance
Events That Changed the World
Great Artists
History Through Art: Renaissance

Ideas That Changed the World
Inside the Vatican
Le Louvre: The Palace and Its Paintings
Renaissance of Florence

Stowaway!
Teach Your Kids World History

Video

Art and Splendor: Michelangelo and the Sistine Chapel
Biography: William Shakespeare—Life of Drama
Budapest
Ferdinand and Isabella
France: History and Culture
Galileo: The Solar System
Granada, 1492
Hernán Cortés
The History of Orthodox Christianity

John Locke
London: City of Majesty
Martin Frobisher's Gold Mine
Martin Luther: Beginning of the Reformation
Martin Luther: Translating the Bible
Painted Princess
Pilgrims and Puritans: The Struggle for Religious Freedom in England
Pirates: Passion and Plunder
The Polish Experience

Reformation Overview
Spain: History and Culture
This Just In . . . Columbus Has Landed
Trees Cry for Rain: A Sephardic Journey
Trompe L'Oeil: Paintings That Fool the Eye
The Vistula
Voyage of Martin Frobisher: A Quest for Gold
Zwingli & Calvin

GRADE TEN

Historical Fiction

Conrad. *Pedro's Journal*
De Treviño. *I, Juan de Pareja*
Dhondy. *Black Swan*
Dillon. *The Seekers*
Haugaard. *Cromwell's Boy*
Hunter. *You Never Knew Her As I Did!*
Llywelyn. *The Last Prince of Ireland*
Matas. *The Burning Time*
Otto. *The Passion Dream Book*
Willard. *A Cold Wind Blowing*
Willard. *The Eldest Son*
Willard. *A Flight of Swans*
Willard. *Harrow and Harvest*
Willard. *The Iron Lily*
Willard. *The Lark and the Laurel*
Willard. *The Sprig of Broom*

Biography

Bard. *Sir Francis Drake*
Bernhard. *Pizarro, Orellana, and the Exploration of the Amazon*
Bush. *Elizabeth I*
Butson. *Ivan the Terrible*
Columbus. *The Log of Christopher Columbus*
Dolan. *Juan Ponce de León*
Dwyer. *Henry VIII*
Dwyer. *James I*
Erickson. *The First Elizabeth*
Erickson. *Mistress Anne: Anne Boleyn*
Fraser. *Shakespeare*
Glossop. *Cardinal Richelieu*
Goldberg. *Miguel de Cervantes*
Haney. *Cesare Borgia*
Hargrove. *Ferdinand Magellan*
Hitzeroth. *Galileo Galilei*
Kaplan. *Oliver Cromwell*
Lilley. *Hernando Cortés*
Marrin. *The Sea King: Sir Francis Drake*
McLanathan. *Leonardo Da Vinci*
McLanathan. *Michaelangelo*
Parker. *Galileo and the Universe*
Pescio. *Rembrandt and Seventeenth Century Holland*
Reti. *The Unknown Leonardo*
Stepanek. *Martin Luther*
Stepanek. *Mary Queen of Scots*
Stevens. *Ferdinand and Isabella*
Wepman. *Hernán Cortéz*
West. *Christopher Columbus*
Wilford. *The Mysterious History of Columbus*

Collective Biography

Anderson. *Explorers Who Found New Worlds*
Axelrod. *Dictators and Tyrants*
Burton. *Journeys of the Great Explorers*
Duffy. *Czar: Russia's Rulers*
Lomask. *Great Lives: Exploration*
Wilkinson. *Generals Who Changed the World*
Wilkinson. *People Who Changed the World*
Wilkinson. *Scientists Who Changed the World*
Wilkinson. *Statesmen Who Changed the World*

History

Ardley. *Music: An Illustrated Encyclopedia*
Bachrach. *The Inquisition*
Cooper. *Renaissance*
Davis. *Man-Made Catastrophes*
Flowers. *The Reformation*
Fradin. *Medicine: Yesterday, Today, and Tomorrow*
Hernandez. *Barmi*
Hibbert. *Cavaliers and Roundheads*
Kort. *Russia*
Kronenwetter. *Northern Ireland*
Lace. *Defeat of the Spanish Armada*
Lace. *England*
Levy. *Women in Society: Britain*
Levy. *Women In Society: Ireland*
Marshall. *Ocean Traders*
McHugh. *Western Art 1600-1800*
Mulcahy. *Diseases: Finding the Cure*
Mysticism: The Experience of the Divine
Osman. *The Italian Renaissance*
Pickford. *The Atlas of Shipwrecks and Treasure*
Ross. *Elizabethan Life*
Ross. *Monarchs of Scotland*
Singman. *Daily Life in Elizabethan England*
Spangenburg. *The History of Science from the Ancient Greeks to the Scientific Revolution*
Strom. *The Expulsion of the Jews*
Yancey. *Life in the Elizabethan Theater*

Multimedia

CD-ROM

Art & Music: The Renaissance
Events That Changed the World
Great Artists
Ideas That Changed the World
Inside the Vatican
Le Louvre: The Palace and Its Paintings
Renaissance of Florence
Stowaway!
Teach Your Kids World History

Video

Art and Splendor:
  Michelangelo and the
  Sistine Chapel
The Artist
Biography: William
  Shakespeare—Life of Drama
Budapest
The Dissenter
Ferdinand and Isabella
Granada, 1492
Hernán Cortés

The History of Orthodox
  Christianity
The Longest Hatred: The
  History of Anti-Semitism
Martin Frobisher's Gold Mine
Painted Princess
Pilgrims and Puritans: The
  Struggle for Religious
  Freedom in England
The Polish Experience
The Prince

Reformation Overview
The Scientist
Spain: History and Culture
Trees Cry for Rain: A
  Sephardic Journey
Trompe L'Oeil: Paintings
  That Fool the Eye
Voyage of Martin Frobisher:
  A Quest for Gold
The World Reborn
Zwingli & Calvin

GRADES ELEVEN AND TWELVE

Historical Fiction

Buckley. To Shield the Queen
Chisholm. A Famine of
  Horses
Chisholm. A Season of Knives
Conrad. Pedro's Journal
Cowell. Nicholas Cooke
De Treviño. I, Juan de Pareja
Dhondy. Black Swan
Dillon. The Seekers
Emerson. Face Down in the
  Marrow-Bone Pie
Eyre. Dirge for a Doge
Garrett. Death of the Fox
Garrett. The Succession

Grace. The Book of Shadows
Herman. The Tears of the
  Madonna
Langenus. Mission West
Llywelyn. The Last Prince of
  Ireland
Marston. The Laughing
  Hangman
Marston. The Mad Courtesan
Marston. The Merry Devils
Marston. The Nine Giants
Marston. The Queen's Head
Marston. The Roaring Boy
Marston. The Silent Woman

Marston. The Trip to
  Jerusalem
Maxwell. The Secret Diary of
  Anne Boleyn
Otto. The Passion Dream
  Book
Willard. A Cold Wind Blowing
Willard. The Eldest Son
Willard. A Flight of Swans
Willard. Harrow and Harvest
Willard. The Iron Lily
Willard. The Lark and the
  Laurel
Willard. The Sprig of Broom

Biography

Bard. Sir Francis Drake
Bernhard. Pizarro, Orellana,
  and the Exploration of the
  Amazon
Bush. Elizabeth I
Butson. Ivan the Terrible
Columbus. The Log of
  Christopher Columbus
Dolan. Juan Ponce de León
Dwyer. Henry VIII
Dwyer. James I
Erickson. The First Elizabeth
Erickson. Mistress Anne:
  Anne Boleyn
Fernandez-Armesto.
  Columbus
Fraser. Shakespeare

Glossop. Cardinal Richelieu
Goldberg. Miguel de
  Cervantes
Haney. Cesare Borgia
Hargrove. Ferdinand
  Magellan
Hibbert. The Virgin Queen:
  Elizabeth I
Hitzeroth. Galileo Galilei
Kaplan. Oliver Cromwell
Lilley. Hernando Cortés
McLanathan. Leonardo Da
  Vinci
McLanathan. Michaelangelo
Pescio. Rembrandt and
  Seventeenth Century
  Holland

Reti. The Unknown Leonardo
Schwartz. Rembrandt
Stepanek. Martin Luther
Stepanek. Mary Queen of
  Scots
Stevens. Ferdinand and
  Isabella
Taviani. Columbus: The
  Great Adventure.
Weir. The Six Wives of Henry
  VIII
Wepman. Hernán Cortéz
Wilford. The Mysterious
  History of Columbus

Collective Biography

Anderson. Explorers Who
  Found New Worlds
Axelrod. Dictators and
  Tyrants

Boorstin. The Creators
Burton. Journeys of the Great
  Explorers
Duffy. Czar: Russia's Rulers

Lomask. Great Lives:
  Exploration
Rabb. Renaissance Lives
Wills. Certain Trumpets

History

Ardley. *Music: An Illustrated Encyclopedia*
Aymar. *Men in the Air*
Bachrach. *The Inquisition*
Beckett. *The Story of Painting*
Berleth. *The Twilight Lords*
Bremness. *Herbs*
Brown. *Christianity*
Castello. *The Jews and Europe*
Cole. *Perspective*
Cooper. *Renaissance*
Davidson. *Everyday Life Through the Ages*
Davis. *Man-Made Catastrophes*
Fernandez-Armesto. *Atlas of World Exploration*
Flowers. *The Reformation*
Gottlieb. *The Family in the Western World*

Hernandez. *Barmi*
Hibbert. *Cavaliers and Roundheads*
Hibbert. *Florence*
Hibbert. *Rome*
Hughes. *Barcelona*
Keegan. *History of Warfare*
Lace. *Defeat of the Spanish Armada*
Lace. *England*
Levy. *Women in Society: Britain*
Levy. *Women in Society: Ireland*
Marshall. *Ocean Traders*
McLynn. *Famous Trials*
Mysticism: The Experience of the Divine
Ozment. *The Bürghermeister's Daughter*

Paiewonsky. *Conquest of Eden*
Pickford. *The Atlas of Shipwrecks and Treasure*
Porter. *London, a Social History*
Ross. *Elizabethan Life*
Ross. *Monarchs of Scotland*
Singman. *Daily Life in Elizabethan England*
Smith. *Fascinating People and Astounding Events from the History of the Western World*
Strom. *The Expulsion of the Jews*
Weir. *The Princes in the Tower*
Wilson. *The Circumnavigators*

Multimedia

CD-ROM

Art & Music: The Renaissance
Events That Changed the World
Great Artists
History Through Art: Renaissance

Ideas That Changed the World
Inside the Vatican
Le Louvre: The Palace and Its Paintings
Renaissance of Florence
Stowaway!

Teach Your Kids World History

Video

Art and Splendor: Michelangelo and the Sistine Chapel
The Artist
Biography: William Shakespeare—Life of Drama
The Dissenter
Ferdinand and Isabella
Granada, 1492
Hernán Cortés

The History of Orthodox Christianity
The Longest Hatred: The History of Anti-Semitism
Martin Frobisher's Gold Mine
Pilgrims and Puritans: The Struggle for Religious Freedom in England
The Polish Experience
The Prince
The Reformation

Reformation Overview
The Renaissance and the New World
The Scientist
Trompe L'Oeil: Paintings That Fool the Eye
Voyage of Martin Frobisher: A Quest for Gold
The Wars of Religion
The World Reborn
Zwingli and Calvin

Europe and the British Isles, 1650-1788

Historical Fiction

Almedingen. *The Crimson Oak*
Almedingen. *Young Mark*
Anderson. *The Druid's Gift*
Beatty. *Campion Towers*
Burton. *Beyond the Weir Bridge*
Burton. *To Ravensrigg*
Calvert. *Hadder MacColl*
Carter. *Children of the Book*
Dick. *False Coin, True Coin*
Forman. *Prince Charlie's Year*
Garfield. *Black Jack*
Garfield. *The December Rose*

Garfield. *Devil-in-the-Fog*
Garfield. *Drummer Boy*
Garfield. *The Empty Sleeve*
Garfield. *Footsteps*
Garfield. *Jack Holborn*
Garfield. *The Night of the Comet*
Garfield. *Smith*
Garfield. *Young Nick and Jubilee*
Greene. *One Foot Ashore*
Greene. *Out of Many Waters*
Harnett. *The Great House*
Hautzig. *Riches*
Hawes. *The Dark Frigate*

Hendry. *Quest for a Kelpie*
Hersom. *The Half Child*
Hunter. *The Ghosts of Glencoe*
Hunter. *The Lothian Run*
McGraw. *Master Cornhill*
Morrison. *Neptune's Fountain: A Young Sculptor in Renaissance Italy*
Sonnleitner. *The Cave Children*
Sutcliff. *Flame-Colored Taffeta*
Wulffson. *The Upside-Down Ship*

Biography

Anderson. *Carl Linnaeus: Father of Classification*
Anderson. *Isaac Newton: The Greatest Scientist of All Time*
Blakely. *Wolfgang Amadeus Mozart*
Blumberg. *The Remarkable Voyages of Captain Cook*
Dolan. *Junípero Serra*
Hargrove. *René-Robert Cavelier Sieur de la Salle*

Hitzeroth. *Sir Isaac Newton*
Langley. *The Expeditions of James Cook*
McGuire. *Catherine the Great*
McTavish. *Isaac Newton*
Noonan. *Captain Cook*
Parker. *Isaac Newton and Gravity*
Sherman. *Henry Stanley and the European Explorers of Africa*
Switzer. *The Magic of Mozart*

Thompson. *Wolfgang Amadeus Mozart*
Twist. *James Cook*
Vernon. *Introducing Bach*
Vernon. *Introducing Mozart*
Yount. *Antoni Van Leeuwenhoek: First to See Microscopic Life*

Collective Biography

Anderson. *Explorers Who Found New Worlds*
Cohen. *Real Vampires*
Cush. *Artists Who Created Great Works*
Fritz. *Around the World in a Hundred Years*
Glubok. *Great Lives: Painting*

Hoobler. *French Portraits*
Hoobler. *Italian Portraits*
Hoobler. *Russian Portraits*
Jacobs. *Great Lives: World Religions*
Krull. *Lives of the Artists*
Krull. *Lives of the Musicians*
Krull. *Lives of the Writers*

Wilkinson. *Generals Who Changed the World*
Wilkinson. *People Who Changed the World*
Wilkinson. *Scientists Who Changed the World*
Wilkinson. *Statesmen Who Changed the World*

History

Biel. *The Black Death*
Child. *The Rise of Islam*
Clare. *Industrial Revolution*

Clements. *An Illustrated History of the World*
Corzine. *The Black Death*

Davies. *Transport*
Evans. *Freedom of Speech*
Evans. *Freedom of the Press*

Fradin. *Medicine: Yesterday, Today, and Tomorrow*
Garfunkel. *On Wings of Joy: Ballet*
Giblin. *Be Seated: A Book About Chairs*
Giblin. *When Plague Strikes*
Greene. *Child Labor*
Hernandez. *Barmi*
Kerr. *Keeping Clean*
Kort. *Russia*
Kotlyarskaya. *Women in Society: Russia*
Kramer. *Exploration and Empire: Science*
Kronenwetter. *Northern Ireland*
Lace. *England*
Levy. *Women in Society: Britain*

Levy. *Women in Society: Ireland*
MacDonald. *Cities*
Marrin. *The Sea Rovers*
Marshall. *Ocean Traders*
Maurer. *Airborne*
McHugh. *Western Art 1600-1800*
Meltzer. *How Our Youngest Workers Are Exploited and Abused*
Morley. *Clothes*
Morley. *Exploring North America*
Mulcahy. *Diseases: Finding the Cure*
Perl. *Why We Dress the Way We Do*
Platt. *Pirate*
Platt. *The Smithsonian Visual Timeline of Inventions*

Reynoldson. *Conflict and Change*
Ross. *Conquerors and Explorers*
Spencer. *Germany: Then and Now*
Steele. *Kidnapping*
Steele. *Smuggling*
Stein. *Witches: Opposing Viewpoints*
Swisher. *The Glorious Revolution*
Ventura. *Clothing*
Ventura. *Food*
Wetterau. *World History*
Wilkinson. *Amazing Buildings*
Williams. *The Age of Discovery*
Woolf. *Picture This: A First Introduction to Paintings*

Multimedia

CD-ROM

Art & Music: The Baroque
Art & Music: The Eighteenth Century
Art & Music: The Renaissance
Eyewitness Encyclopedia of Science

Great Artists
History Through Art: Baroque
History Through Art: Renaissance
Le Louvre: The Palace & Its Paintings

Stowaway!
Teach Your Kids World History

Video

The Age of Reason: Europe After the Renaissance
The British Way of Life
Budapest
Europe: Insular Region
France: History and Culture

The Industrial Revolution
London: City of Majesty
Painted Princess
Pirates: Passion and Plunder
Poland: A Proud Heritage
Spain: History and Culture

Trompe L'Oeil: Paintings That Fool the Eye
Two Hundred Years of Mozart
Ukraine: Kiev and Luov
The Vistula

GRADE EIGHT

Historical Fiction

Almedingen. *The Crimson Oak*
Almedingen. *Young Mark*
Anderson. *The Druid's Gift*
Beatty. *Campion Towers*
Burton. *Beyond the Weir Bridge*
Burton. *To Ravensrigg*
Calvert. *Hadder MacColl*
Forman. *Prince Charlie's Year*
Garfield. *Black Jack*
Garfield. *The December Rose*

Garfield. *Devil-in-the-Fog*
Garfield. *Drummer Boy*
Garfield. *The Empty Sleeve*
Garfield. *Footsteps*
Garfield. *Jack Holborn*
Garfield. *The Night of the Comet*
Garfield. *Smith*
Greene. *One Foot Ashore*
Greene. *Out of Many Waters*
Harnett. *The Great House*
Hautzig. *Riches*
Hawes. *The Dark Frigate*

Hendry. *Quest for a Kelpie*
Hersom. *The Half Child*
Hunter. *The Ghosts of Glencoe*
Hunter. *The Lothian Run*
McGraw. *Master Cornhill*
Sonnleitner. *The Cave Children*
Sutcliff. *Flame-Colored Taffeta*
Wulffson. *The Upside-Down Ship*

Biography

Anderson. *Carl Linnaeus: Father of Classification*
Anderson. *Isaac Newton: The Greatest Scientist of All Time*
Blakely. *Wolfgang Amadeus Mozart*
Blumberg. *The Remarkable Voyages of Captain Cook*
Carson. *Maximilien Robespierre*
Christianson. *Isaac Newton and the Scientific Revolution*
Dolan. *Junípero Serra*

Hargrove. *René-Robert Cavelier Sieur de La Salle*
Hitzeroth. *Sir Isaac Newton*
Horn. *King Louis XIV*
Kaplan. *Oliver Cromwell*
Kittredge. *Frederick the Great: King of Prussia*
Langley. *The Expeditions of James Cook*
Lilley. *Hernando Cortés*
Marrin. *The Sea King: Sir Francis Drake*
Mason. *Leonardo Da Vinci: An Introduction*

Mason. *Michelangelo: An Introduction*
McDermott. *Peter the Great*
McGuire. *Catherine the Great*
Noonan. *Captain Cook*
Sherman. *Henry Stanley and the European Explorers of Africa*
Switzer. *The Magic of Mozart*
Thompson. *Wolfgang Amadeus Mozart*
Twist. *James Cook: Across the Pacific to Australia*

Collective Biography

Anderson. *Explorers Who Found New Worlds*
Cohen. *Real Vampires*
Cush. *Artists Who Created Great Works*
Glubok. *Great Lives: Painting*
Hoobler. *French Portraits*

Hoobler. *Italian Portraits*
Hoobler. *Russian Portraits*
Krull. *Lives of the Artists*
Krull. *Lives of the Musicians*
Krull. *Lives of the Writers*
Wilkinson. *Generals Who Changed the World*

Wilkinson. *People Who Changed the World*
Wilkinson. *Scientists Who Changed the World*
Wilkinson. *Statesmen Who Changed the World*

History

Biel. *The Black Death*
Carrion. *The Empire of the Czars*
Child. *The Rise of Islam*
Clare. *Industrial Revolution*
Clements. *An Illustrated History of the World*
Corzine. *The Black Death*
Cush. *Disasters That Shook the World*
Davies. *Transport*
Evans. *Freedom of Speech*
Evans. *Freedom of the Press*
Fradin. *Medicine: Yesterday, Today, and Tomorrow*
Garfunkel. *On Wings of Joy: Ballet*
Giblin. *Be Seated: A Book About Chairs*
Giblin. *When Plague Strikes*
Greene. *Child Labor*
Hernandez. *Barmi*
Kort. *Russia*

Kotlyarskaya. *Women in Society: Russia*
Kramer. *Exploration and Empire: Science*
Kronenwetter. *Northern Ireland*
Lace. *England*
Levy. *Women in Society: Britain*
Levy. *Women in Society: Ireland*
Macaulay. *Ship*
MacDonald. *Cities*
Marrin. *The Sea Rovers*
Marshall. *Ocean Traders*
Maurer. *Airborne*
McHugh. *Western Art 1600-1800*
Meltzer. *How Our Youngest Workers Are Exploited and Abused*
Morley. *Clothes*

Mulcahy. *Diseases: Finding the Cure*
Osman. *The Italian Renaissance*
Perl. *Why We Dress the Way We Do*
Platt. *Pirate*
Platt. *The Smithsonian Visual Timeline of Inventions*
Spencer. *Germany: Then and Now*
Stein. *Witches: Opposing Viewpoints*
Swisher. *The Glorious Revolution*
Ventura. *Clothing*
Ventura. *Food*
Wetterau. *World History*
Williams. *The Age of Discovery*
Woolf. *Picture This: A First Introduction to Paintings*

Multimedia

CD-ROM

Art & Music: The Baroque
Art & Music: The Eighteenth Century
Art & Music: The Renaissance
Eyewitness Encyclopedia of Science

Great Artists
History Through Art: Baroque
History Through Art: Renaissance
Le Louvre: The Palace & Its Paintings

Stowaway!
Teach Your Kids World History

Video

The Age of Reason: Europe
   After the Renaissance
The British Way of Life
Budapest
France: History and Culture
The Industrial Revolution

London: City of Majesty
Painted Princess
Pirates: Passion and Plunder
Poland: A Proud Heritage
The Soviet Union
Spain: History and Culture

Trompe L'Oeil: Paintings
   That Fool the Eye
Two Hundred Years of Mozart
Ukraine: Kiev and Luov
The Vistula

GRADE NINE

Historical Fiction

Almedingen. *The Crimson
   Oak*
Almedingen. *Young Mark*
Anderson. *The Druid's Gift*
Bartos-Hoppner. *The
   Cossacks*
Beatty. *Campion Towers*
Burton. *Beyond the Weir
   Bridge*
Burton. *To Ravensrigg*
Calvert. *Hadder MacColl*

Carter. *Children of the Book*
Dick. *False Coin, True Coin*
Forman. *Prince Charlie's
   Year*
Garfield. *Black Jack*
Garfield. *The December Rose*
Garfield. *Drummer Boy*
Garfield. *Jack Holborn*
Garfield. *Smith*
Hawes. *The Dark Frigate*
Hendry. *Quest for a Kelpie*

Hersom. *The Half Child*
Hess. *In Search of Honor*
Hunter. *The Ghosts of
   Glencoe*
Paton Walsh. *A Parcel of
   Patterns*
Sonnleitner. *The Cave
   Children*
Sutcliff. *Bonnie Dundee*

Biography

Blumberg. *The Remarkable
   Voyages of Captain Cook*
Campion. *Mother Ann Lee:
   Morning Star of the Shakers*
Carson. *Maximilien
   Robespierre*
Christianson. *Isaac Newton
   and the Scientific
   Revolution*
Dolan. *Junípero Serra*

Erickson. *Bonnie Prince
   Charlie*
Erickson. *Great Catherine*
Erickson. *To the Scaffold:
   Marie Antoinette*
Hitzeroth. *Sir Isaac Newton*
Horn. *King Louis XIV*
Kaplan. *Oliver Cromwell*
Kittredge. *Frederick the
   Great: King of Prussia*

McDermott. *Peter the Great*
McGuire. *Catherine the Great*
Sherman. *Henry Stanley and
   the European Explorers of
   Africa*
Thompson. *Wolfgang
   Amadeus Mozart*
Yount. *Antoni Van
   Leeuwenhoek: First to See
   Microscopic Life*

Collective Biography

Anderson. *Explorers Who
   Found New Worlds*
Burton. *Journeys of the Great
   Explorers*
Cush. *Artists Who Created
   Great Works*
Glubok. *Great Lives: Painting*

Hoobler. *French Portraits*
Hoobler. *Italian Portraits*
Hoobler. *Russian Portraits*
Lomask. *Great Lives:
   Exploration*
Wilkinson. *Generals Who
   Changed the World*

Wilkinson. *People Who
   Changed the World*
Wilkinson. *Scientists Who
   Changed the World*
Wilkinson. *Statesmen Who
   Changed the World*

History

Child. *The Rise of Islam*
Clare. *Industrial Revolution*
Cush. *Disasters That Shook
   the World*
Dale. *Early Cars*
Evans. *Freedom of Speech*
Evans. *Freedom of the Press*
Fradin. *Medicine: Yesterday,
   Today, and Tomorrow*
Garfunkel. *On Wings of Joy:
   Ballet*
Giblin. *When Plague Strikes*
Greene. *Child Labor*

Hernandez. *Barmi*
Kort. *Russia*
Kotlyarskaya. *Women in
   Society: Russia*
Kronenwetter. *Northern
   Ireland*
Lace. *England*
Levy. *Women in Society:
   Britain*
Levy. *Women in Society:
   Ireland*
Macaulay. *Ship*
Marshall. *Ocean Traders*

McHugh. *Western Art
   1600-1800*
Meltzer. *How Our Youngest
   Workers Are Exploited and
   Abused*
Mulcahy. *Diseases: Finding
   the Cure*
Perl. *Why We Dress the Way
   We Do*
Platt. *The Smithsonian Visual
   Timeline of Inventions*

Spangenburg. *The History of Science from the Ancient Greeks to the Scientific Revolution*

Spangenburg. *The History of Science in the Eighteenth Century*

Spencer. *Germany: Then and Now*

Stein. *Witches: Opposing Viewpoints*

Swisher. *The Glorious Revolution*

Wetterau. *World History*

Multimedia

CD-ROM

Art & Music: The Baroque
Art & Music: The Eighteenth Century
Events That Changed the World

History Through Art: Baroque
Ideas That Changed the World
Inside the Vatican
Le Louvre: The Palace & Its Paintings

Stowaway!
Teach Your Kids World History

Video

The Age of Reason: Europe After the Renaissance
Budapest
France: History and Culture
The History of Orthodox Christianity

The Industrial Revolution
John Locke
London: City of Majesty
Painted Princess
Pirates: Passion and Plunder
The Polish Experience

Spain: History and Culture
Trompe L'Oeil: Paintings That Fool the Eye
Two Hundred Years of Mozart
The Vistula

GRADE TEN

Historical Fiction

Almedingen. *The Crimson Oak*
Almedingen. *Young Mark*
Bartos-Hoppner. *The Cossacks*
Beatty. *Campion Towers*
Burton. *Beyond the Weir Bridge*

Burton. *To Ravensrigg*
Carter. *Children of the Book*
Dick. *False Coin, True Coin*
Forman. *Prince Charlie's Year*
Hawes. *The Dark Frigate*
Hendry. *Quest for a Kelpie*
Hess. *In Search of Honor*

Paton Walsh. *A Parcel of Patterns*
Sonnleitner. *The Cave Children*
Sutcliff. *Bonnie Dundee*

Biography

Campion. *Mother Ann Lee: Morning Star of the Shakers*
Carson. *Maximilien Robespierre*
Christianson. *Isaac Newton and the Scientific Revolution*

Dolan. *Junípero Serra*
Erickson. *Bonnie Prince Charlie*
Erickson. *Great Catherine*
Erickson. *To the Scaffold: The Life of Marie Antoinette*
Hitzeroth. *Sir Isaac Newton*

Horn. *King Louis XIV*
Kaplan. *Oliver Cromwell*
McDermott. *Peter the Great*
McGuire. *Catherine the Great*
Thompson. *Wolfgang Amadeus Mozart*

Collective Biography

Anderson. *Explorers Who Found New Worlds*
Axelrod. *Dictators and Tyrants*
Burton. *Journeys of the Great Explorers*

Duffy. *Czar: Russia's Rulers*
Lomask. *Great Lives: Exploration*
Wilkinson. *Generals Who Changed the World*

Wilkinson. *People Who Changed the World*
Wilkinson. *Scientists Who Changed the World*
Wilkinson. *Statesmen Who Changed the World*

History

Ardley. *Music: An Illustrated Encyclopedia*
Dale. *Early Cars*
Davis. *Man-Made Catastrophes*

Fradin. *Medicine: Yesterday, Today, and Tomorrow*
Greene. *Child Labor*
Hernandez. *Barmi*
Hibbert. *Cavaliers and Roundheads*

Kort. *Russia*
Kotlyarskaya. *Women in Society: Russia*
Kronenwetter. *Northern Ireland*
Lace. *England*

Levy. *Women in Society: Britain*
Levy. *Women in Society: Ireland*
Marshall. *Ocean Traders*
McHugh. *Western Art 1600-1800*

Mulcahy. *Diseases: Finding the Cure*
Mysticism: *The Experience of the Divine*
Pickford. *The Atlas of Shipwrecks & Treasure*
Spangenburg. *The History of Science from the Ancient*

Greeks to the Scientific Revolution
Spangenburg. *The History of Science in the Eighteenth Century*
Swisher. *The Glorious Revolution*

Multimedia

CD-ROM

Art & Music: The Baroque
Art & Music: The Eighteenth Century
Events That Changed the World

Great Artists
History Through Art: Baroque
Ideas That Changed the World
Inside the Vatican

Le Louvre: The Palace & Its Paintings
Stowaway!
Teach Your Kids World History

Video

The Age of Reason: Europe After the Renaissance
Budapest
The History of Orthodox Christianity

The Industrial Revolution
John Locke
The Longest Hatred: The History of Anti-Semitism
Painted Princess

The Polish Experience
Spain: History and Culture
Trompe L'Oeil: Paintings That Fool the Eye
Two Hundred Years of Mozart

GRADES ELEVEN AND TWELVE

Historical Fiction

Alexander. *Blind Justice*
Alexander. *Murder in Grub Street*
Alexander. *Person or Persons Unknown*
Alexander. *Watery Grave*
Anand. *The Cherished Wives*
Anand. *The Faithful Lovers*

Bartos-Hoppner. *The Cossacks*
Byrd. *Jefferson: A Novel*
Carr. *Daughters of England*
Carter. *Children of the Book*
Dick. *False Coin, True Coin*
Follett. *A Place Called Freedom*
Hess. *In Search of Honor*

Houston. *Running West*
Laker. *Circle of Pearls*
Laker. *The Golden Tulip*
Laker. *The Silver Touch*
Laker. *The Venetian Mask*
Paton Walsh. *A Parcel of Patterns*
Riley. *The Oracle Glass*
Sutcliff. *Bonnie Dundee*

Biography

Campion. *Mother Ann Lee: Morning Star of the Shakers*
Carson. *Maximilien Robespierre*
Christianson. *Isaac Newton and the Scientific Revolution*

Dolan. *Junípero Serra*
Erickson. *Bonnie Prince Charlie*
Erickson. *Great Catherine*
Erickson. *To the Scaffold: Marie Antoinette*
Hitzeroth. *Sir Isaac Newton*

Horn. *King Louis XIV*
Kaplan. *Oliver Cromwell*
McDermott. *Peter the Great*
McGuire. *Catherine the Great*
Thompson. *Wolfgang Amadeus Mozart*

Collective Biography

Anderson. *Explorers Who Found New Worlds*
Axelrod. *Dictators and Tyrants*

Boorstin. *The Creators*
Burton. *Journeys of the Great Explorers*
Duffy. *Czar: Russia's Rulers*

Lomask. *Great Lives: Exploration*
Rabb. *Renaissance Lives*
Wills. *Certain Trumpets*

History

Ardley. *Music: An Illustrated Encyclopedia*
Aymar. *Men in the Air*
Beckett. *The Story of Painting*
Bremness. *Herbs*

Brown. *Christianity*
Castello. *The Jews and Europe*
Cole. *Perspective*
Dale. *Early Cars*

Davidson. *Everyday Life Through the Ages*
Davis. *Man-Made Catastrophes*
Ewing. *Women in Uniform*

Fernandez-Armesto. *Atlas of World Exploration*

Gottlieb. *The Family in the Western World*

Hernandez. *Barmi*

Hibbert. *Cavaliers and Roundheads*

Hibbert. *Florence*

Hibbert. *Redcoats and Rebels*

Hibbert. *Rome*

Hughes. *Barcelona*

Keegan. *History of Warfare*

Kotlyarskaya. *Women in Society: Russia*

Lace. *England*

Levy. *Women in Society: Britain*

Levy. *Women in Society: Ireland*

Marshall. *Ocean Traders*

McLynn. *Famous Trials*

Mysticism: The Experience of the Divine

Pickford. *The Atlas of Shipwrecks & Treasure*

Porter. *London, a Social History*

Smith. *Fascinating People and Astounding Events from the History of the Western World*

Sobel. *Longitude: The True Story of a Lone Genius*

Spangenburg. *The History of Science in the Eighteenth Century*

Wilson. *The Circumnavigators*

Multimedia

CD-ROM

Art & Music: The Baroque

Art & Music: The Eighteenth Century

Events That Changed the World

Great Artists

History Through Art: Baroque

Ideas That Changed the World

Inside the Vatican

Le Louvre: The Palace & Its Paintings

Stowaway!

Teach Your Kids World History

Video

Absolutism and the Social Contract

The Age of Absolutism

The Age of Reason: Europe After the Renaissance

The Death of the Old Regime

The Enlightened Despots

The Enlightenment

The Enlightenment and Society

The History of Orthodox Christianity

The Industrial Revolution

The Industrial World

John Locke

The Longest Hatred: The History of Anti-Semitism

The Polish Experience

Trompe L'Oeil: Paintings That Fool the Eye

Two Hundred Years of Mozart

Europe and the British Isles, 1789-1859

GRADE SEVEN

Historical Fiction

Aiken. *Bridle the Wind*

Aiken. *The Teeth of the Gale*

Avi. *Beyond the Western Sea, Book One: The Escape from Home*

Avi. *Beyond the Western Sea, Book Two: Lord Kirkle's Money*

Cameron. *The Court of the Stone Children*

Clements. *The Treasure of Plunderell Manor*

Conlon-McKenna. *Fields of Home*

Conlon-McKenna. *Under the Hawthorn Tree*

Conlon-McKenna. *Wildflower Girl*

Hunter. *Pistol in Greenyards*

Matas. *Sworn Enemies*

Mooney. *The Stove Haunting*

Morpurgo. *Twist of Gold*

Overton. *The Ship from Simnel Street*

Paton Walsh. *A Chance Child*

Schur. *The Circlemaker*

Segal. *The Place Where Nobody Stopped*

Winter. *Klara's New World*

Biography

Allman. *Her Piano Sang: A Story About Clara Schumann*

Altman. *Mr. Darwin's Voyage*

Anderson. *Charles Darwin: Naturalist*

Brophy. *John Ericsson and the Inventions of War*

Bryant. *Louis Braille: Teacher of the Blind*

Carroll. *Napoleon Bonaparte*

Chaney. *Aleksandr Pushkin: Poet for the People*

Chiflet. *Victoria and Her Times*

Collins. *Tales for Hard Times: A Story About Charles Dickens*

Evans. *Charles Darwin: Revolutionary Biologist*

Freedman. *Louis Braille*

Gaines. *Alexander von Humboldt: Colossus of Exploration*

Guzzetti. *A Family Called Brontë*

Hyndley. *The Voyage of the Beagle (Darwin)*

Kamen. *Hidden Music: Fanny Mendelssohn*

Klare. *Gregor Mendel: Father of Genetics*

Larroche. *Corot from A to Z*

Loewen. *Beethoven*

Nardo, Don. *Charles Darwin*

Parker. *Charles Darwin and Evolution*

Sellier. *Corot from A to Z*

Shearman. *Queen Victoria*

Shuter. *Helen Williams and the French Revolution*

Smith. *Louis Pasteur: Disease Fighter*

Thompson. *Franz Schubert*

Thompson. *Joseph Hadyn*

Thompson. *Ludwig Van Beethoven*

Twist. *Charles Darwin*

Collective Biography

Aaseng. *Genetics*

Aaseng. *You Are the General II: 1800-1899*

Anderson. *Explorers Who Found New Worlds*

Cush. *Women Who Achieved Greatness*

Glubok. *Great Lives: Painting*

Hoobler. *French Portraits*

Hoobler. *Italian Portraits*

Hoobler. *Russian Portraits*

Italia. *Courageous Crimefighters*

Jacobs. *Great Lives: Human Rights*

Jacobs. *Great Lives: World Religions*

Jacobs. *World Government*

Krull. *Lives of the Artists*

Krull. *Lives of the Musicians*

Krull. *Lives of the Writers*

Mayberry. *Leaders Who Changed the 20th Century*

Weitzman. *Great Lives: Human Culture*

Wilkinson. *People Who Changed the World*

Wilkinson. *Scientists Who Changed the World*

Wilkinson. *Statesmen Who Changed the World*

History

Anderson. *Battles That Changed the Modern World*
Bachrach. *The Charge of the Light Brigade*
Balkwill. *Trafalgar*
Banfield. *The French Revolution*
Biesty. *Man-of-War*
Bowler. *Trains*
Carrion. *The Empire of the Czars*
Clements. *An Illustrated History of the World*
Corzine. *The French Revolution*
Cush. *Disasters That Shook the World*
Davies. *Transport*
Fradin. *Medicine: Yesterday, Today, and Tomorrow*
Garfunkel. *On Wings of Joy: Ballet*
Giblin. *Be Seated: A Book About Chairs*
Harris. *Mummies*
Humble. *Ships*

Kerr. *Keeping Clean*
Kort. *Russia*
Lace. *England*
Levy. *Women in Society: Britain*
Levy. *Women in Society: Ireland*
Markham. *Inventions That Changed Modern Life*
Marshall. *Ocean Traders*
Meltzer. *How Our Youngest Workers Are Exploited and Abused*
Morley. *Clothes*
Mulcahy. *Diseases: Finding the Cure*
Nardo. *The Irish Potato Famine*
Perl. *Why We Dress the Way We Do*
Pietrusza. *The Battle of Waterloo*
Platt. *The Smithsonian Visual Timeline of Inventions*

Pollard. *The Nineteenth Century*
Reynoldson. *Conflict and Change*
Sauvain. *Waterloo*
Spencer. *Germany: Then and Now*
Steele. *Kidnapping*
Stein. *Witches: Opposing Viewpoints*
Stewart. *Life During the French Revolution*
Van der Linde. *The White Stallions*
Ventura. *Clothing*
Ventura. *Food*
Warburton. *Railroads: Bridging the Continents*
Wetterau. *World History*
Wilkinson. *Amazing Buildings*
Woolf. *Picture This: A First Introduction to Paintings*

Multimedia

CD-ROM

Air and Space Smithsonian Dreams of Flight
Art & Music: Impressionism
Art & Music: Romanticism
Exploring the Titanic

Eyewitness Encyclopedia of Science
Great Artists
History Through Art: Pre-Modern Era

Le Louvre: The Palace & Its Paintings
Science Navigator
Teach Your Kids World History

Video

The British Way of Life
Budapest
Charles Darwin: Species Evolution
France: History and Culture
The French Revolution

The German Way of Life
Germany: Past and Present
Jane Austen and Her World
Johann Strauss
London: City of Majesty
Poland: A Proud Heritage

Sight by Touch
The Soviet Union
Spain: History and Culture
Trees Cry for Rain: A Sephardic Journey
The Vistula

GRADE EIGHT

Historical Fiction

Aiken. *Bridle the Wind*
Aiken. *The Teeth of the Gale*
Avi. *Beyond the Western Sea, Book One: The Escape from Home*
Avi. *Beyond the Western Sea, Book Two: Lord Kirkle's Money*

Cameron. *The Court of the Stone Children*
Clements. *The Treasure of Plunderell Manor*
Conlon-McKenna. *Under the Hawthorn Tree*
Conlon-McKenna. *Wildflower Girl*

Hunter. *Pistol in Greenyards*
Matas. *Sworn Enemies*
Mooney. *The Stove Haunting*
Morpurgo. *Twist of Gold*
Overton. *The Ship from Simnel Street*
Paton Walsh. *A Chance Child*
Pullman. *The Tin Princess*

Biography

Altman. *Mr. Darwin's Voyage*
Brophy. *John Ericsson*
Bryant. *Louis Braille*

Carroll. *Napoleon Bonaparte*
Carson. *Maximilien Robespierre*

Chaney. *Aleksandr Pushkin*
Chiflet. *Victoria and Her Times*

Collins. *Tales for Hard Times: Charles Dickens*
Evans. *Charles Darwin*
Gaines. *Alexander von Humboldt*
Guzzetti. *A Family Called Brontë*
Hyndley. *The Voyage of the Beagle (Darwin)*
Kamen. *Hidden Music: Fanny Mendelssohn*
Klare. *Gregor Mendel: Father of Genetics*

Larroche. *Corot from A to Z*
Marrin. *Napoleon and the Napoleonic Wars*
Martin. *Charles Dickens*
Nardo. *Charles Darwin*
Parker. *Charles Darwin*
Richardson. *Francisco José de Goya*
Sellier. *Corot from A to Z*
Shearman. *Queen Victoria*
Shuter. *Helen Williams and the French Revolution*

Smith. *Louis Pasteur: Disease Fighter*
Thompson. *Franz Schubert*
Thompson. *Joseph Hadyn*
Thompson. *Ludwig Van Beethoven*
Twist. *Charles Darwin*
Von der Heide. *Klemens von Metternich*
Waldron. *Francisco Goya*
Weidhorn. *Napoleon*

Collective Biography

Aaseng. *Genetics*
Aaseng. *You Are the General II: 1800-1899*
Anderson. *Explorers Who Found New Worlds*
Cush. *Artists Who Created Great Works*
Cush. *Women Who Achieved Greatness*
Glubok. *Great Lives: Painting*

Hoobler. *French Portraits*
Hoobler. *Italian Portraits*
Hoobler. *Russian Portraits*
Italia. *Courageous Crimefighters*
Krull. *Lives of the Artists*
Krull. *Lives of the Musicians*
Krull. *Lives of the Writers*
Mayberry. *Leaders Who Changed the 20th Century*

Weitzman. *Great Lives: Human Culture*
Wilkinson. *People Who Changed the World*
Wilkinson. *Scientists Who Changed the World*
Wilkinson. *Statesmen Who Changed the World*

History

Anderson. *Battles That Changed the Modern World*
Bachrach. *The Charge of the Light Brigade*
Balkwill. *Trafalgar*
Banfield. *The French Revolution*
Biesty. *Man-of-War*
Carrion. *The Empire of the Czars*
Clements. *An Illustrated History of the World*
Corzine. *The French Revolution*
Cush. *Disasters That Shook the World*
Davies. *Transport*
Fradin. *Medicine: Yesterday, Today, and Tomorrow*
Garfunkel. *On Wings of Joy: Ballet*
Giblin. *Be Seated: A Book About Chairs*

Harris. *Mummies*
Kort. *Russia*
Kotlyarskaya. *Women in Society: Russia*
Lace. *England*
Levy. *Women in Society: Britain*
Levy. *Women in Society: Ireland*
Markham. *Inventions That Changed Modern Life*
Marshall. *Ocean Traders*
Maurer. *Airborne*
Meltzer. *How Our Youngest Workers Are Exploited and Abused*
Morley. *Clothes*
Mulcahy. *Diseases: Finding the Cure*
Nardo. *The Irish Potato Famine*
Perl. *Why We Dress the Way We Do*

Pietrusza. *The Battle of Waterloo*
Platt. *The Smithsonian Visual Timeline of Inventions*
Sauvain. *Waterloo*
Spencer. *Germany: Then and Now*
Stein. *Witches: Opposing Viewpoints*
Stewart. *Life During the French Revolution*
Van der Linde. *The White Stallions*
Ventura. *Clothing*
Ventura. *Food*
Warburton. *Railroads: Bridging the Continents*
Wetterau. *World History*
Woolf. *Picture This: A First Introduction to Paintings*

Multimedia

CD-ROM

Air and Space Smithsonian Dreams of Flight
Art & Music: Romanticism
Eyewitness Encyclopedia of Science

Great Artists
Le Louvre: The Palace & Its Paintings
Science Navigator

Teach Your Kids World History

Video

The British Way of Life

Budapest

France: History and Culture

The French Revolution
The German Way of Life
Germany: Past and Present
Jane Austen and Her World

Johann Strauss
London: City of Majesty
Poland: A Proud Heritage
Sight by Touch

Spain: History and Culture
The Vistula

GRADE NINE

Historical Fiction

Aiken. *Bridle the Wind*
Aiken. *The Teeth of the Gale*
Austen-Leigh. *Later Days at Highbury*
Burton. *The Henchmans at Home*
Burton. *Riders of the Storm*
Burton. *Time of Trial*

Cameron. *The Court of the Stone Children*
Clements. *The Treasure of Plunderell Manor*
Conlon-McKenna. *Wildflower Girl*
Hunter. *Pistol in Greenyards*
Matas. *Sworn Enemies*

Morpurgo. *Twist of Gold*
Overton. *The Ship from Simnel Street*
Paton Walsh. *Grace*
Yates. *Hue and Cry*
Yates. *The Journeyman*

Biography

Altman. *Mr. Darwin's Voyage*
Carroll. *Napoleon Bonaparte*
Carson. *Maximilien Robespierre*
Chaney. *Aleksandr Pushkin*
Chiflet. *Victoria and Her Times*
Erickson. *To the Scaffold: Marie Antoinette*
Evans. *Charles Darwin*
Gaines. *Alexander von Humboldt*
Guzzetti. *A Family Called Brontë*

Hyndley. *The Voyage of the Beagle (Darwin)*
Larroche. *Corot from A to Z*
Marrin. *Napoleon and the Napoleonic Wars*
Martin. *Charles Dickens*
Muhlberger. *What Makes a Goya a Goya?*
Nardo. *Charles Darwin*
Parker. *Charles Darwin*
Richardson. *Francisco José de Goya*
Shearman. *Queen Victoria*

Shuter. *Helen Williams and the French Revolution*
Skelton. *Charles Darwin*
Tames. *Frederic Chopin*
Thompson. *Franz Schubert*
Thompson. *Joseph Hadyn*
Thompson. *Ludwig Van Beethoven*
Von der Heide. *Klemens von Metternich*
Waldron. *Francisco Goya*
Weidhorn. *Napoleon*

Collective Biography

Aaseng. *Genetics*
Aaseng. *You Are the General II: 1800-1899*
Anderson. *Explorers Who Found New Worlds*
Burton. *Journeys of the Great Explorers*
Cush. *Artists Who Created Great Works*
Cush. *Women Who Achieved Greatness*

Glubok. *Great Lives: Painting*
Hoobler. *French Portraits*
Hoobler. *Italian Portraits*
Hoobler. *Russian Portraits*
Italia. *Courageous Crimefighters*
Lomask. *Great Lives: Exploration*
Mayberry. *Leaders Who Changed the 20th Century*

Weitzman. *Great Lives: Human Culture*
Weitzman. *Great Lives: Theater*
Wilkinson. *People Who Changed the World*
Wilkinson. *Scientists Who Changed the World*
Wilkinson. *Statesmen Who Changed the World*

History

Anderson. *Battles That Changed the Modern World*
Bachrach. *The Charge of the Light Brigade*
Balkwill. *Trafalgar*
Banfield. *The French Revolution*
Corzine. *The French Revolution*
Cush. *Disasters That Shook the World*

Dale. *Early Railways*
Fradin. *Medicine: Yesterday, Today, and Tomorrow*
Garfunkel. *On Wings of Joy: Ballet*
Kirchberger. *The French Revolution*
Kort. *Russia*
Kotlyarskaya. *Women in Society: Russia*
Lace. *England*

Levy. *Women in Society: Britain*
Levy. *Women in Society: Ireland*
Markham. *Inventions That Changed Modern Life*
Marshall. *Ocean Traders*
Meltzer. *How Our Youngest Workers Are Exploited and Abused*

Mulcahy. *Diseases: Finding the Cure*
Nardo. *The Irish Potato Famine*
Perl. *Why We Dress the Way We Do*
Pietrusza. *The Battle of Waterloo*

Platt. *The Smithsonian Visual Timeline of Inventions*
Singer. *Structures That Changed the Way the World Looked*
Spangenburg. *The History of Science in the Nineteenth Century*

Spencer. *Germany: Then and Now*
Stewart. *Life During the French Revolution*
Warburton. *Railroads: Bridging the Continents*
Wetterau. *World History*

Multimedia

CD-ROM

Air and Space Smithsonian Dreams of Flight
Art & Music: Romanticism
Events That Changed the World

Great Artists
Ideas That Changed the World
Inside the Vatican
Le Louvre: The Palace & Its Paintings

Science Navigator
Teach Your Kids World History

Video

Budapest
France: History and Culture
The French Revolution
Germany: Past and Present

Jane Austen and Her World
Johann Strauss
Lenin According to Lenin
The Polish Experience

Sight by Touch
Spain: History and Culture
The Vistula

GRADE TEN

Historical Fiction

Aiken. *Bridle the Wind*
Aiken. *The Teeth of the Gale*
Austen-Leigh. *Later Days at Highbury*

Burton. *Riders of the Storm*
Burton. *Time of Trial*
Hunter. *Pistol in Greenyards*
Paton Walsh. *Grace*

Yates. *Hue and Cry*
Yates. *The Journeyman*

Biography

Brophy. *John Ericsson*
Carson. *Maximilien Robespierre*
Chaney. *Aleksandr Pushkin: Poet for the People*
Erickson. *Her Little Majesty: The Life of Queen Victoria*
Erickson. *To the Scaffold: Marie Antoinette*
Evans. *Charles Darwin: Revolutionary Biologist*

Gaines. *Alexander von Humboldt*
Larroche. *Corot from A to Z*
Marrin. *Napoleon and the Napoleonic Wars*
Martin. *Charles Dickens*
Nardo. *Charles Darwin*
Richardson. *Francisco José de Goya*
Shearman. *Queen Victoria*
Skelton. *Charles Darwin*

Tames. *Frederic Chopin*
Thompson. *Franz Schubert*
Thompson. *Joseph Hadyn*
Thompson. *Ludwig Van Beethoven*
Von der Heide. *Klemens von Metternich*
Waldron. *Francisco Goya*
Weidhorn. *Napoleon*

Collective Biography

Aaseng. *Genetics*
Aaseng. *You Are the General II: 1800-1899*
Anderson. *Explorers Who Found New Worlds*
Axelrod. *Dictators and Tyrants*

Burton. *Journeys of the Great Explorers*
Duffy. *Czar: Russia's Rulers*
Lomask. *Great Lives: Exploration*
Weitzman. *Great Lives: Theater*

Wilkinson. *People Who Changed the World*
Wilkinson. *Scientists Who Changed the World*
Wilkinson. *Statesmen Who Changed the World*

History

Ardley. *Music: An Illustrated Encyclopedia*
Bachrach Deborah. *The Charge of the Light Brigade*

Banfield. *The French Revolution*
Dale. *Early Railways*

Davis. *Man-Made Catastrophes*
Fradin. *Medicine: Yesterday, Today, and Tomorrow*

Haythornthwaite. *The Napoleonic Source Book*
Kirchberger. *The French Revolution*
Kort. *Russia*
Kotlyarskaya. *Women in Society: Russia*
Kristy. *Coubertin's Olympics*
Lace. *England*

Levy. *Women in Society: Britain*
Levy. *Women in Society: Ireland*
Marrin. *The United States in the First World War*
Marshall. *Ocean Traders*
Mulcahy. *Diseases: Finding the Cure*

Pickford. *The Atlas of Shipwrecks & Treasure*
Ross. *The Origins of World War I*
Ross. *The Russian Revolution*
Spangenburg. *The History of Science in the Nineteenth Century*
Stewart. *Life During the French Revolution*

Multimedia

CD-ROM

Air and Space Smithsonian Dreams of Flight
Art & Music: Romanticism
Events That Changed the World

Great Artists
Ideas That Changed the World
Inside the Vatican
Le Louvre: The Palace & Its Paintings

Science Navigator
Teach Your Kids World History

Video

Budapest
Germany: Past and Present
Jane Austen and Her World

Johann Strauss
The Longest Hatred: The History of Anti-Semitism

The Polish Experience
Spain: History and Culture

GRADES ELEVEN AND TWELVE

Historical Fiction

Aiken. *Bridle the Wind*
Aiken. *Eliza's Daughter*
Aiken. *The Teeth of the Gale*
Austen-Leigh. *Later Days at Highbury*
Barrett. *The Third Sister*
Barron. *Jane and the Man of the Cloth*
Barron. *Jane and the Unpleasantness at Scargrave Manor*
Burton. *Riders of the Storm*
Burton. *Time of Trial*
Chesney. *Back in Society*
Chesney. *Colonel Sandhurst to the Rescue*
Chesney. *Deborah Goes to Dover*
Chesney. *Finessing Clarissa*
Chesney. *Lady Fortescue Steps Out*
Chesney. *Miss Tonks Turns to Crime*
Chesney. *Mrs. Budley Falls from Grace*
Chesney. *Sir Philip's Folly*
Cookson. *The Rag Nymph*

Flanagan. *The Year of the French*
Heaven. *The Wind from the Sea*
Hodge. *Windover*
Holt. *The Captive*
Hughes. *The Rape of the Rose*
Hunter. *Pistol in Greenyards*
Jones. *Emily's Secret*
Laker. *Sugar Pavilion*
McCutchan. *Apprentice to the Sea*
O'Brian. *The Commodore*
O'Brian. *The Golden Ocean*
O'Brian. *The Ionian Mission*
O'Brian. *The Letter of Marque*
O'Brian. *Master and Commander*
O'Brian. *Men-Of-War: Life in Nelson's Navy*
O'Brian. *Nutmeg of Consolation*
O'Brian. *Post Captain*
O'Brian. *The Reverse of the Medal*
O'Brian. *The Unknown Shore*
Paton Walsh. *Grace*

Perry. *Belgrave Square*
Ross. *A Broken Vessel*
Ross. *Cut to the Quick*
Ross. *Whom the Gods Love*
Stewart. *The Magnificent Savages*
Stirling. *Shadows on the Shore*
Tennant. *Pemberley, or, Pride and Prejudice Continued*
Tennant. *An Unequal Marriage, or, Pride and Prejudice Twenty Years Later*
Veryan. *Ask Me No Questions*
Veryan. *Had We Never Loved*
Veryan. *Never Doubt I Love*
Veryan. *The Riddle of Alabaster Royal*
Veryan. *A Shadow's Bliss*
Williams. *Daughter of the Storm*
Williams. *The Island Harp*
Yates. *Hue and Cry*
Yates. *The Journeyman*

Biography

Brophy. *John Ericsson*
Carson. *Maximilien Robespierre*
Chaney. *Aleksandr Pushkin*
Erickson. *Her Little Majesty: The Life of Queen Victoria*
Erickson. *To the Scaffold: Marie Antoinette*
Gaines. *Alexander von Humboldt*
Gordon. *Charlotte Brontë*
Hovey. *A Mind of Her Own: George Sand*

Larroche. *Corot from A to Z*
Markus. *Dared and Done: Elizabeth Barrett and Robert Browning*
Marrin. *Napoleon and the Napoleonic Wars*
Martin. *Charles Dickens*
Richardson. *Francisco José de Goya*
Shearman. *Queen Victoria*
Skelton. *Charles Darwin*
Sunstein. *Mary Shelley*
Tames. *Frederic Chopin*

Thompson. *Franz Schubert*
Thompson. *Joseph Hadyn*
Thompson. Wendy. *Ludwig Van Beethoven*
Von der Heide. *Klemens von Metternich*
Wade. *Ada Byron Lovelace*
Waldron. *Claude Monet*
Welton. *Monet*
Wright. *Manet*

Collective Biography

Aaseng. *Genetics*
Aaseng. *You Are the General II: 1800-1899*
Anderson. *Explorers Who Found New Worlds*

Axelrod. *Dictators and Tyrants*
Boorstin. *The Creators*
Burton. *Journeys of the Great Explorers*

Duffy. *Czar: Russia's Rulers*
Lomask. *Great Lives: Exploration*
Weitzman. *Great Lives: Theater*

History

Ardley. *Music: An Illustrated Encyclopedia*
Bachrach. *The Charge of the Light Brigade*
Beckett. *The Story of Painting*
Castello. *The Jews and Europe*
Cole. *Perspective*
Crowe. *A History of the Gypsies of Eastern Europe and Russia*
Dale. *Early Railways*
Davidson. *Everyday Life Through the Ages*
Davis. *Man-Made Catastrophes*
Gottlieb. *The Family in the Western World*

Haythornthwaite. *The Napoleonic Source Book*
Hibbert. *Florence*
Hibbert. *Rome*
Hibbert. *Venice*
Hughes. *Barcelona*
Keegan. *History of Warfare*
Kirchberger. *The French Revolution*
Kotlyarskaya. *Women in Society: Russia*
Lace. *England*
Levy. *Women in Society: Britain*
Levy. *Women in Society: Ireland*
Marshall. *Ocean Traders*
McLynn. *Famous Trials*

Pickford. *The Atlas of Shipwrecks & Treasure*
Porter. *London, a Social History*
Schama. *Citizens: The French Revolution*
Smith. *Fascinating People and Astounding Events from the History of the Western World*
Spangenburg. *The History of Science in the Nineteenth Century*
Windrow. *Uniforms of the French Foreign Legion*

Multimedia

CD-ROM

Air and Space Smithsonian Dreams of Flight
Art & Music: Romanticism
Events That Changed the World

Great Artists
Ideas That Changed the World
Inside the Vatican
Le Louvre: The Palace & Its Paintings

Science Navigator
Teach Your Kids World History

Video

The Age of the Nation-States
The French Revolution
Germany: Past and Present
Image Before My Eyes

Jane Austen and Her World
Johann Strauss
The Longest Hatred: The History of Anti-Semitism

The Polish Experience
William Blake

Europe and the British Isles, 1860-1918

GRADE SEVEN

Historical Fiction

Anderson. *Black Water*
Avery. *A Likely Lad*
Avery. *Maria Escapes*
Avery. *Maria's Italian Spring*
Bunting. *SOS Titanic*
Burks. *Soldier Boy*
Burton. *The Henchmans at Home*
Cameron. *The Court of the Stone Children*
Clements. *The Treasure of Plunderell Manor*
Cole. *The Dragon in the Cliff*
Conlon-McKenna. *Under the Hawthorn Tree*
Conlon-McKenna. *Wildflower Girl*
Dalokay. *Sister Shako and Kolo the Goat*
Doherty. *Street Child*
Foreman. *War Game*
Geras. *Voyage*
Green. *The Throttlepenny Murder*

Howker. *Isaac Campion*
Lasky. *The Night Journey*
Matas. *Sworn Enemies*
McCutcheon. *Summer of the Zeppelin*
Mooney. *The Stove Haunting*
Morpurgo. *Butterfly Lion*
Morpurgo. *Twist of Gold*
Morpurgo. *Why the Whales Came*
Newman. *The Case of the Baker Street Irregular*
Newman. *The Case of the Etruscan Treasure*
Newman. *The Case of the Frightened Friend*
Newman. *The Case of the Indian Curse*
Newman. *The Case of the Somerville Secret*
Newman. *The Case of the Threatened King*
Newman. *The Case of the Vanishing Corpse*

Newman. *The Case of the Watching Boy*
O'Hara. *The Hiring Fair*
Overton. *The Ship from Simnel Street*
Paton Walsh. *A Chance Child*
Peyton. *The Maplin Bird*
Pitt. *Beyond the High White Wall*
Posell. *Homecoming*
Pullman. *Shadow in the North*
Pullman. *Spring-Heeled Jack*
Schur. *The Circlemaker*
Segal. *The Place Where Nobody Stopped*
Shiefman. *Good-Bye to the Trees*
Williams. *Titanic Crossing*
Winter. *Klara's New World*
Woodruff. *The Orphan of Ellis Island*
Yarbro. *Floating Illusions*
Zei. *The Sound of Dragon's Feet*

Biography

Aller. *J.M. Barrie*
Allman. *Her Piano Sang: A Story About Clara Schumann*
Bentley. *Albert Schweitzer*
Birch. *Marie Curie*
Bjork. *Linnea in Monet's Garden*
Brophy. *John Ericsson and the Inventions of War*
Brown. *Charlie Chaplin*
Brown. *Father Damien*
Brown. *Henry Dunant*
Bryant. *Henri de Toulouse-Lautrec, Artist*

Carpenter. *Robert Louis Stevenson: Finding Treasure Island*
Chiflet. *Victoria and Her Times*
Colver. *Florence Nightingale: War Nurse*
Dommermuth-Costa. *Agatha Christie: Writer of Mystery*
Gay. *Emma Goldman*
Gherman. *Robert Louis Stevenson: Teller of Tales*
Goldberg. *Albert Einstein: The Rebel Behind Relativity*
Habsburg-Lothringen. *Carl Fabergé*

Jacobs. *Nansen's Arctic Adventures*
Kherdian. *The Road from Home*
Klare. *Gregor Mendel: Father of Genetics*
Larroche. *Corot from A to Z*
Levine. *Anna Pavlova*
Loumaye. *Degas*
Loumaye. *Van Gogh*
Lucas. *Vincent Van Gogh*
Martin. *H. G. Wells*
Mason. *Cézanne: An Introduction*
Mason. *Monet: An Introduction*

Mason. *Van Gogh: An Introduction*
Montgomery. *Marie Curie*
Morgan. *Guglielmo Marconi*
Morgan. *Louis Pasteur*
Muhlberger. *What Makes a Degas a Degas?*
Muhlberger. *What Makes a Goya a Goya?*
Muhlberger. *What Makes a Monet a Monet?*
Nardo, Don. *Charles Darwin*
Nardo, Don. *H. G. Wells*
Netzley. *Queen Victoria*

Newfield, Marcia. *The Life of Louis Pasteur*
Parker. *Louis Pasteur and Germs*
Parker. *Marie Curie and Radium*
Pescio. *Van Gogh*
Pollard. *Marie Montessori*
Pozzi. *Chagall*
Resnick. *Lenin: Founder of the Soviet Union*
Rich. *Louis Pasteur*
Sellier. *Cézanne from A to Z*
Sellier. *Chagall from A to Z*

Sellier. *Corot from A to Z*
Sellier. *Matisse from A to Z*
Shearman. *Queen Victoria*
Simon. *Richard Burton*
Smith. *Louis Pasteur: Disease Fighter*
Tanaka. *Anastasia's Album*
Thompson. *Claude Debussy*
Thompson. *Pyotr Ilyich Tchaikovsky*
Twist. *Stanley and Livingstone*

Collective Biography

Aaseng. *Genetics*
Aaseng. *You Are the General II: 1800-1899*
Anderson. *Explorers Who Found New Worlds*
Cush. *Women Who Achieved Greatness*
Glubok. *Great Lives: Painting*
Hoobler. *French Portraits*
Hoobler. *Italian Portraits*
Hoobler. *Russian Portraits*

Italia. *Courageous Crimefighters*
Jacobs. *Great Lives: Human Rights*
Jacobs. *Great Lives: World Religions*
Jacobs. *World Government*
Krull. *Lives of the Artists*
Krull. *Lives of the Musicians*
Krull. *Lives of the Writers*
Mayberry. *Leaders Who Changed the 20th Century*

Schraff. *Women of Peace: Nobel Peace Prize Winners*
Weitzman. *Great Lives: Human Culture*
Wilkinson. *People Who Changed the World*
Wilkinson. *Scientists Who Changed the World*
Wilkinson. *Statesmen Who Changed the World*
Wolf. *Focus: Five Women Photographers*

History

Anderson. *Battles That Changed the Modern World*
Armenia
Ballard. *Exploring the Titanic*
Bosco. *World War I*
Bowler. *Trains*
Brown. *Conflict in Europe and the Great Depression*
Carrion. *The Empire of the Czars*
Cavan. *The Irish-American Experience*
Clare. *First World War*
Clements. *An Illustrated History of the World*
Cohen. *The Alaska Purchase*
Cosner. *War Nurses*
Cush. *Disasters That Shook the World*
Davies. *Transport*
Dunn. *The Russian Revolution*
Fradin. *Medicine: Yesterday, Today, and Tomorrow*
Gallant. *The Day the Sky Split Apart*
Garfunkel. *On Wings of Joy: Ballet*
Gay. *World War I.*
Giblin. *Be Seated: A Book About Chairs*

Granfield. *In Flanders Fields*
Hoare. *The Modern World*
Hudson. *Poetry of the First World War*
Hull. *A Prose Anthology of the First World War*
Humble. *Ships*
Kent. *World War I*
Kerr. *Keeping Clean*
Kort. *Marxism in Power*
Kort. *Russia*
Kotlyarskaya. *Women in Society: Russia*
Kristy, Davida. *Coubertin's Olympics: How the Games Began*
Lace. *England*
Langstaff. *"I Have a Song to Sing O!"*
Levy. *Women in Society: Britain*
Levy. *Women in Society: Ireland*
Macdonald. *A 19th Century Railway Station*
Markham. *Inventions That Changed Modern Life*
Marrin. *The United States in the First World War*
Marshall. *Ocean Traders*

Mason. *Peary and Amundsen: Race to the Poles*
Maurer. *Airborne*
Meltzer. *How Our Youngest Workers Are Exploited and Abused*
Morley. *Clothes*
Mulcahy. *Diseases: Finding the Cure*
Perl. *Why We Dress the Way We Do*
Platt. *The Smithsonian Visual Timeline of Inventions*
Pollard. *The Nineteenth Century*
Pollard. *The Red Cross and the Red Crescent*
Reynoldson. *Conflict and Change*
Ross. *The Origins of World War I*
Ross. *The Russian Revolution*
Salvi. *The Impressionists*
Sauvain. *Waterloo*
Singer. *Structures That Changed the Way the World Looked*
Spencer. *Germany: Then and Now*
Stacey. *The Titanic*

Steele. *Kidnapping*
Stein. *Witches: Opposing Viewpoints*
Stewart. *World War I*
Van der Linde. *The White Stallions*

Ventura. *Clothing*
Ventura. *Food*
Warburton. *Railroads: Bridging the Continents*
Wetterau. *World History*
Wilkinson. *Amazing Buildings*

Woolf. *Picture This: A First Introduction to Paintings*

Multimedia

CD-ROM

Air and Space Smithsonian Dreams of Flight
Art & Music: Impressionism
Art & Music: Romanticism
Daring to Fly!
Exploring the Titanic

Eyewitness Encyclopedia of Science
Great Artists
History Through Art: Pre-Modern Era

Le Louvre: The Palace & Its Paintings
Science Navigator
Teach Your Kids World History

Video

The British Way of Life
Budapest
Charles Darwin: Species Evolution
England's Historic Treasures
France: History and Culture
The French Revolution
The German Way of Life
Germany: Past and Present
Herzl

Jane Austen and Her World
Johann Strauss
Lenin According to Lenin
Lenin and His Legacy
Linnea in Monet's Garden
London: City of Majesty
The October 1917 Revolution and After
Poland: A Proud Heritage
Sight by Touch

The Soviet Union
Spain: History and Culture
Trees Cry for Rain: A Sephardic Journey
Trotsky
Tsiolkovski: The Space Age
The Vistula
Ziveli: Medicine for the Heart

GRADE EIGHT

Historical Fiction

Anderson. *Black Water*
Avery. *A Likely Lad*
Avery. *Maria Escapes*
Avery. *Maria's Italian Spring*
Bunting. *SOS Titanic*
Burks. *Soldier Boy*
Burton. *The Henchmans at Home*
Dalokay. *Sister Shako and Kolo the Goat*
Doherty. *Street Child*
Foreman. *War Game*

Geras. *Voyage*
Green. *The Throttlepenny Murder*
Howker. *Isaac Campion*
Lasky. *The Night Journey*
McCutcheon. *Summer of the Zeppelin*
O'Hara. *The Hiring Fair*
Peyton. *The Maplin Bird*
Pitt. *Beyond the High White Wall*
Posell. *Homecoming*

Pullman. *The Ruby in the Smoke*
Pullman. *Shadow in the North*
Pullman. *Spring-Heeled Jack*
Pullman. *The Tiger in the Well*
Pullman. *The Tin Princess*
Segal. *The Place Where Nobody Stopped*
Shiefman. *Good-Bye to the Trees*
Williams. *Titanic Crossing*
Yarbro. *Floating Illusions*
Zei. *The Sound of Dragon's Feet*

Biography

Bentley. *Albert Schweitzer*
Berman. *Paul Von Hindenburg*
Bernstein. *Albert Einstein and the Frontiers of Physics*
Birch. *Marie Curie*
Bober. *Marc Chagall*
Brand. *William Gladstone*
Brophy. *John Ericsson*
Brown. *Charlie Chaplin*
Brown. *Father Damien*
Brown. *Henry Dunant*

Bryant. *Henri de Toulouse-Lautrec*
Carpenter. *Robert Louis Stevenson: Finding Treasure Island*
Chiflet. *Victoria and Her Times*
Dommermuth-Costa. *Agatha Christie: Writer of Mystery*
Gay. *Emma Goldman*
Goldberg. *Albert Einstein: The Rebel Behind Relativity*
Greenfield. *Paul Gauguin*

Habsburg-Lothringen. *Carl Fabergé*
Haney. *Vladimir Ilich Lenin*
Jacobs. *Nansen's Arctic Adventures*
Kherdian. *The Road from Home*
Klare. *Gregor Mendel: Father of Genetics*
Kline. *Elizabeth Blackwell: A Doctor's Triumph*
Levine. *Anna Pavlova*
Loumaye. *Degas*

Loumaye. *Van Gogh*
Lucas. *Vincent Van Gogh*
Martin. *H. G. Wells*
Mason. *Cézanne: An Introduction*
Mason. *Monet: An Introduction*
Mason. *Van Gogh: An Introduction*
Meyer. *Edgar Degas*
Montgomery. *Marie Curie*
Morgan. *Louis Pasteur*
Muhlberger. *What Makes a Degas a Degas?*

Muhlberger. *What Makes a Goya a Goya?*
Muhlberger. *What Makes a Monet a Monet?*
Nardo. *H. G. Wells*
Netzley. *Queen Victoria*
Pescio. *Van Gogh*
Pollard. *Marie Montessori*
Pozzi. *Chagall*
Resnick. *Lenin*
Rich. *Louis Pasteur*
Sellier. *Cézanne from A to Z*
Sellier. *Chagall from A to Z*
Sellier. *Corot from A to Z*

Sellier. *Matisse from A to Z*
Shearman. *Queen Victoria*
Simon. *Richard Burton*
Smith. *Louis Pasteur: Disease Fighter*
Tanaka. *Anastasia's Album*
Thompson. *Claude Debussy*
Thompson. *Pyotr Ilyich Tchaikovsky*
Twist. *Stanley and Livingstone*
Van Habsburg. *Carl Fabergé*
Waldron. *Claude Monet*

Collective Biography

Aaseng. *Genetics*
Aaseng. *You Are the General II: 1800-1899*
Anderson. *Explorers Who Found New Worlds*
Cush. *Artists Who Created Great Works*
Cush. *Women Who Achieved Greatness*
Glubok. *Great Lives: Painting*
Hoobler. *French Portraits*

Hoobler. *Italian Portraits*
Hoobler. *Russian Portraits*
Italia. *Courageous Crimefighters*
Krull. *Lives of the Artists*
Krull. *Lives of the Musicians*
Krull. *Lives of the Writers*
Mayberry. *Leaders Who Changed the 20th Century*
Schraff. *Women of Peace: Nobel Peace Prize Winners*

Weitzman. *Great Lives: Human Culture*
Wilkinson. *People Who Changed the World*
Wilkinson. *Scientists Who Changed the World*
Wilkinson. *Statesmen Who Changed the World*
Wolf. *Focus: Five Women Photographers*

History

Anderson. *Battles That Changed the Modern World*
Armenia
Bosco. *World War I*
Brown. *Conflict in Europe and the Great Depression*
Carrion. *The Empire of the Czars*
Clare. *First World War*
Clements. *An Illustrated History of the World*
Cohen. *The Alaska Purchase*
Cosner. *War Nurses*
Cush. *Disasters That Shook the World*
Davies. *Transport*
Dunn. *The Russian Revolution*
Finkelstein. *Captain of Innocence: Dreyfus Affair*
Fradin. *Medicine: Yesterday, Today, and Tomorrow*
Gallant. *The Day the Sky Split Apart*
Garfunkel. *On Wings of Joy: Ballet*
Gay. *World War I*
Giblin. *Be Seated: A Book About Chairs*
Granfield. *In Flanders Fields*

Hudson. *Poetry of the First World War*
Hull. *A Prose Anthology of the First World War*
Kent. *World War I*
Kort. *Marxism in Power*
Kort. *Russia*
Kotlyarskaya. *Women in Society: Russia*
Kristy. *Coubertin's Olympics*
Lace. *England*
Levy. *Women in Society: Britain*
Levy. *Women in Society: Ireland*
Markham. *Inventions That Changed Modern Life*
Marrin. *The United States in the First World War*
Marshall. *Ocean Traders*
Mason. *Peary and Amundsen: Race to the Poles*
Maurer. *Airborne*
Meltzer. *How Our Youngest Workers Are Exploited and Abused*
Morley. *Clothes*
Mulcahy. *Diseases: Finding the Cure*

Perl. *Why We Dress the Way We Do*
Platt. *The Smithsonian Visual Timeline of Inventions*
Pollard. *The Red Cross and the Red Crescent*
Ross. *The Origins of World War I*
Ross. *The Russian Revolution*
Salvi. *The Impressionists*
Singer. *Structures That Changed the Way the World Looked*
Spencer. *Germany: Then and Now*
Stein. *Witches: Opposing Viewpoints*
Stewart. *World War I*
Van der Linde. *The White Stallions*
Ventura. *Clothing*
Ventura. *Food*
Warburton. *Railroads: Bridging the Continents*
Wetterau. *World History*
Woolf. *Picture This: A First Introduction to Paintings*

Multimedia

CD-ROM

Air and Space Smithsonian
  Dreams of Flight
Art & Music: Impressionism
Art & Music: Romanticism
Daring to Fly!
Exploring the Titanic

Eyewitness Encyclopedia of
  Science
Great Artists
History Through Art:
  Pre-Modern Era

Le Louvre: The Palace & Its
  Paintings
Science Navigator
Teach Your Kids World
  History

Video

1914-1918: World War I
The British Way of Life
Budapest
England's Historic Treasures
France: History and Culture
The German Way of Life
Germany: Past and Present
Herzl

Johann Strauss
Lenin According to Lenin
Lenin and His Legacy
Linnea in Monet's Garden
London: City of Majesty
The October 1917 Revolution
  and After
Poland: A Proud Heritage

The Soviet Union
Spain: History and Culture
Trotsky
Tsiolkovski: The Space Age
The Vistula
Ziveli: Medicine for the Heart

GRADE NINE

Historical Fiction

Anderson. Black Water
Avery. A Likely Lad
Bunting. SOS Titanic
Burks. Soldier Boy
Burton. The Henchmans at
  Home
Forman. Ring the Judas Bell
Geras. Voyage
Green. The Throttlepenny
  Murder
Howker. Isaac Campion

Hunter. Pistol in Greenyards
Lasky. The Night Journey
Matas. Sworn Enemies
McCutcheon. Summer of the
  Zeppelin
Peyton. The Edge of the Cloud
Peyton. Flambards
Peyton. Flambards in Summer
Peyton. The Maplin Bird
Pitt. Beyond the High White
  Wall

Posell. Homecoming
Pullman. The Ruby in the
  Smoke
Pullman. Shadow in the North
Pullman. The Tiger in the Well
Pullman. The Tin Princess
Wheeler. A Fanfare for the
  Stalwart
Zei. The Sound of Dragon's
  Feet

Biography

Bentley. Albert Schweitzer
Berman. Paul Von
  Hindenburg
Bernstein. Albert Einstein and
  the Frontiers of Physics
Birch. Marie Curie
Bober. Marc Chagall
Brand. William Gladstone
Brombert. Édouard Manet
Brown. Charlie Chaplin
Brown. Father Damien
Brown. Henry Dunant
Bryant. Henri de
  Toulouse-Lautrec
Carpenter. Robert Louis
  Stevenson: Finding
  Treasure Island
Chiflet. Victoria and Her
  Times
Dommermuth-Costa. Agatha
  Christie: Writer of Mystery
Gay. Emma Goldman

Goldberg. Albert Einstein:
  The Rebel Behind Relativity
Greenfield. Paul Gauguin
Habsburg-Lothringen. Carl
  Fabergé
Haney. Charles Stewart
  Parnell
Haney. Vladimir Ilich Lenin
Howard. Gauguin
Jacobs. Nansen's Arctic
  Adventures
Kherdian. The Road from
  Home
Kline. Elizabeth Blackwell: A
  Doctor's Triumph
Levine. Anna Pavlova
Martin. H. G. Wells
Mason. Cézanne: An
  Introduction
Mason. Monet: An
  Introduction

Mason. Van Gogh: An
  Introduction
Meyer. Edgar Degas
Morgan. Louis Pasteur
Muhlberger. What Makes a
  Degas a Degas?
Muhlberger. What Makes a
  Monet a Monet?
Nardo. H. G. Wells
Netzley. Queen Victoria
Pescio. Van Gogh
Pollard. Marie Montessori
Pozzi. Chagall
Rich. Louis Pasteur
Shearman. Queen Victoria
Smith. Garibaldi
Tanaka. Anastasia's Album
Thompson. Claude Debussy
Thompson. Pyotr Ilyich
  Tchaikovsky
Van Habsburg. Carl Fabergé
Waldron. Claude Monet

Collective Biography

Aaseng. *Genetics*
Aaseng. *You Are the General II: 1800-1899*
Anderson. *Explorers Who Found New Worlds*
Burton. *Journeys of the Great Explorers*
Cush. *Artists Who Created Great Works*
Cush. *Women Who Achieved Greatness*
Glubok. *Great Lives: Painting*

Hoobler. *French Portraits*
Hoobler. *Italian Portraits*
Hoobler. *Russian Portraits*
Italia. *Courageous Crimefighters*
Lomask. *Great Lives: Exploration*
Mayberry. *Leaders Who Changed the 20th Century*
Schraff. *Women of Peace: Nobel Peace Prize Winners*

Weitzman. *Great Lives: Human Culture*
Weitzman. *Great Lives: Theater*
Wilkinson. *People Who Changed the World*
Wilkinson. *Scientists Who Changed the World*
Wilkinson. *Statesmen Who Changed the World*
Wolf. *Focus: Five Women Photographers*

History

Anderson. *Battles That Changed the Modern World*
Armenia
Bosco. *World War I*
Brown. *Conflict in Europe and the Great Depression*
Cush. *Disasters That Shook the World*
Dale. *Early Railways*
Dunn. *The Russian Revolution*
Finkelstein. *Captain of Innocence: Dreyfus Affair*
Fradin. *Medicine: Yesterday, Today, and Tomorrow*
Gallant. *The Day the Sky Split Apart*
Garfunkel. *On Wings of Joy: Ballet*
Gay. *World War I*
Granfield. *In Flanders Fields*
Hudson. *Poetry of the First World War*
Hull. *A Prose Anthology of the First World War*

Kent. *World War I*
Kort. *Marxism in Power*
Kort. *Russia*
Kotlyarskaya. *Women in Society: Russia*
Kristy. *Coubertin's Olympics*
Lace. *England*
Levy. *Women in Society: Britain*
Levy. *Women in Society: Ireland*
Markham. *Inventions That Changed Modern Life*
Marrin. *The United States in the First World War*
Marshall. *Ocean Traders*
Meltzer. *How Our Youngest Workers Are Exploited and Abused*
Mulcahy. *Diseases: Finding the Cure*
Perl. *Why We Dress the Way We Do*

Platt. *The Smithsonian Visual Timeline of Inventions*
Ross. *The Origins of World War I*
Ross. *The Russian Revolution*
Salvi. *The Impressionists*
Singer. *Structures That Changed the Way the World Looked*
Spangenburg. *The History of Science from 1895 to 1945*
Spangenburg. *The History of Science in the Nineteenth Century*
Spencer. *Germany: Then and Now*
Stewart. *World War I*
Vail. *A History of the Russian Revolution*
Warburton. *Railroads: Bridging the Continents*
Wetterau. *World History*

Multimedia

CD-ROM

Air and Space Smithsonian Dreams of Flight
Art & Music: Impressionism
Art & Music: Romanticism
Daring to Fly!

Events That Changed the World
Great Artists
History Through Art: Pre-Modern Era
Ideas That Changed the World

Inside the Vatican
Le Louvre: The Palace & Its Paintings
Science Navigator
Teach Your Kids World History

Video

1914-1918: World War I
1917: Revolution in Russia
Aces: A Story of the First Air War
And We Knew How to Dance, the Women of World War One
Budapest
England's Historic Treasures
France: History and Culture

Germany: Past and Present
Herzl
Image Before My Eyes
Johann Strauss
Lenin According to Lenin
Lenin and His Legacy
Lenin and Me, Parts 1 & 2
London: City of Majesty
The October 1917 Revolution and After

The Polish Experience
The Soviet Union
Spain: History and Culture
Trotsky
Tsiolkovski: The Space Age
The Vistula
World War I
Wonders of Man's Creation
Ziveli: Medicine for the Heart

GRADE TEN

Historical Fiction

Anderson. *Black Water*
Burton. *The Henchmans at Home*
Forman. *Ring the Judas Bell*
Green. *The Throttlepenny Murder*
Howker. *Isaac Campion*
King. *A Letter of Mary*
Peyton. *The Edge of the Cloud*
Peyton. *Flambards*
Peyton. *Flambards in Summer*
Peyton. *The Maplin Bird*
Pullman. *The Ruby in the Smoke*
Pullman. *Shadow in the North*
Pullman. *The Tiger in the Well*
Pullman. *The Tin Princess*
Seil. *Sherlock Holmes and the Titanic Tragedy: A Case to Remember*
Wheeler. *A Fanfare for the Stalwart*

Biography

Berman. *Paul Von Hindenburg*
Bernstein. *Albert Einstein and the Frontiers of Physics*
Bober. *Marc Chagall: Painter of Dreams*
Brand. *William Gladstone*
Brombert. *Édouard Manet*
Brophy. *John Ericsson*
Bryant. *Henri de Toulouse-Lautrec*
Chiflet. *Victoria and Her Times*
Erickson. *Her Little Majesty: The Life of Queen Victoria*
Gay. *Emma Goldman*
Goldberg. *Albert Einstein: The Rebel Behind Relativity*
Greenfield. *Paul Gauguin*
Habsburg-Lothringen. *Carl Fabergé*
Haney. *Charles Stewart Parnell*
Haney. *Vladimir Ilich Lenin*
Howard. *Gauguin*
Kherdian. *The Road from Home*
Kline. *Elizabeth Blackwell: A Doctor's Triumph*
Mann. *Sigmund Freud*
Meyer. *Edgar Degas*
Nardo. *H. G. Wells*
Pozzi. *Chagall*
Tanaka. *Anastasia's Album*
Thompson. *Claude Debussy*
Thompson. *Pyotr Ilyich Tchaikovsky*
Shearman. *Queen Victoria*
Smith. *Garibaldi*
Van Habsburg. *Carl Fabergé*
Waldron. *Claude Monet*

Collective Biography

Aaseng. *Genetics*
Aaseng. *You Are the General II: 1800-1899*
Anderson. *Explorers Who Found New Worlds*
Axelrod. *Dictators and Tyrants*
Burton. *Journeys of the Great Explorers*
Duffy. *Czar: Russia's Rulers*
Lomask. *Great Lives: Exploration*
Weitzman. *Great Lives: Theater*
White. *Impressionists Side by Side: Their Friendships, Rivalries, and Artistic Exchanges*
Wilkinson. *People Who Changed the World*
Wilkinson. *Scientists Who Changed the World*
Wilkinson. *Statesmen Who Changed the World*
Wolf. *Focus: Five Women Photographers*

History

Ardley. *Music: An Illustrated Encyclopedia*
Bosco. *World War I*
Clare. *First World War*
Cosner. *War Nurses*
Dale. *Early Railways*
Davis. *Man-Made Catastrophes*
Finkelstein. *Captain of Innocence: Dreyfus Affair*
Fradin. *Medicine: Yesterday, Today, and Tomorrow*
Granfield. *In Flanders Fields*
Gray. *Chronicle of the First World War*
Hudson. *Poetry of the First World War*
Hull. *A Prose Anthology of the First World War*
Kirchberger. *The First World War*
Kort. *Marxism in Power*
Kort. *Russia*
Kotlyarskaya. *Women in Society: Russia*
Kristy. *Coubertin's Olympics*
Lace. *England*
Levy. *Women in Society: Britain*
Levy. *Women in Society: Ireland*
Marrin. *The United States in the First World War*
Marshall. *Ocean Traders*
Mulcahy. *Diseases: Finding the Cure*
Pickford. *The Atlas of Shipwrecks & Treasure*
Ross. *The Origins of World War I*
Ross. *The Russian Revolution*
Spangenburg. *The History of Science from 1895 to 1945*
Spangenburg. *The History of Science in the Nineteenth Century*
Stewart. *World War I*
Vail. *A History of the Russian Revolution*
Welton. *Impressionism*

Multimedia

CD-ROM

Air and Space Smithsonian Dreams of Flight
Art & Music: Impressionism
Art & Music: Romanticism
Daring to Fly!

Events That Changed the World
Great Artists
History Through Art: Pre-Modern Era
Ideas That Changed the World

Inside the Vatican
Le Louvre: The Palace & Its Paintings
Science Navigator
Teach Your Kids World History

Video

1914-1918: World War I
1917: Revolution in Russia
Aces: A Story of the First Air War
And We Knew How to Dance, the Women of World War One
Budapest
England's Historic Treasures
Germany: Past and Present

Herzl
Image Before My Eyes
Johann Strauss
Lenin According to Lenin
Lenin and His Legacy
Lenin and Me, Parts 1 & 2
The Longest Hatred: The History of Anti-Semitism
Munch and Ensor: Fathers of Expressionism

The October 1917 Revolution and After
The Polish Experience
Rise and Fall of the Soviet Union
The Soviet Union
Spain: History and Culture
Trotsky
Wonders of Man's Creation
World War I

GRADES ELEVEN AND TWELVE

Historical Fiction

Anderson. *Black Water*
Baricco. *Silk*
Burton. *The Henchmans at Home*
Cookson. *The Harrogate Secret*
Cookson. *The Moth*
Cookson. *The Parson's Daughter*
Cookson. *The Wingless Bird*
Cooperstein. *Johanna: A Novel of the Van Gogh Family*
Douglas. *Good Morning, Irene*
Douglas. *Irene at Large*
Douglas. *Irene's Last Waltz*
Edgarian. *Rise the Euphrates*
Forman. *Ring the Judas Bell*
Green. *The Throttlepenny Murder*
Gunn. *Young Art and Old Hector*
Harrison. *Patently Murder*
Heaven. *The Craven Legacy*
Heaven. *The Raging Fire*

Holt. *The Silk Vendetta*
Holt. *Snare of Serpents*
Howker. *Isaac Campion*
King. *A Letter of Mary*
Leonard. *Parnell and the Englishwoman*
Linscott. *Crown Witness*
Linscott. *An Easy Day for a Lady*
Linscott. *Hanging on the Wire*
Linscott. *Sister Beneath the Sheet*
Linscott. *Stage Fright*
Maalouf. *Samarkand*
MacDonald. *The Trevarton Inheritance*
Perry. *Belgrave Square*
Perry. *Defend and Betray*
Perry. *The Face of a Stranger*
Perry. *Farriers' Lane*
Perry. *The Hyde Park Headsman*
Perry. *The Sins of the Wolf*
Perry. *A Sudden, Fearful Death*

Peters. *The Deeds of the Disturber*
Peters. *The Last Camel Died at Noon*
Peters. *Lion in the Valley*
Peters. *The Mummy Case*
Peters. *The Snake, the Crocodile, and the Dog*
Peyton. *The Edge of the Cloud*
Peyton. *Flambards*
Peyton. *Flambards in Summer*
Peyton. *The Maplin Bird*
Pullman. *Shadow in the North*
Pullman. *The Ruby in the Smoke*
Pullman. *The Tiger in the Well*
Pullman. *The Tin Princess*
Roberts. *Louisa Elliott*
Seil. *Sherlock Holmes and the Titanic Tragedy: A Case to Remember*
Uris. *Trinity*
Wheeler. *A Fanfare for the Stalwart*

Biography

Berman. *Paul Von Hindenburg*
Bernard. *Van Gogh*
Bernstein. *Albert Einstein and the Frontiers of Physics*
Bober. *Marc Chagall*

Brand. *William Gladstone*
Brombert. *Édouard Manet*
Brophy. *John Ericsson*
Bryant. *Henri de Toulouse-Lautrec*

Erickson. *Her Little Majesty: The Life of Queen Victoria*
Feinberg. *Marx and Marxism*
Gay. *Emma Goldman*
Greenfield. *Paul Gauguin*

Habsburg-Lothringen. *Carl Fabergé*
Haney. *Charles Stewart Parnell*
Haney. *Vladimir Ilich Lenin*
Hovey. *A Mind of Her Own: George Sand*
Howard. *Gauguin*
Kline. *Elizabeth Blackwell: A Doctor's Triumph*
Mann. *Sigmund Freud*

Markus. *Dared and Done: Elizabeth Barrett and Robert Browning*
Meyer. *Edgar Degas*
Pflaum. *Grand Obsession: Madame Curie*
Pozzi. *Chagall*
Shearman. *Queen Victoria*
Smith. *Garibaldi*
Tanaka. *Anastasia's Album*
Taylor. *The Art of Kate Greenaway*

Thompson. *Claude Debussy*
Thompson. *Pyotr Ilyich Tchaikovsky*
Thompson. *Queen Victoria*
Van Habsburg. *Carl Fabergé*
Volkogonov. *Trotsky*
Von der Heide. *Klemens von Metternich*
Waldron. *Claude Monet*
Welton. *Monet*
Wright. *Manet*

Collective Biography

Aaseng. *Genetics*
Aaseng. *You Are the General II: 1800-1899*
Adams. *The World of the Impressionists*
Anderson. *Explorers Who Found New Worlds*

Axelrod. *Dictators and Tyrants*
Boorstin. *The Creators*
Burton. *Journeys of the Great Explorers*
Duffy. *Czar: Russia's Rulers*
Lomask. *Great Lives: Exploration*

Weitzman. *Great Lives: Theater*
White. *Impressionists Side by Side: Their Friendships, Rivalries, and Artistic Exchanges*
Wolf. *Focus: Five Women Photographers*

History

Ardley. *Music: An Illustrated Encyclopedia*
Aymar. *Men in the Air*
Beckett. *The Story of Painting*
Bosco. *World War I*
Castello. *The Jews and Europe*
Cole. *Perspective*
Crowe. *A History of the Gypsies of Eastern Europe and Russia*
Dale. *Early Railways*
Davidson. *Everyday Life Through the Ages*
Davis. *Man-Made Catastrophes*
Ewing. *Women in Uniform*
Finkelstein. *Captain of Innocence: Dreyfus Affair*
Foss. *Poetry of the World Wars*
Gottlieb. *The Family in the Western World*
Granfield. *In Flanders Fields*

Gray. *Chronicle of the First World War*
Hansen. *Gentlemen Volunteers: American Ambulance Drivers*
Hibbert. *Florence*
Hibbert. *Rome*
Hibbert. *Venice*
Hudson. *Poetry of the First World War*
Hughes. *Barcelona*
Keegan. *History of Warfare*
Kirchberger. *The First World War*
Kotlyarskaya. *Women in Society: Russia*
Kristy. *Coubertin's Olympics*
Lace. *England*
Levy. *Women in Society: Britain*
Levy. *Women in Society: Ireland*
Lourie. *Russia Speaks*
Marshall. *Ocean Traders*

McLynn. *Famous Trials*
Pickford. *The Atlas of Shipwrecks & Treasure*
Porter. *London, a Social History*
Ross. *The Russian Revolution*
Schneider. *American Women Overseas in World War I*
Smith. *Fascinating People and Astounding Events from the History of the Western World*
Spangenburg. *The History of Science from 1895 to 1945*
Spangenburg. *The History of Science in the Nineteenth Century*
Vail. *A History of the Russian Revolution*
Welton. *Impressionism*
Windrow. *Uniforms of the French Foreign Legion*

Multimedia

CD-ROM

Air and Space Smithsonian Dreams of Flight
Art & Music: Impressionism
Art & Music: Romanticism
Daring to Fly!

Events That Changed the World
Great Artists
History Through Art: Pre-Modern Era
Ideas That Changed the World

Inside the Vatican
Le Louvre: The Palace & Its Paintings
Science Navigator
Teach Your Kids World History

Video

1914-1918: World War I
1917: Revolution in Russia
Aces: A Story of the First Air War
The Age of the Nation-States
And We Knew How to Dance, the Women of World War One
England's Historic Treasures
Fin de Siecle
Germany: Past and Present

Herzl
Image Before My Eyes
Johann Strauss
Lenin According to Lenin
Lenin and His Legacy
Lenin and Me, Parts 1 & 2
The Longest Hatred: The History of Anti-Semitism
Munch and Ensor: Fathers of Expressionism
A New Public

The October 1917 Revolution and After
The Polish Experience
Revolution and the Romantics
Rise and Fall of the Soviet Union
Trotsky
World War I
Wonders of Man's Creation

Europe and the British Isles, 1919-1945

GRADE SEVEN

Historical Fiction

Anderson. *Paper Faces*
Anderson. *Searching for Shona*
Atlan. *The Passersby*
Bawden. *Carrie's War*
Bawden. *Henry*
Benchley. *Bright Candles*
Bergman. *Along the Tracks*
Bishop. *Twenty and Ten*
Booth. *War Dog: A Novel*
Bunting. *Spying on Miss Müller*
Burgess. *An Angel for May*
Cooper. *Dawn of Fear*
Dillon. *Children of Bach*
Douglas. *The Broken Mirror*
Forman. *Ceremony of Innocence*
Forman. *My Enemy My Brother*
Forman. *The Survivor*
Forman. *The Traitors*
Frank. *No Hero for the Kaiser*
Gallaz. *Rose Blanche*
Gardam. *A Long Way from Verona*
Gehrts. *Don't Say a Word*
Härtling. *Crutches*
Hartman. *War Without Friends*
Haugaard. *Chase Me, Catch Nobody*
Haugaard. *The Little Fishes*
Hautzig. *The Endless Steppe*
Heneghan. *Wish Me Luck*

Hesse. *Letters from Rifka*
Heuck. *The Hideout*
Holm. *North to Freedom*
Holman. *The Wild Children*
Hunter. *Hold on to Love*
Hunter. *A Sound of Chariots*
Kerr. *When Hitler Stole Pink Rabbit*
Kordon. *Brothers Like Friends*
Laird. *But Can the Phoenix Sing?*
Laird. *Shadow of the Wall*
Levitin. *Journey to America*
Lindgard. *Tug of War*
Lowry. *Number the Stars*
Magorian. *Good Night, Mr. Tom*
Magorian. *Not a Swan*
Marvin. *Bridge to Freedom*
Matas. *Code Name Kris*
Matas. *Daniel's Story*
Matas. *Lisa's War*
McSwigan. *Snow Treasure*
Morpurgo. *Waiting for Anya*
Napoli. *Stones in Water*
Nivola. *Elisabeth*
Orgel. *The Devil in Vienna*
Orlev. *The Island on Bird Street*
Orlev. *The Man from the Other Side*
O'Sullivan. *Melody for Nora*
Paton Walsh. *The Dolphin Crossing*

Paton Walsh. *Fireweed*
Pelgrom. *The Winter When Time Was Frozen*
Ray. *To Cross a Line*
Rees. *The Exeter Blitz*
Reiss. *The Upstairs Room*
Richter. *Friedrich*
Richter. *I Was There*
Roth-Hano. *Touch Wood*
Schur. *Sacred Shadows*
Sender. *The Cage*
Serraillier. *The Silver Sword*
Sevela. *We Were Not Like Other People*
Shaw. *A Wider Tomorrow*
Treseder. *Hear O Israel*
Turnbull. *Room for a Stranger*
Turnbull. *Speedwell*
Van Dijk. *Damned Strong Love*
Van Kirk. *A Promise to Keep*
Vos. *Anna Is Still Here*
Vos. *Dancing on the Bridge at Avignon*
Vos. *Hide and Seek*
Westall. *Blitzcat*
Westall. *Echoes of War*
Westall. *The Kingdom by the Sea*
Westall. *The Machine-Gunners*
Westall. *The Promise*
Westall. *Time of Fire*
Zei. *Petro's War*
Zei. *Wildcat Under Glass*

Biography

Aller. *J.M. Barrie*
Altman. *Mr. Darwin's Voyage*
Amdur. *Anne Frank*
Amdur. *Chaim Weizmann*
Ayer. *Adolf Hitler*
Baillet. *Matisse*
Beardsley. *Pablo Picasso*

Bentley. *Albert Schweitzer*
Birch. *Marie Curie*
Berman. *Paul Von Hindenburg*
Bernheim. *Father of the Orphans: Janusz Korczak*
Besson. *October 45*

Bradley. *Hitler and the Third Reich*
Brown. *Charlie Chaplin*
Caulkins. *Joseph Stalin*
Cech. *Jacques-Henri Lartigue*
Corkett. *Norman Bethune*
Dahl. *Boy: Tales of Childhood*

Dahl. *Going Solo*
Davidson. *Hillary and Tenzing*
Dommermuth-Costa. *Nikola Tesla*
Driemen. *Winston Churchill*
Drucker. *Kindersport*
Dunn. *Marie Curie*
Ford. *Howard Carter: Searching for King Tut*
Frank. *The Diary of a Young Girl*
Gay. *Emma Goldman*
Gold. *Memories of Anne Frank: Reflections of a Childhood Friend*
Goldberg. *Albert Einstein: The Rebel Behind Relativity*
Goldenstern. *Albert Einstein*
Gourley. *Beryl Markham: Never Turn Back*
Grady. *Marie Curie*

Gray. *Manya's Story*
Greenfield. *Marc Chagall*
Hargrove. *Pablo Casals*
Heyes. *Adolf Hitler*
Ireland. *Albert Einstein*
Linnéa. *Raoul Wallenberg*
Loumaye. *Chagall*
Lyttle. *Il Duce: Benito Mussolini*
MacDonald. *Pablo Picasso*
Marrin. *Stalin*
Mason. *Picasso: An Introduction*
McPherson. *Ordinary Genius: Albert Einstein*
Meadows. *Pablo Picasso*
Muhlberger. *What Makes a Picasso a Picasso?*
Nicholson. *Raoul Wallenberg*
Otfinoski. *Joseph Stalin: Russia's Last Czar*

Parker. *Guglielmo Marconi and Radio*
Pozzi. *Chagall*
Roberts. *The Importance of Oskar Schindler*
Ross. *Miró*
Selfridge. *Pablo Picasso*
Sellier. *Chagall from A to Z*
Sellier. *Matisse from A to Z*
Shephard. *Maria Montessori*
Shuter. *Christabel Bielenberg and Nazi Germany*
Siegal. *Upon the Head of a Goat*
Swisher. *Pablo Picasso*
Vasileva. *Hostage to War: A True Story*
Verhoeven. *Anne Frank: Beyond the Diary*
Whitelaw. *Charles de Gaulle*
Whitelaw. *Joseph Stalin*
Wiesel. *Night*

Collective Biography

Aaseng. *Genetics*
Aaseng. *You Are the General*
Anderson. *Explorers Who Found New Worlds*
Cohen. *Prophets of Doom*
Cush. *Women Who Achieved Greatness*
Glubok. *Great Lives: Painting*
Hazell. *Heroines: Great Women Through the Ages*

Hoobler. *French Portraits*
Hoobler. *Russian Portraits*
Jacobs. *Great Lives: Human Rights*
Jacobs. *Great Lives: World Religions*
Jacobs. *World Government*
Krull. *Lives of the Artists*
Krull. *Lives of the Musicians*
Krull. *Lives of the Writers*

Mayberry. *Leaders Who Changed the 20th Century*
Schraff. *Women of Peace: Nobel Peace Prize Winners*
Weitzman. *Great Lives: Human Culture*
Wilkinson. *Scientists Who Changed the World*
Wolf. *Focus: Five Women Photographers*

History

Aaseng. *Paris*
Adler. *We Remember the Holocaust*
Anderson. *Battles That Changed the Modern World*
Ayer. *Berlin*
Ayer. *Parallel Journeys*
Ballard. *Exploring the Bismarck*
Black. *Battle of Britain*
Black. *Battle of the Atlantic*
Black. *Battle of the Bulge*
Black. *Blitzkrieg*
Black. *Bombing Fortress Europe*
Black. *D-Day*
Black. *Desert Warfare*
Black. *Flattops at War*
Black. *Invasion of Italy*
Black. *Russia at War*
Black. *Victory in Europe*
Black. *War Behind the Lines*
Boas. *We Are Witnesses*

Borden. *The Little Ships: The Heroic Rescue at Dunkirk in World War II*
Brown. *Conflict in Europe and the Great Depression*
Carroll. *The Battle of Stalingrad*
Cavan. *The Irish-American Experience*
Chaikin. *A Nightmare in History*
Cosner. *War Nurses*
Cross. *Children and War*
Cross. *Technology of War*
Devaney. *America on the Attack: 1943*
Devaney. *America Storms the Beaches: 1944*
Devaney. *America Triumphs: 1945*
Dunnahoo. *Pearl Harbor*
Epler. *The Berlin Wall*
Estonia
Foreman. *War Boy*

Fradin. *Medicine: Yesterday, Today, and Tomorrow*
Friedman. *Escape or Die*
Friedman. *The Other Victims*
Garfunkel. *On Wings of Joy: Ballet*
Gay. *World War II*
Giblin. *When Plague Strikes*
Greenberg. *Letters From a World War II GI*
Greene. *Child Labor*
Greenfeld. *The Hidden Children*
Haas. *Tracking the Holocaust*
Handler. *Surviving the Holocaust in Hungary*
Hanmer. *Leningrad*
Heyes. *Children of the Swastika*
Hoare. *The Modern World*
Hull. *A Prose Anthology of the Second World War*
Humble. *Ships*

Humble. *A World War Two Submarine*
Ippisch. *Sky: Resistance During World War II*
Isserman. *World War II*
Kerr. *Keeping Clean*
Koehn. *Mischling, Second Degree*
Kort. *Marxism in Power*
Kort. *Russia*
Kotlyarskaya. *Women in Society: Russia*
Kronenwetter. *London*
Kronenwetter. *Northern Ireland*
Lace. *England*
Landau. *The Warsaw Ghetto Uprising*
Landau. *We Survived the Holocaust*
Lawson. *The Abraham Lincoln Brigade*
Leitner. *Isabella: From Auschwitz to Freedom*
Levy. *Women in Society: Britain*
Levy. *Women in Society: Ireland*
Marrin. *OVERLORD: D-Day*

Marrin. *Spies, Counterspies, and Saboteurs in World War II*
Marrin. *World War II in the Sky*
Marshall. *Ocean Traders*
Marx. *Echoes of World War II*
Meltzer. *How Gentiles Saved Jews in the Holocaust*
Meltzer. *How Our Youngest Workers Are Exploited and Abused*
Morley. *Clothes*
Mulcahy. *Diseases: Finding the Cure*
Perl. *Four Perfect Pebbles: A Holocaust Story*
Perl. *Why We Dress the Way We Do*
Pettit. *True Stories of Wartime Resistance*
Pietrusza. *The Invasion of Normandy*
Platt. *The Smithsonian Visual Timeline of Inventions*
Resnick. *The Holocaust*
Reynoldson. *Women and War*
Rochman. *Bearing Witness*
Rogasky. *Smoke and Ashes*
Rosenberg. *Hiding to Survive*

Ross. *The USSR Under Stalin*
Sauvain. *El Alamein*
Sherrow. *Amsterdam*
Spencer. *Germany: Then and Now*
Steele. *Food and Feasts Between the Two World Wars*
Steins. *The Allies Against the Axis*
Stewart. *Hitler's Reich*
Stewart. *Life in the Warsaw Ghetto*
Strahinich. *The Holocaust: Understanding and Remembering*
Toll. *Behind the Secret Window: World War II*
Vail. *World War II: The War in Europe*
Ventura. *Clothing*
Ventura. *Food*
Wetterau. *World History*
Wilkinson. *Amazing Buildings*
Woolf. *Picture This: A First Introduction to Paintings*
Zeinert. *The Warsaw Ghetto Uprising*
Zyskind. *Struggle*

Multimedia

CD-ROM

Art & Music: Surrealism
Art & Music: The Twentieth Century
Eyewitness Encyclopedia of Science

History Through Art: 20th Century
Lest We Forget: A History of the Holocaust
Science Navigator

Teach Your Kids World History
World War II, Global Conflict

Video

Albert Einstein: The Education of a Genius
Anzio and the Italian Campaign
The Battle of the Bulge and the Drive to the Rhine
The British Way of Life
Child in Two Worlds
Children of the Holocaust
Children Remember the Holocaust
D-Day and the Battle for France
D-Day Omaha Beach
Diamonds in the Snow
Europe: Insular Region
The German Way of Life

Germany: Past and Present
Hitler's Assault on Europe
The Holocaust: A Teenager's Experience
The Holocaust as Seen Through the Eyes of a Survivor
The Holocaust Wall Hangings
How the Nazis Came to Power
A Little Tailor's Christmas Story
London: City of Majesty
Lost Childhood: The Boys of Birkenau
Married with a Star
Operation: Dragoon
Poland: A Proud Heritage

The Road to Wannsee: Eleven Million Sentenced to Death
Schindler: The Documentary
Shtetl
Spain: History and Culture
The Surreal Eye: On the Threshold of Dreams
Trinity and Beyond: The Atomic Bomb Movie
Trotsky
Tsiolkovski: The Space Age
The Vistula
A Wall of Silence
We Must Never Forget: The Story of the Holocaust

GRADE EIGHT

Historical Fiction

Anderson. *Paper Faces*
Anderson. *Searching for Shona*
Atlan. *The Passersby*
Benchley. *Bright Candles*
Bergman. *Along the Tracks*
Bishop. *Twenty and Ten*
Bitton-Jackson. *I Have Lived a Thousand Years: Growing Up in the Holocaust*
Booth. *War Dog: A Novel*
Carter. *The Hunted*
Cooper. *Dawn of Fear*
Dillon. *Children of Bach*
Forman. *Ceremony of Innocence*
Forman. *My Enemy My Brother*
Forman. *The Survivor*
Forman. *The Traitors*
Frank. *No Hero for the Kaiser*
Gallaz. *Rose Blanche*
Gardam. *A Long Way from Verona*
Gehrts. *Don't Say a Word*
Härtling. *Crutches*
Hartman. *War Without Friends*
Haugaard. *Chase Me, Catch Nobody*
Haugaard. *The Little Fishes*
Hautzig. *The Endless Steppe*

Heneghan. *Wish Me Luck*
Hesse. *Letters from Rifka*
Holman. *The Wild Children*
Hunter. *Hold On to Love*
Hunter. *A Sound of Chariots*
Kordon. *Brothers Like Friends*
Laird. *But Can the Phoenix Sing?*
Laird. *Shadow of the Wall*
Lindgard. *Tug of War*
Magorian. *Good Night, Mr. Tom*
Magorian. *Not a Swan*
Marvin. *Bridge to Freedom*
Matas. *Code Name Kris*
Matas. *Lisa's War*
Morpurgo. *Waiting for Anya*
Napoli. *Stones in Water*
Orgel. *The Devil in Vienna*
Orlev. *The Island on Bird Street*
Orlev. *The Man from the Other Side*
O'Sullivan. *Melody for Nora*
Paton Walsh. *The Dolphin Crossing*
Paton Walsh. *Fireweed*
Pausewang. *The Final Journey*
Pelgrom. *The Acorn Eaters*
Pelgrom. *The Winter When Time Was Frozen*

Ray. *To Cross a Line*
Rees. *The Exeter Blitz*
Reiss. *The Upstairs Room*
Reuter. *The Boys from St. Petri*
Richter. *Friedrich*
Richter. *I Was There*
Roth-Hano. *Touch Wood*
Schur. *Sacred Shadows*
Sender. *The Cage*
Serraillier. *The Silver Sword*
Sevela. *We Were Not Like Other People*
Shaw. *A Wider Tomorrow*
Treseder. *Hear O Israel*
Turnbull. *Speedwell*
Van Dijk. *Damned Strong Love*
Van Kirk. *A Promise to Keep*
Vos. *Dancing on the Bridge at Avignon*
Vos. *Hide and Seek*
Westall. *Blitzcat*
Westall. *Echoes of War*
Westall. *The Kingdom by the Sea*
Westall. *The Machine-Gunners*
Westall. *The Promise*
Westall. *Time of Fire*
Yolen. *Briar Rose*
Zei. *Petro's War*
Zei. *Wildcat Under Glass*

Biography

Aller, Susan Bivin. *J.M. Barrie*
Altman. *Mr. Darwin's Voyage*
Amdur. *Anne Frank*
Amdur. *Chaim Weizmann*
Ayer. *Adolf Hitler*
Baillet. *Matisse*
Banfield. *Charles De Gaulle*
Beardsley. *Pablo Picasso*
Bentley. *Albert Schweitzer*
Bernstein. *Albert Einstein and the Frontiers of Physics*
Berman. *Paul Von Hindenburg*
Bernheim. *Father of the Orphans: Janusz Korczak*
Besson. *October 45*
Birch. *Marie Curie*
Bober. *Marc Chagall*
Bradley. *Hitler and the Third Reich*

Brown. *Charlie Chaplin*
Carter. *George Santayana*
Carter. *Salvador Dali*
Caulkins. *Joseph Stalin*
Cech. *Jacques-Henri Lartigue*
Corkett. *Norman Bethune*
Dahl. *Going Solo*
Dommermuth-Costa. *Nikola Tesla*
Driemen. *Winston Churchill*
Drucker. *Kindersport*
Dunn. *Marie Curie*
Ford. *Howard Carter: Searching for King Tut*
Frank. *The Diary of a Young Girl*
Garza. *Francisco Franco*
Garza. *Pablo Casals*
Gay. *Emma Goldman*

Gold. *Memories of Anne Frank: Reflections of a Childhood Friend*
Goldberg. *Albert Einstein: The Rebel Behind Relativity*
Goldenstern. *Albert Einstein*
Gourley. *Beryl Markham: Never Turn Back*
Grady. *Marie Curie*
Gray. *Manya's Story*
Greenfield. *Marc Chagall*
Hargrove. *Pablo Casals*
Hartenian. *Benito Mussolini*
Heyes. *Adolf Hitler*
Hoobler. *Joseph Stalin*
Ireland. *Albert Einstein*
Linnéa. *Raoul Wallenberg*
Loumaye. *Chagall*
Lyttle. *Il Duce: Benito Mussolini*
MacDonald. *Pablo Picasso*

Marrin. *Stalin*
Mason. *Picasso: An Introduction*
McPherson. *Ordinary Genius: Albert Einstein*
Muhlberger. *What Makes a Picasso a Picasso?*
Mulvihill. *Mussolini and Italian Fascism*
Nicholson. *Raoul Wallenberg*
Novac. *Beautiful Days of My Youth*

Otfinoski. *Alexander Fleming: Conquering Disease with Penicillin*
Otfinoski. *Joseph Stalin: Russia's Last Czar*
Pozzi. *Chagall*
Roberts. *The Importance of Oskar Schindler*
Rogers. *Churchill*
Ross. *Miró*
Selfridge. *Pablo Picasso*
Sellier. *Matisse from A to Z*
Sellier. *Chagall from A to Z*
Shephard. *Maria Montessori*

Shuter. *Christabel Bielenberg and Nazi Germany*
Siegal. *Upon the Head of a Goat*
Swisher. *Pablo Picasso*
Tachau. *Kemal Atatürk*
Vasileva. *Hostage to War: A True Story*
Verhoeven. *Anne Frank: Beyond the Diary*
Whitelaw. *Charles de Gaulle*
Whitelaw. *Joseph Stalin: From Peasant to Premier*
Wiesel. *Night*

Collective Biography

Aaseng. *Genetics*
Aaseng. *Twentieth-Century Inventors*
Aaseng. *You Are the General*
Anderson. *Explorers Who Found New Worlds*
Cohen. *Prophets of Doom*
Cush. *Artists Who Created Great Works*

Cush. *Women Who Achieved Greatness*
Glubok. *Great Lives: Painting*
Hazell. *Heroines: Great Women Through the Ages*
Hoobler. *French Portraits*
Hoobler. *Russian Portraits*
Krull. *Lives of the Artists*
Krull. *Lives of the Musicians*
Krull. *Lives of the Writers*

Mayberry. *Leaders Who Changed the 20th Century*
Schraff. *Women of Peace: Nobel Peace Prize Winners*
Weitzman. *Great Lives: Human Culture*
Wilkinson. *Scientists Who Changed the World*
Wolf. *Focus: Five Women Photographers*

History

Aaseng. *Paris*
Adler. *We Remember the Holocaust*
Anderson. *Battles That Changed the Modern World*
Ayer. *Berlin*
Ayer. *Parallel Journeys*
Ballard. *Exploring The Bismarck*
Black. *Battle of Britain*
Black. *Battle of the Atlantic*
Black. *Battle of the Bulge*
Black. *Blitzkrieg*
Black. *Bombing Fortress Europe*
Black. *D-Day*
Black. *Desert Warfare*
Black. *Flattops at War*
Black. *Invasion of Italy*
Black. *Russia at War*
Black. *Victory in Europe*
Black. *War Behind the Lines*
Boas. *We Are Witnesses*
Brown. *Conflict in Europe and the Great Depression*
Carroll. *The Battle of Stalingrad*
Chaikin. *A Nightmare in History*
Cosner. *War Nurses*

Devaney. *America on the Attack: 1943*
Devaney. *America Storms the Beaches: 1944*
Devaney. *America Triumphs: 1945*
Dunnahoo. *Pearl Harbor*
Epler. *The Berlin Wall*
Estonia
Fradin. *Medicine: Yesterday, Today, and Tomorrow*
Friedman. *Escape or Die*
Friedman. *The Other Victims*
Garfunkel. *On Wings of Joy: Ballet*
Gay. *World War II*
Giblin. *When Plague Strikes*
Greenberg. *Letters From a World War II GI*
Greene. *Child Labor*
Greenfeld. *The Hidden Children*
Haas. *Tracking the Holocaust*
Handler. *Surviving the Holocaust in Hungary*
Hanmer. *Leningrad*
Heyes. *Children of the Swastika*
Hull. *A Prose Anthology of the Second World War*
Ippisch. *Sky: Resistance During World War II*

Isserman. *World War II*
Koehn. *Mischling, Second Degree*
Kort. *Marxism in Power*
Kort. *Russia*
Kotlyarskaya. *Women in Society: Russia*
Kronenwetter. *London*
Kronenwetter. *Northern Ireland*
Lace. *England*
Landau. *The Warsaw Ghetto Uprising*
Landau. *We Survived the Holocaust*
Lawson. *The Abraham Lincoln Brigade*
Leitner. *Isabella: From Auschwitz to Freedom*
Levy. *Women in Society: Britain*
Levy. *Women in Society: Ireland*
Marrin. *OVERLORD: D-Day*
Marrin. *Spies, Counterspies, and Saboteurs in World War II*
Marrin. *World War II in the Sky*
Marshall. *Ocean Traders*
Marx. *Echoes of World War II*

Meltzer. *How Gentiles Saved Jews in the Holocaust*

Meltzer. *How Our Youngest Workers Are Exploited and Abused*

Morley. *Clothes*

Mulcahy. *Diseases: Finding the Cure*

Perl. *Four Perfect Pebbles: A Holocaust Story*

Perl. *Why We Dress the Way We Do*

Pettit. *True Stories of Wartime Resistance*

Pietrusza. *The Invasion of Normandy*

Platt. *The Smithsonian Visual Timeline of Inventions*

Reynoldson. *Women and War*

Rochman. *Bearing Witness*

Rogasky. *Smoke and Ashes*

Rosenberg. *Hiding to Survive*

Ross. *The USSR Under Stalin*

Sauvain. *El Alamein*

Sherrow. *Amsterdam*

Spencer. *Germany: Then and Now*

Steele. *Food and Feasts Between the Two World Wars*

Stein. *World War II in Europe*

Steins. *The Allies Against the Axis*

Stewart. *Hitler's Reich*

Stewart. *Life in the Warsaw Ghetto*

Strahinich. *The Holocaust: Understanding and Remembering*

Toll. *Behind the Secret Window: World War II*

Vail. *World War II: The War in Europe*

Ventura. *Clothing*

Ventura. *Food*

Wetterau. *World History*

Woolf. *Picture This: A First Introduction to Paintings*

Zeinert. *The Warsaw Ghetto Uprising*

Zyskind. *Struggle*

Multimedia

CD-ROM

Art & Music: Surrealism

Art & Music: The Twentieth Century

Eyewitness Encyclopedia of Science

History Through Art: 20th Century

Lest We Forget: A History of the Holocaust

Science Navigator

Teach Your Kids World History

World War II, Global Conflict

Video

1945-1989: The Cold War

Albert Einstein: The Education of a Genius

Anzio and the Italian Campaign

The B-24 Trilogy: The Victory Bombers

The Battle of the Bulge and the Drive to the Rhine

The British Way of Life

Child in Two Worlds

Children of the Holocaust

Children Remember the Holocaust

D-Day and the Battle for France

D-Day Omaha Beach

Diamonds in the Snow

Europe: Insular Region

The German Way of Life

Germany: Past and Present

Grave of the Fireflies

Hitler's Assault on Europe

The Holocaust: A Teenager's Experience

The Holocaust as Seen Through the Eyes of a Survivor

The Holocaust Wall Hangings

How the Nazis Came to Power

A Little Tailor's Christmas Story

London: City of Majesty

Lost Childhood: The Boys of Birkenau

Married with a Star

Operation: Dragoon

Poland: A Proud Heritage

The Road to Wannsee: Eleven Million Sentenced to Death

Schindler: The Documentary

Shtetl

Spain: History and Culture

The Surreal Eye: On the Threshold of Dreams

Survivors of the Holocaust

Trinity and Beyond: The Atomic Bomb Movie

Trotsky

Tsiolkovski: The Space Age

The Vistula

A Wall of Silence

We Must Never Forget: The Story of the Holocaust

GRADE NINE

Historical Fiction

Baklanov. *Forever Nineteen*

Benchley. *Bright Candles*

Bergman. *Along the Tracks*

Bishop. *Twenty and Ten*

Bitton-Jackson. *I Have Lived a Thousand Years:*

Growing up in the Holocaust

Booth. *War Dog: A Novel*

Carter. *The Hunted*

Durrell. *White Eagles over Serbia*

Forman. *Ceremony of Innocence*

Forman. *Horses of Anger*

Forman. *My Enemy My Brother*

Forman. *The Survivor*

Forman. *The Traitors*
Frank. *No Hero for the Kaiser*
Friedman. *Nightfather*
Gallaz. *Rose Blanche*
Gardam. *A Long Way from Verona*
Gehrts. *Don't Say a Word*
Goldstein. *Mazel*
Hackl. *Farewell Sidonia*
Hartman. *War Without Friends*
Haugaard. *Chase Me, Catch Nobody*
Haugaard. *The Little Fishes*
Hautzig. *The Endless Steppe*
Hesse. *Letters from Rifka*
Holman. *The Wild Children*
Hunter. *Hold on to Love*
Hunter. *A Sound of Chariots*
Hunter. *The Third Eye*
Kordon. *Brothers Like Friends*
Laird. *But Can the Phoenix Sing?*
Laird. *Shadow of the Wall*
Lindgard. *Tug of War*
Magorian. *Good Night, Mr. Tom*
Magorian. *Not a Swan*
Marvin. *Bridge to Freedom*

Matas. *Code Name Kris*
Matas. *Lisa's War*
Napoli. *Stones in Water*
Nolan. *If I Should Die Before I Wake*
Norling. *Patty's Journey: From Orphanage to Adoption and Reunion*
Orlev. *The Island on Bird Street*
Orlev. *The Man from the Other Side*
O'Sullivan. *Melody for Nora*
Paton Walsh. *The Dolphin Crossing*
Paton Walsh. *Fireweed*
Pausewang. *The Final Journey*
Pelgrom. *The Acorn Eaters*
Pelgrom. *The Winter When Time Was Frozen*
Peyton. *Flambards Divided*
Ray. *To Cross a Line*
Raymond. *Daniel and Esther*
Rees. *The Exeter Blitz*
Reiss. *The Upstairs Room*
Reuter. *The Boys from St. Petri*

Richter. *Friedrich*
Richter. *I Was There*
Roth-Hano. *Touch Wood*
Schur. *Sacred Shadows*
Sender. *The Cage*
Serraillier. *The Silver Sword*
Sevela. *We Were Not Like Other People*
Shaw. *A Wider Tomorrow*
Treseder. *Hear O Israel*
Turnbull. *Speedwell*
Van Dijk. *Damned Strong Love*
Van Kirk. *A Promise to Keep*
Vos. *Dancing on the Bridge at Avignon*
Westall. *Blitzcat*
Westall. *Echoes of War*
Westall. *The Kingdom by the Sea*
Westall. *The Machine-Gunners*
Westall. *The Promise*
Yolen. *Briar Rose*
Yolen. *The Devil's Arithmetic*
Zei. *Petro's War*
Zei. *Wildcat Under Glass*

Biography

Amdur. *Anne Frank*
Amdur. *Chaim Weizmann*
Atkinson. *In Kindling Flame: Hannah Senesh*
Ayer. *Adolf Hitler*
Baillet. *Matisse*
Banfield. *Charles De Gaulle*
Beardsley. *Pablo Picasso*
Bentley. *Albert Schweitzer*
Berman. *Paul Von Hindenburg*
Bernheim. *Father of the Orphans: Janusz Korczak*
Bernstein. *Albert Einstein and the Frontiers of Physics*
Bierman. *Righteous Gentile: Raoul Wallenberg*
Birch. *Marie Curie*
Bober. *Marc Chagall*
Bradley. *Hitler and the Third Reich*
Brown. *Charlie Chaplin*
Carter. *George Santayana*
Carter. *Salvador Dali*
Casals. *Joys and Sorrows*
Caulkins. *Joseph Stalin*
Cech. *Jacques-Henri Lartigue*
Corkett. *Norman Bethune*
Dahl. *Going Solo*
Dommermuth-Costa. *Nikola Tesla*

Driemen. *Winston Churchill*
Dunn. *Marie Curie*
Flynn. *George Orwell*
Frank. *The Diary of a Young Girl*
Garza. *Francisco Franco*
Garza. *Pablo Casals*
Gay. *Emma Goldman*
Gelistsen. *Rena's Promise*
Gold. *Memories of Anne Frank: Reflections of a Childhood Friend*
Goldberg. *Albert Einstein: The Rebel Behind Relativity*
Goldenstern. *Albert Einstein*
Gourley. *Beryl Markham: Never Turn Back*
Grady. *Marie Curie*
Gray. *Manya's Story*
Greenfield. *Marc Chagall*
Hargrove. *Pablo*
Hartenian. *Benito Mussolini*
Heyes. *Adolf Hitler*
Hoobler. *Joseph Stalin*
Ireland. *Albert Einstein*
Lewis. *Tomá Masaryk*
Linnéa. *Raoul Wallenberg*
Lyttle. *Il Duce: Benito Mussolini*
Lyttle. *Pablo Picasso*
MacDonald. *Pablo Picasso*

Marrin. *Hitler*
Marrin. *Stalin*
Mason. *Picasso: An Introduction*
Muhlberger. *What Makes a Picasso a Picasso?*
Mulvihill. *Mussolini and Italian Fascism*
Nicholson. *Raoul Wallenberg*
Novac. *Beautiful Days of My Youth*
Otfinoski. *Alexander Fleming*
Otfinoski. *Joseph Stalin*
Pozzi. *Chagall*
Roberts. *The Importance of Oskar Schindler*
Rogers. *Churchill*
Selfridge. *Pablo Picasso*
Shephard. *Maria Montessori*
Shuter. *Christabel Bielenberg and Nazi Germany*
Siegal. *Upon the Head of a Goat*
Tachau. *Kemal Atatürk*
Vasileva. *Hostage to War: A True Story*
Verhoeven. *Anne Frank: Beyond the Diary*
Whitelaw. *Charles de Gaulle*
Whitelaw. *Joseph Stalin*
Wiesel. *Night*

Collective Biography

Aaseng. *Genetics*
Aaseng. *Twentieth-Century Inventors*
Aaseng. *You Are the General*
Cohen. *Prophets of Doom*
Cush. *Artists Who Created Great Works*
Cush. *Women Who Achieved Greatness*

Glubok. *Great Lives: Painting*
Hoobler. *French Portraits*
Hoobler. *Russian Portraits*
Mahoney. *Women in Espionage*
Mayberry. *Leaders Who Changed the 20th Century*
Schraff. *Women of Peace: Nobel Peace Prize Winners*

Oleksy. *Military Leaders of World War II*
Weitzman. *Great Lives: Human Culture*
Wilkinson. *Scientists Who Changed the World*
Wolf. *Focus: Five Women Photographers*

History

Aaseng. *Paris*
Adler. *We Remember the Holocaust*
Anderson. *Battles That Changed the Modern World*
Ayer. *Berlin*
Ayer. *Parallel Journeys*
Boas. *We Are Witnesses*
Brown. *Conflict in Europe and the Great Depression*
Carroll. *The Battle of Stalingrad*
Childers. *Wings of Morning*
Chrisp. *The Rise of Fascism*
Cosner. *War Nurses*
Dale. *Early Cars*
Devaney. *America on the Attack: 1943*
Devaney. *America Storms the Beaches: 1944*
Devaney. *America Triumphs: 1945*
Epler. *The Berlin Wall*
Estonia
Fradin. *Medicine: Yesterday, Today, and Tomorrow*
Friedman. *Escape or Die*
Friedman. *The Other Victims*
Garfunkel. *On Wings of Joy: Ballet*
Gay. *World War II*
Greenberg. *Letters From a World War II GI*
Greene. *Child Labor*
Handler. *Surviving the Holocaust in Hungary*
Hanmer. *Leningrad*

Heyes. *Children of the Swastika*
Hull. *A Prose Anthology of the Second World War*
Ippisch. *Sky: Resistance during World War II*
Isserman. *World War II*
Koehn. *Mischling, Second Degree*
Kort. *Marxism in Power*
Kort. *Russia*
Kotlyarskaya. *Women in Society: Russia*
Kronenwetter. *London*
Kronenwetter. *Northern Ireland*
Lace. *England*
Landau. *The Warsaw Ghetto Uprising*
Landau. *We Survived the Holocaust*
Lawson. *The Abraham Lincoln Brigade*
Leitner. *Isabella: From Auschwitz to Freedom*
Levy. *Women in Society: Britain*
Levy. *Women in Society: Ireland*
Marrin. *OVERLORD: D-Day*
Marshall. *Ocean Traders*
Meltzer. *How Gentiles Saved Jews in the Holocaust*
Meltzer. *How Our Youngest Workers Are Exploited and Abused*
Meltzer. *The Jews of the Holocaust*

Mulcahy. *Diseases: Finding the Cure*
Perl. *Four Perfect Pebbles: A Holocaust Story*
Perl. *Why We Dress the Way We Do*
Pettit. *True Stories of Wartime Resistance*
Pietrusza. *The Invasion of Normandy*
Platt. *The Smithsonian Visual Timeline of Inventions*
Rice. *The Final Solution*
Rochman. *Bearing Witness*
Ross. *The USSR Under Stalin*
Sauvain. *El Alamein*
Sherrow. *Amsterdam*
Spangenburg. *The History of Science from 1895 to 1945*
Spencer. *Germany: Then and Now*
Steele. *Food and Feasts Between the Two World Wars*
Stein. *World War II in Europe*
Stewart. *Hitler's Reich*
Stewart. *Life in the Warsaw Ghetto*
Strahinich. *The Holocaust: Understanding and Remembering*
Toll. *Behind the Secret Window: World War II*
Vail. *World War II: The War in Europe*
Wetterau. *World History*
Zeinert. *The Warsaw Ghetto Uprising*
Zyskind. *Struggle*

Multimedia

CD-ROM

Art & Music: Surrealism
Art & Music: The Twentieth Century
Complete Maus
Events That Changed the World

History Through Art: 20th Century
Ideas That Changed the World
Lest We Forget: A History of the Holocaust

Our Times: The Multimedia Encyclopedia of the Twentieth Century
Science Navigator
Teach Your Kids World History
World War II, Global Conflict

Video

1945-1989: The Cold War

The 20's: From Illusion to Disillusion

Anzio and the Italian Campaign

The B-24 Trilogy: The Victory Bombers

The Battle of the Bulge and the Drive to the Rhine

Birth of the Bomber: The Story of the B-24 Liberator

Camp of Home and Despair: Westerbork Concentration Camp 1939-1945

Child in Two Worlds

Children of the Holocaust

Children Remember the Holocaust

Choosing One's Way

D-Day and the Battle for France

D-Day Omaha Beach

Dateline: 1943 Europe

Diamonds in the Snow

Disgraced Monuments

Estonia: A Story of Survival

Father's Return to Auschwitz

Forever Activists: Stories From the Veterans of the Abraham Lincoln Brigade

Germany: Past and Present

Grave of the Fireflies

The Hindenburg

Hitler's Assault on Europe

The Holocaust: A Teenager's Experience

The Holocaust as Seen Through the Eyes of a Survivor

The Holocaust Wall Hangings

How the Nazis Came to Power

Image Before My Eyes

The Last Seven Months of Anne Frank

Lenin and Me, Parts 1 & 2

A Little Tailor's Christmas Story

Lodz Ghetto

London: City of Majesty

The Lonely Struggle: Marek Edelman, Last Hero of the Warsaw Ghetto Uprising

Lost Childhood: The Boys of Birkenau

The Lucky Ones: Allied Airmen and Buchenwald

Married with a Star

Memories of Childhood and War

Operation: Dragoon

The Polish Experience

The Power of Conscience: The Danish Resistance and the Rescue of the Jews

Psychology of Neo-Nazism: Another Journey by Train to Auschwitz

The Road to Wannsee: Eleven Million Sentenced to Death

Schindler: The Documentary

The Second World War

Shtetl

Siberia: Land of the Future

Sorrow: The Nazi Legacy

Spain: History and Culture

Stalin

The Surreal Eye: On the Threshold of Dreams

Survivors of the Holocaust

Trinity and Beyond: The Atomic Bomb Movie

Trotsky

Tsiolkovski: The Space Age

The Visas That Saved Lives

The Vistula

A Wall of Silence

War Years: Britain in World War Two—The Phoney War

We Must Never Forget: The Story of the Holocaust

Women's Stories of the Holocaust

World War Two

GRADE TEN

Historical Fiction

Baklanov. *Forever Nineteen*

Benchley. *Bright Candles*

Bergman. *Along the Tracks*

Bitton-Jackson. *I Have Lived a Thousand Years: Growing up in the Holocaust*

Carter. *The Hunted*

Durrell. *White Eagles over Serbia*

Forman. *Ceremony of Innocence*

Forman. *Horses of Anger*

Forman. *My Enemy My Brother*

Forman. *The Survivor*

Forman. *The Traitors*

Frank. *No Hero for the Kaiser*

Friedman. *Nightfather*

Gallaz. *Rose Blanche*

Gehrts. *Don't Say a Word*

Goldstein. *Mazel*

Hackl. *Farewell Sidonia*

Hartman. *War Without Friends*

Hautzig. *The Endless Steppe*

Hunter. *Hold on to Love*

Hunter. *A Sound of Chariots*

Hunter. *The Third Eye*

Laird. *But Can the Phoenix Sing?*

Laird. *Shadow of the Wall*

Magorian. *Good Night, Mr. Tom*

Magorian. *Not a Swan*

Matas. *Code Name Kris*

Matas. *Lisa's War*

Michaels. *Fugitive Pieces: A Novel*

Nolan. *If I Should Die Before I Wake*

Norling. *Patty's Journey: From Orphanage to Adoption and Reunion*

Orlev. *The Man from the Other Side*

O'Sullivan. *Melody for Nora*

Paton Walsh. *The Dolphin Crossing*

Paton Walsh. *Fireweed*

Pausewang. *The Final Journey*

Pelgrom. *The Acorn Eaters*

Pelgrom. *The Winter When Time Was Frozen*

Peyton. *Flambards Divided*

Ray. *To Cross a Line*

Raymond. *Daniel and Esther*

Reuter. *The Boys from St. Petri*

Sender. *The Cage*

Sevela. *We Were Not Like Other People*
Treseder. *Hear O Israel*
Van Dijk. *Damned Strong Love*

Wesley. *Part of the Furniture*
Westall. *Blitzcat*
Westall. *Echoes of War*
Westall. *The Machine-Gunners*

Yolen. *Briar Rose*
Yolen. *The Devil's Arithmetic*

Biography

Adelson. *The Diary of Dawid Sierakowiak*
Amdur. *Chaim Weizmann*
Atkinson. *In Kindling Flame: Hannah Senesh*
Ayer. *Adolf Hitler*
Banfield. *Charles De Gaulle*
Beardsley. *Pablo Picasso*
Berman. *Paul Von Hindenburg*
Bernstein. *Albert Einstein and the Frontiers of Physics*
Bierman. *Righteous*
Bober. *Marc Chagall*
Bradley. *Hitler and the Third Reich*
Carter. *George Santayana*
Carter. *Salvador Dali*
Casals. *Joys and Sorrows*
Caulkins. *Joseph Stalin*
Dahl. *Going Solo*
Deschamps. *Spyglass: An Autobiography*
Driemen. *Winston Churchill*

Flynn. *George Orwell*
Frank. *The Diary of a Young Girl*
Fuchs. *The Hitler Fact Book*
Garza. *Francisco Franco*
Garza. *Pablo Casals*
Gay. *Emma Goldman*
Gelistsen. *Rena's Promise*
Goldberg. *Albert Einstein: The Rebel Behind Relativity*
Gottfried. *Enrico Fermi*
Gourley. *Beryl Markham: Never Turn Back*
Grady. *Marie Curie*
Gray. *Manya's Story*
Greenfield. *Marc Chagall*
Hartenian. *Benito Mussolini*
Heyes. *Adolf Hitler*
Hoobler. *Joseph Stalin*
Lewis. *Tomá Masaryk*
Linnéa. *Raoul Wallenberg*
Lyttle. *Il Duce: Benito Mussolini*
Lyttle. *Pablo Picasso*

Mann. *Sigmund Freud*
Marrin. *Hitler*
Mulvihill. *Mussolini and Italian Fascism*
Novac. *Beautiful Days of My Youth*
Otfinoski. *Alexander Fleming*
Otfinoski. *Joseph Stalin*
Pozzi. *Chagall*
Roberts. *The Importance of Oskar Schindler*
Rogers. *Churchill*
Shephard. *Maria Montessori*
Siegal. *Upon the Head of a Goat*
Tachau. *Kemal Atatürk*
Vasileva. *Hostage to War: A True Story*
Watkins. *Zoli's Legacy I: Inheritance*
Whitelaw. *Charles de Gaulle*
Whitelaw. *Joseph Stalin*
Wiesel. *Night*

Collective Biography

Aaseng. *Genetics*
Aaseng. *Twentieth-Century Inventors*
Aaseng. *You Are the General*
Anderson. *Explorers Who Found New Worlds*

Axelrod. *Dictators and Tyrants*
Mahoney. *Women in Espionage*
Oleksy. *Military Leaders of World War II*

Weitzman. *Great Lives: Theater*
Wilkinson. *Scientists Who Changed the World*
Wolf. *Focus: Five Women Photographers*

History

Adler. *We Remember the Holocaust*
Ardley. *Music: An Illustrated Encyclopedia*
Astor. *Operation Iceberg*
Ayer. *Berlin*
Ayer. *Parallel Journeys*
Boas. *We Are Witnesses*
Burgess. *The Longest Tunnel*
Carroll. *The Battle of Stalingrad*
Childers. *Wings of Morning*
Chrisp. *The Rise of Fascism*
Dale. *Early Cars*
Davis. *Man-Made Catastrophes*
Devaney. *America on the Attack: 1943*
Devaney. *America Storms the Beaches: 1944*

Devaney. *America Triumphs: 1945*
Eichengreen. *From Ashes to Life*
Epler. *The Berlin Wall*
Fradin. *Medicine: Yesterday, Today, and Tomorrow*
Gilbert. *The Day the War Ended: May 8, 1945*
Gill. *German Resistance to Hitler*
Greenberg. *Letters From a World War II GI*
Greene. *Child Labor*
Hillesum. *Etty Hillesum*
Hull. *A Prose Anthology of the Second World War*
Ippisch. *Sky: Resistance During World War II*
Isserman. *World War II*

Koehn. *Mischling, Second Degree*
Kort. *Marxism in Power*
Kort. *Russia*
Kronenwetter. *Northern Ireland*
Lace. *England*
Landau. *The Warsaw Ghetto Uprising*
Landau. *We Survived the Holocaust*
Lawson. *The Abraham Lincoln Brigade*
Levy. *Women in Society: Britain*
Levy. *Women in Society: Ireland*
Marrin. *OVERLORD: D-Day*
Marshall. *Ocean Traders*

Marx. *The Search for Sunken Treasure*

Meltzer. *How Gentiles Saved Jews in the Holocaust*

Meltzer. *The Jews of the Holocaust*

Mulcahy. *Diseases: Finding the Cure*

Pettit. *True Stories of Wartime Resistance*

Perl. *Four Perfect Pebbles: A Holocaust Story*

Pickford. *The Atlas of Shipwrecks & Treasure*

Pietrusza. *The Invasion of Normandy*

Rice. *The Final Solution*

Rochman. *Bearing Witness*

Ross. *The USSR Under Stalin*

Spangenburg. *The History of Science from 1895 to 1945*

Steidl. *Lost Battalions: Going for Broke in the Vosges, Autumn, 1944*

Stewart. *Hitler's Reich*

Stewart. *Life in the Warsaw Ghetto*

Strahinich. *The Holocaust: Understanding and Remembering*

Toll. *Behind the Secret Window: World War II*

Vail. *World War II: The War in Europe*

Zeinert. *The Warsaw Ghetto Uprising*

Multimedia

CD-ROM

Art & Music: Surrealism

Art & Music: The Twentieth Century

Complete Maus

Events That Changed the World

History Through Art: 20th Century

Ideas That Changed the World

Lest We Forget: A History of the Holocaust

Normandy: The Great Crusade

Our Times: The Multimedia Encyclopedia of the Twentieth Century

Science Navigator

Teach Your Kids World History

World War II, Global Conflict

Video

Anzio and the Italian Campaign

The B-24 Trilogy: The Victory Bombers

The Battle of the Bulge and the Drive to the Rhine

Birth of the Bomber: The Story of the B-24 Liberator

Camp of Home and Despair: Westerbork Concentration Camp 1939-1945

Children of the Holocaust

Choosing One's Way

D-Day and the Battle for France

D-Day Omaha Beach

D-Day + 50. . .Normandy

Dateline: 1943 Europe

Diamonds in the Snow

Disgraced Monuments

Estonia: A Story of Survival

Facing Hate

Father's Return to Auschwitz

Forever Activists: Stories from the Veterans of the Abraham Lincoln Brigade

Germany: Past and Present

Grave of the Fireflies

The Hindenburg

Hitler's Assault on Europe

The Holocaust: A Teenager's Experience

The Holocaust as Seen Through the Eyes of a Survivor

The Holocaust Wall Hangings

How the Nazis Came to Power

Image Before My Eyes

The Last Seven Months of Anne Frank

Lenin and Me, Parts 1 & 2

A Little Tailor's Christmas Story

Lodz Ghetto

The Lonely Struggle: Marek Edelman, Last Hero of the Warsaw Ghetto Uprising

Lost Childhood: The Boys of Birkenau

The Lucky Ones: Allied Airmen and Buchenwald

Married with a Star

Memories of Childhood and War

1945-1989: The Cold War

Operation: Dragoon

The Polish Experience

The Power of Conscience: The Danish Resistance and the Rescue of the Jews

Psychology of Neo-Nazism: Another Journey by Train to Auschwitz

Rise and Fall of the Soviet Union

Schindler: The Documentary

The Second World War

Siberia: Land of the Future

Sigrid Undset--A Portrait

Sorrow: The Nazi Legacy

Spain: History and Culture

Stalin

The Surreal Eye: On the Threshold of Dreams

Survivors of the Holocaust

Trinity and Beyond: The Atomic Bomb Movie

Trotsky

The 20's: From Illusion to Disillusion

The Visas That Saved Lives

War Years: Britain in World War Two—the Phoney War

We Must Never Forget: The Story of the Holocaust

Women's Stories of the Holocaust

World War Two

GRADES ELEVEN AND TWELVE

Historical Fiction

Baklanov. *Forever Nineteen*
Benchley. *Bright Candles*
Binchy. *The Glass Lake*
Bitton-Jackson. *I Have Lived a Thousand Years: Growing up in the Holocaust*
Carter. *The Hunted*
Crosby. *The Haldanes*
de Hartog. *The Lamb's War*
Durrell. *White Eagles over Serbia*
Forman. *Ceremony of Innocence*
Forman. *Horses of Anger*
Forman. *My Enemy My Brother*
Forman. *The Survivor*
Forman. *The Traitors*
Friedman. *Nightfather*
Gilbert. *The Treachery of Time*
Glasco. *Slow Through Eden*
Goldstein. *Mazel*
Hackl. *Farewell Sidonia*

Harris. *Enigma*
Hunter. *The Third Eye*
King. *A Monstrous Regiment of Women*
Laird. *But Can the Phoenix Sing?*
Laird. *Shadow of the Wall*
Magorian. *Good Night, Mr. Tom*
Magorian. *Not a Swan*
McCutchan. *Cameron and the Kaiserhof*
McCutchan. *Cameron Comes Through*
McCutchan. *Cameron in Command*
McCutchan. *Cameron's Commitment*
McCutchan. *Cameron's Crossing*
McCutchan. *Cameron's Raid*
McCutchan. *Cameron's Troop Lift*
Michaels. *Fugitive Pieces: A Novel*

Nolan. *If I Should Die Before I Wake*
Norling. *Patty's Journey: From Orphanage to Adoption and Reunion*
Paton Walsh. *The Dolphin Crossing*
Pausewang. *The Final Journey*
Pelgrom. *The Acorn Eaters*
Peyton. *Flambards Divided*
Ray. *To Cross a Line*
Raymond. *Daniel and Esther*
Reuter. *The Boys from St. Petri*
Richter. *I Was There*
Sender. *The Cage*
Sevela. *We Were Not Like Other People*
Van Dijk. *Damned Strong Love*
Wesley. *Part of the Furniture*
Westall. *Blitzcat*
Yolen. *Briar Rose*
Yolen. *The Devil's Arithmetic*

Biography

Adelson. *The Diary of Dawid Sierakowiak*
Aline. *The Spy Went Dancing*
Amdur. *Chaim Weizmann*
Atkinson. *In Kindling Flame: Hannah Senesh*
Ayer. *Adolf Hitler*
Banfield. *Charles De Gaulle*
Beardsley. *Pablo Picasso*
Berman. *Paul Von Hindenburg*
Bernstein. *Albert Einstein and the Frontiers of Physics*
Bierman. *Righteous Gentile: Raoul Wallenberg*
Bober. *Marc Chagall*
Bradley. *Hitler and the Third Reich*
Carter. *George Santayana*
Carter. *Salvador Dali*
Casals. *Joys and Sorrows*
Caulkins. *Joseph Stalin*
Dahl. *Going Solo*
Deschamps. *Spyglass*

Driemen. *Winston Churchill*
Edvardson. *Burned Child Seeks the Fire: A Memoir*
Flynn. *George Orwell*
Frank. *The Diary of a Young Girl*
Fuchs. *The Hitler Fact Book*
Garza. *Francisco Franco*
Garza. *Pablo Casals*
Gay. *Emma Goldman*
Gelistsen. *Rena's Promise*
Gottfried. *Enrico Fermi*
Gray. *Manya's Story*
Greenfield. *Marc Chagall*
Hartenian. *Benito Mussolini*
Heyes. *Adolf Hitler*
Hoobler. *Joseph Stalin*
Lewis. *Tomá Masaryk*
Lyttle. *Il Duce: Benito Mussolini*
Lyttle. *Pablo Picasso*
Manchester. *Winston Spencer Churchill: 1874-1932*

Manchester. *Winston Spencer Churchill:1932-1940*
Mann. *Sigmund Freud*
Marrin. *Hitler*
Meyers. *Doors to Madame Marie*
Mulvihill. *Mussolini and Italian Fascism*
Novac. *Beautiful Days of My Youth*
Otfinoski. *Alexander Fleming*
Pozzi. *Chagall*
Radzinsky. *Stalin*
Roberts. *The Importance of Oskar Schindler*
Rogers. *Churchill*
Tachau. *Kemal Atatürk*
Vasileva. *Hostage to War: A True Story*
Volkogonov. *Trotsky*
Watkins. *Zoli's Legacy I: Inheritance*
Wiesel. *Night*

Collective Biography

Aaseng. *Genetics*
Aaseng. *Twentieth-Century Inventors*

Aaseng. *You Are the General*
Anderson. *Explorers Who Found New Worlds*

Axelrod. *Dictators and Tyrants*
Boorstin. *The Creators*

Mahoney. *Women in Espionage*
Landrum. *Profiles of Female Genius*

Landrum. *Profiles of Genius: Thirteen Creative Men*
Oleksy. *Military Leaders of World War II*

Weitzman. *Great Lives: Theater*
Wolf. *Focus: Five Women Photographers*

History

Adler. *We Remember the Holocaust*
Ardley. *Music: An Illustrated Encyclopedia*
Astor. *Operation Iceberg*
Ayer. *Berlin*
Ayer. *Parallel Journeys*
Aymar. *Men in the Air*
Beckett. *The Story of Painting*
Bles. *Child at War*
Boas. *We Are Witnesses*
Breznitz. *Memory Fields*
Burgess. *The Longest Tunnel*
Castello. *The Jews and Europe*
Childers. *Wings of Morning*
Chrisp. *The Rise of Fascism*
Cole. *Perspective*
Crowe. *A History of the Gypsies of Eastern Europe and Russia*
Dale. *Early Cars*
Davidson. *Everyday Life Through the Ages*
Davis. *Man-Made Catastrophes*
Devaney. *America on the Attack: 1943*
Devaney. *America Storms the Beaches: 1944*
Devaney. *America Triumphs: 1945*
Douglas. *The World War, 1939-1945*
Dwork. *Children with a Star*
Eichengreen. *From Ashes to Life*
Ewing. *Women in Uniform*

Fluek. *Memories of My Life in a Polish Village*
Fogelman. *Rescuers of Jews During the Holocaust*
Foss. *Poetry of the World Wars*
Friedman. *Flying Against the Wind*
Fulbrook. *The Divided Germany*
Gilbert. *The Day the War Ended: May 8, 1945*
Gill. *German Resistance to Hitler*
Greenberg. *Letters from a World War II GI*
Hibbert. *Venice*
Hillesum. *Etty Hillesum*
Hoare. *The Modern World*
Holliday. *Children in the Holocaust and World War II*
Ippisch. *Sky: Resistance During World War II*
Keegan. *History of Warfare*
Koehn. *Mischling, Second Degree*
Lace. *England*
Leckie. *Okinawa: The Last Battle of World War II*
Levy. *Women in Society: Britain*
Levy. *Women in Society: Ireland*
Lindwer. *The Last Seven Months of Anne Frank*
Marshall. *Ocean Traders*

Marx. *The Search for Sunken Treasure*
Meltzer. *The Jews of the Holocaust*
Miller. *The Oral History of D-Day*
Perl. *Four Perfect Pebbles: A Holocaust Story*
Pickford. *The Atlas of Shipwrecks & Treasure*
Pimlott. *The Elite: The Special Forces of the World*
Porter. *London, a Social History*
Posner. *Hitler's Children*
Rice. *The Final Solution*
Ross. *The USSR Under Stalin*
Rotem. *Memoirs of a Warsaw Ghetto Fighter*
Spangenburg. *The History of Science from 1895 to 1945*
Steidl. *Lost Battalions: Going for Broke in the Vosges, Autumn, 1944*
Steinhoff. *Voices from the Third Reich*
Terkel. *The Good War*
Vogel. *Bad Times, Good Friends*
Weintraub. *The End of World War II*
Wicks. *No Time to Wave Goodbye*
Wiesel. *From the Kingdom of Memory*
Windrow. *Uniforms of the French Foreign Legion*

Multimedia

CD-ROM

Art & Music: Surrealism
Art & Music: The Twentieth Century
Complete Maus
Events That Changed the World

History Through Art: 20th Century
Ideas That Changed the World
Lest We Forget: A History of the Holocaust
Normandy: The Great Crusade

Our Times: The Multimedia Encyclopedia of the Twentieth Century
Science Navigator
Teach Your Kids World History
World War II, Global Conflict

Video

1945-1989: The Cold War
The 20's: From Illusion to Disillusion
The B-24 Trilogy: The Victory Bombers

Birth of the Bomber: The Story of the B-24 Liberator
Camp of Home and Despair: Westerbork Concentration Camp 1939-1945
Children of the Holocaust

Choosing One's Way
D-Day and the Battle for France
D-Day Omaha Beach
D-Day + 50. . .Normandy
Dateline: 1943 Europe

Diamonds in the Snow
Disgraced Monuments
Estonia: A Story of Survival
Facing Hate
Father's Return to Auschwitz
The First World War and the
    Rise of Fascism
Forever Activists: Stories
    from the Veterans of the
    Abraham Lincoln Brigade
Germany: Past and Present
Grave of the Fireflies
The Hindenburg
The Holocaust: A Teenager's
    Experience
The Holocaust as Seen
    Through the Eyes of a
    Survivor
The Holocaust Wall Hangings
How the Nazis Came to Power
Image Before My Eyes
The Last Seven Months of
    Anne Frank

Lenin and Me, Parts 1 & 2
Lodz Ghetto
The Lonely Struggle: Marek
    Edelman, Last Hero of the
    Warsaw Ghetto Uprising
Lost Childhood: The Boys of
    Birkenau
The Lucky Ones: Allied
    Airmen and Buchenwald
Married with a Star
Memories of Childhood and
    War
Operation: Dragoon
The Personal File of Anna
    Akhmatova
The Polish Experience
The Power of Conscience:
    The Danish Resistance and
    the Rescue of the Jews
Psychology of Neo-Nazism:
    Another Journey by Train
    to Auschwitz

Rise and Fall of the Soviet
    Union
Schindler: The Documentary
The Second World War
Siberia: Land of the Future
Sigrid Undset—A Portrait
Sorrow: The Nazi Legacy
Stalin
The Surreal Eye: On the
    Threshold of Dreams
Survivors of the Holocaust
The Technological Revolution
Trinity and Beyond: The
    Atomic Bomb Movie
The Visas That Saved Lives
War Years: Britain in World
    War Two—the Phoney War
We Must Never Forget: The
    Story of the Holocaust
Women's Stories of the
    Holocaust
World War Two

Europe and the British Isles, 1946 to the Present

Historical Fiction

De Treviño. *Turi's Poppa*
Degens. *Freya on the Wall*
Degens. *On the Third Ward*
Elmer. *Touch the Sky*
Fenton. *The Morning of the Gods*
Geras. *The Tower Room*
Goodman. *Songs from Home*
Kossman. *Behind the Border*

Layton. *The Swap*
Lorbiecki. *From My Palace of Leaves in Sarajevo*
Magorian. *Back Home*
Matas. *After the War*
Mead. *Adem's Cross*
Mooney. *The Voices of Silence*
Morpurgo. *Mr. Nobody's Eyes*

Morpurgo. *The War of Jenkins' Ear*
Reiss. *The Journey Back*
Roper. *In Caverns of Blue Ice*
Rosen. *Andi's War*
Rowlands. *Milk and Honey*
Sender. *To Life*
Szablya. *The Fall of the Red Star*

Biography

Allen. *The Windsor Secret*
Auerbach. *Queen Elizabeth II*
Ayer. *Boris Yeltsin*
Beardsley. *Pablo Picasso*
Bentley. *Albert Schweitzer*
Caulkins. *Joseph Stalin*
Cech. *Jacques-Henri Lartigue*
Courtney. *Sir Peter Scott*
Craig. *Lech Walesa*
Craig. *Lech Walesa and His Poland*
Ebon. *Nikita Khrushchev*
Foster. *Margaret Thatcher*
Gourley. *Beryl Markham: Never Turn Back*
Gray. *Bob Geldof*
Greenfield. *Marc Chagall*
Hargrove. *Pablo Casals*
Hole. *Margaret Thatcher*

Hughes. *Madam Prime Minister: Margaret Thatcher*
Kaye. *Lech Walesa*
Kort. *Mikhail Gorbachev*
Kristy. *George Balanchine*
Lambroza. *Boris Yeltsin*
Lazo. *Elie Wiesel*
Lazo. *Lech Walesa*
Loumaye. *Chagall*
MacDonald. *Pablo Picasso*
Marrin. *Stalin*
Mason. *Picasso: An Introduction*
Muhlberger. *What Makes a Picasso a Picasso?*
Otfinoski. *Joseph Stalin*
Perl. *Isaac Bashevis Singer*
Pozzi. *Chagall*

Roberts. *Dian Fossey*
Ross. *Miró*
Schecter. *Boris Yeltsin*
Schiffman. *Josip Broz Tito*
Selfridge. *Pablo Picasso*
Senn. *Jane Goodall: Naturalist*
Severance. *Winston Churchill*
Sheldon. *Dag Hammarskjöld*
Shephard. *Maria Montessori*
Sproule. *Mikhail Gorbachev*
Stefoff. *Lech Walesa*
Stewart. *Sir Edmund Hillary*
Swisher. *Pablo Picasso*
Twist. *Gagarin and Armstrong*
Winner. *Peter Benenson*

Collective Biography

Aaseng. *Genetics*
Aaseng. *You Are the General*
Blue. *People of Peace*
Cohen. *Prophets of Doom*
Cush. *Women Who Achieved Greatness*
Hoobler. *French Portraits*
Hoobler. *Russian Portraits*
Italia. *Courageous Crimefighters*

Jacobs. *Great Lives: Human Rights*
Jacobs. *Great Lives: World Religions*
Krull. *Lives of the Artists*
Krull. *Lives of the Musicians*
Martin. *The Beatles*
Mayberry. *Leaders Who Changed the 20th Century*

Newton. *James Watson & Francis Crick*
Schraff. *Women of Peace: Nobel Peace Prize Winners*
Wilkinson. *Scientists Who Changed the World*
Wolf. *Focus: Five Women Photographers*
Woog. *The Beatles*

History

Anderson. *Battles That Changed the Modern World*
Ashabranner. *Discovering Chinese Central Asia*
Bachrach. *The Korean War*
Bachrach. *Tell Them We Remember*
Belarus
Bortz. *Catastrophe!*
Bradley. *Kazakhstan*
Capek. *Artistic Trickery: Trompe L'Oeil Art*
Chaikin. *A Nightmare in History*
Clark. *The Commonwealth of Independent States*
Cross. *Aftermath of War*
Cumming. *Russia*
Cush. *Disasters That Shook the World*
Deltenre. *Russia*
Epler. *The Berlin Wall*
Estonia
Finkelstein. *The Cuban Missile Crisis*
Flint. *The Baltic States*
Flint. *The Russian Federation*
Garfunkel. *On Wings of Joy: Ballet*
Georgia
Giblin. *Be Seated: A Book About Chairs*
Giblin. *When Plague Strikes*
Gosnell. *Belarus, Ukraine, and Moldova*
Harbor. *Conflict in Eastern Europe*
Heater. *The Cold War*
Kazakhstan

King. *The Gulf War*
Koral. *An Album of War Refugees*
Kort. *The Cold War*
Kort. *Marxism in Power*
Kort. *Russia*
Kotlyarskaya. *Women in Society: Russia*
Kronenwetter. *The New Eastern Europe*
Kyrgyzstan
Lace. *England*
Landau. *Nazi War Criminals*
Langone. *Spreading Poison*
Latvia
Levy. *Women in Society: Britain*
Levy. *Women in Society: Ireland*
Lithuania
Lynch. *Great Buildings*
Meltzer. *Gold*
Moldova
Morley. *Clothes*
Mulcahy. *Diseases: Finding the Cure*
Nardo. *Chernobyl*
Patterson. *Book of the United Nations*
Perl. *Why We Dress the Way We Do*
Pietrusza. *The End of the Cold War*
Platt. *The Smithsonian Visual Timeline of Inventions*
Rice. *The Nuremberg Trials*
Roberts. *Georgia, Armenia, and Azerbaijan*

Ross. *Conquerors and Explorers*
Ross. *The United Nations*
Ross. *The USSR Under Stalin*
Russia
Sawyer. *Refugees*
Seymour-Jones. *Refugees*
Sifakis. *Hoaxes and Scams*
Smith. *The Collapse of the Soviet Union*
Spencer. *Germany: Then and Now*
Steele. *Censorship*
Steele. *Riots*
Steele. *Smuggling*
Strahinich. *The Holocaust: Understanding and Remembering*
Strom. *Searching for the Gypsies*
Sunk! Exploring Underwater Archaeology
Tajikistan
Tchudi. *Lock and Key*
Thomas. *The Central Asian States*
Turkmenistan
Turvey. *Inventions*
Ukraine
Uzbekistan
Westerfeld. *The Berlin Airlift*
Wetterau. *World History*
Wilkinson. *Amazing Buildings*
Wilkinson. *Building*
Woolf. *Picture This: A First Introduction to Paintings*
Yancey. *The Reunification of Germany*

Multimedia

CD-ROM

Art & Music: The Twentieth Century
Eyewitness Encyclopedia of Science

Religions of the World
Science Navigator
Teach Your Kids World History

The Way Things Work

Video

Albert Einstein: The Education of a Genius
The Baltic States: Finding Independence
The Berlin Airlift
The British Way of Life
The Cold War, Part 3
Czechoslovakia: 1968
Discovering Russia
Europe: Insular Region
The Fall of Soviet Communism (Part 4)

Germany: From Partition to Reunification, 1945-1990
Germany: Past and Present
The Hungarian Uprising: 1956
The Illegals
Legacy of the Mound Builders
London: City of Majesty
Lost Childhood: The Boys of Birkenau

Mirror, Mirror: Northern Ireland
Other Voices, Other Songs: The Armenians
Siberia: Land of the Future
Solidarity
Spain: History and Culture
Trompe L'Oeil: Paintings That Fool the Eye
Ukraine: Kiev and Luov

GRADE EIGHT

Historical Fiction

De Treviño. *Turi's Poppa*
Degens. *Freya on the Wall*
Degens. *On the Third Ward*
Elmer. *Touch the Sky*
Fenton. *The Morning of the Gods*
Geras. *The Tower Room*
Goodman. *Songs from Home*

Layton. *The Swap*
Lorbiecki. *From My Palace of Leaves in Sarajevo*
Magorian. *Back Home*
Matas. *After the War*
Mead. *Adem's Cross*
Morpurgo. *Mr. Nobody's Eyes*

Morpurgo. *The War of Jenkins' Ear*
Reiss. *The Journey Back*
Rosen. *Andi's War*
Sender. *To Life*
Szablya. *The Fall of the Red Star*

Biography

Auerbach. *Queen Elizabeth II*
Banfield. *Charles De Gaulle*
Beardsley. *Pablo Picasso*
Bentley. *Albert Schweitzer*
Carter. *Salvador Dali*
Caulkins. *Joseph Stalin*
Cech. *Jacques-Henri Lartigue*
Courtney. *Sir Peter Scott*
Craig. *Lech Walesa*
Craig. *Lech Walesa and His Poland*
Ebon. *Nikita Khrushchev*
Foster. *Margaret Thatcher*
Garza. *Francisco Franco*
Garza. *Pablo Casals*
Gourley. *Beryl Markham: Never Turn Back*
Gray. *Bob Geldof*
Greenfield. *Marc Chagall*

Hargrove. *Pablo Casals*
Hole. *Margaret Thatcher*
Hughes. *Madam Prime Minister: Margaret Thatcher*
Kaye. *Lech Walesa*
Kort. *Mikhail Gorbachev*
Kristy. *George Balanchine*
Lambroza. *Boris Yeltsin*
Lazo. *Elie Wiesel*
Lazo. *Lech Walesa*
Loumaye. *Chagall*
MacDonald. *Pablo Picasso*
Marrin. *Stalin*
Mason. *Picasso: An Introduction*
Muhlberger. *What Makes a Picasso a Picasso?*
Otfinoski. *Joseph Stalin*

Pozzi. *Chagall*
Roberts. *Dian Fossey*
Ross. *Miró*
Schecter. *Boris Yeltsin*
Schiffman. *Josip Broz Tito*
Selfridge. *Pablo Picasso*
Severance. *Winston Churchill*
Sheldon. *Dag Hammarskjöld*
Shephard. *Maria Montessori*
Sproule. *Mikhail Gorbachev*
Stefoff. *Lech Walesa*
Stewart. *Sir Edmund Hillary*
Swisher. *Pablo Picasso*
Twist. *Gagarin and Armstrong*
Walch. *Pope John XXIII*
Winner. *Peter Benenson*

Collective Biography

Aaseng. *Genetics*
Aaseng. *You Are the General*
Blue. *People of Peace*
Cohen. *Prophets of Doom*
Cush. *Artists Who Created Great Works*
Cush. *Women Who Achieved Greatness*
Hoobler. *French Portraits*

Hoobler. *Russian Portraits*
Italia. *Courageous Crimefighters*
Krull. *Lives of the Artists*
Krull. *Lives of the Musicians*
Martin. *The Beatles*
Matthews. *Power Brokers*
Mayberry. *Leaders Who Changed the 20th Century*

Newton. *James Watson & Francis Crick*
Schraff. *Women of Peace: Nobel Peace Prize Winners*
Wilkinson. *Scientists Who Changed the World*
Wolf. *Focus: Five Women Photographers*
Woog. *The Beatles*

History

Anderson. *Battles That Changed the Modern World*
Bachrach. *The Korean War*
Bachrach. *Tell Them We Remember*
Belarus
Bortz. *Catastrophe!*
Capek. *Artistic Trickery: Trompe L'Oeil Art*
Chaikin. *A Nightmare in History*
Clark. *The Commonwealth of Independent States*
Cumming. *Russia*

Cush. *Disasters That Shook the World*
Deltenre. *Russia*
Epler. *The Berlin Wall*
Estonia
Finkelstein. *The Cuban Missile Crisis*
Garfunkel. *On Wings of Joy: Ballet*
Georgia
Giblin. *Be Seated: A Book About Chairs*
Giblin. *When Plague Strikes*

Harbor. *The Breakup of the Soviet Union*
Harbor. *Conflict in Eastern Europe*
Heater. *The Cold War*
Kazakhstan
King. *The Gulf War*
Koral. *An Album of War Refugees*
Kort. *The Cold War*
Kort. *Marxism in Power*
Kort. *Russia*
Kotlyarskaya. *Women in Society: Russia*

Kronenwetter. *The New Eastern Europe*
Kyrgyzstan
Lace. *England*
Landau. *Nazi War Criminals*
Langone. *Spreading Poison*
Latvia
Lawson. *The Iran Hostage Crisis*
Levy. *Women in Society: Britain*
Levy. *Women in Society: Ireland*
Lithuania
Lynch. *Great Buildings*
Meltzer. *Gold*
Moldova
Morley. *Clothes*
Mulcahy. *Diseases: Finding the Cure*
Nardo. *Chernobyl*

Patterson. *Book of the United Nations*
Perl. *Why We Dress the Way We Do*
Pietrusza. *The End of the Cold War*
Platt. *The Smithsonian Visual Timeline of Inventions*
Rice. *The Nuremberg Trials*
Ross. *The United Nations*
Ross. *The USSR Under Stalin*
Russia
Sawyer. *Refugees*
Sifakis. *Hoaxes and Scams*
Smith. *The Collapse of the Soviet Union*
Spencer. *Germany: Then and Now*
Strahinich. *The Holocaust: Understanding and Remembering*

Strom. *Searching for the Gypsies*
Sunk! Exploring Underwater Archaeology
Tajikistan
Tchudi. *Lock and Key*
Turkmenistan
Turvey. *Inventions*
Ukraine
Uzbekistan
The War Against Terrorism
Westerfeld. *The Berlin Airlift*
Wetterau. *World History*
Wilkinson. *Building*
Woolf. *Picture This: A First Introduction to Paintings*
Yancey. *The Reunification of Germany*

Multimedia

CD-ROM

Art & Music: The Twentieth Century
Eyewitness Encyclopedia of Science

Religions of the World
Science Navigator
Teach Your Kids World History

The Way Things Work

Video

Albanian Journey: End of an Era
Albert Einstein: The Education of a Genius
The Baltic States: Finding Independence
The Berlin Airlift
The British Way of Life
The Cold War, Part 3
Czechoslovakia: 1968
Discovering Russia
Europe: Insular Region

The Fall of Soviet Communism (Part 4)
Germany: Past and Present
The Hungarian Uprising: 1956
The Illegals
Legacy of the Mound Builders
London: City of Majesty
Lost Childhood: The Boys of Birkenau
Mirror, Mirror: Northern Ireland

Other Voices, Other Songs: The Armenians
The Reunification of Germany
The Revolution in Eastern Europe
Siberia: Land of the Future
Solidarity
Spain: History and Culture
Stalin
Survivors of the Holocaust
Trompe L'Oeil: Paintings That Fool the Eye
Ukraine: Kiev and Luov

GRADE NINE

Historical Fiction

De Treviño. *Turi's Poppa*
Degens. *Freya on the Wall*
Degens. *On the Third Ward*
Geras. *The Tower Room*
Goodman. *Songs from Home*
Hendry. *Double Vision*

Magorian. *Back Home*
Matas. *After the War*
Mead. *Adem's Cross*
Morpurgo. *The War of Jenkins' Ear*
Reiss. *The Journey Back*

Rosen. *Andi's War*
Schlink. *The Reader*
Sender. *To Life*
Szablya. *The Fall of the Red Star*

Biography

Banfield. *Charles De Gaulle*
Beardsley. *Pablo Picasso*
Bentley. *Albert Schweitzer*

Bradford. *Elizabeth*
Carter. *Salvador Dali*
Casals. *Joys and Sorrows*

Caulkins. *Joseph Stalin*
Cech. *Jacques-Henri Lartigue*
Courtney. *Sir Peter Scott*

Craig. *Lech Walesa and His Poland*
Craig. *Lech Walesa*
Ebon. *Nikita Khrushchev*
Foster. *Margaret Thatcher*
Garza. *Francisco Franco*
Garza. *Pablo Casals*
Gourley. *Beryl Markham: Never Turn Back*
Greenfield. *Marc Chagall*
Hargrove. *Pablo Casals*
Hole. *Margaret Thatcher*
Hughes. *Madam Prime Minister*

Kaye. *Lech Walesa*
Kort. *Mikhail Gorbachev*
Kristy. *George Balanchine*
Lambroza. *Boris Yeltsin*
Lyttle. *Pablo Picasso*
MacDonald. *Pablo Picasso*
Madden. *Fidel Castro*
Marrin. *Stalin*
Mason. *Picasso: An Introduction*
Muhlberger. *What Makes a Picasso a Picasso?*
Otfinoski. *Alexander Fleming*
Otfinoski. *Joseph Stalin*

Pozzi. *Chagall*
Roberts. *Dian Fossey*
Schecter. *Boris Yeltsin*
Schiffman. *Josip Broz Tito*
Selfridge. *Pablo Picasso*
Severance. *Winston Churchill*
Sheldon. *Dag Hammarskjöld*
Shephard. *Maria Montessori*
Sproule. *Mikhail Gorbachev*
Stefoff. *Lech Walesa*
Walch. *Pope John XXIII*
Winner. *Peter Benenson*

Collective Biography

Aaseng. *Genetics*
Aaseng. *Twentieth-Century Inventors*
Aaseng. *You Are the General*
Cohen. *Prophets of Doom*
Cush. *Artists Who Created Great Works*
Cush. *Women Who Achieved Greatness*
Hoobler. *French Portraits*

Hoobler. *Russian Portraits*
Italia. *Courageous Crimefighters*
Martin. *The Beatles*
Matthews. *Power Brokers*
Mayberry. *Leaders Who Changed the 20th Century*
Newton. *James Watson & Francis Crick*

Schraff. *Women of Peace: Nobel Peace Prize Winners*
Sherrow. *James Watson & Francis Crick: Decoding the Secrets of DNA*
Wilkinson. *Scientists Who Changed the World*
Wolf. *Focus: Five Women Photographers*
Woog. *The Beatles*

History

Anderson. *Battles That Changed the Modern World*
Ashton. *The Cold War*
Bachrach. *The Korean War*
Bachrach. *Tell Them We Remember*
Belarus
Bortz. *Catastrophe!*
Capek. *Artistic Trickery: Trompe L'Oeil Art*
Cush. *Disasters That Shook the World*
Epler. *The Berlin Wall*
Estonia
Finkelstein. *The Cuban Missile Crisis*
Garfunkel. *On Wings of Joy: Ballet*
Georgia
Harbor. *The Breakup of the Soviet Union*
Harbor. *Conflict in Eastern Europe*
Heater. *The Cold War*
Kazakhstan
King. *The Gulf War*
Koral. *An Album of War Refugees*
Kort. *The Cold War*
Kort. *Marxism in Power*

Kort. *Russia*
Kotlyarskaya. *Women in Society: Russia*
Kronenwetter. *The New Eastern Europe*
Kyrgyzstan
Lace. *England*
Landau. *Nazi War Criminals*
Langone. *Spreading Poison*
Latvia
Lawson. *The Iran Hostage Crisis*
Levy. *Women in Society: Britain*
Levy. *Women in Society: Ireland*
Lithuania
Moldova
Morin. *The World War II War Crimes Trials*
Mulcahy. *Diseases: Finding the Cure*
Patterson. *Book of the United Nations*
Perl. *Why We Dress the Way We Do*
Pietrusza. *The End of the Cold War*
Platt. *The Smithsonian Visual Timeline of Inventions*

Rice. *The Nuremberg Trials*
Ross. *The United Nations*
Ross. *The USSR Under Stalin*
Russia
Sawyer. *Refugees*
Sifakis. *Hoaxes and Scams*
Smith. *The Collapse of the Soviet Union*
Spangenburg. *The History of Science from the 1946 to the 1990s*
Spangenburg. *Opening the Space Frontier*
Spencer. *Germany: Then and Now*
Strahinich. *The Holocaust: Understanding and Remembering*
Tajikistan
Tchudi. *Lock and Key*
Turkmenistan
Ukraine
Uzbekistan
The War Against Terrorism
Westerfeld. *The Berlin Airlift*
Wetterau. *World History*
Wilkinson. *Building*
Yancey. *The Reunification of Germany*

Multimedia

CD-ROM

Art & Music: The Twentieth Century

Events That Changed the World

Ideas That Changed the World

Religions of the World

Science Navigator

Teach Your Kids World History

The Way Things Work

Video

Albanian Journey: End of an Era

The Artists' Revolution: 10 Days in Prague

The Baltic States: Finding Independence

The Berlin Airlift

Breaking Barriers: A History of the Status of Women and the Role of the United Nations

The Cold War, Part 3

Czechoslovakia: 1968

Discovering Russia

Disgraced Monuments

Dosvedanya Means Good-Bye

Estonia: A Story of Survival

The Fall of Soviet Communism (Part 4)

From Vienna to Jerusalem: The Century of Teddy Kollek

Germany: Past and Present

Heart of the Warrior

The Hungarian Uprising: 1956

The Illegals

London: City of Majesty

Lost Childhood: The Boys of Birkenau

Mirror, Mirror: Northern Ireland

The Modern Philosophers

November's Children: Revolution in Prague

Other Voices, Other Songs: The Armenians

Pilgrimage of Remembrance: Jews in Poland Today

Return to My Shtetl Delatyn

The Reunification of Germany

The Revolution in Eastern Europe

Siberia: Land of the Future

Simon Wiesenthal: Freedom Is Not a Gift from Heaven

Solidarity

Spain: History and Culture

Trompe L'Oeil: Paintings That Fool the Eye

Unknown Secrets: Art and the Rosenberg Era

GRADE TEN

Historical Fiction

Degens. Freya on the Wall

Degens. On the Third Ward

Geras. The Tower Room

Hendry. Double Vision

Magorian. Back Home

Mead. Adem's Cross

Michaels. Fugitive Pieces: A Novel

Schlink. The Reader

Sender. To Life

Biography

Banfield. Charles De Gaulle

Beardsley. Pablo Picasso

Bradford. Elizabeth

Carter. Salvador Dali

Casals. Joys and Sorrows

Caulkins. Joseph Stalin

Ebon. Nikita Khrushchev

Foster. Margaret Thatcher

Garza. Francisco Franco

Garza. Pablo Casals

Gottfried. Enrico Fermi

Gourley. Beryl Markham: Never Turn Back

Greenfield. Marc Chagall

Hole. Margaret Thatcher

Kaye. Lech Walesa

Kort. Mikhail Gorbachev

Lyttle. Pablo Picasso

Otfinoski. Alexander Fleming

Otfinoski. Joseph Stalin

Pozzi. Chagall

Roberts. Dian Fossey

Schiffman. Josip Broz Tito

Severance. Winston Churchill

Sheldon. Dag Hammarskjöld

Shephard. Maria Montessori

Stefoff. Lech Walesa

Walch. Pope John XXIII

Watkins. Zoli's Legacy II: Bequest

Collective Biography

Aaseng. Genetics

Aaseng. Twentieth-Century Inventors

Aaseng. You Are the General

Martin. The Beatles

Newton. James Watson & Francis Crick

Sherrow. James Watson & Francis Crick: Decoding the Secrets of DNA

Wilkinson. Scientists Who Changed the World

Wolf. Focus: Five Women Photographers

Woog. The Beatles

History

Ashton. The Cold War

Bachrach. The Korean War

Capek. Artistic Trickery: Trompe L'Oeil Art

Davis. Man-Made Catastrophes

Epler. The Berlin Wall

Finkelstein. *The Cuban Missile Crisis*

Harbor. *The Breakup of the Soviet Union*

Heater. *The Cold War*

Hull. *Breaking Free: Human Rights Poetry*

King. *The Gulf War*

Kort. *Marxism in Power*

Kort. *The Cold War*

Kort. *Russia*

Kotlyarskaya. *Women in Society: Russia*

Kronenwetter. *The New Eastern Europe*

Lace. *England*

Landau. *Nazi War Criminals*

Langone. *Spreading Poison*

Lawson. *The Iran Hostage Crisis*

Levy. *Women in Society: Britain*

Levy. *Women in Society: Ireland*

Morin. *The World War II War Crimes Trials*

Mulcahy. *Diseases: Finding the Cure*

Nudel. *A Hand in the Darkness*

Patterson. *Book of the United Nations*

Rice. *The Nuremberg Trials*

Ross. *The United Nations*

Ross. *The USSR Under Stalin*

Sawyer. *Refugees*

Sifakis. *Hoaxes and Scams*

Smith. *The Collapse of the Soviet Union*

Smith. *The Frugal Gourmet on Our Immigrant Ancestors*

Spangenburg. *The History of Science from the 1946 to the 1990s*

Spangenburg. *Opening the Space Frontier: Space Exploration*

Strahinich. *The Holocaust: Understanding and Remembering*

Tchudi. *Lock and Key*

The War Against Terrorism

Wilkinson. *Building*

Yancey. *The Reunification of Germany*

Multimedia

CD-ROM

Art & Music: The Twentieth Century

Events That Changed the World

Ideas That Changed the World

Religions of the World

Science Navigator

Teach Your Kids World History

The Way Things Work

Video

Albanian Journey: End of an Era

Are We Winning Mommy? America and the Cold War

The Artists' Revolution: 10 Days in Prague

The Berlin Airlift

Breaking Barriers: A History of the Status of Women and the Role of the United Nations

The Changing Faces of Communist Poland

The Cold War, Part 3

Czechoslovakia: 1968

Discovering Russia

Disgraced Monuments

Dosvedanya Means Good-Bye

Estonia: A Story of Survival

The Fall of Soviet Communism (Part 4)

From Vienna to Jerusalem: The Century of Teddy Kollek

Germany: Past and Present

Heart of the Warrior

The Hungarian Uprising: 1956

The Illegals

Lost Childhood: The Boys of Birkenau

November's Children: Revolution in Prague

Pilgrimage of Remembrance: Jews in Poland Today

Return to My Shtetl Delatyn

The Reunification of Germany

The Revolution in Eastern Europe

Simon Wiesenthal: Freedom Is Not a Gift from Heaven

Solidarity

Spain: History and Culture

Stalin

Survivors of the Holocaust

Trompe L'Oeil: Paintings That Fool the Eye

Unknown Secrets: Art and the Rosenberg Era

GRADES ELEVEN AND TWELVE

Historical Fiction

Degens. *Freya on the Wall*

Doyle. *Paddy Clarke, Ha Ha Ha*

Friedman. *The Shovel and the Loom*

Hendry. *Double Vision*

Kennedy. *The Bitterest Age*

Michaels. *Fugitive Pieces*

Roberts. *Morning's Gate*

Schlink. *The Reader*

Sender. *To Life*

Biography

Banfield. *Charles De Gaulle*

Beardsley. *Pablo Picasso*

Bradford. *Elizabeth*

Carter. *Salvador Dali*

Casals. *Joys and Sorrows*

Caulkins. *Joseph Stalin*

Ebon. *Nikita Khrushchev*

Garza. *Francisco Franco*

Garza. *Pablo Casals*

Gottfried. *Enrico Fermi*

Greenfield. *Marc Chagall*

Hole. *Margaret Thatcher*

House. *George and Joy Adamson*

Kaye. *Lech Walesa*

Kort. *Mikhail Gorbachev*

Lyttle. *Pablo Picasso*

O'Halloran. *Pure Heart
Enlightened Mind*
Otfinoski. *Alexander Fleming*
Radzinsky. *Stalin*

Roberts. *Dian Fossey*
Schiffman. *Josip Broz Tito*
Sheldon. *Dag Hammarskjöld*
Stefoff. *Lech Walesa*

Walch. *Pope John XXIII*
Watkins. *Zoli's Legacy II:
Bequest*

Collective Biography

Aaseng. *Genetics*
Aaseng. *Twentieth-Century
Inventors*
Aaseng. *You Are the General*
Boorstin. *The Creators*
Landrum. *Profiles of Female
Genius*

Landrum. *Profiles of Genius:
Thirteen Creative Men*
Martin. *The Beatles*
Matthews. *Power Brokers*
Pozzi. *Chagall*

Sherrow. *James Watson &
Francis Crick: Decoding
the Secrets of DNA*
Smith. *Women Who Write*
Wolf. *Focus: Five Women
Photographers*
Woog. *The Beatles*

History

Ashton. *The Cold War*
Aymar. *Men in the Air*
Bachrach. *The Korean War*
Beckett. *The Story of Painting*
Capek. *Artistic Trickery:
Trompe L'Oeil Art*
Cole. *Perspective*
Crowe. *A History of the
Gypsies of Eastern Europe
and Russia*
Davis. *Man-Made
Catastrophes*
Ewing. *Women in Uniform*
Finkelstein. *The Cuban
Missile Crisis*
Fulbrook. *The Divided Germany*
Hoffman. *Archimedes' Revenge*
Hull. *Breaking Free: Human
Rights Poetry*

Kauffman. *The European
Community*
Keegan. *History of Warfare*
Lace. *England*
Langone. *Spreading Poison*
Levy. *Women in Society: Britain*
Levy. *Women in Society:
Ireland*
Maass. *Love Thy Neighbor: A
Story of War*
Morin. *The World War II
War Crimes Trials*
Nudel. *A Hand in the Darkness*
Porter. *London, a Social History*
Rice. *The Nuremberg Trials*
Ross. *The USSR Under Stalin*
Schimmel. *Mystery of Numbers*
Sifakis. *Encyclopedia of
Assassinations*

Smith. *The Frugal Gourmet on
Our Immigrant Ancestors*
Snyder. *The European
Women's Almanac*
Spangenburg. *The History of
Science from the 1946 to
the 1990s*
Spangenburg. *Opening the
Space Frontier: Space
Exploration*
Strahinich. *The Holocaust:
Understanding and
Remembering*
Wiesel. *From the Kingdom of
Memory*
Wilkinson. *Building*
Windrow. *Uniforms of the
French Foreign Legion*

Multimedia

CD-ROM

*Art & Music: The Twentieth
Century*
*Events That Changed the
World*

*Ideas That Changed the World
Religions of the World
Science Navigator*

*Teach Your Kids World
History
The Way Things Work*

Video

*Albanian Journey: End of an
Era*
*Are We Winning Mommy?
America and the Cold War*
*The Artists' Revolution: 10
Days in Prague*
*Breaking Barriers: A History
of the Status of Women and
the Role of the United
Nations*
*The Changing Faces of
Communist Poland*
The Cold War, Part 3
The Cold War
Czechoslovakia: 1968
Discovering Russia
Disgraced Monuments
Dosvedanya Means Good-Bye

Estonia: A Story of Survival
*The Fall of Soviet
Communism (Part 4)*
*From Vienna to Jerusalem:
The Century of Teddy
Kollek*
Germany: Past and Present
Heart of the Warrior
*The Hungarian Uprising:
1956*
The Illegals
*Lost Childhood: The Boys of
Birkenau*
*November's Children:
Revolution in Prague*
*The Personal File of Anna
Akhmatova*

*Pilgrimage of Remembrance:
Jews in Poland Today*
Return to My Shtetl Delatyn
The Reunification of Germany
*The Revolution in Eastern
Europe*
Semanta Santa in Seville
*Simon Wiesenthal: Freedom
Is Not a Gift from Heaven*
Solidarity
Stalin
Survivors of the Holocaust
The Technological Revolution
Toward the Future
*Trompe L'Oeil: Paintings
That Fool the Eye*
*Unknown Secrets: Art and the
Rosenberg Era*

Africa and South Africa

BEFORE 1900

Historical Fiction

Carter. *The Sentinels*

Hansen. *The Captive*

Rupert. *The African Mask*

Collective Biography

Hoobler. *African Portraits*
Simon. *Richard Burton*

Stanley. *Shaka: King of the Zulus*

History

Africa and the Origin of Humans
Anda. *Yoruba*
Bangura. *Kipsigis*
Barboza. *Door of No Return: Gorée Island*
Bianchi. *The Nubians*
Boateng. *Asante*
Corbishley. *Secret Cities*
De Bruycker. *Africa*
Feelings. *The Middle Passage*
Franck. *Around Africa and Asia by Sea*
Gordon. *Islam*
Jenkins. *Ancient Egypt, Ethiopia, and Nubia*
Koslow. *Dahomey: The Warrior Kings*

Koslow. *The West African Kingdoms 750-1900*
Mann. *Oyo, Benin, Ashanti: The Guinea Coast*
Medearis. *A History of African Americans*
Meltzer. *Gold*
Millar. *The Kingdom of Benin West Africa*
Murray. *Africa*
Nardo. *Braving the New World*
Ndukwe. *Fulani*
Ofosu-Appiah. *People in Bondage*
Ojo. *Mbuti*
Oluikpe. *Swazi*
Palmer. *The First Passage*

Parris. *Rendille*
Reynoldson. *Conflict and Change*
Ricciuti. *Somalia*
Rissik. *Women in Society: South Africa*
Sallah. *Wolof*
Street Smart! Cities of the Ancient World
Sullivan. *Slave Ship*
Udechukwu. *Herero*
Van Wyk. *Basotho*
Wangari. *Ameru*
Wilkinson. *The Magical East*
Zeleza. *Maasai*
Zeleza. *Mijikenda*

Multimedia

CD-ROM

Teach Your Kids World History

Video

Abubakari: The Explorer King of Mali
Africa: History and Culture

Ghana
The Roots of African Civilization

A Son of Africa

GRADES NINE THROUGH TWELVE

Historical Fiction
Achebe. *Things Fall Apart*
Carter. *The Sentinels*

Haley. *Roots*
O'Brian. *The Wine-Dark Sea*

Biography
Equiano. *The Kidnapped Prince: Olaudah Equiano*

Hoobler. *African Portraits*

Collective Biography

History
Africa and the Origin of Humans
Boateng. *Asante*
Feelings. *The Middle Passage*
Jenkins. *Ancient Egypt, Ethiopia, and Nubia*
Jones. *Africa, 1500-1900*
Gordon. *Islam*
Koslow. *The West African Kingdoms 750-1900*

Mann. *Oyo, Benin, Ashanti: The Guinea Coast*
Ndukwe. *Fulani*
Ofosu-Appiah. *People in Bondage*
Ojo. *Mbuti*
Palmer. *The First Passage*
Ricciuti. *Somalia*

Rissik. *Women in Society: South Africa*
Sallah. *Wolof*
Thompson. *A History of South Africa*
Time-Life. *Africa's Glorious Legacy*
Udechukwu. *Herero*
Van Wyk. *Basotho*

Multimedia

CD-ROM
Teach Your Kids World History

Video
Dark Passages
Ghana

The Roots of African Civilization

A Son of Africa

AFTER 1900

GRADES SEVEN AND EIGHT

Historical Fiction
Farmer. *A Girl Named Disaster*
Gordon. *The Middle of Somewhere*

Morpurgo. *Butterfly Lion*
Sacks. *Beyond Safe Boundaries*

Weaver-Gelzer. *In the Time of Trouble*

Biography
Bentley. *Archbishop Tutu of South Africa*
Denenberg. *Nelson Mandela*
Eide. *Robert Mugabe*
Feinberg. *Nelson Mandela*

Hoobler. *Mandela*
Hughes. *Nelson Mandela*
Kellner. *Kwame Nkrumah*
Mathabane. *Kaffir Boy in America*

Otfinoski. *Nelson Mandela*
Pogrund. *Nelson Mandela*
Wepman. *Jomo Kenyatta*
Winner. *Desmond Tutu*

Collective Biography
Blue. *People of Peace*

Hazell. *Heroes: Great Men Through the Ages*

Hoobler. *African Portraits*
Matthews. *Power Brokers*

History
Berg. *An Eritrean Family*
Boateng. *Asante*
Cheney. *The Land and People of Zimbabwe*

Halliburton. *Africa's Struggle for Independence*
Langone. *Spreading Poison*

Liptak. *Endangered Peoples*
Lynch. *Great Buildings*

Medearis. *A History of African Americans*
Meltzer. *Gold*
Millar. *The Kingdom of Benin West Africa*
Murray. *Africa*
Ndukwe. *Fulani*

Ojo. *Mbuti*
Parris. *Rendille*
Reynoldson. *Conflict and Change*
Ricciuti. *Somalia*
Rissik. *Women in Society: South Africa*

Sallah. *Wolof*
Swinimer. *Pokot*
Udechukwu. *Herero*
Van Wyk. *Basotho*
Wangari. *Ameru*
Zeleza. *Maasai*
Zeleza. *Mijikenda*

Multimedia

CD-ROM

Teach Your Kids World History

Video

Africa
Africa: Land and People
Archbishop Desmond Tutu Addresses Apartheid

Defiance in the Townships
Ghana
Mandela: From Prison to President

Nelson Mandela: The Man
North Africa and the Global War

GRADES NINE THROUGH TWELVE

Historical Fiction

Sacks. *Beyond Safe Boundaries*

Weaver-Gelzer. *In the Time of Trouble*

Biography

Eide. *Robert Mugabe*
Hoobler. *Mandela*
Kellner. *Kwame Nkrumah*

Mandela. *Long Walk to Freedom: Nelson Mandela*
Mathabane. *Kaffir Boy in America*

Otfinoski. *Nelson Mandela*
Wepman. *Desmond Tutu*
Wepman. *Jomo Kenyatta*

Collective Biography

History

Barnes. *Aman: A Somali Girl*
Boateng. *Asante*
Busby. *Daughters of Africa*
Cheney. *The Land and People of Zimbabwe*
Feelings. *The Middle Passage*
Holland. *The Struggle*
Hull. *Breaking Free: Human Rights Poetry*
Langone. *Spreading Poison*

McLynn. *Famous Trials*
Ndukwe. *Fulani*
Ojo. *Mbuti*
Ricciuti. *Somalia*
Rissik. *Women in Society: South Africa*
Sallah. *Wolof*
Sparks. *The Mind of South Africa*

Sparks. *Tomorrow is Another Country*
Swinimer. *Pokot*
Thompson. *A History of South Africa*
Time-Life. *Africa's Glorious Legacy*
Udechukwu. *Herero*
Van Wyk. *Basotho*

Multimedia

CD-ROM

Teach Your Kids World History

Video

Africa
Archbishop Desmond Tutu Addresses Apartheid
Bishop Desmond Tutu: Apartheid in South Africa

Defiance in the Townships
Europe and the Third World
Ghana
Mandela: From Prison to President

Nelson Mandela and the Struggle to End Apartheid
North Africa and the Global War
We Jive Like This

Australia, New Zealand, Pacific Islands, and Antartica

Historical Fiction

Baillie. *The Secrets of Walden Rising*
Beatty. *Jonathan Down Under*
Bond. *Truth to Tell*
Bosse. *Deep Dream of the Rain Forest*
Disher. *The Bamboo Flute*
Duder. *Alex in Rome*
Duder. *In Lane Three, Alex Archer*

Dunlop. *The Poetry Girl*
French. *Somewhere Around the Corner*
Gee. *The Champion*
Gee. *The Fat Man*
Gee. *The Fire-Raiser*
Klein. *All in the Blue Unclouded Weather*
Klein. *Dresses of Red and Gold*

Klein. *The Sky in Silver Lace*
Mayne. *Low Tide*
Noonan. *McKenzie's Boots*
Pople. *A Nugget of Gold*
Pople. *The Other Side of the Family*
Sperry. *Call it Courage*
Taylor. *The Bomb*

Biography

Brown. *Father Damien*
Chua-eoan. *Corazon Aquino*
Gaffney. *Edmund Hillary*
Haskins. *Corazon Aquino*

McCurdy. *Trapped by the Ice! Shackleton's Amazing Antarctic Adventure*
Nadel. *Corazon Aquino*

Ward. *Wandering Girl*

Collective Biography

History

Bandon. *Filipino Americans*
Black. *Bataan and Corregidor*
Black. *Guadalcanal*
Black. *Island Hopping in the Pacific*
Black. *Iwo Jima and Okinawa*

Black. *Pearl Harbor!*
Duggleby. *Impossible Quests*
Liptak. *Endangered Peoples*
Lynch. *Great Buildings*
Macdonald. *Maori*
Marrin. *Victory in the Pacific*

Nardo. *Krakatoa*
Rice. *The Battle of Midway*
Stein. *World War II in the Pacific*

Multimedia

CD-ROM

Teach Your Kids World History

Video

Guadalcanal and the Pacific Counterattack
Indonesia: The Jeweled Archipelago

Iwo Jima, Okinawa and the Push on Japan
Pearl Harbor to Midway
Tarawa and the Island War

GRADE EIGHT

Historical Fiction

Baillie. *The Secrets of Walden Rising*
Beatty. *Jonathan Down Under*
Bond. *Truth to Tell*
Bosse. *Deep Dream of the Rain Forest*
Disher. *The Bamboo Flute*
Duder. *Alex in Rome*
Duder. *In Lane Three, Alex Archer*

Dunlop. *The Poetry Girl*
French. *Somewhere Around the Corner*
Gee. *The Champion*
Gee. *The Fat Man*
Gee. *The Fire-Raiser*
Klein. *All in the Blue Unclouded Weather*
Klein. *Dresses of Red and Gold*
Klein. *The Sky in Silver Lace*

Noonan. *McKenzie's Boots*
Pople. *A Nugget of Gold*
Pople. *The Other Side of the Family*
Rathe. *The Wreck of the Barque Stefano*
Taylor. *The Bomb*

Biography

Brown. *Father Damien*
Chua-eoan. *Corazon Aquino*
Gaffney. *Edmund Hillary*

Haskins. *Corazon Aquino*
Nadel. *Corazon Aquino: Journey to Power*

Ward. *Wandering Girl*

Collective Biography

History

Bandon. *Filipino Americans*
Black. *Bataan and Corregidor*
Black. *Guadalcanal*
Black. *Island Hopping in the Pacific*

Black. *Iwo Jima and Okinawa*
Black. *Pearl Harbor!*
Liptak. *Endangered Peoples*
Lynch. *Great Buildings*
Macdonald. *Maori*

Marrin. *Victory in the Pacific*
Nardo. *Krakatoa*
Rice. *The Battle of Midway*
Stein. *World War II in the Pacific*

Multimedia

CD-ROM

Teach Your Kids World History

Video

Guadalcanal and the Pacific Counterattack
Indonesia: The Jeweled Archipelago

Iwo Jima, Okinawa and the Push on Japan
Pearl Harbor to Midway
Tarawa and the Island War

GRADE NINE

Historical Fiction

Baillie. *The Secrets of Walden Rising*
Bainbridge. *The Birthday Boys*
Beatty. *Jonathan Down Under*
Bond. *Truth to Tell*
Bosse. *Deep Dream of the Rain Forest*
Collins. *Jacob's Ladder*

Duder. *Alex in Rome*
Duder. *In Lane Three, Alex Archer*
Gee. *The Champion*
Gee. *The Fat Man*
Gee. *The Fire-Raiser*
Hickman. *Voyage of the Exiles*
Klein. *All in the Blue Unclouded Weather*

Klein. *Dresses of Red and Gold*
Noonan. *McKenzie's Boots*
Pople. *A Nugget of Gold*
Pople. *The Other Side of the Family*
Rathe. *The Wreck of the Barque Stefano*
Southall. *Blackbird*
Taylor. *The Bomb*

Biography

Brown. *Father Damien*
Chua-eoan. *Corazon Aquino*
Gaffney. *Edmund Hillary*

Haskins. *Corazon Aquino: Leader of the Philippines*

Nadel. *Corazon Aquino: Journey to Power*
Ward. *Wandering Girl*

History

Liptak. *Endangered Peoples*
Marrin. *Victory in the Pacific*

Nardo. *World War II in the Pacific*
Rice. *The Battle of Midway*

Stein. *World War II in the Pacific*

Multimedia

CD-ROM

Teach Your Kids World History

Video

Act of War: The Overthrow of the Hawaiian Nation
Illuminated Lives: A Brief History of Women's Work in the Middle Ages
Indonesia: The Jeweled Archipelago

Into the Deep Freeze
Iwo Jima, Okinawa and the Push on Japan
The Mystic Lands Series: Australia: Dreamtime

The Mystic Lands Series: Bali: Island of a Thousand Temples
Pearl Harbor to Midway
Tarawa and the Island War

GRADE TEN

Historical Fiction

Bainbridge. *The Birthday Boys*
Bond. *Truth to Tell*
Bosse. *Deep Dream of the Rain Forest*

Collins. *Jacob's Ladder*
Duder. *Alex in Rome*
Duder. *In Lane Three, Alex Archer*
Hickman. *Voyage of the Exiles*

Noonan. *McKenzie's Boots*
Rathe. *The Wreck of the Barque Stefano*
Southall. *Blackbird*
Taylor. *The Bomb*

Biography

Chua-eoan. *Corazon Aquino*
Haskins. *Corazon Aquino*

Nadel. *Corazon Aquino: Journey to Power*

Paulsen. *Eastern Sun, Winter Moon*
Ward. *Wandering Girl*

Collective Biography

History

Astor. *Operation Iceberg*
Marrin. *Victory in the Pacific*

Nardo. *World War II in the Pacific*
Rice. *The Battle of Midway*

Stein. *World War II in the Pacific*

Multimedia

CD-ROM

Teach Your Kids World History

Video

Act of War: The Overthrow of the Hawaiian Nation
Illuminated Lives: A Brief History of Women's Work in the Middle Ages
Indonesia: The Jeweled Archipelago

Into the Deep Freeze
Iwo Jima, Okinawa and the Push on Japan
The Mystic Lands Series: Australia: Dreamtime

The Mystic Lands Series: Bali: Island of a Thousand Temples
Pearl Harbor to Midway
Tarawa and the Island War

GRADES ELEVEN AND TWELVE

Historical Fiction

Attanasio. *Wyvern*
Bainbridge. *The Birthday Boys*
Bosse. *Deep Dream of the Rain Forest*
Collins. *Jacob's Ladder*
Hickman. *Voyage of the Exiles*
Holt. *The Road to Paradise Island*
O'Brian. *Desolation Island*
O'Brian. *Thirteen Gun Salute*
O'Brian. *The Truelove*
Rathe. *The Wreck of the Barque Stefano*
Southall. *Blackbird*
Taylor. *The Bomb*

Biography

Chua-eoan. *Corazon Aquino*
Nadel. *Corazon Aquino: Journey to Power*
Paulsen. *Eastern Sun, Winter Moon*
Ward. *Wandering Girl*

History

Astor. *Operation Iceberg*
Leckie. *Okinawa: The Last Battle of World War II*
Nardo. *World War II in the Pacific*
Stein. *World War II in the Pacific*

Multimedia

CD-ROM

Teach Your Kids World History

Video

Act of War: The Overthrow of the Hawaiian Nation
America in Asia
From the Barrel of a Gun
Indonesia: The Jeweled Archipelago
Illuminated Lives: A Brief History of Women's Work in the Middle Ages
Into the Deep Freeze
Iwo Jima, Okinawa and the Push on Japan
The Mystic Lands Series: Australia: Dreamtime
The Mystic Lands Series: Bali: Island of a Thousand Temples
Pearl Harbor to Midway
Tarawa and the Island War

Canada

GRADE SEVEN

Historical Fiction

Anderson. *The Journey of the Shadow Bairns*
Anderson. *Pioneer Settlers in New France*
Bond. *Another Shore*
Boraks-Nemetz. *The Old Brown Suitcase*
Doyle. *Uncle Ronald*
Dubois. *Abenaki Captive*
Durbin. *The Broken Blade*
Ellis. *Next-Door Neighbors*
Garrigue. *The Eternal Spring of Mr. Ito*

Harris. *Raven's Cry*
Holeman. *Promise Song*
Hudson. *Dawn Rider*
Hudson. *Sweetgrass*
Katz. *Out of the Dark*
Levin. *Brother Moose*
Lindgard. *Between Two Worlds*
Lunn. *Shadow in Hawthorn Bay*
Major. *Blood Red Ochre*
Marko. *Away to Fundy Bay*

Pearson. *The Lights Go on Again*
Pearson. *Looking at the Moon*
Reed. *The Kraken*
Rice. *The Year the Wolves Came*
Roe. *Circle of Light*
Rylant. *I Had Seen Castles*
Speare. *Calico Captive*
Sterling. *My Name is Seepeetza*
Treece. *Westward to Vinland*
Turner. *The Haunted Igloo*

Biography

Xydes. *Alexander Mackenzie*

Collective Biography

Cohen. *The Ghosts of War*

Italia. *Courageous Crimefighters*

Wilkinson. *Generals Who Changed the World*

History

Alexander. *Inuit*
Beattie. *Buried in Ice*
Berrill. *Mummies, Masks, & Mourners*
Bonvillain. *The Haidas*
Brown. *The Search for the Northwest Passage*

Gorrell. *North Star to Freedom*
Granfield. *In Flanders Fields*
Harris. *Mummies*
Liptak. *Endangered Peoples*
Lynch. *Great Buildings*
Minks. *The French and Indian War*

Osborn. *The Peoples of the Arctic*
Ray. *Gold! The Klondike Adventure*
West. *Vikings, the Cabots, and Jacques Cartier*
Wood. *Ancient America*

Multimedia

CD-ROM

Adventure Canada
Canadian Treasures

One Tribe

Teach Your Kids World History

Video

Canada: People and Places
Canada's Maple Tree: The Story of the Country's Emblem

The Canadian Way of Life
Martin Frobisher's Gold Mine
Rendezvous Canada, 1606
Where the Spirit Lives

GRADE EIGHT

Historical Fiction

Anderson. *The Journey of the Shadow Bairns*
Bond. *Another Shore*
Boraks-Nemetz. *The Old Brown Suitcase*
Brooks. *Two Moons in August*
Doyle. *Uncle Ronald*
Dubois. *Abenaki Captive*
Durbin. *The Broken Blade*
Ellis. *Next-Door Neighbors*
Harris. *Raven's Cry*
Holeman. *Promise Song*
Hudson. *Dawn Rider*
Hudson. *Sweetgrass*
Katz. *Out of the Dark*
Levin. *Brother Moose*
Lindgard. *Between Two Worlds*
Lunn. *Shadow in Hawthorn Bay*
Major. *Blood Red Ochre*
Marko. *Away to Fundy Bay*
Pearson. *The Lights Go on Again*
Pearson. *Looking at the Moon*
Reed. *The Kraken*
Rice. *The Year the Wolves Came*
Roe. *Circle of Light*
Rylant. *I Had Seen Castles*
Speare. *Calico Captive*
Sterling. *My Name is Seepeetza*
Treece. *Westward to Vinland*

Biography

Xydes. *Alexander Mackenzie*

Collective Biography

Cohen. *The Ghosts of War*
Italia. *Courageous Crimefighters*
Wilkinson. *Generals Who Changed the World*

History

Alexander. *Inuit*
Beattie. *Buried in Ice*
Bonvillain. *The Haidas*
Brown. *The Search for the Northwest Passage*
Gorrell. *North Star to Freedom*
Granfield. *In Flanders Fields*
Harris. *Mummies*
Liptak. *Endangered Peoples*
Minks. *The French and Indian War*
Osborn. *The Peoples of the Arctic*
Ray. *Gold! The Klondike Adventure*
West. *Vikings, the Cabots, and Jacques Cartier*
Wood. *Ancient America*

Multimedia

CD-ROM

Adventure Canada
Canadian Treasures
Klondike Gold: An Interactive History
One Tribe
Teach Your Kids World History

Video

Canada: People and Places
Canada's Maple Tree: The Story of the Country's Emblem
The Canadian Way of Life
Martin Frobisher's Gold Mine
Rendezvous Canada, 1606
Where the Spirit Lives

GRADE NINE

Historical Fiction

Anderson. *The Journey of the Shadow Bairns*
Bond. *Another Shore*
Boraks-Nemetz. *The Old Brown Suitcase*
Brooks. *Two Moons in August*
Dubois. *Abenaki Captive*
Ellis. *Next-Door Neighbors*
Harris. *Raven's Cry*
Holeman. *Promise Song*
Hudson. *Dawn Rider*
Hudson. *Sweetgrass*
Katz. *Out of the Dark*
Levin. *Brother Moose*
Lindgard. *Between Two Worlds*
Lunn. *Shadow in Hawthorn Bay*
Major. *Blood Red Ochre*
Marko. *Away to Fundy Bay*
Newth. *The Abduction*
Pearson. *Looking at the Moon*
Rice. *The Year the Wolves Came*
Rylant. *I Had Seen Castles*
Speare. *Calico Captive*
Treece. *Westward to Vinland*

Biography

Humble. *The Voyages of Jacques Cartier*

Mowat. *Born Naked*
Mowat. *My Father's Son*

Xydes. *Alexander Mackenzie*

Collective Biography

Italia. *Courageous Crimefighters*

Wilkinson. *Generals Who Changed the World*

History

Alexander. *Inuit*
Brown. *The Search for the Northwest Passage*
Granfield. *In Flanders Fields*
Liptak. *Endangered Peoples*

Lynch. *Great Buildings*
Minks. *The French and Indian War*
Osborn. *The Peoples of the Arctic*

Ray. *Gold! The Klondike Adventure*
West. *Vikings, the Cabots, and Jacques Cartier*
Wood. *Ancient America*

Multimedia

CD-ROM

Adventure Canada
Klondike Gold: An Interactive History

One Tribe
Teach Your Kids World History

Video

Canada: People and Places
The Canadian Way of Life
Colonial Canada

Martin Frobisher's Gold Mine
Rendezvous Canada, 1606

Speak It! From the Heart of Black Nova Scotia
Where the Spirit Lives

GRADE TEN

Historical Fiction

Anderson. *The Journey of the Shadow Bairns*
Atwood. *Alias Grace*
Atwood, Margaret. *Alias Grace*
Bond. *Another Shore*

Boraks-Nemetz. *The Old Brown Suitcase*
Brooks. *Two Moons in August*
Ellis. *Next-Door Neighbors*
Harris. *Raven's Cry*
Hudson. *Dawn Rider*

Newth. *The Abduction*
Rylant. *I Had Seen Castles*
Speare. *Calico Captive*
Treece. *Westward to Vinland*

Biography

Humble. *The Voyages of Jacques Cartier*

Mowat. *Born Naked*
Mowat. *My Father's Son*

Collective Biography

Wilkinson. *Generals Who Changed the World*

History

Granfield. *In Flanders Fields*

Multimedia

CD-ROM

Adventure Canada
Klondike Gold: An Interactive History

One Tribe
Teach Your Kids World History

Video

Colonial Canada
In the Reign of Twilight
Kanehsatake: 270 Years of Resistance

Martin Frobisher's Gold Mine
Rendezvous Canada, 1606
Speak It! From the Heart of Black Nova Scotia

Where the Spirit Lives

GRADES ELEVEN AND TWELVE

Historical Fiction

Anderson-Dargatz. *The Cure for Death by Lightning*
Atwood. *Alias Grace*
Bond. *Another Shore*

Brooks. *Two Moons in August*
Ellis. *Next-Door Neighbors*
Michener. *Journey*
Newth. *The Abduction*

Rylant. *I Had Seen Castles*
Treece. *Westward to Vinland*

Biography

Humble. *The Voyages of Jacques Cartier*

Mowat. *Born Naked*
Mowat. *My Father's Son*

History

Granfield. *In Flanders Fields*

Multimedia

CD-ROM

Adventure Canada
Klondike Gold: An Interactive History

One Tribe
Teach Your Kids World History

Video

Colonial Canada
In the Reign of Twilight

Kanehsatake: 270 Years of Resistance
Martin Frobisher's Gold Mine

Speak It! From the Heart of Black Nova Scotia
Where the Spirit Lives

China

Historical Fiction

Bell. *Forbidden City*
Bosse. *The Examination*
Chang. *In the Eye of War*
DeJong. *The House of Sixty Fathers*

Dickinson. *Tulku*
Jicai. *Let One Hundred Flowers Bloom*
Russell. *Lichee Tree*

Vander Els. *The Bomber's Moon*
Vander Els. *Leaving Point*

Biography

Foster. *Nien Cheng*
Fritz. *China Homecoming*

Jiang. *Red Scarf Girl: A Memoir of the Cultural Revolution*

Marrin. *Mao Tse-tung*
Stefoff. *Mao Zedong*

Collective Biography

Cohen. *Real Vampires*
Hazell. *Heroines: Great Women Through the Ages*
Hoobler. *Chinese Portraits*
Jacobs. *Great Lives: World Religions*

Jacobs. *World Government*
Newark. *Medieval Warlords*
Wilkinson. *Generals Who Changed the World*
Wilkinson. *People Who Changed the World*

Wilkinson. *Scientists Who Changed the World*
Wilkinson. *Statesmen Who Changed the World*

History

Bandon. *Chinese Americans*
Berrill. *Mummies, Masks, & Mourners*
Beshore. *Science in Ancient China*
Burke. *Food and Fasting*
China from the 7th to the 19th Century
Civilizations of Asia
Compton. *Marriage Customs*
Corbishley. *Secret Cities*
Cotterell. *Ancient China*
Daley. *The Chinese Americans*
Dauber. *China*
Davies. *Transport*
Fritz. *China's Long March*
Gravett. *Arms and Armor*
Harris. *Mummies*

Kort. *China: Under Communism*
Lazo. *The Terra Cotta Army of Emperor Qin*
Lynch. *Great Buildings*
Major. *The Silk Route*
Mann. *The Great Wall: The Story of 4,000 Miles of Earth and Stone That Turned a Nation into a Fortress*
Martell. *The Ancient Chinese*
McNeese. *The Great Wall of China*
Michaelson. *Ancient China*
Millar. *China's Tang Dynasty*
Newark. *Medieval Warlords*
Odijk. *The Chinese*
Prior. *Initiation Customs*

Prior. *Pilgrimages and Journeys*
Reynoldson. *Conflict and Change*
Ross. *China Since 1945*
Rushton. *Birth Customs*
Rushton. *Death Customs*
Singer. *Structures That Changed the Way the World Looked*
Steele. *Smuggling*
Tan. *Women in Society: China*
Warburton. *The Beginning of Writing*
Wilkinson. *Amazing Buildings*
Wilkinson. *The Magical East*
Williams. *Ancient China*
Williams. *Forts and Castles*

Multimedia

CD-ROM

Fine Arts of China
Religions of the World

Teach Your Kids World History

Video

*The Changing Face of Asia:
China, Part I: The Ancient
Empire*
*The Changing Face of Asia:
China, Part II: Revolution!*

*The Changing Face of Asia:
China, Part III: The Fifth
Millennium!*
China: The Ancient Land
China: A History
*China—Festival Celebration
of Ancient Traditions*

China: The Fifth Millennium
*China: From President Sun to
Chairman Mao*
*The Silk Road: A Thousand
Kilometers Beyond the
Yellow River*

GRADE EIGHT

Historical Fiction

Bell. *Forbidden City*
Bosse. *The Examination*

DeJong. *The House of Sixty
Fathers*
Dickinson. *Tulku*

Jicai. *Let One Hundred
Flowers Bloom*

Biography

Dolan. *Chiang Kai-Shek*
Fritz. *China Homecoming*
Garza. *Mao Zedong*
Hoobler. *Zhou Enlai*

Jiang. *Red Scarf Girl: A
Memoir of the Cultural
Revolution*
Marrin. *Mao Tse-tung*

Stefoff. *Mao Zedong*

Collective Biography

Cohen. *Real Vampires*
Hazell. *Heroines: Great
Women Through the Ages*
Hoobler. *Chinese Portraits*
Newark. *Medieval Warlords*

Wilkinson. *Generals Who
Changed the World*
Wilkinson. *People Who
Changed the World*

Wilkinson. *Scientists Who
Changed the World*
Wilkinson. *Statesmen Who
Changed the World*

History

Bandon. *Chinese Americans*
Beshore. *Science in Ancient
China*
Burke. *Food and Fasting*
*China from the 7th to the 19th
Century*
Civilizations of Asia
Compton. *Marriage Customs*
Dauber. *China*
Davies. *Transport*
Fritz. *China's Long March*
Harris. *Mummies*
Kort. *China: Under
Communism*

Lazo. *The Terra Cotta Army
of Emperor Qin*
Lynch. *Great Buildings*
Mann. *The Great Wall: The
Story of 4,000 Miles of Earth
and Stone That Turned a
Nation into a Fortress*
Martell. *The Ancient Chinese*
McNeese. *The Great Wall of
China*
Michaelson. *Ancient China*
Millar. *China's Tang Dynasty*
Newark. *Medieval Warlords*
Prior. *Initiation Customs*

Prior. *Pilgrimages and
Journeys*
Ross. *China Since 1945*
Rushton. *Birth Customs*
Rushton. *Death Customs*
Singer. *Structures That
Changed the Way the
World Looked*
Tan. *Women in Society: China*
Warburton. *The Beginning of
Writing*
Wilkinson. *The Magical East*
Williams. *Ancient China*
Williams. *Forts and Castles*

Multimedia

CD-ROM

Fine Arts of China
Religions of the World

*Teach Your Kids World
History*

Video

*The Changing Face of Asia:
China, Part I: The Ancient
Empire*
*The Changing Face of Asia:
China, Part II: Revolution!*

*The Changing Face of Asia:
China, Part III: The Fifth
Millennium!*
China: The Ancient Land
*China—Festival Celebration
of Ancient Traditions*
China: The Fifth Millennium

*China: From President Sun to
Chairman Mao*
China: A History
*The Silk Road: A Thousand
Kilometers Beyond the
Yellow River*
Windows to the World: China

GRADE NINE

Historical Fiction

Bell. *Forbidden City*
Bosse. *The Examination*
Dickinson. *Tulku*

Jicai. *Let One Hundred Flowers Bloom*

Paterson. *Rebels of the Heavenly Kingdom*

Biography

Dolan. *Chiang Kai-Shek*
Fritz. *China Homecoming*
Garza. *Mao Zedong*
Hoobler. *Zhou Enlai*

Jiang. *Red Scarf Girl: A Memoir of the Cultural Revolution*
Marrin. *Mao Tse-tung*

Spence. *God's Chinese Son: Hong Xiuquan*
Stefoff. *Mao Zedong*

Collective Biography

Hoobler. *Chinese Portraits*
Lomask. *Great Lives: Exploration*
Newark. *Medieval Warlords*

Wilkinson. *Generals Who Changed the World*
Wilkinson. *People Who Changed the World*

Wilkinson. *Scientists Who Changed the World*
Wilkinson. *Statesmen Who Changed the World*

History

Carter. *China Past China Future*
China from the 7th to the 19th Century
Civilizations of Asia
Fritz. *China's Long March*
Kort. *China: Under Communism*

Lazo. *The Terra Cotta Army of Emperor Qin*
Millar. *China's Tang Dynasty*
Pietrusza. *The Chinese Cultural Revolution*
Ross. *China Since 1945*
Singer. *Structures That Changed the Way the World Looked*

Tan. *Women in Society: China*
Time-Life. *China's Buried Kingdoms*
Warburton. *The Beginning of Writing*
Williams. *Ancient China*
Williams. *Forts and Castles*

Multimedia

CD-ROM

Fine Arts of China.
Religions of the World

Teach Your Kids World History

Video

The Changing Face of Asia: China, Part I: The Ancient Empire
The Changing Face of Asia: China, Part II: Revolution!
The Changing Face of Asia: China, Part III: The Fifth Millennium!
China: The Ancient Land
China: The Fifth Millennium
China: From President Sun to Chairman Mao

China: The History and the Mystery
China Moon: Returning Swallows
China Moon: Thread of History
China Rising
The First Emperor of China
The Great Wall of Iron
Illuminated Lives: A Brief History of Women's Work in the Middle Ages

More Than Rice
The Silk Road: Glories of Ancient Chang-An
The Silk Road: A Heat Wave Called Turfan
The Silk Road: A Thousand Kilometers Beyond the Yellow River
Windows to the World: China
Wonders of Man's Creation

GRADE TEN

Historical Fiction

Bell. *Forbidden City*
Bosse. *The Examination*
Dickinson. *Tulku*

Jicai. *Let One Hundred Flowers Bloom*

Paterson. *Rebels of the Heavenly Kingdom*

Biography

Dolan. *Chiang Kai-Shek: Chinese Nationalist*
Fritz. *China Homecoming*
Garza. *Mao Zedong*
Hoobler. *Zhou Enlai*

Jiang. *Red Scarf Girl: A Memoir of the Cultural Revolution*
Lord. *Legacies: A Chinese Mosaic*

Marrin. *Mao Tse-tung and His China*
Spence. *God's Chinese Son: Hong Xiuquan*
Stefoff. *Mao Zedong*

Collective Biography

Axelrod. *Dictators and Tyrants*
Hoobler. *Chinese Portraits*
Lomask. *Great Lives: Exploration*

Newark. *Medieval Warlords*
Wilkinson. *Generals Who Changed the World*
Wilkinson. *People Who Changed the World*

Wilkinson. *Scientists Who Changed the World*
Wilkinson. *Statesmen Who Changed the World*

History

Carter. *China Past China Future*
China from the 7th to the 19th Century
Ching. *Probing China's Soul Civilizations of Asia*
Fritz. *China's Long March*

Kort. *China: Under Communism*
Marx. *The Search for Sunken Treasure*
Millar. *China's Tang Dynasty*
Pickford. *The Atlas of Shipwrecks & Treasure*

Pietrusza. *The Chinese Cultural Revolution*
Ross. *China Since 1945*
Tan. *Women in Society: China*
Time-Life. *China's Buried Kingdoms*
Tong. *Almost a Revolution*

Multimedia

CD-ROM

Fine Arts of China
Religions of the World

Teach Your Kids World History

Video

The Changing Face of Asia: China, Part I: The Ancient Empire
The Changing Face of Asia: China, Part II: Revolution!
The Changing Face of Asia: China, Part III: The Fifth Millennium!
China: The Ancient Land
China: The Fifth Millennium
China: From President Sun to Chairman Mao

China: The History and the Mystery
China Moon: Returning Swallows
China Moon: Thread of History
China Rising
The First Emperor of China
The Great Wall of Iron
Half the Sky: The Women of the Jiang Family
Illuminated Lives: A Brief History of Women's Work in the Middle Ages

More Than Rice
The Silk Road: Glories of Ancient Chang-An
The Silk Road: A Heat Wave Called Turfan
The Silk Road: A Thousand Kilometers Beyond the Yellow River
Windows to the World: China
Wonders of Man's Creation

GRADES ELEVEN AND TWELVE

Historical Fiction

Ballard. *Empire of the Sun*
Bell. *Forbidden City*
Chin. *The Dream of the Red Chamber*

Clavell. *Noble House*
Dickinson. *Tulku*
Jicai. *Let One Hundred Flowers Bloom*

Li. *Farewell to My Concubine*
Paterson. *Rebels of the Heavenly Kingdom*
Sledge. *Empire of Heaven*

Biography

Dolan. *Chiang Kai-Shek*
Garza. *Mao Zedong*
Hoobler. *Zhou Enlai*

Lord. *Legacies*
Spence. *God's Chinese Son: Hong Xiuquan*

Stefoff. *Mao Zedong*

Collective Biography

Axelrod. *Dictators and Tyrants*

Hoobler. *Chinese Portraits*

Lomask. *Great Lives: Exploration*

Newark. *Medieval Warlords*

History

Carter. *China Past China Future*

China from the 7th to the 19th Century

Ching. *Probing China's Soul*

Fritz. *China's Long March*

Mackerras. *Handbook of Contemporary China*

Marx. *The Search for Sunken Treasure*

Pickford. *The Atlas of Shipwrecks & Treasure*

Pietrusza. *The Chinese Cultural Revolution*

Ross. *China Since 1945*

Simmie. *Tiananmen Square*

Spence. *The Search for Modern China*

Tan. *Women in Society: China*

Time-Life. *China's Buried Kingdoms*

Tong. *Almost a Revolution*

Multimedia

CD-ROM

Fine Arts of China

Religions of the World

Teach Your Kids World History

Video

Big Business and the Ghost of Confucius

The Changing Face of Asia: China, Part I: The Ancient Empire

The Changing Face of Asia: China, Part II: Revolution!

The Changing Face of Asia: China, Part III: The Fifth Millennium!

China: The Ancient Land

China: The Fifth Millennium

China: From President Sun to Chairman Mao

China: The History and the Mystery

China Moon: Returning Swallows

China Moon: Thread of History

China Rising

The Fight for Democracy

The First Emperor of China

From the Barrel of a Gun

The Future of the Pacific Basin

The Great Wall of Iron

Half the Sky: The Women of the Jiang Family

Illuminated Lives: A Brief History of Women's Work in the Middle Ages

More Than Rice

The Silk Road: Glories of Ancient Chang-An

The Silk Road: A Heat Wave Called Turfan

The Silk Road: A Thousand Kilometers Beyond the Yellow River

The Two Coasts of China: Asia and the Challenge of the West

Windows to the World: China

Wonders of Man's Creation

Writers and Revolutionaries

India, Tibet, and Burma

Historical Fiction

Bosse. *Tusk and Stone*

Morpurgo. *King of the Cloud Forests*

Biography

Bush. *Mohandas K. Gandhi*
Butler. *Indira Gandhi*
Clucas. *Mother Teresa*
Faber. *Mahatma Gandhi*
Gibb. *The Dalai Lama*
Lazo. *Mahatma Gandhi*

Lazo. *Mother Teresa*
Parenteau. *Prisoner for Peace: Aung Suu Kyi*
Perez. *The Dalai Lama*
Severance. *Gandhi, Great Soul*

Sherrow. *Mohandas Gandhi*
Stewart. *Aung San Suu Kyi: Fearless Voice of Burma*
Stewart. *The 14th Dalai Lama*

Collective Biography

Blue. *People of Peace*
Cush. *Women Who Achieved Greatness*

Hazell. *Heroes: Great Men Through the Ages*
Jacobs. *Great Lives: World Religions*

Jacobs. *World Government*
Wilkinson. *Generals Who Changed the World*

History

Bandon. *Asian Indian Americans*
Black. Blashfield. *Jungle Warfare*
Braquet. *India*
Burke. *Food and Fasting*
Cervera. *The Mughal Empire*
Charley. *Tombs and Treasures Civilizations of Asia*
Compton. *Marriage Customs*

Cush. *Disasters That Shook the World*
De Bruycker. *Tibet*
Franck. *Around Africa and Asia by Sea*
Ghose. *India: Women in Society*
Haskins. *India under Indira and Rajiv Gandhi*
Kendra. *Tibetans*

Lynch. *Great Buildings*
Macmillan. *Diwali: Hindu Festival of Lights*
Prior. *Initiation Customs*
Prior. *Pilgrimages and Journeys*
Rushton. *Birth Customs*
Rushton. *Death Customs*

Multimedia

CD-ROM

Religions of the World

Teach Your Kids World History

Historical Fiction

Bosse. *Tusk and Stone*

Morpurgo. *King of the Cloud Forests*

Biography

Bush. *Mohandas K. Gandhi*
Butler. *Indira Gandhi*
Clucas. *Mother Teresa*
Faber. *Mahatma Gandhi*
Finck. *Jawaharlal Nehru*
Gibb. *The Dalai Lama*

Lazo. *Mahatma Gandhi*
Lazo. *Mother Teresa*
Parenteau. *Prisoner for Peace: Aung San Suu Kyi*
Perez. *The Dalai Lama*

Severance. *Gandhi, Great Soul*
Sherrow. *Mohandas Gandhi*
Stewart. *Aung San Suu Kyi: Fearless Voice of Burma*
Stewart. *The 14th Dalai Lama*

Collective Biography

Blue. *People of Peace*
Cush. *Women Who Achieved Greatness*

Hazell. *Heroes: Great Men Through the Ages*

Wilkinson. *Generals Who Changed the World*

History

Bandon. *Asian Indian Americans*
Black. Blashfield. *Jungle Warfare*
Braquet. *India*
Burke. *Food and Fasting Civilizations of Asia*
Compton. *Marriage Customs*

Cush. *Disasters That Shook the World*
De Bruycker. *Tibet*
Franck. *Around Africa and Asia by Sea*
Ghose. *India: Women in Society*
Haskins. *India under Indira and Rajiv Gandhi*

Kendra. *Tibetans*
Lynch. *Great Buildings*
Macmillan. *Diwali: Hindu Festival of Lights*
Prior. *Initiation Customs*
Prior. *Pilgrimages and Journeys*
Rushton. *Birth Customs*
Rushton. *Death Customs*

Multimedia

CD-ROM

Religions of the World

Teach Your Kids World History

GRADE NINE

Historical Fiction

Bosse. *Tusk and Stone*

Morpurgo. *King of the Cloud Forests*

Biography

Bush. *Mohandas K. Gandhi*
Butler. *Indira Gandhi*
Clucas. *Mother Teresa*
Faber. *Mahatma Gandhi*
Finck. *Jawaharlal Nehru*

Gibb. *The Dalai Lama*
Parenteau. *Prisoner for Peace: Aung San Suu Kyi*
Severance. *Gandhi, Great Soul*

Sherrow. *Mohandas Gandhi*
Stewart. *Aung San Suu Kyi: Fearless Voice of Burma*

Collective Biography

Cush. *Women Who Achieved Greatness*

Wilkinson. *Generals Who Changed the World*

History

Braquet. *India Civilizations of Asia*
Cush. *Disasters That Shook the World*

Franck. *Around Africa and Asia by Sea*
Ghose. *India: Women in Society*

Haskins. *India under Indira and Rajiv Gandhi*
Time-Life. *Ancient India: Land of Mystery*

Multimedia

CD-ROM

Religions of the World

Teach Your Kids World History

Video

The Mystic Lands Series:
Bhutan: Land of the
Thunder Dragon

The Mystic Lands Series:
Burma: Triumph of the
Spirit
The Mystic Lands Series: Taj
Mahal: Heaven on Earth

The Mystic Lands Series:
Varanasi: City of Light
Ocean of Wisdom
Windows to the World: India
Wonders Sacred & Mysterious

GRADE TEN

Historical Fiction

Bosse. *Tusk and Stone*

Morpurgo. *King of the Cloud
Forests*

Biography

Bush. *Mohandas K. Gandhi*
Butler. *Indira Gandhi*
Clucas. *Mother Teresa*
Faber. *Mahatma Gandhi*

Finck. *Jawaharlal Nehru*
Parenteau. *Prisoner for
Peace: Aung San Suu Kyi*
Sherrow. *Mohandas Gandhi*

Stewart. *Aung San Suu Kyi:
Fearless Voice of Burma*

Collective Biography

Wilkinson. *Generals Who
Changed the World*

History

Civilizations of Asia
Ghose. *India: Women in
Society*

Pickford. *The Atlas of
Shipwrecks & Treasure*

Time-Life. *Ancient India:
Land of Mystery*

Multimedia

CD-ROM

Religions of the World

Teach Your Kids World History

Video

Inside Burma: Land of Fear
The Mystic Lands Series:
Bhutan: Land of the
Thunder Dragon

The Mystic Lands Series:
Burma: Triumph of the
Spirit
The Mystic Lands Series: Taj
Mahal: Heaven on Earth

The Mystic Lands Series:
Varanasi: City of Light
Ocean of Wisdom
Windows to the World: India
Wonders Sacred & Mysterious

GRADES ELEVEN AND TWELVE

Historical Fiction

Holt. *The India Fan*
Holt. *Secret for a Nightingale*
O'Brian. *H. M. S. Surprise*

O'Brian. *The Mauritius
Command*
Scott. *The Day of the Scorpion*
Scott. *A Division of the Spoils*

Scott. *The Jewel in the Crown*
Scott. *The Towers of Silence*
Wiggins. *John Dollar*

Biography

Bush. *Mohandas K. Gandhi*
Butler. *Indira Gandhi*
Clucas. *Mother Teresa*

Finck. *Jawaharlal Nehru*
Sherrow. *Mohandas Gandhi*

Stewart. *Aung San Suu Kyi:
Fearless Voice of Burma*

History

Ghose. *India: Women in
Society*

Pickford. *The Atlas of
Shipwrecks & Treasure*

Time-Life. *Ancient India:
Land of Mystery*

Multimedia ——

CD-ROM

Religions of the World

Teach Your Kids World History

Video

Inside Burma: Land of Fear

The Mystic Lands Series: Bhutan: Land of the Thunder Dragon

The Mystic Lands Series: Burma: Triumph of the Spirit

The Mystic Lands Series: Taj Mahal: Heaven on Earth

The Mystic Lands Series: Varanasi: City of Light

Ocean of Wisdom

Windows to the World: India

Wonders Sacred & Mysterious

Israel and the Arab Countries

GRADE SEVEN

Historical Fiction

Almagor. *Under the Domim Tree*
Bergman. *The Boy from over There*
Gilmore. *Remembrance of the Sun*
Maalouf. *Samarkand*
Matas. *The Garden*
Orlev. *The Lady with the Hat*
Orlev. *Lydia, Queen of Palestine*
Semel. *Becoming Gershona*
Semel. *Flying Lessons*

Biography

Adler. *Our Golda Meir*
Amdur. *Chaim Weizmann*
Claypool. *Saddam Hussein*
Cockcroft. *Mohammed Reza Pahlavi: Shah of Iran*
Cytron. *Myriam Mendilow: Mother of Jerusalem*
Diamond. *Anwar Sadat*
Ferber. *Yasir Arafat: A Life of War and Peace*
Finkelstein. *Theodor Herzl: Architect of a Nation*
Gordon. *Ayatollah Khomeini*
Gordon. *The Gemayels*
Gurko. *Theodor Herzl: The Road to Israel*
McAuley. *Golda Meir*
Slater. *Rabin of Israel*
Slater. *Warrior Statesman: Moshe Dayan*
Solecki. *Hosni Mubarak*

Collective Biography

Jacobs. *Great Lives: World Religions*
Jacobs. *World Government*
Weitzman. *Great Lives: Human Culture*

History

Ayoub. *Al Umm El Madayan Azerbaijan*
Beshore. *Science in Early Islamic Culture*
Civilizations of the Middle East
Cooper. *The Dead Sea Scrolls*
Corzine. *The Palestinian-Israeli Accord*
Cozic. *Israel: Opposing Viewpoints*
Cush. *Disasters That Shook the World*
De Bruycker. *Egypt and the Middle East*
Gay. *Persian Gulf War*
Gordon. *Islam*
Husain. *Mecca*
Hussein. *What Do We Know About Islam?*
King. *The Gulf War*
King. *Kurds*
Long. *The Middle East in Search of Peace*
MacDonald. *A 16th Century Mosque*
Major. *The Silk Route*
Moktefi. *The Arabs in the Golden Age*
Morrison. *Middle East*
Pollard. *The Red Cross and the Red Crescent*
Reische. *Arafat and the Palestine Liberation Organization*
Ross. *Causes and Consequences of the Arab-Israeli Conflict*
Samaan. *Women in Society: Egypt*
Singer. *Structures That Changed the Way the World Looked*
Stein. *The Iran Hostage Crisis*
Street Smart! Cities of the Ancient World
Uval. *Women in Society: Israel*

Multimedia

CD-ROM

Jerusalem: Interactive Pilgrimage to the Holy City
Religions of the World
Teach Your Kids World History

102

Video

The Arab World
Biography: Moshe Dayan
Golda Meir
Herzl
The Illegals
Israel

Jordan, the Desert Kingdom
Judaism: The Religion of the
People
Middle East: History and
Culture

Morocco: The Past and
Present of Djemma El Fna
Story of Islam: The Coming
of the Prophet
Weizmann

GRADE EIGHT

Historical Fiction

Almagor. Under the Domim
Tree
Bergman. The Boy from over
There

Gilmore. Remembrance of the
Sun
Matas. The Garden
Orlev. The Lady with the Hat

Orlev. Lydia, Queen of
Palestine
Semel. Becoming Gershona

Biography

Amdur. Chaim Weizmann
Aufderheide. Anwar Sadat
Claypool. Saddam Hussein
Cockcroft. Mohammed Reza
Pahlavi
Cytron. Myriam Mendilow

Diamond. Anwar Sadat
Ferber. Yasir Arafat
Finkelstein. Theodor Herzl
Kyle. Muammar El-Qaddafi
Matusky. King Hussein
McAuley. Golda Meir

Renfrew. Saddam Hussein
Slater. Rabin of Israel
Slater. Warrior Statesman:
Moshe Dayan
Solecki. Hosni Mubarak
Stefoff. Faisal

Collective Biography

Weitzman. Great Lives:
Human Culture

History

Ayoub. Al Umm El Madayan
Beshore. Science in Early
Islamic Culture
Civilizations of the Middle
East
Cooper. The Dead Sea Scrolls
Corzine. The Palestinian-
Israeli Accord
Cozic. Israel: Opposing
Viewpoints
Cush. Disasters That Shook
the World
De Bruycker. Egypt and the
Middle East
Gay. Persian Gulf War
Gordon. Islam

Husain. Mecca
King. The Gulf War
King. Kurds
Lawless. The First Day of the
Six Day War
Lewis. The World of Islam
Long. The Middle East in
Search of Peace
MacDonald. A 16th Century
Mosque
Moktefi. The Arabs in the
Golden Age
Morrison. Middle East
Pollard. The Red Cross and
the Red Crescent

Reische. Arafat and the
Palestine Liberation
Organization
Ross. Causes and
Consequences of the
Arab-Israeli Conflict
Samaan. Women in Society:
Egypt
Singer. Structures That
Changed the Way the
World Looked
Stein. The Iran Hostage Crisis
Street Smart! Cities of the
Ancient World
Uval. Women in Society:
Israel

Multimedia

CD-ROM

Jerusalem: Interactive
Pilgrimage to the Holy City

Religions of the World

Teach Your Kids World
History

Video

The Arab World
Biography: Moshe Dayan
Golda Meir
Herzl
The Illegals
Israel

Jerusalem: Gates to the City
Jordan, the Desert Kingdom
Judaism: The Religion of the
People
Middle East: History and
Culture

Morocco: The Past and
Present of Djemma El Fna
Story of Islam: The Coming
of the Prophet
Weizmann

GRADE NINE

Historical Fiction

Almagor. *Under the Domim Tree*
Chedid. *The Multiple Child*
Gilmore. *Remembrance of the Sun*

Maalouf. *Samarkand*
Matas. *The Garden*
Orlev. *The Lady with the Hat*
Oz. *Soumchi*
Reboul. *Thou Shalt Not Kill*

Welch. *Knight Crusader*
Westall. *Gulf*

Biography

Amdur. *Chaim Weizmann*
Aufderheide. *Anwar Sadat*
Claypool. *Saddam Hussein*
Cockcroft. *Mohammed Reza Pahlavi*
Cytron. *Myriam Mendilow*
Diamond. *Anwar Sadat*

Ferber. *Yasir Arafat*
Finkelstein. *Theodor Herzl*
Gordon. *Ayatollah Khomeini*
Gordon. *The Gemayels*
Kyle. *Muammar El-Qaddafi*
Matusky. *King Hussein*
McAuley. *Golda Meir*

Renfrew. *Saddam Hussein*
Slater. *Rabin of Israel*
Slater. *Warrior Statesman: Moshe Dayan*
Solecki. *Hosni Mubarak*
Stefoff. *Faisal*

Collective Biography

Weizman. *Great Lives: Human Culture*

Weizman. *Great Lives: Theater*

History

Ayoub. *Al Umm El Madayan Civilizations of the Middle East*
Cooper. *The Dead Sea Scrolls*
Corzine. *The Palestinian-Israeli Accord*
Cozic. *Israel: Opposing Viewpoints*
Cush. *Disasters That Shook the World*
Gay. *Persian Gulf War*
Gordon. *Islam*
Gottfried. *Libya: Desert Land in Conflict*
Husain. *Mecca*
King. *The Gulf War*

Lawless. *The First Day of the Six Day War*
Lawless. *The Middle East Since 1945*
Lewis. *Islam in History*
Lewis. *The Middle East*
Lewis. *Race and Slavery in the Middle East*
Lewis. *Semites and Anti-Semites*
Lewis. *The World of Islam*
Morrison. *Middle East*
Reische. *Arafat and the Palestine Liberation Organization*

Robinson. *The Cambridge Illustrated History of the Islamic World*
Ross. *Causes and Consequences of the Arab-Israeli Conflict*
Samaan. *Women in Society: Egypt*
Singer. *Structures That Changed the Way the World Looked*
Time-Life. *The Holy Land*
Uval. *Women in Society: Israel*

Multimedia

CD-ROM

Jerusalem: Interactive Pilgrimage to the Holy City

Religions of the World

Teach Your Kids World History

Video

Biography: Moshe Dayan
444 Days to Freedom: What Really Happened in Iran
Golda Meir
Herzl
The Illegals
Jerusalem: Gates to the City
Jordan, the Desert Kingdom

Judaism: The Religion of the People
Middle East
Morocco: The Past and Present of Djemma El Fna
The Mystic Lands Series: Jerusalem: Mosaic of Faith
Paradise Postponed

The Road to War in the Person Gulf
Story of Islam: The Coming of the Prophet
The Summer of Aviya
Weizmann

GRADE TEN

Historical Fiction

Almagor. *Under the Domim Tree*
Chedid. *The Multiple Child*
Gilmore. *Remembrance of the Sun*

Maalouf. *Samarkand*
Matas. *The Garden*
Orlev. *The Lady with the Hat*
Oz. *Soumchi*
Reboul. *Thou Shalt Not Kill*

Welch. *Knight Crusader*
Westall. *Gulf*

Biography

Amdur. *Chaim Weizmann*
Aufderheide. *Anwar Sadat*
Cockcroft. *Mohammed Reza Pahlavi*
Diamond. *Anwar Sadat*
Ferber. *Yasir Arafat*

Gordon. *Ayatollah Khomeini*
Gordon. *The Gemayels*
Kyle. *Muammar El-Qaddafi*
Matusky. *King Hussein*
McAuley. *Golda Meir*
Renfrew. *Saddam Hussein*

Slater. *Rabin of Israel*
Slater. *Warrior Statesman: Moshe Dayan*
Stefoff. *Faisal*

Collective Biography

Weitzman. *Great Lives: Theater*

History

Civilizations of the Middle East
Corzine. *The Palestinian-Israeli Accord*
Cozic. *Israel: Opposing Viewpoints*
Gordon. *Islam*
Gottfried. *Libya: Desert Land in Conflict*
Hull. *Breaking Free: Human Rights Poetry*
King. *The Gulf War*
Lawless. *The First Day of the Six Day War*

Lawless. *The Middle East Since 1945*
Lewis. *Islam in History*
Lewis. *The Middle East*
Lewis. *Race and Slavery in the Middle East*
Lewis. *Semites and Anti-Semites*
Lewis. *The World of Islam*
Reische. *Arafat and the Palestine Liberation Organization*

Robinson. *The Cambridge Illustrated History of the Islamic World*
Ross. *Causes and Consequences of the Arab-Israeli Conflict*
Samaan. *Women in Society: Egypt*
Time-Life. *The Holy Land*
Uval. *Women in Society: Israel*

Multimedia

CD-ROM

Jerusalem: Interactive Pilgrimage to the Holy City

Religions of the World

Teach Your Kids World History

Video

The Arab World
Biography: Moshe Dayan
444 Days to Freedom: What Really Happened in Iran
Golda Meir
Greetings from Iraq
Gulf War, Parts 1 and 2
Herzl
The Illegals
Iran / Iraq Afghanistan
Jerusalem: Gates to the City

Jordan, the Desert Kingdom
Judaism: The Religion of the People
The Longest Hatred: The History of Anti-Semitism
Middle East
Morocco: The Past and Present of Djemma El Fna
The Mystic Lands Series: Jerusalem: Mosaic of Faith
Paradise Postponed

The Road to War in the Person Gulf
The Six Day War/Yom Kippur
Story of Islam: The Coming of the Prophet
The Summer of Aviya
Terrorism/Lebanon
Weizmann

GRADES ELEVEN AND TWELVE

Historical Fiction

Chedid. *The Multiple Child*
Maalouf. *Samarkand*
O'Brian. *Treason's Harbour*
Oz. *Soumchi*

Peters. *The Hippopotamus Pool*
Reboul. *Thou Shalt Not Kill*
Uris. *Exodus*

Welch. *Knight Crusader*
Westall. *Gulf*

Biography

Amdur. *Chaim Weizmann*
Aufderheide. *Anwar Sadat*
Cockcroft. *Mohammed Reza Pahlavi*
Diamond. *Anwar Sadat*
Ferber. *Yasir Arafat*

Gordon. *Ayatollah Khomeini*
Gordon. *The Gemayels*
Kyle. *Muammar El-Qaddafi*
Matusky. *King Hussein*
McAuley. *Golda Meir*
Renfrew. *Saddam Hussein*

Slater. *Rabin of Israel*
Slater. *Warrior Statesman: Moshe Dayan*
Stefoff. *Faisal*

Collective Biography

Weitzman. *Great Lives: Theater*

History

Cozic. *Israel: Opposing Viewpoints*
Friedman. *From Beirut to Jerusalem*
Gordon. *Islam*
Gottfried. *Libya: Desert Land in Conflict*
Hourani. *A History of the Arab Peoples*
Hull. *Breaking Free: Human Rights Poetry*
Lawless. *The First Day of the Six Day War*

Lawless. *The Middle East Since 1945*
Lewis. *Islam in History*
Lewis. *The Middle East*
Lewis. *Race and Slavery in the Middle East*
Lewis. *Semites and Anti-Semites*
Lewis. *The World of Islam*
Mackey. *Lebanon: Death of a Nation*
McDowall. *A Modern History of the Kurds*

Robinson. *The Cambridge Illustrated History of the Islamic World*
Sahebjam. *The Stoning of Soraya M*
Samaan. *Women in Society: Egypt*
Time-Life. *The Holy Land*
Uval. *Women in Society: Israel*

Multimedia

CD-ROM

Jerusalem: Interactive Pilgrimage to the Holy City

Religions of the World

Teach Your Kids World History

Video

The Arab-Israeli Struggle for Peace
The Arab World
Biography: Moshe Dayan
444 Days to Freedom: What Really Happened in Iran
Golda Meir
Greetings from Iraq
Gulf War, Parts 1 and 2
Herzl

The Illegals
Iran / Iraq Afghanistan
Jerusalem: Gates to the City
Jordan, the Desert Kingdom
The Longest Hatred: The History of Anti-Semitism
Middle East
The Mystic Lands Series: Jerusalem: Mosaic of Faith
Paradise Postponed

The Road to War in the Person Gulf
The Six Day War/Yom Kippur
Story of Islam: The Coming of the Prophet
The Summer of Aviya
Terrorism/Lebanon
Weizmann

Japan

GRADE SEVEN

Historical Fiction

Coerr. *Mieko and the Fifth Treasure*
Crofford. *Born in the Year of Courage*
Dalkey. *Little Sister*
Haugaard. *The Boy and the Samurai*
Haugaard. *The Revenge of the Forty-Seven Samurai*
Haugaard. *The Samurai's Tale*
Maruki. *Hiroshima, No Pika*
Namioka. *The Coming of the Bear*
Namioka. *Island of Ogres*
Paterson. *The Master Puppeteer*
Paterson. *Of Nightingales That Weep*
Paterson. *The Sign of the Chrysanthemum*

Biography

Severns. *Hirohito*

Collective Biography

Cohen. *The Ghosts of War*
Hazell. *Heroines: Great Women Through the Ages*
Hoobler. *Japanese Portraits*
Krull. *Lives of the Writers*
Wilkinson. *Generals Who Changed the World*

History

Black. *Hiroshima and the Atomic Bomb*
Civilizations of Asia
Cross. *Technology of War*
Gravett. *Arms and Armor*
Hoobler. *Showa: The Age of Hirohito*
Langone. *In the Shogun's Shadow*
Lynch. *Great Buildings*
MacDonald. *A Samurai Castle*
Martell. *The Age of Discovery*
Nardo. *Traditional Japan*
Newton. *Tokyo*
Odijk. *The Japanese*
Reynoldson. *Conflict and Change*
Ross. *Rise of Japan and the Pacific Rim*
Sherrow. *Hiroshima*
Wilkinson. *Amazing Buildings*
Wilkinson. *The Magical East*
Williams. *Forts and Castles*

Multimedia

CD-ROM

Religions of the World
Teach Your Kids World History

Video

Barefoot Gen
The Changing Face of Asia: Japan, Part 1: The Divine Land
The Changing Face of Asia: Japan, Part 2: A Nation Reborn
The Changing Face of Asia: Japan, Part 3: Superpower in the Pacific
Genbaku Shi: Killed by the Atomic Bomb
Growing up in Japan
Hiroshima Maiden
Japan: Japan Today
Japan: Nation Reborn
Japan: The Sacred Islands

GRADE EIGHT

Historical Fiction

Dalkey. *Little Sister*
Haugaard. *The Boy and the Samurai*
Haugaard. *The Revenge of the Forty-Seven Samurai*
Haugaard. *The Samurai's Tale*

Namioka. *The Coming of the Bear*
Namioka. *Island of Ogres*
Paterson. *Of Nightingales That Weep*

Paterson. *The Master Puppeteer*
Paterson. *The Sign of the Chrysanthemum*

Biography

Severns. *Hirohito*

Collective Biography

Cohen. *The Ghosts of War*
Hazell. *Heroines: Great Women Through the Ages*

Hoobler. *Japanese Portraits*
Krull. *Lives of the Writers*

Wilkinson. *Generals Who Changed the World*

History

Black. *Hiroshima and the Atomic Bomb*
Civilizations of Asia
Hoobler. *Showa: The Age of Hirohito*

Langone. *In the Shogun's Shadow*
Lynch. *Great Buildings*
MacDonald. *A Samurai Castle*
Nardo. *Traditional Japan*
Newton. *Tokyo*

Ross. *Rise of Japan and the Pacific Rim*
Sherrow. *Hiroshima*
Wilkinson. *The Magical East*
Williams. *Forts and Castles*

Multimedia

CD-ROM

Religions of the World

Teach Your Kids World History

Video

Barefoot Gen
The Changing Face of Asia: Japan, Part 1: The Divine Land
The Changing Face of Asia: Japan, Part 2: A Nation Reborn

The Changing Face of Asia: Japan, Part 3: Superpower in the Pacific
Genbaku Shi: Killed by the Atomic Bomb
Growing up in Japan
Hiroshima Maiden

Japan: Japan Today
Japan: Nation Reborn
Japan: The Sacred Islands

GRADE NINE

Historical Fiction

Dalkey. *Little Sister*
Haugaard. *The Boy and the Samurai*
Haugaard. *The Revenge of the Forty-Seven Samurai*
Haugaard. *The Samurai's Tale*

Matsubara. *Cranes at Dusk*
Namioka. *The Coming of the Bear*
Namioka. *Island of Ogres*
Paterson. *Of Nightingales That Weep*

Paterson. *The Master Puppeteer*
Paterson. *The Sign of the Chrysanthemum*

Biography

Severns. *Hirohito*

Collective Biography

Hoobler. *Japanese Portraits*

Wilkinson. *Generals Who Changed the World*

History

Civilizations of Asia
Hoobler. *Showa: The Age of Hirohito*
Langone. *In the Shogun's Shadow*

Nardo. *Traditional Japan*
Newton. *Tokyo*
Perkins. *Encyclopedia of Japan*
Ross. *Rise of Japan and the Pacific Rim*

Sherrow. *Hiroshima*
Williams. *Forts and Castles*

Multimedia

CD-ROM

Religions of the World

Teach Your Kids World History

Video

After the Cloud Lifted: Hiroshima's Stories of Recovery
The Changing Face of Asia: Japan, Part 1: The Divine Land

The Changing Face of Asia: Japan, Part 2: A Nation Reborn
The Changing Face of Asia: Japan, Part 3: Superpower in the Pacific
Genbaku Shi: Killed by the Atomic Bomb

Japan: Japan Today
Japan: Nation Reborn
Japan: The Sacred Islands
Nagasaki Journey
Our Hiroshima
The Road to War: Japan
U.S.A. vs. "Tokyo Rose"
Windows to the World: Japan

GRADE TEN

Historical Fiction

Dalkey. *Little Sister*
Haugaard. *The Samurai's Tale*
Matsubara. *Cranes at Dusk*
Namioka. *The Coming of the Bear*

Namioka. *Island of Ogres*
Paterson. *Of Nightingales That Weep*
Paterson. *The Master Puppeteer*

Paterson. *The Sign of the Chrysanthemum*

Biography

Severns. *Hirohito*

Collective Biography

Hoobler. *Japanese Portraits*

Wilkinson. *Generals Who Changed the World*

History

Ardley. *Music: An Illustrated Encyclopedia*
Civilizations of Asia

Hoobler. *Showa: The Age of Hirohito*
Nardo. *Traditional Japan*
Perkins. *Encyclopedia of Japan*

Ross. *Rise of Japan and the Pacific Rim*
Sherrow. *Hiroshima*

Multimedia

CD-ROM

Religions of the World

Teach Your Kids World History

Video

After the Cloud Lifted: Hiroshima's Stories of Recovery
The Changing Face of Asia: Japan, Part 1: The Divine Land

The Changing Face of Asia: Japan, Part 2: A Nation Reborn
The Changing Face of Asia: Japan, Part 3: Superpower in the Pacific
Genbaku Shi: Killed by the Atomic Bomb

Japan: Japan Today
Japan: Nation Reborn
Japan: The Sacred Islands
Nagasaki Journey
Our Hiroshima
The Road to War: Japan
U.S.A. vs. "Tokyo Rose"
Windows to the World: Japan

GRADES ELEVEN AND TWELVE

Historical Fiction

Clavell. *Shogun*
Dalkey. *Little Sister*
Deford. *Love and Infamy*
Matsubara. *Cranes at Dusk*

Namioka. *The Coming of the Bear*
Paterson. *Of Nightingales That Weep*

Paterson. *The Master Puppeteer*
Paterson. *The Sign of the Chrysanthemum*
Rowland. *Shinju*

Biography

Severns. *Hirohito*

Collective Biography

Hoobler. *Japanese Portraits*

Landrum. *Profiles of Genius: Thirteen Creative Men*

History

Ardley. *Music: An Illustrated Encyclopedia*

Hoobler. *Showa: The Age of Hirohito*
Keegan. *History of Warfare*

Perkins. *Encyclopedia of Japan*

Multimedia

CD-ROM

Religions of the World

Teach Your Kids World History

Video

After the Cloud Lifted: Hiroshima's Stories of Recovery
The Changing Face of Asia: Japan, Part 1: The Divine Land
The Changing Face of Asia: Japan, Part 2: A Nation Reborn
The Changing Face of Asia: Japan, Part 3: Superpower in the Pacific

The Fight for Democracy
From the Barrel of a Gun
The Future of the Pacific Basin
Genbaku Shi: Killed by the Atomic Bomb
Inside Japan, Inc
Japan: Nation Reborn
Japan: The Sacred Islands
Japan: Japan Today
Meiji: Asia's Response to the West

Nagasaki Journey
Our Hiroshima
Reinventing Japan
Ripples of Change: Japanese Women's Search for Self
The Road to War: Japan
Sentimental Imperialists
U.S.A. vs. "Tokyo Rose"
Windows to the World: Japan
Writers and Revolutionaries

Vietnam, Korea, Cambodia, and Thailand

Historical Fiction

Baillie. *Little Brother*
Choi. *Echoes of the White Giraffe*
Choi. *Gathering of Pearls*
Choi. *Year of Impossible Goodbyes*
Fritsch. *A Part of the Ribbon*
Giles. *Breath of the Dragon*
Ho. *The Clay Marble*
Ho. *Rice Without Rain*
Pettit. *My Name Is San Ho*
Watkins. *My Brother, My Sister, and I*
White. *The Road Home*

Biography

Huynh Quang Nhuong. *The Land I Lost*
Kuckreja. *Prince Norodom Sihanouk*
Lloyd. *Ho Chi Minh*

Collective Biography

Scheller. *Amazing Archaeologists*

History

Bachrach. *The Korean War*
Balaban. *Vietnam*
Bandon. *Korean Americans*
Bandon. *Vietnamese Americans*
Chalberg. *The Land and People of Cambodia*
Civilizations of Asia
Cosner. *War Nurses*
Detzer. *An Asian Tragedy*
Gay. *Korean War*
Gay. *Vietnam War*
Gibson. *The War in Vietnam*
Hoobler. *Vietnam, Why We Fought*
Isserman. *The Korean War*
Lynch. *Great Buildings*
Murphy. *A Hmong Family*
Nash. *North Korea*
Nickelson. *Vietnam*
Rice. *The Tet Offensive*
Singer. *Structures That Changed the Way the World Looked*
Smith. *The Korean War*
Stein. *The Korean War*
Wilkinson. *The Magical East*
Wormser. *Three Faces of Vietnam*

Multimedia

CD-ROM

Passage to Vietnam
Religions of the World
Teach Your Kids World History
The War in Vietnam

Video

Rising Above: Women of Vietnam
South Korea, Land of the Morning Calm

Historical Fiction

Choi. *Echoes of the White Giraffe*
Choi. *Gathering of Pearls*
Choi. *Year of Impossible Goodbyes*
Garland. *Song of the Buffalo Boy*
Ho. *The Clay Marble*

Ho. *Rice Without Rain*
Myers. *Fallen Angels*

Pettit. *My Name Is San Ho*
Watkins. *My Brother, My Sister, and I*

White. *The Road Home*

Biography

Kuckreja. *Prince Norodom Sihanouk*

Lloyd. *Ho Chi Minh*
Stefoff. *Pol Pot*

Collective Biography

Scheller. *Amazing Archaeologists*

History

Bachrach. *The Korean War*
Bandon. *Korean Americans*
Bandon. *Vietnamese Americans*
Chalberg. *The Land and People of Cambodia*
Civilizations of Asia
Cosner. *War Nurses*
Denenberg. *Voices from Vietnam*

Detzer. *An Asian Tragedy*
Gay. *Korean War*
Gay. *Vietnam War*
Gibson. *The War in Vietnam*
Hoobler. *Vietnam, Why We Fought*
Isserman. *The Korean War*
Lynch. *Great Buildings*
Nash. *North Korea*
Nickelson. *Vietnam*

Rice. *The Tet Offensive*
Singer. *Structures That Changed the Way the World Looked*
Smith. *The Korean War*
Stein. *The Korean War*
Wilkinson. *The Magical East*
Wormser. *Three Faces of Vietnam*

Multimedia

CD-ROM

Passage to Vietnam
Religions of the World

Teach Your Kids World History

The War in Vietnam

Video

Rising Above: Women of Vietnam

South Korea, Land of the Morning Calm

GRADE NINE

Historical Fiction

Choi. *Echoes of the White Giraffe*
Choi. *Gathering of Pearls*
Choi. *Year of Impossible Goodbyes*

Garland. *Song of the Buffalo Boy*
Ho. *The Clay Marble*
Ho. *Rice without Rain*
Myers. *Fallen Angels*

Watkins. *My Brother, My Sister, and I*
White. *The Road Home*

Biography

Kuckreja. *Prince Norodom Sihanouk*

Lloyd. *Ho Chi Minh*
Stefoff. *Pol Pot*

Collective Biography

Scheller. *Amazing Archaeologists*

History

Bachrach. *The Korean War*
Chalberg. *The Land and People of Cambodia*
Civilizations of Asia
Cosner. *War Nurses*
Denenberg. *Voices from Vietnam*
Gay. *Korean War*

Gay. *Vietnam War*
Hoobler. *Vietnam, Why We Fought*
Isserman. *The Korean War*
Marrin. *America and Vietnam*
Nickelson. *Vietnam*
Rice. *The Tet Offensive*

Singer. *Structures That Changed the Way the World Looked*
Stein. *The Korean War*
Summers. *Korean War Almanac*
Wormser. *Three Faces of Vietnam*

Multimedia

CD-ROM

Passage to Vietnam
Religions of the World

Teach Your Kids World
* History*

The War in Vietnam

Video

Cambodia: The Struggle for
* Peace*
Kontum Diary
Korea/Vietnam

Rising Above: Women of
* Vietnam*
South Korea, Land of the
* Morning Calm*
Vietnam: After the Fire

Windows to the World:
* Thailand*
Windows to the World:
* Vietnam*

GRADE TEN

Historical Fiction

Choi. *Gathering of Pearls*
Garland. *Song of the Buffalo*
* Boy*

Ho. *Rice Without Rain*
Myers. *Fallen Angels*

Watkins. *My Brother, My*
* Sister, and I*
White. *The Road Home*

Biography

Hodgins. *Reluctant Warrior:*
* A True Story of Duty and*
* Heroism in Vietnam*

Kuckreja. *Prince Norodom*
* Sihanouk*
Lloyd. *Ho Chi Minh*

Stefoff. *Pol Pot*

History

Bachrach. *The Korean War*
Balaban. *Remembering*
* Heaven's Face*
Chalberg. *The Land and*
* People of Cambodia*
Civilizations of Asia
Cosner. *War Nurses*

Denenberg. *Voices from Vietnam*
Hoobler. *Vietnam, Why We*
* Fought*
Hull. *Breaking Free: Human*
* Rights Poetry*
Isserman. *The Korean War*
Marrin. *America and Vietnam*

Nickelson. *Vietnam*
Rice. *The Tet Offensive*
Summers. *Korean War*
* Almanac*
Wormser. *Three Faces of*
* Vietnam*

Multimedia

CD-ROM

Passage to Vietnam
Religions of the World

Teach Your Kids World History
The War in Vietnam

Video

As Seen by Both Sides:
* American and Vietnamese*
* Artists Look at the War*
Cambodia: The Struggle for
* Peace*
Kontum Diary

Korea/Vietnam
Rising Above: Women of
* Vietnam*
South Korea, Land of the
* Morning Calm*
Vietnam: After the Fire

Windows to the World:
* Thailand*
Windows to the World:
* Vietnam*

GRADES ELEVEN AND TWELVE

Historical Fiction

Berent. *Eagle Station*
Berent. *Phantom Leader*
Berent. *Rolling Thunder*
Berent. *Steel Tiger*
Choi. *Gathering of Pearls*

Garland. *Song of the Buffalo*
* Boy*
Hickey. *Chrysanthemum in*
* the Snow*
Ho. *Rice Without Rain*

Huong. *Paradise of the Blind*
Myers. *Fallen Angels*
Somtow. *Jasmine Nights*
White. *The Road Home*

Biography

Hodgins. *Reluctant Warrior: A True Story of Duty and Heroism in Vietnam*

Kuckreja. *Prince Norodom Sihanouk*
Lloyd. *Ho Chi Minh*

Stefoff. *Pol Pot*

History

Bachrach. *The Korean War*
Balaban. *Remembering Heaven's Face*
Brady. *The Coldest War*
Chalberg. *The Land and People of Cambodia*
De Benedetti. *The Antiwar Movement of the Vietnam Era*

Denenberg. *Voices from Vietnam*
Engelmann. *Tears Before the Rain*
Hull. *Breaking Free: Human Rights Poetry*
Marrin. *America and Vietnam*
Nickelson. *Vietnam*
Seymour-Jones. *Refugees*

Summers. *Korean War Almanac*
Wormser. *Three Faces of Vietnam*

Multimedia

CD-ROM

Passage to Vietnam
Religions of the World

Teach Your Kids World History

The War in Vietnam

Video

As Seen by Both Sides: American and Vietnamese Artists Look at the War
Big Business and the Ghost of Confucius
Cambodia: The Struggle for Peace
From the Barrel of a Gun

Kontum Diary
Korea/Vietnam
The Fight for Democracy
The Future of the Pacific Basin
Rising Above: Women of Vietnam

South Korea, Land of the Morning Calm
Vietnam: After the Fire
Windows to the World: Thailand
Windows to the World: Vietnam

South and Central America and the Caribbean

Historical Fiction

Baker. *The Blood of the Brave*
Baker. *Walk the World's Rim*
Berry. *Ajeemah and His Son*
Blair. *Fear the Condor*
De Treviño. *El Güero*
De Treviño. *Leona*
Dorris. *Morning Girl*
Finley. *Soaring Eagle*

Garland. *Cabin 102*
Head. *Culebra Cut*
Howard. *When Daylight Comes*
O'Dell. *Carlota*
O'Dell. *My Name Is Not Angelica*
O'Dell. *The Amethyst Ring*

O'Dell. *The Captive*
O'Dell. *The Feathered Serpent*
Raspail. *Who Will Remember the People?*
Slaughter. *The Dirty War*
Stanley. *Elena*
Taylor. *The Cay*

Biography

Appel. *José Martí*
Arnold. *Alicia Alonso*
Bernier-Grand. *Don Luis Muñoz Marín*
Braun. *A Weekend with Diego Rivera*
Brill. *Journey for Peace: The Story of Rigoberta Menchú*
Brown. *Fidel Castro*
Carroll. *Pancho Villa*
Chrisman. *Hernando de Soto*
Chrisman. *Luis Muñoz Marín*
Cockcroft. *Daniel Ortega*
Cockcroft. *Diego Rivera*
Cruz. *Frida Kahlo: Portrait of a Mexican Painter*
de Ruiz. *To Fly with the Swallows*

de Varona. *Bernardo de Gálvez*
DeStefano. *Chico Mendes*
Drucker. *Frida Kahlo*
Garza. *Frida Kahlo*
Gleiter. *Diego Rivera*
Gleiter. *José Martí*
Gleiter. *Junípero Serra*
Gleiter. *Miguel Hidalgo y Costilla*
Gleiter. *Simón Bolívar*
Gleiter. *Benito Juárez*
Goldstein. *The Journey of Diego Rivera*
Gonzales. *Diego Rivera: His Art, His Life*
Goodnough. *Jose Marti*

Hoobler. *Toussaint L'Ouverture*
Kellner. *Ernesto "Che" Guevara*
Lazo. *Rigoberta Menchú*
Myers. *Toussaint L'Ouverture*
Neimark. *Diego Rivera*
Shuter. *Exquemelin and the Pirates of the Caribbean 1666*
Sumption. *Carlos Finlay*
Thompson. *Pedro Menéndez de Avilés*
Thompson. *Sor Juana Inés de la Cruz*
West. *José Martí*

Collective Biography

Blue. *People of Peace*
Cush. *Women Who Achieved Greatness*
Hazell. *Heroes: Great Men Through the Ages*
Hazell. *Heroines: Great Women Through the Ages*

Hoobler. *Mexican Portraits*
Hoobler. *South American Portraits*
Sills. *Inspirations: Stories About Women Artists*
Wilkinson. *People Who Changed the World*

Wilkinson. *Statesmen Who Changed the World*
Wolf. *Focus: Five Women Photographers*
Scheller. *Amazing Archaeologists*

History

Anthony. *West Indies*
Bandon. *Dominican Americans*
Bandon. *Mexican Americans*

Bandon. *West Indian Americans*
Bierhorst. *The Hungry Woman: The Aztecs*

Blair. *The Land and People of Bolivia*
Burrell. *Life in the Time of Moctezuma and the Aztecs*
Capek. *Murals*

Carter. *The Mexican War*
Carter. *The Spanish-American War*
Charley. *Tombs and Treasures*
Civilizations of the Americas
Corbishley. *Secret Cities*
Cordoba. *Pre-Columbian Peoples of North America*
Dawson. *Food and Feasts with the Aztecs*
Deltenre. *Peru and the Andean Countries*
Dolan. *Panama and the United States*
Galvin. *The Maya of Central America*
Gay. *Spanish American War*
Gow. *The Cuban Missile Crisis*
Halliburton. *The West Indian-American Experience*
Harris. *Mummies*

Hernandez. *San Rafael*
Jacobs. *The Tainos*
Jacobs. *War with Mexico*
Koral. *An Album of War Refugees*
Lankford. *Quinceañera*
Liptak. *Endangered Peoples*
Marrin. *Aztecs and Spaniards*
Marrin. *Inca and Spaniard*
Marrin. *The Spanish-American War*
Martell. *The Age of Discovery*
Mason. *Aztec Times*
Meyer. *The Mystery of the Ancient Maya*
Noblet. *The Amazon and the Americas*
Odijk. *The Aztecs*
Odijk. *The Mayas*
Pascoe. *Mexico and the United States: Cooperation and Conflict*
Putnam. *Mummy*

Rice. *The Cuban Revolution*
Steele. *The Aztec News*
Steele. *The Incas and Machu Picchu*
Stein. *The Aztec Empire*
Stein. *The Mexican Revolution: 1910-1920*
Street Smart! Cities of the Ancient World
The Americas in the Colonial Era
Ventura. *1492*
Warburton. *Aztec Civilization*
Warburton. *The Beginning of Writing*
Winter. *Women in Society: Brazil*
Wood. *Ancient America*
Wood. *The Aztecs*
Wood. *The Incas*

Multimedia

CD-ROM

Exploring Ancient Cities
Maya Quest

One Tribe

Teach Your Kids World History

Video

Art and Architecture of Precolumbian Mexico
The Art and Architecture of the Maya
The Aztec
Biography: Evita the Woman Behind the Myth
Christopher Columbus
The Caribbean
Central America
Central Americans
Christopher Columbus

The Columbian Way of Life
Cuba
Ernesto Che Guevara the Bolivian Diary
In the Land of the Inca
Introducing South America
Juan and Evita Peron
Machu Picchu Revealed
The Maya
The Mayans and Aztecs
Mexico: The Heritage
Mexico: The People of the Sun

Mexico: Yesterday and Today
Middle America: Mexico to Venezuela and the Caribbean Islands
The Moon Woman's Sisters—Highland Guatemala Maya Weaving
Mystery of the Maya
Pancho Villa
Peru's Treasure Tombs
Simon Bolivar

GRADE EIGHT

Historical Fiction

Baker. *The Blood of the Brave*
Baker. *Walk the World's Rim*
Berry. *Ajeemah and His Son*
Blair. *Fear the Condor*
De Treviño. *El Güero*
De Treviño. *Leona*
Finley. *Soaring Eagle*

Garland. *Cabin 102*
Howard. *When Daylight Comes*
O'Dell. *Carlota*
O'Dell. *My Name Is Not Angelica*
O'Dell. *The Amethyst Ring*

O'Dell. *The Captive*
O'Dell. *The Feathered Serpent*
Raspail. *Who Will Remember the People?*
Slaughter. *The Dirty War*
Taylor. *The Cay*

Biography

Arnold, Sandra Martín. *Alicia Alonso: First Lady of the Ballet*

Appel. *José Martí*
Bernier-Grand. *Don Luis Muñoz Marín*

Braun. *A Weekend with Diego Rivera*
Brown. *Fidel Castro*

Carroll. *Pancho Villa*
Cockcroft. *Daniel Ortega*
Cockcroft. *Diego Rivera*
Cruz. *Frida Kahlo: Portrait of a Mexican Painter*
de Ruiz. *To Fly with the Swallows*
DeChancie. *Juan Perón*
Dolan. *Gabriel García Márquez*
Drucker. *Frida Kahlo*
Garza. *Frida Kahlo*

Goldstein. *The Journey of Diego Rivera*
Gonzales. *Diego Rivera: His Art, His Life*
Goodnough. *Jose Marti*
Hoobler. *Toussaint L'Ouverture*
Jones. *Frida Kahlo*
Kellner. *Ernesto "Che" Guevara*
Lazo. *Rigoberta Menchú*

O'Brien. *Antonio López de Santa Anna*
O'Brien. *Pancho Villa*
Ragan. *Emiliano Zapata*
Roman. *Pablo Neruda*
Shuter. *Exquemelin and the Pirates of the Caribbean 1666*
Wepman. *Bolívar*
West. *José Martí*

Collective Biography

Blue. *People of Peace*
Cush. *Women Who Achieved Greatness*
Hazell. *Heroes: Great Men Through the Ages*
Hazell. *Heroines: Great Women Through the Ages*

Hoobler. *Mexican Portraits*
Hoobler. *South American Portraits*
Scheller. *Amazing Archaeologists*
Sills. *Inspirations: Stories About Women Artists*

Wilkinson. *People Who Changed the World*
Wilkinson. *Statesmen Who Changed the World*
Wolf. *Focus: Five Women Photographers*

History

Anthony. *West Indies*
Bandon. *Dominican Americans*
Bandon. *Mexican Americans*
Bandon. *West Indian Americans*
Bierhorst. *The Hungry Woman: The Aztecs*
Blair. *The Land and People of Bolivia*
Burrell. *Life in the Time of Moctezuma and the Aztecs*
Capek. *Murals*
Carter. *The Mexican War*
Carter. *The Spanish-American War*
Cheney. *El Salvador*
Civilizations of the Americas
Deltenre. *Peru and the Andean Countries*
Dolan. *Panama and the United States*

Galvin. *The Maya of Central America*
Gay. *Spanish American War*
Gow. *The Cuban Missile Crisis*
Halliburton. *The West Indian-American Experience*
Harris. *Mummies*
Hernandez. *San Rafael*
Jacobs. *The Tainos*
Jacobs. *War with Mexico*
Koral. *An Album of War Refugees*
Lawson. *The Iran Hostage Crisis and Iran-Contra*
Liptak. *Endangered Peoples*
Marrin. *Aztecs and Spaniards*
Marrin. *Inca and Spaniard*
Marrin. *The Spanish-American War*
Meyer. *The Mystery of the Ancient Maya*

Noblet. *The Amazon and the Americas*
Pascoe. *Mexico and the United States: Cooperation and Conflict*
Putnam. *Mummy*
Rice. *The Cuban Revolution*
Steele. *The Aztec News*
Stein. *The Aztec Empire*
Stein. *The Mexican Revolution: 1910-1920*
Street Smart! Cities of the Ancient World
The Americas in the Colonial Era
Warburton. *Aztec Civilization*
Warburton. *The Beginning of Writing*
Winter. *Women in Society: Brazil*
Wood. *Ancient America*
Wood. *The Incas*

Multimedia

CD-ROM

Exploring Ancient Cities
Maya Quest

One Tribe

Teach Your Kids World History

Video

Art and Architecture of Precolumbian Mexico
The Art and Architecture of the Maya
The Aztec
Biography: Evita the Woman Behind the Myth
Christopher Columbus
The Caribbean
Central America
Central Americans

Christopher Columbus
The Columbian Way of Life
Cuba
Ernesto Che Guevara the Bolivian Diary
In the Land of the Inca
Introducing South America
Juan and Evita Peron
Machu Picchu Revealed
The Maya
The Mayans and Aztecs

Mexico: The Heritage
Mexico: Yesterday and Today
The Moon Woman's Sisters— Highland Guatemala Maya Weaving
Mystery of the Maya
Pancho Villa
Peru's Treasure Tombs
Simon Bolivar

GRADE NINE

Historical Fiction

Baker. *The Blood of the Brave*
Baker. *Walk the World's Rim*
Berry. *Ajeemah and His Son*
Blair. *Fear the Condor*
De Jenkins. *The Honorable Prison*
De Treviño. *El Güero*
Finley. *Soaring Eagle*

Foster. *No Man in the House*
Garland. *Cabin 102*
Howard. *When Daylight Comes*
O'Dell. *Carlota*
O'Dell. *My Name Is Not Angelica*
O'Dell. *The Amethyst Ring*

O'Dell. *The Captive*
O'Dell. *The Feathered Serpent*
Raspail. *Who Will Remember the People?*
Taylor. *The Cay*

Biography

Appel. *José Martí*
Bell-Villada. *García Márquez*
Arnold. *Alicia Alonso*
Brown. *Fidel Castro*
Carroll. *Pancho Villa*
Cockcroft. *Daniel Ortega*
Cockcroft. *Diego Rivera*
Cruz. *Frida Kahlo: Portrait of a Mexican Painter*
de Ruiz. *To Fly with the Swallows*
DeChancie. *Juan Perón*
Dolan. *Gabriel García Márquez*

Drucker. *Frida Kahlo*
Garza. *Frida Kahlo*
Goldstein. *The Journey of Diego Rivera*
Gonzales. *Diego Rivera: His Art, His Life*
Goodnough. *Jose Marti: Cuban Patriot and Poet*
Hoobler. *Toussaint L'Ouverture*
Jones. *Frida Kahlo*
Kellner. *Ernesto "Che" Guevara*
Lennon. *Jorge Luis Borges*

Madden. *Fidel Castro*
O'Brien. *Antonio López de Santa Anna*
O'Brien. *Pancho Villa*
Ragan. *Emiliano Zapata*
Roman. *Pablo Neruda*
Roman. *Octavio Paz*
Shuter. *Exquemelin and the Pirates of the Caribbean 1666*
Wepman. *Bolívar: Latin Revolutionary*

Collective Biography

Cush. *Women Who Achieved Greatness*
Hoobler. *Mexican Portraits*
Hoobler. *South American Portraits*

Scheller. *Amazing Archaeologists*
Wilkinson. *People Who Changed the World*

Wilkinson. *Statesmen Who Changed the World*
Wolf. *Focus: Five Women Photographers*

History

Anthony. *West Indies*
Bierhorst. *The Hungry Woman: The Aztecs*
Capek. *Murals*
Cheney. *El Salvador*
Civilizations of the Americas
Frost. *The Mexican Revolution*
Gay. *Spanish American War*
Gow. *The Cuban Missile Crisis*
Hernandez. *San Rafael*
Jacobs. *The Tainos*
Jenkins. *Nicaragua and the United States*
Koral. *An Album of War Refugees*
Lawson. *The Iran Hostage Crisis and Iran-Contra*

Liptak. *Endangered Peoples*
Marrin. *Inca and Spaniard*
Marrin. *The Spanish-American War*
Meyer. *The Mystery of the Ancient Maya*
Nardo. *The Mexican-American War*
Pascoe. *Mexico and the United States: Cooperation and Conflict*
Pascoe. *Neighbors at Odds*
Rice. *The Cuban Revolution*
Steele. *The Aztec News*
Stein. *The Mexican Revolution: 1910-1920*
The Americas in the Colonial Era

Time-Life. *Aztecs: Reign of Blood & Splendor*
Time-Life. *Incas: Lords of Gold and Glory*
Time-Life. *The Magnificent Maya*
Time-Life. *The Search for El Dorado*
Warburton. *The Beginning of Writing*
Winter. *Women in Society: Brazil*
Wood. *Ancient America*
Wood. *The Incas*

Multimedia

CD-ROM

Exploring Ancient Cities
Maya Quest

One Tribe

Teach Your Kids World
History

Video

The Aztec
Biography: Evita the Woman
Behind the Myth
Bolivia: Then and Now
The Caribbean
Central America
Central Americans
The Columbian Way of Life
Columbus and the Age of
Discovery: The Crossing
Columbus: Gold, God and
Glory
Cuba
Enigma of the Ruins
Ernesto Che Guevara the
Bolivian Diary

Haiti: Kom Sa Ta Dweye
The Hunt for Pancho Villa
In the Land of the Inca
Introducing South America
Invasion
Juan and Evita Peron
Legacy
The Lines
Machu Picchu Revealed
The Maya
Mexico: Yesterday and Today
Mystery of the Maya
The Mystic Lands Series:
Haiti: Dance of the Spirit
The Mystic Lands Series:
Maya: Messages in Stone

The Mystic Lands Series:
Peru: Kingdom in the
Clouds
Pablo Neruda
Pancho Villa
Peru's Treasure Tombs
Return of the Maya
Simon Bolivar
Unheard Voices
The Virgin and the Bull
Wonders of Man's Creation
The Yidishe Gauchos

GRADE TEN

Historical Fiction

Baker. *The Blood of the Brave*
Berry. *Ajeemah and His Son*
Blair. *Fear the Condor*
De Jenkins. *The Honorable*
Prison
Foster. *No Man in the House*

Mastretta. *Lovesick*
O'Dell. *Carlota*
O'Dell. *My Name Is Not*
Angelica
O'Dell. *The Amethyst Ring*
O'Dell. *The Captive*

O'Dell. *The Feathered*
Serpent
Raspail. *Who Will Remember*
the People?

Biography

Arnold. *Alicia Alonso*
Bell-Villada. *García Márquez*
Brown. *Fidel Castro*
Carroll. *Pancho Villa*
Cockcroft. *Daniel Ortega*
Cockcroft. *Diego Rivera*
DeChancie. *Juan Perón*
Dolan. *Gabriel García*
Márquez
Drucker. *Frida Kahlo*

Garza. *Frida Kahlo*
Goldstein. *The Journey of*
Diego Rivera
Hoobler. *Toussaint*
L'Ouverture
Jones. *Frida Kahlo*
Kellner. *Ernesto "Che"*
Guevara
Lennon. *Jorge Luis Borges*
Madden. *Fidel Castro*

O'Brien. *Antonio López de*
Santa Anna
Wepman. *Bolívar: Latin*
Revolutionary
O'Brien. *Pancho Villa*
Ragan. *Emiliano Zapata*
Roman. *Pablo Neruda*
Roman. *Octavio Paz*

Collective Biography

Axelrod. *Dictators and*
Tyrants
Hoobler. *Mexican Portraits*

Hoobler. *South American*
Portraits
Wilkinson. *People Who*
Changed the World

Wilkinson. *Statesmen Who*
Changed the World
Wolf. *Focus: Five Women*
Photographers

History

Ardley. *Music: An Illustrated*
Encyclopedia
Bierhorst. *The Hungry*
Woman: The Aztecs
Capek. *Murals*
Cheney. *El Salvador*

Civilizations of the Americas
Frost. *The Mexican Revolution*
Gow. *The Cuban Missile*
Crisis
Hernandez. *San Rafael*

Heyck. *Life Stories of the*
Nicaraguan Revolution
Hull. *Breaking Free: Human*
Rights Poetry
Jenkins. *Nicaragua and the*
United States

Lawson. *The Iran Hostage Crisis and Iran-Contra*
Marrin. *Inca and Spaniard*
Marrin. *The Spanish-American War*
Meyer. *The Mystery of the Ancient Maya*
Nardo. *The Mexican-American War*

Pascoe. *Mexico and the United States: Cooperation and Conflict*
Pascoe. *Neighbors at Odds*
Stein. *The Mexican Revolution: 1910-1920*
The Americas in the Colonial Era
Time-Life. *Aztecs: Reign of Blood & Splendor*

Time-Life. *Incas: Lords of Gold and Glory*
Time-Life. *The Magnificent Maya*
Time-Life. *The Search for El Dorado*
Winter. *Women in Society: Brazil*

Multimedia

CD-ROM

Exploring Ancient Cities
Maya Quest

One Tribe

Teach Your Kids World History

Video

The Aztec
Biography: Evita the Woman Behind the Myth
Bolivia: Then and Now
The Caribbean
Central America
Central Americans
Columbus and the Age of Discovery: The Crossing
Columbus: Gold, God and Glory
Cuba
Enigma of the Ruins
Ernesto Che Guevara the Bolivian Diary

Haiti: Kom Sa Ta Dweye
The Hunt for Pancho Villa
In the Land of the Inca
Introducing South America
Invasion
Juan and Evita Peron
Legacy
The Lines
Machu Picchu Revealed
The Maya
Mexico: Yesterday and Today
Mystery of the Maya
The Mystic Lands Series: Haiti: Dance of the Spirit

The Mystic Lands Series: Maya: Messages in Stone
The Mystic Lands Series: Peru: Kingdom in the Clouds
Pablo Neruda
Pancho Villa
Return of the Maya
Simon Bolivar
Unheard Voices
The Virgin and the Bull
Where Is Patagonia?
Wonders of Man's Creation
The Yidishe Gauchos

GRADES ELEVEN AND TWELVE

Historical Fiction

Alvarez. *In the Time of the Butterflies*
Benitez. *Bitter Grounds*
Berry. *Ajeemah and His Son*
De Jenkins. *The Honorable Prison*
Foster. *No Man in the House*
Mastretta. *Lovesick*

O'Brian. *The Far Side of the World*
O'Brian. *The Fortune of War*
O'Brian. *The Surgeon's Mate*
O'Dell. *Carlota*
O'Dell. *My Name Is Not Angelica*
O'Dell. *The Amethyst Ring*

O'Dell. *The Captive*
O'Dell. *The Feathered Serpent*
Raspail. *Who Will Remember the People?*

Biography

Bell-Villada. *García Márquez*
Brown. *Fidel Castro*
Carroll. *Pancho Villa*
Cockcroft. *Daniel Ortega*
Cockcroft. *Diego Rivera*
DeChancie. *Juan Perón*
Dolan. *Gabriel García Márquez*
Drucker. *Frida Kahlo: Torment and Triumph in Her Life*

Garza. *Frida Kahlo*
Goldstein. *The Journey of Diego Rivera*
Hoobler. *Toussaint L'Ouverture*
Jones. *Frida Kahlo*
Kellner. *Ernesto "Che" Guevara*
Lennon. *Jorge Luis Borges*
Madden. *Fidel Castro*

O'Brien. *Antonio López de Santa Anna*
O'Brien. *Pancho Villa*
Wepman. *Bolívar: Latin Revolutionary*
Ragan. *Emiliano Zapata*
Roman. *Pablo Neruda*
Roman. *Octavio Paz*

Collective Biography

Axelrod. *Dictators and Tyrants*
Hoobler. *Mexican Portraits*
Hoobler. *South American Portraits*
McCullough. *Brave Companions*
Wolf. *Focus: Five Women Photographers*

History

Ardley. *Music: An Illustrated Encyclopedia*
Bierhorst. *The Mythology of Mexico and Central America*
Bunson. *Encyclopedia of Ancient Mesoamerica*
Calderwood. *Mexico: A Higher Vision*
Capek. *Murals*
Cheney. *El Salvador*
Frost. *The Mexican Revolution*
Gow. *The Cuban Missile Crisis*
Hernandez. *San Rafael*
Heyck. *Life Stories of the Nicaraguan Revolution*
Hull. *Breaking Free: Human Rights Poetry*
Jenkins. *Nicaragua and the United States*
Nardo. *The Mexican-American War*
Pascoe. *Mexico and the United States: Cooperation and Conflict*
Pascoe. *Neighbors at Odds*
Salmoral. *America 1492*
Stein. *The Mexican Revolution: 1910-1920*
Time-Life. *Aztecs: Reign of Blood & Splendor*
Time-Life. *Incas: Lords of Gold and Glory*
Time-Life. *The Magnificent Maya*
Time-Life. *The Search for El Dorado*
Winter. *Women in Society: Brazil*

Multimedia

CD-ROM

Exploring Ancient Cities
Maya Quest
One Tribe
Teach Your Kids World History

Video

Biography: Evita the Woman Behind the Myth
Bolivia: Then and Now
The Caribbean
Central America
Columbus and the Age of Discovery: The Crossing
Columbus: Gold, God and Glory
Cuba
Enigma of the Ruins
Ernesto Che Guevara the Bolivian Diary
Haiti: Kom Sa Ta Dweye
The Hunt for Pancho Villa
In the Land of the Inca
Introducing South America
Invasion
Juan and Evita Peron
Legacy
The Lines
Machu Picchu Revealed
Mystery of the Maya
The Mystic Lands Series: Haiti: Dance of the Spirit
The Mystic Lands Series: Maya: Messages in Stone
The Mystic Lands Series: Peru: Kingdom in the Clouds
Pablo Neruda
Pancho Villa
Return of the Maya
Simon Bolivar
Unheard Voices
The Virgin and the Bull
Where Is Patagonia?
Wonders of Man's Creation
The Yidishe Gauchos

Books: An Annotated Bibliography

A

1. Aaseng, Nathan. **Genetics: Unlocking the Secrets of Life**. Minneapolis, MN: Oliver Press, 1996. 144p. $14.95. ISBN 1-881508-27-7. 6 up

The study of genetics has been a science for only 100 years. Not until the work of Charles Darwin in the nineteenth century and his publication of *The Origin of Species* was an explanation for heredity given other than what Aristotle had posited during the fifth century B.C. The text looks at the nineteenth- and twentieth-century figures who developed the theories behind this science. They include Gregor Mendel and the discovery of dominant and recessive traits, Thomas Hunt Morgan and the chromosome, Oswald Avery and the transforming principle, James Watson and Francis Crick with their work on the double helix of DNA, and Har Gobind Khorana and synthetic genes. Nobel Prize Winners, Glossary, Bibliography, and Index.

2. Aaseng, Nathan. **Paris**. New York: New Discovery, 1992. 96p. $14.95. ISBN 0-02-700010-9. (Cities at War). 6-9

In World War II, German troops entered Paris, France, and occupied the city from 1940 to 1944. Although no fighting occurred in the city, Nazi soldiers abused people, persecuted the city's Jews, and enforced curfews. The French had mixed feelings about their own conduct because of collaboration with the Germans during the war in order to save themselves. Photographs, Notes, Further Reading, and Index.

3. Aaseng, Nathan. **Twentieth-Century Inventors**. New York: Facts on File, 1991. 132p. $17.95. ISBN 0-8160-2485-5. (American Profiles). 8-12

Ten twentieth-century inventors created such things as plastics, airplanes, rockets, lasers, televisions, and pacemakers. Aaseng places the Wright brothers, Robert Goddard, Gordon Gould, Leo Baekeland, Vladimir Zworykin, Ernest Lawrence, Chester Carlson, and William Shockley in the times they worked by showing political, social, and economic influences on their lives. Bibliography and Index.

4. Aaseng, Nathan. **You Are the General**. Minneapolis, MN: Oliver Press, 1994. 160p. $14.95. ISBN 1-881508-11-0. (Great Decisions). 6 up

The text presents the decisions that several twentieth-century generals had to make in the middle of battle. Readers can decide what they would do in the same situation. What they decide will help them understand those who had to make real and life-threatening decisions in the past. Generals include those from the Kaiser's army in August 1914, the German Reich in the summer of 1940, the Imperial Japanese Navy in June 1942, the Allied Forces in June 1944, the United Nations Forces in July 1950, the Vietnamese Communist Forces in July 1967, and the Coalition Forces of Operation Desert Storm in February 1991. Source Notes, Bibliography, and Index.

5. Aaseng, Nathan. **You Are the General II: 1800-1899**. Minneapolis, MN: Oliver Press, 1995. 160p. $14.95. ISBN 1-881508-25-0. (Great Decisions). 6 up

Battles are carefully created patterns of military strategy to gain territory, erode an enemy army's morale, and win a broader war. The text presents eight battles and the generals who fought them. The battles are the British Army at New Orleans in 1815, the Prussian Army at Waterloo in 1815, the U.S. Army in Mexico in August of 1847, the Allied Army in Crimea in September 1854, the Army of Northern Virginia at Chancellorsville in May 1863, the U.S. Army at Little Bighorn in June 1876, and the Boer Army in Natal in December 1899. Source Notes, Bibliography, and Index.

6. Achebe, Chinua. **Things Fall Apart**. 1958. New York: Knopf, 1995. 150p. $15. ISBN 0-679-44623-0. New York: Anchor Books, 1994. 150p. $5.95pa. ISBN 0-385-47454-7pa. YA

When Okonkwo's family starts listening to the Christian missionaries who have come to convert the Ibo tribe of Nigeria in the late nineteenth century, Okonkwo becomes disturbed. When he tries to assert his superiority, the tribe exiles him. While he is gone, the Christians work to ban certain tribal customs and they open schools in which to teach their own beliefs. When Okonkwo returns, he discovers that his own son has turned away from the tribe's traditions.

7. Adams, Steven. **The World of the Impressionists**. 1989. Philadelphia: Courage, 1994. 207p. $17.98. ISBN 1-561-38175-6. YA

Maligned by the traditional art critics and refused places in art exhibits in Paris, the Impressionists, a group of eleven major painters plus others who were born between 1830 and 1841 and who studied in Paris, exhibited their own work for the first time in 1874. The strong, vibrant colors of such men as Monet, Manet, Renoir, Sisley, Seurat, Pissarro, and the American woman Mary Cassatt eventually won a place in the art world. Music, politics, and place influenced them all somewhat, but they stayed with their artistic roots to develop their painting style. Photographs and reproductions decorate the informative text. Index.

8. Adelson, Alan, ed. **The Diary of Dawid Sierakowiak: Five Notebooks from the Lodz Ghetto**. New York: Oxford University Press, 1996. 288p. $27.50. ISBN 0-19-510450-1. YA

Dawid Sierakowiak, an intellectual young man, lived in the slave camp of the Lodz Ghetto and kept diaries about his experiences before his death. Two of the seven diaries were used as fuel in 1945, and the Polish government almost destroyed the remaining five in the 1960s when attempting to eradicate evidence about the ghetto conditions. Dawid at first mocked Hitler, but as food disappeared, he began recording facts, dates, his emotions, the privilege enjoyed by ghetto leaders, and incidents of destruction during his time in the ghetto from 1939 until he was too emaciated to continue after August of 1943. A gentile Polish citizen found the notebooks in the ghetto after the war ended.

9. Adkins, Lesley, and Roy A. Adkins. **Handbook to Life in Ancient Rome**. New York: Facts on File, 1994. 404p. $40. ISBN 0-8160-2755-2. YA

The text covers the 1,200 years of Roman rule, from the eighth century B.C. to the fifth century A.D. It presents information thematically on the Republic and the Empire, military affairs, geography of the Roman world, towns and countryside, travel and trade, literature and the arts, religion, economy and industry, and everyday life. Photographs, line drawings (including floor plans and architectural diagrams), and maps complement the entries. Bibliography and Index.

10. Adler, David A. **Our Golda: The Story of Golda Meir**. Donna Ruff, illustrator. New York: Viking, 1984. 52p. $4.99pa. ISBN 0-14-032104-7pa. 3-7

Golda Meir (1898-1978) lived in Kiev, Russia, outside the Pale of Settlement where only skilled Jews, like her carpenter father, were allowed. At five, Golda had to return to the Pale when her father left for America. In Pinsk, amid the Cossacks and pogroms, they heard talk of a Jewish homeland. Meir's family went to Milwaukee to join her father, and she left for Denver to live with her sister before she and her husband went to Palestine in the 1920s. Meir spoke to crowds about Jewish causes from the time she was 11, and during the rest of her life she led others in the fight for Israel. In 1956, she became the Foreign Minister, and then Prime Minister in 1969. Before her death in 1978, she met with Anwar Sadat in one of many attempts to find peace between the Arabs and the Jews.

11. Adler, David A. **We Remember the Holocaust**. New York: Henry Holt, 1989. 144p. $18.95; $9.95pa. ISBN 0-8050-0434-3; 0-8050-3715-2pa. 6 up

Interviews with Holocaust survivors recount the horrors of Hitler from the time he came to power, through *Kristallnacht* on November 9, 1938, to the Polish killing of Jews in 1947, after the war ended. Millions of people were exterminated for no reason except that they had Jewish blood. The guilt of those who survived, as well as their need to keep the traditions of their forebears alive, permeate this book. Photographs of people and places enhance the impact of these accounts of heinous crimes. Bibliography, Chronology, Glossary, Index, and Suggested Reading.

12. **Africa and the Origin of Humans**. Francis Balistreri, illustrator. Austin, TX: Raintree/Steck-Vaughn, 1992. 80p. $17.97. ISBN 0-8172-3301-6. (History of the World). 7 up

This overview uses informative illustrations and clear maps to complement the text. Each topic, starting with the earliest information known about humans, covers a two-page spread; the book's time span ends around A.D. 300. Topics include the search for human origins, southern African expansion, tribes of the north, Egypt and the birth of its society through the Middle and New Kingdoms, Carthage, the Kingdom of Kush and its capital Meroe, the Kingdom of Aksum, Greeks in Libya and Egypt, Roman control, and Christianity. Glossary and Index.

13. Aiken, Joan. **Bridle the Wind**. New York: Delacorte, 1983. 242p. $14.95. ISBN 0-385-29301-1. 7 up

In the early 1800s, Felix, age thirteen, wakes up in a monastery on the border of France and Spain near the coast; he has been ill for three months following a shipwreck. He has to escape into Spain when he realizes that the monastery's abbot is trying to detain him. Various persons pursue him at the behest of the abbot, and he barely escapes. Felix is especially surprised to discover that the boy with whom he escaped is actually a girl.

14.   Aiken, Joan. **Eliza's Daughter**. New York: St. Martin's Press, 1994. 316p. $20.95. ISBN 0-312-10972-5. YA

In Jane Austen's *Sense and Sensibility,* Colonel Brandon's sister has an illegitimate daughter. The daughter has no social bounds, and after being maltreated in a foster home, she finds refuge with Elinor and Edward Ferrar. They send her to school in Bath, and then she goes to search for her parents in Portugal.

15.   Aiken, Joan. **The Teeth of the Gale**. New York: HarperCollins, 1988. 307p. $14.95. ISBN 0-06-020045-6. 7-10

In the 1820s, Felix, a college student in Salamanca, Spain, gets a letter from his grandfather requesting that he return home to help Dona Conchita find her three children, kidnapped by her felon husband. He rushes home so that he will also have a chance to see his friend Juana, whom he met in *Bridle the Wind*, who is preparing to take her religious vows. During his search for the children, villains pursue Felix for the money they think he has hidden but realize that he is honest in his denials. He succeeds in his quest.

16.   **Alchemy: The Art of Knowing**. San Francisco: Chronicle, 1994. 62p. $9.95. ISBN 0-8118-0473-9. (Little Wisdom Library-Medieval Wisdom). YA

Alchemists were concerned with turning base metals into gold. Not until the eighteenth century, when the Greek classification of the elements was discredited, did alchemy lose its believability. Illustrated with copies of illuminated manuscripts, the text gives a history of alchemy's proponents. It probably began in Egypt around 2500 B.C. with Hermes Trismegistus, when Egypt's name was "Khem" for its black soil (thus al-chem-y). Alchemy was most likely the first experimental science, leading from Roger Bacon's creation of gunpowder in Europe, in 1292, to the mathematical physics of Galileo and Newton. Other contemporaries of Bacon were Albertus Magnus (1193-1280) and two of his students, Thomas Aquinas and Arnald de Villanova in Spain, who found a method to counteract poisons. Other important names are Bernard of Treves and Nicholas Flamel (fourteenth century), George Ripley (fifteenth century), and Nostradamus (c. 1642). Alchemy was based on philosophical and spiritual concepts predating Christianity; its main ingredients were mercury, sulphur, salt, and the mysterious "life principle" that the alchemist had to contribute. Bibliography and Further Reading.

17.   Alder, Elizabeth. **The King's Shadow**. New York: Farrar, Straus & Giroux, 1995. 257p. $17. ISBN 0-374-34182-6. 6-9

Evyn, a young Welsh serf, wants to be a traveling storyteller. But ruffians destroy his dream by killing his parents and cutting out his tongue before his uncle sells him into slavery. Although he cannot speak to the people with whom he works, he learns to read and write, and eventually he begins to serve Harold Godwinson, the charismatic man who becomes the King of England. Evyn loves Harold like his own father, and he stays by Harold until his death at the Battle of Hastings in 1066, where William defeats Harold and becomes king. Harold's widow takes Evyn home and nurses him back to health so that Evyn can write about his master, the king whose shadow he had been. *American Library Association Best Books for Young Adults.*

18.   Alexander, Bruce. **Blind Justice**. New York: Putnam, 1994. 254p. $19.95. ISBN 0-399-13978-8. YA

Sir John Fielding helps to create London's first police force even though he is blind. This mystery involves Fielding's investigation of a murder in eighteenth-century London with the help of Jeremy Proctor.

19.   Alexander, Bruce. **Murder in Grub Street**. New York: Putnam, 1995. 288p. $21.95. ISBN 0-399-14085-9. YA

Jeremy Proctor, age thirteen, teams up with Sir John Fielding, the blind magistrate and creator of London's first police force. They investigate the murder of the printer Ezekiel Grabb, his family, and two employees on the day before Jeremy was to become apprenticed to him. As Sir John's eyes, Jeremy eventually earns a place in the household. In the course of their investigations, the pair go throughout eighteenth-century London, from Covent Garden to the Bedlam madhouse, as they search for answers.

20.   Alexander, Bruce. **Person or Persons Unknown**. New York: Putnam, 1997. 288p. $22.95. ISBN 0-399-14309-2. YA

In 1770, prostitutes are dying in Covent Garden. Sir John Fielding of Bow Street and Jeremy Proctor, the boy who "sees" for the blind judge, search for the killer. Since the first two murders are different from the others, they worry about two killers instead of one. Among the intrigues of London are anti-Semites and class differences.

21.   Alexander, Bruce. **Watery Grave**. New York: Putnam, 1996. 265p. $22.95. ISBN 0-399-14155-3. YA

The blind magistrate Sir John Fielding wants to find out who murdered Captain Josiah Markham at sea. He uses his "eyes," his fourteen-year-old apprentice Jeremy Proctor, to help him find the evidence that will convict the real killer.

22. Alexander, Bryan, and Cherry Alexander. **Inuit**. Austin, TX: Raintree/Steck-Vaughn, 1993. 48p. $15.96. ISBN 0-8114-2301-8. (Threatened Cultures). 4-9

The Inuit (Eskimos) from Arctic Canada and Greenland have many traditions, but they must strive to preserve their way of life and maintain their cultural identity in the modern world. Bibliography and Index.

23. Aline, Countess of Romanones. **The Spy Went Dancing: My Further Adventures as an Undercover Agent**. New York: Putnam, 1990. 319p. $19.95. ISBN 0-399-13509-X. New York: Jove, 1991. 319p. $5.95pa. ISBN 0-515-10507-4pa. YA

In this sequel to *The Spy Wore Red* (1987), the Countess tells about being recruited and trained by the Office of Strategic Services during World War II. She went to spy in Spain under the code name of "Tiger." At the end of the war, she helped to uncover assets taken by the Third Reich. The story, supposedly true, includes anecdotes of people of renown who lived or socialized on large estates that the Countess visited. Her career ended in 1947 when she married into one of Spain's oldest families.

24. Allen, Peter. **The Windsor Secret: New Revelations of the Nazi Connection**. New York: Stein and Day, 1984. 304p. $17.95. ISBN 0-8128-2975-1. YA

Allen posits that in 1940, the Duke of Windsor had secret communications with Hitler, through Adolph Hess, and that after the war ended, British intelligence officers went into Germany to find and destroy any documents that might refer to those meetings. Allen discovered this information when researching documents for another book. In a report by someone named Schellenberg, Allen thinks he has found a reference to an attempted kidnap of the Duke in Portugal, which might have been a cover for other activities in which the Duke was engaged. Allen gives the background of the Duke's abdication and situations leading to this conclusion. Bibliography and Index.

25. Aller, Susan Bivin. **J.M. Barrie: The Magic Behind Peter Pan**. Minneapolis, MN: Lerner, 1994. 128p. $22.95. ISBN 0-8225-4918-2. (Lerner Biographies). 5 up

The author of *Peter Pan*, James Matthew Barrie (1860-1937), was a journalist before his story about a boy who refused to grow up made him famous. Bibliography and Index.

26. Allman, Barbara. **Her Piano Sang: A Story About Clara Schumann**. Shelly O. Haas, illustrator. Minneapolis, MN: Carolrhoda, 1996. 64p. $18.95. ISBN 1-57505-012-9. (Creative Minds). 3-7

Clara Schumann (1819-1896) made her professional debut as a pianist when she was only nine years old. Her father demanded much of her, and when she married Robert Schumann against her father's wishes and after a long courtship, she had to raise the family as he developed mental illness. She continued to compose and perform. The story presents a woman who pursued a formerly masculine career and succeeded. Illustrations highlight the text. Index.

27. Almagor, Gila. **Under the Domim Tree**. Hillel Schenker, translator. New York: Simon & Schuster, 1995. 164p. $15. ISBN 0-671-89020-4. 6-10

After World War II, in 1953, Aviya, Yola, and Mira live at Udim, a youth village on Israel's coast. They all have survived the Holocaust. Each eventually tells of personal tragedy, while they all hope that a family member will someday appear. Mira cannot remember her family, and when two people take her to court because they say she is their child, the others realize that adults may take advantage of all of them. Not until the trial in the courtroom can Mira remember her repressed past in Poland and her name. She escapes the clutches of the two impostors who want her reparation money.

28. Almedingen, E. M. **The Crimson Oak**. New York: Putnam, 1983. 112p. $9.95. ISBN 0-698-20569-3. 7 up

Around 1739, the peasant Peter rescues a woman from a bear. She gives him an oak twig, says that she will help him one day, and identifies herself as the exiled Russian Princess Elizabeth. Peter then petitions the Empress Anna to allow him to learn to write, but authorities arrest and imprison him because laws forbid peasants to get an education. However, a man Peter meets while in prison teaches him. When he is freed, a friend writes to Elizabeth, recently restored to her throne as czarina, telling her about Peter's ability to write. She gives him work and gifts for his destitute village.

29. Almedingen, E. M. **Katia**. Victor Ambrus, illustrator. New York: Farrar, Straus & Giroux, 1967. 207p. $3.95. ISBN 9-99750-148-9. 6-9

As a girl of five, Katia goes to live with her cousin after her mother's death. During the six years she lives with her cousin (1836-1842), she learns to speak French, German, and English along with her Russian while she studies many other subjects. Her most important lesson is learning that she must respect other humans, regardless of class. When Katia returns to her father's house, finding that her stepmother accepts and likes her is a surprise.

30. Almedingen, E. M. **Young Mark: The Story of a Venture**. New York: Farrar, Straus & Giroux, 1968. 146p. $3.75. ISBN 0-374-38745-1. 7-10

The author's great-great-grandfather, Mark Poltoratzky, left the Ukraine in 1742 to sing for the Hetman, Tsarina Elizabeth's intended husband, in St. Petersburg. He has several adventures on his journey—some rather frightening—but he eventually arrives. Mark hears tales of the Hetman's horrible actions, but then meets him unexpectedly after someone steals the Hetman's breakfast in the Tsarina Meadow. After the Hetman hears Mark sing, he introduces Mark to Elizabeth. She retains his service throughout his life, giving him material rewards for his efforts to use God's gift of music for service to others.

31. Alper, Ann Fitzpatrick. **Forgotten Voyager: The Story of Amerigo Vespucci**. Minneapolis, MN: Carolrhoda, 1991. 80p. $11.95. ISBN 0-87614-442-3. 4-8

This biography of Amerigo Vespucci (1451-1512) discusses his discoveries and explorations for Spain. In 1499, he sailed to the West Indies and discovered the mouth of the Amazon. Later (1501) he sailed along the northern coast of South America and proved that the land was one continent. Bibliography and Index.

32. Altman, Linda Jacobs. **Mr. Darwin's Voyage**. New York: Dillon Press, 1995. 160p. $13.95; $7.95pa. ISBN 0-87518-609-2; 0-382-24962-3pa. (People in Focus). 6-9

Charles Darwin (1809-1882) expected to become a country parson, but on his way to divinity school, Captain Robert FitzRoy of the survey ship, HMS *Beagle,* offered to take him on a voyage around the globe as its resident naturalist. He went through the rain forests of Brazil, the waste of Tierra del Fuego, and the Galapagos Islands. His research showed that slow change over time had formed the earth and the species on it, including humans. As a scientist, he thought the theory was good, but his own humanity inherently rejected it. Photographs and reproductions enhance the text. Selected Bibliography, Notes, and Index.

33. Alvarez, Julia. **In the Time of the Butterflies**. Chapel Hill, NC: Algonquin, 1994. 344p. $21.95. ISBN 1-56512-038-8. YA

The three Mirabel sisters—Minerva, Patria, and Maria Teresa—become martyrs of the movement during the liberation of the Dominican Republic from Trujillo in 1960 when they are murdered while returning from visiting their husbands in prison. Their sister Dede remembers their unique attributes as young girls.

34. Amdur, Richard. **Anne Frank**. New York: Chelsea House, 1993. 111p. $18.95; $7.95pa. ISBN 0-7910-1641-2; 0-7910-1645-5pa. (Library of Biography). 5 up

This story traces the life of the young Jewish girl, Anne Frank (1929-1945), whose diary tells of the years during which she and her family hid from the Nazis in an Amsterdam attic. Bibliography and Index.

35. Amdur, Richard. **Chaim Weizmann**. New York: Chelsea House, 1988. 112p. $18.95. ISBN 0-87754-446-8. (World Leaders Past and Present). 5 up

Chaim Weizmann (1874-1952), born in czarist Russia, grew up to become the president of Israel. As a student he became interested in Zionism and the movement for the Jews to establish their own country in Palestine. Weizmann, a scientist by profession, helped England in World War I and convinced Britain to support the idea of a new Jewish nation. For twenty years, he served as president of the World Zionist Organization and raised funds for this endeavor. He tried to found a country peacefully but was unable to resolve conflicts between militant Zionists and Palestinian Arabs. When Israel became a reality after World War II, Weizmann served as its first president. Photographs enhance the text. Chronology, Further Reading, and Index.

36. **The Americas in the Colonial Era**. Remo Berselli, illustrator. Austin, TX: Raintree/Steck-Vaughn, 1993. 82p. $17.97. ISBN 0-8114-3326-9. (History of the World). 7 up

This overview uses informative illustrations and clear maps to complement the text. The two-page spreads begin with the pre-Columbian civilizations' encounters with European explorers and continues through the American Revolution. Topics refer to the discovery of America; the explorers who came afterward; Native Americans; Spanish colonization; the Portuguese, French, and Dutch in America; Creoles; and other aspects of the civilizations. Glossary and Index.

37. Anand, Valerie. **The Cherished Wives**. New York: St. Martin's Press, 1996. 341p. $23.95. ISBN 0-312-13943-8. (Bridges over Time 5). YA

Lucy-Anne Brown marries into the Whitmead family in 1742. Her husband, George Whitmead, is a merchant in the East India Company, and although he is a distant cousin, she barely knows him. Lucy-Anne's great-aunt wishes for her to have power and freedom in her marriage, two unusual and uncommon states of marriage in that time. Her great-aunt's wish helps Lucy-Anne as she becomes a mother and a grandmother in the latter half of the eighteenth century.

38. Anand, Valerie. **Crown of Roses**. New York: St. Martin's Press, 1989. 404p. $19.95. ISBN 0-312-03315-X. YA

King Edward IV marries Bess Woodville, beautiful but below his station, and thus loses the support of many of his followers. Among those he can trust are his brother Richard of Gloucester and Petronel Faldene, married at the age of fourteen in 1466 to a wealthy man, Lionel Eynesby. Edward sends Petronel and her husband on an undercover mission in France. Petronel's husband mistreats her and wants a son and heir, blaming her for his lack. She has a child by Lionel's nephew Geoffrey, and Lionel thinks the child is his. Other events bring Richard of Gloucester to the throne, and Petronel and her son become part of the turbulence in the court leading to the battle of Bosworth Field in August 1485 when Henry defeats Richard III.

39. Anand, Valerie. **The Disputed Crown**. New York: Scribners, 1982. 297p. $10. ISBN 0-684-17629-7. YA

William attempts to unite the Normans with the English after he wins the British crown in 1066. His wife, Mathilde, spends her time raising their children and becoming involved in her own intrigues. His enemies continue their attempts to assassinate him while he encourages Normans to intermarry with the English to avoid further wars.

40. Anand, Valerie. **The Faithful Lovers**. New York: St. Martin's Press, 1994. 373p. $22.95. ISBN 0-312-10979-2. (Bridges over Time 4). YA

In his seaside Cornish estate, Ninian Whitmead lives alone. The wreck of a pirate ship off the coast leaves the Indian girl Parvati stranded as its only survivor. Whitmead takes her to his home, falls in love with her, marries her, and has a son with her. Parvati adopts a Christian name and is baptized, but the Puritan community will not accept her. The English Civil War, the Glorious Revolution, the plague, and the Great Fire of London in 1666 come into their lives and those of their descendants.

41. Anand, Valerie. **Gildenford**. New York: Scribners, 1977. 392p. $10. ISBN 0-684-14896-X. YA

Cnut, the Viking king in England, has a son by Emma in 1018; he declares this boy his heir even though he has an older son and Emma has two other sons. Eighteen years later, Cnut's older son decides to claim the throne, and the massacre at Gildenford occurs. Edward, one of Emma's other sons, becomes the king. Because Edward has no heir, he chooses William of Normandy as his successor rather than Harold Godwin, because Harold has falsely accused Emma of misdeeds. The loyal servant Brand helps guard Godwin's sons and protect the kingship.

42. Anand, Valerie. **King of the Wood**. New York: St. Martin's Press, 1989. 468p. $18.95. ISBN 0-312-02939-X. YA

Born in Normandy as the son of an English father and a Norman mother in 1068, Ralph des Aix becomes part of William Rufus's court. William, known as the Conqueror, adopts Ralph and designates him heir, because Ralph's mother died at his birth. Rufus gives Ralph land as promised, and although it is not the land Ralph wanted, Ralph works to show that he is worthy. When Rufus dies an untimely death while hunting, Henry, the third son, grabs a chance to succeed and usurps Ralph's position.

43. Anand, Valerie. **The Norman Pretender**. New York: Scribners, 1979. 410p. $12.50. ISBN 0-684-16099-4. YA

After Harold Hardraada tries to take control of England, William sails from Normandy. The two meet at the Battle of Hastings in 1066. At Harold's death, William claims the throne. The people under the new rule worry about its effect on their lives in this view of England in the eleventh century. Some worry about supporting William because they think that Harold's forces will retake the throne. Others vow to support William in any circumstances.

44. Anand, Valerie. **The Proud Villeins**. New York: St. Martin's Press, 1992. 310p. $19.95. ISBN 0-312-08282-7. (Bridges over Time 1). YA

Those who massacred citizens at Gildenford in 1036 spared the life of the Norman Ivon, but Ivon has had to spend his life as a thrall to the British lords. His grandson refuses to acknowledge his Norman blood and loses his rights, as well as those of his children, as a freeman after the Normans return to power. Though Ivon's line continues in thrall up to 1215, they still retain their heritage.

45. Anand, Valerie. **The Ruthless Yeomen**. New York: St. Martin's Press, 1993. 342p. $19.95. ISBN 0-312-08884-1. (Bridges over Time 2). YA

Among the historical events that serve as a background for this story are the battle at Crécy in 1346, during which the English fight the French and the Black Death. Richard II's poll taxes cause ruin and lead Wat Tyler to instigate the Peasants' Revolt against Richard in 1381.

46. Anand, Valerie. **Women of Ashdon**. New York: St. Martin's Press, 1993. 373p. $21.95. ISBN 0-312-09417-5. (Bridges over Time 3). YA

This story about England in the late fourteenth and early fifteenth centuries presents the women of the Whitmead family, who have kept together in Ashdon. It gives a strong sense of time and place.

47.   **Anatolia: Cauldron of Cultures**. Alexandria, VA: Time-Life, 1995. 168p. $18.95. ISBN 0-8094-9108-7. (Lost Civilizations). YA

As one of the most ancient homes of humanity, Turkey has a varied history and culture. Chatal Hoyuk in south central Turkey, excavated in the 1960s, is one of the first known cities with agriculture, trade, and religion, dating back to the Stone Age. Another important group rediscovered is the Hittites, who lived from 2000 to 1200 B.C. The text also covers other aspects of this country's civilization. Bibliography, Chronology, and Index.

48.   Anda, Michael O. **Yoruba**. New York: Rosen, 1995. 64p. $15.95. ISBN 0-8239-1988-9. (Heritage Library of African Peoples, West Africa). 7-10

The text focuses on the Yoruba, one of the largest ethnic groups in sub-Saharan Africa. The slave trade dramatically affected their numbers and spread their culture to the New World, especially Brazil. Their current problems, including those of Yorubans in Nigeria, also appear in the text. Further Reading, Glossary, and Index.

49.   Anderson, Dale. **Battles That Changed the Modern World**. Austin, TX: Raintree/Steck-Vaughn, 1994. 48p. $15.96. ISBN 0-8114-4928-9. (20 Events Series). 6 up

Since the beginning of the nineteenth century, twenty battles have had a great impact on the world. In two-page spreads, Anderson presents the important aspects of these battles. They are Waterloo (1812), Antietam (1862), Gettysburg (1863), Sedan (1870), Little Bighorn (1875), Tsushima Strait (1905), the Marne (1914), Guernica (1937), Nanking (1937), Britain (1940), El Alamein (1942), Midway (1942), Stalingrad (1941-1943), Normandy (1944), the Chinese Civil War (1947-1949), Inchon (1950), Dien Bien Phu (1954), the Six-Day War (1967), the Tet Offensive (1968), and Desert Storm (1991). Glossary, Suggested Readings, and Index.

50.   Anderson, Dale. **Explorers Who Found New Worlds**. Austin, TX: Raintree/Steck-Vaughn, 1994. 48p. $15.96. ISBN 0-8114-4931-9. (20 Events Series). 6 up

In two-page spreads, Anderson presents profiles of twenty explorers who found places that changed the lives of people throughout the world. The explorers discussed here start with Marco Polo (Venice) in the thirteenth century. In the fifteenth century, Christopher Columbus (Portugal) and Vasco da Gama (Portugal) set forth. Their work continued in the sixteenth century with Vasco Nuñez de Balboa (Spain), Ferdinand Magellan (Portugal), Francisco Vasquez de Coronado (Spain), and Jacques Cartier (France). In the seventeenth century, Henry Hudson (England), Louis Joliet and Jacques Marquette (France), and René-Robert Cavelier, Sieur de La Salle (France) explored North America. The eighteenth-century explorers covered are Vitus Bering (Denmark), James Cook (England), and Alexander Mackenzie (Scotland). Nineteenth-century adventurers profiled are Americans Meriwether Lewis and William Clark, David Livingstone (Scotland), Richard Francis Burton and John Hanning Speke (England), John McDouall Stuart (Scotland and Australia), Sven Hedin (Sweden), and Robert Peary (America). The twentieth century boasts Roald Amundsen (Norway). Glossary, Suggested Readings, and Index.

51.   Anderson, Joan. **Pioneer Settlers in New France**. George Ancona, photographs. New York: Lodestar, Dutton, 1990. 60p. $15.95. ISBN 0-525-67291-5. 4-7

Jean François lives with his aunt and uncle in Louisbourg, Nova Scotia, in 1763. An orphaned French noble, he prefers sailing to working in his uncle's store. One day he slips away with a peasant fisherman's son to enjoy an afternoon on the sea. But the French and the British have recently declared war, and he jeopardizes his freedom by being in unsafe waters.

52.   Anderson, Margaret. **Carl Linnaeus: Father of Classification**. Springfield, NJ: Enslow, 1997. 128p. $18.95. ISBN 0-89490-786-7. (Great Minds of Science). 4-8

Carl von Linne (1707-1778), a Swedish botanist, invented the binomial nomenclature for classifying plants and animals. Photographs of places where he lived and worked illustrate the text, which includes much about him and his scientific expeditions. Chronology, Further Reading, Glossary, and Index.

53.   Anderson, Margaret. **Charles Darwin: Naturalist**. Springfield, NJ: Enslow, 1994. 128p. $17.95. ISBN 0-89490-476-0. (Great Minds of Science). 4-7

Charles Darwin (1809-1882) shared his birth date with Abraham Lincoln, but rather than trying to stop a civil war, he almost caused one when he published *On the Origin of Species* in 1859. His book claimed that, over time, small differences among similar plants and animals can cause new species to evolve. He did much of his research on a five-year trip around the world on the HMS *Beagle*. His three main ideas were that plants and animals have more offspring than needed; that, overall, numbers of each kind of plant and animal remain stable; and that all offspring are not alike. The offspring survive based on natural selection. People who believed that all species had been created and "fixed" by God were horrified by this theory. Notes, Chronology, Glossary, Further Reading, and Index.

54. Anderson, Margaret. **The Druid's Gift**. New York: Knopf, 1989. 211p. $12.95. ISBN 0-394-91936-X. 6-9

Three historical periods—the Vikings, the eighteenth century, and the twentieth century—fuse in this historical fantasy set on Hirta, an island off the coast of Scotland. Caitlin, also called Cathan, Catie, and Catriona, uses her ability to see into the future as a basis for urging the druids to forgo their Samhain human sacrifices and form a truce with the villagers who need their blessings. She finds that changing centuries of ritual needs a supernatural force.

55. Anderson, Margaret. **Isaac Newton: The Greatest Scientist of All Time**. Springfield, NJ: Enslow, 1996. 128p. $18.95. ISBN 0-89490-681-X. (Great Minds of Science). 5-8

Isaac Newton (1642-1727) made enormous scientific advances, but they did not keep him from skipping meals or holding grudges against his colleagues. The text places Newton within the context of his time and shows the relationship of his life to his work. Photographs, Reproductions, Further Reading, Glossary, Notes, and Index.

56. Anderson, Margaret. **The Journey of the Shadow Bairns**. Patricia H. Lincoln, illustrator. New York: Knopf, 1980. 177p. $8.99. ISBN 0-394-94511-5. 7 up

After Elspeth's parents save money to immigrate to Canada from Glasgow, Scotland, in 1902, they both die. Elspeth, age thirteen, and her brother leave anyway, fearful that authorities will send them to different homes. When they arrive, they cannot find their relatives, and they become separated. After Elspeth works at a hotel for a difficult employer, they reunite with people they met on board the ship, who help them create a surrogate family.

57. Anderson, Margaret. **Searching for Shona**. New York: Knopf, 1979. 159p. $6.95; $3.95pa. ISBN 0-394-93724-4; 0-394-82587-Xpa. 5-8

Marjorie's wealthy uncle leaves her at the Edinburgh, Scotland, train station in 1939, on the first leg in her journey to Canada as a war evacuee. She meets a girl whom she had known at the orphanage. The two girls decide to trade places, so Shona goes to Marjorie's relatives in Canada and Marjorie takes Shona's place. After the war, when Shona returns to Edinburgh and her parents appear, she does not want to return to her real identity. Marjorie continues living happily as Shona with Shona's family.

58. Anderson, Rachel. **Black Water**. New York: Henry Holt, 1995. 168p. $14.95. ISBN 0-8050-3847-7. New York: Paper Star, 1996. 168p. $4.95pa. ISBN 0-698-11421-3pa. 6-10

People think that Albert is freaky or mad because of his lapses of consciousness. His mother searches frantically for a cure, but when she fails, Albert has to rely on his own resources as he copes with his epilepsy in Victorian England. On a train he meets Edward Lear, also a victim of epilepsy, and Lear gives Albert a curious recipe for the malady after Albert has a seizure. The objectivity and humor of this book make an intriguing story.

59. Anderson, Rachel. **Paper Faces**. New York: Henry Holt, 1993. 150p. $14.95. ISBN 0-8050-2527-8. 6-8

World War II in London is difficult for Dot and her mother, but the end of the war and the changes it brings, especially the anticipated arrival of a father she has never known, are almost overwhelming.

60. Anderson-Dargatz, Gail. **The Cure for Death by Lightning**. Boston: Houghton Mifflin, 1996. 297p. $21.95. ISBN 0-395-77184-6. YA

In 1941, Beth Weeks, fifteen, lives on a Canadian farm where she and her family struggle with the shortages of World War II. She tries to escape the advances and beatings of her abusive father, mentally deranged from World War I, but she cannot. She visits a Native American friend on a nearby reservation, and the sense that a coyote's evil spirit permeates the area stays with them even though she finds respite away from the farm.

61. Anthony, Suzanne. **West Indies**. New York: Chelsea House, 1989. 127p. $15.95. ISBN 1-55546-793-8. 5 up

This general overview of the West Indies introduces the Greater and Lesser Antilles. The Great Antilles islands include Cuba, Jamaica, the Dominican Republic, Haiti, and Puerto Rico; the Lesser Antilles contains the rest of the islands loosely associated with Columbus's arrival. These islands are also famous for such figures as Henry Morgan, a buccaneer made governor of Port Royal, Jamaica, around 1675; Toussaint Louverture, who led the slave revolt on Haiti in 1804; and Joséphine de Beauharnais, wife of Napoléon Bonaparte. Clearly, tourism helps these islands to overcome poverty and the legacies of some of their former rulers—England, Spain, France, and the Netherlands—although they are basically united in a common Creole bond. Facts at a Glance, History at a Glance, Glossary, Index, and Map.

62. Appel, Todd M. **José Martí**. New York: Chelsea House, 1992. 110p. $18.95. ISBN 0-7910-1246-8. (Hispanics of Achievement). 5 up

In Cuba, José Martí (1853-1895) is one of the most revered figures. He was a communicator, an organizer, a political theorist, and a guerrilla fighter. When he was sixteen, the Spanish imprisoned him for organizing against them and exiled him to Spain, where he studied at Madrid's Central University. He returned to Cuba and led an insurrection in 1878. Again he was exiled, this time to the United States, where he spent fifteen years working for Cuban independence. In 1892, he founded the Cuban Revolutionary Party and went to Cuba to fight the Second War of Independence. He died before his party won. Photographs enhance the text. Chronology, Further Reading, and Index.

63. Ardley, Neil. **Music: An Illustrated Encyclopedia**. New York: Facts on File, 1986. 192p. $18.95. ISBN 0-8160-1542-0. YA

In this comprehensive overview, a reader can find an answer to almost any general, and some detailed, questions about music. A collection of articles presents all types of instruments, kinds of music, performers, and specific works. A brief look at music in Japan, Indonesia, Australia, Africa, Europe, and North, South, and Central America helps the reader see the cultural differences in music. A history of music presents Egypt, Greece, Rome, and Asia. Additionally, material covers how artists and technicians make various types of recordings. Annotated Bibliography of "Music Makers" and Index.

64. **Armenia**. Minneapolis, MN: Lerner, 1993. 56p. $19.95. ISBN 0-8225-2806-1. (Then and Now). 5-9

Timur and the Mongolian hordes came into Armenia in the late 1300s and massacred much of the population. Other countries have done the same throughout the centuries. This text discusses these massacres and other problems the country faces as it tries to succeed since becoming independent in 1991. Photographs and maps enhance additional information about economics, geography, politics, and ethnography. Glossary and Index.

65. Arnold, Sandra Martín. **Alicia Alonso: First Lady of the Ballet**. New York: Walker, 1993. 100p. $14.95. ISBN 0-8027-8242-6. 4 up

Alicia Alonso (b. 1917), although plagued by serious eyesight problems, was, from 1941 to 1960, one of the principal stars of the American Ballet Theatre. She was particularly famous in the role of Giselle. In 1948, she formed the Ballet Alicia Alonso (renamed Ballet de Cuba in 1955 and the Ballet Nacional de Cuba in 1959). Her school has been admired for the quality of its training. Bibliography and Index.

66. Ash, Maureen. **Alexander the Great: Ancient Empire Builder**. Chicago: Childrens Press, 1991. 128p. $28.20. ISBN 0-516-03063-9. (The World's Great Explorers). 3 up

Photographs, reproductions, maps, and text tell the story of Alexander the Great (356-323 B.C.), the general who directed the Macedonian expansion. The chapters look at his background, his father, Philip of Macedonia, his subjugation of the Grecian states, and the invasion of Persia. They also discuss Darius, Issus, the siege of Tyre, and conquests on Alexander's way to Egypt and India. Appendices, Timeline, Glossary, and Bibliography.

67. Ash, Maureen. **Vasco Núñez de Balboa**. Chicago: Childrens Press, 1990. 126p. $28.20. ISBN 0-516-03057-4. (The World's Great Explorers). 3 up

Beautiful color photographs and reproductions illustrate this introduction to Balboa (1475-1519), the Spaniard who discovered the Pacific Ocean. Balboa had trained to be a soldier, but the advent of peace led him to search for other ways to gain fame. He became an explorer and left for the New World when he was twenty-six. The text looks at his conflicts with other leaders at Dárien and how he tried to defend his purpose before they executed him. Timeline, Glossary, Bibliography, and Index.

68. Ashabranner, Brent. **Land of Yesterday, Land of Tomorrow: Discovering Chinese Central Asia**. Paul, David, and Peter Conklin, photographs. New York: Cobblehill/Dutton, 1992. 84p. $16. ISBN 0-525-65086-5. 4-7

Although Ashabranner is the author, the text concerns a trip that the photographers took into China's Xinjiang Province, which was open to foreigners between 1984 and 1990. The main city of Kashgar lies on the trade route of the ancient Silk Road, where Marco Polo visited in the thirteenth century. The basically non-Chinese population of this area continues to live as it has for many years. Especially interesting are photographs of *buz kashi*, a polo match, and the bazaars. Bibliography and Index.

69. Ashton, S. R. **The Cold War**. London: Batsford, 1990. 64p. $19.95. ISBN 0-7134-5817-8. (Living Through History). 9 up

The Cold War had real personalities behind it who made the decisions for the countries involved. The people discussed here make this book as much a collective biography as a history of the time period. Those who were influential at the beginning of the Cold War are the American George Frost Kennan (b. 1904) and the Russian Andrei Zhdanov (1896-1948) for Stalin. In Eastern Europe, Stanislaw Mikolajczyk (1901-1966) fled Poland in 1947. Two significant Czechoslovakians were Eduard Bene (1884-1948) and Jan Masaryk (1886-1948). The Yugoslavian Milovan Djilas (b. 1911) also participated. In Germany, Lucius D. Clay (1897-1978) was the American general in Berlin who dealt with Konrad Adenauer (1876-1967) and Walter Ulbricht (1893-1973). The American Robert Julius Oppenheimer (1904-1967) and Klaus Fuchs (1911-1988), who left Germany for England, worked on the atomic bomb. During the Cuban crisis, Russian Nikita Sergeyevich Khrushchev (1894-1971), Cuban Fidel Castro (b. 1927), and American John Fitzgerald Kennedy (1917-1963) were the important figures. Photographs enhance the text. Date List, Books for Further Reading, and Index.

70. Astor, Gerald. **Operation Iceberg: The Invasion and Conquest of Okinawa in World War II**. New York: Donald I. Fine, 1995. 480p. $24.95. ISBN 1-55611-425-7. New York: Dell, 1996. 480p. $5.99pa. ISBN 0-440-22178-1pa. YA

This account of Okinawa is an oral history. After presenting the background of the battle, Astor reports the responses of witnesses on opposing sides to give a balanced view. Okinawa was an especially complex fight, with an invasion, a land battle, an air battle, and a sea battle. Photographs complement the text. Index.

71. Atkinson, Linda. **In Kindling Flame: The Story of Hannah Senesh (1921-1944)**. New York: Lothrop, Lee & Shepard, 1985. 214p. $14.95. ISBN 0-688-02714-8. 9 up

Hannah Senesh grew up in Hungary prior to World War II. Because she was Jewish, she suffered under a 1938 Hungarian law that limited Jews in the professions they could practice and banished them from public life. She decided to defend herself, her family, and her people against this unspeakable prejudice. She went to Palestine in 1939, and then she began to try to rescue Jews by parachuting behind the lines. She was caught, imprisoned, and then executed in a Hungarian prison in 1944. Suggestions for Further Reading and Index.

72. Atlan, Liliane. **The Passersby**. Rochelle Owens, translator; Lisa Desimini, illustrator. New York: Henry Holt, 1993. 80p. $13.95. ISBN 0-8050-3054-9. 6-8

No, anorectic after World War II, has to learn to understand why a human should want to live. She interacts with members of her family, but her adopted brother, an Auschwitz survivor, finally helps her realize that she has qualities to help others.

73. Attanasio, A. A. **Kingdom of the Grail**. New York: HarperCollins, 1992. 500p. $23. ISBN 0-06-017965-1. YA

Around 1140, Ailena Valaise's son banishes her from the Welsh family home. Ten years later, she returns, attributing her youthfulness to a drink from the Holy Grail. Because she can recognize and converse with everyone, they begin to believe that she is actually Ailena. When she has become secure in her disguise, she admits that she is a Jewess impostor who has come to defeat Ailena's evil son.

74. Attanasio, A. A. **Wyvern**. New York: Ticknor & Fields, 1988. 422p. $19.95. ISBN 0-89919-409-5. YA

Because he has fair skin and blond hair, Jaki is an outcast in his Borneo tribe. Only one person will associate with him, the tribal seer. When pirates kidnap Jaki from the island, they carry him with them around the world. Not until he reaches the shores of North America does he find a home where he feels that he can be a part of the community.

75. Atwood, Margaret. **Alias Grace**. New York: Doubleday, 1996. 464p. $24.95. ISBN 0-385-47571-3. YA

Grace Marks, sixteen, was accused of the murders of her employer and his pregnant mistress and housekeeper in Canada in the 1840s. Her partner was hanged, and she received a life imprisonment sentence after relating three different versions of the murder. In Atwood's novel, Grace endures the verbal probing of a doctor who tries to determine if she is guilty or innocent after sixteen years in prison. His questions and her answers as he tries to hypnotize her into remembering the truth bring more complexities to light about the rights of and injustices to women during the nineteenth century.

76. Auerbach, Susan. **Queen Elizabeth II**. Vero Beach, FL: Rourke, 1993. 112p. $16.95. ISBN 0-86625-481-1. (World Leaders). 5-8

Queen Elizabeth II (b. 1926) became queen of England in 1953 after the death of her father. She has ruled for the latter half of the twentieth century. The text looks at her life and the influences on her decisions as the titular head of England. Photographs and reproductions enhance the text. Time Line, Glossary, Bibliography, Media Resources, and Index.

77. Aufderheide, Patricia. **Anwar Sadat**. New York: Chelsea House, 1985. 112p. $18.95. ISBN 0-87754-560-X. (World Leaders Past and Present). 8 up

Although born into an Egyptian peasant family, Anwar Sadat (1919-1981) used his abilities as soldier and statesman to become one of the leaders for peace in the Middle East. After three wars with Israel—two of which he lost—Sadat realized that he needed to change his country's policy. He braved disagreement to meet with Israel's leaders and begin peace negotiations; he won the Nobel Peace Prize for his efforts in 1978. Photographs enhance the text. Chronology, Further Reading, and Index.

78. Austen-Leigh, Joan. **Later Days at Highbury**. New York: St. Martin's Press, 1996. 160p. $19.95. ISBN 0-312-14642-6. YA

Mrs. Goddard, a school mistress with twin boarders, lives in the town where Emma of Jane Austen's *Emma* lives. Mrs. Goddard corresponds with her London sister and tells her about the events in Highbury while her sister relates stories of teas, balls, and junkets in London. Jane Austen lovers will enjoy the possibilities of meeting Emma's neighbors although Emma never actually visits.

79.   Avery, Gillian. **A Likely Lad**. 1971. New York: Simon & Schuster, 1994. $16. ISBN 0-671-79867-7. YA

Willy's father is pleased when Willy, who is only six years old, tells the local gardener that because his father pays for the upkeep, he should be able to have a flower. Willy runs away when he is twelve because his father wants him to stop school and start working "up the ladder" in his father's insurance company. A family intrigue finally causes Willy's father to agree with him. *Guardian Award*.

80.   Avery, Gillian. **Maria Escapes**. Scott Snow, illustrator. New York: Simon & Schuster, 1992. 258p. $15. ISBN 0-671-77074-8. 4-8

Maria, an orphan bundled off to boarding school in 1875, hates the people and the lessons and runs away. She goes to her uncle in Oxford, England, who decides to let her stay when he hears that she wants to study Latin and Greek and be an Oxford professor. She and the three boys next door work with a tutor, and Maria is learning to do her own research in the Oxford Bodleian Library when she becomes interested in the story of a local boy from the seventeenth century. Although the four neighbors get into trouble, Maria's uncle remains kindly and helpful.

81.   Avery, Gillian. **Maria's Italian Spring**. Scott Snow, illustrator. New York: Simon & Schuster, 1993. 265p. $15. ISBN 0-671-79582-1. 4-8

Maria's uncle, from *Maria Escapes*, dies in 1877. Maria's only living relative lives in Italy, and because Maria likes Greek and Latin, the relative takes her back to Italy. Maria hates having to visit all of the buildings and see all the famous pictures, especially because she is unable to speak Italian. She pretends to be ill and then sneaks out of the house to visit with an English girl nearby. With her, Maria explores the town as she would like to see it.

82.   Avi. **Beyond the Western Sea, Book One: The Escape from Home**. New York: Jackson, Orchard, 1996. 304p. $18.95. ISBN 0-531-09513-4. 5-8

Patrick and his sister, Maura, have to escape from Ireland in 1851 after their landlord destroys their hovel. Also trying to catch the *Robert Peel* from Liverpool, England, on January 24 is Laurence, age eleven, the son of an English lord; Laurence is running away from abuse and his own guilt. The three have various difficulties getting to the ship because of people who wish to keep them off it; the novel spans the five days before they finally get on board and start their trip. *Booklist Starred Review, Bulletin Blue Ribbon Book,* and *American Library Association Best Books for Young Adults*.

83.   Avi. **Beyond the Western Sea, Book Two: Lord Kirkle's Money**. New York: Jackson, Orchard, 1996. 380p. $18.95. ISBN 0-531-09520-7. 5-8

Patrick O'Connell and his sister Maura, along with their friends Mr. Horatio Drabble and Laurence Kirkle, sail on the *Robert Peel* from England to Boston in 1851. After arrival, they all go to Lowell, Massachusetts, where they find out that the O'Connell father has died. The characters must endure prejudice and hardship, but they eventually overcome these evil forces.

84.   Avi-Yonah, Michael. **Piece by Piece! Mosaics of the Ancient World**. Minneapolis, MN: Runestone Press, 1993. 64p. $22.95. ISBN 0-8225-3204-2. (Buried Worlds). 5 up

Mosaics reveal what the people who made them wanted to show. The subject might be a story from the classical world, an illustration of a myth, or merely a pleasing picture. This book follows archaeologists' investigations of ancient mosaics, which have told them about the Greek, Roman, and Byzantine worlds. Glossary and Index.

85.   Axelrod, Alan, and Charles Phillips. **Dictators and Tyrants: Absolute Rulers and Would-Be Rulers in World History**. New York: Facts on File, 1995. 340p. $45. ISBN 0-8160-2866-4. YA

The biographical capsules in this collection cover the main points of the lives of 600 tyrants who "ruled illegitimately by the terms of [their] societies." Subjects include Jean-Claude Duvalier and Deng Xiaoping. Many entries end with brief bibliographies. Index.

86.   Ayer, Eleanor H. **Adolf Hitler**. San Diego, CA: Lucent, 1996. 128p. $16.95. ISBN 1-56006-072-7. (The Importance Of). 7 up

Adolf Hitler (1889-1945) came into power when Germany's image of itself was at a low point after World War I. He was not a German by birth, but Germany and Austria had once been united under the Hapsburgs, and he wanted to reunite the Germanic peoples. After he gained power, each year he staged a seven-day gathering in Nuremberg where the Nazis and the Hitler Youth came together to worship him. His success was based on his charismatic presentation of ideas that the German people wanted to hear. They wanted to know that conditions in the country would improve, that their lives would be better, and that they would become the most powerful country on earth. One way they planned to achieve these goals was by exterminating all those who would dilute the race. The text looks at this man and what he did to make an everlasting impression on the history of the world. Photographs and boxed topics augment the text. Notes, For Further Reading, Works Consulted, and Index.

87. Ayer, Eleanor. **Berlin**. New York: New Discovery, 1992. 96p. $14.95. ISBN 0-02-707800-0. (Cities at War). 6 up

The text looks at the effects of World War II on the people who lived in Berlin. Eyewitnesses, diaries, and other primary sources tell about the rise of Nazism, what having a bomb drop in the street outside was like, what the victims of the Holocaust looked like, how the Holocaust victims were treated, and the response to Hitler's fall. Documentary photographs accentuate the text. Bibliography and Index.

88. Ayer, Eleanor H. **Boris Yeltsin: Man of the People**. New York: Macmillan, 1992. 144p. $13.95. ISBN 0-8751-8543-6. (People in Focus). 4-7

Born in 1931, Boris Nikolayevich Yeltsin went from his childhood on a collective farm, through his education as a civil engineer, to his election as the first president of Russia after it became a republic in 1991. He has had the difficult task of trying to turn the country from a socialist economy into a capitalist economy.

89. Ayer, Eleanor H., with Helen Waterford. **Parallel Journeys**. New York: Atheneum, 1995. 220p. $15. ISBN 0-689-31830-8. 7 up

When Adolf Hitler came to power in Germany in 1933, he affected two young Germans in drastically different ways. Alfons Heck was a member of the Hitler Youth and admired everything about Hitler. Helen Waterford was forced to flee from Germany to Holland and go into hiding; eventually the Gestapo sent her to the Auschwitz death camp in Poland. Alfons and Helen met forty years later and found that they shared the common purpose of showing that if there can be peace between a Jew and a Nazi, then the world can also achieve peace. The stories of their experiences during the war give much insight into the attitudes of those who caused pain and those who had to endure it. Notes, Bibliography, and Index. *Flora Stieglitz Straus Award, Notable Children's Trade Books in the Field of Social Studies*, and *American Library Association Best Books for Young Adults*.

90. Aymar, Brandt, ed. **Men in the Air: The Best Flight Stories of All Time from Greek Mythology to the Space Age**. New York: Crown, 1990. 557p. $24.95; $12.99pa. ISBN 0-517-57403-9; 0-517-14656-8pa. YA

Both fiction and nonfiction, these stories give insight into the hardships accompanying the humans who have risked their lives to fly. Diary entries from Leonardo da Vinci, the Wright brothers, Louis Blériot, Charles Lindbergh, Eddie Rickenbacher, Amelia Earhart, and others complement the fictional accounts of danger coupled with daring, inherent in the desire to fly.

91. Ayoub, Abderrahman, ed. **Al Umm El Madayan: An Islamic City Through the Ages**. Kathleen Leverich, translator; Francesco Corni, illustrator. Boston: Houghton Mifflin, 1994. 61p. $16.95. ISBN 0-395-65967-1. 5 up

Accompanied by detailed drawings and text, this story traces a fictional city in North Africa from its Islamic beginnings. It shows the social life and customs as they have developed and as they are practiced today. Index.

92. **Azerbaijan**. Minneapolis, MN: Lerner, 1993. 56p. $19.95. ISBN 0-8225-2810-X. (Then and Now). 5-9

With its history linked to that of Armenia and Persia, Azerbaijan has been subsumed by the Persians, Mongols, and the Communists. This text discusses these and other problems for the country in its struggle since becoming independent in 1991. Photographs and maps enhance additional information about economics, geography, politics, and ethnography. Glossary and Index.

B

93.   Bachrach, Deborah. **The Charge of the Light Brigade**. San Diego, CA: Lucent, 1997. 111p. $19.95. ISBN 1-56006-455-2. 7 up

During the Crimean War, on October 25, 1854, the British army's Light Brigade charged the Russian army. The battle was a major military misfire with poor commanding causing disaster. The text looks at the battle along with its historical and political background and includes well-placed box excerpts and a careful chronology. Bibliography, Chronology, Further Reading, and Index.

94.   Bachrach, Deborah. **The Inquisition**. San Diego, CA: Lucent, 1995. 127p. $14.95. ISBN 1-56006-247-9. (World History). 8 up

In 1233, Pope Gregory IV established the papal Inquisition to combat heresy—but it usually imprisoned people. In 1542, Paul III wanted the Inquisition to become part of the Holy Office to combat Protestantism. In 1478, the independent Spanish Inquisition, established by the Spanish monarchs and headed by Tomás de Torquemada, punished Jews and Muslims, often with the death penalty. It was not abolished until 1834. Bibliography and Index.

95.   Bachrach, Deborah. **The Korean War**. San Diego, CA: Lucent, 1991. 96p. $16.95. ISBN 1-56006-409-9. (America's Wars). 7 up

The text looks at the Korean War, which lasted from 1950 to 1953, and explains how America was involved; it also discusses the war's events and legacy.

96.   Bachrach, Susan D. **Tell Them We Remember: The Story of the Holocaust**. Boston: Little, Brown, 1994. 109p. $19.95. ISBN 0-316-07484-5. 5-9

Bachrach uses the same format that the United States Holocaust Museum uses for visitors. She starts with a series of photographs of children and traces their experiences throughout the Holocaust—where they went and, in some cases, where they died. The other photographs also come from the museum's collection. The text follows the chronology of the Holocaust, beginning with life before the Holocaust and Hitler's rise to power in 1933, and follows the survivors through the Nuremberg Trials in 1945 and 1946. Chronology, Suggestions for Further Reading, Glossary, and Index.

97.   Baillet, Yolande. **Matisse: Painter of the Essential**. John Goodman, translator; Bernadette Theulet-Luzie, illustrator. New York: Chelsea House, 1995. 53p. $14.95. ISBN 0-7910-2812-7. (Art for Children). 5-9

Henri Matisse (1869-1954) was a French painter whose use of pure colors and simple shapes on canvas and in collage have delighted his viewers. Reproductions enhance the text.

98.   Baillie, Allan. **Little Brother**. New York: Viking, 1992. 144p. $14. ISBN 0-670-84381-4. 3-7

Vithy and his brother, Mang, try to cross the Cambodian border into Thailand after escaping from the Big Paddy where they had been held for nearly a year following the Vietnamese war. Although they manage to evade the Khmer Rouge soldiers, they are separated, and Vithy must travel alone. He has to cross jungles, mountains, and landscape where enemies hide throughout, and where the rules that he has known throughout his life no longer exist. He eventually realizes that he must trust someone to help him escape and search for his brother, because he can do neither alone. People help him get to Australia, and there he finds what he was looking for.

99.   Baillie, Allan. **The Secrets of Walden Rising**. New York: Viking, 1997. 168p. $13.99. ISBN 0-670-87351-9. 7-9

When Brendan moves to Australia from England, he hates the small town of Jacks Marsh, and his peers reciprocate. In his loneliness, he goes to nearby Fetter Lake, a reservoir, and draws the scene. He begins to see something in the water, and he and his adversary, Bago, join to search for treasure in the old mining town, which is rising from the lake because of severe drought. They discover that others want the possible treasure as well, and their hunt becomes dangerous.

100.   Bainbridge, Beryl. **The Birthday Boys**. New York: Carroll & Graf, 1994. 189p. $18.95. ISBN 0-7867-0071-8. YA

In this fictionalized account of British explorer Robert Falcon Scott's trek to the Antarctic, the story comes from the diaries of five men on the journey: Evans, Wilson, Bowers, Oates, and Scott himself. Oates tells of the final segment, walking to the Pole when they see Roald Amundsen's black flag announcing that he has already arrived and that they are not first. He notes that Scott had disregarded the strength, superiority, and terrain of the enemy Antarctic, and ignored the fact that dogs were the only feasible transport. Then Oates welcomes the disorientation before his death.

101.   Baker, Betty. **The Blood of the Brave**. New York: Harper, 1966. 165p. $4.79. ISBN 0-06-020326-9. 7-10

In 1518, Juan comes from Castile, Spain, to Cuba with his father and joins Cortez's expedition to Mexico as the priest's translator. A slave, Doña Marina, knows Spanish and translates for Cortez. When Cortez hears that natives have raided Vera Cruz, a city he has claimed, he imprisons Montezuma, Mexico's ruler. Juan learns that Montezuma has sacrificed humans because he believes that only blood will make the sun rise each morning. Montezuma thinks that Cortez may be Quetzalcoatl, the god expected to return in the year of One Reed; therefore, he declares his allegiance to the Spanish King Charles and to Cortez. But his people rise against Cortez, who returns the following year to destroy them. Juan and his father start their own farm while other men use the city's ruins to build their churches.

102.   Baker, Betty. **Walk the World's Rim**. New York: HarperCollins, 1965. 80p. $14.89. ISBN 0-06-020381-1. 5-9

Of 600 men who sailed from Cuba to Florida in 1527, only 4 survived. One, the black slave Esteban, encourages a young Indian, Chako, to go with him to Mexico. While their leaders petition for money to go to the seven cities of Cíbola, they wait separately in the city; Chako is disturbed that Esteban has not come to tell him what will happen. When Cortez tells Chako to feed his horse, Chako finds Esteban, the slave, confined to the stables. Although taught not to respect slaves, Chako soon realizes that Esteban tells the truth, and when the Cíbolans murder Esteban, Chako dejectedly returns to his Florida home.

103.   Baker, Rosalie F., and Charles F. Baker. **Ancient Greeks**. New York: Oxford University Press, 1997. 280p. $35. ISBN 0-19-509940-0. (Oxford Profiles). 7 up

The text is divided into five chronological sections, with biographies about several Greeks of the time period and information about their professions and backgrounds, revealing Greek culture as well. Subjects include politicians, philosophers, mathematicians, dramatists, authors, and soldiers. Commentary shows both disagreement and accord from scholars who have written about the subjects. Chronology, Further Reading, Glossary, and Index.

104.   Baklanov, Grigory. **Forever Nineteen**. Antonina Bouis, translator. New York: Lippincott, 1989. 168p. $13.95. ISBN 0-397-32297-6. 9 up

Volodya, age nineteen, is a Russian soldier fighting the Germans in 1941. He escapes several battles, albeit with some wounds, and falls in love. But machine-gun fire fells him in a trench, and thirty years later, actors planning a reenactment of World War II discover his body.

105.   Balaban, John. **Remembering Heaven's Face: A Moral Witness in Vietnam**. New York: Poseidon Press, 1991. 334p. $21.95; $11pa. ISBN 0-671-69065-5; 0-671-77969-9pa. YA

Balaban, a conscientious objector during the Vietnam War, traveled to Vietnam during the war to work for the International Voluntary Services. In 1971, he returned to collect traditional songs. He kept notebooks for 20 years as a duty, but refused to open them because "their contents [were] unbearable." In 1989, he went to North Vietnam; afterward, he returned to open the notebooks and to relate the terrible things that happened.

106.   Balaban, John. **Vietnam: The Land We Never Knew**. Geoffrey Clifford, photographer. San Francisco: Chronicle, 1989. 144p. $29.95. ISBN 0-87701-597-X. 5-7

A land of rice and monsoons; of four religions—Taoism, Buddhism, Confucianism, and now Christianity; and of numerous foreign invasions during its 3,000-year history, Vietnam has kept its traditions. Beautiful photographs of everyday life enhance the text of this book. One sees the country's natural beauty, the people, the government, the remnants of war, and the hope for the future.

107.   Balkwill, Richard. **Trafalgar**. Fred Anderson, illustrator. New York: New Discovery, 1993. 32p. $13.95. ISBN 0-02-726326-6. (Great Battles and Sieges). 5 up

Sixteen miles west of Cape Trafalgar, near Cadiz, Spain, on Monday, October 21, 1805, twenty-seven ships of the British Royal Navy met a combined French and Spanish fleet of thirty-three ships. Seventeen thousand British sailors and more than 2,000 guns served under Admiral Lord Nelson from his flagship, the HMS *Victory*. The French and Spanish fleet had more men and more guns, but after a five-hour battle in which 5,000 men died, the British won, without losing any ships, whereas the French and Spanish lost nineteen. Discussion follows on Horatio Nelson, Napoleon, the ships, the sailor's life, fighting at sea, the preparation for the battle, and the events after Trafalgar. Glossary and Index.

108.   Ballard, J. G. **Empire of the Sun**. New York: Buccaneer, 1987. 279p. $24.95. ISBN 1-56849-663-X. New York: Pocket Books, 1987. 384p. $5.99pa. ISBN 0-671-64877-2pa. YA

Jim lives in Shanghai with his parents during World War II. What he sees is not a world war but a battle between the Japanese and the starving Chinese peasants and refugees. He is accidentally separated from his parents after the bombing of Pearl Harbor, and he tries to surrender, as he was told to do if captured. Neither the guards nor the British will take him seriously, and he barely survives the ravages of the war. When he sees the excess of the West in comparison with the lack of goods in the East, he worries about the future for all.

109. Ballard, Robert D. **Exploring the Bismarck**. New York: Scholastic, 1991. 64p. $15.95. ISBN 0-590-44268-6. (Time Quest). 3-8

Robert Ballard and his assistants recovered the shipwreck of the German battleship *Bismarck* in 1989. Photographs of the ship complement the story of the battle during which it sank in World War II. Recommended Further Reading. *American Library Association Recommended Book for the Reluctant Young Reader* and *Outstanding Science Trade Books for Children*.

110. Ballard, Robert D. **Exploring the Titanic**. Ken Marschall, illustrator. New York: Madison, Scholastic, 1988. 96p. $14.95; $6.95pa. ISBN 0-590-41953-6; 0-590-41952-8pa. 4-7

Dr. Robert Ballard became fascinated with the story of the *Titanic*. When the tiny submarine *Alvin*'s tether was extended to 13,000 feet, Ballard realized that he could reach the wreck two and one-half miles under the sea. In July 1986, he saw the ship that had last been above the water on April 14, 1912. On that night, only 705 of the 2,220 people on board the magnificent ship reached the safety of a rescue vessel, the *Carpathia*, after an iceberg tore through the hull. Ballard returned to the *Titanic* eight times, going inside and reliving the scene based on what he had read or heard from survivors of that doomed voyage. Further Reading, Glossary, and *Titanic* Timeline. *American Library Association Best Books for Young Adults*, *School Library Journal Best Books of the Year*, and *Horn Book Fanfare*.

111. Ballard, Robert D., with Rich Archbold. **The Lost Wreck of the Isis**. Ken Marshall and Wesley Lowe, illustrators. New York: Scholastic, 1990. 63p. $15.95; $6.95pa. ISBN 0-590-43852-2; 0-590-43853-0pa. (Time Quest). 2-8

When Ballard located the wreck of the *Isis* off the coast of Italy, he found artifacts of the Roman world. The text describing the "find" alternates with a story set at the time when the *Isis* actually sailed so that the reader can connect more readily with the people who might have been on the *Isis* and what they would have transported. The book is, therefore, both historical fiction and information. It gives excellent insight as to how modern tools (underwater vehicles, cameras, and computers) can find ancient ones. Glossary and Recommended Further Reading. *Outstanding Science Trade Books for Children*.

112. Bandon, Alexandra. **Asian Indian Americans**. New York: New Discovery, Silver Burdett, 1994. 112p. $14.95. ISBN 0-02-768144-0. (Footsteps to America). 5-8

Bandon examines the lives of Asian Indian Americans after they began to arrive in America around 1965. For them to leave their country was a major decision; therefore, Bandon tries to identify what in the history of the country would have precipitated such a move. Using personal narratives as a basis, she shows what the journey to America was like, what life in America has been like for those who came, the prejudice they faced, and the opportunities they found. For Further Reading and Index.

113. Bandon, Alexandra. **Chinese Americans**. New York: New Discovery, Silver Burdett, 1994. 112p. $14.95. ISBN 0-02-768149-1. (Footsteps to America). 5-8

Bandon examines the lives of Chinese Americans. For them to leave their country was a major decision; therefore, Bandon tries to identify what in the history of the country would have precipitated such a move. Using personal narratives as a basis, she shows what the journey to America was like, what life in America has been like for those who came, the prejudice they faced, and the opportunities they found. For Further Reading and Index.

114. Bandon, Alexandra. **Dominican Americans**. New York: New Discovery, Silver Burdett, 1994. 112p. $14.95. ISBN 0-02-768152-1. (Footsteps to America). 5-8

Bandon examines the lives of Dominican Americans after they began to arrive in America around 1965. For them to leave their country was a major decision, so Bandon tries to identify what in the history of their country would have precipitated such a move. Using personal narratives as a basis, she shows what the journey to America was like, what life in America has been like for those who came, the prejudice they faced, and the opportunities they found. For Further Reading and Index.

115. Bandon, Alexandra. **Filipino Americans**. New York: New Discovery, Macmillan, 1993. 112p. $14.95. ISBN 0-02-768143-2. (Footsteps to America). 5-8

Bandon examines the lives of Filipino Americans. For them to leave their country was a major decision; therefore, Bandon tries to identify what in the history of their country would have precipitated such a move. Using personal narratives as a basis, she shows what the journey to America was like, what life in America has been like for those who came, the prejudice they faced, and the opportunities they found. For Further Reading and Index.

116. Bandon, Alexandra. **Korean Americans**. New York: New Discovery, Silver Burdett, 1994. 111p. $14.95. ISBN 0-02-768147-5. (Footsteps to America). 5-8

Bandon examines the lives of Korean Americans. For them to leave their country was a major decision; therefore, Bandon tries to identify what in the history of their country would have precipitated such a move. Using personal narratives as a basis, she shows what the journey to America was like, what life in America has been like for those who came, the prejudice they faced, and the opportunities they found. For Further Reading and Index.

117. Bandon, Alexandra. **Mexican Americans**. New York: New Discovery, Macmillan, 1993. 110p. $14.95. ISBN 0-02-768412-4. (Footsteps to America). 5-8

Bandon examines the lives of Mexican Americans. For them to leave their country was a major decision; therefore, Bandon tries to identify what in the history of their country would have precipitated such a move. Using personal narratives as a basis, she shows what the journey to America was like, what life in America has been like for those who came, the prejudice they faced, and the opportunities they found. For Further Reading and Index.

118. Bandon, Alexandra. **Vietnamese Americans**. New York: New Discovery, Silver Burdett, 1994. 112p. $14.95. ISBN 0-02-768146-7. (Footsteps to America). 5-8

Bandon examines the lives of Vietnamese Americans. For them to leave their country was a major decision; therefore, Bandon tries to identify what in the history of their country would have precipitated such a move. Using personal narratives as a basis, she shows what the journey to America was like, what life in America has been like for those who came, the prejudice they faced, and the opportunities they found. For Further Reading and Index.

119. Bandon, Alexandra. **West Indian Americans**. New York: New Discovery, Silver Burdett, 1994. 112p. $14.95. ISBN 0-02-768148-3. (Footsteps to America). 5-8

In this text, Bandon examines the lives of West Indian Americans. For them to decide to leave their country was a major decision; therefore, Bandon tries to identify what in the history of their country would have precipitated such a move. Using personal narratives as a basis, she shows what the journey to America was like, what life in America has been like for those who have come, the prejudices they faced, and the opportunities they found. For Further Reading and Index.

120. Banfield, Susan. **Charlemagne**. New York: Chelsea House, 1986. 112p. $18.95. ISBN 0-87754-592-8. (World Leaders Past and Present). 5 up

Charlemagne (742-814) came to the Frankish throne in 771 and fought savage Christian crusades against the Germans and the Moorish infidels in Spain. His politics and his religious zeal gained him a coronation as Emperor of the West in 800. As a lawmaker, a warrior, and a lover of learning, he helped revive Europe during his rule in the Carolingian Renaissance. He became the first great monarch of medieval Europe. Reproductions and maps enhance the text. Chronology, Further Reading, and Index.

121. Banfield, Susan. **Charles de Gaulle**. New York: Chelsea House, 1985. 112p. $18.95. ISBN 0-87754-551-0. (World Leaders Past and Present). 8 up

Charles de Gaulle (1890–1970) led France while Nazis occupied the country and after World War II. He saved France from civil war in Algeria while restoring strength to the country and retaining its international prestige. Some consider him to be one of the greatest leaders of the century. Photographs and reproductions enhance the text. Chronology, Further Reading, and Index.

122. Banfield, Susan. **Joan of Arc**. New York: Chelsea House, 1985. 112p. $18.95. ISBN 0-87754-556-1. (World Leaders Past and Present). 5 up

With little formal education, Joan of Arc (1412-1431) helped the French overcome the English occupation. She heard voices from St. Michael, St. Catherine, and St. Margaret, which convinced her that she had to help France. She persuaded the Dauphin Charles to give her an army, and in 1429, she led the French to victory at Orléans. She was eventually captured, imprisoned, tried, and executed. The Catholic Church declared her a saint in 1920, and her bravery is still legend. Photographs and reproductions enhance the text. Chronology, Further Reading, and Index.

123. Banfield, Susan. **The Rights of Man, The Reign of Terror: The Story of the French Revolution**. New York: Lippincott, 1989. 213p. $15. ISBN 0-397-32353-0. 7 up

Banfield begins the story of the French Revolution by contrasting the morning rituals of Marie Antoinette and Louis XVI with those of peasants and Parisian laborers. Brocades and free bread do not match tatters and bread costing four days of work. Revolution was fomented long before 1789. Writers such as Voltaire, who died in 1778; Montesquieu; and Jean-Jacques Rousseau raged at injustice, lambasted intolerance, and lauded the common man. Their work and the hostility of the commoners led to the downfall of the nobility and the clergy at the

Bastille on July 14, 1789. Jean-Paul Marat, a journalist; the Jacobins and Girondins; and leaders such as La-fayette, Danton, and Robespierre kept the revolution alive until commoners guillotined Robespierre. Banfield suggests that this was the beginning of such uprisings as the Russian Revolution, occurring more than a century later. Further Study and Index.

124. Bangura, Abdul Karim. **Kipsigis**. New York: Rosen, 1995. 64p. $15.95. ISBN 0-8239-1765-7. (Heritage Library of African Peoples). 5-8

The Kipsigis, now in the western portion of Kenya, migrated from Egypt through the Sudan. Their proud his-tory shows that they were able to govern themselves with equality. Topics discussed in addition to general history are the organization of their society, initiation, marriage and family, European contact and rule, and a view of their future. Photographs, boxed information, and maps enhance the text. Glossary, Further Reading, and Index.

125. Barboza, Steven. **Door of No Return: The Legend of Gorée Island**. New York: Cobblehill, Dutton, 1994. 42p. $14.99. ISBN 0-525-65188-8. 5 up

As early as 1433, Africans captured other Africans and sold them to Portuguese traders. They assembled the captured slaves on Gorée Island, two miles west of Dakar, Senegal. According to records in Lisbon, 3,589 slaves arrived there between 1486 and 1493. In 1619, a Dutch ship sailed into Jamestown, Virginia, with 20 slaves. Many Africans also owned slaves, and by the late 1800s slaves comprised two-thirds of many African societies. On Gorée, the wealthy kept slave houses. Anne Pepin, a *signare* who acted as the wife of the French governor of Senegal (although unmarried to him), had more than 35 slaves. The island today is a place of pil-grimage for Americans wanting to see where their ancestors started their long journey to servitude. Index.

126. Bard, Roberta. **Sir Francis Drake and the Struggle for an Ocean Empire**. New York: Chelsea House, 1992. 128p. $19.95. ISBN 0-7910-1302-2. (World Explorers). 5 up

Francis Drake (1540?-1596), the son of Protestants who had fled from Catholic persecution in 1549, be-gan working aboard ship when he was still a teenager. He traveled to the Caribbean and the Spanish West In-dies several times before he returned to raid Spanish treasure. He became the first Englishman to circumnavigate the globe, was elected to the House of Commons, attacked Spain in Cadiz harbor, battled the Spanish Armada, and died at sea. Photographs and reproductions enhance the text. Glossary, Bibliography, and Index.

127. Baricco, Alessandro. **Silk**. Guido Waldman, translator. New York: Farrar, Straus & Giroux, 1997. 96p. $22.95. ISBN 0-399-14309-2. YA

Joncour meets a woman without oriental-shaped eyes while buying silkworms on his journeys from France to Japan in the 1860s. They never speak to each other, but they begin and carry on an affair.

128. Barnes, Virginia Lee, and Janice Boddy. **Aman: The Story of a Somali Girl**. New York: Pantheon, 1994. 336p. $23; $13pa. ISBN 0-679-43606-5; 0-679-76209-4pa. YA

The authors retell the story of Aman, the daughter of a Somali woman in the late 1950s who lived apart from her husband and earned her own living. Aman spends her youth needing money and trying to stay a virgin for marriage, undergoing ceremonial genital surgery at age nine. She falls in love with a forbidden male, and she breaks the taboo when she is thirteen, a decision that ruins her reputation and her ability to make money. By the time she is nineteen, at the end of the book, she has faced a difficult marriage, war, risk, and poverty in her determination to survive.

129. Barrett, Julia. **The Third Sister**. New York: Donald I. Fine, 1996. 256p. $22.95. ISBN 1-55611-496-6. YA

Margaret, seventeen, is the youngest sister in Jane Austen's *Sense and Sensibility*, and after her sisters have married, she fears that no one will marry her without a dowry. But she meets two men who fall in love with her; one has secrets, and the other is a cad. She chooses the wrong one, but last-minute information saves her.

130. Barron, Stephanie. **Jane and the Man of the Cloth**. New York: Bantam, 1997. 274p. $21.95. ISBN 0-553-10203-6. YA

Jane, her sister, Cassandra, and their parents travel from Bath to Lyme in a coach that overturns in the rain and injures Cassandra. When Jane goes to a nearby house for help, she meets Geoffry Sidmouth. Cassandra re-turns to London, and Jane hears about the events on the coast, which seem to point to Sidmouth as a smuggler of luxury items from France. After two murders, Jane begins to investigate the suspect.

131. Barron, Stephanie. **Jane and the Unpleasantness at Scargrave Manor**. New York: Bantam, 1996. 302p. $19.95. ISBN 0-553-10196-X. YA

Jane Austen visits her friend Isobel, Countess of Scargrave, when she and her older husband return from their honeymoon in the early 1800s. At a ball, Isobel's husband is found dead from poisoning, and when Isobel and her husband's handsome nephew are accused of the murder, Jane knows she must investigate and clear them of the unwarranted charges.

132. Bartos-Hoppner, Barbara. **The Cossacks**. Stella Humphries, translator. 1963. New York: Henry Z. Walck, Random House, 1972. 295p. $6.50. ISBN 0-8098-3046-9. YA

Mitya leaves his home in 1579 to follow Yermak Timofeyev, the chieftain of the Cossacks whose band of Christians unlawfully fights the horrible acts of Ivan the Terrible. When Yermak was a young boy, Ivan's soldiers had strangled Yermak's parents while he watched. While Mitya fights, he realizes that soldiers need treatment after battles, so he begins transporting medicine and herbs instead of killing. But when Yermak drowns, Mitya, after more than five years, returns home and becomes a doctor, trying to help others.

133. Baumann, Hans. **The Barque of the Brothers: A Tale of the Days of Henry the Navigator**. I. McHugh & F. McHugh, translators. New York: Henry Z. Walck, Random House, 1958. 245p. $6. ISBN 0-8098-3019-1. YA

After the orphans Tinoco and Aires join the army of the Infante Henrique (Henry the Navigator), they meet the conquered young black Lopo, who will not speak to them until he hears Aires play the guitar. They fight in Tangier and continue to the Ivory Coast in Africa, where the financier of the fleet decides to transport "black ivory"—slaves. Tinoco and Aires leave the ship, but natives kill Tinoco before they can escape. Aires goes home to Portugal, but realizes that without his brother, he will be much happier sharing his life with Lopo in Africa.

134. Baumann, Hans. **I Marched with Hannibal**. K. Potts, translator. New York: Henry Z. Walck, Random House, 1972. 226p. $6. ISBN 0-8098-3042-6. YA

An old man relates his story to two teenagers in the ruins of Saguntum. He tells of Hannibal destroying the town, but says that Hannibal's elephant, Suru, and its driver saved him, a boy of twelve. As one of thousands of mercenaries, he joined the horses and elephants traversing the Alps to fight the Romans. Seventeen thousand mercenaries and 2,000 horsemen died during the nine days crossing the Alps, but the remaining soldiers stayed loyal because they thought that Hannibal cared. After Suru died, Roman soldiers captured the man, but Hannibal's Greek secretary befriended him and taught him to read and to appreciate nature, two things that helped him survive until he could return home. He noted that Hannibal took everything except what they needed most, their pure water.

135. Bawden, Nina. **Carrie's War**. Colleen Browning, illustrator. 1973. New York: HarperCollins, 1992. 159p. $14.89. ISBN 0-397-31450-7. 4-7

Evacuated from London in 1939, an eleven-year-old girl and her younger brother stay in a small Welsh town. They and another evacuee befriend a young boy who is unable to speak clearly, and are in turn protected by the woman caring for him. Carrie sees their house afire from the train as she returns to her family, but has no way to contact or warn them. She thinks that her misbehavior before her departure caused the fire. Thirty years later, Carrie's son finds out that she had nothing to do with the fire, but her guilt and fears have controlled her life. *Carnegie Commendation* and *Phoenix Award*.

136. Bawden, Nina. **Henry**. Joyce Powzyk, illustrator. New York: Lothrop, Lee & Shepard, 1988. 119p. $15. ISBN 0-688-07894-X. New York: Yearling, Dell, 1990. 119p. $3.25pa. ISBN 0-440-40309-Xpa. 3-7

The first-person female narrator, her mother, and two brothers evacuate to Wales from England during World War II while her father fights. They find and tend a baby squirrel whom they name Henry. Soon she and the two boys are slightly jealous of the attention their mother gives to Henry. They try to adjust during the long separation by focusing on their schoolwork, the people who own the farm on which they live, and the farm animals. They realize that their mother is trying to cope with the absence of their father, but all of them have a similar problem. *Parenting's Reading Magic Award* and *American Library Association Notable Books for Children*.

137. Baxter, Nicola. **Invaders and Settlers: Facts—Things to Make—Activities**. New York: Franklin Watts, 1994. 32p. $18.50. ISBN 0-531-14338-4. (Craft Topics). 5-8

The text covers the Romans, Britain, Anglo-Saxons, Alfred, later British kings, and William the Conqueror. Accompanying the illustrations and history are ideas for crafts. For example, coupled with the discussion of the Roman invasion of Britain are directions to create a Celtic shield. Glossary, Resources, and Index.

138. Baxter, Nicola. **Romans: Facts—Things to Make—Activities**. Nigel Longden, illustrator. New York: Franklin Watts, 1992. 32p. $18.50. ISBN 0-531-14143-8. (Craft Topics). 5-8

In addition to describing the daily life of Romans, the text gives ideas for making items that help in the comprehension of how something might have been done. Patterns and suggestions for materials to make a Roman villa, a mosaic, a victor's wreath, a theater mask, a writing tablet, a tunic and toga, and a statue are included. Glossary, Resources, and Index.

139. Beardsley, John. **Pablo Picasso**. New York: Harry N. Abrams, 1991. 92p. $19.95. ISBN 0-8109-3713-1. (First Impressions). 7 up

Pablo Picasso (1881–1973), born in Spain, had amazing energies as an artist during his long life. Beardsley, a museum curator, discusses Picasso's relationships and their effect on his art. These people include women he loved or mistreated, as well as other painters and poets of pre–World War II. The reproductions within the text show the evolution of Picasso's art, and Beardsley explains Picasso's involvement in Cubism and his influence on avant-garde trends. Additionally, Beardsley relates why Picasso is such an important artist. List of Illustrations and Index.

140. Beattie, Owen, and John Geiger. **Buried in Ice: The Mystery of a Lost Arctic Expedition**. Janet Wilson, illustrator. New York: Scholastic, Madison Press, 1992. 64p. $15.95. ISBN 0-590-43848-4. (Time Quest). 4 up

In 1845, Sir John Franklin led an expedition of 128 men to find the Northwest Passage between the Atlantic and Pacific Oceans. No one returned. In 1984, Owen Beattie, an archaeologist, found three graves of crewmen on a remote island in the Canadian Arctic, which have given insight into the voyage and its failure. The results of the find are reported, with photographs of the scene. Glossary, The Search for the Northwest Passage History, and Recommended Further Reading. *Notable Children's Trade Books in the Field of Social Studies, American Library Association Best Books for Young Adults, American Library Association Quick Picks for Reluctant Young Adult Readers,* and *Outstanding Science Trade Books for Children.*

141. Beatty, John, and Patricia Beatty. **Campion Towers**. New York: Macmillan, 1965. 293p. $4.95. ISBN 0-02-708670-4. 7 up

When Penitence Hervey arrives in England from Salem colony in 1651 to receive an inheritance from her deceased mother's mother, a man awaits her at the docks. He wants her to help him reveal the family's papist background in Cromwell's world. Penitence at first supports Cromwell and reveals that Charles Stuart plans to hide in the family home, Campion Towers. But when Stuart's men capture her and she talks with Charles Stuart, she realizes that she understands and supports his view more. She helps Charles escape and returns to Salem to await the arrival of her new love, Julian Killingtree, after relinquishing the family jewels to the Cavaliers' cause.

142. Beatty, John, and Patricia Beatty. **Master Rosalind**. New York: Morrow, 1974. 221p. $11.25. ISBN 0-688-21819-9. 5-9

Rosalind, age twelve in 1598, dresses as a boy and walks to Oxford, England, to borrow a valuable book from her grandfather's friend. A man who knows the value of the book pretends to be crazy and kidnaps her. When she shows no talent for helping the man and his accomplice steal, they release her. Instead of returning home, she spends a year traveling with Shakespeare's players. After various events, someone finds out that she is not male, but in the interim she has received an inheritance and can return to her grandfather without ignominy.

143. Beatty, Patricia. **Jonathan Down Under**. New York: Morrow, 1982. 219p. $10.25. ISBN 0-688-01467-4. 5-9

Jonathan Cole's father, crazy for gold in 1851, goes to Australia after little success in California and takes Jonathan with him. After Jonathan recovers from "sandy blight," a disease during which he stayed inside for several months and had his eyes scraped daily to keep him from going blind, he hears that his father's partner has left with their gold. Then a mine cave-in kills his father. Jonathan begins working for an Irish woman who has come to Australia to escape the potato famine, but she soon dies. When he helps others find gold, they give him money to return home because he is interested in neither gold nor Australia.

144. Beckett, Wendy. **The Duke and the Peasant: Life in the Middle Ages**. New York; Prestel, 1997. 30p. $14. ISBN 0-7913-1813-6. (Adventures in Art). 5-9

Paintings from the late medieval period recreate the lives of dukes, courtiers, and peasants. Index.

145. Beckett, Wendy. **The Story of Painting**. New York: Dorling Kindersley, 1994. 400p. $39.95. ISBN 1-56458-615-4. YA

This book is an overview of western painting from the Lascaux cave painters to the present, with the main emphasis on the last 800 years. The material is chronological, with chapters grouped according to trends or movements. Each chapter contains leaders of the period, their most famous works, information about the artists' lives, and the political, religious, and social influences on their work. Index.

146. **Belarus**. Minneapolis, MN: Lerner, 1993. 56p. $19.95. ISBN 0-8225-2811-8. (Then and Now). 5-9

Known as "White Russia," Belarus lies east of Poland, south of Latvia and Lithuania, and north of Ukraine. Originally inhabited by the Slavs, the country is trying to succeed after becoming independent in 1991. Photographs and maps enhance additional information about economics, geography, politics, and ethnography. Glossary and Index.

147. Bell, William. **Forbidden City**. New York: Bantam, 1991. 200p. $14.95; $3.50pa. ISBN 0-553-07131-9; 0-553-28864-4pa. 7 up

With his news-cameraman father in Beijing, Alex, age seventeen, expects to enjoy his interest in Chinese history, and he makes friends with some Chinese who admire leaders of the People's Liberation Army. When the army turns on the students and massacres them in Tiananmen Square in the spring of 1989, these friends realize that the people they respected have lied to them. Although not definitive historical fiction, this novel tells a story about a situation important in Chinese history.

148. Bell-Villada, Gene H. **García Márquez: The Man and His Work**. Chapel Hill: University of North Carolina Press, 1990. 247p. $15.95pa. ISBN 0-8078-4264-8pa. YA

This biography introduces the politics of Colombia, as well as the life and works of García Márquez, by interweaving them in the text. The information on García's *One Hundred Years of Solitude* and *The Autumn of the Patriarch* are invaluable to persons interested in those extraordinary works. The influence of writers such as Faulkner and Joyce on García Márquez becomes clear in the discussions. Bell-Villada sees the works as histories rather than merely *magical realism*, a term that he sees as a limitation on their magnitude. Bibliography and Index.

149. Benchley, Nathaniel. **Bright Candles: A Novel of Danish Resistance**. New York: Harper, 1974. 256p. $5.50. ISBN 0-06-020461-3. 7 up

When Gens was sixteen, during the German occupation of Denmark, he joined the resistance movement. He could not understand why his father did not obviously oppose the German rule. But what the family discovers after the war is that each went a separate way in their work with the underground to save the Danish Jews, including being caught and imprisoned.

150. Bender, Michael, author/illustrator. **Waiting for Filippo: The Life of Renaissance Architect Filippo Brunelleschi**. San Francisco: Chronicle, 1996. Unpaged. $19.95. ISBN 0-8118-0181-0. 3-7

This book details the life of Filippo Brunelleschi (1377-1446) of Florence, Italy, with pop-ups of some of the buildings he designed. *Parents Choice Honor Book.*

151. Benitez, Sandra. **Bitter Grounds**. New York: Hyperion, 1997. 445p. $22.95. ISBN 0-7868-6157-6. YA

Between 1933 and 1977, three generations of El Salvadoran women face political upheaval. In their different social classes, they have unequal economic benefits and educational opportunities, but are united in their fear of the future.

152. Bentley, James. **Albert Schweitzer**. Milwaukee, WI: Gareth Stevens, 1989. 68p. $16.95. ISBN 0-55532-823-7. (People Who Have Helped the World). 7-9

Albert Schweitzer (1875–1965) was an accomplished organist (and organ builder), theologian, philosopher, and physician. Although already trained as a minister, with his own congregation, he decided to become a doctor after hearing a plea for medical missionaries to come to Africa. He served in Lambaréné in the Republic of Gabon for fifty years, excluding his imprisonment by the French for being a German in a French colony during World War I and times of poor health. He built a hospital, unlike western hospitals, that would make patients feel comfortable. It contained rows of huts where families could stay with patients and cook their own preferred food. One of the ways he made money to improve the hospital was by giving organ concerts. By the end of his service, the hospital had more than 70 rows of huts and treated up to 600 people each day. In 1952, when Schweitzer won the Nobel Peace Prize, he used the money to build a hospital section for those with leprosy. For More Information, Glossary, Chronology, and Index.

153. Bentley, Judith. **Archbishop Tutu of South Africa**. Springfield, NJ: Enslow, 1988. 96p. $16.95. ISBN 0-89490-180-X. 5-7

This book predates changes in South Africa to abolish apartheid, but it gives good background about this severe problem. In introducing Tutu's parents, the author presents historical information about their tribes, the Xhosa and the Tswana, and their encounters with the Boers. Tutu's educated father taught school and paid for Tutu (b. 1931) to attend mission schools, whereas white children were able to attend segregated public schools for free. Tutu gained admittance to medical school, but the family did not have enough money to pay for it. Instead, he began teaching. When he was twenty-five, however, his school closed, and he decided to become an Anglican priest, because a clergyman who opposed apartheid had treated him and his people with respect. As a black adult, Tutu had to carry a pass, and he as well as Nelson Mandela, who spoke for the African National Congress, were against such laws. In 1960, initial black protests against the white government caused deaths and shocked the world. Tutu soon qualified to attend King's College in England, and the government finally gave him permission to leave for four years. The taste of freedom made him refuse to accept his prior status, and he returned to England to work for the World Council of Churches. He received the Nobel Peace Prize for his efforts against apartheid, but not until the 1990s did apartheid end. Further Reading and Index.

154. Berent, Mark. **Eagle Station**. New York: Putnam, 1992. 396p. $22.95. ISBN 0-399-13722-X. New York: Jove, 1993. 396p. $5.99pa. ISBN 0-515-11208-9pa. YA

Air force pilots continue their work in 1968 Vietnam as they protect Eagle Station and its radar in this sequel to *Rolling Thunder, Steel Tiger,* and *Phantom Leader*. Finally, one person makes contact with the prisoners in Hanoi to let them know that the government is working on their release. However, not all Americans sympathize with their difficulties during the war.

155. Berent, Mark. **Phantom Leader**. New York: Putnam, 1991. 414p. $21.95. ISBN 0-399-13603-7. New York: Jove, 1992. 414p. $5.99pa. ISBN 0-515-10785-9pa. YA

When the Viet Cong down Flak's plane in 1967, they imprison him in Hanoi. The Tet Offensive leads to more captures, and other pilots join Flak in prison. When a pilot helps him escape, the French return him to the Viet Cong. Flak realizes that those thought to be friends may be enemies and vice versa.

156. Berent, Mark. **Rolling Thunder**. New York: Putnam, 1989. 382p. $15.95. ISBN 0-399-13439-5. New York: Jove, 1989. 382p. $5.99pa. ISBN 0-515-10190-7pa. YA

In 1965, three air force pilots do their job in Vietnam by participating in the bombing raids and by trying to escape death. They instead have to face the deaths of friends. When they return to the United States, they have to face hostile hippies who oppose the war in Vietnam and splatter red dye on their bodies.

157. Berent, Mark. **Steel Tiger**. New York: Putnam, 1990. 399p. $19.95. ISBN 0-399-13538-3. New York: Jove, 1994. 399p. $5.99pa. ISBN 0-515-10467-1pa. YA

Air force officers from *Rolling Thunder* meet in Vietnam in 1967. When the Viet Cong later catch Bannister, a Russian pilot helps him escape, but the pilot dies in an ensuing battle. The other pilots have to deal with a variety of wartime situations, not all of them military.

158. Berg, Lois A. **An Eritrean Family**. Minneapolis, MN: Lerner, 1997. 64p. $16.13; $8.95pa. ISBN 0-8225-3405-3; 0-8225-9755-1pa. (Journey Between Two Worlds). 5-7

Yordanos Kiflu, fourteen, flees with her family from Eritrea, an African country at war with Ethiopia, because of the famine and injustice in their country. Further Reading and Index.

159. Bergman, Tamar. **Along the Tracks**. Michael Swirsky, translator. Boston: Houghton Mifflin, 1991. 245p. $14.95. ISBN 0-395-55328-8. 6-10

Yankele is seven when World War II begins, and his family journeys from Lodz, Poland, toward the Urals in Russia. His father joins the Russian army. As Yankele and his mother travel by train, Yankele gets off during a bombing raid but does not get back on before the train leaves. Thus Yankele begins four years of wandering through Uzbekistan, surviving starvation and incarceration with petty theft and careful hiding. He eventually finds his mother and, miraculously, his father, who had been missing in action, alive in Poland. *Bulletin Blue Ribbon Book.*

160. Bergman, Tamar. **The Boy from Over There**. Hillel Halkin, translator. Boston: Houghton Mifflin, 1988. 181p. $12.95. ISBN 0-395-43077-1. 5-8

When Rami's father brings an orphaned Jewish refugee from Poland to the kibbutz after World War II, some of the people welcome the newcomer and some do not. The boy has to learn to deal with his mother's death, and Rina, his best friend, has to cope with the loss of her father. After they accept the fact that they cannot bring back their parents, they begin to look forward to their life in the Jordan Valley after Israel's recognition as a country in 1948.

161. Berleth, Richard J. **The Twilight Lords: An Irish Chronicle**. New York: Knopf, 1978. 316p. $12.95. ISBN 0-394-49667-1. YA

Sixteenth-century Ireland was a place of clans and chieftains, feudal relationships and tribes, and regional and hereditary conflicts. The English, under Queen Elizabeth, thought that the Irish were an inferior race, and they decided to take the land for themselves between 1579 and 1599. The feudal barons of Ireland (Gerald Fitzgerald, Earl of Desmond; James Fitzmaurice, Captain of Desmond; and Hugh O'Neill, Earl of Tyrone) tried to defend themselves against Peter Carew, Warham St. Leger, Edmund Spenser, Walter Raleigh, Francis Walsingham, and others. The queen's men won after they decimated the population of southern Ireland. They destroyed any of the people standing in their way to wealth and control. Genealogies, Select Chapter Bibliographies, and Index.

162. Berman, Russell. **Paul von Hindenburg**. New York: Chelsea House, 1987. 112p. $18.95. ISBN 0-87754-532-4. (World Leaders Past and Present). 8 up

In 1914, Paul von Hindenburg (1847–1934), as commander of German troops at Tannenberg, defeated the Russian tsar's army. Although von Hindenburg retired from military service in 1911, Kaiser Wilhelm II recalled him and asked him to take charge during World War I. Although the Germans lost World War I, von

Hindenburg became known throughout the world. He did not want to be a politician, but he was twice elected president of the new German republic. In 1933, he made the choice of Adolf Hitler as the chancellor and unwittingly began the horror of Nazi dictatorship. Photographs enhance the text. Chronology, Further Reading, and Index.

163.   Bernard, Bruce. **Van Gogh**. New York: Dorling Kindersley, 1992. 64p. $16.95. ISBN 1-56458-069-5. (Eyewitness Art). 12 up
    Vincent van Gogh (1853–1890) never made money from his art. He never planned to be an artist until he decided to follow that career in his late twenties. The text uses reproductions to give a sense of his life and his art and the influences that shaped both.

164.   Bernhard, Brendan. **Pizarro, Orellana, and the Exploration of the Amazon**. New York: Chelsea House, 1991. 110p. $18.95; $7.95pa. ISBN 0-7910-1305-7; 0-7910-1529-7pa. (World Explorers). 5 up
    Francisco de Orellana (d. c. 1546) and Francisco Pizarro (c. 1475-1541) journeyed through the Amazon Basin in the early sixteenth century. The text also discusses the Inca and the Spanish conquest of South America. Bibliography and Index.

165.   Bernheim, Mark. **Father of the Orphans: The Story of Janusz Korczak**. New York: Lodestar, 1988. 139p. $14.95. ISBN 0-525-67265-6. 6-9
    As a child in Poland, Korczak (born Henryk Goldszmit) was intensely lonely because his parents would not allow him to play with children below their social class. His father then went insane, adding to Korczak's alienation. After Korczak became a doctor, he devoted his time to orphans. He followed many of them to Treblinka in World War II, where they all died. Photographs, Bibliography, and Index.

166.   Bernier-Grand, Carmen T. **Poet and Politician of Puerto Rico: Don Luis Muñoz Marín**. New York: Orchard, 1995. 118p. $15.95. ISBN 0-531-06887-0. 5-8
    Don Luis Muñoz Marín (1898-1980), educated in the United States, wanted to be a poet. But his father's commitment to improving Puerto Rico influenced him so that he too became a politician. After the Liberal Party expelled him, he founded the Popular Democratic Party based on enhancing the lives of ordinary Puerto Rican families. He used aid from the United States to improve Puerto Rican facilities in Operation Bootstrap with his governing principle being "Give a man a fish, and he will have a single meal. Teach him to fish and he can eat the rest of his life." Later Muñoz Marín became the first governor of Puerto Rico in its new status as a commonwealth. Photographs enhance the text. Afterword, Appendix, Sources and Other Information, and Index.

167.   Bernstein, Jeremy. **Albert Einstein and the Frontiers of Physics**. New York: Oxford University Press, 1996. 189p. $19.95. ISBN 0-19-509275-9. (Oxford Portraits in Science). 8 up
    Albert Einstein (1879-1955) revolutionized physics, and Bernstein discusses his theories of relativity, quantum mechanics, and gravitation along with their relevant mathematical formulas. The text also covers his life as the son of Jewish parents born in Germany, his education in Germany and Switzerland, the politics of his time, and other details about his work. He won the Nobel Prize in 1921, and in 1932 he left Europe for the United States and Princeton, before Hitler began his ultimate extermination of the Jews. Further Reading, Chronology, and Index.

168.   Berrill, Margaret. **Mummies, Masks, & Mourners**. Chris Molan, illustrator. New York: Lodestar, Dutton, 1990. 48p. $14.95. ISBN 0-525-67282-6. (Time Detectives). 4-7
    The "grave goods" that archaeologists find buried with the dead often reveal something about the culture and its burial customs. Berrill presents an unusual group of "finds." First are two Stone Age excavations: Çatal Hüyük in Turkey, found in 1958, and Haddenham, near Ely in England, the oldest wooden building ever discovered. From investigations of the pyramids in Egypt come mummies searching for the Field of Reeds. Recent excavations reveal Sumerians in 2500 B.C. Other places excavated include the Siberian Altai horsemen from 400 B.C.; the Lindow Man, who died 2,000 years ago and was recently discovered in a peat bog; the Lady Dai from the Han Dynasty in China, buried 2,100 years previously; Roman memorials in Ephesus; Basket Makers in the American Southwest at Four Corners; Hopewell mounds in the Ohio/Tennessee area; Viking Ship burials; Qilakitsoq of the Inuits, buried in 1475 and found in Greenland; and the Kalabar Ijaw funeral screens from Africa. Fact boxes give additional information about each burial place and its culture. Drawings and photographs, one of a piece of 2,000-year-old preserved tattooed skin, augment the text. Glossary and Index.

169.   Berry, James. **Ajeemah and His Son**. New York: HarperCollins, 1992. 84p. $13.89; $3.95pa. ISBN 0-06-021044-3; 0-06-440523-0pa. 7 up
    Atu, age eighteen, and his father are captured in 1807 in Africa while walking to visit Atu's intended bride. They are sold into slavery and transported to Jamaica. There they become separated, and each spends the rest of his life trying to regain his freedom and reunite with the other. Atu survives until the Jamaican slaves are freed,

on August 1, 1838, but his father does not. *American Library Association Notable Children's Book, American Library Association Best Books for Young Adults, Horn Book Fanfare Honor List, Booklist Books for Youth Editors' Choices, Notable Children's Trade Books in the Field of Social Studies, Bulletin Blue Ribbon Book, Boston Globe-Horn Book Fiction Award,* and *New York Public Library Books for the Teen Age.*

170. Beshore, George. **Science in Ancient China**. New York: Franklin Watts, 1988. 95p. $16.60. ISBN 0-531-10596-2. (First Book). 5-8

An introduction to China and its science precedes chapters on different developments from this culture. They include scanning the heavens, basic science and mathematics, healing and herbal medicine, finding food for the people, roads and canals, tools and technology, and contemporary debt to the culture for its discoveries. Photographs and drawings enhance the text. Glossary, Further Reading, and Index.

171. Beshore, George. **Science in Early Islamic Culture**. New York: Franklin Watts, 1988. 70p. $16.60. ISBN 0-531-10596-2. (First Book). 5-8

An introduction to early Islamic culture and its science precedes chapters on different developments. They include mathematics, astronomy, the study of optics or light and vision, alchemy, and contemporary debt to the culture for its discoveries. Drawings and Reproductions supplement the text. Glossary, Further Reading, and Index.

172. Besson, Jean-Louis, author/illustrator. **October 45: Childhood Memories of the War**. Carol Volk, translator. San Diego, CA: Creative Editions, Harcourt Brace, 1995. 94p. $22. ISBN 0-15-200955-8. 4-8

Jean-Louis Besson, age seven, and his family take a vacation to Normandy in 1939, which the Germans interrupt with the beginning of World War II. The family moves to a small Brittany village from Paris to avoid anticipated bombing and returns during the occupation, during which they face food shortages, rationing, hiding in subway stations during air raids, and the deportation of Jewish friends. To hear about the outside world, they have to secretly listen to British broadcasts. Because his family did not experience the horrors of the war that many faced, Besson's viewpoint in this story is that of a young boy whose main concern is the unpleasant and uncomfortable train ride to Brittany. Each page indicates a month and a year as he tells of the lovely German uniforms and the American ballpoint pens, along with other observations during the period. *Prix Octognone, International Center of Children's Literature, France.*

173. Bianchi, Robert Steven. **The Nubians: People of the Ancient Nile**. Brookfield, CT: Millbrook Press, 1994. 63p. $15.90. ISBN 1-56294-356-1. 5-8

The Nubian civilization developed in southern Egypt about 10,000 years ago, along the banks of the Nile River between the modern cities of Aswan, Egypt, and Khartoum, Sudan, while the pharaohs were building their pyramids to the north. The Egyptians often mentioned the Nubians, but the Nubian written language, Meroitic, did not develop until 250 B.C. They did carve pictures in sandstone, and archaeologists study these along with artifacts discovered in the area to find other clues about the civilization. Important Dates in the History of Ancient Nubia, Find Out More, and Index.

174. Biel, Timothy L. **Charlemagne**. San Diego, CA: Lucent, 1997. 127p. $17.96. ISBN 1-56006-074-3 (The Importance Of). 6 up

Primary and secondary sources help tell the history of the Frankish kingdom and reveal Charlemagne (768-814) and his achievements. The text explores the negative and positive aspects of Charlemagne's character and clearly asserts his influence on the future of Europe. Bibliography, Chronology, Further Reading, Glossary, and Index.

175. Biel, Timothy L. **Pompeii**. San Diego, CA: Lucent, 1989. 64p. $12.95. ISBN 1-56006-000-X. (World Disasters). 5-8

In A.D. 79, Vesuvius erupted and destroyed the ancient city of Pompeii, south of Rome, Italy. Seventeen hundred years later, archaeologists uncovered many of its secrets and exposed the life of the people in the Roman Empire, in general and specifically on that day. Bibliography and Index.

176. Biel, Timothy Levi. **The Black Death**. Maurie Manning and Michael Spackman, illustrators. San Diego, CA: Lucent, 1989. 64p. $12.95. ISBN 1-56006-001-8. 5-7

The title fails to reveal the myriad details included in this book about life in England during the Middle Ages around 1347. Important terms appear in bold type for easy identification of information about the feudal system, the church hierarchy, the growth of cities, the plague itself, and its treatment. Documents from the years 1347 to 1350 chronicle the spread of the plague from the Tatars to Messina, Italy, and up to England via Europe; eventually, the Black Death killed 25 million of the 60 million living in Europe, taking more lives than both World Wars I and II combined. Plague outbreaks continued every decade or so, including a serious outbreak in England during 1665. Not until 1894 did a Swiss scientist, investigating an outbreak in Hong Kong, connect the disease to rats. Glossary, Further Reading, Other Works Consulted, and Index.

177. Biel, Timothy Levi. **The Crusades**. San Diego, CA: Lucent, 1995. 128p. $14.95. ISBN 1-56006-245-2. (World History). 6 up

The text gives a thorough treatment of the crusades, starting with a chronology of the most important dates beginning in 1027 and continuing through 1270. It looks at the different classes of people who went on the journeys and the roles of leaders, including Pope Leo IX, Urban II, Godfrey of Bouillon, Bernard of Clairvaux, King Louis VII, Eleanor of Aquitaine, and Richard the Lionheart. Photographs and reproductions enhance the text. Glossary, Further Reading, Primary Sources, and Index.

178. Bierhorst, John, ed. **The Hungry Woman: Myths and Legends of the Aztecs**. New York: Morrow, 1984. 148p. $11.95; $9pa. ISBN 0-688-02766-0; 0-688-12301-5pa. 5-10

Aztec legends began with the Toltec civilization in its capital, Tula, center of the arts and sciences, which flourished from 150 B.C. through A.D. 850 as Teotihuacán. When the city fell, northern tribes intermarried, and they all became known as Aztecs. Eventually Mexicans founded their capital on the remaining, though undesirable, land, but their armies gained a reputation for fierceness. Thus, by 1440, Mexico, Texcoco, and Tlacopan had formed an alliance. The empire took shape under the fourth ruler, Itzcoatl, and reached its zenith under the ninth ruler, Montezuma II. In the myths two important spirits, Quetzalcoatl (creator) and Tezcatlipoca (destroyer) oppose each other. Because the bearded Quetzalcoatl was supposed to return in the year 1 Reed (Aztec calendar), Montezuma greeted the bearded Cortés in 1519 as if a returning god. Two other important figures in the legends are Tonantzin (Our Mother), identified now with the Lady of Mercy at Guadalupe, and *la llorona*, the weeping woman who lures men to their deaths after she murdered her children. In the stories, separating history from legend is often impossible. Guide to Terms and References.

179. Bierhorst, John. **The Mythology of Mexico and Central America**. New York: Morrow, 1990. 190p. $17. ISBN 0-688-06721-2. YA

Using history as a reference for the stories that have been handed down, the author emphasizes that the term *mythology* does not define what these characters and their exploits mean to the Mesoamerican cultures. Such figures as the Aztec gods Quetzalcoatl and Tlaloc (the rain god), and Chac, the Maya equivalent to Tlaloc, are household words with broad artistic, literary, and even social applications. Bierhorst categorizes the stories within each type identified and discusses their significance. Further References, Glossary, Index.

180. Bierman, John. **Righteous Gentile: The Story of Raoul Wallenberg, Missing Hero of the Holocaust**. 1981. New York: Penguin, 1996. 218p. $11.95pa. ISBN 0-14-024664-9pa. YA

While Adolf Eichmann was boasting of having sent 5 million Jews to their Final Solution, Raoul Wallenberg found his mission in life when the Swedish government summoned him to go to Budapest, Hungary, to help the Jews there. His concern and his actions included creating official-looking Swedish passports that were internationally worthless but that fooled Hungarian Nazi authorities and allowed Jews to leave Hungary. After the war, the Russians imprisoned him but refused to acknowledge that he was still alive. In the late 1970s, information from a recently released political prisoner indicated that a Swede had been in the prison for thirty years. Wallenberg's fate, however, is still uncertain. Bibliography.

181. Biesty, Stephen, and Richard Platt. **Man-of-War**. Boston: Dorling Kindersley, Houghton Mifflin, 1993. 27p. $16.95. ISBN 1-56458-321-X. (Cross-Sections). 4 up

This British warship from the time of Napoleon was a complex building. Detailed illustrations give the cross-sections of the ship. Among the topics covered, along with appropriate pictures, are health, leisure, discipline, navigating, work, cooking and eating, battle stations, sleeping, officers, and admiral's privileges. Glossary and Index.

182. Binchy, Maeve. **The Glass Lake**. New York: Delacorte, 1995. 584p. $23.95. ISBN 0-385-31354-3. New York: Bantam, 1996. 584p. $7.50pa. ISBN 0-440-22159-5pa. YA

In the 1950s in Ireland, Kit McMahon and her friend continue to have differences in their values and emotions. A parallel plot involves Kit's mother, who supposedly drowned when Kit was younger, but who really went to London with a lover. Successful in business, Kit's mother pretends to be the mother's friend and begins communicating with Kit, wanting to be near her as Kit passes through her teen years.

183. Birch, Beverley. **Marie Curie**. Milwaukee, WI: Gareth Stevens, 1988. 68p. $16.95. ISBN 0-55532-818-0. (People Who Have Helped the World). 7-9

When Marie Curie (1867–1934) was a young girl in Warsaw, Poland, Polish law forbade education of women past secondary school. Marie Sklodowska's family had little money, because several family members had become ill. Therefore, Marie and her sister worked so that the sister could go to Paris to study; Marie was to join her later. Marie went to Paris when she was twenty-three, learned French and physics simultaneously, and became first in her class. She met the chief of labs at the Sorbonne, Pierre Curie, and they began to work together and soon married. Curie read about Henri Becquerel's work on x-rays and decided to use it as a basis for her doctor of science research (she was the first female doctor of science in Europe). She used an electrometer to find that Becquerel's x-rays came from uranium and thorium, but also from unidentified sources. She discovered two new elements, polonium and radium. She and Pierre had to sift through tons of pitchblende to collect enough radium to prove its existence. They also discovered *induced radioactivity;* that is, anything put near radium becomes radioactive. What they did not realize was that they were suffering from radiation sickness themselves, which preyed on their health as it did to other researchers who were unaware of its dangers. Marie Curie won a Nobel Prize for Physics in 1903 and one for Chemistry in 1912; her daughter and her husband won a third for the family. After Pierre's early death, after he was run over by a horse and carriage, Marie Curie became the first female professor at the Sorbonne. Then, during World War I, she created a portable x-ray machine to take to the front so that doctors could more quickly locate shrapnel in soldiers' bodies. Radiation sickness eventually killed her in 1934. To Find Out More, List of New Words, Important Dates, and Index.

184.   **The Birth of Modern Europe**. Remo Berselli, illustrator; Mary DiIanni, translator. Austin, TX: Raintree/Steck-Vaughn, 1993. 72p. $17.97. ISBN 0-8114-3325-0. (History of the World). 7 up
    This overview uses informative illustrations and clear maps to complement the text, which discusses history beginning with the early 1300s and continuing through the mid-1500s. Two-page topics cover the political, economic, and cultural changes of the times, including the end of the Byzantine Empire, the Mongols and Turks, the Hundred Years' War, Italy's changes, art, the church and its troubles, England and France after 1450, the Rhine, the Renaissance, Charles V, the "New World," and the Protestant Reformation. Glossary and Index.

185.   Bisel, Sara C. **The Secrets of Vesuvius: Exploring the Mysteries of an Ancient Buried City**. New York: Scholastic, 1990. 64p. $6.95pa. ISBN 0-590-43851-4pa. (Time Quest Book). 4-7
    Alternating chapters of historical fiction and of history present the story of an archaeologist who, in 1982, first began exhuming the bones of people buried in Herculaneum by the sixty-five feet of volcanic material blown from Mount Vesuvius in A.D. 79. Pliny recorded his view of the volcano from twenty miles across the bay, and his uncle, who had tried to get closer, died in it. At Pompeii, on the other side of the mountain, twelve feet of ash and pumice buried the inhabitants. Bisel's careful assessment of the bones and the artifacts surrounding them weave an interesting story of what the life of a slave girl serving in a wealthy family might have been—including her sore gums with two recently pulled teeth. Glossary, Recommended Further Reading, and pictures of the Buried Town through the Ages. *Outstanding Science Trade Books for Children.*

186.   Bishop, Claire Huchet. **Twenty and Ten**. William Pène du Bois, illustrator. 1952. New York: Peter Smith, 1984. 76p. $17.75. ISBN 0-8446-6168-6. New York: Puffin, Penguin, 1991. 76p. $3.99pa. ISBN 0-14-031076-2pa. 5-9
    During World War II in France, Janet and twenty of her classmates are evacuated to the countryside with the Catholic sister who teaches them. When ten Jewish children arrive and hide in a nearby cave, all risk their lives by denying any knowledge of the children to the Nazis who come questioning. They continue to feed the children as long as needed. *Child Study Children's Book Committee at Bank Street College Award.*

187.   Bitton-Jackson, Livia. **I Have Lived a Thousand Years: Growing Up in the Holocaust**. New York: Simon & Schuster, 1997. 224p. $17. ISBN 0-689-81022-9. 7-10
    When Hungarian Jew Elli Friedmann is thirteen in 1944, she and her family are deported to Auschwitz. Since she is tall and has blond braids, she is not sent immediately to the crematorium. Instead, she and her mother survive much trauma and horror with their courage and ingenuity.

188.   Bjork, Christine, and Lena Anderson, author/illustrators. **Linnea in Monet's Garden**. Joan Sandin, translator. Stockholm, Sweden: R&S/New York: Farrar, Straus & Giroux, 1987. 53p. $15. ISBN 91-29-58314-4. 4-7
    Linnea and her friend Mr. Bloom go from Sweden to Paris to visit the Marmottan Museum, where many of Monet's paintings hang. Then they go to Giverny, Monet's garden outside Paris, where Linnea sees some of the lovely scenes he painted. The text also includes information about Monet's life as an Impressionist painter (1840–1926). What Happened When.

189.   Black, Wallace B., and Jean F. Blashfield. **Bataan and Corregidor**. New York: Crestwood House, 1991. 48p. $12.95. ISBN 0-89686-557-6. (World War II 50th Anniversary). 5-8
    After the attack on Pearl Harbor, the Japanese went to the Philippines. Japanese air attacks led the United States to use Corregidor in Manila Bay as the command post while Bataan, part of the island of Luzon across from Manila, was the stronghold for troops to hold off the invading Japanese. The Battle of Bataan under General MacArthur failed, and on April 9, 1942, the Allies surrendered it to the Japanese. Then Corregidor was surrendered on May 6, 1942. Black-and-white photographs supplement the text. Glossary and Index.

190. Black, Wallace B., and Jean F. Blashfield. **Battle of Britain**. New York: Crestwood House, 1991. 48p. $12.95. ISBN 0-89686-553-3. (World War II 50th Anniversary). 5-8

When the German *Luftwaffe* bombed Great Britain for three months in 1940, it fortunately made some errors. A Channel battle ensued from July 10 until August 12. Then the Eagle Attack occurred from August 13 to September 6, followed by the Blitz from September 7 to 30. The courage of both the British public and the British flyers contributed to the *Luftwaffe*'s failure to achieve its goals. Black-and-white photographs highlight the text. Glossary and Index.

191. Black, Wallace B., and Jean F. Blashfield. **Battle of the Atlantic**. New York: Crestwood House, 1991. 48p. $12.95. ISBN 0-89686-558-4. (World War II 50th Anniversary). 4-9

This account of the Battle of the Atlantic tells of the struggle that the Allied forces had in trying to keep the North Atlantic free of German U-boats, or submarines, during World War II. On September 3, 1939, when the Germans torpedoed the *Athenia*, a British ocean liner with 1,300 passengers, they claimed that they thought it was an armed merchant ship. Photos and diagrams show the blitzkrieg at sea. U-boats and bombers, along with convoys to Russia, appeared before the U.S. Navy joined the battle, and the Allies fought back. Although U-boats were discovered off the coast of New York, antisubmarine warfare helped control them. Black-and-white photographs augment the text. Closer Look at German U-Boats and Allied Ships and Planes, Glossary, and Index.

192. Black, Wallace B., and Jean F. Blashfield. **Battle of the Bulge**. New York: Crestwood House, 1992. 48p. $12.95. ISBN 0-89686-568-1. (World War II 50th Anniversary). 5-8

The road to Ardennes started in 1944. The Watch on the Rhine was Hitler's plan to divide the American and British attack before the Battle of the Bulge, December 16, 1944. He failed, but with Bastogne under siege, the German commander asked for an Allied surrender. The Allied commander, McAuliffe, replied, "Nuts!" On December 26, General Patton broke through the German lines and stopped the siege. Nordwind and Bodenplatte were two plans of the German offense that failed, and the Germans withdrew by January 22, 1945. The Bridge at Remagen was where the Allies crossed into German territory on March 7, 1945. Black-and-white photographs highlight the text. Glossary and Index.

193. Black, Wallace B., and Jean F. Blashfield. **Blitzkrieg**. New York: Crestwood House, 1991. 48p. $12.95. ISBN 0-89686-552-5. (World War II 50th Anniversary). 5-8

In 1939, the Germans attacked Poland. In the "lightning war" of the *Blitzkrieg,* they used tanks to swoop across the countryside with aircraft and artillery supporting them. Names such as *Panzer* (tanks), *Luftwaffe* (air force), *Wehrmacht* (German army), and *Stuka* (dive bombers) became common words. Two days later, on September 3, 1939, England and France declared war on Germany, because they had promised to support Poland. War in Scandinavia followed, first against the Soviets and then against the Germans. The battle for France began when the Germans invaded Holland in 1940. People were rescued from France through Dunkirk on May 26, after the Germans arrived on May 19; France surrendered on June 6, 1940. Black-and-white photographs supplement the text. Glossary and Index.

194. Black, Wallace B., and Jean F. Blashfield. **Bombing Fortress Europe**. New York: Crestwood House, 1992. 48p. $12.95. ISBN 0-89686-562-2. (World War II 50th Anniversary). 5 up

Hitler's "Fortress Europe" was to take back lands Germany had lost during World War I, such as the Saar (the Rhineland bordering France and Memel on Germany's northern border) and Poland. By the end of 1940, Hitler controlled all of central and most of western Europe. Great Britain's only recourse was to bomb the Fortress, beginning in 1941; thus the Eighth Air Force was born. After four disastrous missions, the Ploesti raid, Operation Pointblank, Schweinfurt, and Regensburg, Britain began preparations for D-Day and the Battle for Berlin. Black-and-white photographs augment the text. Glossary and Index.

195. Black, Wallace B., and Jean F. Blashfield. **D-Day**. New York: Crestwood House, 1992. 48p. $12.95. ISBN 0-89686-566-6. (World War II 50th Anniversary). 5 up

In planning for D-Day, the Allies decided to invade the Normandy beaches to retake France. Operation Neptune called for naval operations to land on the Normandy beaches while protected from the air by the Allied forces. The Germans delayed in their pursuit, and the June 6, 1944, Allied invasion was successful. Black-and-white photographs supplement the text. Glossary and Index.

196. Black, Wallace B., and Jean F. Blashfield. **Desert Warfare**. New York: Crestwood House, 1992. 48p. $12.95. ISBN 0-89686-561-4. (World War II 50th Anniversary). 5 up

Italy had a disaster in Africa when the British took control of East Africa in February 1941. The German army, with Rommel, the Desert Fox, in charge, came to rescue the Italian forces. The British retreated to El Alamein, 240 miles from Egypt, but Montgomery took charge and defeated Rommel. The Allied Operation Torch invasion led to the race for Tunis. Next was the Battle of Kasserine Pass, which the British won because the Germans could not agree on the best plan of attack. Victory at Hill 609 prepared the way for the May 13, 1943, invasion of Italy. Black-and-white photographs supplement the text. Glossary and Index.

197. Black, Wallace B., and Jean F. Blashfield. **Flattops at War**. New York: Crestwood House, 1992. 48p. $12.95. ISBN 0-89686-559-2. (World War II 50th Anniversary). 5 up

After Pearl Harbor, the Battle of Coral Sea took place in February 1942. The Battle of Midway followed in June 1942. In these battles, the flattops (aircraft carriers) were most important. They continued to escort U-boats and participated in the Marianas "Turkey Shoot," June 19-21, 1944. Photographs of the war with flattops and planes of the U.S. Navy correlate with the text. Glossary and Index.

198. Black, Wallace B., and Jean F. Blashfield. **Guadalcanal**. New York: Crestwood House, 1992. 48p. $12.95. ISBN 0-89686-560-6. (World War II 50th Anniversary). 5 up

The Japanese attacked Midway Island on June 4, 1942. Following the attack, the Allies decided to invade Guadalcanal in August. Land battles ensued, as did sea battles, culminating with the Battle of the Solomon Islands on November 12, 1942. The Air Force helped, and the Japanese finally withdrew from Guadalcanal in February 1943. Black-and-white photographs augment the text. Index.

199. Black, Wallace B., and Jean F. Blashfield. **Hiroshima and the Atomic Bomb**. New York: Crestwood House, 1993. 48p. $12.95. ISBN 0-89686-571-1. (World War II 50th Anniversary). 5 up

In 1942, the Manhattan Project in Los Alamos and uranium manufacturing at Oak Ridge, Tennessee, simultaneously allowed the creation of the atomic bomb. After Iwo Jima and Okinawa, the Allies firebombed Tokyo in March 1945. Although the Japanese were starving, they kept fighting. The *Enola Gay* dropped "Little Boy," the first atomic bomb ordered by President Truman, on August 6, 1945, at 8:16 A.M. After the second bomb ("Fat Man") on Nagasaki three days later, Japan surrendered. Black-and-white photographs supplement the text. Glossary and Index.

200. Black, Wallace B., and Jean F. Blashfield. **Invasion of Italy**. New York: Crestwood House, 1992. 48p. $12.95. ISBN 0-89686-565-7. (World War II 50th Anniversary). 5 up

In 1943, Operation Husky marked the invasion of Sicily to gain control of the Mediterranean Sea. The Allied forces landed there on July 10, 1943, under British Field Marshal Sir Harold Alexander, and Italy surrendered on September 1. Then the Allies invaded southern Italy. The Italian fleet surrendered, and the Germans retreated toward Rome. The Allies became temporarily trapped at Anzio because of misunderstandings and delays. The Battle for Monte Cassino occurred in late 1944, and Rome finally fell on June 4, 1944. The Germans made their new line 150 miles north of Rome before they surrendered Italy on April 29, 1945, after Mussolini's assassination. Black-and-white photographs augment the text. Glossary and Index.

201. Black, Wallace B., and Jean F. Blashfield. **Island Hopping in the Pacific**. New York: Crestwood House, 1992. 48p. $12.95. ISBN 0-89686-567-3. (World War II 50th Anniversary). 5 up

Japan threatened Australia in 1942, and the first encounter with naval forces occurred at the Battle of the Coral Sea. The strategy of island-hopping began from Guadalcanal and Papua, New Guinea. The Japanese had Rabaul, a fortress on the island of New Britain, that the Allies decided to capture after taking the Solomons and New Guinea. In 1944, the Allies' target date for retaking Philippines and Formosa (Taiwan) was February 1945, but they succeeded by June 1944. General MacArthur returned to the Philippines in October 1944 and plotted to take Iwo Jima. Black-and-white photographs augment the text. Glossary and Index.

202. Black, Wallace B., and Jean F. Blashfield. **Iwo Jima and Okinawa**. New York: Crestwood House, 1993. 48p. $12.95. ISBN 0-89686-569-X. (World War II 50th Anniversary). 5 up

The battles of Coral Sea and Midway occurred in 1945 before the Marines began landing on Iwo Jima beaches. They captured Mount Suribachi on February 23, 1945. Then they continued until victory on June 20 with Operation Iceberg. The Allied forces needed Okinawa for a base from which to launch other attacks on the Japanese. Black-and-white photographs highlight the text. Glossary and Index.

203. Black, Wallace B., and Jean F. Blashfield. **Jungle Warfare**. New York: Crestwood House, 1992. 48p. $12.95. ISBN 0-89686-563-0. (World War II 50th Anniversary). 5 up

In January 1942, Japan invaded Burma. The Allied commanders Vinegar Joe Stillwell, Chiang Kai-Shek, and Claire Chennault of the Flying Tigers in France, disagreed about approaches to the difficult jungle terrain. Then Wingate's Chindit Raiders, British guerrilla forces, completed daring missions so that Wingate earned the label of "half genius and half mad." Merrill's Marauders were America's jungle fighters. Also in this area were the U.S. Air Force and the OSS, forerunner of the CIA. The last campaigns in the China-India-Burma area occurred in 1945. Black-and-white photographs supplement the text. Glossary and Index.

204. Black, Wallace B., and Jean F. Blashfield. **Pearl Harbor!** New York: Crestwood House, 1991. 48p. $12.95. ISBN 0-89686-555-X. (World War II 50th Anniversary). 5-8

In 1941, when the Japanese bombed the Pacific fleet at Pearl Harbor, America was ill-prepared for combat but still declared war on Japan. This account discusses the Japanese strategy and tactics and why the American forces were surprised by the attack. Black-and-white photographs complement the text. Glossary and Index.

205. Black, Wallace B., and Jean F. Blashfield. **Russia at War**. New York: Crestwood House, 1991. 48p. $12.95. ISBN 0-89686-556-8. (World War II 50th Anniversary). 4-8

The Germans attacked Russia on June 22, 1941, although Joseph Stalin and Adolf Hitler were supposedly friends. The major points of engagement included Barbarossa, where the Germans invaded; the Siege of Leningrad, which lasted 900 days; Operation Typhoon, during which Moscow awaited attack; the Battle of Stalingrad; and the beginning of the end at Kursk. Other information on partisans and guerrilla warfare also appears. Glossary and Index.

206. Black, Wallace B., and Jean F. Blashfield. **Victory in Europe**. New York: Crestwood House, 1992. 48p. $12.95. ISBN 0-89686-570-3. (World War II 50th Anniversary). 5 up

The text gives an overview of World War II in Europe, the trek eastward from the Rhine, the Russian thousand-mile front, Germany surrounded, the Battle of Berlin in 1945, and the unconditional German surrender on May 7, 1945. The book also covers the Holocaust, starting with *Kristallnacht* (Crystal Night), as it looks at the cost of the war to all. Capsule biographies of Allied leaders end the information. Black-and-white photographs supplement the text. Glossary and Index.

207. Black, Wallace B., and Jean F. Blashfield. **War Behind the Lines**. New York: Crestwood House, 1992. 48p. $12.95. ISBN 0-89686-564-9. (World War II 50th Anniversary). 5 up

During World War II, battles behind the lines helped win the war. The text looks at the British Secret Services, the OSS of the Americans, the organization of the Resistance against the Nazis, the *Maquis* or Resistance heroes, women and the underground war, the Resistance in Norway, *Chetniks* (Yugoslavians) and Partisans (Communists against Hitler in other countries), and Russian Partisans. Heroes of the Resistance include Major General William Donovan, Marshal Tito, and General Charles de Gaulle. Glossary and Index.

208. Blair, David Nelson. **Fear the Condor**. New York: Lodestar, 1992. 138p. $15. ISBN 0-525-67381-4. 7 up

While her father fights in the Chaco War during 1932, Bartolina, age ten, gets new duties at the patrón's hacienda and also has to help her grandparents on their farm. She speaks only Aymara, but she learns "ink weaving" (writing) by the time her father returns from fighting. Then she is able to help him prepare for meetings of men who are planning to unionize so they can get fair rights to their lands. Bartolina knows that education is the one thing that can help her family escape from its bonds.

209. Blair, David Nelson. **The Land and People of Bolivia**. New York: Lippincott, 1990. 208p. $15.89. ISBN 0-397-32383-2. (Portraits of the Nations). 5-8

A combination of current information and historical background shows that Bolivia was an important site of the Tiahuanaco culture between 400 B.C. and A.D. 1200 on Lake Titicaca. The Incas rose to power in the area by the 1520s, with an empire of 6 million people stretching over 2,500 miles. The Spanish explorers Cortés and later Pizarro arrived and conquered the Incas. Simon Bolívar freed the Bolivians from Spanish rule by 1825. In 1952, the Chaco War erupted, with workers challenging their employers. By 1979, Bolivia had a female president, Lydia Tejada. Further Reading, Filmography, Diskography, and Index.

210. Blakely, Roger K. **Wolfgang Amadeus Mozart**. San Diego, CA: Lucent, 1993. 112p. $16.95. ISBN 1-56006-028-X. (The Importance Of). 5-8

Wolfgang Amadeus Mozart (1756-1791) rarely used his middle name, preferring Amadée or no middle name. Sometimes he composed as he played; other times he seemed to be merely writing down the music that was all in his head. Mozart produced music both for his own pleasure and for money. His music reflected his era, and he wrote sacred music as well as the orderly secular music expected during the Enlightenment. He enjoyed parties and had a sense of humor, but he realized the gift of each day and the burden of bringing renown to Austria, his country, through his music. Notes, Glossary, For Further Reading, Works Consulted, and Index.

211. Blassingame, Wyatt. **Ponce de León**. Russ Hoover, illustrator. New York: Chelsea Juniors, 1991. 100p. $14.95. ISBN 0-7910-1493-2. (Discovery Biography). 3-7

Juan Ponce de León (1474-1521) learned to be a soldier as a boy so that he could fight the Moors in Spain. He decided to join Columbus's second voyage, and he and his family spent the rest of his life in the New World. He is still credited with discovering Florida, although John Cabot may have been there fifteen years previously, or the Norsemen 500 years before.

212. Bles, Mark. **Child at War: The True Story of a Young Belgian Resistance Fighter**. San Francisco: Mercury House, 1991. 301p. $20.95. ISBN 1-56279-004-8. YA

Hortense Daman was a Belgium partisan who survived imprisonment at the Ravensbruck concentration camp in Germany. Bles, who served in the British Army during World War II, adds information about Flemish collaborators and daily life under the Nazis, along with relevant photographs. Daman began to work with the Resistance when she was thirteen years old. She survived dangerous missions, but was finally caught, imprisoned, tortured, and made to do slave labor. How she survived is a story of bravery. Bibliography.

213. Blue, Rose, and Corrine Naden. **People of Peace**. Brookfield, CT: Millbrook Press, 1994. 80p. $18.90. ISBN 1-56294-409-6. 5-8

Because some people refused to compromise with the status quo and instead worked for peace, they made the world better than before. Some of these people won the Nobel Peace Prize for their efforts, but they have all saved lives. The people presented here are Andrew Carnegie (United States, 1835-1919), Jane Addams (United States, 1860-1935), Woodrow Wilson (United States, 1856-1924), Mohandas Gandhi (India, 1869-1948), Ralph Bunche (United States, 1904-1971), Dag Hammarskjöld (Sweden, 1905-1961), Jimmy Carter (United States, b. 1924), Desmond Tutu (South Africa, b. 1931), Oscar Arias Sanchez (Costa Rica, b. 1941), Betty Williams (Northern Ireland, b. 1943), and Mairead Corrigan Maguire (Northern Ireland, b. 1944). Conclusion, For Further Reading, and Index.

214. Blumberg, Rhoda. **The Remarkable Voyages of Captain Cook**. New York: Bradbury, 1991. 137p. $18.95. ISBN 0-02-711682-4. 6 up

James Cook (1728-1779) took three voyages around the world. Possible riches in the southern continents lured him to take the first two; on the third he was searching for the Northwest Passage between the Atlantic and the Pacific Oceans. He traveled from the heat of Tahiti to the cold of Antarctica and to other places around the globe. He stayed in Hawaii on his last voyage, departed with gifts, and returned after a storm. The Hawaiians were unhappy to see him return, and they killed him. Photographs augment the text. Notes, Bibliography, and Index. *Bulletin Blue Ribbon Book.*

215. Boas, Jacob, ed. **We Are Witnesses: Five Diaries of Teenagers Who Died in the Holocaust**. New York: Edge, Henry Holt, 1995. 196p. $15.95. ISBN 0-8050-3702-0. 6 up

Teenagers who did not survive the World War II Holocaust wrote the diaries presented in this book. They are David Rubinowicz in Poland, Yitzhak Rudashevski in Lithuania, Moshe Ze'ev Flinker in Belgium, Éva Heyman in Hungary, and Anne Frank in Holland. The diaries all give insight into the fears and hopes that these young people had during their short lives. Notes and Index. *American Library Association Notable Books for Young Adults* and *Notable Children's Trade Books in the Field of Social Studies.*

216. Boateng, Faustine Ama. **Asante**. New York: Rosen, 1996. 64p. $15.95. ISBN 0-8239-1975-7. (The Heritage Library of African People). 7 up

The text examines the history of the Asante in Ghana along with the social life and customs, religion, education, and arts. Further Reading, Glossary, and Index.

217. Bober, Natalie S. **Marc Chagall: Painter of Dreams**. Vera Rosenberry, illustrator. Philadelphia: Jewish Publication Society, 1991. 142p. $14.95. ISBN 0-8276-0379-7. (Young Biography). 8 up

The Hasidic movement of Judaism did not condone the painting of images, but Marc Chagall overcame this prohibition because of his intense love of paint and color. His family endured pogroms while living in St. Petersburg, and he went to Paris in 1921 with his wife and daughter. In 1937, he became a French citizen, but in 1940 he had to escape from France to New York. He tried new art forms throughout his life and worked with stained glass in the latter half of his career, but the Jewish influence was always an underlying theme. Glossary of Art Terms, Important Dates, Index, and Works by Marc Chagall.

218. Bond, Nancy. **Another Shore**. 1988. New York: Margaret K. McElderry, 1991. 384p. $5pa. ISBN 0-689-50463-2pa. 7 up

In this historical fantasy, Lyn, age seventeen, goes to Louisbourg on Nova Scotia in Canada with her mother. She gets a job as an animator (costumed guide) portraying one of the eighteenth-century residents, Elizabeth Bernard. Lyn finds herself in Elizabeth's family with the family thinking she is Elizabeth, although her mistakes irritate them. Another animator also finds himself in the past with her, and he becomes more and more frightened at not being able to get away. When Lyn finds that she cannot return to the present, she decides to make a new life with the eighteenth-century Frenchman she has come to love.

219. Bond, Nancy. **Truth to Tell**. New York: Margaret K. McElderry, 1994. 336p. $17.95. ISBN 0-689-50601-5. 7 up

In 1958, Alice, age fourteen, and her mother move from Cambridge, England, to New Zealand, where her mother has accepted a job writing the family history of an old woman. Alice's stepfather follows after he finishes his summer job on the Channel ferry. Alice resents her mother's decision, but the old woman's real story, as well as Alice's, is unexpected.

220. Bonvillain, Nancy. **The Haidas: People of the Northwest Coast**. Brookfield, CT: Millbrook Press, 1994. 64p. $15.90. ISBN 1-56294-491-6. (Native Americans). 5-8

The Haida ancestors settled on the Queen Charlotte Islands in British Columbia, Canada, c. 1000. Many died in Alaska after 1750 from smallpox. Part of their culture was the celebration of potlatches and ceremonial dances that Canada outlawed in 1884. In the twentieth century, the Haidas joined with the Tlingits to file a land claim against the United States in Alaska, which they won. As they have become integrated into Alaskan and Canadian life, they have tried to preserve their identity through their traditions and artifacts. Important Dates, Glossary, Bibliography, and Index.

221. Boorstin, Daniel J. **The Creators: A History of Heroes of the Imagination**. New York: Random House, 1992. 811p. $30. ISBN 0-394-54395-5. New York: Vintage, 1993. 811p. $17pa. ISBN 0-679-74375-8pa. YA

This sequel to *The Discoverers* (1984) investigates people who have accomplished something new in the arts. Most of the chapters are essays within themselves, but their themes connect. Boorstin covers an enormous range of information, from ancient history to the present and across countries, as he examines what being creative means. Annotated Chapter Bibliographies and Index.

222. Booth, Martin. **War Dog: A Novel**. New York: Simon & Schuster, 1997. 133p. $15. ISBN 0-689-81380-5. 6-9

The owner of the black Labrador, Jet, has trained Jet to poach. After her owner is arrested, she begins to serve the British army in World War II by finding wounded soldiers and casualties in bombed cities. When she accompanies the military to Italy, she encounters her original owner.

223. Boraks-Nemetz, Lillian. **The Old Brown Suitcase: A Teenager's Story of War and Peace**. Port Angeles, WA: Ben-Simon, 1994. 148p. $9.50pa. ISBN 0-914539-10-8pa. 6-10

In alternating chapters, the reader follows Slava's story as a child in the Warsaw ghetto and as a teenager safe in Canada. By starting with a Canadian segment, the author alleviates readers' fears that Slava might die in World War II's Nazi camps. Slava's parents change her name to Elizabeth, but wealthy, unfeeling children who have no idea what she has endured still persecute her for being Jewish and for being unable to speak English well. Her father, trained to be a lawyer, finally buys a delicatessen, but never enjoys the work. Slava remembers her little sister who did not survive the war, but one boy is kind to her, and she soon realizes that she cares for him more than just as a friend. *Shelia A. Egoff's Children's Literature Prize of Canada.*

224. Bortz, Fred. **Catastrophe! Great Engineering Failure—and Success**. New York: W. H. Freeman, 1995. 80p. $19.95; $13.95pa. ISBN 0-7167-6538-1; 0-7167-6539-Xpa. (Scientific American's Mystery of Science). 5-9

Six engineering debacles have changed the lives of people who experienced them and lived as well as the families of those who died. The six discussed in the text are the collapse of the Kansas City Hyatt skywalk in 1980; the Tacoma Narrows Bridge in 1940; the crash of Eastern Airlines Flight 401 in Florida in 1972; the U.S. Space Shuttle *Challenger* disaster in 1986; nuclear power plant accidents (Three-Mile Island in 1979 and Chernobyl in 1986); and "The Great Northeast Blackout" of 1965. By explaining the science behind each disaster, the text shows how inadequate planning caused the problems and how engineers have corrected them. Photographs and Index.

225. Bosco, Peter. **World War I**. New York: Facts on File, 1991. 124p. $17.95. ISBN 0-8160-2460-X. (America at War). 7-12

Before World War I, the United States had established a policy of isolationism. Bosco tells why America changed its policy to enter World War I and discusses military logistics, political maneuvering, and the terrors of battle. He focuses on several conflicts such as Belleau Wood and the Argonne. Bibliography and Index.

226. Bosse, Malcolm. **Captives of Time**. New York: Delacorte, 1987. 255p. $14.95. ISBN 0-385-29583-9. 8 up

Anne, age sixteen, and her mute brother Niklas, age twelve, survive a fourteenth-century raid on their farm, but they see soldiers kill their mother after raping her and find their father dead in the family paper mill. They journey to find an uncle; when they arrive, he is working on an invention. Anne's abilities help him develop the clock, an item that provokes fear and anger among citizens. Among the other incidents with which Anne must cope are her own rape, the murder of her love, and the plague. Many of the attitudes and problems inherent in the Middle Ages become clear in this story.

227. Bosse, Malcolm. **Deep Dream of the Rain Forest**. New York: Farrar, Straus & Giroux, 1993. 179p. $15. ISBN 0-7862-0145-2. 7 up

Harry Windsor, age fifteen, accompanies his uncle on a 1920 expedition to the jungles of Borneo. Bayang, a young Iban tribesman, captures Harry because he thinks that Harry can help him and an outcast lame Iban girl called Duck Foot. Bayang wants Harry to support a "dream quest" to become the tribal leader.

228. Bosse, Malcolm. **The Examination**. New York: Farrar, Straus & Giroux, 1994. 296p. $17. ISBN 0-374-32234-1. 6-10

Around 1448, in China, Hong Chen decides to sell his prized fighting crickets to finance his brother's trip to Beijing to take the government examinations that can earn both brothers fame and lifelong wealth. Troubles and tests of varied kinds—rains, famine, locusts, and pirates—occur on the journey. They eventually arrive, and Hong delivers to a barber a mysterious letter that he has carried throughout the trip. Hong finds that he must take his own "exam" in Beijing while his brother exhibits his knowledge of and belief in Confucius. Both succeed, with Chen being welcomed inside the Forbidden City and Hong finding his future.

229. Bosse, Malcolm. **Tusk and Stone**. Emeryville, CA: Front Street, 1995. 244p. $15.95. ISBN 1-886910-01-4. 6-10

As Arjun travels across India in the seventh century, bandits attack the caravan, kill people, kidnap his sister, and drug him before selling him into the army. Arjun humbly begins to rebuild his life, saying that he will serve those well who bought his soldiering. He rises in the military to become an elephant handler and then a mounted soldier. His Brahmin pride wins over his concept of karma when he is a warrior and faces a rival who almost destroys him. Then he must again rebuild his life, this time as a stonecutter and carver. In that profession, he becomes introspective about his spiritual beliefs.

230. Bowler, Mike. **Trains**. Steve Herridge, Paul Higgens, and Martin Woodward, illustrators. Austin, TX: Raintree/Steck-Vaughn, 1995. 32p. $13.98. ISBN 0-8114-6192-0. (Pointers). 3-7

The first locomotive ran along tracks in 1804. Two-page spreads of text and illustration present the history of trains. Topics and trains discussed are early railroads (c. 1825), the first inter-city railroad (1829), American locomotives (mid-nineteenth century), long-distance express trains (c. 1900), express steam trains, the largest steam engine, long-distance diesels, diesel-electric trains, high-speed diesels, subways, and the fastest trains currently in use. Glossary and Index.

231. Bradford, Karleen. **There Will Be Wolves**. New York: Lodestar, 1996. 195p. $15.99. ISBN 0-525-67539-6. 7-10

Ursula has learned the skill of healing with herbs from her father, an apothecary. When the community accuses her of witchcraft, she leaves, deciding to travel from her home in Germany to Constantinople as part of the People's Crusade in the eleventh century. Along with falling in love with Bruno, she experiences the difficulties of a pilgrimage and the often hostile interactions among those in the group.

232. Bradford, Sarah. **Elizabeth: A Biography of Britain's Queen**. New York: Farrar, Straus & Giroux, 1996. 564p. $30. ISBN 0-374-14749-3. YA

After living quietly with her family until her father George VI unexpectedly became king, Queen Elizabeth herself came to the throne in 1952 at his death. Her subjects see her as decent and loyal. She has raised her four children as well as she can while fulfilling the responsibilities of the crown and trying to ignore her husband's peccadilloes. This biography relies on informers, friends, and relatives as sources. Within the realm, women still take the role of second-class citizens, with men generally forming the circle of power around the queen. Her biography can only be an interim account, because the story as yet has no ending. Bibliography and Index.

233. Bradley, Catherine. **Hitler and the Third Reich**. New York: Franklin Watts, Gloucester, 1990. 62p. $13.95. ISBN 0-531-17228-7. (World War II Biographies). 6 up

Although Adolf Hitler (1889-1945) created many myths about his childhood to support his rise to greatness, he was particularly ordinary. When he served in the army during World War I, he was not promoted because his superiors did not think he had leadership qualities. This nondescript beginning to the career of a man who almost controlled the world twenty years later indicates that Hitler was very good at covering his real intentions until horrendous economic times allowed him to begin his program to "purify" Germany. Photographs, Chronology, Glossary, Further Reading, and Index.

234. Bradley, Catherine. **Kazakhstan**. Brookfield, CT: Millbrook Press, 1992. 32p. $15.90. ISBN 1-56294-308-1. (Former Soviet States). 4-7

The text discusses the cultural background, politics, economics, and history of the former Soviet republic of Kazakhstan. Rock pictures, stone tools, and cave paintings dated as 40,000 years old have been found in the area. Kazakhstan's current peoples are mainly Muslim, though some follow Sufism. Glossary and Index.

235.   Bradley, Marion Zimmer. **Forest House**. New York: Viking, 1994. 476p. $21.95. ISBN 0-670-84454-3. New York: New American Library, 1995. 476p. $14.95pa. ISBN 0-451-45424-3pa. YA

In Roman Britain, Eilan, a Druid, falls in love with Gaius, a Roman whose mother was a Druid and whose father is an important officer in the Roman legions. The inevitable clash between the two cultures occurs with Eilan's belief in the cult of the Goddess, where the priestess has the power, and Gaius's belief in a patriarchal society. Their son offers hope of unification.

236.   Bradshaw, Gillian. **The Beacon at Alexandria**. 1986. New York: Soho, 1994. 374p. $14pa. ISBN 1-56947-010-3pa. YA

Claris, age fifteen, faces a prearranged marriage to the cruel governor of Ephesus in A.D. 371, but her brother helps her escape to Alexandria, Egypt. Pretending to be a eunuch, she begins to study medicine as she has always wanted. She graduates and becomes a respected physician, but events expose her background. During her second escape, she finds herself with the man she has loved for several years.

237.   Bradshaw, Gillian. **The Bearkeeper's Daughter**. Boston: Houghton Mifflin, 1987. 310p. $18.95. ISBN 0-395-43620-6. YA

As his father dies of plague, John, age twenty-four, finds out that his mother is the Empress Theodora of Constantinople. He goes to reconcile with her, and she gets him a job so that he will not reveal their relationship. He has no ambition, but when Justinian accuses him of lying about his relationship with his mother, he refuses to speak against her.

238.   Brady, James. **The Coldest War: A Memoir of Korea**. New York: Orion, Crown, 1990. 248p. $19.95. ISBN 0-517-57690-2. New York: Pocket Books, 1995. 248p. $6.50pa. ISBN 0-671-72525-4pa. YA

In a highly personal memoir, Brady discusses his participation in the war, which began in 1950 with North Korea's trespass of the 38th Parallel. The war ended in 1953 after 54,000 Americans had been killed. Brady suggests that Korea was the last campaign of World War II and the first battle of Vietnam. He was 23 during his year in Korea, and he carefully details his experience. Index.

239.   Bragg, Melvin. **The Sword and the Miracle**. New York: Random House, 1997. 688p. $20. ISBN 0-375-50003-0. YA

The Celtic princess Bega flees with Padric, a British prince, in A.D. 657 from Ireland to Britain. Although they are in love, each has responsibilities to fulfill before committing to each other.

240.   Brand, Eric. **William Gladstone**. New York: Chelsea House, 1986. 114p. $18.95. ISBN 0-87754-528-6. (World Leaders Past and Present). 8 up

Known as the conscience of nineteenth-century Britain, William Gladstone (1809–1898) served four terms as prime minister in a career spanning sixty years. He always fought for liberal reform. At first, he was intolerant of differing religions and supported slavery in the British colonies. As he matured, he realized that the lower classes had rights too. He challenged and defeated Benjamin Disraeli and helped to reform the electoral system while creating a national system of education. He never attained home rule for Ireland, but he tried to help the less fortunate. Photographs and reproductions enhance the text. Chronology, Further Reading, and Index.

241.   Braquet, Anne, and Martine Noblet. **India**. Maureen Walker, translator. Hauppauge, NY: Barron's, 1994. 77p. $11.95; $6.95pa. ISBN 0-8120-6427-5; 0-8120-1866-4pa. (Tintin's Travel Diaries). 5 up

The text asks thirty questions about India, covering a variety of topics such as whether the term "Hindu" or "Indian" is correct, the definition of "untouchable," why monsoons are both good and bad, why cows are sacred to Hindus, cremation, the maharajas, and who was Gandhi. Illustrations and photographs complement the simple question text on the lefthand pages and the more thorough and scholarly answer on the righthand pages. Glossary, Chronological Chart, Map, Bibliography, and Index.

242.   Braun, Barbara. **A Weekend with Diego Rivera**. New York: Rizzoli, 1994. 63p. $19.95. ISBN 0-8478-1749-0. (Weekend with the Artist). 5-8

Diego Rivera (1886-1957) tells about his life and career as if the reader were talking with him. He says that he tells the story of Mexico in his work—its history, its Revolution, its Indian past, and its popular traditions. Because of his devotion, Mexico considers Rivera one of its three greatest painters. He has been collecting pre-Columbian artifacts since his return to Mexico in 1920, after spending fourteen years in Paris where he knew Picasso, Modigliani, Mondrian, and Delaunay. Pictures of his paintings decorate the pages of his story. Where to See Rivera, Important Dates in Rivera's Life, and List of Illustrations.

243.   Bremness, Lesley. **Herbs**. New York: Dorling Kindersley, 1994. 304p. $17.95pa. ISBN 1-56458-496-8pa. (Eyewitness Handbooks). YA

Although not a history book, the text is an excellent reference for the types of herbs that people have used throughout history as cures or for other reasons. For example, belladonna dilates the eye pupils, "an effect once thought by Italian women to look seductive," but it is poisonous. Glossary and Index.

244.   Brennan, J. H. **Shiva: An Adventure of the Ice Age**. New York: Lippincott, 1990. 184p. $13.95. ISBN 0-397-32453-7. 5 up

By the time she reaches eleven years of age, Shiva has survived as an orphan and as a left-handed member of her Ice Age tribe. When she finds a circle of stones and the skull of a sabre-toothed tiger—magical items in the eyes of her tribe—the tribe gains respect for her. She warns the tribe to stay away from the "ogres," a different species, to protect the ogres who once saved her life.

245.   Breznitz, Shlomo. **Memory Fields: The Legacy of a Wartime Childhood in Czechoslovakia**. New York: Knopf, 1993. 179p. $21. ISBN 0-679-40403-1. YA

Breznitz grew up in Czechoslovakia during World War II. In the text, he recalls his life during that time and how the war affected him. He feared being detected as a Jew while pretending to be a good Catholic living in a Catholic orphanage. When the Germans were sending the last Jews to Auschwitz, a Catholic sister "hid" him by having him work as an aide in the hospital where Nazis could see him. The stratagem worked and he survived. Because Breznitz is a psychology professor, he interjects an understanding of how his experiences during that time have affected him through the years.

246.   Brier, Bob. **Egyptian Mummies: Unraveling the Secrets of an Ancient Art**. New York: Morrow, 1994. 352p. $23; $14pa. ISBN 0-688-10272-7; 0-688-14624-4pa. YA

Most concerns with mummies seem to be in the unwrapping of them. This author is more intrigued with the process of mummification and why it occurred. One premise is that, based on the Osiris/Isis myth, mummification evolved to stop cannibalism. A study of all available information on the procedures used in ancient Egypt helped the author to mummify a cadaver in 1994. He talks about how to make mummies, what they are, what to expect when unwrapping a mummy, animal mummies, grave robbers, and the representation of the mummy in contemporary fiction and film. Notes, Selected Bibliography, and Index.

247.   Brill, Marlene Targ. **Journey for Peace: The Story of Rigoberta Menchú**. Rubén De Anda, illustrator. New York: Lodestar, 1996. 64p. $14.99. ISBN 0-525-67524-8. 4-7

Rigoberta Menchú believed her father's political stance, and after he was murdered, she became a leader of the Mayan people as they struggled against an oppressive government. In 1992, she received the Nobel Peace Prize for her efforts. The text draws on information in Menchú's biography, information from United Nations' publications, and interviews with people in the international peace movement. Her life is a testimony of what one human can do for others.

248.   Briquebec, John. **The Ancient World: From the Earliest Civilizations to the Roman Empire**. New York: Warwick Press, Franklin Watts, 1990. 48p. $19.86. ISBN 0-531-19073-0. (Historical Atlas). 3-8

In looking at civilizations known to exist before the establishment of the Roman Empire, the text gives information about historical and social events from prehistoric peoples up through the fall of the Roman Empire. Index.

249.   Brombert, Beth Archer. **Édouard Manet: Rebel in a Frock Coat**. Boston: Little, Brown, 1996. 505p. $29.95. ISBN 0-316-10947-9. YA

Édouard Manet (1832–1883) exhibited his painting of "Le Déjeuner sur l'Herbe" in the 1863 Salon des Refusés. Then he exhibited a nude, "Olympia," at the Salon of 1865, and started a scandal among Parisian critics. However, he refused to join the Impressionists when they exhibited in the 1870s separate from the Salons. Brombert says that Manet was neither radical nor revolutionary; he simply wanted to go "through the main door" of the Salon. After inheriting money at the death of his father, Manet brought his mistress and their son into his house with his mother, and they lived as a bourgeois family from that point on. The text uses diaries, letters, documents, and memoirs to give a sense of the political and social timbre of the day, including the influence of mistresses on composers' and artists' creative work. Bibliography and Index.

250.   Brooks, Martha. **Two Moons in August**. Boston: Joy Street/Little, Brown, 1992. 199p. $14.95. ISBN 0-316-10979-7. 8 up

Sidonie, aged sixteen in 1959, has lost her mother, seen her father withdraw from society, and had a friend die in an accident. As she wonders what will happen next, she must also deal with a sister who is less interested in helping than in mistreating Sidonie and her own Chinese boyfriend. Sidonie begins the healing process when another physician's son comes to her Canadian town with his own problems. Helping him cope with his parents' abuse of each other and divorce allows her to dwell less in her own grief.

251.   Brooks, Polly Schoyer. **Beyond the Myth: The Story of Joan of Arc**. New York: Lippincott, 1990. 176p. $16. ISBN 0-397-32422-7. 8 up

With a beginning discussion on the disarray of the fifteenth century, Brooks shows how people could believe in a young girl, Joan, who thought that she could rid France of the British and set the rightful heir on the French throne. Born in Domremy in 1412, she heard voices that convinced her that she should save France. She persuaded others, including Charles, the heir apparent, to give her an army. She defeated the British at Orléans, but after she accomplished what she had promised, she was tried and burned at the stake in 1431. The text gives extensive background on this unusual female. Bibliography and Index. *Bulletin Blue Ribbon Book*.

252.   Brooks, Polly Schoyer. **Cleopatra: Goddess of Egypt, Enemy of Rome**. New York: HarperCollins, 1995. 151p. $15.95. ISBN 0-06-023607-8. 7 up

Cleopatra, a warrior queen, ruled her country by making necessary alliances with would-be conquerors. She was the last Ptolemy ruler in Egypt and mother to both Julius Caesar's and Mark Antony's children. Because so little has been found that might have been written about her while she lived, much of her life must be speculation. However, Plutarch, one of her enemies, noted that "the contact of her presence . . . was irresistible . . . the attraction of her person . . . was something bewitching." She kept the respect of her enemies because she committed suicide rather than allowing herself to be conquered. Chronology, Notes, Bibliography, and Index.

253.   Brooks, Polly Schoyer. **Queen Eleanor: Independent Spirit of the Medieval World**. New York: Harper-Collins, 1983. 182p. $14.89. ISBN 0-397-31995-9. 7 up

Born in 1122, Eleanor inherited the Duchy of Aquitaine in 1137 and married Louis, who became the king of France. She dedicated the abbey church of St. Denis, the first Gothic building in 1144; the next year, she had the first of her ten children. In 1147, she joined Louis on the Second Crusade. Four years later, she met Duke Henry of Normandy, whom she married the next year after divorcing Louis. In 1153, she bore the first of Henry's five sons, William. In 1154, Henry and Eleanor became king and queen of England, ruling from the borders of Scotland to the borders of Spain. In 1166, as a result of Henry's affair with "Fair Rosamond," Eleanor returned to France and established the court of love in Poitiers. Eleanor's sons, with her support, rebelled against Henry in 1173, and he imprisoned her. In 1189, Henry died, and Richard, as crowned King of England, freed his mother. In 1194, after Germans captured Richard, Eleanor traveled across the Alps to ransom him. In 1199, Richard died and John became king. She died in 1204 before the English made John sign the Magna Carta. *American Library Association Notable Book, School Library Journal Best Book, NCSS/CBC Notable Children's Trade Books in the Field of Social Studies,* and the *Boston Globe-Horn Book Honor Book*.

254.   Brophy, Ann. **John Ericsson and the Inventions of War**. Englewood Cliffs, NJ: Silver Burdett, 1991. 126p. $12.95; $7.95pa. ISBN 0-382-09943-5; 0-382-24052-9pa. (The History of the Civil War). 5 up

John Ericsson (1803-1889) was a Swedish-born inventor who spent time in England, where he designed one of the world's first steam locomotives, before he arrived in the United States. He neglected to get patents on many of his inventions, but he made a major contribution to the Union forces during the Civil War. He created a propeller for moving ships and built the ironclad warship, the *Monitor*. In a famous naval duel, the *Monitor* engaged the Confederate ship, the *Merrimack,* and Ericsson's creation was strong enough to win. Photographs and drawings highlight the text. Timetables, Suggested Reading, Selected Sources, and Index.

255.   Brown, Gene. **Conflict in Europe and the Great Depression: World War I (1914-1940)**. New York: Twenty-First Century, 1994. 64p. $15.98. ISBN 0-8050-2585-5. (First Person American). 5-9

Brown posits that the time between World Wars I and II was when modern America was born. He discusses the rugged individualism that characterized many Americans at the time, but notes that the government became a major force in everyday lives during and after the Great Depression of the 1930s. Most Americans were moving to cities, and mass media were growing in importance. From being a nation of ballplayers and performers, Americans became watchers. Among persons presented are John Reed, Gordon Parks, Al Capone, Marcus Garvey, and Lillian Gish. Photographs enhance the text. Timeline, For Further Reading, and Index.

256.   Brown, Pam. **Charlie Chaplin**. Milwaukee, WI: Gareth Stevens, 1991. 68p. $16.95. ISBN 0-55532-838-5. (People Who Have Helped the World). 7-9

Charles Chaplin began performing at the age of five, taking over for his mother when she lost her voice on stage. Although he, his half brother, and his mother had no money, his mother entertained them by miming expressions and actions of people on the street. Charlie left school at age nine to join a clog dancing troupe, but he eventually outgrew it. His mother had serious mental lapses, and the two boys tried to support themselves. Chaplin approached a theatrical agent when he was fourteen, and he got a job. In May 1913, while he was touring America, two men in the movies saw his work and hired him. He created the Little Tramp character, whom Americans adored, and between 1917 and 1941, focused his films on injustices that people like immigrants and abandoned children had to face. In 1950, McCarthyism infiltrated the American mind, and Chaplin's defense of Communists as human beings like any others made him seem guilty. He went to England and was refused reentry into the United States. He lived in Switzerland for twenty years until his death in 1977. Organizations, Books, Glossary, Chronology, and Index.

257.   Brown, Pam. **Father Damien**. Milwaukee, WI: Gareth Stevens, 1988. 68p. $16.95. ISBN 0-55532-815-6. (People Who Have Helped the World). 7-9

Born Josef de Veuster-Wouters in 1840 in the Flemish area of Belgium, Father Damien trained for business but decided that he wanted to help people. After becoming a priest, he went first to the Pacific Islands and then on to Molokai, a leper colony. By 1865, the disease, brought by the Chinese, was rapidly spreading among islanders, who had no immunity. The horrible conditions distressed Father Damien, but he worked calmly and eventually brought both law and decency to the people afflicted. By 1885, Father Damien himself had contracted the disease, which did not yet have a cure. Photographs of persons scarred by leprosy show the terrible effect of this disease. Organizations, Books, List of New Words, Important Dates, and Index.

258.   Brown, Pam. **Henry Dunant**. Milwaukee, WI: Gareth Stevens, 1989. 68p. $16.95. ISBN 0-55532-824-5. (People Who Have Helped the World). 7-9

Henry Dunant's wealthy Swiss family was religious, and expected Dunant (1828–1910) to help people less fortunate than he. Henry proposed and supported a worldwide Young Men's Christian Association (YMCA) in 1855 and was against slavery in America. The battle of Solferino, to unite the separate Italian states, in 1859, changed Dunant, who was in Italy on business at the time; the loss of 200 lives on the day of battle and the subsequent loss of 20,000 lives because of inadequate supplies haunted him for five years. He wrote a book about the experience in which he questioned why no organization had helped the soldiers. Many responded, including Florence Nightingale, who said that an organization should exist for both war- and peacetime. On August 22, 1864, fourteen nations met and signed the articles forming the first Geneva Convention. Dunant lost his personal fortune (probably through lack of attention), had to claim bankruptcy, leave the Red Cross and Geneva, and wander through Europe trying to survive. Eventually he settled in Heiden, Switzerland, the home of his grandparents, in a hospital where he recovered from tuberculosis. After a journalist heard of him and wrote an article about him, money flowed in to him from all over the world. He was awarded the first Nobel Prize for Peace in 1901 for his work. He had many ideas well before the public was ready to accept them, so his ideas did not become realities in his lifetime. Organizations, Books, Glossary, Chronology, and Index.

259.   Brown, Stephen F. **Christianity**. New York: Facts on File, 1991. 128p. $17.95. ISBN 0-8160-2441-3. (World Religions). YA

The text includes a detailed overview of the origin of Christianity and follows with its history. It notes the branches and basic beliefs of Christian groups as well as their organizational structures. Rites and passages such as baptism, marriage, and confirmation help formulate the impact of Christianity and its place in the modern world as its most widespread religion. For Further Reading, Glossary, and Index.

260.   Brown, Warren. **Fidel Castro: Cuban Revolutionary**. Brookfield, CT: Millbrook Press, 1994. 128p. $16.40. ISBN 1-56294-385-5. 7 up

Fidel Castro (b. 1927) rose to power in 1959 as the revolutionary leader who opposed the corruption and violence of the Batista regime in Cuba. He has ruled a Communist government in Cuba spanning the last five decades. Castro became an ally of the Soviet Union and thus an enemy of the United States. Bibliography and Index.

261.   Brown, Warren. **The Search for the Northwest Passage**. New York: Chelsea House, 1991. 111p. $18.95. ISBN 0-7910-1297-2. (World Explorers). 5 up

From approximately 1497, with John Cabot, until 1850, with Sir John Franklin, men searched for a passage along the top of the North American continent between Europe and China. The text includes personal accounts of these searches along with maps and color photographs. Bibliography and Index.

262.   Bruns, Roger. **Julius Caesar**. New York: Chelsea House, 1987. 112p. $18.95. ISBN 1-87754-514-6. (World Leaders Past and Present). 5 up

Julius Caesar (b. 100 B.C.) spent his life working toward the highest position in Rome, first as an emerging politician who appealed directly to the people in 59 B.C. and later as part of a governing triumvirate with Pompey and Crassus. With the Gauls, from 58 to 51 B.C., he used brutality to gain what he wanted. In 49 B.C., he declared war on an elite group of conservative senators and wrested power from them. On the Ides of March, 44 B.C., he went to the Roman Senate, where his men stabbed him to death because they thought he wanted too much power. Yet he brought glory to Rome, along with elaborate celebrations of it and many reforms. Photographs and reproductions enhance the text. Chronology, Further Reading, and Index.

263.   Bryant, Jennifer. **Henri de Toulouse-Lautrec, Artist**. New York: Chelsea House, 1994. 128p. $18.95. ISBN 0-7910-2408-3. (Great Achievers: Lives of the Physically Challenged). 5 up

In his early teens, Henri de Toulouse-Lautrec (1864–1901) had two falls that crippled him and caused his legs to stop growing. While he was recovering from the injuries, he began to draw familiar subjects; at age seventeen, he went to Paris to study art. Although he learned academic painting, he developed his own style and used the unorthodox lifestyle of Montmartre, with its prostitutes, patrons, and performers, as his subject matter. His big chance came when the Moulin Rouge nightclub commissioned him to create an advertising poster for the club. Originally scorned in the art world, he is now admired for his realistic themes and careful technique. Photographs and reproductions augment the text. Chronology, Further Reading, and Index.

264.   Bryant, Jennifer Fisher. **Louis Braille: Teacher of the Blind**. New York: Chelsea House, 1994. 111p. $18.95; $7.95pa. ISBN 0-7910-2077-0; 0-7910-2090-8pa. (Great Achievers: Lives of the Physically Challenged). 4-8

Louis Braille (1809-1852) spent many years at the Royal Institute for Blind Youth in Paris. After becoming blind as a youth, he developed his "braille" touch system for reading when he was fifteen, but political disagreements kept those who could promote it from accepting it for many years. Drawings, reproductions, and historical photographs complement the text. Bibliography and Index.

265.   Buckley, Fiona. **To Shield the Queen**. New York: Scribners, 1997. 273p. $21. ISBN 0-684-83841-9. YA

Ursula Blanchard is the lady-in-waiting to Queen Elizabeth in 1600. She goes to visit the wife of Sir Robert Dudley who is ill and whom people suspect of slowly being poisoned so that Dudley can marry Elizabeth. But while Ursula is with her, she dies of a broken neck, and expectations change rapidly.

266.   Buechner, Frederick. **Godric**. New York: Atheneum, 1980. 178p. $10.95. ISBN 0-689-11086-3. New York: HarperCollins, 1983. 178p. $12pa. ISBN 0-06-061162-6pa. YA

Godric travels to Rome and Jerusalem, beginning in 1065, before becoming a hermit. He experiences the life of the Middle Ages as the Normans take over England. After consummating his love with the one woman he adores, both feel guilty for a variety of reasons and separate immediately. As a hermit, Godric realizes that the important things in life are those that money cannot buy, including his friendships with two snakes that stay by his fire.

267.   Bunson, Matthew. **Encyclopedia of the Middle Ages**. New York: Facts on File, 1995. 512p. $45. ISBN 0-8160-2456-1. YA

When the Western Roman Empire collapsed, other forms of government had to take its place. The new systems that arose then lasted until the Renaissance. Included here are essays on the major writers of the period, Dante and Chaucer; the feudal society that allowed a stable economy to exist; the development of Christianity and the ensuing Crusades; the growth of the Islamic empire; and the Magna Carta, signed under duress but a beginning for the rights of the individual. Line drawings, maps, family trees, and appendices of ruling dynasties help to clarify the time. Bibliography, Glossary, and Index.

268.   Bunson, Matthew. **Encyclopedia of the Roman Empire**. New York: Facts on File, 1994. 494p. $45. ISBN 0-8160-2135-X. YA

This comprehensive reference includes both short citations and long essays on any topic or person associated with the Roman Empire. General categories in which one will find many listings are the government, society, literature and art, law, trade and commerce, warfare, and religion. Longer essays discuss art and architecture, coinage, education, gods and goddesses, the military, Rome, and taxes. Other features are a chronology and more than sixty line drawings and maps. Appendices include a list of emperors and diagrams of family trees. Glossary of Governmental, Military, and Social Titles, Selected Readings, and Index.

269.   Bunson, Stephen, and Margaret Bunson. **Encyclopedia of Ancient Mesoamerica**. New York: Facts on File, 1996. 416p. $45. ISBN 0-8160-2402-2. YA

The broad scope of this text covers the people of Mesoamerica from the rise of the early cultures at the end of the last Ice Age (around 11,000 B.C.) through the fall of the Aztecs to Spanish conquerors in the 1500s. Civilizations discussed include the Aztecs, Olmecs, Zapotecs, Tehtihuacáns, and the Mayans. Essays on art and architecture, social life, belief systems, and the military balance entries on rulers, sites, and events. Drawings and maps help to pinpoint information. Bibliography, Chronology, Glossary, and Index.

270.   Bunting, Eve. **SOS Titanic**. San Diego, CA: Harcourt Brace, 1996. 256p. $12; $6pa. ISBN 0-15-200271-5; 0-15-201305-9pa. 6-9

Barry, an upper-class Irish boy of fifteen, prepares to join his parents in America after living with his grandparents while his parents worked in China. On board the ship are Frank and Jonnie, who blame Barry's grandfather for forcing their departure from Ireland via steerage. Frank threatens Barry for having a relationship with Frank's sister. After the *Titanic*'s collision with an iceberg on April 14, 1912, Barry tries to save Frank; he cannot, but he does save Frank's sister. The *Carpathia* rescues both of them the following morning.

271.   Bunting, Eve. **Spying on Miss Müller**. New York: Clarion, 1995. 181p. $13.95. ISBN 0-395-69172-9. 5-7

Jessie and her friends in her Belfast, Ireland, school think their German teacher, Miss Müller, is wonderful. After World War II begins, they change their minds and start rumors. When they see her climb the stairs to the roof one night, they wonder if she is a spy. Jessie wants to prove her teacher's innocence, so she begins watching her. What she discovers is a tryst between Miss Müller and Mr. Bolton, the Latin teacher. But another friend, Greta, is angry that her father has been killed, and she exposes the lovers. Because it is against the rules for teachers to be married, Miss Müller is fired, and Mr. Bolton joins the army. Jessie hopes they will be happy, but doubts that they will see each other again.

272.   Burch, Joann J. **Isabella of Castile: Queen on Horseback**. New York: Franklin Watts, 1991. 63p. $18.43. ISBN 0-531-20033-7. (First Books). 4-8

When Isabella I (1451-1504) was Queen of Spain, ruling with her husband Ferdinand from 1479 until 1504, she rode through the countryside on horseback garnering support for their works. Her horsewomanship helped to bring political and religious unity to their kingdom. Its prosperity allowed her to support Columbus in his quest for the Indies. Bibliography and Index.

273.   Burgess, Alan. **The Longest Tunnel: The True Story of World War II's Great Escape**. New York: Grove Weidenfeld, 1990. 288p. $19.95. ISBN 1-55584-033-7. YA

In March 1944, seventy-six Allied prisoners of war crawled through a tunnel nicknamed "Harry" that they had dug underneath the prison at Sagan, Stalag Luft III. Only three survived after the Gestapo caught the others and murdered them without trial—acts against the Geneva Convention. By interviewing the three who survived and checking documents, Burgess reveals a stark saga of World War II. Index.

274.   Burgess, Melvin. **An Angel for May**. New York: Simon & Schuster, 1995. 154p. $15. ISBN 0-671-89004-2. 5-7

In this historical fantasy, Tam roams around a ruined farm in the English countryside after his parents divorce, and the dog of a homeless woman he sees there leads him through the fireplace into the time of World War II, when the farm is thriving. Mr. Nutter, the owner, wants Tam to stay and be friends with May, a traumatized girl who refuses to eat or sleep indoors. When Tam returns to the present, he sees that a fire will destroy the farm and Mr. Nutter, and he tries to find a way to go back in time again to warn them.

275.   Burke, Deirdre. **Food and Fasting**. New York: Thomson Learning, 1993. 32p. $13.95. ISBN 1-56847-034-7. (Comparing Religions). 4-8

Six major religions—Buddhism, Christianity, Hinduism, Judaism, Islam, and Sikhism—have rules about what some foods mean and which foods they may eat. The text looks at what they eat, how they eat it, what and when they cannot eat, what foods appear at religious festivals, and what foods (e.g., bread and wine) appear in places of worship. Photographs enhance the information. Glossary, Books to Read, and Index.

276.   Burks, Brian. **Soldier Boy**. San Diego, CA: Harcourt Brace, 1997. 154p. $12. ISBN 0-15-201218-4. 6-9

When Johnny "The Kid" McBane flees from his Chicago boxing promoter, he enlists in the cavalry after lying about his age. When he arrives at Custer's Seventh Cavalry at Fort Lincoln, he prepares to fight the Indians in the spring. The story mainly describes the escapades in camp before Johnny dies in battle at the end of the book.

277.   Burrell, Roy. **The Greeks**. Peter Connolly, illustrator. New York: Oxford University Press, 1990. 112p. $16.95. ISBN 0-19-917161-0. 5-7

This overview of the ancient Greeks presents their life, culture, and customs, with an emphasis on their military strategies, especially the armies and navies of Alexander the Great. By having the narrator converse with someone living at the time, Burrell gives a sense of immediacy to the information. Illustrations highlight the text. Chronology.

278.   Burrell, Roy. **Life in the Time of Moctezuma and the Aztecs**. Angus McBride, illustrator. Austin, TX: Raintree/Steck-Vaughn, 1993. 63p. $16.98. ISBN 0-8114-3351-X. (Life in the Time Of). 4-8

During the early 1500s, Moctezuma ruled the Aztecs in Tenochtitlán. The text presents the people who supported and fought for him, how they did it, religious rituals, women and girls and their maturation customs, life in the town and countryside, crafts and trades, and myths. But Cortés arrived with his soldiers and destroyed the Aztec civilization by 1521. Each chapter covers a specific topic, using illustrations to clarify. Glossary and Index.

279.   Burton, Hester. **Beyond the Weir Bridge**. Victor G. Ambrus, illustrator. New York: Crowell, 1970. 227p. $4.95. ISBN 0-690-14052-5. 7-10

As young people, Richard, Richenda, and Thomas dare each other to cross a rickety *(weir)* bridge. In 1651, they separate: Richard goes to Oxford and squanders his opportunity, while the physically weak Thomas must stay at home, his father having spent all the family's money on drink. Richenda meets Margaret Fell, a Quaker, who influences her. She marries Thomas, who shares her Quaker beliefs, and they restore his father's property. Later, Thomas meets and helps Richard in London during the plague. Thomas dies, the Great Fire destroys the city, and Richenda realizes that Richard needs her love so she marries him. *Boston Globe-Horn Book Award.*

280. Burton, Hester. **The Henchmans at Home**. New York: Crowell, 1972. $4.50. 182p. ISBN 0-690-37706-1. 6-10

In English Victorian society of the 1890s, Rob, Ellen, and William mature over a period of eleven years. They experience various events, observe prejudice, and find that their beliefs change when they look at situations from new perspectives. What they realize most is that each has to accept the individuality of the other and that their parents have reasons for the decisions they make.

281. Burton, Hester. **Riders of the Storm**. New York: Crowell, 1973. 200p. $7.95. ISBN 0-690-70074-1. YA

A sequel to *The Rebel,* this book begins in 1793 with the protagonist, Stephen, helping his friend in Manchester at a school for workers' children. He and others think that parliamentary reform is mandatory, but they face false charges of sedition from those who would keep the status quo to protect their economic position. Stephen and two others are forced to spend all their money on defense. After acquittal, however, they return to the countryside and realize that the use of water power will help them rebuild the mill and restart the school.

282. Burton, Hester. **Time of Trial**. 1963. New York: Yearling, 1970. 216p. $1.50pa. ISBN 0-440-48901-6pa. YA

In 1803, Margaret can do nothing while a mob, angry at her father for writing in favor of reforms and money for the poor rather than war in France, burns his bookstore, his printing press, and their home above the shop. A student staying with the family arranges for Margaret and the housekeeper to go to the Essex coast while her father serves a prison term for his beliefs. Later, a brother humiliated by the father's plight reconciles with the family, and Margaret finds happiness with the student who helped her find sanctuary on the coast. *Carnegie Medal.*

283. Burton, Hester. **To Ravensrigg**. New York: Crowell, 1977. 148p. $10.78. ISBN 0-690-01354-X. 7-10

Although slavery has been outlawed by 1786 in England, Emmie, age fourteen, finds that slave trading still occurs. She helps a slave escape by persuading her sea captain father to take him away from England on the next trip. Emmie survives a subsequent shipwreck during which her father, before he drowns, tells her to go to Ravensrigg and say that she is "Mary's daughter." Quakers help her succeed in her mission, and Emmie meets the grandmother she has never known. She discovers the family secrets and why a man tried to kidnap her on her journey. To escape his claims, she marries one of the Quaker sons as soon as possible.

284. Burton, Rosemary, Richard Cavendish, and Bernard Stonehouse. **Journeys of the Great Explorers**. New York: Facts on File, 1992. 224p. $34.95. ISBN 0-8160-2840-0. YA

The text looks at the voyages of thirty explorers who set out to find remote parts of the world. A timeline compares six regions of the globe and relates the significant discoveries and events in each segment. Anecdotes about unusual animals or events highlight the information. Illustrations include magazine photographs, souvenirs, portraits, and equipment pictures. Bibliography and Index.

285. Busby, Margaret. **Daughters of Africa: An International Anthology of Words and Writing by Women of African Descent from Ancient Egypt to the Present**. New York: Random House, 1992. 1089p. $35. ISBN 0-679-41634-X. New York: Ballantine, 1994. 1089p. $19.95pa. ISBN 0-345-38268-4pa. YA

In this anthology appear the works of 200 Black women writing over four centuries from Africa, North America, the Caribbean, Latin America, Europe, and Asia. They have written in many genres including autobiography, memoirs, oral history, letters, diaries, short stories, novels (experimental, historical, science fiction), poetry, drama, humor, nonfiction (political, feminist, anthropological), journalism, speeches, essays, and folklore. This collection allows Black women to speak for themselves, and they all speak with different voices. Biographical Headnotes, Bibliography, Further Reading, and Index.

286. Bush, Catherine. **Elizabeth I**. New York: Chelsea House, 1988. 112p. $18.95. ISBN 0-87754-579-0. (World Leaders Past and Present). 5 up

The unwanted daughter of Henry VIII, Elizabeth I (1533-1603) grew up without her mother, Anne Boleyn, whom Henry had executed. Elizabeth had a lonely childhood while watching her half-sister Mary misrule England. Elizabeth acceded to the throne in 1558, where she showed her political skill and united her country. She was a scholar, a believer in religious tolerance, and a patron of the arts. She refused to allow anyone to gain power over her, and her country flourished while she ruled. Photographs and reproductions enhance the text. Chronology, Further Reading, and Index.

287. Bush, Catherine. **Mohandas K. Gandhi: Indian Nationalist Leader**. New York: Chelsea House, 1985. 112p. $18.95. ISBN 0-87754-555-3. (World Leaders Past and Present). 5 up

For two generations, Gandhi (1869-1948) was the conscience of India. He returned to India, after being educated in England and working in South Africa, to forward the cause of independence from Britain through nonviolent means. He succeeded, but one of his own countrymen assassinated him. Photographs and reproductions enhance the text. Chronology, Further Reading, and Index.

288. Butler, Francelia. **Indira Gandhi**. New York: Chelsea House, 1986. 116p. $18.95. ISBN 0-87754-596-0. (World Leaders Past and Present). 5 up

Indira Gandhi (1917-1984) became prime minister of India after Jawaharlal Nehru, her father. She fought for economic progress and social reform in India, the country with the second largest population in the world. She believed in democracy, but she also used dictatorial tactics if nothing else worked. She suspended civil rights during a "state of emergency" between 1975 and 1977, but she was overwhelmingly reelected in 1980. The text looks at her life and the forces that shaped it, including the constant support for Indian independence from Britain that she heard at home as a child. Photographs enhance the text. Chronology, Further Reading, and Index.

289. Butson, Thomas G. **Ivan the Terrible**. New York: Chelsea House, 1987. 112p. $18.95. ISBN 0-87754-534-0. (World Leaders Past and Present). 8 up

Ivan the Terrible (1530–1584) was the first tsar of Russia. As he attempted to establish a strong state, with Moscow as the central authority, he almost destroyed his realm. Orphaned at age eight, he discarded his guardian when he was thirteen, and then four years later adopted the title of tsar. He worked for reforms in local government, law code, and the church. After his wife died in 1564, he began his seven-year reign of terror, during which he tortured and murdered thousands. In 1570, he slaughtered the inhabitants of Novgorod and burned the city. In 1581, he murdered his son and heir. He himself died, without peace, in 1584. Even with his excesses, Ivan left a strong state. Photographs and reproductions enhance the text. Chronology, Further Reading, and Index.

290. Byrd, Max. **Jefferson: A Novel**. New York: Bantam, 1993. 424p. $22.95; $5.99pa. ISBN 0-553-09470-X; 0-553-56867-1pa. YA

In 1784, Thomas Jefferson's young secretary in Paris tries to figure out his employer. Jefferson and his enigmatic ways baffle the man as he observes Jefferson dealing with the French, debating with his American colleagues, and becoming friends with married women. The secretary does his best to understand Jefferson, but all he can do is report what he sees.

C

291. Calderwood, Michael, and Gabriel Brena. **Mexico: A Higher Vision: An Aerial Journey from Past to Present**. Michael Calderwood, photographs. La Jolla, CA: Alti, 1990. 192p. $35. ISBN 0-9625399-0-2. YA

Although seemingly a coffee-table book of photographs shot high above Mexico, the book is a stunning overview of the historical and geographical sites in the country, with text about the history of the area. Although Mexico was probably settled more than 24,000 years ago, the documented history seems to begin with the Mayans around A.D. 350, during their first golden age at Chichen. In A.D. 750, the Toltecs rebuilt the area as Chichen-Itza. Teotihuacán ("home of the gods"), another settlement in A.D. 700, was an Aztec city of over 100,000 persons. Mexico-Tenochtitlán, founded by the Aztecs in A.D. 1325, is the city Cortés destroyed and then rebuilt. Today, as Mexico City, its population is over 15 million. The Baja peninsula has one of the largest collections of cave paintings known in the world created before A.D. 1100. The Photography Index also functions as a place for notes that make historical comparisons. For example, the Pyramids of the Moon and the Sun are at Teotihuacán. The Pyramid of the Sun, according to the note, is only half as tall as the Pyramid of Cheops in Egypt, but is almost the same size.

292. Calvert, Patricia. **Hadder MacColl**. New York: Scribners, 1985. 160p. $12.95. ISBN 0-684-18447-8. 5-9

In 1745, Hadder MacColl looks forward to her brother's return from the university at Edinburgh, Scotland. Disappointed that he brings a friend home with him, and concerned that he no longer wants the clans to fight each other, she discounts him when he refuses to kill a mountain lion that is threatening their dogs. But he has to fight at Culloden to help restore the Jacobites to Scotland's throne, and at his death, Hadder realizes that she and her father are the ones with misplaced values. After her father's death, others help Hadder in her decision to emigrate to America.

293. Cameron, Eleanor. **The Court of the Stone Children**. 1973. Magnolia, MA: Peter Smith, 1983. 208p. $18.05. ISBN 0-8446-6757-9. New York: Puffin, 1992. $4.99pa. ISBN 0-14-034289-3pa. 4 up

Nina wants to become a museum curator because she finds solace in San Francisco's French Museum, a place where Chagall's painting *Time Is a River Without Banks* greets her. In this historical fantasy, Nina meets Dominique, a figure in an early-nineteenth-century painting. Dominique says that she dreamed about Nina as a girl and wants Nina to help her find out what happened to her father. Nina solves the puzzle by guessing about a painting and shows Dominique that her father was innocent of charges made against him by Napoleon's army. *American Book Award*.

294. Campion, Nardi Reeder. **Mother Ann Lee: Morning Star of the Shakers**. Hanover, NH: University Press of New England, 1990. 180p. $13.95pa. ISBN 0-87451-527-0pa. 9 up

Ann Lee (1736-1784) founded one of the most successful communal living environments in the world with the Shaker community. She believed that she was the second coming of Christ; her followers believed that she was the Word of God made manifest. She preached in the streets (women were not allowed in the pulpit) and led evangelical services in Manchester, England (where people publicly confessed sin, spoke in tongues, and danced ecstatically) until she was put in jail. After marriage, she used her own name instead of her husband's in a time when women were merely a husband's property. Then she founded the United Society of Believers in Christ's Second Appearing—the Shakers. She took her group on a 59-day voyage to the colonies, and during the American Revolution she preached nonresistance. Few facts about her life remain, but she became a leader for many who wanted to escape from competition, materialism, sexism, and self-gratification. People spoke of her blue eyes and inner beauty, but no likeness remains of her. Bibliography and Index.

295. Capek, Michael. **Artistic Trickery: The Tradition of the Trompe L'Oeil Art**. Minneapolis, MN: Lerner, 1995. Unpaged. $21.50. ISBN 0-8225-2064-8. (Art Beyond Borders). 5 up

An enjoyable presentation of *trompe l'oeil* art—paintings that confuse the eye so that viewers think they are seeing something when they are not. *Trompe l'oeil* is not realism, which tries to represent objects truthfully; *trompe l'oeil* is a visual game. The text looks at several contemporary artists who make *trompe l'oeil* paintings and the subjects that have intrigued artists through the years. These themes include damaged goods, money and stamps, food, people, animals and bugs, slates and letter racks, doors, landscapes, and murals. The earliest illustration comes from 1475, and other illustrations cover each century since. Glossary and Index. *IRA Children's Choices*.

296. Capek, Michael. **Murals: Cave, Cathedral, to Street**. Minneapolis, MN: Lerner, 1996. 72p. $17.21. ISBN 0-8225-2065-6. (American Pastfinder). 5 up

The text looks at murals, huge drawings that decorate caves, walls, ceilings, and the sides of buildings. In an unusual order, the text looks at contemporary murals first and goes backward in history; the last chapter examines cave paintings. Among the topics are contemporary community murals, historical murals in the United States, Mexican murals, Italian Renaissance murals, early Christian murals, murals of ancient Rome and Egypt, and cave paintings. Glossary, For Further Reading, and Index.

297.   Carpenter, Angelica S., and Jean Shirley. **Robert Louis Stevenson: Finding Treasure Island**. Minneapolis, MN: Lerner, 1997. 144p. $17.95. ISBN 0-8225-4955-7. 6-9

Robert Louis Stevenson (1850-1894) grew up in Scotland and traveled in France and the United States. At thirty-seven, he traveled in the South Seas with his family and eventually settled on the Samoan island of Upolu. These experiences served as the settings for his novels, such as *Treasure Island*. Bibliography and Index.

298.   Carr, Philippa. **Daughters of England**. New York: Putnam, 1995. 308p. $22.95. ISBN 0-399-14023-9. YA

Twenty years after Oliver Cromwell's rule in the Restoration, Sarah falls in love with Lord Rosslyn and marries him. He, however, is already married, and when she finds out, she feels intense guilt. She leaves him immediately and goes to friends, who help her raise her daughter Kate. When Sarah dies, Kate tells about living on her father's estate with a stepbrother as the times in which they live become more unstable.

299.   Carrion, Esther. **The Empire of the Czars**. Chicago: Childrens Press, 1994. 34p. $20. ISBN 0-516-08319-0. (The World Heritage). 3 up

Russia is so diverse that one must look at many facets to get a glimpse into its history and its people. In the sixth and seventh centuries, Kiev was founded, and from this city grew the current country. Muscovy became heir to Kiev's power in the fourteenth and fifteenth centuries. Sites shown in photographs include St. Petersburg, Moscow's Kremlin and Red Square, Petcherskaya Lavra of Kiev, Kizhi Pogost, and the historic city of Itchan Kala in the heart of Asia. Glossary and Index.

300.   Carroll, Bob. **The Battle of Stalingrad**. San Diego, CA: Lucent, 1997. 95p. $19.95. ISBN 1-56006-452-8. (Battles of World War II). 6-10

The German Sixth Army held the Russian defenders from the end of August 1942 until the end of January 1943 at the city of Stalingrad. Carroll notes that this battle was one of the important turning points in World War Two, and proves his point by expounding upon the battle of wills between the two dictators, Stalin and Hitler. Boxed text and archival photographs augment the information. Bibliography, Chronology, Further Reading, and Index.

301.   Carroll, Bob. **Napoleon Bonaparte**. San Diego, CA: Lucent, 1994. 112p. $16.95. ISBN 1-56006-021-2. (The Importance Of). 6-9

Napoleon Bonaparte (1769-1821) rose to become the greatest military leader of France and perhaps of the world. After the French Revolution, he used the concepts of equality, liberty, and brotherhood as the basis for the *Code Napoleon* (the basis of law in France and much of Europe today); centralized the government (a model for dictatorships everywhere); and pursued foreign policy that led to the creation of modern Italy, Germany, and Poland, and the expansion of the United States into a powerful nation. At the same time, he killed millions of people and enriched France by stealing treasures from other countries (such as da Vinci's *Mona Lisa*, which hangs in the Louvre rather than in Italy). He preached freedom but enslaved many. In 1799, at thirty-five, he had himself designated the "First Consul for Life"; in 1804, he crowned himself emperor of France. When his beloved wife Josephine did not bear him an heir, he divorced her and married Marie Louise of Austria. Napoleon II was born in 1811, but Napoleon I continued to visit Josephine. His conquest of Egypt made him feel equal to Alexander the Great and Julius Caesar; it was in Egypt that his men found the Rosetta Stone. Eventually he lost power and was exiled to Elba. But he came back, started amassing an army, and fought Wellington at the Battle of Waterloo in 1815, suffering a stunning loss. His final exile was to the isolated St. Helene where he died, perhaps poisoned by arsenic. Notes, For Further Reading, Additional Works Consulted, and Index.

302.   Carroll, Bob. **Pancho Villa**. San Diego, CA: Lucent, 1996. 112p. $16.95. ISBN 1-56006-069-7. (The Importance Of). 7 up

Pancho Villa (1878–1923) was an outlaw and a revolutionary who rebelled against Mexico's cruel landowners. Without him, the Mexican Revolution might not have been successful. He was a complex and uneducated man who often let his emotions rule; he shot first and then asked questions. He was brave to the point of being foolhardy, but he took risks that inspired his followers and rewarded loyalty. He was also a master of guerrilla tactics, but had difficulty with technology. He kept money for himself, but he was basically a patriot for Mexico. Notes, For Further Reading, Works Consulted, and Index.

303.   Carson, S. L. **Maximilien Robespierre**. New York: Chelsea House, 1988. 112p. $18.95. ISBN 0-87754-549-9. (World Leaders Past and Present). 8 up

Robespierre (1758–1794), a leader of the French Revolution, tried to steer France toward an ideal "Republic of Virtue." He sent many innocent people to the guillotine while he created a dictatorship. Although a lawyer with high principles, he led the powerful Jacobin Club early in his career so that it would reflect his principles, and made himself the spokesman for France's urban workers. He had enough influence when elected to the Commune of Paris that his desire to execute the king was fulfilled. The Committee of Public

Safety developed a policy known as "the Terror," and Robespierre began methodically executing his political opponents. When he tried to replace Christianity in France with a religion based on the Revolution's values—which were actually his own—his opponents finally arrested him in 1794. Soon after, at the age of thirty-six, he fell under the guillotine. Reproductions enhance the text. Chronology, For Further Reading, and Index.

304.   Carter, Alden. **China Past—China Future**. New York: Franklin Watts, 1994. 143p. $21.10. ISBN 0-531-11161-X. 9 up

Knowledge about the prehistory of China extends back at least 400,000 years. Written history begins with the Shang Dynasty, which came to power between 1766 and 1576 B.C. The craftsmen of this dynasty created bronze statues using techniques not equaled in Europe for another 2,500 years. The dynasty eventually lost energy. The Zhou emperors incorporated their feudal system, followed by the Qin Dynasty under Shi Huangdi (d. 209 B.C.), who started the Great Wall of China. The Han emperors and the mandarin scholar-officials began to rule in 202 B.C., before China split into three kingdoms—the Wei, the Wu, and Shu-Han. It reunited, and the Mongols arrived under Temujin (1162?–1227). The last dynasty, the Qing, decayed with the beginning of the 1800s. In the modern era, China has undergone the Nationalist revolution, the Japanese invasion, the Communist triumph, the Great Leap Forward, the Cultural Revolution, and the suppression of democracy with the Tiananmen Square event. Understanding who and why about the Chinese remains imperative for contemporary peoples. Source Notes, Suggested Reading, and Index.

305.   Carter, Alden R. **The Mexican War: Manifest Destiny**. New York: Franklin Watts, 1992. 63p. $12.40. ISBN 0-531-20081-7. (First Books). 4-8

With a general focus on military and political strategies, the text gives the history of the Mexican War, which lasted from 1846 to 1848. It discusses events, personalities, and the aftermath of the war as well. Reproductions enhance the text. Bibliography and Index.

306.   Carter, Alden R. **The Spanish-American War: Imperial Ambitions**. New York: Franklin Watts, 1992. 64p. $12.40. ISBN 0-531-20078-7. (First Books). 4-8

The text tells of the ten-week war in 1898 between the United States and Spain over the liberation of Cuba. Theodore Roosevelt and his Rough Riders gained stature when the fight ended the Spanish colonial empire, and other countries recognized the United States as a world power. Bibliography and Index.

307.   Carter, David. **George Santayana**. New York: Chelsea House, 1992. 110p. $18.95. ISBN 0-7910-1254-9. (Hispanics of Achievement). 8 up

George Santayana (1863–1952) came to the United States from Spain when he was eight years old. Educated at Harvard, he stayed there to teach. After he inherited money at his mother's death, he went abroad to write and to travel. His philosophy, poetry, and criticism revealed his depth of knowledge. Photographs enhance the text. Chronology, Further Reading, and Index.

308.   Carter, David A. **Salvador Dali**. New York: Chelsea House, 1994. 119p. $18.95; $7.95pa. ISBN 0-7910-1778-8; 0-7910-3015-6pa. (Hispanics of Achievement). 8 up

Salvador Dali (1904–1989), a talented artist, often used theatrics to gain attention. The text presents a study of his works from 1926 through 1970 to show the development of his style. His wife's demands over fifty years of marriage caused him to compromise some of his artistic efforts in order to earn money. Chronology, Further Reading, and Index.

309.   Carter, Dorothy S. **His Majesty, Queen Hatshepsut**. Michele Chessare, illustrator. Philadelphia: Lippincott, 1987. 248p. $13.95. ISBN 0-397-32178-3. 6-9

Having to share the reign with her young half-nephew annoys Hatshepsut, so she maneuvers to declare herself the only ruler of Egypt by saying that her father told her in a dream that she was the Pharaoh. She rules for twenty-two years, surviving the schemes of the priesthood to kill her until an advisor serves her poisoned wine. Although fictionalized, this book is based on facts about Hatshepsut, the woman who ruled in Egypt from 1503 B.C. to 1482 B.C. She advanced the civilization by renovating portions of Karnak and building the beautiful temple of Dayr al-Bahrı on the Nile near Thebes. By the time of her death, a viper had bitten and killed her daughter and her confidant had been murdered. Carter supposes that Hatshepsut was tired of fighting her subordinates when her own life ended.

310.   Carter, Peter. **Children of the Book**. 1982. London: Oxford University Press, 1987. 272p. $13.95. ISBN 0-19-271456-2. YA

Three sixteen-year-olds, the Polish Stefan, the Austrian Anna, and the Turk Timur, are in Vienna during the summer of 1683 when the Turks break their treaty with Austria and attack. Timur accompanies Vasif, the Janissary leader, in his attempt to take the city, and Stefan tries to defend it. Timur kills Stefan, and Stefan's father retaliates. Anna almost starves inside the city walls. The story gives various views of the "infidel" according to each group in its attempt to understand human motivations. *The Observer Award* (Great Britain) and *Leseratten Award* (Germany).

311. Carter, Peter. **The Hunted**. New York: Farrar, Straus & Giroux, 1994. 309p. $17. ISBN 0-374-33520-6. 8 up

In 1943, Corporal Vito Salvani tries to return to Italy when it surrenders to the Allies. He takes with him an orphaned Jewish child, Judah. They become lost in French territory, still controlled by the Germans and the Gestapo, and have to escape. Their ordeal is especially treacherous because one man has decided that he must capture them.

312. Carter, Peter. **The Sentinels**. New York: Oxford University Press, 1980. 199p. $10.95. ISBN 0-19-271438-4. 7-9

John, shipwrecked from an antislave patrol ship, and Lyapo, a Yoruba captured to be sold into slavery, find themselves together on the African coast trying to survive in 1840. They attempt to learn each other's languages and begin to use each other's strengths during their ordeal. When the British Royal Navy rescues John, he returns to his ship, but Lyapo decides to stay in Africa. *Guardian Award* and *Premio di Lettaratura d'Italie*.

313. Casals, Pablo. **Joys and Sorrows**. New York: Simon & Schuster, 1970. 314p. $9.95pa. ISBN 0-671-21774-7pa. 9 up

Written when Casals was ninety-three, this autobiography gives insight into the life of an extraordinarily talented man. His mother recognized his musical ability and carefully watched his maturity so that he went to the right teacher at the right time. Casals was a humanist, concerned about the state of the world. Having met John Kennedy several times, Casals felt that Kennedy was a good man who was trying to make life better for others. Casals's young wife, to whom he was devoted, knew that Kennedy's death would affect Casals greatly, so she tried to keep him from hearing the news as long as possible. Casals says very clearly that young people with talent should not succumb to vanity because what they have is not something over which they have any control. What they do with their talent is the only thing that is important. Casals shows that if a person has talent and works hard with it, others will want to help with success. Index.

314. Castello, Ellena Romero, and Urie Marcus Kapon. **The Jews and Europe: 2000 Years of History**. New York: Henry Holt, 1994. 239p. $50. ISBN 0-8050-3526-5. YA

The text gives a history of European Jews, from the early Greek and Roman times to the Holocaust, to highlight their uniqueness, although it tends to focus more on hardship than accomplishment. Included are a variety of subjects under the general areas of history, culture, and intellectual life, such as religion, holidays, ritual clothing and food, architecture, illuminated manuscripts, painting, music, cinema, ancient and modern languages, and religious and secular languages. Photographs, Glossary, Bibliography, and Index.

315. Caulkins, Janet. **Joseph Stalin**. New York: Franklin Watts, 1990. 160p. $13.90. ISBN 0-87518-557-6. (Impact Biography). 7 up

Iosif Dzhugashvili (1879–1953), at age fifteen, took the first steps toward becoming a priest. Five years later, he was expelled from seminary school for trying to overthrow the tsar's government. Born into poverty in a peasant Georgian family, he hated authority and rebelled against it while rising through the Bolshevik Party after the 1917 revolution. When Lenin died in 1924, Stalin plotted for power; by 1927, he controlled the Soviet Union. He tried to increase food production and to industrialize the country, but he brought hardship, starvation, and death to many instead. He had anyone who disagreed with him tortured, exiled, or killed. His Five-Year plans liquidated an entire class of *kulaks* (farmers) and his famine starved millions of peasants. He killed nearly 500,000 intellectuals and executed his own supporters. Glossary, Time Line, Bibliography, and Index.

316. Cavan, Seamus. **The Irish-American Experience**. Brookfield, CT: Millbrook Press, 1993. 64p. $14.90. ISBN 1-56294-218-2. 5-7

The text presents the history of Ireland with an emphasis on the last two centuries, when the Irish suffered the potato famine, and many had to leave Ireland in order to survive. Among the topics included are the Irish at sea on the way to America, tenement life in America, and the way that men started to take leadership roles in politics. Photographs, Bibliography, Notes, and Index. *Child Study Association Children's Books of the Year*.

317. Cech, John. **Jacques-Henri Lartigue: Boy with a Camera**. New York: Four Winds, 1994. 32p. $15.95. ISBN 0-02-718136-7. 4-9

From the age of seven in 1902, when he received his first camera, Jacques-Henri Lartigue (1894-1986) knew how to capture the best moment to record on his film. He kept a diary throughout his life, and his reasons for and responses to the photographs in the text are featured. Among the many unique images he caught was one of a pilot at the takeoff of an attempt to cross the English Channel from England to France.

318. Cervera, Isabel. **The Mughal Empire**. Chicago: Childrens Press, 1994. 34p. $20. ISBN 0-516-08392-9. (The World Heritage). 4-7

In 1526, Zahir ud-din, nicknamed Babur (Persian for "panther"), conquered the sultanate of Dehli, India, after a battle at Panipat. His empire became known as the Mughal (Persian for "Mongol") Empire. The Mughals governed for more than 300 years and tried to unify Hindus and Muslims. Two of Babur's successors were Akbar (1556-1605) and Shah Jahan (1627-1658). These two built the greatest works of Indo-Islamic architecture: the Red Fort of Agra, Fatehpur Sikri, the Shalimar Gardens and Fortress of Lahore (Pakistan), and the Taj Mahal. Photographs of these sites complement the text. Glossary and Index.

319.   Ceserani, Gian Paolo. **Marco Polo**. New York: Philomel, 1982. 33p. $9.95. ISBN 0-399-20843-7. 5-8

Marco Polo (1254-1323?), a thirteenth-century Venetian merchant, traveled to Asia and lived for a while in the court of Kublai Khan. His account of his travels influenced many explorers, notably Christopher Columbus. Maps complement the text.

320.   Chaikin, Miriam. **Menorahs, Mezuzas, and Other Jewish Symbols**. Erika Weihs, illustrator. New York: Clarion, 1990. 102p. $15.95. ISBN 0-899-19856-2. 5-8

Starting with the rise of a new tribe in the Middle East around 1800 B.C.E. (Before the Christian Era) and Abraham and Sarah's belief that one God rules all, Chaikin traces Jewish symbols through history. Abraham's circumcision of himself and his followers was the first symbolic act of these Jews. Chaikin covers symbolic acts and ideas; symbolic garments and dress; symbols in Jewish worship; symbols of the state of Israel; and home, number, and holiday symbols. The information will be of special aid to non-Jewish readers who need explanations of terms. Notes, Bibliography, and Index.

321.   Chaikin, Miriam. **A Nightmare in History**. New York: Clarion, 1987. 128p. $15.95. ISBN 0-89919-461-3. New York: Clarion, 1992. 128p. $7.95pa. ISBN 0-395-61579-8pa. 5 up

The Nazis murdered 6 of 9 million Jews who lived in Europe before World War II. They also murdered 5 million more people—Gypsies, Russians, Poles, Slavs, and others. Chaikin traces Judaism from Abraham and Sarah through the centuries in Europe and relates how various "hate" groups formed, eventually leading to *pogroms* and then to Hitler's atrocities. She says that the book is to keep people from forgetting. She includes many facts about the Warsaw Ghetto, Auschwitz-Birkenau, and the help that non-Jews gave to fight against the inhumanity of Hitler's "final solution." Photographs clarify the facts related. Books about the Holocaust and Index.

322.   Chalberg Chandler, David P. **The Land and People of Cambodia**. New York: HarperCollins, 1991. 210p. $17.95. ISBN 0-06-021129-6. (Portraits of Nations). 6-12

After placing Cambodia in modern times, much of this text covers its history. Although somewhat laborious to read, it offers information not readily available elsewhere about this particular country. The first historical mention of Cambodia occurred around 200 B.C. Jayavarman, who reigned from A.D. 802 to 834, founded Angkor. He and the twenty-five other Angkorean kings ruled until approximately A.D. 1300. King Suryavarman II built Angkor, the largest religious building in the world, in the twelfth century. Beginning in the fifteenth century, the Thais invaded Angkor, and the capital shifted southward to Phnom Penh. In 1863, France proclaimed a protectorate over Cambodia and made a treaty with King Norodom. The protectorate lasted until 1953. Other leaders included the Communist Saloth Sar, who took the name Pol Pot; his government, the Democratic Kampuchea (D.K.) Regime, murdered over a million Cambodians from 1976 to 1978 by starving or overworking them. In 1979, the Vietnamese Communists invaded and Pol Pot fled. In 1989, the People's Republic of Kampuchea (P.D.K.) changed its name to the State of Cambodia. Photographs, maps, and drawings augment the text. Bibliography, Filmography, Discography, and Index.

323.   Chaney, J. R. **Aleksandr Pushkin: Poet for the People**. Minneapolis, MN: Lerner, 1991. 112p. $14.95. ISBN 0-8225-4911-5. 7-12

Aleksandr Sergeevich Pushkin (1799–1837) was the first Russian writer to work in the Russian language (other poets chose French). Because of his ability to recreate the Russian cultural attitude, his country calls him the "Father of Russian Literature." He lived in St. Petersburg and got involved in various escapades before dying in a duel. Bibliography and Index.

324.   Chang, Margaret, and Raymond Chang. **In the Eye of War**. New York: Margaret K. McElderry, 1990. 198p. $14.95. ISBN 0-689-50503-5. 5-7

During Shao-Shao's tenth year, 1945, until the war ends, his family continues its routine in Shanghai, with his father working for Chiang Kai-shek's Nationalist Underground and the man across the courtyard helping the Japanese invaders. Little by little, Shao-Shao understands why his father wants him to excel at his schoolwork and why he does not like the children to keep pets. The concern of the various generations of the family for each other allows them to continue their traditions, including celebration of the New Year, though not as elaborately as in the past.

325.   Charley, Catherine. **Tombs and Treasures**. New York: Viking, 1995. 48p. $15.99. ISBN 0-670-85899-4. (See Through History). 5-7

Some of the world's greatest archaeological discoveries have included pyramids, hidden burial mounds, sunken treasure ships, mausoleums, and cities of gold. See-through cutaways of an ancient Sumerian "death pit," the tomb of Philip of Macedonia, the grave of a Moche warrior-priest, and the *Mary Rose* (a warship of Tudor

England) highlight the text. Topics on two-page spreads cover Tutankhamen (1323 B.C.), the cemetery at Ur (c. 2500 B.C.), the Etruscans (c. 600-500 B.C.), Scythian tombs (c. 500 B.C.), the first mausoleum (353 B.C.), Philip of Macedonia (336 B.C.), the Jade prince (113 B.C.), Pompeii (A.D. 79), lords of Sipán (A.D. 300), the terra cotta Chinese army (210 B.C.), the tomb of Pacal (A.D. 683), Sutton Hoo (A.D. 625), Tamerlane (A.D. 1405), El Dorado (A.D. 1544), the *Mary Rose* (A.D. 1545), and the Taj Mahal (A.D. 1632). Key Dates, Glossary, and Index. *Notable Children's Trade Books in the Field of Social Studies.*

326. Chedid, Andree. **The Multiple Child**. San Francisco: Mercury House, 1995. 177p. $12.95. ISBN 1-56279-079-X. YA

In Lebanon during the 1980s, Omar-Jo loses his arm and his parents in a car bombing outside his home. His grandfather sends him to Paris to live with relatives, but they are disinterested in him. He forms an extended family with a jazz musician and a merry-go-round operator and owner. As the story of his family emerges, the setting moves from Beirut to Cairo to Paris, and Omar-Jo shows such inner strength that he improves the lives of those who have become his friends.

327. Cheney, Glenn Alan. **El Salvador: Country in Crisis**. New York: Franklin Watts, 1990. 127p. $19.14. ISBN 0-531-04423-8. (Impact). 8 up

After El Salvador gained independence from Spain in 1821, only fourteen families owned almost all of the coffee-growing land and controlled bank and export companies. Today, although 300 families have most of the power, they are still called "fourteen families." Because people made more money exporting coffee and importing food, agriculture has never been important in the country. The feeling of helplessness after 1929 in the lower economic classes opened the way for leftist thinkers. During the Depression, few people drank coffee, so the fortunes of the wealthy also decreased, and communism began to thrive. This text is somewhat disjointed, as it intermingles historical concepts with current problems, but few accessible texts exist about El Salvador.

328. Cheney, Patricia. **The Land and People of Zimbabwe**. New York: Lippincott, 1990. 242p. $15.89. ISBN 0-397-32393-X. (Portraits of the Nations). 7-12

In a detailed discussion of the creation of modern Zimbabwe, Cheney traces its history from 30,000 B.C. when Stone Age hunter-gatherers settled on the plain. The first Bantu-speaking settlers arrived around A.D. 500 and the Shona ethnic group around A.D. 1000. The author defines *Bantu* not as a race or ethnic group but as a group of more than 400 languages spoken by Negroid peoples populating Africa south of the Sahara. Shona bases its heritage on genealogical relationships and land rights presented in an oral tradition. In 1895, the territory became Rhodesia, and by 1930 separate areas of "black" and "white" became law. Finally in 1979, Zimbabwe reemerged as a state governed by its own native settlers. The story becomes especially powerful in the firsthand personal experiences that Cheney relates. Photographs, map, and text information boxes augment the story. Bibliography and Index.

329. Chesney, Marion. **Back in Society**. New York: St. Martin's Press, 1994. 152p. $18.95. ISBN 0-312-10932-6. YA

Lady Jane Remney tries to commit suicide in the early 1880s at the Poor Relations Hotel because she cannot pay her bills. Having run away from home to avoid an arranged marriage, she soon has a choice of an Englishman or a Frenchman.

330. Chesney, Marion. **Colonel Sandhurst to the Rescue**. New York: St. Martin's Press, 1994. 152p. $17.95. ISBN 0-312-10444-8. YA

To avoid an arranged marriage with old Lord Bewley, Frederica Gray stays at the Poor Relations Hotel in the early nineteenth century, and Colonel Sandhurst decides to demand a ransom for her since her parents owe large sums to the hotel. A variety of mistaken identities eventually allow the right people to make permanent matrimonial matches.

331. Chesney, Marion. **Deborah Goes to Dover**. New York: St. Martin's Press, 1992. 151p. $16.95. ISBN 0-312-06952-9. YA

Lady Deborah Western wants to travel to a prize fight via coach in the early nineteenth century, and the only way she can go unescorted is to pretend that she is a man. On the trip to Dover, she meets Miss Pym, a matchmaker, who decides to take her case.

332. Chesney, Marion. **Finessing Clarissa**. New York: St. Martin's Press, 1989. 168p. $14.95. ISBN 0-8161-5013-3. YA

Clarissa Vevian is especially uncoordinated, but when she goes to London for the season in the early nineteenth century, the Tribble sisters decide that they will help her refine her social graces and abilities. She shows them that she can survive independently as well.

333. Chesney, Marion. **Lady Fortescue Steps Out**. New York: St. Martin's Press, 1992. 152p. $17.95. ISBN 0-312-08231-2. YA

Distressed at her situation of being a poor aristocrat, Lady Fortescue decides to rectify her situation. She persuades five other persons in her same condition to join her in opening a hotel so that they may increase their income during the early nineteenth century.

334. Chesney, Marion. **Miss Tonks Turns to Crime**. New York: St. Martin's Press, 1993. 152p. $16.95. ISBN 0-312-08846-9. YA

When the hotel that she and five others are running in the early nineteenth century needs repair, Miss Tonks decides that she will get the money wherever she can. A likely candidate is her wealthy sister, but instead of asking for a loan, Miss Tonks decides to steal from her.

335. Chesney, Marion. **Mrs. Budley Falls from Grace**. New York: St. Martin's Press, 1993. 152p. $16.95. ISBN 0-312-09342-X. YA

In the early nineteenth century, the other proprietors of the Poor Relations Hotel encourage Mrs. Budley to go to the home of a doddering marquess and take enough trinkets to support them for awhile. When she arrives, she discovers that his handsome nephew is in residence, and that he has unexpected plans for her.

336. Chesney, Marion. **Sir Philip's Folly**. New York: St. Martin's Press, 1993. 148p. $17.95. ISBN 0-312-09912-6. YA

Sir Philip Sommerville falls in love with an unsuitable woman staying at the hotel run by the Poor Relations early in the nineteenth century. They decide that they will get rid of her, and to help a young guest, whose widowed mother keeps her from going out, to find a husband.

337. Chiflet, Jean-Loup, and Alain Beaulet. **Victoria and Her Times**. George Wen, translator. New York: Henry Holt, 1996. $19.95. ISBN 0-8050-5084-1. (Who, What, When, Where, Why). 6-9

The text describes the life of Queen Victoria (1819-1901) and her era in double-page spreads. A variety of topics, including information on Sherlock Holmes and Victoria's handwriting, enliven the information. Index.

338. Child, John. **The Crusades**. Nigel Kelly, illustrator. New York: Peter Bedrick, 1996. 64p. $17.95. ISBN 0-87226-119-0. 5 up

The Crusades began in 1095 when Pope Urban II called for the first one; they did not end until the fall of Acre, the last Crusader stronghold, in 1291. Among those closely associated with the Crusades are Richard the Lionheart, Saladin, Eleanor of Acquitaine, and Saint Louis IX, King of France. Understanding the Crusades helps to interpret the continuing conflict between Christian Europe and America and Islam. Index.

339. Child, John. **The Rise of Islam**. New York: Peter Bedrick, 1995. 64p. $16.95. ISBN 0-87226-116-6. (Biographical History). 6-9

The text presents a history of Islam from the birth of Muhammad in 570 to the present. It describes the spread of the religion and its culture in the Middle East, Asia, and Europe. In two-page chapters covering a variety of topics, Child uses quotes from Islamic leaders, the Koran, and scholarly texts important to the faith. He also notes the contributions throughout history to science, literature, art, and politics from people of Islamic heritage. Index.

340. Childers, Thomas. **Wings of Morning: The Story of the Last American Bomber Shot Down over Germany in World War II**. Boston: Addison-Wesley, 1995. 276p. $23; $12pa. ISBN 0-201-48310-6; 0-201-40722-1pa. YA

In World War II, Childers's uncle was one of the 10 (two survived) who never returned from the Black Cat, the last American bomber shot down in Germany. By using letters and interviews, including the German villagers who lived near the crash, he has investigated and found that ground flak may have led the bomber off course on what turned out to be an unnecessary mission. The two who survived may or may not have been tortured. One may have died because a parachute opened too close to the ground; another may have been trapped inside the plane. In addition to the story of the crash, information about the tension and interminable waiting between flights is also provided. Index. *American Library Association Best Books for Young Adults*.

341. Chin, Tsao Hsueh. **The Dream of the Red Chamber**. Florence McHugh & Isabel McHugh, translators. 1958. Westport, CT: Greenwood Press, 1975. 582p. $37.50. ISBN 0-8371-8113-5. New York: Doubleday, 1958. 582p. $11.95pa. ISBN 0-385-09379-9pa. YA

Pao Yu, age eleven, enjoys the life of the upper class in the earlier Ching Dynasty of China, around 1729. He makes best friends with one of his cousins, Black Jade, but his parents decide that he will marry another, even though they tell him that he may marry Black Jade. Distressed when he has to marry Precious Clasp, Pao Yu becomes ill after the wedding, and Black Jade dies. After Pao Yu improves, he passes his examinations and disappears. He reappears with two monks, still wearing the jade stone around his neck that he has worn since birth. His father understands that he is from the spirit world, preferring it to the material.

342. **China from the 7th to the 19th Century**. Remo Berselli and Giorgio Bacchin, illustrators; Mary Di-Ianni, translator. Austin, TX: Raintree/Steck-Vaughn, 1994. 72p. $17.97. ISBN 0-8114-3329-3. (History of the World). 7 up

This overview uses informative illustrations and clear maps to complement the text, which is divided into two-page topics. The topics discussed are the Tang, Song, and Ming Dynasties; Mongols; Marco Polo; the birth of Vietnam; Jesuits in China; Tibet under Chinese rule; social and religious practices; and the opium trade. Glossary and Index.

343. Ching, Julia. **Probing China's Soul: Religion and the Body Politic in the People's Republic**. New York: HarperCollins, 1990. 269p. $18.95. ISBN 0-06-250139-9. YA

In 1989, Deng Xiaoping refuted democracy at Tiananmen Square by challenging demonstrating students and then massacring them. Ching writes that Deng mixed Stalin's methods with Oriental ways to gain a kind of revolutionary immortality, as did Mao Zedong who died in 1976. The author presents information on centuries of Chinese religion and philosophy and how it relates to the events during China's forty-year history of communism. Some of the sources are mainland intellectuals who have been "silenced," some under arrest. Bibliography and Index.

344. Chisholm, P. F. **A Famine of Horses**. New York: Walker, 1995. 271p. $20.95. ISBN 0-8027-3252-6. YA

Sir Robert Carey becomes the new warden in Elizabethan England and helps to solve the murder of Sweetmilk Graham before a clan war develops. Carey has to go undercover as a peddler to infiltrate an enemy's castle during his investigation.

345. Chisholm, P. F. **A Season of Knives**. New York: Walker, 1996. 231p. $19.95. ISBN 0-8027-3276-3. YA

Sir Robert Carey's servant, Barnabus, has been accused of a murder and awaits trial in the castle dungeon when Carey returns to Carlisle town during Elizabethan times. Because Barnabus had been a thief before going to work for Carey, he is a good suspect. However, Carey's knowledge of the laws of inheritance helps him deduce who might have killed the man, and he helps expose both the motive and the killer during the town square trial.

346. **Chivalry: The Path of Love**. San Francisco: Chronicle, 1994. 62p. $9.95. ISBN 0-8118-0464-X. (Little Wisdom Library—Medieval Wisdom). YA

Chivalry is the ideal code of behavior for men at arms, nobility who aspired to fame in the new European world of the twelfth and later centuries. The code of chivalry combined courage and steadfastness with personal honor, modesty, loyalty, and courtly love for one lady. After the instability of the sixth through the tenth centuries, with the exceptions of Charlemagne, Otto, monastic orders, and the priesthood, Pope Urban declared the first crusade to free Jerusalem from the heathen Saracens in 1095. He reminded men of the nobility of fighting for Christ. In 1118, the Knights of the Temple, or the Templars, formed after the Hospitalliers, seemed to represent what Urban wanted when they fought fiercely but with the characteristics deemed appropriate for a chivalrous knight. Bibliography and Further Reading.

347. Choi, Sook Nyul. **Echoes of the White Giraffe**. Boston: Houghton Mifflin, 1993. 137p. $13.95. ISBN 0-395-64721-5. New York: Yearling, 1995. 137p. $3.50pa. ISBN 0-440-40970-5pa. 6-9

Sookan, age fifteen, her mother, and her brother leave their Korean home in 1952 to seek refuge in Pusan. In this sequel to *The Year of Impossible Goodbyes*, they live in a shack near other refugee huts on a mountain covered with slick mud. Sookan makes friends with a young man but cannot pursue the relationship because her culture forbids such liaisons. She knows that when she leaves for America, after passing her exams and winning a scholarship, she will see him no more. Among the characters in the story, one refugee stands outside his hut near the top of the mountain each day and yells "Good morning"; his attitude delights Sookan. Near the end of the story, she finally reunites with the older brothers whom she and the others have longed to find. *American Library Association Notable Books for Children*.

348. Choi, Sook Nyul. **Gathering of Pearls**. Boston: Houghton Mifflin, 1994. 163p. $13.95. ISBN 0-395-67437-9. 7-12

Sookan leaves Seoul, Korea, for New York City, very concerned about her first year of school in a foreign country. She must simultaneously learn a new language and a new culture in the sequel to *The Year of Impossible Goodbyes* and *Echoes of the White Giraffe*. Her sister's responses to her letters berate her changes from her old attitudes. Sookan feels guilty for her thoughts, but her college friend suggests that Sookan not let her sister run her life. But when Sookan receives news of her mother's death, she grieves and knows that she must continue her own strand of "pearls."

349. Choi, Sook Nyul. **The Year of Impossible Goodbyes**. Boston: Houghton Mifflin, 1991. 171p. $15.95. ISBN 0-395-57419-6. New York: Yearling, 1993. $3.99pa. ISBN 0-440-40759-1pa. 5-9

Sookan, who is ten years old in 1945 when World War II ends, faces the Russian invasion after the Japanese leave North Korea. She, her mother, and her brother are separated from her father and three older brothers. The Russians capture people trying to escape across the Thirty-Eighth Parallel and detain her mother, but Sookan and her brother successfully escape to the south. The story tells about the Japanese occupation and what the soldiers did to the people, including their taking girls from work in the knitting factories to the war front to become prostitutes. *Bulletin Blue Ribbon Book* and *School Library Journal Best Book*.

350. Chrisman, Abbott. **Hernando de Soto**. Rick Whipple, illustrator. Austin, TX: Raintree/Steck-Vaughn, 1993. 32p. $13.98; $5.95pa. ISBN 0-8172-2903-5; 0-8114-6753-8pa. (Hispanic Stories). 4-7

Hernado de Soto (1500-1542) left Spain when he was fourteen to serve as a page to Don Pedro Arias de Ávila, known as Pedrarias. There de Soto met Balboa, who taught him the art of soldiering and helped him train to become a knight by the age of seventeen. He lost a battle against Cortés, a countryman he foolishly trusted, and watched Pisarro kill the Incan Atahualpa. De Soto returned to Spain and married, but he came back to the New World and explored the Mississippi before he died of malaria. Glossary. English and Spanish text.

351. Chrisman, Abbott. **Luis Muñoz Marín**. Dennis Matz, illustrator. Austin, TX: Raintree/Steck-Vaughn, 1993. 32p. $13.98; $5.95pa. ISBN 0-8114-8477-7; 0-8114-6760-0pa. (Hispanic Stories). 4-7

Luis Muñoz Marín (1898-1980), educated in the United States, wanted to be a writer, but his father's desire to see life in Puerto Rico improve became a family concern. In 1938, Muñoz Marín started a new political party in Puerto Rico and got people to support him. In 1947, the people elected him the first governor when Puerto Rico became a commonwealth. After a time in office, Muñoz Marín resigned, saying that he had helped them start and that they must continue without him. Glossary. English and Spanish text.

352. Chrisp, Peter. **The Rise of Fascism**. New York: Bookwright/Franklin Watts, 1991. 64p. $19.14. ISBN 0-531-18438-2. (Witness History). 9 up

By surveying the origins and causes of European fascism in Italy, Nazi Germany, Spain, and Romania, the text seeks both the common characteristics of the nationalistic fascist movements and the differences among them. Bibliography and Index.

353. Christianson, Gale E. **Isaac Newton and the Scientific Revolution**. New York: Oxford University Press, 1996. 155p. $19.95. ISBN 0-19-509224-4. (Oxford Portraits in Science). 8 up

This book discusses not only the theories of Isaac Newton (1642-1727) but also his life in detail. Newton was a difficult personality who could be vengeful and arrogant, but he did make important contributions to the history of science. Christianson relates Newton to his time from the beheading of Charles I and depicts his experiments in alchemy as those of a scientist utilizing the best tools and ideas known to him. Bibliography, Chronology, and Index.

354. Chua-eoan, Howard. **Corazon Aquino**. New York: Chelsea House, 1988. 112p. $18.95; $7.95pa. ISBN 1-55546-825-X; 0-7910-0553-4pa. (World Leaders Past and Present). 5 up

Although very intelligent, Corazon Aquino (b. 1933) spent her early married life as a typical Filipino housewife, raising her family and watching television. In 1986, her life changed. Her husband, a member of the opposition political party against Marcos, was murdered when he returned from the United States. The Catholic Church backed Aquino and her honesty, helping her to overthrow Marcos. In 1986, Marcos defeated her, but the military began to change its support, and its members later ousted Marcos, giving Aquino control of the government. Her help brought democracy to the Philippines. Photographs highlight the text. Chronology, Further Reading, and Index.

355. **Civilizations of Asia**. Francis Balistreri, illustrator. Austin, TX: Raintree/Steck-Vaughn, 1992. 80p. $17.97. ISBN 0-8172-3302-4. (History of the World). 7 up

This overview uses informative illustrations and clear maps to complement the text. Each two-page topic covers information from the beginnings of time until approximately A.D. 600 in China, Japan, India, Indochina, Indonesia, Australia, and Oceania. Topics about the countries contain the Paleolithic and Neolithic periods; Middle Joman Period; Indus Valley civilization; Hinduism; Asoka and Buddhism; Jainism; Shang and Zhou Dynasties; Mauray, Satavahana, and Guptan Empires; Kushan Period; Tibet; Qin and Han Empires; Yayoi Epoch in Japan; Long Bronze Age in Southeast Asia; and the birth of Indochina. Glossary and Index.

356. **Civilizations of the Americas**. Francis Balistreri, illustrator. Austin, TX: Raintree/Steck-Vaughn, 1992. 80p. $17.97. ISBN 0-8172-3306-7. (History of the World). 7 up

This overview uses informative illustrations and clear maps to complement the information about North America, Mesoamerica, and South America. Two-page discussions present North America's cultures of the West and Northwest coast, ancient peoples, Anasazi, Great Plains, Mississippi people, Arctic, and people of the

Subarctic. In Mesoamerica appear the Teotihuacan, Toltecs, Aztecs, Olmecs, Zapotecs, Mixtecs, Maya and Chichén Itzá, and Veracruz. In South America, discussions concern the Andean civilization, Incas, Caribbean, Amazon basin, Brazil, Chaco, Pampa, Uruguay, Chile, Patagonia, and Tierra del Fuego. Glossary and Index.

357. **Civilizations of the Middle East**. Francis Balistreri, illustrator. Austin, TX: Raintree/Steck-Vaughn, 1992. 80p. $17.97. ISBN 0-8172-3303-2. (History of the World). 7 up

This overview uses informative illustrations and clear maps to complement two-page discussions on Sumeria, Babylon, Assyria, Israel, Persia, Greece, and Rome, from the Neolithic Age until the spread of Christianity with Constantine in approximately A.D. 313. Cultures, people, and sites here are Obeid, Uruk, Akkadians, Susa and Elam, Hammurabi, Hittites, Hurrites, Mari, Ebla, Ugarit, Byblos, Phoenicians, Urartu, Anatolia, Achaemenid, Hebrews, Seleucids, Pergamum, Parthian, Sassanians, and the teachings of Jesus. Glossary and Index.

358. Clare, John D., ed. **Ancient Greece**. San Diego, CA: Gulliver, Harcourt Brace, 1994. 64p. $16.95. ISBN 0-15-200516-1. (Living History). 6-9

Complemented with posed photographs depicting Greece, the text looks at life in Greece from about 800 B.C. until 146 B.C. Short discussions of various topics present the Greek world, farming in Attica, Sparta, gods and goddesses, heroes, the Olympic games, Greek colonies, Marathon, Thermopylae and Salamis, Athenian democracy and empire, art and architecture, theater, knowledge and philosophy, doctors and medicine, rituals of men, craftspeople and traders, the agora, old age and death, plague and war, Philip and Alexander, Alexandria, and the rise of Rome, as well as women's roles during the period. A concluding essay explores the ways in which people today benefit from knowing what happened during that time period. Index. *Notable Children's Trade Books in the Field of Social Studies.*

359. Clare, John D., ed. **Classical Rome**. San Diego, CA: Gulliver, Harcourt Brace, 1993. 64p. $16.95. ISBN 0-15-200513-7. (Living History). 6-10

Complemented with posed photographs, the text presents the beginning and development of Rome in two-page coverage of topics. It shows everyday life, politics and government, and the achievements of Rome's architects and engineers. Index.

360. Clare, John D. **First World War**. San Diego, CA: Gulliver, Harcourt Brace, 1995. 64p. $16.95. ISBN 0-15-200087-9. (Living History). 5-8

Both real and reenactment photographs augment the text, giving an overview of World War I from its beginning, when Archduke Ferdinand and his wife Sophie were murdered in Sarajevo on June 28, 1914, until its end, on November 11, 1918. The text establishes a sense of the war by discussing why men joined the armed forces, life in the trenches, the use of gas and tanks, the fight from the air and the sea, shortages that occurred, women in the war, and the Treaty of Versailles in 1919. A concluding essay explores the ways that people today benefit from knowing what happened during that time. Index. *Notable Children's Trade Books in the Field of Social Studies.*

361. Clare, John D., ed. **Fourteenth-Century Towns**. San Diego, CA: Gulliver, Harcourt Brace, 1993. 64p. $16.95. ISBN 0-15-200515-3. (Living History). 6-10

The two-page topic spreads include photographs of persons in settings that recreate the Middle Ages. An overview of the time precedes discussions of everyday life, food, the role of the church, commerce, guilds and apprenticeships, contrasts between rich and poor, plague and famine, and social customs. A concluding essay explores the ways in which people today benefit from knowing what happened during that time period. Index.

362. Clare, John D., ed. **Industrial Revolution**. San Diego, CA: Gulliver, Harcourt Brace, 1994. 64p. $16.95. ISBN 0-15-200514-5. (Living History). 4-8

Complemented with posed photographs depicting the Industrial Revolution in Europe and America, along with photographs and prints of works created throughout the time, this text looks at the changes in life from 1712 until the end of the nineteenth century. Short discussions of various topics chronologically present the preceding economic system, trade and growth, the rise of the first factories, coal, the first railways, machines, changes in city life, iron and steel, bridges and tunnels, the men with the money, the second revolution and the attempt to gain power as a result, unions and politics, laws, medicine and health, education, philanthropy, and women's roles. A concluding essay explores the ways in which people today benefit from knowing what happened during that time period. Index. *Notable Children's Trade Books in the Field of Social Studies.*

363. Clare, John D. **Italian Renaissance**. San Diego, CA: Gulliver/Harcourt Brace, 1995. 64p. $16.95. ISBN 0-15-200088-7. (Living History). 7-9

Complemented with posed photographs depicting Renaissance times and prints of works created during the Renaissance, the text looks at life in Italy from approximately 1268 until 1559. Short discussions of various topics present the Humanists of Florence; the courts of Italy; the artists in a variety of fields, including

Leonardo da Vinci, Michelangelo, and Raphael; and comments on courtiers' and women's roles during the period. A concluding essay explores the ways in which people today benefit from knowing what happened during that time period. Index.

364.   Clare, John D. **Knights in Armor**. San Diego, CA: Gulliver/Harcourt Brace, 1996. 64p. $9pa. ISBN 0-15-201308-3pa. (Living History). 7-9
    Complemented with posed photographs depicting medieval times, the text looks at life in Europe during the eleventh, twelfth, and early thirteenth centuries. Short discussions of various topics include the difficult training for becoming a knight, the tournaments, the lengthy crusades to stop the Infidels, the long pilgrimages to worship at religious shrines, and the roles of women during the time. A concluding essay explores the ways in which people today benefit from knowing what happened during that time period. Index.

365.   Clare, John D., ed. **The Vikings**. San Diego, CA: Gulliver, Harcourt Brace, 1996. 64p. $9pa. ISBN 0-15-201309-1pa. (Living History). 6-10
    Complemented with posed photographs depicting Viking times and prints of works created during the Viking period, the text looks at Viking life, including religion, peoples, clothes, homes, and customs, as well as how Viking families spent the long Scandinavian winters. A concluding essay explores the ways in which people today benefit from knowing what happened during that time period. Index. *Notable Children's Trade Books in the Field of Social Studies.*

366.   Clark, Mary Jane Behrends. **The Commonwealth of Independent States**. Brookfield, CT: Millbrook Press, 1992. 64p. $16.40. ISBN 1-56294-081-3. (Headliners). 4-8
    Eleven countries that were once part of the Soviet Union declared their independence in 1991. Their backgrounds indicate that, in addition to their common problem of surviving through the reign of Stalin and the Communist regime, they have had and will have diverse problems as part of a loosely federated commonwealth. The text discusses the countries, histories. and peoples of Russia, Ukraine, Belarus, Moldova, Armenia, Azerbaijan, Uzbekistan, Kazakhstan, Turkmenistan, Kyrgyzstan, and Tajikistan. Chronology, For Further Reading, and Index. *Society of School Librarians International Best.*

367.   Clavell, James. **Noble House**. 1981. New York: Dell, 1993. 1200p. $6.99pa. ISBN 0-440-16484-2pa. YA
    In 1841, the first *tai-pan* (corporate head) of Noble House, a Hong Kong trading company, said that he would do anything for the person who could present the other half of a specific coin. When two Americans arrive in 1963, they do not understand the history behind Hong Kong business or the unwritten rules of trade. The Chinese know how to get as much as possible from their deals, and the British control everything. Competition between Noble House and its rival causes intrigues to develop at various levels of the corporation's society.

368.   Clavell, James. **Shogun**. 1975. New York: Dell, 1993. 803p. $6.99pa. ISBN 0-440-17800-2pa. YA
    In 1600, John Blackthorne shipwrecks in Japanese waters. Jealous Spanish and Portuguese Jesuits in Japan translate for him and misrepresent his intentions. But Toranaga, the man positioning himself to become shogun of all Japan, realizes that Blackthorne is honest, and he frees Blackthorne from prison. He matches Blackthorne with a trustworthy Japanese instructor, with whom Blackthorne falls in love. After watching Blackthorne's progress, Toranaga realizes that the former ship's pilot is the one man in Japan who will not conspire against him.

369.   Claypool, Jane. **Saddam Hussein**. Vero Beach, FL: Rourke, 1993. 110p. $22.60. ISBN 0-86625-477-3. (World Leaders). 5-9
    Saddam Hussein (b. 1937) fought a war with the United States in 1991 and lost. To place him within his world, the text gives an overview of Islam (beginning with Mohammed) as it discusses the resurgence of Iraq, the rise of Arab nationalism, the assassinations associated with the Arab nations, Saddam's exile in Egypt, his battle with the Kurds on the Turkish border, and the war with the United States over Kuwait. Photographs, Sunni and Shiite: The Two Main Branches of Islam, Time Line, Glossary, Bibliography, Media Resources, and Index.

370.   Clements, Bruce. **The Treasure of Plunderell Manor**. New York: Farrar, Straus & Giroux, 1987. 180p. $12.95. ISBN 0-374-37746-4. 6-9
    Laurel, age fourteen, abandoned in England as a baby, becomes maid to mistress Alice at Plunderell Manor in 1853. Orphaned Alice lives in the house with her aunt and uncle, who have locked her in a tower room and would like for her to disappear before she turns eighteen and inherits her fortune. Laurel helps Alice solve the riddle that reveals where her parents hid the family treasure; in the process, she saves Alice's life. Laurel, however, decides that she would rather go to America than be wealthy in a society she does not like.

371.   Clements, Gillian, author/illustrator. **An Illustrated History of the World: How We Got to Where We Are**. New York: Farrar, Straus & Giroux, 1992. 62p. $16. ISBN 0-374-33258-4. 6-8

Clements presents single- and double-spread cartoon segments that cover the events in a period of world history, beginning with theories about the origin of the universe. She continues into the 1970s and ends with a timeline noting different epochs of history. Chronology.

372.   Clucas, Joan Graff. **Mother Teresa**. New York: Chelsea House, 1988. 112p. $18.95; $7.95pa. ISBN 1-55546-855-1; 0-7910-0602-6pa. (World Leaders Past and Present). 5 up

Mother Teresa (1910–1997) grew up in Skopje in what was then Yugoslavia. When she was eighteen, she joined the Loreto order of missionary nuns in India and took her final vows nine years later. After nine more years passed, she began work with the destitute by establishing her own order, the Missionaries of Charity. In Calcutta, she found shelters for the homeless, the sick, and the dying. In 1965, she began her world travels to establish other centers like this one. By 1969, she had started the International Association of Co-Workers of Mother Teresa as an organization for lay supporters to work with her programs. In 1979, she received the Nobel Peace Prize. Photographs enhance the text. Chronology, Further Reading, and Index.

373.   Cockcroft, James. **Daniel Ortega**. New York: Chelsea House, 1991. 112p. $18.95. ISBN 1-55546-846-2. (World Leaders Past and Present). 5 up

While in prison for eight years, Daniel Ortega (b. 1945) organized his fellow inmates to overthrow the oppressive Somoza regime in Nicaragua once they were released. They succeeded in 1979 and installed a provisional government on the Day of Joy. One year later, the United States backed rebels who launched an attack against the new Sandinista government. In 1984, the people elected Ortega president, but the fighting, backed with U.S. money, continued for ten more years. In 1990, elections named a new president. Ortega's subversive activities during the 1960s allowed the more democratic government to become a reality in the 1990s. Photographs enhance the text. Chronology, Further Reading, and Index.

374.   Cockcroft, James. **Diego Rivera**. New York: Chelsea House, 1991. 120p. $18.95; $7.95pa. ISBN 0-7910-1252-2; 0-7910-1279-4pa. (Hispanics of Achievement). 5 up

Diego Rivera (1886-1957) studied art in Europe, but decided not to paint in the European tradition. He worked to develop a uniquely Mexican—and uniquely Rivera—style. After living in Paris for ten years, he returned to Mexico and began painting frescoes and murals. In his work, he treated religious subjects irreverently. Because he condemned social injustice and wanted to celebrate the spirit of the ordinary person, he experimented with communism. His leftist politics, as well as his lifestyle, threatened the wealthy, but he refused to let their opinions rule his life. Photographs and reproductions enhance the text. Chronology, Further Reading, and Index.

375.   Cockcroft, James. **Mohammed Reza Pahlavi: Shah of Iran**. New York: Chelsea House, 1988. 112p. $18.95. ISBN 1-55546-847-0. (World Leaders Past and Present). 5 up

Mohammed Reza Pahlavi (1919-1980) became the Shah of Iran in 1940 and led his country for thirty-seven years in a tyrannical reign. He quelled an uprising in 1953, but the Islamic clergy, under the leadership of the Ayatollah Khomeini, forced him out in 1979 after he murdered unarmed protesters in the streets during 1978. Some historians see him as one of the most brutal leaders in history; others think that his leadership introduced modern technology into Iran. Photographs enhance the text. Chronology, Further Reading, and Index.

376.   Codye, Corinn. **Luis W. Alvarez**. Bob Masheris, illustrator. Austin, TX: Raintree/Steck-Vaughn, 1993. 32p. $13.98; $5.95pa. ISBN 0-8114-8467-X; 0-8114-6750-3pa. (Hispanic Stories). 4-7

Luis Alvarez (1911-1988) grew up in California, where he started his scientific career as a youngster by building a radio. He became especially interested in physics, and when the atom bomb fell on Hiroshima in 1945, he and a team of men flew around the area to measure its impact. Later, he and colleagues built a hydrogen bubble chamber in which they discovered many new atomic particles. His work won him the Nobel Prize in Physics in 1968. A new interest in his later life was geology. He and his son studied rocks and hypothesized that a meteor crashing into the Earth had destroyed the dinosaurs because they identified iridium that would not otherwise have been found in Earth's rocks. Glossary.

377.   Codye, Corinn. **Queen Isabella I**. Rick Whipple, illustrator. Austin, TX: Raintree/Steck-Vaughn, 1993. 32p. $13.98; $5.95pa. ISBN 0-8172-3380-6; 0-8114-6758-9pa. (Hispanic Stories). 4-7

Isabella (1451-1504), daughter of the king and queen of Castile, near Ávila in Spain, never expected to be queen because her brother was next in the line of succession. Her brother, however, was not a good king, and Castilian nobles urged her to assume the throne. To keep from war, she suggested that Henry be king but that he designate her as his heir. She married Ferdinand, crown prince of Aragón, because she wanted Spain united as a Catholic country. All of her decisions worked to this end, including the one that provided Columbus with money to go to the New World; he had to promise that he would take the Catholic religion to those he met. The Inquisition occurred under her reign, but many speculate that she was unaware of the horrors inflicted by the priests on Muslims, Jews, and alleged heretics. Glossary.

378. Coerr, Eleanor. **Mieko and the Fifth Treasure**. New York: Putnam, 1993. 79p. $13.95. ISBN 0-399-22434-3. 4-7

Meiko, age ten, has four tangible treasures—a sable brush, an inkstick, an inkstone, and a roll of rice paper. She remembers her art teacher telling her, before the bomb dropped on Nagasaki, Japan, in 1945, that she had a fifth treasure—beauty in her heart. But the bomb hurt her hand, and she can no longer paint as she did before. In her new school near her grandparents' farm, she feels isolated, and the children tease her about her scar. She must search deeply to regain the fifth treasure.

379. Cohen, Daniel. **The Alaska Purchase**. Brookfield, CT: Millbrook Press, 1996. 64p. $15.90. ISBN 1-56294-528-9. (Spotlight on American History). 4-8

In 1867, the United States bought from Russia the land that became the 49th state, Alaska. The text looks at the events from 1728 through 1864 that led to the completion of the purchase. Other topics cover the discovery of Alaska, the sea-otter trade, the land of Alaska under Russian rule, the American takeover of the land, and what happened to Alaska after its purchase. Primary sources help to tell Alaska's story along with photographs and reproductions. Chronology, Bibliography, Further Reading, and Index.

380. Cohen, Daniel. **The Ghosts of War**. New York: Putnam, 1990. 95p. $13.95. ISBN 0-399-22200-6. New York: Minstrel, 1993. 95p. $2.99pa. ISBN 0-671-74086-5pa. 5-8

Reports of ghosts near battlefields have occurred in all times. The text recounts samurai ghosts from 1180 to 1185, the angel of Mons in 1914, a Polish mercenary of the Revolutionary War, Steven Decatur's ghost after 1820 in Washington, D.C., and Lieutenant Muir in Canada in 1812. Other ghosts also appear in these thirteen ghost tales, which Cohen says are "true" to the people who related them. Whether the stories can be verified is perhaps not as important as the concepts of realism and the history they impart.

381. Cohen, Daniel. **Prophets of Doom**. Brookfield, CT: Millbrook Press, 1992. 144p. $15.90. ISBN 1-56294-068-6. 6-9

Taking a skeptical view that anyone can accurately predict the future, the text covers the Millerites, Jehovah's Witnesses, the Greek oracles, the Cumaean Sybil, Mother Shipton, the Bible, Nostradamus, and Edgar Cayce. By noting various prophecies and their failures, Cohen supports his thesis. Bibliography and Index.

382. Cohen, Daniel. **Real Vampires**. New York: Cobblehill, Dutton, 1995. 114p. $13.99. ISBN 0-525-65189-6. 6-8

Cohen presents vampires in various time periods throughout the world. He includes a German vampire from the early eighteenth century, Hungarian vampires in 1715 and 1725, Chinese and Russian vampires from various centuries, and English vampires since the twelfth century, including nineteenth-century vampires in Oxford and at Highgate. Selected Bibliography.

383. Coldsmith, Don. **Runestone**. New York: Bantam, 1995. 489p. $21.95; $5.99pa. ISBN 0-553-09643-5; 0-553-57280-6pa. YA

Because blond, blue-eyed Native Americans live in Oklahoma today, Coldsmith speculates who might have been their forefathers and mothers in this fictional work. The protagonist, Nils Thorsson, a Viking shipmaster, lands in Newfoundland, Canada, and begins exploring the continent. He and his friend have problems that they cannot solve without the help of Odin, a Native American. The two become assimilated into Odin's tribe and father offspring. Their exciting story may or may not answer the original question.

384. Cole, Alison. **Perspective**. New York: Dorling Kindersley, 1992. 64p. $16.95. ISBN 1-56458-068-7. (Eyewitness Art). 12 up

In 27 minichapters, Cole gives a guide to the theory and techniques of perspective, from its beginnings in the Renaissance in the thirteenth century to pop art and its flatness in the twentieth. Chronology, Glossary, and Index.

385. Cole, Sheila. **The Dragon in the Cliff: A Novel Based on the Life of Mary Anning**. T. C. Farrow, illustrator. New York: Lothrop, Lee & Shepard, 1991. 211p. $12.95. ISBN 0-688-10196-8. 5-7

Mary Anning, age seven, begins climbing the cliffs surrounding the beaches of Lyme Regis, England, to find fossils that her father can clean and sell to tourists. In 1910, her father dies and Mary works to support her family. In 1812, she discovers a fossil ichthyosaurus, or "crocodile," as she called it, that measures seventeen feet. She makes other discoveries, but because women of that time were not archaeologists and never wrote scientific papers, no one mentions her work. Although poor and uneducated, she is very intelligent and teaches herself about her discoveries.

386. Collins, Alan. **Jacob's Ladder**. New York: Dutton, 1989. 151p. $13.95. ISBN 0-525-67272-9. 9 up

Jacob, age thirteen, angrily refuses help during the Australian Depression after his father dies in an "accident" that was probably the result of anti-Semitic laborers pushing him off a cliff. Jacob's stepmother also rejects him and his younger brother. A social worker takes them to a Jewish orphanage in Sydney where other Jewish children wait for their parents to escape Hitler's Holocaust. Jacob continues to feel alienated from these children, whose backgrounds are so different from his, but the Zionist youth and the Communist community begin to interest him after his brother is arrested for stealing.

387.   Collins, David R. **Tales for Hard Times: A Story About Charles Dickens**. David Mataya, illustrator. Minneapolis, MN: Carolrhoda, 1990. 64p. $9.95. ISBN 0-87614-433-4. (Creative Minds). 4-8

Writing about times in the nineteenth century, Charles Dickens (1812-1870) drew on his own poverty-stricken past, and delighted his audiences around the world. Drawings complement the text. Bibliography.

388.   Columbus, Christopher. **The Log of Christopher Columbus**. Robert H. Fuson, translator. Camden, ME: International Marine/TAB, 1987. 272p. $29.95. ISBN 0-87742-951-0. YA

The translation of the log that Columbus kept on his voyages, beginning on August 3, 1492, and ending on March 15, 1493, forms the main body of the text. Additional material about the background of the log; about Columbus, the man; and descriptions of the ships and the sailors' navigational abilities makes the book much more informative. Appendices include theories of landfall, crews of the expedition, Columbus's voyages before 1492, roots and tubers, and Columbus's first days. Bibliography and Index.

389.   Colver, Anne. **Florence Nightingale: War Nurse**. New York: Chelsea House, 1992. 80p. $14.95. ISBN 0-7910-1466-5. (Discovery Biography). 3-7

Florence Nightingale (1820-1910) enjoyed playing "nurse" as a child and graduated to tending animals before she began nursing humans in her village. Her wealthy family disapproved of her career choice, but she refused to give up her work for marriage. She became skilled enough that the British government sent her to help in the Crimean War. In England, she became a heroine, and returned to found the Nightingale School for training nurses.

390.   Compton, Anita. **Marriage Customs**. New York: Thomson Learning, 1993. 32p. $13.95. ISBN 1-56847-033-9. (Comparing Religions). 4-8

Six major religions—Buddhism, Christianity, Hinduism, Judaism, Islam, and Sikhism—have specific ceremonies for marriage. Some have signed contracts and ways of affirming the promises connected to the marriage. In all, marriage has its basis in the family's life. Photographs enhance the information. Glossary, Books to Read, and Index.

391.   Conlon-McKenna, Marita. **Fields of Home**. New York: Holiday House, 1997. 189p. $15.95. ISBN 0-8234-1295-4. 5-7

The third and final segment of the O'Driscoll family trilogy following *Under the Hawthorn Tree* (1990) and *Wildflower Girl* (1992) occurs twelve years after the Irish potato famine almost destroyed the children. Eily remains in Ireland on a tenant farm with her husband and children, Michael trains to be a horseman, and Peggy continues to work as a housemaid in Boston. All have serious problems to face and difficult decisions to make as they remain concerned about each member of their family.

392.   Conlon-McKenna, Marita. **Under the Hawthorn Tree**. Donald Teskey, illustrator. New York: Holiday House, 1990. 153p. $13.95. ISBN 0-8234-0838-8. 5 up

During the Irish famine of the 1840s, twelve-year-old Eily looks after her younger siblings, Michael and Peggy, while their mother goes to find their father, who is working on the roads. While the children's mother is gone, the bailiff repossesses the house, and the children have to find some way to survive without going to the workhouse. Remembering their mother's story of her childhood, the children walk to the far-off town where two aunts may still live. They succeed after having seen many whom they consider even worse off than they during this terrible time. *IRA Teachers' Award.*

393.   Conlon-McKenna, Marita. **Wildflower Girl**. New York: Holiday House, 1992. 173p. $14.95. ISBN 0-8234-0988-0. 5-7

In this sequel to *Under the Hawthorn Tree*, Peggy, the youngest in her family at thirteen, decides to leave Ireland and her siblings to go to America. After suffering through forty days in steerage class on a ship crossing the Atlantic, she reaches Boston. She first works for an alcoholic who beats her. She finds another position with a wealthy family where the work is hard but fair. Her relationship with her fellow workers makes her feel as if she has some family around her again.

394.   Connolly, Peter, author/illustrator. **Pompeii**. New York: Oxford University Press, 1990. 77p. $19.95; $11.95pa. ISBN 0-19-917159-9; 0-19-917158-0pa. 6-8

The text describes the eruption of Mt. Vesuvius, the volcano that destroyed Pompeii in A.D. 79, by examining the excavation finds at the site. Connolly includes detailed drawings recreating the scenes that might have been caught in the lava on that day. Maps, Glossary, and Index.

395. Connolly, Peter, author/illustrator. **The Roman Fort**. New York: Oxford University Press, 1991. 32p. $19.95. ISBN 0-19-917108-4. (Rebuilding the Past). 6-10

Topographical maps and drawings clearly show the aspects of a Roman fort along Hadrian's Wall in England on the northwest frontier in A.D. 43. The fort is Vindolanda, where the Batavians and Tungrians fought with the Romans. Among the topics presented are the division of soldiers into cohorts and centuries, the headquarters, morning reports, the day's work, toilets, water and waste, baths, the village around the fort, and death and burial practices. Index.

396. Connolly, Peter. **Tiberius Claudius Maximus: The Cavalryman**. New York: Oxford University Press, 1989. 32p. $12.95. ISBN 0-19-917106-8. 5-9

A Roman soldier who served over thirty years for the Emperor Trajan in the Seventh Legion, Tiberius Claudius Maximus lived from approximately A.D. 70. His story appears on his tombstone, discovered in northern Greece in 1965. He captured Decebalus, the Dacian leader who lived in Romania beyond the Danube. This text presents the second part of his career as he returned to Tapae, helped bring about the fall of Sarmizegethusa, and was rewarded for his bravery and his devotion to duty as a member of the cavalry. Photographs, Illustrations, and Index.

397. Connolly, Peter. **Tiberius Claudius Maximus: The Legionary**. New York: Oxford University Press, 1989. 32p. $12.95. ISBN 0-19-917105-X. 5-9

A Roman soldier who served over thirty years for the Emperor Trajan in the Seventh Legion, Tiberius Claudius Maximus lived from approximately A.D. 70. His story appears on his tombstone, discovered in northern Greece in 1965. He captured Decebalus, the Dacian leader who lived in Romania beyond the Danube. Topics in this text discuss the first part of his career and include his life as a soldier, from his sore feet through weapons training to bridging the Danube. The text also looks at the camp in enemy territory, the armor and weapons used, and the battle itself. Photographs, Illustrations, and Index.

398. Conrad, Pam. **Pedro's Journal: A Voyage with Christopher Columbus**. Peter Koeppen, illustrator. Honesdale, PA: Caroline House, 1991. 81p. $13.95. ISBN 1-878093-17-7. New York: Scholastic, 1992. 81p. $2.95pa. ISBN 0-590-46206-7pa. 3-7

Pedro accompanies Christopher Columbus on the *Santa Maria* in 1492 because he can read and write. He records the crew's frustration, Columbus's responses to events, their encounters with the natives, and the fierceness of storms on their return to Spain.

399. Cookson, Catherine. **The Harrogate Secret**. New York: Summit, 1988. 352p. $18.95. ISBN 0-671-65941-3. YA

Freddie lives in a small coal-mining and shipbuilding English town where he works for people in The Towers. He falls in love with Belle, but has to use his talents to escape poverty so that he can win her in marriage. His blind sister uses her ability to hear and smell to warn people in times of danger, and she helps Freddie to escape his own dangers.

400. Cookson, Catherine. **The Moth**. New York: Summit, 1986. 294p. $17.95. ISBN 0-671-44076-4. YA

Robert's father dies in 1913 when Robert is in his early twenties, and Robert begins building furniture for his uncle's British business. He meets Agnes, an upper-class woman, with whom he falls in love, but her brothers threaten to disown her if she marries him. Robert's unexpected inheritance of his uncle's wealth removes the brothers' hostility toward him.

401. Cookson, Catherine. **The Parson's Daughter**. New York: Summit, 1987. 390p. $19.95. ISBN 0-671-63293-0. YA

Mary Ann is twelve years old when she meets David as he sits near a river bordering her family's parsonage. She finds out that he is illegitimate, but he becomes her friend. She eventually marries, is widowed twice, and her daughter runs away before she meets David again. He has become wealthy from his inheritance, and she finds happiness by returning with him to Australia.

402. Cookson, Catherine. **The Rag Nymph**. New York: Simon & Schuster, 1993. 351p. $22. ISBN 0-671-86477-7. YA

In 1854, Millie, age seven, goes to live with "Raggie Aggie," a woman who sells rags in an undesirable part of town. Aggie changes her life to protect Millie so that she will grow up safely.

403.   Cookson, Catherine. **The Wingless Bird**. New York: Summit, 1991. 383p. $19.95. ISBN 0-671-66620-7. YA

Agnes, aged twenty-two, knows that she must escape the demands that her father places on her to manage his business. In 1913, she meets and plans to marry a wealthy, upper-middle-class man. Both her selfish father and Charles's father try to prevent the marriage. After Charles dies from tuberculosis, Agnes meets his brother, who was wounded in World War I, and finds happiness with him.

404.   Coolidge, Olivia. **The Golden Days of Greece**. Enrico Arno, illustrator. 1968. New York: HarperCollins, 1990. 224p. $14.89. ISBN 0-690-04795-0. 4-7

First the Achaeans and then the Dorians arrived in the land that became Greece. Coolidge gives a solid overview of Greek history, beginning with Heinrich Schliemann's discovery of the treasures of Troy and Agamemnon's gold at Mycenae, which seem to verify Homer's stories in *The Iliad*. The other chapters include the origins of the Olympic games, Aristodemos the Spartan, the Persians' attack and the ensuing Greek victories, Pericles, Socrates, Plato, Philip, and Alexander. Greek Words and Proper Names and Index.

405.   Coolidge, Olivia. **Marathon Looks on the Sea**. Erwin Schachner, illustrator. Boston: Houghton Mifflin, 1967. 248p. $3.50. ISBN 0-395-06724-3. 7-10

Metiochos, the son of a Greek general early separated from him, becomes the favorite of Darius, the Persian king. When Persia and Athens meet at Marathon in 490 B.C., Metiochos worries about his part in deciding the outcome of the battle. He has to decide how to face both his father and his benefactor.

406.   Cooper, Ilene. **The Dead Sea Scrolls**. John Thompson, illustrator. New York: William Morrow, 1997. 64p. $15. ISBN 0-688-14300-8. 5-9

In 1947, a young boy found some crumbling scrolls in a cave near the Dead Sea. What the scrolls contained has caused controversy since the boy sold them. Cooper tells of the quest to own the scrolls, the rivalry among Biblical scholars to interpret them, and the coincidences and scientific advances that have shown their age and importance. Index.

407.   Cooper, Susan. **Dawn of Fear**. Margery Gill, illustrator. 1970. New York: Aladdin, 1989. $3.95pa. ISBN 0-689-71327-4pa. 5 up

Derek lives with his family outside London during World War II, and they have to go to the local shelters almost every night during air raids. When a bomb hits his friend's house one night and kills his friend, the war takes on a different meaning. Derek has to adjust to the huge hole in his own life.

408.   Cooper, Tracy E. **Renaissance**. New York: Abbeville Press, 1995. 95p. $12.95. ISBN 0-7892-0023-6. (Abbeville Stylebooks). YA

Beginning with an overview of the Age of Exploration, the text focuses on Renaissance architecture and design. Buildings (inside and outside), furnishings of palaces and apartments, churches, gardens, theaters, piazzas, and cities all appear. Photographs and reproductions augment the text. Index.

409.   Cooperstein, Claire. **Johanna: A Novel of the van Gogh Family**. New York: Scribners, 1996. 256p. $22. ISBN 0-684-80234-1. YA

The sister-in-law of Vincent van Gogh and wife of Theo, Vincent's beloved brother, accepted Vincent as a member of the family. At Vincent's death, Theo collapsed mentally and never recovered. Johanna, left as a widow with a young son, had little money and a collection of Vincent's paintings. After her father suggested that she sell the paintings for firewood, she devoted her life to gaining recognition for Vincent's genius. She helped him gain a place in the art world while she also became an activist for women's rights in Holland. *School Library Journal Best Adult Books for Young Adults.*

410.   Corbishley, Mike. **Ancient Rome**. New York: Facts on File, 1989. 96p. $17.95. ISBN 0-8160-1970-3. (Cultural Atlas for Young People). 6-9

The text describes all areas of the Roman Empire: Rome itself, other areas of Italy, Africa, Spain, Gaul, Greece, Britain, and Asia Minor. Sidebars and beautiful color illustrations reveal the Rome of the Caesars, the Greek influence on poets and dramatists, and other aspects of daily life during Roman times. Bibliography, Chronology, Glossary, Gazetteer, and Index.

411.   Corbishley, Mike. **Everyday Life in Roman Times**. Peter Kesteven, illustrator. New York: Franklin Watts, 1994. 32p. $18. ISBN 0-531-14288-4. (Clues to the Past). 4-8

The Roman civilization and the daily lives of its people are the subjects of this book. The text reveals the strictly observed social strata and the customs of the times; illustrations show examples of the buildings, the dress, the foods, and the items people used for various activities. Index.

412. Corbishley, Mike. **The Medieval World: From the Fall of Rome to the Discovery of America**. New York: Peter Bedrick, 1993. 64p. $18.95. ISBN 0-87226-362-2. (Timelink). 5 up

The text surveys the known world between A.D. 450 and 1500. In detailed time charts, one sees what was happening simultaneously in Africa, Europe, Asia, and the Americas. Among the topics presented are Buddhism, Islam, the Vikings, the Crusades, the plague, and medieval towns. Photographs, maps, and charts highlight the text. Glossary and Index.

413. Corbishley, Mike. **The Middle Ages**. New York: Facts on File, 1990. 96p. $17.95. ISBN 0-8160-1973-8. (Cultural Atlas for Young People). 6-9

Beginning with an overview of medieval Europe, the text then covers the barbarians, Crusades, and empires of the time. Sidebars include information on topics such as stained glass design and the Bayeux Tapestry, which illustrates William's landing in England in 1066. The second section covers the history of each region of Europe, including Scandinavia and Russia. Informative color illustrations augment the text. Bibliography, Chronology, Glossary, Gazetteer, and Index.

414. Corbishley, Mike. **Rome and the Ancient World**. New York: Facts on File, 1993. 78p. $17.95. ISBN 0-8160-2786-2. (Illustrated History of the World). 4-7

The first section of text covers the rise of Rome, the Empire, and everyday life in the Empire. The second segment looks at the world outside the Empire. In this world is ancient China, ancient India, the Kushars, the Parthian and Sassanian Empires, and Africa's Nok, Axum, and Petra. Beautiful illustrations highlight the text. Glossary, Further Reading, and Index.

415. Corbishley, Mike. **Secret Cities**. Roger Walker, illustrator. New York: Lodestar, 1989. 47p. $14.95. ISBN 0-525-67275-3. (Time Detectives). 4-7

Covering a span of 8,000 years, the text speculates about the lives in cities that have been excavated or restored. The cities covered (with approximate dates) are Skara Brae in Scotland (3000 B.C.), Biskupin in Poland (750 B.C.), Jorvik in England (A.D. 800), Çatal Hüyük in Turkey (6500 B.C.), the Pyramid of Khufu in Egypt (2700 B.C.), Knossos in Greece (1500 B.C.), Pompeii and Herculaneum in Italy (A.D. 100), Mohenjo-Daro in China (A.D. 1400), Great Zimbabwe in Zimbabwe (A.D. 1400), Ch'in Shi-huang-ti in China (200 B.C.), Mesa Verde in the United States (A.D. 1200), Machu Picchu in Peru (A.D. 1400), and Williamsburg in the United States (A.D. 1800). Glossary and Index.

416. Corbishley, Mike. **What Do We Know About the Romans?** New York: Peter Bedrick, 1992. 45p. $16.95. ISBN 0-87226-352-5. (What Do We Know About . . .?). 3-7

In an attempt to give a sense of Roman life, the text covers school, work, food, family, clothes, gods, medicine, government, the arts, inventions, travel, and military obligations. Illustrations complement the text. Index.

417. Cordoba, Maria. **Pre-Columbian Peoples of North America**. Chicago: Childrens Press, 1994. 34p. $20. ISBN 0-516-08393-7. (The World Heritage). 4-7

Photographs clearly augment the text in this discussion of the people who lived in North America before Columbus arrived. The main sites presented in Canada are Bison Cliff, where bison jumped; Anthony Island, where the Haida Indians built totem poles; and L'Anse aux Meadows National Historic Park, which holds definitive proof that the Vikings settled in America before Columbus. Two sites in the United States are Mesa Verde National Park, home to the Anasazi nearly 700 years ago, and Cahokia Mounds Historic Site, where remains of mounds that denoted the Mississippian culture are found. Glossary and Index.

418. Corkett, Anne. **Norman Bethune**. Milwaukee, WI: Gareth Stevens, 1990. 68p. $16.95. ISBN 0-8368-0373-6. (People Who Have Helped the World). 7-9

Born in 1890 into a Canadian minister's home, Norman Bethune very early asserted his independence by his activities and his interests. He went to college, left school to go to work, returned to school, worked, enlisted in World War I, and finished his medical training in England. He was very disturbed that the Canadian health system did not give poor people adequate health care. After a failed marriage, tuberculosis, and a failed remarriage to the same woman, he decided to go to Spain to help the Loyalists against Franco. There he developed mobile blood transfusion units that were widely used during World War II. But Bethune did not live to see his success. He died in China in 1939, where he had gone to help Mao Zedong's Eighth Route Army fight the Japanese. Medical conditions were so poor that he was one of few qualified doctors for 13 million civilians and 15,000 troops. He learned to improvise and, most importantly, taught the Chinese so that they could teach others how to give medical aid. Only recently has he been acknowledged in Canada for his actions, but he has been a hero in China since his death. Organizations, Books, Glossary, Chronology, and Index.

419.	Cornwell, Bernard. **Enemy of God**. New York: St. Martin's Press, 1997. 416p. $24.95. ISBN 0-312-15523-9. YA

Derfel tells about Arthur as one of his closest friends in the sequel to *The Winter King*. Arthur tries to unite the Britons against the Saxons who want their land and to support Christianity, while Merlin's followers want to preserve the Celtic Druid ways. Arthur also tries to save the throne for nasty Mordred before Guinevere and Lancelot betray him.

420.	Cornwell, Bernard. **The Winter King: A Novel of Arthur**. New York: St. Martin's Press, 1996. 431p. $14.95. ISBN 0-312-15696-0. YA

Derfel Cadarn, one of Merlin's foundlings in the sixth century, tells the story of fighting with Arthur, his hero. Since Arthur is illegitimate, he has no political clout that he does not earn, and he works hard to rid the country of the invading Saxons. Unfortunately, he chooses to marry the scheming Guinevere instead of the intended Ceinwyn, and he must deal with her as well as the cowardly Lancelot.

421.	Corrain, Lucia. **Giotto and Medieval Art: The Lives and Works of the Medieval Artists**. Sergio Ricciardi and Andrea Ricciardi, illustrators. New York: Peter Bedrick, 1995. 64p. $19.95. ISBN 0-87226-315-0. 4 up

As painter, architect, and engineer, Giotto (1267-1337) was the most influential artist of medieval Europe. The text recounts his life, his techniques, and his masterpiece frescoes, wood-panel paintings, and mosaics. Included in the text are many reproductions of his work and pictures of the times. Index.

422.	Corrick, James A. **The Byzantine Empire**. San Diego, CA: Lucent, 1996. 112p. $16.95. ISBN 1-56006-307-6. (World History). 7-10

The text, with boxed excerpts from primary and secondary sources and visual accents, tells an interesting story of the Byzantines who came to power after the fall of the Roman Empire. Their mystery becomes a little clearer in the text. Bibliography, Chronology, Further Reading, and Index.

423.	Corzine, Phyllis. **The Black Death**. San Diego, CA: Lucent, 1996. 112p. $16.95. ISBN 1-56006-299-1. (World History). 5-8

The bubonic plague permeated Europe, killing millions. This text discusses its spread from Asia on ships trading throughout the known world. Overpopulation and lack of sanitation in Europe incited it. Changes resulted from the rapid decrease in population such as the breakdown of the feudal system, revised attitudes toward religion, and different farming methods. Photographs, maps, and reproductions augment the text. Bibliography, Chronology, Further Reading, and Index.

424.	Corzine, Phyllis. **The French Revolution**. San Diego, CA: Lucent, 1995. 112p. $14.95. ISBN 1-56006-248-7. (World History). 7 up

The French Revolution began with the storming of the Bastille on July 14, 1789. The text looks at the events leading to this momentous occasion and the ensuing battles that occurred as the common peoples destroyed the nobility. It continues through the reign of terror and the legacy of the Revolution. Notes, For Further Reading, Works Consulted, and Index.

425.	Corzine, Phyllis. **The Palestinian-Israeli Accord**. San Diego, CA: Lucent, 1996. 112p. $16.95. ISBN 1-56006-181-2. (Overview). 6-10

Corzine looks at the history preceding the contemporary Palestinian-Israeli accord. She describes the creation of the state of Israel, a perceived opportunistic role played by the British, and the various wars that have occurred as the Arabs have shown hostility about the new state. The history ends in mid-1996 and gives a good background for the long-standing conflict. Bibliography, Further Reading, Glossary, and Index.

426.	Cosner, Shaaron. **War Nurses**. New York: Walker, 1988. 106p. $16.95. ISBN 0-8027-6826-1. 5-9

The text includes chapters on war nurses and their activities in the Civil War, the Crimean War, the Spanish-American War, World Wars I and II, the Korean War, and the Vietnam War. Letters and stories about the various personalities, among them Clara Barton and Florence Nightingale, show what the nurses had to face in their quest to help the wounded. Among the other topics included are a brief history of war weapons, the wounds from each, and the medical developments that evolved from these types of wounds. These nurses were clearly war veterans, a status for which nurses have had to petition. Index.

427.	Cotterell, Arthur. **Ancient China**. Allen Hills and Geoff Brightling, illustrators. New York: Knopf, 1994. 63p. $16. ISBN 0-679-96167-4. (Eyewitness). 4-7

China is the world's oldest civilization and was controlled under one empire from 221 B.C. until A.D. 1912. The first great dynasty lasted from 1650 to 1027 B.C. The dynasties include the Shang, Zhon, Qin, Han, Sui, Tang, Song, Yuan, Ming, Quing, and then the People's Republic in 1949. The text, with photographic highlights, covers the health, farm life, waterways, cities, homes, foods, clothes, and beliefs of the Chinese people. Index.

428.   Coulter, Catherine. **Lord of Falcon Ridge**. New York: Jove Books/Berkeley, 1995. 365p. $6.50pa. ISBN 0-515-11584-3pa. (Viking Trilogy). YA

In the third novel of the Viking trilogy, after *Lord of Raven's Peak* and *Lord of Hawkfell Island*, Cleve goes to Chessa, queen of Ireland, to arrange Chessa's marriage to William of Normandy. She is interested in neither William nor Ragnor of York—she wants to marry Cleve himself. In a dream, Cleve realizes that he has land in Scotland and wants to claim it. The two fall in love, but Cleve has to save her from Ragnor and others, and his father's magic helps him.

429.   Courtney, Julia. **Sir Peter Scott: Champion for the Environment and Founder of the World Wildlife Fund**. Milwaukee, WI: Gareth Stevens, 1989. 68p. $16.95. ISBN 0-55532-819-9. (People Who Have Helped the World). 7-9

Peter Scott's father tried to be the first to reach the South Pole from England, but Roald Amundsen, a Norwegian, had arrived one month earlier. Scott's father wrote in his diary, found with him after his death at the South Pole, that Peter's mother should teach him to love nature. She did, and Peter Scott (1909–1989) became the founder of the World Wildlife Fund (now Worldwide Fund for Nature). At Cambridge, Scott studied natural history but found that he hated dead things; he was more interested in the living. He changed to art and spent much of his life creating beautiful paintings of the wildlife he loved. He spent much time outdoors, was an Olympic medalist in sailing, and was much affected by World War II. After the war, he began to act on his belief that killing things, including wildlife, needed to be stopped. He began his conservancy in 1946, and it grew, with him winning awards and being knighted by Queen Elizabeth for his work. Achievements of the Worldwide Fund for Nature, Organizations, Books, List of New Words, Important Dates, and Index.

430.   Cowell, Stephanie. **Nicholas Cooke: Actor, Soldier, Physician, Priest: A Novel**. New York: Norton, 1993. 440p. $24. ISBN 0-393-03543-3. New York: Ballantine, 1994. 440p. $12pa. ISBN 0-345-39016-4pa. YA

To escape his life in Canterbury, where his father has been hanged and his mother is a prostitute, Nick, age thirteen, goes to London in 1592. There he meets Kit Morley (Christopher Marlowe), who apprentices him to John Heminges, an actor among whose friends is one Will "Shagspere." These people become Nick's family, but he loses interest in acting and moves through the professions of soldier, physician, and priest while trying to find what he wants.

431.   Cowley, Marjorie. **Dar and the Spear-Thrower**. New York: Clarion, 1994. 118p. $13.95. ISBN 0-395-68132-4. 4-7

Around 15,000 years ago in France, during the Cro-Magnon period, Dar, age thirteen, undergoes his clan's initiation into manhood. He hears about a spear-thrower, a device that will enable him to throw with greater power and therefore be the warrior his tribe expects, and he goes on a dangerous journey in search of the item. What he finds is much more than he could have imagined.

432.   Cozic, Charles P. **Israel: Opposing Viewpoints**. San Diego, CA: Greenhaven, 1994. 288p. $19.95; $14.44pa. ISBN 1-56510-133-2; 1-56510-132-4pa. (Opposing Viewpoints). 7-12

The text looks at the questions that people have asked about the Palestinians and the Jewish state of Israel through the years since the British sanctioned the country of Israel in 1945. The focus covers both sides of six questions. Topics question whether Jews need a homeland, whether Israel needs Zionism, the prospects for Arab-Israeli peace, Palestinian rights violations, Israel giving up some of its land for peace, and U.S. support of Israel. Editorial commentary gives background for essays so that they can be seen in their original context. Such personages as the Zionist founder Theodore Herzl and Sami Hadawi, the Palestinian scholar, speak within the pages of the text. Bibliography, Chronology, and Index.

433.   Craig, Mary. **Lech Walesa**. Milwaukee, WI: Gareth Stevens, 1990. 68p. $16.95. ISBN 0-55532-821-0. (People Who Have Helped the World). 7-9

In 1939, Hitler wanted the lands of Poland but not its people. He encouraged the murders of Polish citizens, and one in five Poles were killed, including Lech Walesa's father, who died when Lech was two in 1945. With the German defeat, Stalin and his Communists marched into Poland. The Poles revolted in 1956 but were defeated. After school and training, Walesa went to Gdansk and became a ship's electrician. There the working conditions appalled him. He supported student protests in 1968, but other workers accepted the government's view that the students were lazy and undisciplined. In 1970, the government raised food prices but not wages. The shipworkers had a strike, but some were killed in Gdansk and many massacred in another town. Walesa was eventually fired three times because of his activism. Among those who joined in the cry for freedom was the Cardinal of Cracow, Karol Wojtyla, later Pope John Paul II. In 1980, the strike reached its height, with the government making agreements but soon reneging after the workers returned. Walesa was imprisoned but then freed when the government said he was no longer important. The world and the workers disagreed; he received the Nobel Peace Prize in 1983, and in 1990, after the government failed, the people elected Walesa president. Organizations, Books, Glossary, Chronology, and Index.

434.   Craig, Mary. **Lech Walesa and His Poland**. New York: Continuum, 1987. 326p. $18.95. ISBN 0-826-40390-5. 5-10

Although circumstances have changed in Poland, with Walesa actually becoming its leader, since Craig wrote the book, the text tells about the twentieth-century trials of Poland under communism and Gomuka. The book is half-biography, half-history, in its telling. Walesa, an intelligent man who passed exams to enter technological school, did not have enough money to attend, but he refused to complain about his fate and became a skilled worker instead. His decisions in his dealings with both the communists and his friends show his strong morality. When he won the Nobel Peace Prize in 1983 for his work in organizing the Solidarity movement in Poland, many felt that he represented all Poles trying to lift themselves out of an untenable situation. Bibliography and Index.

435.   Crofford, Emily. **Born in the Year of Courage**. Minneapolis, MN: Carolrhoda, 1992. 160p. $19.95. ISBN 0-87614-679-5. (Adventures in Time). 4-7

In 1841, Manjiro, age fifteen, finds himself shipwrecked. An American whaling ship rescues him, and he is surprised to find that the Americans are not all barbarians as his Japanese heritage has taught him. He decides to work toward opening trade between the two countries by taking a whaling boat back to Japan to begin his work.

436.   Crosby, Caroline. **The Haldanes**. New York: St Martin's Press, 1993. 344p. $21.95. ISBN 0-312-09303-9. YA

In the early twentieth century, Pauline, age fifteen, has to leave London for a Scottish boarding school when her father's financial losses force him to go abroad during the reign of George V (1910–1936). She hears from a cold-hearted cousin that her mother, who abandoned Pauline as a young child, has remarried and is pregnant. Pauline has to deal with her family ties by helping her mother find the youngest child and coping with her unsavory stepfather. Pauline, however, enjoys her school with its sports and academics, and the teachers there help her mature.

437.   Crosher, Judith. **Ancient Egypt**. New York: Viking, 1993. 48p. $14.99. ISBN 0-670-84755-0. (See Through History). 5-8

Around 3000 B.C., the Egyptians expanded along the Nile and became the first unified nation. Egypt developed a complex civilization, culminating with the construction of the vast pyramids for their dead rulers. See-through cutaways of a town house, the palace of Akhenaten, the tomb of Sennedjem, and the temple of Khons augment the text. Two-page topical spreads include information on the Nile, the God-King of Egypt, medicine and the law, women, childhood, the home, writing and calculation, arts and crafts, fashion, the palace, peasant farmers, trade and tribute, education, tombs, pyramids, gods and goddesses, death and the afterlife, temples, war, and the last days of the civilization. Key Dates, Glossary, and Index.

438.   Cross, Donna Woolfolk. **Pope Joan**. New York: Crown, 1996. 432p. $25. ISBN 0-517-59365-3. YA

In the ninth century, a female pope named Joan of Ingelheim (born in 814) may have risen from being the daughter of a village canon, to the highest church office. Several men betray her, including her father, who will not let her study after her brothers teach her to read and write. She dresses as a man when her family dies in a Viking raid and enters the Benedictine monastery at Fulda. After years of work, she recovers from the plague, goes to Rome, and saves Pope Sergius, using her healing skills. She encounters a man with whom she had fallen in love before entering the monastery, and they work together after the people elect her as pope. As plotters try to kill her, she learns that she is pregnant, and eventually dies a woman's death. *School Library Journal Best Adult Books for Young Adults.*

439.   Cross, Robin. **Aftermath of War**. New York: Thomson Learning, 1994. 48p. $14.95. ISBN 1-56847-178-5. (World War II). 5-7

Many books cover World War II, but this book looks at what happened after the war's end. It reports on the Nuremberg trials of Nazi war criminals, the division of Germany and the Berlin airlift, the contrast in power between the United States and Britain, the beginning of the "cold war," and Japanese factories' shift from producing war goods to making peacetime items. An interesting aspect of the year immediately after the war is the forces of nature: In 1946-1947, Britain had the coldest winter in fifty-three years, with snows melting to flood the island in the spring and the following summer producing a drought. Such natural trials following those inflicted by humans must have been especially frustrating. Glossary, Books to Read, Chronology, and Index.

440.   Cross, Robin. **Children and War**. New York: Thomson Learning, 1994. 48p. $14.95. ISBN 1-56847-180-7. (World War II). 5-7

By using the experiences of young people during the war, Cross presents a view of World War II. His subjects include a Polish boy imprisoned by Soviet police, a French girl who fought in the Resistance, a messenger boy in Britain during bombing attacks, a child from Hiroshima, and an American who had no direct contact except through newsreels. Further Reading, Glossary, and Index.

441. Cross, Robin. **Technology of War**. New York: Thomson Learning, 1994. 48p. $14.95. ISBN 1-56847-177-7. (World War II). 5-7

Many weapons used in World War II had been introduced in World War I, with the submarine almost winning both wars for Germany. Between 1918 and 1939, radio communications improved, and the civil aviation industry expanded. Cathode ray tubes appeared, vital for radar screens, and research into the nature of the atom progressed. In 1936-1939, the Soviet Union, Germany, and Japan tested their new weapons, fighter planes, dive bombers, and tanks. The ultimate weapon became the atom bomb that the Americans developed. Glossary, Books to Read, Chronology, and Index.

442. Crowe, David. **A History of the Gypsies of Eastern Europe and Russia**. New York: St. Martin's Press, 1996. 317p. $14.95. ISBN 0-312-12946-7. YA

The text looks at Gypsy history by looking at each eastern European country and discussing the roles of the Gypsies from the Middle Ages to the present. The Rom people, according to scarce historical evidence, began migrating from India over 1,000 years ago. Additional background from Bulgaria, Czechoslovakia (before division), Hungary, Romania, Russia, and Yugoslavia (before division) gives a historical overview of each country as well. Among the facts that come forth are that at the time of the Emancipation Proclamation in 1863, Gypsies in Romania were slaves, bought and sold for life. Upper classes, especially in Russia, used Gypsy talents such as music for relaxation, even when the official policy was to shun them. The Romish persecution continued into the twentieth century during the Holocaust, when Gypsies were often the subjects of Nazi medical experimentation. In recent years, Grattan Puxon, a Rom, has encouraged Gypsies to identify themselves and demand rights that governments have denied them for centuries. Bibliography and Index.

443. Cruz, Barbara C. **Frida Kahlo: Portrait of a Mexican Painter**. Springfield, NJ: Enslow, 1996. 112p. $18.95. ISBN 0-89490-765-4. 6-9

As a Mexican painter, Frida Kahlo (1907-1954) gained much of her reputation after her death. The text looks at her devotion to her art and her more intense commitment to her husband, Diego Rivera. It also discusses her political beliefs and pride in her Mexican heritage. Further Reading and Index.

444. Cumming, David. **Russia**. New York: Thomson Learning, 1995. 48p. $15.95. ISBN 1-56847-240-4. (Modern Industrial World). 5-8

As the text discusses the current situation in Russia, it also includes Russian history. To understand the Russia of today, one must know the culture and economics of its past. Photographs, tables, and sidebars relay additional information. Glossary, Further Information, and Index.

445. Cush, Cathie. **Artists Who Created Great Works**. Austin, TX: Raintree/Steck-Vaughn, 1995. 48p. $15.96. ISBN 0-8114-4993-5. (20 Events Series). 6 up

In two-page spreads, Cush creates a mini-history of art by presenting profiles on twenty artists spanning from Leonardo Da Vinci (Italy, 1452-1519) to Salvador Dali (Spain, 1904-1989). Photographs of famous paintings accompany the text. Other artists included are Albrecht Dürer (Germany, 1471-1528), Michelangelo Buonarroti (Italy, 1475-1564), Gian Lorenzo Bernini (Italy, 1598-1680), Rembrandt van Rijn (Netherlands, 1606-1669), Christopher Wren (England, 1632-1723), Francisco Goya (Spain, 1746-1828), Joseph M. W. Turner (England, 1775-1851), Eugène Delacroix (France, 1798-1863), Auguste Rodin (France, 1840-1917), Claude Monet (France, 1840-1926), Henri Matisse (France, 1869-1954), Pablo Picasso (Spain, 1881-1973), Diego Rivera (Mexico, 1886-1957), Ludwig Mies van der Rohe (Germany, 1886-1969), Georgia O'Keeffe (United States, 1887-1986), Alexander Calder (United States, 1898-1976), Henry Moore (England, 1898-1986), and Ansel Adams (United States, 1902-1984). Glossary, Suggested Readings, and Index.

446. Cush, Cathie. **Disasters That Shook the World**. Austin, TX: Raintree/Steck-Vaughn, 1994. 48p. $15.96. ISBN 0-8114-4929-7. (20 Events Series). 6 up

Some of the major changes in perception that have occurred in the world have come as a result of a disaster. In two-page spreads, Cush discusses twenty situations that were never expected to happen. They are the explosion of Vesuvius (A.D. 79 in Pompeii, Italy), the Black Death (fourteenth-century Europe), the destruction of the Native Americans (fifteenth through nineteenth centuries), the Great London Fire (1666), the Irish Potato Famine (1845-1849), the Great Chicago Fire (1871), Krakatoa's eruption (Indonesia, 1883), the San Francisco earthquake (1906), the *Titanic* sinking (1912), the world flu epidemic (1917-1919), the Bangladesh cyclone (1970), famine in Ethiopia and Somalia (1984-1985; 1992), the AIDS epidemic (1980s), the Bhopal chemical disaster (India, 1984), the *Challenger* explosion (United States, 1986), the Chernobyl nuclear meltdown (Russia, 1986), the *Exxon Valdez* oil spill (1989), the death of the Aral Sea (between Kazakhstan and Uzbekistan, 1960-1990), the Gulf War oil disaster (Kuwait, 1991), and hurricanes Andrew (Atlantic, 1992) and Iniki (Hawaii, 1992). Glossary, Suggested Readings, and Index.

447. Cush, Cathie. **Women Who Achieved Greatness**. Austin, TX: Raintree/Steck-Vaughn, 1995. 48p. $15.96. ISBN 0-8114-4938-6. (20 Events Series). 6 up

Women have achieved greatness in a variety of ways, and some, though not all, have received recognition for it. In two-page spreads, Cush profiles some of these women. The women included are Maria Montessori (Italy, 1870-1952), Helen Keller (1880-1968) and Annie Sullivan (d. 1936), Eleanor Roosevelt (1884-1962), Amelia Earhart (1899-1937), Golda Meir (Israel, 1898-1978), Margaret Mead (1901-1978), Barbara McClintock (1902-1992), Marian Anderson (1900-1993), Margaret Bourke-White (1906-1971), Rachel Carson (1907-1964), Mother Teresa (Albania and India, 1910-1997), Indira Gandhi (India, 1917-1984), Katharine Meyer Graham (b. 1917), Maya Angelou (b. 1928), Violeta Chamorro (Nicaragua, b. 1929), Jane Goodall (England, b. 1934), Barbara Jordan (1936-1996), Aung San Suu Kyi (Burma, b. 1944), Wilma Mankiller (b. 1945), and Oprah Winfrey (b. 1954). Glossary, Suggested Readings, and Index.

448. Cushman, Karen. **Catherine Called Birdy**. New York: Clarion, 1994. 174p. $14.95. ISBN 0-395-68186-3. New York: Trophy, 1995. 174p. $4.50pa. ISBN 0-06-440584-2pa. 7-10

In diary form, Catherine, age thirteen, writes about her life in 1290, as her favorite brother has suggested. Meanwhile, her father is trying to marry her to the man offering the most money for her hand. Each entry starts with the name of the saint celebrated for the day and the reason the person is worshipped as a saint. Catherine thinks that all the women are saints because they kept their chastity and did the things of which men approve. She hates women's work, and one of her brothers loves drawing and the idea of fighting in the Crusades. She clearly shows the role of women in the Middle Ages. *American Library Association Best Books for Young Adults, Carl Sandburg Award for Literary Excellence, American Library Association Notable Children's Books, YASD Best Books for Young Adults, Booklist Children's Editors' Choice, Parenting Magazine Ten Best, School Library Journal Best Books, Golden Kite Award,* and *Newbery Honor.*

449. Cushman, Karen. **The Midwife's Apprentice**. New York: Clarion, 1995. 122p. $10.95. ISBN 0-395-69229-6. New York: Trophy, 1995. 122p. $4.50pa. ISBN 0-06-440640-Xpa. 5-9

After the midwife finds Brat, aged twelve or thirteen, hiding in a dung heap, she renames the girl Beetle and gives her a job as an assistant. As Beetle becomes more confident and more articulate, she renames herself Alyce, and soon realizes that midwifery is the profession for her. In the twelfth century, she works to become more proficient as she copes with those around her. *American Library Association Notable Children's Books, American Library Association Best Books for Young Adults, Booklist Books for Youth Editors' Choices, American Booksellers' Pick of the Lists, Horn Book Fanfare Honor List, School Library Journal Best Books,* and *Newbery Medal.*

450. Cytron, Barry, and Phyllis Cytron. **Myriam Mendilow: Mother of Jerusalem**. Minneapolis, MN: Lerner, 1994. 128p. $22.95. ISBN 0-8225-4919-0. 5 up

Myriam Mendilow (1909-1989) grew up in a Jewish home with a mother who did not believe that the old ways were the best. Mendilow became a teacher, and one of her skills was seeing when others needed something; she always tried to find what that something was to improve their lives. She saw that the elderly of Jerusalem had no money, no friends, and no esteem. She created places for them to go where they could make crafts for sale and feel as if they were contributing to life instead of merely existing. Epilogue, Source Notes, and Index.

D

451. Dahl, Roald. **Boy: Tales of Childhood**. New York: Farrar, Straus & Giroux, 1984. 160p. $16. ISBN 0-374-37374-4. 3 up

Dahl lived his early childhood in Wales and England, son of a Norwegian mother and a father who had gone to Wales to start a business supplying ships. His father's early death, soon after Dahl's sister died at age seven, did not seem to cause economic distress, because Dahl's mother was able to give the family whatever it needed, including private school (public, in England) education. Dahl's stories of childhood during the 1920s in England show children fascinated with the local store's candy, hiding a dead mouse in one of the candy jars, and admiring the stunning ride of an older boy on his bicycle. Dahl spent summers in Norway and vividly remembers the summer when a doctor removed his adenoids without using anesthesia. His nose was almost severed in a motor car accident, with his mother driving. While he was in school, the Cadbury candy factory sent bars of unmarked candy for the boys to test. Dahl's mother offered him education at Oxford or Cambridge, but with his application for and receipt of a coveted position with Shell Oil, he ends this book.

452. Dahl, Roald. **Going Solo**. New York: Farrar, Straus & Giroux, 1986. 208p. $14.95. ISBN 0-374-16503-3. 7 up

In 1938, Roald Dahl found himself traveling by ship to Dar es Salaam for a job with Shell Oil. He realized that the British subjects who chose to live and work in this part of the world, and were accompanying him on the ship, were slightly "dotty." He learned a lot about them and himself during the voyage. After his arrival, he learned about being aware of things—like the snakes that might be crawling by. Inspired by an incident in which a lion grabbed a cook's wife, took her toward the jungle, and then dropped her unharmed at the sound of a gunshot into the air, Dahl wrote his first article. When the war with Germany began, he joined the Royal Air Force. His recollection of his severe wounds received in a crash, his long recovery, and his reentry into the Greek theater of the war, flying a plane in combat although he barely knew how the plane worked, gives a clear picture of the universal uncertainty and confusion in wartime as well as the warmth of humans who help each other.

453. Dale, Rodney. **Early Cars**. New York: Oxford University Press, 1994. 64p. $18; $10.95pa. ISBN 0-19-521002-6; 0-19-521006-9pa. (Discoveries & Inventions). 9 up

From early self-moving carriages through cars on the road, the text discusses steam omnibuses, the engines and chassis of cars, the Nuremberg carriage in 1649, and steam carriages in the eighteenth and early nineteenth centuries. Pioneers and their contributions include Walter Hancock (1749-1852), Sir Goldsworthy Gurney (1793-1875), Otto and Langen's "free piston" engine in 1866, Dr. Rudolf Diesel's engine in the late nineteenth century, Dunlop's pneumatic bicycle tires, and Wankel's rotary engine in the mid-1950s. Names important for private cars are Lenoir, Marcus, Delamare-Deboutteville, Hammel, and Carl Benz (around 1885). Daimler, Butler, Peugeot and Panhard, John Knight, and Lanchester and Austin were also working around that time. Henry Ford's first car appeared in 1896 while the Renault brothers were experimenting in France. Rolls tells the story of the first cars while diagrams and photographs reinforce the text. Chronology, Further Reading, and Index.

454. Dale, Rodney. **Early Railways**. New York: Oxford University Press, 1994. 64p. $18; $10.95pa. ISBN 0-19-521003-4; 0-19-521007-7pa. (Discoveries & Inventions). 9 up

The world's first railway station opened in Stockton, England, in 1825, after George Stephenson and others had worked to build steam engines and devise rails on which the trains could run. The originators did not foresee that the railway would entice people who had never traveled to use them, and they replaced many coaches in the process. The text traces development in England and the United States, using diagrams, drawings, and photographs to illustrate salient points. Chronology, Further Reading, and Index.

455. Daley, William. **The Chinese Americans**. New York: Chelsea House, 1995. 93p. $19.95; $8.95pa. ISBN 0-7910-3357-0; 0-7910-3379-1pa. (The Peoples of North America). 4-7

The immigration of Chinese into the United States began to rise when the first Opium War between China and England (1839-1842) gave Hong Kong to England in the Treaty of Nanking and opened four other Chinese ports. The corrupt Manchu (Ch'ing Dynasty) rulers imposed higher taxes, causing the people to revolt in 1850 under the leadership of Hung Hsiu-ch'uan, a convert to Christianity, in the Taiping "Great Peace" Rebellion. But the Taipings were defeated in 1864. A second Opium War fought at the same time, from 1856 to 1860, caused even more turmoil. By 1848, only seven Chinese were recorded as living in San Francisco, but by 1851 the gold rush had attracted 25,000. The Chinese immigrants were prevented from voting, holding public office, and practicing certain trades. For these reasons, they started laundries and worked to build the railroads across the United States. Immigration laws tightened in 1882, keeping out many women who had stayed behind to look after their husbands' parents. In the twentieth century, other problems in China caused emigration. Sun Yat-Sen ruled from 1866 to 1925, when the Japanese began to trouble the Chinese. In 1949, Mao Zedong declared victory over Chiang and established his brand of communism. Chinese Americans developed the Bing cherry and were the first to hatch eggs with artificial heat. They have cultural depth through their religions—Confucianism, Taoism, and Buddhism—and their artists and inventors, such as Wang, Yo-Yo Ma, Maya Lin, Maxine Hong Kingston, Lawrence Yep, and David Hwang. Selected References and Index.

456.   Dalkey, Kara. **Little Sister**. San Diego, CA: Harcourt Brace, 1996. 200p. $17. ISBN 0-15-201392-X. 7 up

Fujiwara no Mitsuko, or Little Puddle, age thirteen, lives in the imperial court of Japan during the Heian period, around 1100. Her kimono hides her body shape, and its sleeves hide her face in public. But outlaws attack her village, murdering her brother-in-law. Then the warlord takes her family away. She sheds her traditional role and asks a *tengu* (shape-shifter) and other creatures from Japanese myths to help her family regain its honor.

457.   Dalokay, Vedat. **Sister Shako and Kolo the Goat: Memories of My Childhood in Turkey**. Güner Ener, translator. New York: Lothrop, Lee & Shepard, 1994. 96p. $13. ISBN 0-688-13271-5. 5-8

In this tale, Dalokay remembers an old woman from his childhood whose family had been murdered during a vendetta. She kept a white goat, Kolo, in his father's old stable. Sister Shako saw signs and omens in the goat's positions, such as raised ears indicating a wolf or a gendarme's arrival. Sister Shako's understanding of nature, close relationship to the goat, and wise advice to Dalokay show the tendencies of rural Turkish people before television infiltrated the land. When Sister Shako died, he knew that she was part of the earth, or, as she said, "I shall enter the blood of whoever drinks Kolo's milk." *Mildred L. Batchelder Honor Book.*

458.   Dana, Barbara. **Young Joan**. New York: Zolotow, HarperCollins, 1991. 384p. $17.95. ISBN 0-06-021422-8. 5-9

Joan of Arc (1412?-1431) supposedly heard her name being spoken aloud in a garden where no other human was present. After a time, she allowed herself to think that she might be the maid of whom Merlin had spoken, the one who would help France. The text looks at Joan of Arc's early life, seeing her as a mystic in her time rather than someone who was either hysterical or a feminist. Joan's favorite activity was praying, and although she enjoyed her family and her pets, God was the center of her life. With this focus, she convinced the Dauphin that she could save France—and she did. Bibliography and Index. *Bulletin Blue Ribbon Book.*

459.   Dauber, Maximilien, and Martine Noblet. **China**. Maureen Walker, translator. Hauppauge, NY: Barron's, 1994. 77p. $11.95; $6.95pa. ISBN 0-8120-6426-7; 0-8120-1865-6pa. (Tintin's Travel Diaries). 5 up

The text asks thirty questions about China, covering a variety of topics such as what the Chinese used to build their houses, what are the "ten thousand small trades," what is the silk road, what are the powers of the dragon, and who was Mao. Illustrations and photographs complement the simple text on the lefthand pages and the more scholarly answers on the righthand pages. Glossary, Chronological Chart, Map, Bibliography, and Index.

460.   Davidson, Bob. **Hillary and Tenzing Climb Everest**. New York: Dillon Press, Macmillan, 1993. 32p. $13.95. ISBN 0-87518-534-7. (Great Twentieth Century Expeditions). 4-7

Many failed attempts to climb Mount Everest occurred in the 1920s and 1930s before Sir Edmund Hillary and Norkey Tenzing decided to attack Everest from the south. They eventually succeeded in 1953. The text details the plans for the ascent, the icefall they encountered, and the "roof of the world," which they finally reached. Also included are descriptions of later expeditions and the North face climb of Ronald Messner in 1980. Photographs and drawings enhance the text. Glossary and Index.

461.   Davidson, Michael Worth, ed. **Everyday Life Through the Ages**. Pleasantville, NY: Reader's Digest, 1992. 384p. $30. ISBN 0-276-42035-7. YA

The text, divided into three parts that cover ancient worlds, old worlds and new worlds, and the modern world, looks at different peoples throughout 30,000 years of history and how they lived their days. Russian peasants, Venetian merchants, English coal miners, and Australian aborigines appear. Also included are insights on Viking housekeeping, being a slave on a tobacco plantation, and how the Medicis treated people who lived in Florence. The illustrations try to show what words cannot say in this social history. An "A-Z of Everyday Things" mentions 100 inventions such as adhesive, beds, birth control, silk, and yokes. Index.

462.   Davies, Eryl. **Transport: On Land, Road and Rail**. New York: Franklin Watts, 1992. 47p. $7.95pa. ISBN 0-531-15741-5pa. (Timelines). 5-8

Illustrations interspersed with text show a history of transport. The text covers the first wheels, Roman roads, ancient China, Vikings, medieval Europe, animal power, coaches, steam pioneers, the railroad age, pedal power, the first motorcycles, automobiles, underground trains, streetcars, delivery modes, racing cars, and the future in transportation. Timeline, Glossary, and Index.

463.   Davis, Lee Allyn. **Man-Made Catastrophes: From the Burning of Rome to the Lockerbie Crash**. New York: Facts on File, 1993. 352p. $40. ISBN 0-8160-2035-3. YA

The text covers 284 incidents caused by humans. The various situations include railway disasters, space disasters, fires, explosions, air crashes, terrorism, riots, nuclear accidents, and maritime disasters. Bibliography and Index.

464.   Davis, Lindsey. **The Iron Hand of Mars**. New York: Crown, 1993. 305p. $20. ISBN 0-517-59240-1. New York: Ballantine, 1994. 305p. $4.99pa. ISBN 0-345-38024-Xpa. YA

Marcus Didius Falco, private detective for the Emperor Vespasian (A.D. 69–79), goes to Germania, the land of Tactius, to find out what happened to the rebel leader Civilis and Munius Lupercus, the "gift" sent to Veleda, the beautiful German prophetess who spearheaded the rebellion. He also needs to find out how to silence Veleda. When he arrives, he has the further problem of finding the Fourteenth Legion's commander. Falco's unassuming attitude makes his search especially entertaining.

465.   Davis, Lindsey. **Last Act in Palmyra**. New York: Mysterious Press, 1996. 400p. $22.95. ISBN 0-89296-625-4. YA

Marcus Didius Falco and his love, Helena, leave Nero's circus in Rome during the first century A.D. with a troop of actors as they try to solve a crime. They eventually perform with the troop in one of Falco's plays, and their performance helps them catch the criminal.

466.   Davis, Lindsey. **Poseidon's Gold**. New York: Crown, 1994. 336p. $22. ISBN 0-517-59241-X. New York: Ballantine, 1995. 336p. $5.99pa. ISBN 0-345-38025-8pa. YA

Marcus Didius Falco becomes embroiled in a problem created by his late brother, Festus. An ex-legionnaire claims that Festus owed him and many others a great deal of money. When Falco is charged with Festus's murder, and his love Helena is arrested as his accomplice, he must work to find the real criminal during the rule of Vespasian around A.D. 75.

467.   Davis, Lindsey. **Shadows in Bronze**. New York: Crown, 1991. 343p. $19. ISBN 0-517-57612-0. New York: Ballantine, 1993. 343p. $4.99pa. ISBN 0-345-37426-6pa. YA

In A.D. 70, Marcus Didius Falco works for the Roman Emperor Vespasian as a detective. He hears that Barnabus has instigated a plot to overthrow Vespasian and kill Marcus. Marcus, in disguise, trails Barnabus and finds that the path also leads him to his only love.

468.   Davis, Lindsey. **Silver Pigs**. New York: Crown, 1989. 258p. $18.95. ISBN 0-517-57363-6. New York: Ballantine, 1992. 258p. $4.99pa. ISBN 0-345-36907-6pa. YA

In A.D. 70, Marcus Didius Falco helps to uncover a Roman plot against Nero's successor, the Emperor Vespasian. Falco must find the men chasing a senator's daughter because she knows where traitors have hidden the "silver pigs" (lead ingots with silver inside) that they smuggled into the capital as part of their plot against the emperor.

469.   Davis, Lindsey. **Venus in Copper**. New York: Crown, 1992. 277p. $19. ISBN 0-517-58477-8. New York: Ballantine, 1993. 277p. $4.50pa. ISBN 0-345-37390-1pa. YA

Marcus Didius Falco decides to return to his business of private detective, around A.D. 71, because he does not think that the Emperor Vespasian is paying him enough money. Marcus needs more to support the woman he wants to marry. His case concerns a real estate magnate's intended bride, whom he must follow to see if she is interested only in the magnate's money. When the man suddenly dies, the case leads to the woman and to other unexpected concerns.

470.   Dawson, Imogen. **Food and Feasts in Ancient Greece**. New York: New Discovery, Silver Burdett, 1995. 32p. $14.95. ISBN 0-02-726329-0. (Food & Feasts). 4-7

The text looks at the ways food was grown and prepared by people living in ancient Greece from approximately 2500 B.C. to 30 B.C. by focusing on the crops in the countryside and the types of food that had to be shipped to the cities and suburbs. Food from the sea was important in ancient Greece as well. If one traveled, one had to eat, so the text covers food in taverns and inns and aboard ship. Additional information about cooking utensils and recipes from ancient Greece gives a good sense of the times. Photographs and reproductions highlight the text. Glossary, Further Reading, and Index.

471.   Dawson, Imogen. **Food and Feasts in the Middle Ages**. New York: New Discovery, 1994. 32p. $14.95. ISBN 0-02-726324-X. (Food & Feasts). 4-7

The text looks at the ways food was grown and prepared during the Middle Ages, from the end of the Roman Empire until approximately A.D. 1500, by focusing on the crops in the countryside and the types of food that had to be shipped to the cities and suburbs. If one traveled, one had to eat, so the text covers food in taverns, inns, and aboard ship. Additional information about cooking utensils and recipes from the medieval period gives a good sense of the times. Photographs and reproductions enhance the text. Glossary, Further Reading, and Index.

472. Dawson, Imogen. **Food and Feasts with the Aztecs**. New York: New Discovery, Silver Burdett, 1995. 32p. $14.95. ISBN 0-02-726318-5. (Food & Feasts). 4-7

The text looks at the ways Aztecs grew and prepared food, from approximately A.D. 1300 to 1500, by focusing on the crops in the countryside and the types of food that had to be shipped to the cities. If one traveled, one had to eat, so the text covers food offered in taverns and inns and served to the armies. Additional information about cooking utensils and recipes gives a good sense of the times. Photographs and reproductions enhance the text. Glossary, Further Reading, and Index.

473. Day, David. **The Search for King Arthur**. New York: Facts on File, 1995. 176p. $24.95. ISBN 0-8160-3370-6. YA

A question that scholars and fans have wanted to answer for years is whether King Arthur actually existed. No one can be absolutely certain, but archaeologists have uncovered enough historical evidence to make it plausible that he was real. The text looks at *Artorius Dux Bellorum* (Lord of Battles) and examines fact, myth, politics, religion, literature, and art about Arthur and those with whom he associated, such as Morgan le Fay, Merlin, Guinevere, and Lancelot. The text traces these people, as well as places and items, so that they have a historical context. Reproductions, Bibliography, Chronology, and Index.

474. **Dazzling! Jewelry of the Ancient World**. Minneapolis, MN: Runestone Press, 1995. 64p. $22.95. ISBN 0-8225-3203-4. (Buried Worlds). 6 up

Archaeologists have discovered jewelry, made from precious and semiprecious stones, gold, silver, and other metals, in ancient grave sites. Some of these important finds reveal the Ur in Mesopotamia since 2500 B.C.; the Egyptians since 3100 B.C.; the Chinese since 2000 B.C.; Taxila in ancient Pakistan since the first century B.C.; Southeast Asia since 2000 B.C.; Priam of Troy's treasure of 1400 B.C., discovered by Schliemann in the nineteenth century; the Minoan peoples since 1800 B.C.; the Celts since 700 B.C.; the Romans; and the American peoples. Photographs of finds reveal the styles indigenous to these different sites and cultures. Pronunciation Guide, Glossary, and Index.

475. De Angeli, Marguerite. **Black Fox of Lorne**. New York: Doubleday, 1956. 191p. $4.43. ISBN 0-385-08300-9. 7-10

In A.D. 950, Jan and Brus, thirteen-year-old twins, go with their father Harald Redbeard to the Scottish coast. Gavin the Black Fox kills Harald and takes Jan captive. Brus hides but changes places with Jan at various times. They want to avenge their father's death, but the couple with whom Jan stays suggests that better ways than murder exist to solve problems. Their Christian ideas interest him, and when he tells his brother, Brus too thinks about this other way. They find their mother in Edin's boro, where she also has been exposed to this new religion. Happily reunited, they are more able to cope with their adversities. *Newbery Honor.*

476. De Angeli, Marguerite, author/illustrator. **The Door in the Wall: A Story of Medieval London**. 1949. Magnolia, MA: Peter Smith, 1996. 111p. $17.75. ISBN 0-8446-6834-6. New York: Dell, 1990. 111p. $3.99pa. ISBN 0-440-40283-2pa. 3-7

In 1325, Robin becomes ill after his parents have left to serve King Edward III and his queen. A monk takes him to a hospice for his long recovery, patiently teaching him to carve, to write, to read, to play music, and to swim to strengthen his arms. They travel to another area to await Robin's parents, but soon after they arrive at the castle, the Welsh attack it. Robin's ability to swim allows him to go for reinforcements, and ultimately the castle defenders defeat the Welsh soldiers. When his parents and King Edward III return, Edward knights Robin for his bravery. Robin has learned from the monk that one must do one's best with what one has. *Newbery Medal.*

477. De Benedetti, Charles, and Charles Chatfield. **An American Ordeal: The Antiwar Movement of the Vietnam Era**. Syracuse, NY: Syracuse University Press, 1990. 495p. $17.95pa. ISBN 0-8156-0245-6pa. YA

De Benedetti divides the period of the Vietnam War into four parts: 1955-1963, 1963-1965, 1965-1970, and 1970-1975. After the war in Indochina began, its influence spread to America, and with the war grew a massive antiwar sentiment that challenged cultural norms such as scientific objectivity, religious beliefs, white male dominance, adult standards, acceptance of poverty, the Cold War mission, and consensus. This scholarly book discusses the revaluation of these norms and asserts that the antiwar movement was more about America than Vietnam. Notes, Bibliography, and Index.

478. De Bruycker, Daniel, and Maximilien Dauber. **Africa**. Maureen Walker, translator. Hauppauge, NY: Barron's, 1994. 77p. $11.95; $6.95pa. ISBN 0-8120-6425-9; 0-8120-1864-8pa. (Tintin's Travel Diaries). 5 up

The text asks thirty questions about Africa, covering a variety of topics such as the origin of the continent's name, the first explorers, the slavers, and where King Solomon's mines were located. Illustrations and photographs complement the simple text on the lefthand pages and the more scholarly answers on the righthand pages. Glossary, Chronological Chart, Map, Bibliography, and Index.

479.   De Bruycker, Daniel, and Maximilien Dauber. **Egypt and the Middle East**. Maureen Walker, translator. Hauppauge, NY: Barron's, 1995. 77p. $11.95; $6.95pa. ISBN 0-8120-6488-7; 0-8120-9159-0pa. (Tintin's Travel Diaries). 5 up

The text asks thirty questions about Egypt and the Middle East, covering a variety of topics such as what the function of a pyramid was, who the pharaohs were, which queens were famous, who invented writing, and who the Phoenicians were. Illustrations and photographs complement the simple text on the lefthand pages and the more scholarly answers on the righthand pages. Glossary, Chronological Chart, Map, Bibliography, and Index.

480.   De Bruycker, Daniel, and Maximilien Dauber. **Tibet**. Hauppauge, NY: Barron's, 1995. 80p. $11.95; $6.95pa. ISBN 0-8120-6504-2; 0-8120-9237-6pa. (Tintin's Travel Diaries). 5 up

Tibet, at the "top of the world," is home to the Dalai Lama, the *yak*, and the *yeti* or "abominable snowman." The text combines facts about Tibet, set in large type, with separate segments on facing pages incorporating history and anecdotes relating to the facts. Illustrating these two-page spreads are a combination of the cartoon figure Tintin and photographs of the landscape and the people. Glossary, Chronological Chart, Map, Index, and Bibliography for Readers from 7 to 77.

481.   De Carvalho, Mário. **A God Strolling in the Cool of the Evening**. Gregory Rabassa, translator. Baton Rouge: Louisiana State University Press, 1997. 265p. $26.95. ISBN 0-8071-2235-1. YA

In Portugal, Lucius Valerius Quintius rules Tarcisis, a small city. His hero is Marcus Aurelius, and all he wants to do is to make just decisions for his people. Problems become dilemmas, however, which he must solve to the best of his ability. *Pegasus Prize.*

482.   De Hartog, Jan. **The Lamb's War**. New York: HarperCollins, 1979. 461p. $13.95. ISBN 0-06-010995-5. New York: Fawcett, 1982. 461p. $3.95pa. ISBN 0-449-20019-1pa. YA

Laura, 15, goes to Schwalbenbach death camp, where Nazis have imprisoned her Dutch father for trying to save Jewish babies. An officer, irked by her father, ties him up and rapes Laura in front of him. Her father's rage and ensuing death haunt Laura after she survives the camp, marries an American for entrance into the United States, goes to medical school, and attempts to save the babies in the Southwest. She becomes increasingly fat as she tries to live with the intense guilt that she feels over her father's death.

483.   De Jenkins, Lyll. **The Honorable Prison**. New York: Lodestar, Dutton, 1988. 201p. $14.95. ISBN 0-525-67238-9. New York: Penguin, 1989. 201p. $4.99pa. ISBN 0-14-032952-8pa. 9 up

A South American military regime arrests Marta, age seventeen, and her family because her father has criticized the regime in his newspaper stories. They have to live in isolation, far from the city, where they are hungry and her father has no treatment for his tuberculosis. Marta and her younger brother look forward to their weekly trip to market, until they can no longer get food. Then Marta falls in love with a local boy, but as she thinks about going with him against her family, she knows that she may be sacrificing herself and her family. Although the General eventually loses, Marta's family suffers excessively for its belief in the truth. *Scott O'Dell Award.*

484.   De Ruiz, Dana Catharine. **To Fly with the Swallows: A Story of Old California**. Debbe Heller, illustrator. Austin, TX: Raintree/Steck-Vaughn, 1993. 53p. $15.49; $5.95pa. ISBN 0-8114-7234-5; 0-8114-8074-7pa. (Stories of America—Personal Challenge). 5-9

In 1806, Concha, 15, lived with her family in San Francisco, where her father was commander of the presidio defending Spain's New World empire on the northern border of Alta California. Nikolai Petrovich Rezanov arrived from St. Petersburg requesting supplies for his ship. He stayed long enough for Concha and him to want to marry, but Rezanov was not Catholic. He left, as requested, to get the permission of the czar, the King of Spain, and the pope in Italy. Concha waited, but after five years she received word of his death. She never married but spent her life dedicated to Saint Francis and helping those who needed her in childbirth, sickness, and death. At 60, she became California's first nun in Santa Catalina. Epilogue, Afterword, and Notes.

485.   de Treviño, Elizabeth. **El Güero: A True Adventure Story**. Leslie W. Bowman, illustrator. New York: Farrar, Straus & Giroux, 1989. 112p. $12.95. ISBN 0-374-31995-2. 6-9

After a military coup deposes the government of Lerdo de Tejada, El Güero's father is sent into exile from Mexico to the outpost of Ensenada during the late nineteenth century. There his father, a judge, tries to establish a justice system, but the military commander puts him in jail. El Güero and two friends travel across the desert to Baja California to tell the *commandante* of his father's difficulties. His effort gets his father released and the power-hungry Captain Alanis arrested.

486.   de Treviño, Elizabeth. **I, Juan de Pareja**. New York: Farrar, Straus & Giroux, 1965. 192p. $16; $3.95pa. ISBN 0-374-33531-1; 0-374-43525-1pa. 7 up

In the seventeenth century, Juan is Diego Velasquez's slave while Velasquez serves King Philip IV in Spain. Juan loves to watch the painter at work, and although slaves are banned by law from painting, Juan secretly does so. He sees Peter Paul Rubens during a court visit in 1628 and hears that he uses nudes as models. Juan goes with Velasquez to Italy in 1649 to paint nobles and to collect artworks for the king. At the age of forty, Juan tells Velasquez and the king that he has been painting, and Velasquez frees him immediately so that he will not suffer punishment of any kind. Juan learns the value of truth in life and in painting according to Velasquez. *Newbery Medal.*

487. de Treviño, Elizabeth. **Leona: A Love Story**. New York: Farrar, Straus & Giroux, 1994. 142p. $15. ISBN 0-374-34382-9. 5-8

Before Leona Vicario became the wife of the Mexican patriot, Andres Quintana Roo, she was honored by her government after Mexico's War for Independence in the 1800s. Her guardian, loyal to the Spanish crown, would not let her leave the house when he realized that she was in love with Roo. She escaped and traveled, with great risk and difficulty, to join Roo and the Insurgent cause, because she wanted to fight for the Criollos, for the abolition of slavery, and for the suppression of the Inquisition. Through it all, she had a debilitating illness.

488. de Treviño, Elizabeth. **Turi's Poppa**. New York: Farrar, Straus & Giroux, 1968. 186p. $3.95. ISBN 0-374-37887-8. 6-9

When Turi is eight, World War II ends, and he and his father walk from Budapest to Cremona, Italy, site of his father's new job as the Violin Institute director. To get the job, though, Turi's father has to prove that he is the premier violin maker by making a violin that will please a violinist used to a Stradivari. Turi undergoes a role reversal, because he has to keep encouraging his father, in whom he has total faith, that the endeavors will be successful. *Boston Globe-Horn Book Award.*

489. De Varona, Frank. **Bernardo de Gálvez**. Tom Redman, illustrator. Austin, TX: Raintree/Steck-Vaughn, 1993. 32p. $13.98; $5.95pa. ISBN 0-8172-3379-2; 0-8114-6756-2pa. (Hispanic Stories). 4-7

As a Spanish soldier, Bernardo de Gálvez (1746-1786) was assigned first to duty in Mexico, where he fought the Apaches, and then the Louisiana Territory, where he fought France. He ordered the British to leave the territory and gave Americans freedom to use it. His greatest victory was in Pensacola (now Florida) in 1781, when he defeated the British. Glossary. English and Spanish text.

490. DeChancie, John. **Juan Perón**. New York: Chelsea House, 1987. 112p. $18.95. ISBN 0-87754-548-0. (World Leaders Past and Present). 8 up

Juan Perón (1895–1974) served as president and dictator of Argentina from 1946 to 1955. He first came to power in a coup d'état and won popularity with the workers as secretary of labor. As president, he eliminated his opponents to gain total power. He initiated ambitious programs of industrialization and reform while attempting to break Argentina's economic dependence on Europe. He was not as popular with the military, and a rebellion in 1955 forced him to resign rather than fight a civil war. In 1973, he came back to power, but he died soon after. Photographs enhance the text. Chronology, Further Reading, and Index.

491. Deem, James M. **How to Make a Mummy Talk**. True Kelley, illustrator. Boston: Houghton Mifflin, 1995. 184p. $14.95. ISBN 0-395-62427-4. 4-8

Entertaining illustrations and boxed questions guide the reader through this text about mummies. With the premise that mummies "talk" through what archaeologists discover about them, Deem explores fact and myth about how mummies were and are made, what mummies "say," and where to find them. Some of the more famous mummies discussed are the 5,000-year-old Iceman of Europe; Elmer McCurdy, an Oklahoma outlaw; mummies from California; a Bigfoot mummy from Minnesota; and an Egyptian mummy. Bibliography and Index.

492. Deford, Frank. **Love and Infamy**. New York: Viking, 1993. 516p. $5.99. ISBN 0-670-82995-1. YA

Cotton Drake grows up in Japan after World War I with his missionary parents and makes friends with Kiyoshi. As adults, Cotton becomes a missionary, and Kiyoshi works in Honolulu in an international shipping firm. There Admiral Yamamoto recruits Kiyoshi as an intelligence officer, and he finds that the admiral is planning to bomb Pearl Harbor without informing the Imperial Army beforehand. He tells Cotton, and Cotton tries to convince American officials of the plan. Some of the historical accuracy in this story must be questioned, but it shows the Japanese culture and perceptions of work, honor, sex, religion, family, and duty, which are valuable assets in a story featuring believable characters.

493. Degens, T. **Freya on the Wall**. San Diego, CA: Browndeer, Harcourt Brace, 1997. 288p. $17. ISBN 0-15-200210-3. 7 up

Freya lives in East Germany just before the fall of the Berlin Wall in 1989. She imagines fleeing across the border to West Germany just as her grandmother fled from the Soviet army in 1945 while wondering if small local events would influence larger events, as the chaos theory suggests. When her American cousin visits her after the Wall opens, Freya tells her the stories. As Freya explores her family's history and the separations that sent her grandmother's sister abroad, she finds that her grandmother has omitted significant details from her version of their escape.

494. Degens, T. **On the Third Ward**. New York: Harper, 1990. 243p. $14.95. ISBN 0-06-021428-7. 7-10

Wanda survives the monotony of her confinement in the German (Hessian) State Hospital for Children with Tuberculosis in 1951 by telling tales to and with the other patients. The tales become their lives as they strive to escape the hospital where only death seems a constant.

495. DeJong, Meindert. **The House of Sixty Fathers**. Maurice Sendak, illustrator. 1956. New York: Harper-Collins, 1990. 189p. $14.89; $4.50pa. ISBN 0-06-021481-3; 0-06-440200-2pa. 5-8

The sampan on which Tien Pao is sleeping washes downriver from Hengyang where his parents work at the American airfield. When he comes ashore, he and his pig begin the long walk back to the area through the Japanese-occupied territory of China. When an American airman crashes his plane nearby, Tien Pao helps him, and the Americans in turn look after him. All sixty of the airmen in the area want to adopt him, but he wants to find his family. *Newbery Honor Book, American Library Association Notable Books for Children, International Board of Books for Young People,* and *Child Study Association Children's Book Award.*

496. Deltenre, Chantal, and Martine Noblet. **Peru and the Andean Countries**. Maureen Walker, translator. Hauppauge, NY: Barron's, 1995. 77p. $11.95; $6.95pa. ISBN 0-8120-6490-9; 0-8120-9161-2pa. (Tintin's Travel Diaries). 5 up

The text asks thirty questions about Peru and the Andean countries, covering a variety of topics such as the mystery of the Nazca, the origin of the Indians, where Machu Picchu is, how the Incas traveled and wrote, and where the giant statues on Easter Island might have come from. Illustrations and photographs complement the simple text on the lefthand pages and the more scholarly answers on the righthand pages. Glossary, Chronological Chart, Map, Bibliography, and Index.

497. Deltenre, Chantal, and Martine Noblet. **Russia**. Maureen Walker, translator. Hauppauge, NY: Barron's, 1995. 77p. $11.95; $6.95pa. ISBN 0-8120-6491-7; 0-8120-9162-2pa. (Tintin's Travel Diaries). 5 up

The text asks thirty questions about Russia, covering a variety of topics such as who the horsemen of the steppes were, what an icon is, the origin of the Russians, who the great Russian novelists were, and what happened at Chernobyl. Illustrations and photographs complement the simple text on the lefthand pages and the more scholarly answers on the righthand pages. Glossary, Chronological Chart, Map, Bibliography, and Index.

498. Denenberg, Barry. **Nelson Mandela: "No Easy Walk to Freedom."** New York: Scholastic, 1991. 164p. $12.95; $3.50pa. ISBN 0-590-44163-9; 0-590-44154-Xpa. 5-8

Denenberg divides this biography of Mandela into three parts: "Roots," "Afrikaners and Apartheid," and "The Struggle." Within these parts, he includes information about Africa, about the Boers and the British, and about the various groups and events that led to Mandela's imprisonment. In 1980, after the Soweto uprising, the white citizens realized that they must either "adapt or die." When they finally seemed to adapt, Mandela was freed from prison after twenty-seven years. Chronology, Bibliography, and Index.

499. Denenberg, Barry. **Voices from Vietnam**. New York: Scholastic, 1995. 251p. $16.95. ISBN 0-590-44267-8. 8 up

From the mid-1800s until after World War II, the French controlled Vietnam, exploiting its people and its resources. In May 1954, Ho Chi Minh's Communists defeated the French, who had been supported by Americans fearful of Communist control of the area. Americans began to support Diem, and the war that ended with the final offensive of the North Vietnamese in 1975 began in earnest. Denenberg uses direct quotes by persons involved in all aspects of the war in telling what the war was about and what it did. His story makes the reasons for and results of war in Vietnam understandable. *American Library Association Best Books for Young Adults* and *American Library Association Booklist Editors' Choices.*

500. Descamps-Lequime, Sophie, and Denise Vernerey. **The Ancient Greeks: In the Land of the Gods**. Mary Kae LaRose, translator; Veronique Ageorges, illustrator. Brookfield, CT: Millbrook Press, 1992. 64p. $16.40. ISBN 1-56294-069-4. (Peoples of the Past). 5-8

The Greeks, unusually curious about themselves and their world, had a sense of adventure and a desire to know the truth. Evidence of Greek achievement has survived through the centuries. The text looks at the ancient Greek world, growing up in Greece, Greek styles of dress and ways of life, the rights of the citizen, wars, Panhellenic games, Greek theater, and religion. The Family of Gods, Find Out More, Glossary, and Index.

501. Deschamps, Helene. **Spyglass: An Autobiography**. New York: Henry Holt, 1995. 308p. $16.95. ISBN 0-8050-3536-2. 10 up

In 1940, France surrendered to Germany, and Helene Deschamps, age seventeen, joined the French Resistance. Later, during World War II, she worked for the American Office of Strategic Services (OSS) as a spy. In the book, she flirts, hides, exchanges passwords, guides gunned-down American pilots, and runs from the Gestapo. While narrowly escaping death, she lives her life passionately both in her work and in her romances. Index.

502. DeStefano, Susan. **Chico Mendes: Fight for the Forest**. Larry Raymond, illustrator. New York: Twenty-First Century, 1992. 76p. $14.98. ISBN 0-8050-2501-4. (Earth Keepers). 4-7

Chico Mendes (d. 1988) was a rubber tapper in the Amazon rain forest who tried to stop the destruction of the forest. For his concerns, he was murdered. The text also looks at the history of the rain forest and its ecological importance to the rest of the world. Glossary and Index.

503. Detzer, David. **An Asian Tragedy: America and Vietnam**. Brookfield, CT: Millbrook Press, 1992. 160p. $16.90. ISBN 1-56294-066-X. 7-9

By using "tragedy" in the title, the author shows the view of the Vietnam War from 1961 to 1975 presented in the text. In chronological order, the text details many decisions that caused difficulties for both Americans and Vietnamese after war was declared. Not too many could be called heroes in this conflict. Bibliography and Index.

504. Devaney, John. **America on the Attack: 1943**. New York: Walker, 1992. 224p. $18.85. ISBN 0-8027-8194-2. (World War II). 7 up

The beginning of 1943 was a humiliating defeat for Eisenhower at Kasserine Pass in Tunisia, but his forces returned to drive Rommel back. Patton helped contain the Germans and Italians along the beaches of the Mediterranean. In England, bombers flew to Dresden and Hamburg. In Stalingrad, Germans surrendered. Hitler stopped the Soviets but began to stall so that by 1943's end, Russians had pushed the Germans out of most of the Soviet Union. The text looks at the entire year of the war in detail. For Further Reading and Index.

505. Devaney, John. **America Storms the Beaches: 1944**. New York: Walker, 1993. 201p. $17.95. ISBN 0-8027-8244-2. (World War II). 7 up

Fighter planes and battleships filled the Pacific theater as 1944 began. Allied troops broke Germans in Italy and worked their way toward Central Europe. Eisenhower sent invading troops into Normandy in June. Original source materials help show this year of the war, including the Japanese kamikaze pilots and a failed assassination attempt on Hitler. For Further Reading and Index.

506. Devaney, John. **America Triumphs: 1945**. New York: Walker, 1995. 199p. $18.95. ISBN 0-8027-8347-3. 7 up

In his prologue, Devaney briefly summarizes the progression of World War II from its beginning in 1939 through 1944. The text, beginning on January 1, 1945, presents accounts from individuals as they face different battles, including Iwo Jima and Okinawa. Their comments show the motivations and the philosophical forces driving their choices to fight for their countries. He presents Eisenhower's first encounter with a German death camp as well as the ceremonies when the Japanese surrendered to General Douglas MacArthur. He includes photographs and biographical sketches of Chiang Kai-shek, Winston Churchill, Charles de Gaulle, Dwight Eisenhower, Emperor Hirohito, Adolf Hitler, Douglas MacArthur, George C. Marshall, Erwin Rommel, Franklin Delano Roosevelt, Josef Stalin, Hideki Tojo, and Harry S. Truman. Important Dates, Maps, For Further Reading, and Index.

507. Dhondy, Farrukh. **Black Swan**. Boston: Houghton Mifflin, 1993. 217p. $14.95. ISBN 0-395-66076-9. 7 up

When her mother is sick, Rose, age eighteen, helps her employer by copying an astronomer/astrologer's diaries from 1592, during the time of Shakespeare. Political enemies from his Caribbean island home hunt the employer, a West Indian, and Rose's real life begins to seem like the diaries. The diarist asserts that Christopher Marlowe and his black lover, an ex-slave, wrote plays under the name of a useless actor, William Shakespeare. Both Rose, of mixed heritage, and the slave suffered for their racial background, and the political intrigue also has parallel action.

508. Di Franco, J. Philip. **The Italian Americans**. New York: Chelsea House, 1988. 94p. $18.95; $7.95pa. ISBN 0-87754-886-2; 0-7910-0268-3pa. (Peoples of North America). 5 up

Although this book professes to discuss only Italian Americans, it recounts a brief history of Italy through its revolutions and the Italian unification movement, *Risorgimento*, led by Guiseppe Mazzini, G. Garibaldi, and Camillo Benso di Cavour. In the nineteenth century, however, the greed of the wealthy led to a difficult life for many southern Italians. The northern Italians emigrated first, with the southern Italians following them. The peak immigration years were 1900 to 1914, when more than 2 million Italians arrived in the United States. Not all of them remained, but by 1980, 12 million Italians had settled in the United States. Among those who influenced American life was Filippo Mazzei, a physician philosopher whom Thomas Jefferson translated and whose words closely resembled the Bill of Rights. In 1832, Lorenzo de Ponte brought opera to America. Wine growers from Italy established the Swiss Colony winery, and fruit growers began the Del Monte company. Famous Italian Americans include Fiorello La Guardia, Geraldine Ferraro, Mario Cuomo, Mother Cabrini (America's first saint), Joe DiMaggio, Mario Lanza, Frank Sinatra, Marconi, Fermi, Toscanini, Anne Bancroft, and Lee Iacocca. Selected References and Index.

509. Diamond, Arthur. **Anwar Sadat**. San Diego, CA: Lucent, 1994. 112p. $16.95. ISBN 1-56006-020-4. (The Importance Of). 7 up

Anwar Sadat (1918–1981) spent two years in jail for his role in anti-British activities; then he took part in the 1952 coup when Nasser ousted King Farouk. At Nasser's death in 1956, Sadat became president. At first he fought Israel, but he then began peace talks with Menachem Begin in 1977, with the Camp David Accords following in 1978. Militant Muslims, disapproving of his peace initiatives, assassinated him during a military parade. Notes, For Further Reading, Works Consulted, and Index.

510. Dick, Lois Hoadley. **False Coin, True Coin**. Greenville, SC: Bob Jones University Press, 1993. 172p. $6.49pa. ISBN 0-89084-664-2pa. (Light Line). 6-10

Cissy Nidd's father, the Bedford jailer, also trafficks in counterfeit coins in London around 1660 during the Stuart reign. Cissy meets John Bunyan, a Dissenter against the monarchy's state religion who has been jailed, and he helps her to see that life offers more than drudgery and deceit. She suffers, but because she has been kind to others, they in turn try to help her through her trials.

511. Dickinson, Peter. **The Dancing Bear**. Boston: Little, Brown, 1973. 244p. $6.95. ISBN 0-316-18426-8. 7 up

In A.D. 558, the Kutrigur Huns invade Justinian's Byzantium and capture Addie, the teenage daughter of a wealthy family. Her slave Silvester, the household priest Holy John, and a pet dancing bear Bubba go to rescue her. In their travels, they help a dying Hun and find out that Addie's uncle wants Silvester captured and returned. They eventually reach the Hun camp, where the Huns think Bubba is a totem, especially after he smells and kills the Hun who gored him during the initial attack. After the three retrieve and escape with Addie during the confusion of a surprise ambush on the camp, they choose to live with an exiled Roman away from the city, where they do not have to worry about social rank.

512. Dickinson, Peter. **Tulku**. 1979. Magnolia, MA: Peter Smith, 1995. 288p. $17.55. ISBN 0-8446-6830-3. New York; Laurel, 1993. $3.99pa. ISBN 0-440-21489-0pa. 7 up

As the Boxer Rebellion takes hold of China in 1900, Theo's missionary father sends him a message telling him to leave. He does, but feels guilty for deserting. He meets Mrs. Jones, a British collector of exotic plants, who returns to their village and confirms the death of Theo's father. The two travel out of China through Tibet, the only route open. After they reach the Dong Pe monastery, a lama thinks that Theo is a reincarnated religious leader named Tulku. He decides instead that the unborn child Mrs. Jones carries, after Lung, her guide, impregnates her, could be Tulku. Mrs. Jones decides to remain in Tibet to hear more of the lama's teachings after sending Theo to England. *Whitbread Award, Carnegie Medal,* and *International Board of Books for Young People.*

513. Dillon, Eilís. **Children of Bach**. New York: Scribners, 1992. 164p. $13.95. ISBN 0-684-19440-6. 5-8

When four children return to their Budapest, Hungary, home one afternoon at the beginning of World War II, a neighbor, Mrs. Nagy, tells them that Nazi soldiers have taken away their musician parents and their aunt. Their aunt returns. She, the children, and Mrs. Nagy, who is part Jewish, then hide in a van behind furniture for a trip into Italy to find their cousin in the mountains. There they may play their music without worry, but Mrs. Nagy continues her irritating habits. Although the children are safe, they have to face the possibility that they will never see their parents again.

514. Dillon, Eilís. **The Seekers**. New York: Scribners, 1986. 136p. $12.95. ISBN 0-684-18595-4. 7 up

In 1632, Edward and his family leave England for Plymouth, Massachusetts, when his fiancée's father decides that he and his daughter Rebecca are resettling. In their new home, they all try to adjust to the religious zealots, the illnesses, and the hard work in the area. Edward and Rebecca decide that they prefer to live in England, so they return home.

515. Disher, Garry. **The Bamboo Flute**. New York: Ticknor & Fields, 1993. 96p. $10.95. ISBN 0-395-66595-7. 5-8

During the Depression of 1932 in Australia, Paul wants his family to return to the music that they loved before the economic troubles. His parents warn him to stay away from the men called swagmen, who roam about seeking food or work, but when he meets Eric the Red, who plays a flute and steals sheep, Paul learns how to bring music back into his family's life. With Eric's help, Paul makes his own flute from bamboo.

516. Dodge, Stephen. **Christopher Columbus and the First Voyages to the New World**. New York: Chelsea House, 1990. 128p. $19.95. ISBN 0-7910-1299-9. (World Explorers). 5 up

Columbus departed on August 2, 1492, from Genoa, and arrived in San Salvador two months later. The text describes his life, this voyage, and Columbus's three additional voyages before his death. Photographs and reproductions enhance the text. Chronology, Further Reading, and Index.

517. Doherty, Berlie. **Street Child**. New York: Orchard, 1994. 149p. $14.95. ISBN 0-531-06864-1. 5-8

The opening chapter helps the reader cope with the pain of Jim Jarvis's story, because the reader learns immediately that Jim does find protection in the end. Around 1886 in London, Jim's mother dies after getting her daughters positions as maids, but Jim has to go to the workhouse, a horrible place from which he escapes. He helps his mother's friend until her grandfather sells him to a man who nearly works him to death. Then he meets Dr. Barnardo, who wants to help him and the other homeless boys on the street.

518. Doherty, Katherine, and Craig A. Doherty. **Benazir Bhutto**. New York: Franklin Watts, 1990. 144p. $13.90. ISBN 0-531-10936-4. (Impact Biography). 5 up

Benazir Bhutto, the first woman to head a Muslim state, became Pakistan's prime minister when she was thirty-five years old. She attended Harvard and Oxford in preparation for a political career. During her attempts to restore democracy in Pakistan, she was imprisoned, placed in solitary confinement, and became ill. She eventually lost her position to another president. Bibliography and Index.

519. Doherty, P. C. **An Ancient Evil: The Knights' Tale of Mystery and Murder as He Goes on a Pilgrimage from London to Canterbury**. New York: St. Martin's Press, 1994. 248p. $21. ISBN 0-312-11740-X. YA

Each pilgrim on the journey to Canterbury tells a story; the Knight tells of a vampire cult that thrived during the time of William the Conqueror in the Oxfordshire wilderness. Two hundred years later, mysterious student and citizen deaths in Oxford baffle the sheriff and the authorities, but Lady Constance, Abbess of the Convent of St. Anne's, thinks that the murders relate to the cult and petitions the king's help. Sir Godfre Evesden and Alexander McBain come to investigate. A third person, the blind exorcist Dame Edith Mohun, who had an experience with the cult as a young girl, goes with them. Their careful work helps them solve the mystery, but they cannot destroy the cult.

520. Doherty, P. C. **A Tapestry of Murders**. New York: St. Martin's Press, 1996. 247p. $21.95. ISBN 0-312-14052-5. YA

When designated to tell his tale at night, the Man of Law from Chaucer tells of the murder of Vallence, a French courtier on the way back to France after the death of the Dowager Queen Isabella in 1358. The Sheriff of London asks Nicholas Chirke, the young lawyer telling the tale, to find out what secret Vallence was carrying that would cause his death. With his mysterious assistant Scathelocke, Chirke discovers shadows of the underworld and a female assassin.

521. Doherty, P. C. **A Tournament of Murders**. New York: St. Martin's Press, 1997. 256p. $21.95. ISBN 0-312-17048-3. YA

Franklin tells his story on a pilgrimage to Canterbury about a knight, Sir Gilbert Savage, who while dying, tells family secrets to his squire, Richard Greenele. Greenele rushes back to England to confer with a lawyer who will reveal his true parentage and how five trusted knights betrayed his father. On his pilgrimage, outlaws pursue him before he finds the truth.

522. Doherty, Paul C. **King Arthur**. New York: Chelsea House, 1987. 115p. $18.95. ISBN 0-87754-506-5. (World Leaders Past and Present). 5 up

Whether Arthur was a tribal leader or a great king in British history, the many legends about his life leave no doubt that someone of great influence once reigned in the British Isles. The text looks at the archaeological research that seems to prove Arthur's existence, as well as legends about his reign during the Anglo-Saxon period of A.D. 449 to 1066. Photographs and reproductions enhance the text. Further Reading, Chronology, and Index.

523. Dolan, Edward F. **Panama and the United States: Their Canal, Their Stormy Years**. New York: Franklin Watts, 1990. 160p. $19.86. ISBN 0-531-10911-9. 5 up

When Columbus arrived in what is now Panama on his fourth voyage in 1503, probably 750,000 people, from the Cuna tribe and others, lived there. But Balboa arrived first, in 1501. Not until 1513 did Balboa cross Panama to see the great body of water on the other side, the Pacific. Balboa realized that a waterway would make the journey much easier; thus, the idea of a canal began very early in Panama's recorded history. From 1799 to 1804, Alexander von Humbolt surveyed the area and found nine reasonable routes to cut across land to the Pacific. Because of battles, treaties, and misfortune, the United States was not free to complete the canal until the beginning of the twentieth century. The man who made it most possible was William Crawford Gorgas; he discovered that mosquitoes caused malaria and yellow fever and saved the lives of many workers. On August 15, 1913, the canal opened. A further series of treaties and disagreements between Panama and the United States have peppered the canal's history. Finally, Torrijos made an agreement with President Carter to take possession of the canal on December 31, 1999. Panama's new ruler at Torrijos's death, Noreiga, did nothing to further good relationships. Photographs show the progress of the canal's construction. Source Notes, Bibliography, and Index.

524. Dolan, Sean. **Chiang Kai-Shek: Chinese Nationalist**. New York: Chelsea House, 1988. 112p. $18.95. ISBN 0-87754-517-0. (World Leaders Past and Present). 8 up

Chiang Kai-shek (1887–1975) established his government in Taiwan in 1949 when the Communists took control of the mainland. History remembers him as the man who lost China because of the corruption in his government and his use of military force to stop his enemies. The Qing Dynasty mistreated his family, a wrong he never forgot. Their overthrow in 1912 led him to join Sun Yat-sen, a Chinese revolutionary, and after Sun's death in 1925, he became the leader of the Nationalist Party and head of the united China in 1928. But his massacres of Chinese forces at Shanghai and other cities started twenty years of civil war. He fled in 1949 to Taiwan, where he ruled for thirty years. Photographs enhance the text. Chronology, Further Reading, and Index.

525. Dolan, Sean. **Gabriel García Márquez**. New York: Chelsea House, 1993. 128p. $18.95. ISBN 0-7910-1243-3. (Hispanics of Achievement). 8 up

Some have called Gabriel García Márquez (b. 1928) the most powerful man in Latin America, but he has never held political office. His influence comes from his book, *One Hundred Years of Solitude*, translated into more than twenty-six languages. In the book, using magic realism, he tells the story of Colombia, his country. He wrote the book by working nonstop for eighteen months. This book and others won him the 1982 Nobel Prize for Literature. The text looks at his life and his work. Photographs enhance the text. Chronology, Further Reading, and Index.

526. Dolan, Sean. **Juan Ponce de León**. New York: Chelsea House, 1995. 110p. $18.95. ISBN 0-7910-2023-1. (Hispanics of Achievement). 5 up

While searching for the fountain of youth, Juan Ponce de León (1474-1521) became the first European to reach the area he later named Florida. When he came to the New World with Columbus, on Columbus's second voyage in 1493, de León decided to settle in Hispaniola with his family, where he ruled as the military commander and deputy governor. He began exploring Puerto Rico (Borinquén) and became its governor in 1508. He always wanted more wealth than he had, and when he heard of a place that sounded as if it had money, he went. In Florida, the Calusa Indians fought with and killed him. Engravings and reproductions enhance the text. Chronology, Further Reading, and Index.

527. Dolan, Sean. **Junípero Serra**. New York: Chelsea House, 1991. 110p. $18.95; $7.95pa. ISBN 0-7910-1255-7; 0-7910-1282-4pa. (Hispanics of Achievement). 5 up

Miguel José Serra (1713-1784), born in Majorca, began his religious training at fifteen. He became a Franciscan and in 1748 left his home and family to become a missionary in the New World. He served the Spanish missions built by the conquerors trying to convert Indians to Catholicism by either persuasion or force. In 1769, he joined the expeditions exploring California and established the string of missions that still stand today from San Diego to San Francisco. In 1988, the church began the process of making him a saint, although Native Americans accuse him of trying to destroy their culture. Engravings and reproductions enhance the text. Chronology, Further Reading, and Index.

528. Dommermuth-Costa, Carol. **Agatha Christie: Writer of Mystery**. Minneapolis, MN: Lerner, 1997. 112p. $17.21. ISBN 0-8225-4954-9. (Biographies). 5-9

Dame Agatha Christie (1890-1976), the "First Lady of Crime," had the support of family and servants before she married a World War I pilot who left her for another woman. She had begun to write detective fiction, and her second marriage to an archaeologist, Max Mallowan, was successful as were her creations Hercule Poirot and Miss Marple. Photographs highlight the text. Bibliography and Index.

529. Dommermuth-Costa, Carol. **Nikola Tesla: A Spark of Genius**. Minneapolis, MN: Lerner, 1994. 144p. $17.21. ISBN 0-8225-4920-4. 5-9

Nikola Tesla (1856-1943), born in Croatia, was the true inventor of radio. He developed the technology that harnessed alternating-current electricity. He was a friend to George Westinghouse and a rival of Thomas Edison. He became a millionaire whose fortune evaporated when he bought equipment that burned up. Marconi rather than Tesla received credit for inventing the radio, and Tesla claimed that Marconi was using seventeen of Tesla's patents. Since Tesla's death, scientists have continued to discover the scope of his achievements and to establish awards in his name in the field of electricity. Sources, Bibliography, and Index.

530. Dorris, Michael. **Morning Girl**. New York: Hyperion, 1992. 74p. $12.95; $3.50pa. ISBN 1-56282-285-3; 1-56282-661-1pa. 3-7

In 1492, Morning Girl and Star Boy live with their parents on a Bahamian island. Their world changes when Columbus finds them and imposes new concepts of culture on their society. *Scott O'Dell Award.*

531. Douglas, Carole N. **Good Morning, Irene**. New York: TOR, 1991. 374p. $19.95. ISBN 0-312-93211-1. YA

After trying to escape from the King of Bohemia, Irene and her husband are reported to have died in the Alps. Around 1890, however, Sherlock Holmes discovers that they are living in Paris with Irene's friend Nell, as they try to solve a mystery surrounding a man dredged from the Seine and tattooed with a design that Irene has previously seen.

532. Douglas, Carole N. **Irene at Large**. New York: TOR, 1992. 381p. $19.95; $4.99pa. ISBN 0-312-85223-1; 0-8125-1702-4pa. YA

Irene, her husband, and her friend Nell rescue Quentin in 1890 when he falls in front of them on a Paris street. Thinking that he might have been poisoned, they proceed to save him. Quentin had been on his way to warn Dr. Watson that someone was trying to kill Watson because he had been kind to Quentin in India ten years before. After they identify Dr. Watson's enemy, Quentin disappears.

533. Douglas, Carole N. **Irene's Last Waltz**. New York: Forge, 1994. 480p. $22.95. ISBN 0-312-85224-X. YA

Irene, her husband Geoffrey, and her friend Nell have a murder to solve in the 1890s.

534. Douglas, Kirk. **The Broken Mirror**. New York: Simon & Schuster, 1997. 88p. $13. ISBN 0-689-81493-3. 4-7

Moishe's mother thinks that the Nazi hooligans will disappear, and his father moves the family to a farm in Germany during 1939. A worker reveals them to the Nazis, and they go to a concentration camp. Moishe is the only one to survive; he claims Catholicism and ends up in an American orphanage before declaring his Jewishness.

535. Douglas, Roy. **The World War, 1939-1945: The Cartoonists' Vision**. New York: Routledge, 1990. 300p. $16.95pa. ISBN 0-415-07141-0pa. YA

The political cartoon encapsulates the mood of a group of people in history and reveals how subtle propaganda can be. A page of commentary and perspective accompanies each of these political cartoons collected from World War II. Included are cartoons that show how the war appeared to people in different nations and to diverse groups within those nations. Many are British; some are Italian and French; a few are German or Russian; and none are Japanese.

536. Doyle, Brian. **Uncle Ronald**. Buffalo, NY: Firefly Books, 1997. 144p. $16.95. ISBN 0-88899-266-1. 6-8

Mickey McGuire, 112, recalls his life in Ottawa in 1895 when he began bed-wetting at age twelve. His mother sent him to his uncle's farm, and Uncle Ronald is the opposite of Mickey's abusive father. His mother follows after his father beats her severely, and the two expect him to follow. The story includes a conflict between the area and the federal troops over the collection of back taxes.

537. Doyle, Roddy. **Paddy Clarke, Ha Ha Ha**. New York: Viking, 1993. 282p. $20.95. ISBN 0-670-85345-3. YA

Ten-year-old Paddy Clarke lives with his family in the Dublin neighborhood of Barrytown in the late 1960s. He wants to be tough like his friends and spends his time engaging in malicious but harmless acts such as writing in hardening cement and torturing his little brother. He also has to listen to his parents fight at night. Paddy tries to understand the adult world and to figure out his place in it. *Booker Prize*.

538. Dramer, Kim. **Kublai Khan: Mongol Emperor**. New York: Chelsea House, 1990. 112p. $18.95; $7.95pa. ISBN 0-7910-0697-2; 1-55546-812-8pa. (World Leaders Past and Present). 5 up

Grandson of Genghis the Conqueror, Kublai Khan (1215-1294) was the emperor of China and its states and the head of the Mongol army. He greeted and supposedly welcomed Marco Polo to his court in 1275, urging Polo to stay for many years. Kublai was at times a patron of the arts and sciences and generally the fair and wise ruler of a group of nomadic farmers. The Mongols, a nomadic culture, were military giants who conquered territory from the western area of Russia to Indochina, though they failed against Japan and Java (Indonesia), and Kublai's army protected merchants traveling on the great Silk Route. But his love of luxury eventually bankrupted his court, and after his death the dynasty deteriorated. Marco Polo wrote about Kublai Khan when he returned from his travels. Photographs and reproductions enhance the text. Chronology, Further Reading, and Index.

539. Driemen, J. E. **Winston Churchill: An Unbreakable Spirit**. New York: Dillon Press, 1990. 128p. $13.95. ISBN 0-87518-434-0. (People in Focus). 5 up

Sir Winston Churchill (1874-1965) grew up in an upper-class British family but had to overcome his poor school record with action. His many achievements prepared him for his position as Britain's prime minister during World War II, when Hitler threatened the country. Churchill said that he had nothing to offer but "blood, toil, tears, and sweat." People often remember him with his fingers formed in the "V for Victory" sign. Appendix, Selected Bibliography, and Index.

540. Drucker, Malka. **Frida Kahlo: Torment and Triumph in Her Life**. New York: Bantam, 1991. 159p. $7pa. ISBN 0-553-35408-6pa. (Barnard Biography). 7 up

Frida Kahlo (1907–1954), daughter of a Mexican mother and a Hungarian Jewish father, was Mexico's best known female artist, but a woman relatively unknown outside her country. She painted self-portraits that showed her suffering, pain, and feelings of betrayal. Her husband, Diego Rivera, Mexico's leading artist, introduced her to expressionism, nationalism, and political activism. She once said, "I have suffered two accidents in my life . . . one in which a streetcar ran over me. The other is Diego." The bus accident when she was eighteen left her disabled for life. Kahlo's work absorbed her, and her character as a strong woman comes through her creations. Chronology and Index.

541. Drucker, Olga Levy. **Kindersport**. New York: Henry Holt, 1992. 145p. $14.95. ISBN 0-8050-1711-9. 5-8

Born in Germany in 1927, Ollie Levy enjoyed the life of a publisher's daughter. The German government had honored her father's service in World War I, but in 1938, on *Kristallnacht*, he and the family realized that their Jewish origin would allow them no future honor. Ollie's parents sent her to England on a children's train with other Jewish children. She lived there for six years, enduring a different kind of prejudice, but was able to reunite with her parents in the United States in 1945. This autobiographical story depicts life for a young girl exiled from her family and her home during World War II.

542. Dubois, Muriel L. **Abenaki Captive**. Minneapolis, MN: Carolrhoda, 1994. 180p. $14.96. ISBN 0-87614-753-8. 5-8

In 1752, the St. Francis Abenaki of eastern Canada capture John Stark and his friend, Amos Eastman, while killing a third person who was with them. Because whites had killed a young Abenaki man, Ogistin's brother, Ogistin at first hates Stark, but the other Abenakis like him. Stark stays with the tribe for some time before he decides to leave. Differences between the beliefs of the Abenaki and the Europeans become clear when Ogistin depends on his guardian spirit, a lynx. What also becomes clear are the divisions between settlers at the time: the hostilities between the Catholics and the Protestants and between the French and the English.

543. Duder, Tessa. **Alex in Rome**. Boston: Houghton Mifflin, 1992. 166p. $12.95. ISBN 0-395-62879-2. 6 up

Swimming for New Zealand in the 1960 Olympic Games in Rome, Alex, age sixteen, wins a bronze medal. During the games, she meets an "Italian" who finally admits that he is really from New Zealand and is in Italy to study opera. Alex's experiences, both in the pool and out of it, give her added insight into the confusing world of international cultures. *New Zealand's AIM Children's Book Award* and *Esther Glen Medal* (New Zealand).

544. Duder, Tessa. **In Lane Three, Alex Archer**. Boston: Houghton Mifflin, 1989. 176p. $13.95. ISBN 0-395-50927-0. New York: Bantam, 1991. 175p. $3.99pa. ISBN 0-553-29020-7pa. 7-10

Alex, age fifteen, prepares in 1959 to swim in the 1960 Olympics in Rome on the New Zealand team. She refuses to limit herself to swimming, although she faces stiff competition from another swimmer who wins more races than Alex does. Alex performs in the dance and theater events at her school, plays on the hockey team, and has a full-time boyfriend. But several complications make her year more soul-searching than she might have wanted. *New Zealand's AIM Children's Book Award* and *Esther Glen Medal* (New Zealand).

545. Duffy, James P., and Vincent L. Ricci. **Czar: Russia's Rulers for More than One Thousand Years**. New York: Facts on File, 1996. 288p. $35. ISBN 0-8160-2873-7. YA

The text traces the monarchy of the Russian Empire from Rurik (d. 879), a Viking who established the empire, to its end with the execution of Nicholas II in 1918. It looks at each monarch in detail, including those from the House of Rurik (Ivan III the Great, Vasily III, Ivan IV the Terrible, Feodor I); the House of Godunov (Boris Godunov and Feodor II); the Usurpers (Dmitri, Vasily IV, and the interim); and the House of Romanov (Michael, Alexis, Feodor III, Ivan V, Peter I the Great, Catherine I, Peter II, Anna, Ivan VI, Elizabeth, Peter III, Catherine II the Great, Paul I, Alexander I, Nicholas I, Alexander II, Alexander III, and Nicholas II). Bibliography and Index.

546. Duggleby, John. **Impossible Quests**. Allan Eitzen, illustrator. New York: Crestwood House, 1990. 48p. $10.95. ISBN 0-89686-509-6. (Incredible History). 4 up

Various quests have attempted to prove the existence of Bigfoot in the Pacific Northwest of the United States and Canada, the Loch Ness Monster in Scotland, Noah's Ark in Turkey, Atlantis in the Mediterranean, and the lost continent of gold in the South Pacific. The text discusses these quests and illustrates them with black-and-white drawings. Bibliography and Index.

547. Dunlop, Betty. **The Poetry Girl**. Boston: Houghton Mifflin, 1989. 209p. $13.95. ISBN 0-395-49679-9. 6-8

Natalia, age twelve, moves with her Russian parents to another town in New Zealand during 1946. Her father, suicidal and harsh, argues with her mother constantly. Natalia feels alone and is often absent from school. Classmates and teachers seem to persecute her, and her only outlet is the poetry she writes for herself. Her brother tells her two years later that she is growing up, and she decides that she will try to fulfill her own needs.

548. Dunn, Andrew. **Marie Curie**. New York: Gloucester, 1991. 48p. $17.71. ISBN 0-531-18375-0. (Pioneers of Science). 5 up

Marie Curie's (1867-1934) work led to an understanding of the atom. Radioactivity is helpful in medicine and in industry; it gives power in nuclear reactors, but it can cause the destruction of humans if misused. Photographs, Date Chart, Glossary, and Index.

549. Dunn, John. **The Russian Revolution**. San Diego, CA: Lucent, 1994. 112p. $14.95. ISBN 1-56006-234-7. (World History Series). 6 up

Until 1917, the Romanovs had ruled Russia for 330 years. In 1917, over 140 million people from fiercely independent ethnic groups, such as Armenians, Balts, Finns, Jews, Germans, Poles, Ukranians, and others, lived within Russia's boundaries. But the country had stagnated, in part because of the lasting influences of the Mongol invasion during the thirteenth century. This absorbing history of the changes in Russia uses sources written during the period and the research of recognized scholars in its clear and concise evocation of the time. In the nineteenth century, the serfs, who had always been considered the property of their owners, started rebelling. Between 1825 and 1854, more than 500 uprisings occurred; each time, the czar's troops brutally beat the participants. In 1861, serfdom was abandoned, but Karl Marx's *Communist Manifesto* of 1848 had swayed Lenin toward equalization of the masses. Although he was exiled in 1895 for his activities, his advocates continued to fight. In 1905, hundreds died on "Bloody Sunday." In 1914, Russia entered World War I, and Rasputin's sinister influence over Czar Nicholas II, his family, and the government angered the populace. After Rasputin's murder in 1916, Lenin returned to St. Petersburg in 1917 to incite the Bolshevik Revolution and the eventual taking of the Winter Palace. By 1918, Lenin had signed the Treaty of Brest-Litovsk to take the Russians out of World War I and had begun ruling; Nicholas and his family were executed. In 1922, the Soviet Union began, but by 1924, Lenin was dead, and Stalin struggled to win leadership by stripping Trotsky of power. From 1929 to 1932, Stalin starved at least 5 million peasants who refused to obey his collectivization; three years later, from 1935 to 1938, he presided over the Great Purge during which another 15 million Soviets were killed. Stalin said, "You cannot make a revolution with silk gloves." His legacy of oppression continued after his death in 1953 until the Soviet Union ceased to exist in 1991. Notes, For Further Reading, Works Consulted, and Index.

550. Dunnahoo, Terry. **Pearl Harbor: America Enters the War**. New York: Franklin Watts, 1991. 112p. $21.10. ISBN 0-531-11010-9. (Twentieth Century American History). 7-12

Dunnahoo discusses the Japanese attack on Pearl Harbor at Oahu, Hawaii, on December 7, 1941. He gives background about the buildup of the Japanese military, the move of America's Pacific fleet to Hawaii, and the relationship between the United States and Japan before the attack. Dunnahoo focuses on the politics and the diplomacy of the situation rather than on the military aspect. Bibliography and Index.

551. Durbin, William. **The Broken Blade**. New York: Delacorte, 1997. 160p. $14.95. ISBN 0-385-32224-0. 5-8

Pierre, thirteen, has to go to work for his father's company in 1800 when his father injures himself in a wood-chopping accident in Canada. He becomes a voyager, a French-Canadian canoeman. On his first canoe trip to Grand Portage, Pierre ages in many ways and becomes a man. While he has to deal with an unsavory character and mourn the drowning of one of the crew, he also sees the natural beauty of his environment.

552. Durrell, Lawrence. **White Eagles over Serbia**. 1957. New York: Arcade, 1995. 200p. $19.95. ISBN 1-55970-312-1. 9 up

The British spy Meuthen works in a mountainous area of Serbia when the Communists and Tito take over Serbia and Croatia. He looks for clues to the murder of another spy. As a Serbian speaker who has survival skills, he finds out about the White Eagles, a Royalist group trying to overthrow the new government. The plot fails, but Meuthen escapes before the group kills him.

553. Dwork, Deborah. **Children with a Star: Jewish Youth in Nazi Europe**. New Haven, CT: Yale University Press, 1991. 354p. $18pa. ISBN 0-300-05447-5pa. YA

This oral history presents the lives of Jewish children in the Holocaust of World War II as they lived at home, in transit camps, in hiding, in ghettos, and in death and labor camps. Dwork relies on primary sources of diaries, letters, and interviews, and reiterates that only 10 percent of the Jewish children survived. Some of those who shared their stories for this book had never before told anyone of their almost unspeakable experiences. Glossary, Bibliography, and Index.

554. Dwyer, Frank. **Henry VIII**. New York: Chelsea House, 1987. 112p. $18.95. ISBN 0-87754-530-8. (World Leaders Past and Present). 5 up

Called "Great Henry" when he came to the English throne in 1509, Henry VIII (1491-1547) had many positive qualities. In the 1530s, when a desire for church reform arose, Henry declared himself as the Supreme Head of the Church. He ordered the dissolution of monasteries, levied heavy taxes, suppressed opposition, and demanded that all pledge loyalty to him. By the time he died, he had had six wives (some of whom he had executed), beheaded his able minister Thomas More, expanded the power of Parliament, and used up most of his country's funds. But the overall result of his reign was the creation of England as a nation; Henry was the link between medieval and modern England. Reproductions enhance the text. Chronology, Further Reading, and Index.

555.   Dwyer, Frank. **James I**. New York: Chelsea House, 1988. 112p. $18.95. ISBN 1-55546-811-X. (World Leaders Past and Present). 8 up

When Elizabeth I died in 1603, James I (1566–1625), the founder of the Stuart royal line, became king. The son of Mary, Queen of Scots, James was a scholar, but he insisted on recognition of the divine right of kingship from Parliament and refused to moderate his religious views. This stance angered the Puritans, and the Catholics attempted to kill him in the 1605 Gunpowder plot. Protestant England came to despise him for his alliance with Catholic Spain, his corrupt court, and his inability to work with Parliament. Photographs and reproductions enhance the text. Chronology, Further Reading, and Index.

556.   Dyson, John. **Westward with Columbus**. Ken Marschall and Peter Christopher, illustrators. New York: Scholastic, 1991. 64p. $15.95. ISBN 0-590-43846-8. (Time Quest). 3-7

When Christopher Columbus (1451-1506) discovered the New World, he might have taken a more southerly route than previously thought. One scholar, Luís Miguel Coin, took the journey and believes that Columbus had a secret map. Living history photographs illustrate the fifteenth century, and a parallel fiction story about Pedro, a deckhand on the *Santa Maria*, relates the conditions on board the ship. Bibliography and Glossary. *Notable Children's Trade Books in the Field of Social Studies.*

E

557. **The Early Middle Ages**. Remo Berselli and Antonio Molino, illustrators. Austin, TX: Raintree/Steck-Vaughn, 1990. 72p. $17.97. ISBN 0-8172-3307-5. (History of the World). 7 up

This survey of the history of Europe and the Middle East, from the fall of the Western Roman Empire in A.D. 476 to 1000, uses informative illustrations and clear maps to complement the text. Two-page topics include Christianity during the fourth and fifth centuries A.D., the Huns, Justinian, monks, Franks and Lombards, Islam, Slavs, Carolingians, Charlemagne, Byzantium, Vikings, Hungarians, Saracens, and the Holy Roman Empire. Glossary and Index.

558. Ebon, Martin. **Nikita Khrushchev**. New York: Chelsea House, 1990. 112p. $18.95. ISBN 0-87754-562-6. (World Leaders Past and Present). 5 up

In 1956, Nikita Khrushchev (1894-1971) denounced the crimes of the Soviet leader Joseph Stalin. These statements began the relaxation of political repression in the U.S.S.R. Although born a peasant, Khrushchev rose within the Communist party after joining in 1918, because he was a skillful organizer. In 1961, he almost caused a nuclear war by refusing the demands of the United States to remove missiles he had ordered installed in Cuba. By the time he lost power in 1964, he had begun establishing relations with the western world. Photographs enhance the text. Chronology, Further Reading, and Index.

559. Edgarian, Carol. **Rise the Euphrates**. New York: Random House, 1994. 370p. $22. ISBN 0-679-42601-9. YA

Although Seta lives in the present, she must come to terms with the legacy of her grandmother who survived when Turks killed her entire Armenian family in 1915. Her grandmother emigrated to the United States and married another Armenian, but her mother has denied her past, refusing to take part in her mother's survivor guilt. Seta realizes that she cannot do the same.

560. Edvardson, Cordelia. **Burned Child Seeks the Fire: A Memoir**. Joel Agee, translator. Boston, MA: Beacon Press, 1997. 106p. $18. ISBN 0-8070-7094-7. YA

As a child, Cordelia Edvardson was raised Catholic, but in 1943, the Gestapo discovers that she is partially Jewish, a fact her mother has been hiding. To keep her mother from being tried for treason, Cordelia goes to Auschwitz where her faith helps her. But after she survives the camp, she does not have the same attitude toward her faith as she had before.

561. Eichengreen, Lucille. **From Ashes to Life: My Memories of the Holocaust**. San Francisco: Mercury House, 1994. 217p. $17.95. ISBN 1-56279-052-8pa. YA

In 1933, Cecilia Landau, age eight, had to move from her Hamburg neighborhood because people began jeering at her family. Her father was deported and the Nazis returned his ashes to the family in 1941. Cecilia, her mother, and her sister were deported to Lodz, Poland, where her mother died of starvation and her sister disappeared. Cecilia survived in Lodz for three years before being sent to Auschwitz. At the Sasel work camp, she worked in an office where she memorized the names and addresses of forty-two Germans who ran the camp. She became the chief witness against them when the British came to arrest the Nazis. After death threats, she came to the United States with a new name, married a man whose parents had died in Lodz, and had children. When she returned as Hamburg's official guest in 1991, she found that disdain toward Jews still lingered.

562. Eide, Lorraine. **Robert Mugabe**. New York: Chelsea House, 1988. 112p. $18.95. ISBN 1-55546-845-4. (World Leaders Past and Present). 5 up

In 1980, Robert Mugabe (b. 1924) became the leader of Zimbabwe, ending ninety years of racist, white-minority rule in the country formerly called Rhodesia. He had been a leader in the resistance while also working as a teacher and political organizer. Arrested in 1963, he stayed in jail for eleven years. After his release, he led guerrillas against the white government until a cease-fire was declared. He tried to keep the tribes from fighting as he brought changes in education, women's rights, and health care. Photographs enhance the text. Chronology, Further Reading, and Index.

563. Ellis, Sarah. **Next-Door Neighbors**. New York: Macmillan, 1990. 154p. $13.95. ISBN 0-689-50495-0. 4-7

In 1957, Peggy, age twelve, and her family move to Vancouver where her father is a minister. She finally makes friends with George, a young Russian immigrant, and Sing, Mrs. Manning's gardener and houseboy. They help her overcome her shyness, and she learns that the device of pretending to be a puppet is one way to meet new people. *School Library Journal Best Book.*

564. Elmer, Robert. **Touch the Sky**. Minneapolis, MN: Bethany, 1997. 172p. $5.99pa. ISBN 1-55661-661-9pa. (Young Underground). 5-8

Danish twins Peter and Elise and their Jewish friend Henrik hear about a plan to blow up a ship taking Jewish refugees to Palestine in 1946. They encounter a series of adventures as they try to stop a Syrian from carrying out the plan.

565. Emerson, Kathy Lynn. **Face Down in the Marrow-bone Pie: An Elizabethan Mystery**. New York: St. Martin's Press, 1997. 218p. $21.95. ISBN 0-312-15123-3. YA

Lady Susanna manages Leigh Abbey, her home with her husband during the sixteenth century. She works on collecting and growing herbs while her husband spends time abroad for Queen Elizabeth. He receives a letter that his steward at his home manor died eating a marrow-bone pie, and Susanna goes north to find that other servants have left and that the house is neglected. Her subtle investigations tell her that the steward was poisoned, and she decides to find out who killed him.

566. Engelmann, Larry. **Tears Before the Rain: An Oral History of the Fall of South Vietnam**. New York: Oxford University Press, 1990. 375p. $22.95. ISBN 0-19-505386-9. YA

Engelmann gathered this collection of powerful stories from people in 1985 about the ending of the Vietnam War, 10 years after North Vietnam took over South Vietnam and Saigon was renamed Ho Chi Ming City. In each section of the book is a series of firsthand stories. The topics discussed with Americans are the last flight from Danang, orphans, congressional delegations, the American Embassy, the Central Intelligence Agency, the Defense Attaché Office, the joint military team, the Military Sealift Command, marines, POWs, the media, civilians, and the presidency. Those topics that Engelmann covered with the Vietnamese he interviewed are the military, civilians, children, and victors. A final part looks at the Bui Doi (dust of the earth) and the Vietnamese as a whole. Glossary of Abbreviations and Acronyms and Index.

567. Epler, Doris M. **The Berlin Wall: How It Rose and Why It Fell**. Brookfield, CT: Millbrook Press, 1992. 128p. $15.90. ISBN 1-56294-114-3. 7 up

After beginning with the problems in the Weimar Republic that led to the acceptance of Nazism and the onset of World War II, this history of the Berlin Wall ends with the German reunification. It shows the tensions that arose after the war that led to the Wall's construction and the difficulties that the Wall itself caused for the Germans. Photographs, Notes, Chronology, Bibliography, Further Reading, and Index.

568. Equiano, Olaudah. **The Kidnapped Prince: The Life of Olaudah Equiano**. Ann Cameron, adapter. New York: Knopf, 1995. 133p. $16. ISBN 0-679-85619-6. 7-10

When prince Olaudah Equiano was a young boy, slavers captured him and took him from his home. He realized that knowledge might save him and learned to box, to cut hair, to navigate a ship, to ride a horse, to load a gun, to do accounts, to trade in order to buy his freedom, and, most important, to read and to write. He survived to write his story. He wanted to show that those who said that the lives of slaves were happy were wrong; these people were only interested in protecting their economic welfare. His book became a best-seller soon after its publication in 1789. Eight editions were published within three years in England and America.

569. Erickson, Carolly. **Bonnie Prince Charlie: A Biography**. New York: Morrow, 1989. 331p. $19.95. ISBN 0-688-06087-0. YA

Charles Edward (1720–1788), known as Bonnie Prince Charlie and the Young Pretender to the Stuart throne, was the grandson of James II, King of England. With those loyal to him, he began the Jacobite Rebellion in 1745–46 in Edinburgh with 2,000 men. Because the Jacobite sentiment was strong only in the highlands of Scotland, they never got further than Derby in England. The British defeated the Scots at the Battle of Culloden, and Bonnie Prince Charlie fled to France. Nobles who participated were executed, and another 1,000 were condemned to death in this bloody crushing of "The Forty-Five." Bonnie Prince Charlie was the last hope for the Stuarts and their followers to regain power. Bibliography and Index.

570. Erickson, Carolly. **The First Elizabeth**. New York: Summit/Simon & Schuster, 1983. 446p. $19.95. ISBN 0-671-41746-0. YA

Queen Elizabeth (1533–1603) learned as a child to be careful about her words and her actions, because others always had ulterior motives in their relationships with her. She ruled England for forty years, refusing to marry. She was a diplomat who improved the lives of her subjects as the Renaissance came north from Italy, and she kept Spain out of the country in 1588. Bibliography and Index.

571. Erickson, Carolly. **Great Catherine**. New York: Crown, 1994. 392p. $25. ISBN 0-517-59091-3. New York: St. Martin's Press, 1995. 392p. $14.95pa. ISBN 0-312-13503-3pa. YA

Catherine of Russia (1729–1796) wrote autobiographies, which Erickson uses as some of the sources for this text. Catherine wanted to be a Western-style ruler, but her subjects saw her as an enlightened despot. Catherine drafted laws, reformed her government, and improved conditions for her people. She also had a reputation for forming liaisons with the men in her court. The text reveals much about this complex and powerful woman. Index.

572. Erickson, Carolly. **Her Little Majesty: The Life of Queen Victoria**. New York: Simon & Schuster, 1997. 288p. $23. ISBN 0-684-80765-3. YA

Victoria (1819-1901) became queen at eighteen after a lonely childhood in the care of a dictatorial mother. She fell in love with her cousin Albert, and together they ruled and raised children until his death. Afterward, she had to adjust to his absence with the help of advisors and family. During her reign, England and the world changed dramatically.

573. Erickson, Carolly. **Mistress Anne: The Exceptional Life of Anne Boleyn**. New York: Summit/Simon & Schuster, 1984. 288p. $17.95. ISBN 0-671-41747-9. YA

Anne Boleyn (1507–1536), the second of Henry VIII's six wives, courted Henry for six years before she secretly married him. After their marriage and Henry's divorce from Catherine, Anne was crowned queen. She encouraged the split with the Church of Rome, and her child, a girl, became Elizabeth I, Queen of England. After Anne had a miscarriage, she was accused of incest and adultery, tried, and condemned to death. Her head hung from the London Bridge as an example of unacceptable morals. Through the years, her reputation has been tarnished because of the unreliable sources upon which biographical material has been based. Bibliography and Index.

574. Erickson, Carolly. **To the Scaffold: The Life of Marie Antoinette**. New York: Morrow, 1991. 384p. $22.95. ISBN 0-688-07301-8. YA

In this biography, Erikson presents Marie Antoinette (1755–1793), the queen-consort of Louis XVI of France from 1774 to 1792, as a person who was too naive to appropriately assess the events occurring around her. A beautiful woman with average intelligence, she was disinterested in developing qualities to make her a better queen. The text looks closely at her daily activities and gives a special view of this woman whose name is often associated with the reasons that the French peasants revolted in 1789.

575. **Estonia**. Minneapolis, MN: Lerner, 1992. 56p. $19.95. ISBN 0-8225-2803-7. (Then and Now). 5-9

The text covers the history, economics, geography, politics, ethnography, and possible future of Estonia, a Baltic country, which the Soviet Union annexed in 1940 and which gained freedom in 1991. Maps and photographs complement the text. Glossary and Index.

576. **Europe at the Time of Greece and Rome**. Francis Balistreri, illustrator. Austin, TX: Raintree/Steck-Vaughn, 1992. 80p. $17.97. ISBN 0-8172-3305-9. (History of the World). 7 up

This overview uses informative illustrations and clear maps to complement the text. Each topic covers two pages, with various points revealing Greek and Roman cultures from approximately 800 B.C. to A.D. 305. Discussion examines Athens and Sparta; the Persian wars; Greek religion, social life, art, theater, and philosophy; Alexander; Roman religion and society; imperial Rome and its provinces; Gauls; Germans; the Eastern provinces; and Byzantium. Glossary and Index.

577. Evans, J. Edward. **Charles Darwin: Revolutionary Biologist**. Minneapolis, MN: Lerner, 1993. 112p. $21.50. ISBN 0-8225-4914-X. 5 up

When Charles Darwin (1809-1882) left the Galápagos Islands, he realized that he had been making serious mistakes in his categorization of plants and animals. He began to ask why some species inhabited some islands and not others, and why different species appeared on the same island. His reformulation of questions led to his major work, *The Origin of Species*, published many years later in 1859. His work shocked many, but others recognized it as a major contribution about the beginnings of life. Bibliography and Index. *Outstanding Science Trade Book for Children* and *John S. Burroughs Nature Book for Young Readers*.

578. Evans, J. Edward. **Freedom of Speech**. Minneapolis, MN: Lerner, 1990. 72p. $9.50. ISBN 0-8225-1753-1. 7 up

In this interesting history of the concept of free speech, Evans begins with the Athenians killing Socrates because he asked too many questions. His values, however, prevailed, as did those of Galileo in Italy, who suffered for saying the world was round. Printing presses led government and church officials to impose censorship throughout the sixteenth and seventeenth centuries because seditious libel supposedly hurt rulers. A big debate on free speech in the United States occurred in 1798 when Federalists passed the Sedition Act. As soon as Jefferson became President, he repealed the act and freed those who had been imprisoned under it. Another Sedition Act in 1918 decreed that people could not speak against the government about World War I and the draft. Then in 1919, the Supreme Court became involved. The Court heard cases and established that a "clear and present danger" must be apparent before speech may be silenced. The Fourteenth Amendment protected people under both state and federal laws. Appendix with the Bill of Rights, For Further Reading, Important Words, and Index.

579. Evans, J. Edward. **Freedom of the Press**. Minneapolis, MN: Lerner, 1990. 72p. $9.95. ISBN 0-8225-1753-1. 7-10

From the development of the Gutenberg printing press around 1436 through the Pentagon Papers release in 1971, the text traces the history of the concept of freedom of speech by discussing how the Supreme Court has interpreted this constitutional amendment and why the issue is controversial. Illustrations add to the information. Bibliography and Index.

580. Ewing, Elizabeth. **Women in Uniform Through the Centuries**. Totowa, NJ: Rowman & Littlefield, 1975. 160p. $21.50. ISBN 0-87471-690-X. YA

Photographs and drawings help emphasize the points that Ewing makes about uniforms, be they for military service or for a religious convent. Within the topics, she uses a historical approach to show how clothing has revealed status. The topics are service and servitude, women in a man's world, Florence Nightingale and the start of a modern age, youth, the time in war, developments between the wars, new looks for traditional uniforms, and women out of uniform. Bibliography and Index.

581. Eyre, Elizabeth. **Dirge for a Doge**. New York: St. Martin's Press, 1997. 320p. $23.95. ISBN 0-312-15109-8. YA

The Renaissance detective Sigismondo is in Venice for the funeral of a friend when Vettor Darin hires him to investigate the murder of his deceased daughter's husband. Niccolo has died in his study, and Sigismondo discovers that many people could have reason to want his demise.

F

582. Faber, Doris, and Harold Faber. **Mahatma Gandhi**. New York: Julian Messner, 1986. 122p. $10.98. ISBN 0-671-60176-8. 5 up

Mahatma, the name given to Mohandas Gandhi (1869-1948), means "Great Soul." He was warm, unassuming, and sometimes comic. He also wrote his own autobiography when he was fifty, in which he set forth his philosophical and religious beliefs. The Fabers have used this autobiography to give insights into various situations in Gandhi's life. A husband at the age thirteen, he was surprised to find that his preoccupation with his young wife was detracting from his concentration in other areas. Another time he became physically ill after eating meat, a practice that his religion forbade. Other pieces of information reveal the character of this man who helped India to gain its freedom from Britain in 1947 through mainly nonviolent means. Source Note, Suggested Further Readings, and Index.

583. Farmer, Nancy. **A Girl Named Disaster**. New York: Jackson, Orchard, 1996. 309p. $19.95. ISBN 0-531-09539-8. 6-9

With her grandmother's blessing, Nhamo, eleven, escapes from a horrible marriage in Mozambique during 1981 to her father's family in Zimbabwe. A two-day journey extends to a year when the boat goes astray. Baboons look after her on an island for a while, and when she finally reaches Zimbabwe, she lives with scientists and learns to survive in civilization before she finds her father's family. The background gives information on the Shona and on South Africa in this unusual novel. *American Library Association Notable Books for Children*, *American Library Association Best Books for Young Adults*, *Booklist Best Books for Young Adults*, *Booklist Notable Children's Books*, *School Library Journal Best Book*, and *Newbery Honor Book*.

584. Feelings, Tom, author/illustrator. **The Middle Passage: White Ships, Black Cargo**. New York: Dial Press, 1995. 80p. $40. ISBN 0-8037-1804-7. 7 up

Feelings describes his search for his African past, and John Henrik Clarke's overview of the slave trade follows it. A series of illustrations depicts the events that people forced into slavery had to endure. The strong, truthful scenes include capture, transport on land and sea, rape, murder, life on shipboard, and rats gnawing on a dead body. *Bulletin Blue Ribbon Book*, *American Library Association Notable Books for Children*, *American Library Association Best Books for Young Adults*, and *Coretta Scott King Illustrator Award*.

585. Feinberg, Barbara. **Marx and Marxism**. New York: Franklin Watts, 1985. 122p. $12.90. ISBN 0-531-10065-0. YA

Karl Marx (1818–1883) was a German philosopher who started the concept of communism with his book *Das Kapital*. His theories influenced Lenin and others and became the basis of the Soviet Union's government during the twentieth century. Bibliography and Index.

586. Feinberg, Brian. **Nelson Mandela and the Quest for Freedom**. New York: Chelsea Juniors, 1992. 80p. $14.95. ISBN 0-7910-1569-6. (Junior World Biographies). 3-7

The text relates Nelson Mandela's story of fighting to win equal rights for blacks in South Africa. He spent twenty-seven years in prison because he believed that people should be free regardless of color. Chronology, Further Reading, Glossary, and Index.

587. Feldman, Eve B. **Benjamin Franklin: Scientist and Inventor**. New York: Franklin Watts, 1990. 64p. $19.90. ISBN 0-531-10867-8. (First Books). 5-8

The text about Benjamin Franklin (1706-1790) emphasizes his ideas and inventions before and after he discovered electricity with his kite experiment. They include the lightning rod, the Franklin stove, the harmonica, bifocals, writing tables, and public libraries. Experiments You Can Do with Electricity, Glossary, For Further Reading, and Index.

588. Fenton, Edward. **The Morning of the Gods**. New York: Delacorte, 1987. 184p. $14.95. ISBN 0-385-29550-2. 6-8

In 1974, Carla, age twelve, comes to a small Greek village to stay with her great-aunt Tiggie (Antigone) and great-uncle Theo, the people who had raised her orphan mother. With her mother recently dead in a car accident, Carla absorbs all of the atmosphere about which her mother had told her. She finds that life in the village is more complex than she had imagined when comments about the political situation let her know that all is not well with the Greek junta. While she is there, she helps to save a poet, a national hero, from the military, and she learns about Greek Orthodoxy, including the Easter rituals.

589.   Ferber, Elizabeth. **Yasir Arafat: A Life of War and Peace**. Brookfield, CT: Millbrook Press, 1995. 144p. $17.40. ISBN 1-56294-585-8. 6 up

Although Yasir Arafat claims to have been born in Jerusalem in 1929, many persons suspect that he was born in Cairo, Egypt, where his family was living at the time. His mother died when he was a boy, and then a favorite uncle, who led the Muslim Brotherhood for young Palestinian boys, was murdered. Arafat's father probably ordered the assassinations. In the 1950s, Arafat emerged as a leader of the Muslim Brotherhood and then of his own group, the *Fatah*. In 1969, he took over the leadership of the Palestinian Liberation Organization (PLO). The text tries to reveal the man known as Arafat with accompanying photographs. Chronology, Bibliography, and Index.

590.   Fernandez-Armesto, Felipe. **Columbus**. New York: Oxford University Press, 1991. 218p. $30; $11.95pa. ISBN 0-19-215898-8; 0-19-285260-4pa. YA

The text looks at Columbus and sees a man whose main motivations for finding a route to India were monetary gain and social advancement. Instead of being a visionary, he mirrored the thinking of his times and gathered the good opinions of people who could lobby for his cause with Queen Isabella. Columbus made many mistakes and was a terrible administrator, but his descriptions of his voyages enticed others to follow him. Bibliography and Index.

591.   Fernandez-Armesto, Felipe. **The Spanish Armada: The Experience of the War in 1588**. New York: Oxford University Press, 1988. 300p. $35. ISBN 0-19-822926-7. YA

Fernandez-Armesto discusses the 1588 naval battle between Spain and England and sees it as an unexceptional fight when compared to other sixteenth-century battles. He wonders how the English could consider it a glorious victory when they barely defeated a group of Spaniards who had been weakened by disease and battered by storms. In his opinion, the Spaniards missed a major opportunity by not attacking. Bibliography and Index.

592.   Fernandez-Armesto, Felipe, ed. **The Times Atlas of World Exploration: 3,000 Years of Exploring, Explorers, and Mapmaking**. New York: HarperCollins, 1991. 286p. $75. ISBN 0-06-270032-4. YA

The 136 maps in this book start with 1700 B.C., when the Chinese were exploring, and extend to recent space satellites. The first section looks at world exploration up to A.D. 1500. The remaining eleven sections show various maps of regions such as the central Atlantic. Antique maps and illustrations of important paintings complement the text containing the latest scholarship. Glossary, Biographies, Chronology, and Index.

593.   Finck, Lila, and John P. Hayes. **Jawaharlal Nehru**. New York: Chelsea House, 1987. 112p. $18.95. ISBN 0-87754-543-X. (World Leaders Past and Present). 8 up

Jawaharlal Nehru (1889–1964) became the independent India's first prime minister in 1947. Born into a wealthy Kashmiri Brahmin family, he studied in England, but he worried about his less fortunate countrymen. He worked with Mohandas Gandhi in the nonviolent struggle for Indian independence. Nehru placed national problems within an international framework so that India could follow a policy of nonalignment. He embodied the most honorable traditions of East and West. Photographs enhance the text. Chronology, Further Reading, and Index.

594.   Finkelstein, Norman H. **Captain of Innocence: France and the Dreyfus Affair**. New York: Putnam, 1991. 160p. $15.95. ISBN 0-399-22243-X. 8 up

Alfred Dreyfus, a quiet Jewish army captain, was "degraded" in January of 1895 after exemplary military service. The question remains as to whether he was guilty of his alleged crime or if he was a victim of anti-Semitism. Émile Zola, a well-known French writer, wrote an article about the "Dreyfus affair," titled *J'accuse,* which stunned the world. Zola noted various discrepancies in the evidence presented at the court martial. This text explores the events that led to Dreyfus's arrest, imprisonment, and subsequent trial. Time Line, Who's Who, Selected Bibliography, and Index.

595.   Finkelstein, Norman H. **The Other 1492: Jewish Settlement in the New World**. 1989. New York: Beechtree, 1992. 100p. $4.95pa. ISBN 0-688-11572-1pa. 5-9

For many Jewish people, the year 1492 brings thoughts of discrimination, persecution, and expulsion. In the same year that Isabella and Ferdinand sent Columbus toward the New World, they expelled the vibrant and intellectual Jewish community that had grown in Spain. The text covers the trials of the Sephardic Jews by looking at their contributions to Spanish culture, their years of persecution, their forced conversion and exile, and the ensuing travels that finally sent them to Columbus's New World to establish Jewish communities in the original colonies. Reproductions supplement the text. Bibliography and Index.

596.   Finkelstein, Norman H. **Theodor Herzl: Architect of a Nation**. Minneapolis, MN: Lerner, 1992. 128p. $22.95. ISBN 0-8225-4913-1. 5-9

Although Theodor Herzl (b. 1860) died in 1904, he was reburied with honors in Israel on August 17, 1949. He had worked on the possibility of a homeland for the Jews during most of his lifetime in Austria, almost fifty years before the state was founded. He was a journalist and playwright who believed that the only way to escape the torment of anti-Semitism was to have a place for Jews to live together in Israel. He worked tirelessly with Jewish leaders to establish a base for a new nation. He helped with the First Zionist Congress, which met in 1897. Notes, Glossary, and Index.

597.   Finkelstein, Norman H. **Thirteen Days! Ninety Miles: The Cuban Missile Crisis**. New York: Julian Messner, 1994. 101p. $15. ISBN 0-671-86622-2. 7 up

Using information recently declassified, Finkelstein tells the story of the events that led to the discovery that the Soviet Union had placed missiles in Cuba and John F. Kennedy's resulting blockade of the country. Because communication was much less rapid at that time, tension developed that could have led to a nuclear war. Finkelstein recreates that tension. Bibliography and Index.

598.   Finley, Mary Peace. **Soaring Eagle**. New York: Simon & Schuster, 1993. 166p. $14. ISBN 0-671-75598-6. 4-9

Julio Montoya wonders who his family is, because he is blond-haired and green-eyed in Mexico during 1845. When Julio's father returns to Taos, the two go on the trail to Bent's Fort. After Apaches kill his father, Julio must survive a snowstorm, a wolf attack, and then snowblindness. Cheyenne Indians find him, nurse him back to health, and claim him as one of their own. While wondering about his childhood, Julio adapts to this new tribe and earns his own name, Soaring Eagle. He never answers his questions, but he finds surrogate family support.

599.   Fisher, Leonard Everett. **William Tell**. New York: Farrar, Straus & Giroux, 1996. Unpaged. $16. ISBN 0-374-38436-3. 3-7

Hermann Gessler, governor for King Albert of Hapsburg in 1307, demanded that the citizens of Aldorf kneel before his hat, placed in the town square. Three people forgot to do so and were imprisoned. William Tell and his son, however, refused. Gessler was furious and demanded that Tell, a superb hunter, either split an apple set on his son's head or go to prison. Tell succeeded; the next week, he shot Gessler so that the town would also be free.

600.   Flanagan, Thomas. **The Year of the French**. New York: Henry Holt, 1989. 528p. $14.95. ISBN 0-8050-1020-3pa. YA

In August and September of 1798, French soldiers come to Vinegar Hill in Ireland to help the Irish with their rebellion against the English. Five narrators—a Protestant clergyman, a solicitor, a wife, a schoolmaster, and a soldier—tell about the event from their individual perspectives. A poet named Owen also becomes involved in the rebellion because he feels an affinity with his Irish past and is *fey*. The rebellion, planned by people with personal motives, fails.

601.   Fleischman, Paul. **Dateline: Troy**. Gwen Frankfeldt and Glenn Morrow, illustrators. Bergenfield, NJ: Candlewick Press, 1996. 80p. $15.99. ISBN 1-56402-469-5. 7-12

Fleischman compares contemporary news to the Battle of Troy and shows the similarities between the Troy of 3,000 years ago and today. He compares people through beliefs in astrology, child abandonment, beauty pageants, and all phases of war. The presentation reveals that neither things nor people have changed much. *Booklist Best Books for Young Adults*.

602.   Flint, David. **The Baltic States**. Brookfield, CT: Millbrook Press, 1992. 32p. $15.90. ISBN 1-56294-310-3. (Former Soviet States). 4-7

The text discusses the cultural background, politics, economics, and histories of the former Soviet republics of Estonia, Lithuania, and Latvia. These states, annexed to the Soviet Union in 1940, have had a long history of invasion because of their arable lands and desirable locations. Glossary and Index.

603.   Flint, David. **The Russian Federation**. Brookfield, CT: Millbrook Press, 1992. 32p. $15.90. ISBN 1-56294-305-7. (Former Soviet States). 4-7

The text discusses the cultural background, politics, economics, and history of the former Soviet republic of Russia. In this country, by the fifth century A.D., Slavic tribes had begun migrating from the west. In the ninth century, the Scandinavian chieftains founded the first Russian state, centered in Novgorod and Kiev. In the thirteenth century, the Mongols overran the country. It recovered under the grand dukes and princes of Muscovy, or Moscow, and by 1480 it had freed itself from the Mongols. Ivan the Terrible became the first formally proclaimed Tsar (1547). Peter the Great (1682-1725) extended the domain and, in 1721, founded the

Russian Empire. After the rule of communism in the twentieth century, Russia declared freedom. Glossary and Index.

604.   Flowers, Sarah. **The Reformation**. San Diego, CA: Lucent, 1995. 128p. $16.95. ISBN 1-56006-243-6. (World History). 8 up

The text looks at the Reformation, which began with Martin Luther's posting of the *Ninety-Five Theses* on the church door at Wittenburg in 1517, through eyewitness accounts and other primary sources. It covers the causes as well as the effects of this momentous decision to question the Catholic sale of indulgences. Bibliography, Chronology, Further Reading, Notes, and Index.

605.   Fluek, Toby Knobel, author/illustrator. **Memories of My Life in a Polish Village**. New York: Knopf, 1990. 110p. $19.95. ISBN 0-394-58617-4. YA

In this book, Fluek has created extraordinary paintings and drawings to describe her life—her family, Polish customs, the school where she was the only Jew, her dressmaker sister and her apprentices, and holiday traditions. In her small town of only ten families, classes were still obvious—the rich man, the Bible-educated man, the respectable middle class, and the poor. But on September 1, 1939, when the Russians came, life changed. It was not too bad, except for the pressure to become Communist, until the Germans arrived in 1941. Her family's experiences of trying to hide from the Germans, being interned, and then escaping were like those of many others. Only Fluek and her mother escaped. In a displaced persons camp, Fluek met her husband, and they emigrated to America, following Fluek's mother.

606.   Flynn, Nigel. **George Orwell: Life and Works**. Vero Beach, FL: Rourke, 1990. 112p. $22.60. ISBN 0-86593-018-X. YA

Eric Blair (1903–1950) took the name George Orwell when he began selling his writing. His experiences fighting in the Spanish Civil War and World War II, as well as hearing what leaders were doing to gain power, influenced his satires, *Animal Farm* and *1984*. Photographs in the book depict the times and his life. Glossary, List of Dates, Further Reading, and Index.

607.   Fogelman, Eva. **Conscience and Courage: Rescuers of Jews During the Holocaust**. New York: Anchor, 1994. 393p. $23.95; $14pa. ISBN 0-385-42027-7; 0-385-42028-5pa. YA

Fogelman discusses those people who rescued Jews during the Holocaust of World War II. The book, divided into three parts, looks at "The Rescuers," "The Motivation," and "Postwar." She separates the rescuers into five categories: those who helped because of moral or ethical reasons, those who had a special relationship with the Jewish people, those who opposed the Third Reich and its policies, those in medicine or social work, and children who became involved because of their families. Among well-known helpers were Oskar Schindler, Raoul Wallenberg, and Miep Gies. The text also includes many who were unknown outside their personal circle of friends. Photographs and Index.

608.   Follett, Ken. **A Place Called Freedom**. New York: Crown, 1995. 407p. $25. ISBN 0-517-70176-6. New York: Fawcett, 1996. 608p. $6.99pa. ISBN 0-449-22515-1pa. YA

Mack lives in Scotland during the 1770s, where he must mine coal to survive. He wants freedom from this drudgery, and the only choice he has is to leave. He travels to America via London and arrives in Virginia. There he begins to work in tobacco fields owned by the Jamisson family, who also owned the Scottish mine where he worked previously. The interchange between Mack, the spoiled Jamisson son Jay, and Jay's more compassionate fiancée, Lizzie, give a sense of place and of social status.

609.   Ford, Barbara. **Howard Carter: Searching for King Tut**. Janet Hamlin, illustrator. New York: Freeman, 1995. 63p. $14.95. ISBN 0-7167-6587-X. (Science Superstars). 4-8

Howard Carter (1873-1939) assisted others at the excavation at Tell el-Amarna in Egypt in the 1890s. In 1922, in the Valley of the Tombs of the Kings in Luxor, Egypt, he and George Herbert discovered the tomb of Tutankhamen, a pharaoh who reigned in the fourteenth century BC. Because it was untouched by grave robbers or other archaeologists, it held numerous treasures that Carter cataloged for 10 years. He also discovered the tombs of the pharaoh Thutmose IV and Queen Hatshepsut. Afterword, Index, Glossary, and Further Reading.

610.   Foreman, Michael, author/illustrator. **War Boy: A Country Childhood**. New York: Arcade, 1990. 96p. $16.95. ISBN 1-55970-049-1. 3-7

Foreman opens this memoir of childhood on April 21, 1941, when bombers strafed his Pakefield village home on the east coast of England. The Germans ignited the church in order to have enough light to find the nearby Lowestoft Airbase, but a huge mist suddenly rolled in from the sea and obscured the fire. He recounts life in the village, where his mother owned a small store during World War II and where soldiers came to drink tea and escape the pervasive fear. Watercolor illustrations augment the poignant text.

611. Foreman, Michael, author/illustrator. **War Game**. New York: Arcade, 1994. 72p. $16.95. ISBN 1-55970-242-7. 5-8

Will, an avid soccer player, has to go to the front lines of World War I, in the French trenches, for Britain in 1914. The daily routine is boring and frightening; war is not the glamorous calling that posters and appeals to serve would have potential soldiers believe. At Christmas, Will participates in a spontaneous carol-fest and soccer game between the German and English troops. But after Christmas, a new group of Germans fills the trenches, and Will dies.

612. Forman, James D. **Ceremony of Innocence**. New York: Dutton, 1970. 249p. $7.95. ISBN 0-8015-1140-2. 7 up

In 1943, the Gestapo take Hans and Sophi Scholl from a university building to a Munich prison. Hans, age twenty-four, faces accusations of treason for distributing pamphlets condemning Hitler. He reflects on the previous years; his attempts to help Jews, only to see them shot; and the responses that people had in and out of battle during the tense times. When a guard offers him a gun and freedom, Hans knows that if he accepts he will be indebted to this man, so he refuses and waits to die. *Lewis Carroll Shelf Award.*

613. Forman, James D. **Horses of Anger**. New York: Farrar, Straus & Giroux, 1967. 249p. $3.95. ISBN 0-374-33333-5. 9 up

As a boy of ten in the Germany of 1939, Hans admires Hitler and wants to follow him to war. The book looks at Hans and his attitudes on successive birthdays until 1944 after he has seen people go off to war and the results of war on those around him. He no longer has any of the patriotic zeal of a youngster, as he loses his first love to a soldier whose young Jewish wife does not return from her imprisonment.

614. Forman, James D. **My Enemy My Brother**. 1969. New York: Dutton, 1981. 250p. $10.25. ISBN 0-525-66735-0. 7 up

Daniel, age sixteen, has difficulty adjusting to life outside the concentration camp at the end of World War II in Poland. He and his grandfather return to the Warsaw ghetto where they last saw their family, gather the buried family treasures, and begin to reestablish their lives. Daniel meets young people going to Palestine, and he follows them. He becomes friends with an Arab sheepherder and saves him from drowning in a flash flood. Then Daniel has to kill the boy's father while Daniel is on guard duty. Although they know themselves to be similar, their warring cultures will not allow them to be friends.

615. Forman, James D. **Prince Charlie's Year**. New York: Scribners, 1991. 136p. $12.95. ISBN 0-684-19242-X. 7-10

As Colin Macdonald prepares for a 1780 battle against the English in North Carolina, he remembers the last battle he fought against the English in 1745. He was 14 at Culloden, Scotland, when he fought for Prince Charlie. After defeat, the British took him prisoner and transported him to America, where he was bound out for seven years. After his love, Peggy, joined him, he survived. The story recounts the 1745 Jacobite rebellion and the clan system that supported a man who could not win the fight.

616. Forman, James D. **Ring the Judas Bell**. 1965. New York: Dell, 1977. 218p. $1.25pa. ISBN 0-440-97488-7pa. YA

In 1917, the Andartes rebel group contests the Greek government by capturing children and marching them to Yugoslavia. Nicholos and his sister escape from the camp with twenty children and take them through the cold and over thin ice back to Greece. Once home, Nicholos sees that his once-pacifist father has changed, but Nicholos realizes that fighting solves nothing. He thinks the most positive thing they can do is rehang the church bell torn down by the Andartes, which was supposedly made from one of the coins for which Judas sold Christ.

617. Forman, James D. **The Survivor**. 1976. New York: Farrar, Straus & Giroux, 1985. 272p. $11.95. ISBN 0-374-37312-4. 7 up

David and his family leave their home in Amsterdam and try to hide from the Nazis, but only one of them escapes. The Nazis catch the others inside the coffins where a Catholic priest has hidden them. David goes to Westerbork and Auschwitz, but survives the horrors to return to his family home in Amsterdam at the age of twenty. He retrieves his grandfather's diary of the times after they left through 1942, and he knows that he must find his sister, who escaped the Nazis alone. He finds the cave where she hid and sees a note saying that she has left for Palestine. He follows.

618. Forman, James D. **The Traitors**. New York: Farrar, Straus & Giroux, 1968. 238p. $3.95. ISBN 0-374-37722-7. 8 up

Paul naively invites his Jewish friend to go with him and his brother to a meeting of the Hitler Youth in Nuremburg during 1938. The friend declines, but when *Kristallnacht* occurs the next month, Paul becomes aware of the problem of anti-Semitism and his brother's fanaticism for Hitler. His brother becomes a soldier and accuses Paul of being a coward every time he returns home. Paul and his father, however, hide Paul's Jewish friend and his family. They also crawl through sewers to defuse Nazi explosives so that the Americans will be able to cross the bridge into their German town. Paul's brother finally admits that he was the coward, because he deliberately became wounded so that he could leave the front lines of the fighting.

619. Foss, Michael, ed. **Poetry of the World Wars**. New York: Peter Bedrick, 1990. 292p. $18.95. ISBN 0-87226-336-3. YA

Poets needed to express their horror of war in words. In World War I, the "Great War," they were stunned by the inhumanity and cruelty. When war began again in 1939, they could only look inward with a private grief. The text anthologizes poems written about World War I, the time between the two wars, and World War II.

620. Foster, Cecil. **No Man in the House**. New York: Ballantine, 1991. 280p. $17; $10pa. ISBN 0-345-38067-3; 0-345-38899-2pa. YA

In 1964, Howard and his two brothers remain in Barbados with their grandmother while their parents search for a better life in England. When a new headmaster arrives, he changes the school's approach to discipline and learning. He helps Howard survive the taunts from other boys about living in a fatherless home by showing that an education helps people anticipate a better future.

621. Foster, Leila Merrell. **Margaret Thatcher: First Woman Prime Minister of Great Britain**. Chicago: Childrens Press, 1990. 120p. $18.60. ISBN 0-516-03269-0. (People of Distinction). 6 up

The text begins with the race for Margaret Thatcher (b. 1925) to take leadership of the Conservative Party in Parliament in 1975. A discussion of the opposition and the way ballots were counted gives an unexpected suspense to the process which one knows Thatcher won. The remainder of the text looks at her childhood, her choice of career, her family, her race for Parliament, her service as Leader of the Opposition and as Prime Minister during the Falklands War, as well as the difficulties of getting reelected. Notes, Time Line, and Index.

622. Foster, Leila Merrell. **Nien Cheng: Courage in China**. Chicago: Childrens Press, 1992. 111p. $19.30; $5.95pa. ISBN 0-516-03279-8; 0-516-43279-6pa. (People of Distinction). 4-7

Nien Cheng (b. 1915) faced the Red Guards, a group of teenagers and young people organized by Mao Ze-dong to raid the wealthy after 1966. They destroyed her belongings and then harassed and imprisoned her for seven years, a period she wrote about in *Life and Death in Shanghai*. This text presents some information about her youth but concentrates mostly on her experiences after the Red Guard became a force in China. Photographs, Time Line, and Index.

623. Fradin, Dennis Brindell. **Medicine: Yesterday, Today, and Tomorrow**. Chicago: Childrens Press, 1989. 222p. $26.60. ISBN 0-516-00538-3. 7-10

The text gives an overview of the history of medicine. Among the topics covered in part 1 on "Yesterday," are ancient medicine, the Middle Ages, the Renaissance, the seventeenth and eighteenth centuries, the nineteenth century, and from 1900 to the present. In the segment on "Today," the text looks at the human body, why and how things go wrong, and modern medicine. Among the topics in "Tomorrow" are cancer, cardiovascular disease, transplants and artificial organs, genetic engineering, and better life for the elderly. Glossary, Bibliography, and Index.

624. Fradon, Dana, author/illustrator. **Harald the Herald: A Book About Heraldry**. New York: Dutton, 1990. Unpaged. $14.95. ISBN 0-525-44634-6. 4-7

With clear explanations of terms used in heraldry during the medieval period (from 1066 until 1485), the text shows the duties of heralds, which were to develop, record, and monitor the symbols on coats of arms. The fictional Miss Quincy and her class incorporate the information.

625. Franck, Irene M., and David M. Brownstone. **Around Africa and Asia by Sea**. New York: Facts on File, 1990. 111p. $17.95. ISBN 0-8160-1875-8. (Trade and Travel Routes). 7 up

The text looks at the history of the Spice Route, the first major link between East and West. The Spice Route linked the great civilizations of the Mediterranean, India, and Southeast Asia, beginning over 5,000 years ago. The Cape of Good Hope Route, forged in 1487 with the Portuguese entry into exploration, was also a major source of East-West trade as was the Modern Spice Route. Much has happened in history because of trade in spices. Index.

626. Frank, Anne. **The Diary of a Young Girl**. B. M. Mooyaart-Doubleday, translator. 1952. New York: Doubleday, 1996. 308p. $25. ISBN 0-385-47378-8. 6 up

Anne Frank (1929-1945) and her family lived a normal life in Holland during the 1930s until Hitler came to power in Germany. Her businessman father looked after the family, but when the Nazis entered Holland and occupied it, the Franks had to hide in the abandoned half of an old office; Anne was then thirteen. Others came to join them, and soon eight people shared two tiny rooms. No one could leave nor be seen from the outside. The few people who knew where they were had to get food to them without being detected. The diary reveals Anne Frank's thoughts and feelings as she copes with this inhumane constraint on her life. *American Library Association Notable Books for Young Adults.*

627. Frank, Rudolf. **No Hero for the Kaiser**. Patricia Crampton, translator; Klaus Steffens, illustrator. New York: Lothrop, Lee & Shepard, 1986. 222p. $13. ISBN 0-688-06093-5. 7-10

Jan, a Polish boy of fourteen in 1914, adopts an invading German military unit after his father leaves to join the Polish army and his mother dies. He stays with them for two years, guiding them through the countryside that he knows so well, but his experiences distress him enough that he runs away on the day that the Kaiser plans to award him citizenship and military honors. *Preis der Leseratten, Buxtehuder Bulle, Gustav Heinemann Friedenspreis, Mildred L. Batchelder Award,* and *American Library Association Notable Children's Book.*

628. Fraser, Russell A. **Shakespeare: The Later Years**. New York: Columbia University Press, 1992. 380p. $34.50; $17.50pa. ISBN 0-231-06766-6; 0-231-06767-4pa. YA

Fraser's *Young Shakespeare* (1989) ends in 1594; this book begins there and continues to Shakespeare's death in 1616. By looking at the works and the times in which Shakespeare wrote them, Fraser shows how Shakespeare incorporated the events of the day into his plays. He suggests that Shakespeare used much that happened in his earlier life as source material, and turned these ordinary details into an extraordinary and timeless body of work. Bibliography and Index.

629. French, Jackie. **Somewhere Around the Corner**. New York: Henry Holt, 1995. 230p. $14.95. ISBN 0-8050-3889-2. 5-8

In this historical fantasy, Barbara tries to escape a political demonstration in contemporary Australia by imagining that she is "around the corner." She finds herself in a Depression demonstration during 1932 instead. A young man takes her to Poverty Gully, a "susso camp" where the unemployed live. She becomes friends with several people who help her cope with the situation and with whom she can share dancing and building a school. When she tells stories about "around the corner," the adults listen more closely than the young people. Barbara eventually returns to the present, where she discovers that she can have the best of both past and present.

630. Friedman, Carl. **Nightfather**. Arnold Pomerans and Erica Pomerans, translators. New York: Persea, 1994. 130p. $18.50; $7.95pa. ISBN 0-89255-193-3; 0-89255-210-7pa. YA

The narrator and her brother Simon know the life of two worlds—theirs and their father's. Their father associates everything with the concentration camp from which he was liberated at the end of World War II. The children feel guilty for all they have, but they also fear that something so irrational could happen to them. When their father has finally told them about his entire experience, their mother is still waiting for him, as she was on the day he returned home to their Dutch town after the war. *Bulletin Blue Ribbon Book.*

631. Friedman, Carl. **The Shovel and the Loom**. Jeannette Ringold, translator. New York: Persea, 1996. 176p. $20. ISBN 0-89255-216-6. YA

When Chayah, a college student, becomes a nanny for a three-year-old in Antwerp during the 1970s, she cares so much for the child that she begins to investigate her heritage. She classifies the three types of responses to her Jewishness by thinking of her father's continual reference to being a Holocaust survivor, her mother's refusal to recall, and a family friend's belief that religion is the only sense in a chaotic world.

632. Friedman, Ina. **Escape or Die**. 1982. Cambridge, MA: Yellow Moon, 1991. 146p. $10.95pa. ISBN 0-938756-34-6pa. 6 up

Thirty-five million people died in World War II. Six million Jews died in the death camps, but five million non-Jews also met death there. The text looks at survivors, twelve men and women from Africa, Asia, Europe, and North and South America, who under the age of twenty, had both courage and luck. Some of them had never before told their stories of escaping form Germany, Austria, Czechoslovakia, Poland, Holland, Belgium, Ukraine, France, and Hungary. Glossary and Index.

633. Friedman, Ina R. **Flying Against the Wind: The Story of a Young Woman Who Defied the Nazis**. Brookline, MA: Lodgepole, 1995. 216p. $11.95pa. ISBN 0-886721-00-9pa. YA

Cato Bonjes van Beek (1920–1943) grew up in Nazi Germany. Though not a Jew, she defied Hitler's plans and worked actively for the restoration of individual rights and human dignity. Because she refused to follow the Nazis, she paid the ultimate price. Glossary, Chronology, Further Reading, and Index. *Notable Children's Trade Books in the Field of Social Studies.*

634.   Friedman, Ina R. **The Other Victims: First-Person Stories of Non-Jews Persecuted by the Nazis**. Boston: Houghton Mifflin, 1990. 180p. $14.95; $5.95pa. ISBN 0-395-50212-8; 0-395-74515-2pa. 5-9

In addition to the millions of Jews persecuted in World War II's Holocaust, 5 million Christians were also deliberately murdered. They included gypsies, blacks, many Slavs, homosexuals, ministers, and Jehovah's Witnesses. This book is a collection of personal interviews with survivors, detailing what they and their families and friends experienced. Other Books of Interest to the Reader and Index.

635.   Friedman, Thomas. **From Beirut to Jerusalem**. New York: Farrar, Straus & Giroux, 1991 (rev. ed.). 576p. $25. ISBN 0-374-15895-9. New York: Doubleday, Anchor, 1990. $12.95pa. ISBN 0-385-41372-6pa. 11-12

A newspaper correspondent, Thomas Friedman, tells the story of his experiences with his Arab and Israeli friends during his days as a journalist in their countries. In telling the anecdotes of people he has met, he gives a clear indication of the turmoil in the country of Lebanon. Why people continue to fight becomes understandable but not acceptable. Index.

636.   Fritz, Jean. **Around the World in a Hundred Years: From Henry the Navigator to Magellan**. Anthony Bacon Venti, illustrator. New York: Putnam, 1994. 128p. $17.95. ISBN 0-399-22527-7. 4-7

In 1400, mapmakers named the space around the edge of the areas they had drawn as the Unknown. Later that century, explorers ventured into the Unknown searching for routes to the gold of China. The text discusses explorations, beginning with Prince Henry the Navigator (1394-1460) and ending with Magellan (1480?-1521), whose ship (after he had died in the Philippines) continued around the world. The explorers include Bartholomew Diaz exploring from 1487 to 1500, Christopher Columbus (1492-1504), Vasco da Gama (1497-1502), Pedro Álvares Cabral (1500-1501), John Cabot (1497-1498), Amerigo Vespucci (1499-1501), Juan Ponce de León (1513), and Vasco Núñez de Balboa (1513). Notes, Bibliography, and Index.

637.   Fritz, Jean. **China Homecoming**. New York: Putnam, 1985. 144p. $16.95. ISBN 0-399-21182-9. 5 up

As an adult, Fritz wanted to return to China, the place where she was born and lived for the first 10 years of her life. The Chinese government finally permitted her visit, and she describes the changes as well as the constancy that is Chinese life in the 1980s, after Mao's Cultural Revolution. Her ability to speak Chinese gave her insights during the continued Communist rule to which most Westerners are not privileged. Notes from the Author, Brief Outline of Chinese History, and Bibliography.

638.   Fritz, Jean. **China's Long March: 6000 Miles of Danger**. New York: Putnam, 1988. 128p. $16.95. ISBN 0-399-21512-3. 7 up

During 1934 and 1935, members of the Communist Army, mainly men, followed Mao Zedong across China in a 6,000-mile-long march—much longer than any had anticipated—to defeat the Nationalists under Chiang-Kai-shek. The peasants in the army knew that they must win if they were to keep the few shreds of self-respect they had gained with the defeat of the wealthy. After lives of poverty and injustice, they had had regular food and shelter. In the years after, while Mao grew older, a new wife ill-advised him to start the Cultural Revolution so that people would remember what the original revolution had done for them. Mao killed intellectuals and artists from 1966 to 1976 in his attempt to get the people to return to the peasant ways. After his death, his compatriots on the Long March and through his rule told Fritz that Mao had been wrong in his later life. Maps, Notes, Bibliography, and Index.

639.   Frost, Mary Pierce, and Susan Keegan. **The Mexican Revolution**. San Diego, CA: Lucent, 1996. 128p. $16.95. ISBN 1-56006-292-4. (World History). 9 up

The text looks at Mexican history from Porfirio Diaz's fall in 1911 to the end of Lazaro Cardenas's term in 1940. They discuss the political unrest in the country with its poverty, racist attitudes, and corrupt government, and recall the leaders who have tried to change the situation. Bibliography, Chronology, Further Reading, and Index.

640.   Fuchs, Thomas. **The Hitler Fact Book**. Los Angeles: Fountain, 1990. 255p. $14.95. ISBN 0-9623202-9-3. YA

Fuchs attempts to dispel myths about Hitler by looking at his decisions and habits on a variety of subjects, including appearance, choice of symbols, views, personal choices, and attitudes. Sample chapter headings contain such phrases as "Hitler's Moustache," "Hitler Laughs," "Backstage Hitler," "I Was Hitler's Dentist," and "Games the *Fuhrer* Played." They assemble an unsettling view of a demented man. Bibliography, Chronology, and Index.

641.   Fulbrook, Mary. **The Divided Nation: A History of Germany, 1918–1990**. New York: Oxford University Press, 1992. 416p. $18.95pa. ISBN 0-19-507571-4pa. YA

The smaller section of this text presents the Weimar Republic and the Third Reich. Over half of the book discusses the two Germanies since 1945. Fulbrook shows the importance of the elite groups from 1918 to 1990, the roles and interaction of various classes, the economy, the place of dissenting groups in the societies, and the international connections. She also reviews the events that led to the end of the divided Germanies. Bibliography and Index.

642.   Furlong, Monica. **Juniper**. New York: Knopf, 1991. 192p. $12.95. ISBN 0-394-83220-5. 5-8

This prequel to *Wise Child* tells how Juniper learned the secret teachings of the *dorans,* which she later imparted to Wise Child during the early Christian times. Euny teaches Juniper with a fierceness that Juniper refuses to use later in her life when she in turn imparts the knowledge of herbs, spells, and rituals to Wise Child.

643.   Furlong, Monica. **Wise Child**. New York: Knopf, 1987. 228p. $11.95. ISBN 0-394-99105-2. 6-8

Juniper, an outcast, looks after Wise Child, age nine, after Wild Child's mother deserts her and her father does not return from sea. In early Christian times, the Scottish village mistrusts Juniper's powers of healing, and they need a scapegoat to blame for an outbreak of smallpox. Wise Child sees that Juniper's magic is nothing more than her close attention to detail, which helps her observe illnesses and remember the appropriate cures.

G

644. Gaffney, Timothy. **Edmund Hillary**. Chicago: Childrens Press, 1990. 128p. $28.20. ISBN 0-516-03052-3. (World's Great Explorers). 5-9

From New Zealand, where he learned to love snow, Edmund Hillary (b. 1919) traveled the globe attempting to go places no other human had been. In 1953, he reached the top of Mt. Everest in the Himalayas, at 29,028 feet (8,848 meters) the highest point on earth. In 1960, he went on an expedition in the Himalayas to search for the Abominable Snowman, or *yeti*, which he never found. By living at high altitude for a long time, he helped scientists study the effects of oxygen deficiency. His wife and a daughter died in an airplane crash on their way to be with him while he helped build a hospital in the Himalayas. Timeline of Events, Glossary, Bibliography, and Index.

645. Gaines, Ann. **Alexander von Humboldt: Colossus of Exploration**. New York: Chelsea House, 1990. 112p. $19.95. ISBN 0-7910-1313-8. (World Explorers). 5 up

Alexander von Humboldt (1769-1859) was a naturalist, botanist, mineralogist, marine biologist, volcanologist, anthropologist, explorer, geographer, philosopher, teacher, and writer. He was so interested in the natural world that he left Prussia when he was thirty to travel in South America exploring the rain forests and rivers. The rest of his life he devoted to publishing the data he had collected. His final publication, *Cosmos,* which he worked on for thirty years, appeared one year before he died; it was his attempt to say in plain language all that he had observed. Photographs, engravings, and reproductions enhance the text. Chronology, Further Reading, and Index.

646. Gallant, Roy. **The Day the Sky Split Apart: Investigating a Cosmic Mystery**. New York: Atheneum, 1995. 156p. $16. ISBN 0-689-80323-0. 6 up

On June 30, 1908, in the Tunguska wilderness of Siberia, a series of explosions occurred. Witnesses said that fire seemed to pour out of the sky, and seismographic instruments around the world registered impacts. In the 1920s, an anthropologist talked to natives and then began to investigate the event. Foreign researchers were kept from the area until 1992. Research there by Gallant and others indicates that this blast, which devastated an area half the size of Rhode Island, was probably an exploding meteorite. The question remains as to whether these kinds of destruction can be foreseen. The text looks at the initial investigations and asks questions about the future. Further Reading and Index.

647. Gallaz, Christophe. **Rose Blanche**. Roberto Innocenti, illustrator; Martha Coventry, translator. 1986. Mankato, MN: Creative Editions, Harcourt Brace, 1996. 28p. $17; $8pa. ISBN 0-15-200918-3; 0-15-200917-5pa. 6 up

One day during World War II, Rose Blanche follows an army truck through her German town, after she sees the mayor push a little boy inside it who did not want to go. When she discovers barbed wire with starving people behind it, she feeds the hungry prisoners her rations throughout the winter. One day she discovers the wire cut; in the fog, foreign soldiers see her and shoot her, thinking she is the enemy. She symbolizes the Germans who wanted to stop the war. *Mildred L. Batchelder Award* and *American Library Association Notable Books for Children.*

648. Galvin, Irene F. **The Maya of Central America**. Tarrytown, NY: Benchmark, 1996. 80p. $19.95. ISBN 0-7614-0091-5. 6-8

Galvin presents the Mayan culture through its art, poetry, religion, language, and way of life. Among the topics are hieroglyphs, the three separate Mayan calendars, and the study of astronomy that the Mayans pursued. Illustrations aid the text. Bibliography, Chronology, Further Reading, Glossary, and Index.

649. Gardam, Jane. **A Long Way from Verona**. 1972. New York: Macmillan, 1988. 192p. $13.95. ISBN 0-02-735781-3. 6-9

At age nine, Jessica hears an author talk at her school, and she knows that she wants to write. When she is thirteen, during World War II, and her poem wins a *London Times* contest, all of the difficulties of the school year fade away. *Phoenix Award.*

650. Garden, Nancy. **Dove and Sword: A Novel of Joan of Arc**. New York: Farrar, Straus & Giroux, 1995. 304p. $17. ISBN 0-374-34476-0. 7-10

While Jeanne d'Arc (1412?–1431} raises an army in Tours, a friend accompanying Jeanne d'Arc's mother on a pilgrimage to Le Puy asks to join Jeanne. Gabrielle dresses in male clothing and serves as a page and medic to the soldiers. However, she also manages a passionate romance with a male. Gabrielle becomes the foil or "dove" to Jeanne's image of the sword as they try to save France, each in her own way.

651. Garfield, Leon. **Black Jack**. Antony Maitland, illustrator. New York: Random House, 1969. 192p. $4.50. ISBN 0-394-80713-8. 6-9

An orphaned boy and a hanged-man-come-back-to-life hold up a coach. After an insane girl on the coach escapes, she and the boy join a caravan, where she regains her sanity and they fall in love. After other events, the two stow away on the boy's uncle's ship and escape their eighteenth-century life in London.

652. Garfield, Leon. **The December Rose**. New York: Viking, 1987. 208p. $12.95. ISBN 0-670-81054-1. 6-9

Barnacle, a filthy sweep, is also a biter, a liar, and a thief in late-eighteenth-century London. After he steals a locket, the police come after him, but a barge owner pities him and takes him in. Further intrigues, espionage, and treason help to reveal information about a boat, *The December Rose*. Eventually, Barnacle reforms. *School Library Journal Best Book*.

653. Garfield, Leon. **Devil-in-the-Fog**. 1966. Magnolia, MA: Peter Smith, 1991. 205p. $15. ISBN 0-8446-6452-9. 5-8

George Treet, age fourteen, finds out that his family name is actually Dexter. He moves to Sir John Dexter's, but there he hears that Mr. Treet is a villain. After much confusion, George comes to understand that Mr. Treet has sold him to the Dexters to act as their heir. He fills the role well enough to irritate Sir John, but Lady Dexter likes him immensely. *Guardian Award for Children's Fiction*.

654. Garfield, Leon. **The Drummer Boy**. Antony Maitland, illustrator. New York: Random House, 1969. 154p. $5.69. ISBN 0-394-90855-4. 7-9

When Charlie Sampson returns from France to England, he goes to tell Sophia Lawrence that her intended, James Digby, died honorably in battle. At her house, Charlie finds that her father, General Lawrence, is to be hanged for poor leadership of his troops. Charlie falls in love with Sophia but escapes when he realizes that she thrives on death. He then warns Lawrence's son-in-law, Maddox, that the general plans to kill him because the general blames Maddox for his troubles. *Carnegie Medal Citation*.

655. Garfield, Leon. **The Empty Sleeve**. New York: Delacorte, 1988. 207p. $14.95. ISBN 0-440-50049-4. 6-8

Peter and Paul are twins in eighteenth-century England. At age fourteen, Peter becomes a locksmith's apprentice in London; his angelic opposite, Paul, plans to stay at home. Before Peter leaves, an old man gives them two carved sailing ships encased in bottles, but Paul switches them so that he gets Peter's. As Peter becomes entangled in various difficulties in London, the ship that Paul has decays, and the old man cannot repair it. *School Library Journal Best Book*.

656. Garfield, Leon. **Footsteps**. 1980. New York: Yearling, 1988. 272p. $3.25pa. ISBN 0-440-40102-Xpa. 5-8

On his deathbed, William's father tells William, age twelve, that he cheated his business partner, Alfred Diamond. William rushes to London and searches for Diamond, or his son, at an address hidden inside his father's gold watch so that he can confess the deed. After several meetings with a man named John Robinson, William realizes that John Robinson is Diamond's son and that he is William's enemy. William saves John, however, when John almost dies in the fire he sets to destroy William's home. When all is resolved, William no longer hears the footsteps of his father's pacing as he has each night since his father's death. *Whitbread Book of the Year*.

657. Garfield, Leon. **Jack Holborn**. Antony Maitland, illustrator. New York: Random House, 1965. 250p. $5.99. ISBN 0-394-91323-X. 6-9

Abandoned as a baby, Jack Holborn stows away on the *Bristol* when he is thirteen. Pirates capture the ship, and the pirate captain tells Jack that he will identify Jack's mother if Jack saves him three times. Among the characters they meet as the result of shipwrecks and rescues are men who help make Jack rich and help him find his mother, in a variety of strange but believable ways.

658. Garfield, Leon. **The Night of the Comet**. New York: Delacorte, 1979. 149p. $8.95. ISBN 0-385-28753-4. 5-8

In the mid-eighteenth century, on April 6, Pigott's comet comes into the sky, and lovers prepare to have a party in its honor. Bostock tries to attract his friend's sister, but she ignores him. Others also have various difficulties with their partners during the celebration.

659. Garfield, Leon. **Smith**. 1967. New York: Peter Smith, 1991. 218p. $16. ISBN 0-8446-6455-3. New York: Dell, 1987. 218p. $4.95pa. ISBN 0-440-48044-2pa. 6-9

Just before a man is murdered, Smith pickpockets the murderer and finds a document, which he cannot read. A blind man he meets has a daughter who will teach him to read, so Smith consents to live with the man and help him. After he learns how, he reads the document, but he refuses to give it up even though he is imprisoned for it. Smith and his blind benefactor eventually claim reward money for the document. *Carnegie Commendation* and *Phoenix Award.*

660. Garfield, Leon. **The Sound of Coaches**. John Lawrence, illustrator. 1974. New York: Viking, 1985. 265p. $2.95pa. ISBN 0-14-030961-6pa. 7 up

Sam, a foundling child whose adoptive father is a coachman, wants to become a driver himself. On one of his first jobs, he has an accident as he comes into London. He wanders away from this profession after he becomes enamored with the theater, and he performs in a Shakespearian drama. He continues to search for his real parents, and finds out about his father, as he also falls in love with Jenny.

661. Garfield, Leon. **Young Nick and Jubilee**. New York: Delacorte, 1989. 137p. $13.95. ISBN 0-385-29777-7. 5-7

Nick, age ten, and Jubilee, age nine, survive in London during the eighteenth century as orphans living in parks and stealing their food. A thief, Mr. Owens, helps them get into a charity school by pretending to be their father. But part of the deal is that the schoolmaster makes surprise visits to the homes of his students. Thus, Nick and Jubilee have to live with Mr. Owens while waiting for the visit. Instead of throwing them out afterward, Mr. Owens finds he likes being their father, and he is a good one.

662. Garfunkel, Trudy. **On Wings of Joy: The Story of Ballet from the 16th Century to Today**. Boston: Little, Brown, 1994. 194p. $18.95. ISBN 0-316-30412-3. 6 up

Ballet began more than 400 years ago in the courts of Europe. In the seventeenth century, the English masque and the five positions of classical ballet were established. Although some changes occurred in the eighteenth century, Jean-Georges Noverre (1727-1810), the father of modern ballet, was the theorist of the times. Dancers received training commensurate with their body types. In the nineteenth century, Romanticism and Romantic ballet began. Famous dancers included Marie Taglioni, Jules Perrot, Carlotta Grisi, and Carlotta Brianza. During the twentieth century, modern dance arrived. Still, famous dancers preferred classical ballet. Names that dominate this century are Anna Pavlova and George Balanchine. Coda, Glossary, Bibliography, and Index.

663. Garland, Sherry. **Cabin 102**. San Diego, CA: Harcourt Brace, 1995. 243p. $11; $5pa. ISBN 0-15-238631-9; 0-15-200662-1pa. 5-9

Although set in the present, this historical fantasy couples the contemporary Dusty, twelve, with Tahni, an Arawak Indian girl who is in the cabin next door to Dusty's on a cruise ship. Through a series of inquiries and situations where people think he is crazy, Dusty finds out that Tahni drowned when the Spanish galleon *Estrella Vespertina* capsized in 1511. Now she is trying to return to her island of Bogati. With her story comes historical background on the Spanish conquest in the Caribbean and the end of the Arawak Indians.

664. Garland, Sherry. **Song of the Buffalo Boy**. San Diego: Harcourt Brace, 1992. 249p. $15.95; $5pa. ISBN 0-15-277107-7; 0-15-200098-4pa. 8 up

At age seventeen, Loi remembers an American from her childhood in 1973, who gave Loi's mother a picture of the three of them before disappearing from her life. Loi, a *con-lai* (half-breed), and her mother suffer the insults of the neighbors until Loi decides to leave for America with a boy who loves her but whose parents have forbidden him to marry her. Before she leaves, her mother tells her that the man she remembers is not her father. Her mother had to prostitute herself to find food for her own mother during the Vietnam War, and Loi is the result of her decision. *American Library Association Best Books for Young Adults, Notable Children's Trade Books in the Field of Social Studies,* and *New York Public Library's Books for the Teen Age.*

665. Garrett, George P. **Death of the Fox: A Novel of Elizabeth and Raleigh**. San Diego, CA: Harcourt Brace, 1991. 744p. $14.95pa. ISBN 0-15-625233-3pa. YA

Sir Walter Ralegh hates James I, and he plans the last two days of his life before James executes him. He thinks of all he has done, and even though he considers his memories to be foolish, he is content with what he has been able to accomplish.

666. Garrett, George P. **The Succession: A Novel of Elizabeth and James**. San Diego, CA: Harcourt Brace, 1991. 679p. $12.95. ISBN 0-15-686303-0. YA

As he rides from Scotland to London, William Cecil's spy disguises himself several times so that no one will know he is carrying the message of James's birth to Elizabeth I. As he changes costumes, he moves through the social strata. He hears what people in various groups say about Elizabeth and realizes that Elizabeth must keep many different kinds of people happy in her kingdom. Elizabeth refuses to name James as her heir until just before her death, perhaps as a way of keeping her subjects waiting for the unexpected. When she dies in 1603, he becomes king.

667.　Garrigue, Shelia. **The Eternal Spring of Mr. Ito**. 1985. New York: Aladdin, 1994. 163p. $3.95pa. ISBN 0-689-71809-8pa. 5-7

While living with Canadian relatives during World War II, after evacuation from England, Sara becomes friends with her uncle's gardener and World War I companion, Mr. Ito. He helps her start a bonsai plant, but the Japanese bomb Pearl Harbor in 1941, and the government interns Mr. Ito's family while he hides in a cave. Sara finds him and saves his bonsai tree, which has already been passed down through many generations, so that it can continue its long life.

668.　Garwood, Julie. **Saving Grace**. New York: Pocket/Simon & Schuster, 1993. 372p. $22; $5.99pa. ISBN 0-671-74422-4; 0-671-87011-4pa. YA

Although inconsistencies with Scottish customs may appear in the detail, this book nevertheless spins a worthy tale. Lady Johanna, widowed by the age of sixteen, marries a Scot instead of the cruel baron whom King John of England has chosen for her. The Scottish lord delights in the land she brings into the marriage, but Johanna has to gain respect from his people while she adjusts to the different way of life.

669.　Garwood, Julie. **The Secret**. New York: Pocket, 1992. 379p. $5.99pa. ISBN 0-671-74221-6pa. YA

In 1200, Judith goes from her home in Britain to the wild highlands of Scotland. She unexpectedly falls in love, decides to marry and stay in the village, and finds the father whom she has never known. She asserts her rights and surprises the village.

670.　Garza, Hedda. **Francisco Franco—Spanish Dictator**. New York: Chelsea House, 1987. 112p. $18.95. ISBN 0-87754-524-3. (World Leaders Past and Present). 8 up

Francisco Franco (1892–1975) graduated from a military academy in 1910, and in 1923 became the commander of the Spanish Foreign Legion. The Spanish Republic came into being in 1931, but by 1936 Franco and his men were ready to overthrow it because it was moving toward Marxism. With the help of Germany's Adolf Hitler and Italy's Benito Mussolini, Franco and his Nationalists won the bloody Spanish Civil War, and Franco began his thirty-six years of dictatorship. He restricted civil liberties, censored the press, and imprisoned or killed political opponents while supposedly modernizing his country. Afraid that democracy in Europe would end, hundreds of Americans went to fight in Spain even though the United States government passed laws to make their participation illegal. The text looks at these and other aspects of Franco's rule in Spain. Photographs and reproductions enhance the text. Chronology, Further Reading, and Index.

671.　Garza, Hedda. **Frida Kahlo**. New York: Chelsea House, 1994. 120p. $18.95; $7.95pa. ISBN 0-7910-1698-6; 0-7910-1699-4pa. (Hispanics of Achievement). 5 up

In 1925, Frida Kahlo (1907-1954) was one of the survivors of a bus crash in Mexico City in which several people died. She had a long recovery during which she began painting. She dreamed of becoming a doctor, but the crash kept her from walking without pain. She then married an artist, Diego Rivera, but continued struggling for recognition of the intensely personal paintings that she created. Although little known outside Mexico at her death, she is now known internationally for her unique style. Photographs and reproductions enhance the text. Chronology, Further Reading, and Index.

672.　Garza, Hedda. **Mao Zedong**. New York: Chelsea House, 1988. 112p. $18.95. ISBN 0-87754-564-2. (World Leaders Past and Present). 8 up

Mao Zedong (1893–1976) proclaimed the People's Republic of China at the Gate of Heavenly Peace in Beijing in October 1949. He ruled China for twenty-seven years, asserting his own type of communism. After studying the works of Karl Marx, he helped found the Chinese Communist Party in 1921. He had joined with Chiang Kai-shek's Nationalist Party in the 1920s to resist foreign invasion and China's warlords, but he and Chiang disagreed thereafter. Although nearly defeated, Mao formed his Red Army and developed the principles that inspired the Long March during 1934 and 1935, a 6,000-mile trek to establish Mao as the Communists' supreme leader. His programs, including the Great Leap Forward and the Great Proletarian Cultural Revolution, failed, but he did begin the modernization of China. Photographs enhance the text. Chronology, Further Reading, and Index.

673.　Garza, Hedda. **Pablo Casals**. New York: Chelsea House, 1995. 112p. $18.95; $7.95. ISBN 0-7910-1237-9; 0-7910-1264-6pa. (Hispanics of Achievement). 8 up

As cello virtuoso, composer, and conductor, Pablo Casals (1876–1973) gained a well-deserved reputation for excellence during the twentieth century. He studied in Spain, Belgium, and France and founded an orchestra in the 1920s. Because of his strong political conscience, he gave benefit concerts during the Spanish Civil War to aid those being displaced by Franco, whom he hated. Known internationally, he founded other important festivals and benefits to allow all to hear the beauty of music. Photographs and reproductions enhance the text. Chronology, Further Reading, and Index.

673a.   Gay, Kathlyn, and Martin Gay. **Emma Goldman**. San Diego, CA: Lucent, 1997. 128p. $16.95. ISBN 1-56006-024-7. (The Importance Of). 7 up.

Emma Goldman (1869-1940) immigrated to the United States from Russia when she was sixteen after her tyrannical father determined that she would marry a man whom she despised. The sight of child labor, terrible working conditions, and low pay led her to fight for workers' rights and win herself the title of anarchist. She spent much of her life abroad while she was exiled from the United States. Bibliography, Chronology, Further Reading, and Index.

674.   Gay, Kathlyn, and Martin Gay. **Korean War**. New York: Twenty-First Century, 1996. 64p. $15.98. ISBN 0-8050-4100-1. (Voices from the Past). 7-9

Letters, diaries, and newspaper accounts help to give an overview of the Korean War in which America fought for South Korea as part of United Nations troops from 1950 to 1953. Photographs, Maps, Further Reading, Notes, and Index.

675.   Gay, Kathlyn, and Martin Gay. **Persian Gulf War**. New York: Twenty-First Century, 1996. 64p. $15.98. ISBN 0-8050-4102-8. (Voices from the Past). 7-9

Letters, diaries, and newspaper accounts help to give an overview of the Persian Gulf War in which the United States fought to help Kuwait and Saudi Arabia overcome aggression from Sadam Hussein of Iraq in January and February of 1991. Photographs, Maps, Further Reading, Notes, and Index.

676.   Gay, Kathlyn, and Martin Gay. **Spanish-American War**. New York: Twenty-First Century, 1995. 64p. $15.98. ISBN 0-8050-2847-1. (Voices from the Past). 7-9

Letters, diaries, and newspaper accounts help to give an overview of the causes, the battles, and the results of the Spanish-American War in which the Americans fought in 1898 against Spain. Photographs, Maps, Further Reading, Notes, and Index.

677.   Gay, Kathlyn, and Martin Gay. **Vietnam War**. New York: Twenty-First Century, 1996. 64p. $15.98. ISBN 0-8050-4101-X. (Voices from the Past). 7-9

Letters, diaries, and newspaper accounts help to give an overview of the Vietnam War in which the United States became involved in 1961 to fight against communism in Southeast Asia. It lasted until 1975. Photographs, Maps, Further Reading, Notes, and Index.

678.   Gay, Kathlyn, and Martin Gay. **World War I**. New York: Twenty-First Century, 1995. 64p. $15.98. ISBN 0-8050-2848-X. (Voices from the Past). 7-9

Letters, diaries, and newspaper accounts help to give an overview of World War I, which the Americans entered in 1917 and fought until 1918. Photographs, Maps, Further Reading, Notes, and Index.

679.   Gay, Kathlyn, and Martin Gay. **World War II**. New York: Twenty-First Century, 1995. 64p. $15.98. ISBN 0-8050-2849-8. (Voices from the Past). 7-9

Letters, diaries, and newspaper accounts help to give an overview of World War II, which the Americans entered in 1941 and fought until 1945. Photographs, Maps, Further Reading, Notes, and Index.

680.   Gedge, Pauline. **Child of the Morning**. New York: Sophia, 1993. 300p. $14. ISBN 0-939149-85-0. YA

Hatshepsut's father tells her that she must learn the arts of war and government because his heir and her intended husband, Thothmes, is incompetent. She becomes knowledgeable and rules Egypt for twenty years while diplomatically controlling priests who do not want to listen to a woman's commands. When her stepson decides to take back his throne, he first has Hatshepsut's trusted companion, Senmut, murdered. Finally, Thothmes assassinates Hatshepsut by having servants give her poisoned wine.

681.   Gee, Maurice. **The Champion**. New York: Simon & Schuster, 1993. 212p. $16. ISBN 0-671-86561-7. 6-9

Rex, aged twelve in 1943, anticipates the arrival of an American soldier who will stay with his family in New Zealand to recuperate. When the soldier arrives, Rex is shocked that he is black. Once Rex adjusts to Jack, Jack helps him become friends with other children who have had experiences like Jack's, a half-Maori boy and a Dalmatian immigrant. Then Rex and his friends in turn help Jack when white American soldiers recklessly pursue him.

682.   Gee, Maurice. **The Fat Man**. New York: Simon & Schuster, 1997. 192p. $16. ISBN 0-689-81182-9. 6-9

Colin, twelve, lives in New Zealand during the Depression when the fat man, Herbert Muskie, encourages him to steal. Muskie leaves and returns with a wife, stepdaughter, and money made in Canada bootlegging. He continues his vicious ways with the adults not seeming to notice and Colin worried about the results. *School Library Journal Best Book.*

683.   Gee, Maurice. **The Fire-Raiser**. Boston: Houghton Mifflin, 1992. 172p. $14.95. ISBN 0-395-62428-2. 5-9

In 1915, someone sets a fire in Kitty's New Zealand town. No one knows the culprit, but the children suspect one man of the deed. Although the adults disagree, the children also find benzene cans and rags near his home. When he repeats the arson, the children prove to be correct.

684. Gehrts, Barbara. **Don't Say a Word**. New York: Macmillan, 1986. 170p. $11.95. ISBN 0-689-50412-8. 7-10

At the beginning of World War II, Anna lives with her family outside Berlin. But as the war progresses, the Gestapo arrests her father, a *Luftwaffe* officer, for giving information to the Allies. Her best friend, a Jew, commits suicide. Her boyfriend dies on the Russian front, and during military training, her brother gets an infection that kills him. Her home is bombed and her mother ages prematurely. Hitler's regime destroys families regardless of race and background. *American Library Association Notable Children's Book* and *International Board on Books for Young People.*

685. Gelissen, Rena, and Heather Dune Macadam. **Rena's Promise**. New York: Beacon Press/Farrar, Straus & Giroux, 1996. 288p. $14pa. ISBN 0-8070-7071-8pa. YA

Rena Kornreich went to Auschwitz on the first Jewish transport, and she and her sister survived the Nazi death camps for three more years. The text tells her story of trying to stay alive and to keep her sister with her during that time in World War II.

686. George, Margaret. **The Memoirs of Cleopatra**. New York: St. Martin's Press, 1997. 976p. $27.95. ISBN 0-312-15430-5. YA

Cleopatra is an intelligent and compassionate woman who knows that she must play politics to stay alive. She saw her mother die when she was three, and she knew that she wanted to prepare for her demise with her own hands. She shares her life and her loves inextricably tied to Rome, although her home was in North Africa.

687. **Georgia**. Minneapolis, MN: Lerner, 1992. 56p. $19.95. ISBN 0-8225-2807-X. (Then and Now). 5-9

Georgia, on the coast of the Black Sea, has a known history dating from the fourth century B.C., and it reached the height of its power during the twelfth and thirteenth centuries. The text covers the history, economics, geography, politics, ethnography, and possible future of Georgia. Maps and photographs complement the text. Glossary and Index.

688. Geras, Adele. **The Tower Room**. San Diego, CA: Harcourt Brace, 1992. 150p. $15.95. ISBN 0-15-289627-9. 7-10

Her parents die after Megan starts boarding school, and she falls in love with the new laboratory instructor when she is a senior in 1962. After she runs away with him to London, she realizes that the bloom of love is much more appealing without the responsibility of work and the need for shelter.

689. Geras, Adele. **Voyage**. New York: Atheneum, 1983. 194p. $12.95. ISBN 0-689-30955-4. 5-9

Mina, age fourteen, and her family leave Russia in the early twentieth century for America, to escape the pogroms against Jews. On board the ship, Mina uses her energy to help those on board who can barely survive from the seasickness, the hunger, and the filth that surrounds them. The omniscient point of view exposes the diverse responses of those on board ship to this difficult experience.

690. Getz, David. **Frozen Man**. Peter McCarty, illustrator. New York: Redfeather, Henry Holt, 1994. 68p. $14.95. ISBN 0-8050-3261-4. 4-7

A body found in the Alps between Austria and Italy seemed unexceptional until an archaeologist examined it and discovered that the man had died more than 5,000 years ago. From his body, archaeologists have learned what life in Europe might have been like during that time, including the type of clothing worn, the food eaten, and what the people looked like. Glossary, Bibliography, and Index.

691. Gherman, Beverly. **Robert Louis Stevenson: Teller of Tales**. New York: Atheneum, 1996. 144p. $16. ISBN 0-689-31985-1. 3-7

Robert Louis Stevenson (1859-1894) lived in a strict Scottish household and studied law to please his father. But he wanted to write, and his love of adventure took him across France on a donkey and across America chasing his true love to California. He wrote books to entertain his stepson, and after the success of *Treasure Island* he wrote other adventure stories. His family then went to the South Pacific, where he spent his final years living on Samoa. Index.

692. Ghose, Vijaya. **India: Women in Society**. New York: Marshall Cavendish, 1994. 128p. $21.95. ISBN 1-85435-564-3. (Women in Society). 7-12

After introducing the women of India through the myth of Savitri, the woman who outwitted the gods, the author discusses the roles of women in India by interweaving historical and contemporary practices. She presents the expectations imposed upon women: rural and urban, religious and secular, poor and wealthy. The chapters cover milestones, women in society, what being a woman means in the culture, and the life of a woman from birth to old age. Short biographies of Indira Gandhi (1917–1984); Raziya Sultan (d. 1240); Mirabai (c. 1504–c. 1550); Laxmibai, rani of Jhansi (1835–1858); Sarojini Naidu (1879–1949); and Ela Bhatt (d.

1933) show what Indian women have done. Photographs complement the text. Women Firsts, Glossary, Further Reading, and Index.

693.   Gibb, Christopher. **The Dalai Lama**. Milwaukee, MN: Gareth Stevens, 1990. 68p. $16.95. ISBN 0-8368-0224-1. (People Who Have Helped the World). 7-9

The fourteenth Dalai Lama of Tibet, Tenzin Gyatso (1935), was identified and tested by Tibetan monks at the age of two to succeed the previous Dalai Lama. This biography includes information about the country of Tibet, its Buddhist beliefs, and its struggle against the Chinese that led to the exile of the Dalai Lama in India. It also shows the independence of the Tibetan people and the tragedy of the Chinese invasion and destruction of the culture. The Dalai Lama has taught and continues to teach that world peace begins with each individual taking responsibility for self and for others. "The Way of Buddha," Bibliography, Glossary, Chronology, and Index.

694.   Giblin, James. **Be Seated: A Book About Chairs**. New York: HarperCollins, 1993. 136p. $15. ISBN 0-06-021537-2. 4-8

The text gives a history of chairs beginning with the three-legged stools and chairs of the Egyptians, which were mortise- and tenon-joined. It includes the thrones of kings such as Solomon and the *klismos* of the Greeks with their curved lines. Giblin also discusses the Sheridan chair and the Shaker rocker. The chair becomes a part of social custom, art, and politics in the society that uses it. Bibliography, Notes, and Index.

695.   Giblin, James. **When Plague Strikes: The Black Death, Smallpox, AIDS**. New York: HarperCollins, 1995. 212p. $14.95. ISBN 0-06-025854-3. 5-9

Three major plagues have hit the known world in the past 1,000 years: the Black Death, smallpox, and AIDS. They have killed millions of people and have left social, economic, and political havoc. Although each plague has helped to increase knowledge about the human body, each new one must be researched and tested for a cure. The text first recounts the Plague of Athens that struck in the summer of 430 B.C. Those who lived had terrible scars or lost their eyesight or their memory. Today no one is sure what the disease might have been, although typhus, smallpox, and the bubonic plague are candidates. The sure thing is that doctors did not know how to treat it. Giblin continues with information about the three plagues that have ravaged the world since. Source Notes, Bibliography, and Index. *American Library Association Best Books for Young Adults, Notable Children's Trade Books in the Field of Social Studies*, and *American Library Association Notable Books for Children*.

696.   Giblin, James Cross. **The Riddle of the Rosetta Stone: Key to Ancient Egypt**. New York: Crowell, 1990. 85p. $15.89. ISBN 0-690-04799-1. New York: Trophy, 1993. 85p. $5.95pa. ISBN 0-06-446137-8pa. 5-7

In 1799, Napoleon's soldiers found a black stone in an old fort north of Alexandria, Egypt, and sent it to Cairo to be examined by scholars whom Napoleon had brought on his campaign. They could not decipher the three languages inscribed on the stone before the British routed Napoleon and claimed the stone for the British Museum. Several other scholars who worked on the problem discovered that the three languages on the stone were Greek (Alexander ruled during its creation), Demotic (of the people), and hieroglyphic (sacred). A few years later, a poor young French student, Champollion, met some of the men who had been with Napoleon. He dedicated himself to finding the connection among the languages. In 1824, his book showed that the hieroglyphs were both sound and symbol and he correlated the three segments of the stone. Afterword about the Demotic Translation, Bibliography, and Index. *Notable Children's Trade Books in the Field of Social Studies* and *American Library Association Notable Books for Children*.

697.   Giblin, James Cross. **The Truth About Unicorns**. Michael McDermott, illustrator. New York: HarperCollins, 1991. 113p. $15; $6.95pa. ISBN 0-06-022478-9; 0-06-446147-5pa. 5 up

Although the unicorn is a mythical animal, it has appeared throughout history. The Chinese saw it as representing nobility and virtue, and many Christians have seen it as a symbol of Jesus Christ. Some have thought that the unicorn possesses magical powers; that it was the swiftest of beasts, so that no other beast could catch it; and that only the purest female could tame it. Photographs of the Unicorn Tapestries complement the text, which looks at the myths and legends of this being. Bibliography, Reading List, and Index. *American Library Association Notable Books for Children* and *School Library Journal Best Book*.

698.   Gibson, Michael. **The War in Vietnam**. New York: Bookwright Press, Franklin Watts, 1992. 63p. $19.14. ISBN 0-531-18408-0. (Witness History). 5-8

The text traces the history of Vietnam from 1887 until the French left in 1954. It discusses the United States's entry into the conflict after it began in 1961 and the country's exit before the fighting ended in 1975, as well as the current situation within the country. Black-and-white and a few color photographs highlight the text. Chronology, Glossary, and Index.

699.   Gilbert, Anna. **The Treachery of Time**. New York: St. Martin's Press, 1996. 444p. $24.95. ISBN 0-312-14055-X. YA

When Esther and Daniel find an orphaned girl before World War I, they show pity for her. And when she returns years later, she vows to retaliate. She lures Daniel away from Esther, and after Esther marries an older widower, the girl, Clarice, appears and claims that the widower is her father and that she wants her inheritance. *Cookson Award.*

700. Gilbert, Martin. **The Day the War Ended: May 8, 1945—Victory in Europe**. New York: Henry Holt, 1995. 473p. $30; $16.95pa. ISBN 0-8050-3926-0; 0-8050-4735-2pa. YA

This book records the day that World War II ended in Europe by reporting on the feelings and responses of people who experienced it on all sides of the conflict. Index.

701. Gill, Anton. **An Honourable Defeat: A History of German Resistance to Hitler, 1933–1945**. New York: Henry Holt, 1994. 293p. $25; $14.95pa. ISBN 0-8050-3514-1; 0-8050-3515-Xpa. YA

Among the groups and the individuals who opposed Hitler and his National Socialism were some in the church, the Foreign Office, Hitler's general staff, Communists, aristocrats, Social Democrats, and students in Munich's White Rose group. Another group, the Edelweiss Pirates, opposed the Hitler Youth. Gill's book is based on interviews with resistance survivors and relatives of those who were executed for their dissension. Bibliography and Index.

702. Gilmore, Kate. **Remembrance of the Sun**. Boston: Houghton Mifflin, 1986. 250p. $13.95. ISBN 0-395-41104-1. 7-10

Jill, age seventeen, lives in Tehran, Iran, where her American father is working, when the first demonstration against the shah occurs in the late 1970s. Jill falls in love with an Iranian boy who wants the oppression to end and, as a student, joins the demonstrators. But none of them foresee the results of a radical group of Islamic zealots taking control. Because of the government shift, Jill must leave the enjoyable expatriate life she describes in her narration, including her boyfriend.

703. Glasco, Gordon. **Slow Through Eden**. New York: Poseidon, 1992. 259p. $23. ISBN 0-671-62305-2. YA

Katherine and David, both physicists, start to develop the atomic bomb in Berlin during World War II. David, however, is Jewish, and they know they must escape as soon as possible to London. But in London, a Russian spy kills David. Katherine takes their son and goes to New York, where she begins another life by joining the team working on the Manhattan Project, a bomb for the United States.

704. Glassman, Bruce. **Mikhail Baryshnikov**. Englewood Cliffs, NJ: Silver Burdett, 1991. 128p. $14.95. ISBN 0-382-09907-9. (Genius: Artist and Process). 7-9

In 1966, Mikhail Baryshnikov (b. 1948) stunned his viewers with his dancing, and he quickly became a star in the Kirov Ballet. His unique talent and technique, developed after he had seen his first ballet at the age of six, led him to defect from the Soviet Union in 1974. In the United States, he has continued to dance and to choreograph, believing that the dance can say what he thinks. Photographs highlight the text. Chronology, Glossary, Bibliography, and Index.

705. Gleiter, Jan. **Benito Juárez**. Francis Balistreri, illustrator. Austin, TX: Raintree/Steck-Vaughn, 1993. 32p. $19.97; $4.95pa. ISBN 0-8172-3381-4; 0-8114-6759-7pa. (Hispanic Stories). 4-7

Born a Zapotec Indian in Oaxaca, with few of the rights of the Spanish, Benito Juárez (1806-1871) worked his way through school and finally became a lawyer who defended the poor. He became Mexico's president before the French invaded in the 1860s and returned when they left. Several times he overcame heavy opposition and passed laws that took power away from the church. Throughout his career, he tried to govern with compassion. Glossary. English and Spanish text.

706. Gleiter, Jan, and Kathleen Thompson. **Diego Rivera**. Yoshi Miyake, illustrator. Austin, TX: Raintree/Steck-Vaughn, 1993. 32p. $19.97; $4.95pa. ISBN 0-8172-2908-6; 0-8114-6764-3pa. (Hispanic Stories). 4-7

As a child, Diego Rivera (1886-1957) drew pictures on everything he could reach, so his father restricted him to drawing in his room, but allowed him to draw on anything. As a young man, he went from Mexico, his home, to Spain and then Paris and later Italy. Among his friends was Picasso. Rivera's style developed, and when he returned to Mexico, he wanted to create art that everyone could see. He painted murals that featured workers. As a Communist, he spoke actively against Hitler in World War II. Glossary.

707. Gleiter, Jan, and Kathleen Thompson. **José Martí**. Les Didier, illustrator. Austin, TX: Raintree/Steck-Vaughn, 1993. 32p. $19.97; $4.95pa. ISBN 0-8172-2906-X; 0-8114-6761-9pa. (Hispanic Stories). 4-7

José Martí (1853-1895) was born in Cuba while the Spanish controlled it. At age sixteen, he was imprisoned for an article he wrote agitating against the Spanish, and he was eventually deported to Spain. There he studied law, and the Spanish government allowed him to go to Mexico. From Mexico, Guatemala, Spain, and New York, he continued to fight for Cuban freedom through his writing. He led the revolution of 1895 but was killed as soon as it began. His colleagues did not see Cuban freedom until 1902. Glossary. English and Spanish text.

708.   Gleiter, Jan, and Kathleen Thompson. **Junípero Serra**. Charles Shaw, illustrator. Austin, TX: Raintree/Steck-Vaughn, 1993. 32p. $13.98; $5.95pa. ISBN 0-8172-2909-4; 0-8114-6765-1pa. (Hispanic Stories). 4-7

As a Franciscan teacher and scholar in Spain, Junípero Serra (1713-1784) decided to go to the New World and help the natives. He and a friend went to California and began to build missions—San Diego, San Francisco, San Antonio, and San Luis Obispo. He wanted to make Spanish settlement in the area easier. He convinced the viceroy that soldiers protecting the missions needed to have their families join them, which created the towns surrounding the missions. Glossary.

709.   Gleiter, Jan, and Kathleen Thompson. **Miguel Hidalgo y Costilla**. Rick Karpinski, illustrator. Austin, TX: Raintree/Steck-Vaughn, 1993. 32p. $19.97; $4.95pa. ISBN 0-8172-2905-1; 0-8114-6757-0pa. (Hispanic Stories). 4-7

Miguel Hidalgo y Costilla (1753-1811) has been called the "Father of Mexican Independence" for two reasons. First, he was a Catholic priest. Secondly, he led his Indian followers in battle against the Spanish for independence. Because he did not have the leadership skills for battle, he lost. After he was tried and shot, the fight continued for another ten years until Mexico became free. Glossary. English and Spanish text.

710.   Gleiter, Jan, and Kathleen Thompson. **Simón Bolívar**. Tom Redman, illustrator. Austin, TX: Raintree/Steck-Vaughn, 1993. 32p. $19.97; $4.95pa. ISBN 0-8172-2902-7; 0-8114-6751-1pa. (Hispanic Stories). 4-7

Born of very rich parents in Venezuela, Simón Bolívar (1782-1830) became an orphan, and a tutor taught him the ideas of European thinkers, such as Jean-Jacques Rousseau, who believed in liberty and equality. In Rome, Bolívar dedicated himself to freeing Venezuela from Spain. After two revolutions and many years, he succeeded, but his other dreams were never totally realized. Glossary. English and Spanish text.

711.   Glossop, Pat. **Cardinal Richelieu**. New York: Chelsea House, 1990. 112p. $18.95. ISBN 1-55546-822-5. (World Leaders Past and Present). 8 up

Armand-Jean du Plessis de Richelieu (1585–1642) dominated the intellectual world in seventeenth-century Europe. He used the Catholic Church as a way to ascend to political authority; Pope Paul V named him a cardinal and King Louis XIII designated him the first minister of France. He thus imposed his will on the French monarchy, France, and Europe. He succeeded in establishing France as the foremost political, cultural, and military power in Europe. He also began a tradition of despotism and oppression that exploded a century later with the revolution. He once said that "[o]ne must sleep like a lion, with open eyes," because he believed that everyone was plotting against him—and he was probably right. Engravings and reproductions enhance the text. Chronology, Further Reading, and Index.

712.   Glubok, Shirley. **Great Lives: Painting**. New York: Scribners, 1994. 238p. $24.95. ISBN 0-684-19052-4. (Great Lives). 5-9

Places where they live and experiences they have influence the subjects that artists choose to paint. Biographical profiles of 23 major painters appear in the text: Mary Cassatt, American (1844-1926); Marc Chagall, Russian (1887-1985); Frederick E. Church, American (1826-1900); Jacques-Louis David, French (1748-1825); Edgar Degas, French (1834-1917); Albrecht Dürer, German (1471-1528); Thomas Gainsborough, English (1727-1788); Paul Gaugin, French (1848-1903); El Greco, Greek (1541-1614); Winslow Homer, American (1836-1910); Leonardo da Vinci, Italian (1452-1519); Michelangelo, Italian (1475-1564); Claude Monet, French (1840-1926); Georgia O'Keeffe, American (1889-1986); Pablo Picasso, Spanish (1881-1973); Rembrandt van Rijn, Dutch (1606-1669); Diego Rivera, Mexican (1886-1957); Peter Paul Rubens, Flemish (1577-1640); Titian, Venetian (?-1576); Vincent van Gogh, Dutch (1853-1890); Diego de Veláquez, Spanish (1599-1660); Johannes Vermeer, Dutch (1632-1675); and James McNeill Whistler, American (1834-1903). Further Reading and Index.

713.   Gold, Alison Leslie. **Memories of Anne Frank: Reflections of a Childhood Friend**. New York: Scholastic, 1997. 135p. $16.95. ISBN 0-590-90722-0. 6-9

Hannah Pick-Goslar was Anne Frank's childhood friend from the ages of four to thirteen. She was also incarcerated in Bergen-Belsen although a fence separated them, and they talked to each other through the barbed wire. Like many young people, they were developing in different ways as they matured, and the text looks at their experiences. Photographs.

714.   Goldberg, Jake. **Albert Einstein: The Rebel Behind Relativity**. New York: Franklin Watts, 1996. 128p. $22. ISBN 0-531-11251-9. (Impact Biographies). 7 up

In this biography, Goldberg gives the background and accomplishments of Albert Einstein (1879-1955) as well as his major theories in a readable text with chapter inserts and diagrams to explain them. He also shows how Einstein's theories evolved from those of Planck and Bohr. Further Reading, Glossary, and Index.

715.   Goldberg, Jake. **Miguel de Cervantes**. New York: Chelsea House, 1993. 112p. $18.95. ISBN 0-7910-1238-7. (Hispanics of Achievement). 8 up

Miguel de Cervantes (1547–1616), imprisoned for five years in Algiers by pirates after the naval battle of Lepanto, found himself imprisoned again in Spain for supposedly keeping irregular accounts for the Spanish crown. After his release, he devoted his life to writing. His masterpiece, *Don Quixote,* was published in two parts, one in 1805 and the second in 1815. The text looks at Cervantes, the time in which he lived, and *Don Quixote,* a novel whose protagonist's beliefs still influence anyone who reads about him. Reproductions enhance the text. Chronology, Further Reading, and Index.

716.   Goldenstern, Joyce. **Albert Einstein: Physicist and Genius**. Springfield, NJ: Enslow, 1995. 128p. $17.95. ISBN 0-89490-480-9. (Great Minds of Science). 6-9

Albert Einstein (1879-1955) formulated one of the most important ideas of the twentieth century, the General Theory of Relativity. He won the 1921 Nobel Prize in Physics, and his genius became famous. It saved his life when Hitler began killing Jews in World War II. From his Princeton, New Jersey, home, Einstein helped others to flee Europe, but he refused to become president of Israel. He wanted to continue work on scientific questions, many of which remained unanswered at his death. Photographs, Chronology, Further Reading, Glossary, and Index.

717.   Goldstein, Ernest. **The Journey of Diego Rivera**. Minneapolis, MN: Lerner, 1995. 104p. $17.21. ISBN 0-8225-2066-4. (Art Beyond Borders). 7 up

This biography of Diego Rivera (1886–1957) looks mainly at his work rather than at his personal life. It shows the influence of his Cubist painter days in Paris and the development of his political ideas of inclusion. His desire to reach the masses meshes with his decision to paint murals of the people. Reproductions, Further Reading, and Index.

718.   Goldstein, Rebecca. **Mazel**. New York: Viking, 1996. 357p. $23.95; $11.95pa. ISBN 0-670-85648-7; 0-14-023905-7pa. YA

"Luck" (*mazel* in Yiddish) helps Sasha escape both her Polish village and Warsaw's ghetto during World War II. Her story influences her daughter and her granddaughter as it intertwines with Yiddish folktales and fairy tales. Whether one can ever escape one's past or one's ancestors—or if one would want to—becomes the question.

718a.   Gonen, Rivka. **Charge! Weapons and Warfare in Ancient Times**. Minneapolis, MN: Runestone Press, 1993. 72p. $22.95. ISBN 0-8225-3201-8. (Buried Worlds). 5 up.

In documenting the development of armor and weapons, the text presents early artillery such as the ballista. It describes other weapons including spears, swords, bows and arrows, catapults and their use in warfare along with protective helmets, body armor, and shields. Excellent photographs and drawings of artifacts enhance the information. Glossary and Index.

719.   Gonen, Rivka. **Fired Up: Making Pottery in Ancient Times**. Minneapolis, MN: Runestone Press, 1993. 72p. $22.95. ISBN 0-8225-3202-6. (Buried Worlds). 5 up

In an explanation of theories about the origins of pottery, the text presents the development of the potter's wheel and methods of dating pottery, which help archaeologists decide how old a site might be. Designs on pottery also help to distinguish its origins. Glossary and Index.

720.   Gonzales, Doreen. **Diego Rivera: His Art, His Life**. Springfield, NJ: Enslow, 1996. 128p. $18.95. ISBN 0-89490-764-6. 6-9

Gonzales sees Diego Rivera as an egotistical man, absorbed in himself and letting his art interfere with his marriage to Frida Kahlo, another Mexican painter; his children; and his extramarital love affairs. The text also discusses his political beliefs and pride in his Mexican heritage. Further Reading and Index.

721.   Goodman, Joan Elizabeth. **Songs from Home**. San Diego, CA: Harcourt Brace, 1994. 213p. $10.95; $4.95pa. ISBN 0-14-203590-7; 0-15-203591-5pa. 5-9

Anna, aged twelve in 1969, lives in Rome with her father in a *pensione* (a dilapidated boardinghouse) and sings with him in restaurants at night for pay. She hates it and lies to people at her school about her life. When a friend moves nearby, she has to tell the truth. She finally decides to leave her father in Europe, because he still cannot face her mother's tragic death, and go to his family in America, although she has never met any of them.

722.   Goodman, Joan Elizabeth. **The Winter Hare**. Boston: Houghton Mifflin, 1996. 255p. $15.95. ISBN 0-395-78569-3. 6-9

Will Belet, twelve, is small for his age after a bout with pox during the twelfth century in England. He has the nickname of Rabbit, and is happy to become a page to his uncle because he wants to emulate King Arthur and become a knight during England's civil war of 1140. He discovers, however, that war is almost unbearable as he bravely helps the Empress Matilda escape from Oxford Castle and finds himself in the middle of a fight between his father and his uncle.

723. Goodnough, David. **José Martí: Cuban Patriot and Poet**. Springfield, NJ: Enslow, 1996. 128p. $17.95. ISBN 0-89490-761-1. (Hispanic Biographies). 5-9

José Martí (1853-1895) promoted Cuban independence and kept the United States from dominating politics and economics in the Caribbean. The text also looks at Martí's cultural legacy; he wrote the song "Guantanamera" and founded the modernist literary movement in Latin America. The Spanish killed Martí when he returned to Cuba after years in exile. Chronology, Further Reading, Notes, and Index.

724. Goodwin, Maire D. **Where the Towers Pierce the Sky**. New York: Macmillan, 1989. 185p. $13.95. ISBN 0-02-736871-8. 7-10

Lizzie, surprised when a French boy shows up in her room one night, is more shocked when the two of them end up in France during 1429. A wizard wants to know if Joan of Arc was able to get Charles VII on the throne, so he can tell the English. What they decide to do is work for Joan of Arc, and Lizzie watches the ensuing discussions and hears about Joan of Arc's visions from the viewpoint of the twentieth century. Lizzie's attitude contrasts with Joan's courage and sincerity.

725. Gordon, Lyndall. **Charlotte Brontë: A Passionate Life**. New York: Norton, 1995. 416p. $27.50; $17pa. ISBN 0-393-03722-3; 0-393-31448-0pa. YA

According to Gordon, Charlotte Brontë (1816–1855), the author of *Jane Eyre* and *Villette,* was a very resourceful woman committed to her writing. She survived during a time inhospitable to women and incorporated autobiographical elements in her novels. Gordon also explores the relationship between Brontë and the publisher George Smith. Chronology, Bibliography, and Index.

726. Gordon, Matthew S. **Ayatollah Khomeini**. New York: Chelsea House, 1986. 120p. $18.95. ISBN 0-87754-559-6. (World Leaders Past and Present). 5 up

For many of his Iranian countrymen, Ayatollah Khomeini (1902-1989) restored his nation's pride and independence, although many Westerners saw him as a fanatical tyrant. In 1941, he published a book that attacked the regime of Reza Pahlavi, the Shah of Iran. Khomeini hated the idea of modernization and detested the corruption of the shah's regime. Khomeini was arrested and exiled but continued to lead the millions who wanted to overthrow the shah. In 1979, he returned and established himself as the leader of Iran, with a government based on Islamic principles. His ideals give an insight into the Middle Eastern psyche. Photographs enhance the text. Chronology, Further Reading, and Index.

727. Gordon, Matthew S. **The Gemayels**. New York: Chelsea House, 1988. 112p. $18.95. ISBN 1-55546-834-9. (World Leaders Past and Present). 5 up

The Gemayel family members have been leaders in Lebanon since the 1930s. Pierre Gemayel, who gained recognition at the 1936 Berlin Olympics, wanted to form an orderly political organization like that of the Nazis in Germany. He formed Kataib, a fascist military organization that eventually became a legitimate political party. His son, Bashir (1947-1982), became the Kataib commander and then the head of the Lebanese forces in 1976. In August 1982, Bashir was elected president, but a month later he was assassinated. Bashir's older brother, Amin, became president. He has been moderate, but he still has problems maintaining peace in his country. Photographs and reproductions enhance the text. Chronology, Further Reading, and Index.

728. Gordon, Matthew S. **Islam**. New York: Facts on File, 1991. 128p. $18.95. ISBN 0-8160-2443-X. (World Religions). 7-12

To understand Islam, knowledge of its origins and its history helps. The text looks first at the modern Islamic world before returning to the past. General topics covered are Muhammad and the founding of Islam, the spread of Islam, the Koran, Hadith and the law, the variety of religious life in Islam, the Muslim ritual life, and the patterns of Islamic life. Glossary, For Further Reading, and Index.

729. Gordon, Shelia. **The Middle of Somewhere**. New York: Jackson, Orchard, 1990. 154p. $13.95. ISBN 0-531-05908-1. 5-7

The stories of forced removals in South Africa, at a time before Nelson Mandela was freed from prison, are important slices of history. Rebecca and Noni, both age nine, keep hearing about Pofadderkloof, a place supposedly nicer than their current home. However, the government has lied to their people before, and the adults try to stay where they are. Noni's family leaves, and Rebecca must adjust to the loss of her friend while waiting for her mother's biweekly visits and for Papa's release from prison. The story ends in 1990, when the government releases both Rebecca's papa and Mandela.

730. Gorrell, Gena K. **North Star to Freedom: The Story of the Underground Railroad**. New York: Delacorte, 1997. 168p. $17.95. ISBN 0-385-32319-0. 6-8

The focus of this book, unlike other texts on the Underground Railroad, is Canada. Many of the slaves who took the railroad ended their journey in Canada with the help of abolitionists and Quakers along the way. Individual accounts from slaves who settled in Canada add new insights about this ordeal of American history. Reproductions, Bibliography, Further Reading, Notes, and Index.

731.   Gosnell, Kelvin. **Belarus, Ukraine, and Moldova**. Brookfield, CT: Millbrook Press, 1992. 32p. $15.90. ISBN 1-56294-306-5. (Former Soviet States). 4-7

The text discusses the cultural background, politics, economics, and histories of the former Soviet republics of Belarus, Ukraine, and Moldova. Originally inhabited by Slavs, Belarus lies east of Poland and north of Ukraine. Ukraine has had human inhabitants at least since 6000 B.C., because it sits on a major trade route; Moldova is more closely connected to Romania through its language and culture. Glossary and Index.

732.   Gottfried, Ted. **Enrico Fermi: Pioneer of the Atomic Age**. New York: Facts on File, 1992. 138p. $17.95. ISBN 0-8160-2623-8. (Makers of Modern Science). YA

Enrico Fermi (1901–1954), an Italian, won the Nobel Prize in Physics for his work leading to the first nuclear chain reaction and the creation of the atomic bomb. He understood the atom and its potential for creating energy, and he wanted humans to use that energy responsibly. When the first atomic bomb exploded at its test site on July 16, 1945, south of Albuquerque, New Mexico, he tried a simple "ripple effect" experiment, using papers placed on the ground at a measured distance from the drop, so that he could calculate the strength of the explosion. Later, his calculations, measured against more sophisticated developments, proved to be accurate. He always told his students that simple experiments were best. The text looks at this man and his life. Afterword, Glossary, Further Reading, and Index.

733.   Gottfried, Ted. **Libya: Desert Land in Conflict**. Brookfield, CT: Millbrook Press, 1994. 159p. $16.90. ISBN 1-56294-351-0. 9 up

The Phoenicians started three colonies in the area now known as contemporary Libya—Oea (Tripoli), Sabratha (Sabratah), and Labqui (Leptis Magna)—in the ninth century B.C. When Carthage fell to Rome in 146 B.C., the region of Libya became open for conquest, and Rome ruled Libya for 500 years. The Vandals, then the Byzantines, and finally the Arabs came into the area. Other powers and leaders have been in control, but Muammar al-Qaddafi took power in 1969. Libya's turbulent history continues, and Gottfried tries to make sense of all the influences in this Islamic country. Source Notes, Chronology, Facts About Libya, Recommended Reading, and Index.

734.   Gottlieb, Beatrice. **The Family in the Western World from the Black Death to the Industrial Age**. New York: Oxford University Press, 1993. 309p. $30; $12.95pa. ISBN 0-19-507344-4; 0-19-509056-Xpa. YA

The text looks at the role of the family during the period between the Black Death in the fourteenth century to the Industrial Age of the eighteenth century. Among the topics covered are what *family* means, how one determines what constitutes a household, and what it means to be related to someone else. Also included are marriage arrangements, sexuality, child rearing, and the family's economic, social, and political responsibilities. Bibliography and Index.

735.   Gourley, Catherine. **Beryl Markham: Never Turn Back**. Berkeley, CA: Conari Press, 1997. 224p. ISBN 1-57324-073-7. (Barnard Biography). 6-10

Beryl Markham (1903-1986) spent most of her life in Kenya, although she was born in England. She became a pilot in the early days of aviation, setting a record with her trans-Atlantic flight; was a horse trainer; and spent time in Hollywood after publishing a book. The text examines her life and the risks that she took without regard to being female. Bibliography and Index.

736.   Gow, Catherine Hester. **The Cuban Missile Crisis**. San Diego, CA: Lucent, 1997. 112p. $16.95. ISBN 1-56006-289-4. (World History Series). 8 up

Half of the text covers background about the Cuban Revolution and the deterioration of the relationship between the United States and Cuba when Castro took over and began to cozy with the Communists. The Bay of Pigs invasion failed, then the missile crisis with Khrushchev threatened to cause a war, but John Kennedy allowed a period of reflection before action. The second half of the book analyzes the event and the input of those involved. Photographs, Bibliography, Chronology, Further Reading, and Index.

737.   Grace, C. L. **The Book of Shadows**. New York: St. Martin's Press, 1996. 195p. $20.95. ISBN 0-312-14287-0. YA

Tenebrae, a necromancer, has spells and secrets in his journal during the fifteenth century, which frighten Kathryn Swinbrooke, a physician. Someone else kills Tenebrae inside a locked room and steals his Book of Shadows. Kathryn and her Irish friend Colum Murtagh must find the murderer and the book, at the request of Elizabeth I.

738.   Grace, C. L. **The Eye of God**. New York: St. Martin's Press, 1994. 198p. $18.95. ISBN 0-312-10978-4. YA

Kathryn Swinbrooke, a physician and chemist in England during 1471, must look at the dead body of Brandon, a trusted soldier for Richard Neville, Earl of Warwick, who disappeared while transporting a royal relic, the Eye of God, to Canterbury's monks. Edward IV has commanded another soldier, Colum Murtagh, to find the relic. The two endanger themselves when another murder occurs in Canterbury and Colum realizes that he is being followed. Their knowledge of Chaucer and "The Pardoner's Tale" helps them solve the crime.

739.   Grace, C. L. **A Shrine of Murders**. New York: St. Martin's Press, 1993. 195p. $17.95. ISBN 0-312-09388-8. YA

As a physician and chemist during the time of Chaucer in the fifteenth century, Kathryn Swinbrooke must solve the murders of people who have been identified by notes tacked on the doors of Canterbury Cathedral. Her partner, Colum Murtagh, an Irish soldier who supports the crown, helps her because he can enter places in which a woman is not allowed. Kathryn solves the murder with her wits and familiarity with Chaucer, and Murtagh helps her.

740.   Grady, Sean M. **Marie Curie**. San Diego, CA: Lucent, 1992. 111p. $16.95. ISBN 1-56006-003-6. (The Importance Of). 7-10

A scientific pioneer, Marie Curie (1867–1934) was one of the first to investigate radioactivity, and the first to recognize that radioactivity is the result of changes in the atoms of an element. She discovered the radioactive elements radium and polonium, which exist naturally only in microscopic quantities, and helped open the field of atomic physics. She won one Nobel Prize for Physics in 1903 and one for Chemistry in 1911, thus becoming one of only three people to have the distinction of winning in different fields. Notes, For Further Reading, Works Consulted, and Index.

741.   Graham, Harriet. **A Boy and His Bear**. New York: Simon & Schuster, Margaret K. McElderry, 1996. 196p. $16. ISBN 0-689-80943-3. 6-9

Dickon becomes apprenticed to a tanner after his widowed mother remarries in medieval England. He hates having to work on the skins of animals that he loves, and when he goes on an errand to the bear pits where bears fight dogs, he rescues a cub and flees. He sails to France with entertainers, and the Bear Catcher follows him. In some scenes, the bear cub gives its view of the situation, and eventually, Dickon does what he must, which is to set the bear free.

742.   Graham-Campbell, James, et al. **Cultural Atlas of the Viking World**. New York: Facts on File, 1994. 240p. $45. ISBN 0-8160-3004-9. YA

Divided into four parts, the text, after a chronology, discusses the origins of the Vikings, the Viking Age in Scandinavia, the Vikings overseas, and the end of the Viking world. Within each broad category, photographs of sites and artifacts and illustrations help clarify information about the land, climate, society, daily life, towns, trade, crafts, religion, and places the Vikings visited. Glossary, Bibliography, Gazetteer, and Index.

743.   Granfield, Linda. **In Flanders Fields: The Story of the Poem by John McCrae**. Janet Wilson, illustrator. New York: Doubleday, 1996. Unpaged. $15.95. ISBN 0-385-32228-3. 5 up

Using the poem "In Flanders Fields" as a base, the text discusses the poem, gives an overview of World War I, and briefly capsulizes the life of the Canadian poet John McCrae. Sketches, photographs, and memorabilia add to the illustrations.

744.   Gravett, Chris. **Arms and Armor**. Richard Hook, Chris Rothero, and Peter Sarson, illustrators. Austin, TX: Raintree/Steck-Vaughn, 1995. 32p. $13.98. ISBN 0-8114-6190-4. (Pointers). 3-7

Two-page spreads on types of arms and armor explain their effectiveness and give historical information as well as illustrations. The periods and items covered include Early Bronze weapons (through 612 B.C.), Chinese crossbowmen (1500-500 B.C.), armies of iron (500 B.C.-A.D. 100), the age of mail armor (A.D. 300-1300), Eastern warriors (A.D. 1200-1500), medieval foot soldiers (A.D. 1300-1500), steel plates for soldiers (A.D. 1100-1600), Japanese samurai (A.D. 400-1600), muskets and powder (A.D. 1700-1900), firearms (A.D. 1800s), and today's armor made of Kevlar. Glossary and Index.

745.   Gravett, Christopher. **Knight**. Geoff Dann, photographs. New York: Knopf, 1993. 63p. $19. ISBN 0-679-83882-1. (Eyewitness). 4-8

Text and photographs give detailed information about the history of knights, the ritual of knighthood, their training, and their armor. Two-page spreads include such topics as the first knights, the Normans, armor, arms, horses, castles at war and under siege, battle, castles in peace, lords and ladies of the manor, chivalry, tournaments and jousts, foot combat, heraldry, hunting and hawking, faith and pilgrimage, the Crusades, Knights of Christ, Knights of the Rising Sun, professional knights, and the decline of chivalry by the seventeenth century. Index.

746. Gravett, Christopher. **The World of the Medieval Knight**. Brett Breckon, illustrator. New York: Peter Bedrick, 1997. 64p. $19.95. ISBN 0-87226-277-4. 5-10

Among the topics covered in double-page spreads are horses, weapons, castle life, hunting, and jousting. For each main topic, Gravett includes more specific information in subsequent pages. Glossary and Index.

747. Gray, Bettyanne. **Manya's Story**. 1978. Minneapolis, MN: Runestone Press, 1995. 128p. $14.21. ISBN 0-8225-3156-9. 7 up

Manya and her husband Israel escaped from the Russian Ukraine in 1921 and came to the United States, where they hoped to practice their Jewish faith freely. They had survived at least two pogroms in their homeland while the Bolshevik Red Army, the anti-Bolshevik White Army, and the forces fighting for Ukrainian independence battled each other. The author is the American-born daughter of the couple, and she recounts their story in memory of the many other members of her family who perished both in the pogroms and in the Holocaust.

748. Gray, Charlotte. **Bob Geldof**. Milwaukee, WI: Gareth Stevens, 1988. 68p. $16.95. ISBN 0-55532-814-8. (People Who Have Helped the World). 7-8

Bob Geldof has refused to change many of the undesirable habits he acquired in his teen years, but he has used other talents to collect money for the starving children of Ethiopia. During his final year in a Dublin high school, Geldof volunteered with the Simon Communities, where he worked with the poor, the homeless, alcoholics, and drug addicts. Bored after school, he went to England and then Canada, where he wrote music columns for a newspaper. Back in Ireland in 1975, his friends started a band called the Boomtown Rats, of which he became the lead singer and manager. Bad luck followed their good fortune in 1984, but Geldof happened to see the starving Ethiopian children on television and realized that he was fine compared to those children. He organized Band Aid—a record of top British rock stars—which earned $9 million for aid to Ethiopia. He went to Ethiopia, where he met Mother Teresa. Americans also made a record, and then Geldof organized a concert for July 13, 1985. One and a half billion people went to concerts all over the world, with the main ones being in Philadelphia and London. Phil Collins sang in both concerts by flying on the Concorde between cities. In 1985, Geldof collected $92 million for the cause. Organizations, Books, Glossary, Chronology, and Index.

749. Gray, Randal, and Christopher Argyle. **Chronicle of the First World War—Vol. I: 1914-1916**. New York: Facts on File, 1991. 420p. $45. ISBN 0-8160-2139-2. YA

To give the day-by-day events of World War I in its first two years, the text uses two-page spreads in parallel columns with the headings, "Western Front," "Eastern Front," "Southern Front," "Turkish Front," "African Operations," "Sea War," "Air War," "International Events," and "Home Fronts." Statistical tables tell of troops engaged, losses, aircraft, ships, and other pertinent information. The "Home Fronts" column helps the reader connect national events and attitudes with battles happening in other places. Glossary, Bibliography, and Index.

750. Green, Robert. **Tutankhamun**. New York: Franklin Watts, 1996. 64p. $20.95; $5.95pa. ISBN 0-531-20233-X; 0-531-15802-0pa. (First Books—Ancient Biographies). 5-7

The text looks at Howard Carter's exciting discovery of King Tut's tomb in 1922 and gives a biography of this young pharaoh (c. 1358 B.C.) culled from information about artifacts found in the tomb. It also includes a list of Internet sources with other information on King Tutankhamun. Chronology and Index.

751. Green, Roger J. **The Throttlepenny Murder**. New York: Oxford University Press, 1989. 197p. $14.95. ISBN 0-19-271601-8. 7-10

Jessie, age thirteen, works for the miser Mr. Dobson in 1885. Authorities arrest her for his death, but five other people saw the murder, though each was unaware of the others. Jessie is sentenced to hang, but after she gains a reprieve, someone else unjustly suffers for the deed. Those of a lower social or economic class may suffer because only the wealthy can afford to buy their innocence.

752. Greenberg, Judith E., and Helen Carey McKeever. **Letters from a World War II GI**. New York: Franklin Watts, 1995. 144p. $13.93. ISBN 0-531-11212-8. (In Their Own Words). 7 up

During World War II, Keith Winston sent letters to his wife that show the way one enlistee felt about the war. Because his letters were subject to censorship, he could not discuss the war itself. He shows the rumors, misinformation, and changes in orders to which enlisted personnel were subject. He gives a different view of the war and one that shows how unsettling army life could be. Photographs and drawings highlight the text. Epilogue, For Further Reading, and Index.

753. Greene, Jacqueline Dembar. **One Foot Ashore**. New York: Walker, 1994. 196p. $16.95. ISBN 0-8027-8281-7. 5-8

When she is ten in 1648, during the Portuguese Inquisition, Maria Ben Lazar and her sister Isobel (age six) are taken from their Jewish parents to Brazil, where they are made to work as slaves and learn the Catholic religion. Maria escapes in 1654 and stows away on a ship to Amsterdam, in search of her parents and her sister from whom she has been separated. In Amsterdam, the Dutch painter, Rembrandt, who lives in the Jewish quarter, keeps her in his house until she has the unexpected happiness of being reunited with her parents and later finding that her sister is in New Amsterdam. Isobel's story appears in *Out of Many Waters* (Walker, 1988).

754. Greene, Jacqueline, Dembar. **Out of Many Waters**. New York: Walker, 1988. 200p. $16.95; $8.95pa. ISBN 0-8027-6811-3; 0-8027-7401-6pa. 5-8

After being kidnapped by Portuguese Catholics during the Portuguese Inquisition in 1548, Isobel (age twelve) and Maria (age sixteen) try to escape from Brazil during 1654 by stowing away on different ships. Isobel reaches New Amsterdam rather than Amsterdam, as she had hoped and where she thinks her parents and Maria might be. After enduring storms and pirates, she becomes one of the twenty-three immigrants to be New Amsterdam's first Jewish refugees. *One Foot Ashore* (Walker, 1994) tells Maria's story. *Sydney Taylor Honor Book* and *New York Public Library Book for the Teen Age.*

755. Greene, Laura Offenhartz. **Child Labor: Then and Now**. New York: Franklin Watts, 1992. 144p. $20.60. ISBN 0-531-13008-8. (Impact). 5-10

Ever since the British, with their chimney sweeps in the 1700s, and the Industrial Revolution, with children working in factories, child labor has been a serious problem. In the early twentieth century, Lewis Hine photographed children, especially immigrants, working in the terrible conditions of mines, mills, factories, sweatshops, and farms. A change in the laws has helped the United States, but child labor still exists in countries from which America gets many goods. Engravings enhance the text. Selected Bibliography and Index.

756. Greenfeld, Howard. **The Hidden Children**. New York: Ticknor & Fields, 1993. 118p. $15.95. ISBN 0-395-66074-2. 4 up

Many children in the Holocaust lived with strangers who risked their lives to protect the children. All Jewish children learned to lie and conceal their true identities. They learned when they could laugh or cry and when they must be silent. Among the places they hid were attics, basements, haylofts, underground passages, orphanages, and convents. All lost their childhood years. For Further Reading and Index.

757. Greenfield, Howard. **Marc Chagall**. New York: Harry N. Abrams, 1990. 92p. $13.95. ISBN 0-8109-3152-4. (First Impressions). 7 up

As a boy, Marc Chagall (1887–1985) loved to draw and paint, but no one in his Russian village could teach him. He eventually convinced his family to let him go from Vitebsk to St. Petersburg in 1906 to learn about art. He eventually traveled all over the world, where he had gained prior fame through his unusual figures painted with unexpected colors. Reproductions and Index.

758. Greenfield, Howard. **Paul Gauguin**. New York: Harry N. Abrams, 1993. 92p. $13.95. ISBN 0-8109-3376-4. (First Impressions). 7 up

Born in Peru and raised in France, Paul Gauguin (1848–1903) worked as a sailor before settling in Paris to become a businessman. After he lost his job, he began painting seriously, but he could not support his family. He traveled to various places looking for the right light and color, and he finally abandoned his family and traveled to Tahiti, where he thought the light would be best. He struggled with poverty and illness for the rest of his life while he refined his original style. List of Illustrations and Index.

759. Gregory, Tony. **The Dark Ages**. New York: Facts on File, 1993. 78p. $17.95. ISBN 0-8160-2787-0. (Illustrated History of the World). 4-7

When Roman dominance ended, new cultures and tribes, such as the Anglo-Saxons, Celts, and Vikings, appeared. Charlemagne gained power in France. New empires and cultures rose to power with the Byzantines and Islam. Part of the text discusses the eastern world of the Silk Road, the Americas, the Mayan culture, and the Pacific. Beautiful illustrations highlight the text. Glossary, Further Reading, and Index.

760. Grosjean, Didier, and Claudine Roland. **Rousseau: Still Voyages**. Francine De Boeck, illustrator; John Goodman, translator. New York: Chelsea House, 1995. 60p. $14.95. ISBN 0-7910-2816-X. (Art for Children). 3-7

An eleven-year-old boy becomes interested in pictures, supposedly painted by a customs officer, that show jungles and wild animals. He begins reading a boring book and finds out that Henri Rousseau (1844-1910), called "Le Douanier," was a "Sunday" painter who had a full-time job during the week. The boy goes with his parents to Paris to investigate some of the information he discovered in the book, and their explorations reveal many interesting facts about Rousseau, his life, and the influences on his paintings. Reproductions, Glossary, and Chronology.

761.   Guittard, Charles. **The Romans: Life in the Empire**. Mary Kae LaRose, translator; Annie-Calude Martin, illustrator. Brookfield, CT: Millbrook Press, 1992. 64p. $16.40; $7.95pa. ISBN 1-56294-200-X; 0-7613-0097-Xpa. (Peoples of the Past). 5-8

The Romans constructed buildings, roads, and bridges so that they would endure; because of this, archaeologists and historians have been able to trace and reveal Roman culture. The text looks at the formation of the Roman Empire, Roman cities, the provinces, a child's life, dress, food and drink, entertainment, arts and sciences, and the Roman gods. Dates to Remember, Map, Find Out More, Glossary, and Index.

762.   Gunn, Neil. **Young Art and Old Hector**. New York: Walker, 1991. 255p. $21.95. ISBN 0-8027-1177-4. YA

· When Young Art, age eight, meets Old Hector, a neighbor, Art's family has been frustrating him too much. In this tale set in the nineteenth-century Scottish highlands, Old Hector begins to share his wisdom with Art. Although Young Art does not quite understand, he feels secure with Old Hector and honored to be allowed to stay with him. Young Art does not understand why people who have money can decide who will be allowed to fish in their streams, but he realizes that family and friends help to combat the difficulties that society imposes.

763.   Gurko, Miriam. **Theodor Herzl: The Road to Israel**. Erika Weihs, illustrator. Philadelphia, PA: Jewish Publication Society, 1988. 89p. $14.95. ISBN 0-8276-0312-6. 3-7

When he was growing up in Vienna, Theodor Herzl (1860-1904) was not particularly interested in Jewish matters, as his family was rather erratic in its practice of the religion. But he became increasingly aware of the anti-Semitic atmosphere of late-nineteenth-century Europe. The trial of Alfred Dreyfus, the Jewish army officer unjustly accused of treason in France, disturbed him. He realized that Jews needed their own homeland. His ceaseless efforts led to the foundation of the World Zionist Organization, but he sometimes neglected his own family because of his social concerns. He was unable to see a Jewish state established during his lifetime, but without his work, Israel might never have come into being. Important Dates and Index.

764.   Guzzetti, Paula. **A Family Called Brontë**. New York: Dillon Press, 1994. 128p. $13.95. ISBN 0-87518-592-4. (People in Focus). 6-9

The text looks at the lives of the Brontës—Charlotte, Emily, Anne, and Branwell—as they grew up in rural nineteenth-century England. They made tiny hand-stitched books, about the size of postage stamps, from scraps of paper and wrote in them. They spent early years caring for children, but they failed as governesses and teachers and began writing instead. In 1847, the three sisters published *Jane Eyre, Wuthering Heights*, and *Agnes Grey* under male pen names (Currer Bell, Ellis Bell, and Acton Bell) so that the novels would be more readily received in literary circles. Their lives were shadowed by tuberculosis and the failed career of their brother, who died at age thirty-one. Chronology, Bibliography, and Index.

$$\boxed{\text{H}}$$

765. Haas, Gerda. **Tracking the Holocaust**. Minneapolis, MN: Runestone Press, 1995. 176p. $22.95. ISBN 0-8225-3257-7. 5 up

When Gerda Haas's American-born children did not understand why some things that happened were important to her, Haas decided that she must recount her own youth so that her children would know what she had experienced by the age of twenty-three. She traces the stories of eight persons caught in the Holocaust, six of whom survived. The text gives a history from the beginning of Nazi rule in Germany in the 1930s. Haas covers Germany, Poland, Denmark, Norway, Holland, Belgium, Luxembourg, France, Italy, Hungary, and the Balkan countries. In most of these countries, she places one of the people and describes their experiences. Sentencing, Sources, Documentary Material, Map Citation, The Testimonies of Survivors and Victims, and Index.

766. Habsburg-Lothringen, Geza von. **Carl Fabergé**. New York: Harry N. Abrams, 1994. 92p. $19.95. ISBN 0-8109-3324-1. (First Impressions). 7 up

Peter Carl Fabergé (1846–1920) created beautiful jewelry designs for two czars in Russia. Among the works for which he is best known are the jeweled Easter eggs, many of which are on display in St. Petersburg and Moscow. A few reside in the United States (some in Richmond, Virginia). The text also includes history of the times during the reigns of Russia's last two czars. Photographs highlight the text. Index.

767. Hackl, Erich. **Farewell Sidonia**. Edna McCown, translator. New York: Fromm International, 1991. 135p. $16.95; $8.95pa. ISBN 0-88064-124-X; 0-8806-4135-5pa. YA

An infant abandoned on the steps of a hospital in 1933, Sidonia has a note attached to her saying that she needs parents. Foster parents take her, but as Hitler's hostility permeates Austria, Sidonia's darker skin reveals that she has the hated gypsy blood. Taken to the gypsy headquarters and placed on the last transport to Auschwitz, she dies there from grief, according to her brother's account years after the events.

768. Haley, Alex. **Roots**. New York: Doubleday, 1976. $25; $6.99pa. ISBN 0-385-03787-2; 0-440-17464-3pa. YA

In this book, Alex Haley traces the background of an African American whose ancestor was transported to America as a slave. He finds his African home and his position as tribal royalty. Index.

769. Halliburton, Warren. **The West Indian-American Experience**. Brookfield, CT: Millbrook Press, 1994. 64p. $16.40. ISBN 1-56294-340-5. (Coming to America). 4-8

European settlers eradicated the Arawaks, original inhabitants of the Caribbean, but traces of the culture remain. In the centuries after Columbus, many of the inhabitants died from diseases or became slaves to their conquerors. Between 1640 and 1713 more than seven slave revolts occurred in the British islands. In 1760, Tacky's Rebellion broke out in Jamaica, and in 1831 another revolt led to the abolishment of slavers in 1833. More recent inhabitants of the islands have immigrated to the United States, looking for economic opportunities. They found them, along with racial discrimination, unlike any they had experienced in the West Indies. Between 1952 and the 1960s, few islanders were admitted to the country, but after that the laws changed. More About West Indian Americans and Index.

770. Halliburton, Warren J., and Kathilyn Solomon Probosz. **Africa's Struggle for Independence**. New York: Crestwood House, 1992. 48p. $13.95. ISBN 0-89686-679-3. (Africa Today). 5-10

Africa as a continent has struggled with the slave trade and colonialism. The text examines the history of the independence movement in Africa from the European colonization of the continent to the present, with photographs to complement the text. Index.

771. Hanawalt, Barbara. **Growing up in Medieval London**. Wayne Howell, illustrator. New York: Oxford University Press, 1993. 300p. $35; $12.95pa. ISBN 0-19-508405-5; 0-19-509384-4pa. YA

Using extant information such as court documents, wills, advice manuals, and literary works, Hanawalt argues that childhood and adolescence in thirteenth- and fourteenth-century London were recognized and distinct stages in the lives of young people. She looks at birth, the establishment of social and family connections, the social and educational activities during early childhood, the broader range of connections in later childhood, and adolescence as the last stage before adulthood. She includes London orphans and their situations, apprentices and their relationships to their masters, children as they began jobs as servants, and the upper class. Bibliography and Index.

772.   Handler, Andrew, and Susan V. Meschel. **Young People Speak: Surviving the Holocaust in Hungary**. New York: Franklin Watts, 1993. 160p. $13.40. ISBN 0-531-11044-3. 6-9

Eleven Jews who survived their childhoods in Hungary during World War II tell their stories. None seemed to realize that death was a possibility, even though they lost homes, friends, and family members. One commented that injecting spinach under Hitler's skin after the war would be a good way to punish him. Another tells of a grandmother who stole his birthday candy and blamed a servant; the servant subsequently reported the grandmother to the Nazis. Photographs, Bibliography, and Index.

773.   Haney, John. **Cesare Borgia**. New York: Chelsea House, 1987. 112p. $18.95. ISBN 0-87754-595-2. (World Leaders Past and Present). 8 up

Cesare Borgia (1475–1506) embodied the dark side of the Renaissance ideal that persons who had capacity for self-development and individualism were more desirable than others. He used whatever means necessary to advance his own ends, including deceit, murder, and manipulation, and was the model for Machiavelli's *The Prince*. Born illegitimate, his father became Pope Alexander VI and appointed him archbishop. Later freed from this position to advance the family fortunes, he formed an alliance with the king of France and then began military campaigns to conquer Italy. When Cesare's father died, a hostile pope took over; after his imprisonment and escape in 1506, he died the next year in battle. Maps and reproductions enhance the text. Chronology, Further Reading, and Index.

774.   Haney, John. **Charles Stewart Parnell**. New York: Chelsea House, 1989. 112p. $18.95. ISBN 1-55546-820-9. (World Leaders Past and Present). 9 up

Charles Stewart Parnell (1846–1891) became the leader of the Irish Catholic nationalist movement between 1877 and 1890. He went to the British Parliament's House of Commons at age twenty-nine and became a formidable politician. He led a movement for the end of Ireland's oppression, and by 1885 his Home Rule party had won enough seats in the House of Commons so that a balance of power existed between the two British parties. Although Gladstone's Home Rule bill met defeat in 1886, Parnell remained an Irish leader until he was named in a divorce suit in 1890. He died a year later, distressed about the public sentiment against him, and the public lost an able statesman. Photographs and engravings enhance the text. Chronology, Further Reading, and Index.

775.   Haney, John. **Vladimir Ilich Lenin**. New York: Chelsea House, 1988. 112p. $18.95. ISBN 0-87754-570-7. (World Leaders Past and Present). 8 up

With powerful intellect and commitment to his cause, Vladimir Lenin (1870–1924) led the Russian Revolution of 1917. As a young man, he was first arrested for inciting factory workers to strike, and he spent three years in Siberian exile. He worked in the background, and in 1917 seized power from the weak provisional government that had taken over from Tsar Nicholas II. He created a socialist democracy at first, but by 1924, he had changed it to a Communist state. He was at the center of a struggle for economic and social justice. Photographs and reproductions enhance the text. Chronology, Further Reading, and Index.

776.   Hanmer, Trudy J. **Leningrad**. New York: New Discovery, 1992. 96p. $14.95. ISBN 0-02-742615-7. (Cities at War). 6-9

The Russian city of Leningrad refused to submit to the German invasion in World War II. The Germans decided to surround the city in the winter of 1941 and keep any supplies from reaching the people, in hopes of starving and freezing them into submission. For nearly three years (900 days), no fuel or food reached the people, while Nazi bombers patrolled the skies. Two million people died during the siege. Photographs, Notes, Further Reading, and Index.

777.   Hansen, Arlen J. **Gentlemen Volunteers: The Story of the American Ambulance Drivers in the Great War: August 1914-September 1918**. New York: Arcade, 1996. 254p. $27.95. ISBN 1-55970-313-X. YA

In World War I, Americans, mainly from Ivy League schools, went to Flanders to drive ambulances. There they took the "Lizzies," or ambulances, through mud and fire while they transported the wounded. Although most of them returned, their experiences gave them a sense of comaraderie that they could not retain at home. Index.

778.   Hansen, Joyce. **The Captive**. New York: Scholastic, 1994. 195p. $13.95; $3.50pa. ISBN 0-590-41625-1; 0-590-41624-3pa. 5-8

Slavers capture Kofi, 12, when a family servant betrays him, and take him from his African home to America in 1788. There he works for a New England family of somber Puritans. Then he meets Paul Cuffe, an African American shipbuilder who wants to take Africans back to their homeland. He becomes a first mate on Cuffe's ship, which gives him a chance to go home. *Coretta Scott King Honor* and *Notable Children's Trade Books in the Field of Social Studies*.

779. Harbor, Bernard. **The Breakup of the Soviet Union: Opposing Viewpoints**. San Diego, CA: Greenhaven, 1994. 264p. $19.95. ISBN 1-56510-068-9. (Opposing Viewpoints). YA

The text looks at the breakup of the Soviet Union in 1990. Different and opposing views exist as to the reasons. The questions argued are why it happened, how it will affect the world, how the United States should respond, what policies would strengthen the new republics' economies, and what measures would reduce ethnic conflict in the republics. For Further Discussion, Bibliography, and Index.

780. Harbor, Bernard. **Conflict in Eastern Europe**. New York: New Discovery, 1993. 48p. $13.95. ISBN 0-02-742626-2. (Conflicts). 6-9

The text looks at the revolutions that occurred in Eastern Europe in 1989, after which communism fell. Included is information about the fall of the Berlin Wall; the role of Gorbachev; the death of Romania's Ceauescu; and the changes in Czechoslovakia, Hungary, Poland, and Albania. Economics and privatization, ethnic conflicts, the differences between East and West, and religion all come into the discussion. Glossary, Further Information, and Index.

781. Harding, Paul. **Red Slayer: Being the Second of the Sorrowful Mysteries of Brother Athelstan**. New York: Morrow, 1994. 238p. $20. ISBN 0-688-12569-7. YA

In a prologue dated June 1362, Janissaries come aboard a vessel and seemingly kill all those aboard. However, the fate of a knight and an orphan boy for whom he is caring is not revealed. The story proper begins during December of 1377 in London, when Brother Athelstan and his helper, Cranston, are attempting to solve the murder of the nasty Constable of the Tower of London and two of his Crusader colleagues. They succeed, and the prologue closely relates to the ending.

782. Hargrove, Jim. **Ferdinand Magellan**. Chicago: Childrens Press, 1989. 128p. $23.93. ISBN 0-516-03051-5. (World's Great Explorers). 8 up

The text looks at the world before Ferdinand Magellan (1480?–1521) made his voyage during the Age of Discovery. As he crossed the Atlantic after departing Spain in 1519, he had a variety of troubles, but he did find a passage between the Atlantic and Pacific Oceans, which became known as the Strait of Magellan. The text continues with Magellan's arrival in the Philippines, his death, and the completion of the voyage after he died. The remaining ship from his convoy arrived in Spain with enough spices to pay for the entire expedition. Appendices, Maps, Timeline, Glossary, Bibliography, and Index.

783. Hargrove, Jim. **Pablo Casals: Cellist of Conscience**. Chicago: Childrens Press, 1991. 127p. $19.30; $5.95pa. ISBN 0-516-03272-0; 0-516-43272-9pa. (People of Distinction). 6-9

Pablo Casals (1876-1973) became an extraordinary cellist during his life, playing around the world. The text looks at his childhood, after his birth in Catalonia; his struggle to take music lessons; his subsequent fame; the difficulties of war in Spain and World War II, which shattered the dreams of so many; and his exile from Spain during the rise of Franco. Quotes from Casals help to validate the information. Photographs, Notes, and Index.

784. Hargrove, Jim. **René-Robert Cavelier Sieur de La Salle**. Chicago: Childrens Press, 1990. 128p. $17.95. ISBN 0-516-03054-X. (World's Great Explorers). 4-8

La Salle (1643-1687) traveled along the Illinois River to the mouth of the Mississippi River during winter, when he had to carry his canoes along the frozen water rather than ride in them. He planned to follow all 4,300 miles of the river, building forts for the French soldiers. He acquired for France and Louis XIV all of the land that France later sold to Thomas Jefferson in the Louisiana Purchase. Timeline, Glossary, Bibliography, and Index.

785. Harnett, Cynthia, author/illustrator. **The Cargo of the Madalena**. 1959. Minneapolis, MN: Lerner, 1984. 236p. $13.50. ISBN 0-8225-0890-7. 5 up

In 1482, William Caxton brings the printing press to England and hires Bendy to help him produce a manuscript of King Arthur's tales. Because scribes will lose their jobs to this machine, which prints a hundred copies to their one, they plot to keep away from Caxton the one thing he needs. Bendy discovers that his brothers, both scriveners, have hidden Caxton's paper, which disappeared from the cargo of the *Madalena*. Oddly, Bendy's father, also a scrivener, looks forward to the progress signaled by the printing press and disapproves of his sons' deceit because it also supports the Red Rose Henry Tudor's plan to dethrone Edward IV. *Carnegie Commendation*.

786. Harnett, Cynthia, author/illustrator. **The Great House**. 1949. Minneapolis, MN: Lerner, 1984. 180p. $9.95. ISBN 0-8225-0893-1. 5 up

Geoffrey's father, a friend of Sir Christopher Wren in London, moves Geoffrey and his sister Barbara to the country in 1690. Although Elizabeth is happy that the country client has a daughter, no one will let them play together, though they meet by accident. Geoffrey thinks that the house should be repositioned to overlook the river, and the adults eventually realize that he has the best idea. The client decides to send Geoffrey to Oxford.

787.   Harnett, Cynthia, author /illustrator. **The Merchant's Mark**. 1951. Minneapolis, MN: Lerner, 1984. 192p. $9.95. ISBN 0-8225-0891-5. 5 up

Nicholas, age fifteen, trains to take over the Fetterlock wool business from his father. In 1493, their wool has a high reputation with foreign buyers. At the same time, he has to plan for his arranged marriage to Cecily, a girl whom he has never met. When they meet, they fortunately become friends, and they help to stop the distribution of mysterious inferior wool with the Fetterlock mark on it. *Carnegie Medal.*

788.   Harnett, Cynthia, author/illustrator. **The Sign of the Green Falcon**. 1953. Minneapolis, MN: Lerner, 1984. 219p. $9.95. ISBN 0-8225-0888-5. 5 up

In 1415, Dickon finds out that he will be apprenticed to his godfather, Richard Whittington, a London mercer. He knows that it is a great honor, but he wanted to be a grocer like his father and brother. He and his other brother find themselves involved with the Lollards in a plot against Henry V when other mercer apprentices trap them. Because they are honest and Adam tries to help others at Agincourt, the two escape charges.

789.   Harnett, Cynthia, author/illustrator. **Stars of Fortune**. 1956. Minneapolis, MN: Lerner, 1984. 288p. $9.95. ISBN 0-8225-0892-3. 5 up

Four of the Washington children in Sulgrave Manor become involved in a plot to help the young Princess Elizabeth flee from England to Italy. She lives nearby in Woodstock, held prisoner by her elder sister, Mary Tudor. A subplot reveals how the priests survived while Henry VIII tried to annihilate all of the Catholics and their property. Fortunately, Elizabeth did not escape; if she had, she probably would have lost her chance at the throne.

790.   Harnett, Cynthia. **The Writing on the Hearth**. Gareth Floyd, illustrator. 1971. Minneapolis, MN: Lerner, 1984. 300p. $13.50. ISBN 0-8225-0889-3. 5 up

Stephen and his sister, Lys, are orphans who live with their stepfather in rural England during the fifteenth century. Because Stephen's father died in service to the earl, Stephen will be allowed to learn to read and write. If he does well, he might even be sent to Oxford for study. One day during a storm, Stephen takes shelter with Meg, a woman some people accuse of being a witch. Meg has a visitor, and when Stephen listens to the conversation, he begins to think the rumors are true. After encountering a series of problems, including the plague in London, Henry VI's accusations, and William Caxton's concerns, Stephen realizes that he has made a mistake. His honesty gains him the position at Oxford that he so badly wants.

791.   Harpur, James, and Elizabeth M. Hallam. **Revelations: The Medieval World**. New York: Henry Holt, 1995. 120p. $35. ISBN 0-8050-4140-0. YA

The text surveys history from the end of the western Roman Empire, with the fall of Rome, to the beginning of the Age of Exploration in Europe. The four sections cover castles, nobles, and knights; urban decline and increased commerce in the eleventh century; the 80 cathedrals and 500 churches built between 1050 and 1400; and warfare. Present-day towns and places such as Dover Castle, Constantinople, and Florence are pictured in fold-overs that show them now and during medieval times. Additional information on topics such as courtly love, St. Francis of Assisi, and El Cid also appear. Bibliography and Index. *School Library Journal Best Adult Books for Young Adults.*

792.   Harris, Christie. **Raven's Cry**. Bill Reid, illustrator. 1966. Seattle, WA: University of Washington Press, 1992. 193p. $14.95pa. ISBN 0-295-97221-1pa. 5-10

When the white men find the Haida people in 1775, they take the sea otter that is the Haidas' livelihood. In addition to greed, the hunters bring smallpox, consumption, death, and vile treatment. By 1884, only 600 of the tribe remained, having suffered horribly at the hands of these outsiders who destroyed their culture and defiled their religion.

793.   Harris, Geraldine. **Ancient Egypt**. New York: Facts on File, 1990. 96p. $17.95. ISBN 0-8160-1971-1. (Cultural Atlas for Young People). 6-9

This oversize book groups its topics into two segments, one on Egypt before the pharaohs and one going down the Nile. Illustrations augment the history with cartouches of pharaoh's names, human forms of Egyptian deities, maps, and photographs. The text concentrates on archaeological information gleaned from ancient Egyptian sites in Karnak and Abu Simbel. It discusses mummy preparation, the construction of the pyramids, and many other topics that reveal the lives of the ancient Egyptians. Chronology, Glossary, Gazetteer, and Index.

794.   Harris, Jacqueline L. **Science in Ancient Rome**. New York: Franklin Watts, 1988. 72p. $16.10. ISBN 0-531-10595-4. (First Book). 5-8

An introduction to ancient Rome and its science precedes chapters on different developments from this culture. Subjects include Roman builders of arches, concrete, and homes; Roman miners of brass and gold;

Roman physicians; public health through sewers and aqueducts; the Roman calendar; and contemporary debt to the culture for its discoveries. Photographs supplement the text. Glossary, Further Reading, and Index.

795. Harris, Nathaniel. **Mummies: A Very Peculiar History**. David Salariya, illustrator. New York: Franklin Watts, 1995. 48p. $21.40; $5.95pa. ISBN 0-531-14354-6; 0-531-15271-5pa. (Very Peculiar History). 4-8

Drawings and text tell the story of mummies, from Egyptian times to the present, in two-page spreads. Using the definition of *mummy* as a corpse that has been preserved to keep it from decaying, the text notes that preservation may be either planned or a fluke of nature. The mummies here include Egyptians, English sailors, Danes, Inuits, Incas, Scythians, Sicilians, a Chinese court lady, and an Alpine traveler. Oliver Cromwell, Lord Nelson, Jeremy Bentham, Eva Perón, and Lenin are some of the famous figures whose bodies or body parts have been kept for posterity. Glossary and Index.

796. Harris, Robert. **Enigma**. New York: Random House, 1995. 320p. $23. ISBN 0-679-42887-9. YA

In 1943, mathematicians and cryptologists gather in England's Bletchley Park, where they begin trying to decode a German cipher that has stymied both British and American intelligence. Tom Jericho, after a nervous breakdown and a wrecked romance, is still the best code-breaker, and the group needs his mastery if they are to have any possibility of succeeding. Jericho still hopes to patch up his romance, but the woman he loves may have passed classified information to the enemy. Jericho must work to meet his professional and personal challenges. *School Library Journal Best Adult Books for Young Adults*.

797. Harrison, Ray. **Patently Murder**. New York: St Martin's Press, 1992. 255p. $18.95. ISBN 0-312-07058-6. YA

When Catherine Marsden decides to give a girl sitting in a London doorway some money, she finds that the girl is dead. Catherine, a newspaper reporter in 1890, and her police friends try to solve the murder. Their investigation leads them to connect the girl, a child prostitute, with another recent murder.

798. Hart, George. **Ancient Egypt**. New York: Knopf, 1990. 64p. $19. ISBN 0-679-90742-X. (Eyewitness Books). 4-7

Although very "busy," with from two to ten carefully labeled photographs on each page and some general text, Hart's book covers many topics. The contents include Egypt before the pharaohs, practices in life and after-life, gods and goddesses, religion, writing, war, the Nile, various trades, daily habits, leisure activities, and a brief look at Egypt after the pharaohs. Index.

799. Hartenian, Larry. **Benito Mussolini**. New York: Chelsea House, 1988. 112p. $18.95. ISBN 0-87754-572-3. (World Leaders Past and Present.) 8 up

Benito Mussolini (1883–1945) ruled Italy from 1922 to 1943 as its fascist leader, crushing any who opposed him. He took whatever view was most advantageous, from socialist to nationalist, imperialist, and beneficiary of the wealthy. He later had his black-shirted thugs assault socialists, striking workers, and offices of opposition newspapers. He became an absolute dictator in 1925, with the Italian parliament's approval. He joined Hitler in starting World War II even though Italy was not ready to fight a major war. After he was deposed, he was captured and shot, and his body was displayed upside down in a public square. Photographs enhance the text. Chronology, Further Reading, and Index.

800. Härtling, Peter. **Crutches**. New York: Lothrop, Lee & Shepard, 1988. 163p. $12. ISBN 0-688-07991-1. 5-8

Thomas, age twelve, becomes separated from his mother on a transport from Koln, Germany, to Vienna, Austria. After he discovers that his aunt is gone and her house has been bombed, he attaches himself to a one-legged man on crutches, who stays with him until they locate his mother. The man tries to avoid relationships, but he begins to care about Thomas and does not want to tell him when the Red Cross locates Thomas's mother. The man's integrity, his growing love for Thomas, and his concern for Thomas's well-being, however, force him to take Thomas back to Germany. *Mildred L. Batchelder Award* and *American Library Association Notable Books for Children*.

801. Hartman, Evert. **War Without Friends**. Patricia Crampton, translator. New York: Crown, 1982. 218p. $10.95. ISBN 0-517-54754-6. 7-10

Arnold Westervoort, age fifteen, lives in Holland with his family while the Germans occupy it. He is a fanatical Hitler supporter who bullies everyone, including his family. When schoolmates mock him, the girl he likes spurns him, and others accuse him of being a spy and an informer, he begins to understand that he must think independently.

802. Haskins, James. **Corazon Aquino: Leader of the Philippines**. Springfield, NJ: Enslow, 1988. 127p. $17.95. ISBN 0-89490-152-4. (Contemporary Women). 7-10

The text looks at the life and unexpected political career of Corazon Aquino (b. 1933) during her rise to become president of the Philippines. Her husband was first imprisoned for his activities and then the victim of severe heart trouble. They went to America for health care, and while they were there, Marcos exiled him. When Aquino returned to the Philippines, he was assassinated, and his wife Corazon replaced him as the presidential candidate, winning the election. Index.

803. Haskins, James. **India under Indira and Rajiv Gandhi**. Hillside, NJ: Enslow, 1989. 104p. $15.95. ISBN 0-89490-146-X. 7-10

Beginning with detail about the lives of Mohandas Gandhi and Jawaharlal Nehru, this text clarifies why Nehru's daughter would have become the choice for prime minister of India. Because the book covers Indian politics only to 1987, it does not tell about Rajiv's subsequent leadership or assassination. Bibliography and Index.

804. Haslam, Andrew, and Alexandra Parsons. **Ancient Egypt**. New York: Thomson Learning, 1995. 64p. $18.95. ISBN 1-56847-140-8. (Make It Work!). 3-7

The text presents information on ancient Egypt interspersed with suggestions about creating various projects, from clothing to dioramas to food. Topics include clothes, landscape, beliefs, artwork, boats, and pyramids. Glossary and Index.

805. Haugaard, Erik. **The Boy and the Samurai**. Boston: Houghton Mifflin, 1991. 221p. $14.95. ISBN 0-395-56398-4. 6-9

The orphan Saru, or "monkey," is both homeless and friendless, surviving by begging and living near a temple shrine. Saru becomes friends with a kind samurai and helps him rescue his wife from the warlord's castle in sixteenth-century Japan. His plan saves the three of them plus a priest who has acted as his mentor. Saru realizes that he must always tell the truth, because it will keep him free. *Parents' Choice*.

806. Haugaard, Erik. **A Boy's Will**. 1983. Boston: Houghton Mifflin, 1990. 41p. $5.95pa. ISBN 0-395-54962-0pa. 4-7

When Patrick overhears a British navy captain say that he plans to capture John Paul Jones off the southern coast of Ireland in 1779, he goes to Skellig Michael, an island that St. Patrick made famous. From the island, Patrick sails to meet Jones and warn him of the plot.

807. Haugaard, Erik. **Chase Me, Catch Nobody**. Boston: Houghton Mifflin, 1980. 209p. $7.95. ISBN 0-395-29208-5. 6-9

Erik, age fourteen, goes with a school group from Denmark to Germany during his spring vacation in 1937. When a man asks Erik to take a package off the ferry for him, Erik agrees, but realizes that he must also deliver the package when the Gestapo meet the man and escort him from the ferry. After Erik delivers the passports in the package, he becomes involved in helping a Jewish girl get to Denmark after hiding in an attic for a year. Before any of the plot resolves, Erik and his one friend have to escape on a leaky little boat.

808. Haugaard, Erik. **Cromwell's Boy**. 1978. Boston: Houghton Mifflin, 1990. 214p. $7.96pa. ISBN 0-395-54975-2pa. 7 up

As he rides through Boston one night in 1686 to encourage his friends to curtail King James's power in the colonies, Oliver remembers his service under the Oliver Cromwell of England during the English Civil War. At that time he also rode one night so that he would not be caught as a spy. He knows that despots of any kind in any country should not be tolerated.

809. Haugaard, Erik. **The Little Fishes**. Milton Johnson, illustrator. Magnolia, MA: Peter Smith, 1967. 214p. $17.80. ISBN 0-8446-6245-3. 7 up

Guido, age twelve, lives by begging and stealing during World War II in Italy after his mother dies. He and two others leave Naples to find food elsewhere, but the adults they meet are in the same condition. He attempts to help others, including a woman desperate for food to feed her newborn child. *Jane Addams Book Award, Boston Globe-Horn Book Award, New York Herald Tribune Award*, and *Danish Cultural Ministries Award*.

810. Haugaard, Erik. **A Messenger for Parliament**. Boston: Houghton Mifflin, 1976. 218p. $6.95. ISBN 0-395-24392-0. 6-9

Oliver, named for Oliver Cromwell when he was only a plowman in 1630, spends time with his father as a camp follower of the Parliamentary Army after his mother dies in 1641. Oliver meets a variety of people and becomes a messenger for Cromwell himself during the English civil war. Oliver tells this story as an old man who has lived in America for many years.

811. Haugaard, Erik. **The Revenge of the Forty-Seven Samurai**. Boston: Houghton Mifflin, 1995. 240p. $14.95. ISBN 0-395-70809-5. 6-9

Jiro, a lowly servant in a deceased samurai's household during the fourteenth year of Genroku (1701) under the shogun Tokugawa Tsunayoshi, observes the plans for revenge against Lord Kira, the man whose demands on Lord Asano caused him to commit ritual suicide. Jiro assists in preparing for the final fight against Lord Kira, although he wonders why the samurai retainers want to sacrifice themselves. Because he is not a samurai, he can question their values and be glad that he does not have to make a life-and-death decision on such a seemingly insignificant point. *American Library Association Notable Books for Children* and *American Library Association Notable Books for Young Adults.*

812. Haugaard, Erik. **The Rider and His Horse**. Leo Dillon and Diane Dillon, illustrators. Boston: Houghton Mifflin, 1968. 243p. $3.95. ISBN 0-395-06801-0. 7 up

Eleasar ben Ya'ir and the Zealots die at Masada rather than submit to the Romans. David ben Joseph tells the story because the historian Joseph ben Matthias, a Jew, has taken the side of the Romans in his rendition of the event. David goes to Masada and promises Eleasar that he will not commit suicide there, but will stay alive to tell the real details. After the battle, David meets with the other historian, who has changed his name to Josephus, to give him the true record. *Phoenix Award.*

813. Haugaard, Erik. **The Samurai's Tale**. Boston: Houghton Mifflin, 1984. 256p. $14.95; $5.95pa. ISBN 0-395-34559-6; 0-395-54970-1pa. 7-10

As he reflects on his past, Taro remembers his life in Japan around 1550 when he served his master, Lord Akiyama, as a servant's servant, a stable boy, a secret messenger, and finally as a samurai. After he learned to write, he sent a servant with his love poems to a nobleman's daughter with whom he had fallen in love. He and the girl had to escape the enemy by disguising themselves. *American Library Association Notable Children's Book.*

814. Haugaard, Erik. **A Slave's Tale**. Keith Eros, illustrator. Boston: Houghton Mifflin, 1965. 217p. $7.95. ISBN 0-395-06804-5. 8 up

When Hakon gives her freedom, Helga wants to do everything she can, including stowing away on a ship bound for Frankland in 997. After the ship arrives, and she disembarks with the others, they sustain a vicious attack. Only four of the men survive, and they do so under the care of priests who practice a new religion. This religion interests Helga and she begins to investigate its advantages.

815. Hautzig, Esther. **The Endless Steppe: A Girl in Exile**. 1968. New York: HarperCollins, 1995. 243p. $4.50pa. ISBN 0-06-440577-Xpa. 7 up

Esther, age ten, lives in Vilna, Poland, in 1941. But Russians arrive and deport her family to Siberia because they have been capitalists. She lives in desolation with her parents and her grandmother, who must work in either the field or the mine. Esther goes to school, works at home, and does little jobs for a crust of bread to eat. They have to survive in Siberia for five years before they can find a way out of their predicament. *American Library Association Notable Children's Books, Boston Globe-Horn Book Honor Book, Jane Addams Award, Sydney Taylor Book Award, New York Times Outstanding Children's Books, Horn Book Fanfare, Lewis Carroll Shelf Award, National Book Award for Children's Literature Nominee,* and *Deutsche Jugendliteraturpreis "Honorable List."*

816. Hautzig, Esther. **Riches**. Donna Diamond, illustrator. New York: HarperCollins, 1992. 44p. $14. ISBN 0-06-022260-3. 4-8

When a couple from a small European town retire from their hard work, in the nineteenth century, the husband asks a rabbi what to do in his leisure time. The rabbi suggests that he drive a cart around the countryside for three months while his wife stays at home studying as she wants. After he does, he realizes that many things in life are more important than material objects. *Notable Children's Trade Books in the Field of Social Studies* and *Jewish Book Award Finalist.*

817. Hawes, Charles Boardman. **The Dark Frigate**. 1924. Boston: Little, Brown, 1971. 264p. $19.95; $6.95pa. ISBN 0-316-35096-6; 0-316-35009-5pa. 7 up

Philip Marsham, an orphan in seventeenth-century England, has to flee London after an accident for which he is blamed. He signs up to sail on the *Rose of Devon*, a frigate leaving for Newfoundland. The ship rescues a group of men from a shipwreck, but they make the crew accompany them on their pirate expeditions. Philip becomes an outlaw and knows that he can only face a hangman when he returns to England. *Newbery Medal.*

818.   Hayner, Linda K. **The Foundling**. Charleston, SC: Bob Jones University Press, 1997. 341p. $9.95pa. ISBN 0-89084-941-2pa. 7 up

In 1644, a destitute mother abandons her child in front of a London church. A constable finds him and places him in a caring foster home, and when he grows up, he becomes an ironmonger. At the same time, Cromwell and the Parliamentarians are fighting the Royalists in the English Civil War.

819.   Haythornthwaite, Philip J. **The Napoleonic Source Book**. New York: Facts on File, 1991. 414p. $40. ISBN 0-8160-2547-9. YA

For students of Napoleon, this handbook includes military and naval armament, uniform color, forces, disciplines, and much other information on the sixty kingdoms, duchies, republics, or countries that fought in the Napoleonic wars between 1791 and 1815. Other sections highlight campaigns, beginning with the French Revolution; biographies; and "Miscellanea." Illustrations, Glossary, Chapter Bibliographies, Bibliography, and Index.

820.   Hazell, Rebecca, author/illustrator. **Heroes: Great Men Through the Ages**. New York: Abbeville, 1997. 80p. $19.95. ISBN 0-7892-0289-1. 5-8

In this collective biography, Hazell chooses twelve men whose contributions to society made changes in politics, art, or daily life. Among the men she includes are Mohandas Gandhi (1869-1948), Indian leader; Mansa Kankan Musa, a Muslim leader in West Africa during the 1300s; Leonardo da Vinci (1452-1519), Renaissance artist; William Shakespeare (1564-1616), Elizabethan dramatist; and Jorge Luis Borges (1899-1986), Argentinian author. Further Reading.

821.   Hazell, Rebecca, author/illustrator. **Heroines: Great Women Through the Ages**. New York: Abbeville, 1996. 79p. $19.95. ISBN 0-7892-0289-1. 5-8

The text covers twelve women from ancient Greece to contemporary times. Additional to the information about each life are backgrounds on the culture and times in which these heroines lived. Among those included are Lady Murasaki Shikibu (c. 973-c. 1025), Sacagawea (c. 1787-1812), Agnodice of ancient Greece (3rd century BC), Anna Akhmatova (1888-1966), Madame Sun Yat-Sen (1893-1931), Frida Kahlo (1907-1954), Eleanor of Aquitaine (1122-1202), Joan of Arc (c. 1412-1431), Queen Elizabeth I (1533-1603), Harriet Tubman (c. 1820-1913), Marie Curie (1867-1934), and Amelia Earhart (1897-1937). Further Reading.

822.   Head, Judith. **Culebra Cut**. Minneapolis, MN: Carolrhoda, 1995. 153p. $14.96. ISBN 0-87614-878-X. (Adventures in Time). 4-7

William, age eleven, lives in Panama with his father, a physician, during 1911, when workers are constructing the Panama Canal. He learns as much as possible about the canal and loves living close to it, so that he can visit the most difficult portion of the project, Culebra Cut. He gets a friend, Victoria, however, who gives him a different perspective on the canal. He learns about the jungle and a Jamaican healer, and sees the work of a racist bully, Bud. More About the Panama Canal.

823.   Heater, Derek. **The Cold War**. New York: Bookwright Press, Franklin Watts, 1989. 63p. $12.90. ISBN 0-531-18275-4. (Witness History). 7 up

Short chapters present different aspects of the Cold War, which followed World War II between the western capitalist and eastern socialist countries. Brief biographies of leading figures and quotes further the information. Heater believes that the Cold War began with the Bolshevik Revolution in 1917. Maps and other illustrations enhance the text. Bibliography, Chronology, Glossary, and Index.

824.   Heaven, Constance. **The Craven Legacy**. New York: Putnam, 1986. 328p. $18.95. ISBN 0-399-13235-X. YA

In the 1800s, after authorities arrest Della's father for a murder he did not commit, Della moves from London to the Yorkshire Dales to live with her father's family. She begins teaching, and she finds out the family secrets. Soon she also falls in love with a married mill owner whose wife deserts him regularly to spend weeks in London. Eventually her father proves his innocence, and the mill owner's wife dies in London, giving Della the possibility of happiness.

825.   Heaven, Constance. **The Raging Fire**. New York: Putnam, 1987. 503p. $19.95. ISBN 0-399-13395-X. YA

In 1915, Galina studies at the university under a nonpracticing English doctor in St. Petersburg, Russia. The doctor helps one of Galina's fellow revolutionaries, and she falls in love with him. During the Russian transition to a Bolshevik regime, a fanatic who loves Galina follows her; as she waits to escape from the newly formed Soviet Union, this man gains a position that allows him to control her future.

826. Heaven, Constance. **The Wind from the Sea**. New York: St. Martin's Press, 1993. 502p. $23.95. ISBN 0-312-08921-X. YA

Isabelle and her brother, Guy, escape from France to England in 1793 during the unrest following the French Revolution. They live with their mother's brother while Guy becomes involved in raids to France. Isabelle meets and decides to marry Robert, who also does secret work. After the war ends, she and Robert go to St. Petersburg, Russia, to represent the English government.

827. Hendry, Diana. **Double Vision**. Cambridge, MA: Candlewick, 1993. 271p. $14.95. ISBN 1-56402-125-4. 9 up

Eliza, age fifteen, wants to be either sophisticated like her friend Jo or romantic like her older sister Rosa, in England during the early 1950s. She falls in love with an older boarder, Jake, at Jo's house, although she is also dating a boy her own age. After Jake leaves for Ecuador, Rosa marries, and Jo becomes pregnant and also marries. Jake sends Eliza a gift, and she realizes that she must establish her own life without wanting to be like the others.

828. Hendry, Frances. **Quest for a Kelpie**. New York: Holiday House, 1988. 153p. $12.95. ISBN 0-8234-0680-6. 7-10

In 1743, Jean, age eleven, becomes caught in the struggle between Prince Charlie's Highland rebels and William of Cumberland. For the next four years, she helps her people and the Gypsies by riding through the forest on a huge horse, a *kelpie*, on which Prince Charlie can later escape another of Cumberland's vicious attacks. When Jeannie tells her story, she is a great-great-grandmother remembering her youth and the pain of British hostility.

829. Hendry, Frances Mary. **Quest for a Maid**. New York: Farrar, Straus & Giroux, 1992. 273p. $14.95; $4.95pa. ISBN 0-374-36162-2; 0-374-46155-4pa. 5 up

Meg, age nine, thinks that her sister killed King Alexander of Scotland with witchcraft to help a woman who wanted to claim the throne for her son. As a helper in the home of Sir Patrick Spens in the thirteenth century, Meg gets to accompany Sir Spens to Norway to return with Margaret, the rightful heir to the throne. Meg discovers that her sister should not be accused of this crime because she did not commit it. *Bulletin Blue Ribbon Book* and *American Library Association Notable Books for Children*.

830. Heneghan, James. **Wish Me Luck**. New York: Farrar, Straus & Giroux, 1997. 196p. $16. ISBN 0-374-38453-3. 5-8

Jamie Monaghan wonders about his new classmate, Tom Bleeker, instead of being concerned for the German bombs that might fall on Liverpool. When the bombing begins, however, he has to leave home for Canada on the *City of Benares*. Bleeker and his sister are also on the ship, and when torpedos cause it to begin sinking in the mid-Atlantic, Bleeker saves the wounded Jamie and his sister. Bleeker is swept away in the water, and Jamie thinks he is dead, although he knows that Bleeker is resilient. Bleeker does survive, and they become friends involved in several adventures.

831. Herman, George. **The Tears of the Madonna**. New York: Carroll & Graf, 1996. 288p. $22.95. ISBN 0-7867-0243-5. YA

In Mantua during 1499, Leonardo da Vinci paints the portrait of Isabella d'Este, Marquesa of Mantua. When someone beheads a courier and a priceless diamond necklace disappears, Leonardo and his helper, the dwarf Niccolo, must use their intelligence and knowledge of the human body to find the criminal. Lucretia Borgia in Rome, Isabella, and Caterina Sforza in Imola all appear in public wearing the necklace after the murder. They must decide if counterfeit copies exist as well.

832. Hernandez, Xavier. **San Rafael: A Central American City Through the Ages**. Jordi Ballonga and Josep Escoffet, illustrators. Boston: Houghton Mifflin, 1992. 61p. $14.95. ISBN 0-395-60645-4. 7-12

This book details the history of the city of San Rafael from its rise from the land as a Mayan agricultural and religious center, through the Spanish American colonial age, to the present. Although the city is fictional, its history gives an excellent view of what one would expect a city between Mexico's Yucatan Peninsula and Guatemala's Sierra de las Minas to be. The detailed drawings show how the city would have grown and changed. Index.

833. Hernandez, Xavier, and Jordi Ballonga. **Lebek: A City of Northern Europe Through the Ages**. Kathleen Leverich, translator; Francesco Corni, illustrator. Boston: Houghton Mifflin, 1991. 64p. $14.95. ISBN 0-395-57442-0. 7-12

The fictional Lebek, a Hanseatic city based on a combination of northern European cities such as Hamburg, Amsterdam, and Lubeck, earned its wealth from the economic league of ship traders. Its development, beginning in 1000 B.C. as a timbered village on a North Sea island, covers fourteen stages, each introduced by a double-page spread followed by another with details of economic and political history at the time. Included is background as to the choice of locale, the environmental resources available, and the needs of the society as it grew and changed the town. In the current city, evolved through the centuries, dikes and canals protect the people and their possessions. Index.

834. Hernandez, Xavier, and Pilar Comes. **Barmi: A Mediterranean City Through the Ages**. Jordi Ballonga, illustrator. Boston: Houghton Mifflin, 1990. Unpaged. $14.95. ISBN 0-395-54227-8. 7-12

Although not a real city, the history of Barmi illustrates how cities begin, grow, and change through the centuries. Farmers and herders were on the land in the fourth century B.C. Then, in the second century B.C., a Roman legionary camp arrived; from it, a large Roman city had evolved by the fourth century A.D. The age of the barbarians in the sixth century A.D. led to feudalism in the eleventh century, which continued through the thirteenth century. Commercial expansion in the mid-fifteenth century changed the city again, and the sixteenth-century Renaissance city became the seventeenth-century fortified city. By the mid-eighteenth century, factories had been built, and more factories appeared by the mid-nineteenth century. Expansion and urban growth continued the commercial and industrial base of the twentieth century. Drawings.

835. Hersom, Kathleen. **The Half Child**. New York: Simon & Schuster, 1991. 176p. $13.95. ISBN 0-671-74225-6. 5-9

Lucy, age ten, has a flashback to 1650, when her four-year-old sister disappeared in the moors near Durham, England, after the birth of another child. Sarah seemed to be dim-witted, and the family thought she was a changeling who would return to the fairies one day. Lucy kept searching for her sister, knowing that Sarah understood the hostility toward her. Lucy says that she married the man who found Sarah and placed her in a foster home during the difficult times of the English civil war and Cromwell's cause.

836. Hess, Donna Lynn. **In Search of Honor**. Greenville, SC: Bob Jones University, 1991. 153p. $6.49pa. ISBN 0-89084-595-6pa. 9 up

When Jacques Chenier's father wants to give his wife a gift in 1787, he poaches a pigeon outside Paris. Jacques watches the warden murder his father for the deed. Afterward, Jacques continues to make sculptures of stone and wax until he is captured for helping a friend collect money that is rightfully his. After Jacques escapes from the Bastille, he takes part in the French Revolution with Danton and Robespierre. The Bastille's oldest prisoner is his friend, and through this man he begins to realize that inner peace makes life worthwhile.

837. Hesse, Karen. **Letters from Rifka**. New York: Henry Holt, 1992. 148p. $14.95. ISBN 0-8050-1964-2. New York: Puffin, 1993. 148p. $3.99pa. ISBN 0-14-036391-2pa. 5-9

Rifka, age twelve in 1919, flees Russia with her family to escape the Jewish pogroms. She carries with her a beloved volume of poetry by Alexander Pushkin. In the book, she writes letters to her cousin, Tovah, to tell about her experiences on the journey. Rifka has to endure the humiliation of doctors' examinations, typhus, ringworm treatment in Belgium (during which she loses her hair), and being detained at Ellis Island because of her baldness. Her ability to speak other languages allows her to help a young Russian peasant (her enemy) and an orphaned Polish baby at Ellis Island.

838. Heuck, Sigrid. **The Hideout**. Rika Lesser, translator. New York: Dutton, 1988. 183p. $5pa. ISBN 0-525-44343-6pa. 4-7

An old woman finds Rebecca, age nine, in a bombed air raid shelter during 1944, but Rebecca does not remember her own identity. The woman registers her with a Missing Persons Bureau and sends her to an orphanage. There she makes friends with a boy hiding in a nearby cornfield, and he tells her fantastic stories. When she hears an enemy air raid, she suddenly remembers her name, and at the end of the war, she is able to reunite with her parents.

839. Heyck, Denis Lynn Daly. **Life Stories of the Nicaraguan Revolution**. New York: Routledge, 1990. 355p. $16.95pa. ISBN 0-415-90211-8pa. YA

Nicaraguan history began in 1520 when the Spanish pushed south from Mexico to conquer Central America and founded (in 1524) the colonial cities of León and Granada. The country was autonomous from 1838 until 1855, when an American adventurer, William Walker, declared himself president and ruled for two years until he was deposed. However, with his arrival, American infiltration of the country began. Somoza, as head of an American-supported National Guard, became the ruler in 1936 and began the corruption that did not end until 1979, although he was assassinated in 1956. His guard ruled by intimidation, extortion, torture, and murder. From owning one pathetic coffee plantation in 1936, his family used government to amass a fortune of $500 million by 1979. They also allowed pesticides to sicken the populace. By the early 1970s, some Catholics had broken away from the church in supporting the government to form a "popular church," and this group cooperated with the Sandinista National Liberation Front in a broad revolutionary movement. The ensuing struggle cost 50,000 lives. Through interviews, this book recounts life stories of twenty-six persons in three general groupings—political, religious, and survivors.

840. Heyes, Eileen. **Adolf Hitler**. Brookfield, CT: Millbrook Press, 1994. 160p. $17.40. ISBN 1-56294-343-X. 7 up

The debate continues as to why Germany let itself be led for twelve years by the mass murderer, Adolf Hitler (1889–1945). Hitler answered a need in the people who elected him; they thought he could reenergize the economy and stop inflation. But what he really wanted was for people to believe the myth that Germans were a master race, and that Germany had been infiltrated by Jews and others who had to be exterminated so that the master race could remain undiluted. Heyes presents Hitler after careful research. Notes, Further Reading, Chronology, and Index.

841. Heyes, Eileen. **Children of the Swastika: The Hitler Youth**. Brookfield, CT: Millbrook Press, 1993. 96p. $14.90. ISBN 1-56294-237-9. 7 up

During his regime from 1933 to 1945, Hitler created youth groups that were fanatically loyal to him. These state-sponsored youth organizations trained boys and girls age ten and older to serve Hitler's government without question. Interviews with former members, quotes from *Mein Kampf* (Hitler's book), and scholarly sources show the immense control that Hitler had over these children, who would do anything their Nazi superiors requested. Bibliography, Chronology, and Index. *Child Study Association Children's Books of the Year* and *New York Public Library Books for the Teen Age.*

842. Hibbert, Christopher. **Cavaliers and Roundheads: The English Civil War, 1642–1649**. New York: Scribners, 1993. 337p. $27.50. ISBN 0-684-19557-7. YA

On January 30, 1649, Oliver Cromwell's government beheaded Charles I after waging war against the Cavaliers for seven years. In 1642, Charles tried to arrest those men in Parliament who disagreed with him, and the English civil war officially began. Hibbert describes the events during those years with anecdotes and vivid battle scenes. He relates the horrors of the war that occurred when soldiers from both sides unlawfully raided the civilians—the Royalists for money and the Puritans to purge them of worldly evils. Hibbert includes biographical portraits of Cromwell and the Stuart kings. Maps, Illustrations, Bibliography, and Index.

843. Hibbert, Christopher. **Florence: The Biography of a City**. New York: Norton, 1993. 398p. $35. ISBN 0-393-03563-8. YA

Whether Florence was a town that the Romans invaded to conquer the Etruscans, or whether the Romans established it in 59 B.C., is unclear. Little of the Roman town remains except for place names and the right-angled, Roman-style streets. However the city came to be, Florence was initially unimportant; it was small with no background. The text looks at the beginning of the history of Florence from 59 B.C. through the flood and restoration of 1966 to 1992. Among the topics covered are the Guelphs and Ghibellines of 1115–1280; the Blacks and Whites from 1280 to 1348; the rise of the House of Medici from 1420 to 1439; the Pazzi conspiracy in 1478; Lorenzo the Magnificent from 1478 to 1492; the Grand Duke Cosimo I from 1537 to 1574; the Grand Duke Peter Leopold from 1765 to 1791; and facets of the nineteenth and twentieth centuries. Bibliography and Index.

844. Hibbert, Christopher. **Redcoats and Rebels: The American Revolution Through British Eyes**. New York: Avon, 1991. 375p. $12.50pa. ISBN 0-380-71544-9pa. YA

A different way to look at the American Revolution is from the British point of view. Hibbert discusses the blunders and decisions that the British could have changed to win the war. He also shows that the colonists were as hostile toward the Loyalist or Tory neighbors as the British had been toward the Scots. The biographical sketches here are not those of American military figures but of the British leaders such as Thomas Gage, Francis Smith, Huge Percy, William Howe, John Burgoyne, Nathaniel Green, and Charles Cornwallis. Bibliography and Index.

845. Hibbert, Christopher. **Rome, The Biography of a City**. New York: Norton, 1985. 387p. $25. ISBN 0-393-01984-5. 9 up

Hibbert divides this history of the city of Rome into two parts. Part One begins with the legend of Romulus and Remus and continues to the sack of Rome in 1527. Part Two ends with World War II and is followed by an Epilogue. These two sections contain much information about the cycles of the city as it grew, after the mythical rape of the Sabine women, until the Allies won the war, including all of its intrigue. Index and Bibliography.

846. Hibbert, Christopher. **Venice: The Biography of a City**. New York: Norton, 1989. 435p. $45. ISBN 0-393-02676-0. 8 up

Hibbert begins the history of the city of Venice with the story of two ninth-century merchants who transported a body, supposedly that of St. Mark, from Egypt to Venice, where the Doge reverently received it. The first part of the history covers A.D. 500 to 1814 after Napoleon, and the second part covers 1814, when the Austrians arrived, through 1987. Photographs illustrate subjects such as travelers, defeats and triumphs, artists and architects, ambassadors and visitors, the Romantic response, and tourists and exiles. Glossary, Sources, and Index.

847.   Hibbert, Christopher. **The Virgin Queen: Elizabeth I, Genius of the Golden Age**. Reading, MA: Addison-Wesley, 1991. 287p. $25; $15pa. ISBN 0-201-15626-1; 0-201-60817-0pa. YA

This biography of Queen Elizabeth I (1533–1603) tries to reveal Elizabeth the person rather than Elizabeth the queen. Hibbert details Elizabeth's whims and interests, although it is difficult to ascertain what is personal and what is political when he discusses her attitudes toward men, marriage, and religion. As queen, always in the public eye and almost liquidated as a child, she must have known that she could never be completely honest. Index.

848.   Hickey, James. **Chrysanthemum in the Snow: The Novel of the Korean War**. New York: Crown, 1990. 333p. $19.95. ISBN 0-517-57402-0. YA

Robertson is so gravely wounded in the Korean War during 1952 that his recovery gives him celebrity status in the hospital. One of the nurses falls in love with his manners, but he decides to leave Korea and the war with a Korean man who also does not want to face a future that includes a memory of the difficult past.

849.   Hickman, Patricia. **Voyage of the Exiles**. Minneapolis, MN: Bethany House, 1994. 320p. $8.99pa. ISBN 1-55661-541-8pa. (Land of the Far Horizon). YA

In 1786, George Prentice is convicted to hang in London as a pickpocket, but his sentence is changed to seven years of hard labor in New South Wales. He and 700 other convicts board ships to make the 16,000-mile journey. He expects never to see his family again. What he does not know is that his daughter Katy has found work with the fleet's captain and that his wife has been falsely accused of stealing and is being transported to the same place on another ship. Their harrowing journey takes them to Sydney Bay, where with God's help, they hope to create a better life.

850.   Hillesum, Etty. **Etty Hillesum: An Interrupted Life and Letters from Westerbork**. Arnold J. Pomerans, translator. New York: Henry Holt, 1996. 376p. $27.50. ISBN 0-8050-4894-4. YA

Etty Hillesum was older than twenty when she was taken to Westerbork, the transit camp before Auschwitz. The first half of the book contains her diaries in which she wonders about the situation and shows her continued faith in God. In the second half are letters recounting details of camp horrors. Throughout, she manages to rise above the situation and keep her courage.

851.   Hinds, Kathryn. **The Ancient Romans**. Tarrytown, NY: Benchmark, 1996. 80p. $19.95. ISBN 0-7614-0090-7. (Cultures of the Past). 7 up

Among the topics presented are Roman character traits of practicality, their ability to construct aqueducts and buildings, their sources of entertainment such as gladiators and chariot races, and their religious views. Color photographs and reproductions augment the text. Chronology, Further Reading, Glossary, and Index.

852.   Hinds, Kathryn. **The Celts of Northern Europe**. Tarrytown, NY: Benchmark, 1996. 80p. $19.95. ISBN 0-7614-0092-3. (Cultures of the Past). 7-10

Although the Celts never ruled an empire, they exerted a major influence in Europe. The text examines their attitudes toward religion, their social structure, their art, and their oral tradition. Color photographs and reproductions highlight the text. Chronology, Further Reading, Glossary, and Index.

853.   Hirsch, Charles. **Taxation: Paying for Government**. Austin, TX: Blackbirch/Steck-Vaughn, 1993. 48p. $15.49. ISBN 0-8114-7356-2. (Good Citizenship). 5-9

After defining what taxes are, the text tells what the government uses taxes for and the kinds of taxes. A history shows that taxes were first mentioned in 3500 B.C. in Sumer (currently Iraq). Egyptians, Greeks, and Romans all paid taxes. Spanish taxes financed Columbus's trip to the New World. However, many have complained about unfair taxes, one of the major reasons that the American Revolution began. A final presentation on the Internal Revenue Service completes the information. Photographs and drawings supplement the text. Further Reading, Glossary, and Index.

854.   Hitzeroth, Deborah, and Sharon Heerboth. **Galileo Galilei**. San Diego, CA: Lucent, 1992. 96p. $16.95. ISBN 1-56006-027-1. (The Importance Of). 7 up

Galileo (1564–1642) was one of the most important figures in the world with his inventions, scholarship, and research. He refused to accept the notions of his day, and he criticized the most powerful people in the church and the universities. His nickname became the "Wrangler" because he always asked questions about "truths" that people thought to be immutable. He constructed and used the telescope, and published attacks on Aristotle while supporting Copernicus. Even after the Inquisition sentenced him in 1632, he is rumored to have remarked that nevertheless, "the earth does move." He died under house arrest. Photographs and reproductions enhance the text. Notes, For Further Reading, Works Consulted, and Index.

855.   Hitzeroth, Deborah, and Sharon Heerboth. **Sir Isaac Newton**. San Diego, CA: Lucent, 1994. 96p. $16.95. ISBN 1-56006-046-8. (The Importance Of). 7 up

An inventor, scholar, and researcher, the British subject Isaac Newton (1642–1727) formulated the basis for all modern science. In *Mathematical Principles of Natural Philosophy* (the *Principia*), he created the framework for physics, developed laws of motion, and outlined laws of universal gravitation. First intrigued by the fall of an apple from a tree, he eventually conceived the law of gravity. His theories of gravity, light, and motion and his insights on calculus are still important in radio, television, space travel, and telescopy. He built upon the work of Copernicus, Galileo, and Kepler. He taught at Cambridge University, and in 1705 became the first scientist to be knighted. Notes, For Further Reading, Additional Works Consulted, and Index.

856.   Ho, Minfong. **The Clay Marble**. New York: Farrar, Straus & Giroux, 1991. 163p. $13.95. ISBN 0-374-31340-7. 6-9

Dara, age twelve, and her family have to leave their Cambodian farm in 1980 after Communists kill her father in the war. Dara's brother, Sarun, becomes militaristic and shoots her friend by mistake. They finally reach a Thai border refugee camp where they find food and shelter; there they also get rice plants to start over at the war's end, to reform their "clay marble."

857.   Ho, Minfong. **Rice Without Rain**. New York: Lothrop, Lee & Shepard, 1990. 236p. $12.95. ISBN 0-688-06355-1. 7 up

In Thailand, Jinda, age seventeen, and her family wonder about the university students who come to their village in 1973, saying that they want to learn about farming. Because the villagers are having a poor rice harvest, they hope for help, and they agree when Ned, the student leader, suggests that they give one-third instead of one-half of their rice to the landlord. Because of his decision, Jinda's father is arrested and goes to prison. When Jinda goes to Bangkok, having fallen in love with Ned, she discovers that he makes speeches supporting Communist ideals. Ned uses her father as an example of governmental oppression. The ending of their story is realistic.

858.   Hoare, Stephen. **The Modern World**. New York: Facts on File, 1993. 78p. $17.95. ISBN 0-8160-2792-7. (Illustrated History of the World). 4-7

A history of the twentieth century must discuss the decline of European colonial empires and give a background for World War I, which in turn led to World War II. The postwar world, with the cold war between East and West, stayed in the forefront until the end of the 1980s. Human rights, religious struggles, and space travel continued to be important to societies. Illustrations highlight the text. Glossary, Further Reading, and Index.

859.   Hodge, Jane Aiken. **Windover**. New York: St. Martin's Press, 1992. 266p. $17.95. ISBN 0-312-07884-6. YA

In 1789, after Kathryn falls in love with the man tutoring her half brothers, her enraged stepfather banishes the man from the house. The stepfather has an unnatural interest in Kathryn, and he pursues it until she marries someone just to avoid him. After her husband commits suicide, she flees to London where she reunites with the tutor whom she thought had died.

860.   Hodgins, Michael C. **Reluctant Warrior: A True Story of Duty and Heroism in Vietnam**. New York: Fawcett, 1997. 400p. $24. ISBN 0-449-91059-8. YA

Hodgins served as a lieutenant in Vietnam, and he tells of a soldier's experiences in the rice paddies and the jungles of that war. Additionally, he describes the methods of motivating men to do as well as they could under the unpleasant and adverse conditions.

861.   Hoffman, Paul. **Archimedes' Revenge: The Joys and Perils of Mathematics**. 1988. New York: Crest, 1995. 285p. $5.99pa. ISBN 0-449-21750-7pa. YA

In an attempt to make mathematics accessible to the numerically illiterate, this text presents essays on mathematical topics such as tiling problems, artificial intelligence, voting paradoxes, computational complexity, and Turing machines. Among the puzzles with which mathematicians play are the unbreakable code, the traveling-salesman problem, the perfect Easter egg, Mobius molecules, and Archimedes's "revenge" question to a third-century B.C. mathematical rival about cattle grazing on a field—which a supercomputer did not solve until 1981. These and other ideas make the concept of mathematics intriguing. Annotated Bibliography and Index.

862.   Hole, Dorothy. **Margaret Thatcher: Britain's Prime Minister**. Springfield, NJ: Enslow, 1990. 128p. $17.95. ISBN 0-89490-246-6. (Contemporary Women). 7 up

The former world leader, Margaret Thatcher (b. 1925), began her adulthood as did many other women, with her work revolving around the home, study, and church. At Oxford University, she became active in politics. By 1979, she had worked her way through the political system to become prime minister of Great Britain. She led her country through strikes, inflation, and the Falkland Islands war against Argentina in 1982. Her intelligence and hard work gained her a place in history. Further Reading and Index.

863.   Holeman, Linda. **Promise Song**. Plattsburg, NY: Tundra, 1997. 260p. $7.95. ISBN 0-88776-387-1. 6-9

Rosetta and her sister Flora lose everything when their parents die, including their country when they are sent to Canada in 1900. They arrive in Nova Scotia, and different families adopt them. Rosetta becomes an indentured servant, and her master steals her money, but she eventually forms a bond with his wife, and they both escape his harshness to find Flora.

864.   Holland, Cecelia. **Jerusalem**. New York: Forge, 1996. $23.95; $6.99pa. ISBN 0-312-85956-2; 0-615-00546-2pa. YA

After the illiterate Norman knight Rannulf Fitzwilliam has a conversion experience, he joins the Knights Templar and becomes the narrator of this story about the Christian attempt to take Jerusalem, from Saladin and the Infidels in A.D. 1187. Rannulf must fight a personal battle between his vows of chastity and love for Sibylla, the woman who plans to become the Queen of Jerusalem when her brother, Baudouin, dies from leprosy. Another knight has similar conflicts over his love for Saladin's son. The story presents the time and the place with intensity and excitement.

865.   Holland, Cecelia. **The Lords of Vaumartin**. Boston: Houghton Mifflin, 1988. 344p. $18.95. ISBN 0-395-48828-1. YA

Although the heir to the castle of Vaumartin, Everard, age fourteen, prefers study to knighthood. A jealous uncle tricks him into going to war, and in 1346 he survives the battle of Crécy. Afterward, he goes to Paris in disguise, where he reunites with his books. He helps to save Paris from Etienne Marcel so that the dauphin may take his rightful throne, but happily refuses to return to his own title.

866.   Holland, Heidi. **The Struggle: A History of the African National Congress**. New York: G. Braziller, 1990. 256p. $19.95; $10.95pa. ISBN 0-8076-1238-3; 0-8076-1255-3pa. YA

Using interviews with major participants in the fight against apartheid in South Africa and other sources, Holland presents the history of the African National Congress and Nelson Mandela's importance as its ideological head. She divides the history into three sections. The first section covers the founding of the organization in 1912 to the National Party victory in 1948 when apartheid was established. The second covers 1948 to 1960 when the Sharkeville massacre occurred; leaders not imprisoned had to go into exile, and the organization reluctantly changed its policy to include violence if necessary. The third part accounts for 1960 to 1989, when blacks and Afrikaners had many confrontations. Blacks in South Africa merely wanted their rights, but whites were outwardly hostile and repressed them more instead. Index.

867.   Holliday, Laurel. **Children in the Holocaust and World War II: Their Secret Diaries**. New York: Pocket, 1995. 409p. $20. ISBN 0-671-52054-7. YA

The text is a composite of diaries that twenty-three young people, ages ten through eighteen, kept during the Holocaust in World War II. Holliday comments that Anne Frank and her diary are atypical of the diaries and children in the Holocaust because she stayed in hiding and did not experience the Gestapo harassment or the constant daily search for food and supplies. These children realized that one way to keep their sanity was by writing about their situations. They could say what they thought about the Germans in writing, although they could never say anything aloud. They were also lonely, and the writing gave them a friend. Some of these children died after carefully hiding their private thoughts. The children quoted lived in Poland, Holland, Germany, Czechoslovakia, Austria, Hungary, Lithuania, Russia, Belgium, England, and Denmark. Bibliography and Sources.

868.   Holm, Ann. **North to Freedom**. L. W. Kingsland, translator. 1965. New York: Peter Smith, 1984. 190p. $17.55. ISBN 0-8446-6156-2. San Diego, CA: Harcourt Brace, 1990. 239p. $4.95pa. ISBN 0-15-257553-7pa. 3-7

David, age twelve, escapes from a camp somewhere in the Soviet Union by jumping over a fence during a thirty-second electricity interruption. He travels via Salonika through Italy on his way to Denmark. He has been in the camp most of his life, but a man befriended him and taught him several languages. He can converse, but he does not remember laughter, colors, or oranges. Music amazes him. He eventually reaches Denmark and reunites with his mother. *Gyldendal Prize for Best Scandinavian Children's Book, American Library Association Notable Books for Children, Gold Medal Winner of Boys' Club of America, Junior Book Award,* and *Lewis Carroll Shelf Award.*

869.   Holman, Felice. **The Wild Children**. New York: Scribners, 1983. 160p. $13.95. ISBN 0-684-17970-9. New York: Puffin, 1985. 160p. $4.99pa. ISBN 0-14-031930-1pa. 6-9

Alex, age twelve, walks over 100 miles to Moscow after the Russian Revolution ends, and he is the only member of his family not arrested. During the 1920s, he becomes one of the homeless *bezprizoni*, a band of children who search for food and shelter. They travel illegally on trains to the south in hopes of finding better provisions. Alex makes a contact that helps them reach Finland on their way to America. *American Library Association Notable Books for Young Adults.*

870. Holt, Victoria. **The Captive**. New York: Doubleday, 1989. 357p. $18.95. ISBN 0-385-26332-5. New York: Crest, 1990. 357p. $5.95pa. ISBN 0-449-21817-1pa. YA

Rosetta, age eighteen, sails with her parents and Lucas, all Egyptologists, and a man named John to Africa in the late eighteenth century, but the ship wrecks off the Cape. Rosetta, Lucas, and John escape, but pirates capture them and sell Rosetta to a Turkish pasha. After the pasha frees her, she returns to England where she finds that John has been falsely accused of murder. She works for his freedom.

871. Holt, Victoria. **The India Fan**. New York: Doubleday, 1988. 404p. $18.95. ISBN 0-385-24600-5. New York: Crest, 1996. 404p. $5.99pa. ISBN 0-449-21697-7pa. YA

When Drusilla is a child living in the rectory, she plays with the wealthy children Lavinia and Fabian, who live in the largest village house. As adults, Lavinia marries, and both she and Fabian go to India. Drusilla also goes to India, where she finds Lavinia murdered. She looks after Lavinia's children, which gives Fabian a reason to marry her although she is in a lower social class.

872. Holt, Victoria. **The Road to Paradise Island**. New York: Doubleday, 1985. 368p. $16.95. ISBN 0-385-19110-3. New York: Crest, 1993. 368p. $5.99pa. ISBN 0-449-20888-5pa. YA

In 1890, at the age of eighteen, Annalice finds a diary written by her namesake over 100 years earlier. In the diary appears a map of an island near Australia. Her brother Philip decides to investigate the place, but he does not return as expected, and when Annalice journeys to Australia to find him, she uncovers surprising entanglements.

873. Holt, Victoria. **Secret for a Nightingale**. New York: Doubleday, 1986. 371p. $16.95. ISBN 0-385-23621-2. New York: Fawcett, 1991. 371p. $5.95pa. ISBN 0-449-21296-3pa. YA

While a child in India, Susanna finds that she has an ability to heal people. However, she has less success with her own life, making an unfortunate marriage and having a child die. Yet when she goes to the Crimea to help nurse the soldiers, she finds fulfillment as well as love with a physician whom she had previously and wrongly mistrusted.

874. Holt, Victoria. **The Silk Vendetta**. New York: Doubleday, 1987. 425p. $17.95. ISBN 0-385-24299-9. New York: Fawcett, 1988. 425p. $5.95pa. ISBN 0-449-21548-2pa. YA

In the late nineteenth century, Lenore and her grand'mère work as seamstresses and weavers in the country home of a wealthy British silk merchant. When Lenore refuses the advances of the merchant's upper-class son, he retaliates by causing enough problems that her husband, his brother, and his sister are murdered before a French count realizes the deadly connection.

875. Holt, Victoria. **Snare of Serpents**. New York: Doubleday, 1990. 373p. $23.95. ISBN 0-385-41385-8. New York: Fawcett, 1991. 373p. $5.99pa. ISBN 0-449-21928-3pa. YA

During the Boer War in 1899, Davinia, age sixteen, lives in Edinburgh. After her mother dies, her father accuses a new governess of theft, fires her, and hires another. When he dies soon thereafter, authorities charge Davinia with the murder, and she has to leave for Africa when she is found to be "not proven" as the murderer. After she marries and returns to Scotland, she finds the truth behind the situation.

876. Hoobler, Dorothy, and Thomas Hoobler. **African Portraits**. John Gampert, illustrator. Austin, TX: Raintree/Steck-Vaughn, 1993. 96p. $16.98. ISBN 0-8114-6378-8. (Images Across the Ages). 6 up

The text gives short biographical profiles of persons from the possible birthplace of the human race, Africa. The sub-Saharan figures are: Piankhy, King of Kush who invaded Egypt (751?-716 B.C.); King Ezana (fourth century A.D.) of ancient Ethiopia; King Lalibela (twelfth century) of Zagwe; King Mansa Musa, Mali Muslim leader (d. 1332); Ahmed Baba, Timbuktu scholar (1556-1627); Euware the Great, mighty warrior (d. 1473); Ann Nzinga, warrior-queen of Angola (1583-1663); Cinque, slave from Sierra Leone (c. 1811-1879); Menelik II, king of Shoa in Ethiopia (1844-1913) and Taitu, his wife (d. 1918); Kwame Nkrumah, who freed Ghana (1909-1972); Wole Soyinka, writer (b. 1934); Kipchoge Keino, Olympic runner (b. 1940); and Miriam Makeba (b. 1932) and Joseph Shabalala (c. 1945), South African musicians. Glossary, Bibliography, Sources, and Index.

877. Hoobler, Dorothy, and Thomas Hoobler. **Chinese Portraits**. Victoria Bruck, illustrator. Austin, TX: Raintree/Steck-Vaughn, 1993. 96p. $16.98. ISBN 0-8114-6375-3. (Images Across the Ages). 6 up

The text gives short biographical profiles of prominent persons in Chinese civilization for the past 3,000 years. They are: Confucius, the hidden orchid (551-479 B.C.); Shi Huang Di, the first emperor (259-210 B.C.); the Ban Family, the tigers (640-604? B.C.); Empress Wu, only female son of heaven (A.D. 625-705); Li Bo, vagabond (701-762); Du Fu, candidate (712-770); Ma Yuan, one-corner Ma (twelfth century); Zheng He, admiral of the western seas (1371-1433?); Yuan Mei, the poetic gourmet (1716-1796?); Lin Xezu, antidrug crusader (1785-1850); and Soong Family, makers of a new China (twentieth century). Spelling of Chinese Names in English, Glossary, Bibliography, Sources, and Index.

878. Hoobler, Dorothy, and Thomas Hoobler. **Cleopatra**. New York: Chelsea House, 1985. 115p. $18.95. ISBN 0-87754-589-8. (World Leaders Past and Present). 5 up

Cleopatra (69-30 B.C.) knew that she had to protect herself, so she made liaisons—first with her brother, then with Caesar, and finally with Mark Antony—in order to keep her position. She had skill and courage and the will to survive. The text looks at this woman whom historians have represented in various lights through the centuries: seductive, cunning, clever, manipulative, and malevolent. Photographs and reproductions enhance the text. Chronology, Further Reading, and Index.

879. Hoobler, Dorothy, and Thomas Hoobler. **French Portraits**. Bill Farnsworth, illustrator. Austin, TX: Raintree/Steck-Vaughn, 1994. 96p. $16.98. ISBN 0-8114-6382-6. (Images Across the Ages). 6 up

The text gives short biographical profiles of persons who helped to shape the history of France. They are: Charlemagne, king and emperor (742?-814); Joan of Arc, woman warrior (1412?-1431); Jacques Cartier, explorer (1491-1557); Molière, playwright (1622-1673); Madame Geoffrin, *salon* hostess (1699-1777); Maximilien Robespierre, revolutionary zealot (1758-1794); Antonin Carême, French chef (1784-1833); George Sand, author (1804-1876); Pierre Auguste Renoir, painter (1841-1919); Charles de Gaulle, French leader (1890-1970); and Catherine Deneuve, actress (b. 1943). Glossary, Bibliography, Sources, and Index.

880. Hoobler, Dorothy, and Thomas Hoobler. **Italian Portraits**. Kim Fujiwari, illustrator. Austin, TX: Raintree/Steck-Vaughn, 1993. 96p. $16.98. ISBN 0-8114-6377-X. (Images Across the Ages). 6 up

The text gives short biographical profiles of figures from Italy's history. They are: Julius Caesar, conqueror (100-44 B.C.); Suetonius, Roman gossip (A.D. 69-140); St. Francis of Assisi, contemplative leader (1182-1226); Dante, writer (1265-1321); Isabella (1474-1539) and Beatrice d'Este (1475-1497), feminists; Leonardo da Vinci (1452-1519) and Michelangelo Buonarroti (1475-1564), artists; Galileo Galilei, astronomer and physicist (1564-1642); Alessandro di Cagliostro, magician and alchemist (1743-1795); Giuseppe Verdi, musician and composer (1813-1901); and Maria Montessori, educator (1870-1952). Glossary, Bibliography, Sources, and Index.

881. Hoobler, Dorothy, and Thomas Hoobler. **Japanese Portraits**. Victoria Bruck, illustrator. Austin, TX: Raintree/Steck-Vaughn, 1993. 96p. $16.98. ISBN 0-8114-6381-8. (Images Across the Ages). 6 up

The text gives short biographical profiles of prominent persons from both ancient and modern Japanese civilization. They are: Shotoku Taichi, the prince of sacred virtue (574-623); Murasaki Shikibu (978?-1031?) and Sei Shonagon (962?-1013), writers; Yoritomo (1147-1199) and Yoshitsune (1159-1189), the tragic Minamoto brothers; Nichiren, "the pillar of Japan" (1222-1282); Sen No Rikyu, the tea master (1522-1591); Okuni, female founder of kabuki (1571-1610?); Mitsui Shuho, businesswoman (1590-1676); Bash, poet (1644-1694); Hokusai, artist (1760-1849); Saigo Takemori, the last samurai (1827-1877); Hani Motoko, woman reporter and school founder (1873-1957); and Ako Morita, salesman to the world (b. 1921). Glossary, Bibliography, Sources, and Index.

882. Hoobler, Dorothy, and Thomas Hoobler. **Joseph Stalin**. New York: Chelsea House, 1985. 112p. $18.95. ISBN 0-87754-576-6. (World Leaders Past and Present). 8 up

Joseph Stalin (1879–1953) was an absolute ruler who enforced land reforms and, in the 1930s, purged all opposition by killing millions. Many more died under his leadership in World War II. His successors denounced him after his 1953 death, but they continued to follow his brutal methods of government. Photographs enhance the text. Chronology, Further Reading, and Index.

883. Hoobler, Dorothy, and Thomas Hoobler. **Mandela: The Man, the Struggle, the Triumph**. New York: Franklin Watts, 1992. 143p. $13.95. ISBN 0-531-15245-6. 8 up

Nelson Mandela said to the judge who sentenced him to life imprisonment, "If I had my time over I would do the same again. So would any who dares to call himself a man." Mandela served in prison for twenty-seven years because he wanted to free his people from the apartheid policies of South Africa, where blacks were forbidden to go into certain areas or live in certain places. The text covers his life. Notes, Bibliography, For Further Reading, and Index.

884. Hoobler, Dorothy, and Thomas Hoobler. **Mexican Portraits**. Robert Kuester, illustrator. Austin, TX: Raintree/Steck-Vaughn, 1993. 96p. $16.98. ISBN 0-8114-6376-1. (Images Across the Ages). 6 up

The text gives short biographical profiles of figures from Mexico's ancient and modern, as well as religious, cultures. They are: King Nezahualcoyotl, poet and engineer of Texcoco (1402-1472); Moctezuma II, Aztec leader (1467-1520); Malinche, translator to Cortés (1501-1550); Juan Diego, religious visionary (1474-1548); Diego de la Cruz, slave (mid-1700s); Juana Inés de la Cruz, poet (1651-1695); Miguel Hidalgo y Costilla, priest (1753-1811); Benito Juárez, political leader (1806-1872); Pancho Villa (1877-1923) and Emiliano Zapata (1879-1919), revolutionaries; Diego Rivera (1886-1957) and Frida Kahlo (1907-1954), painters; and Amalia Hernández, dancer (b. 1919?). Glossary, Bibliography, Sources, and Index.

885. Hoobler, Dorothy, and Thomas Hoobler. **Russian Portraits**. John Edens, illustrator. Austin, TX: Raintree/Steck-Vaughn, 1994. 96p. $16.98. ISBN 0-8114-6380-X. (Images Across the Ages). 6 up

The text gives short biographical profiles of persons important throughout the history of Russia. They are: Alexander Nevsky, repeller of Mongol and Swedish invaders (1220?-1263); Yermak, Cossack leader (d. 1584); Avvakum, Russian Orthodox priest (1620-1682); Feodosia Morozova, noble woman (1630-1675); Peter the Great, founder of St. Petersburg (1672-1725); Catherine the Great, empress (1729-1796); Alexander Pushkin, poet (1799-1837); Leo Tolstoy, novelist (1828-1910); Peter Tchaikovsky, composer and musician (1840-1893); Anna Pavlova, ballet dancer (1882-1931); Vera Zasulich, revolutionary (1849-1919); Sergei Eisenstein, movie maker (1898-1948); and Andrei Sakharov, scientist and human rights activist (1921-1989) and his wife, Elena Bonner, nurse and human rights activist (b. 1923). Glossary, Bibliography, Sources, and Index.

886. Hoobler, Dorothy, and Thomas Hoobler. **Showa: The Age of Hirohito**. New York: Walker, 1990. 176p. $15.95. ISBN 0-8027-6966-7. 6-12

As the 124th emperor of Japan, Hirohito of the Showa reign supposedly declared war on the United States and then decided to surrender. Whether he actually had any choice in the matter is unclear; through the centuries, the emperor of Japan has been the titular head, descended from the gods, but not the decision maker. The Hooblers begin the story in 1853, when Admiral Perry entered Edo Bay to ask for admittance to Japanese ports. They note that although the emperor's signature was on the treaty agreement, the shogun was the person with the real power and who made the decision. Since 1600, the members of the Tokugawa family had been the shoguns, but after the treaty, the *daimyo*, other families, took power from the Tokugawa family in 1868. A new emperor was enthroned and the samurai class's rights and privileges were abolished. In 1877, Saigo, a former samurai, led a rebellion but was defeated. Finally a constitution was written in 1889. Hirohito was born in 1901 and trained by a former samurai who had to know calligraphy, *bonsai, ikebana* (flower arranging), and the tea ceremony. Thus Hirohito knew many things; he especially loved marine biology. Always frustrated by the isolation of his role, he said before his death in 1989 that the favorite time in his life was his visit to Great Britain when he was a young man. This book, very informative and very interesting, gives insights into rarely discussed areas of a culture.

887. Hoobler, Dorothy, and Thomas Hoobler. **South American Portraits**. Stephen Marchesi, illustrator. Austin, TX: Raintree/Steck-Vaughn, 1994. 96p. $16.98. ISBN 0-8114-6383-4. (Images Across the Ages). 6 up

The text gives short biographical profiles of persons who helped to shape the history of South America. They are: Garcilaso de la Vega, Peruvian-born Spanish soldier, historian, and translator (1539?-1616); Rose of Lima, saint from Lima, Peru (1586-1617); Antônio Francisco Lisboa, architect and sculptor (1738-1814); Simón Bolívar (1783-1830) and José de San Martín (1778-1850), liberators; Maria Antônio Muniz, head of a Brazilian family with a tragic cycle (1762-1870); Domingo Faustino Sarmiento, Argentinian president (1811-1888); Simón I. Patiño, Bolivian tin mine owner (1865-1947); Gabriela Mistral, Chilean author, (1889-1957); Heitor Villa-Lobos, Brazilian musician (1887-1959); Evita Perón, Argentinian leader (1919-1952); Pelé, soccer star (b. 1940); and Gabriel García Márquez, Columbian novelist (b. 1928). Glossary, Bibliography, Sources, and Index.

888. Hoobler, Thomas, and Dorothy Hoobler. **Toussaint L'Ouverture**. New York: Chelsea House, 1989. 111p. $18.95. ISBN 1-55546-818-7. (World Leaders Past and Present). 5 up

Toussaint L'Ouverture (1744-1803) led the one rebellion in which slaves succeeded in overthrowing their masters and assuming leadership of their own country. A slave for forty-seven years, he had read widely and become a medic, and he used his knowledge to become a general, a diplomat, and a leader uniting his people into a nation after the slaves rebelled in 1791. The slaves claimed victories over armies from France, Spain, and Britain so that St. Domingue could eventually transform itself into Haiti, the second independent nation in the Western Hemisphere. Engravings and illustrations enhance the text. Chronology, Further Reading, and Index.

889. Hoobler, Dorothy, and Thomas Hoobler. **Vietnam, Why We Fought: An Illustrated History**. New York: Knopf, 1990. 160p. $17.95. ISBN 0-394-81943-2. 7-10

By briefly relating Vietnam's history since 111 B.C., the Hooblers note that the Vietnamese often called themselves "the smaller dragon," whereas China was the "larger dragon." But to them, the dragon is the water god, giver of life and food and representative of royalty, prosperity, and good luck. The text, illustrated with photographs of the people and the soldiers, relates the chronology of the war from the time of French occupation, through the United States intervention, to the final withdrawal when the Communists renamed Saigon as Ho Chi Minh city. The book ends with a discussion of the inception and dedication of the Vietnam Memorial, designed by Maya Lin. Maps, Glossary, Further Reading, and Index.

890. Hoobler, Dorothy, and Thomas Hoobler. **Zhou Enlai**. New York: Chelsea House, 1986. 116p. $18.95. ISBN 0-87754-516-2. (World Leaders Past and Present). 8 up

Zhou Enlai (1898–1976) became the first premier for the People's Republic of China. He showed restraint in an era when people had fierce ideological ideas. His family was middle-class Mandarin, and he received a traditional Chinese education before joining the Communist Party in 1921. He tried to ally the Communists with

Chiang Kai-shek's Nationalists, but war broke out in 1927. He then directed the Communist's Red Army, first against the Nationalists and then against the Japanese in the 1930s and 1940s. Under Mao Zedong, in 1949, Zhou became the country's premier and foreign minister. Photographs and reproductions enhance the text. Chronology, Further Reading, and Index.

891.   Horn, Pierre L. **King Louis XIV**. New York: Chelsea House, 1986. 116p. $18.95. ISBN 0-87754-591-X. (World Leaders Past and Present). 8 up

France's King Louis XIV (1638–1715) was clever and arrogant. He strengthened the power of the monarchy, waged wars, and promoted French culture during his fifty-four-year reign. He believed that God had given him the divine right to rule, and his personal enemies received the brunt of his decisions. He claimed that he, rather than the pope, was the head of the French Catholic Church, and he persecuted the Protestants. He built Versailles, a palace that earned him the name of "Sun King." At his death, France had endured wars that had decimated its treasury, and many of his subjects wanted him gone. Photographs, engravings, and reproductions enhance the text. Chronology, Further Reading, and Index.

892.   Hourani, Albert. **A History of the Arab Peoples**. Cambridge, MA: Belknap Press/Harvard University Press, 1991. 551p. $27.50. ISBN 0-674-39565-4. New York: Warner, 1992. 551p. $15.99pa. ISBN 0-446-39392-4pa. YA

This text looks at Arab history and culture for the past twelve centuries in an attempt to show its complexities. Parts of the text cover the beginnings of Islam in the seventh to tenth centuries, Arab Muslim societies in the eleventh to fifteenth centuries, the Ottoman Age from the sixteenth to the eighteenth centuries, the age of European empires from 1800 to 1939, and the age of nation-states since 1939. Maps, Genealogies and Dynasties, Notes, Bibliography, and Index.

893.   House, Adrian. **The Great Safari: The Lives of George and Joy Adamson**. New York: Morrow, 1993. 464p. $25. ISBN 0-688-10141-0. YA

Joy Adamson was a wild and gifted Austrian artist who found animals and many men, including her British publisher, irresistible. With her husband George in Kenya, she raised and freed both a cheetah and a leopard. She also produced more than 400 exquisite paintings of wildflowers, 80 of coral fish, and more than 570 tribal studies. George Adamson, her husband, released over twenty-five lions into the jungle. Although they gained fame as the adopted parents of the lioness Elsa, who served as a surrogate for the child they never had, they had a stormy marriage. Both were original proponents of the Green Movement. A Turkana tribesman whom Joy Adamson had dismissed from service shot her when she was seventy years old, and Somali bandits shot George as he tried to rescue a German woman whom they were robbing and molesting.

894.   Houston, James. **Running West**. 1990. New York: Kingston, 1996. 320p. $14pa. ISBN 1-575-66044-Xpa. YA

When William wins a duel in 1714 against a boy from another Scottish clan, he has to leave to protect himself and his family. He goes to Canada, and there he meets a woman from the Dene nation with whom he falls in love.

895.   Hovey, Tamara. **A Mind of Her Own: A Life of the Writer George Sand**. New York: HarperCollins, 1977. 211p. $8.95. ISBN 0-06-022616-1. YA

A gifted novelist and playwright, George Sand (1804–1876), or Mme. Dudevant, shocked people by wearing men's pants and smoking cigars in public. Her role in the Romantic revolution that swept across Europe in the nineteenth century earned her the name "Great Woman of the Opposition." She refused to acquiesce to society's norms, preferring to practice free love, like her male friends, but she supported workers' and women's rights. Among her friends were Balzac, Flaubert, Delacroix, Chopin, and Liszt. However, she influenced many outside her circle with her ideas of equality. Bibliography and Index.

896.   Howard, Ellen. **When Daylight Comes**. New York: Atheneum, 1985. 192p. $14.95. ISBN 0-689-31133-8. 5-9

Helena, the daughter of a wealthy St. Jan (John)'s plantation owner in the Caribbean, watches slaves revolt on the island in 1733. They capture her, make her work in the fields, and demand that she serve a former slave who was once an African queen. She learns how to accept responsibility and to understand real love while in this unexpectedly difficult situation.

897.   Howard, Michael. **Gauguin**. New York: Dorling Kindersley, 1992. 63p. $16.95. ISBN 1-56458-066-0. (Eyewitness Art). YA

This brief biography of Gauguin (1848–1903) looks at his life and his place in his times. Also appearing are reproductions of his work, his palette and tools, the objects he painted in Tahiti and other places, preliminary sketches, photographs, and documents. Small segments of some of the paintings have been enlarged to show brush-stroke techniques. Gauguin Collections, Glossary, and Index.

898. Howker, Janni. **Isaac Campion**. New York: Greenwillow, 1987. 83p. $10.25. ISBN 0-688-06658-5. 7 up

In the spring of 1901, Isaac Campion's brother dies in an accident in which he is impaled on fence spikes; thereafter, Isaac has to help his bitter father raise horses. As an old man, Isaac remembers the hatred that his father had for the father of the boy who made the dare that caused Dan to die. When Isaac's uncle asks him to come to America with him, Isaac knows that he must if he is ever going to escape from his father's hostility.

899. Hudson, Edward. **Poetry of the First World War**. Minneapolis, MN: Lerner, 1990. 128p. $16.95. ISBN 1-85210-667-0. 7 up

In a month-by-month sequence through World War I, these poems about the war show the attitudes at the beginning of the war and the shifts that occurred as the war progressed. The early poems show a patriotism that the later ones reject. Death, the horrors of battle and the trenches, and the ironic twists of fate in wartime come forth as the war continues. Of the thirty-seven poets presented, fifteen died in uniform. Photographs augment the text.

900. Hudson, Jan. **Dawn Rider**. New York: Philomel/Putnam, 1990. 175p. $14.95. ISBN 0-399-22178-6. 6 up

In 1750, Kit Fox, age sixteen, does not feel special until she sees a horse. She knows that she wants to ride this powerful animal, but her Blackfeet tribe does not think that women should be involved in horse training. She sneaks away from home every morning and earns the confidence of the horse. When the Snakes invade the tribe and the men have to leave to fight them, she proves her value by racing to a nearby tribe for guns. *Writer's Guild of Alberta Awards for Excellence* (Canada).

901. Hudson, Jan. **Sweetgrass**. New York: Philomel, 1989. 160p. $13.95. ISBN 0-399-21721-5. 6-9

Sweetgrass, age fifteen, a Blackfoot in the nineteenth century, worries about not being married when most of the younger girls have already become wives. She also worries about whether the boy she loves will have enough horses for her father to approve him and whether her stepmother will decide that Sweetgrass is responsible enough to be a wife. Her people struggle in their lives on the Canadian prairie, and after she nurses both her brother and her stepmother through smallpox by feeding them fish (a forbidden food), her father decides that she may marry. *Canadian Library Association Book of the Year, Governor General's Literary Awards, International Board of Books for Young People, American Library Association Notable Books for Children, School Library Journal Best Book,* and *Canada Council Children's Literature Prize.*

902. Hughes, Glyn. **The Rape of the Rose**. New York: Simon & Schuster, 1993. 319p. $21. ISBN 0-671-72516-5. YA

In 1812, Mor Greave, a handloom weaver and schoolmaster in Yorkshire, England, becomes involved in the Luddite rebellion. As he flees a failed attack on a mill, a prostitute rescues him. He lives in a time when wealthy owners abused working children and the poor wished for better lives. Instead of being hotheaded, he is educated and thoughtful. What he learns from his experience is that the poor suffer because of the rich, not because of divine providence.

903. Hughes, Libby. **Madam Prime Minister: A Biography of Margaret Thatcher**. New York: Dillon Press, 1989. 144p. $13.95. ISBN 0-87518-410-3. (People in Focus). 6-9

Although she pursued chemistry at Oxford University, Margaret Thatcher (b. 1925) decided to study law after graduation because of her interest in politics. She showed that she was willing to work as a child of eleven. She won a speech contest, asserting to someone that she was not "lucky" to win because she had carefully prepared the speech and deserved the credit. She first ran to become a member of Parliament and then became the head of her Conservative Party. Several years later, the people elected her as the first woman Prime Minister. During the ten years she served, Britons nicknamed her the "Iron Lady." Selected Bibliography and Index.

904. Hughes, Libby. **Nelson Mandela: Voice of Freedom**. New York: Dillon Press, 1992. 144p. $12.95. ISBN 0-87518-484-7. 6-9

Nelson Mandela (b. 1918) has had a major impact on race relations in South Africa, partly by suffering personal deprivation. He helped to establish the African National Congress and the anti-apartheid movements that struggled to give blacks their rights, but he was incarcerated as a political prisoner for twenty-seven years. He became president of South Africa after the period covered in this book ends. Bibliography and Index.

905. Hughes, Robert. **Barcelona**. New York: Knopf, 1992. 575p. $27.50; $15pa. ISBN 0-394-58027-3; 0-679-74383-9pa. YA

The text tells the story of Barcelona, Spain, the capital of Catalonia, from its founding in 230 B.C. during Roman times through the times of the Moors and Charlemagne to the twentieth century. Hughes relates information on the arts, including literature and painting, the politics the personalities, the religion, and the business of this vibrant city so that anyone can see both the ordinary and the exceptional. Extras such as translations of local expressions, Catalan verse, and popular songs reveal Barcelona's cultural and societal norms as well as idiosyncrasies associated with such artists as Gaudí and Mir. Illustrations, Bibliography, and Index.

905a.   Hull, Mary. **The Travels of Marco Polo**. San Diego, CA: Lucent Books, 1995. 96p. $14.95. ISBN 1-56006-238-X. (World History). 6-10

With a background on the world politics at the time of Marco Polo (1254-1323?), Hull then tells of the Polo family's two journeys to the East. On the second, Marco Polo went; he related his journey, beginning in 1271, in his diaries. During Polo's experiences, he became a favorite of the Great Khan in Khan-Balik, the city now known as Beijing. After much time and money, the family decided to leave, and after 15,000 miles, they returned to Venice in 1295. There they had to face the cultural changes that had occurred during their absence. Reproductions enhance the text. Further Reading, Notes, and Index.

906.   Hull, Robert, sell. **Breaking Free: An Anthology of Human Rights Poetry**. New York: Thomson Learning, 1994. 64p. $17.95. ISBN 1-56847-196-3. All ages

This anthology of international poems written over several centuries presents such themes as imprisonment, liberation, slavery, hunger, education, and family and human relations. Photographs and drawings illustrate the text. Poet Biographies, Glossary, Bibliography, and Index.

907.   Hull, Robert, ed. **A Prose Anthology of the First World War**. Brookfield, CT: Millbrook Press, 1993. 64p. $14.40. ISBN 1-56294-222-0. 7 up

World War I becomes personal when seen through the eyes of people who lived it day by day. Thoughts from their memoirs, diaries, and letters, accompanied by photographs, give an immediacy to the war unavailable from dry history dates. Chapters include the beginning of the war, soldiers, ordinary people, at sea and in the air, back at home, looking after the wounded and dying, and endings. Glossary, Further Reading, and Index.

908.   Hull, Robert, ed. **A Prose Anthology of the Second World War**. Brookfield, CT: Millbrook Press, 1993. 64p. $14.40. ISBN 1-56294-223-9. 7 up

World War II becomes personal when seen through the eyes of people who lived it day by day. Thoughts from their memoirs, diaries, and letters, accompanied by photographs, give an immediacy to the war unavailable from dry history dates. Chapters include the Nazis and the Jews, fighting in Western Europe, refugees and "aliens," bombing the cities, women in the war, war in the Pacific, and endings. Glossary, Further Reading, and Index.

909.   Humble, Richard. **Ships**. Peter Cornwall, illustrator. Austin, TX: Raintree/Steck-Vaughn, 1994. 32p. $21.40. ISBN 0-8114-6158-0. (Pointers). 3-7

Two-page spreads on each type of ship tell its structure and give historical information and an illustration. The types of ships presented are Egyptian warships, Greek triremes, Viking long ships, man-of-war ships, ships of the Line, early steamships, clipper ships, ironclads, turret rams, submarines, aircraft carriers, and ocean liners. Glossary and Index.

910.   Humble, Richard. **The Voyages of Jacques Cartier**. New York: Franklin Watts, 1992. 32p. $12.40. ISBN 0-531-14216-7. YA

The French navigator, Jacques Cartier (1491–1557), discovered the St. Lawrence River, now a border between the United States and Canada, as well as the fertile land beyond. His explorations led to the establishment of the first French colony in the Americas. Photographs and reproductions enhance the text. Time Chart, Glossary, and Index.

911.   Humble, Richard. **A World War Two Submarine**. Mark Bergin, illustrator. New York: Peter Bedrick, 1991. 48p. $18.95. ISBN 0-87226-351-7. (Inside Story). 4-7

The very first submarine used in the United States was in 1776, when the *Turtle* was put to service to explode British ammunition. It failed, but it caused engineers to began searching for a submarine that would work. The text looks at submarine warfare during the World Wars and how they were designed and built. Diagrams and drawings show the midships, bow tubes, sleeping and eating arrangements, sonar, torpedoes and guns, and uniforms worn by the crew. A brief discussion of the Battle of the Atlantic from 1940 to 1943 describes subs in action. Chronology, Glossary, and Index.

912.   Humphrey, Judy. **Genghis Khan**. New York: Chelsea House, 1987. 112p. $18.95. ISBN 0-87754-527-8. (World Leaders Past and Present). 5 up

Genghis Khan (1162-1227) established the world's largest empire by using intimidation to supplement his political and military strategies. He spent his childhood traveling with his father's nomads, but when he was thirteen, his father died and the clan deserted. His people eventually recognized the resourceful Genghis as their leader, or khan, in 1183. He began raiding, which consolidated his local power, but then he began attacking the neighbors to add to his wealth. In 1227, his empire crossed the Asian continent. He established trade routes and laws that remained long after his death. Photographs and reproductions enhance the text. Chronology, Further Reading, and Index.

913. Hunter, Erica C. D. **First Civilizations: Cultural Atlas for Young People**. New York: Facts on File, 1994. 96p. $19.95. ISBN 0-8160-2976-8. 6 up

In this book, text and photographs of artifacts and ruins complement one another as they give an overview of history from its beginnings to 323 B.C. in the Middle East. The broad categories are: early peoples to 11,000 B.C.; the first farmers (11,000-9300 B.C.); movement toward civilization (7000-4000 B.C.); states in conflict (3000-2350 B.C.); kings of Agade (2350-2000 B.C.); rival kingdoms (2000-1500 B.C.); the Kassite empire (1600-1200 B.C.); changing kingdoms (1200-900 B.C.); the late Assyrian empire (1000-750 B.C.); Assyria triumphant (750-626 B.C.); Babylonian revival (626-560 B.C.); the rise of the Persian empire (560-521 B.C.); the empire of Darius (521-486 B.C.); and the end of the ancient Near East (486-323 B.C.). Glossary, Further Reading, Gazetteer, and Index.

914. Hunter, Mollie. **The Ghosts of Glencoe**. 1969. Edinburgh, Scotland: Canongate, 1995. 191p. $7.95pa. ISBN 0-86241-467-9pa. 6-9

In 1692, Ensign Stewart finds out that some of the Scottish-born officers in the British army are in sympathy with the British cause and plan to massacre Scots at Glencoe. He decides to warn the rebels that the army will attack. His warning is too late to save the Macdonalds, but he escapes from his situation as a traitor.

915. Hunter, Mollie. **Hold On to Love**. New York: Harper, 1984. 288p. $12.89. ISBN 0-06-022688-9. 7-10

Bridie, age fifteen, works at her grandfather's Edinburgh flower shop while attending night school to learn how to be a writer. She meets Peter in one of her classes, treats him rudely because of her anger at an instructor, and does not see him again for a year. After the second meeting, they begin a relationship, but Bridie does not like Peter's possessive attitude. After he has to leave to fight in World War II in 1939, she realizes, in this sequel to *A Sound of Chariots*, that love is more important than pettiness, and they marry after he returns safely from the difficult Battle of Dunkirk.

916. Hunter, Mollie. **The Lothian Run**. 1970. Edinburgh, Scotland: Canongate, 1990. 221p. $4.95pa. ISBN 0-86241-069-Xpa. 5-8

In 1736, Sandy, age sixteen, discovers a Scottish smuggling gang. They take documents to Jacobites in France who plan to overthrow the ruling Hanoverians. The lawyer who employs Sandy is delighted with the investigation because it enables him to capture several people who are part of the plot.

917. Hunter, Mollie. **Pistol in Greenyards**. 1968. Edinburgh, Scotland: Canongate, 1990. 192p. $6.95pa. ISBN 0-86241-175-0pa. 7-10

Connal, age fifteen, threatens a sheriff who tries to evict his family from their highland Scottish home because lowlanders want better grazing land. In 1854, he and his clan have to protect their rights from those who would take them away. Unfortunately, they are not strong enough to resist the well-armed attackers.

918. Hunter, Mollie. **A Sound of Chariots**. New York: HarperCollins, 1972. 241p. $12.89; $4.95pa. ISBN 0-06-022669-2; 0-06-440235-5pa. 7-10

Bridie, age nine, hears that her father has died, and as his favorite, she is overcome with grief and the fragile nature of life in the 1930s in Scotland. She loves words, and she can tell stories that fascinate her classmates. As she matures, she realizes that she has no money to attend college, so she leaves home to work so that she can pay for classes to help her be a better writer. *Phoenix Award, American Library Association Notable Children's Books of 1971–1975, Horn Book Fanfare Honor List, New York Times Outstanding Children's Books,* and *Child Study Association Children's Book Committee at Bank Street College Award.*

919. Hunter, Mollie. **The Spanish Letters**. Elizabeth Grant, illustrator. 1964. Edinburgh, Scotland: Canongate, 1990. 173p. $6.95pa. ISBN 0-86241-057-6pa. 5-8

Jamie is a "caddie," or guide, in Edinburgh during 1589. At age fifteen, he helps discover a Spanish plot to capture Scotland and England when he overhears various conversations in his job. After his report reaches Queen Elizabeth, and King James escapes capture, he earns the chance for a better job.

920. Hunter, Mollie. **The Stronghold**. 1974. New York: Avon, 1977. 204p. $3.50pa. ISBN 0-380-00834-3pa. YA

When Romans come up the coast of the Orkney Islands to capture members of the tribe as slaves, Coll, age eighteen, designs a unique tower to protect the people. The tribal leader refuses to accept the plan and the Romans almost destroy the tribe. Others realize that protecting themselves from insiders may be as important as protection from outsiders. *Carnegie Medal.*

921. Hunter, Mollie. **The Third Eye**. 1973. New York: Harper, 1979. 224p. $12.89. ISBN 0-06-022677-3. YA

When Jinty is thirteen years old, in 1935, she takes a weekend job at an earl's house near Edinburgh. Jinty has been called *fey* and is reputed to have the "second sight," and she uses her gift to realize that the earl has decided to break the family curse of the oldest son dying before inheriting the title by taking his own life. She also knows that to reveal his plan would cost him his position in society. She has to decide how to handle her knowledge.

922. Hunter, Mollie. **The 13th Member**. 1971. Magnolia, MA: Peter Smith, 1988. 214p. $19.55. ISBN 0-8446-6362-X. 6-9

In 1590, Adam Lawrie, age sixteen, follows Gilly, the kitchen maid, after she leaves the house. She goes into the dark of a Scottish night to participate in a thirteen-member witches' coven from which she is trying to free herself. After Adam and Gilly, with the help of a trusted scholar, discover the plot to murder James I, they walk to England, where they hope to start new lives using Gilly's ability to heal people and Adam's innate intelligence.

923. Hunter, Mollie. **You Never Knew Her As I Did!** New York: HarperCollins, 1981. 216p. $13.95. ISBN 0-06-022678-1. 7-10

Will, aged seventeen in 1567, falls in love with Mary, Queen of Scots, when he is assigned to watch over her. The Earl of Moray exiles her at the island castle of Lochleven while he enjoys acting as regent. Will, the servant and unrecognized illegitimate son of Sir William Douglas, remembers the time twenty years later when he hears about her execution. He had gotten to know her and thought that she was too much maligned. To show his concern, he helped her plan an unsuccessful escape from the castle; as an adult, he never married.

924. Huong, Duong Thu. **Paradise of the Blind**. Phan Huy Duong and Nina McPherson, translators. New York: Morrow, 1993. 270p. $20. ISBN 0-688-11445-8. YA

Hang, a young woman from the slums of Hanoi in modern Vietnam, rebels against her mother and feels pressure from her Aunt Tam, who tries to pass both wealth and bitterness to her. She travels to Moscow to see her sick uncle, the man who separated her parents with his zealous political campaign in 1953 when he returned to their village and accused her father of being an enemy of the state. Hang slowly realizes that she must look to the future if she is ever to find inner peace.

925. Hussein, Shahrukh. **Mecca**. New York: Dillon Press, 1993. 46p. $13.95. ISBN 0-87518-572-X. (Holy Cities). 5-9

Mecca, Islam's most sacred city, has been important to the Middle East since Ibrahim discovered the Zam-zam spring there. Muhammad, born in the city in approximately A.D. 570, had a revelation from God that followers of Islam should pray toward *Kaaba*, the most sacred Islamic sanctuary inside the Great Mosque, the Haram. Contemporary Muslims look forward to their *hajj* or pilgrimage to the city as an affirmation of their faith. Non-Muslims may not enter the city. The text looks at the religion and the people who follow it. Photographs enhance the text. Timeline, Further Reading, and Index.

926. Hussein, Shahrukh. **What Do We Know About Islam?** New York: Peter Bedrick, 1997. 40p. $18.95. ISBN 0-87226-388-6. (What Do We Know About . . .). 4-7

After summarizing a history of Islam, Hussein discusses holidays, the pilgrimage to Mecca, dietary restrictions, art, and other topics. In the timeline, modern leaders receive acknowledgement. Chronology, Glossary, and Index.

927. Huynh Quang Nhuong. **The Land I Lost: Adventures of a Boy in Vietnam**. Vo-dinh Mai, illustrator. 1982. Magnolia, MA: Peter Smith, 1992. 115p. $17.75. ISBN 0-8446-6586-X. New York: Trophy, 1986. 115p. $3.95pa. ISBN 0-06-440183-9pa. 4-7

Huynh Quang Nhuong grew up in Vietnam during the 1960s and was drafted into the army. A gunshot paralyzed him, and he came to the United States for treatment and further schooling in chemistry. In this book he tells the story of his childhood and the things he remembers. On the list are his beautiful grandmother, crocodiles, horse snakes, killer wild hogs, a 200-pound catfish, taming pythons, fishing in flooded rice fields, and his pet water buffalo. *American Library Association Notable Books for Children, Notable Children's Trade Books in the Field of Social Studies, NCTE Teachers' Choices,* and *Booklist Editors' Choices.*

928. Hyndley, Kate. **The Voyage of the *Beagle* (Darwin)**. Peter T. Bull, illustrator. New York: Bookwright Press, Franklin Watts, 1989. 32p. $11.90. ISBN 0-531-18272-X. (Great Journeys). 5-9

Charles Darwin (1809-1882) went aboard the HMS *Beagle* for a voyage that lasted for five years, from 1831 to 1836. During this trip, he observed natural habitats not available in England, which gave him additional information on which to base his theory of the evolution of species expressed in *On the Origin of Species* and *The Descent of Man*. The text covers this experience in two-page chapters. Illustrations augment the text. Bibliography and Index.

I

929. Ippisch, Hanneke. **Sky: A True Story of Resistance During World War II**. New York: Simon & Schuster, 1996. 128p. $16. ISBN 0-689-80508-X. 7 up

Hanneke Ippisch remembers her life during World War II when she was a Dutch resistance worker. The first chapters recall her childhood before the war; the rest recreates the German invasion of the Netherlands on May 10, 1942, and covers the period until the end of the occupation in 1945. Hanneke became a messenger for the underground and a guide for Jews escaping into the forest before the Nazis captured her as a political prisoner. She relates the story behind the railway workers' strike, which slowed the German transport of prisoners, and admits that she enjoyed watching a crowd persecuting those who had helped the Nazis. Her commitment, courage, and self-control allowed her to achieve her goals through surprising and dangerous methods. Notes, Further Reading, and Index. *Bulletin Blue Ribbon Book.*

930. Ireland, Karin. **Albert Einstein**. Englewood Cliffs, NJ: Silver Burdett, 1989. 109p. $13.98. ISBN 0-382-09523-5. (Pioneers in Change). 5-9

Albert Einstein (1879-1955) refused to talk until he was three years old, and many thought that he might be retarded. He hated the discipline in German schools and would not study as required, preferring to investigate the laws of physics. He transferred to schools in Switzerland and discovered that not all schools were as mindless as the German schools, where questions were discouraged and rote memory applauded. He renounced his German citizenship, but as an adult, he was considered Jewish first and had to endure the difficulties of this background. He became an American citizen, warned President Roosevelt about the possibility of a German atomic bomb, and spent the last years of his life at Princeton. He was distraught when the American atomic bomb killed people in Japan, and he was disturbed that his son had to remain in a mental hospital. He did not have enough time to complete his unified field theory, but otherwise he lived a full and happy life. Photographs, Bibliography, and Index.

931. **The Islamic World: From Its Origins to the 16th Century**. Giacinto Gaudenzi and Giorgio Bacchin, illustrators; Pamela Swinglehurst, translator. Austin, TX: Raintree/Steck-Vaughn, 1994. 72p. $17.97. ISBN 0-8114-3328-5. (History of the World). 7 up

This overview uses informative illustrations and clear maps to complement the text. Among the two-page topic spreads presented here are Islamic conquests, Sunnis, Shiites, the Umayyad Empire, Abbasids, Iran, Fatimids and Saladin, Seljuk Turks, the Maghrib, the Almoravids, the Almohads, Mongols, Mamluks, Ottomans, Tamerlane and Suleiman, Constantinople and Istanbul, Islam in India, Africa south of the Sahara, and the larger Islamic world. Glossary and Index.

932. Isserman, Maurice. **The Korean War: America at War**. New York: Facts on File, 1992. 117p. $17.95. ISBN 0-8160-2688-2. (America at War). 7 up

The Korean War (1950-1953), called by some the "forgotten" war, was the first "undeclared" war fought under the United Nations flag. The text tells about the miscalculation of military personnel who believed that the invading North Koreans would not fight, followed by a chronological account of the war. Pertinent quotes from participants show what this war was like. Bibliography and Index.

933. Isserman, Maurice. **World War II**. New York: Facts on File, 1991. 184p. $17.95. ISBN 0-8160-2374-3. (America at War). 7 up

This volume gives an overview of World War II, beginning with Leo Szilard's concern in 1939 that the best people working on nuclear fission were in Hitler's Germany. Szilard was a Hungarian scientist who had recently come to America. His advice led to the Manhattan Project and the development of the atomic bomb later used in Japan. The text presents the major events of the war, the major objectives and strategies of the war's leaders, and significant innovations in weapons and tactics. Biographical references to many of the leaders also appear. Recommended Reading and Index.

934. Italia, Robert. **Courageous Crimefighters**. Minneapolis, MN: Oliver Press, 1995. 160p. $14.95. ISBN 1-881508-21-8. (Profiles). 6-9

People who lived the adventures that make mystery and detective books so appealing risk their lives to catch criminals. The text looks at eight of these people: Sir Robert Peel (1788-1850) of Scotland Yard in England; Allan Pinkerton (1819-1884), the original private eye in America; Samuel Steele (1851-1919), a Canadian mountie; Leander H. McNelly (1844-1877), captain of the Texas Rangers; Melvin Purvis (1903-1960) and Eliot Ness (1902-1957), top agents in the Federal Bureau of Investigation; Estes Kefauver (1903-1963), a crusader in Congress; and Simon Wiesenthal (b. 1908), hunter of Nazis. Bibliography and Index.

J

935. Jacobs, Francine. **A Passion for Danger: Nansen's Arctic Adventures**. New York: Putnam, 1994. 160p. $17.95. ISBN 0-399-22674-5. 5-9

Fridtjof Nansen (1861-1930) of Norway was an explorer, statesman, scientist, and humanitarian. In 1882, he took a sealer into the seas of Greenland and began explorations in the area. In 1893, he spent seventeen months attempting to cross the Arctic Ocean to find the North Pole. The text looks at his journeys as he related them in his memoirs and presents the numerous dangers he encountered. He was unsuccessful in reaching the Pole, but his information on oceanography, meteorology, and diet helped those who came after him. In 1906, he became Norway's first minister to England. That Nansen received the Nobel Prize in 1922 for his work with World War I refugees shows his interest in helping others. Photographs, Bibliography, Notes, and Index.

936. Jacobs, Francine. **The Tainos: The People Who Welcomed Columbus**. Patrick Collins, illustrator. New York: Putnam, 1992. 103p. $15.95. ISBN 0-399-22116-6. 5-9

The Indians who met Christopher Columbus and his crews in 1492 were called Tainos. They had no written language, so all that survives about them are the writings made during the time of Columbus and pictographs discovered in caves on the islands. They were peaceful farming people whose ancestors had come from South America hundreds of years before. Although the Tainos welcomed Columbus and his men, the visitors called them Indians because they thought they were in India. Then they destroyed the Taino culture in their greed for gold. In fifty years, the Tainos became extinct. Notes, Museums, Bibliography, and Index.

937. Jacobs, William. **War with Mexico**. Brookfield, CT: Millbrook Press, 1994. 64p. $15.90; $5.95pa. ISBN 1-56294-366-9; 1-56294-776-1pa. (Spotlight on American History). 5-8

War between Mexico and the United States started in 1846 over territories that both claimed. Battles occurred at Monterey and Buena Vista as the United States drove toward Mexico City. When the United States won the war, many thought the boundaries of the country would extend with the Treaty of Guadalupe Hidalgo. What ensued after 1848 was anything but peaceful because of the bills in Congress to keep slavery from being legal in the new territories. The text discusses these various aspects of this war. Chronology, Further Reading, Bibliography, and Index.

938. Jacobs, William Jay. **Great Lives: Human Rights**. New York: Scribners, 1990. 278p. $22.95. ISBN 0-684-19036-2. 4-7

People concerned with the rights of all humans have been expressing their beliefs throughout history. The text uses a chronological organization to profile some of these people who have spoken out for others. In the New World setting, human rights advocates included Anne Hutchinson and Roger Williams. In the nineteenth century, such people as Dorothea Dix and Frederick Douglass professed their beliefs. In the industrial age, Susan B. Anthony and Andrew Carnegie are examples; in the twentieth century are such figures as Emma Goldman, Jacob Riis, Cesar Chavez, and Martin Luther King, Jr. For Further Reading and Index.

939. Jacobs, William Jay. **Great Lives**: **World Religions**. New York: Atheneum, 1996. 280p. $23. ISBN 0-689-80486-5. 4-7

The text covers religions and religious leaders throughout world history. Beginning with the religions of ancient Egypt and Persia, it continues with Asian religions, Judaism, Christianity, and Islam. Among the figures presented are Amenhotep IV, Zarathustra, Confucius, Buddha, Muhammad, Mahavira, Gandhi, Jesus, Khomeini, Moses, Jeremiah, Meir, Erasmus, Thomas Aquinas, John Calvin, John Wesley, George Fox, Roger Williams, Anne Hutchinson, Martin Luther King, Jr., Mother Teresa, and Joseph Smith. If appropriate, a brief interpretation of a person's theology also appears. Further Reading and Index.

940. Jacobs, William Jay. **La Salle: A Life of Boundless Adventure**. New York: Franklin Watts, 1994. 64p. $19.90. ISBN 0-531-20141-4. (First Book Explorer). 5-8

Robert Cavelier La Salle (1643–1687) placed the flag of France and a wooden Christian cross at the mouth of the Mississippi River on April 9, 1682. This claim for Louis XIV covered all of the land with rivers flowing into the Mississippi. Because Louisiana was so large, it added an enormous amount of territory to France. La Salle loved grand adventures, and he and his party explored the interior of the continent around the Great Lakes, the Ohio River, and the Gulf of Mexico. La Salle's main interests were in finding a water route to China, taking Mexico from Spain, and helping France to triumph over its enemies; gold did not entice him. For Further Reading and Index.

941. Jacobs, William Jay. **World Government**. New York: Scribners, 1992. 288p. $22.95. ISBN 0-684-19285-3. (Great Lives). 7 up

The text includes short biographies of up to 14 pages on such leaders as Napoleon Bonaparte (1769-1821), Vladimir Lenin (1870-1924), Adolf Hitler (1889-1945), Winston Churchill (1874-1965), Mohandas Gandhi (1869-1948), Mao Tse-tung (1893-1976), Charles de Gaulle (1890-1970), Golda Meir (1898-1978), Ruholla Khomeini (1900-1989), and Mikhail Gorbachev (b. 1931). Each entry presents the early lives of these people and shows what events led them to become leaders. Among the resources Jacobs used are diary entries, excerpts from published writings, and quotations. Photographs and For Further Reading.

942.   Jaro, Benita Kane. **The Door in the Wall**. Sag Harbor, NY: Permanent Press, 1994. 220p. $24. ISBN 1-877946-39-7. YA

Marcus Caelius Rufus (a real soldier for Caesar who lived 82–48 B.C.) writes in his diary about his reaction to his recent life as he takes control of a small country in Rome's civil war between Pompey and Caesar. He recalls his life in Rome as he came of age, rose to a position of respect, commanded an army, and, most recently, wondered about who to support—the man Caesar, with whom his life has become entwined, or Pompey, to whom Cicero turns. Marcus rejects the moral for Caesar's attentions, affections, and awards. Notes.

943.   Jenkins, Earnestine. **A Glorious Past: Ancient Egypt, Ethiopia, and Nubia**. New York: Chelsea House, 1994. 118p. $19.95; $7.95pa. ISBN 0-7910-2258-7; 0-7910-2684-1pa. (Milestones in Black American History). 5 up

The past of African-Americans can be traced to the African civilizations of Egypt, Nubia, and Ethiopia. Older than Egypt, which began in approximately 3100 B.C., Nubia, starting in about 3800 B.C., lasted longer than 5,000 years and possessed uncountable wealth. The Nubians were builders and creators of beautiful artifacts in gold, ebony, bronze, glass, and silver, and they developed their own alphabet. In the first century A.D., Ethiopia, originally known as Axum or Abyssinia, began a thousand-year history during which it controlled much of northern Africa and the wealthy Red Sea trade. Ezana, a strong king of the third century A.D., established Christianity and increased the kingdom's wealth. Among the Axumite literature is the story of the queen of Sheba and her visit to Solomon. Index.

944.   Jenkins, Tony. **Nicaragua and the United States: Years of Conflict**. New York: Franklin Watts, 1989. 187p. $21.29. ISBN 0-531-10795-7. 9 up

Eleven chapters give the history of the relationship between the United States and Nicaragua, from William Walker and the Manifest Destiny of 1848 up to the Bush and Ortega administrations in 1989. Among the thoughtful topics included are the Sandinistas, Contras, the non-Communists' fear of total suppression, the internal polarization in the church, and liberation theology. Bibliography, Chronology, and Index.

945.   Jiang, Ji-Li. **Red Scarf Girl: A Memoir of the Cultural Revolution**. New York: HarperCollins, 1997. 285p. $14.95. ISBN 0-06-027585-5. 6-10

When Ji-Li Jiang was twelve in 1966, she was intelligent and assertive, but the Cultural Revolution changed her life. No longer were intelligence, talent, or wealth respected. She had always believed that the Communist Party was kind and that Chairman Mao was dearer than her parents. When her father is detained, she must decide whether to renounce him or the Party.

946.   Jicai, Feng. **Let One Hundred Flowers Bloom**. Christopher Smith, translator. New York: Viking, 1996. 106p. $13.99. ISBN 0-670-85805-6. 7 up

After he graduates from the Beijing Academy of Fine Arts in the early 1960s, authorities send Hia Xiayu to a provincial pottery factory as punishment for his political crimes in the Cultural Revolution. Although he does not know what his crimes are, he decides to adjust and learn about pottery from the master potters with whom he works. The head of a section in the factory loves the woman that Hia marries, so he suffers various harassments for that as well. His wife thinks he is a counterrevolutionary after he is sent to hard labor in a quarry, and she aborts their child. The one thing that keeps him going is his dog, which tries to protect him.

947.   Jones, Constance. **Africa, 1500–1900**. New York: Facts on File, 1993. 140p. $16.95. ISBN 0-8160-2774-9. (World History Library). YA

The text gives an overview of Africa from 1500 to 1900. Chapters include information on the slave trade, European colonization and partition, and the beginning of apartheid. Topics cover the city-states, kingdoms, cultures, and traditions of the groups who lived in Africa at this time. Bibliography, Chronology, and Index.

948.   Jones, Jane Anderson. **Frida Kahlo**. Vero Beach, FL: Rourke, 1993. 111p. $14.95. ISBN 0-86625-485-4. (Arts). 8 up

Frida Kahlo (1907–1954) was involved in a terrible accident at age eighteen, but she kept her passionate interest in art, communism, her husband Diego Rivera, and her Mexican heritage. Her surrealist and symbolic paintings appear in color reproductions, and the story of her life interests and entertains. Chronology, Glossary, Bibliography, and Index.

949.   Jones, Jill. **Emily's Secret**. New York: St. Martin's Press, 1995. 355p. $4.99pa. ISBN 0-312-95576-6pa. YA

One of her descendants looks at the life of Emily Brontë (1818–1848) by combining a modern-day love story with flashbacks to the writer's life. The insights about the times make the reader wonder about the circumstances surrounding Emily's death.

950.   Jones, Terry, and Alan Ereira. **Crusades**. New York: Facts on File, 1995. 256p. $24.95. ISBN 0-8160-3275-0. YA

The text traces the Crusades and those who went on them in an overly zealous attempt to strike down the infidels in the name of moral and religious beliefs. Leaders such as Richard the Lionhearted and Philip Augustus are highlighted, along with the Crusaders' triumphs and defeats. Photographs, illustrations, and maps complement the text. Bibliography and Index.

951.   Jordan, Sherryl. **Wolf Woman**. Boston: Houghton Mifflin, 1994. 162p. $13.95. ISBN 0-395-70932-6. 7-10

A tribal chieftain in early Christian Britain finds Tanith living with wolves. When he takes her into the tribe, some of the members believe that she is filled with evil because of her association with the wolves. She must choose between a wolf clan that has accepted her and a human who loves her. What she knows is that wolves, unlike humans, only kill when their prey "chooses" to be killed. Her choice defies what the humans expect.

$$\boxed{\mathbb{K}}$$

952. Kamen, Gloria. **Hidden Music: The Life of Fanny Mendelssohn**. New York: Atheneum, 1996. 82p. $15. ISBN 0-689-31714-X. 5-8

Fanny Mendelssohn's (1805-1847) father told her that her music could be only an ornament; unlike her brother, Felix, she could not have a career in music. Yet, she composed more than 400 scores, and she had the chance to direct an orchestra in her home on one occasion. She supposedly did not even complain when her brother played some of her compositions and claimed them as his own. The text looks at her life and that of her family in the context of the times. Glossary, Bibliography, and Index.

953. Kaplan, Lawrence. **Oliver Cromwell**. New York: Chelsea House, 1986. 114p. $18.95. ISBN 0-87754-580-4. (World Leaders Past and Present). 8 up

Oliver Cromwell (1599–1658) fought for religious freedom in England as a Puritan while persecuting Catholics in Ireland. He supported parliamentary government but disbanded it when people challenged his methods. He denied that he had political ambition but rose to the pinnacle of political power in England. After leading the civil war against Charles I, he became the "Lord Protector" of Great Britain in 1653, declining the title of king. Photographs and reproductions enhance the text. Chronology, Further Reading, and Index.

954. Kaplan, Zoë Coralnik. **Eleanor of Aquitaine**. New York: Chelsea House, 1986. 114p. $18.95. ISBN 0-87754-552-7. (World Leaders Past and Present). 5 up

Eleanor of Aquitaine (1122-1204) was wife of two kings and mother of two others. She married her first husband, Louis Capet (Louis VII of France), when she was fifteen. She divorced him in 1152 to marry Henry Plantagenet, who became king of England two years later. She returned to France after this marriage soured to establish the court of love. In 1174, Henry disbanded her court and had her jailed for causing her children to rise against him. He held her captive for fifteen years until her favorite son, Richard the Lionhearted, came to power at Henry's death. She went on a crusade with her first husband, and she continued to travel well into her seventies when she crossed the Alps. Photographs and reproductions enhance the text. Chronology, Further Reading, and Index.

955. Katz, Welwyn Wilton. **Out of the Dark**. New York: Margaret K. McElderry, 1996. 192p. $16. ISBN 0-689-80947-6. 6-9

Ben Elliot and his younger brother, Keith, have to move to their father's boyhood home in a tiny Newfoundland village after their mother dies. Ben hates leaving all his friends, and the children in the new town resent his attitude toward them. As he spends time in a nearby Viking settlement, Ben imagines that he is Tor, a Viking shipbuilder. His pretenses become reality in this historical fantasy when Ben finds himself inside the Viking world.

956. Kauffman, Mark A. **The European Community: An Essential Guide Toward Knowing and Understanding the EC**. Denver, CO: Stone & Quill, 1993. 235p. $25.95. ISBN 1-883377-16-1. YA

The European Community is organized around concepts that may be unfamiliar to most Americans. The text explains why the countries of Western Europe have decided to begin cooperating, the real significance of the 1992 single European market program, the differences between the European Community and the United States, the European Community's ambitions, its plan to create a common currency, information about each member nation, how the EC makes and enforces its laws, its relationship with nonmember European nations, and its history. Chronology, Glossary, and Index.

957. Kaye, Tony. **Lech Walesa**. New York: Chelsea House, 1989. 112p. $18.95; $7.95pa. ISBN 1-55546-856-X; 0-7910-0689-1pa. (World Leaders Past and Present). 5 up

Although not able to go to college, Lech Walesa (b. 1943) showed his intelligence and capability in his jobs, and his disgust at labor conditions in Poland made him organize workers to complain. He was fired from three jobs for his social agitations, beginning in 1968. In 1980, he began the Solidarity movement, and for his efforts he won the Nobel Peace Prize in 1983. When communism failed in 1990, the people of Poland elected him to be their first president. Photographs enhance the text. Further Reading, Glossary, and Index.

958. **Kazakhstan**. Minneapolis, MN: Lerner, 1993. 56p. $19.95. ISBN 0-8225-2815-0. (Then and Now). 5-9

the Mongolian hordes invaded and influenced Kazakhstan for centuries. This text discusses this history and other problems the country now faces in its struggle for success since becoming independent in 1991. Photographs and maps enhance additional information about economics, geography, politics, and ethnography. Glossary and Index.

959.   Keegan, John. **History of Warfare**. New York: Knopf, 1993. 432p. $30; $15pa. ISBN 0-394-58801-0; 0-679-73082-6pa. YA

This survey of warfare starts with the beginning of history and continues to the atomic bomb's explosions in Hiroshima and Nagasaki during 1945. Keegan believes not that war is an extension of politics, as Clausewitz does, but that war is an extension of a culture. He draws on various resources from history, anthropology, ethnology, and psychology to express his theories that the threats to peace today are countries who wage war as they did before government or politics were invented. Bibliography and Index.

960.   Kellner, Douglas. **Ernesto "Che" Guevara**. New York: Chelsea House, 1988. 112p. $18.95. ISBN 1-55546-835-7. (World Leaders Past and Present). 7 up

By birth an Argentinean, Guevara (1928–1967) traveled throughout Latin America, where he lived among the impoverished peasants of the countryside and with exiled activists in the cities. He saw the failures of agrarian reform in Bolivia and watched U.S. intervention help overthrow the elected socialist government in Guatemala. In Mexico, he met Cuban exiles who wanted to oust the corrupt military regime. He went to Cuba and became a guerrilla fighter in the mountains and jungles, as well as Fidel Castro's head of industrialization. But the failure of his economic plan and a split with Castro made him leave Cuba to fight in the Congo and then in Bolivia, where he died. Photographs enhance the text. Chronology, Further Reading, and Index.

961.   Kellner, Douglas. **Kwame Nkrumah**. New York: Chelsea House, 1987. 112p. $18.95. ISBN 0-87754-546-4. (World Leaders Past and Present). 5 up

Kwame Nkrumah (1909-1972) founded modern Ghana and was a leader in the pan-African movement to promote African unity and overthrow colonial rule. He studied in the United States and England but returned to his country to serve in 1947. He sponsored nonviolent protests which led to his imprisonment, but he was freed in 1951. The Gold Coast obtained sovereignty from the British in 1957 and was renamed Ghana. Nkrumah transformed Ghana into a modern nation, but could not quell its different factions. His programs fought tribalism, but the poor economy and corruption kept many groups from supporting him, and he eventually left office in 1966. He lived in Guinea and died in Rumania. Photographs enhance the text. Chronology, Further Reading, and Index.

962.   Kelly, Eric. **The Trumpeter of Krakow**. Janina Domanska, illustrator. 1928. New York: Macmillan, 1968. 224p. $15.95; $3.95pa. ISBN 0-02-750140-X; 0-689-71571-4pa. 7 up

When Joseph is fifteen years old, in 1461, he and his parents leave their Ukranian farm after someone burns it and go to Krakow, Poland. They begin their new lives with the help of people they meet, but the alchemists in their neighborhood almost destroy the family in their repeated attempts to make gold. Joseph's forefathers had made a promise to the Polish king hundreds of years earlier, and his father wants to fulfill the promise to Casimir IV. He needs to do it before whoever destroyed their home finds them and the treasure they keep. *Newbery Medal.*

963.   Kendra, Judith. **Tibetans**. New York: Thomson Learning, 1994. 48p. $24.21. ISBN 1-56847-152-1. (Threatened Cultures). 5-8

Cultures with traditional ways of life unlike anything in the modern world are threatened with extinction when they come face to face with newer, more powerful societies. In 1950, the Chinese invaded Tibet. Since then the Tibetans have struggled to maintain their identity. The text integrates the past and the present as it shows Tibetan customs. A major concern is the continued exile of the greatest Buddhist leader, the Dalai Lama. Glossary, Further Reading, Further Information, and Index.

964.   Kennedy, Raymond A. **The Bitterest Age**. New York: Ticknor & Fields, 1994. 218p. $22.95. ISBN 0-395-68629-6. YA

Ingebord Maas moves with her mother and brother to Potsdam from Berlin to wait for her father to return from the Russian front during World War II. When her mother's letters return from the front unopened, Ingebord refuses to believe that her father might be dead.

965.   Kent, Peter, author/illustrator. **A Slice Through a City**. Brookfield, CT: Millbrook Press, 1996. 32p. $16.90. ISBN 0-7613-0039-2. 4-8

The text presents a European city that resembles London and other places in England as it might have evolved during the ages. Cross-sections show the site during the time periods of the Stone Age, the Romans, and later times in history, with eleven two-page spreads.

966.   Kent, Zachary. **World War I: "The War to End Wars."** Springfield, NJ: Enslow, 1994. 128p. $17.95. ISBN 0-89490-523-6. (American War). 6 up

Starting with the sinking of the *Lusitania* in 1915, the text relates the progress of World War, I from its beginning in Sarajevo in August 1914 until its end in November 1918. It presents the major battles starting with the Hindenburg Line marked by the Germans, Belleau Wood, the Marne, Saint-Mihiel, and the

Meuse-Argonne offensive. Among the leaders on both sides were Captain Baron Manfred von Richthofen, "The Red Baron"; Sergeant York; General Douglas MacArthur; and General John J. (Black Jack) Pershing. During the war, more than 116,000 American soldiers died, and 4 million more from other nations. Afterward, President Woodrow Wilson tried to start the League of Nations, but American isolationism defeated his plan. Photographs complement the text. Chronology, Notes, Further Reading, and Index.

967. Kerr, Daisy. **Keeping Clean**. New York: Franklin Watts, 1995. 48p. $14.42. ISBN 0-531-15353-8. 4-7

This text relates a history of bathing, plumbing, and waste removal. Each two-page spread deals with a different time or region as they cover such topics as the ancient world, the Middle Ages, Roman baths, spaceship hygiene, and lavatories on board ships. Illustrations augment the text. Glossary and Index.

968. Kerr, Judith, author/illustrator. **When Hitler Stole Pink Rabbit**. New York: Putnam, 1972. 192p. $14.95. ISBN 0-698-20182-5. New York: Yearling, 1974. 192p. $3.99pa. ISBN 0-440-49017-0pa. 4-7

Anna's Jewish family leaves Berlin for Switzerland in 1933 after her father disappears. At the border, she has to leave her pink rabbit, her favorite stuffed animal. The family joins her father and goes to France, but as the war comes to France, they escape to England. Anna, age nine when she leaves Berlin, has to learn new languages and attend new schools while her family runs from the war.

969. Kherdian, David. **The Road from Home: The Story of an Armenian Girl**. New York: Greenwillow/ Morrow, 1979. 238p. $14.93; $4.95pa. ISBN 0-688-84205-4; 0-688-14425-Xpa. 7 up

In a first-person point of view biography, Kherdian tells the story of his mother, an Armenian girl who endured the wrath of the Turkish government to survive. The historical background shows that modern Turkey continued the persecution of the Armenians begun by "Red" Sultan Abdul Hamid in the 1895–1896 massacres. Although the modern constitution said that the government was founded on liberty, equality, justice, and fraternity, the government decided to settle the "Armenian Question" in 1915. Veron Dumehjian, born to a wealthy Armenian family, enjoyed the material comforts gleaned from her father's poppy gum exporting business. But the Turkish soldiers arrived one day and made the family, except for the grandmother whose two sons were serving in the Turkish army, leave within two hours. Almost every member of the family died of cholera in a camp, and Veron's mother died of despair soon after. Veron eventually reunited with her father and then her grandmother, but the Turks then ran her and the other Armenians out of yet another town. After she arrived in Athens with a favorite aunt, a family succeeded in getting her to come to America with them to marry their son, the father of the author. *Newbery Honor.*

970. King, Celia. **Seven Ancient Wonders of the World**. San Francisco: Chronicle, 1990. Unpaged. $9.95. ISBN 0-87701-707-7. 3 up

The seven ancient wonders of the world pop up in this book. They are the Pyramids of Egypt, the Pharos lighthouse at Alexandria, the Hanging Gardens of Babylon, the Temple of Diana at Ephesus, the Colossus of Rhodes, the Statue of Zeus at Olympia, and the Mausoleum at Halicarnassus.

971. King, John. **The Gulf War**. New York: Dillon Press, Macmillan, 1991. 48p. $13.95. ISBN 0-87518-514-2. 5-10

Questions arise as to why the United States fought the Gulf War in 1991. The text looks at geography in the area, history, the role of oil, and Saddam Hussein's Iraq as it asks why Hussein initially invaded Kuwait. The crisis began in August 1990 and escalated to the attack in January 1991. Glossary, Key Events, Further Reading, and Index.

972. King, John. **Kurds**. New York: Thomson Learning, 1994. 48p. $15.95. ISBN 1-56847-149-1. (Threatened Cultures). 5-8

The text presents three people—one in Turkey, one in Iraq, and one in Iran—who have no homeland. They are Kurds who have been displaced. By addressing the history and politics of these people, the text illustrates the problems they face. Photographs and maps enhance the text. Further Reading, Glossary, and Index.

973. King, Laurie R. **A Letter of Mary**. New York: St. Martin's Press, 1997. 288p. $23.95. ISBN 0-312-14670-1. YA

Mary Russell, an Oxford theologian, lives with her husband, Sherlock Holmes, in Sussex. Her friend Dorothy Ruskin brings her a document from a Palestinian dig that seems to be a letter from Mariam of Magdala, a woman who calls herself an apostle of Jesus. After Ruskin gives Russell the letter, she dies in a traffic accident that proves to be a murder. Russell and Holmes investigate.

974. King, Laurie R. **A Monstrous Regiment of Women**. New York: St. Martin's Press, 1995. 326p. $22.95. ISBN 0-312-13565-3. YA

Mary Russell, the assistant to Sherlock Holmes from *The Beekeeper's Apprentice*, has her own situation in Oxford, England, after World War I. She still likes Holmes, but her interest in women's rights and her concern for furthering her studies keeps her in Oxford. When she meets Margery Childe, a spiritual advisor to several young women, she wonders why so many of Childe's protégés die and leave their estates to Childe. Her investigation takes her to the back streets of London and various encounters with Holmes.

975.   King, Perry Scott. **Pericles**. New York: Chelsea House, 1988. 112p. $18.95. ISBN 0-87754-547-2. (World Leaders Past and Present). 5 up

Pericles (499-429 B.C.), a general, was such an influential member of the governing council of Athens that his time is called the "age of Pericles." He was the son of Xanthippus, a Greek war hero, and Agaristes, a descendent of Cleisthemes, the founder of Athenian democracy. Pericles entered public life when he sponsored the chorus for performances of *The Persians*. He was an orator who advocated democracy and additional rights for the lower classes. In his attempt to establish the Athenian empire, he led Athens into frequent wars against rivals who were unwilling to accept Athenian dominance, and defeated them with naval power. He built the temples on the Acropolis, such as the Parthenon, as monuments to Athenian glory. Photographs and reproductions enhance the text. Chronology, Further Reading, and Index.

976.   Kirchberger, Joe H. **The First World War**. New York: Facts on File, 1992. 402p. $45. ISBN 0-8160-2552-5. (Eyewitness History). YA

In 1914, Austria-Hungary and Serbia had a disagreement that, with the assassination of Archduke Francis Ferdinand of Austria, escalated into a major war involving Russia, Germany, France, Britain, Japan, and Turkey. By 1917, the United States had joined. This war, also known as the Great War, changed European history. The text includes many firsthand accounts of the war from memoirs, speeches, newspapers, and letters. Some of the commentaries come from T. E. Lawrence (Lawrence of Arabia), Woodrow Wilson, Otto von Bismarck, and Vladimir Lenin. Each chapter includes an essay about the area of the war it presents and a chronology of events. Appendices, Bibliography, and Index.

977.   Kirchberger, Joe H. **The French Revolution and Napoleon**. New York: Facts on File, 1989. 376p. $45. ISBN 0-8160-2090-6. (Eyewitness History). YA

The French Revolution of 1789 has been called the first revolution of the modern world. It inspired people in other nations to rebel and assert themselves. The text looks at all aspects of the Revolution through speeches, letters, newspaper articles, diaries, and memoirs to show how people in all levels of society interpreted the events of the Revolution as they occurred. Essays, chronicles of events, more than 50 historical documents, and nearly 100 contemporary illustrations, as well as brief biographies of nearly 200 people, tell the story. Bibliography and Index.

978.   Kisling, Lee. **The Fool's War**. New York: HarperCollins, 1992. 166p. $14. ISBN 0-06-020836-8. 5-8

Clemmy, age fifteen, must take charge of the family farm in the Middle Ages after his father dies. The farm, although successful, does not challenge his capabilities, and he becomes involved in various other endeavors. He saves the village idiot from his father's abuse and learns to read Latin with a monk's help. He leaves to serve the king and keeps him from having to fight against "the Turk," Suleiman the Magnificent. A touch of fantasy saves them from the Turks, but the history of the mid-sixteenth century is apparent throughout the tale.

979.   Kittredge, Mary. **Frederick the Great: King of Prussia**. New York: Chelsea House, 1987. 112p. $18.95. ISBN 0-87754-525-1. (World Leaders Past and Present). 8 up

Frederick II (1740–1786) ruled the kingdom of Prussia from 1740 until his death; even his own subjects called him "Frederick the Great." He reformed his country, modernized it, set the standards for war in eighteenth-century Europe, and followed the intellectual thinking of the Enlightenment. He supported human equality and freedom and thought that a king's power was based on diplomatic and military success rather than divine right. His many interests also earned him the title of the "philosopher king." Photographs and reproductions enhance the text. Chronology, Further Reading, and Index.

980.   Kittredge, Mary. **Marc Antony**. New York: Chelsea House, 1988. 112p. $18.95; $7.95pa. ISBN 0-87754-505-7; 0-7910-0610-7pa. (World Leaders Past and Present). 5 up

Marc Antony (83?-30 B.C.) rose briefly above the political tumult in Rome to become its leader in 44 B.C. He first served in Syria and Egypt and acquired riches enough to buy influence and win election to his first public office in 52 B.C. He took Julius Caesar's position in 44 B.C., and after appropriating Caesar's fortune, gained control of the army and drove Caesar's assassins into exile. Soon, however, he had to share power with Octavian and Lepidus in the Second Triumvirate. In 41 B.C., he met and fell in love with Cleopatra of Alexandria and married her. In 32 B.C., Rome declared war on them, and when Octavian won control in 30 B.C., Antony committed suicide. Reproductions highlight the text. Further Reading, Chronology, and Index.

981.   Klare, Roger. **Gregor Mendel: Father of Genetics**. Springfield, NJ: Enslow, 1997. 128p. $18.95. ISBN 0-89490-789-1. (Great Minds of Science). 5-8

Gregor Mendel (1822-1884) discovered the concept of how genes become dominant and recessive. The text looks at his personal and professional life. Photographs, Diagrams, Chronology, Further Reading, Glossary, and Index.

982.   Klein, Robin. **All in the Blue Unclouded Weather**. New York: Viking, 1991. 162p. $11.95. ISBN 0-670-83909-4. 5-9

In rural Australia, after World War II, four sisters, the Melling girls, have individual interests and goals, but have to cope collectively with their cousin's troublemaking. Grace wants to leave home; Heather, age thirteen, acts superior to the others; Cathy wants approval from a wealthy girl in school; and Vivienne, the youngest, hates the hand-me-downs that she must wear. Vivienne decides to spend all her money in a second-hand store on a china plate that matches her mother's wedding plate, and her mother is very pleased with her sacrifice.

983.   Klein, Robin. **Dresses of Red and Gold**. New York: Viking 1992. 177p. $12.50. ISBN 0-670-84733-X. 5-9

This sequel to *All in the Blue Unclouded Weather* takes place in the autumn after World War II has ended. The Melling girls continue living in their small Australian town while their father looks for work. One sister has gone to the city to study dressmaking, but Heather, age fourteen, and the younger girls have various experiences; Cathy brags about a large birthday party, which she has to stage when guests show up, and Vivienne stays in the hospital with a tonsillectomy after her elderly roommate dies. Grace comes to visit but looks forward to leaving. Their snobbish cousin comes to visit often without an invitation.

984.   Klein, Robin. **The Sky in Silver Lace**. New York: Viking, 1996. 178p. $13.99. ISBN 0-670-86692-X. 5-8

The Melling sisters (Vivienne, Heather, Cathy, and Grace) and their mother, from *All in the Blue Unclouded Weather* and *Dresses of Red and Gold,* have to find a place to live because their father has left home in the midst of marital problems. During this time in the 1940s, they move three times in the suburb of an Australian city. But the dreams of each girl seem a little closer to coming true, and their annoying cousin, Isobel, has an experience that somewhat chastens her irritating attitude.

985.   Kline, Nancy. **Elizabeth Blackwell: A Doctor's Triumph**. Berkeley, CA: Conari Press, 1997. 224p. $6.95pa. ISBN 1-57324-057-5pa. (Barnard Biography). 8 up

Elizabeth Blackwell (1821-1910), considered the first American female doctor, emigrated from England with her family of Dissenters. She pursued her quest for a medical school to admit her until finally Geneva Medical College of Western New York did so as the result of a joke. She succeeded after much to deter her, and Kline places the reader in Blackwell's time so that her achievements are even more apparent. Bibliography, Chronology, and Index.

986.   Koehn, Ilse. **Mischling, Second Degree: My Childhood in Nazi Germany**. New York: Greenwillow/Morrow, 1977. 240p. $12.88. ISBN 0-688-84110-4. 7 up

When the Nuremberg Laws for protection were decreed in Germany on September 15, 1935, the author, age six, had one Jewish grandparent, which meant that she was designated a "*mischling*, second degree." Her parents were free thinkers and anti-Nazi, but they had not told her that she had a Jewish grandmother. During the war years, she became a Hitler Youth. She did not know until after the Nazi defeat that she was partially Jewish.

987.   Koenig, Viviane. **The Ancient Egyptians: Life in the Nile Valley**. Mary Kae LaRose, translator; Veronique Ageorges, illustrator. 1992. Brookfield, CT: Millbrook Press, 1996. 64p. $7.95pa. ISBN 0-7613-0099-6pa. (Peoples of the Past). 5-8

Over 5,000 years ago, the Egyptian culture, which lasted for 2,000 years, began to form. Only in the past two or three centuries has information about this civilization begun to materialize. Archaeologists have found artifacts that have helped them learn something about the towns, the temples, and the tombs of these people. The text discusses the importance of the Nile, daily life, craftsmen and artists, scribes and scholars, and pharaohs. Find Out More, Glossary, and Index.

988.   Konigsburg, E. L. **A Proud Taste for Scarlet and Miniver**. New York: Atheneum, 1973. 202p. $14.95. ISBN 0-689-30111-1. New York: Dell, 1989. 202p. $3.99pa. ISBN 0-440-47201-6pa. 6 up

As she waits for Henry II to arrive in heaven, Eleanor of Aquitaine (c. 1122-1204) and her companions remember her life. They recall incidents from the twelfth century in France and England in which she was involved. She was the mother of two kings, King Richard the Lionheart and King John, and the wife of two kings, Henry II of England and Louis VII of France. *Phoenix Honor Book.*

989.   Koral, April. **An Album of War Refugees**. New York: Franklin Watts, 1989. 96p. $13.90. ISBN 0-531-10765-5. (Picture Album). 6-9

The text presents refugees from different countries who have come to the United States since the Armenians arrived in 1915. The latest refugees have come from Central America. Personal stories bring immediacy to situations in which people have had to leave their homes, usually having lost all material items, in order to save their lives. In their land of exile, they have faced new political, social, and economic problems. Bibliography and Index.

990.   Kordon, Klaus. **Brothers Like Friends**. Elizabeth D. Crawford, translator. New York: Philomel, 1992. 206p. $14.95. ISBN 0-399-22137-9. 5 up

Frank, age seven, lives in Berlin, Germany, in the Russian sector during 1950. His two favorite things are his half-brother, Burkie the soccer star, and his own dream world. His life changes, however, when his mother decides to marry a man who has little interest in the children and his brother dies from an unusual injury in a soccer game. Fortunately, he has kindly neighbors who try to support him. *German Youth Literature Award Runner-up.*

991.   Kort, Michael. **China: Under Communism**. Brookfield, CT: Millbrook Press, 1995. 175p. $17.40. ISBN 1-56294-450-9. 7 up

China has one-fifth of the world's population and its third largest economy. Although this history of China focuses on the time period since Mao Zedong formed the People's Republic of China on October 1, 1949, it also gives a brief history of Chinese culture through the centuries. Kort looks at the Chinese Empire, the Chinese Republic, Socialist China, the Great Leap Forward, the Cultural Revolution, and China under Deng Xiaoping. Glossary, Recommended Reading, and Index.

992.   Kort, Michael. **Mikhail Gorbachev**. New York: Franklin Watts, 1990. 128p. $13.90. ISBN 0-531-10941-0. (Impact Biography). 7 up

Because of the changes he made in the Soviet Union, Mikhail Gorbachev (b. 1931) must be considered one of the most important leaders of the twentieth century. He helped to end the forty-five-year-old Cold War, allowed the Berlin Wall to fall, and fomented the rise of democracy in Eastern Europe. His reforms had names such as *glasnost, perestroika,* and *democratizatsiya.* By looking at his life in relationship to Soviet history, the text shows how remarkable the changes he wrought were. It also covers the withdrawal of Russian troops from Afghanistan, the Chernobyl nuclear disaster, the Armenian earthquake, the INF nuclear arms agreement, and the restructuring of the Communist Party. Source Notes, Further Reading, and Index.

993.   Kort, Michael. **Russia**. New York: Facts on File, 1995. 168p. $17.95. ISBN 0-8160-3061-8. (Nations in Transition). 7 up

The text looks at the history of Russia from its beginnings through the Soviet period. It discusses how the various government policies have affected the ordinary citizens who have had to live with those rules, and carefully explains the difficulties in the transition after the demise of the Soviet Union. Quotes from Russians living through this period give authenticity to the text. Among the chapter topics are politics, government, the new economy, and daily life. Photographs, Chronology, Further Reading, Notes, and Index.

994.   Kort, Michael G. **The Cold War**. Brookfield, CT: Millbrook Press, 1994. 160p. $17.40. ISBN 1-56294-353-7. 7 up

From 1945 to 1990, the United States was involved in a rivalry of ideologies between the capitalist countries of the West and the Communist nations led by the Soviet Union. The text looks at the origins of the conflict and the buildup of nuclear weapons with which each side could destroy the other. The two sides encouraged spying and other secret activities. The topics covered are the rise of the Berlin Wall; Soviet Russia and communism; the Korean War; the Cold War underground and in the United States; adjustments to new leaders; the Cuban Missile Crisis with Kennedy, Khrushchev, and Castro; Vietnam; détente; and the end of the Cold War in 1990 with the fall of the Berlin Wall. For Further Reading and Index.

995.   Kort, Michael G. **Marxism in Power: The Rise and Fall of a Doctrine**. Brookfield, CT: Millbrook Press, 1993. 176p. $16.90. ISBN 1-56294-241-7. 7 up

Karl Marx (1818–1883) believed in the rights of the proletariat, and his philosophy became the central tenet for the governments of Lenin, Stalin, and Mao. These men, however, adapted the beliefs to their own ideas and purposes, and the evolution away from the pure doctrine espoused by Marx eventually caused the demise of Chinese cultural life and the collapse of the Soviet government in the late 1980s and early 1990s. Bibliography, Chronology, and Index.

996. Koslow, Philip. **Centuries of Greatness: The West African Kingdoms 750–1900**. New York: Chelsea House, 1995. 118p. $14.95; $7.95pa. ISBN 0-7910-2266-8; 0-7910-2692-2pa. (Milestones in Black American History). 5 up

Covering over 1,000 years of history in Africa, the text presents information from the Ghanian Empire through the slave trade. Military, economic, and political background helps clarify the history of Africa's groups, and several first-person accounts give an immediacy to some of the information. Black-and-white photographs show the area. Further Reading, Chronology, and Index.

997. Koslow, Philip. **Dahomey: The Warrior Kings**. New York: Chelsea House, 1996. 63p. $15.95; $8.95pa. ISBN 0-7910-3137-3; 0-7910-3138-1pa. (The Kingdoms of Africa). 5-8

In the seventeenth and eighteenth centuries, Dahomey was a powerful West African kingdom. The five chapters cover its history from the establishment of the empire; the rule of the warring kings; the kingdom's political and social structure; to its culture, religion, art, and technology. The rulers of Dahomey prospered by trading slaves, and the text covers this aspect of the history. Photographs, Chronology, Further Reading, Glossary, and Index.

998. Koslow, Philip. **El Cid**. New York: Chelsea House, 1993. 111p. $18.95. ISBN 0-7910-1239-5. (Hispanics of Achievement). 5 up

As Spain's national hero, Rodrigo Díaz (d. 1099) was given the name "El Cid" (derived from the Arabic word for "lord") for his exploits. In the eleventh century, at age seventeen, he took command of the Castilian army. Later, King Alfonso VI banished him, but during fifteen years of exile, he led a private army to victories over Christians and Muslims alike. In 1094, he captured Valencia and became its ruler. Then he crushed a Muslim army on the plains of Cuarte, the beginning of the "Reconquest" to reclaim land from Muslims. Photographs and reproductions enhance the text. Chronology, Further Reading, and Index.

999. Kossman, Nina. **Behind the Border**. New York: Lothrop, Lee & Shepard, 1994. 96p. $14. ISBN 0-688-13494-7. 4-7

Nina's family decides to leave Russia in the 1960s, but her teacher hears about it before they get permission and calls Nina's father a traitor. Nina has been taught to love Lenin and to fear foreign tourists who might put a small bomb in candy or chewing gum. When she loses her beach ball on the Black Sea, it floats behind the border where she cannot go to retrieve it. When the teacher says that Nina's father will die of a heart attack on the plane, Nina realizes that the teacher spreads lies. Notes.

1000. Kotlyarskaya, Elena. **Women in Society: Russia**. New York: Marshall Cavendish, 1994. 128p. $21.95. ISBN 1-85435-561-9. (Women in Society). 7 up

After introducing the women of Russia through the story of Yaroslavna, the twelfth-century wife of Prince Igor whose love and loyalty helped her husband escape disgrace and defeat, the author discusses the roles of Russian women by interweaving historical and contemporary practices. She presents the expectations imposed upon rural and urban dwellers, religious and secular believers, and the poor or wealthy. The chapters cover milestones, what being a woman means in the culture, and the life of a woman from birth to old age. Short biographies of Valentina, the first woman in space; Parasha the Pearl, a singer (1768–1803); Valkyrie or Alexandra Kollontai, Marxist revolutionist (1872–1952); Catherine the Great (1729–1796); and Galina Ulanova, ballerina (b. 1910) show what some women have done. Photographs complement the text. Women Firsts, Glossary, Further Reading, and Index.

1001. Kramer, Ann, and Simon Adams. **Exploration and Empire: Empire-Builders, European Expansion and the Development of Science**. New York: Warwick Press, Franklin Watts, 1990. 48p. $13.90. ISBN 0-531-19074-9. (Historical Atlas). 3-8

The text looks at world history from the Renaissance to the Industrial Revolution in five chapters, the first establishing the world situation in 1450 and the others presenting different regions of the world. Topics include the development of printing, the roles of women, slavery, the end of the Aztec and Incan empires, growth of worldwide trade, early settlement of the Americas, the rise of the Chinese and Japanese empires, European expansion, and the growth of science. Illustrations enhance the text. Index.

1002. Kristy, Davida. **Coubertin's Olympics: How the Games Began**. Minneapolis, MN: Lerner, 1995. 128p. $17.21. ISBN 0-8225-3327-8. 5 up

Baron Pierre de Coubertin (1863-1937) decided to reestablish the Olympics, last held in A.D. 388 in Greece, more than 1,500 years later. He was successful in 1896. He gave speeches, arranged alliances, and organized an international conference on amateur sports where he slyly changed the topic to the Olympics. Not given recognition in 1896, he was eventually named President for Life of the Olympic Games. The torch ritual began in 1936, and it took twelve days to transport the torch from Olympia, Greece, to Berlin, Germany. De Coubertin seems to have sacrificed his personal life for this dream that he made into reality. Sources of Information and Index. *New York Public Library Books for the Teen Age.*

1003. Kristy, Davida. **George Balanchine: American Ballet Master**. Minneapolis, MN: Lerner, 1996. 128p. $17.21. ISBN 0-8225-4951-4. (Lerner Biographies). 5 up

Gyorgy Balanchivadze (1904-1983) never wanted to be a dancer, and after his mother enrolled him in ballet school, he ran away. Yet he returned and discovered that the rigorous training gave him ideas for new movements and new stories to tell through dance. Later he traveled throughout Europe, where he met an American who thought that Americans would like ballet. He changed his Russian name to George Balanchine and created popular dances for Broadway, film, and the circus before forming his own ballet company. The text looks at his life and his accomplishments. Sources, Bibliography, and Index.

1004. Kronenwetter, Michael. **London**. New York: New Discovery, 1992. 96p. $14.95. ISBN 0-02-751050-6. (Cities at War). 7-10

The text gives an account of World War II in London through eyewitness quotes from interviews, diaries, and other primary sources. Accompanying documentary photographs reveal the actions of ordinary citizens trying to survive. Covering the Blitz and the experiences of the young evacuees, the text emphasizes the daily lives of ordinary Londoners rather than the unusual. Bibliography and Index.

1005. Kronenwetter, Michael. **The New Eastern Europe**. New York: Franklin Watts, 1991. 160p. $13.90. ISBN 0-531-11066-4. 7 up

The text includes a history of Czechoslovakia (now the Czech Republic and Slovakia), Poland, Hungary, Bulgaria, Romania, and the former German Democratic Republic. This background creates a necessary base for an explanation of the importance of the breakup of old alliances and the creation of new ones into 1991. Photographs and maps enhance the text. Further Reading and Index.

1006. Kronenwetter, Michael. **Northern Ireland**. New York: Franklin Watts, 1990. 160p. $13.90. ISBN 0-531-10942-9. 7 up

The text looks at the history of Northern Ireland and Ireland and shows the basis of contemporary conflicts in the dual battles between the Irish and the English and the Protestants and the Catholics. Kronenwetter indicates that the Irish people have been taking sides against each other for so long that they think a compromise would mean that others had lost their lives and gained nothing. Both sides have used terrorist attacks to break the other, and many of these incidents are cited in this clear account of the Troubles. Notes, Further Reading, and Index.

1007. Kronenwetter, Michael. **The War Against Terrorism**. Englewood Cliffs, NJ: Julian Messner, 1989. 130p. $13.98. ISBN 0-671-69050-7. 7 up

Since the mid-1960s, international terrorism has escalated. With instant communication, people throughout the globe know immediately when a terrorist act occurs. The text discusses the history of terrorism and includes overviews of terrorist and antiterrorist groups. Terrorism comes in varied forms, and the United States has had to create a policy and a response toward the acts that sometimes seem appropriate to everyone except those directly involved in the situation. Among the specific situations noted are the Munich Olympic Game murders and terrorism in Latin America, Northern Ireland, and the Middle East. Bibliography and Index.

1008. Krull, Kathleen. **Lives of the Artists: Masterpieces, Messes (and What the Neighbors Thought)**. Kathryn Hewitt, illustrator. San Diego, CA: Harcourt Brace, 1995. 96p. $19. ISBN 0-15-200103-4. 4-8

Vignettes on artists, arranged chronologically, give interesting insights into their lives and sometimes their relationships to each other. The artists are Leonardo da Vinci (Italy, 1452-1519), Michelangelo Buonarroti (Italy, 1475-1564), Peter Bruegel (Netherlands, 1525-1569), Sofonisba Anguissola who served King Philip II of Spain although Italian (1532-1625), Rembrandt van Rijn (Holland, 1606-1669), Katsushika Hokusai (Japan, 1760-1849), Mary Cassatt (American relocated in France, 1845-1926), Vincent van Gogh (Holland, 1853-1890), Käthe Kollwitz (Germany, 1867-1945), Henri Matisse (France, 1869-1954), Pablo Picasso (Spain 1881-1973), Marc Chagall (Russia, 1887-1985), Marcel Duchamp (France, 1887-1968), Georgia O'Keeffe (United States, 1887-1986), William H. Johnson (United States, 1901-1970), Salvador Dali (Spain, 1904-1989), Isamu Noguchi (United States, 1904-1988), Diego Rivera (Mexico, 1886-1957), Frida Kahlo (Mexico, 1907-1954), and Andy Warhol (United States, 1928-1987). Artistic Terms, Index of Artists, and For Further Reading and Looking. *IRA Teachers' Choices, American Bookseller Pick of the Lists*, and *New York Public Library Books for the Teen Age*.

1009. Krull, Kathleen. **Lives of the Athletes: Thrills, Spills (and What the Neighbors Thought)**. Kathryn Hewitt, illustrator. San Diego, CA: Harcourt Brace, 1997. 96p. $19. ISBN 0-15-200806-3. 4-7

In capsule biographies, Krull tells a little about the lives of some international athletes. She includes commentaries on Jim Thorpe (1888-1953), Duke Kahanamoku (1890-1968), Babe Ruth (1895-1948), Red Grange (1903-1991), Johnny Weissmuller (1903-1984), Gertrude Ederle (b. 1906), Babe Didrikson Zaharias (1911-1956), Sonja Henie (1912-1969), Jesse Owens (1913-1980), Jackie Robinson (1919-1972), Sir Edmund Hillary (b. 1919), Maurice Richard (b. 1921), Maureen Connolly (1934-1969), Roberto Clemente (1934-1972), Wilma Rudolph (1940-1994), Arthur Ashe (1943-1993), Pete Maravich (1947-1988), Bruce Lee (1940-1973), Pelé (b. 1940), and Flo Hyman (1954-1986). Selected Bibliography.

1010. Krull, Kathleen. **Lives of the Musicians: Good Times, Bad Times (and What the Neighbors Thought)**. Kathryn Hewitt, illustrator. San Diego, CA: Harcourt Brace, 1993. 96p. $18.95. ISBN 0-15-248010-2. 4-8

Vignettes on musicians, arranged chronologically, give interesting insights into their lives and sometimes their relationships to each other. The musicians included are Antonio Vivaldi (Italy, 1876-1741), Johann Sebastian Bach (Germany, 1685-1750), Wolfgang Amadeus Mozart (Austria, 1756-1791), Ludwig van Beethoven (Germany, 1770-1827), Frédéric Chopin (Poland, 1810-1849), Giuseppe Verdi (Italy, 1813-1901), Clara Schumann (Germany, 1819-1896), Stephen Foster (America, 1826-1864), Johannes Brahms (Germany, 1833-1897), Peter Ilich Tchaikovsky (Russia, 1840-1893), William Gilbert (England, 1836-1911) and Arthur Sullivan (England, 1842-1900), Erik Satie (France, 1866-1925), Scott Joplin (America, 1868-1917), Charles Ives (1874-1954), Igor Stravinsky (Russia, 1882-1971), Nadia Boulanger (France, 1887-1979), Sergei Prokofiev (Ukraine, 1891-1953), George Gershwin (America, 1898-1937), and Woody Guthrie (America, 1912-1967). Musical Terms, Index of Composers, and For Further Reading and Listening. *Boston Globe-Horn Book Honor, American Library Association Notable Books for Children, Notable Children's Trade Books in the Field of Social Studies, PEN Center USA West Literary Award, IRA Teachers' Choices, New York Public Library's Books for the Teen Age*, and *Golden Kite Honor*.

1011. Krull, Kathleen. **Lives of the Writers: Comedies, Tragedies (and What the Neighbors Thought)**. Kathryn Hewitt, illustrator. San Diego, CA: Harcourt Brace, 1994. 96p. $19. ISBN 0-15-248009-9. 4 up

Vignettes on writers, arranged chronologically, give interesting insights into their lives and sometimes their relationships to each other. Writers covered are Murasaki Shikibu (Japan, 973?-1025?), Miguel de Cervantes (Spain, 1547-1616), William Shakespeare (England, 1564-1616), Jane Austen (England, 1775-1817), Hans Christian Anderson (Denmark, 1805-1875), Edgar Allan Poe (America, 1809-1849), Charles Dickens (England, 1812-1870), Charlotte Brontë (England, 1816-1855) and Emily Brontë (England, 1818-1848), Emily Dickinson (America, 1830-1886), Louisa May Alcott (America, 1832-1888), Mark Twain (America, 1835-1910), Frances Hodgson Burnett (England, 1849-1924), Robert Louis Stevenson (Scotland, 1850-1894), Jack London (America, 1876-1916), Carl Sandburg (America, 1878-1967), E. B. White (America, 1899-1985), Zora Neale Hurston (America, 1901?-1960), Langston Hughes (1902-1967), and Isaac Bashevis Singer (Poland and America, 1904-1991). Literary Terms, Index of Writers, and For Further Reading and Writing. *American Bookseller Pick of the Lists, NCTE Notable Children's Trade Books in the Language Arts*, and *IRA Teachers' Choices*.

1012. Kuckreja, Madhavi. **Prince Norodom Sihanouk**. New York: Chelsea House, 1990. 110p. $18.95. ISBN 1-55546-851-9. (World Leaders Past and Present). 5 up

The leader of the Southeast Asian nation of Cambodia, who freed it from France without war, is Prince Norodom Sihanouk (b. 1922). He tried to keep Cambodia on a neutral course, but the war in Vietnam moved into his country, and Pol Pot's Khmer Rouge rebels overthrew him in 1970. He watched from abroad as war tore his nation, but he had no power to stop the rebels as they killed over 2 million people through execution or overwork. In 1979, Vietnam drove out the Khmer Rouge, and for ten years, Sihanouk allied with Pol Pot's murderers. Photographs enhance the text. Chronology, Further Reading, and Index.

1013. Kyle, Benjamin. **Muammar el-Qaddafi**. New York: Chelsea House, 1987. 112p. $18.95. ISBN 0-87754-446-8. (World Leaders Past and Present). 5 up

Muammar el-Qaddafi (b. 1942) seized power in 1969 at the age of twenty-seven. He was a Bedouin despot who resented the centuries of Greek, Roman, Turkish, French, and British control over the Middle East. He believed in Gamal Abdel Nasser's call for a unified Arab nation based on Islam and the desire to destroy Israel. In 1969, he overthrew King Idris I, the man Western nations installed in power after World War II. El-Qaddafi has nationalized industries, brought Islamic law into the political system, and used oil wealth for roads, hospitals, schools, factories, and mosques. Photographs enhance the text. Chronology, Further Reading, and Index.

1014. **Kyrgyzstan**. Minneapolis, MN: Lerner, 1993. 56p. $19.95. ISBN 0-8225-2814-2. (Then and Now). 5-9

The Kyrgyz (or Kirghiz), a nomadic, Turkic-speaking, Sunni Muslim people with Mongol strains, comprise a little over half the population of Kyrgyzstan. Their huge differences from their twentieth-century captors, the Soviet Union communists, along with other problems, are the focus of this text covering the history, economics, geography, and politics of the country. Maps and photographs complement the text. Glossary and Index.

L

1015. Lace, William. **Defeat of the Spanish Armada**. San Diego, CA: Lucent, 1997. 96p. $19.95. ISBN 1-56006-458-7. (Battles of the Middle Ages). 7 up

In 1588, Elizabeth I supported the British navy's attempt to defeat the Spanish fleet as it sailed into the British channel. The battle was the first on the sea, and the tactics established here remained in practice until World War II when aircraft carriers entered service. The text discusses the political, religious, and historical situation that led to the battle and the subsequent Spanish defeat. Bibliography, Chronology, Further Reading, and Index.

1016. Lace, William W. **England**. San Diego, CA: Lucent, 1997. 128p. $17.96. ISBN 1-56006-194-4. (Overview: Modern Nations of the World). 7 up

Illustrations and photographs complement the six chapters of text, each based on a theme through which Lace shows that England has changed from a world leader to a supporting player. He includes sidebars with stories of English history such as Hengist and Horsa and backgrounds about Henry VIII's six wives to make the book both anecdotal and scholarly. Bibliography, Chronology, Further Reading, and Index.

1017. Lace, William W. **The Little Princes in the Tower**. San Diego, CA: Lucent, 1996. 112p. $16.95. ISBN 1-56006-262-2. (Mysterious Deaths). 7 up

Richard III has been accused of murdering the two princes who could have hindered his ambitions. The text recounts the research on this historic event and covers the politics of the fifteenth century that surrounded the deaths. Additional information in boxes livens the presentation as well. Bibliography, Further Reading, and Index.

1018. Laird, Christa. **But Can the Phoenix Sing?** New York: Greenwillow, 1995. 224p. $15. ISBN 0-688-13612-5. 7 up

Misha Edelman survives Dr. Janusz Korczak's orphanage in the Warsaw ghetto, as related in *Shadow of the Wall*, and forest partisans look after him while they struggle to survive. He joins the underground resistance, but the Wehrmacht captures him after the 1944 Warsaw Uprising. He lives to become a refugee when the Allies liberate the camp, but he has to learn to live in a different world, where he is not as successful with relationships as he might like.

1019. Laird, Christa. **Shadow of the Wall**. New York: Greenwillow, 1990. 144p. $12.95. ISBN 0-688-09336-1. 7 up

Misha, age thirteen, watches each member of his family either leave or die in the Warsaw ghetto during 1942. He decides that he must escape, and another orphan leads him through the slimy sewers under the city. With his false papers and his convincing Aryan looks, Misha has hopes of surviving on the other side. *Janusz Korczak Award*.

1020. Laker, Rosalind. **Circle of Pearls**. New York: Doubleday, 1990. 519p. $19.95. ISBN 0-385-26305-8. YA

Because he is fighting for the Royalists against the Parliamentarians, around 1650, Julia's father is gone while she is young. As she matures, she falls in love with the son of the man responsible for her father's death and decides to marry him instead of her brother's best friend, Christopher Wren. Julia survives both the plague and the Great Fire of London in 1666, and she lives to be old enough to mourn Wren when he dies.

1021. Laker, Rosalind. **The Golden Tulip**. New York: Doubleday, 1991. 585p. $20. ISBN 0-385-41560-5. YA

Francesca, the daughter of a temperamental but talented painter in Amsterdam during the 1660s, likes to visit Rembrandt's studio. Later she goes to Delft to become Vermeer's apprentice. When her mother dies, Francesca's father's debts lead him to arrange a marriage between her and an older wealthy man. Her intended husband is also disagreeable, and she loves someone else. When the French invade Holland, her fiancé is revealed as a traitor, and he dies before she has to marry him.

1022. Laker, Rosalind. **The Silver Touch**. New York: Doubleday, 1987. 356p. $16.95. ISBN 0-385-23745-6. YA

Heather, an orphan at age twelve in 1721, works in her uncle's London tavern. John, age eighteen, sees her secretly sketching a cat and begins a relationship that results in their marriage and establishment of a silversmithing business. They endure both hard and happy times as they raise their family and their reputation through their work.

1023. Laker, Rosalind. **Sugar Pavilion**. New York: Doubleday, 1994. 370p. $22.50. ISBN 0-385-46826-1. YA

In 1793, Sophie Delcourt escapes from France to England with her four-year-old charge, Antoine de Juneau, heir to his father's title and ruined estates. After they arrive in Brighton, Sophie finds work in the confectionery trade, which she learned from her father. She also keeps Antoine's identity secret so that one day he can return to France and claim his inheritance. Sophie becomes successful in her profession, and two men woo her. She has to decide whether to choose the captain who catches smugglers on the coast or the cavalier who engages in illegal activities. In the background is the relationship of George, Prince of Wales, and his wife, Maria Fitzherbert. The highlight of Sophie's confectionery career comes when she makes a copy of Brighton's Pavilion in sugar to display at its reopening in 1823.

1024. Laker, Rosalind. **The Venetian Mask**. New York: Doubleday, 1993. 422p. $22.50. ISBN 0-385-42190-7. YA

After Marietta's mother, a Venetian carnival mask maker, dies in 1775, Marietta goes to live in the orphan housing for children with musical talent. She trains there, makes friends, and grows up. She and her two close friends become involved in a feud between two noble families. Before they have happier lives, they are further separated from loved ones by both death and imprisonment.

1025. Lambert, Joan Dahr. **Circles of Stone**. New York: Pocket Books, 1997. 416p. $23. ISBN 0-671-55285-6. YA

The Zenas carry their goddess tradition from Africa to southern France throughout the centuries. The first Zena's mother dies in a flood, and when she finds an orphan whose parents were killed by lions, she is adopted into the orphan's clan. There she becomes the leader and creates the first sacred stone circle. Other Zenas span thousands of years as they come to earth to lead.

1026. Lambroza, Shlomo. **Boris Yeltsin**. Vero Beach, FL: Rourke, 1993. 110p. $22.60. ISBN 0-86625-482-X. (World Leaders). YA

Boris Yeltsin (b. 1931) became president of the new federation of Russia in June 1991, taking over from Mikhail Gorbachev after the dissolution of the Soviet Union. He has tried to rule during a time when he has had to direct vast economic changes in a formerly closed economy. Yeltsin signed a nuclear arms reduction agreement with U.S. President Bush. Time Line, Glossary, Bibliography, Media Resources, and Index.

1027. Landau, Elaine. **The Curse of Tutankhamen**. Brookfield, CT: Millbrook Press, 1996. 48p. $14.90. ISBN 0-7613-0014-7. (Mysteries of Science). 4-7

Landau offers a variety of causes for the so-called curse on those who went into Tutankhamen's Egyptian tomb. Although Lord Carnarvon and at least six other people suffered tragedies afterward, others did not. The possibilities that Landau offers make this speculative subject more intriguing. Glossary, Notes, and Index.

1028. Landau, Elaine. **Nazi War Criminals**. New York: Franklin Watts, 1990. 159p. $12.95. ISBN 0-531-15181-6. 7 up

This graphic text, enhanced by photographs, describes the atrocities committed by several men later convicted as Nazi war criminals. In addition to persons not in charge of death camps like John (Ivan) Demjanjuk, Landau exposes Dr. Josef Mengele, Adolf Eichmann, and Klaus Barbie (the Butcher of Lyons). For Further Reading and Index.

1029. Landau, Elaine. **The Warsaw Ghetto Uprising**. New York: New Discovery, 1992. 143p. $14.95. ISBN 0-02-751392-0. 7 up

During World War II, Nazis in Warsaw, Poland, forced nearly half a million Jews to live in a small ghetto. When Jews in the ghetto learned in 1943 that the Nazis were planning to destroy them as a birthday present for Adolph Hitler, they rebelled. They fought for twenty-eight days against the Nazi forces while people outside the ghetto ignored the gunshots and the fires. The Jews successfully defeated the Germans before they ran out of ammunition. The Nazis who destroyed this ghetto and the beautiful synagogue in Warsaw received the death sentence in the Nüremberg trials after the war. Notes, For Further Reading, and Index.

1030. Landau, Elaine. **We Survived the Holocaust**. New York: Franklin Watts, 1991. 144p. $13.95. ISBN 0-531-15229-4. 7 up

The people in this book all went through and survived the Holocaust. Five of the survivors come from Germany, one from both Germany and Poland, four from Poland, one from Austria, two from Holland, one from Hungary and Transylvania, one from Czechoslovakia and Hungary, and one from Transylvania. Glossary, For Further Reading, and Index.

1031. Landrum, Gene N. **Profiles of Female Genius: Thirteen Creative Women Who Changed the World**. Amherst, NY: Prometheus, 1994. 437p. $24.95. ISBN 0-87975-892-9. YA

In looking at female genius, Landrum examines self-esteem, birth order, childhood transience, role models, education, intelligence, crisis, personality traits, and temperament. With strict criteria for selection, he presents the profiles of 13 women who helped make significant changes in their fields. The women are Mary Kay Ash in cosmetics (b. 1917), Maria Callas in opera (1923-1977), Liz Claiborne in women's clothes (b. 1929), Jane Fonda in video and movies (b. 1937), Estée Lauder in cosmetics (b. 1908), Madonna in entertainment (b. 1958), Golda Meir in politics (1898-1978), Ayn Rand in philosophical literature (1905-1982), Gloria Steinem in women's issues (b. 1934), Margaret Thatcher in politics (b. 1925), Lillian Vernon in catalog sales (b. 1928), Linda Wachner in lingerie (b. 1946), and Oprah Winfrey in television talk (b. 1954). References and Index.

1032.   Landrum, Gene N. **Profiles of Genius: Thirteen Creative Men Who Changed the World**. Amherst, NY: Prometheus, 1993. 263p. $24.95. ISBN 0-87975-832-5. YA

By examining innovation, change, and personality, Landrum suggests 10 reasons why traditional managers are not innovative. Using strict criteria for selection, he chooses 13 innovators and discusses their characteristics. He presents Steven Jobs (b. 1955) and Apple Computers, Fred Smith (b. 1944) and Federal Express, Tom Monaghan (b. 1937) and Domino's Pizza, Nolan Bushnell (b. 1943) and Atari and Pizza Time Theater, William Gates III (b. 1955) and Microsoft, Marcel Bich (b. 1914) and Bic Pens, Solomon Price (b. 1916) and Price Club, Howard Head (1914-1991) and Head Ski and Prince Tennis, William Lear (1902-1978) and Learjet, Soichiro Honda (1906-1991) and Honda Motors, Akio Morita (b. 1921) and Sony, Arthur Jones (b. 1923) and Nautilus, and Ted Turner (b. 1938) and Turner Broadcasting. Bibliography and Index.

1033.   Langenus, Ron. **Mission West**. Willem van Velzen, illustrator; Niesje C. Horsman-Delmonte, translator. Chester Springs, PA: Wolfhound, Dufour, 1990. 144p. $8.95pa. ISBN 0-86327-239-8pa. 7 up

Rory, age seventeen, walks across Ireland to take a parchment to a monastery while the English, under Cromwell in 1649, systematically try to destroy his country. They have brutally murdered his foster father, a priest, and although Rory wants to avenge the priest's death, he has promised to get the parchment—contents unknown—to a safe place. What he discovers is that the document contains vital information about Ireland that will help the country in the future. *Belgian Book Prize.*

1034.   Langley, Andrew. **Discovering the New World: The Voyages of Christopher Columbus**. Paul Crompton, illustrator. New York: Chelsea House, 1994. 32p. $14.95. ISBN 0-7910-2821-6. (Great Explorers). 4-8

The text presents Columbus's life and his desire to go east. It describes the process of setting out from Spain and what life would have been like aboard the Santa Maria. It also covers Columbus's second and third voyages. Glossary and Index.

1035.   Langley, Andrew. **Exploring the Pacific: The Expeditions of James Cook**. David McAllister, illustrator. New York: Chelsea House, 1994. 32p. $14.95. ISBN 0-7910-2819-4. (Great Explorers). 4-8

As a boy, James Cook (1728-1779) wanted to be a sailor, but his father discouraged him and urged him to become a shopkeeper. He left, learned about the sea, joined the Royal Navy, and was determined to be a success. In 1758, he first commanded a warship. He made important trips in the Pacific Ocean, was the father of Antarctic exploration, and mapped coastlines and islands. He tried to be honorable to the native peoples he met, and he became distressed that Europeans had brought diseases that destroyed many of the natives. He claimed Australia as a British colony. Glossary and Index.

1036.   Langley, Andrew. **The Industrial Revolution**. New York: Viking, 1994. 48p. $15.99. ISBN 0-670-85835-8. 6-8

In two-page spreads, Langley discusses some of the many subjects constituting the Industrial Revolution. In addition to typical illustrations are four transparent overlays which, when lifted, reveal the inside of a coal miner's home, a railroad station, a cotton factory, and the crew's quarters on an immigrant ship. Beginning with the world in 1700, Langley continues with other topics: the need to grow more food, machines on land, spinning and weaving, cotton, iron, coal, steam, inventions, canals, railroads, the joining of continents, country life, town life, factories, health and disease, social reform, riots and hunger, immigrants, art and architecture, and electric power. Key Dates, Glossary, and Index.

1037.   Langley, Andrew. **Medieval Life**. Geoff Dann and Geoff Brightling, photographs. New York: Knopf, 1996. 63p. $19. ISBN 0-679-98077-6. (Eyewitness Books). 5-8

The profuse illustrations augmenting the text give an overview of medieval life. Topics covered in double-page spreads include the structure of society, daily life in different societal levels, the role and influence of religion, health and disease, jobs, and culture and the arts. Index.

1038.   Langley, Andrew, and Philip de Souza. **The Roman News**. New York: Candlewick, 1996. 32p. $15.99. ISBN 0-7636-0055-5. 5 up

The approach to the Romans through newspaper style highlights fashion, sports, trade, food, and the military. Each page has headlines, sometimes with classifieds advertising such things as reusable wax tablets. Highly readable and slightly sensational, the news under a headline such as "Caesar Stabbed" seems much more accessible than in a textbook. Maps and Index.

1039. Langone, John. **In the Shogun's Shadow: Understanding a Changing Japan**. Steve Parton, illustrator. Boston: Little, Brown, 1994. 202p. $16.95. ISBN 0-316-51409-8. 6-9

For Americans, understanding a culture as different as Japanese society takes a change in mindset. Langone gives pointers in his text, divided into three main parts: Japan's geography and history, modern Japanese society, and United States-Japanese relations. Within these general areas, he discusses religion, daily life, sex and sex roles, work, youth, and cultural expectations. An appendix gives information on spoken and unspoken language. Notes and Index.

1040. Langone, John. **Spreading Poison: A Book About Racism and Prejudice**. Boston: Little, Brown, 1993. 192p. $15.95. ISBN 0-316-51410-1. 7 up

By looking at various incidents in history, the text shows how prejudice can spread. Specific events include the Holocaust, Ku Klux Klan lynchings of Blacks, the internment of Japanese Americans, and the mistreatment of Native Americans. Specific topics include racism, anti-Semitism, homophobia, ethnic intolerance for immigrants, discrimination against the disabled, and sexism. Notes and Index.

1041. Langstaff, John, selector and editor. **"I Have a Song to Sing O!": An Introduction to the Songs of Gilbert and Sullivan**. Emma Chichester Clark, illustrator. New York: Margaret K. McElderry, 1994. 74p. $17.95. ISBN 0-689-50591-4. 4 up

This collection of songs includes both piano and vocal scores for ten songs from Gilbert and Sullivan musicals, including *The Mikado* and *The Pirates of Penzance*.

1042. Lankford, Mary. **Quinceañera: A Latina's Journey to Womanhood**. Brookfield, CT: Millbrook Press, 1994. 47p. $15.40. ISBN 1-56294-363-4. 4-7

Although the text describes the celebration of *quinceañera* in the life of a modern girl, the ritual is ages old, tracing back to the ancient native American cultures of Central and Latin America, particularly Mexico. After the Spanish conquered the Aztecs in 1521, the traditions of the Spaniards' Catholic religion meshed with the initiation rites of the Aztecs. At fifteen, a young woman had to choose between a lifetime of service to the church or marriage. The quinceañera marks the passage from childhood to adulthood and affirms religious faith. Photographs illustrate the text. Further Reading and Index. *New York Public Library Books for the Teen Age.*

1043. Larroche, Caroline. **Corot from A to Z**. Claudia Bedrick, translator. New York: Peter Bedrick, 1996. 59p. $14.95. ISBN 0-87226-477-7. 4-10

Jean-Baptiste-Camille Corot's life (1796-1875) and work in chapters titled with thematic words in alphabetical order describe him in an artistic context as well as a historical time. The table of contents page exhibits miniature reproductions of Corot's paintings.

1044. Lasky, Kathryn. **The Night Journey**. Trina S. Hynam, illustrator. New York: Viking, 1986. 152p. $12.95. ISBN 0-670-80935-7. New York: Penguin, 1986. 152p. $4.99pa. ISBN 0-14-032048-2pa. 5-9

Not until she is thirteen does Rache hear the story of Jewish pogroms and her grandmother's escape from Russia with her family in 1900. Her grandmother hid under chicken crates, paraded as a Purim player, and crossed the border with her cookies. The cookies held the family's gold. *National Jewish Awards, American Library Association Notable Books for Children, Association of Jewish Libraries Award*, and *Sydney Taylor Book Award.*

1045. **The Late Middle Ages**. Cath Polito, illustrator. Austin, TX: Raintree/Steck-Vaughn, 1990. 72p. $17.97. ISBN 0-8172-3308-3. (History of the World). 7 up

This overview uses informative illustrations and clear maps to complement the text, which presents European life between A.D. 1000 and 1300. It focuses on the growth of cities, the beginning of a money-based economy, the emergence of a shared religion, and increased trade. Topics include the Western Empire and the Church, Romanesque and Gothic styles, Venice and Byzantium, England and France, Hohenstaufen emperors, Turks and Mongols, Russia, Capetian kings, Wales and Scotland, Florentine Republic, Christian Spain, and Greek and Roman cultures during the times. Glossary and Index.

1046. **Latvia**. Minneapolis, MN: Lerner, 1992. 56p. $19.95. ISBN 0-8225-2802-9. (Then and Now). 5-9

The text covers the history, economics, geography, politics, ethnography, and possible future of Latvia, a Baltic country that the Soviet Union annexed in 1940. Latvia gained its freedom in 1991. Maps and photographs complement the text. Glossary and Index.

1047. Lawless, Richard, and Heather Bleaney. **The First Day of the Six Day War**. London: Dryad Press, 1990. 64p. $19.95. ISBN 0-85219-820-5. (A Day That Made History). 8 up

The text gives an account of the first day of the Israeli war against Egypt, on June 5, 1967. The Israeli air force attacked Egypt early in the morning by flying below radar and effectively destroying Egypt's air power, which was lined up at bases where Egyptian intelligence had figured Israeli planes could not reach. The text continues by looking at the last five days of the war and at the events that led to it. Photographs, Further Reading, and Index.

1048.   Lawless, Richard, and Heather Bleaney. **The Middle East Since 1945**. Batsford, NH: David and Charles, 1990. 72p. $19.95. ISBN 0-7134-5991-3. (Post-War World). 9 up

The text looks at the Middle East since the end of World War II, but it also includes background events leading to Arab nationalism and the conflicting Zionism that supported and eventually established the Jewish settlement in Palestine. After the war came the state of Israel, Arab-Israeli wars, Nassar and Sadat in Egypt wielding influence, conflicts over oil production and sale, and violence in both Lebanon and Iran. With information from a variety of sources, the text tries to show why the conflicts continue in this area of the world. Bibliography, Chronology, and Index.

1049.   Lawson, Don. **The Abraham Lincoln Brigade: Americans Fighting Fascism in the Spanish Civil War**. New York: Crowell, 1989. 176p. $11.95. ISBN 0-690-04697-9. 7-10

After a background on the history of Spain and its losses in the past 200 years, the text discusses General Franco and his seizure of military and political power from the Loyalists in 1937 during the Spanish civil war. Volunteers from the United States went to Spain and joined the Abraham Lincoln Brigade, but got no support from the United States because the government suspected that the Loyalists were receiving support from the U.S.S.R. Lawson details the battles in which the brigade fought and profiles its leaders. Bibliography and Index.

1050.   Lawson, Don. **America Held Hostage: The Iran Hostage Crisis and the Iran-Contra Affair**. New York: Franklin Watts, 1991. 128p. $12.90. ISBN 0-531-11009-5. 8-10

The text looks at the background to the hostage situation that occurred in Iran during the late 1970s. The men were freed on January 20, 1981, after 444 days in captivity. In 1986, government officials were accused of selling arms to Iran and using the profit to fund Contra rebels in Nicaragua, although Congress had voted not to support the rebels. Although not a happy book, this is an important look at recent history. Notes, Chronology, Bibliography, and Index.

1051.   Layton, George. **The Swap**. New York: Putnam, 1997. 192p. $16.95. ISBN 0-399-23148-X. 5-8

The narrator, a boy of eleven living in northern England during the 1950s, undergoes the difficulties of growing up, taunted by his classmates for his beliefs. After spending a week in London on an exchange with a wealthy family, he regrets his working-class background but eventually realizes that he is happy with his mother and his aunt in their town.

1052.   Lazo, Caroline. **Elie Wiesel**. New York: Dillon Press, 1994. 64p. $13.95. ISBN 0-87518-636-X. (Peacemakers). 4-8

When Elie Wiesel (b. 1928) lived in Sighet, Rumania, after the Nazis started rounding people up and taking them away, a man returned to town and said that the Nazis had killed everyone. He had been shot in the leg and had pretended to be dead when he fell into the pit with the others, but he escaped after the Nazis left. No one believed the man's stories, even after the Nazis returned. Wiesel went into a concentration camp as a young man with his father and helplessly watched his father die, a situation he wrote about in *Night*. His father's last questions were "Where is God? Where is Man?" The text gives a brief overview of anti-Semitism before telling Wiesel's story. He survived, but 6 million Jews did not, and Wiesel continues to write about them. He received the Nobel Peace Prize in 1986. For Further Reading and Index.

1053.   Lazo, Caroline. **Lech Walesa**. New York: Dillon Press, 1993. 64p. $13.95. ISBN 0-87518-525-8. (Peacemakers). 4-8

Lech Walesa (b. 1943) risked his job and his life by organizing workers in the Gdansk, Poland, shipyards. In 1980, he called the workers to join in the Solidarity movement, an effort to gain better working conditions in their Communist country. When he won the Nobel Peace Prize, he could not go to accept it for fear that he would not be allowed to reenter Poland. After the fall of communism in 1989, Walesa was elected the first president of Poland. For Further Reading and Index.

1054.   Lazo, Caroline. **Mother Teresa**. New York: Dillon Press, 1993. 64p. $13.95. ISBN 0-87518-559-2. (Peacemakers). 4-8

Mother Teresa (1910-1997) founded the Missionaries of Charity after she left her Albanian home as a teenager to join a convent and teach the poor. Her work, which continues today, led to the Nobel Peace Prize in 1979. Photographs, For Further Reading, and Index.

1055.   Lazo, Caroline. **Rigoberta Menchú**. New York: Dillon Press, 1994. 64p. $13.95. ISBN 0-87518-619-X. (Peacemakers). 4 up

Rigoberta Menchú realized the power of the spoken word as a young girl of Mayan ancestry in Guatemala during the 1970s. She saw that the Indian dialects allowed the people to talk without the Spanish-speaking minority of wealthy landowners and military leaders understanding them. However, the poor could not understand the Spanish either. She taught herself Spanish and began to try to secure human rights for the Indians of

Guatemala. Her parents were murdered when she was a teenager, and she went into exile in Mexico in 1981 to keep herself alive. From there she worked, and she won the Nobel Peace Prize for her efforts in 1992. For Further Reading and Index.

1056. Lazo, Caroline. **The Terra Cotta Army of Emperor Qin**. New York: New Discovery, Macmillan, 1993. 80p. $14.95. ISBN 0-02-754631-4. (Timestop). 5-9

In 1974, men digging near the city of Xian in China unearthed the life-size figure of an ancient warrior. What they subsequently discovered was a field of over 7,500 warriors made of terra-cotta, each one individually created. Some held spears, others knelt with their bows and arrows, and still others rode horseback. They had been in the same spot for over 2,000 years, guarding the tomb of China's first emperor, Qin. The text looks at the story of Qin and the creation of this army. For Further Reading and Index.

1057. Lazo, Caroline Evensen. **Mahatma Gandhi**. New York: Dillon Press, 1993. 64p. $13.95. ISBN 0-87518-526-6. (Peacemakers). 4 up

Mahatma Gandhi (1869-1948) returned to India after education abroad and eventually became its leader. His policy of nonviolent resistance helped to free his country from British rule. He was assassinated by one of his countrymen. Bibliography and Index.

1058. Leckie, Robert. **Okinawa: The Last Battle of World War II**. New York: Viking, 1995. 220p. $24.95; $13.95pa. ISBN 0-670-84716-X; 0-14-017389-7pa. YA

The text presents all aspects of the Okinawa landing, from its planning to its execution, as well as the ground fighting and the fierce action of the Japanese at sea with their kamikaze planes and ships. Leckie believes that Japan would have surrendered without either bomb or invasion and that Truman dropped the bomb to show Stalin his power. However, Okinawa was decisive because a Japanese victory would have heightened the conviction of the Japanese military inner sanctum that Japan should never accept an Allied surrender offer, even with Hirohito's influence to the contrary. Bibliography and Index.

1059. Leitner, Isabella, and Irving A. Leitner. **Isabella: From Auschwitz to Freedom**. 1978. New York: Anchor, 1994. 240p. $12.95pa. ISBN 0-385-47318-4pa. 6 up

In the text, Leitner describes the deportation of her family to Auschwitz where they were imprisoned for a year. Her sister and mother went to their deaths as soon as they arrived, and the rest of the family of four sisters had to struggle to survive. They also were sent to the concentration camp at Birnbaumel. The Russians rescued them, and they emigrated to New York. What one finds is that in the despair perhaps the only saving emotion can be love.

1060. Lennon, Adrian. **Jorge Luis Borges**. New York: Chelsea House, 1992. 110p. $18.95. ISBN 0-7910-1236-0. (Hispanics of Achievement). 7 up

The Argentinean writer Jorge Luis Borges (1899–1986) became the first author from Latin America to achieve worldwide fame. He went to school in Switzerland during World War I and absorbed European culture. His magical blend of fact, fantasy, and philosophy puts him in a class by himself. Although he lost his eyesight in the 1950s, he continued his work. Photographs enhance the text. Chronology, Further Reading, and Index.

1061. Leonard, Hugh. **Parnell and the Englishwoman**. New York: Atheneum, 1991. 265p. $19.95. ISBN 0-689-12127-X. YA

In 1880, Kitty O'Shea tries to help her Irish husband's political career by talking to Charles Stewart Parnell. Instead of helping her husband, she begins an affair with Parnell and has three children by him, though each is accepted by her husband as his own child. News of the affair becomes public, and after Mr. O'Shea dies, Kitty marries Parnell. But the public will not accept this abuse of their Catholic religion, and the people kill Parnell by breaking his heart and exhausting him.

1062. Levin, Betty. **Brother Moose**. New York: Greenwillow, 1990. 214p. $12.95. ISBN 0-688-09266-7. 5-9

Louisa and Nell meet in a Canadian orphanage, which they leave in the 1870 to live with people who have offered to take them. Various problems erupt after they separate. Louisa goes with an old Indian and his grandson to search for Nell's benefactor.

1063. Levine, Ellen. **Anna Pavlova: Genius of the Dance**. New York: Scholastic, 1995. 132p. $14.95. ISBN 0-590-44304-6. 6-9

Anna Pavlova, born the daughter of a laundress in 1881, saw a ballet when she was eight and knew from then on that she must dance. Not able to enter the ballet school in St. Petersburg, Russia, until she was ten, she quickly learned and excelled. Throughout her life she wanted to dance for everyone, not just the wealthy who could afford the front-row seats. She traveled extensively, usually accompanied by a troupe that performed with her. During the second half of her life, she spent much time abroad teaching students and trying to make her dance a gift. She even danced when ill. When she could no longer go on stage, her friends knew that her illness was serious, and she died in 1931. Glossary, Selected Bibliography, and Index.

1064.   Levinson, Nancy Smiler. **Christopher Columbus: Voyager to the Unknown**. New York: Lodestar, Dutton, 1990. 118p. $17. ISBN 0-525-67292-3. 5-9

Illustrated with reproductions of paintings and manuscripts from museums throughout the world, Levinson presents Columbus, noting the influence of his reading—Toscanelli and Marco Polo—on his decision to find a route to the riches of the east. Levinson shows the relationships of Columbus to Isabel and her cold husband, Ferdinand, and to the people with whom he sailed, in the well-documented text. Clear maps of the four voyages show exactly where Columbus's logs indicate that he stopped. Chronology, Articles of Capitulation, Letter of Introduction, Crew on First Voyage, Suggested Reading, and Index.

1065.   Levitin, Sonia. **Escape from Egypt**. Boston: Little, Brown, 1994. 267p. $16.95. ISBN 0-316-52273-2. 7 up

Jesse, a teenage slave in Egypt before the twelfth century B.C., has been apprenticed to a goldsmith, an honor that will keep him out of the pharaoh's quarries. In the shop, he sees Jennat, a half-Egyptian, half-Syrian slave girl of higher rank whose mistress has decided that Jennat should also learn these skills. Jesse's parents arrange his engagement to a pious cousin, Talia, and the family decides to leave Egypt with the rebel Moses in search of a better life. In the new land, Talia sees Jesse with Jennat and realizes that she will not be able to make him happy.

1066.   Levitin, Sonia. **Journey to America**. Charles Robinson, illustrator. 1970. New York: Atheneum, 1993. 160p. $13.95. ISBN 0-689-31829-4. New York: Macmillan, 1986. 160p. $3.95pa. ISBN 0-689-71130-1pa. 3-7

In 1938, Lisa's father goes on a "vacation" to Switzerland from their home in Berlin. He then leaves for America, and Lisa, her two sisters, and her mother wait for him to send for them. Because the Nazis will not allow them to take any of their belongings when they hear from Lisa's father, they leave for Switzerland carrying nothing. Then they have to remain in Zurich for almost a year before they can arrange passage to America and reunite. *National Jewish Awards*.

1067.   Levy, Patricia. **Women in Society: Britain**. New York: Marshall Cavendish, 1993. 128p. $22.95. ISBN 1-85435-555-4. (Women in Society). 7 up

After introducing the women of Britain through British myths, the author discusses the roles of women in Britain by interweaving historical and contemporary practices. She presents the expectations imposed upon women—rural and urban, religious and secular, poor and wealthy. The chapters cover milestones, women in society, what being a woman means in the culture, and the life of a woman from birth to old age. Women Firsts, Glossary, Further Reading, and Index.

1068.   Levy, Patricia. **Women in Society: Ireland**. New York: Marshall Cavendish, 1994. 128p. $21.95. ISBN 1-85435-563-5. (Women in Society). 7 up

Grace O'Malley, also known as Granuaile, became a pirate in the sixteenth century and defied the English before joining them. The author presents Grace's story as she discusses the roles of women in Ireland by interweaving historical and contemporary practices. She presents the expectations imposed upon women—rural and urban, religious and secular, poor and wealthy. The chapters cover milestones, women in society, what being a woman means in the culture, and the life of a woman from birth to old age. Short biographies of Mary Robinson, who became president of Ireland after attending Harvard in the United States; Sinead O'Connor, a rock music star; Kathleen Lynn, a physician (1874–1955); Bernadette Devlin, a civil rights activist; Constance Markievicz (1868–1927); and Mrs. Justice Susan Denham, the first woman on the Irish Supreme Court, show what women have done. Photographs complement the text. Women Firsts, Glossary, Further Reading, and Index.

1069.   Lewin, Rhoda G., ed. **Witnesses to the Holocaust: An Oral History**. Boston: Twayne, 1990. 240p. $20.95; $12.95pa. ISBN 0-8057-9100-0; 0-8057-9126-4pa. YA

Lewin presents the accounts of Holocaust survivors now living in Minnesota. She also includes accounts of those who liberated the Jews from the concentration camps. The words of the liberators tend to be more vivid because they use emotions to tell their experiences; the victims seem to be almost clinically detached from their ordeals. How they tell the story may be as important as what they say. Index.

1070.   Lewis, Bernard. **Islam in History: Ideas, People, and Events in the Middle East**. 1974. Chicago: Open Court, 1993. 487p. $59.95; $27.95pa. ISBN 0-8126-9216-0; 0-8126-9217-9pa. YA

Thirty-two essays present Lewis's assessment of such topics as the Salman Rushdie threat, Anwar Sadat's assassination, Khomeini's power in Iran, and the support for Sadam Hussein. He has been researching the Middle East for many years, and his insights help Westerners begin to understand some of the complex attitudes in this part of the world. Bibliography and Index.

1071. Lewis, Bernard. **The Middle East: A Brief History of the Last 2,000 Years**. New York: Scribners, 1996. 448p. $30. ISBN 0-684-80712-2. YA

In this comprehensive history, beginning with the seventh century in the Middle East, Lewis makes two major points. He believes, first, that everything that happens in the Arab world has parallels in past history and second, that the West is winning its struggle with Islam, and has been winning since the Ottomans had to sign the Treaty of Carlowitz in 1699. A major reason for the Western victory is that Muslim indifference to the technology and innovation that began in the West as early as the sixteenth century has kept Islam from being able to compete on either sea or land. Among Lewis's proofs of Islam's decline are Napoleon's quick defeat of Egypt in 1798, the Ottoman Empire's dissolution after World War I, and the survival of Israel. He also asserts that Saddam Hussein's attempt to seize Kuwait in 1990 was typical of Middle Eastern behavior since the beginning of recorded time. Other information fills this valuable book. Bibliography and Index.

1072. Lewis, Bernard. **Race and Slavery in the Middle East: An Historical Enquiry**. New York: Oxford University Press, 1990. 184p. $30; $10.95pa. ISBN 0-19-506283-3; 0-19-505326-5pa. YA

Lewis shows how slavery spread in the Islamic world even though people denied that the Islamic world had ever been connected to slavery. He says that racial consciousness became racial prejudice in the Islamic world, but that slavery was not the demeaning system that existed in the United States. He gives examples from every period of Islamic history to support his thesis and the idea of the economic function of slavery and of the social function of racism. Bibliography and Index.

1073. Lewis, Bernard. **Semites and Anti-Semites: An Inquiry into Conflict and Prejudice**. New York: Norton, 1986. 283p. $7.95pa. ISBN 0-393-30420-5pa. YA

A Jew, according to rabbinic law, is one born to a Jewish mother or converted to the Jewish religion. To the Nazis, a Jew was a member of a specific race. Lewis investigates the origin of the hostilities in the Middle East between Arabs and Jews and sees that it stems from three kinds of prejudice. One is a conflict of peoples and nations over territory. Another is the disagreement between neighboring peoples who have different cultural traditions and backgrounds. The third, and the one most prevalent in the past decade, is a case of anti-Semitism in which Arabs see Jews or Israelis as the embodiment of evil. They have separated the concept of Zionism from that of Judaism. Additionally, in intellectual circles, anti-Semitism has been the accepted view, though scholars have met privately and personably to discuss their common interests. The views that Lewis discusses in detail give insight into the problems of the Middle East. Notes and Index.

1074. Lewis, Bernard, ed. **The World of Islam: Faith, People, Culture**. New York: Thames & Hudson, 1992. 360p. $29.95. ISBN 0-500-27624-2. 8 up

When the Prophet Muhammad died in 632, he had established a Muslim state in a large part of Arabia. The practice of Islam has continued since that time. The text includes essays with accompanying color photographs on the following topics: the faith and the faithful, the art and architecture, the growth and culture of urban Islam, the Sufi tradition, Islamic literature, Islamic music, contributions to science, warfare, Moorish Spain in the golden age of Cordoba and Granada, the flowering of Iranian civilization, the Ottoman Empire and the rise and fall of Turkish dominance, Muslim India, and Islam today. Chronology, Select Bibliography, and Index.

1075. Lewis, Gavin. **Tomáš Masaryk**. New York: Chelsea House, 1989. 110p. $18.95. ISBN 1-55546-816-0. (World Leaders Past and Present). 8 up

Born the son of a coach driver in Austria-Hungary, Tomáš Masaryk (1850–1937) learned to hate the authoritarian rule of the Hapsburgs. As a professor of philosophy in Prague, he searched for truth and tried to start a democratic relationship between the Czechs and the neighboring Slovaks. After World War II, he convinced Woodrow Wilson to support his idea, and Masaryk returned to Prague as the president-liberator of Czechoslovakia. He is one of the few individuals in the world to create a nation. Photographs and engravings enhance the text. Chronology, Further Reading, and Index.

1076. Lewis, Hilda. **The Ship That Flew**. 1939. Chatam, NY: S. G. Phillips, 1958. 246p. $22.95. ISBN 0-87599-067-3. 5-7

When Peter sees a six-inch ship in a shop, he spends all his money to buy it. The ship magically enlarges and carries Peter and his three siblings through time. They have experiences in Asgard, Robin Hood's England, Egypt during the reign of Amenemhot the First, and the time of William the Conqueror. In this historical fantasy, as the children grow up, they travel less frequently; finally, Peter returns the ship and becomes a writer, using his words on which to travel.

1077. Li, Pi-hua. **Farewell to My Concubine**. New York: Morrow, 1993. 255p. $10. ISBN 0-06-097644-6. YA

As young boys, Duan Xialou and Cheng Dieyi train to sing at the Peking Opera before the Japanese invade China. With much work and punishment, they become stars with their interpretation of the two roles in the opera, *Farewell to My Concubine*. Cheng, however, becomes the character from the opera who loves Duan, and when Duan marries in real life, Cheng is intensely jealous of his wife.

1078. Lilley, Stephen R. **Hernando Cortés**. San Diego, CA: Lucent, 1996. 112p. $16.95. ISBN 1-56006-066-2. (The Importance of). 7 up

In the sixteenth century, Hernando Cortés (1485–1547) was a hero. In three years, he conquered most of Mexico and added 25 million new subjects to the Spanish empire. He seized enough Aztec gold and precious gems to change the world economy. He also made America seem mythic to many more explorers, who came to its shores to share in the wealth that Cortés had found. The Aztecs believed that he was the god Quetzalcoatl returning home, so they helped him in his quest, not knowing what he would do in the end. The text looks at his expeditions and his life. Photographs and boxed topics augment the text. Notes, For Further Reading, Works Consulted, and Index.

1079. Lindgard, Joan. **Between Two Worlds**. New York: Dutton, 1991. 186p. $14.95. ISBN 0-525-67360-1. 7-9

The Petersons come to Canada from Latvia via Germany after World War II, sponsored by a Toronto family, in this sequel to *Tug of War*. Father becomes ill, and Astra and Hugo, the eighteen-year-old twins, have to find jobs to keep the family together. They also take courses at night so that they can learn the language as well. Their diligence helps them save enough money to buy land.

1080. Lindgard, Joan. **Tug of War**. New York: Dutton, 1990. 194p. $14.95. ISBN 0-525-67306-7. 7-9

Hugo, age fourteen, becomes separated from his twin Astra and the rest of the family as they travel through Poland during 1944 from Latvia to Leipzig. Someone knocks off Hugo's glasses in the crowded train station, and he cannot find the family. They must leave him. Difficult years follow as the family wanders through Germany, with the father finally getting a teaching job in Canada after writing over 2,000 letters. As the family leaves the country via Hamburg, by chance Astra sees Hugo, who has been living with a kind German family, and he joins them.

1081. Lindwer, Willy. **The Last Seven Months of Anne Frank**. Alison Marsschaert, translator. 1991. New York: Anchor, 1992. 204p. $12.95pa. ISBN 0-385-42360-8pa. YA

Lindwer interviewed and filmed six Dutch Holocaust survivors who told about their backgrounds, their captures by the Nazis, their experiences in the camps, and what happened to them when they were liberated. Each knew Anne Frank, and each tells about her final days. In this book, Lindwer gives the complete texts of the interviews, including information omitted from her documentary of 1988.

1082. Linnéa, Sharon. **Raoul Wallenberg: The Man Who Stopped Death**. Philadelphia, PA: Jewish Publication Society, 1993. 151p. $17.95; $9.95pa. ISBN 0-8276-0440-8; 0-8276-0448-3pa. 6 up

Raoul Wallenberg was a Swedish diplomat who went to Budapest, Hungary, during World War II to try to help free the Jews there. He issued passports that he said the Swedish government had authorized for Jews so that they could leave. He also offered diplomatic immunity under the Swedish flag and dared the Nazis to defy him. He disappeared soon after the Soviets came into the city, and stories about his last days are contradictory and uncertain. He was in a prison, but it is uncertain whether he died when the Russians said he did. Index.

1083. Linscott, Gillian. **Crown Witness**. New York: St. Martin's Press, 1995. 218p. $20.95. ISBN 0-312-13456-8. YA

Emma Pankhurst requests that Nell Bray come with her to the precoronation parade for George V in 1910, because she has heard that antisuffragists will be threatening her group of women favoring the right to vote. Nell Bray sees a float with a king being beheaded and realizes that it symbolizes another problem with the parade. When the son of a prominent cabinet member is shot instead, Bray goes on a search that wanders from Holloway prison to a commune of Russian anarchists.

1084. Linscott, Gillian. **An Easy Day for a Lady**. New York: St. Martin's Press, 1995. 210p. $19.95. ISBN 0-312-11811-2. YA

Mountain climbers use the phrase "an easy day for a lady" to denote an effortless path. In 1910, Nell Bray travels to Chamonix in the French Alps after Britain's House of Commons defeats a bill to give women the vote, hoping to have a vacation that will help her forget her frustration. Two days after her arrival, a rescue team discovers a man in the ice who disappeared three decades previously, and Nell becomes the interpreter for the Englishman's family as she continues her detective work during the early twentieth century. What she finds is that the man's death was not accidental.

1085. Linscott, Gillian. **Hanging on the Wire**. New York: St. Martin's Press, 1993. 215p. $17.95. ISBN 0-312-08806-X. YA

Nell Bray continues her detective work during World War I in England when she helps her old friend Jenny Chesney, who is working at the Nantgarrew military hospital. A woman there is upset over Freud's theories and is trying to disprove them with sabotage. When someone is killed, Nell Bray goes to the hospital and helps find the murderer.

1086. Linscott, Gillian. **Sister Beneath the Sheet**. New York: St. Martin's Press, 1991. 224p. $17.95. ISBN 0-312-06464-0. YA

Nell Bray's detective work takes her from her home in England to Biarritz, France, during the early twentieth century when Emma Pankhurst tells her that a prostitute has left the suffragettes 50,000 pounds. In Biarritz, Nell discovers that Topaz Brown did not commit suicide; instead, someone murdered her. When Nell figures out who did it and accuses him, he tries to kill her before he fails and kills himself instead. Nell returns to London, where she is again arrested and jailed for demonstrating against the government.

1087. Linscott, Gillian. **Stage Fright**. New York: St. Martin's Press, 1993. 188p. $17.95. ISBN 0-312-09812-X. YA

In the early twentieth century, George Bernard Shaw hears that Nell Bray, a suffragette who has served two terms in prison, has solved two murders as well. He hires Nell to watch the leading actress, Belle, in his new play because her husband, who married her for her money, has promised to keep her from performing. During rehearsals, Belle has a variety of unexpected problems, and finally someone wearing her costume is murdered. Bray solves the mystery.

1088. Liptak, Karen. **Endangered Peoples**. New York: Franklin Watts, 1993. 160p. $13.40. ISBN 0-531-10987-9. (Impact). 6-9

The text examines five ethnic groups around the world who maintain tribal existences and have been studied in the twentieth century. These tribes are the Yanomani of the Amazon rain forest, the San (Bushmen) of the Kalahari Desert, the Bambuti (pygmies) of the Ituri Forest, the Aborigines of Australia, and the Inuits (Eskimos) of the Arctic. Their histories and habits, and the things that threaten them, complete the information. Photographs and drawings enhance the text. Further Reading, Glossary, Notes, and Index.

1089. **Lithuania**. Minneapolis, MN: Lerner, 1992. 56p. $19.95. ISBN 0-8225-2804-5. (Then and Now). 5-9

This text covers the history, economics, geography, politics, ethnography, and possible future for Lithuania, including its environmental problems. Maps and photographs complement the text. Glossary and Index.

1090. Litowinsky, Olga. **The High Voyage: The Final Crossing of Christopher Columbus**. New York: Delacorte, 1991. 147p. $14.95. ISBN 0-385-30304-1. 5-8

In 1502, Fernando, thirteen, joins his father on another voyage trying to find India. They reach Jamaica instead. Several crew members mutiny against Columbus, but the others defeat them. Columbus eventually gets a ship to sail back to Spain. Fernando decides that he wants to stay in Spain rather than explore the world.

1091. Llorente, Pilar Molina. **The Apprentice**. Juan Ramon Alonso, translator. New York: Farrar, Straus & Giroux, 1993. 101p. $4.95pa. ISBN 0-374-40432-1pa. 6-9

Arduino wants to become a painter's apprentice in Florence, Italy, during the Renaissance. He gets the chance, but finds that his dream of painting frescoes does not match the reality of cleaning and mixing pigments. He also finds that the Maestro is keeping the previous apprentice chained in the attic because his talent promised to be greater than the Maestro's. When the Maestro becomes sick, Arduino convinces him to free Donato from the attic and let him complete an important commission. He does, and Donato and Arduino save the Maestro's reputation. A serving woman, also annoyed by various situations, and a duchess show the female point of view and demonstrate that women never had a chance to be apprentices in the Renaissance. *Mildred L. Batchelder Award.*

1092. Lloyd, Dana Ohlmeyer. **Ho Chi Minh**. New York: Chelsea House, 1986. 112p. $18.95. ISBN 0-87754-571-5. (World Leaders Past and Present). 5 up

Ho Chi Minh (1890-1968) was head of the long struggle to liberate Vietnam from foreign control. He led an army against the French and became president of Communist North Vietnam. He traveled to Europe as a young man to request independence from the French at the Versailles Peace conference, but after he was denied, he traveled to the Soviet Union in 1923 to study their revolution and the developing Communist system. He returned and defeated the French, with settlement made at the 1954 Geneva Convention. Some think him great; others think of him as betraying his country to communism. Photographs enhance the text. Chronology, Further Reading, and Index.

1093. Llywelyn, Morgan. **Brian Boru: Emperor of the Irish**. Chester Springs, PA: O'Brien Press, Dufor Editions, 1991. 160p. $8.95pa. ISBN 0-86278-230-9pa. 6-9

In the tenth century, Brian Boru becomes determined to free and rule Ireland by either overcoming or contenting the Viking raiders. As a child, Boru watches the Vikings as they raid his Munster home and kill his mother, brothers, and servants. At Clonmacnois, while studying with the monks, Boru reviews battle plans of Alexander the Great and Julius Caesar and learns ways to build, make music, and do mathematics so that he will be prepared to conquer and rule. His honesty and his commitment earn the respect of thousands who follow him and help him achieve his goal. *Irish Children's Book Trust Book of the Year.*

1094. Llywelyn, Morgan. **Druids**. New York: Morrow, 1991. 456p. $19.95. ISBN 0-688-08819-8. YA

Ainvar eventually becomes a Druid after being fascinated by the Order of the Wise as a child. His belief in the immortal soul interests Vercingetorix of Gaul, and Ainvar becomes his servant. They try to unite the tribes of Gaul so that they will be ready to fight the encroaching Roman troops, but Caesar invades and wins in 58 B.C. After watching Vercingetorix keep his dignity as a defeated king, while the Romans spit at him and treat him like an object, Ainvar escapes to continue his Druidic life.

1095. Llywelyn, Morgan. **The Last Prince of Ireland**. New York: Morrow, 1992. 368p. $22. ISBN 0-688-10794-X. YA

Donal Cam O'Sullivan decides that he will defend Ireland against the British after he finds his son murdered. He and his clan flee their wet and cold countryside in 1602 after the Battle of Kinsale to find protection inland at the stronghold of Brian O'Rourke. There they wait for a better opportunity to defeat the British.

1096. Llywelyn, Morgan. **Xerxes**. New York: Chelsea House, 1987. 112p. $18.95. ISBN 0-87754-447-6. (World Leaders Past and Present). 5 up

Xerxes (c. 519-465 B.C.), king of Persia, thought that his empire was the center of civilization. The accounts of his life conflict. Some show that he was easily manipulated and an indecisive coward, and others portray him as a sensitive ruler, reformer, and strong warrior. When he ascended the throne in 486 B.C., he suppressed revolts in Egypt and Marathon. Then he started to invade Greece. Xerxes beat the quickly consolidated Greek city-states at Thermopylae, but mistakenly engaged the Greek fleet at Salamis, where it defeated and disgraced him. As he grew older, he became more involved in court intrigue, annoying his wives and children and irritating his generals enough so that someone murdered him in his chambers. Oddly, Xerxes is probably responsible for the rise of Greek civilization, because his encroachment upon Greek lands seemed to be the only cause that could unite the city-states. Photographs and engravings enhance the text. Chronology, Further Reading, and Index.

1097. Loewen, Nancy. **Beethoven**. Vero Beach, FL: Rourke, 1989. 111p. $22.60. ISBN 0-86592-609-3. (Profiles in Music). 4-7

When he was only four, Ludwig van Beethoven (1770-1827) began composing his own songs. From that time on, he had a stunning career in music composition and performance. He premiered the ninth of his symphonies, conducting while deaf before an appreciative Viennese audience in 1824. Photographs highlight the text. Glossary, Index, and Listening Choices.

1098. Lomask, Milton. **Great Lives: Exploration**. New York: Scribners, 1988. 258p. $23. ISBN 0-684-18511-3. YA

The text looks at famous explorers who have changed the world. Included are Pytheas (4th c. B.C.) and his discovery that the pull of the moon controls the tides in the ocean; Hoei-shin (5th c. B.C.), one of the first Asians to find and explore portions of North and Central America; Leif Erikson (10th c. A.D.) and his exploration of the North American coast; Prince Henry the Navigator (1394-1460) of Portugal; Christopher Columbus (1451-1506); John Cabot (1450-1499) and his claim of North America for England; Vasco da Gama (1460?-1524) and his sea-lane to the Orient going to the east from Portugal; Marco Polo (1254-1324) to Asia; Amerigo Vespucci's (1454-1512) discovery of Brazil; Fernão de Magalhães, known as Magellan (c. 1480-1521) and his circumnavigation of the globe; Jacques Cartier (1491-1557) and the St. Lawrence River claimed for France; Balboa (1475-1519) and the discovery of the Pacific Ocean; La Salle (1643-1687) and his expedition up the Mississippi River to its mouth; Orellana (c. 1490-1546) and his navigation of the Amazon River; Meriwether Lewis (1774-1809) opening the American West; Roald Amundsen (1872-1928) and the North and South Poles; Nordenskiöld (1832-1901) and the Northeast Passage; James Cook (1728-1779) with Australia and the Antarctic Circle; Alexander MacKenzie (1764-1820) and the first expedition to cross North America; Robert O'Hara Burke (1820-1861) and the first expedition to cross the continent of Australia; Sir Richard Francis Burton (1821-1890) as one of the few non-Muslims to enter Mecca in Arabia, and the first to enter Harar in Africa, another Muslim shrine; David Livingstone (1813-1873), discoverer of Africa's Victoria Falls, several central African lakes, and the source of the Congo River; Mary Henrietta Kinglsey (1862-1900) and her trips to Africa; Robert Edwin Peary (1856-1920) and the North Pole; and Richard Evelyn Byrd (1888-1957) and trips to both the North and South Poles. Photographs, Important Dates in the History of Geographical Exploration, Further Reading, and Index.

1099. Long, Cathryn. **The Middle East in Search of Peace**. Brookfield, CT: Millbrook Press, 1996. 64p. $16.90. ISBN 0-761-30105-4. (Headliners). 4-8

The text explores the origins of the Israeli-Arab conflict; previous peace plans; and the peace plan initiated in 1993 between Yitzhak Rabin, then prime minister of Israel, and Yasir Arafat, Palestine Liberation Organization chairman. It includes the peace plan provisions; secret meetings; the *Intifada,* begun in 1987; and *Hamas.* Chronology, For Further Reading, and Index.

1100.   Lopez-Medina, Sylvia. **Siguiriya**. New York: HarperCollins, 1997. 320p. $23. ISBN 0-06-017271-1. YA

In fifteenth-century Spain, during Isabella and Ferdinand's fanatically Catholic reign, a Muslin general marries an independent Jewish woman. He helps her find ways for other Jews to leave the country, but their own children, products of a mixed heritage, suffer as outsiders.

1101.   Lorbiecki, Marybeth. **From My Palace of Leaves in Sarajevo**. Herbert Tauss, illustrator. New York: Dial Press, 1997. 64p. $14.99. ISBN 0-8037-2033-5. 5-8

Nadja, ten, writes letters to her American cousin Alex before the war begins in Sarajevo, Bosnia. After the war, her letters become more desperate as she begins to hear bombs and guns instead of the music she loves. She has to live without electricity, and the availability of enough food or water is never certain. She keeps hoping that things will be better, and this emotion also fills her letters.

1102.   Lord, Bette Bao. **Legacies: A Chinese Mosaic**. New York: Knopf, 1990. 242p. $19.95. ISBN 0-394-58325-6. YA

While Lord lived in China from 1985 to 1989, she interviewed many Chinese persecuted by Mao's Cultural Revolution. This book relates those interviews while also describing her experiences and her family's history. Among the accounts included are those of a veteran of Mao's Long March in 1934, an artist, an actress, a teacher, an entrepreneur, a journalist, and a peasant. Chronology.

1103.   Lord, Bette Bao. **The Middle Heart**. New York: Knopf, 1996. 372p. $25. ISBN 0-394-53432-8. YA

In the 1930s, a motley group forms a friendship in China. They include Steel Hope, the second son of the fallen House of Li; Mountain Pine, Steel Hope's crippled servant; and Firecrackers, a grave keeper's daughter disguised as a boy. As China enters war, they separate. Firecrackers becomes an opera singer who learns to perform while bombs fall nearby, and Steel Hope becomes an engineer who participates in the underground fighting the Japanese while revering the revolution. Mountain Pine becomes a writer and a hermit. When they meet again, their different paths and different ideologies test their friendship.

1104.   Loumaye, Jacqueline. **Chagall: My Sad and Joyous Village**. Veronique Boiry, illustrator; John Goodman, translator. New York: Chelsea House, 1994. 57p. $14.95. ISBN 0-7910-2807-0. (Art for Children). 4-8

Marc Chagall (1887-1985) was born in Russia in Vitebsk, where he began creating his unusual paintings with their dreamlike style. The text, with a story line of two persons discussing Chagall's paintings and his life, gives insight into the man, who had to leave his country, and into his work. He spent the latter half of his life in Nice, France, where the light influenced his work, including stained-glass designs. Color reproductions augment the text. Glossary and Chronology.

1105.   Loumaye, Jacqueline. **Degas: The Painted Gesture**. Nadine Massart, illustrator; John Goodman, translator. New York: Chelsea House, 1994. 57p. $14.95. ISBN 0-7910-2809-7. (Art for Children). 4-8

Students look at and discuss the life and work of Edgar Degas (1834-1917). By examining his paintings almost as if they were characters themselves, the text reveals the man and his time. Chronology and Glossary.

1106.   Loumaye, Jacqueline. **Van Gogh: The Touch of Yellow**. Claudine Roucha, illustrator; John Goodman, translator. New York: Chelsea House, 1994. 57p. $14.95. ISBN 0-7910-2817-8. (Art for Children). 4-8

When a child visits Uncle Paul, his uncle introduces him to van Gogh, and they visit places where the paintings are displayed. Reproductions show the variety in van Gogh's work, and information about his life complements the discussion of his paintings and their depictions of the places where he lived. Glossary and Chronology.

1107.   Lourie, Richard. **Russia Speaks: An Oral History from the Revolution to the Present**. New York: Burlingame/HarperCollins, 1991. 396p. $25. ISBN 0-06-016449-2. YA

Lesser-known episodes from Russia after the Revolution appear in the text as the result of interviews with Soviets. Among the topics are the Soviet participation in the Spanish Civil War, the 1940 invasion of Finland, the postwar crimes in Leningrad, and sketches of leaders such as Lenin and Stalin. The thirty survivors span the history of the Soviet Union's twentieth century and include Andrei Sakharov's mother-in-law and a White Army officer. As members of the masses, they can only hint at what happened outside their sphere, but they can all tell what happened to them personally. Index.

1108.   Loverance, Rowena, and Tim Wood. **Ancient Greece**. New York: Viking, 1993. 48p. $14.99. ISBN 0-670-84754-2. (See Through History). 5-8

See-through illustrations of a town house, public buildings in the Athenian marketplace, an open-air theater, and a warship reveal aspects of ancient Greece. Two-page spreads give information on topics concerning the origin of the Greeks and their land and sea, family life, food and festivals, houses, city-states and government, work, public life, science and philosophy, sports and games, the theater, gods and goddesses, temples and oracles, death and burial, ships, war, and the Greek legacy. Key Dates, Glossary, and Index.

1109. Lowry, Lois. **Number the Stars**. Boston: Houghton Mifflin, 1989. 169p. $14.95. ISBN 0-395-51060-0. New York: Dell, 1989. 169p. $4.50pa. ISBN 0-440-40327-8pa. 4-7

Annemarie and her friend Ellen pretend to be sisters one night when the Nazis come to Ellen's Copenhagen home to arrest her parents, who have already gone into hiding. Ellen's family and others get to Annemarie's uncle's fishing boat, and Annemarie saves them all from the Nazis by taking a handkerchief covered with blood and cocaine to the boat after it was accidentally left behind. The handkerchief deadens the Nazis' search dogs' sense of smell and saves the Jews from being discovered under a vat of fish. *Newbery Medal, National Jewish Awards, Association of Jewish Libraries Award, Sydney Taylor Book Award, American Library Association Notable Books for Children,* and *School Library Journal Best Book.*

1110. Lucas, Eileen. **Vincent van Gogh**. New York: Franklin Watts, 1991. 63p. $18.43. ISBN 0-531-20024-8. (First Books). 4-8

Vincent van Gogh (1853-1890) tried several professions before he decided that he wanted to be a painter. He moved to France, and the pictures he saw in Paris greatly influenced him. He lived mainly in the Provence area of France, where he painted many of his pictures. Six months after van Gogh died, his brother, Theo, to whom he was very close, also died. Theo's wife had them buried side by side. Van Gogh had a mental disease for which he was hospitalized, although doctors have never been sure what it was. Reproductions of van Gogh's paintings complement the text. Masterpieces of Vincent van Gogh, For Further Reading, and Index.

1111. Lunn, Janet. **Shadow in Hawthorn Bay**. New York: Scribners, 1987. 192p. $13.95. ISBN 0-684-18843-0. New York: Penguin, 1988. 192p. $3.95pa. ISBN 0-14-032436-4pa. 5-9

Mairi, who lives in Scotland around 1800, has *an dà shelladh* or the "second sight." She hears her cousin Duncan calling to her from Canada to tell her to come where he has emigrated. She goes and finds that he has recently drowned. Instead of letting the experience disturb her, she decides to marry and begin a new life. *Canada Council Children's Literature Prize, Canada Children's Book of the Year Award,* and *International Board on Books for Young People.*

1112. Lynch, Anne. **Great Buildings**. Alexandria, VA: Time-Life, 1996. 64p. $16. ISBN 0-8094-9371-3. 5-8

Chronological coverage of twenty-six buildings thoughout history display their construction and unusual aspects. Photographs and drawings, some with cross-sectional views, add to the value of the text. Buildings include a Trobriand woven hut, a Mayan pyramid in Mexico, Ishtar's Gate in Babylon, the Baths of Caracalla in Rome, a Hindu temple in India, a Buddhist shrine in Indonesia, the hall of Supreme Harmony in Beijing, the Horyuji Temple Complex in Japan, the Hagia Sophia in Istanbul, the Alhambra in Granada, Notre Dame in Paris, St. Peter's in Rome, Versailles, Casa Milá in Barcelona, the Toronto SkyDome, and the Sydney Opera House. Photographs, Glossary, and Index.

1113. Lynch, Daniel. **Yellow: A Novel**. New York: Walker, 1992. 211p. $19.95. ISBN 0-8027-1226-6. YA

During the Spanish-American War of 1898, journalist Richard Davis and artist Frederic Remington travel to meet Cuban resistance fighters while trying to get a story for William Randolph Hearst's "scandal" newspaper. The dying writer Ambrose Bierce tells the story of the adventure as a prostitute told it to him.

1114. Lyttle, Richard B. **Il Duce: The Rise and Fall of Benito Mussolini**. New York: Atheneum, 1987. 256p. $13.95. ISBN 0-689-31213-X. 7 up

Benito Mussolini (1883–1945), the prime minister of the Italian government, wanted to expand the country. In 1939, he formalized an alliance with Germany and then took Italy into World War II on Hitler's side in 1940. His Fascist Brown Shirts terrorized the people, and in 1943 Victor Emmanuel III dismissed him. He continued to lead a puppet Nazi government in northern Italy until someone assassinated him in 1945. The text looks at the crises in his life, both personal and political. Bibliography and Index.

1115. Lyttle, Richard B. **Pablo Picasso: The Man and the Image**. New York: Atheneum, 1989. 246p. $15.95. ISBN 0-689-31393-4. YA

Pablo Picasso (1881–1973) created paintings, lithographs, etchings, drawings, book illustrations, ceramic designs, and stage settings. The text gives details about his life, including his relationships with women and his family. Bibliography and Index.

M

1116. Maalouf, Amin. **Samarkand: A Novel (Emerging Voices)**. Russell Harris, translator. New York: Interlink, 1995. 304p. $35; $14.95pa. ISBN 1-56656-200-7; 1-56656-194-9pa. YA

The story begins in eleventh-century Persia and ends when the *Titanic* sinks in 1912. The narrator, an American in the twentieth century, pursues the fate of *The Rubaiyat* of Omar Khayyam. Khayyam was an astronomer, mathematician, and poet who did the best he could under the strictures of Muslim dogmatism. During his lifetime, his poetry was not recognized, but Edward Fitzgerald later discovered it and arranged it into sections. Samarkand and its exoticism creates an intriguing background with empires rising and falling—as Khayyam said, a "chessboard of the world."

1117. Maass, Peter. **Love Thy Neighbor: A Story of War**. New York: Knopf, 1996. 305p. $25. ISBN 0-679-44433-5. YA

What Maass saw as a correspondent in Bosnia was fascist Serbian thugs with well-equipped armies slaughtering a group of unarmed civilians who were trying to start their nation on a basis of tolerance. In the rural areas, the genocidal attacks destroyed huge groups of non-Serbs. Serbs captured and detained thousands of Muslims in concentration camps. Inmates begged Maass not to ask questions, because answering would cause their deaths after he left. The text tells what happened in Bosnia factually as it asks philosophically how humans can let such things happen. Index.

1118. Macaulay, David, author/illustrator. **Castle**. Boston: Houghton Mifflin, 1977. 80p. $16.95; $7.95pa. ISBN 0-395-25784-0; 0-395-32920-5pa. 5 up

The castle that Macaulay builds is imaginary, but is based on the concept, structural process, and physical appearance of several castles constructed to help the English conquer Wales between 1277 and 1305. These castles and the towns around them were the culmination of over two centuries of development, in Europe and the Holy Land, of the castle as a way to keep military forces together. Glossary. *Caldecott Honor Book.*

1119. Macaulay, David, author/illustrator. **Cathedral: The Story of Its Construction**. Boston: Houghton Mifflin, 1973. 77p. $16.95. ISBN 0-395-17513-5. 3 up

Macaulay builds an imaginary cathedral based on the French cathedral at Reims. The text discusses the people's reasons for wanting a cathedral, how they got the money to build it, and how long it took them to complete such a huge building in the twelfth century. Illustrations and diagrams reveal what an enormous accomplishment building a cathedral was and also the prestige that it brought to the village in which it was constructed.

1120. Macaulay, David, author/illustrator. **Ship**. Boston: Houghton Mifflin, 1993. 96p. $19.95. ISBN 0-395-52439-3. 6 up

The space shuttles of the fifteenth century were small ships called caravels. No drawings remain to show what these ships looked like or how they were built. The text looks at a caravel recovered by archaeologists from the Caribbean waters and recreates it piece by piece. Then it uses a diary format to tell of the ship's last voyage from Seville to its sinking.

1121. MacDonald, Fiona. **Cities: Citizens and Civilizations**. New York: Franklin Watts, 1992. 48p. $13.95; $7.95pa. ISBN 0-531-15247-2; 0-531-15287-1pa. (Timelines). 5-8

In two-page topic spreads, the text covers many cities, with detailed illustrations showing each city's character. The sites covered are the first cities (Sumer, ancient Egypt, and Thebes); Greek city-states (Athens and Sparta); Rome; the Viking Hedeby in Denmark; early American Mesa Verde; Córdoba, Spain; Paris; Venice; Florence; Nurenberg; Constantinople; Amsterdam; Vienna; St. Petersburg, Russia; New York; industrial cities like Pittsburgh and Leeds, England; and London. It also discusses suburbs; inner cities; cityscapes of Paris, France, and Sydney, Australia; and what future cities might resemble. Timeline, Glossary, and Index.

1122. MacDonald, Fiona. **A Greek Temple**. Mark Bergin, illustrator. New York: Peter Bedrick, 1992. 48p. $18.95. ISBN 0-87226-351-4. (Inside Story). 4-8

This survey illustrates the construction and history of the Parthenon in ancient Greece, as well as including other information. Two-page topics and diagrams discuss homes for the gods, prayers and sacrifices, festival games, temple design, proportions of buildings, site preparation, citizens and workers, columns and walls, roofs, Parthenon sculptures, the craftsman's day, inside the Parthenon and on the Acropolis, Athena's birthday, memorials, the past and the present, and contemporary Greek influence. Glossary and Index.

1123. MacDonald, Fiona. **A Medieval Castle**. Mark Bergin, illustrator. New York: Peter Bedrick, 1990. 48p. $16.95. ISBN 0-87226-340-1. (Inside Story). 5-7

With text and cutaway illustrations, the author and illustrator reveal the civilization and expectations of people who lived and worked in castles during the Middle Ages. Index.

1124.   MacDonald, Fiona. **A Medieval Cathedral**. John James, illustrator. New York: Peter Bedrick, 1991. 48p. $18.95; $8.95pa. ISBN 0-87226-350-9; 0-87226-266-9pa. (Inside Story). 5-8

Most cathedrals were built during the Middle Ages, between 550 and 1450. With detailed and informative illustrations accompanying the text, topics covered are choice of site, cathedral architecture, stone quarrying, the foundation, craftsmen, stone tracery, the worker's day, wall building, types of drains, gargoyles and roofs, floors and vaults, bell towers and spires, priests and people, pilgrims, miracle plays, monasteries, and other facts. Glossary and Index.

1125.   MacDonald, Fiona. **The Middle Ages**. New York: Facts on File, 1993. 78p. $17.95. ISBN 0-8160-2788-9. (Illustrated History of the World). 4-7

In the western world, during the Middle Ages, life focused on government, religion, chivalry, and survival. More people began to live in towns as trade developed. The crises of the Black Death, the Mongol advance, and the Ottomans touched many, with exploration and foreign voyages signaling the end of the Middle Ages and the beginning of the Renaissance. Outside of the western world, other orders prevailed. Islamic government and society ruled the Near East, and in the Far East, China's Sing empire was in power. Illustrations highlight the text. Glossary, Further Reading, and Index.

1126.   MacDonald, Fiona. **A 19th Century Railway Station**. John James, illustrator. New York: Peter Bedrick, 1990. 48p. $16.95. ISBN 0-87226-341-X. (Inside Story). 5-7

The text explains how nineteenth-century railway stations were financed, built, decorated, and managed. Detailed pictures augment the text and give information about the people who worked in the stations and the activities undertaken there. Glossary and Index.

1127.   MacDonald, Fiona. **A Roman Fort**. Gerald Wood, illustrator. New York: Peter Bedrick, 1983. 48p. $18.95; $8.95pa. ISBN 0-87226-370-3; 0-87226-259-6pa. (Inside Story). 6-8

Two-page spreads present various topics related to a Roman fort. The discussions include army legions and organization, Roman roads and construction, camps, searching for sites to build forts, the expansion of a fort into a village, food and water, illness and injury, gods and spirits, soldiers on parade and off-duty, and types of warfare. Clear drawings, diagrams, and maps highlight the text. Glossary and Index.

1128.   MacDonald, Fiona. **A Samurai Castle**. John James and David Antram, illustrators. New York: Peter Bedrick, 1995. 48p. $18.95. ISBN 0-87226-381-9. (Inside Story). 5-8

The text covers samurai castles of the seventeenth and eighteenth centuries in Japan. It gives information on their construction, history, and inhabitants. The double-page spreads offer diverse topics such as women's lives, interiors, towns around the castles, methods of entertaining visitors, and arms. Glossary and Index.

1129.   MacDonald, Fiona. **A 16th Century Mosque**. Mark Bergin, illustrator. New York: Peter Bedrick, 1994. 48p. $18.95. ISBN 0-87226-310-X. 5 up

In two-page spreads, text and vivid illustrations cover such topics as the spread of Islam and the faith, the first mosque, various styles of mosques, the lives of the workers who built them, the Ottoman Empire, Suleyman the Magnificent and his mosque, the domed roofs, the call to prayer, mihrab and minbar, woodwork and tiles, carpets and rugs, light and color, the people of the mosque, schools and colleges, and medicine and charity, as well as mosques around the world. Glossary, Dates in This Book, and Index.

1130.   MacDonald, Malcolm. **The Trevarton Inheritance**. New York: St. Martin's Press, 1996. 395p. $24.95. ISBN 0-312-14748-1. YA

Crissy Moore's parents and grandfather die, all within a few days. She wants her family of six siblings to stay together, but she must request help from the grandmother, who has refused to speak to her mother since she ran away with Crissy's father, a coachman. Crissy becomes a maid in her grandmother's home during the late 1800s in Cornwall, and she and Jim, the man she eventually marries, plan to start a business photographing tourists at the seaside. Both endeavors help her reach her goal.

1131.   MacDonald, Patricia A. **Pablo Picasso**. Englewood Cliffs, NJ: Silver Burdett, 1990. 128p. $12.95. ISBN 0-382-09903-6. (Genius! The Artist and the Process). 7-10

Pablo Picasso (1881–1973), born in Malaga and educated at art school in Barcelona, experimented in both art and life. He helped develop Cubism but abandoned it after feeling that it had gone as far as it could. During the war years, especially those of the Spanish civil war, he painted to show his anguish. He spent his later years on the Riviera, in the sun, and said about his work that "[n]othing is more important than to create enthusiasm." Chronology, Glossary, Bibliography, and Index.

1132. MacDonald, Robert. **Maori**. New York: Thomson Learning, 1994. 48p. $24.21. ISBN 1-56847-151-3. (Threatened Cultures). 4-8

Cultures such as that of the Maori in New Zealand, which maintain traditional ways of life unlike anything in the modern world, are threatened with extinction when they come face to face with technology. The text shows how the Maoris have tried to integrate their ancient traditions into contemporary situations through looking at both the past and the present of the Maori tribe. Glossary of Maori Words, Glossary of English Words, Further Reading, Further Information, and Index.

1133. Mackerras, Colin, and Amanda Yorke. **The Cambridge Handbook of Contemporary China**. New York: Cambridge University Press, 1991. 266p. $22.95pa. ISBN 0-521-38342-0pa. YA

The text presents information on the People's Republic of China from its beginning in 1949 through the spring of 1990. It includes a chronology of events from 1900 through 1990, with broad subject subheadings and biographies of major figures. Other chapters are essays on politics, foreign relations, the economy, the population, the education, the culture and society, and ethnic minorities living in China. Charts, Tables, Graphs, Annotated Bibliography, Appendices, Gazetteer, and Index.

1134. Mackey, Sandra. **Lebanon: Death of a Nation**. New York: Doubleday, 1989. 304p. $12.95pa. ISBN 0-385-41381-5pa. YA

By 1983, when terrorists bombed the American embassy in Beirut, Lebanon, the Lebanese civil war had reportedly been raging since 1975. Mackey posits that although the discontent had begun festering centuries before, the Western money that filtered into Beirut, making it the "Paris of the East," and other Middle Eastern events finally moved the Shiite Muslims to action. She notes that each Lebanese citizen practiced a hierarchy of loyalty— first to family, then to village, and then to religion, before fighting as a nation. The most affluent Lebanese were the Marronite Christians, although a minority; next wealthiest were the Muslims, the renegade Druze, the Sunni, and lastly the lowly servant class Shiites. Many felt that the American University in Beirut—begun in 1866 as a Christian institution, and continued as a place where Arabs could learn Western ideas while keeping their Arab beliefs—was a major concern, because many of its graduates became leaders of the country. This account of Lebanon, a small country of no more than 4,000 square miles, gives insight into its problems. Selected Bibliography and Index.

1135. Macmillan, Dianne M. **Diwali: Hindu Festival of Lights**. Springfield, NJ: Enslow, 1977. 48p. $16.95. ISBN 0-89490-817-0. 4-8

Hindu beliefs are portrayed in this description of an important festival and presentation of the important books, legends, and other traditions associated with the religion. Glossary and Index.

1136. Madden, Paul. **Fidel Castro**. Vero Beach, FL: Rourke, 1993. 111p. $22.60. ISBN 0-86625-479-X. (World Leaders). YA

In 1959, Fidel Castro took over the government of Cuba by overthrowing a hated dictator. Some call him a demagogue; others think that he has tried to bring social justice and a decent standard of living to Cuba. He has also tried to keep others from exploiting Third World countries. The text, with photographs, examines Castro's life and what he has done to change his country. Major Achievements, Time Line, Glossary, Bibliography, Media Resources, and Index.

1137. Magorian, Michelle. **Back Home**. 1984. New York: HarperCollins, 1992. 352p. $4.95pa. ISBN 0-06-440411-0pa. 7 up

Rusty returns to England in 1945 after being evacuated to America. She dislikes the lack of goods, her boarding school, and her father's dictatorial attitude. After several difficulties, Rusty's mother leaves her husband, and Rusty, her mother, and her little brother go to live in a house recently inherited when her mother's close friend died. *American Library Association Best Books for Young Adults* and *New York Public Library Children's Books*.

1138. Magorian, Michelle. **Good Night, Mr. Tom**. New York: HarperCollins, 1982. 318p. $15.89; $4.50pa. ISBN 0-06-024079-2; 0-06-440174-Xpa. 7 up

Willie Beech, age eight, evacuates from London in 1939 to a small village, where he stays with Mr. Tom, an old man still mourning the deaths of his wife and son many years before. Willie is fearful of almost everything, but Mr. Tom helps him, and Willie even learns to read. When Willie makes friends with Zach, he discovers laughter. He has to return to his mother in London, but when Mr. Tom does not hear from Willie for several weeks, Mr. Tom goes to London to search for him. Mr. Tom finds Willie locked in the closet where his mentally unbalanced mother has left him. Mr. Tom takes Willie home to adopt him as his son. *IRA Children's Book Award, American Library Association Notable Children's Book, American Library Association Best Books for Young Adults, Horn Book Fanfare Honor List, Booklist Young Adult Editors' Choices, NCTE Teachers' Choices, Notable Children's Trade Books in the Field of Social Studies, Guardian Award, American Library Association Notable Children's Book,* and *Association of Booksellers for Children's Choices.*

1139.   Magorian, Michelle. **Not a Swan**. New York: HarperCollins, 1992. 407p. $18. ISBN 0-06-024215-9. 7 up

When Rose, age seventeen, and her two older sisters stay in an English coastal village after evacuation from London in 1944, Rose anticipates the summer. By the end of the time, she has learned to accept herself and her feelings of inferiority have dissipated. When a magazine accepts her first short story for publication, she is especially pleased with the influence of her summer's experience of working in a bookshop.

1140.   Mahoney, M. H. **Women in Espionage: A Biographical Dictionary**. Santa Barbara, CA: ABC-CLIO, 1993. 253p. $65. ISBN 0-87436-743-3. 9 up

As a former CIA operative, Mahoney presents alphabetical entries on 150 women who have been involved in espionage. She includes Delilah in the Bible as well as those from the American Revolution and the Civil War. Most of the women are American or European, but some come from other countries. In the introduction, Mahoney lists some of the roles that women have played as spies. Bibliography and Index.

1141.   Major, John S. **The Silk Route: 7000 Miles of History**. Stephen Fieser, illustrator. New York: Harper-Collins, 1995. 32p. $14.95. ISBN 0-06-022924-1. 4-7

Silk has long been a symbol of riches and luxury, and a 7,000-mile-long trade route flourished for centuries by which silk traveled from China throughout the East. The story begins in A.D. 700 with the Tang Dynasty. The trade journey began in Chang'an (city), with traders stopping to pray at Dunhauang (monastery), crossing the Taklamakan (desert), stopping at Kashgar (oasis), traveling over Pamirs (mountains), stopping in Tashkent (market), going through Transoxiana (wild country with nomads), and visiting Herat (Persian city), Baghdad (greatest Islamic city), Damascus, Tyre, and Byzantium. *American Booksellers' Pick of the Lists.*

1142.   Major, Kevin. **Blood Red Ochre**. New York: Delacorte, 1989. 148p. $14.95. ISBN 0-385-29794-7. 7-9

David, age fifteen, narrates half of the chapters in this historical fantasy; Dauoodaset of the extinct Beothuk tribe tells the others. When David, the twentieth-century character, starts a school project about this tribe, whose members painted themselves with red ochre, he finds out that Nancy, an aloof classmate, is working on the same subject. Dauoodaset worries about his people starving and about finding his lost love Shanawdithit in 1829. When David and Nancy go to the uninhabited island where the tribe lived, Nancy goes off as Shanawdithit after she and Dauoodaset reunite. David returns home.

1143.   Malterre, Elona. **The Last Wolf of Ireland.** New York: Clarion, 1990. 127p. $13.95. ISBN 0-395-54381-9. 5-7

Around 1786 in Ireland, Devin and his friend, Katey, see the Squire kill a mother wolf, and they save the litter. They feed them until a village boy tells what they are doing. Devin saves one male, but the society hates wolves, and when the wolf is grown, someone mortally wounds it. Devin has cared for it and it returns to Devin before dying.

1144.   Manchester, William. **The Last Lion: Winston Spencer Churchill: Alone, 1932–1940**. Boston: Little, Brown, 1988. 756p. $40. ISBN 0-316-54512-0. New York: Dell, 1989. 756p. $17.95pa. ISBN 0-385-31331-4pa. YA

From 1932 until 1940, Winston Churchill (1874–1965) could not garner the attention necessary for people to thwart Hitler. Churchill had his own failings, and he saw in Hitler's methods the seeds of the war before it began. He said that he warned British and French leaders four times, and that the war would not have occurred if they had listened to him on just one of those occasions. In the text, Manchester shows the weak and the strong in Churchill. He was a country squire, a journalist, a historian, a painter, a bricklayer, a father, a husband, a self-advertiser, an insensitive employer, and a megalomaniac. At the same time, he was exceedingly intelligent, magnanimous, and loyal, and a charismatic leader. But he was also out of power between the two wars. Index.

1145.   Manchester, William. **The Last Lion: Winston Spencer Churchill: Visions of Glory, 1874–1932**. Boston: Little, Brown, 1983. 800p. $35. ISBN 0-316-54503-1. New York: Dell, 1989. 800p. $16.95pa. ISBN 0-385-31348-9pa. YA

The first part of a biography of Winston Churchill (1874–1965) presents his early life and his preparation for England's participation in World War II. Churchill was a rather poor student, but as he matured, and went to India to serve England, he began to polish important character traits. Index.

1146.   Mandela, Nelson. **Long Walk to Freedom: The Autobiography of Nelson Mandela**. Boston: Little, Brown, 1994. 558p. $24.95. ISBN 0-316-54585-6. YA

Nelson Mandela's fight against opposition in South Africa won him the Nobel Peace Prize and the presidency of his country. But he did not win these prizes without major personal sacrifice. Raised in the traditional tribal way, he became a student and law clerk in Johannesburg. He headed the African National Congress, and through it, spoke for human rights and racial equality. He was sentenced to life imprisonment at the Rivonia Trial of 1964, and he stayed in prison for twenty-seven years before his release in 1990. He tells of the years in prison and of the negotiations to free him. Index.

1147. Manley, John. **Atlas of Prehistoric Britain**. David Lyons, photographs. New York: Oxford University Press, 1989. 160p. $39.95. ISBN 0-19-520807-2. YA

Photographs of grave mounds, standing stones, and tombs, as well as maps noting their locations, highlight this extensive text on archaeological finds from prehistoric humans in the British Isles. Descriptions of artifacts and their uses reveal possible lifestyles of tribes, from 500,000 B.C. through the Romans in A.D. 43. Timelines, Sites to Visit, Select Bibliography, and Index.

1148. Mann, Barry. **Sigmund Freud**. Vero Beach, FL: Rourke, 1993. 112p. $22.60. ISBN 0-86625-491-9. (Pioneers). YA

Mann places Sigmund Freud (1856–1939) within his time and shows how innovative his work was. He investigates Freud's theories and discusses his relationships with various individuals in his life, including Jung. Some of Freud's important work involved the unconscious, free association, and self-analysis. Even though others may discount Freud and his emphasis on sexuality, he began researching a part of life that had not been charted by another. Photographs, Books by Sigmund Freud, Time Line, Glossary, Bibliography, Media Resources, and Index.

1149. Mann, Elizabeth. **The Great Wall: The Story of 4,000 Miles of Earth and Stone That Turned a Nation into a Fortress**. New York: Mikaya Press, 1997. 48p. $18.95. ISBN 0-96504-932-9. (Wonders of the World). 7-8

The first attempts at building a wall in China occurred as early as 200 B.C., although success did not occur until after Kublai Khan began to rule. When the wall was completed, it was a giant attempt at keeping enemies out of the country. Chronology and Index.

1150. Mann, Kenny. **Oyo, Benin, Ashanti: The Guinea Coast**. New York: Dillon Press, 1996. 105p. $15.95; $7.95pa. ISBN 0-87518-657-2; 0-382-39177-2pa. (African Kingdoms of the Past). 6-10

In this text, African legends become part of the history of the area. The text covers environment, kingdom building, and the slave trade in Oyo, Benin, and Ashanti. Information on the history of each area, along with the individual cultures found there, gives each an identity. An epilogue covers the areas' history from colonization to the present. Photographs, Chronology, Further Reading, and Index.

1151. Markham, Lois. **Inventions That Changed Modern Life**. Austin, TX: Raintree/Steck-Vaughn, 1994. 48p. $15.96. ISBN 0-8114-4930-0. (20 Events Series). 6 up

In the late eighteenth century, James Watt's steam engine was produced for sale, Nicolas Appert began working with food preservation, and Eli Whitney designed interchangeable parts for guns. In the nineteenth century, Richard Trevithick and George Stephenson worked with locomotives. Photography began with experiments in France and England by Josiah Wedgwood, Joseph-Nicéphore Niepce, Louis Daguerre, and W. H. Fox Talbot. Cyrus McCormick began work on the combine harvester, and Isaac Singer patented the sewing machine begun by Elias Howe. Work on refrigeration, plastics, the telephone, electric light, and the automobile ended the century. In 1901, Marconi's radio worked. Also in the twentieth century, the airplane, assembly line, rocket, nuclear fission, television, computers, and lasers have changed the way people live. Each topic covers two pages. Glossary, Suggested Readings, and Index.

1152. Marko, Katherine. **Away to Fundy Bay**. New York: Walker, 1985. 145p. $11.95. ISBN 0-8027-6594-7. 5-9

During 1775, Doone, age thirteen, tries to escape the British press gangs in Halifax, Nova Scotia, by going to his mother's friends' farm near Fundy Bay. After a time, his uncle dies, and he is able to rescue his mother and sister, who had had to remain as servants to the man. When he saves the farm owner's son from hanging after the son is accused of treason, the owner gives Doone land for his family.

1153. Markus, Julia. **Dared and Done: The Marriage of Elizabeth Barrett and Robert Browning**. New York: Knopf, 1995. 382p. $30. ISBN 0-679-41602-1. YA

Elizabeth Barrett (1806–1861) and Robert Browning (1812–1889) courted by letter after he first wrote her, an internationally known poet, that he loved her work and her. Barrett's father had forbidden any of his twelve children ever to marry, and she had been an invalid most of her life who relied on morphine. After twenty months of writing to each other, Barrett and Browning ran away to Italy and a marriage in which they both thrived. Markus tells the story of this marriage and these two talented people. Notes, Selected Bibliography, and Index.

1154. Marrin, Albert. **The Airman's War: World War II in the Sky**. New York: Atheneum, 1982. 213p. $11.95. ISBN 0-689-30907-4. 5 up

In 1939, German Reichsmarshal Hermann Goering boasted that no one would ever bomb Germany. He thought that Germany controlled the skies. He was wrong. The text looks at the importance of air power in World War II after many leaders of the American armed services had ignored the value of an air force in the early 1930s. Three men, "Hap" Arnold, "Tooey" Spaatz, and Ira Eaker, fulfilled "Billy" Mitchell's goal for a strong air fleet. The text tells their stories; the stories of pilots in the war flying bombers and fighter planes; the stories of the planes they flew, such as the B-17s, the Liberators, the Spitfires, and the Messerschmitts; and the battles they fought, some of them bombing raids that lasted around the clock. Photographs, Maps, Some More Books, and Index.

1155.   Marrin, Albert. **America and Vietnam: The Elephant and the Tiger**. New York: Viking, 1992. 256p. $16. ISBN 0-670-84063-7. 9 up

The text presents a background history of Vietnam followed by a capsule biography of Ho Chi Minh before telling how the war affected both Vietnam and the United States. Marrin attempts to show both the atrocities and the admirable acts on both sides of the battlefield as he explains the motivations and mistakes behind the war. Glossary, Bibliography, and Index.

1156.   Marrin, Albert. **Aztecs and Spaniards: Cortés and the Conquest of Mexico**. New York: Atheneum, 1986. 212p. $12.95. ISBN 0-689-31176-1. 5-8

The legend goes that in 1168 a god commanded the Aztecs to move south in search of a better home. They did, and they settled in the valley of Mexico, where they built their city on islands in a large lake. They grew, in less than two centuries, to a vast empire. In 1519, when Cortés arrived, no city in Europe could match the size of Tenochtitlán. The Spaniards had come to get wealth and they decided to take it from the Aztecs. When Cortés marched on the city, the final Aztec uprising led to the Night of Tears, when so many died by Spanish swords. Some More Books and Index.

1157.   Marrin, Albert. **Hitler**. New York: Viking, 1987. 249p. $13.95. ISBN 0-670-81546-2. YA

Among the achievements of Adolf Hitler (1889–1945) were that he influenced the mind-set of a country, built an unstoppable army out of one that had recently lost a major war, and murdered an astounding number of people. As a World War I foot soldier, he developed a passion for war and began to develop his ideas for blitzkrieg tactics. The text looks at his life and the battles he directed as he set out to destroy anyone who opposed him on his way to ruling the world. Some More Books and Index.

1158.   Marrin, Albert. **Inca and Spaniard: Pizarro and the Conquest of Peru**. New York: Atheneum, 1989. 211p. $15.95. ISBN 0-689-31481-7. 7-10

The text gives a background on the Incas, an Indian group who took control of their Peruvian area of Cuzco around A.D. 1100 and continued that control by taking tribute from the surrounding peoples. When the Spaniards arrived, their luck changed. Francisco Pizarro (1476–1541), wanting to be important and wealthy, brought an army into their area and decimated their culture, taking whatever his greed could gather. Bibliography and Index.

1159.   Marrin, Albert. **Mao Tse-tung and His China**. New York: Viking, 1989. 282p. $14.95. ISBN 0-670-82940-4. 7 up

Mao Tse-tung (1893–1976) spread Chinese communism to the masses and almost destroyed his country with his purges during the Cultural Revolution. The text looks at the man and at Chinese history from 1911, at the overthrow of the Manchu Dynasty, the rise of the Chinese Communist Party, and the end of the Cultural Revolution. Glossary, Bibliography, and Index.

1160.   Marrin, Albert. **Napoleon and the Napoleonic Wars**. New York: Viking, 1991. 224p. $14.95. ISBN 0-670-83480-7. 8 up

Napoleon Bonaparte (1769–1821) always wanted to be a soldier, but because he was living during a time of revolution, he became much more. His ability to seize opportunities allowed him to rise to the rank of general by the age of twenty-four. By breaking many military rules, he conquered Europe with the first mass army and the first mass graves. The text looks at his accomplishments and conquests, and at his failure when he tried to take Russia during the middle of winter. Some More Books and Index.

1161.   Marrin, Albert. **OVERLORD: D-Day and the Invasion of Europe**. New York: Atheneum, 1982. 176p. $12.95. ISBN 0-689-30931-7. 7 up

In 1942, Winston Churchill flew to the United States to meet with Franklin Roosevelt about ways to stop Adolf Hitler from taking over Europe. What evolved was a plan called Operation OVERLORD, the Allied plan for freeing Europe and winning the war. The project took extraordinary planning, with supplies collected in England along with ships, tanks, planes, and gliders. Dummy airfields with fake tanks and planes had to be prepared as lures for Hitler's air force. Germany knew the invasion would occur and fortified the coast of France along the English Channel closest to England. The landing at Omaha Beach along with Juno and Utah on June 6, 1944, was difficult. Photographs, Maps, Some More Books, and Index.

1162.   Marrin, Albert. **The Sea King: Sir Francis Drake and His Times**. New York: Atheneum, 1995. 168p. $18. ISBN 0-689-31887-1. 6-10

Instead of telling Francis Drake (1540?-1596) that she planned to knight him, Queen Elizabeth I implied that she was going to use the sword she had laid on his neck to cut off his head. She knighted him, though, because she was indebted to this man, who had gained a position for England in the New World after Spain and Portugal had seemed to control it. He was a great mariner and navigator as well as commander. He was a leader, a preacher, and a lover of children. He usually freed his prisoners and gave them gifts. But he was also demanding, insistent on obedience, and ruthless when necessary. The text covers his life and the times, including the Spanish Inquisition and the Spanish Armada, and the difficulties of life at sea. Some More Books, Notes, and Index. *School Library Journal Starred Review.*

1163.   Marrin, Albert. **The Sea Rovers: Pirates, Privateers, and Buccaneers**. New York: Atheneum, 1984. 173p. $15.95. ISBN 0-689-31029-3. 5 up

In the early history of Europeans coming to American shores, pirates rode the seas in search of other peoples' wealth. English sea dogs such as Jack Hawkins and Francis Drake helped Queen Elizabeth declare war on Spain. Henry Morgan, Blackbeard, and Captain Kidd looked for booty on all the ships sailing the Atlantic. On the Mediterranean, the Barbary pirates patrolled the northern coast of Africa, but the U.S. Navy proved itself by thwarting their progress. The text looks at these pirates as well as women who also sailed under the pirate flag, the Jolly Roger. Some More Books and Index.

1164.   Marrin, Albert. **The Secret Armies: Spies, Counterspies, and Saboteurs in World War II**. New York: Atheneum, 1985. 239p. $13.95. ISBN 0-689-31165-6. 5 up

Spies and counterspies worked in Europe during World War II under code names, such as Hedgehog, Zigzag, and Tricycle, to gather information behind German lines and pass misinformation to Nazi intelligence. People participated in the Resistance movement, in the Maquis in France, in the Netherlands, and in other conquered countries where people risked their lives. These undercover agents cracked the German secret code with the Enigma machine and helped ensure an Allied victory. The text looks at all aspects of these important participants in the war. Photographs, More Books, and Index.

1165.   Marrin, Albert. **The Spanish-American War**. New York: Atheneum, 1991. 182p. $15.95. ISBN 0-689-31663-1. 7 up

In 1898, the United States fought "a splendid little war" according to diplomat John Hay. Using inconclusive data to blame the Spanish for an attack on the USS *Maine*, a battleship, the United States joined the war to free Cuba from Spain. Marrin uses the facts along with biographical sketches of figures important in the decision to fight the war, such as William Randolph Hearst, whose newspaper blamed the Spanish for the deaths of the 260 men on the *Maine;* George Dewey, the man who destroyed the Spanish fleet in Manila Bay, the Philippines; and Theodore Roosevelt, the hero of San Juan Hill in Puerto Rico. Although the United States won in Puerto Rico and the Philippines, Marrin shows through text and photographs that jingoists, expansionists, and yellow journalists encouraged the country to intervene in the war for the wrong reasons. Bibliography and Index.

1166.   Marrin, Albert. **Stalin: Russia's Man of Steel**. New York: Viking, 1988. 256p. $13.95; $5.99pa. ISBN 0-670-82102-0; 0-14-032605-7pa. 7-9

As leader of the Soviet state, Joseph Stalin (1879–1953) was the only free person of over 190 million in his country. No one told him what to do, and he did what he wanted. He created cities from nothing; dictated what people would read, see, and do; and rid himself of dissenters by either shooting them or starving them. Over 20 million of his people died at his command during peacetime, and other tens of millions toiled in the *gulags* where he had exiled them. He initially admired Hitler, and Hitler returned the favor. Stalin was the greatest mass murderer of all time. Some More Books and Index.

1167.   Marrin, Albert. **Victory in the Pacific**. New York: Atheneum, 1983. 217p. $12.95. ISBN 0-689-30948-1. 7 up

When the Japanese attacked Pearl Harbor on December 7, 1941, 96 U.S. warships were in the harbor for the weekend with only a few people looking after them. The text looks at the events leading to that defeat and the battles afterward in the Pacific. Those included are Midway, Guadalcanal, Betio, and the movement toward Japan to the Caroline and Mariana Islands and the Philippines. Taking Iwo Jima and Okinawa allowed the Allied bombing of mainland Japan. Among the other topics are the basic structures of the ships, the torpedo charges, and how the big guns fired aboard ship. Photographs, Some More Books, and Index.

1168.   Marrin, Albert. **The Yanks Are Coming: The United States in the First World War**. New York: Atheneum, 1986. 248p. $14.95. ISBN 0-689-31209-1. 7 up

Furious that German U-boats had sunk an American passenger ship, the *Lusitania,* in 1915, Americans began to think that they should enter World War I. President Wilson believed in peace, but finally, on April 2, 1917, he declared war. The United States had to mobilize rapidly by coordinating industry, training doughboy soldiers, and promoting the war to those who did not want to fight. The text recounts these achievements; the battles on the front line such as Chateau Thierry and Belleau Woods, where more U.S. Marines died in one day than in their entire history; and Meuse-Argonne, where the Lost Battalion became trapped behind German lines. Leaders such as Foch, Pershing, Mitchell, and Marshall appear within the pages as they tried to give morale and direction to their men. Some More Books and Index.

1169.   Marshall, Michael W. **Ocean Traders: From the Portuguese Discoveries to the Present Day**. New York: Facts on File, 1990. 192p. $24.95. ISBN 0-8160-2420-0. 7 up

From 2600 B.C., when Pharaoh Sneferu supposedly sent 40 ships to Phoenicia, until the present, ships for ocean trading have kept countries wealthy. Not until the Portuguese in the 1400s, however, was a ship designed that was fast enough to actually trade. Previously, ships carried cargo rather than salable goods. Chapters emphasize the long dawn of trading ships, the ocean trader coming of age from 1400 to 1600, the ocean highways developing from 1500 to 1700, the wars at sea from 1700 to 1800, the rise and fall of the sailing trader from 1800 to 1910, and the compound engine and container ships that evolved from 1890 through the twentieth century. Diagrams complement photographs and text on life aboard as well as the design of all these ships. Selected Bibliography and Index.

1170.   Marston, Edward. **The Dragons of Archenfield**. New York: St. Martin's Press, 1995. 256p. $21.95. ISBN 0-312-13472-X. (Domesday, 3). YA

Ralph Delchard and the lawyer Gervase Bret go to the Welsh border to investigate land claims in the eleventh century. In Archenfield, they find much more than borders in the conflicts among the Norman, Welsh, and Saxon inhabitants, and they have to solve a crime.

1171.   Marston, Edward. **The Laughing Hangman: A Novel**. New York: St. Martin's Press, 1996. 248p. $21.95. ISBN 0-312-14305-2. YA

When Lord Westfield's men decide to present Jonas Applegarth's irreverent play, *The Misfortunes of Marriage*, they disturb their rival, the Blackfriars, and attract all of Applegarth's many enemies. After his murder, they understand the play in a different way, and perform it stunningly. Nick Bracewell must keep the troupe together throughout the affair while watching for the murderer.

1172.   Marston, Edward. **The Lions of the North**. New York: St. Martin's Press, 1996. 227p. $21.95. ISBN 0-312-14671-X. (Domesday, 4). YA

Ralph Delchard and Gervase Bret lead a group into Yorkshire to settle land claims while they compile the Domesday Book for William the Conqueror. Lions around the castle of Aubrey Maminot eat an intruder, and the two begin to investigate why someone would seek such a horrible suicide. They discover that Maminot has been consorting with enemies and is prepared to help the country offering him the most money. His lions have guarded his secret, but at least one of them retaliates at his "justice."

1173.   Marston, Edward. **The Mad Courtesan**. New York: Fawcett, 1994. 252p. $4.99pa. ISBN 0-449-22246-2pa. YA

Nicholas Bracewell, stage manager for Lord Westfield's Men in London, has several problems. The leading man of Nick's troupe has fallen in love with a beauty; the health of Elizabeth I, Good Queen Bess, is in decline; a rival company begins to do well; and someone axe-murders the gentleman player Sebastian Carrick. Bracewell wonders why he feels as if a shadow has fallen over him and the time.

1174.   Marston, Edward. **The Merry Devils: An Elizabethan Whodunit**. New York: St. Martin's Press, 1990. 237p. $16.95. ISBN 0-312-03863-1. YA

Lord Westfield's Men, an actors' troupe, loses one of their devils in the second performance of *The Merry Devils*. The leader, Nicholas Bracewell, has to investigate the mystery. He is able to pull the pieces together when the troupe goes to Parkbrook to perform the play for Francis Jordan. He finds out that Jordan has tried to get rid of the estate's real heir but failed.

1175.   Marston, Edward. **The Nine Giants: An Elizabethan Theater Mystery**. New York: St. Martin's Press, 1991. 236p. $17.95. ISBN 0-312-06426-8. YA

Nicholas Bracewell, the stage manager for Lord Westfield's Men, an acting troupe in Elizabethan England, must look after the logistics as well as the men. The company's star has an affair, someone assaults an apprentice, Bracewell and the local waterman find a body in the Thames, and the troupe faces possible expulsion from their theater if its ownership changes hands. The problems come to a head at the Lord Mayor's Show, when people line the streets and the Thames for parade and pomp.

1176.   Marston, Edward. **The Queen's Head: An Elizabethan Whodunit**. New York: St. Martin's Press, 1988. 236p. $16.95. ISBN 0-312-02970-5. YA

In 1588, Nicholas Bracewell, stage manager of Lord Westfield's Men in London, has to find a replacement for the company's leading actor and to keep his promise to a dying man that he will find the murderer. Accidents, robberies, and other misfortunes occur to the company, but they receive an invitation to appear at the court of Queen Elizabeth. At the court performance, Bracewell identifies the murderer.

1177.   Marston, Edward. **The Ravens of Blackwater**. New York: St. Martin's Press, 1994. 245p. $20.95. ISBN 0-312-11330-7. New York: Fawcett, 1996. 245p. $5.99pa. ISBN 0-449-22410-4pa. (Domesday, 2). YA

While William the Conqueror's men travel to Blackwood Hall around 1085 to count holdings and enter them in the Domesday book, they hear of the eldest FitzCorbucion son's murder. Almost anyone in the town had reason to kill him, so Gervase Bret, the king's lawyer, has to carefully assess the situation before he can find the murderer. From those most likely to have committed the deed, a young man in love with the FitzCorbucion daughter and a wronged slave, he carefully extracts necessary information. An additional complication involves the prioress in a nearby abbey.

1178.   Marston, Edward. **The Roaring Boy**. New York: St. Martin's Press, 1995. 272p. $21.95. ISBN 0-312-13155-0. YA

Nicholas Bracewell, the Elizabethan stage manager, helps to create a new kind of play based on a murder case. When Westfield's men play it, Bracewell has to deal with the result. *Edgar Nomination*.

1179.   Marston, Edward. **The Silent Woman: An Elizabethan Theater Mystery**. New York: St. Martin's Press, 1994. 312p. $21.95. ISBN 0-312-11115-0. YA

When fire destroys the London home of Lord Westfield's Men, the troupe has to go on tour to make money. Before they leave, a woman trying to deliver a message to Nicholas Bracewell, the troupe's stage manger, is killed before she sees him. He realizes that he must return to his childhood home to solve the murder, and there he meets his past.

1180.   Marston, Edward. **The Trip to Jerusalem: An Elizabethan Whodunit**. New York: St. Martin's Press, 1990. 223p. $15.95. ISBN 0-312-05174-3. YA

Nicholas Bracewell and the acting troupe Lord Westfield's Men leave London during the Black Plague to tour the North. But one of their members dies before they are able to leave, and after they depart, they discover that Banbury's Men, a rival troupe, has been stealing their best plays. In York, while they present a play, the threads of a murderous plot come together.

1181.   Marston, Edward. **The Wolves of Savernake**. New York: St. Martin's Press, 1993. 256p. $19.95. ISBN 0-312-09942-8. (Domesday, 1). YA

After William the Conqueror comes to England as the king, he sends surveyors to find out who owns land and record the holding in William's Domesday book. Ralph Delchard and Gervase Bret are two of those designated to survey. When they go to Savernake in 1086, they discover that a wolf has killed the wealthy miller. But they suspect more, and their investigation shows that their suspicion is correct.

1182.   Marston, Elsa. **The Ancient Egyptians**. New York: Marshall Cavendish, 1996. 80p. $19.95. ISBN 0-7614-0073-7. (Cultures of the Past). 5-8

The text looks at the artifacts, monuments, domestic scenes, and historical aspects of ancient Egypt while telling about the evolution of the Egyptian dynasties. It also presents a competent explanation of the complex Egyptian religious beliefs. Photographs, Drawings, Bibliography, Chronology, Further Reading, Glossary, and Index.

1183.   Martell, Hazel Mary. **The Age of Discovery**. New York: Facts on File, 1993. 78p. $17.95. ISBN 0-8160-2789-7. (Illustrated History of the World). 4-7

The Reformation changed the western world. Also during this time, printing was developed, another stunning shift. Russia emerged as a power under Peter the Great, Japan flourished with its shoguns, and the Spanish and Portuguese colonized the Americas. Illustrations highlight the text. Glossary, Further Reading, and Index.

1184.   Martell, Hazel Mary. **The Ancient Chinese**. New York: New Discovery, Macmillan, 1993. 64p. $14.95. ISBN 0-02-730653-4. (Worlds of the Past). 4-8

The double-page topics on ancient China include government, social structure, everyday life, food, arts and crafts, and brief dynastic histories. Photographs and color reproductions augment the text. Chronology, Glossary, and Index.

1185. Martell, Hazel Mary. **The Celts**. New York: Viking, 1996. 48p. $16.99. ISBN 0-670-86558-3. (See Through History). 5-8

The text gives information about the Celts, people who inhabited Ireland and England before the Romans came. It looks at their daily lives, government, foods, weapons, and houses with full illustrations and see-through overlays of fortress interiors, homes, and burial sites. Chronology, Glossary, and Index.

1186. Martell, Hazel Mary. **Food and Feasts with the Vikings**. New York: New Discovery, 1995. 32p. $14.95. ISBN 0-02-726317-7. 4-7

The text looks at the ways food was grown and prepared during Viking times, from approximately A.D. 700 to 1000, by focusing on the crops in the countryside and the types of food that had to be shipped to the towns. One had to eat when traveling, so the text covers food that travelers ate, especially aboard ship. Additional information about cooking utensils and recipes from the Viking period give a good sense of the times. Photographs and reproductions enhance the text. Glossary, Further Reading, and Index.

1187. Martell, Hazel Mary. **The Vikings and Jorvik**. New York: Dillon Press, Macmillan, 1993. 32p. $13.95. ISBN 0-87518-541-X. (Hidden Worlds). 4-7

One record of the Vikings' first arrival in England, in the *Anglo-Saxon Chronicle*, says that they came in A.D. 789. In A.D. 793, they raided the monastery at Lindisfarne on the coast of Northumberland, stealing the monastery's treasures and killing some of the monks. Recently archaeologists have found information that shows Vikings' skills in shipbuilding and metalworking and their endeavors as traders and farmers. They captured the English town of Eoforwic (York) in A.D. 867 and established a major trading center there, which flourished until the Norman Conquest in 1066. The text, with photographs, illustrations, and maps, tells about these people. Glossary and Index.

1188. Martell, Hazel Mary. **What Do We Know About the Celts?** New York: Peter Bedrick, 1993. 45p. $18.95. ISBN 0-87226-363-0. (What Do We Know About . . .). 3 up

With illustrations or photographs of ancient sites and artifacts on each page, the text tells about Celtic life in the times before the Romans in Ireland and England—the history, daily routine, social structure, and culture. Holidays, getting food, clothing, and travels are part of the information. Glossary and Index.

1189. Martell, Hazel Mary, and Paul G. Bahn. **The Kingfisher Book of the Ancient World: From the Ice Age to the Roman Empire**. New York: Kingfisher, 1995. 160p. $19.95. ISBN 1-85697-565-7. 5-7

After telling how archaeologists discover information about prehistoric cultures, the text then summarizes the major cultures between 10,000 B.C. and A.D. 600. They include the Fertile Crescent, Egypt to Asia, Greece and Rome, Europe, Africa, the Americas, and the Pacific Islands. Maps, Photographs, Chronology, Glossary, and Index.

1190. Martell, Helen M. **What Do We Know About the Vikings?** New York: Peter Bedrick, 1992. 40p. $18.95. ISBN 0-87226-355-X. (What Do We Know About . . .). 4-7

With illustrations or photographs of ancient sites and artifacts on each page, the text tells about Viking life during the eleventh and twelfth centuries: the history, daily routine, social structure, and culture. Holidays, getting food, clothing, and travels are part of the information. Glossary and Index.

1191. Martin, Christopher. **Charles Dickens: Life and Works**. Vero Beach, FL: Rourke, 1990. 112p. $22.60. ISBN 0-86593-016-3. 8 up

Charles Dickens (1812–1870) observed the life of debtors' prison by going to visit his father after they had come to London from a pleasant home in the countryside. Dickens had to quit school and work while still a youngster. He eventually returned to school, but his experiences led him to hate the self-importance of lawyers and judges. His first article, a fictional sketch of London life and people, appeared in *Monthly Magazine,* a Fleet Street publication, in 1833. As a clerk in the House of Commons, he saw passage of the Reform Bill of 1832, which abolished an unfair voting system; the Factory Act, banning employment of children under the age of nine; the abolition of slavery; and the New Poor Law. He was writing during the "Hungry forties"—the 1840s, a bleak decade in which corn laws kept food prices high while people starved, and the potato crop failed in Ireland. He became a social critic, and the text coordinates passages from Dickens's novels with experiences from his personal life. Glossary, List of Dates, Further Reading, and Index.

1192. Martin, Christopher. **H. G. Wells: Life and Works**. Vero Beach, FL: Rourke, 1988. 112p. $22.60. ISBN 0-86592-297-7. 5-9

H. G. Wells (1866-1946) described himself as the ugly duckling who found out he was a swan. Born into the Victorian lower middle class, he had to struggle for the science education he wanted. He wanted to live in a utopia, and he created these worlds in his work. In his realistic science fiction writing, he exposed what he saw as the horrors of the twentieth century. Glossary, List of Dates, Further Reading, and Index.

1193.   Martin, Marvin. **The Beatles: The Music Was Never the Same**. New York: Franklin Watts, 1996. 207p. $22.70. ISBN 0-531-11307-8. 6 up

In this collective biography, Martin recalls the role of the Beatles in changing music. He includes details from history, the members' careers, and their influence on music today. Discography and Index.

1194.   Maruki, Toshi, author/illustrator. **Hiroshima, No Pika**. New York: Lothrop, Lee & Shepard, 1982. 48p. $16. ISBN 0-688-01297-3. 4-7

In 1945, Mii is seven. She and her parents experience the chaos following the blast of the atomic bomb dropped by the American airplane, the *Enola Gay*. In shock, Mii carries her chopsticks for several days before she realizes that they are still in her hand. After some time, her father dies, and Mii never gets any larger than she was when the bomb fell. The expressionist illustrations heighten the fury of the scene without overly realistic gore. *Mildred L. Batchelder Award, Jane Addams Children's Book Award,* and *American Library Association Notable Books for Children.*

1195.   Marvin, Isabel R. **Bridge to Freedom**. Philadelphia: Jewish Publication Society, 1991. 136p. $14.95. ISBN 0-8276-0377-0. 5-9

In March of 1945, Kurt, age fifteen and German, has deserted his army unit and fears recapture by the retreating Germans as well as by the advancing Americans. He enters a cave where Rachel, age sixteen and Jewish, has hidden after escaping from Berlin. They have to trust each other in order to cross a bridge over the Rhine River into Belgium. Aided by American soldiers and Belgian farmers, they both reach Liège, and find each other on May 8, Victory in Europe Day.

1196.   Marx, Robert F., and Jennifer Marx. **The Search for Sunken Treasure: Exploring the World's Great Shipwrecks**. Buffalo, NY: Firefly Books, 1996. 196p. $19.95. ISBN 1-55013-788-3. YA

The text looks at some of the well-known shipwrecks throughout history, beginning with ancient Phoenician merchant ships and including Roman galleys, Chinese trading vessels, the *Bismarck*, and others. Bibliography and Index.

1197.   Marx, Trish. **Echoes of World War II**. Minneapolis, MN: Lerner, 1994. 96p. $14.96. ISBN 0-8225-4898-4. 5-8

In pictures of war, one often sees soldiers. The children are less visible, but what happens to the children during a war has a huge impact on the future. Marx follows the paths of six children, four in Europe and two in Asia, through World War II. Some left their parents and others had parents leave them. These six survived, which is why their stories can be told. Photographs augment the text. Index.

1198.   Mason, Antony. **Aztec Times**. Michael White, illustrator. New York: Simon & Schuster, 1997. 29p. $16.95. ISBN 0-689-81199-3. (If You Were There). 4-7

Eleven topics on double-page spreads include origins of the Aztec civilization, daily life and customs, the Spanish conquests, and games the people played. Photographs, Chronology, and Index.

1199.   Mason, Antony. **Cézanne: An Introduction to the Artist's Life and Work**. Hauppauge, NY: Barron's, 1994. 32p. $14.95; $8.50pa. ISBN 0-8120-6459-3; 0-8120-1293-3pa. (Famous Artists). 5 up

Born in the south of France, Cézanne (1839-1906) left the area as a young man to attend art school in Paris, where he met Pissarro, Renoir, Monet, Sisley, and other Impressionists. He exhibited with them, and after his father died and left him money, he never had to worry about selling his paintings. He continued to investigate the form, color, and structure of objects and their relationships to each other. Beautifully clear reproductions highlight the text, which has helpful comments about composition. Chronology, Art History, Museums, Glossary, and Indexes.

1200.   Mason, Antony. **Leonardo da Vinci: An Introduction to the Artist's Life and Work**. Hauppauge, NY: Barron's, 1994. 32p. $14.95; $8.50pa. ISBN 0-8120-6460-7; 0-8120-1997-0pa. (Famous Artists). 5 up

As one of Italy's most gifted painters, Leonardo da Vinci (1452-1519) was famous while he lived. He made detailed studies of almost everything, including the human body, animals, and mechanical movement. His notebook sketches, written backwards so that they can be read only with a mirror, show that he conceived of military tanks, helicopters, airplanes, and other machines that were not invented until more than 400 years later. He apprenticed himself to Verrocchio in Florence and then worked in Milan at the court of Duke Ludovico Sforza, during which time he painted the *Mona Lisa*. Clear reproductions highlight the text, which includes helpful comments about composition. Chronology, Art History, Museums, Glossary, and Indexes.

1201.   Mason, Antony. **Matisse: An Introduction to the Artist's Life and Work**. Hauppauge, NY: Barron's, 1995. 32p. $14.95; $8.50pa. ISBN 0-8120-6534-4; 0-8120-9426-3pa. (Famous Artists). 5 up

One of the most inventive of twentieth-century artists was Henri Matisse (1869-1954), born in France. He worked in a group with other artists called "Fauves." He worked to achieve a sense of movement, and his bold use of color and simplicity of design made him famous. Some of the influences on his artistic career include Morocco, odalisques, dance themes, jazz, and the Vence Chapel. Beautifully clear reproductions highlight the text, which includes helpful comments about composition. Chronology, Art History, Museums, Glossary, and Indexes.

1202.   Mason, Antony. **Michelangelo: An Introduction to the Artist's Life and Work**. Hauppauge, NY: Barron's, 1994. 32p. $14.95; $8.50pa. ISBN 0-8120-6461-5; 0-8120-1998-9pa. (Famous Artists). 5 up

Michelangelo Buonarroti, born near Florence, Italy, in 1475, died in Rome in 1564. His works, especially the frescoes painted on the Sistine Chapel ceiling in Rome's Vatican and the sculpture *David*, are some of the finest art treasures in the world. He was one of the first artists to be admired for his genius and creativity rather than being considered merely a servant to a patron. Clear reproductions highlight the text, which includes helpful comments about composition. Chronology, Art History, Museums, Glossary, and Indexes.

1203.   Mason, Antony. **Monet: An Introduction to the Artist's Life and Work**. Hauppauge, NY: Barron's, 1994. 32p. $14.95; $8.50pa. ISBN 0-8120-6494-1; 0-8120-9174-4pa. (Famous Artists). 5 up

Claude Monet (1840-1926), today one of the most famous French artists, as a young man refused to use traditional methods of painting. He wanted his pictures to capture the mood of his surroundings by showing the reflection of the light; he and other artists who thought as he did became the Impressionists. He lived by the sea as a young boy, moved to Paris, almost starved while he tried to paint, enjoyed Giverny outside Paris, and developed series of paintings on various subjects, such as Rouen Cathedral and water lilies. Clear reproductions highlight the text, which includes helpful comments about composition. Chronology, Art History, Museums, Glossary, and Indexes.

1204.   Mason, Antony. **Picasso: An Introduction to the Artist's Life and Work**. Hauppauge, NY: Barron's, 1994. 32p. $14.95; $8.50pa. ISBN 0-8120-6496-8; 0-8120-9175-2pa. (Famous Artists). 5 up

Pablo Picasso (1881-1973) may be the greatest artist of the twentieth century. He helped found the Cubist movement and brought new ideas to art. After growing up in Spain, he went through several distinct periods in his artistic development, known as the Blue Period, the Rose Period, Analytical Cubism, Synthetic Cubism, World War I, Guernica, World War II, and the final years. Clear reproductions highlight the text, which includes helpful comments about composition. Chronology, Art History, Museums, Glossary, and Indexes.

1205.   Mason, Antony. **Van Gogh: An Introduction to the Artist's Life and Work**. Hauppauge, NY: Barron's, 1994. 32p. $14.95; $8.50pa. ISBN 0-8120-6462-3; 0-8120-1997-7pa. (Famous Artists). 5 up

As a young man from a middle-class family in the Netherlands, Vincent van Gogh (1853-1890) painted but became interested in religion and becoming a minister. After little success, he began painting seriously, but never made much money. He was often hungry and ill, and these physical problems may have strongly influenced his colorful, bold, passionate paintings. What may seem at first to be pure globs of paint are actually carefully conceived brush strokes in such famous paintings as *The Sunflowers* and *The Starry Night*. Clear reproductions highlight the text, which includes helpful comments about composition. Chronology, Art History, Museums, Glossary, and Indexes.

1206.   Mason, Antony. **Viking Times**. Michael Welply, illustrator. New York: Simon & Schuster, 1997. 29p. $16.95. ISBN 0-689-81198-5. (If You Were There). 4-7

Norman conquerors, exploration and trade, how the Vikings became Christians, and games are four of the eleven topics discussed about the Vikings and their lives. Photographs, Chronology, and Index.

1207.   Mastretta, Ángeles. **Lovesick**. Margaret Sayers Peden, translator. New York: Riverhead, 1997. 292p. $22. ISBN 1-57322-062-0. YA

Daughter of a Mexican physician interested in politics and a mother who is an herbalist, Emilia Sauri, born in 1893, has a happy childhood. When she grows up, she falls in love with with the wanderer Daniel, but knows that he will never stay with her. She makes herself care for the physician Antonio Zavalza, whom she eventually marries, but she makes certain that she always keeps Daniel.

1208.   Matas, Carol. **After the War**. New York: Simon & Schuster, 1996. 128p. $16. ISBN 0-689-80350-8. 6-9

Ruth, age fifteen, survives the Ostroviec ghetto, Auschwitz, Buchenwald, and anti-Semitic pogroms in Poland after the end of World War II, unlike eighty members of her family. She joins a Zionist group preparing to travel via ship and illegally enter Israel. The British attack the ship and take her and the others to Cyprus. In the refugee camp there, she finds her brother and eventually escapes with her boyfriend into Israel.

1209. Matas, Carol. **The Burning Time**. New York: Delacorte, 1994. 113p. $15.95. ISBN 0-385-32097-3. 6-10

Rose Rives, aged fifteen in 1600, helps her mother with herbs and midwifery in France. When her father falls off a horse and dies, her life changes. Her mother saves the life of the wife and child of their chateau owner, but the doctor says that her mother must be evil to be able to do things he cannot. This attitude extends into the village, and Rose's mother and other women are accused of witchcraft by the priest and other men. Rose sees her mother scalded in torture, and she gives her herbs in secret to save her from further suffering before escaping herself. Not for five years are the innocent women cleared, but by then, almost all of them have been burned.

1210. Matas, Carol. **Code Name Kris**. New York: Scribners, 1990. 152p. $12.95. ISBN 0-684-19208-X. 7-10

Jesper, whose code name is "Kris," narrates this sequel to *Lisa's War*. He continues to work as a member of the resistance in Denmark to save the Danish Jews from the German Gestapo while Lisa and her brother Stefan, Jesper's best friend, survive in Sweden. Told as a flashback while Jesper is imprisoned, he reveals the German treatment of the Danes. He finally gains his own freedom on liberation day, May 4, which the Danes celebrate by lighting candles in their windows. *Canadian Lester and Orpen Dennys Award.*

1211. Matas, Carol. **Daniel's Story**. New York: Scholastic, 1993. 136p. $13.95. ISBN 0-590-46920-7. 4-7

Daniel, age fourteen, takes a train with his family in 1941 from Frankfurt, Germany, to the Jewish ghetto in Lodz, Poland. Although his ancestors and family had lived in Frankfurt for more than 600 years, they now have to leave. At Auschwitz and Buchenwald, he recalls photographs from his younger life and contrasts what they meant to him then with his current situation. He and his father survive; other family members do not. *Notable Children's Trade Books in the Field of Social Studies.*

1212. Matas, Carol. **The Garden**. New York: Simon & Schuster, 1997. 102p. $15. ISBN 0-689-80349-4. 7-10

In the sequel to *After the War* (1996), set in 1947, Ruth Mendelson, sixteen, and her boyfriend, Zvi, live on the Kibbutz David in Palestine. She joins Haganah, a Jewish defense group, and her brother Simon is a member of Irgun, a terrorist group, while Jews try to forge the state of Israel. Although Ruth hates the concept of war as a way to gain security, she has to fight in several battles because the kibbutz lies in the paths of both the British and the Arabs.

1213. Matas, Carol. **Lisa's War**. New York: Scribners, 1989. 111p. $12.95. ISBN 0-684-19010-9. 7-10

Lisa, age twelve, is glad that her brother takes part in the Danish Resistance in 1940 when the Germans come to Copenhagen. She tries to convince her cousin that he and his family should also help, because the Nazis threaten all Jews. Her father hears from the rabbi that the Nazis will arrest Jews on Rosh Hashanah. The Resistance helps many to evacuate to Sweden beforehand. *Geoffrey Bilson Award for Historical Fiction for Young People.*

1214. Matas, Carol. **Sworn Enemies**. New York: Bantam, 1993. 132p. $16. ISBN 0-553-08326-0. 6-9

Aaron, a sixteen-year-old yeshiva student whose father has paid to keep him from serving in the Russian army of 1840, suffers the jealousy of Zev, a boy who loves the same girl. Zev gets the military to kidnap Aaron in order to fill their quota, but the recruiters also capture Zev. The two must go on a forced march together; even after they conspire to escape, their dislike of each other continues because of their differing backgrounds and personalities.

1215. Mathabane, Mark. **Kaffir Boy in America: An Encounter with Apartheid**. 1989. New York: New American Library, 1995. 303p. $12.95pa. ISBN 0-452-26471-5pa. 7 up

This sequel to *Kaffir Boy* covers the period in Mathabane's life when he comes to America as a student and writer. He observes American attitudes toward South Africa and is surprisingly sympathetic, because he realizes that some possible punitive behaviors might harm the blacks in South Africa rather than help them. In this volume, he gains self-realization as well as a clearer understanding of the behavior of others. Index.

1216. Matsubara, Hisako. **Cranes at Dusk**. Leila Vennewitz, translator. New York: Dial Press, 1985. 253p. $15.95. ISBN 0-385-27858-6. YA

Saya's father Guji, a Shinto priest, predicts with his *I Ching* in 1945 that the Japanese will lose World War II and that a bomb will not drop on Kyoto. When Saya's little brother Bo dies unexpectedly, Guji laments that he has neglected to chart the lives of his children with the *I Ching* and has therefore not protected them. Saya, age ten, prays for Bo's soul instead.

1217. Matthews, Rupert. **Power Brokers: Kingmakers & Usurpers Throughout History**. New York: Facts on File, 1990. 326p. $27.95. ISBN 0-8160-2156-2. 8 up

Beginning in c. 2875 B.C. with Khufu, or Cheops, who usurped the throne of the Pharaoh Sneferu, the author presents nearly 300 people throughout the world who used power or position to gain more power or position. The most recent listed is Idi Amin, who took power in Uganda in 1971. Many familiar names, both male and female, eastern and western, fill the interesting text. The book is relevant for all historical time periods. Bibliography and Index.

1218.   Matusky, Gregory, and John P. Hayes. **King Hussein**. New York: Chelsea House, 1987. 112p. $18.95. ISBN 0-87754-533-2. (World Leaders Past and Present). 7 up

Hussein ibn Talal (b. 1935) attended British schools prior to the assassination of his grandfather in 1953; thereafter he became the king of Jordan. He has created a sense of nationalism in his country while forging somewhat erratic policies with his Arab nation neighbors. He refused to join the United Arab Republic and recognized the Palestine Liberation Organization while crushing it in his own country. He expelled the British military from Jordan but kept economic ties with England. He is a soldier, a diplomat, and a king, married to an American graduate of Princeton. He has made his country into a flourishing nation. Photographs enhance the text. Chronology, Further Reading, and Index.

1219.   Maurer, Richard. **Airborne: The Search for the Secret of Flight**. New York: Aladdin, 1990. 48p. $5.95pa. ISBN 0-671-69423-5pa. (NOVA). 5-8

A history of flight, the text begins with experiments and designs for various types of aircraft, gliders, and hot-air balloons from the 1600s. It continues through the history of experimentation until the Wright brothers flew their heavier-than-air craft in 1903. Drawings, photographs, and diagrams illustrate the principles of flight that had to be understood before flying became possible. When such terms as *aileron*, *elevator*, *rudder*, and *throttle* became attached to the principles, human flight began. Index.

1220.   Mayberry, Jodine. **Leaders Who Changed the 20th Century**. Austin, TX: Raintree/Steck-Vaughn, 1993. 48p. $15.96. ISBN 0-81144-926-2. (20 Events). 7 up

To understand what happened during the twentieth century, one must know something about those who became leaders and who changed things close to them. Among the leaders presented here in two-page spreads are Woodrow Wilson, Jane Addams, Ho Chi Minh, Lech Walesa, Vladimir Lenin, Mohandas Gandhi, Adolf Hitler, Winston Churchill, Franklin Roosevelt, Joseph Stalin, Mao Zedong, Fidel Castro, Martin Luther King, Jr., Anwar Sadat, Menachem Begin, the Ayatollah Khomeini, Margaret Thatcher, Mikhail Gorbachev, and Nelson Mandela. Photographs and drawings enhance the text. Further Reading, Glossary, and Index.

1221.   Mayne, William. **Low Tide**. New York: Delacorte, 1993. 198p. $14. ISBN 0-385-30904-X. 4-7

While Charlie, his sister Elisabeth, and his Maori friend, Wiremu, fish early one morning in Jade Bay on the coast of New Zealand, an especially low tide reveals a rock in the distance, with a wrecked ship thought to have treasure aboard perched on top. They go to examine the ship, and while they are on it a huge tidal wave sweeps them and the ship into the mountains where the Koroua, a legendary mountain man, lives. He assuages their fears and helps them return home while revealing the truth about himself and the ship.

1222.   Maxwell, Robin. **The Secret Diary of Anne Boleyn**. New York: Arcade, 1997. 288p. $23.95. ISBN 1-55970-375-X. YA

In her secret diary, Anne Boleyn keeps a log of her life and warns her daughter to never let a man control her the way she let Henry finally have control over her. In her childhood, Elizabeth hears only that her mother was an adulterer and a traitor. When Elizabeth gets her mother's diary from an old friend of her mother's after she becomes queen, she learns about the real woman Anne Boleyn was.

1223.   McAuley, Karen. **Golda Meir**. New York: Chelsea House, 1985. 110p. $18.95. ISBN 0-87754-568-5. (World Leaders Past and Present). 5 up

Golda Meir (1898-1978), born into a Russian family that immigrated to Wisconsin, experienced anti-Semitism as a child. As a young adult, she became committed to Zionism and socialism, and in 1921, she moved to Palestine. Finally, in 1948, her dream for the State of Israel came true. She was a kibbutz worker, a social activist, a politician, an ambassador, and finally a prime minister for her country. Photographs enhance the text. Chronology, Further Reading, and Index.

1224.   McCaffrey, Anne. **Black Horses for the King**. San Diego, CA: Harcourt Brace, 1996. 223p. $16. ISBN 0-15-227322-0. 7 up

After Galwyn's father loses his money and dies during the times of the Saxon raids, Galwyn must work on his uncle's ship, although he prefers to work with the horses that he loved on his father's land. His ability to learn languages quickly makes him valuable to one of the ship's passengers, King Arthur. He translates for Arthur when the king buys horses strong enough to breed good stock for his army to challenge the raiding Saxons. Galwyn's knowledge of horses also helps Arthur after his return. Galwyn learns how to put the new iron sandals on the horses' hooves and is ready to go with the armies to war as a blacksmith. Simultaneously, Galwyn must protect the horses from a vindictive young man who was dismissed from service.

1225. McCaughrean, Geraldine. **El Cid**. Victor G. Ambrus, illustrator. New York: Oxford University Press, 1989. 126p. $17.95. ISBN 0-19-276077-7. 6 up

El Cid, or Rodrigo Diaz de Vivar (1040-1099), was a soldier-hero who won glory when he helped to conquer the Moors at Valencia after they had taken much of Spain. He violated all of the conditions of surrender by burning the leader, cadi ibn Djahhaff, at the stake and slaughtering citizens. He then ruled most of Valencia and Murcia. The text includes this and other stories of El Cid's exploits.

1226. McCaughrean, Geraldine. **A Little Lower than the Angels**. New York: Oxford University Press, 1987. 133p. $15. ISBN 0-19-271561-5. 6-9

Gabriel is a bound apprentice to a stonemason, but he escapes and joins a group performing mystery and miracle plays in fourteenth-century England. He thinks that he is healing townspeople who declare that the plays have healed them until he discovers that the troupe's leader pays townspeople to pretend. Although disappointed, he thinks that the plays are important for people to see, and he helps his two friends, a father and daughter, record the words for players in the future. *Whitbread Book of the Year.*

1227. McCullough, Colleen. **Caesar's Women**. New York: Morrow, 1996. 696p. $25; $7.99pa. ISBN 0-688-09371-X; 0-380-71084-6pa. YA

As Caesar rises to power, he deflates his enemies, but they wait for him, planning how to avenge his mistreatments. He consults his mother about his decisions as she manages the household; he loves his daughter, misses his dead wife, but all the while, worries more about his political aspirations than about his family.

1228. McCullough, Colleen. **The First Man in Rome**. 1990. New York: Morrow, 1996. 896p. $22.95. ISBN 0-688-09372-8. New York: Avon Books, 1991. 896p. $7.99pa. ISBN 0-380-71081-1pa. YA

From 110 to 106 B.C., Gaius Marius is part of the intrigue in Rome. He and other government leaders know that all inhabitants, both free citizens and slaves, must be controlled.

1229. McCullough, Colleen. **Fortune's Favorites**. 1993. New York: Avon Books, 1994. 878p. $6.99pa. ISBN 0-380-71083-8pa. YA

After returning from exile, Sulla becomes dictator, but suddenly retires. Pompey designates himself as "Magnus" ("The Great") and begins his climb upward. His rival, however, is Julius Caesar, who rises to power in the first century B.C. in this novel following *The First Man in Rome* and *The Grass Crown*.

1230. McCullough, Colleen. **The Grass Crown**. 1991. New York: Avon, 1992. 756p. $6.99pa. ISBN 0-380-71082-Xpa. YA

The focus in McCullough's second book on Rome, after *The First Man in Rome*, is Lucius Cornelius Sulla. During the first century B.C., he protects his position of leadership as well as he can with the opposition and intrigue surrounding him.

1231. McCullough, David. **Brave Companions: Portraits in History**. 1991. New York: Touchstone, Simon & Shuster, 1992. 240p. $12pa. ISBN 0-671-79276-8pa. YA

The 17 essays and speeches in this book contain portraits throughout the history of the United States of such people as Alexander von Humboldt and his South American explorations, Louis Agassiz and his impact on American families and their education, Teddy Roosevelt and his conservationism, Miriam Rothschild and her work in zoology, and Harriet Beecher Stowe's writing. Others come from the professions of social work, architecture, literature, etymology, and history. They include the Marquis de Morès, Frederick Remington, W. A. Roebling, Beryl Markham, Conrad Richter, Harry Caudill, David Plowden, and Simon Willard. Index.

1232. McCurdy, Michael, author/illustrator. **Trapped by the Ice! Shackleton's Amazing Antarctic Adventure**. New York: Walker, 1997. 41p. $16.95. ISBN 0-8027-8438-0. 4-7

In 1915, Sir Ernest Shackleton tried to cross the Antarctic, but ice stopped and soon sank his ship. Since rescue planes were nonexistent at the time, the crew had to survive without the ship until the ice broke. Their journals tell how they did it without losing a man. Bibliography and Index.

1233. McCutchan, Philip. **Apprentice to the Sea**. New York: St. Martin's Press, 1995. 183p. $17.95. ISBN 0-312-11743-4. YA

Tom Chatto, a young apprentice seaman from the west of Ireland in the nineteenth century, sails on a square-rigged windjammer from Liverpool, England. What he learns is jo-re-du-com, "job, responsibility, duty, and command." His captain shows his character throughout by protecting a stowaway who helps him, but the first mate cannot resist blaming and punishing without proof of guilt.

1234. McCutchan, Philip. **Cameron and the Kaiserhof**. New York: St. Martin's Press, 1984. 188p. $10.95. ISBN 0-312-11443-5. YA

Donald Cameron, a lieutenant-commander in the Royal Naval Reserves, receives orders from an intelligence officer, "Mr. Cambridge," to fly to Gibraltar. He must disguise himself as a Spanish workman and make contact with a seaman picked to board the German merchant vessel, the *Kaiserhof*. Once aboard the ship and out of port, they must take over the bridge and sail the ship to England so that the British can investigate its information about Germany's advanced submarine technology in World War II. The attempt does not work according to plan, and Cameron and the others become prisoners-of-war. They escape, but not without difficulty.

1235. McCutchan, Philip. **Cameron Comes Through**. New York: St. Martin's Press, 1986. 157p. $12.95. ISBN 0-312-11444-3. YA

On the British destroyer *Wharfedale,* deployed to the Mediterranean against the Germans in 1941, Donald Cameron finds that he has the most dangerous task on board: that of rescuing a man from the Nazis who knows about the Nazi attack on Russia. Cameron and several others must enter a German camp, grab the man, escape before the Nazis advance into southern Crete, take a boat from troops on the beach who want to be evacuated, and return to the destroyer, all within a few hours. The destroyer itself must avoid dive-bombing Stukas and Italian warships. The only alternative seems to be to violate Turkish neutrality by going through the Dardanelles, a risky choice.

1236. McCutchan, Philip. **Cameron in Command**. New York: St. Martin's Press, 1984. 163p. $10.95. ISBN 0-312-11446-X. YA

Donald Cameron's first command in World War II is the corvette HMS *Briar,* which receives orders to travel south from Sierra Leone to the Falkland Islands to help stop a Japanese attack on Port Stanley. Cameron skirmishes with a U-boat on the way but reaches his destination. A blinding snowstorm, however, keeps him from seeing the enemy in the air or the sea, and the demolition landing party he has delivered fails. Because Churchill wants to save all involved, he sends cover.

1237. McCutchan, Philip. **Cameron's Commitment**. New York: St. Martin's Press, 1989. 190p. $14.95. ISBN 0-312-02532-7. YA

Not until he hears of the secret mission that Sir Winston Churchill has planned for the crew does Lieutenant-Commander Donald Cameron understand why he has been picked to captain the light cruiser *Castile*, a post that would normally go to a captain in the regular Navy rather than to someone in the Reserve. The strategy for the ship is to go along the darkened coast of occupied France during World War II and bomb Dieppe. Although successful, the ships involved suffer many casualties.

1238. McCutchan, Philip. **Cameron's Crossing**. New York: St. Martin's Press, 1993. 171p. $17.95. ISBN 0-312-09762-X. YA

Donald Cameron, a lieutenant-commander in the Royal Navy, must take the HMS *Charger* to the United States with his crew during World War II to recommission a destroyer, under the lend-lease agreement between Britain and the United States. Cameron expects an easy voyage, but the weather and the abominable captain deny him the pleasure. He must take command of the ship before all end up dead.

1239. McCutchan, Philip. **Cameron's Raid**. New York: St. Martin's Press, 1985. 184p. $11.95. ISBN 0-312-11452-4. YA

Lieutenant-Commander Donald Cameron hears that he has to take his old P-class destroyer, along with two others, into the French port of Brest in Churchill's Operation Scatter. They must deliver marine commandos whose mission is to blow up the German U-boat pens, a task the Air Force has been unable to complete. They face heavy fire, and even with help from the French Resistance, the senior officer's ship is blown up and the commandos fail to return. Cameron takes control and creeps inland in the only move he thinks can achieve the objective.

1240. McCutchan, Philip. **Cameron's Troop Lift**. New York: St. Martin's Press, 1986. 185p. $13.95. ISBN 0-312-01008-7. YA

When World War II shifts to the Pacific after the Battle of the Atlantic, Lieutenant-Commander Donald Cameron of the British Navy captains the destroyer *Caithness*. When the ship rescues a Japanese survivor, Cameron discovers that a convoy is transporting British prisoners-of-war from Singapore to Rangoon to do slave labor in the Burmese jungle. He decides to pursue. But he and the enemy captain have to measure their actions against the possible destruction of crew and prisoners.

1241. McCutcheon, Elsie. **Summer of the Zeppelin**. New York: Farrar, Straus & Giroux, 1985. 168p. $11.95. ISBN 0-374-37294-2. 5-9

When Elvira is twelve, in 1918, a German zeppelin bombs a small English village near her home. She and her friend then meet a German prisoner working nearby who speaks English. Although his people have hurt her nation, she tries to help him return to Germany to find his sister, because she knows that her father, away fighting for three years, would want her to be kind.

1242. McDermott, Kathleen. **Peter the Great**. New York: Chelsea House, 1990. 109p. $18.95. ISBN 1-55546-821-7. (World Leaders Past and Present). 7 up

Peter the Great (1672–1725) had many conflicting roles. He was conqueror, reformer, tyrant, and visionary. But whichever characteristic he expressed, he transformed his country of Russia into one of the great powers of Europe. His interest in the French influenced him to build St. Petersburg with broad, sweeping spaces on the River Neva. He instituted religious, political, social, and economic reforms because he wanted his country to be the equal of his neighbors. With his navy, he won control of the Baltic Sea and access to the Atlantic. Even though an oppressor, his subjects referred to him as "teacher of his people." Photographs and engravings enhance the text. Chronology, Further Reading, and Index.

1243. McDowall, David. **A Modern History of the Kurds**. New York: I. B. Tauris, 1996. 451p. $35. ISBN 1-85043-653-3. YA

In Turkey, Iran, and Iraq, the Kurds have existed as minorities with few rights, and their presence has plagued the governments in those countries. One of the reasons that the Kurds have not successfully fought for their rights is that they fight among themselves. They disagree on religion. Some are Shii and others are Sunni, with the Sunni further dividing into different Sufi brotherhoods; still others follow the Yazidi sect. They support different tribes, speak different dialects of Kurdish, and have national boundaries dividing their populations. The text studies the historical background of the Kurdish struggles in each of the three countries, with emphasis on the last century when the Ottoman Empire and Qajar Iran were the two major Kurdish divisions. The book continues through contemporary times and offers a supposition as to which place gives the Kurds the best possibility of establishing autonomy. Bibliography and Index.

1244. McGowen, Tom. **The Time of the Forest**. Boston: Houghton Mifflin, 1988. 110p. $12.95. ISBN 0-395-44471-3. 5-8

When Wolf and his tribe see strangers in the forest, they are not surprised, but they have difficulty coping with a tribe living only five days of travel away that keeps its animals in pens and plows the ground. The two tribes fight each other, but Wolf saves a girl from the farming tribe. After he helps her, each of their tribes ostracizes them, and they have to leave to form their own group.

1245. McGraw, Eloise. **The Golden Goblet**. 1961. Magnolia, MA: Peter Smith, 1988. 248p. $17. ISBN 0-8446-6342-5. New York: Viking, 1990. 248p. $4.99pa. ISBN 0-14-030335-9pa. 5-9

Ranofer, age twelve, begins to watch his brother's disgusting friend and determines that he is stealing gold from his employer in ancient Egypt. Ranofer's brother not only takes Ranofer's inheritance and refuses to buy Ranofer an apprenticeship, but also is a thief; he steals from a queen's tomb. When Ranofer realizes what is happening, he reports it to the palace, and the guards finally believe him when he identifies the objects. As a result of his loyalty, he becomes a goldsmith's apprentice. *Newbery Honor*.

1246. McGraw, Eloise. **Mara, Daughter of the Nile**. 1953. Magnolia, MA: Peter Smith, 1991. 280p. $16.50. ISBN 0-8446-6536-3. 5-9

Mara, age seventeen, has blue eyes, an unusual characteristic in Egypt during 1550 B.C. Although a slave, she speaks and reads Babylonian. This ability enables her to translate for the wife of Hatshepsut's brother, Thutmose, and to become a spy for evil brothers who are trying to destroy Thutmose. Then she begins to spy on the brothers for Thutmose's brother, Sheftu. After proving her loyalty to Sheftu, she marries him when the evil brothers are apprehended.

1247. McGraw, Eloise. **Master Cornhill**. 1973. New York: Penguin, 1987. 218p. $4.95pa. ISBN 0-14-032255-8pa. 5 up

Michael, aged eleven in 1666, returns to London after having been evacuated because of the plague and finds that all the members of his adoptive family have died. While he hides from press gangs, he begins working for Mr. Maas, the best mapmaker in London. After living through the Great Fire, Michael realizes that to be an artist as he desires, he must take creative risks.

1248. McGraw, Eloise. **The Striped Ships**. New York: Macmillan, 1991. 229p. $15.95. ISBN 0-689-50532-9. 7-9

Juliana, age eleven, watches Norman ships invade the English Channel in 1066. William the Conqueror's men force her into bondage while she mourns her father's loss and hopes that the rest of her family is still alive.

She does meet her younger brother and goes with him to Canterbury, where monks take him in. Juliana moves from doing menial tasks to working on a large tapestry (which becomes the Bayeux Tapestry). She eventually meets her mother, now married to a Norman, and only with counseling from a monk can she accept her mother's decision to marry the enemy.

1249. McGuire, Leslie. **Catherine the Great**. New York: Chelsea House, 1986. 112p. $18.95. ISBN 0-87754-513-8. (World Leaders Past and Present). 5 up

Catherine the Great or Catherine II (1729–1796), the empress of Russia, was an enlightened and progressive ruler. In 1762, after her husband Peter acceded to the throne, she deposed him and declared herself empress. She added millions of miles of territory to the country, increased the efficiency of Russia's administration, and improved the banking system. French philosophy intrigued her, and she corresponded with some of her day's great thinkers. Reproductions enhance the text. Chronology, Further Reading, and Index.

1250. McHugh, Christopher. **Western Art 1600-1800**. New York: Thomson Learning, 1994. 48p. $16.95. ISBN 1-56847-219-6. (Art and Artists). 7-10

In the text, McHugh covers major art movements in the western world by focusing on the Dutch, the Italian Renaissance, Spain, France, and England. Boxes include capsule biographies and commentaries of and on women artists, El Greco (1541-1614), Jan Vermeer (1632-1675), *Commedia dell'arte* (sixteenth-century drama), William Hogarth (1697-1764), Francisco de Goya (1746-1828), the arts of Native Americans, and Greco-Roman painting. Glossary, Further Reading, Where to See Seventeenth and Eighteenth Century Art (United States), and Index.

1251. McLanathan, Richard. **Leonardo da Vinci**. New York: Harry N. Abrams, 1990. 92p. $19.95. ISBN 0-8109-1256-2. (First Impressions). 7 up

Photographs, reproductions, and text tell the story of Leonardo da Vinci (1452–1519). They present Leonardo and his relationship to the Renaissance, his first masterpieces, his time at the court of Milan, his subsequent return to Florence, and his contributions to humanity. Known as a practical man rather than a great artist, his high position in the court allowed him the freedom to follow his interest in architecture and engineering as well. Because he was curious about the future, he kept notebooks, hundreds of pages of which contained sketches and concepts. He devised submarines, tanks, and airplanes. He changed art because he wanted to paint nature as it really looked. He was an inventor, an engineer, a scientist, a musician, and an artist. Index.

1252. McLanathan, Richard. **Michelangelo**. New York: Harry N. Abrams, 1993. 92p. $19.95. ISBN 0-8109-3634-8. (First Impressions). 7 up

Ironically, no accounts of artistry or creativity exist in any of Michelangelo's (1474–1564) family history. But as a young child, he began living with a wet nurse in a stonecutter's family, where he learned to use the stonecutter's tools. When he returned to Florence at the age of ten, he had to learn to read and write (he was later to be Italy's most famous poet). Then he discovered his gift for drawing. In 1488, he finally convinced his father to allow him to become apprenticed to Domenico Ghirlandaio, where he could draw for a living. Among the people with whom he associated in his long career were Lorenzo the Magnificent of the Medici family and Julius, the warrior pope. Index.

1253. McLaren, Clemence. **Inside the Walls of Troy**. New York: Atheneum, 1996. 184p. $15. ISBN 0-689-31820-0. 7 up

Helen of Troy relates the story of her elopement with Paris, during the fourteenth or fifteenth century B.C., from a different perspective than that of Homer and his *Iliad*. She feels that beauty burdens her. Cassandra, Paris's sister, continues the story as she discusses the men in combat outside Troy's city walls and the women struggling within. The women must comfort and nurse the men, supervise their homes, and gather food for their families during this terrible war.

1254. McLynn, F. J. **Famous Trials: Cases That Made History**. New York: Reader's Digest, 1996. 182p. $27.95. ISBN 0-89577-655-3. YA

Although McLynn includes no criteria for selection, the cases here have influenced history. Arranged into groups according to the types of court that heard the case—special, military, church, or jury—those discussed include the trials of Socrates, Jesus, Thomas More, Danton of the French Revolution, Dreyfus in France, the Chinese Gang of Four, Galileo, John Brown, Tojo, Scopes, and Nelson Mandela. Commentary adds information about the importance of each case to history. Bibliography, Chronology, and Index.

1255. McNeese, Tim. **The Great Wall of China**. San Diego, CA: Lucent, 1997. 96p. $16.95. ISBN 1-56006-428-5. (Building History). 6-8

The text and photographs cover the building techniques of the Great Wall and provide the historical background leading to its construction. Chronology, Bibliography, Further Reading, and Index.

1256. McNeill, Sarah. **Ancient Egyptian People**. Brookfield, CT: Millbrook Press, 1997. 48p. $15.90. ISBN 0-7613-0056-2. (People and Places). 5-8

Among the thirteen ancient Egyptian classes discussed in this text are peasants, priests, pharaohs, women, mummy-makers, and servants. For each group, McNeill discusses their rank, roles in society, and community responsibilities. Illustrations of artifacts and landscape highlight the text. Further Reading, Glossary, and Index.

1257. McNeill, Sarah. **Ancient Egyptian Places**. Brookfield, CT: Millbrook Press, 1997. 48p. $15.90. ISBN 0-7613-0057-0. (People and Places). 5-8

McNeill highlights thirteen different important places in Egyptian life. They include the factory, the pyramid, the tomb, the Nile River, and the desert. Illustrations of artifacts and landscape highlight the text. Further Reading, Glossary, and Index.

1258. McPherson, Stephanie Sammartino. **Ordinary Genius: The Story of Albert Einstein**. Minneapolis, MN: Carolrhoda, 1995. 95p. $17.50. ISBN 0-87614-788-0. (Trailblazers). 5-8

Albert Einstein (1879-1955) developed theories of relativity that changed the way people perceive space and time. He hated violence and wanted world peace. He was also proud to be Jewish, and he worked to help Jews have a better life. Black-and-white photographs supplement the text. Bibliography and Index. *Outstanding Science Trade Books for Children.*

1259. McSwigan, Marie. **Snow Treasure**. Andre LeBlanc, illustrator. 1942. New York: Scholastic, 1986. 156p. $3.50pa. ISBN 0-590-42537-4pa. 3-7

In 1940, Peter Lundstrom and the other children of the village fool the Nazis who parachute into their Norwegian village and hold it hostage. Peter's uncle tells him that the children can save the country's gold, hidden in the town, by riding their sleds with the gold bullion under them to the shore of the fjord. There they can bury the gold under snowmen until men working with his uncle can retrieve it for loading onto a camouflaged boat nearby.

1260. McTavish, Douglas. **Isaac Newton**. New York: Bookwright Press, Franklin Watts, 1990. 48p. $17.71. ISBN 0-531-18351-3. (Pioneers of Science). 5-8

Isaac Newton (1642-1727) made important discoveries that have affected history. The text looks at his life growing up in England and the scientists and thinkers who influenced him. He invented differential calculus and formulated the theories of universal gravitation, terrestrial mechanics, and color. Anecdotal information says that the sight of a falling apple led to his treatise on gravitation, which he presented in his work, *Principia Mathematica* (1687). Chronology, Glossary, Bibliography, and Index.

1261. Mead, Alice. **Adem's Cross**. New York: Farrar, Straus & Giroux, 1996. 144p. $15. ISBN 0-374-30057-7. 5 up

In 1993, Adem, age fourteen and of Albanian descent, lives in Kosovo, the poorest province of the former Yugoslavia, which the Serbs occupy. While his sister, Fatmira, stands on a bridge reading a poem, the Serbs shoot her. Adem's family undergoes further suffering for his sister's passive resistance, and three soldiers grab Adem on a lonely road, tear off his shirt, and carve the Serb insignia on his chest. He decides to escape so that the nightmare for his family can end. A Serbian man, supposedly his enemy, and a gypsy, Fikel, help him to cross the border into Albania. *American Library Association Notable Books for Young Adults.*

1262. Medearis, Angela Shelf. **Come This Far to Freedom: A History of African Americans**. New York: Atheneum, 1993. 148p. $14.95. ISBN 0-689-31522-8. 5 up

Medearis divides the history of African Americans into five parts: coming from Africa to the hardships of slavery, the fight for freedom, the fresh start during Reconstruction after the Civil War, the movement for equality, and the people who have continued to break down the barriers in politics, the military, the sciences, and other fields. Important Dates, Bibliography, and Index.

1263. Medeiros, Teresa. **Fairest of Them All**. New York: Fanfare, 1995. 371p. $5.99pa. ISBN 0-553-56333-5pa. YA

When Holly de Chaste, the most beautiful woman in England, discovers that her father has offered her as a prize in a tournament of knights, she decides to disguise her beauty. Then she meets one of the knights, a handsome Welshman, and has to reassess her decision.

1264. Meltzer, Milton. **Cheap Raw Material: How Our Youngest Workers Are Exploited and Abused**. New York: Viking, 1994. 167p. $14.95. ISBN 0-670-83128-X. 7-9

Meltzer looks at the history of child labor since the beginning of civilization to show that children have always worked. He investigates the mills, mines, and sweatshops in which they have labored. He also notes how they have been maligned and abused with no rights as long as no one outside the workplace knew what was happening inside. Accidents have been common, disabling children for the rest of their lives. Bibliography, Source Notes, and Index.

1265.   Meltzer, Milton. **Columbus and the World Around Him**. New York: Franklin Watts, 1990. 192p. $23.40. ISBN 0-531-10899-6. 6 up

Meltzer draws upon Columbus's journal and other contemporary records to understand the man. Meltzer presents the European culture in which Columbus matured as it moved from medievalism to the early Renaissance. Columbus saw people in the New World as inferior and deserving of enslavement, with their lands as prizes for the explorers and Queen Isabella. A Note on Sources and Index.

1266.   Meltzer, Milton. **Gold: The True Story of Why People Search for It, Mine It, Trade It, Steal It, Mint It, Hoard It**. New York: HarperCollins, 1993. 167p. $15. ISBN 0-06-022983-7. 4-8

Photographs complement the text, which tells of humankind's 5,000-year quest for gold. Included are such topics as shekels, bezants, florins, ducats, and guineas. Other chapters look at where to get gold in the mines and the slaves who mined it, African empires built on gold, the gold rush in California, the search from Australia to South Africa, and what people endured when others came to their lands looking for gold. Bibliography and Index.

1267.   Meltzer, Milton. **Rescue: The Story of How Gentiles Saved Jews in the Holocaust**. New York: HarperCollins, 1991. 168p. $6.95pa. ISBN 0-06-446117-3pa. 7 up

In the text, Meltzer includes many stories of Gentiles who defied the Nazis' plan for extermination of the Jews. Among these people, who showed that they would not be cowed by immoral acts, were peasant, policeman, housemaid, countess, bricklayer, priest, industrialist, librarian, washerwoman, pastor, clerk, and priest. Two of the chapters cover Oskar Schindler and the Countess Marushka. Bibliography and Index.

1268.   Meltzer, Milton F. **Never to Forget: The Jews of the Holocaust**. New York: HarperCollins, 1976. 217p. $15.89; $6.95pa. ISBN 0-06-024174-8; 0-06-446119-1pa. YA

By referring to private letters, diaries, memoirs, poems, and songs, Meltzer shows that the 6 million Jews that Hitler destroyed in the Holocaust were real people who had tried to live their lives day by day just to survive. Meltzer recounts all of the legal changes that Hitler instigated as he rose to power and began his systematic anti-Semitic campaign, which eventually led to the ghettos and the death camps. Chronology, Bibliography, and Index. *American Library Association Best of the Best Books for Young Adults 1970–1983, American Library Association Notable Children's Book, Boston Globe-Horn Book Award for Nonfiction, School Library Journal Best Books, New York Times Outstanding Children's Books, Notable Children's Trade Books in the Field of Social Studies, Jane Addams Award, National Book Award for Children's Literature Nominee, IBBY Hans Christian Andersen Honors List,* and *Sidney Taylor Book Award.*

1269.   Meyer, Carolyn, and Charles Gallenkamp. **The Mystery of the Ancient Maya**. 1975. New York: Margaret K. McElderry, 1995. 178p. $15. ISBN 0-689-50619-8. 6-9

Since the mid-1800s, explorers have uncovered evidence showing that the Mayan civilization, which covered 125,000 square miles over parts of modern Mexico, Guatemala, Belize, Honduras, and El Salvador, was very advanced. Archaeologists have found ruins filled with jade, pottery, sculptures, wall paintings, and other beautiful artifacts. The text includes much new and recently discovered information on the Maya, such as advances in the reading of hieroglyphic inscriptions, new interpretations of images in the art, and much about all aspects of the society. In four parts, the text tries to address such points as how the ruins were discovered, what the explorers found, who these people were, and what happened to their civilization. Glossary and Index.

1270.   Meyer, Susan E. **Edgar Degas**. New York: Harry N. Abrams, 1994. 92p. $19.95. ISBN 0-8109-3220-2. (First Impressions). 8 up

Edgar Degas (1834–1917) grew up in a wealthy home but worked hard all his life. He loved families, yet he never married or had children of his own. Although he was a leader of the French Impressionist movement, his art was very different from that of Monet, Renoir, and Pissarro. He worked inside his study, looking at ballet dancers, jockeys, singers, musicians, laundresses, and milliners. He experimented with everything but demanded perfection in his work. Reproductions of his paintings highlight the text. Index.

1271.   Meyers, Odette. **Doors to Madame Marie**. Seattle: University of Washington Press, 1997. 400p. $24.95. ISBN 0-295-97576-8. YA

Odette Meyers moves with her family from Poland to Paris when she is a young girl, but while she is growing up, the Germans occupy Paris. The concierge of the family's apartment is Madame Marie, a woman who helps Odette find refuge in the French countryside as a Jewish child pretending to be Catholic. Meyers later visits those villages and interacts with the people who saved her life.

1272.   Michaels, Anne. **Fugitive Pieces: A Novel**. New York: Knopf, 1997. 304p. $23.50. ISBN 0-679-45439-X. YA

Jakob Beer survives the Holocaust after his entire Polish family dies. Antanasios Roussos, "Athos," a Greek scholar, rescues him and raises him on a Greek island. Jakob learns from him about Nazi attempts to change archaeological discovery results so that they prove Aryan supremacy and other denials of the past. Jakob sees Athens and its suffering during the war and goes with Athos to Toronto where Athos teaches. Athos dies in Toronto, and Jakob continues his work under the influence of the past and the demand of the present. He also becomes a poet, somewhat surprised at the healing power of words after being so hurt by their destruction.

1273.   Michaelson, Carol. **Ancient China**. New York: Time-Life, 1996. 64p. $15. ISBN 0-80949-248-2. (Nature Company Discoveries). 6 up

Among the topics covered in the text are mythology, Confucian and Daoist philosophies, Buddhism, views about death, justification of the ruler's right to govern, living in ancient China, and the creative aspects of the times. Included is information on the social order, peasants, land, clothing, celebrations, medical practices, printing, silk, and writing. A four-page foldout of the Great Wall highlights the text. Chronology, Glossary, and Index.

1274.   Michener, James. **Journey**. New York: Random House, 1989. 245p. $25. ISBN 0-394-57826-0. YA

Lord Luton leaves London in 1897 for the Klondike area of Canada, after he hears that someone has discovered gold there. Surprised by the huge distance across Canada, Luton becomes separated from his group and stays in the Klondike for only a few hours before starting his return journey.

1275.   Millar, Heather. **China's Tang Dynasty**. New York: Benchmark Books, 1996. 80p. $19.95. ISBN 0-7614-0074-5. (Cultures of the Past). 6-10

The text examines the artifacts, monuments, domestic scenes, and historical aspects of China's Tang Dynasty, which lasted from 618 to 907, as it discusses the religion, art, education, and customs of the time. Included is an explanation of Confucian and Buddhist ideals and their legacy. During this era, some of China's most famous poets were working, including Tu Fu, Wang Wei, and Li Po. Photographs, Drawings, Bibliography, Chronology, Further Reading, Glossary, and Index.

1276.   Millar, Heather. **The Kingdom of Benin West Africa**. Tarrytown, NY: Benchmark, 1996. 80p. $19.95. ISBN 0-7614-0088-5. 6-8

Benin was one of the most important kingdoms in West Africa five hundred years ago. The text includes an overview of its history and information about the slavery practiced there before the Europeans ever landed on the coast. Belief systems with witches, ghosts, magic, and sacrificial rites were important then, but the text also includes information about modern life.

1277.   Millard, Anne. **Pyramids**. New York: Kingfisher Books, 1996. 63p. $14.95. ISBN 1-85697-674-2. Brookfield, CT: Copper Beach, 1996. 64p. $6.95pa. ISBN 1-56294-194-1pa. 4 up

The text looks at different types of pyramids, including those built in Egypt at different times and those built by other civilizations. It looks at the process of building an Egyptian pyramid, from cutting the huge stones to moving them onto the pyramid, and discusses how important the pyramids were to Egyptian lifestyle and religion. Among the other pyramids covered are some in North America, South and Central America, the Louvre in Paris, and the Transamerica pyramid in San Francisco. Glossary and Index.

1278.   Miller, Russell. **Nothing Less than Victory: The Oral History of D-Day**. New York: Morrow, 1994. 556p. $27.50; $15pa. ISBN 0-688-10209-3; 0-688-14344-Xpa. YA

Miller compiled information from sources such as letters, diaries, memoranda, and official reports as well as interviews with veterans who fought on D-Day, June 6, 1944, to write a history of that day. What he discovered was that the statistics meant nothing to the individuals who participated in the greatest amphibious operation ever staged. They were only interested in survival and coping with the changes around them. Notes, Select Bibliography, and Index.

1279.   Minks, Benton, and Louise Minks. **The French and Indian War**. San Diego, CA: Lucent, 1995. 112p. $16.95. ISBN 1-56006-236-3. (World History Series). 6 up

In 1754, the French and Indian War began the battle between France and England over control of the New World. John Cabot arrived on the coast of Canada in 1497 and returned to England with positive reports. In 1614, John Smith charted the Atlantic coast from Virginia to Maine. Although other explorers also visited, at the beginning of the eighteenth century only France and England remained interested in owning the land. This absorbing history of the French and British tactics uses sources written during the period, the research of recognized scholars, and recent archaeological evidence. King George's War, begun in 1744, ended with the Treaty of Aix-la-Chapelle in 1748, in which Louisbourg was returned to France. In 1755, the French defeated the British in the Battle of the Wilderness, and in 1756 the formal war began. In 1757, the Marquis de Montcalm destroyed Forts Oswego and

William Henry. In England, William Pitt decided to converge on Quebec, where General Jeffrey Amherst took Louisbourg in 1758, but Montcalm defended Fort Ticonderoga. The British began building Fort Pitt on the site of the burned Fort Duquesne. In 1759, the English captured Quebec, and the French surrendered in 1760. In 1763, Chief Pontiac led the Northwest Territory Indian nations against the English, and when the war officially ended that year, with the Peace of Paris, the British were unable to expand into the Indian territories as they desired. The British also needed money to pay for the war, so they began to tax the American colonists. These and other events led to the next war, the War of Independence. Notes, Glossary, For Further Reading, Additional Works Consulted, Research Bibliography, and Index.

1280.   Mitchell, Barbara. **Pyramids: Opposing Viewpoints**. San Diego, CA: Greenhaven, 1988. 95p. $14.95. ISBN 1-89908-051-0. (Great Mysteries—Opposing Viewpoints). 7 up
     The text examines the mystery surrounding the building of the Egyptian pyramids, incorporating expert opinions and popular theories. Among the topics discussed is the concept that visitors from space built the pyramids. Theories that the pyramids contain knowledge of a superior race still abound. Or the pyramids may merely be tombs that can cause those who enter them to become cursed or die. Photographs and reproductions enhance the text. Glossary, Books for Further Exploration, and Index.

1281.   Moktefi, Mokhtar. **The Arabs in the Golden Age**. Veronique Ageorges, illustrator; Mary Kae LaRose, translator. Brookfield, CT: Millbrook Press, 1992. 64p. $16.40. ISBN 1-56294-201-8. (Peoples of the Past). 4-8
     The Golden Age of the Arabs began in the early eighth century, when Muhammad's teachings began to spread, and lasted into the thirteenth century. Islam was the creative force behind the military, religious, and cultural prominence that the Arabs achieved during this time. Islam was and is a set of laws guiding all aspects of the lives of its believers. During this period, many beautiful artworks, including calligraphic manuscripts, were produced; many people learned to read; and many advances occurred in technology, science, medicine, and mathematics. The text looks at the Islamic world, the caliph's rule, the empire, city and country life, Arab society, and the sharing of knowledge. Dates to Remember, Map, Find Out More, Glossary, and Index.

1282.   **Moldova**. Minneapolis, MN: Lerner, 1993. 56p. $19.95. ISBN 0-8225-2809-6. (Then and Now). 5-9
     With a Romanian culture and language, Moldova has been separate from other former Soviet Union countries. The text covers the history, economics, geography, politics, ethnography, and possible future of Moldova as it continues to assert its freedom. Maps and photographs complement the text. Glossary and Index.

1283.   Monjo, F. N. **Letters to Horseface: Young Mozart's Travels in Italy**. Don Bolognese and Elaine Raphael, illustrators. New York: Viking, 1976. 92p. $10.95. ISBN 0-670-42738-1. 4-7
     During 1769, when he was fourteen, Mozart traveled in Italy for a year with his father. He wrote letters to his sister, Nannerl, affectionately called "Horseface." The text, done as fictionalized letters, tells about his music (including the composition of his first opera), the people he met, and what he did during that time. About This Story and Bibliography.

1284.   Montgomery, Mary. **Marie Curie**. Severino Baraldi, illustrator. Englewood Cliffs, NJ: Silver Burdett, 1990. 104p. $12.95. ISBN 0-382-09981-8. (What Made Them Great). 5-8
     Marie Curie (1867-1934), known as Manya, grew up in Poland before attending school in Paris, where she finished first in her class. She met and married Pierre Curie, and they spent a life together doing scientific research that won her two Nobel Prizes. Appendix, Books for Further Reading, and Index.

1285.   Mooney, Bel. **The Stove Haunting**. Boston: Houghton Mifflin, 1988. 126p. $12.95. ISBN 0-395-46764-0. 5-8
     Daniel and his parents find an ugly old stove behind a wall in the old rectory they renovate after moving from London to the West country. When Daniel, age eleven, looks inside the stove, he finds himself in the rectory during 1835. In this historical fantasy, he assumes the work of a kitchen boy who blacks the stove. He sees the privileged wealthy begin to weaken when faced with agricultural unions and Methodism. Daniel's best friend is one of the secret organizers in these groups against the upper class. Daniel watches the choices that these people make in order to live more fulfilled and purposeful lives.

1286.   Morgan, Nina. **Guglielmo Marconi**. New York: Bookwright Press, Franklin Watts, 1991. 48p. $12.40. ISBN 0-531-18417-X. (Pioneers of Science). 5-7
     When Guglielmo Marconi (1874-1937) was born, a servant remarked that he had large ears. His mother supposedly responded, "He will be able to hear the still small voice of the air." Whether or not she really said it, Marconi did exactly that. His life paralleled the development of wireless communication, and he worked hard to improve it. He patented the wireless telegraph, set up a company, and was the first person to send telegraph messages without wires. His experimentation with radio waves led to the radio and a worldwide system of wireless communication. Photographs, Illustrations, Date Chart, Books to Read, Glossary, and Index.

1287. Morgan, Nina. **Louis Pasteur**. New York: Bookwright Press, Franklin Watts, 1992. 48p. $12.40. ISBN 0-531-18459-5. (Pioneers of Science). 5-9

The text looks at the life of Louis Pasteur (1822-1895) as well as the world before and after him. He worked with chemicals and crystals before he became interested in microbes or germs, which he thought were the possible cause of much disease but also the possible cure for others. He saved the silkworm industry and helped makers of wine and milk with his pasteurization process. His belief was that one should use one's knowledge, share it, and serve one's country. Photographs and Illustrations, Date Chart, Glossary, Books to Read, and Index.

1288. Morin, Isobel. **Days of Judgment: The World War II War Crimes Trials**. Brookfield, CT: Millbrook Press, 1995. 144p. $16.40. ISBN 1-56294-442-8. YA

Before World War II, international agreements had set standards for the treatment of prisoners and civilians during wartime; they had also outlawed "wars of aggression." At the end of World War II, many felt that Germany and Japan had broken these laws. The Nuremberg trials by the International Military Tribunal began in Germany on November 20, 1945, and were followed in 1946 by the trials in Japan. Other war crimes were also tried at different times. Epilogue, Appendices: Defendants at the International Military Tribunal at Nuremberg, Twelve Later Nuremberg Trials, Defendants at the International Military Tribunal at Tokyo. Notes, Bibliography, and Index.

1289. Morley, Jacqueline. **Clothes: For Work, Play and Display**. Vanda Baginskia, Mark Bergin, John James, Carolyn Scrace, and Gerald Wood, illustrators. New York: Franklin Watts, 1992. 48p. $7.95pa. ISBN 0-531-15740-7pa. (Timelines). 5-8

Two-page spreads divide the text into minichapters with many illustrations to show clothes throughout history. The time periods covered are the first clothes people wore; classical clothes of the Minoans, Greeks, and Romans; the Dark Ages; armor and tournament gear; medieval and Renaissance Italy; farthingales with Spanish influence in the sixteenth century; seventeenth-century Cavaliers and Puritans in England; court clothes and politics of France; crinoline petticoats introduced in 1857; folk costumes; dress reforms like bloomers; sportswear; between the World Wars; work clothes; clothes today; and clothes of the future. Timeline, Glossary, and Index.

1290. Morpurgo, Michael. **Butterfly Lion**. New York: Viking, 1997. 96p. $14.99. ISBN 0-670-87461-2. 4-7

When Bertie lives in South Africa at the turn of the century, he rescues a rare white lion cub from hyenas and begins a friendship with the animal. He goes to boarding school in England, and tells the white lion that they will meet again. The lion becomes part of a French circus, but years later, during World War I, Bertie sees the white lion's picture on a circus poster and begins his quest to see him again.

1291. Morpurgo, Michael. **King of the Cloud Forests**. New York: Viking, 1988. 146p. $12.95. ISBN 0-670-82069-5. 5 up

In 1937, the Japanese bomb China, and Ashley, age fourteen, must leave his missionary father for India in the company of a family friend, pretending to be his son. In Tibet, the two become separated when they are trapped by a blizzard, and Ashley awakens to find huge creatures nursing him. He goes with them and realizes that they are the legendary Yetis of the mountains. When he finally reunites with Uncle Sung, he hesitates to relate the experience, but in England he finds the man whose photograph the Yetis gave him and knows that he did not dream his experience.

1292. Morpurgo, Michael. **Mr. Nobody's Eyes**. New York: Viking, 1990. 138p. $12.95. ISBN 0-670-83022-4. 5-8

Harry, age ten, wants to return to the time when he and his mother were the only members of his family, after his father died when he was shot down over the English Channel in World War II. But by 1947, Harry's mother has remarried and had a baby. Harry hides in the basement of the bombed-out house next door and looks after a runaway chimpanzee from the circus, Ocky. The two leave London for Bournemouth. When his stepfather rescues him, Harry realizes that he does care.

1293. Morpurgo, Michael. **Twist of Gold**. New York: Viking, 1993. 246p. $14.99. ISBN 0-670-84851-4. 5-9

When Sean O'Brien's mother is too sick from hunger to travel during the 1850s, he and his sister leave Ireland to join their father in America. They carry with them the symbol of their clan: the golden torc (necklace) of their ancestors. Thieves who know of their possession try to steal it, and twice they lose it. But twice they find it again as they travel from Boston to California to meet their father, and surprisingly, their mother, who has been able to make a quicker, safer journey.

1294. Morpurgo, Michael. **Waiting for Anya**. New York: Viking, 1991. 172p. $12.95. ISBN 0-670-83735-0. 5-8

Jo, age twelve and a shepherd on the border between Spain and France, helps to save Jewish children in World War II by smuggling them over the border. With Germans patrolling and infiltrating the town, several people realize that if the children pretend to be shepherds, they will be able to roam over the mountains without suspicion to escape. *School Library Journal Best Book.*

1295.   Morpurgo, Michael. **The War of Jenkins' Ear**. New York: Philomel, 1995. 178p. $16.95. ISBN 0-399-22735-0. 6-9

In 1952, Toby Jenkins begins the year at Redlands Prep in Sussex, England. A new boy, Christopher, refuses to bow to the headmaster's demands, and tells Toby that he is Jesus Christ reincarnated and plans to save the world. Toby doubts, but a miracle occurs that makes Toby Christopher's first disciple. In a fight between the village boys and the school boys, Christopher advocates peace and tolerance. When authorities find out about Christopher's claims, they expel him and threaten Toby with expulsion unless he recants his support. Although he still believes in Christopher, Toby acquiesces rather than embarrass his parents. *American Library Association Notable Books for Young Adults.*

1296.   Morpurgo, Michael. **Why the Whales Came**. 1987. New York: Apple, Scholastic, 1990. 141p. $2.75pa. ISBN 0-590-42912-4pa. 5-7

Gracie's parents have told her to avoid the Birdman, who lives on the Isles of Sicily, because he is mad. In 1914, Gracie finds herself at his home and discovers that he is merely deaf. He carves lovely birds and knows why the people in Gracie's neighborhood think the nearby island is cursed. One day a whale beaches itself nearby, and he begs the townspeople to help it return to the water. Because the Birdman has given Gracie's mother food while her husband serves in the navy, she understands that he needs their aid. Although she is only ten, Gracie helps the others see the value in this remarkable man.

1297.   Morressy, John. **The Juggler**. New York: Henry Holt, 1996. 261p. $16.95. ISBN 0-8050-4217-2. 7 up

After an introduction in which Count Osostro condemns a traveling juggler and cuts off his right hand, the story turns to Beran, a young peasant boy in medieval times, who wants to be a juggler. He finds another juggler who is willing to take on an apprentice. Later an old man visits and offers him the juggling skill in return for something Beran values not at all. Beran pledges his right hand instead. After Beran finds happiness in various ways, the old man returns, insisting that the debt has not been paid. Beran escapes by going on a pilgrimage to the Holy Land. But he seems to think that sacrificing his hand to Count Osostro is less frightening than fulfilling his promise to the old man.

1298.   Morrison, Ian A. **Middle East**. Austin, TX: Raintree/Steck-Vaughn, 1991. 96p. $16.98. ISBN 0-8114-2440-5. 5-9

This survey of the Middle East gives information on its geography, languages, religions, history, occupations, family life, food, cities, and education. It emphasizes that knowing the history of the area helps one to understand past and present conflicts among the peoples who live there. Index.

1299.   Moss, Carol. **Science in Ancient Mesopotamia**. New York: Franklin Watts, 1988. 72p. $16.60. ISBN 0-531-10594-6. (First Book). 5-8

An introduction to ancient Mesopotamia and its science precedes chapters on different developments from this culture. They include writing, medicine, mathematics, exploration of the skies, surveys of nature, everyday technology, and the contemporary debt to the culture for its discoveries. Photographs supplement the text. Glossary, Further Reading, and Index.

1300.   Mowat, Farley. **Born Naked**. Boston: Houghton Mifflin, 1994. 256p. $21.95. ISBN 0-395-68927-9. YA

A Canadian writer, Farley Mowat grew up loving nature, and he became a registered ornithologist at the age of fourteen. His first efforts to become a writer led to his being fired from a newspaper when he graphically described the underwater mating of the ruddy duck. In this book Mowat, the author of *Never Cry Wolf* and other works, describes his life between the world wars.

1301.   Mowat, Farley, Angus McGill Mowat, and Helen Anne Mowat. **My Father's Son: Memories of War and Peace**. Boston: Houghton Mifflin, 1993. 340p. $24.95. ISBN 0-395-65029-1. YA

In letters home from the European battlefront during World War II and the Italian campaign, Farley Mowat told his father about his hatred of Canadian policy. His father responded as a veteran of World War I, and they kept the exchange going throughout the war. The text looks at these letters and some from Mowat's mother that give insight into the times, the family, and Canadian politics of the 1940s. Glossary.

1302.   Muhlberger, Richard. **What Makes a Bruegel a Bruegel?** New York: Viking, 1993. 48p. $11.99. ISBN 0-670-85203-1. 5-9

Pieter Bruegel the Elder (c. 1525-1569) drew everyday scenes. The stress of living in Belgium under the foreign domination of Spain underlies but is not overt in his work. His subjects reveal themselves in their poses rather than through facial expressions, and he filled his paintings with many details. Paintings reproduced and discussed are *The Fall of Icarus, Children's Games, The Fall of the Rebel Angels, Two Monkeys, The Tower of Babel, The Adoration of the Kings, The Harvesters, Hunters in the Snow, The Land of Cockaigne, The Wedding Banquet, The Peasant Dance*, and *The Parable of the Blind*.

1303. Muhlberger, Richard. **What Makes a Cassatt a Cassatt?** New York: Viking, 1994. 48p. $11.99. ISBN 0-670-85742-4. 5-9

Although born an American, Mary Cassatt (1844-1926) lived most of her life in Paris, painting in the style of the French Impressionists. She traveled to Spain, and her study of the work of Velásquez and Goya led her to focus on people and eliminate almost all background detail. Japanese work inspired her to use contrasting colors and tilted perspective. She used solid lines and clear colors to present relationships between people. Included are reproductions and discussions of *Offering the Panale to the Bullfighter, Little Girl in a Blue Armchair, At the Opéra, Lydia Crocheting in the Garden at Marly, Five O'Clock Tea, Reading Le Figaro, Children Playing on the Beach, The Letter, Baby Reaching for an Apple, The Boating Party, Breakfast in Bed*, and *Mother and Child*.

1304. Muhlberger, Richard. **What Makes a Degas a Degas?** New York: Viking, 1993. 48p. $11.99. ISBN 0-670-85205-8. 5-9

Hilaire-Germain-Edgar Degas (1834-1917) was born in Paris to parents who exposed him to music and art. After a rift with his father over becoming a painter, Degas pursued the traditional route of traveling to Italy to study the masters. He returned to Paris and joined the Impressionists, but he preferred to paint inside, plan his paintings, and base them on strong drawing, unlike his friends. He thus bridged the new and the old in the art of his time. In his work, he cut figures off at the edge of the canvas for a candid effect, tipped the stage upward as if viewed from above, painted patches of brilliant color to augment movement, and opened large spaces in the background to take the eye into the depths. Works reproduced and discussed are *The Bellelli Family, A Woman Seated Beside a Vase of Flowers, Carriage at the Races, The Orchestra at the Opéra, Race Horses at Longchamp, Portraits in an Office (New Orleans), The Dance Class, Miss La La at the Cirque Fernando, Woman Ironing, The Singer in Green, The Millinery Shop*, and *Dancers, Pink and Green*.

1305. Muhlberger, Richard. **What Makes a Goya a Goya?** New York: Viking, 1994. 48p. $11.99. ISBN 0-670-85743-2. 5-9

Francisco José de Goya y Lucientes (1746-1828) moved with his family to Saragossa, Spain, where he became an apprentice in 1760. In Madrid by 1763, he worked with Francisco Bayeu at the royal court and viewed the royal art collection, becoming most inspired by Diego Velázquez from the previous century. Goya's images are simultaneously realistic and fantastic and dreamlike. He blamed injustice and superstition for the wars around him, and he preferred the reason of the Enlightenment in which he lived. As the text discusses Goya's life, it comments on his painting and its evolution. He used quick, loose brushstrokes and black, roughly indicated backgrounds, and liked women dressed in the traditional Spanish costume of a *maja*. Works included are *The Crockery Vendor, Don Manuel Osorio Manrique de Zuñiga, Goya in His Studio, The Duchess of Alba, The Family of Charles IV, Bullfight in a Village, The Burial of the Sardine, The Colossus, The Third of May, 1808, The Forge, Self-Portrait with Doctor Arrieta*, and *The Witches' Sabbath*.

1306. Muhlberger, Richard. **What Makes a Leonardo a Leonardo?** New York: Viking, 1994. 48p. $11.99. ISBN 0-670-85744-0. 5-9

Leonardo da Vinci (1452-1519) became famous during his lifetime; in fact, someone published a biography about him the year before he died. Another biographer, Vasari, wrote about him in 1550 and again in 1568, after interviewing people who had known Leonardo. Leonardo's parents never married, and apparently he spent his childhood with grandparents who willed him their estate. He moved to Florence with his father as a teenager and became apprenticed to Verrocchio, with whom he worked for approximately thirteen years. Leonardo's diaries show his many interests—music, biology, botany, engineering, and invention. He finished few of his paintings, probably because he was a perfectionist. The twelve paintings reproduced and discussed here are *The Baptism of Christ, The Annunciation, Ginevra de' Benci, The Adoration of the Magi, Lady with an Ermine, The Virgin of the Rocks, The Last Supper, The Virgin and Child with Saints Anne and John the Baptist, The Battle of Anghiari, Mona Lisa, The Virgin and Child with Saint Anne*, and *Saint John the Baptist*. Leonardo used deep shadows to show three dimensions with gestures conveying real-life emotions. His aerial or atmospheric perspective make his backgrounds look blurry, pale, and far away.

1307. Muhlberger, Richard. **What Makes a Monet a Monet?** New York: Viking, 1994. 48p. $11.99. ISBN 0-670-85742-4. 5-9

Monet (1840-1926) tried to capture a special moment in each painting by paying more attention to the overall subject than to specific detail. He started his art by doing caricatures of people on the beach at Honfleur. When he began painting seriously, he returned to his studio, but he saw Eugene Boudin's paintings and went with him to paint outside, rather than remaining in the studio where traditional painters thought one should stay. Paintings discussed in the text are *Garden at Sainte-Adresse, The Luncheon, La Grenouillère, Poppy Field, Argenteuil, Gare Saint-Lazare, Bouquet of Sunflowers, Haystacks, Poplars, Rouen Cathedral, Bridge over a Pool of Water Lilies, The Houses of Parliament,* and *Water Lilies*.

1308.   Muhlberger, Richard. **What Makes a Picasso a Picasso?** New York: Viking, 1994. 48p. $11.99. ISBN 0-670-85741-6. 5-9

Pablo Ruiz Picasso (1881-1973) almost single-handedly created modern art with his thousands of works—painting, sculpture, prints, and ceramics. He was a superb draftsman, able to accurately capture almost anything with his pencil. In 1900, he moved from Barcelona, Spain, to Paris, France, and eventually settled there. The color in his early paintings reflects his own emotional life. In his styles, he showed several viewpoints at once, and exaggerated and distorted shapes and colors for emotion while simplifying things into basic shapes (such as circles and triangles) with bold black or color outlines. His works reproduced and discussed are *Harlequin, The Blind Man's Meal, Family of the Saltimbanques, Gertrude Stein, Les Demoiselles d'Avignon, Daniel-Henry Kahnweiler, Violin and Fruit, Three Musicians, Three Women at the Spring, Guernica, Night Fishing at Antibes,* and *First Steps*.

1309.   Mulcahy, Robert. **Diseases: Finding the Cure**. Minneapolis, MN: Oliver Press, 1996. 144p. $14.95. ISBN 1-881508-28-5. 7 up

Why people get sick has been a mystery for centuries. In the eighteenth century, James Lind (1716-1794) conducted the first clinical trials to discover a cure for scurvy. Edward Jenner (1749-1823) worked to find an inoculation against smallpox. Louis Pasteur (1822-1895) suggested finding the germ and turning it into a vaccine to kill itself. Since then, Paul Ehrlich founded chemotherapy, Frederick Banting refined insulin, Alexander Fleming discovered penicillin, and Jonas Salk developed the polio vaccine. Currently, researchers work frantically to find a cure for AIDS. Nobel Prize Winners, Glossary, Bibliography, and Index.

1310.   Mulvihill, Margaret. **Mussolini and Italian Fascism**. New York: Franklin Watts, 1990. 62p. $11.90. ISBN 0-531-17253-8. (World War II Biographies). 8 up

Benito Mussolini (1883–1945) led the fascist state of Italy before and during World War II. The text discusses his life and the origin and ideology of fascism. Photographs and drawings enhance the text. Bibliography, Chronology, Glossary, and Index.

1311.   Murphy, Nora. **A Hmong Family**. Minneapolis, MN: Lerner, 1997. 64p. $16.13; $8.95pa. ISBN 0-8225-3406-1; 0-614-28837-1pa. (Journey Between Two Worlds). 5-7

At eleven, Xiong Pao Vang has to cope with a new culture after he and his family have escaped from Laos and the wars there. Further Reading and Index.

1312.   Murray, Jocelyn. **Africa**. New York: Facts on File, 1990. 96p. $17.95. ISBN 0-8160-2209-7. (Cultural Atlas for Young People). 6-9

The text examines as many facets of Africa as possible, using full-color illustrations and maps. Chronology, Glossary, Gazetteer, and Index.

1313.   Myers, Walter Dean. **Fallen Angels**. New York: Scholastic, 1988. 369p. $14.95; $3.50pa. ISBN 0-590-40942-5; 0-590-40943-3pa. 8 up

Richie, a seventeen-year-old African-American, enlists in the army and leaves for Vietnam in 1967. He plans to use the money he earns to pay for his brother's school clothes. When he arrives on the front, he realizes that war is quite different from what he expected. After hours of doing nothing, he and his squad have to battle the sly Viet Cong, who often kill before the squad knows they are present. Richie has the "good" fortune of being wounded so that he can return home, but what he has seen continues to disturb his thoughts. *Coretta Scott King Award, American Library Association Best Books for Young Adults, American Library Association Quick Picks for Reluctant Young Adult Readers, American Library Association Booklist Editors' Choice, Horn Book Fanfare Honor List,* and *School Library Journal Best Book*.

1314.   Myers, Walter Dean. **Toussaint L'Ouverture: The Fight for Haiti's Freedom**. Jacob Lawrence, illustrator. New York: Simon & Schuster, 1996. 40p. $16. ISBN 0-689-80126-2. 3-7

Toussaint L'Ouverture (1743?-1803), a freed slave who became general of a Haitian slave army, helped to defeat Haiti's French conquerors in 1791. His leadership liberated the island. The text looks at L'Ouverture's early life and how it inspired Jacob Lawrence's artwork in the 1930s and 1940s. *American Library Association Notable Books for Children*.

1315.   **Mysticism: The Experience of the Divine**. San Francisco: Chronicle, 1994. 62p. $9.95. ISBN 0-8118-0484-4. (Little Wisdom Library—Medieval Wisdom). YA

A *mystic experience* is a union with the divine or the transcendent. The text, complemented with copies of medieval illuminations and manuscripts, gives a history of mysticism. In A.D. 251, St. Antony, in Egypt, originated the true monastic life. His chief disciple, Pachomius, continued the tradition at Antony's death. Writing about it was St. Paul's convert at Athens, Dionysius the Areopagite. Plotinus, in the third century, showed the influence of neo-Platonism, and Augustine came forward in the fourth century in an area now known as Algeria. Among the mystics of medieval times, around the twelfth century, were Richard of St. Victor and the devotional mystics Bernard of Clairvaux, Francis of Assisi, Catherine of Siena, Hildegarde of Bingen, and Rupert of Deutz. Ramon Lull of Catalan appeared in the thirteenth century. The German Meister Eckhart, condemned by the Inquisition, had followers in Henry Suso, Jan Ruybroeck, and John Tauler. Heretics in the same century who believed in the Free Spirit teaching were John Scotus Erigena, Amaury of Bene, the Beghards and Beguines, Nicholas of Basle, and Joachim of Fiore. Close to heresy were Teresa of Avila, Francis of Assisi, and John of the Cross. In the seventeenth century, Miguel de Molinos became famous. That early medieval times produced so many mystical thinkers may belie their reputation as the Dark Ages. Bibliography and Further Reading.

N

1316. Nadel, Laurie. **Corazon Aquino: Journey to Power**. New York: Julian Messner, 1987. 128p. $13.98. ISBN 0-671-63950-1. 7 up

Corazon Aquino (b. 1933), after the death of her husband, helped to unseat one of the most entrenched dictators in the Philippines. She became aware of the political situation through her marriage, but that someone who had her background of wealth and isolation from the masses could become president of her country seems amazing. The text uses Aquino's words and interviews with people who know her to recreate her story. Index.

1317. Namioka, Lensey. **The Coming of the Bear**. New York: HarperCollins, 1992. 235p. $14. ISBN 0-06-020288-2. 7 up

The samurai Matsuzo and Zenta and their boat are dashed onto the island of Ezo (Hokkaido) by an unexpected squall at sea. Ainus, a strange, round-eyed people, surround them and look after their wounds. They see how hard the life is for this group, and they realize that they are captives. They have to plan an escape to a Japanese compound on another part of the island. The Japanese, however, are planning war against the Ainus to gain more land. The two captives help to stop the war by identifying the Ainu traitors.

1318. Namioka, Lensey. **Island of Ogres**. New York: HarperCollins, 1989. 197p. $13.89. ISBN 0-06-24373-2. 7 up

When Kajiro, an unemployed samurai, lands on a Japanese island in the sixteenth century, the people think that he is a famous warrior who will save them from the mysterious disappearances of chickens and dogs. He does not correct the villagers and finds himself fulfilling the role they expect of him when he observes the commander and his wife going to visit an unidentified guest, who supposedly is ill, every day. He helps the islanders to quell a revolt in their former daimyo's name.

1319. Napoli, Donna Jo. **Song of the Magdalene**. New York: Scholastic, 1996. 240p. $15.95. ISBN 0-590-93705-7. YA

Miriam loves to run alone into the fields from her home during the early years of the first century A.D. One day, as she enjoys the beauty of nature, she suffers an epileptic fit. Fearful that she has devils within her, she tells no one. Not until she has a second seizure in front of her physically disabled friend Abraham, and he assures her that neither of them have sinned enough to earn their respective afflictions, does she begin to accept herself. She discovers that she loves Abraham, a highly intelligent man who teaches her to read the Torah. After she realizes she loves him and conceives his child, he dies, and a hostile villager rapes her. She leaves the village to go to other relatives, but during her travels, as a woman alone, she is called a prostitute. On this journey she also hears about the man Joshua. After she has another fit at a well near him, he declares that she has no devils in her. *American Library Association Notable Books for Young Adults* and *Booklist Best Books for Young Adults*.

1320. Napoli, Donna Jo. **Stones in Water**. New York: Dutton, 1997. 209p. $15.99. ISBN 0-525-45842-5. 4-9

Roberto, his brother, and two friends sneak into a Venetian movie house during World War II, and during the movie, German soldiers trap those inside and ship them from Italy to a concentration camp as forced labor. One of the friends is Jewish, a fact they try to hide, but after Polish Jews arrive, he is beaten to death for trying to save Roberto's boots.

1321. Nardo, Don. **The Age of Augustus**. San Diego, CA: Lucent, 1996. 112p. $16.95. ISBN 1-56006-306-8. (World History). 5-8

Nardo discusses the rise of Augustus Caesar (63 B.C.-A.D. 14) as emperor of Rome and his accomplishments made by consolidating Rome's power. He also includes commentary about people who were living and working at the time such as the writers Livy, Horace, and Virgil. Photographs, maps, and reproductions augment the text. Bibliography, Chronology, Further Reading, and Index.

1322. Nardo, Don. **The Age of Pericles**. San Diego, CA: Lucent, 1996. 112p. $16.95. ISBN 1-56006-303-3. (World History). 7 up

Primary and secondary sources give the basic historical facts from the points of view of those who lived during the time of Pericles. Pericles (d. 429 B.C.) himself was noted for advancing democracy in Athens and for deciding to construct the Parthenon on the Acropolis. Bibliography, Chronology, Further Reading, Notes, and Index.

1323. Nardo, Don. **Ancient Greece**. San Diego, CA: Lucent, 1994. 112p. $16.95. ISBN 1-56006-229-0. (World History Series). 7-9

This history of ancient Greece uses sources written during the period, the research of recognized scholars, and recent archaeological evidence in its clear and concise evocation of the time. The text begins with the Minoans (2200–1450 B.C.) and their advanced culture on Crete, where women and men were equal and the people revered the Great Mother and worshipped bulls. The Minoans contrast in temperament with the more militaristic Myceneans on the mainland, who eventually invaded Troy around 1200 B.C. The civilization disappeared between 1600 and 1450 B.C., when the volcanic island of Thera exploded in an eruption that affected the entire Mediterranean. (Thera's demise is probably the Atlantis that Plato discusses.) After the Dorians arrived in 1100 B.C. and were overcome, the city-states such as Athens and Sparta began to rise, and the recognition of the worth of the individual (except women, foreigners, and slaves) led to the creation of democracy. In 776 B.C., the Olympic Games began, and Homer wrote *The Iliad* and *The Odyssey*. The Greek and Persian wars followed. When the Greeks won, Athens began its Golden Age and, according to one historian, made Europe itself possible. But the city-states could not coexist; therefore, the Peloponnesian wars between Greek (Sparta) and Greek (Athens) began and lasted for twenty-seven years. The paucity of funds and men allowed the Macedonians under Philip II and Alexander to invade and spread the Greek culture throughout the known world. With Greek decline in the Hellenistic age, the cities of Alexandria and Antioch became the most prestigious in the ancient world. Notes, For Further Reading, Works Consulted, and Index.

1324. Nardo, Don. **The Battle of Marathon**. San Diego, CA: Lucent, 1995. 96p. $19.95. ISBN 1-56006-412-9. (Battles of the Ancient World). 7-9

After examining the causes of the Greek and Persian wars, the text discusses the conflicts and events that directly led to the Battle at Marathon in 490 B.C., when 10,000 Athenians and their allies defeated 50,000 Persian troops. Nardo says that the battle was distantly related to the rise of the Greek Golden Age, basing his assessment on primary and secondary sources that include Herodotus. Bibliography, Chronology, Further Reading, and Index.

1325. Nardo, Don. **The Battle of Zama**. San Diego, CA: Lucent, 1996. 96p. $19.95. ISBN 1-56006-420-X. (Battles of the Ancient World). 7-9

The Battle of Zama ended the seventeen-year conflict between Rome and Carthage in 202 B.C. Scipio Africanus led the Romans against Hannibal's Carthaginians and won victory in this second Punic War. The text shows the struggle between the two powers and the brutality of the war. Bibliography, Chronology, Further Reading, and Index.

1326. Nardo, Don. **Braving the New World: 1619-1784**. New York: Chelsea House, 1994. 117p. $19.95; $7.95pa. ISBN 0-7910-2259-5; 0-7910-2685-Xpa. (Milestones of Black American History). 7-9

In covering the roles of Black Americans from 1619 to 1784, the text and illustrations present the sugar revolution when the slave trade developed, early colonial slavery, the increase in the number of slaves imported as plantation needs grew, the trip from Africa to America, the relationship between master and slave, and the growth of African American culture. Further Reading and Index.

1327. Nardo, Don. **Caesar's Conquest of Gaul**. San Diego, CA: Lucent, 1996. 96p. $16.95. ISBN 1-56006-301-7. (The Importance Of). 7 up

In 52 B.C., the Roman general, Gaius Julius Caesar, defeated the last citadel of Gallic military strength in Alesia. He used superior training, the supply network of the Roman army, and better weapons to defeat his enemy. To the Romans, this campaign signaled a tremendous accomplishment. Caesar's conquest expanded Rome's empire and brought new products into the dominion, among them gold and precious stones. The text discusses urban Rome versus rural Gaul, Gaul's savage frontiers, Caesar's experiences in Britain, the great Gallic rebellion, Caesar's victories, and Rome's legacy in Gaul and Britain. Photographs and boxed topics augment the text. Notes, For Further Reading, Works Consulted, and Index.

1328. Nardo, Don. **Charles Darwin**. New York: Chelsea House, 1993. 112p. $18.95. ISBN 0-7910-1729-X. (Library of Biography). 7 up

When he returned from his five-year voyage around the world, Charles Darwin began to formulate his theory of evolution. He waited twenty-eight years before publishing it, to be sure that he could support it through his investigations of nature. The publication of *On the Origin of Species* infuriated many clergy, who felt that it undermined the teachings in the Bible, but many scientists saw that it made sense. The text, with photographs and reproductions, looks at Darwin's life and work. Further Reading, Chronology, and Index.

1329. Nardo, Don. **Chernobyl**. Brian McGovern, illustrator. San Diego, CA: Lucent, 1990. 64p. $12.95. ISBN 1-56006-008-5. (World Disasters). 5 up

On April 27, 1986, in Pripyat, Ukraine (then the Soviet Union), the nuclear reactor malfunctioned, and the ensuing nuclear accident affected the town and those nearby forever. The Soviet authorities refused to announce the disaster, but Swedish scientists detected the radiation in the air. Although safeguards are supposedly followed at all nuclear plants, the situation showed that the worst can happen when humans err. Photographs, diagrams, and drawings accent the text. Further Reading, Glossary, Works Consulted, and Index.

1330. Nardo, Don. **Cleopatra**. San Diego, CA: Lucent, 1993. 112p. $16.95. ISBN 1-56006-023-9. (The Importance Of). 7 up

Cleopatra (69-30 B.C.) became queen in 51 B.C., but her brother Ptolemy XIII drove her from Alexandria in 49 B.C. Caesar helped her regain the throne the following year. After Caesar was assassinated in 44 B.C., Cleopatra and Antony began their relationship, but Antony left to marry Octavian's sister Octavia. He returned to Cleopatra in 37 B.C. Antony's campaign against Carthia ended in failure in 36 B.C., but he proclaimed Cleopatra "Queen of Kings" in 34 B.C. The two prepared for war against Rome, but Octavian defeated them at Actium in Greece. They then committed suicide. Included are chapters on Egypt and Rome as the world of Cleopatra's childhood, her quest for power by joining Caesar, and the concept of Cleopatra as the new Isis. Among the facts and the fictions discussed in this text is that the Romans hated Cleopatra because she was a foreigner, a woman, and had, according to them, corrupted both Caesar and Antony. Reproductions and photographs augment the text. For Further Reading, Works Consulted, and Index.

1331. Nardo, Don. **Greek and Roman Theater**. San Diego, CA: Lucent, 1995. 112p. $16.95. ISBN 1-56006-249-5. (World History Series). 7 up

This absorbing history of the Greek and Roman theater uses sources written during the period, the research of recognized scholars, and recent archaeological evidence. The world's first theater, in Knossos on Crete, functioned between 2200 and 1450 B.C. The Greek theater's rituals of Dionysius were well developed in the dithyramb by the eighth century B.C. The first known actor, Thespis, showed his skill by winning a *rhapsodia*, in which he gave dramatic renditions of the epics *The Iliad* and *The Odyssey*. Drama reached its heights during the fifth century B.C. through the works of Sophocles, Aeschylus, and Euripides. As Athens lost power, drama also deteriorated into the baudy New Comedy and the popular work of Menander around 350 B.C. The early Roman theater began its rise with ribald farce, in which women as well as men performed. The first full-length Roman play based on Greek models of tragedy was presented during Ludi Romani, the September religious festival of Rome, with the most famous playwrights being Terence and Plautus. By the time of the Roman Republic, the rulers wanted to keep the masses, who had more leisure time while their slaves worked, occupied. They offered free bread and free daily entertainment, including gladiatorial combat and chariot races. The theater had to compete with such fare, and it often lost. The last recorded performance in a Roman theater was in A.D. 533, after the official fall of Rome and the rise of Christianity. The Greek and Roman legacy became Europe's roving minstrels, medieval court jesters, and the French comedy of manners perfected by Molière in the seventeenth century. Notes, For Further Reading, Works Consulted, and Index.

1332. Nardo, Don. **H. G. Wells**. San Diego, CA: Lucent, 1992. 111p. $16.95. ISBN 1-56006-025-5. (The Importance Of). 7 up

H. G. Wells (1866–1946) wanted to use his hard-earned fame and talent to change the world. In his writing, he continually used themes that would expose the world's poverty, waste, and pollution. People did not change, but Wells did not stop trying to create utopias on earth. Photographs, Notes, For Further Reading, Works Consulted, and Index.

1333. Nardo, Don. **The Irish Potato Famine**. Brian McGovern, illustrator. San Diego, CA: Lucent, 1990. 64p. $12.95. ISBN 1-56006-012-3. (World Disasters). 7-9

Ireland seems always to have felt the weight of British dominance, starting with the Celts. In 1798, Theobald Wolfe Tone led a rebellion against the British, which failed. The British kept the good land for themselves, and the tenant farmers had to support themselves on potatoes. In 1843, 1844, and 1845, the potato crops failed when an unknown blight attacked them. Thousands starved, and those who could emigrate did. The British prime minster, Sir Robert Peel, pitied the Irish and sent them aid, but the British treasurer, Charles Trevelyan (1807–1886) hated them and stopped some of the relief from reaching its destination. The famine was a major disaster for Ireland. Drawings augment the text. Glossary, Works Consulted, and Index.

1334. Nardo, Don. **Julius Caesar**. San Diego, CA: Lucent, 1996. 112p. $16.95. ISBN 1-56006-083-2. (The Importance Of). 8 up

The complexity of Caesar (100-44 B.C.) during the Roman Republic becomes clear in this account of his life, from his brutal public acts to his leniency for some of his enemies. Caesar elicited an almost unparalleled loyalty from his soldiers, and he used this influence to gain control over the government. Nardo gives a balanced account of Caesar, his accomplishments, and the shortcomings which led to his assassination. Bibliography, Chronology, Further Reading, and Index.

1335.   Nardo, Don. **Krakatoa**. San Diego, CA: Lucent, 1990. 64p. $12.95. ISBN 1-56006-001-5. (World Disasters). 5-8

The 1883 eruption of Krakatoa, in Indonesia, killed 36,000 people with the resulting tidal waves. It influenced weather and sunsets across the globe for months afterward. The cultural, historical, and geographic contexts of this disaster and how it affected both people and environment appear in the text, with supporting illustrations, diagrams, and maps. Glossary, Further Reading, and Index.

1336.   Nardo, Don. **Life in Ancient Rome**. San Diego, CA: Lucent, 1996. 112p. $16.95. ISBN 1-56006-335-1. (Way People Live). 7-10

Nardo traces the history and life in Rome beginning with its political structure of the Senate and the evolution from republic to empire. Among the groups he presents are soldiers, slaves, freedmen, and citizens. He discusses their activities and entertainment along with other important aspects of their daily life. Bibliography, Chronology, Further Reading, Glossary, and Index.

1337.   Nardo, Don. **The Mexican-American War**. San Diego, CA: Lucent, 1991. 96p. $16.95. ISBN 1-56006-402-1. (America's Wars). 9 up

The Mexican-American War lasted from 1845 to 1848, with the immediate cause of the war being the U.S. annexation of Texas in December 1845. Other factors were the existence of long-standing claims by U.S. citizens against Mexico and the American ambition to acquire California. When the attempt to buy California and Mexico in 1845 failed, President James Polk prepared for war, and in March 1846, General Zachary Taylor began the aggression. The text also presents other historical and cultural backgrounds in the conflict. Diagrams, boxed comments, maps, and black-and-white photographs augment the text. Bibliography, Glossary, Appendix, and Index.

1338.   Nardo, Don. **The Punic Wars**. San Diego, CA: Lucent, 1996. 109p. $16.95. ISBN 1-56006-417-X. (The Importance Of). 7 up

The Punic Wars, fought in the third and second centuries B.C. between Rome and Carthage, the two great military powers of the time, were the first world wars. Both sides used the most advanced weapons available for twenty-four years without a break. The naval losses of the Romans were far larger than those for all countries in World War II. The text looks at the ancient rivalry between Rome and Carthage, the times between wars, Hannibal's invasion of Italy, Rome's rejuvenation, and the end of the wars with Carthage in flames. Photographs and boxed topics augment the text. Notes, For Further Reading, Works Consulted, and Index.

1339.   Nardo, Don. **The Roman Empire**. San Diego, CA: Lucent, 1994. 112p. $16.95. ISBN 1-56006-231-2. (World History Series). 7-9

In A.D. 79, a volcanic eruption destroyed Pompeii and Herculaneum. This disaster was, in a way, a gift to modern people because the volcanic ash caught humans and animals going about their daily lives and preserved a view of the life in the Roman Empire (30 B.C.–A.D. 476) for archaeologists to discover.

The Romans believed that their system, begun with the democratic Roman Republic, was the most logical yet devised on earth, and they imposed it on everyone they ruled. When Octavian took power in 27 B.C., he created a more dictatorial state, but he began the *Pax Romana*, a time when the Romans were not fighting people along the borders. With his death came the rule of the Caesars. Tiberius ruled reasonably, but Caligula, who followed, was cruel, sexually perverse, and extravagant. After Tiberius's murder, Claudius became a surprisingly enlightened ruler, and took the Romans into Britain, an area that Julius Caesar had first visited. By the middle of the first century, women had gained the right to manage their own money and to sue their husbands for divorce. Later dictators such as Nero controlled everyone. Fortunately, five good emperors followed Nero's devastating rule: Nerva, Trajan, Hadrian, Antonius Pius, and Marcus Aurelius. Hadrian decided that the empire was too large when he visited its parts and erected his Wall in Britain to keep out the Scots north of the boundary. A series of weak and selfish rulers succeeded Marcus Aurelius, and by 284 Diocletian took the leadership to keep Rome from reaching total destruction. In A.D. 312, Constantine, while attempting to conquer Maxentius, a coruler in Rome, supposedly saw a cross in the sky. He made his soldiers paint crosses on their shields, and they defeated Maxentius the next day. By A.D. 378, an emperor declared that Christianity was the religion of the empire. Throughout these years, Rome slowly disintegrated, with the final defeat of the western half occurring in A.D. 476 when the German general Odoacer removed Augustus from the throne. The eastern half did not fall until 1453, when the Turks took Constantinople. The Romans left a legacy of their farming system, public works, language, laws, and transmission of Greek culture and ideas. Notes, For Further Reading, Works Consulted, and Index.

1340.   Nardo, Don. **The Roman Republic**. San Diego, CA: Lucent, 1994. 112p. $16.95. ISBN 1-56006-230-4. (World History Series). 7-9

The Romans imitated other cultures and then adjusted the ideas to make them practical, as they honored society rather than the individual. The official date of Rome's appearance on the Tiber River is 753 B.C., although towns dotted the area before; the official legend is that Rome descended from Aeneas, prince of Troy, through

Romulus and Remus. These Romans kept strong family ties and believed that all living things had a spirit, a religion now called *animism*. With the unification of Italy, the Etruscan kings were expelled, and the Roman Republic (510–30 B.C.) gave the people a voice when power became divided among several leaders. Rome eventually won the Punic Wars against Carthage in 201 B.C., after fighting the able generals Hamilcar and his son Hannibal. Rome began its expansion, and the Mediterranean became a "Roman lake." By 48 B.C., the military strength under Sulla had increased, but Spartacus led a slave revolt that Pompey finally quelled just as he defeated the pirates who were ruining Mediterranean trade. Julius Caesar's ambition, ruthlessness, and dishonesty followed, and after he returned from Egypt and Cleopatra's seduction, senators murdered him on the Ides of March, 44 B.C. Because many men wanted his power, the murder turned into an empty victory when three men—Mark Antony, Octavian, and Marcus Lepidus—vied for leadership. Octavian became the victor and assumed the status of Augustus, "the exalted one." Notes, For Further Reading, Works Consulted, and Index.

1341. Nardo, Don. **Traditional Japan**. San Diego, CA: Lucent, 1995. 112p. $16.95. ISBN 1-56006-244-4. (World History Series). 6-10

The strong feeling of group solidarity that defines Japan as a nation is rooted in its political and cultural history, extending from ancient times to its opening to the West in 1854. The Japanese psyche seems to see itself as part of the nation rather than as an individual; the Japanese have always been adept at borrowing from other cultures but making the material distinctly their own. Sources written during the periods presented and research of renowned historians helps to interpret traditional Japan. Shotoku, the first Japanese statesman, came to power in 590. During and after his reign, the Taika Reform and the Taiho Code were instituted, and Nara was declared the capital in 710. In 794, Kyoto became the new capital. By 858, the Fijiwara family firmly controlled the state. During their leadership, Lady Murasaki wrote *The Tale of Genji*. The Taira and Minamoto fought the Genpei War between 1180 and 1185, with Minamoto Yoritomo establishing a military government and becoming shogun in 1192. The Mongols invaded twice during the thirteenth century, but the Emperor Go-Daigo ascended the throne in 1318. His power led to civil war between the north and the south from 1336 until 1392. From 1467 to 1477, the Onin war almost destroyed Kyoto. The Portuguese arrived in 1542, and in 1592, Japan invaded Korea. In 1635, a Japanese edict forbade all foreign travel and isolated the country until 1853, when Commodore Perry arrived; Japan signed the Treaty of Kanagawa in 1854. In the next decade, the Meiji Restoration began as the period of isolation ended. Notes, For Further Reading, Works Consulted, and Index.

1342. Nardo, Don. **The Trial of Joan of Arc**. San Diego, CA: Lucent, 1997. 96p. $17. ISBN 1-56006-466-8. (Famous Trials). 8 up

After reviewing Joan of Arc's life (1412-1431), the text examines her trial for witchcraft, after her success in the Hundred Years' War, in detail. Bibliography, Chronology, Further Reading, and Index.

1343. Nardo, Don. **The Trial of Socrates**. San Diego, CA: Lucent, 1996. 96p. $16.95. ISBN 1-56006-267-3. (Famous Trials). 7-10

The text looks at Socrates (469-399 B.C.) and his life in context of Greek expectations, and focuses on the causes and results of his trial. Bibliography, Further Reading, and Index.

1344. Nardo, Don. **World War II: The War in the Pacific**. San Diego, CA: Lucent, 1991. 96p. $16.95. ISBN 1-56006-408-0. (America's Wars). 9-12

In addition to facts about the progress of World War II in the Pacific, the text also gives information about the Japanese culture before the war began. Because the Japanese government focused on militarism, its choice to bomb Pearl Harbor was understandable although unexpected at the time it occurred. Diagrams, boxed comments, maps, and black-and-white photographs augment the text. Bibliography, Glossary, Appendix, and Index.

1345. Nash, Amy K. **North Korea**. New York: Chelsea House, 1991. 128p. $15.95. ISBN 0-7910-0157-1. (Places and People of the World). 6-8

The text relates both the history of and the present situation in North Korea. A timeline indicates that the Chinese recognized the walled town-state of Old Choson (the present-day Pyongyang) in 300 B.C. In A.D. 58-668, during the Period of the Three Kingdoms of Koguryo, Paekche, and Silla, someone began recording Korean history. During this time, Buddhism and Confucianism became religions. Around the eleventh and twelfth centuries, the Mongols invaded, and Kublai Khan enlisted Korean men to fight Japan. In 1785, the Koreans banned all forms of Western learning. In 1948, Syngman Rhee became the president of the Republic of (South) Korea, and Kim Il Sung became premier of the Democratic People's Republic of Korea. The Korean War began on June 25, 1950, when the North Koreans attacked across the Thirty-Eighth Parallel; it ended in 1953. In the late 1980s, peace talks began once more. Photographs and reproductions enhance the text. Glossary and Index.

1346. Ndukwe, Pat I. **Fulani**. New York: Rosen, 1996. 64p. $15.95. ISBN 0-8239-1982-X. (Heritage Library of African Peoples. West Africa). 7 up

The text focuses on the land, history, social and political life, Fulani religious beliefs, and their relationship with the other people who live in their region of West Africa. The Fulani are mainly Moslem, and the area they inhabit stretches from northern Nigeria to Mali and the Atlantic coast. Further Reading, Glossary, and Index.

1347. Neimark, Anne E. **Diego Rivera: Artist of the People**. New York: HarperCollins, 1992. 116p. $16.89. ISBN 0-06-021784-7. 3-7

Diego Rivera (1886-1957) expressed his concerns for human dignity in his art. In this fictional biography, Neimark has invented some scenes that she cannot verify, just as Rivera himself fictionalized life with his tales about various experiences as he lived and traveled in Spain, France, the U.S.S.R., the United States, and Mexico. He caused controversy, refusing to compromise his beliefs in his work or his life. Reproductions, Murals, Books for Further Reading, and Index.

1348. Netzley, Patricia D. **Queen Victoria**. San Diego, CA: Lucent, 1996. 128p. $16.95. ISBN 1-56006-063-8. (The Importance Of). 7-9

Queen Victoria (1819–1901) of England led the British Empire during its years of major power, but she was not a vocal supporter of women's rights. Excerpts from her own journals reveal her response to the proposition of marriage from her first cousin, Prince Albert; a condolence letter sent to Mary Todd Lincoln after her husband's assassination; and various other interesting items. Victoria had nine children whose marriages linked the British throne to Russia, Germany, Greece, Denmark, and Romania. Chronology, Further Reading, Notes, and Index.

1349. Newark, Timothy. **Celtic Warriors, 400 B.C.–A.D. 1600** New York: Sterling, Blandford Press, 1988. 160p. $16.95pa. ISBN 0-7137-2043-3pa. YA

The Celtic warriors descended on the British Isles, France, Spain, Italy, Macedonia, and Asia Minor from the Germanic area, fought, and gained control of the areas. As a result of their occupation, people in Ireland, the Scottish Hebrides and Islands, the Isle of Man, Wales, Cornwall, and Brittany spoke the Celtic language into the twentieth century. The text looks at the Celts and their battle strategies in this part of Europe's military history. Index.

1350. Newark, Timothy. **Medieval Warlords**. New York: Blandford Press, 1987. 144p. $19.95. ISBN 0-7137-1816-1. 7 up

In this text, Newark has used medieval chronicles to reconstruct the lives and careers of seven medieval warlords. He tells about Aetius (c. 390–454), conqueror of Attila the Hun; Gaiseric (c. 400–477), the Barbarian pirate of the Mediterranean; An Lu-shan (c. 703–757), a Chinese rebel warlord; Owen of Wales (c. 1335–1378), a mercenary in the Hundred Years' War; Betrand du Guesclin (c. 1320–1380), the famed French warlord; Jan Zizka (c. 1360–1424), the blind leader of the Hussites; and Vlad Dracula (c. 1430–1476), the true prince of Wallachia and a crusader against the Turks. Bibliography and Index.

1351. Newfield, Marcia. **The Life of Louis Pasteur**. Antonio Castro, illustrator. New York: Twenty-First Century, 1991. 80p. $13.98. ISBN 0-941477-67-3. (Pioneers in Health and Medicine). 4-7

When Louis Pasteur (1822-1895) found a treatment for rabies, he was hesitant to try it on a human until he realized that it was the last chance for the man to survive. It worked, but Pasteur worried throughout the course of the treatment about the results. He was a successful teacher who shared his knowledge with his students. His motto was "Onward!" but he made his students challenge any belief that would not stand up to scientific inquiry. On his seventieth birthday, he still asked people to question what they had done with their teaching and if they had served their country. He is the father of microbiology. For Further Reading and Index.

1352. Newman, Robert. **The Case of the Baker Street Irregular**. 1978. Magnolia, MA: Peter Smith, 1984. 200p. $18.75. ISBN 0-8446-6762-5. 3-7

After Andrew's aunt dies, he goes from Cornwall to London with his tutor. The tutor disappears, but Andrew meets Sherlock Holmes, who helps him to find the man and also to reunite with his mother. At age fourteen in the 1890s, Andrew realizes that his mother has not enjoyed their separation and that they will try to stay together while she follows her stage career.

1353. Newman, Robert. **The Case of the Etruscan Treasure**. New York: Atheneum, 1983. 173p. $10.95. ISBN 0-689-30992-9. 3-7

Andrew's mother stars in a New York play in the 1890s, and Andrew and Sara come with her. Inspector Wyatt joins them and they become involved with a crime boss who wants them to help him find files that were removed from a building before arsonists destroyed it.

1354. Newman, Robert. **The Case of the Frightened Friend**. New York: Atheneum, 1984. 168p. $11.95. ISBN 0-689-31018-8. 3-7

When Andrew's school friend fears that someone is trying to kill him at home, Andrew tells his friend from Scotland Yard. They investigate the school friend's late-nineteenth-century London home and stepmother and discover a spy working in an important government office.

1355. Newman, Robert. **The Case of the Indian Curse**. New York: Atheneum, 1986. 168p. $11.95. ISBN 0-689-31177-X. 3-7

Beasley, the friend of Andrew's new stepfather, becomes ill, and Andrew and Sara show concern. After they are both kidnapped, they discover that Thugs from India are trying to kill the person who could reveal their activities to others. They have been drugging Beasley so that he will tell them what he knows. After several serious encounters, they discover and reveal the Thug leader to Scotland Yard.

1356. Newman, Robert. **The Case of the Somerville Secret**. New York: Atheneum, 1981. 184p. $12.95. ISBN 0-689-30825-6. 3-7

Inspector Wyatt needs Andrew and Sara's help to solve the London murder of a former military man in the 1890s. They find a sixteen-year-old child who looks like a monster with six toes and no intelligence. The people who killed Inspector Wyatt's friend are also trying to kill the deformed child for their own personal gain.

1357. Newman, Robert. **The Case of the Threatened King**. New York: Atheneum, 1982. 212p. $10.95. ISBN 0-689-30887-6. 3-7

Someone kidnaps Sara, Andrew's friend, along with the daughter of the Serbian ambassador to England. Inspector Wyatt soon finds out that someone wants to kill the King of Serbia during his visit to London in the late nineteenth century.

1358. Newman, Robert. **The Case of the Vanishing Corpse**. 1980. New York: Atheneum, 1990. 221p. $4.95pa. ISBN 0-689-30755-1pa. 3-7

Because Andrew's mother is an actress, he meets George Bernard Shaw as they dine in London during his summer vacation. On one of his walks with his friend, Sara, he meets the local constable, Peter Wyatt. When Andrew's mother's diamonds disappear, Wyatt helps with the investigation. Then Andrew is drawn into the search for the murderer of a man on their street. A strange priest of an Egyptian religion lives nearby and may be involved with the case.

1359. Newman, Robert. **The Case of the Watching Boy**. New York: Atheneum, 1987. 171p. $13.95. ISBN 0-689-31317-9. 3-7

Andrew and Markham, who met at school, decide to help a woman get her child back, only to find out that the boy is not hers. They discover in the 1890s that the boy is the heir to the Rumanian throne and that the woman is an accomplice plotting with people to get the boy's father to abdicate. Andrew realizes that such situations make the history that used to bore him in school.

1360. Newman, Sharan. **Death Comes as Epiphany**. New York: Tor, 1993. 320p. $19.95. ISBN 0-312-85419-6. New York: Forge, 1995. $4.99pa. ISBN 0-812-52293-1pa. (Catherine LeVendeur, 1). YA

Catherine LeVendeur is the most promising student at the paraclete, which Héloïse, former lover of Abelard, heads. Someone alters the text of a psalter that the paraclete has given to the Abbot of Suger. Héloïse sends Catherine to find out who committed the heresy and why. Catherine finds other mysteries as well in this twelfth-century French setting. *Macavity winner* and *Agatha and Anthony nominee*.

1361. Newman, Sharan. **The Devil's Door**. New York: Forge, 1994. 384p. $21.95; $4.99pa. ISBN 0-312-85420-X; 0-8125-2295-8pa. YA

As a novice in Héloïse's Convent of the paraclete in France during 1140, Catherine LeVendeur wants to find the attacker of a wealthy countess who dies after being brought to the convent for help. Catherine suspects the countess's husband of beating her, but when Catherine's betrothed, Edgar, shows up to take her home, she feels torn between finding the attacker and her impending marriage. Héloïse requests that Catherine go on an important journey for her, so Catherine and Edgar go to Abelard and his son Astrolabe while they wait for the heresy trial against Abelard. After the worst occurs, Catherine and Edgar realize that they must continue to go where they are needed.

1362. Newman, Sharan. **Strong as Death**. New York: Forge, 1996. 384p. $23.95. ISBN 0-312-86179-6. (Catherine LeVendeur, 4). YA

After suffering several miscarriages and the birth of a stillborn child, Catherine LeVendeur has a prophetic dream. She sees Edgar, her husband, and herself beginning a pilgrimage to the monastery of Compostela to petition St. James for a child in 1142. During their journey, they encounter mad monks, crafty crusaders, and pilgrims. Some of the pilgrims are murdered, and Catherine and Edgar must find the murderer, although the discovery threatens both Catherine's life and that of the child she carries.

1363. Newman, Sharan. **The Wandering Arm**. New York: Forge, 1995. 352p. $23.95. ISBN 0-312-85829-9. New York: Tor, 1996. $6.99pa. ISBN 0-8125-5089-7pa. (Catherine LeVendeur, 3). YA

Catherine LeVendeur, once a brilliant student in Héloïse's Paraclete in France around 1135, and her husband Edgar, a Scot, become involved in the illegal trade of religious relics. One trader, who might have possessed the arm of St. Aldhelm of England, has been murdered. Catherine's Jewish relatives are concerned about the progress of the trader Natan Ben Judah's investigation. They all wonder who would want a relic badly enough to kill for it, and Catherine and Edgar must find out. *Agatha Nominee.*

1364. Newth, Mette. **The Abduction**. Tina Nunnally and Steve Murray, translators. New York: Farrar, Straus & Giroux, 1989. 248p. $13.95. ISBN 0-374-30008-9. 9 up

Norwegians take the Inuits Osuqo and Poq from Greenland during the seventeenth century, and kill Poq's brother and father while on board ship. They beat Osuqo into submission and rape Poq. When they reach a Dutch port, a crippled girl, Christine, is horrified that the explorers have mistreated other humans so badly. The story, told in alternating chapters from Christine's and Osuqo's points of view, climaxes with an accusation of witchcraft. The two finally decide that the only way out of their situation is to return to sea, where they expect to die. *School Library Journal Best Book.*

1365. Newton, David E. **James Watson & Francis Crick: Discovery of the Double Helix**. New York: Facts on File, 1992. 130p. $17.95. ISBN 0-8160-2558-4. 6 up

Two scientists, one working in England and the other in America, began to work together to discover how molecules in living bodies could determine biological traits. In 1953, in one of the greatest accomplishments in the history of science, Francis Crick (b. 1916) and James Watson (b. 1928) discovered the DNA molecule. The text looks at their lives, the search, and what the discovery means to science. Glossary, Further Reading, and Index.

1366. Newton, David E. **Tokyo**. New York: New Discovery, 1992. 96p. $14.95. ISBN 0-02-768235-8. (Cities at War). 6-9

In World War II, many Japanese young people enlisted in the military because they wanted to bring honor to their families. When the Allies continued to threaten invasion as the war progressed, people became fearful of the result, and pride was rarely the issue. Bombing of Tokyo began in 1944, but it was spared from the atomic bomb. Photographs, Notes, Further Reading, and Index.

1367. Nicholson, Michael, and David Winner. **Raoul Wallenberg**. Milwaukee, WI: Gareth Stevens, 1989. 68p. $16.95. ISBN 0-55532-820-2. (People Who Have Helped the World). 7-9

Raoul Wallenberg (1912–1945?), a Swede, attended architecture school in the United States. Back in Sweden, he used his ability to speak German, French, Russian, English, and Swedish to join a business importing exotic foods. His employer recommended him to the neutral Swedish government when it wanted someone to go to Hungary to negotiate with its government to keep Jews alive. Much of the text explains Hitler's Aryan theory and anti-Semitism. Diary entries describe the gas chambers, the long marches, and the train rides to death for the Jews. The Bulgarians refused to cooperate with the Nazis, as did the Danes and some of Mussolini's Italian citizens. When Wallenberg arrived in Budapest in 1944, Nazis under Adolf Eichmann had already killed 3 million Polish Jews, and only 230,000 of a Budapest community of 750,000 survived. Wallenberg used fake Swedish passports, called "Schutz-Passen," which fooled the Nazis into thinking that those who held them had immunity. He also established safe houses and bought food. His efforts saved more than 100,000 Jews before the Soviets arrived in January of 1945. They were evidently suspicious of Wallenberg's activities because they did not help him. He disappeared on January 17, 1945, when he went for a meeting with them. Although the Soviets denied it, many think that they imprisoned Wallenberg and that he died there. Organizations, Books, Glossary, Chronology, and Index.

1368. Nickelson, Harry. **Vietnam**. San Diego, CA: Lucent, 1989. 96p. $22.59. ISBN 1-56006-110-3. (Overview). 5 up

The text begins with Vietnam's status as French Indochina during the 1950s and ends with the current situation in the country. It shows the tragedy for all in both words and photographs from news sources and describes how the aftermath of the Vietnam War affected American foreign policy. Bibliography and Index.

1369. Nicolle, David. **Medieval Knights**. New York: Viking, 1997. 48p. $16.99. ISBN 0-670-87463-9. (See Through History). 5-7

The world of medieval knights appears in this text, which includes see-through pages of a knight's chain mail suit of armor, a fortified manor house, a cliffside fortress of the crusaders, and the ships of the seabound knights. Key Dates, Glossary, and Index.

1370. Nivola, Claire A., author/illustrator. **Elisabeth**. New York: Farrar, Straus & Giroux, 1997. 32p. $16. ISBN 0-374-32085-3. 5-7

When a Jewish child has to leave everything at her home in Nazi Germany, including her beloved doll Elisabeth, and cannot return for her, she does not understand. She is lonely without the doll, but based on the author's mother's story, she is ecstatic when one day in an antique shop, she finds Elisabeth.

1371. Noblet, Martine, and Chantal Deltenre. **The Amazon and the Americas**. Maureen Walker, translator. Hauppauge, NY: Barron's, 1995. 77p. $11.95; $6.95pa. ISBN 0-8120-6489-5; 0-8120-9160-4pa. (Tintin's Travel Diaries). 5 up

The text asks thirty questions about the Amazon and the Americas, covering a variety of topics such as what is the "Igapo" and the "Green Hell," who are the Indians, where is the carnival, who were the filibusters, and where did the Caribs live. Illustrations and photographs complement the simple text that appears on the lefthand page and the more scholarly answers on the righthand pages. Glossary, Chronological Chart, Map, Bibliography, and Index.

1372. Nolan, Han. **If I Should Die Before I Wake**. San Diego, CA: Harcourt Brace, 1994. 288p. $16.95. ISBN 0-15-238040-X. 9 up

Hilary, a neo-Nazi, has a motorcycle accident and ends up in a "Jew" hospital, where she is blown back in time to the Holocaust and inhabits the body of someone named Chana. Chana (Hilary) faces the hopelessness and terror of the concentration camps and sees Jews betray other Jews when they think themselves better. After Hilary experiences the Holocaust, she has a different perspective when she returns to the present.

1373. Noonan, Jon. **Captain Cook**. Yoshi Miyake, illustrator. New York: Crestwood House, 1993. 48p. $12.95. ISBN 0-89686-709-9. (Explorers). 4-8

Captain James Cook (1728-1779) made three voyages to the South Seas. He went to Tahiti and Australia on the *Endeavor*, to the Antarctic circle on a second voyage, and to Alaska and Hawaii on his last voyage. When he returned to Hawaii after having been given many gifts upon his first departure, he irritated the islanders, and they attacked him. If Cook had been able to swim, he might have escaped, but he could not, and the islanders killed him. Glossary and Index.

1374. Noonan, Jon. **Ferdinand Magellan**. Yoshi Miyake, illustrator. New York: Crestwood House, 1993. 48p. $12.95. ISBN 0-89686-706-4. (Explorers). 4-8

Ferdinand Magellan (1480?-1521) was always brave as a child and even saved his cousin's life. His character served him well as he sailed from Spain, lost his command, and then found South America. He survived mutiny only to die after reaching the Philippines, but his ship and crew continued the journey around the world. Glossary and Index.

1375. Noonan, Jon. **Marco Polo**. New York: Crestwood House, 1993. 48p. $12.95. ISBN 0-89686-704-8. (Explorers). 4-8

Marco Polo (1254-1324) grew up in Venice while his father, whom he had never met, traveled in the East. After his father returned to Venice, he decided to take Marco with him on the next trip to the East. The text tells of their problems en route to the City of Peace before Polo met the Great Khan in 1275. Polo became an honored member of the household, followed the Mongol customs, and learned to write in four of the languages that the 12,000 members of the household spoke. At that time, China's Great Wall was nearly 1,200 miles long. Polo served the Khan for seventeen years, visiting all areas of Cathay. Glossary and Index.

1376. Noonan, Michael. **McKenzie's Boots**. New York: Orchard, Franklin Watts, 1988. 249p. $13.95. ISBN 0-531-08348-9. 7-10

Rod Murray, age fourteen, enlists in the Australian army in 1941, pretending to be older. He needs to get away from his alcoholic mother and a girl who does not love him as he does her. He has difficulty getting boots large enough as he keeps growing, and he meets a butterfly hunter who also happens to be a Japanese soldier. When Rod takes the man prisoner, he receives an award, but he is uninterested in the award or in hurting anyone. Later, another Japanese soldier kills him and writes on his boot that he was a hero.

1377. Norling, Donna S. **Patty's Journey: From Orphanage to Adoption and Reunion**. Minneapolis, MN: University of Minnesota Press, 1996. 208p. $17.95. ISBN 0-8166-2866-1. YA

When she is four, the state government separates Patty from her indigent mother after her father is caught robbing a store during the Depression to get food for his wife and three children. Patty tries to see her brother and sister, but they go to foster homes where they are maltreated; and she, too, faces serious situations as she grows up, and changes her name. As an adult, she searches for her past and, through the journey, reveals the horrendous lives offered to orphans in the mid-twentieth century.

1378.   Novac, Ana. **Beautiful Days of My Youth**. New York: Henry Holt, 1997. 314p. $15.95. ISBN 0-8050-5018-3. 8 up

During World War II, Novac secretly kept a diary while in the concentration camps of Auschwitz and Plaszow. At fifteen, she was determined to accurately record the horrors of the situation, even if she were the only person ever to read her accounts. Throughout all, she maintained her will to live.

1379.   Nudel, Ida. **A Hand in the Darkness**. Stefani Hoffman, translator. New York: Warner, 1990. 314p. $13.99pa. ISBN 0-446-39325-8pa. YA

After hearing Voice of Israel broadcasts on the radio, Nudel realized that Soviet jails housed Jewish political prisoners and that she wanted to go to Israel. She and her family applied for exit visas to Israel in 1971. They, along with other "Refuseniks," became scapegoats for the Soviet government's problems and suffered harassment. Nudel worked to aid the Jewish prisoners and their families. After she was exiled to Siberia in 1978, her case came to the attention of Armand Hammer, a wealthy American with Soviet ties, who helped her emigrate to Israel. Index.

O

1380. Oakes, Catherine. **The Middle Ages**. Stephen Biesty, illustrator. San Diego, CA: Gulliver, Harcourt Brace, 1989. 28p. $14.95. ISBN 0-15-200451-3. (Exploring the Past). 3-7

Striking color illustrations reveal life during the Middle Ages. The text covers such topics as education and universities; religion and pilgrimages; the life of the nobility with feasts and tournaments; life in the country with the lord and his peasants; life in the towns with people and their homes, clothes, and health; and what was happening in navigation and exploration. Time Chart and Index.

1381. O'Brian, Patrick. **The Commodore**. New York: Norton, 1995. 288p. $22.50; $11.95pa. ISBN 0-393-03760-6; 0-393-31459-6pa. YA

Captain Jack Aubrey and his friend, Stephen Maturin, a surgeon and a spy, spend more time on land than at sea during the early nineteenth century, as they try to find the root of family secrets. Aubrey's wife begins to assert her independence, while Maturin sees his young daughter for the first time. He discovers that she is autistic and that his wife has left him. Aubrey is promoted to commodore and given a fleet of ships, ostensibly to stop slavers out of Africa, although his real mission is to keep the French from Ireland.

1382. O'Brian, Patrick. **Desolation Island**. New York: Norton, 1991. 325p. $22.50; $11.95pa. ISBN 0-393-03705-3; 0-393-30812-Xpa. YA

Captain Jack Aubrey and his friend, Stephen Maturin, a surgeon and a spy, sail on the *Leopold* to Australia during the days of Lord Nelson in the early nineteenth century. In the hold are convicts; above is a beautiful woman who also happens to be a spy.

1383. O'Brian, Patrick. **The Far Side of the World**. New York: Norton, 1992. 366p. $22.50; $11.95pa. ISBN 0-393-03710-X; 0-393-30862-6pa. YA

Captain Jack Aubrey and his friend, Stephen Maturin, a surgeon and a spy, set sail for the Great South Sea and the rounding of Cape Horn in the early nineteenth century during the time of Lord Nelson. Their enemy awaits them.

1384. O'Brian, Patrick. **The Fortune of War**. New York: Norton, 1991. 329p. $22.50; $11.95pa. ISBN 0-393-03706-1; 0-393-30813-8pa. YA

At the outbreak of the War of 1812, Captain Jack Aubrey and his friend, Stephen Maturin, a surgeon and a spy, rush from the Dutch East Indies to England. From there, they go to meet their enemy.

1385. O'Brian, Patrick. **The Golden Ocean: A Novel**. New York: Norton, 1994. 285p. $22.50. ISBN 0-393-03630-8. YA

In this adventure, Peter Palafox faces the perils of the sea in the early nineteenth century.

1386. O'Brian, Patrick. **H. M. S. *Surprise***. New York: Norton, 1991. 379p. $22.50; $11.95pa. ISBN 0-393-03703-7; 0-393-30761-1pa. YA

Captain Jack Aubrey and his friend, Stephen Maturin, a surgeon and a spy, sail on the Indian Ocean during the days of Lord Nelson in the early nineteenth century. There they have to save themselves from a local pirate almost as cunning as they.

1387. O'Brian, Patrick. **The Ionian Mission**. New York: Norton, 1991. 367p. $22.50; $11.95pa. ISBN 0-393-03708-8; 0-393-30821-9pa. YA

Captain Jack Aubrey and his friend, Stephen Maturin, a surgeon and a spy, go to the Greek islands on a serious mission for the British navy in the early nineteenth century. They find their assignment quite hazardous.

1388. O'Brian, Patrick. **The Letter of Marque**. New York: Norton, 1992. 284p. $22.50; $11.95pa. ISBN 0-393-02874-7; 0-393-30905-3pa. YA

Captain Jack Aubrey and his friend, Stephen Maturin, a surgeon and a spy, sail on a mission against the French for the British Navy, during the early nineteenth century, in hope of redeeming Aubrey from disgrace.

1389. O'Brian, Patrick. **Master and Commander**. New York: Norton, 1990. 412p. $22.50; $11.95pa. ISBN 0-393-03701-0; 0-393-30705-0pa. YA

Captain Jack Aubrey and his friend, Stephen Maturin, a surgeon and a spy, fight in the Napoleonic Wars of the early nineteenth century with Lord Nelson. This is the first episode in their exploits.

1390.   O'Brian, Patrick. **The Mauritius Command**. New York: Norton, 1991. 348p. $22.50; $11.95pa. ISBN 0-393-03704-5; 0-393-30762-Xpa. YA

Captain Jack Aubrey of the British Navy and his friend, Stephen Maturin, a surgeon and a spy, go to the Indian Ocean to capture the islands of Reunion and Mauritius from the French. There they face unexpected difficulties in the early nineteenth century.

1391.   O'Brian, Patrick. **Men-of-War: Life in Nelson's Navy**. New York: Norton, 1995. 95p. $23. ISBN 0-393-03858-0. YA

The text gives a factual as well as anecdotal discussion of life in the British Navy during the time of Lord Nelson in the early nineteenth century. Not only does it describe life for the recruit, but it also tells about the daily activities of the highest commander. Index.

1392.   O'Brian, Patrick. **Nutmeg of Consolation**. New York: Norton, 1991. 315p. $22.50; $11.95pa. ISBN 0-393-03032-6; 0-393-30906-1pa. YA

Captain Jack Aubrey and his friend, Stephen Maturin, a surgeon and a spy, along with their crew, are shipwrecked on a remote island in the early nineteenth century. They have only their wrecked schooner from which to fashion a seaworthy vessel as their single means of escape.

1393.   O'Brian, Patrick. **Post Captain**. New York: Norton, 1990. 496p. $22.50; $11.95pa. ISBN 0-393-03702-9; 0-393-30706-9pa. YA

After Captain Jack Aubrey escapes from debtors' prison in France, he and his friend Stephen Maturin, a surgeon and a spy, avoid a mutiny as they pursue their enemies into a harbor held by the French during the days of Lord Nelson in the early nineteenth century.

1394.   O'Brian, Patrick. **The Reverse of the Medal**. New York: Norton, 1992. 287p. $22.50; $11.95pa. ISBN 0-393-03711-8; 0-393-30960-6pa. YA

Captain Jack Aubrey needs the help of his friend, Stephen Maturin, a surgeon and a spy, in the early nineteenth century to escape from the London criminal underground while involved in British government espionage.

1395.   O'Brian, Patrick. **The Surgeon's Mate**. New York: Norton, 1992. 382p. $22.50; $11.95pa. ISBN 0-393-03707-X; 0-393-30820-0pa. YA

In the early nineteenth century, Captain Jack Aubrey and his friend, Stephen Maturin, a surgeon and a spy, find themselves chased by two privateers through the Grand Banks. The fog and the shallow water make their flight especially dangerous.

1396.   O'Brian, Patrick. **Thirteen Gun Salute**. New York: Norton, 1991. 319p. $22.50; $11.95pa. ISBN 0-393-02974-3; 0-393-30907-Xpa. YA

Captain Jack Aubrey and his friend, Stephen Maturin, a surgeon and a spy, sail on the *Diane* as they undertake a British diplomatic mission to keep the Malay princes from joining the French in the early nineteenth century.

1397.   O'Brian, Patrick. **Treason's Harbour**. New York: Norton, 1992. 334p. $22.50; $11.95pa. ISBN 0-393-03709-6; 0-393-30863-4pa. YA

In the early nineteenth century, Captain Jack Aubrey and his friend, Stephen Maturin, a surgeon and a spy, sail in the pirate-infested waters of the Red Sea. When sabotage threatens Aubrey's mission, Maturin uses his cunning to quell the enemy.

1398.   O'Brian, Patrick. **The Truelove**. New York: Norton, 1992. 256p. $22.50; $11.95pa. ISBN 0-393-03109-8; 0-393-31016-7pa. YA

Captain Jack Aubrey and his friend, Stephen Maturin, a surgeon and a spy, rush on the *Surprise* to recapture a British whaler that the French have taken in the Sandwich Islands. Their journey, set in the early nineteenth century, gives them many problems.

1399.   O'Brian, Patrick. **The Unknown Shore**. New York: Norton, 1995. 313p. $23. ISBN 0-393-03859-9. YA

On board the *Wager* are the midshipman Jack Byron and his friend Tobias Barrow. Barrow is so naive that he is unaware of the deep problems they have. This novel details sea life during the early nineteenth century.

1400.   O'Brian, Patrick. **The Wine-Dark Sea**. New York: Norton, 1993. 261p. $22.50; $11pa. ISBN 0-393-03558-1; 0-393-31244-5pa. YA

Captain Jack Aubrey and his friend, Stephen Maturin, a surgeon and a spy, sail across the Great South Sea in pursuit of a valuable prize. What they have to face first are the storms and the icebergs lurking just below the surface of the water.

1401. O'Brien, Steven. **Antonio López de Santa Anna**. New York: Chelsea House, 1992. 100p. $18.95. ISBN 0-7910-1245-X. (Hispanics of Achievement). 8 up

Antonio López de Santa Anna (1794–1876) was a military strategist, politician, and president of Mexico. For thirty years, he was Mexico's most prominent figure. He looked for opportunities and shifted loyalty as necessary to get them. He routed the Texas army at the Alamo, but that army defeated him at San Jacinto in 1836. He then served four terms as president of Mexico, although he was repeatedly ousted and exiled. He may be a traitor, a dictator, or a national hero, depending on the historian one reads. Engravings and reproductions enhance the text. Chronology, Further Reading, and Index.

1402. O'Brien, Steven. **Pancho Villa**. New York: Chelsea House, 1994. 111p. $18.95. ISBN 0-7910-1257-3. (Hispanics of Achievement). 5 up

As one of the Mexican revolutionaries, Pancho Villa (1878–1923) fought to free his country from the Americans during 1910–1920. Some think he was more destructive than constructive in his fight against injustice. The topics include discussions of Villa as desperado, bandit patriot, fugitive, and dictator of the north. Photographs highlight the text. Bibliography, Chronology, and Index.

1403. Ochoa, George. **The Assassination of Julius Caesar**. Englewood Cliffs, NJ: Silver Burdett, 1991. 64p. $16.95. ISBN 0-382-24130-4. (Turning Points in World History). 7 up

Julius Caesar (100–44 B.C.) positioned himself in Rome so that he became the people's choice as leader instead of Pompey. He established a dictatorship while helping Rome to achieve needed physical reforms, but when he wanted to become king, his men decided to murder him. Marc Antony eventually became the new Caesar. Photographs, Reproductions, Suggested Reading, and Index.

1404. O'Dell, Scott. **The Amethyst Ring**. Boston: Houghton Mifflin, 1983. 224p. $14.95. ISBN 0-395-33886-7. 7 up

In the third book of the trilogy beginning with *The Captive* (followed by *The Feathered Serpent*), Carlos (Charles I), the king of Spain, accuses Julian of keeping the king's fifth of gold around 1530. Julian's supporters become lethargic from coca plant chewing, so he cannot defeat Cortés. Julian, however, successfully escapes and joins Pizarro. But Pizarro massacres the followers of the Incan king Atahualpa, and Julian leaves and follows a woman to Machu Picchu, where she rejects him.

1405. O'Dell, Scott. **The Captive**. Boston: Houghton Mifflin, 1979. 244p. $14.95. ISBN 0-395-27811-2. 7 up

In the first of a trilogy, Julian, a seminarian, arrives in the New World from Seville, Spain, in 1506. He realizes that the captain has come for gold rather than to save the heathens, and Julian refuses to keep his share of the loot. The natives, however, think that the blond Julian is the risen Kukulcán, dead for 400 years, come back to life to save them. When Julian sees the power that his disguise gives him over the Mayan priests, the thrill seduces him.

1406. O'Dell, Scott. **Carlota**. 1977. New York: Dell, 1989. 144p. $3.99pa. ISBN 0-440-90928-7pa. 7 up

In 1846, when she is only sixteen years old, Carlota's father dies, and she becomes the mistress of her family's large Mexican ranch. She refuses to continue the family's practice of owning slaves and returns a boy to his Indian tribe; she also refuses to hate the "gringos," knowing that the emotion killed her father.

1407. O'Dell, Scott. **The Feathered Serpent**. Boston: Houghton Mifflin, 1981. 224p. $16.45. ISBN 0-395-30851-8. 7 up

In the second book of the trilogy after *The Captive* and before *The Amethyst Ring*, Julian begins to revive the Mayan City of the Seven Serpents with the advice of the Aztec ruler Montezuma (Montequma) of Tenochtitlán. But Cortés soon arrives, and Julian realizes that Cortés plans to invade the city.

1408. O'Dell, Scott. **The Hawk That Dare Not Hunt by Day**. 1975. Greenville, SC: Bob Jones University Press, 1986. 182p. $6.49pa. ISBN 0-89084-368-6pa. 4-7

Tom and his Uncle Jack smuggle goods into England from Europe. When Tom sells William Tyndale an illegal manuscript of the Bible by Martin Luther in 1524, Tyndale only wants to translate it and let the common people have copies. Tom takes Tyndale to Antwerp to have the translation printed, but another man betrays Tyndale, who is then hung for his crime. After Tyndale's death, the traitor ironically loses everything for his self-serving action.

1409. O'Dell, Scott. **My Name Is Not Angelica**. Boston: Houghton Mifflin, 1989. 130p. $14.95. ISBN 0-395-51061-9. New York: Yearling/Dell, 1990. 130p. $3.99pa. ISBN 0-440-40379-0pa. 5-9

When one of their African tribespeople betrays them, Raisha and her betrothed are captured and taken to St. John's in the Caribbean to be sold into slavery. Her owner gives Raisha the name Angelica, but Raisha hates the name as well as the servitude. In 1733, she joins the slave revolt but refuses to jump off a cliff as the others, including her husband, do when the plantation owners stop the revolt, because she does not want to kill the child growing within her.

1410. O'Dell, Scott. **The Road to Damietta**. Boston: Houghton Mifflin, 1985. 256p. $14.95. ISBN 0-395-38923-2. New York: Fawcett, 1988. 240p. $4.50pa. ISBN 0-449-70233-2pa. YA

In 1225, Ricca is only thirteen years old when she falls in love with Francis. After he transforms into the man known to history as Francis of Assisi, she tries to seduce him, but he refuses. As a speaker of Arabic, she accompanies Francis to Damietta when he tries to negotiate between the Moslems and the Crusaders, and sees that he never wavers from his goal of a better life for the less fortunate.

1411. Odijk, Pamela. **The Aztecs**. Englewood Cliffs, NJ: Silver Burdett, 1990. 47p. $14.95. ISBN 0-382-09887-0. 5-7

As a wandering people, the Aztecs settled Tenocha and the Mexica in the Basin of Mexico around 1168; by the fifteenth and sixteenth centuries, they ruled a large empire in southern Mexico from their capital of Tenochtitlán. Most of the information about them comes from Spanish accounts of Aztec books. The Spanish, however, destroyed any of the documents dealing with the Aztec civilization. Among the topics are the environment, how families lived, food and medicine, clothes, religion and ritual, laws, writing, legends and literature, music and dancing, travel and exploration, wars and battles, inventions and special skills, and the end of the Aztec era. Photographs and reproductions enhance the text. Glossary and Index.

1412. Odijk, Pamela. **The Chinese**. Englewood Cliffs, NJ: Silver Burdett, 1991. 47p. $14.95. ISBN 0-382-09894-3. 5-7

China had one of the most long-lasting and stable civilizations in the world before it changed to Communism in the twentieth century. The Shang and Zhou Dynasties, beginning in 1400 B.C., established China's basic characteristics. Inventions and special skills associated with the culture include silk making, astronomy, metalworking, porcelain, paper, printing, gunpowder, the compass, and the wheelbarrow. Other topics presented include food and medicine, clothes, religion and rituals, law, writing, legends and literature, art and architecture, transportation and communication, and wars and battles. Photographs and reproductions enhance the text. Glossary and Index.

1413. Odijk, Pamela. **The Japanese**. Englewood Cliffs, NJ: Silver Burdett, 1991. 47p. $14.95. ISBN 0-382-09898-6. 5-7

Before the Chinese writing system reached Japan in the fifth century A.D., the Japanese had no written historical records. Information from previous times comes from anthropologists, archaeologists, and legends; the earliest known inhabitants were the Jomon culture in 11,000 B.C. This text looks at life and culture in Japan before it opened to the West in A.D. 1854. Among the topics are the environment, how families lived, food and medicine, clothes, religion and ritual, laws, writing, legends and literature, music and dancing, travel and exploration, wars and battles, inventions and special skills, and the end of this era. Photographs and reproductions enhance the text. Glossary and Index.

1414. Odijk, Pamela. **The Mayas**. Englewood Cliffs, NJ: Silver Burdett, 1990. 48p. $14.95. ISBN 0-382-09890-0. (Ancient World). 5-7

Ancient Mayans lived in what is presently southern Mexico, Belize, Guatemala, Honduras, and western El Salvador. The ancient Mayans were farmers, architects who built pyramids, and artists and goldsmiths. Their social system harmonized with the environment and they believed in and respected the eternity of time. They also had their own calendar. Their formative period occurred from c. 2000 B.C. to A.D. 250 and their classic period from A.D. 250 to A.D. 900. They entered a decline around A.D. 900 and had been in decline for 600 years by the time the Spanish arrived and took power. The text covers a variety of topics about Mayan culture; among them are the environment, how families lived, food and medicine, clothes, religion and ritual, laws, writing, legends and literature, music and dancing, travel and exploration, wars and battles, inventions and special skills, and the end of the civilization. Photographs and reproductions enhance the text. Glossary and Index.

1415. Odijk, Pamela. **The Phoenicians**. Englewood Cliffs, NJ: Silver Burdett, 1989. 47p. $14.95. ISBN 0-382-09891-9. (Ancient World). 5-8

The Phoenicians lived in what is currently Lebanon, parts of Syria, and Israel; their main city was Tyre. The text discusses their civilization, including their land, food, law, arts and architecture, hunting, medicine, clothing, religion, laws, legends, and recreation. Phoenician refugees founded Carthage and fought in the Punic Wars against Rome. Glossary and Index.

1416. Odijk, Pamela. **The Romans**. Englewood Cliffs, NJ: Silver Burdett, 1989. 47p. $14.95. ISBN 0-382-09885-4. (Ancient World). 5-8

The text discusses the civilization of ancient Rome, including hunting, medicine, clothing, religion, laws, legends, recreation, transportation, music, dancing, inventions and special skills, and why the civilization declined. Photographs, diagrams, maps, and reproductions accent the text. Glossary and Index.

1417.   Odijk, Pamela. **The Sumerians**. Englewood Cliffs, NJ: Silver Burdett, 1990. 48p. $14.95. ISBN 0-382-09892-7. (Ancient World). 5-7

The Sumerians, who inhabited the land which today is Iraq, have a history from the beginning of the fourth millennium B.C., the date of the oldest inscribed tablet found at Uruk. This advanced society had much that is still part of civilization today, including libraries. Among the topics in the text are land, flora and fauna of the time, agriculture, how families lived, food and medicine, clothing, religion, laws, writing, legends, art and architecture, transportation and communication, music, wars, and inventions and special skills. Names and places associated with the Sumerians are Ur, Nippur, King Gudea, Ur-Nammu, Girsu, Lugal-Zaggisi, Enheduanna, and Eridu. Photographs and reproductions enhance the text. Glossary and Index.

1418.   Ofosu-Appiah, L. H. **People in Bondage: African Slavery Since the 15th Century**. Minneapolis, MN: Runestone Press, 1993. 112p. $15.95. ISBN 0-8225-3150-X. 7 up

The text begins with ancient civilizations in its historical look at slavery and the position of people who do not have power in a society. It focuses on the African slave trade and its relationship to the New World in the fifteenth century. Churches, governments, and rulers must take the blame for this unsavory practice, because all of them are implicated at one time or another in its advancement. Photographs and drawings augment the text. Index.

1419.   O'Halloran, Maura. **Pure Heart, Enlightened Mind: The Zen Journal and Letters of Maura "Soshin" O'Halloran**. Boston: Charles E. Tuttle, 1994. 311p. $18. ISBN 0-8048-1977-7. YA

Maura O'Halloran took a degree in mathematical economics and sociology from Trinity College, Dublin, Ireland, and then came to America. There she decided to follow the demanding monastic life of Buddhism. In her journal and letters, she does not answer or even question why she made these decisions. Instead, she tells about living this life.

1420.   O'Hara, Elizabeth (Eilís Ní Dhuibhne). **The Hiring Fair**. Chester Springs, PA: Poolbeg, DuFour Editions, 1994. 159p. $8.95pa. ISBN 1-85371-275-2pa. 5-8

In 1890, Sally is twelve and the oldest and most scatterbrained of three children. Her father drowns while fishing, as the rest of the family is enjoying a party. After his death, the family has no income with which to pay the rent on their land in Donegal, Ireland. The mother takes Sally and her sister to a hiring fair where two men hire them to work for six months. Although their situation is unexpected and difficult, their masters generally treat them well, and they save their land. *Bisto Book of the Year Merit Award* and *Irish Children's Book Trust*.

1421.   Ojo, Onukaba A. **Mbuti**. New York: Rosen, 1996. 64p. $15.95. ISBN 0-8239-1998-6. (Heritage Library of African Peoples—Central Africa). 7 up

The text focuses on the land, history, social and political life, and religious beliefs of the pygmy Mbuti, and their relationships with the other people who live in their region of central Africa near the Ituri Forest of northeast Zaire. Further Reading, Glossary, and Index.

1422.   Oleksy, Walter. **Mikhail Gorbachev: A Leader for Soviet Change**. Chicago: Childrens Press, 1989. 152p. $17.27. ISBN 0-516-03265-8. 4 up

Mikhail Gorbachev (b. 1931) came to power in the Soviet Union in 1985 at the death of Konstantin Chernenko. The son of peasants, he ascended to power with little opposition. He was not like the former leaders influenced by Joseph Stalin, and the world expected life to be slightly different in the Soviet Union with his leadership. He was more willing to discuss human rights and was concerned about the economic base of the area. He introduced social, political, and economic reforms that offered people their first hope of change. But the change, which came with difficulty, is still occurring. The text looks at Gorbachev's life and his rise to the top of the Soviet Union. Time Line, Notes, and Index.

1423.   Oleksy, Walter. **Military Leaders of World War II**. New York: Facts on File, 1994. 154p. $17.95. ISBN 0-8160-3008-1. (American Profiles). 8 up

Because World War II involved every major power in the world, the decisions of those who led the U.S. military units became very important. In the Pacific, leaders were Colonel Claire Lee Chennault of the "Flying Tigers"; Lieutenant Colonel Evans Carlson of "Carlson's Raiders"; General Douglas MacArthur of the United States Far East Command; Admiral Chester W. Nimitz, Commander of the United States Pacific Fleet; and Admiral William F. "Bull" Halsey, Commander of the Third Fleet. In Europe were General Dwight D. Eisenhower, Supreme United States Commander in Europe; Jacqueline Cochran, Director of the Women's Air Force Service pilots; General Omar Bradley, Commander of the Second Army and Twelfth Army Corps; Captain Curtis E. LeMay, Army Air Corps Commander in Europe and the Pacific; and General George S. Patton, Jr., Commander, 2nd Armored Division and Third Army. Index.

1424. Oliphant, Margaret. **The Earliest Civilizations**. New York: Facts on File, 1993. 78p. $17.95. ISBN 0-8160-2785-4. (Illustrated History of the World). 4-7

The earliest civilizations of the world included the nomadic hunters of the Stone Age, the Golden Age of Egypt, Troy, and the Mycenaean world, as well as the Minoan society on Crete. The Aryan Indians, further inside Asia, also developed a system of writing. Beautiful illustrations highlight the text. Glossary, Further Reading, and Index.

1425. Oluikpe, Benson O. **Swazi**. New York: Rosen, 1997. 64p. $15.95. ISBN 0-8239-2012-7. (Heritage Library of the African Peoples). 5-8

The Swazi kingdom has a varied history, and the text covers some of the culture, the customs, and the people who have helped the kingdom survive. In the government, the king, queen mother, and the councils have a "checks and balances" system, which keeps one of the groups from having too much power. But a traditional land tenure system no longer seems to work properly. Photographs, Further Reading, Glossary, and Index.

1426. O'Neal, Michael. **King Arthur: Opposing Viewpoints**. San Diego, CA: Greenhaven, 1992. 112p. $14.95. ISBN 0-89908-095-2. (Great Mysteries—Opposing Viewpoints). 6-9

The earliest reference to King Arthur occurs around 600. The question remains as to whether he was real or legendary. The text examines the conflicting evidence about the existence and historical basis of this man. Bibliography and Index.

1427. O'Neal, Michael. **Pyramids: Opposing Viewpoints**. San Diego, CA: Greenhaven, 1995. 96p. $16.95. ISBN 1-56510-216-9. (Great Mysteries—Opposing Viewpoints). 6-9

The first known expedition to explore the Great Pyramid at Giza was that of Al Mamun from the Persian city of Baghdad in A.D. 820. The Great Pyramid, which King Khufu ("Cheops" to the Greeks) had built in the twenty-fifth century B.C., is one of three at this location. Khafre ("Khephren" to the Greeks), Khufu's successor, built a second, and Menkaure ("Mycerinus" to the Greeks) built the third, along with three smaller pyramids for his queens. Topics covered in the text give the various views of scholars and archaeologists about why the pyramids were built—as tombs, public works projects, or scientific instruments. Another curiosity is how they were built. A third concern is the dangers encountered by those who enter them. Many different theories have arisen through the centuries about these immense structures.

1428. Orgel, Doris. **The Devil in Vienna**. 1978. Magnolia, MA: Peter Smith, 1995. 246p. $18.05. ISBN 0-8446-6797-8. New York: Viking, 1988. 246p. $4.99pa. ISBN 0-14-032500-Xpa. 6-8

When Inge is thirteen, in 1938, she misses her best friend, who has recently moved to Munich with her Nazi storm trooper father. When Inge's letters are returned, she does not understand why. Then, when Liselotte comes back to Vienna, after Hitler gains power over the Austrian leader, Schuschnigg, she lets Inge know how serious the situation is for the Jews. Inge begins to see other signs while her mother furtively plans for them to leave the country. *Child Study Children's Book Committee at Bank Street College Award, Association of Jewish Libraries Award, Golden Kite Honor Book,* and *Sydney Taylor Book Award.*

1429. Orlev, Uri. **The Island on Bird Street**. Hillel Halkin, translator. Boston: Houghton Mifflin, 1984. 162p. $14.95; $5.95pa. ISBN 0-395-33887-5; 0-395-61623-9pa. 5 up

Alex, age eleven, hides in the ruins of the Warsaw ghetto after police take his father away during World War II. He has to use his ingenuity to stay alive by searching for food and supplies in empty apartments, and he survives until his father returns almost a year later. *Sydney Taylor Book Award, American Library Association Notable Books for Children,* and *Association of Jewish Libraries Award.*

1430. Orlev, Uri. **The Lady with the Hat**. Hillel Halkin, translator. Boston: Houghton Mifflin, 1995. 183p. $14.95. ISBN 0-395-69957-6. 6 up

Yulek, aged seventeen in 1947, survives in an Italian Zionist training camp, although the rest of his family dies in concentration camps during World War II. Yulek decides to return to his former home in Poland, but when he arrives, he discovers that anti-Semitism still pervades the town. He also hears that an English woman has inquired about his family. He thinks that his Aunt Malka, who left years before to marry a Christian, must be searching for him. He knows neither her married name nor her location. After he tries to find her, he ends up in Palestine running the British blockade. Among the characters who flesh out the novel are residents of the kibbutz where Yulek goes and a Jewish girl who, after hiding in a convent during the war, decides that she wants to become a nun in Jerusalem. *American Library Association Notable Books for Children, American Library Association Notable Books for Young Adults,* and *Mildred L. Batchelder Award.*

1431. Orlev, Uri. **Lydia, Queen of Palestine**. Hillel Halkin, translator. Boston: Houghton Mifflin, 1993. 170p. $13.95. ISBN 0-395-65660-5. New York: Puffin, 1995. 170p. $3.99pa. ISBN 0-14-037089-7pa. 4-8

During World War II, Lydia, age ten, goes from her mother's home in Bucharest, Romania, to Palestine to join her father, after he sends a message to let them know that he has arrived safely. Although the Nazi threat is real, Lydia is more upset that her father has remarried. She has to adjust to her new status with him as well as to life on the kibbutz. When her mother finally arrives safely via Turkey, Lydia has to face her mother's new husband as well. By 1944, Lydia realizes that her situation is unpleasant but not the worst that could happen.

1432.　Orlev, Uri. **The Man from the Other Side**. Hillel Halkin, translator. Boston: Houghton Mifflin, 1991. 186p. $13.95. ISBN 0-395-53808-4. 7 up

Marek, age fourteen, participates in the anti-Semitism rampant in Poland during World War II, until he finds out that his own father was Jewish. When he hears this, he starts helping Jews instead, and he begins to understand that his anti-Semitic stepfather, a sewer worker, has been covering up his real beliefs so that he can help the Jews. After Marek hides the Jew Jozek in the city, Jozek wants to return to the Warsaw ghetto at the beginning of the uprising. When Marek guides him through the sewers, he finds himself in the fighting. *Bulletin Blue Ribbon Book, Mildred L. Batchelder Award, National Jewish Awards, American Library Association Notable Children's Book,* and *School Library Journal Best Book.*

1433.　Osborn, Kevin. **The Peoples of the Arctic**. New York: Chelsea House, 1990. 111p. $15.95. ISBN 0-87754-875-5. (Peoples of North America). 5 up

Starting with the past, the text and accompanying photographs present information about the Inuits, their lives, and their history as the first Americans. By seeing their landscape, one gains a feeling for the culture and its timelessness. Further Reading and Index.

1434.　Osman, Karen. **The Italian Renaissance**. San Diego, CA: Lucent, 1996. 112p. $16.95. ISBN 1-56006-237-1. (World History). 7 up

The Renaissance in Italy, according to this text, spans a time from 1375 to 1625. The book discusses the seeds of the Renaissance, Humanism, the early Renaissance in Florence, the art and architecture of the early Renaissance, Rome and the French invasions of Italy, three great artists of the High Renaissance (Leonardo da Vinci, Michelangelo, and Raphael), and the late Renaissance. Notes, For Further Reading, Works Consulted, and Index.

1435.　O'Sullivan, Mark. **Melody for Nora**. Chester Springs, PA: Dufour, Wolfhound, 1995. 217p. $8.95pa. ISBN 0-86327-425-0pa. 7-10.

In 1922, after Nora's mother dies, her father divides the children among relatives in Ireland. Nora, at the age of fourteen, has already become a gifted pianist, and resents having to live in Tipperary instead of Dublin. She becomes involved with the hostilities in the area through her uncle, who supports the government forces, and his brother on the opposite side, who prefers the Irregulars. Her story and situation show the civil war in Ireland that resulted after Ireland's independence from England.

1436.　Otfinoski, Steven. **Alexander Fleming: Conquering Disease with Penicillin**. New York: Facts on File, 1992. 116p. $17.95. ISBN 0-8160-2752-8. (Makers of Modern Science). 8 up

In 1922, Alexander Fleming (1881–1955) discovered an antibiotic after experimenting with bacterial cultures. He saw a blue mold growing and killing the bacteria around it. Because the mold's name was *Penicillium*, he called the antibiotic "penicillin." This breakthrough in science did not benefit humans for another twenty years, but its use in World War II saved many lives. Otfinoski indicates that Fleming lived a "tidy" life, a fact that most likely helped him make one of the foremost scientific discoveries in history. Glossary, Further Reading, and Index.

1437.　Otfinoski, Steven. **Joseph Stalin: Russia's Last Czar**. Brookfield, CT: Millbrook Press, 1993. 128p. $15.90. ISBN 1-56294-240-9. 7-10

Even after death, Joseph Stalin (1879–1953) caused chaos. During his funeral procession on March 9, 1953, hundreds of people died in the frenzy surrounding his coffin. During the twenty-five years of his rule, Stalin had decreed the deaths of 40 million people, most of them Soviets. He raised himself to the level of god in his country, and for whatever reasons, many seemed to idolize him. The text looks at this man, once a choirboy, who caused the murders of more people than anyone in history. Chronology, Notes, Bibliography, and Index.

1438.　Otfinoski, Steven. **Nelson Mandela: The Fight Against Apartheid**. Brookfield, CT: Millbrook Press, 1992. 128p. $16.40. ISBN 1-56294-067-8. 7 up

In this biography of Nelson Mandela (b. 1918), Otfinoski also includes background about the practice of apartheid in South Africa, which denied blacks their rights for many years. After World War II, the country tightened its system as other African nations were gaining their freedom. Mandela served in prison for twenty-seven years after trying to aid his people. Chronology, Notes, Bibliography, and Index. *Child Study Association Children's Books of the Year.*

1439. Otto, Whitney. **The Passion Dream Book**. New York: HarperCollins, 1997. 276p. $22. ISBN 0-06-017824-8. YA

In Renaissance Florence, Guilietta Marcel is an artist, trained by her father, who can never be recognized because she is female. Instead, she spies on Michelangelo and relates bits of information to others who pay her for it. A box she designs becomes a memento passed down through the generations until it reaches her descendant, Romy March, who has her own problems with acceptance in the early 1900s when she falls in love with an African American.

1440. Overton, Jenny. **The Ship from Simnel Street**. New York: Greenwillow, 1986. 144p. $10.25. ISBN 0-688-06182-6. 6-9

Polly runs away from her English home during the Peninsula War to find the soldier she loves. Her father goes after her, and her mother and another person have to keep the family bakery working while they are gone. Everything that happens connects to the cakes that the family bakes, such as hot cross buns for Easter, cradle cake for babies, and simnel cake for mother's day. All return safely, with Polly married to her soldier.

1441. Oz, Amos. **Soumchi: A Tale of Love and Adventure**. Quint Buchholz, illustrator; Amos Oz and Penelope Farmer, translators. 1980. San Diego, CA: Harcourt Brace, 1993. 71p. $10pa. ISBN 0-15-600193-4pa. YA

Soumchi, age eleven and living in British-occupied Jerusalem just after World War II, is delighted with the bicycle his uncle gives him, even though it is a girl's bicycle. He ignores the jeers of others and dreams that he is riding toward the heart of Africa. He shows the bicycle to his friend, who wants to trade his new train set for it. Soumchi accepts the trade, and then gets involved with a neighborhood bully, a dog, and locks himself out. At the same time he loves Esthie, who knows that he has written a love poem for her. As he says, things change, and they do before the story ends.

1442. Ozment, Steven. **The Bürghermeister's Daughter: Scandal in a Sixteenth-Century German Town**. New York: St. Martin's Press, 1996. 227p. $23.95. ISBN 0-312-13939-X. YA

Anna Büschler, daughter of a merchant in the town of Hall in Swabia during the sixteenth century, found employment during her later teen years as a servant in a nearby castle. While there, she began a relationship with a younger nobleman that she named Erasmus. When Anna's mother died in 1520, Anna returned home and began to dress in ways questionable to the townspeople—they could see her naked body under her clothes. When her father discovered that she was having not one, but two affairs (one with Erasmus), he turned her out of the house. After several years, she decided to take him to court for her inheritance. Though she accepted his offer of settlement at first, she then decided that she did not like it, and went to court again several more times. She married, and her husband died about the same time as her father. During her earlier years, she carried on a correspondence with her two lovers, and through those letters, the kinds of relationships either possible or not possible because of social status become clear. She and Erasmus had no future because of his superior status, but she and her other lover were equals who shared similar problems. The text shows her in her time and her country. Bibliography and Index.

P

1443. Paiewonsky, Michael. **Conquest of Eden, 1493-1515**. 1991. Chicago: Academy, 1993. 176p. $34.95 ISBN 0-926330-04-7. YA

Paiewonsky uses reports and letters of Spanish explorers to reveal their lust for gold and their willingness to destroy the native life in the New World to get it after Columbus's initial voyage in 1492. The text looks at the significance of Columbus's "discovery," and the resulting destruction of native peoples in St. Croix during 1515. It includes Columbus's letter to Queen Isabella describing the beauty and the wealth of the area as well as the journals and logs of Columbus's sons and brothers telling of the Indians' reactions to intruders, the disappearance of exploring parties, meetings with cannibals, and the cruel treatment of Indians who interfered with the collection of wealth for the Spanish crown. Woodcuts, engravings, and photographs complement the text. Bibliography and Index.

1444. Palmer, Colin A. **The First Passage: Blacks in the Americas, 1502-1617**. New York: Oxford University Press, 1995. 126p. $21. ISBN 0-19-508699-6. (Young Oxford History of African Americans). 7 up

In an attempt to discuss all slaves in the first of an 11-volume series, the text talks about the differences among African cultures and how those who were enslaved had to change their traditions and religions. It centers on slaves in Peru, Brazil, and Mexico who might also have been miners or pearl fishers instead of domestic field hands. Black-and-white reproductions enhance the text. Bibliography and Index.

1445. Parenteau, John. **Prisoner for Peace: Aung San Suu Kyi and Burma's Struggle for Democracy**. Greensboro, NC: Morgan Reynolds, 1994. 151p. $18.95. ISBN 1-883846-05-6. (Champions of Freedom). 7-10

In 1947, Aung San's father was assassinated in Burma (Myanmar); she was two years old. Since then, she has tried to expose the country's corrupt government. Her efforts won her a Nobel Peace Prize before she returned home from England in 1988. Her story, however, has not ended, nor has peace reached her country. Photographs enhance the text. Bibliography, Glossary, and Index.

1446. Paris, Erna. **The End of Days: A Story of Tolerance, Tyranny, and the Expulsion of the Jews from Spain**. Amherst, NY: Prometheus, 1995. 327p. $28.95. ISBN 1-57392-017-7. 7 up

In the fifteenth century, Spain degenerated from a place where Christians, Jews, and Moors could live together into the narrow terror of the Spanish Inquisition. Paris traces 200 years of Spanish history to show the changes that occurred before the plague that killed 30 percent of Europe's population and on which citizens began to blame non-Christians. Paris also discusses the motives of the inquisitors, their actions, and the fates of the accused, along with the actual expulsion of the Jews in 1492. Bibliography and Index.

1447. Parker, Steve. **Aristotle and Scientific Thought**. New York: Chelsea House, 1995. 32p. $14.95. ISBN 0-7910-3004-0. (Science Discoveries). 4-8

In a presentation of Aristotle's life, the text first notes the Greek philosophers who came before Aristotle (384-322 B.C.). Aristotle studied at Plato's academy and became interested in many things, including nature. He was the first naturalist to categorize living things as vertebrates or invertebrates. He studied the sea animals and characterized aspects of human anatomy. He also began his own school at the Lyceum in 334 B.C. The final topic is Aristotle's legacy and the timeline of his world. Photographs and reproductions enhance the text. Glossary and Index.

1448. Parker, Steve. **Charles Darwin and Evolution**. New York: Chelsea House, 1995. 32p. $14.95. ISBN 0-7910-3007-5. (Science Discoveries). 5-9

The text, with complementary photographs and reproductions, looks at the life of Charles Darwin (1809-1882). His early years, spent collecting things in nature, and his five-year trip on the *Beagle* helped him to develop his theory that all things survive because of natural selection. *The Origin of Species* shocked many because it denied the stories in the Bible. Others, however, realized that his research was reasonable, and in ensuing years, his theory became a practical basis for scientists who began to ask about the purpose of everything and how these things might help survival and reproduction. World in Darwin's Time, Glossary, and Index.

1449. Parker, Steve. **Galileo and the Universe**. Tony Smith, illustrator. New York: Chelsea House, 1995. 32p. $14.95. ISBN 0-7910-3008-3. (Science Discoveries). 4-8

When he was seventeen, Galileo thought that he might become a doctor. One day, as he watched a lamp swing back and forth, he realized that whether it swung a long way or only slightly, it took the same amount of time. He then became interested in physics and mathematics and gave up medicine. When he concluded that the sun was not the center of the universe, and refused to stop writing about this discovery, the powerful Church imprisoned him. The text looks at Galileo in the context of his times and at his legacy to astronomy. The World in Galileo's Time, Glossary, and Index.

1450. Parker, Steve. **Guglielmo Marconi and Radio**. New York: Chelsea House, 1995. 32p. $14.95. ISBN 0-791-03009-1. (Science Discoveries). 3-7

Guglielmo Marconi (1874-1937) began experimenting with radio waves in 1890; by 1895, he could send signals with a directional antenna several kilometers away. Because the radio waves traveled through air, the system became known as "wireless communication." Marconi made his equipment more and more powerful, so that by 1920 radio messages could circle the globe. Without his tests of radio waves in the attic of the Bologna, Italy, villa in which his family lived, the development of television and radar might have been delayed. When he died, radio stations around the world went silent for two minutes. The World in Marconi's Time, Glossary, and Index.

1451. Parker, Steve. **Isaac Newton and Gravity**. New York: Chelsea House, 1995. 32p. $14.95. ISBN 0-7910-3010-5. (Science Discoveries). 3-7

Isaac Newton (1642-1727) made revolutionary advances in gravity, forces, motion, mechanics, astronomy, and mathematics. He drew together many theories that had appeared in science and showed that seemingly different events and processes had the same underlying causes. His basic framework for the physical sciences lasted for 200 years. He has been called "the culminating fighter in the Scientific Revolution of the seventeenth century." Glossary and Index.

1452. Parker, Steve. **Louis Pasteur and Germs**. New York: Chelsea House, 1995. 32p. $14.95. ISBN 0-7910-3002-4. (Science Discoveries). 3-7

Louis Pasteur (1822-1895) founded the science of microbiology, which is the study of living things, such as bacteria and viruses, that are visible only with the aid of a microscope. His research made advances possible in medicine, public health, and hygiene; he initiated vaccinations and invented the pasteurization of milk. The text looks at Pasteur in terms of his times and of his work. Glossary and Index.

1453. Parker, Steve. **Marie Curie and Radium**. New York: Chelsea House, 1995. 32p. $14.95. ISBN 0-7910-3011-3. (Science Discoveries). 3-7

Marie Curie (1867-1934) helped to start the atomic age with her work on radioactive elements. She discovered radium while struggling against a lack of money and recognition, illness, and those who believed that women could not be real scientists. The winner of two Nobel Prizes, she is one of the pioneers of science. Photographs and reproductions complement the text. The World in Marie Curie's Time, Glossary, and Index.

1454. Parotti, Phillip. **Fires in the Sky**. New York: Ticknor & Fields, 1990. 250p. $19.95. ISBN 0-89919-930-5. YA

Dymas, age nineteen, is a Trojan warrior who helps Troy win the Mysian Wars with a victory at Cyme. His elevated status enables him to meet Hecuba, the queen of Troy, who involves him in palace intrigues that weaken Troy's defenses. Dymas discovers that Greece has created a supply base on Scyros, which indicates that Greece will soon attack Troy. But Dymas knows that Troy is not yet ready to fight again.

1455. Parris, Ronald. **Rendille**. New York: Rosen, 1994. 64p. $15.95. ISBN 0-8239-1763-0. (Heritage Library of African Peoples). 5-8

As a small group of desert dwellers in Kenya, the Rendille have a reputation for being able to survive in harsh conditions. They divide into two distinct groups, cattle herders or farmers, with each group having its own customs. The text looks at the people, their society, their daily life, customs and rituals, European contact, and social change. Photographs, boxed sidebar information, and maps enhance the text. Glossary, Further Reading, and Index.

1456. Partnow, Elaine, comp. and ed. **The New Quotable Woman**. Rev. ed. New York: Facts on File, 1992. 714p. $40. ISBN 0-8160-2134-1. YA

Some 15,000 quotations represent 2,500 women. The entries are arranged in chronological order according to the birth year of the woman quoted. Within years, entries are alphabetical. Perhaps as helpful and interesting as the quotes are the indices, which include a biographical index, a subject index, an occupation index, and an index of nationality and ethnicity.

1457. Pascoe, Elaine. **Mexico and the United States: Cooperation and Conflict**. New York: Twenty-First Century Books, 1996. 126p. $17.98. ISBN 0-8050-4180-X. 7 up

Pascoe recounts the relations between Mexico and the United States from the Spanish colonial period to 1996. She gives a detailed history of Mexico in a clear narrative that gives much important background for understanding conflicts. Chronology, Further Reading, and Index.

1458. Pascoe, Elaine. **Neighbors at Odds: U.S. Policy in Latin America**. New York: Franklin Watts, 1990. 128p. $21.20. ISBN 0-531-10903-8. YA

Pascoe traces the path of the relationship between the United States and Latin America, beginning with the Monroe Doctrine. She presents various viewpoints, from countries that think the United States has controlled all their policy to those that are thankful for the aid they have received. She shows that Latin America became more discontented while the United States responded inconsistently during the Reagan years. Although the book is outdated, it is a good basis for study of the past few years and any change of stance that has occurred in the U.S. government toward Latin America. Annotated Bibliography and Index.

1459. Paterson, Katherine. **The Master Puppeteer**. Haru Wells, illustrator. 1975. New York: HarperCollins, 1991. 180p. $14.89; $4.50pa. ISBN 0-690-04905-6; 0-06-440281-9pa. 7 up

Jiro, apprentice to the harsh master of the puppet theater, Yoshida, wants to find the identity of Saber, the bandit who robs from the rich to feed the poor during the famine in Japan. In the eighteenth century, Jiro and Acedia's son become friends and share concerns about the starving people outside of the theater. When they see family members among the group, they become especially distressed. *National Book Award for Children's Literature Winner, American Library Association Notable Children's Books of 1976–1980,* and *School Library Journal Best Books.*

1460. Paterson, Katherine. **Of Nightingales That Weep**. Haru Wells, illustrator. 1974. New York: Trophy, HarperCollins, 1989. 172p. $4.50pa. ISBN 0-06-440282-7pa. 5 up

Taiko, age eleven, likes to remember her samurai father instead of the ugly potter that her mother married after her father's death. She is happy to serve the child emperor at the Heike imperial court with her beauty and her lovely singing voice. After several years, her talents intrigue Hideo, an enemy Genji spy, and she refuses to come home to help her pregnant mother and stepfather. When she does return, her mother and brother have died, and an accident scars her face. She can no longer expect to return to Hideo, and she begins to see the inner beauty of the potter. *Phoenix Award* and *American Library Association Notable Children's Books of 1971-1975.*

1461. Paterson, Katherine. **Rebels of the Heavenly Kingdom**. New York: Lodestar, Dutton, 1983. 230p. $14.99. ISBN 0-525-66911-6. New York: Puffin, 1995. 230p. $3.99pa. ISBN 0-14-037610-0pa. YA

Wang Lee finds himself rescued from kidnappers by a group of people dedicated to overthrowing the hated Manchu emperor of China. The group, including women with unbound feet, want to be free in a new age of the Heavenly Kingdom of Great Peace. They instigate the Taiping Rebellion and fight from 1850 to 1853. Wang has to kill when he prefers not to, and Mei Lin has to free herself, first from the imperial soldiers and then from this group whose Christian values change to Communist ideals.

1462. Paterson, Katherine. **The Sign of the Chrysanthemum**. Peter Land, illustrator. 1973. New York: Crowell, 1991. 132p. $14.95. ISBN 0-690-73625-8. New York: Trophy, HarperCollins, 1988. 128p. $4.50pa. ISBN 0-06-440232-0pa. 7 up

Muna wanders around the city in 1170 to find his father after his mother dies. He meets a man whom he likes, but the man is a disreputable, unemployed samurai—a *ronin*. The ronin wants Muna to report to him about the movements of the Gengi and Heike while he works for a sword maker who refuses to arm men deemed unworthy of his efforts. When Muna decides to stop informing the ronin, the sword maker appoints him as an apprentice.

1463. Paton Walsh, Jill. **A Chance Child**. 1978. New York: Sunburst, Farrar, Straus & Giroux, 1991. 192p. $3.95pa. ISBN 0-374-41174-3pa. 5 up

In alternating chapters, Creep's life is contrasted with that of Christopher and his sister, Pauline. Creep lives in the 1820s in the sordid mining community, and Christopher, living in the present, thinks that Creep is his half brother. This view of the 1820s would not be so real to Christopher if his sister Pauline did not also know Creep.

1464. Paton Walsh, Jill. **The Dolphin Crossing**. 1967. New York: Yearling Books/Dell, 1990. 133p. $3.50pa. ISBN 0-440-40310-3pa. 7 up

After John, age seventeen, meets an evacuee from London, they sail John's boat, *The Dolphin*, across the English Channel in World War II to transport soldiers from Dunkirk, France, during a German invasion. John lies unconscious for three days after being shot, and his friend takes the boat back alone. When he does not return, John mourns the loss but realizes that his friend wanted to help others still stranded in Dunkirk.

1465. Paton Walsh, Jill. **The Emperor's Winding Sheet**. 1974. New York: Farrar, Straus & Giroux, 1992. 288p. $4.95pa. ISBN 0-374-42121-8pa. 7 up

When Piers shipwrecks off the coast of Constantinople, he ends up at the court of the Emperor Constantine XI, just before the Turks defeat him and end the Eastern Roman Empire in 1453. Because Piers comes to admire Constantine, he stays with the ex-emperor after the defeat, even though Constantine has given him his freedom.

1466. Paton Walsh, Jill. **Fireweed**. 1970. New York: Farrar, Straus & Giroux, 1988. 144p. $3.50pa. ISBN 0-374-42316-4pa. 6 up

Bill, age fifteen, hates being evacuated to Wales during World War II, so he returns to London. His aunt's house has been bombed, and it is off limits. He meets Julie, a girl whose family thinks she is dead because Germans sank the ship on which she supposedly sailed to Canada. The two sleep in bomb shelters and do odd jobs before setting up house in a bombed area looking after a young orphan boy.

1467. Paton Walsh, Jill. **Grace**. New York: Farrar, Straus & Giroux, 1992. 256p. $16; $5.95pa. ISBN 0-374-32758-0; 0-374-42792-5pa. YA

When Grace and her father see a shipwreck from their lighthouse in 1838, they decide to risk the high waves of the storm to save the people they see hanging from a rock before the next tide washes in. Strangers hear about Grace's heroism and send her money and gifts. She begins to misinterpret her own reasons for the rescue and thinks that she must have done it because she was greedy. The fear that greed might be her motivation weakens her so much that consumption invades her body and kills her.

1468. Paton Walsh, Jill. **A Parcel of Patterns**. New York: Farrar, Straus & Giroux, 1983. 139p. $11.95; $3.95pa. ISBN 0-374-35750-1; 0-374-45743-3pa. YA

Mall, age sixteen, watches helplessly in 1665 as people in her small village die after the plague arrives from London in a damp package of dress patterns. She tries to save her family and friends, as well as her fiancé, by having someone tell him that she has died, so that he will not come to town and contract the disease. Her plan fails when he comes anyway, despondent over her supposed death. He does get sick and die, the very thing that Mall had tried to avoid.

1469. Patterson, Charles. **The Oxford 50th Anniversary Book of the United Nations**. New York: Oxford University Press, 1995. 237p. $40. ISBN 0-19-508280-X. 7 up

The text gives the history of the United Nations by discussing the various attempts in history to establish such a body before the current United Nations was chartered in 1945. Chapters include peacekeeping missions, disarmament and arms control, helping to establish human rights, the appearance of new nations, international law, and the specialized agencies within the body. Photographs highlight the text. Further Reading and Index.

1470. Paulsen, Gary. **Eastern Sun, Winter Moon**. San Diego, CA: Harcourt Brace, 1993. 244p. $11. ISBN 0-15-600203-5pa. YA

Gary Paulsen writes this strong story of his childhood at nine, during World War II, when he went with his mother to live with his military father in the Philippines. The sense of life from a child's microcosmic view of the war raging around him is unsentimental in the telling. Author of books that include *Dogsong*, *Call Me Francis Tucker*, and *The Rifle,* he survived his childhood by realizing that everything stays the same while everything changes. Nothing ever ends.

1471. Pausewang, Gudren. **The Final Journey**. Patricia Crampton, translator. New York: Viking, 1996. 160p. $14.99. ISBN 0-670-86456-0. 8 up

Alice Dubsky, eleven, has spent two years hiding in a basement until Nazis discover her. She boards a train car crammed with fifty people. On the trip, she realizes that her parents must have taken the same journey several months before. Since her parents and grandparents kept her sheltered from the situation, she slowly begins to understand the severity of her situation. In the train car, she sees her grandfather die and watches a baby being born in the excrement. People outside the train do nothing to help when they stop in the local stations, and one passenger in the train is shot for trying to escape. When Alice arrives at Auschwitz, she goes to the left with the children and the old to strip for the showers. *Booklist Best Books for Young Adults, Bulletin Blue Ribbon Book,* and *American Library Association Notable Books for Young Adults*

1472. Paxson, Diana L. **The Dragons of the Rhine**. New York: AvoNova, Morrow, 1995. 371p. $23. ISBN 0-688-13986-8. YA

In the sequel to *The Wolf and the Raven,* Sigfrid Sigmundson, a warrior and shape-shifter, has killed Fafnar, and the court of Burgund (called the Dragons of the Rhine) has welcomed him. Gundohar, the Burgund lord, proclaims Sigfrid to be a blood brother. A witch causes Sigfrid to fall in love with the princess Gudrun and betray his love Brunahild, who waits for him with a girl child born after Sigfrid's departure. Sigfrid returns, defeats Brunahild, and brings her to marry the Burgund king. A Walkyrja, she plots revenge for this insult.

1473. Paxson, Diana L. **The Wolf and the Raven: A Novel**. 1993. New York: Avon, 1994. 320p. $5.99pa. ISBN 0-380-76562-8pa. YA

During the fifth century in Europe, an enemy abducts Brunahild, a Hun princess, and instructs her in the art of sorcery. She meets Sigfrid, a royal family son apprenticed to a smith, in the first of a trilogy retelling the *Nibelungenlied* legend. The historical account of the times, even if the characters have names known in mythology, makes this an intriguing story.

1474. Paxson, Diana L., and Adrienne Martine-Barnes. **Master of Earth and Water**. New York: AvoNova/Morrow, 1993. 395p. $32. ISBN 0-688-12505-0. YA

In the first chronicle of his life, Finn MacCumhaill (Fionn mac Cumhal) is born in Ireland (Eriu), and two women rush to take him away so that the most powerful Druid will not destroy him. He learns from Bodbmall about nature and from Liath Luachra how to survive. On Beltane, when he discovers his parentage, he has to kill, in self-defense, to become the prophet, poet, warrior, and outlaw of third-century Ireland.

1475. Paxson, Diana L., and Adrienne Martine-Barnes. **The Shield Between the Worlds**. New York: AvoNova/Morrow, 1994. 317p. $22. ISBN 0-688-13176-X. YA

At twenty-four, Fionn mac Cumhal has already been the subject of legends in Eriu (Ireland). He falls in love with Sadh, but she must suffer because his grandfather wants to get at him through her. When he escapes the Otherworld after seven years, he finds his son, Oisin, and again thwarts the Dark Druid, in this second chronicle of his third-century life.

1476. Pearson, Anne. **Ancient Greece**. New York: Knopf, 1992. 63p. $20. ISBN 0-679-81682-8. (Eyewitness). 6-9

To give an understanding of Greek art, architecture, and artifacts, illustrations accompany the text. Topics covered in double-page spreads include Minoan and Mycenaean civilization, Athenian politics, mythology, religion, women's lives, childhood, games, food and drink, theater, hygiene, clothing, sports, art, agriculture, trade, crafts, warfare, science and medicine, philosophy, death and the afterlife, Alexander the Great, and Hellenism. Index.

1477. Pearson, Anne. **The Vikings**. New York: Viking, 1994. 48p. $15.99. ISBN 0-670-85834-X. 6-8

Two-page discussions present many subjects that reveal Viking life. In addition to the normal illustrations are four transparent overlays which, when lifted, reveal the inside of a house, a ship, a church, and the location of items in the Oseberg ship find. The topics covered are fame, kings, freemen and slaves, farming and food, hunting and fishing, families, holidays, clothes, arts and crafts, ships, trade, weapons and warfare, death and burial, law, settlers, gods, the coming of Christianity, sagas and runes, and the end of the Viking era. Key Dates, Glossary, and Index.

1478. Pearson, Kit. **The Lights Go on Again**. New York: Viking, 1994. 201p. $13.99. ISBN 0-670-84919-7. 5-8

In this sequel to *The Sky Is Falling* and *Looking at the Moon*, as the end of World War II nears, Norah, age fifteen, and Gavin, age ten, are preparing to return to England from Toronto when they receive word that their parents have been killed by a bomb. Their grandfather comes to Canada to get them, but Gavin decides that he wants to stay with his Aunt Florence, the woman who has cared for him throughout the war and of whom he has grown very fond. When Gavin begins to remember facets of his childhood, though, he changes his mind and returns to England. He finds a country in need, unlike the wealthy Canadian home he has left, but he tries to adjust.

1479. Pearson, Kit. **Looking at the Moon**. New York: Viking, 1992. 212p. $12.95. ISBN 0-670-84097-1. 5-9

In the sequel to *The Sky Is Falling,* Norah and her Canadian "family" spend the summer of 1944 at their lake cottage. She becomes moody and difficult in her third Canadian summer, but she does not realize that her feelings relate to the changes in her body. Otherwise, she has adjusted to this different environment.

1480. Pelgrom, Els. **The Acorn Eaters**. Johanna H. Prins and Johanna W. Prins, translators. New York: Farrar, Straus & Giroux, 1997. 211p. $16. ISBN 0-374-30029-1. 8 up

Santiago leaves school at eight to forage for his family, surviving with other Andalusian cave dwellers after the Spanish Civil War. His jobs for the next six years take him into the countryside, allowing him to contrast the wealthy clergy and the landholders who kill peasants poaching on their lands to the people in his situation.

1481. Pelgrom, Els. **The Winter When Time Was Frozen**. Maryka Rudnik and Raphel Rudnik, translators. New York: Morrow, 1980. 253p. $12.88. ISBN 0-688-32247-6. 6-10

During the winter of 1944-1945, Noortje, age eleven, and her father stay on a Dutch farm with several other people. The food disappears more rapidly than it should for the number of people in the house who are eating it, and Noortje finds out that the farm's owner is feeding a Jewish family hiding in a nearby cave. When a baby is born in the cave, they take it inside before the Nazis discover the family. When the war ends, after a horrible period with V-1 bombs exploding, the baby's uncle says that all of the family died in a concentration camp. *Mildred L. Batchelder Award.*

1482. Pelta, Kathy. **Discovering Christopher Columbus: How History Is Invented**. Minneapolis, MN: Lerner, 1991. 112p. $19.95. ISBN 0-8225-4899-2. 6-9

The text looks at the life of Christopher Columbus and his voyages beginning in 1492 and ending in 1506. Additional chapters examine the historical response to his discovery in the subsequent centuries. An ending chapter titled "You, the Historian" shows how information can be disseminated, even when it is wrong, because historians copy what another historian has written without trying to get the information from as original a source as possible. Sometimes even primary sources are unreliable. Pelta comments about a letter from Columbus that washed ashore in a barrel. It would have been interesting, except that it was written in modern English, a language that was not even spoken during Columbus's lifetime. Sources and Information. *Notable Children's Trade Books in the Field of Social Studies* and *American Library Association Notable Books for Children.*

1483. Penman, Sharon Kay. **Falls the Shadow**. 1988. New York: Ballantine, 1989. 580p. $12.50pa. ISBN 0-345-36033-8pa. YA

In 1231, Simon de Montfort, age twenty-two, asks the Earl of Chester to restore his earldom of Leicester, which had been unjustly taken from his father. Chester agrees. The second in a trilogy beginning with *Here Be Dragons*, this story looks at de Montfort's life and his ability to create either intense loyalty or bitter hatred until his death at the Battle of Evesham in 1266.

1484. Penman, Sharon Kay. **Here Be Dragons**. 1985. New York: Ballantine, 1993. 704p. $12.50pa. ISBN 0-345-38284-6pa. YA

This first book of a trilogy begins with the Plantagenet House at war with itself in 1183. King Henry and his son John have a conflict with Henry's other three sons, Henry, Richard, and Geoffrey. After many battles against the Normans and the English, by 1234, Llewelyn has united Wales.

1485. Penman, Sharon Kay. **The Queen's Man: A Medieval Mystery**. New York: Henry Holt, 1996. 240p. $23. ISBN 0-8050-3885-X. YA

In twelfth-century England, Justin deQuincy discovers a dead goldsmith on the Winchester Road. He finds a letter on the body and takes it to Eleanor of Aquitaine, who waits for her son Richard the Lionhearted to return to his throne. In the letter Eleanor reads that Richard is alive, although imprisoned. She makes Justin her man and asks him to investigate the murder. As he moves from London to Winchester and back, he has a series of adventures with all levels of society.

1486. Penman, Sharon Kay. **The Reckoning**. New York: Henry Holt, 1991. 593p. $24.95. ISBN 0-8050-1014-9. New York: Ballantine, 1991. 592p. $12.50pa. ISBN 0-345-37888-1pa. YA

In the final novel of the trilogy, with *Here Be Dragons* and *Falls the Shadow*, Llewelyn attempts to keep both his brother Davydd and the English king from overcoming the united Wales. When Edward kills Llewelyn and other Welsh men in 1283, he separates the surviving mothers and children and anoints his own firstborn as Prince of Wales.

1487. Penman, Sharon Kay. **The Sunne in Splendor**. 1982. New York: Ballantine, 1990. 936p. $12.50pa. ISBN 0-345-36313-2pa. YA

After 1483, Richard's two nephews never again appear in public, and people accuse Richard of having them murdered in the Tower of London. Tudor historians also report that Richard was deformed, although the claim has never been substantiated. Richard seems to have loved and respected his older brother Edward and his wife Anne as well. This story covers medieval England and its wars from 1459 to 1483 between the Houses of Lancaster and York.

1488. Penman, Sharon Kay. **When Christ and His Saints Slept**. New York: Henry Holt, 1995. 746p. $25. ISBN 0-8050-1015-7. New York: Ballantine, 1996. 746p. $14pa. ISBN 0-345-39668-5pa. YA

As Henry I, the youngest son of William the Conqueror, nears the end of his life and his reign, he names Maude as his heir. Maude's battles to become the ruler, against Stephen, King of England, disturb the twelfth-century countryside for too many years.

1489. Perdrizet, Marie-Pierre. **The Cathedral Builders**. Eddy Krähenbühl, illustrator; Mary Beth Raycraft, translator. Brookfield, CT: Millbrook Press, 1992. 64p. $16.40. ISBN 1-56294-162-3. (Peoples of the Past). 5-8

Gothic cathedrals were planned and constructed in the eleventh and twelfth centuries when almost everyone in the area was Christian. The text looks at the building of the cathedral from stone; architectural details such as buttresses; the stained-glass windows; why the cathedrals were built; what celebrations took place in them; and the legacy of the builders. An interesting addition is the guide on how to experience a cathedral. Illustrations enhance the text. Dates to Remember, Find Out More, Glossary, and Index. *New York Public Library Books for the Teen Age.*

1490.   Perez, Louis G. **The Dalai Lama**. Vero Beach, FL: Rourke, 1993. 112p. $22.60. ISBN 0-86625-480-3. (Biographies of World Leaders). 5-8

A child found in the Tibetan wilderness became the spiritual leader of his people. Tibetan monks believe that babies must be treated in special ways; a baby, reincarnated from a life that helped others, had to be nurtured to ascertain if he were destined to be the next Dalai Lama. This child, Tenzin Gyatso, passed the tests. As an adult, he won the Nobel Peace Prize for his attempts to help free his people from Chinese oppression through nonviolent means. He has been exiled from Tibet since 1959 but continues to press for an end to Chinese aggression. The text, with photographs, examines Buddhist beliefs and the Dalai Lama's life. Time Line, Glossary, Bibliography, Media Resources, and Index.

1491.   Perkins, Dorothy. **Encyclopedia of Japan: Japanese History and Culture from Abacus to Zori**. New York: Facts on File, 1991. 410p. $40. ISBN 0-8160-1934-7. YA

Among the 1,000 alphabetical entries in this encompassing work are Kabuki, Abacus, Tea Ceremony, Biotechnology Industry, Fifth-Generation Advanced Computer Systems, Shinjuku, westerners associated with Japan (such as Douglas MacArthur and Edwin O. Reischauer), Advertising, Tofu, and Sony. Cross References, Bibliography, and Index.

1492.   Perl, Lila. **From Top Hats to Baseball Caps, from Bustles to Blue Jeans: Why We Dress the Way We Do**. New York: Clarion, 1990. 118p. $14.95. ISBN 0-899-19872-4. 5-9

Perl thinks that through the years in Western Europe and the United States such things as social class, women's liberation, war, and technology have influenced styles of clothing. She includes chapters on pants, skirts, shoes, and hats. The text is complemented with photographs and drawings. Bibliography and Index.

1493.   Perl, Lila. **Isaac Bashevis Singer: The Life of a Storyteller**. Donna Ruff, illustrator. Philadelphia, PA: Jewish Publication Society, 1995. 95p. $12.95. ISBN 0-8276-0512-9. 5-7

In 1904, Icek-Hersz Zynger was born in Poland, where his first stories written in Yiddish were published. In 1935, Isaac Bashevis Singer came to the United States, where he continued writing. Singer has won many awards for his work, including a Newbery Honor, a National Book Award, and the Nobel Prize for Literature. At his death in 1991, he received the acclaim worthy of his body of work. Important Dates, Bibliography, Works, and Index.

1494.   Perl, Lila, and Marion Blumenthal Lazan. **Four Perfect Pebbles: A Holocaust Story**. New York: Morrow, 1996. 130p. $15. ISBN 0-688-14294-X. 5-8

Before experiencing the Holocaust in Bergen-Belsen, Marion Blumenthal Lazan had a happy, secure family life in prewar Germany. Her grandparents had run a business since 1894, but Hitler's decrees gradually decreased their rights until they were forced to move from Hoya to Hanover and then to Holland. Before they could leave for America, the Nazis invaded and deported them to Westerbork, then to Bergen-Belsen, and onto a death train to Auschwitz before the Russians liberated them. Marion's father died of typhus after liberation, however, and she, her mother, and her brother had to spend three years as displaced persons before they eventually arrived in the United States. Photographs and Bibliography. *American Library Association Notable Books for Children*.

1495.   Pernoud, Régine. **A Day with a Medieval Troubadour**. Giorgio Bacchin, illustrator; Dominique Clift, translator. Minneapolis, MN: Runestone, 1997. 64p. $16.95. ISBN 0-8225-1915-1. (A Day With). 5-7

A medieval troubadour was a person who wrote or composed anything, and their tradition began in the Provençe region of France at the end of the eleventh century. Introduced by a background about troubadours and their part in pilgrimages to places such as Santiago, the text describes a day with a twelfth-century troubadour named Peire Vidal. Glossary, Further Reading, and Index. *Andersen Prize Europe*.

1496.   Pernoud, Régine. **A Day with a Miller**. Giorgio Bacchin, illustrator; Dominique Clift, translator. Minneapolis, MN: Runestone, 1997. 64p. $16.95. ISBN 0-8225-1914-3. (A Day With). 5-7

The text gives a brief history of the importance of milling for food and follows with the description of a day in the life of a miller during the twelfth century in France. Illustrations enhance his story. Glossary, Further Reading, and Index. *Andersen Prize Europe*.

1497.   Pernoud, Régine. **A Day with a Noblewoman**. Giorgio Bacchin, illustrator; Dominique Clift, translator. Minneapolis, MN: Runestone, 1997. 64p. $16.95. ISBN 0-8225-1916-X. (A Day With). 5-7

A brief description of the nobility in France during the thirteenth century and a discussion of the Crusades precedes the details of a day in the life of the widow Blanche, a thirteenth-century noblewoman who must manage her large landholdings by herself. Glossary, Further Reading, and Index. *Andersen Prize Europe*.

1498. Pernoud, Régine. **A Day with a Stonecutter**. Giorgio Bacchin, illustrator; Dominique Clift, translator. Minneapolis, MN: Runestone, 1997. 64p. $16.95. ISBN 0-8225-1913-5. (A Day With). 5-7

The text begins with a description of the various parts of medieval cathedrals, especially Chartres, and the roles that stonecutters play in their creation. It then tells the story of one day in the life of Yves, a stonecutter who works at the Abbey of St. George in Normandy during the twelfth century. Glossary, Further Reading, and Index. *Andersen Prize Europe.*

1499. Perry, Anne. **Belgrave Square**. New York: Ballantine, Fawcett, 1992. 361p. $18; $5.99pa. ISBN 0-449-90678-7; 0-449-22227-6pa. YA

Around 1890 in London, Weems, a moneylender who blackmails people as a sideline, is murdered. After police identify the murderer, they find an unexpected complication.

1500. Perry, Anne. **Defend and Betray**. New York: Fawcett Columbine, 1992. 385p. $5.99pa. ISBN 0-8041-1188-Xpa. YA

The protagonist of this novel, set during 1857 in London, is Hester Latterly, who served in the Crimean War with Florence Nightingale. Hester suspects that a wife who confessed to the murder of her husband did not do it, and that she is protecting someone else. The detective William Monk investigates the crime. The Victorian time frame of the story allows the author to show the treatment of women, who had few rights, and the hypocritical social, class-oriented attitudes.

1501. Perry, Anne. **The Face of a Stranger**. New York: Fawcett, 1990. 328p. $17.95. ISBN 0-449-90530-6. New York: Ivy/Ballantine, 1995. 328p. $5.99pa. ISBN 0-8041-0858-7pa. YA

Although people tell William Monk that he is a police detective, amnesia after an accident in London during the 1890s will not allow him to verify their statements. He continues to work on cases and tries to find who murdered a Crimean War hero from the upper class. Although he eventually solves the crime, he is uncertain for much of the time as to whether he might be the criminal for whom he looks.

1502. Perry, Anne. **Farriers' Lane**. New York: Fawcett Columbine, 1993. 374p. $20. ISBN 0-449-90569-1. YA

Charlotte Pitt, wife of Thomas Pitt, finds the culprit in this mystery set in London during Victorian times of the nineteenth century.

1503. Perry, Anne. **The Hyde Park Headsman**. New York: Fawcett Columbine, 1994. 392p. $5.99pa. ISBN 0-449-22350-7pa. YA

Charlotte and Thomas Pitt solve a mystery set in London during the nineteenth century.

1504. Perry, Anne. **Pentecost Alley**. New York: Fawcett Columbine, 1996. 405p. $22.95. ISBN 0-449-90635-3. YA

After the reign of Jack the Ripper ends, more terror hits Whitechapel with the murder of a prostitute. Thomas Pitt, head of the Bow Street command, has to find the killer. Pitt is relieved that a gentleman is cleared of the deed, but after someone else has been executed for the crime, an identical murder occurs. Pitt hates the indifference of the upper economic class toward the lower class, and he has to face it in this search for the killer.

1505. Perry, Anne. **The Sins of the Wolf**. New York: Fawcett Columbine, 1994. 374p. $21.50; $6.99pa. ISBN 0-449-90638-8; 0-8041-1383-1pa. YA

In a mystery set in Victorian London, which reveals attitudes and expectations of the mid-nineteenth century, Hester Latterly, a nurse, and the private detective William Monk investigate the murder of a wealthy woman traveling with her nurse. The murdered woman's family accuses the nurse, but Hester Latterly defends her, as does Florence Nightingale with a surprise courtroom visit.

1506. Perry, Anne. **A Sudden, Fearful Death**. New York: Fawcett Columbine, 1993. 338p. $5.99pa. ISBN 0-8041-1283-5pa. YA

After the detective William Monk goes to see a woman in Victorian London to discuss an attack on her sister in their back yard, he becomes involved in another case involving the murder of a nurse in a nearby hospital. Connections between the two crimes appear as the novel develops, and the courtroom scene revelations at the Old Bailey contain surprises. Additionally, Perry gives insight into the social expectations of the mid-nineteenth century.

1507. Pescio, Claudio. **Rembrandt and Seventeenth-Century Holland: The Dutch Nation and Its Painters**. Sergio, illustrator. New York: Peter Bedrick, 1996. 64p. $22.50. ISBN 0-8722-6317-7. (Masters of Art). 7 up

The text looks at Rembrandt's (1606–1669) life in terms of the times in which he lived. It also includes small reproductions of 112 of his paintings, with a thorough analysis of 5 of them (including "The Anatomy Lesson of Dr. Nicholaes Tulp" and "The Night Watch"). Extra information appears about landscape painting and other aspects of seventeenth-century Dutch artwork. Bibliography, Chronology, and Index.

1508. Pescio, Claudio. **Van Gogh**. New York: Peter Bedrick, 1996. 64p. $19.95. ISBN 0-87226-525-0. 7 up

Vincent van Gogh (1853–1890) grew up in Holland but spent many years in France. He trained first to be a minister but realized that he really wanted to paint. He eventually settled in the south of France, in Provence, to work. Because he made no money on his painting while he was alive, his brother Theo, to whom he was especially close, helped support him. Reproductions complement the text. Masterpieces, For Further Reading, and Index.

1509. Peters, Elizabeth. **The Deeds of the Disturber**. New York: Atheneum, 1988. 289p. $5.99pa. ISBN 0-446-35333-7. YA

A priest at the British Museum says that he has cursed someone for desecrating a mummy, but Amelia Peabody refuses to accept this information. Her investigation of the priest uncovers a murderer.

1510. Peters, Elizabeth. **The Hippopotamus Pool**. New York: Warner, 1996. 384p. $22.95. ISBN 0-446-51833-6. YA

Amelia Peabody, the archaeologist, goes to Egypt in the nineteenth century looking for finds at the pyramids. On New Year's Eve in Cairo, a stranger hands her a scarab ring that he says came from the tomb of Queen Tetisheri. In her investigation of its authenticity, she confronts a mystery.

1511. Peters, Elizabeth. **The Last Camel Died at Noon**. New York: Warner, 1991. 352p. $5.99pa. ISBN 0-446-36338-3pa. YA

While in Egypt with her husband and her son Ramses, Amelia Peabody and Ramses search for an archaeologist in the Sudan who disappeared fourteen years before.

1512. Peters, Elizabeth. **Lion in the Valley**. New York: Atheneum, 1986. 291p. $4.99pa. ISBN 0-8125-1242-1pa. YA

When Amelia Peabody and her husband return to Egypt with their eight-year-old son, Ramses, a criminal kidnaps Amelia, and her family has to find her location.

1513. Peters, Elizabeth. **The Mummy Case**. New York: St. Martin's Press, 1995. 313p. $5.99pa. ISBN 0-446-60193-4pa. YA

Amelia Peabody, her husband, and their son Ramses go to Egypt to excavate. A dealer in stolen antiquities is murdered, and Amelia spends her time investigating the case instead.

1514. Peters, Elizabeth. **The Snake, the Crocodile, and the Dog**. New York: Warner, 1992. 340p. $19.95. ISBN 0-446-51585-X. YA

When Amelia Peabody and her husband go to Egypt without their son, they plan to enjoy each other's company romantically. But while they excavate a gravesite in the late 1800s, a criminal causes them much discomfort and ruins their initial plans.

1515. Peters, Ellis. **The Confession of Brother Haluin**. New York: Mysterious Press, 1988. 164p. $15.95. ISBN 0-89296-349-2. YA

The heavy snows of 1142 almost destroy the Shrewsbury Abbey roof, and Brother Haluin's fall almost kills him. While expecting to die, Haluin confesses the serious problems of his past to both the Abbot and Brother Cadfael. After Haluin recovers, he and Brother Cadfael take a journey during which Haluin asks forgiveness for his deeds, and they find a murder to solve.

1516. Peters, Ellis. **Dead Man's Ransom**. New York: Morrow, 1984. 190p. $13.95. ISBN 0-688-04194-9. YA

In 1141, King Stephen and Empress Maud battle at Lincoln for the crown, and their conflict results in a prisoner exchange. One prisoner dies mysteriously, and Brother Cadfael finds that the man died from unnatural causes.

1517. Peters, Ellis. **The Devil's Novice**. New York: Morrow, 1984. 192p. $13.95. ISBN 0-688-03247-8. YA

In 1140, when a novice and a political envoy come to the Shrewsbury Abbey, the envoy is later found murdered. Because he seems disconcerted, the brothers think that the novice is guilty, but Brother Cadfael realizes that the novice did not commit the murder.

1518. Peters, Ellis. **An Excellent Mystery**. New York: Morrow, 1985. 190p. $15.95. ISBN 0-688-06250-4. YA

After King Stephen and Empress Maud draw Henry of Blois, the Bishop of Winchester, into their struggle for the crown, fire destroys Winchester. Two of the brothers from that priory seek refuge at Shrewsbury. When a visitor arrives and talks about the disappearance of a girl, Brother Cadfael has another murder to solve.

1519. Peters, Ellis. **The Heretic's Apprentice**. New York: Mysterious Press, 1990. 186p. $16.95. ISBN 0-89296-381-6. New York: Warner, 1995. 186p. $5.99pa. ISBN 0-446-40000-9pa. YA

When Elave brings his master to Shrewsbury for burial on the abbey grounds in 1143, another visitor accuses him of heresy for saying that everyone will find salvation. The trial leads to a murder that requires Brother Cadfael's talents of investigation.

1520. Peters, Ellis. **The Hermit of Eyton Forest**. New York: Mysterious Press, 1988. 224p. $15.95. ISBN 0-89296-290-9. YA

In 1142, King Stephen demands that Empress Maud surrender her claim to the throne. While they are fighting outside the Shrewsbury abbey, internal political problems are also occurring. When a pupil disappears and the corpse shows up in Eyton Forest, Brother Cadfael must go outside the monastery to solve the murder.

1521. Peters, Ellis. **The Holy Thief**. New York: Mysterious Press, 1993. 246p. $17.95. ISBN 0-89296-524-X. New York: Warner, 1994. 246p. $5.99pa. ISBN 0-446-40363-6pa. YA

After an archer kills Geoffrey de Mandeville, Earl of Essex, in 1144, Brother Herluin begins to solicit funds for repairing the Benedictine Abbey at Ramsay, which the earl had ruined. He and Brother Tutilo arrive at Shrewsbury before two others, a troubadour and a girl singer. When they are all present, someone steals the sacred bones of St. Winifred and commits a murder, which Brother Cadfael must solve.

1522. Peters, Ellis. **The Leper of St. Giles**. 1982. New York: Warner, 1995. 223p. $5.50pa. ISBN 0-446-40437-3pa. YA

When a princess's prospective bridegroom dies in 1139, Brother Cadfael investigates, because the princess actually loved someone else. Brother Cadfael finds both the princess's lost relative, inside the leper house of Saint Giles, and a solution to the murder.

1523. Peters, Ellis. **Monk's Hood**. New York: Morrow, 1981. 224p. $9.95. ISBN 0-688-00452-0. New York: Warner, 1992. 224p. $5.99pa. ISBN 0-446-40300-8pa. YA

Monk's hood, a medicine that poisons if ingested, seems to be the item that has made one of the abbey's guests at Shrewsbury ill. Brother Cadfael's investigation shows that the guest's stepson did not try to poison the man, although he had many reasons to do so.

1524. Peters, Ellis. **A Morbid Taste for Bones**. 1978. New York: Mysterious Press, 1994. 208p. $5.99pa. ISBN 0-446-40015-7pa. YA

When Brother Cadfael and Prior Robert go to Wales to retrieve the bones of Saint Winifred in the twelfth century, a murder occurs while they are in the small town. Brother Cadfael helps to solve the murder, but the fact that the Gwytherin parish enjoys more renown because of the murder and after the bones are removed annoys Prior Robert.

1525. Peters, Ellis. **The Pilgrim of Hate**. New York: Morrow, 1984. 190p. $14.95. ISBN 0-688-04964-8. YA

To honor the bones of Saint Winifred in 1141, four years after their arrival at Shrewsbury, pilgrims come to the abbey. Two of them seem to have a connection with a knight at Winchester who supports the Empress Maud. Brother Cadfael solves the mystery and realizes that one of the men is the husband of the empress.

1526. Peters, Ellis. **The Potter's Field**. 1990. New York: Warner, 1995. 230p. $5.99pa. ISBN 0-446-40058-0pa. YA

After a field given to the Shrewsbury Abbey of St. Peter and St. Paul in 1143 is legally transferred, the monks plow it and find the body of a young woman, who appears to have been dead for over a year. They think that she may be the missing wife of the man who gave the field to the monks. Brother Cadfael investigates with the help of a novice trying to flee the East Anglian civil war brewing outside the monastery.

1527. Peters, Ellis. **The Raven in the Foregate**. New York: Morrow, 1986. 201p. $15.95. ISBN 0-688-06558-9. YA

Ailnoth goes to the parish of the Holy Cross in 1141, and his zeal surprises the parishioners used to the mild Father Adam, his predecessor. On Christmas morning, Ailnoth is found drowned in the mill pond. When Brother Cadfael investigates the murder, he finds a connection to the Empress Maud and her followers. With his friend, Hugh, the sheriff of Shrewsbury, Brother Cadfael finds out what happened.

1528. Peters, Ellis. **The Rose Rent**. 1986. New York: Crest, Fawcett, 1988. 190p. $4.95pa. ISBN 0-449-21495-8pa. YA

Someone murders Brother Eluric, a colleague of Brother Cadfael, in 1142, as he is on his way to pay the yearly rent of one rose to the woman who lets her cottage and garden to Shrewsbury Abbey. Brother Cadfael decides that someone who wanted the rental to stop would be the culprit, but he realizes that several people fit that description. He solves the murder and makes the owner happy as well.

1529.   Peters, Ellis. **The Sanctuary Sparrow**. New York: Morrow, 1983. 222p. $12.50. ISBN 0-688-02252-9. YA

After being accused of robbery and murder, Liliwin, a boy acrobat and jongleur, flees a mob by running inside the Benedictine Abbey of St. Peter and St. Paul in 1140 and claiming sanctuary. While Liliwin uses his forty-day respite before having to be released to the law, Brother Cadfael investigates and finds that the boy is innocent.

1530.   Peters, Ellis. **St. Peter's Fair**. 1981. New York: Warner, 1995. 220p. $5.99pa. ISBN 0-446-40301-6pa. YA

At the annual Saint Peter's Fair in Shrewsbury on July 30, 1139, someone stabs and kills a wealthy merchant. To fulfill her uncle's last wish, his niece then risks her own life. Brother Cadfael rescues her and finds the murderer.

1531.   Peters, Ellis. **The Summer of the Danes**. New York: Mysterious Press, 1991. 251p. $16.95. ISBN 0-89296-448-0. New York: Mysterious Press, 1995. 251p. $5.99pa. ISBN 0-446-40018-1pa. YA

During a time of peace between King Stephen and Empress Maud in 1144, Brother Cadfael grabs a chance to go to Wales with Brother Mark. In Wales, Danish mercenaries fighting for Cadwaladr capture Brother Cadfael and a woman. While he waits to be released, he solves the murder of one of Owain's prisoners, Cadwaladr's brother.

1532.   Peters, Ellis. **The Virgin in the Ice**. New York: Morrow, 1983. 220p. $11.95. ISBN 0-688-01672-3. YA

In 1139, during the civil war between King Stephen and the Empress Maud, two orphans and their chaperone become lost in the winter woods. Their nearest kinsman supports Empress Maud, so he cannot come to look for them without jeopardizing his life. Brother Cadfael becomes involved while on his way to the priory of Bromfield with his herbal medicines. He investigates a murder and finds information about his own son.

1533.   Pettit, Jayne. **My Name Is San Ho**. New York: Scholastic, 1992. 149p. $13.95. ISBN 0-590-44172-8. 5-8

San Ho, age ten, goes from his small Vietnamese village with his mother to a friend's home in Saigon in 1972. She does not come back for three years, and when she returns, she is married to an American. San Ho travels to America with them, where he has to adjust to both his father and his new culture, while trying to learn English and struggling to understand what happened to his country.

1534.   Pettit, Jayne. **A Time to Fight Back: True Stories of Wartime Resistance**. Boston: Houghton Mifflin, 1996. 163p. $15.95. ISBN 0-395-76504-8. 7 up

The text focuses on the courageous acts of eight children of the Resistance in Europe during World War II. They include a Belgian boy of twelve who was a courier for secret messages; a German of nine who endured the Allied bombing raids; Elie Wiesel, who at age fifteen survived Auschwitz-Birkenau; a Japanese-American girl of seven who went with her family to an internment camp; and a deaf-mute boy who helped to rescue and smuggle a Royal Air Force pilot out of France. These individual acts display the heroism that helped to defeat Hitler. Bibliography.

1535.   Peyton, K. M. **The Edge of the Cloud**. 1969. Magnolia, MA: Peter Smith, 1992. 192p. $16.80. ISBN 0-8446-6566-5. New York: Penguin, 1989. 192p. $3.99pa. ISBN 0-14-030905-5pa. 9 up

Christina and Will decide to marry as soon as Will becomes twenty-one, in this second book of the Flambards trilogy. Will begins stunt flying with a friend, but after the friend dies and Will's father dies, he and Christina change their minds and marry before Will goes to fight in World War I as a pilot. *Carnegie Medal* and *Guardian Award*.

1536.   Peyton, K. M. **Flambards**. 1967. Magnolia, MA: Peter Smith, 1991. 224p. $16.50. ISBN 0-8446-6533-9. New York: Penguin, 1989. 224p. $3.95pa. ISBN 0-14-034153-6pa. 9 up

In this first book of the Flambards trilogy, when she is twelve in 1908, the orphan Christina goes to live with her uncle and his two sons. One son loves horses and the other hates them. She grows up with the careless Mark, who impregnates a servant and wants to marry her, but Christina realizes that she prefers Will, the brother enamored of flying. She refuses Mark for Will. *Guardian Award for Children's Fiction* and *Carnegie Commendation*.

1537.   Peyton, K. M. **Flambards Divided**. New York: Philomel, 1982. $10.95. ISBN 0-399-20864-X. 9 up

Christina and Dick marry and try to run Flambards, but Christina cannot control the differences between class structure and expectations set in childhood. The people on the farm will not take orders from Dick. As they have their troubles, Christina's child is stillborn after she falls off a horse. When she goes to a country party, she realizes that she loves Mark after all. Mark's ex-wife introduces Christina to a member of Parliament who says that the law forbidding wives to marry their dead husband's brothers will be changed.

1538.   Peyton, K. M. **Flambards in Summer**. 1969. Magnolia, MA: Peter Smith, 1992. 208p. $16.50. ISBN 0-8446-6567-3. New York: Penguin, 1989. 208p. $3.95pa. ISBN 0-14-034154-4pa. 9 up

This third book in the Flambards trilogy tells of Christina at age twenty-one, in 1916, when she is already a widow and has inherited Will's fortune. When she returns to Flambards, she is pregnant with Will's child. She offers to adopt Mark's son and decides that she and Dick should marry and revive the Flambards land. *Guardian Award*.

1539.   Peyton, K. M. **The Maplin Bird**. Victor Ambrus, illustrator. 1964. New York: Gregg Press, 1980. 237p. $9.95. ISBN 0-8398-2611-7. 7-10

Toby, age sixteen, only has a sailboat remaining from his inheritance in the late 1860s, and he has to sail away in it to keep his uncle from taking it too for his own children. Toby and his sister Emily find work, and a wealthy boy approaches Toby about helping him retrieve a wrecked yacht. The boy had been smuggling, and when they go to the yacht, police arrest the boy, and Toby breaks his leg during the escape. The boy's sister nurses Toby to health, and Toby and Emily survive their travails. *Carnegie Commendation*.

1540.   Pflaum, Rosalynd. **Grand Obsession: Madame Curie and Her World**. New York: Doubleday, 1989. 496p. $22.50. ISBN 0-385-26135-7. YA

Marie Curie (1867–1934) and her husband, Pierre Curie (1859–1906), received a joint Nobel Prize in 1903 for their discovery of radium and polonium and their subsequent work on radioactivity. In 1911, Marie Curie received a second Nobel for her studies of pure radium. Then in 1935, her daughter and son-in-law were awarded a third family Nobel for their synthesis of new radioelements. However, they were all slighted by the elitist French scientific community, because Marie Curie grew up in Poland and was therefore an outsider. The text looks at their lives in their world, including Marie Curie's affair—scandalous at the time, in 1911—five years after her husband's death, and the son-in-law's role in the French resistance during World War II, which was followed by postwar Communist activities. This family, suffering from radiation sickness for much of the time, advanced science and increased the possibilities for modern inventions. Bibliography and Index.

1541.   Phillips, Ann. **The Peace Child**. New York: Oxford University Press, 1988. 150p. $15. ISBN 0-19-271560-7. 5 up

In 1380, Alys, age ten, finds out that she was born into another family. When she was born, the families traded babies as a way to settle a blood feud. She has to devote her energy to keeping the peace between the two groups, and two years later, during the plague, she travels between them and helps them survive. At her own marriage, she plans for all of her children to be "peace children."

1542.   Pickford, Nigel. **The Atlas of Shipwrecks & Treasure**. New York: Dorling Kindersley, 1994. 200p. $29.95. ISBN 1-56458-599-9. YA

Maps identify the locations of ships that were wrecked during a particular period of history. Following these are a description of the find and facts about the history of shipbuilding and cargo gleaned from the recovery of the ruin. Photographs complement the text. Periods covered are the Bronze Age to Byzantium (up to A.D. 1000), the Vikings (beginning in the ninth century A.D.), Chinese junks (early fifteenth century), the Levantine trade (1000-1500), Portuguese carracks (sixteenth century to mid-seventeenth), the Armada (sixteenth century), Spanish plate fleets (sixteenth and seventeenth centuries), pirates and privateers (late sixteenth to eighteenth centuries), East Indiamen (seventeenth and eighteenth centuries), the Age of Revolution (eighteenth and early nineteenth centuries), great collections (eighteenth and nineteenth centuries), the rush for gold (nineteenth century), mail ships and liners (nineteenth and twentieth centuries), and World War II (1940-1945). Gazetteer Maps, Shipwreck Listings, Glossary, Bibliography, and Index.

1543.   Pietrusza, David. **The Battle of Waterloo**. San Diego, CA: Lucent, 1996. 96p. $26.59. ISBN 1-56006-423-4. (Battles of the Nineteenth Century). 6-9

The battle of Waterloo in 1815 set a combination of British, Dutch, and Belgian forces totaling 67,000 against Napoleon's forces of 74,000 French. When Gebhard von Blücher arrived with the Prussian army, Napoleon met defeat. The text looks at this battle as well as at Napoleon's ambitions to control Europe, which drove him to fight so often. One segment also looks at Napoleon's achievement in establishing his Code. Bibliography, Chronology, Further Reading, and Index.

1544.   Pietrusza, David. **The Chinese Cultural Revolution**. San Diego, CA: Lucent, 1996. 96p. $16.95. ISBN 1-56006-305-X. (World History). 9 up

Pietrusza recounts Mao Tse-tung's rise to power in 1949 to his 1958 Great Leap Forward movement, which failed, and his return to power in the 1960s. Pietrusza thinks that life for the working class has improved since the Cultural Revolution, but shows that totalitarian government still controls everything. Bibliography, Chronology, Further Reading, and Index.

1545. Pietrusza, David. **The End of the Cold War**. San Diego, CA: Lucent, 1995. 112p. $16.95. ISBN 1-56006-280-0. (World History). 7–9

To persons familiar with the oppression of the Soviet regime and its tentacles, the fall of the Berlin Wall on November 9, 1989, almost 30 years after its erection in 1961, was an astonishing sight broadcast on international television. The text traces the beginnings of Eastern European communism in the twentieth century and the living conditions of those caught in its clutches. It establishes that the first breach with Communist leaders occurred in 1948 in Yugoslavia, but Stalin quickly quelled the revolt. The text presents Poland's Solidarity stand and subsequent defeat before Gorbachev's rise to leadership and Solidarity's triumph after Gorbachev took office as well as other uprisings and failures throughout the regime. The chipping of the Soviet Bloc led to its collapse and the period afterward—still uncertain, but at least unfettered. Notes, Glossary, For Further Exploration, Works Consulted, and Index.

1546. Pietrusza, David. **The Invasion of Normandy**. San Diego, CA: Lucent, 1995. 110p. $19.95. ISBN 1-56006-413-7. (Battles of World War II). 7 up

Photographs, maps, and sidebars help tell the story of the Allied forces' invasion of Normandy on June 6, 1944. The text discusses the prior catastrophes at Slapton Sands and Dieppe, which gave the Allies reason to think that the invasion might not work. The text gives background on the planning involved and the people who helped it occur. It also discusses the problems that occurred on beaches other than the ones on which the Americans landed, Omaha and Utah. Bibliography, Chronology, Further Reading, Glossary, and Index.

1547. Pimlott, John, ed. **The Elite: The Special Forces of the World, Vol. 1**. New York: Marshall Cavendish, 1987. 160p. $189.95 set. ISBN 0-86307-792-7. YA

Articles laid out as collages of text, photographs of soldiers and battles, maps, and illustrations of equipment tell about the elite forces in the world, which have developed and controlled warfare in the twentieth century. Included in this volume are stories about the Nachtjagdgeschwader 1 in Nüremberg, 1944; the German 7th Armored Division in France, 1940; the 7th Duke of Edinburgh's Own Gurkha Rifles in the Falklands, 1982; the South African Recce Commandos in Namibia, 1980s; training in the Royal Marines; weapons and equipment of British paratroops of World War II; the D-Day landing of the 9th Battalion, The Parachute Regiment, in Normandy, 1944; and the 1st Airborne Division at Arnhem, 1944. Index.

1548. Pimlott, John, ed. **The Elite: The Special Forces of the World, Vol. 2**. New York: Marshall Cavendish, 1987. 160p. $189.95 set. ISBN 0-86307-794-3. YA

Articles laid out as collages of text, photographs of soldiers and battles, maps, and illustrations of equipment tell about the elite forces in the world, which have developed and controlled warfare in the twentieth century. Included in this volume are stories about the Israeli Golani Brigade and the Golan Heights in 1967 and Lebanon in 1982; the No. 11 Squadron of the Pakistan Air Force at Punjab in 1965; Operation Kipling and the SAS in France, 1944, and Germany, 1945; Scorpions and Scimitars in the Falklands, 1982; the French 3rd Colonial Parachute, chasseurs alpins, and 9th Zouave Regiment, Algeria, 1956–1960; the Suffolk Regiment in Malaya, 1949–1953; the Soviet 105th Guards Airborne Division in Afghanistan, 1979; the American Flying Tigers in China, 1941–1942; the Grossdeutschland Regiment in France, 1940, and Soviet Union, 1943; Japanese suicide units, 1944–1945; South Vietnamese marines, 1971; the Explosive Ordnance Disposal Units in Northern Ireland, 1972; Popski's Private Army in the Western Desert and Italy; the 12th Submarine Flotilla of the Royal Navy in Norway, 1943; and the 22nd Special Air Service Regiment in Oman, 1958–1959. Index.

1549. Pimlott, John, ed. **The Elite: The Special Forces of the World, Vol. 3**. New York: Marshall Cavendish, 1987. 160p. $189.95 set. ISBN 0-86307-793-5. YA

Articles laid out as collages of text, photographs of soldiers and battles, maps, and illustrations of equipment tell about the elite forces in the world, which have developed and controlled warfare in the twentieth century. Included in this volume are stories about the German Brandenburgers in Europe, 1939–1940; training and deployment of the Spetsnaz, Soviet Special Forces; the RAF Glider Pilot Regiment at D-Day, 1944; the Israeli 202nd Parachute Brigade in the Sinai, 1967; the Chindits in Burma, 1943; the formation and training of the U.S. Green Berets; the U.S. Special Forces in Vietnam; the formation of the Special Air Service (SAS) in 1941; the Egyptian Commandos in the Yom Kippur War, 1973; and the U.S. 82nd Airborne Division invasion of Grenada, 1983. Index.

1550. Pimlott, John, ed. **The Elite: The Special Forces of the World, Vol. 4**. New York: Marshall Cavendish, 1987. 160p. $189.95 set. ISBN 0-86307-796-X. YA

Articles laid out as collages of text, photographs of soldiers and battles, maps, and illustrations of equipment tell about the elite forces in the world, which have developed and controlled warfare in the twentieth century. Included in this volume are stories about the Royal Netherlands Marine Corps and the South Moluccan hijack in 1977; the U.S. 4th Fighter-Interceptor Wing in Korea, 1950–1953; the USAF 3rd Aerospace Rescue and Recovery Group in Vietnam; the SAS in Yemen, 1963, World War II; World War I; and training for the West German Fallschirmjäger Paratroops. Index.

1551.   Pimlott, John, ed. **The Elite: The Special Forces of the World, Vol. 5**. New York: Marshall Cavendish, 1987. 160p. $189.95 set. ISBN 0-86307-795-1. YA

Articles made up of collages of text, photographs of soldiers and battles, maps, and illustrations of equipment tell about the elite forces in the world that have developed and controlled warfare in the twentieth century. Included in this volume are stories about the Rhodesian SAS in Zambia, 1979; the U.S. 322nd Bombardment Group in Europe during 1943; Kampfgruppe Peiper in Ardennes, 1944; 73rd Hanoverian Fusilieres in World War I, France, 1918; Israeli Defence Force, Entebbe, 1976; USAF 44th Tactical Fighter Squadron in Vietnam, 1964-1971; U.S. 2nd Marine Raider Battalion, Guadalcanal in 1942; No. 249 RAF Squadron in Malta, 1941-1943; U.S. Army Tunnel Rats in Vietnam; 28th Marine Regiment in Iwo Jima, 1945; and the Soviet Air Force 16th Guards Fighter Regiment, 1943. Index.

1552.   Pimlott, John. **Middle East: A Background to the Conflicts**. New York: Gloucester, Franklin Watts, 1991. 36p. $11.90. ISBN 0-531-17329-1. (Hotspots). 3-7

The text starts with a brief summary of the 1991 Gulf War, and then examines the nineteenth-century conflicts leading to this war. Additional information about the Arab-Israeli difficulties shows that the peace process in this area has a history of violence and discord to overcome. Photographs supplement the text. Chronology, Glossary, and Index.

1553.   Pitt, Nancy. **Beyond the High White Wall**. New York: Scribners, 1986. 135p. $11.95. ISBN 0-684-18663-2. 6-9

After Libby sees a foreman on her family's property in the Ukraine murder an innocent Jewish man in 1903, she begins to understand why her family plans to leave the home they love for America. Someone burns their home before they can leave, and other incidents make life uncomfortable. However, the fact that they have decided to take control of their lives by leaving pleases her.

1554.   Platt, Richard. **Castle**. Stephen Biesty, illustrator. New York: Dorling Kindersley, 1994. 27p. $16.95. ISBN 1-56458-467-4. (Stephen Biesty's Cross-Sections). 5-10

Platt and Biesty show what happens both inside and outside a castle by examining it layer by layer and including intriguing bits of information. Lords, for example, needed to get a license to crenellate or they would be accused of having an adulterine castle. Subject segments are defense and siege, garrison and prisoners, building a castle, trades and skills, lifestyles of the lords, food and feasting, entertainment, livestock and produce, weapons, and punishments. Glossary and Index.

1555.   Platt, Richard. **Pirate**. Tina Chambers, illustrator. New York: Knopf, 1995. 64p. $19. ISBN 0-679-87255-8. (Eyewitness). 5-8

Photographs of artifacts and drawings complement the text, presented in two-page spreads that cover different topics. They include the pirates of ancient Greece and Rome, the raiders of the north, the Barbary Coast in the eleventh century, the corsairs of Malta during the sixteenth and seventeenth centuries, and the privateers, buccaneers, and pirates of the Caribbean. Other topics are women pirates like Mary Read, the Jolly Roger flag, pirate life, pirates in the Indian Ocean, American privateers, the French corsairs, and pirates of the China Sea. Index.

1556.   Platt, Richard. **The Smithsonian Visual Timeline of Inventions**. New York: Dorling Kindersley, 1994. 64p. $16.95. ISBN 1-56458-675-8. 5-9

Each segment contains an overview of the period followed by a timeline presenting inventions helpful to counting and communication, daily life and health, agriculture and industry, and travel and conquest. A brief list of world events correlates to the inventions. For example, the closed-eye needle appeared in 1450. Time segments are 600,000 B.C. (Fire, etc.) to A.D. 1299 for the first inventions; 1300-1779 for inventions motivated by printing and the spread of ideas; 1780-1869 and the rise of steam power and the Industrial Revolution; 1870-1939 and the use of electric power in the modern world; and 1940-2000, when transistors and information seem most important. Index of Inventions and Index of Inventors.

1557.   Pogrund, Benjamin. **Nelson Mandela**. Milwaukee, WI: Gareth Stevens, 1991. 68p. $16.95. ISBN 0-8368-0357-4. (People Who Have Helped the World). 7-9

Nelson Mandela (b. 1918), son of a chief of the Tembu tribe in South Africa, went to the local school and on to Johannesburg for college and legal training. There he became involved in the political life of colored people trying to escape apartheid. The history of South Africa is the story of white settlers taking away the rights of a native people because they had a different skin color. The world seemed unaware of the intolerance until 1947, but Mandela's efforts continued, and in 1962 the government imprisoned him. He stayed in prison for twenty-seven years, until 1990, when he was seventy-one years old. Although he had been offered freedom several times, Mandela refused until his race was given the freedoms and rights previously denied. This book ends before Mandela's election as president, but it gives a good overview of the situation that destroyed so many other lives. For More Information, Glossary, Chronology, and Index.

1558. Pollard, Michael. **Maria Montessori**. Milwaukee, WI: Gareth Stevens, 1990. 68p. $16.95. ISBN 0-8368-0217-9. (People Who Have Helped the World). 7-9

In 1907, Dr. Maria Montessori began her educational experiment, with her first students from the San Lorenzo slums outside Rome, Italy. Her path to this point had led through secondary schooling with males in her quest to be a doctor (against her father's wishes), speaking for women's rights, and secretly bearing an illegitimate son. From her research, she concluded that children learn most rapidly between the ages of two and one-half and five. By 1909, Montessori's experiment had attracted requests for her to start other schools. Then she began training others in her Montessori method. The text carefully describes the educational activities that she espoused. Organizations, Books, Glossary, Chronology, and Index.

1559. Pollard, Michael. **The Nineteenth Century**. New York: Facts on File, 1993. 78p. $17.95. ISBN 0-8160-2791-9. (Illustrated History of the World). 4-7

In the nineteenth century, towns and the cities showed changes from the old way of life. The British went into India and Americans went west in attempts to build empires. The slave trade led to the Civil War in the United States. Other changes affected Europe, Africa, Australia, and New Zealand as steamships reshaped travel, the oil age began, and the communication revolution started. Illustrations highlight the text. Glossary, Further Reading, and Index.

1560. Pollard, Michael. **The Red Cross and the Red Crescent**. New York: New Discovery, 1994. 64p. $7.95. ISBN 0-02-774720-4. (Organizations That Help the World). 4-8

The Red Cross and the Red Crescent are two organizations created in the nineteenth century to help soldiers on the battlefield receive help more quickly. Neutral emergency units became available that could offer medical aid without threatening the enemy. In Europe, Jean-Herni Dunant watched the Battle of Solferino in 1859. In 1862, he wrote a book about it in which he suggested ways to alleviate some of the deaths. At the same time, Clara Barton in America had become interested in helping prisoners and the wounded. In 1863, an international conference to launch the Red Cross movement opened in Geneva with representatives from 16 countries. On August 22, 1964, the first Geneva Convention had signatures from 12 countries. During the Franco-Prussian war of 1870-1871, the Red Cross helped trace and report on prisoners of war, and Clara Barton provided relief on the battlefields. In 1873, Barton returned to the United States to begin setting up the Red Cross in America. Various other treaties and disagreements continued to refine the process. Since then, the Red Cross (Red Crescent in Islamic countries) has been a major relief organization. Glossary, Important Dates, How You Can Help, and Index.

1561. Pope, Elizabeth Marie. **The Perilous Gard**. Richard Cuffari, illustrator. Boston: Houghton Mifflin, 1974. 272p. $16.95. ISBN 0-395-18512-2. New York: Puffin, Penguin, 1992. 272p. $5.99pa. ISBN 0-14-034912-Xpa. 6 up

In 1558, Queen Mary sends Kate from Hatfield House to Sir Geoffrey's Elvenwood Hall in Derbyshire, the place known as the "perilous gard." The people are fearful of fairy folk who live in the caves and think that Kate is one of them. She shows that she is not by saving a boy during a flash flood. But when Sir Geoffrey's young daughter disappears, Kate realizes that the fairy folk have kidnapped her for their All Hallows' Eve sacrifice. Kate follows them and tells her friend Christopher where to go to trade places as the sacrifice. Because she learns their rules, Kate claims Christopher before the sacrifice, and the fairy folk must free him. *Newbery Honor*.

1562. Pople, Maureen. **A Nugget of Gold**. New York: Henry Holt, 1989. 183p. $13.95. ISBN 0-8050-0984-1. 7-9

Sally, living in the present, alternates chapters with Ann Bird, who lived around 1870. Sally finds a nugget of gold inset with a diamond and the words "Ann Bird Jem ever." As Sally hears the story of Ann Bird from the people with whom she is staying in Australia, while her parents try to reconcile their differences, Sally finds out what happened to Ann Bird when she was a settler.

1563. Pople, Maureen. **The Other Side of the Family**. New York: Henry Holt, 1988. 167p. $13.95. ISBN 0-8050-0758-X. 5-9

Kate, age fifteen, journeys to Australia during World War II to stay with relatives on both sides of the family. Her mother's parents make no decisions without consulting Kate's grandfather's bowling club, and her father's mother has not spoken to Kate's parents for twenty years. Yet she finds that her father's mother, although deaf and poor rather than glamorous as Kate had heard, has much respect from the neighbors. Kate quickly learns to admire her integrity and intelligence.

1564. Porter, Roy. **London, a Social History**. Cambridge, MA: Harvard University Press, 1995. 431p. $29.95. ISBN 0-674-53838-2. YA

This history of London, from Roman times to Margaret Thatcher's days as Prime Minister, presents the city in its depths and its heights. London has survived fires, wars, plagues, and rulers who would dismantle it. That it is so old, and that it has come into the twentieth century with modernizations, is in itself amazing. It has had to clean its river, find supplies of pure drinking water, overcome class distinction to create universal education, try to keep its population civil, and create and update a public transportation system, while expanding its commerce and industry. London has never been perfect, but the myriad facets of its history make it always exciting. Bibliography and Index.

1565.   Posell, Elsa. **Homecoming**. San Diego, CA: Harcourt Brace, 1987. 230p. $14.95. ISBN 0-15-235160-4. 6-9

Olya and her wealthy family face opposition after the government of Tsar Nicholas falls in 1918, because their Jewish family supported the tsar. Her father escapes to America, but before the others can join him, Olya's mother dies. The children, with financial aid and other help from people they meet, finally arrive in Antwerp where they can take a ship to America.

1566.   Posner, Gerald L. **Hitler's Children: Sons and Daughters of Leaders of Third Reich Talk About Themselves and Their Fathers**. New York: Random House, 1991. 239p. $21. ISBN 0-394-58299-3. YA

Posner interviewed children of Nazi leaders during World War II in Germany to assess their reaction to the war and their relationships with their fathers. The subjects include children of Dr. Josef Mengele, Colonel Claus von Stauffenberg, Hermann Göring, bank president Hjalmar Schacht, Rudolf Hess, and Max Drexel. Bibliography and Index.

1567.   Poulton, Michael. **Life in the Time of Augustus and the Ancient Romans**. Christine Molan, illustrator. Austin, TX: Raintree/Steck-Vaughn, 1993. 63p. $16.98. ISBN 0-8114-3350-1. (Life in the Time Of). 4-8

After members of Julius Caesar's senate murdered him in 44 B.C., Octavian began his rise to power; he completed it with the defeat of Antonius and Cleopatra. The text focuses on religion, the Roman army, ships and trade, life in Rome and the countryside, and the architecture and building of the period. Each chapter covers specifics of the topics with illustrations to clarify. Glossary and Index.

1568.   Poulton, Michael. **Life in the Time of Pericles and the Ancient Greeks**. John James, illustrator. Austin, TX: Raintree/Steck-Vaughn, 1993. 63p. $16.98. ISBN 0-8114-3352-8. (Life in the Time Of). 4-8

Pericles (499-429 B.C.) rose to power after the Greeks fought the Persians and survived the battles at Marathon, Thermopylae, and Salamis. He ascended to leadership during a time when Athenian culture was flourishing—the theater, religious rites, and the Olympic Games. Pericles seemed to become too proud as he grew older and the Athenian battle with Sparta became more open. When the plague broke out, many citizens blamed Pericles, but Pericles died of it himself before Sparta became the victor. Each chapter covers specifics of the topics with illustrations to clarify. Glossary and Index.

1569.   Powell, Anton. **Ancient Greece**. New York: Facts on File, 1989. 96p. $17.95. ISBN 0-8160-1972-X. (Cultural Atlas for Young People). 6-9

As much as possible about ancient Greece appears in this text, complemented by full-color illustrations. Topics that help one to understand the life of the ancient Greeks include the Minoan, Cretan, and Mycenaen civilizations of the fifteenth and fourteenth centuries B.C.; the Trojan War, about which Homer wrote, from 900-700 B.C.; Homer's primitive Greece; Athens and its dramatists, historians, and philosophers; the growth of Athens; the Olympic Games, and much more. Chronology, Glossary, Gazetteer, and Index.

1570.   Powell, Anton, and Philip Steele. **The Greek News**. New York: Candlewick, 1996. 32p. $15.99. ISBN 1-56402-874-7. 5-9

The approach to the Greeks through the style of a newspaper highlights fashion, sports, trade, food, and the military. Each page has headlines, sometimes with classifieds advertising such things as instruments for sale. Highly readable and slightly sensational, the news under a headline such as "Olympic Games Spoiled" seems much more accessible than in a textbook. Maps and Index.

1571.   Powers, Elizabeth. **Nero**. New York: Chelsea House, 1988. 112p. $18.95. ISBN 0-87754-544-8. (World Leaders Past and Present). 7 up

Among the atrocities with which Nero (A.D. 37–68) is charged are burning Rome, feeding Christians to wild animals, murdering his mother and wife, and participating in depraved acts. He was an embodiment of evil. He rose to the throne because of his shrewd mother, Agrippina, who poisoned her husband Claudius so that her son could become the emperor. Finally, Nero committed suicide. Photographs and engravings enhance the text. Chronology, Further Reading, and Index.

1572.   Pozzi, Gianni. **Chagall**. Claudia Saraceni and L. R. Galante, illustrators. New York: Peter Bedrick, 1997. 64p. $22.50. ISBN 0-87226-527-7. (Masters of Art). 7 up

Marc Chagall (1887-1985) lived ninety-seven years, and during that time, enormous changes occurred throughout the world. He grew up in Vitebsk, Russia, before leaving to live and travel throughout the world. His pictures incorporated scenes from his life, his family, and his friends. Chronology and Index.

1573. **Prehistoric and Ancient Europe**. Francis Balistreri, illustrator. Austin, TX: Raintree/Steck-Vaughn, 1992. 80p. $17.97. ISBN 0-8172-3304-0. (History of the World). 7 up

This overview uses informative illustrations and clear maps to complement the text. Each topic covers two pages, beginning with the first hunters of the ancient and middle Paleolithic periods, and moving to the Celts from the beginning to approximately 200 B.C. Other topics are the Copper, Bronze, and Iron Ages; Crete; the Iberians; the Italics; the Etruscans; Hallstatt; and the Scythians. Glossary and Index.

1574. Prior, Katherine. **Initiation Customs**. New York: Thomson Learning, 1993. 32p. $13.95. ISBN 1-56847-035-5. (Comparing Religions). 4-8

Six major religions—Buddhism, Christianity, Hinduism, Judaism, Islam, and Sikhism—have specific ideas about the introduction to adulthood. The text examines the age for initiation ceremonies, how much study and preparation each requires, the special clothing worn, and the symbols that represent the religion. Topics such as baptism and confirmation for Christians, bar mitzvah for Jews, *uanayana* for Hindus, *anint* for Sikhs, and *pravrajya* for Buddhists show these rituals.

1575. Prior, Katherine. **Pilgrimages and Journeys**. New York: Thomson Learning, 1993. 32p. $13.95. ISBN 1-56847-032-0. (Comparing Religions). 4-8

Six major religions—Buddhism, Christianity, Hinduism, Judaism, Islam, and Sikhism—have used pilgrimages and journeys as part of their faith. The text looks at why people go on pilgrimages, where they go, how they behave and dress, and what journeys they took in the past. Photographs of holy sites such as Jerusalem augment the text. Glossary, Books to Read, and Index.

1576. Pryor, Bonnie. **Seth of the Lion People**. New York: Morrow, 1988. 118p. $11.95; $4.95pa. ISBN 0-688-07327-1; 0-688-13624-9pa. 3-7

At the age of thirteen, Seth has to endure the hostility of his peers because he is crippled. A falling rock that killed his mother shattered his leg and permanently wounded him. But Seth has other interests, and learning the tribe's stories from his dying father, the Teller-of-Tales, is one of them. When the leader of the tribe, a hunter, threatens him, he leaves and finds a place for the tribe to move so that its hunters can find food more easily.

1577. Pullman, Philip. **The Ruby in the Smoke**. New York: Knopf, 1987. 230p. $11.95; $4.99pa. ISBN 0-394-98826-4; 0-394-89589-4pa. 8 up

Sally Lockhart, age sixteen, kills a man by merely mentioning words from her dead father's cryptic note, found after his death in 1872. Sally becomes the subject of deceit and ill will at the hands of people who want her dead. Her final confrontation on London Bridge allows her to find out how her father provided for her well-being. *IRA Teachers' Choice, Children's Book of the Year* (Great Britain), and *School Library Journal Best Book.*

1578. Pullman, Philip. **Shadow in the North**. New York: Knopf, 1988. 320p. $12.95; $3.25pa. ISBN 0-394-89453-7; 0-394-82599-3pa. 7 up

Sally *(The Ruby in the Smoke)* goes into business for herself as a financial consultant in London. In 1878, one of her clients loses money based on her advice, and Sally works to recover the loss. After finding the man and knowing that he has caused several deaths, Sally agrees to marry him if he repays. But she destroys the factory housing his unscrupulous business, and he happens to be inside at the time. *American Library Association Best Book for Young Adults, IRA Teacher's Choice, Booklist Editor's Choice,* and *Edgar Allen Poe Award nomination.*

1579. Pullman, Philip. **Spring-Heeled Jack: A Story of Bravery and Evil**. David Mostyn, illustrator. New York: Knopf, 1991. 112p. $10.99. ISBN 0-679-91057-3. 4-8

With their mother dead and their father disappeared at sea, three orphans run away, intending to sail to America. Mack the Knife, however, grabs them. Spring-Heeled Jack, with springs in his shoes and clothes like the devil, comes to rescue them. One of the stories proceeds in cartoons, whereas the other occurs in regular text in this historical fantasy set in the nineteenth century. In the end, their father reappears on the ship sailing to America. *School Library Journal Best Book.*

1580. Pullman, Philip. **The Tiger in the Well**. New York: Knopf, 1990. 407p. $15.95. ISBN 0-679-90214-7. 8 up

Sally from *The Ruby in the Smoke* receives a court summons stating that her husband wants to divorce her and take custody of their daughter. Although Sally has never married or even heard of the man named on the summons, her handwriting appears in the registry at the church. She has to find a way to prove the mistake. What she finds is a man accused of crimes because he is Jewish, whom someone is attempting to extradite. As she falls in love with him, the puzzle pieces begin to fit. The person who is causing the trouble turns out to be Ay Ling, the man Sally thought she had killed in *The Ruby in the Smoke.*

1581.   Pullman, Philip. **The Tin Princess**. New York: Knopf, 1994. 290p. $16. ISBN 0-679-84757-X. 8 up

Adelaide (from *The Ruby in the Smoke*), Becky's language student, has married into the Razkavia royal family. Becky, age sixteen in 1882, participates in this complex plot in which Sally, the heroine of other Pullman books, appears. Much political intrigue involves these characters, as well as others with Middle European backgrounds.

1582.   Putnam, James. **Mummy**. Peter Hayman, illustrator. New York: Knopf, 1993. 63p. $19. ISBN 0-679-83881-3. (Eyewitness). 4 up

Two-page spreads on mummies include a large Egyptian section, which covers Egyptian mummies, how to wrap mummies, mummy masks, Egyptian mythology, Tutankhamen's treasures, and the mummy's curse. Other mummies discussed are those of Greeks, Romans, Sicilians, animals, people in the Andes, the iceman, and the Bog Man. Archaeologists have located still other mummies in several additional places. Photographs and Index.

1583.   Pyle, Howard. **Men of Iron**. 1891. Greenville, SC: Bob Jones University Press, 1993. 220p. $6.49pa. ISBN 0-89084-694-4pa. YA

In 1400, Henry IV was declared king of England when wicked and weak Richard II was dethroned. Knights who rose above their stations when Richard was king plotted to kill Henry IV; they failed and were hunted instead. When Myles is six, his father is blinded at a joust; meanwhile, Lord Falmouth is ruined, but unjustly because although he had been a faithful counselor to Richard, he had not deceived Henry IV. Myles and his family survive, and when Myles is a young man, he defends his father's honor against his enemy in another duel.

Q

1584. Quick, Amanda. **Mystique**. New York: Bantam, 1995. 357p. $21.95; $6.50pa. ISBN 0-553-09698-2; 0-553-57159-1pa. YA

Alice decides that she will marry the knight, Hugh the Relentless, who needs a housekeeper, so that she can escape her controlling uncle and create a better life for her brother. After she settles into the new life, she has to rescue her neighbor, Lady Emma, the wife of Hugh's main enemy. Later Hugh is poisoned but not killed, and no one is sure who could have done it. As the story progresses through Norman England, Alice and Hugh learn to appreciate each other.

R

1585. Rabb, Theodore K. **Renaissance Lives: Portraits of an Age**. New York: Pantheon, 1993. 262p. $27.50. ISBN 0-679-40781-2. YA

The fifteen people presented in this collective biography exemplify, according to the author, the change to the new way of thinking in the Renaissance. As a companion to the public television series, the text arranges the lives thematically according to dissenter, ruler, artist, warrior, and explorer. Among the persons included are Titian, Artemetia Gentileschi, John Milton, Teresa of Avila, John Hus, Catherine de' Medici, Galileo, Walter Raleigh, and Gluckel of Hameln (businesswoman, mother, and defender of her Jewish faith). Index.

1586. Radzinsky, Edvard. **Stalin**. H. T. Willetts, translator. New York: Doubleday, 1996. 607p. $30. ISBN 0-385-47397-4. YA

The institutions that Joseph Stalin (1879–1953) created while he ruled the Soviet Union stayed in place until 1991, even as Khrushchev ordered Stalin's body to be removed from its place next to Lenin and buried underground in 1961. Stalin carefully destroyed all those who knew him before he came to power, and his legacy is a history of mass arrests, purges, deportations, collectivization of Soviet agriculture, and the cold war. Stalin built his system on a basis of secret police and fear, a fear that trickled down to his subordinates because he could and did destroy any of them as necessary. The text looks at the man and his influence. Bibliography and Index.

1587. Ragan, John David. **Emiliano Zapata**. New York: Chelsea House, 1989. 112p. $18.95. ISBN 1-55546-823-3. (World Leaders Past and Present). 7 up

Emiliano Zapata (1879–1919) helped the peasant Mexicans battle their corrupt government and the wealthy landowners who were taking their land. Zapata began fighting the dictator Porfirio Díaz, and with his military prowess and dedication to land reform, he defeated Díaz. Zapata helped win rights for the villagers while becoming embroiled with others who played roles in the Mexican Revolution. Photographs enhance the text. Chronology, Further Reading, and Index.

1588. Raspail, J. **Who Will Remember the People?** Jeremy Leggatt, translator. San Francisco: Mercury House, 1988. 213p. $18.95. ISBN 0-916515-42-7. YA

As the last survivor of the Kaweskar, Ona Indians, Lafko knows that his people have lived in the area of Tierra del Fuego near Cape Horn for centuries. Their features indicate to outsiders that they are descendants of the first people to cross the Bering land bridge by foot. Lafko fears the land beyond the mountains surrounding his home, because missionaries bringing cultures from the outside have changed and destroyed the lives of his people.

1589. Rathe, Gustave. **The Wreck of the Barque Stefano off the North West Cape of Australia in 1875**. New York: Farrar, Straus & Giroux, 1992. 136p. $17. ISBN 0-374-38585-8. 8 up

One of only ten crew members to make it to shore after a shipwreck on the desolate North West Cape of Australia, sixteen-year-old Miho Baccich struggles to survive. He and another teenager have to resort to cannibalism. Members of an aboriginal tribe find them and look after them, until a pearling ship comes ashore during a storm and discovers them. They return to Dubrovnik and tell their story to a Jesuit scholar. This is the story they told as researched by Baccich's grandson. Photographs and reproductions enhance the text. Glossary, Notes, and Index.

1590. Ray, Delia. **Gold! The Klondike Adventure**. New York: Lodestar, 1989. 90p. $14.95. ISBN 0-525-67288-5. 5 up

In 1897, three men spread the word that they had found gold in a remote corner of Canada. Thousands headed north, some not even knowing where Klondike was located. They all hoped to escape the depressed American economy. Their route started with a steamship journey to Alaska. Then they had to go through mountain passes and build boats for a trip of 500 miles up the Dawson River. Highlighting the text are more than 50 photographs of the people who went on this last major North American adventure. Glossary and Index.

1591. Ray, Karen. **To Cross a Line**. New York: Orchard, 1994. 154p. $15.95. ISBN 0-531-06831-5. 7 up

Egon, age seventeen, has no driver's license as a Jew in Germany during 1938, but he is a baker's apprentice who makes deliveries, so he has to drive a motorbike without one. One day a black car runs into him, and he has to escape from arrest because no one will believe that the accident was not his fault. He has to leave Katarina, who works in the local coffee shop, and try to get across a border. Though he is thwarted on his attempt in Holland and barely successful in Denmark, he survives, and the reader finds out in the afterword that he went on to China and then to the United States.

1592. Raymond, Patrick. **Daniel and Esther**. New York: Macmillan, 1990. 165p. $14.95. ISBN 0-689-50504-3. 9 up

In 1936, Daniel and Esther meet at a British boarding school where Daniel begins to compose orchestral music. When World War II is declared, Daniel's father wants him to return to America. Esther's Jewish parents expect her to return to her home in Austria, because they have had their passports taken. Daniel hears that his mentor, the man who encouraged his music, has been killed in the Spanish Civil War, as he tells the story in 1939. One never knows what happens to Esther. *Bulletin Blue Ribbon*.

1593. Reboul, Antoine. **Thou Shalt Not Kill**. Stephanie Craig, translator. New York: S. G. Phillips, 1969. 157p. $17.95. ISBN 0-87599-161-0. YA

Slimane, an Egyptian boy, and Simmy, an Israeli girl, stumble across each other in the dark Sinai Desert after an Israeli-Egyptian battle in June of 1967. Both fourteen years old, they spend the night in a gun duel until Slimane wounds Simmy. As he moves in to kill her, he realizes that she is a young girl. Instead of killing her, he binds up the wound. They struggle to survive thirst, exhaustion, and sandstorms until they discover a radio and report their location. When people arrive to rescue them, they make their rescuers shake hands and eat together. *Grand Prize of the Salon de L'Enfance*.

1594. Reed, Don C. **The Kraken**. Honesdale, PA: Boyds Mills Press, 1995. 217p. $15.95. ISBN 1-56397-216-6. 5-8

When Tom is twelve years old, in Newfoundland during 1872, he has to help his father, recently blinded by his own gun, to support their fishing family. The merchant who buys the yearly catch begins to cheat the fishers, and Tom has to work harder for the money. In the plot is a battle with a huge squid, called the *kraken,* and also with human evil in the guise of the dishonest merchant. Afterword.

1595. This number not used.

1596. This number not used.

1597. Rees, David. **The Exeter Blitz**. New York: Dutton, 1980. 126p. $7.95. ISBN 0-525-66683-4. 5-9

While Colin Lockwood stands on the cathedral tower, he sees the German bombers blitz the town of Exeter in 1942 during a Baedeker raid. He begins to worry about other members of his family—his sister at the cinema, his mother at a local fashion show, and his father and other sister. Their home destroyed but their lives intact, they help to reconstruct the town. The omniscient point of view allows each family member to share emotions and thoughts about the situation. *Carnegie Medal*.

1598. Reeves, Nicholas. **The Complete Tutankhamun: The King, the Tomb, the Royal Treasure**. 1990. New York: Thames & Hudson, 1995. 224p. $17.95pa. ISBN 0-500-27810-5pa. YA

In discussing the significance of the excavation of Tutankhamun's tomb in 1922, Reeves looks at the history of Egypt during Tutankhamun's life; Howard Carter and Lord Carnarvon's excavations in the Valley of the Kings, which led to the tomb's discovery; a pharaoh's burial; the concept of the "Pharaoh's Curse"; and the contents of the tomb. New information and excellent illustrations add to the text's value. Chronology, Chapter Bibliographies, and Index.

1599.   Reische, Diana. **Arafat and the Palestine Liberation Organization**. New York: Franklin Watts, 1991. 160p. $21.90. ISBN 0-531-11000-1. 7 up

Arafat (b. 1929) survived over fifty assassination and ambush attempts, while rarely sleeping in the same place twice, before the peace movement began in the Middle East. He works eighteen-hour days, seven days a week, to manage his Palestinian Liberation Organization. Some see him as a terrorist; others see him as a hero. The text includes a historical framework as it looks at Palestine, Arab nationalists, the use of terrorism, the Intifada, and the future. Appendix, Source Notes, For Further Reading, and Index.

1600.   Reiss, Johanna. **The Journey Back**. 1976. New York: HarperCollins, 1992. 212p. $17.89; $3.95pa. ISBN 0-06-021457-0; 0-06-447042-3pa. 5 up

Annie and her sister return to their Dutch home after World War II ends in 1945, in this sequel to *The Upstairs Room*. Annie misses the couple who kept them, but at the same time, she wants her new stepmother to like her. She finds that life cannot return to the way it was before the war changed everything. *Notable Children's Trade Books in the Field of Social Studies, Newbery Honor, National Jewish Awards,* and *New York Public Library Books for the Teen Age.*

1601.   Reiss, Johanna. **The Upstairs Room**. New York: HarperCollins, 1972. 196p. $15; $4.50pa. ISBN 0-690-85127-8; 0-06-440370-Xpa. 5 up

In 1942, Annie, age ten, and her sister leave their parents and older sister to hide in the upstairs room of a farmhouse in Holland. They expect to be free to leave any day, but the war lasts two more years during which they, as Jews, cannot be seen by anyone without endangering their lives as well as the lives of the generous couple who hides them. The story tells of their two years in the room, including the day when Annie goes outside and hides in the tall wheat, only to be marooned in the hot sun while Nazi soldiers examine the house. *Newbery Honor, American Library Association Notable Children's Books of 1971-1975, New York Times Outstanding Children's Books, Jane Addams Honor Book, Buxtehude Bulla Prize of Germany,* and *Jewish Book Council Children's Book Award.*

1602.   Renault, Mary. **The Bull from the Sea**. 1963. New York: Random House, 1975. 343p. $8pa. ISBN 0-394-71504-7pa. YA

Theseus returns to Athens but forgets to raise the white sail that will tell his father he is safe, and his father kills himself in grief. Theseus tries to atone for his mistake by cleaning up the kingdom and adding Crete to his conquests. He agrees to marry Phaedra, daughter of the dead king Minos, when he comes of age. However, he meets Hippolyta, queen of the Amazons, and falls in love with her. She has his child, named Hippolytos, although they cannot marry. After Theseus marries Phaedra, Hippolyta sacrifices herself in battle, and Phaedra and his heir come to live with Theseus in Athens. Phaedra lusts after Hippolytos and tries to seduce him, but he refuses, and she accuses him of rape. Theseus condemns Hippolytos without asking what happened, and lives remorsefully because a tidal wave drowns Hippolytos just after Theseus curses him.

1603.   Renault, Mary. **Fire from Heaven**. New York: Random House, 1977. 374p. $10. ISBN 0-394-72291-4. YA

Alexander astonishes various Persian ambassadors with his accomplishments from 352 until 336 B.C., when he becomes the king after Philip's assassination. He shows his political and military abilities at age six, unnerves Demosthenes so that he forgets his speech at age ten, and leads troops in combat at Thrace at age fifteen. When he serves as his father's regent, he founds a city and becomes a general at the age of seventeen. Alexander loves competition in athletics, in battle, and in politics. Although he is married, he also has a loving relationship with his military companion, Hephaiston.

1604.   Renault, Mary. **The King Must Die**. 1958. New York: Vintage, 1988. 352p. $10pa. ISBN 0-394-75104-3pa. YA

Theseus comes to Athens when he is seventeen years old, but he soon has to leave for Crete as one of the seven youths sent as yearly tribute to King Minos of Crete. He falls in love with Minos's daughter Ariadne, who gives him string that helps him free himself from the labyrinth and certain death after fighting in the ritual bull dance. He sees Ariadne and other women tear apart the local king in the yearly ritual sacrifice to ensure fertility during the following year. He leaves the island in disgust. In Athens, he changes to belief in a masculine religion rather than the traditional feminine beliefs, as he unites Eleusis, Troizen, and Athens.

1605.   Renault, Mary. **The Last of the Wine**. 1956. New York: Random House, 1975. 389p. $8.95pa. ISBN 0-394-71653-1pa. YA

Alexias becomes a soldier, athlete, citizen, and pupil of Socrates in Athens, along with his schoolmate and male lover. As he tries to understand the ethical and philosophical truths that Socrates teaches, he cannot reconcile the insolence of the men who condemn Socrates in their quest for power and money.

1606.   Renault, Mary. **The Mask of Apollo**. 1966. New York: Vintage, 1988. 384p. $12pa. ISBN 0-394-75105-1pa. YA

Nikeratos, age nineteen, has studied acting with his father, and he understands the power of an actor over the audience. When his father dies, he joins a small troupe in which he gains enough experience to produce his own plays. When he plays Achilles for Alexander in Pella, he becomes for Alexander the definitive Achilles, the man of moderation who refused to kill Agamemnon near the beginning of the Trojan War, but who sees Hector later kill his best friend Patrokolus.

1607.   Renault, Mary. **The Persian Boy**. 1972. New York: Vintage Books, 1988. 432p. $13pa. ISBN 0-394-75101-9pa. YA

When Alexander the Great is twenty-six years old, he meets a Persian slave boy, Bagoas, who becomes his companion and lover. Bagoas once belonged to the Persian king Darius, and he understands Alexander's need for affection and his sympathy for his Persian subjects. Bagoas stays with Alexander until he dies from a fever.

1608.   Renfrew, Nita N. **Saddam Hussein**. New York: Chelsea House, 1992. 112p. $18.95. ISBN 0-7910-1776-1. (Library of Biography). 7 up

Using books from the Bible as titles for the chapters, Renfrew tells the story of one of the most powerful twentieth-century Arab leaders, Saddam Hussein (b. 1937). As a teenager, he hated Western colonization in the Middle East and joined the militant Arab nationalist party Iraqi Baath. He held a number of offices in the group and participated in the 1968 coup against Iraq's oppressive military government. Although he began social and economic reforms, he also started wars, first with Iran and then with the United States. He continues to lead although seemingly isolated from many countries. Photographs enhance the text. Chronology, Further Reading, and Index.

1609.   Resnick, Abraham. **The Holocaust**. San Diego, CA: Lucent, 1991. 128p. $12.95. ISBN 1-56006-124-3. (Overview). 4-7

The text discusses the Holocaust, from its beginning with *Kristallnacht* through its terrors during World War II as the Nazis imprisoned and executed millions of Jews in concentration camps. It also covers the establishment of the Jewish state of Israel in Palestine after the end of the war. Quotes personalize the text, and photographs and drawings augment it. Further Reading, Glossary, and Index.

1610.   Resnick, Abraham. **Lenin: Founder of the Soviet Union**. Chicago: Childrens Press, 1987. 131p. $17.27. ISBN 0-516-03260-7. (People of Distinction). 4-8

Vladimir Lenin (1870-1924) grew up in tsarist Russia and was shocked when he discovered that his older brother had been arrested for being involved in a plot to assassinate Tsar Alexander III. His brother was hanged, and Lenin seemed to think that he must take his brother's place in ridding the country of a rotten system of government. He and his colleagues overthrew the government of Nicholas II in 1917 to begin the Russian Revolution. As Lenin took power and oversaw the beginning of the communist state, people observed that he could be either ruthless or kind, depending on his mood. Timeline and Index.

1611.   Reti, Ladislao, ed. **The Unknown Leonardo**. 1974. New York: Abradale Press/Harry N. Abrams, 1990. 319p. $34.98. ISBN 0-8109-8101-7. 9 up

This oversized text incorporates illustrations and reproductions of Leonardo da Vinci's (1452–1519) work, both from museums and his notebook, with text about his life. The chapters, by a variety of scholars, look at Leonardo as a painter, as a writer, as *il cavallo*, his relationship to music, as a military architect, his designs of machines and weaponry, his understanding of the mechanics of water and stone, horology, and the elements of machines. In the appendix are references to the bicycle and Leonardo's own words. Notes and Index.

1612.   Reuter, Bjarne. **The Boys from St. Petri**. Anthea Bell, translator. 1991. New York: Dutton, 1994. 192p. $15.99; $4.99pa. ISBN 0-525-45121-8; 0-14-037994-0pa. 8 up

In 1942, several young males in Aalborg, on the Jutland Peninsula in Denmark, began harassing German soldiers. Their anger at Nazi behavior increases when the church organist, a Jew, finds that his German beloved has been taken away and the local Nazi spy threatens him. A group that includes Gunnar and Lars, sons of the minister; Luffe, the inventor; and the fearless Otto, a boy working in the brickyard to help his family, captures guns and derails a train shipment of ammunition coming into town. Although four of them are caught, they are delighted to hear Otto's signal, a whistle atop the brickyard, that he has escaped to safety. *Mildred L. Batchelder Award.*

1613. Reynoldson, Fiona. **Conflict and Change**. New York: Facts on File, 1993. 78p. $17.95. ISBN 0-8160-2790-0. (Illustrated History of the World). 4-7

The text looks at the changes in European town and country life after 1650. It examines absolute rulers, such as Peter the Great, along with the rise of science, industry, and the arts. It was an era of revolution in the American colonies and in France. In China, the Manchu ruled, and in Japan, the Tokugawa Shogunate. The Moguls had power in Russia, and in Africa the slave trade was beginning. The Dutch entered South Africa; the aborigines were in Australia and the Maori in New Zealand. Illustrations highlight the text. Glossary, Further Reading, and Index.

1614. Reynoldson, Fiona. **Women and War**. New York: Thomson Learning, 1994. 48p. $14.95. ISBN 1-56847-082-7. (World War II). 5-8

Women participated in various ways during World War II. The text looks at their importance, using eye-witness accounts as sources. Among the topics included are food and supply rationing, jobs, evacuations, resistance, forced labor, imprisonment, and combat. It tells all aspects of women's situations, including the brutality of concentration camps and condescension from males. Photographs and Index.

1615. Ricciuti, Edward R. **Somalia: A Crisis of Famine and War**. Brookfield, CT: Millbrook Press, 1993. 64p. $16.90. ISBN 1-56294-376-6. (Headliners). 6-10

This history of Somalia shows that it emerged in the late nineteenth century as a colonial state under various European countries. As the home of clans, the people remained separate, and in 1967 a revolution began. In the latter half of the twentieth century, Somalia has been the seat of widespread famine and conflict. Photographs augment the text. Chronology, Further Reading, and Index.

1616. Rice, Bebe Faas. **The Year the Wolves Came**. New York: Dutton, 1994. 148p. $14.99. ISBN 0-525-45209-5. 5-9

Wolves frighten Therese, age ten, and her family when they enter their Canadian prairie home during a 1906 snowstorm. A Russian worker realizes that the wolves have come to find their leader, left in the village thirteen years before. Their leader happens to be Therese's mother. The story is a combination of history, fantasy, and folklore.

1617. Rice, Earle, Jr. **The Battle of Midway**. San Diego, CA: Lucent, 1995. 110p. $19.95. ISBN 1-56006-415-3. (Battles of World War II). 7 up

The Battle of Midway was one of World War II's most important battles. In June 1942, Raymond Spruance led the outnumbered Americans against the Japanese naval forces commanded by Isoruko Yamamoto. In relating the American victory, the text uses contemporary observations to enhance knowledge gleaned through historical scholarship. Appendix, Bibliography, Chronology, Further Reading, and Index.

1618. Rice, Earle, Jr. **The Cuban Revolution**. San Diego, CA: Lucent, 1995. 112p. $16.95. ISBN 1-56006-275-4. (World History Series). 6-9

Fidel Castro believes that he was born to change history, and he has attempted to do so in Cuba since the early 1950s. He seized control of the Cuban government in 1959 and became *el líder máximo* (maximum leader). Castro's opportunity to oust the government rulers began when Batista overthrew the democratic government in 1952. Castro was probably successful in 1959 because of political repression, economic imbalance and depression, and a perceived threat of "Yankee imperialism" that resulted from uneven policies begun in 1898. In 1960, Castro reestablished relations with the Soviet Union and nationalized United States holdings on the island. These actions led the United States to sever ties in 1961 and attempt an invasion at the Bay of Pigs in April of that year—an invasion that was a miserable failure. The Cuban missile crisis occurred from October 24 through 29, 1962, when the Soviets attempted to place missiles capable of firing on the United States in Cuba. Castro continues to rule Cuba. The island's future remains uncertain. Notes, Glossary, For Further Reading, Works Consulted, and Index.

1619. Rice, Earle, Jr. **The Final Solution**. San Diego, CA: Lucent, 1997. 112p. $17.96. ISBN 1-56006-095-6. (The Holocaust Library). 9 up

The text looks at four scholarly views of Holocaust researchers, the "intentionalists," the "functionalists," the "eclectics," and Goldhagen's belief that the Germans' own anti-Semitic attitudes allowed the annihilation to begin and spread. The four stages of the final solution on which scholars agree are the exclusion (1933-1935), the persecution (1935-1939), the expulsion (1939-1941), and the annihilation (1941-1945). Rice combines the information carefully, thoroughly, and clearly. Bibliography, Chronology, Further Reading, Glossary, and Index.

1620.   Rice, Earle, Jr. **The Nuremberg Trials**. San Diego, CA: Lucent, 1996. 112p. $16.95. ISBN 1-56006-269-X. (Famous Trials). 7 up

With trial transcripts as a basis, Rice relays the crimes for which Nazis were accused and eventually proven guilty at the Nuremberg trials after World War II. He includes additional information about the events leading up to the trials in a balanced and thorough account. Bibliography, Chronology, Further Reading, and Index.

1621.   Rice, Earle, Jr. **The Tet Offensive**. San Diego, CA: Lucent, 1996. 96p. $19.95. ISBN 1-56006-422-6. (Battles of the Twentieth Century). 7-10

Maps and sidebars aid this discussion of one of the important moments in the Vietnam War. Rice says that the South Vietnamese and the Americans did not believe that the North would strike during an important holiday, and their ability to regroup and fight the enemy after the surprise attack during the Tet Offensive was a major victory. Unfortunately, the media did not report the positive aspects of the situation, and Americans never believed the war could be won. Bibliography, Chronology, Further Reading, and Index.

1622.   Rich, Beverly. **Louis Pasteur**. Milwaukee, WI: Gareth Stevens, 1989. 68p. $16.95. ISBN 0-55532-839-3. (People Who Have Helped the World). 7-9

Louis Pasteur (1822–1895) could not understand why some vats of wine soured and some fermented normally in the same winery. His careful research revealed that germs, called microbes, that existed outside a substance could ruin it once inside. Scientists had known that microbes existed since the invention of the microscope by Anton van Leeuwenhoek in the eighteenth century, but they thought them harmless. In his research on silkworms, beer, and cattle and sheep diseases, Pasteur found otherwise. *Pasteurization*, the process that heats such liquids as milk to kill the microbes, is named for him. As a child, Pasteur wanted to be an artist, but a dynamic teacher made him curious about science. He devoted his life to finding ways to cure diseases and was successful in finding a vaccine against rabies. Two of his own three children died from typhoid. Organizations, Books, Glossary, Chronology, and Index.

1623.   Richardson, Martha. **Francisco José de Goya**. New York: Chelsea House, 1993. 112p. $18.95. ISBN 0-7910-1780-X. (Hispanics of Achievement). 7 up

Among the labels attached to Francisco Goya (1746–1828) during his life were social climber, libertine, family man, rebel, patriot, world citizen, and champion of the people. He painted the royal family as the court painter, while showing the horrors of war and the darker side of life in his private paintings. Reproductions enhance the text. Chronology, Further Reading, and Index.

1624.   Richter, Hans. **Friedrich**. 1970. Magnolia, MA: Peter Smith, 1992. 149p. $18.25. ISBN 0-8446-6573-8. New York: Penguin, 1987. 149p. $4.99pa. ISBN 0-14-032205-1pa. 5-9

Beginning in 1925, Friedrich's prosperous German family begins to lose its money as the narrator's poor family begins to rise in society. Hitler's propaganda about Jews affects Friedrich because of his Jewish family, and the narrator's father becomes a Nazi supporter. Friedrich eventually dies from shrapnel, which hits him outside a bomb shelter. His only "crime" is that he is Jewish. *Mildred L. Batchelder Award*.

1625.   Richter, Hans. **I Was There**. Edite Kroll, translator. New York: Henry Holt, 1972. 205p. $5.95. ISBN 0-03-088372-5. New York: Penguin, 1992. 205p. $4.99pa. ISBN 0-14-032206-Xpa. 7 up

In 1933, three eight-year-old German boys become friends. They are a Nazi official's son, Heinz; a Communist's son, Gunther; and the narrator. After the war starts twelve years later, Heinz enlists and returns wounded. He asserts that the only hero he saw was a man who jumped on a grenade to save the men in his platoon. When all go to war together at a later time, Heinz himself becomes a hero, sacrificing himself to save his friends.

1626.   Ridd, Stephen, ed. **Julius Caesar in Gaul and Britain**. Austin, TX: Raintree/Steck-Vaughn. 1995. 48p. $22.83. ISBN 0-8114-8283-9. (History Eyewitness). 6 up

Taken from the Latin work *De Bello Gallico (About the Gallic War)*, the text relates the story of Caesar's first expeditions into Britain in 55 and 54 B.C. Caesar wrote seven of the eight chapters, and these commentaries (as Caesar called his writings) are the only written source of information extant about the lives and deaths of the Gauls at this time. The idea that the British tribes painted their faces for war with blue paint originated here. This work is one of the major sources for current historical fiction. Glossary and Index.

1627.   Riley, Judith Merkle. **In Pursuit of the Green Lion**. New York: Delacorte, 1990. 440p. $19.95. ISBN 0-385-30089-1. New York: Dell, 1992. 440p. $4.99pa. ISBN 0-440-21103-4pa. YA

After Margaret becomes a widow in 1356, Brother Gregory's father kidnaps her and makes her marry Brother Gregory, whose secular name is Gilbert de Vilers. Margaret shocks Gilbert's family with her opinions, and when Gilbert's father expects him to beat Margaret and keep her quiet. Gilbert refuses. After Gilbert has to go to France to fight in the Hundred Years' War, Margaret goes to retrieve him, bargains for him with loaded dice, and brings him home.

1628. Riley, Judith Merkle. **The Oracle Glass: A Novel of Seventeenth-Century Paris**. New York: Viking, 1994. 510p. $22.95. ISBN 0-670-85054-3. New York: Ballantine, 1995. 510p. $12.50pa. ISBN 0-449-91006-7pa. YA

Geneviève Pasquier, age fifteen in 1675, transforms herself into a fortune-teller with predictions so accurate that she seems infallible. Although somewhat unattractive, she loves to read and has the ability to gaze into the waters of an oracle glass, which supposedly tell the futures of those who want to know. After her family thinks she is dead, La Voisin, an occultist, takes her in and lets her become a member of her secret society of witches, a group of abortionists and poisoners who control the lives of wealthy Parisian socialites. Geneviève takes on the persona of one "Madame de Morville," wearing a black dress and powered face and carrying a cane. She influences others and survives because of what she knows and has.

1629. Riley, Judith Merkle. **A Vision of Light**. New York: Delacorte, 1989. 442p. $19.95; $4.95pa. ISBN 0-440-50109-1; 0-440-20520-4pa. YA

In 1355, when Margaret of Ashbury decides to write a book, she shocks the friar, Brother Gregory, whom she asks to be her chronicler. Since he needs food, he compromises his ethical beliefs and works with her. Margaret's incredible experiences include surviving the plague and inventing forceps to extract children during the birth process. She also has had many positive relationships with other people. After she becomes a wealthy widow, Gregory's practical father demands that she marry his brother, and Gregory finally realizes that he must marry her instead.

1630. Rissik, Dee. **Women in Society: South Africa**. New York: Marshall Cavendish, 1992. 128p. $21.95. ISBN 1-85435-504-X. (Women in Society). 7 up

After introducing the women of South Africa through their myths, the author discusses the roles of women in South Africa by interweaving historical and contemporary practices. She presents the expectations imposed upon women—rural and urban, religious and secular, poor and wealthy. The chapters cover milestones, women in society, what being a woman means in the culture, and the life of a woman from birth to old age. Women Firsts, Glossary, Further Reading, and Index.

1631. Roaf, Michael. **Cultural Atlas of Mesopotamia and the Ancient Near East**. New York: Facts on File, 1990. 238p. $45. ISBN 0-8160-2218-6. (Cultural Atlas). YA

Three sections—"Villages," "Cities," and "Empires"—show the history, geography, anthropology, and archaeology of Mesopotamia and the Near East. Topics include Babylon, Ur, warfare, ivory carving, and the origin of writing. Maps and illustrations augment the text. Bibliography, Chronology, Glossary, and Index.

1632. Robb, Candace M. **The King's Bishop**. New York: St. Martin's Press, 1996. 372p. $23.95. ISBN 0-312-14638-8. YA

In 1367, Edward III wants to win loyalty from English churchmen because he opposes Pope Urban V. He sends Owen Archer on a journey to collect support from two Cistercian abbeys, and during that period three murders occur. Archer's friend Ned Townley is accused, and when Archer stops to help Townley, he finds clues leading to the court and the king's unpopular mistress, Alice Perrers.

1633. Robb, Candace M. **The Lady Chapel**. New York: St. Martin's Press, 1994. 287p. $20.95. ISBN 0-312-11409-5. YA

Owen Archer's patron, the Archbishop of Canterbury, commands him to investigate the murder of Will Crounce in 1365. Archer cannot find the apprentice who witnessed the murder, and Gilbert Ridley, Crounce's wool business partner, is in shock over finding Crounce's severed hand. Ridley's and several other murders occur as Archer tries to answer some strange questions that possible suspects raise.

1634. Robb, Candace M. **The Riddle of St. Leonard's**. New York: St. Martin's Press, 1997. 320p. $21.95. ISBN 0-312-16983-3. YA

In 1369, Owen Archer, the one-eyed spy in the employ of the Archbishop of York, wants to stay out of York because the plague is raging for the third time. Sir Richard, the bishop's nephew, demands his presence to find out who is murdering the older wealthy boarders in the hospital at St. Leonard's so that the hospital will not be financially ruined by their demise.

1635. Roberts, Ann V. **Louisa Elliott**. Chicago: Contemporary, 1989. 650p. $19.95. ISBN 0-8092-4290-7. YA

At her mother's death, Louisa returns to York, England, in the late nineteenth century. There she falls in love with a married man with whom she has children. Eventually she realizes that she loves her cousin, and she reunites with him after her father dies. Family intrigues and connections affect people through the years.

1636. Roberts, Ann V. **Morning's Gate**. New York: Morrow, 1992. 639p. $22. ISBN 0-688-11074-6. YA

Because Zoe feels that she is more like her deceased grandmother than her parents, she comes to York, England, to find out more about that grandmother. She meets a distant cousin who has diaries and photographs of her grandmother's brothers, including one who had fought in France during World War I. She and the cousin fall in love as they discover why her grandmother had so much strength of character.

1637. Roberts, Elizabeth. **Georgia, Armenia, and Azerbaijan**. Brookfield, CT: Millbrook Press, 1992. 32p. $15.90. ISBN 1-56294-309-X. (Former Soviet States). 4-7

The text discusses the cultural background, politics, economics, and histories of the former Soviet republics of Georgia, Armenia, and Azerbaijan. Georgia borders the Black Sea and was the home of Stalin. Armenia borders Turkey, and Turks have often invaded it and persecuted its citizens. Azerbaijan borders both Iraq and the Caspian Sea. Glossary and Index.

1638. Roberts, Jack. **Dian Fossey**. San Diego, CA: Lucent, 1995. 112p. $16.95. ISBN 1-56006-068-9. (The Importance Of). 7 up

Dian Fossey (1932–1985) was murdered in her African home, near corners of Rwanda, Zaire, and Uganda, where she was studying mountain gorillas. From 1966, she had lived in the area and made human contacts with the gorillas. As she noted the gorillas' many human-like characteristics, she became more interested in saving them from extinction. Hunters could make much money on the skins of these animals and continued to kill them even in their protected habitats. Fossey's death probably came at the hands of someone whom she had insulted in her aggressive efforts to keep the gorillas in a sanctuary. The text discusses these and many other aspects of her life as a scientific researcher and conservationist. Photographs, Notes, For Further Reading, Works Consulted, and Index.

1639. Roberts, Jack L. **The Importance of Oskar Schindler**. San Diego, CA: Lucent, 1995. 111p. $16.95. ISBN 1-56006-079-4. 7 up

Oskar Schindler, a Nazi during World War II, saved over 1,000 Jews from being exterminated. The text looks at his early life and then his business through which he started saving Jews. Bibliography, Further Reading, Notes, and Index.

1640. Robinson, Francis, ed. **The Cambridge Illustrated History of the Islamic World**. New York: Cambridge University Press, 1996. 352p. $39.95. ISBN 0-521-43510-2. (Illustrated Histories). YA

This text includes thorough information about the religion of Islam. It looks at the history and practice of its believers along with its economic, social, and intellectual aspects. Boxed text and inserts add more specific information about a variety of issues that face this group of people. Bibliography, Glossary, and Index.

1641. Robinson, Lynda S. **Eater of Souls**. New York: Walker, 1997. 229p. $21.90. ISBN 0-8027-3294-1. YA

After Tutankhamen has ruled for five years, Lord Meren and his adopted son Kysen, eighteen, must find the identity of a serial killer who cuts up his victims and then eats their hearts.

1642. Robinson, Lynda S. **Murder at the Feast of Rejoicing: A Lord Meren Mystery**. New York: Walker, 1996. 229p. $20.95. ISBN 0-8027-3274-7. YA

During Egyptian times of Tutankhamen, around 1350 B.C., Lord Meren, one of the Pharaoh's closest advisors, looks forward to going home for a rest. When he arrives at the estate, he finds that his sister has invited a group of people for a family celebration, and one of the guests is murdered. Lord Meren has to investigate the situation and see how it relates to his position as one of the Pharaoh's favorites.

1643. Rochman, Hazel, and Darlene Z. McCampbell, selectors. **Bearing Witness: Stories of the Holocaust**. New York: Orchard, 1995. 136p. $15.95. ISBN 0-531-09488-X. 7 up

This collection of writings about the Holocaust presents selections from fiction and nonfiction written by people who lived during the Holocaust of World War II. Authors included are Elie Wiesel, Ida Vos, Erika Mumford, Art Spiegelman, Primo Levi, Cynthia Ozick, Claude Lanzmann, Carl Friedman, Ida Fink, Frank O'Conor, Dorothy Rabinowitz, Anna Deavere Smith, and Delbert D. Cooper. Bibliography. *Bulletin Blue Ribbon Book, Chicago Tribune's Year's Best Books,* and *American Library Association Best Books for Young Adults.*

1644. Roe, Elaine Corbeil. **Circle of Light**. New York: HarperCollins, 1989. 248p. $13.95. ISBN 0-06-025079-8. 5-8

Lucy, age thirteen, decides that she will apply for a scholarship to a Catholic high school in Ontario after she sees the boy on whom she has a crush skating with a girl who goes to that school. As she studies for the scholarship competition, she feels isolated because she wants to be with her friends instead. She does not win, but she learns about her self and her relationships.

1645.   Rogasky, Barbara. **Smoke and Ashes**. New York: Holiday House, 1988. 187p. $16.95. ISBN 0-8234-0697-0. 5 up

The text gives a brief history of the roots of Nazi anti-Semitism and some of the reasons for Hitler's rise to power. Then it follows the development of the plan to exterminate the Jews. Quotations from both major and minor Nazi leaders show how they built the ghettos and concentration camps, why they built them, and who built them. Other chapters look at life in the camps for the Jews, their armed resistance in Warsaw, and what the United States and Britain did and did not do about their situation. A final chapter lists the Nazis tried at Nuremberg and what happened to them. Bibliography and Index.

1646.   Rogers, James T. **The Secret War: Espionage in World War II**. New York: Facts on File, 1991. 91p. $16.95. ISBN 0-8160-2395-6. (World Espionage). 7 up

In World War II, espionage was an important activity for the Japanese, the Germans, the Americans, and the British. Not until the British were able to break the German codes with "Ultra" and the Americans break the Japanese codes with "Magic" was the war winnable. The text looks at espionage in these countries. Suggested Reading and Index.

1647.   Rogers, Judith. **Churchill**. New York: Chelsea House, 1986. 112p. $18.95. ISBN 0-87754-563-4. (World Leaders Past and Present). 8 up

Winston Churchill (1874–1965) had a poor academic record, which he had to struggle to overcome as a young man. Among his many achievements were the Nobel Prize for Literature in 1953 and a knighthood from Queen Elizabeth II. Photographs enhance the text. Chronology, Further Reading, and Index.

1648.   Rogerson, John. **Cultural Atlas of the Bible**. New York: Facts on File, 1993. 96p. $17.95. ISBN 0-8160-2903-3. (Cultural Atlas for Young People). 6-9

Much of the Christian book called the Bible is history, and this text tells what portions of the book have been verified through archaeological evidence. Additionally, the text tries to present the forces that caused these stories to be perpetuated through the centuries, from oral tradition down to their first written form during the Babylonian Exile beginning in 597 B.C. Illustrations of sites highlight the text. Chronology, Glossary, Gazetteer, and Index.

1649.   Roman, Joseph. **Octavio Paz**. New York: Chelsea House, 1993. 110p. $18.95. ISBN 0-7910-1249-2. (Hispanics of Achievement). 9 up

Octavio Paz (b. 1914), a poet and essayist, received the Nobel Prize for Literature in 1990. He is a believer in political and artistic freedom as well as an explorer of other cultures. He grew up during the Mexican Revolution, went to Spain during its civil war in the 1930s, and lived in Paris; in the 1940s, he entered the Mexican diplomatic service. He created some of his greatest work while in Europe and India. After the Mexican government massacred students in 1968, he resigned and began writing full time. Photographs and reproductions enhance the text. Chronology, Further Reading, and Index.

1650.   Roman, Joseph. **Pablo Neruda**. New York: Chelsea House, 1992. 111p. $18.95. ISBN 0-7910-1248-4. (Hispanics of Achievement). 8 up

Pablo Neruda (1904–1973) changed his name when he was a teenager to keep his poetry writing secret from his father. He studied in Santiago, Chile, but served his country as a diplomat in the Orient before fighting against fascism in Spain in the 1930s. In the 1940s, he returned to Chile, where he began advocating rights for the poor. He joined the Communist Party and served in the Chilean senate, attacking the government and foreign business interests. He lived in exile for three years, but returned home a hero. In 1969, he ran for the presidency of Chile before supporting Salvador Allende, and was distressed by the military coup that overthrew Allende. Neruda left a life of courage and beauty in his extraordinary poetry, which speaks of people, love, and equality. He received the Nobel Prize for Literature in 1971. Photographs enhance the text. Chronology, Further Reading, and Index.

1651.   Romei, Francesca. **Leonardo da Vinci: Artist, Inventor, and Scientist of the Renaissance**. Andrea Ricciardi and Sergio Ricciardi, illustrators. New York: Peter Bedrick, 1994. 64p. $19.95. ISBN 0-87226-313-4. (Masters of Art). 4 up

Leonardo da Vinci (1452-1519), one of the world's greatest artists, was also interested in many other things. The double-page spreads in the text cover his life in Florence, his contemporaries, his concept of perspective in painting, Verrocchio's workshop where he apprenticed, his painting, machines, bronze casting, his equestrian monument, the Medicis, his life in Milan, anatomy, mathematics, hydraulics, flight, and architecture. His works include *The Annunciation, The Adoration of the Magi, The Virgin of the Rocks, The Last Supper,* and *The Mona Lisa*. Index.

1652. Roop, Peter, and Connie Roop, eds. **I, Columbus: My Journal—1492-3**. Peter E. Hanson, illustrator. New York: Walker, 1990. 58p. $13.95. ISBN 0-8027-6977-2. 4-8

With a beginning in which he addresses the Christian queen and king of Spain, Columbus tells of preparing three vessels for his voyage to India to see the Great Khan, and announces that he plans to record the events of the journey. The text recaps this journal, in which Columbus noted the number of miles traveled each day and the encounters with Native Americans when he reached land. He presented the log to the queen and king when he returned.

1653. Roper, Robert. **In Caverns of Blue Ice**. Boston: Little, Brown, 1991. 188p. $14.95. ISBN 0-316-75606-7. 4-7

When Louise DeMaistre is only twelve years old in her French Alp village during the early 1950s, she guides her older brother out of a tough spot on a sheer mountain face, showing that she is a mountain climber like the rest of her family. She works first as a porter with Edouard Bruzel, a senior guide, and then she makes ascents on some of the most dangerous peaks. She passes difficult exams to become the first woman Alpine guide and eventually climbs the Himalayas in Nepal, where she almost loses her life.

1654. Rosen, Billi. **Andi's War**. 1989. New York: Puffin, 1991. 144p. $3.95pa. ISBN 0-14-034404-7pa. 6-9

While Andi and her brother live with their grandparents in a small village, their Communist guerrilla parents fight in the Greek civil war to gain control over the Monarchists after World War II. Andi, age eleven, fears nothing, but Paul is younger, and the Monarchists lure him into a trap that will help them capture his mother. Paul suffers intensely and eventually dies because he refuses to reveal what he knows.

1655. Rosenberg, Maxine B. **Hiding to Survive: Stories of Jewish Children Rescued from the Holocaust**. New York: Clarion, 1994. 166p. $15.95. ISBN 0-395-65014-3. 6 up

In the text, fourteen people who remember hiding as children during the Holocaust tell their stories. They come from Greece, Belgium, Poland, Holland, Hungary, Lithuania, and France. A farm dog protected one from a German shepherd that was searching a hayloft. Another lay in a tiny hole waiting for her uncle to return and lift the trap door. Some of the survivors have kept up with those who saved them, though others have never seen their rescuers again. They found that those who helped them had a variety of reasons, some perhaps political, but others humane. Glossary and Further Reading. *Bulletin Blue Ribbon Book*.

1656. Ross, Kate. **A Broken Vessel**. New York: Viking, 1994. 289p. $18.95; $5.95pa. ISBN 0-670-84999-5; 0-14-023453-5pa. YA

When cockney Sally Stokes, nearly nineteen years old, practices prostitution in London in the early nineteenth century, she takes something from each of her customers. She mostly steals handkerchiefs. One handkerchief has a letter in it, which Julian Kestrel, her brother's employer, unexpectedly discovers. She and Kestrel search the clues and spend time trying to solve a murder, undergoing some harrowing experiences along the way. The setting gives a view of the London police force in its infancy and how the English courts worked.

1657. Ross, Kate. **Cut to the Quick**. New York: Viking, 1993. 352p. $19; $5.95pa. ISBN 0-670-84847-6; 0-14-023394-6pa. YA

Julian Kestrel, a Regency fop of the 1820s, acts as a private eye in an English manor house where he has gone to be best man at a wedding for a man whom he saved from a gambling debt. There he sees the fighting families distress the couple. The corpse of a young woman appears in Kestrel's bed, and when he tries to find out who killed her, he uncovers several possibilities. The Dipper, Kestrel's manservant and reformed pickpocket, assists.

1658. Ross, Kate. **Whom the Gods Love**. New York: Viking, 1995. 400p. $20.95; $5.95pa. ISBN 0-670-86207-X; 0-14-024767-X. YA

Julian Kestrel becomes involved in solving his third murder in England's 1820s when someone murders one of his old friends in the library while people enjoy a party in another room. Kestrel discovers that many individuals had a motive to kill the man, including his business associates, his servants, and even his wife.

1659. Ross, Nicholas. **Miró**. Hauppauge, NY: Barron's, 1995. 32p. $14.95; $8.50pa. ISBN 0-8120-6535-2; 0-8120-9427-1pa. (Famous Artists). 5 up

Joan Miró (1893-1983), often described as a Spanish surrealist, worked in a variety of media: sculpture, textiles, pottery, theater, public monuments, and painting. The text discusses the influences on Miró's life, such as his Catalonian ancestry, his life in Paris, the Spanish Civil and World Wars, theater, tapestry, and other artists such as Salvador Dali, Pablo Picasso, and Antoni Gaudí, who came from his hometown of Barcelona. Clear reproductions highlight the text. Chronology, Art History, Museums, Glossary, and Indexes.

1660. Ross, Stewart. **Causes and Consequences of the Arab-Israeli Conflict**. Austin, TX: Raintree/Steck-Vaughn, 1995. 80p. $25.68. ISBN 0-8172-4051-9. (Causes and Consequences). 7 up

This text, which traces the history of Middle Eastern conflict, includes an assessment of the British involvement in the creation of the state of Israel in 1948. It also looks at the contributions of other major powers such as the United States, the Soviet Union, and the United Nations, and of the Palestinian contingent. This background shows that reasons for hostility exist on both sides and explains why coming to terms on peace is so difficult. Chronology, Further Reading, Glossary, and Index.

1661. Ross, Stewart. **Causes and Consequences of the Rise of Japan and the Pacific Rim**. Austin, TX: Raintree/Steck-Vaughn, 1995. 80p. $25.68. ISBN 0-8172-4054-3. (Causes and Consequences). 7 up

Since World War II's destruction, Japan has recovered with remarkable speed. The text looks at the social, economic, and political reasons why this change has occurred. Additional economic power has come to other Pacific Rim areas, such as Singapore, Hong Kong, and South Korea; Ross notes the causes here. Although China is most important, Ross thinks that its political instability keeps its future, and that of Hong Kong, cloudy. Chronology, Further Reading, Glossary, and Index.

1662. Ross, Stewart. **China Since 1945**. New York: Bookwright Press/Franklin Watts, 1989. 64p. $13.40. ISBN 0-531-18220-7. (Witness History). 7 up

The text discusses the history of China from Mao Zedong's Communist takeover in 1945, through the Great Leap Forward in 1958 (which failed in 1959), and the Cultural Revolution in 1966-1969. It then notes the changes that have taken place since Mao's death in 1976. Bibliography and Index.

1663. Ross, Stewart. **Elizabethan Life: How It Was**. London: Batsford, 1991. 72p. $19.95. ISBN 0-7134-6356-2. 7-11

The text looks at life during the time of Elizabeth I in England, from 1558 to 1603. The general topics covered are country life, town life, at home, women and children, education and learning, the poor, arts and entertainment, church and faith, government, law and order, plot and rebellion, and war Time Chart, Glossary, Maps, Further Reading, and Index.

1664. Ross, Stewart. **Monarchs of Scotland**. New York: Facts on File, 1990. 192p. $27.95. ISBN 0-8160-2479-0. YA

The text begins with the history of Scotland in about A.D. 841, when the House of Alpin took the throne. A brief biographical capsule of each monarch gives pertinent information about his reign. The monarchs came from the Houses of Dunkeld, Balliol, Bruce, Stewart, and after the Union of the Crowns, Stuart. After the Act of Union, the Jacobites were on the throne. Final information about the clans also appears. Chronology and Index.

1665. Ross, Stewart. **The Origins of World War I**. New York: Bookwright Press/Franklin Watts, 1989. 63p. $11.90. ISBN 0-531-18260-6. (Witness History). 7 up

Maps, short biographical highlights of leading figures, color illustrations, and graphs augment short chapters covering different topics about the beginning of World War I. The conclusion that Ross draws is that the war might not have happened in certain circumstances, but many complexities led to its onset. Chronology, Glossary, Notes, and Index.

1666. Ross, Stewart. **The Russian Revolution, 1914–1924**. New York: Bookwright Press/Franklin Watts, 1989. 64p. $13.40. ISBN 0-531-18221-5. (Witness History). 7 up

The text examines the causes, events, aftermath, and historical significance of the 1917 revolution in Russia, led by Lenin, Trotsky, and Kerensky. Index.

1667. Ross, Stewart. **Shakespeare and Macbeth: The Story Behind the Play**. Tony Karpinski and Victor Ambrus, illustrators. New York: Viking, 1994. 35p. $16.99. ISBN 0-670-85629-0. 7-9

In 1605, Shakespeare announced to Richard Burbage that he was going to stage a play about Macbeth. Ross traces how Shakespeare changed the facts about Macbeth for the play and gives information about staging at the Globe Theater. He also describes the court performance for King James. This background information makes the play much more accessible than it might normally be. William Shakespeare Chronology, The Play, Shakespeare's Works, and Index.

1668. Ross, Stewart. **The United Nations**. New York: Franklin Watts, 1990. 64p. $11.90. ISBN 0-531-18295-9. (Witness History). 7 up

The text examines the history of the United Nations from the days before the discussions about the League of Nations to the present. The responsibilities of the United Nations are peacekeeping, human rights, and human welfare for people around the world. Black-and-white photographs supplement the text. Bibliography, Chronology, Glossary, Notes, and Index.

1669. Ross, Stewart. **The USSR Under Stalin**. New York: Bookwright Press/Franklin Watts, 1991. 64p. $11.90. ISBN 0-531-18409-9. (Witness History). 7 up

Joseph Stalin (1879–1953) seized power in the Soviet Union in 1936 and kept his dictatorship until his death. During his control, social and economic changes occurred that may have contributed to the nation's devastation in World War II. Among other atrocities, Stalin imprisoned or had murdered those whose intelligence threatened his power. Black-and white photographs supplement the text. Bibliography, Chronology, Glossary, Notes, and Index.

1670. Rotem, Simha (Kazik). **Memoirs of a Warsaw Ghetto Fighter**. Barbara Hashay, translator. New Haven, CT: Yale University Press, 1995. 180p. $22. ISBN 0-300-05797-0. YA

In 1943, the Nazis decided to liquidate the Warsaw ghetto in Poland. They did not expect 500 Jewish fighters inside to defy them. After realizing that they could not penetrate the ghetto, the Nazis used cannons and aerial bombings from outside it. When the Jews had lost, Kazik, age nineteen, led the survivors out of the ruins through the sewers. Kazik then spent the rest of the war helping the Jews who remained in Warsaw. The text tells his story. References and Index.

1671. Roth-Hano, Renée. **Touch Wood: A Girlhood in Occupied France**. New York: Four Winds Press, 1988. 297p. $16.95. ISBN 0-02-777340-X. New York: Penguin, 1989. 297p. $5.99pa. ISBN 0-14-034085-8pa. 5-9

On August 22, 1940, Renée Roth's parents send her and her two sisters to a convent in Normandy, where they will stay while the Nazis are in France. They had already escaped from Alsace when Renée was nine. The diary form of the novel tells about the interactions between the sisters, other friends in the convent, and the nuns in charge. They remain safe until the bombing at the front of the Allied invasion, and the family eventually reunites in Paris. *American Library Association Notable Books for Children.*

1672. Rowland, Laura Joh. **Shinju**. New York: Random House, 1994. 367p. $5.99pa. ISBN 0-679-43422-4pa. YA

When Sano, formerly a tutor and samurai but now a police officer, finds a young man bound to a beautiful woman dragged from the Sumida River in Edo during January 1689, he thinks *shinju*, or ritual double suicide. As he follows his routine investigation, he finds deceit that leads to murder instead. His search takes him into the seamy city that will become Tokyo and shows the privileged class, the townspeople, the pleasure district, and the everyday society of late seventeenth-century Japan.

1673. Rowlands, Avril. **Milk and Honey**. New York: Oxford University Press, 1990. 143p. $15. ISBN 0-19-271627-1. 4-7

In 1958, after Nelson, age twelve, and his family arrive in England, he soon becomes homesick for the sunshine and color of his Jamaican homeland. As some of the first immigrants, they find out that British citizens do not welcome them. Nelson, however, makes friends with old Mrs. Waterman, who helps him adjust to this new and hostile place by treating him respectfully and requesting his help with weeding her garden.

1674. Rupert, Janet E. **The African Mask**. New York: Clarion, 1994. 125p. $13.95. ISBN 0-395-67295-3. 6-9

In eleventh-century Africa, Layo, age twelve, goes to the city of Ife to meet her Yoruban husband and learn what job she will have as his wife. Instead of making the pottery for which her grandmother is famous, she finds that she will have to help with bronzes, a medium she does not yet appreciate. She tries to have the agreement broken, but realizes almost too late that her grandmother knows better than she what is best.

1675. Rushton, Lucy. **Birth Customs**. New York: Thomson Learning, 1993. 32p. $13.95; $5.95pa. ISBN 1-56847-034-7; 1-56847-502-0pa. (Comparing Religions). 4-8

Six major religions—Buddhism, Christianity, Hinduism, Judaism, Islam, and Sikhism—have customs surrounding the birth of a child. The text looks at the choosing of a name, the prayers said over the child, the ceremonies, and gifts to the child and family. Photographs enhance the information. Glossary, Books to Read, and Index.

1676. Rushton, Lucy. **Death Customs**. New York: Thomson Learning, 1993. 32p. $13.95; $5.95pa. ISBN 1-56847-031-2; 1-56847-503-9pa. (Comparing Religions). 4-8

Six major religions—Buddhism, Christianity, Hinduism, Judaism, Islam, and Sikhism—have specific rituals for approaching death. The text looks at the practices, the attitudes toward death, mourning customs, and ways to remember the dead. Glossary, Books to Read, and Index.

1677. **Russia**. Minneapolis, MN: Lerner, 1992. 56p. $19.95. ISBN 0-8225-2805-3. (Then and Now). 5-9

As the largest of the countries to gain its freedom in 1991, Russia continues to have severe problems. The text looks at its history, beginning with the arrival of the Mongol hordes through Peter the Great, Ivan, and its other rulers. It also examines the economics, geography, politics, and ethnography of the country. Maps and photographs complement the text. Glossary and Index.

1678.   Rutherford, Edward. **London**. New York: Crown, 1997. 829p. $25.95. ISBN 0-517-59181-2. YA

London is a trading post that grows into a powerful seat of government with control of much of the globe. The characters weaving into its history know Chaucer, see Shakespeare plays, experience the plague, and flee from London's fires.

1679.   Rutherford, Edward. **Russka**. New York: Crown, 1991. 760p. $25. ISBN 0-517-58048-9. YA

Families live in a small Ukrainian village through the centuries from A.D. 180 to the Russian Revolution.

1680.   Rutherford, Edward. **Sarum**. New York: Crown, 1987. 897p. $45.95. ISBN 1-56849-114-X. YA

Five families living in the environs of Salisbury, England, represent the history of the area from the Ice Age through the twentieth century.

1681.   Rylant, Cynthia. **I Had Seen Castles**. San Diego, CA: Harcourt Brace, 1993. 97p. $10.95. ISBN 0-15-238003-5. 7 up

John, 17 in 1941, wants to enlist immediately when the Japanese bomb Pearl Harbor. He meets Ginny, who is against all war, and when he enlists, he sacrifices their relationship. As he reflects 50 years later while he lives alone in Canada, he thinks of his losses, including Ginny and his country. Although he had wanted to see castles since he was nine, and he did see them during the war, he wonders if the sacrifices were worth it. No one in the United States had understood his suffering, and he had had to move to Canada. *New York Public Library Books for the Teen Age.*

$$\boxed{\text{S}}$$

1682. Sacks, David, Oswyn Murray, and Margaret Benson. **Encyclopedia of the Ancient Greek World**. New York: Facts on File, 1996. 306p. $45. ISBN 0-8160-2323-9. YA

The alphabetical entries in this collection of facts about the ancient Greek world give information on politics, warfare, history, weaponry, arts, literature, social organizations, mythology, science and technology, clothing, religion, and almost anything else about which one may wonder. The introduction looks at the influence of Greek culture on the contemporary world. Bibliography and Index.

1683. Sacks, Margaret. **Beyond Safe Boundaries**. New York: Dutton, 1989. 160p. $13.95. ISBN 0-525-67281-1. 5 up

Elizabeth Levin, age fifteen, has every imaginable comfort in her South African home in 1962, even though, as Jews, the family has not had full rights. Then her sister goes to college in Johannesburg, becomes involved with student leaders of mixed race, and begins opposing apartheid. Because of her actions and the family's beliefs, their safe world changes. *School Library Journal Best Book.*

1684. Sahebjam, Freidoune. **The Stoning of Soraya M.** Richard Seaver, translator. New York: Arcade, 1994. 144p. $15.95; $9.95pa. ISBN 1-55970-233-8; 1-55970-270-2pa. YA

A woman, born in 1951 in an Iranian village during the reign of the Shah, was married at the age of thirteen by her parents to a husband who beat her and her seven children. His somewhat questionable business takes him to the city, where he eventually finds another woman. A holy man who comes into the village after the Ayatollah Khomeini comes to power urges him to ask for a divorce, after which the holy man propositions Soraya. Soraya's aunt, however, overhears the suggestion and runs him out of the house. To get back at Soraya, the holy man hints that she has been unfaithful and that the townspeople will be purified if they stone her to death, just as they are when they throw stones at the pillars representing the devil outside of Mecca. In 1986, they did just that. Soraya M. and probably more than 1,000 women like her have been unjustly stoned during this regime. Her aunt told this macabre story to the author, a reporter.

1685. Sallah, Tijan M. **Wolof**. New York: Rosen, 1996. 64p. $15.95. ISBN 0-8239-1987-0. (Heritage Library of African Peoples—West Africa). 7 up

The text focuses on the land, history, politics, and religious beliefs of the Wolof. It also includes their relationship to the other people who live in their region of West Africa on the coast of Senegal. Further Reading, Glossary, and Index.

1686. Salmoral, Manuel Lucena. **America 1492: Portrait of a Continent 500 Years Ago**. New York: Facts on File, 1990. 239p. $50. ISBN 0-8160-2483-9. YA

The text gives details about the Incan, Aztec, and Mayan societies of Latin America as well as the cultures in the southwestern area of the current United States. Among the topics presented are the customs of these people, including birth, death, eating, music, sports, medicine, and stimulants. Also included are the achievements of the people in architecture, art, and science. The rigidity of the societies may have led to their destruction. Photographs and drawings enhance the text. Bibliography, Glossary, and Index.

1687. Salvi, Francesco. **The Impressionists: The Origins of Modern Painting**. Deborah Misuri-Charkham, illustrator. New York: Peter Bedrick, 1995. 64p. $22.50. ISBN 0-87226-314-2. (Masters of Art). 6-9

This book, illustrated with drawings of the artists and reproductions of their work, gives an overview of the Impressionist period in the late nineteenth century, which began and flourished in Paris. Topics such as painting in the open air, the influence of Japanese art, photography, people, and the escape from Realism serve as an introduction to the artists. Those included are Edouard Manet, Claude Monet, Pierre Auguste Renoir, Edgar Degas, Paul Cézanne, Camille Pissarro, Alfred Sisley, Berthe Morisot, Mary Cassatt, Armand Guillaumin, and Gustave Caillebotte. Dates and Index.

1688. Samaan, Angele Botros. **Women in Society: Egypt**. New York: Marshall Cavendish, 1992. 128p. $22.95. ISBN 1-85435-505-8. (Women in Society). 7 up

After introducing the women of Egypt through their myths, the author discusses the roles of women in Egypt by interweaving historical and contemporary practices. She presents the expectations imposed upon women—rural and urban, religious and secular, poor and wealthy. The chapters cover milestones, women in society, what being a woman means in the culture, and the life of a woman from birth to old age. Women Firsts, Glossary, Further Reading, and Index.

1689. Sattler, Helen Roney. **Hominids: A Look Back at Our Ancestors**. Christopher Santoro, illustrator. New York: Lothrop, Lee & Shepard, 1988. 125p. $15.95. ISBN 0-688-06061-7. 4-8

Drawings of early fossil remains decorate this story of our early ancestors: the Australopithecines, Genus Homo, Homo Habilis, Homo Erectus, Homo Sapiens Neanderthalensis, and modern humans (Homo Sapiens). Time Chart, Species Chart, Bibliography, and Index.

1690. Sauvain, Philip. **El Alamein**. Harry Clow, illustrator. New York: New Discovery, 1992. 32p. $13.95. ISBN 0-02-781081-X. (Great Battles and Sieges). 5-9

During World War II, one of the great battles was the Battle of El Alamein in Egypt during 1942, in which the British overcame the Germans. The text looks at the events leading to the battle, the battle itself, and the aftermath. Maps, photographs, and drawings supplement the text. Further Reading, Glossary, and Index.

1691. Sauvain, Philip. **Hastings**. Christopher Rothero, illustrator. New York: New Discovery-Macmillan, 1992. 32p. $13.95. ISBN 0-02-781079-8. (Great Battles and Sieges). 5 up

The text presents the background of William of Normandy's claim to the throne of England and discusses the battle that allowed him to become England's king in 1066 at Hastings. This battle was the beginning of the Norman conquest, and Sauvain adds other interesting bits of information about William and the Normans. Maps, photographs, and drawings supplement the text. Further Reading, Glossary, and Index.

1692. Sauvain, Philip. **Waterloo**. Tony Gibbons and Fred Anderson, illustrators. New York: New Discovery, 1993. 32p. $13.95. ISBN 0-02-781096-8. (Great Battles and Sieges). 5 up

The Battle of Waterloo in 1815 caused Napoleon's demise as a world leader after fifteen years of conquests. The text looks at the events leading to the battle, the battle itself, and the aftermath. Maps, photographs, and drawings supplement the text. Further Reading, Glossary, and Index.

1693. Sawyer, Kem Knapp. **Refugees: Seeking a Safe Haven**. Springfield, NJ: Enslow, 1995. 128p. $17.95. ISBN 0-89490-663-1. (Multicultural Issues). 7-10

Although the text only spends one chapter on the historical aspect of refugees, it includes information about the history of current refugee groups. The United Nations estimates that 1 out of every 125 people is a refugee, forced from home because of human rights violations and loss of freedom. The main groups presented here are refugees from Latin America and the Caribbean, Africa, the Middle East, Asia, and Bosnia. Chapter Notes, Bibliography, and Index.

1694. Saxby, Maurice. **The Great Deeds of Heroic Women**. Robert Ingpen, illustrator. New York: Peter Bedrick, 1992. 151p. $24.95. ISBN 0-87226-348-7. 6-12

The women, both real and legendary, featured in the text have displayed their courage, intelligence, boldness, forcefulness, and strength in whatever task they had to accomplish. Those discussed are Athena, Aphrodite, Demeter, Circe, Medea, Esther, Judith, Scheherazade, the Queen of Sheba (1000 B.C.), Boadicea (50 B.C.), Joan of Arc (1412?-1431), the Hunter Maiden, Vasilissa, Pocahontas (1595?-1617), and Mary Bryant. Bibliography and Index.

1695. Saylor, Steven. **Arms of Nemesis**. New York: St. Martin's Press, 1993. 336p. $19.95; $5.99pa. ISBN 0-312-08135-9; 0-8041-1127-8pa. YA

Gordianus the Finder is called to Baiae on the Bay of Naples during the Spartacus slave revolt in 72 B.C. Two slaves are accused of murdering Lucius Licinius, and Gordianus has been requested to absolve them by finding the real murderer. He has only three days for his investigation before Crassus, Licinius's cousin, will kill all of the slaves on his estate in retribution.

1696. Saylor, Steven. **Catilina's Riddle**. New York: St. Martin's Press, 1993. 448p. $21.95; $5.99pa. ISBN 0-312-09763-8; 0-8041-1269-Xpa. YA

Gordianus inherits an Etruscan farm from his benefactor, Lucius Claudius, and when he moves there he has to fend off relatives and neighbors who want the land. Cicero defends his claim and wants payment so he sends his protégé Marcus Caelius, who has become a spy for Cicero's enemy, to let the enemy stay at the farm so that Caelius can report on him to Cicero. Caelius comes, headless bodies appear, and Gordianus surprisingly begins to respect Caelius.

1697. Saylor, Steven. **A Murder on the Appian Way**. New York: St. Martin's Press, 1996. 384p. $23.95 ISBN 0-312-14377-X. YA

Caesar and Pompey try to control the Roman Empire in 52 B.C. while Titus Milo competes with Publius Clodius for control of Rome itself. But Clodius is murdered on the Appian Way, and the city becomes chaotic. To stop the rioting, Clodius's widow, Fulvia, and Pompey implore Gordianus the Finder to investigate, but only after Cicero's oration at the trial does the truth of a huge cover-up surface.

1698.   Saylor, Steven. **Roman Blood**. New York: St. Martin's Press, 1991. 363p. $18.95. ISBN 0-312-06454-3. YA

In the first century B.C., Cicero hires Gordianus to gather evidence for his defense of Sextus Roscius, a farmer accused of patricide. As he investigates, he finds conspiracy and lies.

1699.   Saylor, Steven. **The Venus Throw**. New York: St. Martin's Press, 1996. 308p. $22.95; $5.99pa. ISBN 0-312-11912-7; 0-312-95778-5pa. YA

When an Egyptian ambassador comes to Rome, he fears that the Egyptian king is trying to have him killed. When someone does murder him after he leaves the home of his friend, Gordianus the Finder, Gordianus helps his sister Clodia Pulcher (later the Lesbia made famous by Catullus) accuse his neighbor Marcus Caelius. Caelius's defender, however, is Marcus Tullius Cicero, the great orator.

1700.   Schama, Simon. **Citizens: A Chronicle of the French Revolution**. New York: Knopf, 1989. 948p. $40. ISBN 0-394-55948-7. YA

Schama examines the French Revolution from 1789 until the execution of Robespierre and other Jacobins in 1794. He calls it a major disaster, with violence becoming an end rather than the means to an end as the Revolution progressed. In the first segment of the text, Schama describes the royal regime and its lack of interest in or use for ordinary people. The rest describes the days after the citizens took control of the government in France, and to some extent, in adjoining European countries. He does not think that their choices were much of an improvement over the regime they replaced. Bibliography and Index.

1701.   Scharfstein, Sol. **Understanding Jewish History: From the Patriarchs to the Expulsion from Spain**. Hoboken, NJ: KTAV, 1996. 168p. $15.95pa. ISBN 0-88125-545-9pa. 7 up

Scharfstein gives a clear history of the Jews beginning in Biblical times and continuing through the expulsion from Spain in 1492. Photographs, maps, and reproductions cover every page, keeping the historical account from being a litany of dates. Chronology and Index.

1702.   Schecter, Kate. **Boris Yeltsin**. New York: Chelsea House, 1993. 110p. $18.95. ISBN 0-7910-1749-4. (Library of Biography). 5 up

Elected president of the Russian republic in 1991, Boris Yeltsin (b. 1931) was the first freely elected president of his country. He was the first to challenge the Soviet government from within, the first Politburo member to reject Communist Party privileges, the first among the ruling elite to take Russia out of the Soviet Union, and the first to remove Lenin's portrait from his office wall. He has had a difficult time with the economic problems confronting the Russians. Photographs enhance the text. Chronology, Further Reading, and Index.

1703.   Scheller, William. **Amazing Archaeologists and Their Finds**. Minneapolis, MN: Oliver Press, 1994. 160p. $14.95. ISBN 1-881508-17-X. (Profiles). 6 up

Because of the ceaseless work of people who are intrigued with the past, some of the secrets to history have been unlocked through archaeology. The people and their finds discussed in this book are: Austen Henry Layard (1817-1884) and Hormuzd Rassam (1826-1910), who found Assyria; Henri Mouhot (1826-1861), discoverer of the Temple of Angkor in present-day Cambodia; Heinrich Schliemann (1822-1890), finder of Troy; Sir Arthur Evans (1851-1941), Knossos; Edward Thompson (1840-1935), the sacred well at Chichén Itzá; Hiram Bingham (1875-1956), the Inca hideaway at Machu Picchu; Howard Carter (1874-1939), the tomb of Tutankhamen in Egypt; and Kathleen Kenyon (1906-1978), the biblical city of Jericho. Time Line of Ancient Civilizations, Bibliography, and Index.

1704.   Schiffman, Ruth. **Josip Broz Tito**. New York: Chelsea House, 1987. 112p. $18.95. ISBN 0-87754-443-3. (World Leaders Past and Present). 7 up

Josip Broz Tito (1892–1980) was a labor leader, revolutionary, guerrilla commander, and renowned statesman. As the leader of Yugoslavia, he rebuffed the Soviet Union's attempt to dominate his country; instead, he established his own type of socialism. He survived World War I, and after leaving a Russian prison, he fought the tsar through the Russian Revolution. In 1920, he returned to Yugoslavia and worked underground for the Yugoslav Communist Party. He escaped Stalin's purge and helped the Partisan army defeat the Nazis. He established a state in which workers had rights, and he minimized their repression. Photographs highlight the text. Chronology, Further Reading, and Index.

1705.   Schimmel, Annemarie, and Franz Carl Endres. **Mystery of Numbers**. New York: Oxford University Press, 1993. 314p. $25; $12.95pa. ISBN 0-19-506303-1; 0-19-508919-7pa. YA

After reading the various interpretations of numbers from 1 to 40 and various numbers from 42 to 10,000 based on "symbolism, religious connotation, and linguistic correlation," one may decide that numbers have more meaning than one would like. Many of the ideas concern numbers in the Judaic, Christian, and Islamic heritages, as Schimmel looks at the origin of Arabic numbers, the evolution of modern superstitions, number games, the Gnostic relationship, and mysticism. Some numbers may be merely lucky, "feminine," or "perfect." Reproductions and drawings complement the text. Bibliography and Index.

1706. Schlein, Miriam. **I Sailed with Columbus**. Tom Newsom, illustrator. New York: HarperCollins, 1991. 136p. $14.95. ISBN 0-06-022513-0. 3-7

Julio, twelve, leaves the monastery in which he was raised and sails with Christopher Columbus (Cristóbal Colón) in 1492 on the *Santa Maria*. As the monks had requested, he keeps a diary in which he records events and facts about the voyage. He never loses faith in Columbus, but he looks forward to returning to Spain and becoming a farmer with money earned on the voyage.

1707. Schlink, Bernhard. **The Reader**. Carol Brown Janeway, translator. New York: Pantheon, 1997. 218p. $21. ISBN 0-679-44279-0. YA

In post–World War II Germany, Michael Berg becomes ill on the way home from school, and a woman of forty takes him home and nurses him through hepatitis. Knowing nothing about her, he becomes her lover, and she encourages his schooling. One day she disappears inexplicably, and not until he is a law student several years later does he realize her darker side. He sits on her case when she is tried as a Nazi criminal and he finds that she is also illiterate.

1708. Schneider, Dorothy, and Carl J. Schneider. **Into the Breach: American Women Overseas in World War I**. New York: Viking, 1991. 368p. $29.95. ISBN 0-670-83936-1. YA

Twenty-five thousand middle-class, educated American women served in Europe during World War I. They were peace activists, journalists, nurses and Red Cross workers, physicians, Salvation Army and YMCA workers, and canteen workers. This account uses primary sources such as written memoirs, diaries, letters, and interviews, with secondary sources such as novels, to tell the story of these women serving in Europe, Asia, and the Middle East, where more than 348 died. An appendix lists the occupations and organizations in which the women served and the number for each. Because their experiences were soon forgotten, women serving in World War II had similar problems in establishing themselves abroad. Bibliography and Index.

1709. Schomp, Virginia. **The Ancient Greeks**. New York: Marshall Cavendish, 1996. 79p. $19.95. ISBN 0-7614-0070-2. (Cultures of the Past). 5-8

The text presents the artifacts, monuments, domestic habits, and historical aspects of ancient Greece as it examines the lifestyle of the people. It covers the chronological and cultural history; the Greek belief system, defined through the twelve Olympian gods and goddesses; the societal mores; and the Greek legacy. To the Greeks, the gods and goddesses were an important part of daily life, and the text develops this idea. Photographs, Drawings, Bibliography, Chronology, Further Reading, Glossary, and Index.

1710. Schraff, Anne. **Women of Peace: Nobel Peace Prize Winners**. Springfield, NJ: Enslow, 1994. 112p. $17.95. ISBN 0-89490-493-0. (Collective Biographies). 5-9

The first Nobel Peace Prize was awarded in 1901, and since then, nine women have been named winners for their attempts to establish peace in the world. They are Baroness von Suttner (1905), Jane Addams (1931), Emily Green Balch (1946), Mairead Corrigan and Betty Williams (1976), Mother Teresa (1979), Alva Myrdal (1982), Daw Aung San Suu Kyi (1991), and Rigoberta Menchu (1992). Index.

1711. Schur, Maxine. **The Circlemaker**. New York: Dial Books, 1994. 192p. $14.99. ISBN 0-8037-1354-1. New York: Puffin, 1996. 192p. $4.99pa. ISBN 0-14-037997-5pa. 5-7

One day in 1852, a sign appears in Mendel's village of Molovsk, Russia, announcing that all Jewish boys over the age of twelve will be conscripted for twenty-five years into the czar's army. Mendel runs to his friend Zalman's hut, but his family has left. Mendel escapes so that his own family will not have to pay a bribe for him to stay out of the army. A man sees him at a train station and guides him to the border. Ironically, the person with whom he must find the border is the boy he has hated throughout his school years. They do succeed, and Mendel journeys to Germany and sails to America via steerage class.

1712. Schur, Maxine. **Sacred Shadows**. New York: Dial Books, 1997. 213p. $14.99. ISBN 0-8037-2295-8. 6-9

Lena Katz's father received military honors for his participation and death at Verdun, but during the thirties, when their city of Poznan returns to Poland, the people are hostile to the German heritage. And since her family is Jewish, no one recognizes past sacrifices to the country. When Lena falls in love with a Zionist who wants her to go to Palestine with him, Lena must decide, not knowing the horrors of the Holocaust to come.

1713. Schwartz, Gary. **Rembrandt**. New York: Harry N. Abrams, 1992. 92p. $19.95. ISBN 0-8109-3760-3. (First Impressions). YA

The text looks at Rembrandt's (1606–1669) life and work as he became an artist in Amsterdam. It shows the various periods of his career and his difficulties in later life, as members of his family died and he lost his money. His paintings showed people the way they actually appeared, with honest expressions, rather than unnaturally attractive. He tried to portray their souls in their portraits. Color Reproductions and Index.

1714.   Scott, Paul. **The Day of the Scorpion**. 1968. New York: Avon Books, 1992. 512p. $11pa. ISBN 0-380-71809-Xpa. (Raj Quartet, Book 2). YA

While their father is a prisoner-of-war in World War II, Susan and Sarah Layton live in Pankot, India. Susan marries, has a child, and becomes a widow, a situation with which she is unable to cope. As Sarah watches Susan and those around her, she meets Merrick, a man who imprisoned a British woman's Indian lover on false premises. She accepts him even with his faults.

1715.   Scott, Paul. **A Division of the Spoils**. 1975. New York: Avon Books, 1992. 640p. $11pa. ISBN 0-380-71811-1pa. (Raj Quartet, Book 4). YA

After World War II ends, Sikhs, Muslims, and Hindus in India begin murdering each other as the British vote to leave. Soldiers who have spent their careers in India have to readjust to a different situation, as do their wives, whose social positions will change when they return to Britain. Sarah and Susan Layton's friends and father are some of those with unexpected upheavals in their lives. Susan's second husband has spent his life destroying the potential for personal success and self-esteem in many Indian lives, and he has difficulty with his loss of power and control.

1716.   Scott, Paul. **The Jewel in the Crown**. 1966. New York: Avon Books, 1992. 480p. $11pa. ISBN 0-380-71808-1pa. (Raj Quartet, Book 1). YA

In August 1942, the liberal and conservative forces among the British and Indian residents in Mayapore, India, battle when the British police accuse Indians of raping a young woman. As various stories come to light, the reader sees that the society cannot tolerate a sexual relationship between an Indian and a British subject.

1717.   Scott, Paul. **The Towers of Silence**. New York: Avon Books, 1992. 400p. $11pa. ISBN 0-380-71810-3pa. (Raj Quartet, Book 3). YA

In 1939, Barbie retires from the Protestant children's mission in Rampur, India, and goes to live with Susan and Sarah Layton's grandmother in Pankot. She becomes distressed enough with the situations that she observes after Mabel's death that she herself dies at the end of the war in 1945. She cannot tolerate what has happened to the people in the country.

1718.   **Scrawl! Writing in Ancient Times**. Minneapolis, MN: Runestone Press, 1994. 72p. $22.95. ISBN 0-8225-3209-3. (Buried Worlds). 6 up

Paleography, the study of writing, gives insights into what ancient civilizations achieved in communication and what they thought was important. The text looks at various ancient scripts and what they reveal. Glossary and Index.

1719.   Sedley, Kate. **Death and the Chapman: A Medieval Mystery**. New York: St. Martin's Press, 1992. 190p. $17.95. ISBN 0-312-06945-6. YA

In 1471, while the York and Plantagenet families continue to fight each other in the English countryside, Roger the Chapman works his way toward London. At age nineteen, recently released from a Benedictine monastery, he wishes to use his talent for solving puzzles. In Bristol, a wealthy alderman wants Roger to help find his son, who has disappeared from the Crossed Hands Inn. Roger's searching leads him to another inn where guests have also mysteriously disappeared, and there he finds his answer.

1720.   Sedley, Kate. **The Eve of Saint Hyacinth**. New York: St. Martin's Press, 1996. 280p. $21.95. ISBN 0-312-14331-1. YA

Roger the Chapman returns to London in 1475, during the Wars of the Roses, expecting to rest after solving two murders. He hears that King Edward IV is planning to invade France. A spy in the house of the Duke of Gloucester, one of Edward's brothers, kills the one person who can identify him. Gloucester trusts no one but Roger, whom he hires to find out who is trying to kill him.

1721.   Sedley, Kate. **The Holy Innocents: A Medieval Mystery**. New York: St. Martin's Press, 1994. 280p. $21. ISBN 0-312-11823-6. YA

Roger the Chapman leaves for Totnes after spending a year in Bristol, England, in 1475. As he approaches town, he has to hide from wanderers who have been stealing and pillaging in the nearby villages. He hears that these people have been terrorizing the area for several weeks and that they may be responsible for the disappearance of two children. The children's nurse, a woman who entices him, tells him about the children. What he discovers when he sees that the mystery should be investigated is a carefully planned crime and an unexpected criminal.

1722. Sedley, Kate. **The Plymouth Cloak: The Second Tale of Roger the Chapman**. New York: St. Martin's Press, 1993. $16.95. ISBN 0-312-08875-2. New York: HarperCollins, 1994. 192p. $4.50pa. ISBN 0-06-104320-6pa. YA

Roger the Chapman encounters Richard, Duke of Gloucester, the younger brother of King Edward. As a loyal member of the House of York, the duke asks Roger to accompany a royal messenger on a mission as the duke tries to stop another Lancastrian conflict. The king's agent is slain, and Roger must find the medieval murderer.

1723. Sedley, Kate. **The Weaver's Tale**. New York: St. Martin's Press, 1994. 256p. $20.95. ISBN 0-312-10474-X. New York: HarperCollins, 1995. $4.50pa. ISBN 0-06-104336-2. YA

Roger the Chapman continues his work as a peddler and crime solver during the Wars of the Roses in England. When he gets sick in Bristol, a widowed wool spinner and her daughter nurse him back to health. He repays them by investigating the mysterious death of a family member. He sees the layers of Bristol's merchant society during his search and uncovers a Lollard plot in Gloucester as well.

1724. Segal, Jerry. **The Place Where Nobody Stopped**. Dav Pilkey, illustrator. New York: Orchard, 1991. 154p. $14.95. ISBN 0-531-05897-2. 5 up

For the years between 1895 and 1906, Yosif the baker never has anyone stop at his place located on the road from Vitebsk to Smolensk. When someone does stop, it is the Cossack sergeant major, and he mistreats Yosif. Others who stop need to be supported or hidden, including Mordecai ben Yahbahbai, who becomes a boarder. Yosif's kindness gains more respect than the Cossack's bullying. *Bulletin Blue Ribbon Book.*

1725. Seil, William. **Sherlock Holmes and the Titanic Tragedy: A Case to Remember**. Chicago, IL: Breese Books, 1996. 253p. $14.95pa. ISBN 0-947533-35-4pa. YA

In 1912, Dr. Watson leaves retirement to accompany his friend Sherlock Holmes on the *Titanic* in a secret government mission. Holmes, disguised in a naval uniform, guards a secret agent taking submarine plans to the United States Navy. Someone steals the plans, and others die as the *Titanic* sinks.

1726. Selfridge, John W. **Pablo Picasso**. New York: Chelsea House, 1993. 112p. $18.95. ISBN 0-7910-1777-X. (Hispanics of Achievement). 5 up

When Pablo Picasso (1881–1973) exhibited *Les Demoiselles d'Avignon* in 1907, the four women who broke the rules of human anatomy shocked the art world. Picasso had created detailed drawings at the age of four, and as a teenage art student declared that he would revolutionize painting—which he did. After he moved from Barcelona to Paris, he collaborated in the development of Cubism and worked in the arts of collage, pottery, and sculpture. He left more than 50,000 works of art at his death. Photographs and reproductions enhance the text. Chronology, Further Reading, and Index.

1727. Sellier, Marie. **Cézanne from A to Z**. Claudia Zoe Bedrick, translator. New York: Peter Bedrick, 1996. 60p. $14.95. ISBN 0-87226-476-9. 4 up

Sellier places information from Cézanne's (1839–1906) life and work in chapters titled with thematic words (in alphabetical order) that describe him in an artistic context as well as a historical one. The table of contents page exhibits miniature reproductions of Cézanne's paintings that show his Cubistic style.

1728. Sellier, Marie. **Chagall from A to Z**. Claudia Zoe Bedrick, translator. New York: Peter Bedrick, 1996. 60p. $14.95. ISBN 0-87226-478-5. 4 up

Sellier places information from Chagall's (1887–1985) life and work in chapters titled with thematic words (in alphabetical order) that describe him in an artistic context as well as a historical one. The table of contents page exhibits miniature reproductions of Chagall's paintings that show how he continued to relate to his Russian-Jewish heritage while working in France.

1729. Sellier, Marie. **Corot from A to Z**. Claudia Zoe Bedrick, translator. New York: Peter Bedrick, 1996. 60p. $14.95. ISBN 0-87226-477-7. 4 up

Sellier places information from Corot's (1769–1875) life and work in chapters titled with thematic words (in alphabetical order) that describe him in an artistic context as well as a historical one. The table of contents page exhibits miniature reproductions of Corot's paintings that show how he valued painting the out-of-doors and his Impressionist style.

1730. Sellier, Marie. **Matisse from A to Z**. Claudia Zoe Bedrick, translator. New York: Peter Bedrick, 1995. 60p. $14.95. ISBN 0-87226-475-0. 4 up

Using paintings and information from Matisse's (1869–1954) life, Sellier places them in alphabetical order to tell the story. The titles of some of the chapters are Appendicitis, Light, Kilometers, Carpets, Faces, Windows, Scarlet, Intimacy, Daily, Reflections, and Zenith.

1731. Semel, Nava. **Becoming Gershona**. Seymour Simckes, translator. New York: Viking, 1990. 128p. $11.95. ISBN 0-670-83105-0. 6-8

As a *sabra* (Israeli born), Gershona, age twelve, is the only child of a mother who survived Auschwitz and a father whose own father abandoned him as a young child to go to the United States. When her grandfather returns to Tel Aviv in 1958 and remarries her grandmother, Gershona must acquaint herself with him while reconciling his decisions. She must also deal with her first love for a new boy who recently arrived from Poland, and she must gain acceptance from peers in her neighborhood.

1732. Semel, Nava. **Flying Lessons**. Hillel Halkin, translator. New York: Simon & Schuster, 1995. 122p. $14. ISBN 0-689-80161-0. 5-7

Monsieur Maurice, a concentration camp survivor, a cobbler, and an Israeli neighbor, tells Hadara that anything is possible. Hadara believes him and jumps from the tallest tree in her father's citrus grove in an attempt to fly. She may be too old to believe him, but she may also want to escape from the various situations around her, such as her grieving widower father, the woman who wants to end his grief and become Hadara's stepmother, and a kind boy who stutters.

1733. Sender, Ruth Minsky. **The Cage**. New York: Macmillan, 1986. 252p. $16.95. ISBN 0-02-781830-6. New York: Bantam, 1988. 209p. $4.50pa. ISBN 0-533-27003-6pa. 7 up

After the war, Nancy's mother tells her about her experiences in the Lodz, Poland, ghetto and several concentration camps from 1939 to 1945. She barely escaped execution, and many in her family died. After seven years, a displaced persons bureau helped her find some of her brothers. The horror of the war becomes more immediate to Nancy through her mother's story.

1734. Sender, Ruth Minsky. **To Life**. New York: Simon & Schuster, 1988. 229p. $14.95. ISBN 0-02-781831-4. 7 up

After being freed from the Nazi labor camp of Grafenort, Riva Minska, age nineteen, has to follow a tortuous path to real freedom from Lodz, Poland. She goes first to Wroclaw, looking for family members who might still be alive. On the way, she has to find food and shelter while hiding from soldiers who might rape her. She meets Moishe Senderowicz, and after they marry, they search for their families together. Although Riva wants her first child to be born in America, the two must endure five years of displaced persons camps before they arrive at their new destination.

1735. Senn, J. A. **Jane Goodall: Naturalist**. Woodbridge, CT: Blackbirch Press, 1993. 64p. $14.95. ISBN 1-56711-010-X. (The Library of Famous Women). 3-7

As a young girl, Jane Goodall (b. 1934) became distressed when she saw a man kill a dragonfly. She decided that she wanted to work with and help animals. She chose to become a secretary because her mother had told her that secretaries could work anywhere, and she wanted to work in Africa where the animals lived. When she went to Africa to visit a friend, she obtained a job with Dr. Lewis Leakey, an archaeologist, who introduced her to the chimpanzees. She watched their habits for many months and learned how to get them to accept her. She continued her research for many years, and the chimpanzees soon treated her as one of them. Her best Christmas present was watching the chimpanzees and their delight over a bunch of bananas that she left them under a tree. The text looks mainly at her life in Africa. Glossary, For Further Reading, and Index.

1736. Serraillier, Ian. **The Silver Sword**. C. Walter Hodges, illustrator. New York: S. G. Phillips, 1959. 187p. $26.95. ISBN 0-87599-104-1. 7-9

In 1940, Ruth, age thirteen, and her three siblings have to find their parents after the Nazis take their mother from their Warsaw, Poland, home. They begin a journey that takes them to Switzerland, where they find their father. Their difficulties and courage throughout their journey mirror similar actions by other children during World War II. *Boy's Club of America Award* and *Carnegie Commendation*.

1737. Service, Pamela F. **The Reluctant God**. New York: Atheneum, 1988. 211p. $13.95. ISBN 0-689-31404-3. 6-9

Lorna, in England, wants to be back in Egypt with her widowed father at his archaeological dig. This historical fantasy also tells about Ameni, training to be a priest in 2000 B.C. while his twin brother prepares to become the pharaoh, Senusert III. After Lorna returns to Egypt, she and Ameni meet in a tomb where Ameni is searching for eternity. She takes him back to England with her to find a relic that he needs to fulfill his destiny.

1738. Sevela, Ephraim. **We Were Not Like Other People**. Antonina Bouis, translator. New York: HarperCollins, 1989. 224p. $14.89. ISBN 0-06-025508-0. 7 up

In 1937, Stalin purged the U.S.S.R. In this book, a young Jewish boy tells his first-person story of his father, an army commander, being imprisoned and of the family being designated "enemy of the people." The boy becomes separated from his family but survives World War II, thinking he is alone. Miraculously, the entire family meets at their grandfather's home, and the boy realizes that as his mother had always said, "we were not like other people." *International Board of Books for Young People*.

1739.   Severance, John. **Winston Churchill: Soldier, Statesman, Artist**. New York: Clarion, 1996. 144p. $17.95. ISBN 0-395-69853-7. 7-10

Winston Churchill (1874–1965) saw three wars during his lifetime and was a significant force in one of them, as well as in important peacetime efforts. The text looks at his life from his boyhood through his Boer War participation, his professional achievements, his political career, and his military decisions during World War II. Quotes from his family and from his writings personalize the text. Photographs, Bibliography, and Index.

1740.   Severance, John B. **Gandhi, Great Soul**. New York: Clarion, 1997. 144p. $15.95. ISBN 0-395-77179-X. 6-9

Mohandas (Sanskrit for Great Soul) K. Gandhi (1869-1947) helped to free India from British colonialism. Severance gives a balanced account of Gandhi's life from his privileged life and attendance at British schools, his unhappy arranged marriage when he was thirteen, his experiences in South Africa, which influenced his concerns for the rights of individuals, through his contributions to the concept of *satyagraha*, or "peaceful resistance." Severance also gives the context of Indian politics that became the focus of Gandhi's protest. Photographs, Bibliography, and Index.

1741.   Severns, Karen. **Hirohito**. New York: Chelsea House, 1988. 112p. $7.95pa. ISBN 0-7910-0574-7pa. (World Leaders Past and Present). 7 up

Hirohito (b. 1901) was the 124th emperor in a legendary succession tracing back to the birth of Japan. As the son of the crown prince and grandson of the Emperor Meiji, he saw Meiji's revered military hero Nogi Maresuke commit ritual suicide when Meiji died. Hirohito thought that this act represented misplaced idealism, and when he became leader in 1926 he named himself "Showa," meaning enlightened peace. Japan's leaders refused to listen to his opposition to involvement in World War II, and they forced the nation into war. The first time he ever spoke directly to his subjects was in the surrender speech of August 15, 1945. He cooperated with the Allied occupiers and aided in the reconstruction of his country. He has remained a symbol of *kokutai*, or the Japanese essence, assuring that Japan would endure. Photographs enhance the text. Chronology, Further Reading, and Index.

1742.   Seymour-Jones, Carole. **Refugees**. New York: New Discovery, 1992. 48p. $12.95. ISBN 0-02-735402-4. (Past and Present). 5-7

People have had to flee their homes because of war, poverty, starvation, or government persecution. Among the historical flights of people included in the text are the dispersions under Genghis Khan and the Mongols around 1214, the Trail of Tears in 1838 when the Cherokees had to leave their homes, the boat people fleeing to Thailand following the fall of Saigon in 1975, and the escape of the Israelites from Egypt around 1280 B.C. The text looks at the way these people coped and how other societies have tried to help. Key Dates, Glossary, and Index.

1743.   Shaw, Margret. **A Wider Tomorrow**. New York: Holiday House, 1990. 130p. $13.95. ISBN 0-8234-0837-X. 7-9

Bobby (Roberta), age sixteen, tries to decide whether to go to college in England or to the United States where her boyfriend has a job. She consults her grandmother, and instead of giving advice, her grandmother tells about her own experiences. As a young girl, she had been a suffragette and an ambulance driver in World War I. Then she had become a Member of the British Parliament. She also reveals that she had been secretly married to a British lord during the war, but that he had died from influenza and she had not told his family of the marriage because they would have disapproved. She shows Bobby that one can be a woman with a career and not sacrifice love.

1744.   Shearman, Deirdre. **Queen Victoria**. New York: Chelsea House, 1986. 114p. $18.95. ISBN 0-87754-590-1. (World Leaders Past and Present). 7 up

Britain's longest reigning monarch, Queen Victoria (1819–1901), ruled for sixty-four years. An independent thinker who saw herself as a liberal, she helped propel Great Britain into the forefront of world politics during the nineteenth century. She married Prince Albert of Saxe-Coburg, who advised her on affairs of state and helped to counter her temperament. They influenced parliamentary decisions on both domestic and foreign issues, unlike modern monarchies. The text looks at her devotion to her family, her dignity, her common sense, and her care for others. Photographs and engravings enhance the text. Chronology, Further Reading, and Index.

1745.   Sheldon, Richard N. **Dag Hammarskjöld**. New York: Chelsea House, 1987. 112p. $18.95. ISBN 0-87754-529-4. (World Leaders Past and Present). 7 up

Dag Hammarskjöld (1905–1961) and his Swedish family believed in justice and human potential. He became a diplomat, administrator, politician, and arbitrator in his job as the secretary-general of the United Nations. Trained as an economist, Hammarskjöld also knew international law, which helped with his United Nations leadership beginning in 1953. He sent peacekeeping forces into Lebanon, wanted to admit nonaligned nations, and believed that United Nations employees should be independent. During his efforts to resolve a crisis in the Congo, his plane crashed mysteriously. He was posthumously awarded the Nobel Peace Prize because he believed that words were always more effective than weapons. Photographs enhance the text. Chronology, Further Reading, and Index.

1746.   Shephard, Marie Tennent. **Maria Montessori: Teacher of Teachers**. Minneapolis, MN: Lerner, 1996. 128p. $17.21. ISBN 0-8225-4952-2. (Lerner Biographies). 5 up

Maria Montessori (1870–1952) began defying tradition as a young girl, and when she was twelve years old, she insisted on attending a boys' technical school of math and science. She was the first woman to enroll in the University of Rome's medical school, and after earning the highest grades in her class, was the first Italian woman to become a doctor. While working with the sick, she saw how mentally ill and poor children barely survived in the slums. As she helped them, she found out that children learn best through their senses. Her method of teaching began the Montessori concept, and she traveled around the world to promote it. Sources, Bibliography, and Index.

1747.   Sherman, Steven. **Henry Stanley and the European Explorers of Africa**. New York: Chelsea House, 1993. 111p. $19.95. ISBN 0-7910-1315-4. (World Explorers). 6-9

In 1788, the African Association in London, England, was founded to begin African exploration. Mungo Park began his first expedition to find the Niger River in 1795, but he failed to reach it, and Gordon Laing first reached Timbuktu in 1824–1825. Other explorers who came to the African continent were Hugh Clapperton, Dixon Denham, Walter Oudney, René Caillié, Richard Lander, David Livingstone, Richard Burton, John Hanning Speke, James Grant, and Samuel and Florence Baker. Henry Stanley (1841–1904) left to find Livingstone in 1869 and succeeded in 1871. Reproductions supplement the text. Chronology, Further Reading, and Index.

1748.   Sherrow, Victoria. **Amsterdam**. New York: New Discovery, 1992. 96p. $14.95. ISBN 0-02-782465-9. (Cities at War). 6 up

The text looks at the effects of World War II on the people who lived in Amsterdam. Eyewitnesses, diaries, and other primary sources tell about the Dutch fascists (NSB), the Nazi invasion, the Resistance, protection of the Jews, and the response to the end of the war. Sherrow also uses quotes from Anne Frank and Ida Vos. Documentary photographs focus and accentuate the text. Bibliography and Index.

1749.   Sherrow, Victoria. **Hiroshima**. New York: New Discovery, 1994. 128p. $14.95; $7.95pa. ISBN 0-02-782467-5; 0-382-24742-6pa. (Timestop). 7 up

By the time the *Enola Gay* dropped the atomic bomb on Hiroshima, on August 6, 1945, World War II had become a war of weapons, through the new destructive technologies inherent in planes, missiles, tanks, guns, and bombs. Since that day, Hiroshima has been a symbol of the beginning of the atomic age and a desire for its end ("no more Hiroshimas"). It represents the importance of peace in the world. The text looks at the history of the city and its recovery from the bomb's devastation; it ends by noting the annual commemoration ritual, on August 6, of floating paper lanterns down the Motoyasu River in memory of the people who were killed or maimed by the explosion. Notes, For Further Reading, and Index.

1750.   Sherrow, Victoria. **James Watson & Francis Crick: Decoding the Secrets of DNA**. Woodbridge, CT: Blackbirch, 1995. 110p. $14.95. ISBN 1-56711-133-5. (Partners). 7-10

In the 1950s, two scientists, one from Britain and one from North America, figured out the mystery of DNA, and other scientists have acclaimed this achievement as the greatest biological discovery in the century. Although the men, James Watson (b. 1928) and Francis Crick (b. 1916) had very different backgrounds, they asked the same scientific questions. From the answers, they were able to construct a model of DNA, which has changed concepts of humanity and genetic coding. Bibliography, Chronology, Glossary, Further Reading, and Index.

1751.   Sherrow, Victoria. **Mohandas Gandhi: The Power of the Spirit**. Brookfield, CT: Millbrook Press, 1994. 128p. $16.40. ISBN 1-56294-335-9. 7 up

After studying law in England, Gandhi (1869–1948) did not experience prejudice resulting from his brown skin until he was riding on a train in South Africa. There he was deemed a "coloured" man unworthy of sitting in certain compartments. This situation changed his life. He eventually returned to India to help the country overcome British rule, but he wanted independence to happen without violence. Finally in 1947, India won its independence. Gandhi became the first prime minister and the spiritual as well as political leader of the country. Notes, Chronology, Bibliography, and Index. *New York Public Library Books for the Teen Age.*

1752.   Shiefman, Vicki. **Good-bye to the Trees**. New York: Atheneum, 1993. 150p. $14.95. ISBN 0-689-31806-5. 4-8

Fagel, aged thirteen in 1907, leaves her widowed mother and family in Slonim, Russia, to go to Chelsea, Massachusetts. She says good-bye to all of the trees, though she is actually saying good-bye to her family. In America, she plans to work enough to pay for the rest of the family to join her. What she finds are new customs and opportunities, but she knows that she will not be happy until the family reunites.

1753.   Shuter, Jane, ed. **Christabel Bielenberg and Nazi Germany**. Austin, TX: Raintree/Steck-Vaughn, 1996. 48p. $15.96. ISBN 0-8114-8285-5. (History Eyewitness). 5-9

When Christabel Bielenberg's husband was sent to a concentration camp, she protested his imprisonment to the Gestapo. Her experience shows the tremendous oppression that individuals endured during Hitler's reign. Photographs, Glossary, and Index.

1754. Shuter, Jane, ed. **Exquemelin and the Pirates of the Caribbean**. Austin, TX: Raintree/Steck-Vaughn, 1995. 48p. $15.96. ISBN 0-8114-8282-0. (History Eyewitness). 6 up

Exquemelin sailed from France to Tortuga in the Caribbean during 1666. Because of his situation there under a despotic master, he became a pirate. He recorded his experiences and the conditions of pirates in an autobiography. The text is a version of his description of pirate customs, including torture. He worked for Captain Henry Morgan, one of the most famous Caribbean pirates, and when the original text was published in 1684, Morgan sued him for libel. Glossary and Index.

1755. Shuter, Jane, ed. **Helen Williams and the French Revolution**. Austin, TX: Raintree/Steck-Vaughn, 1996. 48p. $15.96. ISBN 0-8114-8287-1. (History Eyewitness). 5-9

Helen Williams, an Englishwoman living in Paris in 1793–1794, wrote about the Reign of Terror, during which thousands were killed at the guillotine. She watched the changes and feared for herself and for her family until the frenzied acceleration of executions finally led to the death of the perpetrator. Reproductions, Glossary, and Index.

1756. Siegal, Aranka. **Upon the Head of a Goat: A Childhood in Hungary, 1939–1944**. New York: Farrar, Straus & Giroux, 1981. 214p. $9.95. ISBN 0-374-38059-7. 6 up

Piri had to stay in the Ukraine for a year after World War II broke out, but when she returned home to Beregszász, Hungary, she found that she could not attend school, that her stepfather was in the army, that the family had to use ration coupons, and that Jews had curfews. She had to wear the star of David and the Nazis herded her family into ghettos. In 1944, the Nazis transferred the family to Auschwitz. Siegal is the Piri of the story, who never saw her family again after 1944.

1757. Sifakis, Carl. **Encyclopedia of Assassinations**. New York: Facts on File, 1991. 228p. $35. ISBN 0-8160-1935-5. YA

Among the 350 assassination victims from ancient to modern times presented in the text are Abraham Lincoln (d. 1865); Archduke Francis Ferdinand of Austria (d. 1914); Arsinoe III, Queen of Egypt (d. A.D. 204); Spencer Perceval (d. 1812); and Mohammed Sokolli (d. 1579). Some who had assassination attempts directed at them were Napoleon, Fidel Castro, Queen Victoria, and Adolf Hitler. Dates, places, times, names of victims, their assassins, conspirators if any, and other important information appears in the biographical entries. Index.

1758. Sifakis, Carl. **Hoaxes and Scams: A Compendium of Deceptions, Ruses, and Swindles**. New York: Facts on File, 1993. 308p. $45; $19.95pa. ISBN 0-8160-2569-X; 0-8160-3026-Xpa. 7 up

The text presents 700 entries on topics such as medical quackery, art forgeries, Bigfoot, Piltdown Man, the Tasaday tribe, "Kangaroo Monster Who Terrorized Tennessee," "King Tut's typewriter," and the local automobile repair garage. Biographical entries on infamous con artists describe their "mooches." Swindles and scams that can occur everyday happen in such places as the garage, the computer, or the real estate office. If a scam has been advertised, this text may have it. Personality Index and Subject Index.

1759. Sills, Leslie. **Inspirations: Stories About Women Artists**. Ann Fay, illustrator. Morton Grove, IL: Albert Whitman, 1989. Unpaged. $16.95. ISBN 0-8075-4649-0. 5-8

Georgia O'Keeffe (1887-1986), Frida Kahlo (1907-1954), Alice Neel (1900-1984), and Faith Ringgold (b. 1930) have found different inspirations for their work. O'Keeffe loved nature and repeatedly painted the same subjects. Kahlo looked inward for her inspiration and painted what she thought about. Neel called herself a "collector of souls" and tried to capture the inner life of her subjects as well as the vulnerability of human nature. Ringgold tries to express the sense of community in Harlem, her relationships to other women, and life within her family.

1760. Simmie, Scott, and Bob Nixon. **Tiananmen Square: An Eyewitness Account of the Chinese People's Passionate Quest for Democracy**. Seattle, WA: University of Washington Press, 1989. 212p. $16.95pa. ISBN 0-295-96950-4pa. YA

When the authors began interviewing in China in 1988, they found that people wanted changes in the country where forty years of Mao's leadership had stifled them. Discontent caused many people to appear at the student demonstrations of April and May 1989, who were not students, including hotel workers, teachers, clerks, police, and even military. The Tiananmen Square massacre on June 4, 1989, allows a natural division of this book into two sections, one an account of the events preceding June 4 and the other the series of interviews. People who participated in the demonstrations showed that they knew their protest might have serious consequences, but they were willing to risk danger for change. Chronology and Index.

1761. Simms, George Otto. **St. Patrick: The Real Story of Patrick**. David Rooney, illustrator. Chester Springs, PA: Dufour, 1992. 93p. $13.95. ISBN 0-86278-270-8. 5-9

In a book divided into two parts, Simms first looks at the words Patrick (389?–461?) wrote about his experiences and beliefs. The second part presents the legends and stories that have arisen about his life. Simms discusses St. Patrick's struggles to establish the Christian faith in Ireland. Reproductions and illustrations augment the text.

1762. Simon, Charnan. **Explorers of the Ancient World**. Chicago: Childrens Press, 1990. 128p. $26.20. ISBN 0-516-03053-1. (World's Great Explorers). 4-8

The text looks at the voyages and discoveries of explorers in the ancient world. They include Hanno of Carthage (c. 500 B.C.), Hensi of Egypt (c. 1500 B.C.), Eudoxus of Greece (c. 120 B.C.), Pytheas of Greece (c. 330 B.C.), and Alexander the Great (356-323 B.C.). Timeline, Glossary, Bibliography, and Index.

1763. Simon, Charnan. **Henry the Navigator: Master Teacher of Explorers**. Chicago: Childrens Press, 1993. 128p. $26.60. ISBN 0-5160-3071-X. (World's Great Explorers). 5-8

Henry Infante of Portugal (1394–1460) is called "the Navigator" because his navigational innovations had a significant impact on later explorers. He established a school for navigation, for sea exploration, for observation, and for geographers. His patronage created the basis for Portuguese domination during the Age of Exploration.

1764. Simon, Charnan. **Leif Eriksson and the Vikings**. Chicago: Childrens Press, 1991. 128p. $17.95. ISBN 0-516-03060-4. (World's Great Explorers). 5-8

Leif Eriksson (d. ca. 1020) was a Norse explorer who left Greenland to sail west into uncharted waters searching for a new land. Plants, animals, and natural features that Eriksson described show that he reached the northern shores of the New World centuries before Columbus did. Photographs and drawings augment the text. Bibliography, Chronology, Glossary, and Index.

1765. Simon, Charnan. **Richard Burton**. Chicago: Childrens Press, 1991. 128p. $26.60. ISBN 0-516-03062-0. (World's Great Explorers). 5-8

Reproductions, paintings, and photographs, along with Richard Burton's (1821–1890) own journal entries, help to recreate his life as an explorer. He traversed Africa, became an Islamic scholar who made a pilgrimage to Mecca and Medina, discovered Lake Tanganyika, and translated *The Arabian Nights*. Appendices, Timeline, Glossary, Bibliography, and Index.

1766. Simpson, Judith. **Ancient Greece**. Alexandria, VA: Time-Life, 1997. 64p. $17.95. ISBN 0-7835-4801-X. (Discoveries). 4-7

The text focuses on the Classical and the Hellenistic periods, although it also covers the Cycladic and Minoan times as well as the fall of Greece to Rome. Among the topics covered on the double-spread pages are war, dress, education, professions, and religion. Photographs, Reproductions, Glossary, and Index.

1767. Simpson, Judith. **Ancient Rome**. Alexandria, VA: Time-Life, 1997. 64p. $17.95. ISBN 0-7835-4909-1. (Discoveries). 4-7

Roman history, government, religion, social customs, and people are some of the topics covered in the double-spread pages of this view of Roman life. An interesting addition is a four-page fold of the ancient rock of Masada. Photographs, Reproductions, Glossary, and Index.

1768. Singer, Donna. **Structures That Changed the Way the World Looked**. Austin, TX: Raintree/Steck-Vaughn, 1995. 48p. $15.96. ISBN 0-8114-4937-8. (20 Events Series). 6 up

Humans in recorded history have built structures that have survived to tell something about the people who built them. The structures identified here and discussed in two-page spreads are the Great Pyramid (Cairo, Egypt), the Parthenon (Athens, Greece), the Great Wall of China, the Colosseum (Rome, Italy), Palenque (Chiapas, Mexico), Angkor (near Siem Reap, Cambodia), Great Zimbabwe (near Harare, Zimbabwe), Tower of London (England), Anasazi Cliff Dwellings (Mesa Verda, Colorado), Chartres Cathedral (France), Dikes of the Netherlands, Alhambra (Granada, Spain), Taj Mahal (Agra, India), Suez Canal (between Egypt and Israel), Statue of Liberty (New York), Eiffel Tower (Paris, France), Hoover Dam (near Las Vegas, Nevada), Golden Gate Bridge (San Francisco), Sears Tower (Chicago), and the English Channel Tunnel (between France and England). Glossary, Suggested Readings, and Index.

1769. Singman, Jeffrey L. **Daily Life in Elizabethan England**. New York: Greenwood Press, 1996. 227p. $45. ISBN 0-313-29335-X. (Daily Life Through History). 7 up

The text includes a brief overview and chronology of Elizabethan England. The chapters cover the life cycle, housing, living environment, clothing, food and drink, and entertainment of the people. Other topics include popular songs and fabric patterns, as well as a guide to the costs of items in terms that correspond to contemporary rates of exchange. Diagrams and drawings complement the text. Appendix, Bibliography, Chronology, Glossary, Notes, and Index.

1770. Singman, Jeffrey L., and Will McClean. **Daily Life in Chaucer's England**. New York: Greenwood Press, 1996. 252p. $45. ISBN 0-313-29375-9. (Daily Life Through History). 7 up

The text contains a brief overview and chronology of Chaucer's England. The chapters cover the life cycle, housing, living environment, clothing, food and drink, and entertainment of the people. Other features are popular songs and fabric patterns, as well as a guide to the costs of items in terms that correspond to contemporary rates of exchange. Diagrams and drawings complement the text. Appendix, Bibliography, Chronology, Glossary, Notes, and Index.

1771. Skelton, Renee. **Charles Darwin and the Theory of Natural Selection**. Hauppage, NY: Barron's, 1987. 119p. $5.95pa. ISBN 0-8120-3923-8pa. (Solutions: Profiles in Science for Young People). YA

Charles Darwin (1809–1882) stuck with his theory of evolution for twenty years even though many people said he was wrong. In his youth, he had collected plants, insects, rocks, and birds' eggs, and had wondered about the origin of these things and how they lived. When he went around the world on the *Beagle*, he had a chance to see more interesting items. His idea that living things survive by natural selection disturbed adults, just as his behavior had disturbed them when he was young and preferred to collect things or study nature than to do well in school. Glossary, Topics, Reference, and Index.

1772. Skurzynski, Gloria. **Manwolf**. New York: Clarion, 1981. 177p. $10.95. ISBN 0-395-30079-7. YA

Danush, a Polish serf, accompanies a Knight of the Cross to Vienna as his cook in 1382. The knight wears a leather mask and gloves so that Danush never sees his face. But as he looks at hers, her beauty overcomes him, and he renounces his vow of celibacy. After he impregnates her, she returns home and marries someone else. The child, when born, has light skin that repulses those who see him. When the child is seventeen, the knight returns and sees him. Because the child has the same skin as his true father, the knight knows that the boy belongs to him, and he claims him. *American Library Association Best Books for Young Adults, Child Study Association Books of the Year, Booklist Reviewer's Choice,* and *Notable Trade Books in the Field of Social Studies.*

1773. Skurzynski, Gloria. **What Happened in Hamelin**. 1979. New York: Random House, 1993. 192p. $3.99pa. ISBN 0-679-83645-3pa. 5-9

Gast frees the town of Hamelin from its rat infestation, but the town does not give him his final payment. In retribution, he feeds 130 Hamelin children bread containing purple rye. The rye keeps them from sleeping, and on July 26, 1284, he leads the children away from Hamelin while their parents pray in the church for them to sleep. He plans to sell the children, each for a piece of silver, as his payment. *Christopher Award, Booklist Reviewers' Choice,* and *Horn Book Fanfare Honor List.*

1774. Slater, Robert. **Rabin of Israel**. 1980. New York: HarperCollins, 1993. 486p. $6.99pa. ISBN 0-06-101066-9pa. YA

This update of Yitzhak Rabin's (1922–1995) biography includes his roles as Israel's defense minister, as a leader of his political party, and as prime minister. In addition to various aspects of Rabin's difficult personal periods, Slater discusses Israeli politics, including political positioning for power, the Intifada, and the Middle East peace talks. It ends before Rabin's assassination. Bibliography and Index.

1775. Slater, Robert. **Warrior Statesman: The Life of Moshe Dayan**. New York: St. Martin's Press, 1991. 480p. $27.95. ISBN 0-312-06489-6. YA

Moshe Dayan (1915–1981) was the embodiment of the state of Israel until his death. Actually born near the Sea of Galilee on a kibbutz, he eventually led Israel to military and political dominance of the Middle East through his vision and direction. Although he was closely involved in Israel's wars for twenty-five years, and blamed for the lack of preparation in the 1973 war, he supported the Camp David Accords for peace. He had many complexities and flaws, which the text examines. Bibliography and Index.

1776. Slaughter, Charles H. **The Dirty War**. New York: Walker, 1994. 166p. $15.95. ISBN 0-8027-8312-0. 5-8

In Buenos Aires, Argentina, in 1976, thousands of people disappeared from the streets when the military took over the government from President Isabel Perón. Slaughter starts each chapter with a brief segment from the Buenos Aires newspaper as he describes the effects of this coup on innocent people. Atre, age fourteen, his friend Chino, and his family try to survive by ignoring the situation, but they cannot. The army takes Atre's father, and he and Chino find him. Chino and Atre get Atre's father's story published in the newspaper, which keeps him alive and eventually leads to his freedom. But the army also takes Chino, and he is not as fortunate. The "dirty war" ended in 1983 after the military realized that some parents will fight for their children's rights. Glossary of Spanish Words and Phrases.

1777. Sledge, Linda Ching, and Gary Allen Sledge. **Empire of Heaven**. New York: Bantam, 1990. 576p. $19.95. ISBN 0-553-05755-3. YA

In 1847, Rulan's mother, a Chinese aborigine, goes to Hung, the man claiming to be Jesus' brother, to have a spirit exorcized by him. Hung begins the Taiping Rebellion, which Rulan later joins. Rulan becomes a servant and a mistress in a Manchu house so that she can spy for the rebels. Then she falls in love. She and her beloved have both taken vows of celibacy during the rebellion, but they break those vows before escaping from China. He becomes a slave for six years, and she goes to Hawaii to join missionaries. They make great personal sacrifices in pursing their ideals.

1778.   Smith, Brenda. **The Collapse of the Soviet Union**. San Diego, CA: Lucent, 1994. 112p. $22.59. ISBN 1-56006-142-1. (Overview). 7 up

The text discusses the events and influences leading to the establishment of the Soviet Union, emphasizing the mistreatment of serfs that continued into the middle of the nineteenth century. It examines different periods of Soviet history as defined by the leaders in power at the time—Stalin, Brezhnev, and Khrushchev. Gorbachev, as the last leader of the Soviet Union, led the Second Revolution toward *glasnost* (openness) and survived a failed coup in August 1991. Although the people gained freedom, they now must confront many difficulties while learning how to be free. Glossary, Suggestions for Further Reading, Books Consulted, and Index.

1779.   Smith, Brenda. **Egypt of the Pharaohs**. San Diego, CA: Lucent, 1996. 112p. $16.95. ISBN 1-56006-241-X. (World History Series). 6-9

The text looks at Egypt and the creation of the pyramids in great depth, using quotes as available from both primary and secondary sources. A final chapter examines the significance of the Egyptian culture to world history. Bibliography, Chronology, Further Reading, Notes, and Index.

1780.   Smith, Carter, ed. **The Korean War**. Englewood Cliffs, NJ: Silver Burdett, 1990. 64p. $14.98; $7.95pa. ISBN 0-382-09953-2; 0-382-09949-4pa. (Turning Points in American History). 4-8

The text gives the background as to why the United States was involved in the Korean War and the surprise of the Chinese joining on the side of the North Koreans. It focuses on the battles and the strategy of the war, which lasted from 1950 to 1953. Photographs highlight the text. Bibliography and Index.

1781.   Smith, Jeff. **The Frugal Gourmet on Our Immigrant Ancestors**. New York: Morrow, 1990. 539p. $22. ISBN 0-688-07590-8. YA

Although this is a cookbook, the text extends beyond this limiting definition to include essays about each immigrant group mentioned. Additional notes before each recipe give as much about the foods' origin as possible. For example, a Cuban recipe for yellow rice requires saffron. Saffron, however, is very expensive, and people often made the rice without it by using items with the yellow color of saffron. Other pieces of information appear about 35 different groups who have come to the United States as immigrants. Bibliography, Sources, and Index.

1782.   Smith, Linda W. **Louis Pasteur: Disease Fighter**. Springfield, NJ: Enslow, 1997. 128p. $18.95. ISBN 0-89490-790-5. (Great Minds of Science). 5-8

In his frustration over unexplained diseases, Louis Pasteur (1822-1895) began working with germs. He finally ascertained that germs were causing wine and milk to go bad, and the process of heating that he developed is called "pasteurization" in his honor. Photographs, Diagrams, Chronology, Further Reading, Glossary, and Index.

1783.   Smith, Lucinda Irwin. **Women Who Write: From the Past and the Present to the Future. Volume II**. New York: Julian Messner, 1994. 221p. $15. ISBN 0-671-87253-2. 7 up

The text discusses the nature and significance of authorship and uses interviews and biographical profiles to analyze the contributions of notable women writers. Writers from the past are Jane Austen, George Eliot, Emily Dickinson, Virginia Woolf, Anne Frank, Agatha Christie, and Lorraine Hansberry. Contemporary women are Dawn Garcia, Nikki Giovanni, Jan Goodwin, Beth Henley, Tama Janowitz, Maxine Hong Kingston, Norma Klein, Denise Levertov, Nancy Meyers, Joyce Carol Oates, Carolyn See, and Anne Tyler. Available photographs of writers are included. Suggested Reading and Index.

1784.   Smith, Mack. **Garibaldi**. 1956. Westport, CT: Greenwood Press, 1982. 215p. $55. ISBN 0-313-23618-6. (A Great Life in Brief). YA

According to Smith, Garibaldi (1807–1882) was just over fifty years of age when he ceased to be merely a sailor, pirate, farmer, or radical revolutionary and became the national hero with a place in history textbooks. The text presents Garibaldi's life chronologically, mentioning the places where he fought (including the Rio Grande, Montevideo, Rome, Sicily, and Naples) before he tried to establish his own government in Sicily. Because Garibaldi believed in nationalism, he would have been surprised by Italy's decision in World War II to become an aggressor nation. The text examines all these concepts. Index.

1785. Smith, Norman F. **Millions and Billions of Years Ago: Dating Our Earth and Its Life**. New York: Venture, Franklin Watts, 1993. 127p. $13.40. ISBN 0-531-12533-5. 7 up

Divided into sections according to methodology, the text discusses the processes by which scientists determine the age of their specimens, such as counting the number of tree rings, reading the strata, using chemical analyses, and carbon-14 dating. It also looks at recent findings that estimate the age of the universe. Photographs and drawings enhance the text. Further Reading, Glossary, and Index.

1786. Smith, Ronald D. **Fascinating People and Astounding Events from the History of the Western World**. Santa Barbara, CA: ABC-CLIO, 1990. 208p. $29.95. ISBN 0-87436-544-9. YA

In this text, the author presents a series of short essays and articles about periods in history, starting with the Early Near East and proceeding through the twentieth century. Facts and details fill these articles, which give a sense of the historical times discussed. Chronology and Index.

1787. Snyder, Paula, ed. **The European Women's Almanac**. New York: Columbia University Press, 1992. 399p. $35. ISBN 0-231-08064-6. YA

This almanac discusses the status of women in Europe, their rights, and their advances in areas such as education, employment, and health care, arranged by country. First-person accounts, charts, tables, and diagrams make the text immediate and helpful. Bibliography.

1788. Snyder, Zilpha Keatley. **Song of the Gargoyle**. New York: Delacorte, 1991. 224p. $14.95. ISBN 0-385-30301-7. 5-8

In this medieval setting, Tymmon sees a helmeted knight kidnap his father. He leaves the castle and encounters outlaws, peasants, and greedy lords on his journey with his faithful dog, Troff. Troff is so ugly that he resembles a gargoyle, but Tymmon thinks he is magical and converses with him. Various adventures occur, and at the conclusion, Tymmon knows he would prefer to be a court jester rather than a knight.

1789. Sobel, Dava. **Longitude: The True Story of a Lone Genius Who Solved the Greatest Scientific Problem of His Time**. New York: St. Martin's Press, 1996. 184p. $16.95. ISBN 1-55927-397-6. New York: Penguin, 1996. 184p. $9.95pa. ISBN 0-14-025879-5pa. YA

Because being off course delayed arrival in port, many seamen died from hunger or disease. Through the centuries, finding longitude became a major concern. Some seamen used lunar tables, and inventors worked on clocks that would be accurate regardless of bad weather and ocean swells. The perseverance of John Harrison (1693–1776), despite delays from pettiness and politics, eventually solved the problem. The text also includes anecdotal information, such as the cure for scurvy originally being sauerkraut rather than limes. Bibliography and Index.

1790. **Sold! The Origins of Money and Trade**. Minneapolis, MN: Runestone Press, 1994. 64p. $22.95. ISBN 0-8225-3206-9. (Buried Worlds). 6 up

When archaeologists find ruins of ancient civilizations, they also find the types of coins that people used before 500 B.C. Additionally, they may find items that the ancients sold, and through them create some understanding of ancient commerce. Glossary and Index.

1791. Solecki, John. **Hosni Mubarak**. New York: Chelsea House, 1990. 111p. $18.95. ISBN 1-55546-844-6. (World Leaders Past and Present). 5-9

In 1981, Muhammad Hosni Mubarak became the fourth president of the Egyptian republic, after Islamic fundamentalists assassinated Anwar Sadat. During the ten years of his leadership, he has negotiated with various people in the Arabic world while sustaining the treaty with Israel created under Sadat and maintaining economic and military relationships with the United States. The text looks at his background and his role in Egypt. Photographs supplement the text. For Further Reading, Chronology, and Index.

1792. Somtow, S. P. **Jasmine Nights**. New York: St. Martin's Press, 1995. 379p. $23.95. ISBN 0-312-11834-1. YA

Justin, twelve in 1963, has a best friend, Virgil, an African American from Georgia who also lives in Bangkok. Justin's parents disappear into the darkness of intelligence work in the 1960s before the Vietnam War, and Justin lives with his three spinster aunts. When his great-grandmother appears and suggests that he not live in solitude, he meets girls and other people as he begins to mature.

1793. Sonnleitner, A. T. **The Cave Children**. Katarina Freinthal, illustrator; Anthea Bell, translator. New York: S. G. Phillips, 1971. 139p. $19.95. ISBN 0-87599-169-6. 8 up

In 1683, Eva, age eight, and Peter, age nine, go with their grandmother, whom the town has accused of witchcraft, to the mountains. Their grandmother and uncle die, and a rock slide isolates them from civilization. They have to learn how to survive by hunting for their own food and creating their own tools, as people have had to do through the centuries. Their ingenuity helps them last through the first winter and kill a bear, but they know that they must continue to work.

1794. Southall, Ivan. **Blackbird**. New York: Farrar, Straus & Giroux, 1988. 136p. $12.95. ISBN 0-374-30783-0. 9 up

In 1942, Will, his mother, and his brother move inland to avoid a possible Japanese invasion of the Australian coast where they live. Will plays his own war games by climbing on the roof of their house, but fear seizes him as he tries to descend. While trying to decide how to get down from the roof, he hears a speech in his mind made by a young man who lost two legs. That man said that life does not always turn out the way one expects, and Will confronts his own fears.

1795. Spangenburg, Ray, and Diane K. Moser. **The History of Science from 1895 to 1945**. New York: Facts on File, 1994. 164p. $18.95. ISBN 0-8160-2742-0. (On the Shoulders of Giants). 9 up

In the first half of the twentieth century, research in the physical sciences produced new information about the structure of atoms, the nature of light waves, outer space, and relativity. In the life sciences, the disciplines of microbiology, biochemistry, genetics, and archaeology burgeoned, with many scientists of both sexes making new discoveries. Included in the text are anecdotes about the discoveries, as well as biographical profiles. Photographs, Appendices, Glossary, Bibliography, and Index.

1796. Spangenburg, Ray, and Diane K. Moser. **The History of Science from 1946 to the 1990s**. New York: Facts on File, 1994. 176p. $18.95. ISBN 0-8160-2743-9. (On the Shoulders of Giants). 9 up

This text, the final in the series, discusses the significant scientific discoveries since World War II, including increased specialization and the reliance on computers in research. In the physical sciences during the period, the areas of change include the subatomic world, quarks, the beginning of the universe, stars and the solar system, and space exploration. In the life sciences, DNA, RNA, protein, and a concern as to where humans came from are some of the main topics. Scientists associated with these ideas include Stephen Hawking, Stephen Jay Gould, Richard Feynman, Barbara McClintock, and Linus Pauling. Photographs and illustrations enhance the text. Chronology, Glossary, Further Reading, and Index.

1797. Spangenburg, Ray, and Diane K. Moser. **The History of Science from the Ancient Greeks to the Scientific Revolution**. New York: Facts on File, 1993. 166p. $18.95. ISBN 0-8160-2740-4. (On the Shoulders of Giants). 9 up

Science before the eighteenth century focused on the Copernican system, but the time of reason and revolution changed perceptions. This text looks at the physical and life sciences in the eighteenth century by profiling important researchers of the times and the results of their work, as well as much other information. Among those included are Linnaeus, Buffon, Lamarck, and Cuvier. Topics include the solar system, deep space, geology, the birth of chemistry, heat, electricity, physiology, and the precursors of modern evolutionary theory. Photographs and reproductions enhance the text. Chronology, Glossary, Further Reading, and Index.

1798. Spangenburg, Ray, and Diane K. Moser. **The History of Science in the Eighteenth Century**. New York: Facts on File, 1993. 156p. $18.95. ISBN 0-8160-2740-4. (On the Shoulders of Giants). 9-12

Scientific disciplines in the eighteenth century, the century after Newton, included astronomy, geology, chemistry, electricity, natural history, and the life sciences. The text looks at these disciplines and discusses them in the context of social and political developments and the Industrial Revolution. Leading scientists and thinkers of the time were Voltaire, Kant, Linnaeus, and Lavoisier. Achievements included Jenner creating the smallpox vaccine and Halley seeing a comet. Illustrations, Bibliography, and Index.

1799. Spangenburg, Ray, and Diane K. Moser. **The History of Science in the Nineteenth Century**. New York: Facts on File, 1994. 142p. $18.95. ISBN 0-8160-2741-2. (On the Shoulders of Giants). 9 up

During the Industrial Revolution, science became a popular discipline with discoveries in the areas of atoms, the elements, chemistry, evolution, and energy. Other work in the physical sciences included magnetism, electricity, and light. In the life sciences, Darwin went on the *Beagle* to do his research, and the microscope found germs and cells. John Dalton, William Thomson (Lord Kelvin), Michael Faraday, Thomas Edison, Maria Mitchell, and Louis Pasteur were among the working researchers. Photographs and illustrations enhance the text. Chronology, Glossary, Further Reading, and Index.

1800. Spangenburg, Ray, and Diane K. Moser. **Opening the Space Frontier: Space Exploration**. New York: Facts on File, 1989. 111p. $18.95. ISBN 0-8160-1848-0. (On the Shoulders of Giants). 9-12

The text looks at the history of space flight, beginning with imaginary voyages, then moving to China's invention of the rocket, the V-2 rocket program in Germany during World War II, the X-15, the first unmanned satellites and the space race at the launch of Sputnik, the man-in-space program, and men on the moon. It presents test flight details and spacecraft information. Photographs, Glossary, Chronology, Bibliography, and Index.

1801. Sparks, Allister. **The Mind of South Africa**. New York: Knopf, 1990. 424p. $24.95. ISBN 0-394-58108-3. YA

Sparks tries to give a sense of South Africa through 1990, before it became democratic with the election of Nelson Mandela, by presenting its history and showing how the contemporary situation directly resulted from it. He attempts to understand the blacks and the Boers, the ruling tribe, and gives a good idea of apartheid and how minorities within minorities (such as the English-speaking whites) can have their own difficulties. Index.

1802. Sparks, Allister. **Tomorrow Is Another Country: The Inside Story of South Africa's Road to Change**. New York: Hill & Wang/Farrar, Straus & Giroux, 1995. 254p. $22. ISBN 0-8090-9405-3. YA

From the mid-1980s through April of 1994, South Africa underwent a political transformation. The text discusses the secret discussions among intelligent and patient leaders that transpired during the five years before Nelson Mandela's 1990 release from prison. This book (a sequel to *The Mind of South Africa,* which tells the history of apartheid) presents the events leading to the election of Mandela as the first president of the democratic South Africa in 1994. Additionally, Sparks, a newspaper reporter in South Africa, lists ten reasons why he thinks the South African government will survive. Index.

1803. Speare, Elizabeth George. **The Bronze Bow**. Boston: Houghton Mifflin, 1961. 256p. $15.95; $5.95pa. ISBN 0-395-07113-5; 0-395-13719-5pa. 7 up

Daniel, age eighteen, detests the Roman soldiers in Palestine. They crucified his father and uncle for unpaid taxes and sold him to work for a contemptible blacksmith. He joins an outlaw hiding in the mountains, but then he hears about a man named Jesus who preaches nonviolence. Daniel's new employer leaves Daniel in charge of the forge as he follows Jesus, and Daniel thinks that the man may be able to help his sister, still in mourning for the family. *Newbury Medal* and *International Board of Books for Young People.*

1804. Speare, Elizabeth George. **Calico Captive**. Witold T. Mars, illustrator. Boston: Houghton Mifflin, 1957. 288p. $15.95. ISBN 0-395-07112-7. New York: Dell, 1993. 288p. $4.50pa. ISBN 0-440-41156-4pa. 7-9

In 1754, Indians capture Miriam and her pregnant sister, as well as other members of her sister's family, and sell them to the French in Montreal at the beginning of the French and Indian War. Miriam must support the family, and she does so with her dress designing. She also undergoes an arduous prisoner exchange in which she sails from Montreal to England and back to Boston. She finds that helping others gives her unexpected rewards.

1805. Speed, Peter. **Life in the Time of Harald Hardrada and the Vikings**. Richard Hook, illustrator. Austin, TX: Raintree/Steck-Vaughn, 1993. 63p. $16.98. ISBN 0-8114-3353-6. (Life in the Time Of). 4-8

Harald III Harsrasi (1015-1066), half-brother of Olaf, King of Norway, became king himself after he returned from Byzantium and service in the Varangian guard. His nickname "Hardrada" denoted his ruthlessness. During his lifetime, the Vikings continued to live as traders and warriors, believing in Valhalla and Ragnarok. They invaded England, Ireland, France, and Italy before they went into Russia, America, and Byzantium. Harald went back to invade England in 1066 and captured York, but at the ensuing Battle of Stamford Bridge, he died. Although the Saxons defeated these Vikings, the Saxons soon faced defeat with the arrival of William the Conqueror. Each chapter covers specifics of the topics, with illustrations to clarify. Glossary and Index.

1806. Spence, Jonathan D. **God's Chinese Son: The Taiping Heavenly Kingdom of Hong Xiuquan**. New York: Norton, 1996. 352p. $27.50. ISBN 0-393-03844-0. YA

After taking his Confucian state exams in China and failing twice, Hong Xiuquan (1814) became ill; in his feverish state, he had a dream in which he saw himself as the savior of his people. He declared that the evils of crime and drugs were vices in the Chinese government rather than noting that they had been brought in by the British, and people decided that he was a prophet. They organized militia and collected weapons while placing Hong Xiuquan inside a fortress, and they tried to take over the country. What they began was the Taiping Rebellion, and by the time it ended, 20 million people had died. The text looks at this man who wielded such extraordinary influence in nineteenth-century China. Bibliography and Index.

1807. Spence, Jonathan D. **The Search for Modern China**. New York: Norton, 1990. 867p. $24.95. ISBN 0-393-02708-2. YA

The text gives an overview of Chinese history, beginning with the fall of the last Ming emperor in 1644 and ending with the 1989 Tiananmen Square massacre in Beijing. Spence's accounts of the early Qing Dynasty, the Taiping Revolt beginning in 1850, the 1911 Republic, the 1919 May Fourth Movement, the 1949 People's Republic, and the 1989 incident in Tiananmen Square include the views of various groups of people as they grappled with the changes in their lives from the traditional to the modern. He views Mao as a man who knew what he wanted to do and relentlessly pursued his goal. Spence shows all strata of society in all areas of this vast country, as they socialized and defended against the enemy within as well as the enemy outside. Illustrations, Maps, Glossary, Chapter Bibliographies, and Index.

1808. Spencer, William. **Germany: Then and Now**. New York: Franklin Watts, 1994. 160p. $21.10. ISBN 0-531-11137-7. 7 up

Spencer examines Germany since the fall of the Berlin Wall in 1989 to see what the future holds. But he finds that he must look back over the 2,000 years during which Germany was building a national identity, although it did not become a nation-state for many centuries. He looks at the Germanic tribes that stopped the Roman legions, the Holy Roman Empire, the Hanseatic League, the Reformation, the Thirty Years' War, Frederick the Great's Prussian militarism, Napoleon, the Revolution of 1848, Bismarck's ability to create the German Empire in 1871, Kaiser Wilheim II, and the collapse of the Weimar republic. Source Notes, For Further Reading, and Index.

1809. Sperry, Armstrong. **Call It Courage**. 1940. New York: Macmillan, 1968. 96p. $16. ISBN 0-02-786030-2. New York: Aladdin, 1990. 96p. $3.95pa. ISBN 0-689-71391-6pa. 5-7

Matufu knows that facing the thing he fears most, the sea, is the only way to escape the derision of his Polynesian island people, who call him "Boy Who Was Afraid." Almost drowned as a child with his mother, who saved him as she died, he has not recovered from the fear. He takes his dog into a canoe, and they leave. An albatross guides them through a storm toward land, and Matufu saves himself and the dog by killing a tiger shark, octopus, and wild boar. When they see savages on the island, he and the dog sail away in the canoe he built. As he arrives home and his father declares his pride in his son, he dies. His new name, however, is the tribal name by which he is remembered, "Stout Heart." *Newbery Medal.*

1810. Sproule, Anna. **Mikhail Gorbachev**. Milwaukee, WI: Gareth Stevens, 1991. 68p. $16.95. ISBN 0-8368-0401-5. (People Who Have Helped the World). 7-9

In 1985, Gorbachev became the Soviet leader. His policies opened the way for democracy in Hungary, Czechoslovakia, the Soviet Union, and then East Germany with the destruction of the Berlin Wall on November 9, 1989. He wanted *glasnost* or "openness" and *perestroika* or "rebuilding." A brief history of the Soviet Union since the 1917 Russian Revolution introduces Gorbachev's birth in 1931. For his good work in his home area, Gorbachev earned admission to Moscow State University. His Czechoslovakian roommate taught him much about Western lifestyles. After school, as he worked up the Communist Party ladder, he studied agricultural economics and added this knowledge to his law degree. When Gorbachev was forty-seven, in 1978, party leaders decided to make him the Central Committee secretary for agricultural programs. His concerns about changing the standard of living for the Soviets began an upheaval that changed Soviet society. Organizations, Books, Glossary, Chronology, and Index.

1811. Stacey, Tom. **The Titanic**. Maurie Manning and Michael Spackman, illustrators. San Diego, CA: Lucent, 1990. 64p. $22.95. ISBN 1-56006-006-9. (World Disasters). 5-7

The *Titanic* was advertised as the ship that could not sink, but a few days into its maiden voyage, on April 14, 1912, icebergs sank it. The text recounts the story as it has been pieced together by rescue teams and survivors. In 1985, Robert Ballard and his submarine *Jason* discovered the wreckage of the *Titanic*, thereby allowing new information to become available. Diagrams and drawings augment the text. Further Reading, Glossary, Other Works, and Index.

1812. Stanley, Diane. **Elena**. New York: Hyperion, 1996. 56p. $13.95. ISBN 0-7868-0256-1. 4-7

Elena (a character based on a friend of Stanley's mother) was a widow whose husband died when Pancho Villa's army raided their village. She fled from Mexico to California during the Mexican Revolution in the early 1900s. The text covers her decision to leave with her son so that he would not be drafted into the army and her concern that her other three children escape problems in the war-ravaged country.

1813. Stanley, Diane, author/illustrator. **Leonardo Da Vinci**. New York: Morrow, 1996. 48p. $16. ISBN 0-688-10437-1. 4-7

In addition to presenting the known facts about Leonardo da Vinci (1452-1519), Stanley also creates the time in Florence during which he lived. She describes the preliminary steps for painting and sculpting and the various problems da Vinci had in getting materials and investigating his ideas. She uses da Vinci's own writing to show his intelligence and inquisitiveness. Bibliography. *Booklist Best Books for Young Adults, Bulletin Blue Ribbon Book, American Library Association Notable Books for Children, Orbis Pictus Award for Outstanding Nonfiction for Children,* and *School Library Journal Best Book.*

1814. Stanley, Diane, and Peter Vennema. **Good Queen Bess: The Story of Elizabeth I of England**. Diane Stanley, illustrator. New York: Four Winds Press, 1990. Unpaged. $14.95. ISBN 0-02-786810-9. 5 up

Elizabeth I (1533–1603) of England demonstrated various attributes, including diplomacy, religious tolerance, and love for her subjects. She had learned caution as a young girl, trying to survive when many would have preferred her dead, so she was prepared to rule when she became queen at the age of twenty-five. She played side against side at home and abroad, with countries, advisors, and suitors. Bibliography.

1815. Stanley, Diane, and Peter Vennema. **Shaka: King of the Zulus**. Diane Stanley, illustrator. New York: Morrow, 1988. Unpaged. $13.95. ISBN 0-688-07342-5. 4-7

Shaka (1787?–1828) was outcast as a boy and had to prove himself as a warrior before he became chief of the Zulus, a small clan that he led to dominate an empire. Told in two-page chapters, the story shows his rise to power and explains his actions in the context of his times. Although he was a military genius, he may also have been mentally unstable. Sources.

1816. Steedman, Scott. **The Egyptian News**. New York: Candlewick, 1997. 32p. $15.99. ISBN 0-56402-873-0. 4-9

The approach to the Egyptians through the style of a newspaper highlights fashion, sports, trade, food, and the military. Each page has headlines, sometimes with classifieds advertising such things as used papyrus. Highly readable and slightly sensational, the news under a headline such as "Boy-King Murdered?" seems much more accessible than in a textbook. Maps and Index.

1817. Steele, Philip. **The Aztec News**. New York: Candlewick, 1997. 32p. $15.99. ISBN 0-7636-0115-2. 4-9

The approach to the Aztecs through the style of a newspaper highlights fashion, sports, trade, food, and the military. Each page has headlines, sometimes with classifieds advertising a variety of items that the Aztecs used. Highly readable and slightly sensational, the news under a headline such as "Spanish Flee City" seems much more accessible than in a textbook. Maps and Index.

1818. Steele, Philip, author/illustrator. **Castles**. New York: Kingfisher, 1995. 63p. $14.95. ISBN 1-85697-547-9. 3-7

This presentation of castles includes fold-out illustrations showing cross-sections of a castle's interior. The various chapters include information on the age during which castles were built, the towns surrounding a castle, castle defenses, castle life of all dimensions (food, kitchens, fashions, hunting and hawking, jousting, heraldry), and what happens when a castle is besieged. Castles In History, Glossary, and Index.

1819. Steele, Philip. **Censorship**. New York: New Discovery, 1992. 48p. $12.95. ISBN 0-02-735404-0. (Past and Present). 5-7

The text looks at the history of censorship, including the Chinese emperor who burned books in 213 B.C., Roman censors, religion and the printing press, revolution, and private censorship. It examines the reasons stated for censorship and assesses freedom or control as a motive. Key Dates, Glossary, and Index.

1820. Steele, Philip. **The Egyptians and the Valley of the Kings**. New York: Dillon Press, 1994. 32p. $13.95. ISBN 0-87518-539-8. (Hidden Worlds). 4-7

Photographs and maps give an overview of Egypt. Topics included are the pharaohs, pyramids and tombs, the archaeologists' search for Thebes, the attempts to break the language barrier of hieroglyphics, the mask of Tutankhamen, the rulers and the gods, and other bits of information. Glossary and Index.

1821. Steele, Philip. **Food and Feasts Between the Two World Wars**. New York: New Discovery, 1994. 32p. $14.95. ISBN 0-02-726322-3. 7 up

The text looks at the ways food was grown and prepared in the time period between the two world wars by focusing on the crops in the countryside and the types of food that had to be shipped to the cities and suburbs. If one traveled, one had to eat, and the text notes foods available in restaurants. Additional information about cooking utensils and recipes from the 1920s and 1930s gives a good sense of the times. Photographs and reproductions enhance the text. Glossary, Further Reading, and Index.

1822. Steele, Philip. **Food and Feasts in Ancient Rome**. New York: New Discovery, 1994. 32p. $14.95. ISBN 0-02-726321-5. 7 up

The text looks at the ways food was grown and prepared in the Roman Empire as it evolved from approximately 200 B.C. to A.D. 476 by focusing on the crops in the countryside and the types of food that had to be shipped to the cities and suburbs. If one traveled, one had to eat, and the text mentions food available in taverns and inns. Additional information about cooking utensils and recipes from the Romans gives a good sense of the times. Photographs enhance the text. Glossary, Further Reading, and Index.

1823. Steele, Philip. **The Incas and Machu Picchu**. New York: Dillon Press, 1993. 32p. $13.95. ISBN 0-87518-536-3. (Hidden Worlds). 6-8

The Incan civilization began in ancient Peru about 3,500 years ago. The Incas settled in the Cuzco region, in the Andes, about 900 years ago. In 1438, the ruler, Pachacuti Inca Yupanqui, built a powerful state. His brother, Atahualpa, overthrew him, but then Pizarro came and destroyed Atahualpa. One of the major temples of the area was Machu Picchu. In 1911, Hiram Bingham led an expedition in search of the lost city of the Incas. The text talks about the archaeologists who found these ruins and who reconstructed information about this civilization from the finds they made at the site. Photographs, maps, and illustrations augment the text. Glossary and Index.

1824.   Steele, Philip. **Kidnapping**. New York: New Discovery, 1992. 48p. $12.95 ISBN 0-02-735403-2. (Past and Present). 5-7

The text looks at the history of kidnapping, including the hostages of the Greeks and Romans, Joseph in the Bible, the Children's Crusade, and ransoms for kings. It tries to account for the reasons behind kidnappings and abductions and ways to overcome or avoid them. Key Dates, Glossary, and Index.

1825.   Steele, Philip. **Riots**. New York: New Discovery, 1993. 48p. $12.95. ISBN 0-02-786883-4. YA

Steele defines the term *riot* and then traces these "quarrels" through the centuries. Rioting occurred in ancient Greece during 464 B.C., when an earthquake shook Sparta. In A.D. 532, rioting broke out in Constantinople between political groups, the "Greens" and the "Blues." Riots over money, religion, and politics have continued through the centuries. Steele also looks at the lawfulness of such displays and the ways in which they can be controlled. Key Dates, Glossary, and Index.

1826.   Steele, Philip. **The Romans and Pompeii**. New York: Dillon Press, 1994. 32p. $13.95. ISBN 0-87518-538-X. (Hidden Worlds). 4-7

On August 24, A.D. 79, the wealthy city of Pompeii met a "terrible end," destroyed not by armies but by the mysterious forces of nature in the form of lava spewing from Mount Vesuvius, which most people had believed was extinct. Seventeen years prior, an earthquake had damaged some of the buildings; on the morning of the volcanic eruption, dogs started howling and springs dried up. The eruption blasted material twelve miles into the air. The text looks at this event and what archaeologists have found out about the society it destroyed. Glossary and Index.

1827.   Steele, Philip. **Smuggling**. New York: New Discovery, 1993. 48p. $12.95. ISBN 0-02-786884-2. (Past and Present). 5-7

Smugglers have been working for centuries. One of the first documented smuggling operations was the Trojan Horse that the Greeks took into Troy. Other accounts describe Chinese silk smuggling and illegal trading on the seas. The text discusses the history of smuggling, money as the main motive, drugs today, contraband, and how to detect and deter smugglers. Key Dates, Glossary, and Index.

1828.   Steele, Philip. **Thermopylae**. Roger Payne, illustrator. New York: New Discovery, 1992. 32p. $13.95. ISBN 0-02-786887-7. (Great Battles and Sieges). 5 up

For more than two days in 480 B.C., 300 Greek soldiers from Sparta and Thespiae held back the Persian army, the largest force ever seen in the world, but every Greek eventually died. The text looks at the events that led to the battle and gives background on the two armies that fought in it. Topics include the Immortals of Persia, the hoplites of Greece under Leonidas, the march itself, the battle in the pass, the treachery of the Greek Ephialtes to Xerxes, and then the revenge and conquest when the Greek navy defeated the Persians in a battle at Salamis. Glossary, For Further Reading, and Index.

1829.   Steffens, Bradley. **The Children's Crusade**. San Diego, CA: Lucent, 1991. 64p. $11.95. ISBN 1-56006-019-0. (World Disasters). 4-7

In 1212, hundreds of children marched into France and boarded ships to go to Palestine, where they expected to help regain the city of Jerusalem from the Moslems. They never reached their intended destination. Some died from starvation or exhaustion, and others were sold into slavery when they went ashore. The text looks at their lives in their villages during the thirteenth century, the wars that beckoned them, and the legacy of the Crusades. Glossary, Further Reading, Works Consulted, and Index.

1830.   Stefoff, Rebecca. **Faisal**. New York: Chelsea House, 1989. 112p. $18.95. ISBN 1-55546-833-0. (World Leaders Past and Present). 8 up

King Faisal (1906–1975) of Saudi Arabia, angered by the war between Israel and its Arab neighbors in 1973, banned the sale of Arab oil to the United States and other Israeli allies. Faisal ruled for only eleven years, but he shaped his nation for much longer by creating huge cash reserves. He spoke for Arab concerns to the United Nations and transformed his country from a group of warring desert tribes into a modern state. His nephew shot him, never explaining why, and was beheaded publicly several months later. Photographs and reproductions enhance the text. Chronology, Further Reading, and Index.

1831.   Stefoff, Rebecca. **Ferdinand Magellan and the Discovery of the World Ocean**. New York: Chelsea House, 1990. 128p. $19.95. ISBN 0-7910-1291-3. (World Explorers). 5 up

Ferdinand Magellan (1480?–1521) left Spain in 1519 with no reliable maps or charts—only compass, hourglass, and astrolabe—but he became the first man to chart a route around the earth. Of the original 220 sailors who departed with him, only 18 survived the three years of the journey. He himself was killed and did not return with his ship. His expedition discovered the strait linking the Atlantic and Pacific, now called the Strait of Magellan, and showed the vastness of the Pacific Ocean. Maps, engravings, and reproductions enhance the text. Chronology, Further Reading, and Index.

1832. Stefoff, Rebecca. **Lech Walesa: The Road to Democracy**. New York: Fawcett, 1992. 131p. $4pa. ISBN 0-499-90625-6pa. (Great Lives). 7 up

The text focuses on the events in Lech Walesa's (b. 1943) life since 1980, after the Gdansk, Poland, dock strike that he started. It includes chapters on his early years and a brief history of Poland, as well as an explanation of the importance of Walesa's contributions to thwarting Communist rule in his country.

1833. Stefoff, Rebecca. **Mao Zedong: Founder of the People's Republic of China**. Brookfield, CT: Millbrook Press, 1996. 128p. $16.40. ISBN 1-56294-531-9. 7 up

The text begins with the founding of the People's Republic of China and then shifts its focus to the life of Mao Zedong (1893–1976). Mao founded the Chinese Communist Party in 1921 and led the Long March in 1934 and 1935. Not for fourteen years was he able to found the People's Republic, but he continued to work toward that goal with his peasant army. He became the major influence on modern Chinese history. Bibliography, Chronology, Notes, and Index.

1834. Stefoff, Rebecca. **Pol Pot**. New York: Chelsea House, 1991. 111p. $17.95. ISBN 1-55546-640-0. (World Leaders Past and Present). 7-10

Pol Pot, the man who overthrew the Cambodian government in 1975, has remained elusive, but the atrocities of his regime, the Khmer Rouge, are clear. The text presents a clearer history of the regime (before it was overcome in 1979) than of the man who became Pol Pot. Bibliography, Chronology, and Index.

1835. Stefoff, Rebecca. **Saddam Hussein**. Brookfield, CT: Millbrook Press, 1995. 128p. $15.90. ISBN 1-56294-475-4. 7 up

Although the text covers the life of Saddam Hussein (b. 1937), it also interwines the history of Mesopotamia and the rise of modern Iraq. Additionally, the text looks at Operation Desert Storm in 1991 and the retaliatory raid in 1993 when information about an assassination attempt on George Bush surfaced. Hussein rose from poverty, prison, insurrection, and warfare to keep his place as head of his country. Bibliography, Chronology, and Index.

1836. Stefoff, Rebecca. **The Viking Explorers**. New York: Chelsea House, 1993. 111p. $19.95. ISBN 0-7910-1295-6. (World Explorers). 5 up

In A.D. 793, men from the north, whom their victims called "Norsemen," landed on the peaceful island of Lindisfarne in the North Sea, raided the abbey, and killed the monks who lived there. Survivors watched from hiding places as the plunderers took relics and enslaved clerics before sailing their striped-sail ships into the wind. For the next 300 years, the Viking age flourished as these men terrorized other areas of northern Europe. They went as far as Russia and to the coasts of Greenland and Iceland, and probably visited the coast of North America five centuries before Columbus. Photographs and reproductions highlight the text. Chronology, Further Reading, and Index.

1837. Steidl, Franz. **Lost Battalions: Going for Broke in the Vosges, Autumn, 1944**. San Francisco: Presidio Press, 1997. 226p. $24.95. ISBN 0-89141-622-6. YA

Although not mainly about the Nisei (Japanese Americans) who volunteered and fought for the United States in World War II, the text shows that their behavior in the Vosges Mountains against the Germans led to their regiment becoming the most decorated unit in American military history. Bibliography and Index.

1838. Stein, R. Conrad. **The Aztec Empire**. New York: Marshall Cavendish, 1996. 80p. $19.95. ISBN 0-7614-0072-9. (Cultures of the Past). 5-8

The text examines the artifacts, monuments, domestic scenes, and historical aspects of the Aztecs as it looks at the history, beliefs, and lifestyles of the people. It also notes the influence of the Aztecs on modern Mexico and discusses the discovery of the ruins of Tenochtitlán. Photographs, Drawings, Bibliography, Chronology, Further Reading, Glossary, and Index.

1839. Stein, R. Conrad. **The Iran Hostage Crisis**. Chicago: Childrens Press, 1994. 32p. $15.27. ISBN 0-516-06681-1. (Cornerstones of Freedom). 5 up

On November 4, 1979, Iranian students seized 60 employees in the U.S. embassy in Tehran. They kept most of the hostages for 444 days in various places separated from each other. After Jimmy Carter lost the presidential election, Ronald Reagan took office on the same day the hostages were released, January 20, 1981. People displayed yellow ribbons everywhere so that others would not forget the hostages before the Iranians freed them. Index.

1840. Stein, R. Conrad. **The Korean War: "The Forgotten War."** Hillside, NJ: Enslow, 1994. 128p. $17.95. ISBN 0-89490-526-0. (American War). 6-9

Although 54,000 Americans died in the Korean War, fought from 1950 to 1953, many Americans at home lost interest because they did not understand the threat of Communist control spreading when the North Koreans invaded South Korea. This war did not have the media coverage common today, and no major event such as Pearl Harbor caused it to start. The text, with photographs, looks at the war and its effects on those who fought and on their families. Chronology, Further Reading, and Index.

1841. Stein, R. Conrad. **The Mexican Revolution: 1910–1920**. New York: New Discovery, 1994. 160p. $14.95. ISBN 0-02-786950-4. (Timestop). 7 up

From 1910 to 1920, a Mexican revolution occurred for political control of Mexico against soldier-statesman Porfirio Díaz. The text looks at this period of history in ten chapters, each centering on one of the political figures in the revolution, including Zapata, Pancho Villa, Madero, Huerta, and Carranza. Stein discusses the underlying causes of the revolution, such as inequity in land ownership, the racial and regional differences in the country, attitudes toward the Catholic Church, and the involvement of foreign governments. During the conflict, one in eight Mexicans died in battle, from disease, or from hunger; however, the problems were little known outside the country. Chronology, Further Readings, and Index.

1842. Stein, R. Conrad. **World War II in Europe: "America Goes to War."** Hillside, NJ: Enslow, 1994. 128p. $17.95. ISBN 0-89490-525-2. (American War). 6 up

Stein begins the text on World War II with the story of "Canned Goods." The Germans dressed convicts in Polish army uniforms, then killed them and announced that they were Polish invaders whom they had caught before they infiltrated Germany. Adolf Hitler used this farce to justify his invasion of Poland in 1939. Even though the German people were against war, Hitler declared it anyway. Many Germans were shocked that France and Great Britain supported Poland because they had refused to do anything when Hitler had previously broken the Treaty of Versailles. The other chapters follow the war across Europe. Chronology, Notes, Further Reading, and Index.

1843. Stein, R. Conrad. **World War II in the Pacific: "Remember Pearl Harbor."** Springfield, NJ: Enslow, 1994. 128p. $17.95. ISBN 0-89490-524-4. (American War). 7 up

In chronological order, the text covers World War II in the Pacific from the bombing of Pearl Harbor on December 7, 1941, through the signing of the surrender on the USS *Missouri* on September 2, 1945. Black-and-white photographs and maps enhance the text. Further Reading, Chronology, and Index.

1844. Stein, Wendy. **Witches: Opposing Viewpoints**. San Diego, CA: Greenhaven, 1995. 112p. $19.95. ISBN 1-56510-240-1. (Great Mysteries—Opposing Viewpoints). 6-9

In an attempt to define "witch," the author asserts that witches either destroy or heal, depending upon intent. Some researchers trace the etymology of "witch" to *witan* (to know) in Old English, and others select *wiccian* (to cast a spell). The text presents a history of witches from the Western world, mentioning the Inquisition; a trial in Arras, France, from 1459 to 1460; witchcraft in England, especially Chelmsford in Essex; witch covens in sixteenth-century Scotland (1591); and the Salem witch hunt in the American colonies from 1620 to 1725. Some believe that misogyny (hatred of women) is a leading cause of witch hunts because more than 80 percent of the people persecuted as witches have been female. Contemporary witches worship a goddess that is said to have been worshipped more than 35,000 years ago. In history, the most overt worship of the goddess occurred in Greece from approximately 1500 B.C. to 900 B.C. with Diana, Selene, and Hecate. But sources also indicate other pockets of goddess worship. For Further Exploration, Additional Works Consulted, and Index.

1845. Steinhoff, Johannes, Peter Pechel, and Dennis E. Showalter. **Voices from the Third Reich**. Washington, DC: Regnery Gateway, 1989. 550p. $16.95. ISBN 0-89526-766-7. New York: Da Capo Press, 1994. 550p. $17.95pa. ISBN 0-306-80594-4pa. YA

The authors interviewed 157 West German and Austrian survivors of World War II. In the text, they present excerpts from the interviews, placed under thematic headings such as war, genocide, resistance, survival, daily affairs, women, and children. The interviewees could only give their own experiences of the war, including early excitement over the possibility of victory and the later distress from bombing, the lack of necessities, pogroms, concentration camps, and the Berlin airlift. Bibliography and Index.

1846. Steins, Richard. **The Allies Against the Axis: World War II (1940-1950)**. New York: Twenty-First Century Books, 1994. 64p. $15.95. ISBN 0-8050-2586-3. (First Person America). 5-8

America entered World War II after the Japanese bombed Pearl Harbor in 1941, thus ending its isolationist policy. Steins looks at the war on both oceans and notes such situations as the challenges of army segregation, the fear and paranoia of the county according to a nisei (second-generation Japanese American), the women working in factories, soldiers returning to peacetime, and the descent of the Iron Curtain. Photographs enhance the text. Timeline, For Further Reading, and Index.

1847. Stepanek, Sally. **Martin Luther**. New York: Chelsea House, 1986. 128p. $18.95. ISBN 0-87754-538-3. (World Leaders Past and Present). 5 up

Martin Luther (1483–1546) studied theology and became a brilliant professor, but his conclusions about his faith placed him in conflict with the doctrine and teachings of the Roman Catholic Church. He hated the church's avarice and what he saw as spiritual and intellectual poverty. In 1517, he renounced his Catholic faith. In 1521, he defended his position before the Holy Roman Emperor Charles V, thus marking the beginning of the religious, political, and social upheaval called the Reformation. He was the scholar, teacher, debater, and preacher who started the form of Christianity called Protestantism. Photographs, engravings, and reproductions enhance the text. Chronology, Further Reading, and Index.

1848. Stepanek, Sally. **Mary Queen of Scots**. New York: Chelsea House, 1987. 112p. $18.95. ISBN 0-87754-540-5. (World Leaders Past and Present) 5 up

Scotland's last Catholic ruler was Mary (1542–1587), who became queen one week after her birth. Educated in France in King Henry II's court, she married the French crown prince, Francis, but he died in 1560. She returned to Scotland, where religious problems had grown, and her next two marriages added to scandals that her Protestant relatives loudly and publicly discussed. She abdicated in 1567, and her cousin Elizabeth I of England imprisoned her. Twenty years later, Elizabeth accused Mary of plotting against her and executed her. Most people thought that Mary's worst sin was remaining a Catholic. Photographs and engravings enhance the text. Chronology, Further Reading, and Index.

1849. Sterckx, Pierre. **Brueghel: A Gift for Telling Stories**. John Goodman, translator; Claudine Roucha, illustrator. New York: Chelsea House, 1995. 56p. $14.95. ISBN 0-7910-2806-2. (Art for Children). 5-9

The text, complemented with beautiful reproductions, presents children visiting a Brussels art museum where they see Brueghel's paintings. As they examine the paintings, they discuss what they know of his life and how the pictures reveal the times in which he lived (1526-1569). He created fifty masterpieces while he was between the ages of thirty and forty. Index.

1850. Sterling, Shirley. **My Name Is Seepeetza**. Buffalo, NY: Douglas & McIntyre, Groundwood, 1997. 128p. $14.95. ISBN 0-88899-290-4. 5-8

Seepeetza, better known as Martha at the Indian residential school in British Columbia where she has to live, wets the bed and daydreams about her family ranch on the reservation before the government forced her to attend school. The nuns make her wear the wet bedsheet over her head, and the children taunt her for having green eyes and looking white. The journal format presents Seepeetza in the sixth grade during the 1950s feeling helpless, afraid, and homesick. The nuns, however, are not always bad, nor are Seepeetza's parents always perfect. *Sheila A. Egoff Children's Book Prize.*

1851. Stevens, Paul. **Ferdinand and Isabella**. New York: Chelsea House, 1988. 110p. $18.95. ISBN 0-87754-523-5. (World Leaders Past and Present). 5 up

Ferdinand, son of the king of Aragon, expected to be king. Isabella, daughter of the king of Castile's second wife, had to work to get the throne of Castile. She and Ferdinand married secretly in 1469, and struggled for ten years before they could unite their kingdoms. They had to destroy the base of support for the nobles, begin church and economic reforms, and develop a central royal administration. In 1478, they began the Spanish Inquisition to rid the country of heretics. In 1492, they expelled the Moors and funded Christopher Columbus's voyage to find India. Finally, they married their children to people who would strengthen their European alliances. Family tragedies defeated Isabella, who died in 1504, but Ferdinand continued to work on their plans to take over Italy. Photographs and engravings enhance the text. Chronology, Further Reading, and Index.

1852. Stewart, Fred Mustard. **The Magnificent Savages**. New York: Forge, 1996. 383p. $24.95. ISBN 0-312-86111-7. YA

Nathaniel Savage's last wish in 1851 is for his beloved illegitimate son Justin, twelve, to sail to China as a cabin boy on one of the ships in his fleet. Justin's evil older half brother, Sylvaner, and his wife, Adelaide, hear of the plan, and they pay a crew member to murder Justin at sea so that they will inherit all. A lovely Samantha saves him from his killer, a pirate captures the ship and makes Justin marry her, and he travels around the world, looking for Samantha. He discovers from his mother's diary that he is actually the brother and nephew of Sylvaner, as his mother was Adelaide's sister.

1853. Stewart, Gail. **Alexander the Great**. San Diego, CA: Lucent, 1994. 127p. $16.95. ISBN 1-56006-047-6. (The Importance Of). 8 up

Although Alexander (b. 356 B.C.) died in Babylon in 323 B.C., his people built a funeral car in the form of a golden temple and took two years to transport him back to Macedon. When they arrived in Syria, Alexander's general Ptolemy rerouted the cortege to Alexandria, the city that Alexander had founded, for burial. Alexander came to power when he was twenty years old and stayed at the top until his death at the age of thirty-three. He was a conqueror, a master strategist, a military genius, a leader, and, most likely, a robber. As a youngster, he studied with Aristotle for three years before he continued his father's creative battle methods. Then he defeated the city of Thebes (334); crossed the Hellespont into Asia and fought Darius's Persian Empire (334); cut the Gordian knot (333); defeated Darius and the Persian cities of Susa, Babylon, and Persepolis (331); toppled Tyre (332); crossed the Hindu Kush Mountains (329); invaded India and married Roxanne (327); saw his dear friend Hephestion die (324); and died himself in 323. Notes For Further Reading, Additional Works Consulted, and Index.

1854. Stewart, Gail. **Hitler's Reich**. San Diego, CA: Lucent, 1994. 128p. $16.95. ISBN 1-56006-235-5. (World History Series). 7 up

"Solving the Jewish problem" obsessed Adolf Hitler. His top German officials, such as Jager (stationed in Lithuania), fulfilled his orders through, as Jager said, "actions" or methodical killings of millions of people in an "efficient use of time" so that "no backlog was allowed to build up." How Hitler came to power by offering manna to Germans suffering from the effects of World War I and a severe economic depression is carefully documented and analyzed in this text. Notes, For Further Reading, Works Consulted, and Index.

1855. Stewart, Gail. **Life During the French Revolution**. San Diego, CA: Lucent, 1995. 112p. $22.59. ISBN 1-56006-078-6. (The Way People Live). 7 up

Maps and reproductions complement a text that gives a thorough background of the French Revolution, from why the masses were discontented to the nobility's inability to understand why their way of life threatened those less fortunate. It covers the time before the storming of the Bastille on July 14, 1789, through the terrors afterward and the death of Robespierre in 1794. Reproductions enhance the text. Notes, Further Reading, Works Consulted, and Index.

1856. Stewart, Gail. **Life in the Warsaw Ghetto**. San Diego, CA: Lucent, 1995. 112p. $22.59. ISBN 1-56006-075-1. (The Way People Live). 7 up

Stewart comments that to remove stereotypes, one must see a group of people as individuals—at work, at play, in families, at school. From November 1940 until May 1943, 500,000 Jews lived in the Warsaw ghetto, an area enclosed by the Nazis to keep the Jews together until the time came to load them on trains bound for death camps. The Nazis forbade writing, teaching, studying, and religious ceremonies in the ghetto. Some of the passages Stewart includes are diaries written in the ghetto that somehow survived. Adults recalling the time lament that Hitler took away their childhoods when he decided to realize Martin Luther's anti-Semitic statements from the sixteenth century. One of the main triumphs of the Jews living in this hell was an uprising on January 18, 1943, when the inhabitants fought back using weapons that sympathetic Aryans had smuggled into the ghetto through the sewer systems. The Germans, shocked by this show of strength, completely destroyed the compound by May. Notes, For Further Reading, Works Consulted, and Index.

1857. Stewart, Gail B. **World War I**. San Diego, CA: Lucent, 1991. 112p. $16.95. ISBN 1-56006-406-4. (America's Wars). 7-10

With photographs taken before, during, and after World War I, the text relates the process of war from before Archduke Ferdinand was murdered in Sarajevo through the Treaty of Versailles. It examines the effects of the war on other countries as well as the United States and looks at the armies, weapons, battles, and people who were intimately associated with this war. Works Consulted, Further Reading, and Index.

1858. Stewart, Mary. **The Prince and the Pilgrim**. New York: Morrow, 1996. 292p. $23. ISBN 0-688-14538-8. YA

The story of Alexander and Alice alternates chapters as they meet, fall in love, and get rid of their foe during the times of King Arthur and Camelot. Alexander is a young prince who goes to avenge his father's assassination; Alice accompanies her father on pilgrimages to holy shrines. In the plot are pieces of information from the Arthurian legends and a strong sense of time and place; a map identifies locations.

1859. Stewart, Whitney. **Aung San Suu Kyi: Fearless Voice of Burma**. Minneapolis, MN: Lerner, 1997. 128p. $17.96. ISBN 0-8225-4931-X. (Newsmakers). 5 up

Aung San Suu Kyi is a quiet woman who became the leader of Burma's renewed struggle for democracy. In 1989, the government placed her under house arrest, and from her home she led Burma's National League for Democracy in victory at the polls; however, the military government refused to recognize the election. In 1992, she won the Nobel Prize for Peace, still under house arrest. Stewart interviewed her for this biography. Sources, Bibliography, and Index.

1860. Stewart, Whitney. **The 14th Dalai Lama: Spiritual Leader of Tibet**. Minneapolis, MN: Lerner, 1996. 128p. $17.96. ISBN 0-8225-4926-3. (Newsmakers). 5 up

The fourteenth Dalai Lama, chosen as a small child to lead the people of Tibet, lived a life of isolation in the palace and then had to negotiate with the Chinese Communist leader, Mao, before Mao exiled him to India.

While outside his country, he has promoted nonviolence and the importance of human rights, stances that won him a Nobel Prize for Peace in 1989. He remains a beloved and respected spiritual leader. Photographs, Bibliography, and Index.

1861. Stewart, Whitney. **Sir Edmund Hillary: To Everest and Beyond**. Minneapolis, MN: Lerner, 1996. 128p. $17.96. ISBN 0-8225-4927-1. (Newsmakers). 5 up

In 1953, Sir Edmund Hillary (b. 1919), with Tenzing Norgay, became the first human to reach the summit of Mount Everest. Growing up in New Zealand, Hillary had learned that careful planning and preparation allow success. Later he led an expedition across Antarctica and another to the mouth of India's Ganges River, high in the Himalayan Mountains. Hillary has helped the Sherpas have better lives through improved schools and medical help. In more recent years, he has been working to keep an environmental balance in the Himalayas between their natural resources and the tourists who pay to climb them. Photographs, Bibliography, and Index.

1862. Stirling, Jessica. **Shadows on the Shore**. New York: St. Martin's Press, 1994. 346p. $21.95. ISBN 0-312-10546-0. YA

This sequel to *Lantern for the Dark* shows Clare Kelso Quinn thirteen years later in 1802 as a prosperous salt dealer and widow with a daughter. The cad Frederick Striker reappears and woos Clare while planning how to obtain her estate. Simultaneously, one of Lavoisier's students has come to the estate, charmed Clare's daughter, and begun studying the interaction of gases. Before Clare controls all, several unexpected events occur.

1863. Stolz, Mary. **Bartholomew Fair**. New York: Greenwillow, 1990. 152p. $12.95. ISBN 0-688-09522-4. 5-8

In 1597, six people wake up one August morning looking forward to the last day of the Bartholomew Fair. Elizabeth I, a student, a cloth merchant, an aristocrat, a maid, and an apprentice face mortality in some way— either to think that they are just beginning to enjoy life or that they have experienced most of their life on earth. The day's events meet the expectations of some of the characters and deflate the hopes of others, but all recreate Elizabethan England.

1864. Stolz, Mary. **Pangur Ban**. New York: HarperCollins, 1988. 182p. $13.89. ISBN 0-06-025862-4. 7 up

Expected to be either a farmer or a soldier, Carmac wants to be neither in 814. All he wants to do is draw the animals and nature around him, with his cat, Pangur Ban, by his side. His father finally accepts his son's talent and allows him to enter the Benedictine abbey. Carmac's artwork on the illuminated manuscripts is the best ever seen, and he is finishing his manuscript on the life of St. Patrick, fifteen years later, when the Vikings come. He hides the work, and it lies untouched for 300 years before another monk discovers it and its beauty.

1865. **Stones and Bones: How Archaeologists Trace Human Origins**. Minneapolis, MN: Runestone Press, 1994. 64p. $11.95. ISBN 0-8225-3207-7. (Buried Worlds). 4-9

Archaeology as a science is only a century old. During that time, scientists have learned a lot about prehistoric humans and ancient civilizations. The text explains the methodology of archaeology and gives theories that have sprung from this research. Glossary and Index.

1866. Strahinich, Helen. **The Holocaust: Understanding and Remembering**. Springfield, NJ: Enslow, 1996. 112p. $18.95. ISBN 0-89490-725-5. (Issues in Focus). 6 up

The text follows Hitler's rise to power, his annihilation of the Jews, and the aftermath of the Holocaust. It examines the difficult questions as to why so many Jews remained in Germany, why the Germans neglected to save the Jews, and where anti-Semitism arose. The text also looks at Jews in Italy and the Netherlands as well as other persecuted groups including Gypsies, homosexuals, and the Polish elite. Further Reading, Glossary, and Index.

1867. **Street Smart! Cities of the Ancient World**. Minneapolis, MN: Runestone Press, 1994. 80p. $22.95. ISBN 0-8225-3208-5. (Buried Worlds). 5-8

The text presents cities and their components. Archaeologists designate their finds as "cities" only when at least several thousand people lived there and had control of an area outside the walls where they could grow food. Cities developed for economic reasons, near military outposts for safety reasons, or for religious reasons. The world's first city was probably Uruk in southern Mesopotamia, around 4000 B.C. Other Middle Eastern cities are Babylon (after 2000 B.C.), Zimbabwe (1000 B.C.), and Tell al-Amarna (1400 B.C.). Ancient cities of Asia along rivers include Mohenjo-Daro and Harappa (2400-1650 B.C.), Zhengzhou and An-Yang (1600-1400 B.C.), and Changan (207 B.C.). Ancient cities of the Mediterranean were Athens, Sparta, Knossos, Pompeii, and Rome. In the Americas, cities are still being discovered. The group that established the Olmec civilization's major city has not yet been identified. The Mayan Teotihuacán, destroyed in A.D. 750, was the first true urban center in the Americas. The largest Aztec city was Tenochtitlán, lasting from 1325 until approximately 1521. For the Incas, Cuzco was the great city, but thieves looted it in 1532. Pronunciation Guide, Glossary, and Index.

1868. Strom, Yale. **The Expulsion of the Jews: Five Hundred Years of Exodus**. New York: S.P.I. Books, 1992. 192p. $24.95. ISBN 1-56171-081-4. 8 up

Strom wrote this volume to commemorate the 500th anniversary of the expulsion of 200,000 Jews, called the Sephardim, from Spain. They found new homes in various places while trying to retain their Judeo-Spanish tongue and their culture. Strom interviewed Jews throughout Europe to gather information about the diaspora. The places covered here are Sarajevo, Split, and Skopje, (the former) Yugoslavia; Sofia and Plovdiv, Bulgaria; Istanbul and Izmir, Turkey; Thessaloniki, Larissa, Volos, Trikala, Khalkis, and Athens, Greece; Lisbon, Portugal; and Madrid, Toledo, Sevilla, and Córdoba, Spain. Photographs, Bibliography, and Index.

1869. Strom, Yale. **Uncertain Roads: Searching for the Gypsies**. New York: Four Winds Press, 1993. 111p. $19.95. ISBN 0-02-788531-3. 5 up

Historical summaries, interviews, first-person narratives, and photographs describe the lives of the Rom (Gypsy). Gypsies in both urban and rural areas of Sweden, Romania, Hungary, and the Ukraine tell about their experiences and their ways of life. A musical score appears at the end of each of the four chapters, with lyrics in both English and Romani. The Roms, as they prefer to be called, face continued prejudice in Europe with its new boundaries, as they try to escape attack and find housing. Bibliography.

1870. Sullivan, George. **Slave Ship: The Story of the Henrietta Marie**. New York: Cobblehill, Dutton, 1994. 80p. $15.99. ISBN 0-525-65174-8. 5-8

In 1972, divers found the remains of a sunken ship in the Gulf of Mexico. One of the first items found was a pair of shackles, which indicated that the ship had been a slave ship. On the ship's bell was engraved the name *Henrietta Marie* and the date 1699. Records show that the ship had unloaded its human cargo in Jamaica and had sunk in a storm while returning to London. Background information about slavers and photographs of the items discovered in the ship give an insight into what the people on board might have endured. This ship is the only slaver to have been scientifically studied. Bibliography and Index.

1871. Summers, Harry G, Jr. **Korean War Almanac**. New York: Facts on File, 1990. 330p. $29.95; $14.95pa. ISBN 0-8160-1737-9; 0-8160-2463-4pa. YA

This narrative overview of the Korean War, which lasted from 1950 to 1953, presents alphabetical entries on the war's actions, its weapons, the formations, personalities involved (such as Gen. Douglas MacArthur and his replacement, Lt. Gen. Matthew Ridgway), and the concepts underlying battles such as Old Baldy, Capital, Pork Chop, T-Bone, and Heartbreak Ridge. Photographs, Bibliography, and Index.

1872. Sumption, Christine, and Kathleen Thompson. **Carlos Finlay**. Les Didier, illustrator. Austin, TX: Raintree/Steck-Vaughn, 1991. 32p. $19.97. ISBN 0-8172-3378-4. (Hispanic Stories). 4-7

After Carlos Finlay (1833-1915) was born in Cuba, he studied abroad in France and Germany before he attended medical school in the United States. In Cuba, he began studying the disease yellow fever, which gave people fever, headaches, and backaches. After their skin became yellowish, they began to bleed inside, became unconscious, and often died. Finlay finally determined that mosquitoes transmitted the disease, but doctors would not believe him. When Walter Reed came to Cuba to study the disease, he did not believe Finlay either. But after nothing else showed promise, Reed went to Finlay and found that what he said was true. Reed, however, did not give Finlay credit in his paper, and not until the middle of the twentieth century did Finlay receive acclaim for his accomplishment. Glossary. English and Spanish text.

1873. **Sunk! Exploring Underwater Archaeology**. Minneapolis, MN: Runestone Press, 1994. 72p. $22.95. ISBN 0-8225-3205-0. (Buried Worlds). 5 up

Underwater excavation reveals amazing amounts of information about the past. Archaeologists searching underwater require special implements and diving equipment. Even though underwater, they must also make exact measurements and use careful retrieval methods for artifacts, as if they were on land. Their efforts have recovered cities and ships buried in the water. The text looks at the past hiding underneath the Mediterranean, the scientific value of shipwrecks, and harbors ruined by the rising sea. The first scientific excavation of a 3,000-year-old shipwreck, led by Peter Throckmorton and George Bass, occurred in the 1960s near Cape Gelidonya, off the coast of Turkey. Pronunciation Guide, Glossary, and Index.

1874. Sunstein, Emily W. **Mary Shelley: Romance and Reality**. Boston: Little, Brown, 1989. 478p. $24.95. ISBN 0-316-82246-9. YA

Using letters and writings from Mary Shelley's (1797–1851) family, parents William Godwin and Mary Wollstonecraft, and husband Percy Bysshe Shelley, Sunstein pieces together Mary Shelley's life. She changes many of the views surrounding Shelley during the Romantic period and shows that Shelley deserves much more attention and a more positive attitude than she has previously received. Sunstein worked on this book for almost fifteen years, and in the course of her research she learned much about Shelley that other biographers had not uncovered. Bibliography and Index.

1875. Sutcliff, Rosemary. **Blood Feud**. Charles Keeping, illustrator. New York: Dutton, 1977. 144p. $7.50. ISBN 0-525-26730-1. 7 up

In the tenth century, Thormod captures Jestyn on the British coast and takes him as a thrall to Thormod's Scandinavian home. Thormod's family is having a blood feud with another family, and the chase takes Thormod and Jestyn to Miklagard (Istanbul). After Thormod dies, Jestyn has a chance to avenge his death, but he has become a surgeon who helps people, not one who harms them.

1876. Sutcliff, Rosemary. **Bonnie Dundee**. Magnolia, MA: Peter Smith, 1984. 204p. $21.30. ISBN 0-8446-6363-8. YA

Colonel John Graham of Claverhouse fights against William of Orange in support of King James around 1689. An old man tells his grandson the story of his youth as an orphan stable boy who knew Bloody Claver'se, a kind and faithful man. He also tells about the importance of the mysterious Gypsy "tinklers" who appeared when needed and helped to save his life as well as others.

1877. Sutcliff, Rosemary. **Dawn Wind**. Charles Keeping, illustrator. 1962. New York: Henry Z. Walck, 1973. 321p. $1.95pa. ISBN 0-8098-3403-0pa. YA

Around A.D. 500, Owain awakens in a battlefield where dead bodies surround him. A dog keeps him warm through the night, and they leave for Owain's home. He meets Regina, who needs his help, and to get money Owain sells himself into thralldom to a Saxon. After eight years, Owain saves his master from drowning and earns his freedom. He continues to help the family, but when he goes to look for the dolphin ring that he buried before the war, he finds Regina's hair, and knows that she still waits for him.

1878. Sutcliff, Rosemary. **The Eagle of the Ninth**. C. Walter Hodges, illustrator. 1961. New York: Oxford University Press, 1987. 264p. ISBN 0-19-271037-0. New York: Sunburst/Farrar, Straus & Giroux, 1993. $4.95pa. ISBN 0-374-41930-2pa. YA

Marcus wounds his leg and has to resign from his post as a Roman soldier serving in Britain. He visits his uncle, and when they go to the Saturnalia games, Marcus decides to offer a defeated gladiator a post as his servant. They become friends and travel north to look for information about Marcus's father, lost with the Ninth Legion. When they see the Epidaii tribe flaunting the eagle insignia of the Ninth, they steal it and return home with it. They know the fate of the Legion's men, and can only mourn their loss. *Carnegie Commendation*.

1879. Sutcliff, Rosemary. **Flame-Colored Taffeta**. New York: Farrar, Straus & Giroux, 1986. 120p. $14; $4.95pa. ISBN 0-374-32344-5; 0-374-42341-5pa. 6-8

When Damaris is twelve and Peter is thirteen, in the mid-eighteenth century, they help a wounded man on the Sussex coast of England. Because smugglers fill the area, they suspect that he may be escaping from trouble, and they discover that he is an emissary for Bonnie Prince Charlie. The Wise Woman, a healer, hides and cares for him. Damaris admits that she wants to have a petticoat of flame-colored taffeta. Tom sends her one for her wedding four years after he escapes.

1880. Sutcliff, Rosemary. **Frontier Wolf**. New York: Dutton, 1981. 196p. $11.50. ISBN 0-525-30260-3. YA

In the fourth century, Alexios takes charge of a Roman outpost known for renegade British soldiers. Although the men suspect that Alexios may not have the strength to lead them, he learns that he must work with the local leaders, and he becomes successful.

1881. Sutcliff, Rosemary. **Knight's Fee**. Charles Keeping, illustrator. 1960. New York: Henry Z. Walck/ Random House, 1980. 260p. $6. ISBN 0-8098-3034-5. 9 up

In the tenth century, Randal, a ten-year-old dog keeper, grows to be a twenty-one-year-old knight. During that time, he helps foil a plot against the lord of his manor. He also goes to Normandy to fight beside the son of the manor lord. When the son dies, Randal returns, is knighted, and becomes heir to the land.

1882. Sutcliff, Rosemary. **The Lantern Bearers**. Charles Keeping, illustrator. 1959. New York: Sunburst/ Farrar, Straus & Giroux, 1994. 248p. $5.95pa. ISBN 0-374-44302-5pa. YA

The Romans leave Britain, but Aquila deserts in A.D. 410 because he has never lived in Rome. Saxons capture him, and he goes with them as a slave to their homeland, but they bring him back. He escapes and joins Ambrosius's forces against the Saxon king Vortigern. In a battle, Aquila recognizes his nephew as one of the wounded, and he returns to help the boy, even though he is an enemy, after the battle ends. He sends his sister, married to a Saxon, a ring so that she can return it after his nephew arrives home safely. *Carnegie Medal*.

1883. Sutcliff, Rosemary. **The Mark of the Horse Lord**. 1965. New York: Dell, 1989. 276p. $4.95pa. ISBN 0-440-40161-5pa. 7 up

Phaedrus wins his freedom from being a Roman slave gladiator when he kills his opponent. His most difficult role, however, comes when he must pretend to be Midir, king of the Dalraidian, because he looks like his twin. The real Midir, disfigured, cannot appear to his people because they will equate their strength with his loss. Midir and his advisors carefully instruct Phaedrus about Midir's habits and the secrets shared with his best friend. Phaedrus finds that he must take on the responsibility along with the role, and he gives his life for his chosen people to save them from their Roman enemies. *Phoenix Award.*

1884. Sutcliff, Rosemary. **Outcast**. 1955. New York: Sunburst/Farrar, Straus & Giroux, 1995. 229p. $5.95pa. ISBN 0-374-45673-9pa. YA

Beric, a Roman orphan raised in a British tribe and cast out during a famine, boards a ship sailing for Rome, and the crew sells him into slavery. He escapes, but authorities accuse him of a crime he did not commit, and he serves his sentence as a galley slave. A fight on board causes the overseer to toss Beric into the sea, and he swims ashore to Britain. There he sees people whom he has known before and finds a better life.

1885. Sutcliff, Rosemary. **The Shield Ring**. C. Walter Hodges, illustrator. 1962. New York: Henry Z. Walck, 1972. 251p. $6.95. ISBN 0-8098-3105-8. 9 up

Although a spy, Bjorn fears that he will tell the Saxon secrets if the Normans capture and torture him. But as a harper, he is the only one who can infiltrate the enemy strongholds and learn their plans. The Normans do capture and torture him, and he finds out that he is stronger than he had imagined. *Carnegie Commendation.*

1886. Sutcliff, Rosemary. **The Shining Company**. New York: Farrar, Straus & Giroux, 1990. 304p. $14.95; $6.95pa. ISBN 0-374-36807-4; 0-374-46616-5pa. 6-10

Around A.D. 600, Prosper, age twelve, dreams of becoming Prince Gorthyn's shield bearer; two years later, near Edinburgh, he does. Gorthyn is one of King Mynyddog's 300 men training for battle. In the Saxon battle near York, only Prosper and one other survive. To escape their loneliness, they follow the source of a merchant's tales to Constantinople. *American Library Association Notable Books for Children.*

1887. Sutcliff, Rosemary. **The Silver Branch**. Charles Keeping, illustrator. 1959. Magnolia, MA: Peter Smith, 1994. 231p. $17.80. ISBN 0-8446-6780-3. New York: Sunburst/Farrar, Straus & Giroux, 1993. 231p. $4.95pa. ISBN 0-374-46648-3pa. YA

Feeling unworthy of his father's approval, Justin goes to Britain to serve in the Roman army as a surgeon. He discovers that the legion's finance minster is betraying the group, and the man tries to kill him. Afte a group of soldiers protects Justin, they then destroy the evil man, and Justin gains confidence in his own decisions. Carnegie Commendation.

1888. Sutcliff, Rosemary. **Song for a Dark Queen**. New York: Crowell, 1979. 181p. $12.50. ISBN 0-690-03991-5. YA

The harpist Cadwan tells the story of Boudicca, who became queen of the Iceni. Around A.D. 60, she had to protect her tribe from the Romans, who did not respect the tribe's matriarchal lineage. After the death of Boudicca's husband, the Romans raped her daughters and beat her. She gathered friendly tribes to fight the Romans and almost defeated them after burning London.

1889. Sutcliff, Rosemary. **Sun Horse, Moon Horse**. Shirley Felts, illustrator. New York: Dutton, 1978. 111p. $9.95. ISBN 0-525-40495-3. 7 up

Around 100 B.C., Lubrin, an Iceni, loves to draw pictures of horses. The Attribates capture his people, and their ruler makes a deal with Lubrin: he will free the Iceni if Lubrin will draw a horse. After Lubrin completes the picture, he knows that he will be the sacrifice on the eye of the horse that will save the others.

1890. Sutcliff, Rosemary. **Warrior Scarlet**. Charles Keeping, illustrator. 1958. New York: Random House, 1977. 240p. $6.95. ISBN 0-8098-3024-8. New York: Sunburst/Farrar, Straus & Giroux, 1995. 207p. $5.95pa. ISBN 0-374-48244-6pa. 5-9

In the Bronze Age, Drem looks forward to wearing the scarlet cloak that will identify him as a tribal warrior. But he must first kill a wolf. Because he has only one good arm, he fails in his attempt to kill the wolf, and he is cast out of the tribe. Later, he kills three wolves while trying to protect another outcast, and tribal leaders reconsider their law. They recognize that Drem has more than earned the right to wear a scarlet cloak. *International Board of Books for Young People* and *Carnegie Commendation.*

1891. Sutcliff, Rosemary. **The Witch's Brat**. Robert Micklewright, illustrator. New York: Henry Z. Walck, 1970. $7.95. ISBN 0-8098-3095-7. 5-9

Lovel is cast out from his village after being blamed for the death of a cow. He walks to a monastery where the brothers take him in. He learns about herbs and healing and meets the king's jongleur, Rahere. Several years later, Rahere returns and asks Lovel to go to London with him to start a hospital. They begin building St. Bartholomew's, and Lovel's gifts help the sick and wounded even before the hospital opens.

1892. Swinimer, Ciarunja Chesaina. **Pokot**. New York: Rosen, 1994. 64p. $15.95. ISBN 0-8239-1756-8. (Heritage Library of African Peoples). 5-8

Tracing their origin to the Nile River valley, the Pokots have been cattle herders or farmers throughout their history. They have lived in the Upper Rift Valley of western Kenya in thirty different clans, each identified by a totem animal. The text looks at politics and history, European contact and colonial rule, culture, daily life, and a view of the future, with enhancing photographs and reproductions. Glossary, Further Reading, and Index.

1893. Swisher, Clarice. **The Glorious Revolution**. San Diego, CA: Lucent, 1996. 112p. $16.95. ISBN 1-56006-296-7. (World History). 7 up

The Glorious Revolution in England began in 1688 and ended in 1689. Without a single battle, it ushered in a new and more democratic form of government. Prince William of Orange came into the country and the despotic King James II left the throne. William and Mary, the daughter of James II, took the throne with the understanding that they had to work with Parliament. The revolution brought permanent changes to England. The text looks at the forces leading to this situation, beginning with the Tudor shift to the Stuarts from 1603 to 1640; the civil war and anarchy from 1640 to 1660; the Restoration and the disarray following it from 1660 to 1685; from absolutism to rebellion, 1685–1688; from invasion to rights with the Glorious Revolution itself; and from rights to settlement, 1689–1702. Notes, For Further Reading, Works Consulted, and Index.

1894. Swisher, Clarice. **Pablo Picasso**. San Diego, CA: Lucent, 1995. 112p. $16.95. ISBN 1-56006-062-X. (The Importance Of). 5 up

Pablo Picasso (1881-1973) lived through most of the twentieth century, during which he saw wars and changes in all the arts. The chapters look at his childhood and education from 1881 to 1898; his maturation as an artist from 1898 to 1905; his role in Cubism from 1905 to 1912; his influence on collages and ballet and his turning point from 1912 to 1922; the era of post-Cubism, covering 1922 to 1936; the Spanish civil war and *Guernica* during 1936 to 1945; his fame and wealth from 1945 to 1954; and his old age to 1973. It ends with a discussion of his influence on the art world. Notes, For Further Reading, Additional Works Consulted, and Index.

1895. Switzer, Ellen. **The Magic of Mozart: Mozart, *The Magic Flute,* and the Salzburg Marionettes**. Costas, photographer. New York: Atheneum, 1995. 90p. $19.95. ISBN 0-689-31851-0. 4-8

Beginning with the winter weather in Salzburg when Mozart (1756-1791) was born, Switzer surmises that the neighborhood women who attended the birth wore heavy gloves and much clothing, because the house had only one fireplace. She continues with a biography of Mozart ending with his writing of *The Magic Flute*. Photographs of marionettes performing the action complement the discussion of the story behind this opera. A third section tells about the Salzburg Marionette Theater and the types of puppets used through the years in its performances. Bibliography.

1896. Synge, Ursula. **The People and the Promise**. New York: S. G. Phillips, 1974. 191p. $23.95. ISBN 0-87599-208-0. 7-10

When Ra-Mose, a prince of Egypt, visits the hut of Aaron, he begins a friendship that leads to the murder of an overseer and his own exile. In the desert, he marries Leah, Jethro's daughter. In a revelation from Yahweh, he finds that he must return to Egypt and lead the Hebrews out of their bondage.

1897. Szablya, Helen M., and Peggy King Anderson. **The Fall of the Red Star**. Sherman, CT: Boyds Mills Press, 1996. 166p. $15.95. ISBN 1-56397-419-3. 5-8

Stephen, age fourteen, becomes a freedom fighter in Budapest, Hungary, during the revolution in 1956, after the Soviet Union tries to invade and occupy the country. Eight years before, the Communists had taken his father, but Stephen still hopes that his father is alive. Stephen fights in street battles, makes and throws Molotov cocktails, kills someone, and helps his sister deliver her baby. When the Communists win, he, his sister, and his mother flee, but their journey becomes especially perilous when they try to save other people in the swamp they are crossing by boat to the Austrian border.

$\boxed{\text{T}}$

1898. Tachau, Frank. **Kemal Atatürk**. New York: Chelsea House, 1987. 112p. $18.95; $7.95pa. ISBN 0-87754-507-3; 0-7910-0612-3pa. (World Leaders Past and Present). 8 up

Mustafa Kemal (1881–1938) created modern Turkey according to his own vision and adopted the name Atatürk ("Father Turk") in 1934. He served in the army and won fame for his leadership during World War I's Battle of Gallipoli. Eventually the Allies triumphed, but he set up an opposition government to fight both the Allies and the ethnic minorities within the empire. He negotiated terms in 1923 to create the small but autonomous Turkish Republic out of the remains of the Ottoman Empire. Photographs and reproductions enhance the text. Further Reading, Chronology, and Index.

1899. **Tajikistan**. Minneapolis, MN: Lerner, 1993. 56p. $19.95. ISBN 0-8225-2816-9. (Then and Now). 5-9

This country of west-central Asia borders on Afghanistan and China. The Tajik settled it in the tenth century, and the Mongols conquered it in the thirteenth century. The text covers Tajikistan's history, economics, geography, politics, and ethnography. Maps and photographs complement the text. Glossary and Index.

1900. Tan, Pamela. **Women in Society: China**. New York: Marshall Cavendish, 1993. 128p. $22.95. ISBN 1-85435-556-2. (Women in Society). 7 up

After introducing the women of China through Chinese myths, the author discusses the roles of Chinese women by weaving historical and contemporary practices together. She presents the expectations imposed in rural and urban situations, the religious and secular, and the poor and wealthy. The chapters cover milestones, what being a woman means in the culture, and the life of a woman from birth to old age. Women Firsts, Glossary, Further Reading, and Index.

1901. Tanaka, Shelley, and Hugh Brewster, eds. **Anastasia's Album**. New York: Hyperion, 1996. 64p. $17.95. ISBN 0-7868-0292-8. 6 up

Using quotes from letters and diaries of family members and close friends, the text tells the story of Anastasia, the youngest Romanov daughter, who died during the Russian Revolution by firing squad. The photographs of family and palaces recreate the time in which she lived. Glossary.

1902. Tarr, Judith. **Queen of the Swords**. New York: Tor, 1997. 464p. $25.95. ISBN 0-312-85821-3. YA

Melisende becomes Queen of Jerusalem between the First and Second Crusades. She marries an older French noble because of the few marriageable men and, after he dies in battle, she begins her rule. However, the struggle for power among the knights, relatives, and mistresses is intense. Lady Richildis, who goes to Jerusalem in 1129 to search for her brother, becomes an attendant to Melisende and tells her story.

1903. Tarr, Judith. **Throne of Isis**. New York: Forge, 1994. 349p. $22.95. ISBN 0-312-85363-7. YA

Antony falls in love with Cleopatra, not because she is beautiful but because she is regal and alluring. She also has the ability to keep him with her.

1904. Taviani, Paolo Emilio. **Columbus: The Great Adventure: His Life, His Times, and His Voyages**. Luciano F. Farino and Marc A. Beckwith, translators. New York: Orion, 1991. 273p. $20. ISBN 0-517-58474-3. YA

Taviani thinks that Columbus's voyage in 1492 represented the creative genius of the Renaissance as Italy began to shape the modern world. He reviews the various voyages and discusses the places that Columbus would have known. Because Taviani is an Italian politician who came from Genoa, his view of Columbus has an unusual bias. Annotated Bibliography and Index.

1905. Taylor, Ina. **The Art of Kate Greenaway: A Nostalgic Portrait of Childhood**. Gretna, LA: Pelican, 1991. 128p. $35.95. ISBN 0-88289-867-1. YA

Kate Greenaway (1846–1901) became an important illustrator in late nineteenth-century England using children and idyllic country scenes as subjects. Her abilities and a complementary relationship with a publisher gained her fame and wealth while she was in her thirties. She supported her family as they moved to more stylish homes with gardens like those she used in so many of her drawings. The text, with accompanying reproductions, looks at her life and some of her triumphs and disappointments, including a perceived relationship with the Victorian critic, John Ruskin. It additionally gives an interesting view of life in Victorian England for the unmarried woman with the capability of earning her own income. Bibliography and Index.

1906. Taylor, Theodore. **The Bomb**. San Diego, CA: Harcourt Brace, 1995. 197p. $15. ISBN 0-15-200867-5. 7 up

Introducing each chapter in this novel about 16-year-old Sorry Rinamu's concern about U.S. atomic bomb tests on his Pacific island, Bikini Atoll, are pages containing a single statement about various aspects of the bomb. Sorry does not believe the government when it tells the islanders before displacing them that they will be able to return to the island in two years. Sorry, Grandfather Jonjen, and Tara are the last to leave, thinking that they can be six miles away before the actual drop of Operation Crossroads occurs. They are wrong. The government was also wrong. Almost 50 years after the test, Bikini Atoll will poison anyone who tries to survive on its land. *American Library Association Best Books for Young Adults*, *New York Public Library Books for the Teen Age*, *Notable Children's Trade Books in the Field of Social Studies*, and *Scott O'Dell Award for Historical Fiction*.

1907. Taylor, Theodore. **The Cay**. 1969. New York: Doubleday, 1989. 138p. $15.95. ISBN 0-385-07906-0. New York: Flare, 1995. 138p. $4.50pa. ISBN 0-380-01003-8pa. 6-9

In 1942, Phillip, eleven, sails with his mother from Curaçao to Norfolk after German submarines begin torpedoing ships in the harbor. After Germans sink their ship, an old Black man, Timothy, saves Phillip and a cat. On the raft, Phillip finds that he is blind from a head injury sustained during the ship's explosion. On the island where they wash up, Timothy teaches Phillip how to be independent in spite of his disability so that Phillip can survive if Timothy dies. *Jane Addams Book Award*.

1908. Tchudi, Stephen. **Lock and Key: The Secrets of Locking Things Up, In, and Out**. New York: Scribners, 1993. 113p. $14.95. ISBN 0-684-19363-9. 7-10

This history of locks and keys gives unusual information about their origins and uses. The text discusses security systems from those on Khufu's Tomb in Egypt to Fort Knox and atomic safes. It describes the development of different kinds of locks as well as relating stories about locks in history. Bibliography and Index.

1909. Temple, Frances. **The Beduins' Gazelle**. New York: Jackson, Orchard, 1996. 160p. $15.95. ISBN 0-531-09519-3. 6-9

Halima and Atiyah, betrothed since birth, look forward to a desert wedding in the Middle East in 1302. Uncle Saladeen, however, decides that Atiyah should study the Koran in Fez. Then Halima and her camel become separated from the tribal caravan during a sandstorm as the tribe migrates toward water. An enemy sheik sees her and decides that she will become one of his wives. In this book, the same Etienne presented in *The Ramsay Scallop* meets Atiyah at the university in Fez and helps him rescue Halima from the greedy sheik.

1910. Temple, Frances. **The Ramsay Scallop**. New York: Jackson, Orchard, 1994. 310p. $17.99. ISBN 0-531-06836-6. New York: Trophy, 1995. 310p. $4.95pa. ISBN 0-06-440601-6pa. YA

In 1299 in England, Elenor is fourteen and waiting with trepidation for the return of her betrothed, Thomas, from the Crusade. When he returns, Thomas is unsure of marriage as well. The village priest sends them on a religious pilgrimage to take the village sins to Santiago de Compostela in Spain. The journey itself lets them find themselves as it acquaints them with one another. *Booklist Editor's Choice, Booklinks*, and *American Library Association Best Book for Young Adults*.

1911. Tennant, Emma. **Pemberley, or, Pride and Prejudice Continued**. New York: St. Martin's Press, 1993. 184p. $18.95. ISBN 0-312-10793-5. YA

Elizabeth Bennet Darcy, in a sequel to *Pride and Prejudice*, waits apprehensively for her recently widowed mother, sisters, Wickham, and Lady Catherine de Bourgh to come to Pemberley for one of her first Christmases married to Darcy. She is distressed not to have borne an heir, and her sister Jane is already expecting her second child. Crudity and suspicion, however, mar the gathering.

1912. Tennant, Emma. **An Unequal Marriage, or, Pride and Prejudice Twenty Years Later**. New York: St. Martin's Press, 1994. 186p. $18.95. ISBN 0-312-11533-4. YA

Elizabeth, in a second sequel to Jane Austen's *Pride and Prejudice*, enjoys the company of her daughter Miranda, seventeen, but worries about her son Edward who has gambled away part of the family property and dropped out of Eton to become a second Wickham in London.

1913. Terkel, Studs. **The Good War**. New York: New Press, 1996. 589p. $13. ISBN 1-56584-343-6. YA

Accounts of people who lived during World War II or are responding to what they think resulted from the war fill this book. They tell of going to the Far Pacific or confronting the Germans. One of the Andrews sisters visits a military hospital, and a soldier recounts the fear that General Patton put into his men. Others tell of racial inequalities and of the horror when liberating the first concentration camp. Admirals, politicians, intellectuals, and the average person all contribute their views of the war.

1914. Thomas, Elizabeth Marshall. **The Animal Wife**. Boston: Houghton Mifflin, 1990. 289p. $19.95. ISBN 0-395-52453-9. New York: Pocket, 1991. 289p. $5.99pa. ISBN 0-671-73323-0pa. YA

When Kori's father comes back to his tribe searching for a fourth wife, Kori meets him for the first time. Kori decides to leave with his father, a famous hunter, and enjoys life in his father's tribe, which includes a woman from a supposedly inferior group whom he captures and impregnates. Her people recapture her, and Kori tries to get her and his son back, but her relatives kill Kori's half brother instead. Kori's father's other wives leave him, and he and Kori pretend that they do not need women and their complaining.

1915. Thomas, Paul. **The Central Asian States**. Brookfield, CT: Millbrook Press, 1992. 32p. $15.90. ISBN 1-56294-307-3. (Former Soviet States). 4-7

On the southern border of Kazakhstan lie the central Asian states of Uzbekistan, Kyrgyzstan, Tajikistan, and Turkmenistan. The text discusses the cultural background, politics, economics, and history of these former Soviet republics. Uzbekistan, with its cities of Bukhara and Samarqand, borders Afghanistan on the south. Turkmenistan, the most western of the states, borders Afghanistan and the Caspian Sea. Tajikistan has both Afghanistan and Pakistan on its southern border, while Kyrgyzstan lies next to China. Glossary and Index.

1916. Thompson, Dorothy. **Queen Victoria: The Woman, the Monarchy, and the People**. New York: Pantheon, 1990. 167p. $18.95. ISBN 0-394-53709-2. YA

Victoria (1819–1901) ruled England from 1837 until her death, the longest ruling English monarch. At the death of Prince Albert in 1861, she went into seclusion for three years. However, her mark on the latter half of nineteenth-century English history shows that she changed the concept of both the monarchy and politics. Benjamin Disraeli, who alternated with William Gladstone as Victoria's prime minister, gained her the title Empress of India in 1876. The text looks at her life and how her role as a woman affected her subjects. Annotated Bibliography and Index.

1917. Thompson, Kathleen. **Pedro Menéndez de Avilés**. Charles Shaw, illustrator. Austin, TX: Raintree/Steck-Vaughn, 1991. 32p. $19.97. ISBN 0-8172-3383-0. (Hispanic Stories). 4-7

Pedro Menéndez de Avilés (1519-1574), born in Spain, became a sailor who loved his job. He decided that he would drive the French out of the Spanish colony of Florida, first discovered by Ponce de Léon. In 1565, he entered Florida and forcibly removed the settled French. Glossary. English and Spanish text.

1918. Thompson, Kathleen. **Sor Juana Inés de la Cruz**. Rick Karpinski, illustrator. Austin, TX: Raintree/Steck-Vaughn, 1993. 32p. $19.97. ISBN 0-8172-3377-6. (Hispanic Stories). 4-7

Born near the volcano Popocatépetl in about 1648, Inés de la Cruz was probably the greatest poet born in Mexico. She taught herself by studying wherever she could find books, but she could not marry because, as an orphan, she had no dowry. Someone paid for her to enter the convent, and she went there with her books. She entertained the greatest thinkers and scientists of the times. Throughout her life she wrote poetry in various languages, but the archbishop hated women, especially intelligent ones, and he finally found a way to trick her into not being allowed to write any more. Glossary. English and Spanish text.

1919. Thompson, Leonard. **A History of South Africa**. New Haven, CT: Yale University Press, 1990. 288p. $40; $17pa. ISBN 0-300-04815-7; 0-300-06543-4pa. YA

This overview of South African history recreates the political aspects of the area in terms of race relations. Thompson begins with the early black settlements and their chiefs, who governed by consensus, followed by the arrival of the Dutch East India Company and its establishment of a slave society at the Cape. When Afrikaners, British colonists, and Europeans arrived, they continued the conquest of the African societies. Other subjects include the gold and diamond industries, the South African War, the Union of South Africa under white minority control, the founding and development of the African National Congress, the apartheid era, and the changes with the election of de Klerk in 1989. Chronology and Index.

1920. Thompson, Wendy. **Claude Debussy**. New York: Viking, 1993. 48p. $17.99. ISBN 0-670-84482-9. (Composer's World). 7 up

Claude Debussy (1862–1918) freed music from its German restraints by rejecting the musical forms of symphony and sonata in favor of pieces inspired by poems, landscapes, and emotions. France, politically unstable when Debussy was a child, saw Paris become a mecca for artists of all genres when he was in his adulthood. The text includes photographs and selections from his music, covering all periods in his life. List of Works and Index.

1921. Thompson, Wendy. **Franz Schubert** New York: Viking, 1991. 48p. $17.99. ISBN 0-670-84172-2. (Composer's World). 7 up

Franz Schubert (1797–1828) was the last of the great classical Viennese composers. He was one of the torchbearers at Ludwig van Beethoven's funeral, although he had only met Beethoven the previous week. Symbolically, he was carrying the genius that Beethoven had passed to him and that he exhibited in such pieces as the "Unfinished Symphony" and his *leider*. However, he lived only two years longer than Beethoven, because he had contracted syphilis, a disease for which no cure existed during his lifetime. Glossary and List of Works.

1922. Thompson, Wendy. **Joseph Haydn**. New York: Viking, 1993. 48p. $17.99. ISBN 0-670-84171-4. (Composer's World). 7 up

Joseph Haydn (1732–1809) was a classical composer in Vienna during the lives of both Mozart and Beethoven, both of whom he outlived. His composing developed the classical style of music as it is currently known. His life spanned a period of social and political upheaval as well as of great musical change. Democracy did not exist, and musicians led precarious lives, being treated as servants when they worked for royalty. Haydn spent most of his adult life in the service of the Esterházys; after the French Revolution, the Esterházys gave him both freedom and a pension that allowed him to travel in his old age with relative comfort and prosperity. Pictures and excerpts from the scores of the "Surprise Symphony" and *The Creation*'s "The Heavens Are Telling" appear with the text. Glossary and List of Works.

1923. Thompson, Wendy. **Ludwig van Beethoven**. New York: Viking, 1991. 48p. $17.99. ISBN 0-670-83678-8. (Composer's World). 7 up

After placing Ludwig van Beethoven (1770–1827) in the context of his world, Thompson tells about his life through his career as a concert pianist and then a composer in Vienna. At the age of thirty, he began to go deaf, but he continued composing, although this change in his life devastated him. While Napoleon ruled, life in Vienna was more difficult, but after his exile, the government imposed other restrictions. Through it all, Beethoven continued working, and when he died, over 20,000 people lined the streets as his funeral procession went to St. Stephen's Cathedral. Photographs, illustrations, and reproductions of musical scores augment the text. Glossary and List of Works.

1924. Thompson, Wendy. **Pyotr Ilyich Tchaikovsky**. New York: Viking, 1993. 48p. $17.99. ISBN 0-670-84476-4. (Composer's World). 7 up

Composer of such works as the *1812 Overture* and the "First Piano Concerto," Pyotr Ilyich Tchaikovsky (1840–1893) gained great fame throughout the world. Personally, however, he was moody and melancholy, with an unhappy life as a hypochondriac and a homosexual at a time when homosexuality was disgraceful. He liked to show extreme emotion, and emotion fills his music. The text looks at Tchaikovsky as a product of his country and his times, in segments of his childhood (1840–1854), his search for maturity (1866–1870), as a Nationalist from 1870 to 1875, his life crisis from 1875 to 1877 when he made the mistake of deciding to marry, his recovery from the separation in 1878, his wanderings over Europe from 1878 to 1888, and his last years from 1888 to 1893 when he wrote *The Nutcracker*. Glossary, List of Works, and Index.

1925. Thompson, Wendy. **Wolfgang Amadeus Mozart**. New York: Viking, 1991. 48p. $17.99. ISBN 0-670-83679-6. (Composer's World). 7 up

As a child prodigy, Wolfgang Amadeus Mozart (1756–1791) traveled around Europe on concert tours with his father, Leopold. His father never seemed content with the money he made; this was a problem for the rest of Mozart's life. He wrote twenty operas, including *Don Giovanni* and *Die Zauberflöte;* fifty-five concert arias; seventeen masses; one requiem; forty-eight symphonies; twenty-one serenades; and thirty-nine concertos, plus solo piano music, chamber music, and dance music. Glossary and List of Works.

1926. Thomson, Andy. **Morning Star of the Reformation**. Greenville, SC: Bob Jones University Press, 1988. 134p. $6.49pa. ISBN 0-89084-453-4pa. (Light Line). YA

Around 1345 in medieval England, John Wycliffe attended Oxford University, where he developed his intellectual pursuits while facing the Pestilence. He refused to accept the Catholic Church's abuses of the clergy, transubstantiation, and papal supremacy, and he was branded a heretic. He even instigated the English translation of the Bible, and his followers, the Lollards, took the Bible to those in the countryside and urged them to read it for themselves. Among his friends were such luminaries as John Aston, John Purvey, and Nicholas Hereford, but Wycliffe is called the "Morning Star of the Reformation." The sixteenth-century schism of the church rested on his work.

1927. Time-Life. **Africa's Glorious Legacy**. Alexandria, VA: Time-Life, 1994. 168p. $18.95. ISBN 0-8094-9025-0. (Lost Civilizations). 8 up

In 1871, the German Karl Mauch began to look for ancient cultures in Africa. The text begins with his search, and four photoessays follow on the topics of the search itself, the Nubians and their ascent to greatness, the kings of savanna and forest in West Africa, and the cities of stone and coral built on gold. The Nubians held power from 3900 B.C. until A.D. 1500; their golden age was called Kush. West Africa flourished form 1500 B.C. to A.D. 1500, and the East Coast and Zimbabwe had major cultural development from A.D. 100 to 1500. Photographs, Bibliography, and Index.

1928. Time-Life. **Anatolia: Cauldron of Cultures**. Alexandria, VA: Time-Life, 1995. 168p. ISBN 0-8094-9108-7. (Lost Civilizations). 9 up

Not until the nineteenth century, with the advent of archaeology, did people have any idea of the history of civilization. In Anatolia (current-day Turkey), a civilization flourished nearly 6,000 years before Sumer. One of the oldest known cities in the world is Chatal Höyük, a farming and trading center of 6000 to 5600 B.C. One of the oldest permanent settlements excavated is Nevali Cori, a site dating from 10,000 years ago. Finds during the 1980s and 1990s show its achievements. Ashikli Höyük, dating from 8000 B.C., was a developing village sustained mainly by hunting and gathering, but having burial rituals and an appreciation of jewelry that is evident from recent discoveries. These Hittite people and those who followed have a strong history, and the text, maps, and photographs of finds serve as an entry to their worlds. Bibliography and Index.

1929. Time-Life. **Ancient India: Land of Mystery**. Alexandria, VA: Time-Life, 1994. 168p. $18.95. ISBN 0-8094-9037-4. (Lost Civilizations). 9 up

The Indus Valley's inhabitants 700,000 years ago were the Stone Age people; by 7000 B.C., some of their descendants had settled Mehrgarh on the edge of the valley and begun domesticating animals and growing crops. This civilization eventually produced artifacts and created the basis for the urban cultures that rose later. The cultures of ancient India were the Harappan (2600–1800 B.C.), the Vedic and Epic Ages (1800–600 B.C.), the Pre-Mauryan and Mauryan Period (600–100 B.C.), the Satavahanas and Kushanas (100 B.C.–A.D. 300), and the Gupta Empire (A.D. 300–500), which ended when the White Huns from central Asia attacked. Photographs, Bibliography, and Index.

1930. Time-Life. **Aztecs: Reign of Blood & Splendor**. Alexandria, VA: Time-Life, 1992. 168p. $18.95. ISBN 0-8094-9854-5. (Lost Civilizations). 9 up

Communities in Mesoamerica, in the Valley of Mexico, probably existed by 20,000 B.C. By 1500 B.C., farmers were growing corn and weavers were making baskets. In 1200 B.C., the Olmec had spread through the valley, preceding the eventual glory of the Aztecs, who evolved by A.D. 1250 only to be destroyed by the Spanish explorers. The photoessays and text look at the Early and Middle Preclassic culture (1200–400 B.C.), the Late Preclassic (400 B.C.–A.D. 100), the Classic (A.D. 100–750), the Epiclassic (A.D. 750–900), the Early Postclassic or Toltec (A.D. 900–1250), the Late Postclassic and Aztec (A.D. 1250–1521), and the Early Colonial Period (A.D. 1521). Photographs, Bibliography, and Index.

1931. Time-Life. **Celts: Europe's People of Iron**. Alexandria, VA: Time-Life, 1994. 168p. $18.95. ISBN 0-8094-9029-3. (Lost Civilizations). 9 up

This book begins with the intriguing story of a contemporary man who confessed to murdering his wife when a skull was found nearby—but the skull belonged to a woman from the first century A.D. This presentation of the Celts includes four photoessays about their origins. The essays look at the discovery of the Celts, their power and influence, what their lives were like in the Iron Age, and their struggles against Rome. They descended from Stone Age peoples, and scholars have divided their history into three phases: the Hallstatt Period of 800–450 B.C.; the La Tene Period of 450 B.C. to the Roman conquest; and the Roman Period, extending from the Conquest to the fifth century A.D. Photographs, Bibliography, and Index.

1932. Time-Life. **China's Buried Kingdoms**. Alexandria, VA: Time-Life, 1993. 168p. $18.95. ISBN 0-8094-9891-X. (Lost Civilizations). 9 up

Archaeological discoveries in China help give the basis to the history of the Shang (1500–1000 B.C.), Eastern Zhou (1122–221 B.C.), Qin (259–210 B.C.), and Han (c. 206 B.C.) Dynasties, with photoessays of the art, artifacts, and findings from each historical period. Included is the terra-cotta army of Qin Shihuangdi, China's first emperor, and the two-centuries-old tomb of Lady Xin of the Han Dynasty. Bibliography and Index.

1933. Time-Life. **Early Europe: Mysteries in Stone**. Alexandria, VA: Time-Life, 1995. 168p. $18.95. ISBN 0-8094-9100-1. (Lost Civilizations). 9 up

In 1985, a diver found a previously unknown underwater cave; after subsequent dives, he realized that it contained pictures of animals not seen since the Ice Age in Europe. Activity in the cave probably occurred over 27,000 years ago, before it was abandoned for 8,000 years and then reclaimed by Cro-Magnon animal artists. This and other discoveries increase knowledge about prehistoric life. The four photoessays cover these first Europeans and prehistoric stones, the explorers in the wetlands, the beginning of the age of metals, and the age of insecurity with the development of weapons and the rise of a warrior class. The Ice Age or Old Stone Age covers 2,000,000 to 12,000 B.C. The Middle and New Stone Ages lasted from 13,000 to 2000 B.C. The Bronze Age spans 2000 to 800 B.C., and the Iron Age dates from 800 B.C. to the Roman Empire. Photographs, Bibliography, and Index.

1934. Time-Life. **Egypt: Land of the Pharaohs**. Alexandria, VA: Time-Life, 1992. 168p. $18.95. ISBN 0-8094-9851-0. (Lost Civilizations). 9 up

As late as 1989, statues of major archaeological importance were being found at the 3,400-year-old Luxor Temple in Egypt. Such finds continue to astonish and perplex as they reveal the culture of the pharaohs. Four photoessays cover the topics of mummies, tombs, and treasures; the work and finds near the pyramids; the mummies and what they reveal; and the items found in the tombs and their significance. The Egyptian dynasties and their dates are: Early Dynastic Period, 2920–2575 B.C.; Old Kingdom, 2575–2134 B.C.; First Intermediate Period, 2134–2040 B.C.; Middle Kingdom, 2040–1640 B.C.; Second Intermediate Period, 1640–1550 B.C.; New Kingdom, 1550–1070 B.C.; Third Intermediate Period, 1070–712 B.C.; and the Late Period, 712–332 B.C. Photographs, Bibliography, and Index.

1935. Time-Life. **Etruscans: Italy's Lovers of Life**. Alexandria, VA: Time-Life, 1995. 168p. $18.95. ISBN 0-8094-9045-5. (Lost Civilizations). 9 up

A routine widening of an Italian highway in 1968 revealed gravesites and an especially interesting archaeological find of a grave sealed since 700 B.C. The information that the grave contained has helped to identify some of the first Italians. Photoessays discuss these first Italians, finds in Tuscany, burial customs, and other information discovered about the Etruscans. The Etruscans lived between the Arno and Tiber Rivers for 1,000 years, trading with the Greeks until the Romans captured their city-states one by one. The periods of Etruscan history cover the Villanovan (1000–700 B.C.), the Orientalizing (700–600 B.C.), the Archaic (600–480 B.C.), the Classical (480–300 B.C.), and the Hellenistic (300–89 B.C.). Photographs, Bibliography, and Index.

1936. Time-Life. **Greece: Temples, Tombs, & Treasures**. Alexandria, VA: Time-Life, 1994. 168p. $18.95. ISBN 0-8094-9020-X. (Lost Civilizations). 9 up

This text looks at the ways of discovering Greece's past through the archaeological finds made there. The four photoessays cover these discoveries, the new ideas about Greece's Dark Age, and Athens as the eighth wonder of the ancient world, and examine the treasures that have surfaced in places such as Philip II's tomb. The periods in Greek history include the Early (1050–750 B.C.), the Archaic (750–500 B.C.), the Classical (500–323 B.C.), and the Hellenistic (323–31 B.C.). Photographs, Bibliography, and Index.

1937. Time-Life. **The Holy Land**. Alexandria, VA: Time-Life, 1992. 168p. $18.95. ISBN 0-8094-9867-7. (Lost Civilizations). 9 up

The text looks at the ways archaeology supports information found in the Bible. Four photoessays cover the terrain and the finds; the cities of the promised land, including Ashkelon; the complexity of Jerusalem and the Qumran scrolls; and the paths that Jesus may have taken while Herod added to the Roman Empire. The history of the area, from a combination of scripture and archaeological finds, can be divided into segments. These time frames are the Canaanite Cultures (3000–1200 B.C.), the period of Judges in the United Monarchy (1200–920 B.C.), the Divided Monarchy (920–586 B.C.), the Exile and Return (586–323 B.C.), the Greek and Early Roman Period (323–4 B.C.), and the Early Roman and Christian Period (4 B.C.–A.D. 135). Photographs, Bibliography, and Index.

1938. Time-Life. **Incas: Lords of Gold and Glory**. Alexandria, VA: Time-Life, 1992. 168p. $18.95. ISBN 0-8094-9871-5. (Lost Civilizations). 9 up

Before the Incas came into the Andean region of South America, hunters and fishers had already been there for at least 12,000 years; by 3000 B.C., fishing and farming were common ways to earn a living. By 1,000 years later, larger social groups had moved inland and were using irrigation methods developed on the coast. Populations grew around temple complexes and artisans became increasingly sophisticated. Archaeologists classify Andean artifacts by time period and geographical distribution, with the term *horizons* identifying stylistic unity. The periods of the Incan cultures were the Early Horizon (1400–400 B.C.), Early Intermediate Period (400 B.C.–A.D. 550), Middle Horizon (A.D. 550–900), Late Intermediate or Coastal Period (A.D. 550–900), Late Intermediate or Highland Period (A.D. 900–1476), Late Horizon (A.D. 1476–1532), and Early Colonial Period (A.D. 1532–1572). Bibliography and Index.

1939. Time-Life. **The Magnificent Maya**. Alexandria, VA: Time-Life, 1993. 168p. $18.95. ISBN 0-8094-9879-0. (Lost Civilizations). 9 up

After the last Ice Age, approximately 10,000 years ago, people who inhabited what is now Latin America moved from the north into the Yucatan Peninsula, Guatemala, Belize, and parts of Mexico, Honduras, and El Salvador. Around 1500 B.C., village building marked the beginning of the Preclassic Period, the first period of the Mayan civilization. It ended in A.D. 250 when the early Classic period began. In A.D. 600, the Late Classic period started; the Postclassic Period replaced it in A.D. 900. During the fifteenth century, the civilization began dissipating, and the arrival of the Spaniards in the sixteenth century ended their power. Photographs, Bibliography, and Index.

1940.   Time-Life. **Mesopotamia: The Mighty Kings**. Alexandria, VA: Time-Life, 1995. 168p. $18.95. ISBN 0-8094-9041-2. (Lost Civilizations). 9 up

Sumerian civilization began between the Tigris and Euphrates Rivers around 3500 B.C. After various altercations, Mesopotamian heirs rose to take over the legacy in the great Assyrian empire around 2000 B.C. The periods of Mesopotamian culture are the Old Babylonian and Old Assyrian Period (2000–1600 B.C.), the Middle Assyrian Period (1600–1000 B.C.), the Neo-Assyrian Period (1000–605 B.C.), the Neo-Babylonian Period (605–539 B.C.), and the Persian and Hellenistic Period (539–126 B.C.). Photographs, Bibliography, and Index.

1941.   Time-Life. **Persians: Masters of the Empire**. Alexandria, VA: Time-Life, 1993. 168p. $18.95. ISBN 0-8094-9875-8. (Lost Civilizations). 9 up

The text looks at Persian history and the legacies of Cyrus, Darius, and others. The history is divided into four main periods: Pre-Achaemenid (4000–550 B.C.), Achaemenid (550–330 B.C.), Seleucid and Parthian (330 B.C.–A.D. 224), and Sassanian (A.D. 224–642). From 4000 to 550 B.C., cities such as Susa of Elam and Anshan rose out of the land. The Assyrian king Ashurbanipal sacked Susa in 647 B.C. Then the Persians, under King Cyrus the Great, took over in 550 B.C. Cyrus conquered Syria, Asia Minor, and Mesopotamia. Darius seized the throne at the death of Cyrus's son, and chose Susa as his capital. Xerxes I waged wars against Greece, and in 334 B.C., Alexander the Great took over. But when Alexander died, the Seleucids begin ruling. They did not gain complete control, however, and Persian power and prestige began to erode. The text also includes essays on Persepolis, the Empire of Darius, and Persian artistic creations. Bibliography and Index.

1942.   Time-Life. **Pompeii: The Vanished City**. Alexandria, VA: Time-Life, 1992. 168p. $18.95. ISBN 0-8094-9862-6. (Lost Civilizations). 9 up

The excavations at Pompeii and Herculaneum, the cities buried under Vesuvius when it erupted on August 24 and 25, A.D. 79, have revealed humans caught in the volcanic ash as they tried to make their escapes. From these digs, researchers have been able to recreate the lifestyle of the people, make plaster casts of their bodies, and speculate about volcanic eruptions. The four photoessays cover these topics and other revelations about the first century A.D. These two cities thrived during the Roman times of the Early Roman Republic (509–133 B.C.), the period of the Roman Revolution (133–31 B.C.), and the Early Roman Empire (31 B.C.–A.D. 79). Photographs, Bibliography, and Index.

1943.   Time-Life. **Ramses II: Magnificence on the Nile**. Alexandria, VA: Time-Life, 1993. 168p. $18.95. ISBN 0-8094-9012-9. (Lost Civilizations). 9 up

In the text with its four photoessays, the story of Ramses II comes to light. Even when Ramses II was ruling, the country of Egypt was old. The last golden age of Egypt was during the New Kingdom with its three dynasties. The three were the 18th Dynasty (1550–1307 B.C.) under rulers such as the master builder Amenhotep III, Akhenaten, and the boy-king Tutankhamen; the 19th Dynasty (1307–1196 B.C.), during which Ramses II ruled for ninety years and several other pharoahs (including a woman, Tausert) reigned; and the 20th Dynasty (1196–1070 B.C.), during which Ramses III reigned. Photographs, Bibliography, and Index.

1944.   Time-Life. **Rome: Echoes of Imperial Glory**. Alexandria, VA: Time-Life, 1994. 168p. $18.95. ISBN 0-8094-9016-1. (Lost Civilizations). 9 up

Using photographs and illustrations to accompany information about Rome, the text recounts a history that emphasizes the importance of the forum as a center of Roman life. Also featured are Hadrian's career and personal life, the Romans and their colonial expansion, and the army's role as creator of the buildings and aqueducts that held the Roman Empire together. Bibliography and Index.

1945.   Time-Life. **The Search for El Dorado**. Alexandria, VA: Time-Life, 1994. 168p. $18.95. ISBN 0-8094-9033-1. (Lost Civilizations). 9 up

Lake Guatavita, 8,000 feet high and 30 miles from Bogotá, Colombia, is the site of the legend of El Dorado. People have lost money and life trying to find the gold supposedly dropped into this lake. They found gold, but not much, and they have even tried to drain the lake to find more of it. Artisans probably began working the gold as early as 1500 B.C. When the Spaniards arrived in the sixteenth century A.D., the people living between the two great empires of Aztec, Mexico, and Inca, Peru, belonged to smaller societies, with well-developed artisan classes and centered around massive stone monuments. The cultures in the New World were Central America (A.D. 500-1502), Northern Andes (4000 B.C.–A.D.1600), Andes on the North and Central Coasts (10,000 B.C.–A.D.1476), Andes on the South Coast (4500 B.C.–A.D. 600), and the Andes Highland Region (1400 B.C.–A.D. 1100). Photographs, Bibliography, and Index.

1946.   Time-Life. **Sumer: Cities of Eden**. Alexandria, VA: Time-Life, 1993. 168p. $18.95. ISBN 0-8094-9887-1. (Lost Civilizations). 9 up

In the ancient Near East, around 8000 B.C., humans began to domesticate plants and animals. These practices both allowed and forced humans to settle in one place and give up their lives as hunter-gatherers. The periods of their culture are the Ubaid Period (5900–4000 B.C.), the Uruk Period (4000–3000 B.C.), the Early

Dynastic Period (3000–2350 B.C.), the Akkadian Period (2350–2150 B.C.), and the Neo-Sumerian Period (2150–2000 B.C.). As Sumer lost power, other civilizations such as Babylonia and Assyria prepared to take its place. Photographs, Bibliography, and Index.

1947. Time-Life. **Vikings: Raiders from the North**. Alexandria, VA: Time-Life, 1993. 168p. $18.95. ISBN 0-8094-9895-2. (Lost Civilizations). 9 up

Large mounds with ships buried beneath have revealed much about the Viking culture. The text looks at these finds through four photoessays, one of them about York, England. When the Vikings learned to build these ships, they quickly changed from a farming culture to a seagoing people. The periods of their history are the pre-Viking age (A.D. 5–800); Western Europe, the British Isles, and the East (A.D. 800–1100); and Atlantic Outposts (A.D. 860–1540). Photographs, Bibliography, and Index.

1948. Time-Life. **What Life Was Like on the Banks of the Nile: Egypt 3050-30 B.C.** Alexandria, VA: Time-Life, 1996. 192p. $19.95. ISBN 0-8094-9378-0. 6 up

Using primary documents from the lives of Egyptian citizens, the text recreates their times. A farmer who wrote to his family while away on administrative duties shows some of the domestic problems. The thoughts and concerns of pharaohs, warriors, and commoners also appear as well as the roles of women. This insight into Egyptian times is unusual because of the human emotions that so clearly speak through the text. Photographs, Reproductions, Bibliography, Glossary, and Index.

1949. Time-Life. **Wondrous Realms of the Aegean**. Alexandria, VA: Time-Life, 1993. 168p. $18.95. ISBN 0-8094-9875-8. (Lost Civilizations). 9 up

The Early Bronze Age, from 3500 to 2000 B.C., was the time of the Cycladic development. In the Middle Bronze Age, from 2000 to 1600 B.C., the Minoan civilization of Crete blossomed into a highly sophisticated urban culture that advocated peace. The Late Bronze Age, from 1600 to 1050 B.C., was the time of a militaristic Mycenaean civilization, which took over the palace at Knossos after the earthquake at Thera around 1600 B.C. For whatever reasons, the Mycenaean civilization also began to crumble, and the people were forgotten until Homer revived them in *The Iliad* and *The Odyssey*. Bibliography and Index.

1950. Toll, Nelly S. **Behind the Secret Window: A Memoir of a Hidden Childhood During World War II**. New York: Dial Books, 1993. 176p. $17. ISBN 0-8037-1362-2. 6 up

The Nazis began to occupy the town where Nelly Toll lived in 1941. When she was eight years old, in 1943, Nelly Toll and her mother went into hiding in a Gentile family's Lwów, Poland, home. She kept a journal and made vividly colored paintings to forget her world. Her art and the captions she gave the pictures give a sense of the experience. Other members of the family did not return, but Nelly and her mother survived this difficult time. Color plates of the drawings give insight to the times.

1951. Tong, Shen, and Marianne Yen. **Almost a Revolution**. Boston: Houghton Mifflin, 1990. 342p. $19.95. ISBN 0-395-54693-1. YA

Shen Tong escaped from China to the United States after the massacre in Tiananmen Square on June 3 and 4, 1989. One of the worst spots in the fighting on June 4 happened to be in front of his own home, but he comments that the students could have instituted a better plan that would have stopped the tragedy. Tong, one of the leaders of the political demonstrations that incited the attack, had previously established the Olympic Institute, a student organization to discuss new ideas about science, philosophy, and politics. He tells the story of his family life in China and his education before he had to leave his country.

1952. Townsend, Alecia Carel. **Mikhail Baryshnikov**. Vero Beach, FL: Rourke, 1993. 112p. $22.60. ISBN 0-86625-484-6. (The Arts). 7 up

Townsend begins with a description of ballet and how Mikhail Baryshnikov (b. 1948) came to be a dancer. She continues with the story of his life from his years in his homeland of the Soviet Union, dancing for the Kirov, until his defection in 1974 while he was touring Canada. He has become a leader in dance and choreography in the United States. Photographs complement the text. Glossary, Bibliography, and Index.

1953. Trease, Geoffrey. **A Flight of Angels**. Minneapolis, MN: Lerner, 1989. 117p. $9.95. ISBN 0-8225-0731-5. 4-7

Sheila and her friends decide to search the underground caves in their city of Nottingham when they have to do a local history project for school. When a development planned for the area threatens to close the wine shop over the caves, the children have to work fast. What they discover reveals life in their town during 1550. In the caves they find alabaster statues of great artistic value, which had been hidden for over 400 years. They are also able to save jobs as a result of their investigation.

1954. Treece, Henry. **Men of the Hills**. Christine Price, illustrator. New York: S. G. Phillips, 1958. 182p. $22.95. ISBN 0-87599-115-7. 6-9

Over 4,000 years ago in prehistoric England, Lalo, son of the chief of the Men of the Hills, has to kill a wolf to become a man. On the same day, the nomadic conquerors arrive, and he also has to kill humans. Although the nomads kill his father and others, Lalo escapes. He has to learn to live on his own, so he befriends Cradoc, the boy who would one day be the chief of the wild nomads. Because they are only interested in survival, they realize that helping each other is the best way.

1955. Treece, Henry. **The Road to Miklagard**. Christine Price, illustrator. New York: S. G. Phillips, 1957. 254p. $22.95. ISBN 0-87599-118-1. 6-10

Harald, the Viking hero of *Viking's Dawn*, wants more excitement, so he joins Prince Arkil of Denmark, and they sail to Ireland to take the treasure guarded by the giant Grummoch. They enslave the giant in A.D. 785, but Turkish slavers capture them and sell them to Abu Mazur of Spain. Arkil dies, but Harald rescues Abu Mazur from a traitorous gardener, and Abu Mazur asks Harald to take his daughter Marriba to Miklagard (Istanbul). In Miklagard, Marriba and Irene, Constantine's mother, disagree, and Harald sends Marriba back to Spain while he and Grummoch return home.

1956. Treece, Henry. **Swords from the North**. Charles Keeping, illustrator. New York: Pantheon, 1967. 240p. $3.95. YA

In 1034, Harald serves the Varangian Guard in Miklagard for the Empress Zoe. Because he is betrothed to Elizabeth, the daughter of King Jaroslav of Norway, he refuses to be servile to Zoe. The Guard's leader tries to trick him, but Harald figures out ways to escape his wrath. When the leader imprisons him, the empress's niece Maria, who loves him, sees in a vision that she should lower a ladder into his cell. He escapes, but friends die, and after sending Maria back to Miklagard, he returns to Elizabeth.

1957. Treece, Henry. **Viking's Dawn**. Christine Price, illustrator. Chatham, NY: S. G. Phillips, 1956. 253p. $20.95. ISBN 0-87599-117-3. 7-9

Harald first joins a sailing crew on the *Nameless* when it leaves his Norse Viking home with Thorkell Fairhair, a *berserker,* as captain. Thorkell and others die on the voyage after wrecking off the coast of Ireland and being captured. Harald and four others escape through a tunnel, but only Harald survives. He returns home around A.D. 780 on a Danish ship, but one voyage has excited him enough to make him want to return to sea immediately.

1958. Treece, Henry. **Westward to Vinland**. William Stobbs, illustrator. New York: S. G. Phillips, 1967. 192p. $9.95. ISBN 0-87599-136-X. 7 up

In A.D. 960, Norwegians force Eirik the Red to flee to Iceland. He quarrels again and sails to the west in exile, where he and his followers explore the coast of Greenland and settle. Later, his son, Leif the Lucky, brings home people from a shipwreck, and Eirik dies of the plague that they bring with them. Leif goes to America and lands on the southern coast of New England. The people with him try to start a permanent colony, but the hostile *Skraelings* who already live there, as well as arguments among the settlers, cause the colony to fail. Before they leave, Leif's sister bears Snorri, the first white American, and Leif returns to Norway where he dies in 1013.

1959. Treseder, Terry Walton. **Hear O Israel: A Story of the Warsaw Ghetto**. Lloyd Bloom, illustrator. New York: Atheneum, 1990. 41p. $13.95. ISBN 0-689-31456-6. 6 up

The Gestapo transports Isaac, his older brother, and his father to the Treblinka death camp from the Warsaw ghetto after Isaac's mother, other brothers, and sister have died of typhus. Even as Isaac, who is only twelve years old, and his father walk toward the gas chamber, Isaac keeps his faith.

1960. **Turkmenistan**. Minneapolis, MN: Lerner, 1993. 56p. $19.95. ISBN 0-8225-2813-4. (Then and Now). 5-9

As part of the Persian Empire on the border of Afghanistan, Turkmenistan was ruled by such powers as Genghis Khan and Timur. The text covers the history, economics, geography, politics, and ethnography of this recently freed country. Maps and photographs complement the text. Glossary and Index.

1961. Turnbull, Ann. **Room for a Stranger**. Bergenfield, NJ: Candlewick Press, 1996. 112p. $15.99. ISBN 1-56402-868-2. 5-7

Doreen Dyer, age twelve, after appearances in *Speedwell* and *No Friend of Mine*, is unhappy with an evacuee who comes to live with the family. Rhoda can do everything better than Doreen and she is also attractive. After an official invites Rhoda to perform in a town concert, Doreen can no longer contain her jealousy. She expresses her antagonism, and Rhoda runs away to the mines, where a cave-in injures her. When Doreen meets Rhoda's actress mother, she realizes that Rhoda's life has not been as happy as she has advertised.

1962. Turnbull, Ann. **Speedwell**. Cambridge, MA: Candlewick Press, 1992. 119p. $14.95. ISBN 1-56402-112-2. 5-9

In 1930, Mary's father is away from their English home, looking for work, and Mary's mother has no patience with her dreaming. Mary, however, thinks that the only way she can achieve something is to train the homing pigeon Speedwell. She continues to train that pigeon and the others during her father's absence. When he returns, they are ready for him.

1963.   Turner, Bonnie. **The Haunted Igloo**. Boston: Houghton Mifflin, 1991. 152p. $13.95. ISBN 0-395-57037-7. 4-7

In the early 1930s, Jean-Paul, age ten, has difficulty adjusting to his new life in the Canadian Northwest Territories where his father, a geologist, searches for radium in pitchblende. He fears that the Inuit boys may tease him about his limp. The boys enclose him in an igloo as an initiation, but after he raises a runt into a good sled dog and helps deliver his mother's baby, after getting aid from one of the boys' mothers, he earns their respect.

1964.   Turvey, Peter. **Inventions: Inventors and Ingenious Ideas**. New York: Franklin Watts, 1992. 48p. $13.95. ISBN 0-531-14308-2. (Timelines). 5-8

The text and illustrations combine to give the history of inventions, from the making of fire to the space stations of the future. Included are inventors and ingenious ideas during the classical period of the Greeks and Romans, the Middle Ages, the Renaissance, and the present. Chronology, Glossary, and Index.

1965.   Twist, Clint. **Charles Darwin: On the Trail of Evolution**. Austin, TX: Raintree/Steck-Vaughn, 1994. 46p. $15.96. ISBN 0-8114-7255-8. (Beyond the Horizons). 5-8

Charles Darwin (1809-1882) gained fame for the publication of *The Origin of Species* in 1859. The text looks at the historical background of his times; the means of transportation that were available to him, such as the HMS *Beagle* on which he sailed for five years observing the natural world; his theory of evolution that he developed from what he saw; the effect of his theory of evolution and what happened after that theory shocked the world. Photographs highlight the text. Glossary, Further Reading and Index.

1966.   Twist, Clint. **Christopher Columbus**. Austin, TX: Raintree/Steck-Vaughn, 1994. 46p. $15.96. ISBN 0-8114-7253-1. (Beyond the Horizons). 5-8

The text presents the historical background of Columbus's voyage in 1492 by describing the times in which he lived, including the Renaissance, the Reformation, and the Inquisition. It presents the modes of transportation available, his voyages, the discoveries he made, the Native Americans who lived in the New World, and what happened as a result of his trips. Photographs, paintings, drawings, and maps augment the text. Glossary, Further Reading, and Index.

1967.   Twist, Clint. **Gagarin and Armstrong: The First Steps in Space**. Austin, TX: Raintree/Steck-Vaughn, 1995. 46p. $15.96. ISBN 0-8114-3978-X. (Beyond the Horizons). 5-8

Two men were part of two different races in space. In 1961, the Russian Yuri Gagarin became the first person to travel through space. In 1969, Neil Armstrong became the first person to step on the surface of the moon. The text gives historical background, the technology of transportation, the two actual journeys, the discoveries and achievements of the expeditions, information on space and the lunar environment, and information on what happened as a result of the expeditions. Photographs, paintings, drawings, and maps augment the text. Glossary, Further Reading, and Index.

1968.   Twist, Clint. **James Cook: Across the Pacific to Australia**. Austin, TX: Raintree/Steck-Vaughn, 1995. 46p. $15.96. ISBN 0-8114-3975-5. (Beyond the Horizons). 5-8

James Cook (1728-1799) sailed as far north and as far south as ships could go in his time. He tried to find the Southern continent, but explorers did not find Antarctica until 100 years later. His voyages were for scientific exploration, not for political conquest. He always recognized the local powers of the places he visited, but irritated the Hawaiians so badly that they killed him. Along with historical background, transportation available, and the technology of the time, the text discusses native peoples of the Pacific, such as the Maoris, Kooris, Melanesians, and Easter Islanders. Also included is what happened as a result of Cook's explorations. Photographs, paintings, drawings, and maps augment the text. Glossary, Further Reading, and Index.

1969.   Twist, Clint. **Stanley and Livingstone: Expeditions Through Africa**. Austin, TX: Raintree/Steck-Vaughn, 1995. 46p. $15.96. ISBN 0-8114-3976-3. (Beyond the Horizons). 5-8

Henry Stanley (1841-1904) and David Livingstone (1813-1873) both explored in Africa. Livingstone went to Africa as a medical missionary, but disliked being a doctor. He loved travel, and went as many miles as he could. He wanted to get rid of the slavers and establish a trade center near the middle of the continent, but the slavers were too ruthless for him to succeed. He met Stanley, a newspaperman, and they visited for several months. Stanley's trips to Africa were motivated by self-improvement. He had little regard for the men who helped him carve out the Congo for the Belgian ruler. The text discusses the historical background, the transportation methods and equipment, the people of Africa, and what happened as a result of these explorations. Photographs, paintings, drawings, and maps augment the text. Glossary, Further Reading, and Index.

U

1970.   Udechukwu, Ada Obi. **Herero**. New York: Rosen, 1996. 64p. $15.95. ISBN 0-8239-2003-8. (Heritage Library of African Peoples, Southern Africa). 7-10

The Herero are three distinct subgroups sharing a similar language and culture in the contemporary countries of Botswana, Angola, and Namibia. Information in the text covers their religion and culture while emphasizing the difficult political life under German and then South African colonists. Further Reading, Glossary, and Index.

1971.   **Ukraine**. Minneapolis, MN: Lerner, 1993. 56p. $19.95. ISBN 0-8225-2808-8. (Then and Now). 5-9

This area of the former Soviet Union has known human inhabitants at least since 6000 B.C. As a major trade crossroads, it has been a spot that other countries have tried to control for centuries. In the late sixteenth century, a Cossack state formed in it. These and other concerns appear in the text as it discusses the history, economics, geography, politics, and ethnography of the area. Maps and photographs complement the text. Glossary and Index.

1972.   Uris, Leon. **Exodus**. 1958. New York: Bantam, 1989. 608p. $6.99pa. ISBN 0-553-25847-8pa. YA

Ari Ben Canaan becomes a leader for the establishment of the Jewish state after World War II. He and many others battle to save the orphaned children who have gathered in Palestine after escaping concentration camps at the end of the war. Kitty, an American nurse, realizes that she must stay in Israel to help those who need her. As people sacrifice their lives for a place to be free, others prepare the state to come into being.

1973.   Uris, Leon. **Trinity**. 1976. New York: Bantam, 1989. 144p. $7.99pa. ISBN 0-553-25846-Xpa. YA

Seamus is eleven years old in 1885 when his friend Conor's grandfather, Kilty, dies. Kilty had survived the Irish potato famine and the unrest between the Irish Catholics and the ruling British Protestants. The same year, Seamus and Conor see Catholic homes and businesses destroyed, and they become part of the battle to win Ireland's freedom from England. Conor rises to leadership in the Irish Republican Army, and Seamus becomes a reporter. They tell the story of the hardships of the Irish in their fight for freedom.

1974.   Uval, Beth. **Women in Society: Israel**. New York: Marshall Cavendish, 1992. 128p. $22.95. ISBN 1-85435-503-1. (Women in Society). 7 up

After introducing the women of Israel through their myths, the author discusses the roles of women in Israel by interweaving historical and contemporary practices. She presents the expectations imposed upon women in rural and urban areas, religious and secular practices, and poor and wealthy. The chapters cover milestones, what being a woman means in the culture, and the life of a woman from birth to old age. Women Firsts, Glossary, Further Reading, and Index.

1975.   **Uzbekistan**. Minneapolis, MN: Lerner, 1993. 56p. $19.95. ISBN 0-8225-2812-6. (Then and Now). 5-9

A country of west-central Asia, Uzbekistan was settled in ancient times, before Alexander the Great, Genghis Khan, and Tamerlane, in turn, conquered it. The Uzbek peoples finally overran it in the early sixteenth century. Russia conquered the area in the nineteenth century. The text covers this history as well as economics, geography, politics, and ethnography. Maps and photographs complement the text. Glossary and Index.

$$\boxed{V}$$

1976. Vail, John J. **"Peace, Land, Bread!" A History of the Russian Revolution**. New York: Facts on File, 1996. 148p. $17.95. ISBN 0-8160-2818-4. (World History Library). 9 up

Under the reigns of Russian tsars, through that of Nicholas II, the Russian people suffered, but they reached the point where they could bear no more during World War I. In 1917, spontaneous uprisings began, and the coalition between the Provisional Government and the Petrograd Soviet led to the emergence of Lenin and the influence of the Bolsheviks. Rather than examining the personalities involved, this text looks at the people's needs and their demands as the economic and social factors surrounding the revolution shifted. Bibliography, Chronology, Notes, and Index.

1977. Vail, John J. **World War II: The War in Europe**. San Diego, CA: Lucent, 1991. 128p. $16.95. ISBN 1-56006-407-2. (America's Wars). 7 up

The text examines the causes, effects, events, results, and long-term influences of World War II from the events leading to Germany's invasion of Poland to the death of Adolf Hitler in 1945. Details about persons, battles, and atrocities help the war become real. Maps, timelines, photographs, drawings, and paintings augment the text. Bibliography, Chronology, and Index.

1978. Van der Linde, Laurel. **The White Stallions: The Story of the Dancing Horses of Lipizza**. New York: New Discovery, 1994. 72p. $14.95. ISBN 0-02-759055-0. (Timestop). 5-9

In 1580, Archduke Charles II started a horse farm in the town of Lipizza near the Adriatic Sea. His horses, carefully trained and known as the Lipizzaners, were used by the Hapsburgs and trained at the Spanish Riding School, the court stables. They have been threatened with extinction several times—during the time of Napoleon as he advanced on Austria, during World War I when they became the property of the Italian government, and in World War II when Hitler's Nazis almost destroyed them. The text tells their story and discusses the dancelike movements of dressage. Glossary and Index.

1979. Van Dijk, Lutz. **Damned Strong Love: The True Story of Willi G. and Stefan K.** Elizabeth D. Crawford, translator. New York: Henry Holt/Edge, 1995. 138p. $15.95. ISBN 0-8050-3770-5. 9 up

In World War II, Stefan K., a Polish boy of sixteen, falls in love with a German soldier. When the Gestapo finds out, its representatives torture him and take him to a labor camp. He survives and eventually escapes just before the liberation. The novel, told from the first-person point of view, is based on a true story. Stefan K. said in 1994 that he did not know if his lover survived the war. *American Library Association Best Books for Young Adults*, *American Library Association Notable Books for Children*, and *Mildred L. Batchelder Honor Award*.

1980. Van Habsburg, Geza. **Carl Fabergé**. New York: Harry N. Abrams, 1994. 92p. $19.95. ISBN 0-8109-3324-1. (First Impressions). 7 up

Carl Fabergé (1846–1920) was an artist who worked with gold, silver, diamonds, and other precious stones. After beginning as an apprentice to his father, by 1884 he had begun to create luxurious gifts for the ruling families in Europe; his most famous works were jewel-encrusted Easter eggs for the last two tsars of Russia. He was also a successful businessman who employed more than 500 craftsmen and had shops in major European cities. Today, many of his unique creations are in museum collections around the world. Color photographs of his work show their intricacy and the surprise items that he hid inside the eggs. Index.

1981. Van Kirk, Eileen. **A Promise to Keep**. New York: Lodestar, 1990. 147p. $14.95. ISBN 0-525-67319-9. 7-9

In 1940, Ellie, age fourteen, and her older sister, Joanna, leave London for a relative's farm. They meet Curt, an Austrian refugee, to whom both are attracted. But Curt tells Ellie that he is hiding a wounded German flyer who has parachuted into the area. She does not know if she should report Curt and the flyer to the police or if she should help an enemy. Ellie chooses to be loyal to Curt, who in turn supports the Third Reich.

1982. This number not used.

1983. Van Wyk, Gary A. **Basotho**. New York: Rosen, 1996. 64p. $15.95. ISBN 0-8239-2005-4. (Heritage Library of African People). 7 up

The text examines the history of the Basotho in Lesotho along with the social life and customs, religion, education, and arts. Further Reading, Glossary, and Index.

1984. Vander Els, Betty. **The Bomber's Moon**. New York: Farrar, Straus & Giroux, 1985. 168p. $14. ISBN 0-374-30864-0. 5-7

In 1942, Ruth and her brother separate from their missionary parents, leaving them in China. They go first to another part of the country but then continue to India, where they have to read letters filled with censored text and try to figure out what their parents are telling them. After many problems and four years, they reunite in Shanghai, but the children have changed during this crucial period of their lives.

1985. Vander Els, Betty. **Leaving Point**. New York: Farrar, Straus & Giroux, 1987. 212p. $15. ISBN 0-374-34376-4. 5-7

In the sequel to *The Bomber's Moon*, Ruth is fourteen and living in Kwangchen, China, with her parents. A new Communist regime under Mao Tse-Tung has taken control of the government, and its soldiers are mistreating foreign families. While they wait in 1950 for permission to leave the country, Ruth becomes friends with a Chinese girl. Their relationship threatens the safety of the Chinese girl's family, but Ruth's departure reduces the chance of retaliation for fraternizing with a foreigner.

1986. Várdy, Steven Béla. **Attila**. New York: Chelsea House, 1991. 112p. $18.95. ISBN 1-55546-803-9. (World Leaders Past and Present). 5 up

Attila (d. 453) led the Huns out of the eastern steppes to conquer Romans, barbarians, and anyone else in their path. Questions remain about Attila's character as to whether he was bloodthirsty or the one to bring a new feudal order to a decaying Europe. Some also see him as the grandfather of the Hungarian people. The text, with photographs and reproductions, looks at the career and legacy of this man. Further Reading, Chronology, and Index.

1987. Vasileva, Tatiana. **Hostage to War: A True Story**. New York: Scholastic, 1997. 188p. $15.95. ISBN 0-590-13446-9. 7 up

Tatiana Wassiljewa (Vasileva), a Russian girl of thirteen who starved during World War II while laboring for the Nazi invaders, wrote in her journal about the inhumanities of this ordeal. She lived in Wyritza, a small town sixty kilometers from Leningrad, where no food was available. She had to search many miles on foot to trade the family's possessions for corn, but her father died anyway. After her deportation to Germany, she continued her slave labor for German citizens who saw it as their right. But she still made friends in the work camps and kept her positive approach to life until she was reunited with her mother and sister after this horrendously dehumanizing war.

1988. Ventura, Piero, author/illustrator. **Clothing**. Boston: Houghton Mifflin, 1993. 64p. $16.95. ISBN 0-395-66791-7. 4-8

The text, with illustrations, gives a history of clothing. The periods and topics covered are prehistory, Egypt, the Ancient East, tanning leather, Crete, Greek styles, Rome, classical society, Byzantium, the barbarians, from sheep to cloth, pyramidal societies, late Middle Ages, thirteenth and fourteenth centuries, merchants and tailors in the 1400s, end of the Middle Ages, society in the 1500s, sixteenth century, the early 1600s, the style of the Sun King, the early 1700s and getting dressed in the noble ranks, the French revolution, the early 1800s, nineteenth-century society, a tailor's shop in the early 1900s, and the mid-twentieth century. Glossary.

1989. Ventura, Piero, author/illustrator. **Food: Its Evolution Through the Ages**. Boston: Houghton Mifflin, 1994. 64p. $16.95. ISBN 0-395-66790-9. 4-8

Illustrations and text tell the story of food through the centuries. Included are hunting with pits and snares, bows and arrows, and traps; fishing; gatherers; agriculture in ancient Egypt and Rome; making bread; grain transportation; beekeeping, spices, and cured meats; animals and vegetables in the New World; harvesters; steam engines; freezing; canning; cattle raising and breed selection; pasteurization and sterilization; diet; factory ships; and new foods and products. Glossary.

1990. Ventura, Piero, author/illustrator. **1492: The Year of the New World**. New York: Putnam, 1992. 96p. $19.95. ISBN 0-399-22332-0. 4 up

Illustrations and text present what was happening in the Old World during 1492 in Germany, Flanders, England, France, the Ottoman Empire, Genoa, Portugal, and Spain. It looks at Columbus's voyage and those people found in this world: the Tainos, Aztecs, Maya, and Inca. Other important voyages of discovery after 1492 were to the Orient. Some Important Dates in European History 1493-1558, Important Dates in Italian Renaissance Art, Native North and South Americans, Five Hundred Years Later, and Index.

1991. Verhoeven, Rian, and Ruud Van Der Rol. **Anne Frank: Beyond the Diary, A Photographic Remembrance**. Tony Langham and Plym Peters, translators. New York: Viking, 1993. 112p. $17. ISBN 0-670-84932-4. 5 up

Text and accompanying photographs or illustrations describe Anne Frank's (1929-1945) life before her family went into hiding when the Nazis arrived in Amsterdam, Holland. Her father, an amateur photographer, reveals her happy childhood while the political life around her continued to deteriorate without her knowledge. The text includes excerpts from the diary she wrote while confined in the back rooms during the Nazi occupation, and it continues with explanations of what happened to the family after the Nazis took them to the concentration camps. (This information is available at the Anne Frank House in Amsterdam.) Maps, Chronology, Notes, Sources, and Index of People and Places. *Christopher Award, American Library Association Notable Books for Children, A Publishers Weekly Nonfiction Book of the Year, Booklist Editor's Choice, Mildred L. Batchelder Honor,* and *Bulletin Blue Ribbon Book.*

1992. Vernon, Roland. **Introducing Bach**. Parsippany, NJ: Silver Burdett, 1996. 32p. $14.95; $6.95pa. ISBN 0-382-39155-1. (Famous Composers Series). 5-7

This brief overview of Johann Sebastian Bach (1685-1750) includes full-color drawings, photographs, and engravings as well as sidebar information on events, artistic movements, and people of his time. Glossary and Index.

1993. Vernon, Roland. **Introducing Beethoven**. Englewood Cliffs, NJ: Silver Burdett, 1996. 32p. $13.95; $6.95pa. ISBN 0-382-39154-3; 0-382-39153-5pa. (Famous Composers Series). 3-7

Ludwig van Beethoven (1770-1827), born at a time of change in Europe, wrote his music during the transition from the Classical to the Romantic period. The text looks at his life in double-page topic spreads that include his time at court, his classical training, life in Vienna, the *Eroica* symphony, his opera *Fidelio*, the new order after Napoleon's exile, and his difficulties with his deafness. Photographs and reproductions highlight the text. Time Chart, Glossary, and Index.

1994. Vernon, Roland. **Introducing Mozart**. Parsippany, NJ: Silver Burdett, 1996. 32p. $14.95. ISBN 0-382-39159-4. (Famous Composers Series). 5-7

This brief overview of Wolfgang Amadeus Mozart (1756-1791) includes full-color drawings, photographs, and engravings as well as sidebar information on events, artistic movements, and people of his time. Although short, the text is sophisticated, and it places Mozart in his time. Glossary and Index.

1995. Veryan, Patricia. **Ask Me No Questions**. New York: St. Martin's Press, 1993. 340p. $21.95. ISBN 0-312-08699-7. YA

In Georgian England during the second half of the eighteenth century, Ruth Allington gets a job restoring a Dover mansion fresco. She needs to support her dead brother's twins. What she discovers is that the Jeweled Men were responsible for murdering her brother when he opposed their plans to take over England.

1996. Veryan, Patricia. **Had We Never Loved**. New York: Fawcett, 1993. 310p. $4.99pa. ISBN 0-449-22218-7pa. YA

The Jeweled Men target the family of Lord Horatio Glendenning when they call him a traitor for dealing with the Jacobites in the eighteenth century. However, they want to have their own revolution and defeat the Hanoverians.

1997. Veryan, Patricia. **Never Doubt I Love**. New York: St. Martin's Press, 1995. 345p. $21.95. ISBN 0-312-11864-3. YA

Zoe Grainger comes to London to attend the crass Lady Buttershaw's invalid sister in the late eighteenth century. Zoe slowly falls in love with the man hired to take her around London after he helps her search for her missing brother, Travis. He is a diplomat involved with the Jeweled Men trying to overthrow the Hanoverian king.

1998. Veryan, Patricia. **The Riddle of Alabaster Royal**. New York: St. Martin's Press, 1997. 256p. $23.95. ISBN 0-312-17121-8. YA

Jack Vespa returns to his estate of Alabaster Royal after being wounded in battle, hoping to find peace of mind and relaxation. People think that the place is haunted, and no one wants to work there. After a series of incidents and people coming to the house uninvited and unexpected, he has the opposite experience of what he had anticipated.

1999.   Veryan, Patricia. **A Shadow's Bliss**. New York: St. Martin's Press, 1994. 324p. $21.95. ISBN 0-312-10543-6. YA

Around 1746, Crazy Jack lives in a Cornwall village and has moments of lucidness but seems like a gentleman from his speech. When he becomes the castle coachman of Sir Vinsom, Sir Vinsom's only daughter falls in love with him. Jack, however, has found connections between a local mine and the League of Jeweled Men who want to take over England.

2000.   Vining, Elizabeth Gray. **Adam of the Road**. Robert Lawson, illustrator. New York: Viking, 1942. 320p. $17.99. ISBN 0-670-10435-3. New York: Puffin, 1987. 320p. $5.99pa. ISBN 0-14-032464-Xpa. 4-8

After Adam's minstrel father returns from France, the two walk from place to place in England, but they become separated at a large fair in Winchester, England. Adam falls off a wall and knocks himself unconscious; while he slowly recovers, he and his father do not know where the other is. When he is well enough, Adam goes to London to search for Roger. He does not find him until the following spring when they both return to St. Alban's. *Newbery Medal.*

2001.   Viola, Herman J., and Susan P. Viola. **Giuseppe Garibaldi**. New York: Chelsea House, 1988. 112p. $18.95. ISBN 0-87754-526-X. (World Leaders Past and Present). 8 up

Garibaldi (1807–1882) helped to gain freedom for Italy and also fought as a professional revolutionary in South America. He led Italian groups in Brazil and in Uruguay before returning to Italy in 1848 during the wars occurring then, and he was both a fighter and a fugitive. He even established his own government in Sicily, but by 1870 an independent Italy had emerged. Photographs and reproductions enhance the text. Chronology, Further Reading, and Index.

2002.   Vogel, Ilse-Margaret. **Bad Times, Good Friends: A Personal Memoir**. San Diego, CA: Harcourt Brace, 1992. 239p. $16.95. ISBN 0-15-205528-2. 9 up

Ilse-Margaret Vogel and her five friends lived in Berlin during World War II. They risked their lives by printing false identification papers and fake food coupons, trading on the black market, and sheltering people hunted by the Nazis. When asked why she stayed in Germany, Vogel said that she had believed the war would soon be over; after it had been going on for a while, she and her friends became used to deprivation. They stayed in Berlin rather than in small towns because in the city, they could hide and could avoid supporting Hitler, whom they hated. The text reveals a different view of the war, of Germans who helped to defeat the maniac who had taken over their government. *New York Public Library's Books for the Teen Age.*

2003.   Volkogonov, Dmitri. **Trotsky: The Eternal Revolutionary**. Harold Shukman, translator. New York: Free Press, 1996. 524p. $32.50. ISBN 0-02-874119-6. YA

By the time the Russian Civil War ended in 1921, Lev Trotsky was helping Lenin, with many seeing him as Lenin's heir. He wanted Russia to have equal opportunity and social justice, but ten years later, Stalin had sent him into exile. Stalin killed each of the men who had been with Lenin in 1917. Trotsky was the last when Stalin sent someone to put a pickax through Trotsky's skull in Mexico City during 1940. The text reveals information from secret police files previously closed, showing how much Stalin wanted Trotsky and all of his family and friends dead because Stalin feared that Trotsky would kill him first. Volkogonov posits that Trotsky's concept of class war and dictatorship of the proletariat is what allowed Stalin to take what Lenin had started and make it into "Stalinism." Bibliography and Index.

2004.   Von der Heide, John. **Klemens von Metternich**. New York: Chelsea House, 1988. 112p. $18.95. ISBN 0-87754-541-3. (World Leaders Past and Present). 8 up

Prince Klemens von Metternich (1773–1859) of Austria spent fifty years trying to create a "congress system" among Europe's leading monarchies. While attending school in France, he became aware of the atmosphere resulting from the revolution, and he always thought that monarchy was more desirable than democracy. He opposed Napoleon and Napoleon's attempt to take over the world, but Metternich's way did not succeed either; in 1848, rebellion filled Europe and the age of nationalism emerged. Photographs and engravings enhance the text. Chronology, Further Reading, and Index.

2005.   Vos, Ida. **Anna Is Still Here**. Terese Edelstein and Inez Smidt, translators. Boston: Houghton Mifflin, 1993. 139p. $13.95. ISBN 0-395-65368-1. 3-7

Although World War II has ended, Anna still shudders at the years she spent hidden from the Nazis in Holland and thinks that danger lurks everywhere. As the year continues, she and her parents begin to talk about their experiences apart, and Anna makes friends with a Jewish woman who lost her family. When the woman discovers that her daughter has been adopted by another family, she has to look at life differently. Anna realizes that she must do the same, in this sequel to *Hide and Seek*.

2006.   Vos, Ida. **Dancing on the Bridge at Avignon**. Terese Edelstein and Inez Smidt, translators. Boston: Houghton Mifflin, 1995. 183p. $14.95. ISBN 0-395-72039-7. 5-9

Rosa de Jong, age ten, is a talented violinist living in Holland during World War II. Her family hopes that a German general, once rescued by Rosa's uncle, will sign papers that will save them from deportation to Poland. A depressed Rosa remembers when she could go to school and play in the streets without fear. She takes lessons from a Jewish concertmaster until he is arrested, and her playing of his son's composition finally saves her life, but not the lives of her family.

2007.   Vos, Ida. **Hide and Seek**. Terese Edelstein and Inez Smidt, translators. Boston: Houghton Mifflin, 1991. 133p. $13.95. ISBN 0-395-56470-0. 4-8

Rachel, age eight, tells various incidents from her life during five years after the Nazis arrive in Holland in 1940. She has to give up her bicycle, stay off the tram, not play games, and wear a yellow star on her sleeve. She feels as if she is in a cage, and after the liberation, her sister refuses to go into the street right away because it is not yet dark. Among the unexpected emotions after the war is the guilt felt by Jews without tattoos. Then Rachel and her family have to part from the people who hid and protected them. Perhaps worst is the delayed grief about all that happened.

W

2008. Wade, Mary Dodson. **Ada Byron Lovelace: The Lady and the Computer**. New York: Dillon Press, Macmillan, 1994. 128p. $13.95. ISBN 0-87518-598-3. YA

Ada Byron Lovelace (1815–1852) wrote the first computer program, nearly 100 years before the computer was invented. The daughter of the British poet, Lord Byron, Ada was mechanically inclined, liked geography, and designed model ships. By the age of sixteen, she had taught herself geometry. After marrying, she continued to pursue her interest in mathematics and translated a report by Charles Babbage on a new machine. Her translation became three times longer than the original paper and contained radical ideas far beyond those in Babbage's design. Her life became one of gambling debts and an affair that she tried to hide from her husband. No one knew much about her until 1954, when her papers were discovered. Sources, Bibliography, and Index.

2009. Walch, Timothy. **Pope John XXIII**. New York: Chelsea House, 1986. 112p. $18.95. ISBN 0-87754-535-9. (World Leaders Past and Present). 7 up

Born Angelo Giuseppe Roncalli (1881–1963), the man who became Pope John XXIII began studying for the priesthood while still a boy. He served as a hospital chaplain during World War I, and in 1925, after being elevated to archbishop, he went to Bulgaria. He also represented the Vatican in Turkey, Greece, and France. In World War II, he helped civilians and refugees, especially Jews, to escape from the Nazis. In 1958, he became pope and began to liberalize church policies; this work culminated in 1962 when he convened Vatican II. Photographs and reproductions enhance the text. Chronology, Further Reading, and Index.

2010. Waldron, Ann. **Claude Monet**. New York: Harry N. Abrams, 1991. 92p. $19.95. ISBN 0-8109-3620-8. (First Impressions). 8 up

Claude Monet (1840–1926) was always fascinated with natural light. He experimented endlessly with its effect and pioneered the Impressionist movement as a style emphasizing the points of light on a canvas. The text includes reproductions and explanations of his technique of applying paint to a surface. He struggled to maintain his artistic integrity while painting during a period when art critics were hostile toward his work. List of Illustrations and Index.

2011. Waldron, Ann. **Francisco Goya**. New York: Harry N. Abrams, 1992. 92p. $19.95. ISBN 0-8109-3368-3. (First Impressions). 8 up

Although Francisco Goya (1746–1828) grew up in a poor Spanish farming family, he wanted to draw and paint. He learned his craft by painting religious subjects for churches, then portraits of the lesser nobility, followed by designs for tapestries depicting daily life, and finally portraits of the royal family. He saw that life had a darker side, which led him to create a world of imagination in his pictures with giants, witches, and devils. In his later life, he used all of his ideas in a series called the "Black Paintings." Prints and Index.

2012. Waldstreicher, David. **Emma Goldman**. New York: Chelsea House, 1990. 112p. $18.95. ISBN 1-55546-655-9. (American Women of Achievement). 7 up

Emma Goldman (1869-1940) spent her life advocating personal freedom for every individual. She fled a Jewish ghetto and immigrated to the United States in 1885. When the Haymarket Riot occurred in Chicago, during which four anarchists were hanged when they supported striking laborers, Goldman became active in the radical community of New York City. She spoke out against unemployment during the 1893 Depression and was imprisoned. People called her "Red Emma." She supported the rights of workers, women, and minorities. She lectured throughout the country and began an anarchist magazine named *Mother Earth*. She protested the military draft during World War I and was exiled to the Soviet Union. During the last 20 years of her life, she supported international causes like the antifascist movement in the Spanish Civil War. Photographs and reproductions enhance the text. Chronology, Further Reading, and Index.

2013. Walworth, Nancy Zinsser. **Augustus Caesar**. New York: Chelsea House, 1988. 112p. $18.95; $7.95pa. ISBN 1-55546-804-7; 0-7910-0617-4pa. (World Leaders Past and Present). 5 up

Augustus Caesar (63 B.C.-A.D. 14), adopted son of Julius Caesar, became the first emperor of Rome. He was frail and sickly as a boy, but had great determination and intelligence. These qualities led him to join forces with Mark Antony in 43 B.C. to destroy Caesar's assassins. Later he fought against Antony at the Battle of Actium in 31 B.C. to become the single supreme ruler. He retained all necessary powers of office while staying within the limits of tradition. He streamlined the army, funded roads, and began an imperial administration. All of his achievements and his character developments appear in this text, enhanced by photographs and reproductions. Chronology, Further Reading, and Index.

2014. Walworth, Nancy Zinsser. **Constantine**. New York: Chelsea House, 1989. 112p. $18.95. ISBN 1-55546-805-5. (World Leaders Past and Present). 5 up

Constantine (d. 337) dreamed that he was visited by Jesus Christ. This dream changed the world when he decided that he would convert to Christianity. His decision ended Roman paganism and began the rise of Christianity. He had a vision of greatness for the Roman world which his father helped to instill in him. He was able to inspire the masses, calm the pagans, and return financial strength to the Roman Empire. He changed the public image of Christianity by establishing it as a complex organization. Photographs and reproductions enhance the text. Chronology, Further Reading, and Index.

2015. Wangari, Esther. **Ameru**. New York: Rosen, 1995. 64p. $15.95. ISBN 0-8239-1766-5. (Heritage Library of African Peoples, East Africa). 5-8

Various traditions disagree on the origin of the Ameru, but in one story they had to escape Egypt; in a tradition paralleling the Israelites' leaving Egypt, the Ameru eventually reached Kenya. In Kenya, the Ameru district lies on the equator around the slopes of Mt. Kenya. History about this group, along with information about its social structure, its customs and rituals, colonialism, and its future, appear in the text. Photographs, boxed information, and maps enhance the text. Glossary, Further Reading, and Index.

2016. Warburton, Lois. **Aztec Civilization**. San Diego, CA: Lucent, 1995. 127p. $16.95. ISBN 1-56006-277-0. (World History). 6 up

The information on the Aztecs begins with a description of the current ruins in Mexico City, where the ruins of an ancient Aztec temple are all that remains of the sophisticated city of Tenochititlán, a Toltec construction. The Aztecs overran the Toltecs in the twelfth century. Daily life, religion (including human sacrifice), political views, and wealth are among the topics covered in this book. The Aztec empire ended when Cortés came because Moctezuma probably thought that Cortés was the god Quetzlcoatl returned to save the people. Instead, in 1521, Cortés killed them. Photographs and reproductions enhance the text. Maps, Timeline, Works Consulted, Further Reading, and Index.

2017. Warburton, Lois. **The Beginning of Writing**. San Diego, CA: Lucent, 1990. 128p. $16.95. ISBN 1-56006-113-8. 6-10

Before people had writing, they had to communicate. The text looks at their attempts and how these cultures began to form alphabets in order to write. The text highlights the Egyptian, Mayan, Chinese, and American Indian societies. Photographs enhance the text. Bibliography, Glossary, and Index.

2018. Warburton, Lois. **Railroads: Bridging the Continents**. San Diego, CA: Lucent, 1991. 96p. $16.95. ISBN 1-56006-216-9. 6-9

In the text, period paintings, prints, and photographs from Library of Congress collections illustrate two-page spreads that present various topics. They include the major western trails, early railroads, and the inland and ocean waterways. The text examines the history, development, and technology of the steam engine and railroads; discusses the decline of rail transport in the United States; and describes the growth of railroads in Europe and Japan, focusing on their high-speed trains and magnetic levitation. Chronology and Index.

2019. Ward, Glenyse. **Wandering Girl**. New York: Henry Holt, 1991. 183p. $14.95. ISBN 0-8050-1634-1. 7 up

Because she was an aborigine in Australia, Glenyse Ward was taken from her parents and placed in an orphanage as a baby. She began working in a Catholic mission as a child and became a domestic servant when a teenager. She had to spray disinfectant on things because she had touched them, do daily chores for fifteen hours, and sleep on a shabby cot. She recalls the year 1965 when someone finally helped her escape from this terrible life and get a job in Sydney, away from the farm. As she says in the epilogue, she never looked back.

2020. Watkins, Dawn L. **Zoli's Legacy I: Inheritance**. Greenville, SC: Bob Jones University Press, 1991. 190p. $6.49pa. ISBN 0-89084-596-4pa. YA

From 1919 until the beginning of World War II, Zoltán Galambos works hard for the money to get his education in Hungary. When he decides to delay finishing the university to run a new orphanage, his mother tells him never to return to her home. *Finalist, C. S. Lewis Contest.*

2021. Watkins, Dawn L. **Zoli's Legacy II: Bequest**. Greenville, SC: Bob Jones University Press, 1991. 142p. $6.49pa. ISBN 0-89084-597-2pa. YA

After World War II engulfs Zoli and his family, he has to decide what will be best for his life and for others, as he becomes even more concerned about the children who have lost their parents in Hungary. This volume is the second about Zoltán Galambos. *Finalist, C. S. Lewis Contest.*

2022. Watkins, Richard R., author/illustrator. **Gladiator**. Boston: Houghton Mifflin, 1997. 87p. $17. ISBN 0-395-82656-X. 5-8

Gladiators served as the entertainment for all levels of Roman society. The text examines their history and the training that they had to undergo before they shed the shame of slavery for the confidence of combat. Illustrations show the cruelty of these games and the bloodthirsty spectators who demanded them.

2023. Watkins, Yoko Kawashima. **My Brother, My Sister, and I**. New York: Macmillan, 1994. 275p. $16.95. ISBN 0-02-792526-9. 5 up

In this sequel to *So Far from the Bamboo Grove*, Watkins continues the fictionalized account of her life as the thirteen-year-old Yoko, with her sister Ko and brother Hideyo, after their escape from Korea into Japan after World War II. When the warehouse where they live burns in a fire, they live with Yo in the hospital, who was severely wounded in the fire while trying to retrieve the ashes of their mother and the money she gave them before her death. The warehouse owners' heir accuses them of arson and murder, so they must disprove those charges. Additionally, they are trying to find their father, who the Soviets have captured. Yoko hates her school and her horrid treatment by the other girls, who laugh at her poverty. That a child can survive in such adverse circumstances shows the importance of character and love. A few of the adults they meet help them cope until they eventually find their father, aged from years in a Siberian prison camp. *American Library Association Notable Books for Young Adults, Parenting Magazine Best Book, New York Times Notable Book,* and *Publishers Weekly Best Book.*

2024. Weaver-Gelzer, Charlotte. **In the Time of Trouble**. New York: Dutton, 1993. 275p. $15.99. ISBN 0-525-44973-6. 7 up

Jessie Howells, age fourteen in 1959, attends boarding school with two siblings in one part of Cameroon while her missionary parents live in another section. The native Maquis, who have begun fighting against the French colonists, kidnap her parents, but after several days they are returned. However, Jessie has to be strong during the ordeal and reassure her sister and brother that all the family members will be safe and reunited.

2025. Weidhorn, Manfred. **Napoleon**. New York: Atheneum, 1986. 212p. $16.95. ISBN 0-689-31163-X. 7 up

Napoleon (1769–1821) left Corsica for school in France when he was nine years old. In Paris, his classmates taunted him as a foreigner and an outsider. But he excelled at his studies and became one of the most powerful leaders in history, being crowned the emperor of France in his thirties. He was a complex man who was at first a liberal but became rigidly conservative as he lost touch with his people. His final battle, Waterloo, preceded his last years on St. Helena. Further Reading and Index.

2026. Weintraub, Stanley. **The Last Great Victory: The End of World War II July/August 1945**. New York: Dutton, 1995. 730p. $35; $16.95pa. ISBN 0-525-93687-4; 0-452-27063-4pa. YA

The text reveals the intense racial hatred between the Japanese and Americans near the end of World War II and the barbarism of the fighting between them. By presenting the discussions of the American, Japanese, and Soviet governments day-by-day during July and August 1945, Weintraub shows how amazing the end of the war actually was because it neither destroyed Japan nor allowed the Soviets to occupy its northern part. The facts and the chronology speak loudly. He relates the estimates that the Battle of Tokyo would have cost 268,345 lives when extrapolated from the 82,000 casualties at Okinawa. The Japanese had more than 10 times as many military personnel on the home islands, and no one could estimate the effect of the kamikazes. Such figures support Truman's decision to drop the atomic bomb on Japan. Bibliography and Index.

2027. Weir, Alison. **The Princes in the Tower**. New York: Ballantine, 1993. 287p. $23; $12.50pa. ISBN 0-345-38372-9; 0-345-39178-0pa. YA

The two sons of Edward IV—Edward V, age twelve, and his brother, age ten—disappeared in the Tower of London. In the 1520s, Thomas More accused Richard III of being a murderer, but more contemporary historians think that the Tudors maligned Richard. Weir makes assessments based on primary accounts of More's informants. Richard most likely was directly involved in the young princes' demise, and his treatment of the children made him unpopular during his time. Bibliography and Index.

2028. Weir, Alison. **The Six Wives of Henry VIII**. New York: Grove Press, 1992. 643p. $24.95; ISBN 0-8021-1497-0. New York: Ballantine, 1993. 643p. $12.50pa. ISBN 0-345-38072-Xpa. YA

Six women became queens of England because they married Henry VIII: Catherine of Aragon, Anne Boleyn, Jane Seymour, Anne of Cleves, Catharine Howard, and Catharine Parr. The information in this collective work comes from letters, diaries, papers, and diplomatic sources, so personal aspects of these women become apparent. But the women also reflect the times during which they lived. Chronology, Bibliography, and Index.

2029. Weir, Alison. **Wars of the Roses**. New York: Ballantine, 1996. 462p. $24; $12.95pa. ISBN 0-345-39117-9; 0-345-40433-5pa. YA

Beginning with a short history of the house of Plantagenet and the rule of Richard II, the story continues to the Battle of Tewkesbury and the murder of King Henry VI, covering the years of 1399 to 1500. It includes the family rivalries and personalities that made this period so complex and so interesting. Bibliography and Index.

2030. Weisberg, Barbara. **Coronado's Golden Quest**. Mike Eagle, illustrator. Austin, TX: Raintree/Steck-Vaughn, 1993. 79p. $24.26; $5.95pa. ISBN 0-8114-7232-9; 0-8114-8072-0pa. (Stories of America—Personal Challenge). 5-9

Viceroy Mendoza of Spain spent his personal fortune to send Coronado (1510-1554) and an army to find the seven cities of gold that they had heard so much about. They left in 1540, but after more than a year of searching and treachery, they realized that gold was not to be located in the southwest above Mexico. Coronado was wounded when he fell from a horse, and other incidents doomed the journey. A slave named Turk convinced the party that Quivera, his home, had gold and that he would lead them from Cicuye to their rewards. They discovered that he was lying because he thought this was the only way he could escape his captors. Epilogue, Afterword, and Notes.

2031. Weitzman, David. **Great Lives: Human Culture**. New York: Scribners, 1994. 294p. $22.95. ISBN 0-684-19438-4. (Great Lives). 5-9

Biographical profiles of 27 anthropologists and archaeologists describe their work and their motivations. They are Ruth Benedict (American, 1887-1948); Franz Boas (American, 1858-1942); James Henry Breasted (American, 1865-1935); Howard Carter (English, 1873-1939); Herbert, Fifth Earl of Carnarvon (English, 1866-1923); Jean-François Champollion (French, 1790-1832); Arthur Evans (English, 1851-1941); Alice Cunningham Fletcher (American, 1838-1923); Jane Goodall (English, b. 1934); Georg Fredrich Grotefend (German, 1775-1883); Zora Neale Hurston (American, 1891-1960); Alfred Kroeber (English, 1876-1960); Austen Henry Layard (French, 1817-1894); Louis S. B. Leakey (English, 1903-1972); Mary Nicol Leakey (English, b. 1913); Richard Leakey (Kenyan, b. 1944); Robert Harry Lowie (American, 1883-1957); Max Mallowan (English, 1904-1978); Margaret Mead (American, 1901-1978); Elsie Clews Parsons (American, 1875-1941); Hortense Powdermaker (American, 1900-1970); Mary Kawena Pukui (Hawaiian, 1895-1986); Heinrich Schliemann (German, 1822-1890); Michael Ventris (English, 1922-1956); Robert Eric Mortimer Wheeler (English, 1890-1976); Charles Leonard Woolley (English, 1880-1960); and Yigael Yadin (Israeli, 1917-1984). Further Reading and Index.

2032. Weitzman, David. **Great Lives: Theater**. New York: Atheneum, 1996. 320p. $24. ISBN 0-689-80579-9. 9 up

Among the actors, actresses, and playwrights who have made important contributions to world theater are Sarah Bernhardt, Helen Hayes, Laurence Olivier, Paul Robeson, Henrik Ibsen, and George Bernard Shaw. The text looks at the times in which the artists lived, and the social, historical, and personal influences that affected their work. Bibliography and Index.

2033. Welch, Ronald. **Knight Crusader**. William Stobbs, illustrator. 1954. New York: Oxford University Press, 1979. 246p. $4.95. ISBN 0-19-271060-5. 9 up

Every time Philip D'Aubigny sees someone from Wales, he asks about life there. Although Welsh, he has lived in Outremer (Jerusalem) since birth. By 1187, he has to escape from several tight situations in his adopted home before he helps to defeat the Infidels in Acre. Then Philip is free to go to England and Wales to claim his inherited lands. *Carnegie Medal*.

2034. Welton, Jude. **Impressionism**. New York: Dorling Kindersley, 1993. 64p. $16.95. ISBN 1-56458-173-X. (Eyewitness). YA

Two-page topics, complemented with reproductions of Impressionist paintings and other styles of pictures that help describe the topic, give an overview of this important late nineteenth-century art movement. Discussions include Manet's painting of modern life, painting outdoors, student life, Monet, the Batignolles group, rebellion against the Salon, color, the cafe life, Renoir, Caillebotte, trains, Sisley's landscapes, gardens, Pissarro's workers, patrons and domestic lives, Morisot, Degas, Japanese influence, and Cassatt. Glossary and Index.

2035. Welton, Jude. **Monet**. New York: Dorling Kindersley, 1992. 64p. $16.95. ISBN 1-56458-067-9. (Eyewitness Art). 12 up

The text about Monet (1840–1926) equals the excellent graphics, which reveal the personal belongings and artists' tools that Monet used as he created his canvases. Twenty-seven minichapters follow Monet's development. Chronology, Glossary, and Index.

2036.   Wepman, Dennis. **Alexander the Great**. New York: Chelsea House, 1986. 112p. $18.95. ISBN 0-87754-594-4. (World Leaders Past and Present). 5 up

Alexander succeeded to the Macedonian throne in 336 B.C. and quickly secured military and political supremacy over the states of the Greek peninsula. Between 334 and 323 B.C., he established a reputation as one of the greatest leaders the world has ever seen. His empire included the Balkans, parts of northern Africa, the eastern Mediterranean, southwestern Asia, and much of India. He believed that East and West could be united under a single system of government and grow accustomed to one way of life. He may have been bloodthirsty, or he may have been trying to create peace. Photographs and reproductions enhance the text. Glossary, Chronology, and Index.

2037.   Wepman, Dennis. **Bolívar: Latin Revolutionary**. New York: Chelsea House, 1985. 112p. $18.95. ISBN 0-87754-569-3. (World Leaders Past and Present). 7 up

Símon Bolívar (1783–1830) helped to create social justice in the class systems that the Spanish brought with them to South America from the Old World. Although born to one of the wealthiest families in Venezuela, he sacrificed his wealth and luxury to help liberate South America. He led an untrained army to victory against heavy odds, he freed the slaves, and he outlined a theory of government for the continent. Photographs and reproductions enhance the text. Chronology, Further Reading, and Index.

2038.   Wepman, Dennis. **Desmond Tutu**. New York: Franklin Watts, 1989. 157p. $21.20. ISBN 0-531-10780-9. (Impact Biography). YA

Desmond Tutu (b. 1931), as the fiery archbishop of Cape Town and the highest-ranking Anglican churchman in South Africa, became the spokesperson for South African blacks by tirelessly urging world governments to end their investments in that country as long as it continued the policy of apartheid and the poverty and disease it engendered. He won the 1984 Nobel Peace Prize for his efforts. After going to Britain and seeing the possibilities for treating members of various races as human beings, he returned to South Africa and tried to make them realities. Chronology, Notes, Bibliography, and Index.

2039.   Wepman, Dennis. **Hernán Cortés**. New York: Chelsea House, 1986. 115p. $18.95. ISBN 0-87754-593-6. (World Leaders Past and Present). 7 up

As one of the Spanish *conquistadores*, the men whom gold and glory lured to the New World, Hernán Cortés (1485–1547) achieved what he came for. He left Spain in 1504 to become a colonist on the West Indian island of Hispaniola, but he gained command of his own expedition to Mexico in 1518. From Veracruz on the coast, he fought inland until he reached Tenochtitlán, with its wealth and splendor. After Montezuma welcomed him, thinking he was a god, Cortés took the city and killed Montezuma. Photographs and reproductions enhance the text. Chronology, Further Reading, and Index.

2040.   Wepman, Dennis. **Jomo Kenyatta**. New York: Chelsea House, 1985. 112p. $18.95. ISBN 0-87754-575-8. (World Leaders Past and Present). 5 up

Jomo Kenyatta (b. 1894) resolved to free the Kenyan people from British subjugation. He went to London in 1929 and furthered his political education by watching the British at home. He realized then that the British thought their civilization was the best model for everyone. Kenyatta returned to Kenya in 1946 and united the Kenyan tribes. The British imprisoned him, but he regained his freedom in 1961 to become a respected leader of the country. Photographs enhance the text. Chronology, Further Reading, and Index.

2041.   Wepman, Dennis. **Tamerlane**. New York: Chelsea House, 1987. 112p. $18.95. ISBN 0-87754-442-5. (World Leaders Past and Present). 5 up

Tamerlane (1336–1405) was one of the world's great conquerors. In the fourteenth century, he led his Mongols from the steppes of Russia and India to the Mediterranean. He led marauders near the central Asian city of Samarkand and, after capturing thousands of craftsmen and artists, he brought them to Samarkand to use their skills. He is known as the "Earthshaker" because of the millions of Muslims and other "infidels" he slaughtered. As he marched toward China, he died. His mosque stills soars over the city, but he cast a huge shadow during his century. Photographs and reproductions enhance the text. Chronology, Further Reading, and Index.

2042.   Wesley, Mary. **Part of the Furniture**. New York: Viking, 1997. 256p. $22.95. ISBN 0-670-87363-2. YA

In World War II, Juno Marlowe, seventeen, waits to follow her mother from England to Canada. She goes to London, however, with two friends who take advantage of her innocence and leave her pregnant. But someone helps her secure a job on an estate as land girl, which allows her to develop appropriately.

2043.   West, Alan. **José Martí: Man of Poetry, Soldier of Freedom**. Brookfield, CT: Millbrook Press, 1994. 32p. $13.90. ISBN 1-56294-408-8. (Hispanic Heritage). 5-8

José Martí (1853-1895), son of Spanish parents who lived in poverty, had a teacher, Mendive, near his Cuban home who recognized his abilities and paid for his schooling. Martí wrote his first poem for Mendive's wife upon the death of her child. He continued to compose poetry even as he went to prison at age seventeen for writing a letter against the government, and as he was exiled in Spain, and as he returned to Mexico and other South American countries to work for freedom for Cuba. His poem "La Guantanamera" was set to music and sung throughout Cuba and the rest of the world. He died while leading an uprising against Spain in Cuba at Dos Ríos. Important Dates, Find Out More, and Index.

2044. West, Delno C., and Jean M. West. **Braving the North Atlantic: The Vikings, the Cabots, and Jacques Cartier Voyage to America**. New York: Atheneum, 1996. 86p. $16. ISBN 0-689-31822-7. 5-9

The text details the explorations of John Cabot, a Genoese sailor, and his son, Sebastian, in the New World as they tried to find the Northwest Passage to the Orient. The British king sponsored their explorations, and fifteenth-century sources reveal their journey. France also sent an explorer, Jacques Cartier. He found the St. Lawrence River, and his claim made Canada a colony of France. Index.

2045. West, Delno, and Jean M. West. **Christopher Columbus: The Great Adventure and How We Know About It**. New York: Atheneum, 1991. 136p. $15.95. ISBN 0-689-31433-7. 7 up

Three sections in each chapter give facts, pictures, and maps while discussing Columbus's (c. 1451–1506) dream, his search for support, his adventure as he left Portugal, and his return voyages to the New World. Chronology, Glossary, and Index.

2046. Westall, Robert. **Blitzcat**. New York: Scholastic, 1989. 230p. $12.95. ISBN 0-590-42770-9. 7 up

A cat, Lord Gort, personified in this narrative, goes through England searching for her master during World War II. She goes first to the southern coast near Dunkirk, to Dover, and then to Coventry. She senses a German bombing raid, and her behavior warns the residents. The omniscient point of view allows the people to speak for themselves; the cat's view of them is unknown. She finds her master, but she has changed. *American Library Association Best of the Books, 1966–1992* and *Horn Book Fanfare*.

2047. Westall, Robert. **Echoes of War**. New York: Farrar, Straus & Giroux, 1989. 90p. $13.95. ISBN 0-374-31964-2. 7-10

These five stories show the effects of war on various persons. They include a wounded soldier remembering the fires in Dresden, a dead woman found on the seashore after a bombing raid, a shell-shocked grandfather who took things from the kits of dead men who owed him money, and a boy discovering that mines do not cover the beach as he has been told. Although the setting is Britain, these characters could be of any nationality.

2048. Westall, Robert. **Falling into Glory**. New York: Farrar, Straus & Giroux, 1995. 304p. $18. ISBN 0-374-32256-2. 9 up

Robbie, age seventeen, is in his last year of British grammar school after World War II. He has spent his teen years playing rugby, and a new player from the working class helps his team begin to win. At the same time, Robbie becomes attracted to one of his teachers, Emma Harris. Robbie and Emma finally begin an illicit affair, which eventually ends as Robbie begins to wonder what will be best for his future.

2049. Westall, Robert. **Fathom Five**. 1980. Magnolia, MA: Peter Smith, 1995. 256p. $17.05. ISBN 0-8446-6664-5. New Market, Ontario, Canada: McClelland & Stewart, 1996. 256p. $5.99pa. ISBN 0-330-32230-3pa. 8 up

In 1943, Chas is sixteen years old. In this sequel to *The Machine-Gunners*, he and a friend discover a floating olive oil can containing a message about a ship expected in the harbor. They investigate the message, which leads them to a German soldier living in town who pretends to hate Germans. He has been planning to alert a submerged German submarine about the ship's arrival so that the submarine can torpedo it. Chas and his friend thwart the plan.

2050. Westall, Robert. **Gulf**. New York: Scholastic, 1996. 96p. $14.95. ISBN 0-590-22218-X. YA

Tom and Figgis live with their parents during 1990 in England in this historical fantasy. During the Gulf War, Figgis keeps dreaming about a boy in the desert; when he tells Tom, Tom refuses to tell anyone else, but wants more information about the experience. What Tom decides is that Figgis becomes Latif, an Iraqi fighting under Saddam Hussein, when he sleeps. Tom comes to understand the awful state of war as he stands by helplessly, watching while his brother suffers.

2051. Westall, Robert. **The Kingdom by the Sea**. New York: Farrar, Straus & Giroux, 1990. 176p. $15. ISBN 0-374-34205-9. 6-9

Harry escapes a bomb in 1942, but his family does not reach the bomb shelter, and his house is destroyed. Not knowing if his family is dead, Harry leaves. On the English coast, people help him, but one man suggests that he go home to officially say good-bye to the memory of his family. When he returns, he finds his family, relocated and frustrated at his disappearance. *Guardian Award for Children's Fiction*.

2052. Westall, Robert. **The Machine-Gunners**. New York: Greenwillow, 1976. 186p. $13.93. ISBN 0-688-80055-6. New Market, Ontario, Canada: McClelland & Stewart, 1995. 192p. $5.99pa. ISBN 0-330-33428-Xpa. 7 up

When Chas, age fourteen, cuts the machine gun off a downed German fighter plane in World War II, he asks a wealthy boy who lives nearby to store it for him in an unused bomb shelter. The police think that the Irish Republican Army has stolen the gun until Chas and his friends decide to shoot it themselves. Chas loses his war souvenir to the police. *Carnegie Medal.*

2053. Westall, Robert. **The Promise**. New York: Scholastic, 1991. 176p. $13.95. ISBN 0-590-43760-7. 6-9

During the early part of World War II, Bob, age fourteen, has a crush on Valerie, a sickly girl who stays home as much as she goes to school. When she asks Bob to come and find her if she ever gets lost, he readily agrees. She dies and begins to haunt him, reminding him of his promise. Bob recalls that time and how he became more interested in the war effort and thought less of Valerie, not expecting her to demand solace from the grave.

2054. Westall, Robert. **Time of Fire**. New York: Scholastic, 1997. 176p. $15.95. ISBN 0-590-47746-3. 5-8

Sonny lives in Newcastle during World War II, but the war is just talk to him until a bomb kills his mother. He feels guilty because she was killed on an errand that she had asked him to make, and when his father dies while trying to find the German who bombed her, he feels doubly guilty. When he faces a German pilot stranded in the town, the complexities of war and death become even more immediate.

2055. Westall, Robert. **The Wind Eye**. 1977. New Market, Ontario, Canada: McClelland & Stewart, 1995. 192p. $5.99pa. ISBN 0-330-32234-6pa. 7-10

Beth's father sails their boat, the *Wind Eye,* into the seventh-century world of Cuthbertus, before the Vikings came into the North Sea to Lindisfarne. The family discovers that Cuthbert had a strong personality that helped him establish the island monastery. What he did in the seventh century has a profound effect on Beth's twentieth-century family in this historical fantasy.

2056. Westerfeld, Scott. **The Berlin Airlift**. Englewood Cliffs, NJ: Silver Burdett, 1989. 64p. $16.98. ISBN 0-382-09833-1. (Turning Points). 5 up

Although the title indicates that the text covers the Berlin airlift in 1948 and 1949, it also discusses several other points important to the history of the time. It includes background on the Iron Curtain and on the Marshall Plan, with a biographical commentary on George Marshall, "Operation Vittles," and the rise of the Berlin Wall. Index and Suggested Reading.

2057. Wetterau, Bruce. **World History: A Dictionary of Important People, Places, and Events, from Ancient Times to the Present**. New York: Henry Holt, 1994. 1173p. $60; $35pa. ISBN 0-8050-2350-X; 0-8050-4241-5pa. 7 up

This volume includes more than 10,000 entries in alphabetical order, with 135 historical outlines and chronologies containing another 7,000 items.

2058. Wheeler, Thomas Gerald. **All Men Tall**. New York: S. G. Phillips, 1969. 256p. $21.95. ISBN 0-87599-157-2. 8 up

Thomeline, an orphan at age fifteen in 1323, escapes from the queen's treachery to Sussex, where he joins the household of Hugh the Armourer. There he and several others begin to work with a special powder that needs a particularly designed object in which to work. Their cannon soon functions properly and helps defeat the French at Crécy in 1346. With Hugh, Thomeline begins to understand the values of virtue, intelligence, and skill rather than the superficiality of untrained nobility.

2059. Wheeler, Thomas Gerald. **A Fanfare for the Stalwart**. New York: S. G. Phillips, 1967. 191p. $22.95. ISBN 0-87599-139-4. 8 up

Alain Dieudonné, age nineteen in 1912, becomes a trumpeter in Napoleon's Imperial Guard and begins his march toward Moscow with the Grand Army. After the difficult winter with little food and few supplies, the army retreats, and Alain searches for the rear guard. Cossacks shoot his horse, and he has to walk back to Warsaw, wounded and hungry. He and two refugees, a governess and daughter of a French officer, eventually reach their destination. When he returns to Paris, the army acknowledges his valor.

2060. White, Barbara E. **Impressionists Side by Side: Their Friendships, Rivalries, and Artistic Exchanges**. New York: Knopf, 1996. 304p. $65. ISBN 0-679-44317-7. YA

Members of the Impressionist movement, Degas, Manet, Pissarro, Cézanne, Renoir, Monet, Morisot, and Cassatt, depended on each other for all kinds of support, emotional and financial. White uses diaries and letters to support the interactions of the members of this group and to describe how they helped each other while continuing to believe in their "new" artistic style. He shows the narrower dependencies of Degas and Manet, Monet and Renoir, Cézanne and Pissarro, Manet and Morisot, Cassatt and Degas, and others while also disclosing attachments in the larger group. Reproductions highlight the text. Appendix, Bibliography, Chronology, and Index.

2061.   White, Ellen. **The Road Home**. New York: Scholastic, 1995. 469p. $15.95. ISBN 0-590-46737-9. 7 up

Rebecca Phillips, a triage nurse in Vietnam, faces the horrors of the war when they arrive in the emergency room. An injury returns her to her New England home, where she cannot overcome the emptiness she feels after having to kill a young enemy boy. She has great difficulty relating to her concerned parents and the casual attitude of people who do not understand the intensity of the war. She drinks to forget but eventually goes to Colorado to see an amputee who had rejected her in Vietnam. He too has little direction, and her unannounced arrival gives him a reason to live. They realize that much cannot be forgotten, but a future together, as she plans to go to medical school, may be productive for both. *American Library Association Best Books for Young Adults.*

2062.   Whitelaw, Nancy. **Charles de Gaulle: "I Am France."** New York: Dillon Press, 1991. 112p. $13.95. ISBN 0-87518-486-3. (People in Focus). 7 up

Charles de Gaulle (1890–1970) led the forces of the Free French when the Nazis occupied the country during World War II. He was a professional soldier, trained in military school, and a politician, trained on the job, with a vision for his country. He thought that freedom and security were tantamount to a successful France. Photographs, Selected Bibliography, and Index.

2063.   Whitelaw, Nancy. **Joseph Stalin: From Peasant to Premier**. New York: Dillon Press, 1992. 149p. $12.95. ISBN 0-87518-557-6. (People in Focus). 5 up

At age fifteen, Iosif Dzhugashvili (1879-1953) won a scholarship to a seminary school. Three decades later, he was one of the most powerful and most feared men in the world. He always hated authority and fought against it; this characteristic got him expelled from the seminary. One of the difficulties in writing accurately about Stalin is that he ordered systematic alterations of some records and destruction of others, so the true picture can never be known entirely. The text tries to tell as much truth as possible about Stalin's life. Time Line, Selected Bibliography, and Index.

2064.   Whitman, Sylvia. **Hernando de Soto and the Explorers of the American South**. New York: Chelsea House, 1991. 112p. $19.95. ISBN 0-7910-1301-4. (World Explorers). 5 up

Hernando de Soto (1500-1542) returned to the New World, landing on Florida's coast, to find gold in 1539. He had gained much wealth when Pizarro conquered the Incas in Peru, and he expected the same in experience. He roamed through the American South looking for gold, silver, and pearls, but his expedition deteriorated as the men raped, pillaged, and plundered the Indians. On this horrendous journey, he discovered the Mississippi River. Engravings and reproductions enhance the text. Chronology, Further Reading, and Index.

2065.   Wicks, Ben. **No Time to Wave Goodbye**. New York: St. Martin's Press, 1988. 228p. $15.95. ISBN 0-312-03407-5. YA

Ben Wicks, a cartoonist, tells of his experiences in 1939 and 1940 when he was moved from his home (thought to be vulnerable to bombing raids) to a foster home in the countryside. He solicited letters from others who were also moved from their homes. Some of the experiences of the 8,000 who responded were happy, but others were starved or exploited by their foster parents. Between recollections are reports on the progress of the war during that time. Most of these children, now adults, seemed to remain angry at those who sent them away.

2066.   Wiesel, Elie. **From the Kingdom of Memory: Reminiscences**. New York: Schocken, 1995. 250p. $12pa. ISBN 0-8052-1020-2pa. YA

In a series of essays, Elie Wiesel (b. 1928) asserts his belief that one must remember the past if one is to have the best life in the present. He discusses the Holocaust, religious faith, war crimes, peace, and freedom. Among the collected speeches are his response to President Ronald Reagan during Reagan's Bitburg visit and his Nobel acceptance address for the Peace Prize in 1986. He asserts that all Jews are concerned with humanity, not merely with "getting even."

2067.   Wiesel, Elie. **Night**. 1960. New York: Bantam, 1987. 109p. $4.99pa. ISBN 0-553-27253-5pa. 7 up

Elie Wiesel, born in Hungary in 1928, was deported first to Auschwitz and then to Buchenwald, where his parents and younger sister died. This book tells of his experiences through the death of his father in the camp and then liberation by the Americans. All he and the others could think of was getting food. They had not eaten for more than six days because the Germans had been systematically eliminating as many inmates as they could and had stopped feeding the others. Wiesel says that revenge was not on their minds at the end, only food. This book is a powerful statement on inhumanity.

2068. Wiggins, Marianne. **John Dollar**. New York: HarperCollins, 1989. 214p. $17.95; $12pa. ISBN 0-06-016070-5; 0-06-091655-9pa. YA

After her husband dies in World War I, Charlotte goes to Rangoon, Burma, to become a schoolteacher. She finds another life there and enjoys being with a man she meets, named John Dollar. They visit an island with other British subjects, but the trip turns into a disaster that only Charlotte survives.

2069. Wilford, John Noble. **The Mysterious History of Columbus: An Exploration of the Man, the Myth, the Legacy**. New York: Knopf, 1991. 315p. $12pa. ISBN 0-679-73832-0pa. YA

Wilford tells the story of Columbus while documenting how that story has been transmitted through the past 500 years. He uses recent archaeological findings and relies on historiography for his interpretation of the economic, religious, and political reasons that Columbus left Spain. He looks at the consequences of the meetings between the Europeans and the indigenous Americans, the origin of the name "America," Columbus's mind, and the facets of Columbus's reputation. Annotated Chapter Bibliographies and Index.

2070. Wilkinson, Philip. **Amazing Buildings**. Paolo Donati, illustrator. New York: Dorling Kindersley, 1993. 48p. $16.95. ISBN 1-56458-234-5. (Amazing). 3-7

The text presents illustrations of cross sections, as well as drawings and photographs, of twenty-one buildings throughout the world. Included are the palace of Minos in ancient Crete; the Colosseum in Rome; the Mayan Temple of the Inscriptions; Krak des Chevaliers, built in Syria during the Crusades; the Alhambra in Granada, Spain (thirteenth century); Chartres Cathedral, built during the Middle Ages in France; the Imperial Palace of Beijing (1368-1644); Teatro Olimpico, the sixteenth-century replica of an ancient Roman theater in Vicenza, Italy; Himeji Castle in Japan, built in the seventeenth century; the Taj Mahal in India; Versailles of the French King Louis XIV; Brighton Pavilion in nineteenth-century England; the Houses of Parliament in London; the Paris Opera during the reign of Napoleon III (1852-1870); Germany's Neuschwanstein Castle (1864-1886); the Statue of Liberty in New York; the Van Eetvelde House in Brussels; the Notre-Dame-du-Haut, designed by Le Corbusier, in eastern France; the Guggenheim Museum of Frank Lloyd Wright; the Sydney, Australia, Opera House; and the Toronto Sky Dome, built for the Olympics. Index.

2071. Wilkinson, Philip. **Building**. Dave King and Geoff Dann, illustrators. New York: Knopf, 1995. 61p. $16.95. ISBN 0-679-97256-0. (Eyewitness). 4 up

Photographs and drawings give clear pictures of the various aspects of building. Topics covered in two-page spreads are structural engineering, house construction, and building materials. These include wood, earth, bricks, stone, timber frames, the roof, thatching, columns and arches, vaults, staircases, fireplaces and chimneys, doors and doorways, windows, stained glass, balconies, and building on unusual topography. Index.

2072. Wilkinson, Philip, and Jacqueline Dineen. **The Lands of the Bible**. Robert R. Ingpen, illustrator. New York: Chelsea House, 1994. 92p. $19.95. ISBN 0-7910-2752-X. (Mysterious Places). 6 up

Illustrations and text give background information on ten places noted in the Bible. The places are Ur (Iraq, c. 4000-2000 B.C.), Saqqara (Egypt, c. 2680 B.C.), Babylon (Iraq, c. 1792-1750 B.C. and c. 625-540 B.C.), Boghazköy (Turkey, c. 1700-1200 B.C.), Karnak (Egypt, c. 1480-1080 B.C.), Abu Simbel (Egypt, c. 1305-1200 B.C.), Khorsabad (Iraq, 720-705 B.C.), Persepolis (Iran, c. 520-330 B.C.), Petra (Jordan, c. 170 B.C.-A.D. 100), and Alexandria (Egypt, c. 320 B.C.-A.D. 391). Further Reading and Index.

2073. Wilkinson, Philip, and Jacqueline Dineen. **The Mediterranean**. Robert R. Ingpen, illustrator. New York: Chelsea House, 1994. 92p. $19.95. ISBN 0-7910-2751-1. (Mysterious Places). 5 up

The illustrations and maps, along with the text, tell about places in past history. The places are Tarxien on Malta (3600-2500 B.C.); Knossos on Crete (2000-1450 B.C.); Mycenae in Greece (1600-1100 B.C.); Delphi in Greece (650 B.C.- A.D. 150); Epidaurus in Greece (320 B.C.-A.D. 150); Rhodes, an island of Greece (280-226 B.C.); Leptis Magna in Libya (46 B.C.-A.D. 211); Hagia Sophia in Istanbul, Turkey (A.D. 360-537); Mistra in Greece (A.D. 1262-1460); and the Topkapi in Istanbul, Turkey (A.D. 1465-1853). Further Reading and Index.

2074. Wilkinson, Philip, and Jacqueline Dineen. **People Who Changed the World**. Robert R. Ingpen, illustrator. New York: Chelsea House, 1994. 93p. $19.95. ISBN 0-7910-2764-3. (Turning Points in History). 5-10

Religious leaders, philosophers, and explorers have changed the world. Those presented in the text include Confucius (c. 551-479 B.C.), Gautama Buddha (c. 563-480 B.C.), Pericles (c. 495-429 B.C.), Jesus Christ (c. 6 B.C.-c. A.D. 30), Muhammad (c. A.D. 570-632), St. Benedict of Nursia (c. A.D. 480-550), Marco Polo (1215-1294), Lorenzo de Medici (1449-1492), Christopher Columbus (1451-1506), Martin Luther (1483-1546), Ferdinand Magellan (1480-1521), James Cook (1728-1779), Karl Marx (1818-1883), Henri Dunant (1828-1910), Sigmund Freud (1856-1939), Leopold II of Belgium (1835-1909) who colonized Africa, and Martin Luther King, Jr. (1929-1968). Events included are the Black Plague, the Irish Famine, and the Wall Street stock market crash. Further Reading and Index.

2075.   Wilkinson, Philip, and Jacqueline Dineen. **Statesmen Who Changed the World**. Robert R. Ingpen, illustrator. New York: Chelsea House, 1994. 93p. $19.95. ISBN 0-7910-2762-7. (Turning Points in History). 5-10

Using the definition that a statesperson is someone who influences people around the world rather than only in their own country or neighborhood, the text looks at people who have had a vision of changes whether good or bad. Included are Asoka, the Buddhist emperor (270-232 B.C.); Shih Huang Ti, Emperor of China (259-210 B.C.); Julius Caesar, Consul of Rome (100-44 B.C.); Constantine of Byzantium (A.D. 285-337); King John and the Magna Carta (1167-1216); Isabella of Castille (1451-1504) and Ferdinand II of Aragon (1452-1516); Cortés and the Aztec Empire (1485-1547); Ivan IV of Russia (1530-1584); the Manchu Empire of China under Prince Dorgon (1612-1650); Prague's Frederick V (1596-1632); the fall of the Bastille in 1789 under Louis XVI (1754-1793) and Marie Antoinette of Austria (1755-1793); Simón Bolívar (1783-1830) in South America; Emperor Meiji (1852-1912) opening up Japan; Palmerston (1784-1865) and the opening of India; Bismarck (1815-1898) and German unity; Lenin (1870-1924) and the Russian Revolution; Gandhi (1869-1948) and Indian independence; Mao (1893-1976) and the Chinese Long March; Eleanor Roosevelt (1884-1962) and the United Nations; and Gorbachev (b. 1931) and the Berlin Wall. Further Reading and Index.

2076.   Wilkinson, Philip, R. and Michael Pollard. **Generals Who Changed the World**. Robert Ingpen, illustrator. New York: Chelsea House, 1994. 93p. $19.95. ISBN 0-7910-2761-9. (Turning Points in History). 5-10

Generals have changed the map of the Earth through the battles they have won or lost. The generals discussed in the text cover many centuries. They are Alexander of Macedonia (356-323 B.C.); the Vandals, Huns, and Visigoths under Alaric (c. A.D. 370-410); Viking raiders beginning in the eighth century; William I (c. 1027-1087) conquered England in 1066; Abu Bakr, leader of the Almoravids, who overcame Ghana in 1056; the first crusade in 1095 called by Urban II; Genghis Khan (c. 1162-1227) and the Mongols; Sultan Mehmet II (1432-1481) who overtook Byzantium; Babur (1483-1530), conqueror of India; the revolt of the Netherlands toward Spain under William the Silent (1533-1584); Drake and the defeat of the Spanish Armada in 1588 (1540-1596); John III Sobieski (1624-1696) saving Vienna from the Turks; James Wolfe (1727-1759) capturing Quebec; Washington (1732-1799) after Lexington; Napoleon (1769-1821) attacking Moscow; Robert E. Lee (1807-1870) and Sharpsburg; Paul Kruger's Boers (1825-1904) against Great Britain; the beginning of World War I under Kaiser Wilhelm II (1859-1941); Japan's bombing of Pearl Harbor with Hideki Tojo as prime minister (1884-1948); and Dwight Eisenhower (1890-1969) and D-Day. Further Reading and Index.

2077.   Wilkinson, Philip, and Michael Pollard. **The Magical East**. Robert R. Ingpen, illustrator. New York: Chelsea House, 1994. 92p. $19.95. ISBN 0-7910-2754-6. (Mysterious Places). 6 up

Illustrations along with text tell about places of the East that are important to past and present civilizations. They are Mohenjo-Daro (India, c. 2400-1800 B.C.); the Great Wall (China, c. 300 B.C.-A.D. 40); Yoshinogari (Japan, c. 300 B.C.-A.D. 300); Ellora (India, c. A.D. 600-900); Nara (Japan, c. A.D. 710-795); Angkor (Kampuchea, c. A.D. 900-1150); Easter Island (Oceania, c. A.D. 100-1680); Great Zimbabwe (Zimbabwe, c. A.D. 1200-1450); the Forbidden City (Beijing, China, c. A.D. 1404-1450); and the Taj Mahal (Agra, India, c. A.D. 1632-1643). Further Reading and Index.

2078.   Wilkinson, Philip, and Michael Pollard. **Scientists Who Changed the World**. Robert R. Ingpen, illustrator. New York: Chelsea House, 1994. 93p. $19.95. ISBN 0-7910-2763-5. (Turning Points in History). 4-7

People who have had an interest in why and how things happen have helped shape the world. Brief profiles of some of those scientists or groups appear in the text. They are Kaifung, Johannes Gutenberg (fifteenth century), Galileo Galilei (1564-1642), Isaac Newton (1642-1727), James Watt (1736-1819), Donkin and Hall (early nineteenth-century cannery), Louis Daguerre (1789-1851), Charles Darwin (1809-1882), Joseph Lister (1827-1912), Alexander Graham Bell (1847-1922), Marie Curie (1867-1934), the Wright brothers (early twentieth century), Henry Ford (1863-1947), Albert Einstein (1879-1955), John Logie Baird (1888-1946), Alan Turing (1912-1954), the Manhattan Project (early 1940s), Crick and Watson (twentieth century), Wilkins and Franklin (twentieth century), the launch of Sputnik I in 1957, and astronauts Aldrin, Armstrong, and Collins. Photographs enhance the text. Timeline and Index.

2079.   Willard, Barbara. **A Cold Wind Blowing**. 1973. New York: Laurel, 1989. 175p. $3.25pa. ISBN 0-440-20408-9pa. (Mantlemass, 3).YA

When Henry VIII destroys convents and priories in 1538, Piers, son of Medley and Catherine Mallory from *The Sprig of Broom*, protects a young girl as his priest uncle had requested before he died. Piers, age eighteen, falls in love with the girl and they marry. A former schoolmate accuses the girl of being a nun, although she never took her final vows. Because Henry VIII had never released the nuns from their vows of chastity, she dies of guilt at the birth of their child.

2080.   Willard, Barbara. **The Eldest Son**. 1977. New York: Dell, 1989. 192p. $3.25pa. ISBN 0-440-20412-7pa. (Mantlemass, 4). YA

In 1534, Harry, age eighteen (the brother of Piers from *A Cold Wind Blowing*), wants to be an ironmaster. First, though, he has to learn to work with horses, which he expects to inherit. However, a plague kills the horses as well as his daughter. Distraught, Harry and his wife sever their ties and move to her deceased uncle's land, where Harry works as an ironmaster.

2081.   Willard, Barbara. **A Flight of Swans**. 1980. New York: Dell, 1989. 192p. $3.25pa. ISBN 0-440-20458-5pa. (Mantlemass, 6) YA

Ursula, the daughter of Lilias in *The Iron Lily*, is unhappily married to Robin when a London relative appears whose wife has recently died. He leaves his sons with Ursula, but one disappears to see the Spanish Armada in 1588. The man and Ursula fall in love, but because of their complex family ties, they refrain from consummating their emotions.

2082.   Willard, Barbara. **Harrow and Harvest**. 1975. New York: Laurel, 1989. 174p. $3.25pa. ISBN 0-440-20480-1pa. (Mantlemass, 7). YA

Parliamentarians kill Harry Medley during the 1630s as the English civil war rages. His son Edmund, age fifteen, travels to Mantlemass as his father had told him to do. Cecelia, the granddaughter of Ursula from *A Flight of Swans,* has read Ursula's journal before he arrives and knows that he is the true heir. Her aunt, upset that someone else is the heir, tells a Royalist about Edmund, and the Royalist shoots him. When the others leave for the American colonies, Cecelia stays. She then finds out that the family descends from Richard, the last Plantagenet, but she burns all the evidence so that she can start a life free from the past. *Guardian Award.*

2083.   Willard, Barbara. **The Iron Lily**. 1974. New York: Dell, 1989. 175p. $3.25pa. ISBN 0-440-20434-8pa. (Mantlemass, 5). YA

Lilias, age fifteen in 1570, runs away after her mother dies of plague and her aunt announces that her mother's husband was not Lilias's father. With a crooked shoulder, Lilias feels unattractive, but she learns to work with herbs to heal people. Her employer finds her a husband, and their daughter also has a crooked shoulder. When Lilias's husband dies, a man named Medley buys their home; with his crooked shoulder, he feels a kinship with the daughter. Lilias discovers that Piers Medley was her father but that the age difference between her mother and Piers kept them from marrying. *Guardian Award.*

2084.   Willard, Barbara. **The Lark and the Laurel**. 1970. New York: Dell, 1989. 207p. $3.25pa. ISBN 0-440-20156-Xpa. (Mantlemass, 1). YA

Cecily's father escapes to France in 1485 after the Lancasters defeat the Yorkist king Richard. Cecily, age sixteen, goes to live with an aunt who was mistreated by Cecily's father, who made her marry an immoral, crippled bastard. The aunt teaches Cecily to read and write and manage a rabbit farm. Cecily meets the disinherited Lewis Mallory and falls in love. When her own father returns, Cecily discovers that she has been married to Lewis since she was five years old.

2085.   Willard, Barbara. **The Sprig of Broom**. 1971. New York: Dell, 1989. 184p. $3.25pa. ISBN 0-440-20347-3pa. (Mantlemass, 2). YA

Roger, son of Lewis and Cecily Mallory from *The Lark and the Laurel*, has Medley Plashet as his friend in 1506. Villagers suspect Medley's mother of witchcraft because she uses herbs to heal people, and they stone her. Medley goes to live with Roger and falls in love with Roger's sister. Roger decides to enter the priesthood and wills his inheritance to Medley. Then Medley discovers that his grandfather is King Richard Plantagenet, whose symbol is a sprig of broom.

2086.   Williams, Barbara. **Titanic Crossing**. New York: Dial Press, 1995. 149p. $14.99. ISBN 0-8037-1790-3. 4-8

Albert Trask, age thirteen, has the chance to travel from England to America on the *Titanic* in 1912. He roams the deck with Emily, a friend on the ship who notes that third-class passengers have few lifeboats. When the ship sinks, Albert has to save his six-year-old sister. He does, but his mother dies. He and his sister then have to face their dead father's mother in their new home, and Albert learns to assert himself appropriately.

2087.   Williams, Brian. **Ancient China**. New York: Viking, 1996. 48p. $16.99. ISBN 0-670-87157-5. (See Through History). 6-9

The topics in this look at China, with overlays to show the insides of a typical Chinese house, include farming, religion, architecture, clothing, and other aspects of daily life. The history covers the beginnings of Chinese history through the massacre in Tiananmen Square in 1989. Illustrations highlight the text. Chronology, Glossary, and Index.

2088. Williams, Brian. **Forts and Castles**. New York: Viking, 1994. 48p. $15.99. ISBN 0-670-85898-6. (See Through History). 6-9

People began building forts and castles in prehistoric times when walled towns were important, and they continued through the Middle Ages. They helped kings control lands, protect their subjects, and impress their enemies. Armies tried to capture them and developed complex weapons to achieve their goals. See-through cut-aways of a Mycenaean citadel in Greece, a besieged castle in the Middle Ages, the castle of a Japanese warlord, and a U.S. Army frontier fort highlight the text. Two-page topics cover information on Hattusas, Tiryns, the siege of Lachish, hill forts, the Great Wall of China, Roman forts, Masada, the Normans, Crusader castles, the Moors in Spain, the Renaissance, Japanese castles, Sacsayhuaman, Golconda, Vauban fortresses, cavalry fort, Fort Sumter, and the end of the age. Key Dates and Glossary and Index.

2089. Williams, Brian, and Brenda Williams. **The Age of Discovery: From the Renaissance to American Independence**. James Field, illustrator. New York: Peter Bedrick, 1994. 64p. $18.95. ISBN 0-87226-311-8. (Timelink). 5-8

The text presents history in fifty-year segments and depicts discoveries from all cultures. Various aids such as comparative time charts, maps, charts, and graphs show the major historical events from 1491 to 1789 in the Americas, Asia, and Africa. Illustrations complement the text.

2090. Williams, Jeanne. **Daughter of the Storm**. New York: St. Martin's Press, 1994. 311p. $20.95. ISBN 0-312-10441-3. YA

The orphan Christy always feels unwelcome, because she took the place of her foster mother Mairi's daughter, dead at birth in nineteenth-century Scotland. But she has the love of others in the home—Mairi's grandmother and Mairi's son David. Joy and much pain fill their lives as they try to protect their Scottish lands from owners who take their grazing land and rent it to rich American hunters. Eventually David, crippled at the age of twelve by falling down a cliff, becomes a lawyer and helps the crofters, a group of honest, hard-working, much maligned people. Christy earns her place in the islands by teaching and playing the invaluable harp given her by one of the natives. After many of the islanders are wounded in a hostile encounter with landowners at Greenyards, Mairi begins to accept Christy's gifts, in this sequel to *The Island Harp*.

2091. Williams, Jeanne. **The Island Harp**. New York: St. Martin's Press, 1991. 338p. $19.95; $4.99pa. ISBN 0-312-06570-1; 0-312-95001-2pa. YA

Mairi MacLeod, age seventeen, becomes the *de facto* head of her Scottish clan and inherits the role as harper, after her grandfather dies of burns when the landowner's agents torch her family's homes in 1844. When a member of the gentry, Iain, leases part of the estate, and lets them live there, she is surprised. She eventually falls in love with him, but she refuses to accept the other landowners. After the birth of their son, she hears news of Iain's death in Afghanistan. But he returns and still wants to marry her, even after she sings her song about the landowners deceiving the Celtic clans.

2092. Wills, Garry. **Certain Trumpets: The Call of Leaders**. New York: Simon & Schuster, 1994. 336p. $23. ISBN 0-671-65702-X. New York: Touchstone, 1995. 336p. $14pa. ISBN 0-684-80138-8pa. YA

To examine leadership in people, Wills looks at Cesare Borgia (1476?-1507), Dorothy Day (1897-1980), King David (d. 961 B.C.), Mary Baker Eddy (1821-1910), Martha Graham (1893-1991), Martin Luther King, Jr. (1929-1968), Napoleon (1769-1821), Ross Perot (b. 1930), Franklin D. Roosevelt (1882-1945), Eleanor Roosevelt (1884-1962), Socrates (c. 470-399 B.C.), Carl Stotz (1910?-1992), Harriet Tubman (c. 1820-1913), Andrew Young (b. 1932), and George Washington (1732-1799). He analyzes what these people did, assesses their qualities to find what one should expect of a leader, and decides that good leaders concern themselves with the best situation for all, the "common good." Bibliography and Index.

2093. Wilson, Derek. **The Circumnavigators**. New York: Evans, 1989. 345p. $24.95. ISBN 0-87131-601-3. YA

People who have sailed around the world since Magellan in 1522 appear in these pages. Included in addition to Magellan are Drake, pirates, buccaneers, captains, sailors, and yachtsmen who recorded data later used by explorers. The first person to go around the world for pleasure was Annie Brassey in 1876; she gave dinner parties for 40 en route. Even today a trip around the world is an exciting adventure. Bibliography and Index.

2094. Windrow, Martin. **Uniforms of the French Foreign Legion 1831–1981**. Michel Chappell, illustrator. New York: Blandford Press, 1987. 159p. $9.95. ISBN 0-7137-1914-1. YA

The French Foreign Legion is the only survivor of the medieval tradition of permanent mercenary forces; professionalism and toughness marks these men. During the 150 years of the Legion, the uniforms have changed for various units in the field. The text gives extensive descriptions of the Legion's uniforms, field dress, and equipment in all periods of its history. The periods are Africa and Spain from 1831 to 1854; the Crimea and Italy from 1854 to 1860; Vera Cruz to the Gare du Nord from 1860 to 1972; North Africa from 1871 to 1914; Tonkin, Dahomey, and Madagascar; World War I; the interwar years in Morocco, Syria, and Indochina from 1919 to 1939; World War II and uniforms from 1945 to 1949; and the Legion since 1945 in Indochina, Morocco and Madagascar, Algeria and Tunisia, and since Algeria. Index.

2095. Winner, David. **Desmond Tutu**. Milwaukee, WI: Gareth Stevens, 1989. 68p. $16.95. ISBN 0-55532-822-9. (People Who Have Helped the World). 7-9

After an explanation of what *apartheid* meant in South Africa, this book gives a brief history of racial discrimination in that country. When the British defeated the Boers (slave owners) in 1902, they allowed the Afrikaners (Boers) to make laws. The government continued to mistreat blacks, calling them *kaffirs* (infidels or nonbelievers). Desmond Tutu, born in 1931 into a poor black South African family, met a priest who brought him books when he was fourteen and in the hospital sick with tuberculosis. This learning helped Tutu graduate and go to a university. He became a teacher because he had no money for medical school. A new law forbade blacks to get any education, so Tutu studied theology and became a priest. He went to England and saw that races could live together peacefully. When he returned to South Africa, life was worse. He was able to return to England in 1972 and speak around the world for the Theological Educational Fund. He was elected dean of Johannesburg in 1975, the highest position ever held by a black man in the Anglican church to that point. Many whites in South Africa did not know how the blacks lived, because of government censorship, but Tutu spoke about the conditions, and the entire world heard him. In 1984, he won the Nobel Peace Prize because of his work. Although this book was written before South Africa reformed, he played a major role in its reformation. Organizations, Books, Glossary, Chronology, and Index.

2096. Winner, David. **Peter Benenson: Taking a Stand Against Injustice—Amnesty International**. Milwaukee, WI: Gareth Stevens, 1991. 68p. $16.95. ISBN 0-8368-0400-7. (People Who Have Helped the World). 7-9

In 1960, outraged at a London newspaper report about two students who were arrested, charged, and imprisoned for seven years in Portugal for toasting "liberty," Peter Benenson (b. 1921) started Amnesty International, an endeavor that would become the biggest human rights movement in the world. He won the Nobel Peace Prize in 1977 for his efforts. The response to his first newspaper announcement revealed that many persons felt as he did and that many had friends and relatives who had disappeared for trying to be honorable. From Benenson's time at Eton, he had been involved in trying to help people less fortunate; as a lawyer, he often defended individuals who were unjustly charged. His intent in starting his organization was to free all political prisoners. The organization has not totally succeeded, but it has helped many. The Universal Declaration of Human Rights, For More Information, Glossary, Chronology, and Index.

2097. Winter, Jane Kohen. **Women in Society: Brazil**. Eric Siow, illustrator. New York: Marshall Cavendish, 1993. 128p. $22.95. ISBN 1-85435-558-9. (Women in Society). 7 up

After introducing the women of Brazil through their myths, the author discusses the roles of women in Brazil by interweaving historical and contemporary practices. She presents the expectations imposed upon women in rural and urban areas, religious and secular situations, and the poor and wealthy. The chapters cover milestones, what being a woman means in the culture, and the life of a woman from birth to old age. Women Firsts, Glossary, Further Reading, and Index.

2098. Winter, Jeanette, author/illustrator. **Klara's New World**. New York: Knopf, 1992. 41p. $15.99. ISBN 0-679-90626-6. 2-7

In 1852, Klara, age eight, and her family have to leave Sweden during a famine; they head for America where they hope to grow crops. They sail on an ocean, a river, and a lake as well as riding a train, during the three months that it takes them to reach Minnesota.

2099. Wolf, Joan. **Daughter of the Red Deer**. New York: Dutton, 1991. 420p. $19.95. ISBN 0-525-03379-4. New York: Onyx, 1992. 420p. $5.99pa. ISBN 0-451-40334-7pa. YA

Mar and his peers of the patriarchal Horse Tribe in 12,000 B.C. live in the Cro-Magnon Magdelenian culture near the Vésère Valley of France. After bad water poisons women in their tribe, they kidnap the Mother-designate of the matriarchal Red Deer—Alin, age fifteen—and her peers so that they will have wives. The surprise comes when Mar, who treats Alin kindly, and Alin realize that they actually love each other.

2100. Wolf, Joan. **The Reindeer Hunters**. New York: Dutton, 1994. 368p. $20.95. ISBN 0-525-93848-6. YA

Around 25,000 years ago in the Stone Age, the Cro-Magnon humans, known as the Magdalenians, lived in the height of their civilization. Alane's Norakamo tribe and Nardo's Kindred tribe (Wolf Clan) have their yearly battles over the reindeer, for which they have to hunt further afield as the ice melts. When the Redu threaten their food, the marriage of Alane and Nardo helps the two tribes unite to fight and overcome the common foe.

2101. Wolf, Sylvia. **Focus: Five Women Photographers: Julia Margaret Cameron, Margaret Bourke-White, Flor Garduño, Sandy Skoglund, Lorna Simpson**. Morton Grove, IL: Albert Whitman, 1994. 63p. $18.95. ISBN 0-8075-2531-6. 7 up

In addition to presenting a brief biography and summing up the ideas and work of each of the photographers spotlighted, the text also explains the photographic process and its history. Julia Margaret Cameron (British, 1815-1879) lived much of her life in India but did not begin making photographs until 1863, after she had returned to England and been given an old wooden camera. She found that portraits of people she knew were the most satisfying, and she photographed them with their clothes covered so that the focus would be on faces and not on the class in society their clothes revealed. Margaret Bourke-White (American, 1904-1971) became intrigued with buildings and industrial settings. She gave them prominence in her work and became a major figure in photojournalism, working for *Life* magazine. She also photographed such scenes as the liberation of the Nazi death camps in 1945 and India's Gandhi on his hunger strike. Flor Garduño (Mexican, b. 1957) creates stunning pictures documenting the timeless traditions of her Mexican culture as well as others. Sandy Skoglund (American, b. 1946) builds sets to photograph familiar scenes with startling changes such as a room with figures, two of them alive and covered in raisins. Lorna Simpson (American, b. 1960) wants her pictures to raise questions about how American society functions. Photo Credits and Selected Bibliography.

2102. Wood, Marion. **Ancient America**. New York: Facts on File, 1990. 96p. $17.95. ISBN 0-8160-2210-0. (Cultural Atlas for Young People). 6-9

Wood covers the Americas, from the Inuit in the north to the Inca living in the empire that extended as far south as Chile. With as much information as possible, the text gives a picture of conditions in the Americas before the explorers came from Europe to change everything. Chronology, Glossary, Gazetteer, and Index. *New York Public Library Books for the Teen Age.*

2103. Wood, Tim. **Ancient Wonders**. New York: Viking, 1997. 48p. $16.99. ISBN 0-670-87468-X. (See Through History). 5-7

The text looks at the ancient wonders of the world, and the see-through pages show the insides of the Egyptian pharoahs' tombs, Minoan temples on the island of Knossos, the cliff tombs and temples of Petra in Egypt, and the church of Hagia Sophia in Constantinople. Key Dates, Glossary, and Index.

2104. Wood, Tim. **The Aztecs**. New York: Viking, 1992. 48p. $14.99. ISBN 0-670-84492-6. (See Through History). 4-7

When a small band of Spanish explorers arrived in Mexico, they found the militaristic Aztec empire, which stretched from the Atlantic to the Pacific with over 15 million people living in 500 cities and towns. See-through cutaways of a typical Aztec house, an Aztec knight temple, Montezuma's palace and its hidden gold treasures, and the Great Temple of Tenochtitlán (where human sacrifices occurred) highlight the text. The topics presented in two-page spreads include the people, the empire, Tenochtitlán, the Great Temple, the army, warfare, trade, writing, the emperor, arts and crafts, food and farming, growing up, homes, the calendar, gods, and the end of the empire. Key Dates and Glossary and Index.

2105. Wood, Tim. **The Incas**. New York: Viking, 1996. 48p. $16.99. ISBN 0-670-87037-4. (See Through History). 6-9

The topics in this look at the Incas and Peru, with overlays to show the insides of an Incan temple, include farming, religion, architecture, clothing, and other aspects of daily life. The history covers what is known about the Incan Empire and devotes the final two chapters to the Spanish conquest. Illustrations highlight the text. Chronology, Glossary, and Index.

2106. Wood, Tim. **The Renaissance**. New York: Viking, 1993. 48p. $14.99. ISBN 0-670-85149-3. (See Through History). 6-9

For a thousand years after the fall of the Romans, many of their achievements were forgotten, but in the fifteenth and sixteenth centuries scholars rediscovered many ancient Greek and Roman writings. Artists and scientists, including Michelangelo and Galileo, began to build their own work on the classical base previously established. See-through cutaways of a Florentine town house, Columbus's ship the *Santa Maria*, St. Peter's in Rome, and a printer's workshop highlight the text. The two-page topical spreads include information on the rebirth of learning, city-states, government, trade, exploration, ships, architecture, patrons, palaces, women at court, alchemy and science, technology, printing, astronomy, medical advances, warfare, churches and cathedrals, and the Reformation. Key Dates, Glossary, and Index.

2107. Woodruff, Elvira. **The Disappearing Bike Shop**. New York: Yearling, Dell, 1994. 169p. $13.95. ISBN 0-8234-0933-3. 4 up

When Freckle and Tyler, fifth-graders, meet an unusual bicycle salesman and inventor, they find out through their adventures that he is Leonardo da Vinci traveling through time from his life in 1452 through 1519.

2108. Woods, Geraldine. **Science in Ancient Egypt**. New York: Franklin Watts, 1988. 92p. $16.10. ISBN 0-531-10486-9. (First Book). 5-8

An introduction to Egypt and its science precedes chapters on different developments from this culture. They include the pyramids, mathematics, astronomy and timekeeping, medicine, writing and agriculture, crafts and technology, and contemporary debt to the culture for its discoveries. Photographs and drawings enhance the text. Glossary, Further Reading, and Index.

2109. Woog, Adam. **The Beatles**. San Diego, CA: Lucent, 1997. 128p. $17.96. ISBN 1-56006-088-3. (The Importance Of). 5 up

Boxed sidebars complement the text about the four men who composed The Beatles, a rock group of the 1960s. Anecdotes about their lives and work with photographs complete the text. Bibliography, Chronology, Further Reading, and Index.

2110. Woolf, Felicity. **Picture This: A First Introduction to Paintings**. New York: Doubleday, 1990. 40p. $14.95. ISBN 0-385-41135-9. 4-8

The text looks at the history of painting, from the illuminated manuscript to the twentieth-century action painting of Jackson Pollock. The topics include early oil painting, frescoes, mythological subjects, self-portraits, Dutch painting, eighteenth-century French, Turner, two versions of the Ophelia story, Impressionists, van Gogh, Expressionism, and Surrealism. Glossary, Gallery List, and Index.

2111. Wormser, Richard L. **Three Faces of Vietnam**. New York: Franklin Watts, 1993. 157p. $13.90. ISBN 0-531-11142-3. 7 up

Starting in the 1950s when France occupied Vietnam, the text looks at the war until its end in 1975 through the eyes of three groups of people: the Vietnamese, American military personnel, and protesters at home. Personal anecdotes include the views of a Viet Cong sympathizer as well as many others collected from the aforementioned groups. Photographs, Maps, Notes, Further Reading, and Index.

2112. Wright, Patricia. **Goya**. New York: Dorling Kindersley, 1993. 64p. $16.95. ISBN 1-56458-333-3. (Eyewitness). YA

Francisco Goya (1746–1828) and his painting represent dualities in life—light and dark, beautiful and grotesque, public and private. He became famous early and in his later life created the satirical "Black Paintings." The text looks at Goya's life and his place in his times while examining the development of his painting techniques via diagrams and color wheels. Key Biographies, Goya Collections, Glossary, and Index.

2113. Wright, Patricia. **Manet**. New York: Dorling Kindersley, 1993. 64p. $16.95. ISBN 1-56458-172-1. (Eyewitness). YA

The text looks at Edouard Manet (1832–1883) and his work. The two-page topics cover his headstrong youth, his copying of the masters, his student work, his first rejection, and his life in bohemian Paris. Other topics are Spanish vogue, *Victorien Meurent*, the salon of the rejected, a bourgeois scandal, Suzanne Leenhoff, controversy, an elegant realism, Spain and Japan, the Maximilian affair, Morisot, detachment and intimacy, Impressionist landscapes, the courtesan, final masterpiece, and Manet's death. Color reproductions and comments about the subjects in Manet's paintings augment the text. Glossary and Index.

2114. Wroe, Ann. **A Fool and His Money: Life in a Partitioned Town in Fourteenth-Century France**. New York: Hill & Wang, 1995. 243p. $22. ISBN 0-8090-4595-8. YA

When Wroe wanted to understand how a medieval town—partitioned between the city, ruled by the church bishop, and the Bourg, ruled by the count—worked, she found information about Rodez, a southwestern French town caught in the Hundred Years' War beginning around 1337. The town fell into English hands in 1360 but returned to the French in 1369. In court registers, the author found information about Peyre Marques, an old man who had hidden gold coins (probably to escape the high taxes levied by the count and the bishop to pay for their part in the war) but could not remember where he hid them. His story and that of the town give insight into ordinary lives in this historical period. Bibliography and Index.

2115. Wulffson, Don L. **The Upside-Down Ship**. Niles, IL: Albert Whitman, 1986. 136p. $9.75. ISBN 0-8075-8346-4. 5-8

When Bruce returns to Aberdeen, Scotland, in the 1760s after being shipwrecked for six years in Iceland, he has difficulty accepting the attitudes of civilization. His whaling vessel had become lodged in an iceberg, and he had survived on whale meat and stored supplies while drowned sailors lay frozen in another area of the ship. A polar bear that he had befriended as a cub caught fish for him. Bruce's brother becomes angry at his return because his mother died thinking that Bruce was dead.

X

2116. Xydes, Georgia. **Alexander Mackenzie and the Explorers of Canada**. New York: Chelsea House, 1992. 110p. $19.95. ISBN 0-7910-1314-6. (World Explorers). 5 up

Alexander Mackenzie (c. 1764-1820) was a man of contradictions. He hated the wilderness, but he conquered western Canada. He wanted to be an aristocrat, but he spent many years freezing in wooden structures. Although a loner, he was forced to keep close company with voyagers and Indians. As a fur trader, he sacrificed his health while revolutionizing the Canadian trade system. During his 1789 and 1793 expeditions, he explored Canada to the Pacific and to the Arctic Ocean. One river, a mountain range, and a place in western Canada bear his name. Photographs, engravings, and reproductions enhance the text. Chronology, Further Reading, and Index.

Y

2117. Yancey, Diane. **Life in the Elizabethan Theater**. San Diego, CA: Lucent, 1996. 112p. $16.95. ISBN 1-56006-343-2. (The Way People Live). 6-10

Yancey recreates the times of Shakespeare and Elizabeth I in this history. She quotes scholars and gives specific details, including the blood and livers from butcher shops used as stage props. Such items enliven the subject and make it accessible. Bibliography, Chronology, Further Reading, and Index.

2118. Yancey, Diane. **The Reunification of Germany**. San Diego, CA: Lucent, 1994. 128p. $22.59. ISBN 1-56006-143-X. (Overview). 7 up

After almost forty years of separation, East Germany and West Germany reunited into one Germany on October 3, 1990. The separation began after World War II, when the Soviet Union decided that it wanted to seize the free portion of Berlin that was under the control of France and the United States. The Soviets blocked land access from West Germany. On June 24, 1948, the Berlin airlift began, with the Allies flying food and supplies into West Berlin. The Soviets did not give up the land blockade until May 1949. By that time, separate governments controlled the two areas of Germany: the west under the anti-Communist Konrad Adenauer and the east under Walter Ulbricht, the secretary of the German Democratic Republic's Communist Party. More than 400,000 people escaped from the East in 1953, with many others trying unsuccessfully. The number never dropped below 170,000 per year until the Berlin Wall was erected in 1961; the number had risen to 5,000 per day during that summer. At the reunification of the two Germanys in 1989, everyone on both sides was ecstatic. The realization that these two diverse countries, with unequal economic bases, would have to coalesce into one was much less exciting. The difficulties are thoughtfully documented in the text. Glossary, Suggestions for Further Reading, Works Consulted, and Index.

2119. Yarbro, Chelsea Quinn. **Floating Illusions**. New York: HarperCollins, 1986. 215p. $12.95. ISBN 0-06-026643-0. 6-8

While Millicent, fourteen, crosses the Atlantic on an ocean liner in 1910, several people are murdered. Among the friends she makes during her investigation are a magician, a militant feminist, and Anton, a noble. When the magician's life is threatened, he can no longer be a suspect, and Millicent identifies the criminal.

2120. Yarbro, Chelsea Quinn. **Four Horses for Tishtry**. New York: Harper, 1985. 218p. $2.89. ISBN 0-06-026638-4. 7-10

Tishtry, age thirteen, performs in Roman arenas with her chariot and matched horses. She works hard so that she can earn money to buy freedom for the members of her Armenian family. Her master cheats her, however, and she must find a way to overcome the situation while continuing to perform.

2121. Yates, Elizabeth. **Hue & Cry**. 1953. Greenville, SC: Bob Jones University Press, 1991. 182p. $6.49pa. ISBN 0-89084-536-0pa. (Light Line). YA

In a sequel to *The Journeyman*, Melody, the daughter of Jared and Jennet, is deaf and cannot speak properly. She loves to walk in the woods to a nearby lake. One day, she sees an Irish boy with a horse he has stolen. She can write; however, she does not want to report him to those who are in the Hue and Cry group of men who prosecute horse thieves. The boy merely loves the horses and cannot afford one of his own. Melody and the horse-loving boy become friends, and after he has paid his penitence and she has attended school to learn sign language, they decide to marry.

2122. Yates, Elizabeth. **The Journeyman**. Greenville, SC: Bob Jones University Press, 1990. 161p. $6.49pa. ISBN 0-89084-535-2pa. (Pennant). YA

While Jared is still a boy in 1810, a journeyman painter comes to his home, sees his work, and asks Jared's father to let him be the journeyman's apprentice for the next five years. Jared is delighted because all he wants to do is draw pictures, and now he can begin to draw them on the walls in people's homes. When he returns after his apprenticeship ends, someone carelessly notes that the year Jared was born was uncommonly cold, and that the year 1816, when he returns, is also too cold for crops. The town tries him for witchcraft, but his faith, his friends, and his love for Jennet, a girl he has known all his life, help prove his innocence.

2123. Yolen, Jane. **Briar Rose**. New York: Tor Books, 1992. 190p. $17.95; $5.99pa. ISBN 0-312-85135-9; 0-8125-5862-6pa. 8 up

Becca's grandmother has adamantly declared that she is a princess, and Becca tells her before she dies that Becca will find the prince and the castle of the Briar Rose story that her grandmother told her. In the nursing home room are photographs, newspaper clippings, a ring, and a passport that her grandmother has kept in a box. Becca's investigation leads her to Fort Oswego, New York, a former World War II refugee camp, and to Chelmno, Poland, site of Nazi exterminations. She finds out that a partisan fighter had found her grandmother alive in a mass grave and revived her. They married, but after she became pregnant, Nazis murdered her husband. Such a story was not one that could be easily told.

2124. Yolen, Jane. **The Devil's Arithmetic**. New York: Viking, 1988. 170p. $13. ISBN 0-670-81027-4. YA

In this historical fantasy, Hannah becomes bored every year at the family Passover Seder. But when she is 13, she opens the door to symbolically welcome Elijah to the feast and finds herself in a Polish village *(shtetl)* during the 1940s, where everyone calls her "Chaya." She immediately forgets her past as she becomes involved in village life and its fear of the Nazis. When the Nazis take her family and her to a death camp, she only wants to survive. After she is returned to her former life, she understands the significance of the Seder and her history and knows that she will never forget. *National Jewish Awards, Sydney Taylor Book Award,* and *Association of Jewish Libraries Award.*

2125. Yount, Lisa. **Antoni Van Leeuwenhoek: First to See Microscopic Life**. Springfield, NJ: Enslow, 1996. 128p. $18.95. ISBN 0-89490-680-1. (Great Minds of Science). 4-8

Antoni Van Leeuwenhoek (1632-1723) lacked formal scientific training, but his interest in a variety of things led him from his profession as a cloth merchant to making his own microscopes. When he first saw the lice living on his leg multiply via the microscope, he was rather disturbed. Other aspects of his life appear in the text along with some diagrams and illustrations. Photographs, Further Reading, Glossary, Notes, and Index.

2126. Yount, Lisa. **Louis Pasteur**. San Diego, CA: Lucent, 1994. 96p. $16.95. ISBN 1-56006-051-4. (The Importance Of). 5-8

Louis Pasteur (1822-1895) stressed the importance of testing and experimentation in his science laboratory and devoted much of his time to the needs of farmers and factory owners. His work saved money for wine, beer, and vinegar makers as well as silkworm, chicken, sheep, and cattle raisers. He wanted to control living beings so that they could protect or help human beings. He was especially loyal to France, and his research was also an attempt to help his country. He was the first to realize that microorganisms could cause disease as well as cure it. He improved public health, made surgery safer, and prevented many deaths in war. People who remembered Pasteur after his death noted his kindness, his absorption in his thoughts, and his clear love for people. Photographs, Notes, For Further Reading, Works Consulted, and Index.

2127. Yount, Lisa. **William Harvey: Discoverer of How Blood Circulates**. Springfield, NJ: Enslow, 1994. 128p. $17.95. ISBN 0-89490-481-7. (Great Minds of Science). 4-8

William Harvey (1578-1657) was the first of seven sons born in his Folkestone, England, family. After attending Cambridge, he went to Padua, Italy, for advanced medical training. He heard Fabricius, his anatomy teacher, talk about little flaps or doors on the blood vessels, and he remembered this later as he was trying to understand how blood moved through the body. In 1628, he published his book on the movement of the heart and the blood. During his life, he supported King Charles; when Cromwell defeated the king, Harvey lost everything, but he kept working on his ideas. Afterword: A New Kind of Science, Activities, Chronology, Notes, Glossary, and Index.

2128. Yue, Charlotte, and David Yue. **Christopher Columbus: How He Did It**. David Yue, illustrator. Boston: Houghton Mifflin, 1992. 136p. $13.95. ISBN 0-395-52100-9. 5-8

The details in text and drawings carefully describe the ships that Columbus took with him on his voyage in 1492 and what happened aboard in the tiny living quarters. Descriptions of the people, the tools, the armor, and the strong nautical skills of Columbus give answers not found in other books. Illustrations, charts, maps, and drawings augment the text. Bibliography and Index.

Z

2129. Zei, Alki. **Petro's War**. Edward Fenton, translator. New York: Dutton, 1972. 240p. $8.95. ISBN 0-525-36962-7. 4-9

After Greece declares war on Italy in 1940, Petros, age nine, sees his life change. Previously interested only in turtles, he begins to write slogans on Athenian walls about the lack of food. Then he becomes a member of the underground resistance to the Italians and the Germans. Everyone in the family joins the resistance, and they carry messages, hide people, and distribute information. His uncle fights in the mountains and communicates with the family via British Broadcasting. *Mildred L. Batchelder Award.*

2130. Zei, Alki. **The Sound of Dragon's Feet**. Edward Fenton, translator. New York: Dutton, 1979. 113p. $8.50. ISBN 0-525-39712-4. 4-9

In 1894, Sasha, the daughter of a Russian physician, wants to know how one can hear dragon feet and states her admiration for lion tamers. She asks her new tutor, a man who has served time in prison for trying to gain more rights for workers, and he tells her that courage is more than sticking one's head into the mouth of a lion. He says that people have to jeopardize their own lives for others before they can be considered brave. *Mildred L. Batchelder Award.*

2131. Zei, Alki. **Wildcat Under Glass**. Edward Fenton, translator. New York: Henry Holt, 1968. 177p. $4.50. ISBN 0-03-068005-0. 5-9

Melia and her older sister, Myrto, see that the adults in their Greek home in 1936 have become more thoughtful and are having quiet discussions from which the children are excluded. Then their cousin, Niko, comes to the island where they have a summer home and hides in a deserted windmill. Spanish Fascist spies—"Black Shirts"—come looking for him, imprison a friend's father, and burn their grandfather's books. In Athens, a teacher asks Myrto to spy on her family as a leader of the Youth Organization. Such events show them that their situation is much more serious than they had thought. *Mildred L. Batchelder Award.*

2132. Zeinert, Karen. **The Persian Empire**. Tarrytown, NY: Benchmark, 1996. 80p. $19.95. ISBN 0-7614-0089-3. (Cultures of the Past). 7-10

Although almost all contemporary information about the Persians comes from the work of Herodotus, a Persian script deciphered in 1857 also helps contemporary understanding of the culture living in the area now known as Iran. Its great leaders Cyrus, Darius, and Xerxes as well as chapters about religion and daily life give more background on this important empire of ancient times. Illustrations augment the text. Bibliography, Chronology, Further Reading, Glossary, and Index.

2133. Zeinert, Karen. **The Warsaw Ghetto Uprising**. Brookfield, CT: Millbrook Press, 1993. 112p. $16.40. ISBN 1-56294-282-4. 7 up

When the Nazis invaded Poland in 1939, the Warsaw ghetto started forming. An explanation of the roots of Nazi hostility toward Jews shows their brutality as they moved Jews from their homes to places inside the walls and made many of them work. From primary sources, Zeinert tells how others learned to travel below ground to secure food and take children to safety. Several resistance groups helped to plan and implement the 1943 uprising against the Germans, which led to the burning of the ghetto and the deportation of the remaining Jews. Chronology, Bibliography, and Index. *Child Study Association Children's Books of the Year, Society of School Librarians International Best,* and *New York Public Library Books for the Teen Age.*

2134. Zeleza, Tiyambe. **Maasai**. New York: Rosen, 1994. 64p. $15.95. ISBN 0-8239-1757-6. (Heritage Library of African Peoples, East Africa). 5-8

Maasai, legendary as warriors throughout Africa and the world, have conflicting stories about their origin. They arrived, however, in modern Kenya around the fifteenth century, where some kept cattle and some were farmers. The text covers additional history as well as the complex organization of Maasai society, the neighboring peoples, colonial rule, independence, and the political and social changes that have occurred during the twentieth century. Photographs, boxed information, and maps enhance the text. Glossary, Further Reading, and Index.

2135. Zeleza, Tiyambe. **Mijikenda**. New York: Rosen, 1995. 64p. $15.95. ISBN 0-8239-1767-3. (Heritage Library of African Peoples). 5-8

A population of over 750,000 Mijikenda now live on the coast of Kenya. Nine peoples consider themselves members of this group: Giriama, Kauma, Chonyi, Jibana, Kambe, Ribe, Rabai, Duruma, and Digo. Until the tenth century, the Mijikendan ancestors lived in the area of Somalia; they began migrating toward Kenya in the sixteenth century. In the nineteenth century, they lived in *kayas* or walled-in settlements to protect them from Maasai and Ormo attacks. This information and more on the history of these peoples appear in chapters on customs and ritual, the European conquest, the changes caused by colonial rule, eventual independence, and expected changes. Photographs, boxed information, and maps enhance the text. Glossary, Further Reading, and Index.

2136.   Zyskind, Sara. **Struggle**. Minneapolis, MN: Lerner, 1989. 284p. $16.95. ISBN 0-8225-0772-2. 7-9

Zyskind uses the first-person point of view to tell her husband's story of capture and imprisonment during the Holocaust of World War II. He survived until the Americans came on May 2, 1945. Until the Americans arrived, he thought that he was going to die in the bombing of the Ludwigslust camp. This strong story gives insights and raises questions about Germans who refused to help Jews during this terrible time in history.

2137. **Adventure Canada**. CD-ROM. System requirements: IBM or compatible PC, 486/33 MHz or higher CPU, 8 MB RAM, Microsoft Windows 3.1 or later, CD-ROM drive, sound card, mouse, SVGA 256-color display, loudspeakers or headphones. Macintosh: 6 MB RAM, System 7.0, 13-inch monitor (256 colors), CD-ROM drive. Richmond, British Columbia, Canada: Virtual Reality Systems, 1994. $69.95. 5 up

This CD-ROM provides an overview of Canada's history, geography, and daily life. The program has three levels: national, provincial, and natural region. Slides, video, and maps give the information about each level.

2138. **Air and Space Smithsonian Dreams of Flight**. CD-ROM. System requirements: IBM or compatible PC, 486/25 MHz or higher CPU, 4 MB RAM (8 MB recommended), Microsoft Windows 3.1 or later, CD-ROM drive, sound card, mouse, SVGA 256-color display, loudspeakers or headphones. Portland, OR: Creative Multimedia, 1995. $29.95. 5 up

The four areas to explore in this CD-ROM are "Aviation Pioneers," "Flying Machines," "Milestones," and "Culture." Each section includes multimedia resources, photographs, audio, personal interviews, and aerodynamic demonstrations. It includes the history of flight.

2139. **The Anglo Saxons**. CD-ROM. System requirements: IBM or compatible PC, 286 or higher CPU with 2 MB RAM, Microsoft Windows 3.1 (not Windows 95), CD-ROM drive, sound card, mouse, SVGA 256-color display, loudspeakers or headphones. New York: Cambrix-Chelsea House, 1993. $29.95. 8 up

The British Museum cooperated in the creation of this CD-ROM, which looks at the reign of the Anglo-Saxons. Among the topics covered are archaeological London, making books and manuscripts, artifacts, animal designs, kings and kingdoms, places to find Anglo-Saxon ruins, and other pictures. The scholarly production offers further notes, either by text or sound, on paintings and photographs of time. One may choose a topic or consult the index for the specific selection; movement among screens for referencing is easy.

2140. **Art & Music: The Baroque**. CD-ROM. System requirements: IBM or compatible PC, 386/20 MHz or higher CPU, 4 MB RAM (8 MB recommended), Microsoft Windows 3.1 or later, CD-ROM drive, sound card, mouse, SVGA 256-color display, loudspeakers or headphones. Macintosh: 6 to 8 MB RAM, System 7.0, 13-inch monitor (256 colors), CD-ROM drive. Minneapolis, MN: Gareth Stevens, 1995. $80. 6 up

The modes available to study the paintings and music of the Baroque period are the Feature Presentation, Text, View, Index, Question, and Quiz. Artists range from Caravaggio to Rembrandt and the music from Frescobaldi to Handel; also included is the music and drama of opera.

2141. **Art & Music: The Eighteenth Century**. CD-ROM. System requirements: IBM or compatible PC, 386/20 MHz or higher CPU, 4 MB RAM (8 MB recommended), Microsoft Windows 3.1 or later, CD-ROM drive, sound card, mouse, SVGA 256-color display, loudspeakers or headphones. Macintosh: 6 to 8 MB RAM, System 7.0, 13-inch monitor (256 colors), CD-ROM drive. Minneapolis, MN: Gareth Stevens, 1995. $80. 6 up

The modes available to study the paintings and music of the eighteenth century are the Feature Presentation, Text, View, Index, Question, and Quiz. Developments in painting and sculpture parallel music's changes to comic opera and the Viennese classical style.

2142. **Art & Music: Impressionism**. CD-ROM. System requirements: IBM or compatible PC, 386/20 MHz or higher CPU, 4 MB RAM (8 MB recommended), Microsoft Windows 3.1 or later, CD-ROM drive, sound card, mouse, SVGA 256-color display, loudspeakers or headphones. Macintosh: 6 to 8 MB RAM, System 7.0, 13-inch monitor (256 colors), CD-ROM drive. Minneapolis, MN: Gareth Stevens, 1995. $80. 6 up

The modes available to study the paintings and music of the Impressionist period are the Feature Presentation, Text, View, Index, Question, and Quiz. The information focuses on the artists' use of light and color and how the composers worked to create similar effects with instrumentation. Attitudes toward nature, Oriental art, and traditional forms become clear.

2143. **Art & Music: The Medieval Era**. CD-ROM. System requirements: IBM or compatible PC, 386/20 MHz or higher CPU, 4 MB RAM (8 MB recommended), Microsoft Windows 3.1 or later, CD-ROM drive, sound card, mouse, SVGA 256-color display, loudspeakers or headphones. Macintosh: 6 to 8 MB RAM, System 7.0, 13-inch monitor (256 colors), CD-ROM drive. Minneapolis, MN: Gareth Stevens, 1995. $80. 6 up

The modes available to study the evolution of art in the medieval period are the Feature Presentation, Text, View, Index, Question, and Quiz. Manuscript illumination, the cathedral, and the secularization of music and literature are the main topics of discussion.

2144. **Art & Music: The Renaissance**. CD-ROM. System requirements: IBM or compatible PC, 386/20 MHz or higher CPU, 4 MB RAM (8 MB recommended), Microsoft Windows 3.1 or later, CD-ROM drive, sound card, mouse, SVGA 256-color display, loudspeakers or headphones. Macintosh: 6 to 8 MB RAM, System 7.0, 13-inch monitor (256 colors), CD-ROM drive. Minneapolis, MN: Gareth Stevens, 1995. $80. 6 up

The modes available to study the paintings and music of the Renaissance are the Feature Presentation, Text, View, Index, Question, and Quiz. Humanistic philosophy led Renaissance artists and composers to develop new forms and techniques, including oil painting and four-part polyphony.

2145. **Art & Music: Romanticism**. CD-ROM. System requirements: IBM or compatible PC, 386/20 MHz or higher CPU, 4 MB RAM (8 MB recommended), Microsoft Windows 3.1 or later, CD-ROM drive, sound card, mouse, SVGA 256-color display, loudspeakers or headphones. Macintosh: 6 to 8 MB RAM, System 7.0, 13-inch monitor (256 colors), CD-ROM drive. Minneapolis, MN: Gareth Stevens, 1995. $80. 6 up

The modes available to study the paintings and music of the Romantic Period are the Feature Presentation, Text, View, Index, Question, and Quiz. Artists include Delacroix and music focuses on such works as Berlioz's *Requiem*.

2146. **Art & Music: Surrealism**. CD-ROM. System requirements: IBM or compatible PC, 386/20 MHz or higher CPU, 4 MB RAM (8 MB recommended), Microsoft Windows 3.1 or later, CD-ROM drive, sound card, mouse, SVGA 256-color display, loudspeakers or headphones. Macintosh: 6 to 8 MB RAM, System 7.0, 13-inch monitor (256 colors), CD-ROM drive. Minneapolis, MN: Gareth Stevens, 1995. $80. 6 up

The modes available to study the paintings and music of the surrealist period are the Feature Presentation, Text, View, Index, Question, and Quiz. Freud, Einstein, the French Symbolists, Cubists, and Dadaists show their influence on the music and art of the 1920s.

2147. **Art & Music: The Twentieth Century**. CD-ROM. System requirements: IBM or compatible PC, 386/20 MHz or higher CPU, 4 MB RAM (8 MB recommended), Microsoft Windows 3.1 or later, CD-ROM drive, sound card, mouse, SVGA 256-color display, loudspeakers or headphones. Macintosh: 6 to 8 MB RAM, System 7.0, 13-inch monitor (256 colors), CD-ROM drive. Minneapolis, MN: Gareth Stevens, 1995. $80. 6 up

The modes available to study the paintings and music of the twentieth century are the Feature Presentation, Text, View, Index, Question, and Quiz. Artists covered are Matisse, Picasso, Braque, Kandinsky, and Klee, and the musicians included are Schoenberg, Berg, and Webern.

2148. **Canadian Treasures**. CD-ROM. System requirements: IBM or compatible PC (MPC), 486/33 MHz or higher CPU, 8 MB RAM, Microsoft Windows 3.1 or later, CD-ROM drive, sound card, mouse, SVGA 256-color display, loudspeakers or headphones. Macintosh: 6 MB RAM, System 7.0, 13-inch monitor (256 colors), CD-ROM drive. Seattle, WA: VR Didatech, 1997. $49.95. 4-8

Material from the National Archives of Canada fills the five sections of the program, "Making a Nation," "Discovery," "Portraits," "Nation's Capitol," and "Archive Link." Each section contains three topics. The information covers Canada's history, its people, and its traditions.

2149. **Castle Explorer**. CD-ROM. System requirements: IBM or compatible PC, 486/33 MHz or higher CPU, 8 MB RAM, Microsoft Windows 3.1 or later, CD-ROM drive, sound card, mouse, SVGA 256-color display, loudspeakers or headphones. Macintosh: 6 MB RAM, System 7.0, 13-inch monitor (256 colors), CD-ROM drive. New York: DK Multimedia, 1996. $29.95. 5-12

Students become either a page or a spy as they enter a fourteenth-century manor and move around the castle in cross sections. They see the various rooms, from the garrison to the master's quarters, as they meet visitors and workers during their study of medieval life.

2150. **Complete Maus**. CD-ROM. System requirements: Macintosh with 8 MB RAM, System 7.0, color monitor, CD-ROM drive. MS-DOS/MPC available. New York: Voyager, 1994. $49.95. 9-12

Art Spiegelman created two graphic novels about his father's experiences during World War II and the Holocaust. Various levels allow viewers to look at the books, read articles by and about his family, and read transcripts of the interviews with Spiegelman's father between 1972 and 1979.

2150a. **Daring to Fly! From Icarus to the Red Baron**. CD-ROM. System requirements: IBM or compatible PC, 386SX or higher CPU, 4 MB RAM, Microsoft Windows 3.1 or later, CD-ROM drive, sound card, mouse, SVGA 256-color display, loudspeaker or headphones. Macintosh version available. Sausalito, CA: Arnowitz Studios, 1994. $59.95. 6 up

In the main menu of this CD-ROM, eight topic icons lead to exhibits such as "Science of Flight," "Lighter than Air," "Wings of War," "Women Aloft" as it presents the history of flight from the dreams in myths through the post–World War I era of aviation.

2151. **Events That Changed the World**. CD-ROM. System requirements: IBM or compatible PC, 486/33 MHz or higher CPU, 8 MB RAM, Microsoft Windows 3.1 or later, CD-ROM drive, sound card, mouse, SVGA 256-color display with 512K RAM, loudspeakers or headphones. Macintosh: 5 MB RAM, System 7.0, 13-inch monitor (256 colors), CD-ROM drive. New York: Integrated Communications and Entertainment, 1996. $29.95. 9 up

The topics, featuring hundreds of people and places, are Rulers and Empires, Religious Thought and Practice, Conquest and War, Revolution and Disaster, Exploration, Discovery and Creative Thought, and Politics and Political Philosophy. Access to events is through a listing of people, the topics, or several other methods. All help to create a comprehensive view of world history. For example, to find information on Henry IV, the viewer highlights a topic or Henry IV's name.

2152. **Exploring Ancient Cities**. CD-ROM. System requirements: IBM or compatible PC, 486/33 MHz or higher CPU, 8 MB RAM, Microsoft Windows 3.1 or later, CD-ROM drive, sound card, mouse, SVGA 256-color display, loudspeakers or headphones. Macintosh: 6 MB RAM, System 7.0, 13-inch monitor (256 colors), CD-ROM drive. San Francisco: Sumeria, 1994. $59.95. 6 up

An overview of the art, culture, and history of Crete, Petra, Pompeii, and Teotihuacán. This CD-ROM's content comes from material in *Scientific American* from 1967 to 1985. A timeline from 3000 B.C. to A.D. 1000, interactive maps, an index of slide shows, and sections on each of the four cities help users to find information.

2153. **Exploring the Titanic**. CD-ROM. System requirements: Macintosh LC or better, 4 MB RAM, System 7.0, color monitor (256 colors minimum), hard drive with 2.5 MB free, CD-ROM drive. New York: Scholastic, 1994. $149. 4-8

This CD-ROM is the interactive version of Robert D. Ballard's book, which details the sinking of the *Titanic* in 1912 and its recovery in 1985 by the submarine *Alvin*. A timeline relates the event to other happenings in the world; still other avenues examine the ship, the technology used to locate it, and an exploration of the wreck itself. Twenty-nine synthesized voices give information. Pages from the book are printable, as are text and notes.

2154. **Eyewitness Encyclopedia of Science**. CD-ROM. System requirements: Macintosh or IBM or compatible PC, 386/33 MHz or higher CPU, Windows 3.1 or higher, 4 MB RAM, CD-ROM drive, sound card, mouse, SVGA 256-color display, loudspeakers or headphones. New York: Dorling Kindersley, 1994. $79.95. 5-8

Although the CD-ROM covers much more, it includes a Who's Who of scientists, their contributions, and information about their lives.

2155. **Fine Arts of China**. CD-ROM. System requirements: IBM or compatible PC, 386 MHz or higher CPU recommended, 4 MB RAM, Microsoft Windows 3.1 or later, CD-ROM drive, sound card (optional), mouse, VGA color display, loudspeakers or headphones, CD-ROM drive. Hopkins, TN: Hopkins Technology, 1995. $39.95. 7 up

This library of art from China is grouped into topics of ancient sculpture, painting and architecture, ancient and modern fine arts, and arts and crafts. Historical information and critical commentary by a professor of fine arts, a timeline of the Chinese dynasties, and other information are readily available.

2156. **Great Artists**. CD-ROM. System requirements: MS-DOS/MPC, 386/12 MHz or higher CPU, 4 MB RAM, Windows 3.1 or higher, hard drive with 4 MB free, CD-ROM drive, sound card, mouse, SVGA 256-color monitor (minimum), loudspeakers or headphones. Chatsworth, CA: Cambrix Publishing, 1995. $59.95. 6 up

To introduce forty major European artists, the *Great Artists* uses paintings housed in the National Gallery of London. Six sections of interactive features—Artists, Paintings, Topics, Art Atlas, Timeline, and a Workshop—present biographies of the artists, analyses of segments of the paintings, and an overview of life at the time. Male artists included are Botticelli, Campin, Canaletto, Caravaggio, Cézanne, Chardin, Claude, Constable, David, Dégas, Duccio, van Dyck, van Eyck, Gainsborough, van Gogh, Goya, Hals, Hogarth, Holbein, Ingrés, Leonardo, Monet, Piero, Poussin, Raphael, Rembrandt, Renoir, Rousseau, Rubens, Seurat, Stubbs, Tintoretto, Titian, Turner, Uccello, Velazquez, Vermeer, Wright; females are Judith Leyster (Dutch c. 1630) and Berthe Morisot (French c. 1880).

2157. **History Through Art: Ancient Greece**. CD-ROM. System requirements: IBM or compatible PC, 386/20 MHz or higher CPU, 4 MB RAM (8 MB recommended), Microsoft Windows 3.1 or later, CD-ROM drive, sound card, mouse, SVGA 256-color display, loudspeakers or headphones. Macintosh: 6 to 8 MB RAM, System 7.0, 13-inch monitor (256 colors), CD-ROM drive. Minneapolis, MN: Gareth Stevens, 1995. $75. 6 up

The modes available to study the art of Greek antiquity are the Feature Presentation, Text, View, Index, Question, and Quiz. The humanistic spirit appears in the sculpture and architecture developed during this period, when religion, government, social life, and art were interdependent.

2158. **History Through Art: Baroque**. CD-ROM. System requirements: IBM or compatible PC, 386/20 MHz or higher CPU, 4 MB RAM (8 MB recommended), Microsoft Windows 3.1 or later, CD-ROM drive, sound card, mouse, SVGA 256-color display, loudspeakers or headphones. Macintosh: 6 to 8 MB RAM, System 7.0, 13-inch monitor (256 colors), CD-ROM drive. Minneapolis, MN: Gareth Stevens, 1995. $75. 6 up

The modes available to study the art of the Baroque period are the Feature Presentation, Text, View, Index, Question, and Quiz. The famous sculptors, painters, architects, and musicians of the Baroque show the turmoil of the late sixteenth and seventeenth centuries.

2159. **History Through Art: Pre-Modern Era**. CD-ROM. System requirements: IBM or compatible PC, 386/20 MHz or higher CPU, 4 MB RAM (8 MB recommended), Microsoft Windows 3.1 or later, CD-ROM drive, sound card, mouse, SVGA 256-color display, loudspeakers or headphones. Macintosh: 6 to 8 MB RAM, System 7.0, 13-inch monitor (256 colors), CD-ROM drive. Minneapolis, MN: Gareth Stevens, 1995. $75. 6 up

The modes available to study the art of the late nineteenth century are the Feature Presentation, Text, View, Index, Question, and Quiz. The emergence of Realism and then Impressionism show how artists began to change their views of life in the nineteenth century.

2160. **History Through Art: Renaissance**. CD-ROM. System requirements: IBM or compatible PC, 386/20 MHz or higher CPU, 4 MB RAM (8 MB recommended), Microsoft Windows 3.1 or later, CD-ROM drive, sound card, mouse, SVGA 256-color display, loudspeakers or headphones. Macintosh: 6 to 8 MB RAM, System 7.0, 13-inch monitor (256 colors), CD-ROM drive. Minneapolis, MN: Gareth Stevens, 1995. $75. 6 up

The modes available to study the art of the Renaissance are the Feature Presentation, Text, View, Index, Question, and Quiz. Over fifty Renaissance artists and their studies of nature, anatomy, medicine, and the sciences appear in this CD-ROM. What they created represented their values and beliefs and influenced those of contemporary times.

2161. **History Through Art: 20th Century**. CD-ROM. System requirements: IBM or compatible PC, 386/20 MHz or higher CPU, 4 MB RAM (8 MB recommended), Microsoft Windows 3.1 or later, CD-ROM drive, sound card, mouse, SVGA 256-color display, loudspeakers or headphones. Macintosh: 6 to 8 MB RAM, System 7.0, 13-inch monitor (256 colors), CD-ROM drive. Minneapolis, MN: Gareth Stevens, 1995. $75. 6 up

The modes available to study the art of the twentieth century are the Feature Presentation, Text, View, Index, Question, and Quiz. Urbanization changed artists' views in the twentieth century, and the development of photography reflects these changes.

2162. **Ideas That Changed the World**. CD-ROM. System requirements: IBM or compatible PC, 486/33 MHz or higher CPU, 8 MB RAM, Microsoft Windows 3.1 or later, CD-ROM drive, sound card, mouse, SVGA 256-color display with 512K RAM, loudspeakers or headphones. Macintosh: 5 MB RAM, System 7.0, 13-inch monitor (256 colors), CD-ROM drive. New York: Integrated Communications and Entertainment, 1996. $29.95. 9 up

Twenty-five video segments, thousands of illustrations and photographs, and animations discuss human inventions and discoveries. Hypertext links among biographies, timelines, ideas, and other topics give quick access to the almost limitless information in this program. Music and graphics complement the information. The general topics covered are "The First Inventions," "Improving Our Chance of Survival," "From Flint Tools to Production Lines," "Utilizing the Earth's Resources," "Using Natural and Artificial Materials," and "Shrinking the World." Inventions and architectural designs include such things as the wheel, computers, barrel vaulting, thatch, and myriad other items. Viewers can choose Who, What, and Where for information and slide shows.

2163. **Inside the Vatican**. CD-ROM. System requirements: IBM or compatible PC, 486/33 MHz or higher CPU, 8 MB RAM, Microsoft Windows 3.1 or later, CD-ROM drive, sound card, mouse, SVGA 256-color display, loudspeakers or headphones. New York: Jasmine Media, 1996. $49.95. 9 up

Six libraries of information reveal the complete history of the Vatican and the Catholic Church. The topics are "Upon This Rock," "Visions of Glory," "The Flight from Rome," "The Renaissance," "The Changing Consciousness," and "The Third Millennium." The tour leader is Peter Ustinov.

2164. **Jerusalem: Interactive Pilgrimage to the Holy City**. CD-ROM. System requirements: IBM or compatible PC, 486/33 MHz or higher CPU, 4 MB RAM, Microsoft Windows 3.1 or later, CD-ROM drive, sound card, mouse, SVGA 256-color display, loudspeakers or headphones. Macintosh: 4 MB RAM, System 7.0, 13-inch monitor (256 colors), CD-ROM drive. New York: Simon & Schuster Interactive, 1996. $39.95. 6 up

Three thousand years of history, from Herod's time to the present, fill this look at Jerusalem. Maps, photographs, and video footage augment the thorough information on the disc.

2165. **Klondike Gold: An Interactive History**. CD-ROM. System requirements: IBM or compatible PC (MPC), 486/33 MHz or higher CPU, 8 MB RAM, Microsoft Windows 3.1 or later, CD-ROM drive, sound card, mouse, SVGA 256 color-display, loudspeakers or headphones. Macintosh: 6 MB RAM, System 7.0, 13-inch monitor (256 colors), CD-ROM drive. Seattle, WA: VR Didatech, 1996. $49.95. 8 up

The Yukon gold rush in 1896 is the central module of this three-module program, which also presents the periods before and after the rush. Among the topics are the opening of trade routes, transportation, life at the creek gold sites, boom towns, changes as families arrived and stayed, and the people who came not for the gold but to help the people there. The information presents the growth of Canada and North America.

2166. **Le Louvre: The Palace & Its Paintings**. CD-ROM. System requirements: IBM or compatible PC, 486/33 MHz or higher CPU, 8 MB RAM, Microsoft Windows 3.1 or later, CD-ROM drive, sound card, mouse, SVGA 256-color display, loudspeakers or headphones. Macintosh: 6 MB RAM, System 7.0, 13-inch monitor (256 colors), CD-ROM drive. New York: BMG Entertainment/Montparnasse Multimedia, 1995. $49.95. 6 up

This tour of the Louvre discusses 100 paintings from eight centuries of art history. Two hours of narration and twenty minutes of music accompany the artworks, which are accessed by title, artist, or time period.

2167. **Lest We Forget: A History of the Holocaust**. CD-ROM. System requirements: IBM or compatible PC, 486/33 MHz or higher CPU, 8 MB RAM, Microsoft Windows 3.1 or later, CD-ROM drive, sound card, mouse, SVGA 256-color display, loudspeakers or headphones. Macintosh: 6 MB RAM, System 7.0, 13-inch monitor (256 colors), CD-ROM drive. Oak Harbor, WA: Logos Research, 1995. $59.95. 7 up

This view of Hitler's annihilation of European Jews uses video, audio, and animation. Sources include archival film footage, photographs, speeches, and text in four segments: "The Jewish People," "Hitler's Germany," "The Holocaust," and "The Aftermath."

2168. **Maya Quest**. CD-ROM. System requirements: IBM or compatible PC, 486/33 MHz or higher CPU, 8 MB RAM, Microsoft Windows 3.1 or later, CD-ROM drive, sound card, mouse, SVGA 256-color display, loudspeakers or headphones. Macintosh: 6 MB RAM, System 7.0, 13-inch monitor (256 colors), CD-ROM drive. Minneapolis, MN: MECC, 1995. $79. 6 up

Three-dimensional tours by bicycle help to take the viewer into the Mayan historical sites in Central America. Two games access artifacts and historical information; the Multimedia Resource Tool contains pictures, text, music, and sounds.

2169. **Normandy: The Great Crusade**. CD-ROM. System requirements: IBM or compatible PC, 386SX or higher CPU, 4 MB RAM, CD-ROM drive, sound card, mouse, SVGA 256-color display, loudspeakers or headphones. Bethesda, MD: Discovery, 1994. $49.95. 10 up

Video, audio, radio clips, and still photographs describe the events of the Allied invasion of Normandy during World War II. Maps provide general reference; supporting documents include profiles of war leaders, and letters and diaries of both civilians and enlisted men.

2170. **One Tribe**. CD-ROM. System requirements: Macintosh or MS-DOS/MPC, 486/33 MHz or higher CPU, 4 MB RAM, Windows 3.1 or higher, CD-ROM drive, sound card, mouse, SVGA 256-color display (minimum), loudspeakers or headphones. Los Angeles: Virgin Sound and Vision, 1994. $24. 6-12

The video explores diversity among humans. Twenty-five themed slide shows cover topics such as faces, rituals, and animals; each show includes historical information about the evolution of humans in the areas of North America, Latin America, Europe, Asia, Australia, Africa, and the Arctic/Antarctic.

2171. **Our Times: The Multimedia Encyclopedia of the Twentieth Century**. CD-ROM. System requirements: IBM or compatible PC, 486/33 MHz or higher CPU, 4 MB RAM, Microsoft Windows 3.1 or later, CD-ROM drive, sound card, mouse, SVGA 256-color display, loudspeakers or headphones. Macintosh: 4 MB RAM, System 7.0, 13-inch monitor (256 colors), CD-ROM drive. Redwood City, CA: Vicarious, 1996. $69.95. 9 up

With 52,000 articles, 2,500 images, and two hours of narration by James Earl Jones, this CD-ROM covers the people and events of the twentieth century. Special articles and commentary accompany the discussion on each decade.

2172. **Passage to Vietnam**. CD-ROM. System requirements: IBM or compatible PC, 486/33 MHz or higher CPU, 8 MB RAM, Microsoft Windows 3.1 or later, CD-ROM drive, sound card, mouse, SVGA 256-color display, loudspeakers or headphones. Macintosh: 6 MB RAM, System 7.0, 13-inch monitor (256 colors), CD-ROM drive. Sausalito, CA: Interval Research/Against All Odds, 1995. $39.99. 7 up

This CD-ROM includes more than 400 photographs shot by professional photojournalists, along with an hour of video that gives insight into this culture.

2173. **Religions of the World**. CD-ROM. System requirements: IBM or compatible PC, 386SX or higher CPU, 4 MB RAM, Microsoft Windows 3.1 or later, CD-ROM drive, sound card, mouse, SVGA 256-color display, loudspeakers or headphones. Mississauga, Ontario, Canada: Mentorom Multimedia, 1996. $60. 7 up

Eight major religions, their histories, and their beliefs compose this CD-ROM. The two key sections are "Aspects of Religion" and "Contemporary Issues." In the "Aspects of Religion" section, the festivals, people, scriptures, worship, beliefs, artifacts, places, and communities of each religion appear. In "Contemporary Issues," the views of each faith on war, the environment, crime and punishment, social issues, and domestic issues such as race, marriage, abortion, and wealth can be compared. The eight religions discussed are Buddhism, Christianity, Confucianism, Hinduism, Islam, Judaism, Shinto, and Sikhism. Photographs and text provide hypertext links among the topics presented.

2174. **Renaissance of Florence**. CD-ROM. System requirements: IBM or compatible PC, 386/33 MHz or higher CPU, 4 MB RAM (8 MB recommended), Microsoft Windows 3.1 or later, CD-ROM drive, sound card, mouse, SVGA 256-color display, loudspeakers or headphones. Macintosh: 4 MB RAM, System 7.0, 13-inch monitor (256 colors), CD-ROM drive. Santa Monica, CA: Pantheon, 1996. $39.98. 9 up

"Overview," "History," "Arts," "Catalogs," and "Epilogue" sections allow various entries into the information on this CD-ROM. Photographs of artworks from Florence and other galleries, as well as authentic Renaissance music, give a clear sense of the Italian Renaissance. The disc combines visuals, narration, music, and transcripts to show the history and achievements of the time, including the role of women, starting with the renewal of interest in Greek and Roman antiquity.

2175. **Science Navigator**. CD-ROM. System requirements: Macintosh or IBM or compatible PC, 386 CPU, Windows 3.0 or higher, 4 MB RAM, hard drive with 1.5 MB free, CD-ROM drive, VGA or SVGA. New York: McGraw-Hill, 1995. $149.95. 7 up

In addition to other searchable information, this CD-ROM includes biographical sketches from the *McGraw-Hill Dictionary of Scientific and Technical Terms,* 5th ed.

2176. **Stowaway! Stephen Biesty's Incredible Cross-Sections**. CD-ROM. System requirements: IBM or compatible PC, 386SX or higher CPU, 4 MB RAM, CD-ROM drive, sound card, mouse, SVGA 256-color display, loudspeakers or headphones. New York: Dorling Kindersley, 1994. $59.95. 6 up

By clicking the mouse on any part of an eighteenth-century warship, or on one of its crew members, one gets information about the ship. After learning many details about life on the ship, the viewer eventually finds the stowaway.

2177. **Teach Your Kids World History**. CD-ROM. System requirements: IBM or compatible PC, 386SX or higher CPU, 4 MB RAM, CD-ROM drive, sound card, mouse, SVGA 256-color display, loudspeakers or headphones. New York: Chelsea House, 1995. $79.95. 4 up

This CD-ROM, the same as the one entitled *Multimedia World History*, provides information about books written throughout history by author or title. Other access points include Time Periods, Region, Themes, and the history of each day of the year, as well as other levels such as wars, technology, exploration, and maps. The disc provides slides and video clips of various events and keeps a record of all topics accessed during a session. An accompanying text lists the historical figures included and suggests ways to find information on topics of interest.

2178. **Total History**. 3 CD-ROMs. System requirements: IBM or compatible PC, 386SX or higher CPU, 4 MB RAM, CD-ROM drive, sound card, mouse, SVGA 256-color display, loudspeakers or headphones. New York: Bureau of Electronic Publishing-Chelsea House, 1995. $99.95. 4 up

Multimedia U.S. History, Multimedia World History (same as *Teach Your Kids World History),* and *Multimedia World Factbook,* all available separately, constitute this package. *World History* provides information about books written throughout history by author or title; other access points include Time Periods, Region, Themes, and a history of each day of the year, as well as other levels such as wars, technology, exploration, and maps. *U.S. History* presents American people, American places, the armed forces, exploring the continent, general history, science and technology, government, and wars and conflicts. Both programs provide slides and video clips. The *World Factbook* allows access to facts in several ways, such as searching topics, timelines, and glossaries. All keep a history of topics consulted during a session.

2179.   **The War in Vietnam**. CD-ROM. System requirements: IBM or compatible PC, 486/33 MHz or higher CPU, 8 MB RAM, Microsoft Windows 3.1 or later, CD-ROM drive, sound card, mouse, SVGA 256-color display, loudspeakers or headphones. Macintosh: 6 MB RAM, System 7.0, 13-inch monitor (256 colors), CD-ROM drive. New York: Macmillan Digital, 1996. $49.99. 7 up

The process begins with stories about the French in Indochina during the 1940s, and progresses to the status of Vietnam in recent years. The articles, arranged chronologically, cover various time periods. Photographs and an hour of video cover weapons, biographies, and much more information about this war, giving insight into the reasons it happened and the results of its unsettled ending.

2180.   **The Way Things Work**. CD-ROM. System requirements: IBM or compatible PC, 386SX or higher CPU, 4 MB RAM, Microsoft Windows 3.1 or later, CD-ROM drive, sound card, mouse, SVGA 256-color display, loudspeakers or headphones. (Macintosh version available.) New York: Dorling Kindersley, 1994. $79.95. 6-12

A history timeline, brief biographies of inventors, specifications for the inventions, and animations showing the scientific principles underlying the inventions make this CD-ROM especially informative.

2181.   **World War II, Global Conflict**. CD-ROM. System requirements: IBM or compatible PC, 386SX or higher CPU, 4 MB RAM, Microsoft Windows 3.1 or later, CD-ROM drive, sound card, mouse, SVGA 256-color display, loudspeakers or headphones. Mississauga, Ontario, Canada: Mentorom Multimedia, 1996. $60. 7 up

This CD-ROM presents the personalities and events of World War II through posters, cartoons, photographs, video, audio, and text-based documents from around the world. Two main areas are themes and case studies. The five main themes are "African Americans," "Propaganda," "The Atom Bomb," "D-Day," and "The Holocaust." Each has a detailed analysis. Ten case studies look at battles, attitudes, and life at home through segments on "Pearl Harbor," "G.I.s in Britain," "The War in North Africa," "The Blitz," "Women at War," "The Invasion of Normandy," "Internment of Japanese Americans," "Iwo Jima," "Resistance," and "The End of the War." Movement through the CD-ROM comes via an assortment of hypertext links.

Videotapes: An Annotated Bibliography

$$\boxed{A}$$

2182.   **Absolutism and the Social Contract**. Videocassette. Color. 30 min. WGBH Educational Foundation, distributor. Washington, DC: Annenberg/CPB, 1989. $29.95. (The Western Tradition, Program 32). 11 up

The professor presenting this topic projects his excitement for history as he provides insight into the people, politics, thoughts, and events that have shaped western society. Resources from the Metropolitan Museum of Art illustrate the people's response to those who saw themselves as rulers chosen by their god.

2183.   **Abubakari: The Explorer King of Mali**. Videocassette. Color. 15 min. Jenison, MI: All Media, 1993. $99. 4-8

Abubakari II, king of Mali, sent explorers across the Atlantic almost two centuries before Columbus. He ruled an advanced society in which universities functioned and professions included lawyers, doctors, explorers, and philosophers.

2184.   **Aces: A Story of the First Air War**. Videocassette. Color and B&W. 93 min. National Film Board of Canada, distributor. Bethesda, MD: Acorn Media, 1997. $19.95. 9 up

In World War I, combat pilots in the new airplanes were called aces. This video catalogs their adventures and achievements.

2185.   **Act of War: The Overthrow of the Hawaiian Nation**. Videocassette. Color. 58 min. Honolulu, HI: Na Maka o ka Aina, 1993. $165. 9 up

In the 1890s, the United States acquired the Hawaiian Islands. This video intersperses commentary with readings, reenactments, photographs, and film footage to tell of the events leading to the invasion of Hawaii and its subsequent annexation. *Golden Eagle, Council on Nontheatrical Events; Bronze Plaque, Columbus International Film & Video Festival; Silver, Corporation for Public Broadcasting.*

2186.   **Africa**. 4 Videocassettes. Color. 17-22 min. Chicago: Encyclopaedia Britannica, 1993. $99. 5 up

Four programs present Africa and its peoples interacting and coping with the environment. The individual titles are *Central and Eastern Regions, Northern Region, Southern Region,* and *Western Region.*

2187.   **Africa: History and Culture**. Videocassette. Color. 19 min. Irwindale, CA: Barr Media, 1990. $100. (Africa). 6-9

With views of cave drawings and live-action shots, the video provides an overview of Africa's ancient kingdoms and cultural heritage. The narrator comments that scientists believe that the human race originated in the Olduvai Gorge, where they have found 3-million-year-old fossils. Additional commentary includes information about Africa's geographical exploration and colonization.

2188.   **Africa: Land and People**. Videocassette. Color. 24 min. Irwindale, CA: Barr Media, 1990. $100. (Africa). 6-9

Covering Africa in general, this video presents an introduction to the physical features, natural resources, education, religions, agriculture, languages, industries, climate, and social customs.

2189.   **After the Cloud Lifted: Hiroshima's Stories of Recovery**. Videocassette. Color. 35 min. Virginia Beach, VA: RMS Communications, 1996. $150. 9 up

With historic stills and newsreel footage, the video tells about the survivors of Hiroshima, the *hibakusha,* who helped in the recovery of their city. The unbiased recounting of this horror shows people after the blast and their response to it today.

2190. **The Age of Absolutism**. Videocassette. Color. 30 min. WGBH Educational Foundation, distributor. Washington, DC: Annenberg/CPB, 1989. $29.95. (The Western Tradition, Program 31). 11 up

The professor presenting this topic projects his excitement for history as he provides insight into the people, politics, thoughts, and events that have shaped western society. Resources from the Metropolitan Museum of Art illustrate the seventeenth-century belief of divine right.

2191. **The Age of Charlemagne**. Videocassette. Color. 30 min. WGBH Educational Foundation, distributor. Washington, DC: Annenberg/CPB, 1989. $650 set; $29.95 ea. (The Western Tradition, Program 18). 11 up

The professor presenting this topic projects his excitement for history as he provides insight into the people, politics, thoughts, and events that have shaped western society. Resources from the Metropolitan Museum of Art illustrate the time of Charlemagne, who began ruling in 771 and lived for forty-two more years, reshaping European life.

2192. **The Age of Reason: Europe After the Renaissance**. Videocassette. Color. 23 min. Chariot Productions, distributor. Niles, IL: United Learning, 1995. $95. 6 up

John Locke (1632–1704) and Isaac Newton (1642–1727) provided the foundation for this period of history in the eighteenth century, which espoused rationalism, liberalism, humanitarianism, and scientific thought.

2193. **The Age of the Nation-States**. Videocassette. Color. 30 min. Boston: WGBH Educational Foundation, distributor. Washington, DC: Annenberg/CPB, 1989. $29.95. (The Western Tradition, Program 44). 11 up

The professor presenting this topic projects his excitement for history as he provides insight into the people, politics, thoughts, and events that have shaped western society. Resources from the Metropolitan Museum of Art illustrate the countries that promoted themselves so strongly in the nineteenth century.

2194. **Albanian Journey: End of an Era**. Videocassette. Color. 60 min. New York: The Cinema Guild, 1992. $350. 8 up

The country of Albania was born in 1944 under Communist leadership. Not until 1991 did it have its first multiparty elections. The program uses archival footage and interviews with Albanian citizens to show how this history of governmental control has affected their perceptions of citizenship.

2195. **Albert Einstein: The Education of a Genius**. Videocassette. Color. 13 min. Princeton, NJ: Films for the Humanities and Sciences, 1989. $29.95. (Against the Odds). 4 up

Documentary footage, interviews, and animation help present this profile of the genius Albert Einstein (1879-1955).

2196. **Alexander the Great**. Videocassette. Color. 30 min. WGBH Educational Foundation, distributor. Washington, DC: Annenberg/CPB, 1989. $650 set; $29.95 ea. (The Western Tradition, Program 7). 11 up

The professor presenting this topic projects his excitement for history as he provides insight into the people, politics, thoughts, and events that have shaped western society. Resources from the Metropolitan Museum of Art illustrate the meteoric rise of Alexander, who led his Macedonian troops until his death in 323 B.C.

2197. **America in Asia**. Videocassette. Color. 60 min. Pacific Basin Institute, distributor. Washington, DC: Annenberg/CPB, 1992. $275 series; $29.95 ea. (Pacific Century). 11 up

This series looks at 150 years of the Pacific region's political and economic development, through maps, charts, archival footage, and interviews with journalists and historians. It examines each country's relationship with the United States.

2198. **Ancient Egypt: The Gift of the Nile (3000 BC–30 BC)**. Videocassette. Color. 28 min. Chariot Productions. Niles, IL: United Learning, 1997. $125. 5-8

The video examines the Egyptians and their creation of a written language, acceptance of government under one ruler, and worship of a specific pantheon of gods.

2199. **The Ancient Egyptians**. Videocassette. Color. 30 min. WGBH Educational Foundation, distributor. Washington, DC: Annenberg/CPB, 1989. $650 set; $29.95 ea. (The Western Tradition, Program 2). 11 up

The professor presenting this topic projects his excitement for history as he provides insight into the people, politics, thoughts, and events that have shaped western society. Resources from the Metropolitan Museum of Art illustrate the ancient Egyptian way of life.

2200. **Ancient Rome**. Videocassette. Color. 14.5 min. Chicago: Encyclopaedia Britannica, 1993. $99. ISBN 0-8347-9988-X. 6 up

By beginning with pictures of modern Rome and moving to a model of the ancient city, the video recreates daily life in Rome around A.D. 300. The importance of places such as the Palatine, the Forum, the public baths, the Capitol, and the amphitheaters becomes apparent.

2201. **And We Knew How to Dance, the Women of World War One**. Videocassette. Color. 56 min. National Film Board of Canada, distributor. Santa Monica, CA: Direct Cinema, 1995. $95. 9 up

This documentary shows the Canadian women who went to work and aided the war effort during World War I. It also explores the social changes that the war brought about for women.

2202. **Anzio and the Italian Campaign**. Videocassette. Color and B&W. 45 min. Bethesda, MD: Acorn Media, 1989. $19.95. (V for Victory). 7 up

Newsreel footage and stories from the home front give information about World War II. Features include a discussion of General Patton's successful campaign in Sicily and the bloody Anzio battle.

2203. **The Arab-Israeli Struggle for Peace**. Videocassette. Color. 55 min. ITT Productions, distributor. Falls Church, VA: Landmark Media, 1994. $250. 11 up

This video gives a chronological overview of the warfare that has plagued the Middle East since World War II. Events, groups, and individuals featured include the 1948 Israeli war for independence, the Palestinian question, Nasser, Moshe Dayan, the 1956 war, the Gaza Strip, the PLO, the Yom Kippur War, Anwar Sadat, Black September, Abu Nidal, Golda Meir, the Camp David accords, and the most recent attempts at peace between Yasir Arafat and Yitzhak Rabin.

2204. **The Arab World**. 5 videocassettes. Color. 28 min. ea. Princeton, NJ: Films for the Humanities and Sciences, 1997. $399 series; $89.95 ea. 10 up

The five videos in this series are titled *The Arabs: Who They Are, Who They Are Not*; *The Historic Memory*; *The Image of God*; *The Bonds of Pride*; and *Arabs and the West*. In the series, Bill Moyers discusses Arab history and culture with experts who present topics such as dehumanization of Arabs in the American media; the traditional conflict that divides Arabs, Jews, and the West; and the importance of religion for Arabs.

2205. **The Arab World**. Videocassette. Color. 25 min. Madison, WI: Knowledge Unlimited, 1995. $59.95. 5 up

Anwar Sadat said that the Arabs were a people trying to use their ancient traditions as a basis for constructing a modern civilization. The video covers early civilization and the imperialism that fired the Arab desire for independence. It shows the wide variety among Arab peoples; sometimes their one common trait is their language. It looks at the Sumerian civilization, religions, and economic conflicts with the West and among the Arabs themselves.

2206. **Archbishop Desmond Tutu Addresses Apartheid**. Videocassette. Color. 15 min. Derry, NH: Chip Taylor Communications, 1991. $159.99. 7 up

Little historical information comes from this video, but it does contain an unedited speech by Desmond Tutu, who won the Nobel Peace Prize in 1984. The viewer can understand how important the anti-apartheid movement in South Africa has been.

2207. **Are We Winning, Mommy? America and the Cold War**. Videocassette. Color. 87 min. Cine Information, distributor. New York: Cinema Guild, 1990. $395. 10 up

Although produced in 1986, this film gives a good overview of the undercurrents in the Cold War, through news and film clips, historical footage, interviews, and debates. Six parts of the documentary trace the events during this period: "Grand Alliance," "Uneasy Peace," "Containing the Threat," "Red Menace," "Cold Warriors," and "No Place to Hide."

2208. **Art and Architecture of Precolumbian Mexico**. Videocassette. Color. 50 min. Boulder, CO: Alarion Press, 1994. $124. (History Through Art and Architecture). 5 up

Through art and architecture, the history of Precolumbian Mexico, from 1500 B.C. to A.D. 1500, is revealed. The video includes two segments: "The Jaguar and the Feathered Serpent" examines the Olmec, Zapotec, and Teotihuacán cultures; and "War and Human Sacrifice" looks at the Mixtecs, Toltecs, and Aztecs.

2209. **The Art and Architecture of the Maya**. Videocassette. Color. 53 min. Boulder, CO: Alarion Press, 1995. $124. 5 up

The art and architecture of the Mayan civilization help to reveal Mayan history. Divided into two parts, the video looks first at the "Kings, Glyphs, Temples, and Ballcourts" and then at "The Rise and Mysterious Decline of the Maya Kingdoms." Among the topics are the right to the throne, games, religious sacrifices, gods, calendars, and myths.

2210. **Art and Splendor: Michelangelo and the Sistine Chapel**. Videocassette. Color. 35 min. PDJ Productions. New York: V.I.E.W. Video, 1996. $19.98. ISBN 0-8030-1021-4. 7 up

Narrators recount the history of the Sistine Chapel from its inception when Pope Julius II commissioned Michelangelo to repaint the ceiling through the resulting nine major panels and additional work. They discuss the thematic content along with the political and religious views during Michelangelo's lifetime, as close-ups of the art display.

2211. **The Artist**. Videocassette. Color. 55 min. Medici Foundation, distributor. Irwindale, CA: Barr, 1994. $810 series; $150 ea. (Renaissance: The Origins of the Modern World). 10 up

The research of Theodore Rabb, and interviews with experts and political figures, form the basis of this video, one of six in a series, that studies the lives and works of Caravaggio, da Vinci, Michelangelo, Drer, and Titian. It reviews the movement from craftsman to artist and the control of the guilds, the church, and the patrons over artists. It also looks at the role of the artist in society. *Council on Nontheatrical Events, Golden Eagle*.

2212. **The Artists' Revolution: 10 Days in Prague**. Videocassette. Color. 30 min. New York: Cinema Guild, 1996. $250. 9 up

For ten days in November 1989, artists, students, and dissidents tried to overthrow Czechoslovakia's Communist government. Rod Steiger narrates the story of the Velvet Revolution, providing historical background and focusing on such figures as Vaclav Havel.

2213. **As Seen by Both Sides: American and Vietnamese Artists Look at the War**. Videocassette. Color. 58 min. New York: Cinema Guild, 1995. $350. 10 up

By blending archival footage from the Vietnam War with artwork and interviews with people from different areas, the film's creators show the need to create beauty out of suffering. Words from artists and veterans on both sides of the war help to give a balanced view.

2214. **Athenian Democracy**. Videocassette. Color. 15 min. Chicago: Encyclopaedia Britannica, 1993. $99. 7-12

This video presents a portrait of the historical Athens and its limited democracy, including a profile of Pericles (d. 429 B.C.), who helped to form the democracy. It also includes footage of archaeological digs.

2215. **The Aztec**. Videocassette. Color. 30 min. Schlessinger Video Productions, distributor. Bala Cynwyd, PA: Library Video, 1993. $39.95. (Indians of North America). 4-10

This video tells the history and culture of the Aztecs prior to the Spanish conquest, when the culture was at its height. It focuses on the unique history of the Aztecs, using photographs and film footage. It additionally discusses Aztec government, spiritual life, mythical beliefs, and the role of women.

B

2216. **The B-24 Trilogy: The Victory Bombers**. 3 videocassettes. Color and B&W. 60 min. ea. Prime Cut Productions and Goldhil Home Media, distributor. Thousand Oaks, CA: Goldhil Home Media, 1997. $39.95 series; $19.95 ea. 8 up

The three videos of the series, *Bombers Over Normandy*, *Target Nazi Europe*, and *Target Japan*, cover the story of the B-24 and other bombers used to help the Allies win World War II against the Axis and the Japanese.

2217. **Baltic States: Finding Independence**. Videocassette. Color. 20½ min. InterFilm Sweden, distributor. Irwindale, CA: Barr Media, 1991. $90. 4-9

This video acquaints viewers with the history and problems facing the Baltic peoples in Estonia, Latvia, and Lithuania. An Estonian family shows the lack of products available since the country escaped from Communist rule in 1991, but in this respect the video is dated (products are now readily available to anyone who has the money).

2218. **Barefoot Gen**. Videocassette. Color. 80 min. Madhouse Studios, distributor. San Rafael, CA: Tara Releasing, 1995. $99.95. 6 up

This animation, set in Hiroshima, Japan, during 1945, shows Gen surviving the day-to-day struggles of wartime with his family. After the horrifying atomic bomb explosion, he tries to rebuild his life according to his father's antiwar teachings.

2219. **The Battle of the Bulge and the Drive to the Rhine**. Videocassette. Color and B&W. 45 min. Bethesda, MD: Acorn Media, 1989. $19.95. (V for Victory). 7 up

In World War II, Hitler's last effort was a strike at the Belgium forests. Newsreel footage and stories from the home front present this attempt and the 101st Airborne at Bastogne, as well as the seizure of the Remagen bridge.

2220. **The Beginning Is in the End**. Videocassette. Color. 30 min. Ontario, Canada: TVOntario, 1990. $499 series; $99 ea. (Ancient Civilizations). 6 up

Part of a series examining the origins of civilizations, the video investigates the human needs for food, security, and creativity. This video looks at the beginnings of civilization in China, India, Egypt, and Central America, by first focusing on Sumer, near the junction of the Tigris and Euphrates Rivers in Mesopotamia.

2221. **The Berlin Airlift**. Videocassette. Color and B&W. 17 min. Institut fur Film und Bild, distributor. Chicago: Encyclopaedia Britannica, 1990. $270. 7 up

In March 1948, the Soviets tried to thwart the Allied unification of Berlin, Germany, into a single economic unit. They blockaded the city, deciding that the people could starve or surrender. Black-and-white newsreel footage shows the tension of the time as it documents the Berlin airlift, during which planes laden with food first arrived every two minutes and then every fifty seconds until May 12, 1948, when the Soviets capitulated.

2222. **Big Business and the Ghost of Confucius**. Videocassette. Color. 60 min. Pacific Basin Institute, distributor. Washington, DC: Annenberg/CPB, 1992. $275 series; $29.95 ea. (Pacific Century). 11 up

This series looks at 150 years of the Pacific region's political and economic development, through maps, charts, archival footage, and interviews with journalists and historians. It examines each country's relationship with the United States. The rapid economic development in Taiwan, South Korea, and Singapore concerns the modern world.

2223. **Biography: Evita the Woman Behind the Myth**. Videocassette. Color. 50 min. A & E Television Networks, distributor. Burlington, VT: New Video Group, 1997. $19.95. ISBN 0-76700-029-3. 7 up

Eva Duarte Peron (1919-1952) died from cancer at thirty-three. She was born in poverty, wanted to be an actress, and gained fame as the wife of Argentinian ruler Juan Peron. She influenced laws that seemed to take money from the rich and help the poor. Interviews and commentary reflect the complexity of Argentinian responses to her during her life and after.

2224. **Biography: Moshe Dayan**. Videocassette. Color. 50 min. A & E Home Video Productions. New York: New Video Group, 1996. $19.95. 7 up

Moshe Dayan led the Israeli army from 1948 until the 1970s and had a major part in the victories over Egypt in 1956 and 1967. The film emphasizes that Dayan always advocated peace rather than war with the Arabs, and encouraged negotiation. In addition to covering his life, the film also covers the history of Israel.

2225. **Biography: William Shakespeare—Life of Drama**. Videocassette. Color. 50 min. A & E Television Networks. New York: New Video Group, 1997. $19.95. 7 up

This production, thoroughly researched, can add no new information about Shakespeare's life, but the collection of art, interviews with Shakespearean actors, excerpts, and footage on location at Stratford-upon-Avon reveal much about his work. The theories about Shakespeare add mystery to the overall effect.

2226. **Birth of an Empire**. Videocassette. Color. 50 min. Princeton, NJ: Films for the Humanities and Sciences, 1994. $149. (Mongols: Storm from the East). 10 up

At its peak, the Mongolian empire of Ghenghis Khan stretched for 5,000 miles into northern China, central Asia, Afghanistan, Georgia, and Russia. The Khan united a group of nomadic tribes into warriors with excellent horsemanship and hunting abilities. The video additionally examines his leadership and military tactics.

2227. **Birth of the Bomber: The Story of the B-24 Liberator**. Videocassette. Color and B&W. 60 min. Prime Cut Productions and Goldhil Home Media, distributor. Thousand Oaks, CA: Goldhil Home Media, 1997. $19.95. 9 up

During World War II, the Allies developed the B-24, which helped to destroy the Axis troop threat.

2228. **Bishop Desmond Tutu: Apartheid in South Africa**. Videocassette. Color. 15 min. Pleasantville, NY: Sunburst, 1990. $145. (Nobel Prize). 9 up

In presenting the 1984 winner of the Nobel Peace Prize, Desmond Tutu, this video also provides basic information on the historical background of South Africa's political and racial situation. It includes student notebooks and teacher resources.

2229. **The Black Death, 1361**. Videocassette. Color. 30 min. Maryland Public Television, distributor. Washington, DC: Zenger Video, 1989. $395 series; $69.95 ea. (Timeline, Series I). 9 up

This program presents history as today's television news would relate the events. The narrator, Steve Bell, switches live to battlefield reporters, news analysts, and interviewers for the day's news. For the Black Death, the news comes live on March 27, 1361, as a doctor tries to explain his treatment of it.

2230. **Bolivia: Then and Now**. Videocassette. Color. 25 min. Vargas Sherwood Productions, distributor. Chatsworth, CA: Aims Media, 1995. $99.95. 9 up

In 1880, when Bolivia was trying to become a nation-state, Butch Cassidy and the Sundance Kid arrived there to make their living as robbers.

2231. **Breaking Barriers: A History of the Status of Women and the Role of the United Nations**. Videocassette. Color and B&W. 30 min. Red Bank, NJ: Lasch Media, 1994. 9 up

Using historical black-and-white film footage, this video examines the status of women according to political, religious, and economic perspectives, from ancient times to the present. Among other aspects, it shows that gender bias exists in all world religions.

2232. **The British Way of Life**. Videocassette. Color. 23 min. Chatsworth, CA: Aims Media, 1989. $395. 5 up

This overview of British history begins with the end of the Ice Age and continues through the Roman and Norman invasions, the Vikings, the Empire, the Industrial Revolution, and the world wars and their aftermath. It also discusses the development of British democracy, beginning with the Magna Carta, which became the basis for American law.

2233. **Budapest**. Videocassette. Color. 40 min. Pathe Cinema, distributor. Princeton, NJ: Films for the Humanities and Sciences, 1992. $149. 7 up

This video tells the story of Budapest since Arpad the Magyar founded Obuda and the acquisition of the crown of St. Stephen in the tenth century. It continues with the erection and destruction of Mongol, Turkish, Renaissance, and Baroque monuments, along with the subsequent power struggles, occupations, and wars.

2234. **The Byzantine Empire**. Videocassette. Color. 30 min. WGBH Educational Foundation, distributor. Washington, DC: Annenberg/CPB, 1989. $650 set; $29.95 ea. (The Western Tradition, Program 15). 11 up

The professor presenting this topic projects his excitement for history as he provides insight into the people, politics, thoughts, and events that have shaped western society. Resources from the Metropolitan Museum of Art illustrate life during the Byzantine Empire, beginning in A.D. 330 under Constantine I.

2235. **The Byzantine Empire**. Videocassette. Color. 20 min. Chariot Productions, distributor. Niles, IL: United Learning, 1997. $99. 7 up

The video investigates the origin and influence of the Byzantine Empire.

$$\boxed{\complement}$$

2236. **Cambodia: The Struggle for Peace**. Videocassette. Color. 47 min. Derry, NH: Chip Taylor Communications, 1991. $144.99. 9 up

Although dated, in that it covers information only through 1990, this video gives a clear picture of the ruin the Khmer Rouge of Pol Pot inflicted on the Cambodian people during the 1970s. They killed everyone who might threaten the new regime, including thousands of professionals, military, and government officials. Severe food shortages resulted and lack of trained personnel led to a breakdown in the country's infrastructure. Graphic photographs of the dead and starving underscore the severity of this situation.

2237. **Camp of Home and Despair: Westerbork Concentration Camp 1939–1945**. Videocassette. Color. 70 min. AVA Productions, distributor. Teaneck, NJ: Ergo Media, 1995. $39.95. 9 up

Eyewitness accounts by survivors, as well as photographs and films, tell of daily life at Westerbork, a camp in Eastern Holland that was the last stop for over 100,000 Dutch Jews before they were deported to Nazi concentration camps.

2238. **Canada: People and Places**. Videocassette. Color. 20 min. N.C.S.U./Benchmark, distributor. Briarcliff Manor, NY: Benchmark, 1997. $395. 5-9

This video gives a geographical and historical overview of Canada and its provinces, including background on the divisions between French- and English-speaking areas.

2239. Canada's Maple Tree: The Story of the Country's Emblem. Videocassette. Color. 30 min. Bellingham, WA: DEBEC Educational Video, 1995. $35. 5 up

Among the many topics, which include the process of making maple syrup and maple furniture building, is a look at Canadian settlement. The maple leaf first appeared on coinage; then, on July 1, 1867, when the confederation of Canada came into being, it became a part of the flag.

2240. The Canadian Way of Life. Videocassette. Color. 21 min. Century 21 Video. Chatsworth, CA: Aims Media, 1995. $99.95. 6 up

The video presents a broad overview of Canada, the world's second-largest country, with its rich natural resources and its desire to preserve its distinct national identity.

2241. The Caribbean. Videocassette. Color. 20 min. Chicago: Encyclopaedia Britannica, 1993. $99. 7 up

This thorough history of the Caribbean region looks at the resources, people, art, economy, and industry. It discusses the issues of enslaved Africans and natives exploited by the European settlers, as well as the current widespread problems, including poverty.

2242. Cathedrals with a Project. Videocassette. Color. 16 min. Cos Cob, CT: Double Diamond, 1993. $89. (Glory of the Middle Ages). 5-9

This video describes the structural elements of the cathedrals of Chartres, Bourges, and Notre Dame de Paris by defining terms and comparing the styles of Gothic, Romanesque, and High Gothic. It uses examples to show how to build a cathedral from folded paper.

2243. Central America. Videocassette. Color. 21 min. Chicago: Encyclopaedia Britannica, 1993. $99. 5 up

This video explores the history and political significance of Central America and the Panama Canal.

2244. Central Americans. Videocassette. Color. 30 min. Schlessinger Video, distributor. Bala Cynwyd, PA: Library Video, 1993. $39.95. (Multicultural Peoples of North America). 4-10

Based on the Chelsea House series called Peoples of North America, this video highlights Central American culture. It gives reasons for the immigration of Central Americans to America, explanations of customs and traditions, and a history of their transition; it also presents the important leaders from the culture. Historians and sociologists discuss these aspects, and a Central American family explains its cultural identity, shared memories, and reasons for immigration.

2245. The Changing Face of Asia: China, Part I: The Ancient Empire. Videocassette. Color. 16-17 min. ea. Morris Plains, NJ: Lucerne Media, 1996. $525 series; $195 ea. ISBN 0-7934-0850-4. 7 up

The video, shot in China, recounts China's political, social, and cultural history beginning with the Chang Dynasty in 1766 B.C. and continuing to the last emperor's abdication in 1912. It includes background on Confucian philosophy, Buddhism, science and culture under the Han emperors, the military successes of the Mongols under Genghis and Kublai Kahn, and the western influence underlying the imperial system's demise.

2246. The Changing Face of Asia: China, Part II: Revolution! Videocassette. Color. 16-17 min. ea. Morris Plains, NJ: Lucerne Media, 1996. $525 series; $195 ea. ISBN 0-7934-0851-2. 7 up

When China's first president Sun Yat-sen established a democracy, the country's lack of experience with an open bureaucracy, its lack of modernization, and famine led to fighting in 1927 between the Mao's Communists and Chang Kai-shek's Nationalists. Not until after the Japanese invaded and World War II ended did Mao gain control.

2247. The Changing Face of Asia: China, Part III: The Fifth Millennium! Videocassette. Color. 16-17 min. ea. Morris Plains, NJ: Lucerne Media, 1996. $525 series; $195 ea. ISBN 0-7934-0852-0. 7 up

In the period following Mao's death, China liberalizes its economics, but limits on political and human rights remain. Trade increases as China prepares for its future in its fifth millennium.

2248. The Changing Face of Asia: Japan, Part 1: The Divine Land. Videocassette. Color. 15-17 min. ea. Morris Plains, NJ: Lucerne Media, 1996. $525 series; $195 ea. ISBN 0-7934-0853-9. 7 up

A variety of media describe the Japanese culture, including its religions (mainly Shinto), its arts (calligraphy, kabuki, and flower arranging), and the beginning of its interaction with the West.

2249. The Changing Face of Asia: Japan, Part 2: A Nation Reborn. Videocassette. Color. 15-17 min. ea. Morris Plains, NJ: Lucerne Media, 1996. $525 series; $195 ea. ISBN 0-7934-0853-7. 7 up

The video examines Japan's political history beginning with the Emperor Meiji in 1868, and continuing through World War II and afterward under Hirohito.

2250. The Changing Face of Asia: Japan, Part 3: Superpower in the Pacific. Videocassette. Color. 15-17 min. ea. Morris Plains, NJ: Lucerne Media, 1996. $525 series; $195 ea. ISBN 0-7934-0783-4. 7 up

Japan becomes a world economic power, but continues its more isolated traditional values in family life, education, government, and religion.

2251. The Changing Faces of Communist Poland. Videocassette. Color. 23 min. Washington, DC: National Geographic, 1990. $99.95. 10 up

Although the Communists no longer have power in Poland, this video shows the role that the Solidarity movement had in overcoming communism by documenting its rise, repression, and resurgence. Figures discussed include Karl Marx, Stalin, Lech Walesa, General Jaruzelski, and Pope John Paul II.

2252. Charles Darwin: Species Evolution. Videocassette. Color. 24 min. Irwindale, CA: Barr Media, 1989. $50. 4-7

This video is an animation of Charles Darwin and his theory of evolution with its concept of natural selection.

2253. Child in Two Worlds. Videocassette. Color. 60 min. AVA Productions, distributor. Teaneck, NJ: Ergo Media, 1995. $39.95. 6 up

Many European Jewish parents sent their children to hide in Christian foster homes during World War II. This video presents five Jewish war orphans who survived.

2254. Children of the Holocaust. Videocassette. Color. 51 min. Princeton, NJ: Films for the Humanities and Sciences, 1995. $149. 7 up

This program tells the story of four children who survived the Holocaust.

2255. Children Remember the Holocaust. Videocassette. Color. 46 min. SVE and Churchill Media, distributor. Chicago: Churchill Media, 1996. $150. 4-9

Excerpts from diaries juxtapose to pictures of children who died or suffered during the Holocaust. The documentary, narrated by Keanu Reeves, connects the history of that time with the present. *American Library Association Notable Children's Films and Videos* and *Booklist Notable Children's Films and Videos*.

2256. China: A History. Videocassette. Color. 22 min. Irwindale, CA: Barr Media, 1988. $100. (China). 4 up

This video gives the history of China as it examines the dynasties, the Great Wall, and the contributions of China to the world.

2257. China: From President Sun to Chairman Mao. Videocassette. Color. 15 min. Signet Productions, distributor. Morris Plains, NJ: Lucerne Media, 1995. $195. (The Changing Face of Asia). 6 up

Sun Yat-sen became president of China in 1912, and the program follows Chinese history until Chairman Mao took over leadership of the country in 1949.

2258. China: The Ancient Land. Videocassette. Color. 15 min. Signet Productions, distributor. Morris Plains, NJ: Lucerne Media, 1995. $195. (The Changing Face of Asia). 6 up

This video traces the history of China from the Shang Dynasty, in 1766 B.C., to approximately A.D. 1912, when Sun Yat-sen became president of China.

2259. China: The Fifth Millennium. Videocassette. Color. 15 min. Signet Productions, distributor. Morris Plains, NJ: Lucerne Media, 1995. $195. (The Changing Face of Asia). 6 up

China after Mao has its own set of problems. This video addresses China and its situation.

2260. China: The History and the Mystery. 2 videocassettes. Color. 120 min. Las Vegas, NV: Library Distributors of America, 1992. $89.95. 9 up

Stills and live-action footage give a view of 6,000 years of Chinese history through art, geography, and politics. Maps and graphics clarify, as do animations of battle routes.

2261. China Festival Celebration of Ancient Traditions. Videocassette. Color. 8-23 min. Arlington Heights, IL: J. M. Oriental Arts, 1997. 3-8

A celebration in Kaifeng, China, the capital of the Song Dynasty, presents the ancient customs of the country.

2262. China Moon: Returning Swallows. Videocassette. Color. 48 min. Falls Church, VA: Landmark Films, 1989. $295. 9 up

Until the nineteenth century, immigration from China was illegal, and those who left were refused reentry. That policy changed, and today more than 20 million Chinese live abroad. This program relates the history of Chinese immigration to Indochina, America, Canada, Australia, Burma, France, Great Britain, and Holland. Internal situations, such as civil wars, battles between Nationalists and Communists, the Japanese invasion, and World War II, have all been a part of the history of Chinese immigration.

2263. **China Moon: Thread of History**. Videocassette. Color. 48 min. Falls Church, VA: Landmark Films, 1989. $295. 9 up

The thread of China's history has been silk. The desire to increase the silk trade led the Chinese to open their country to Western influences. What followed were the Opium Wars, the Boxer Rebellion, the 1912 Revolution, civil wars, the Japanese invasion, Communist victory, and the Cultural Revolution. The video shows the physical dangers of the trade routes as well.

2264. **China Rising**. 3 videocassettes. Color. 50 min. each. A&E Television Networks, producer. New York: New Video Group, 1996. $49.95 series. 9 up

This series includes three programs, *Paradise of Adventurers, Change in Heaven,* and *Roads to Freedom.* It looks at the development of modern China and life there today. Among the events recounted are the city of Shanghai where modern China was born, the Japanese invasion in 1932, the White Terror when thousands of suspected communists were murdered, and the Communist Revolution under Mao's leadership.

2265. **Chinese Americans**. Videocassette. Color. 30 min. Schlessinger Video, distributor. Bala Cynwyd, PA: Library Video, 1993. $39.95. (Multicultural Peoples of North America). 4-10

Based on the Chelsea House series called Peoples of North America, this video highlights Chinese culture. It gives reasons for the Chinese immigration to America, explanations of customs and traditions, and a history of their transition; it also presents the important leaders from the culture. Historians and sociologists discuss these aspects, and a Chinese family explains its cultural identity, shared memories, and reasons for immigration.

2266. **Choosing One's Way**. Videocassette. Color. 30 min. Holocaust Memorial Foundation of Illinois, distributor. Teaneck, NJ: Ergo Media, 1995. $39.95. 9 up

This program tells the story of Jewish resistance when the inmates of Auschwitz-Birkenau smuggled gunpowder from a nearby munitions factory into the camp and destroyed Crematorium Number Four.

2267. **Christopher Columbus**. Videocassette. Color. 17 min. Los Angeles: Churchill, 1991. $205. 4-8

Through illustration and dramatization, the video presents Columbus's attempt to reach the New World—finding the money and the first voyage. It also addresses the discoveries he made, using actors to dramatize the situations.

2268. **Cities and Cathedrals of the Middle Ages**. Videocassette. Color. 30 min. WGBH Educational Foundation, distributor. Washington, DC: Annenberg/CPB, 1989. $650 set; $29.95 ea. (The Western Tradition, Program 22). 11 up

The professor presenting this topic projects his excitement for history as he provides insight into the people, politics, thoughts, and events that have shaped western society. Resources from the Metropolitan Museum of Art illustrate the rise of cities and the creation of the peoples' monuments to their God—the soaring Gothic cathedrals, which took many years to build.

2269. **The Cold War**. Videocassette. Color. 30 min. WGBH Educational Foundation, distributor. Washington, DC: Annenberg/CPB, 1989. $650 set; $29.95 ea. (The Western Tradition, Program 49). 11 up

The professor presenting this topic projects his excitement for history as he provides insight into the people, politics, thoughts, and events that have shaped western society. Resources from the Metropolitan Museum of Art illustrate the escalation of ill will between fascist and democratic countries.

2270. **The Cold War (Part 3)**. Videocassette. Color. 30 min. Meridian Communications, distributor. Van Nuys, CA: Churchill Media, 1993. $250. ISBN 0-7932-3085-3. (The Torn Iron Curtain). 7 up

An overview of modern Russian history (including the Revolution and the rise of communism, the fall of Czar Nicholas II, World War I, World War II, Stalin, Khrushchev, and Brezhnev) leads to an explanation of how the Cold War developed, and details the interaction between the Soviet Union and the United States.

2271. **Colonial Canada**. Videocassette. Color. 64 min. New York: National Film Board of Canada, 1995. $99. 9 up

The video uses seven stories to tell the history of Canada from 1800 to 1950. It depicts activities such as village life, occupations, schools, clothes, chores, food, homesteading, and transportation. The groups represented are English, Scottish, and French Canadian. Much of the information also applies to pioneer life in the United States.

2272. **The Columbian Way of Life**. Videocassette. Color. 24 min. Chatsworth, CA: Aims Media, 1993. $99.95. 5 up

In addition to information about modern Colombia, the video talks about Colombia's history and its relationship to the development of its government.

2273. **Columbus: Gold, God and Glory**. Videocassette. Color. 58 min. Princeton, NJ: Films for the Humanities and Sciences, 1991. $149. 9 up

After sixteen years of research, a Spanish professor set off from Cadiz in a sixteenth-century caravel with sixteen inexperienced college students. The Columbus they discovered, both before and after the voyage, was a hustler rather than an explorer, who changed his nationality three times in order to get money for his expedition. He promised Queen Isabella new converts to Christianity, but he also wanted 10 percent of the booty collected in the New World. He kept a false journal of the voyage in case the Portuguese stopped him, and he was also an ineffectual governor.

2274. **Columbus and the Age of Discovery: The Crossing**. Videocassette. Color. 58 min. Princeton, NJ: Films for the Humanities and Sciences, 1993. $149. (WGBH Collection). 9 up

In this video, one of seven produced for the quincentennial of Columbus's voyage to the New World, modern-day sailors retrace the trip with replicas of the *Niña*, *Pinta*, and the *Santa Maria*. The difficulties of this undertaking become apparent as the sailors try to solve problems, and historians review the controversy about Columbus's abilities to lead.

2275. **Common Life in the Middle Ages**. Videocassette. Color. 30 min. WGBH Educational Foundation, distributor. Washington, DC: Annenberg/CPB, 1989. $650 set; $29.95 ea. (The Western Tradition, Program 21). 11 up

The professor presenting this topic projects his excitement for history as he provides insight into the people, politics, thoughts, and events that have shaped western society. Resources from the Metropolitan Museum of Art illustrate the life of people in all classes living during the Middle Ages.

2276. **The Crusades**. Videocassette. Color. 20 min. Chariot Productions. Niles, IL: United Learning, 1997. $99. 7 up

The Christian Crusades affected the people who remained at home as well as those who took the long horseback journeys to destroy the Infidels. This video discusses those influences.

2277. **The Crusades, 1187**. Videocassette. Color. 30 min. Maryland Public Television, distributor. Washington, DC: Zenger Video, 1989. $395 series; $69.95 ea. (Timeline, Series I). 9 up

The program presents history as today's television news would relate the events. The narrator, Steve Bell, switches live to battlefield reporters, news analysts, and interviewers for the day's news. For the Crusades, the news comes live on October 2, 1187; in one episode, the Moslem sultan Salah-El-Din (Saladin) talks just before he takes control of Jerusalem.

2278. **Cuba**. Videocassette. Color. 19 min. Camera Q, distributor. Irwindale, CA: Barr Media, 1990. $90. 7 up

In 1895, Cuba fought to free itself from the Spanish rule that was established with Columbus. The result of the revolution was a harsh dictatorship, which Fidel Castro overthrew for his own harsh Marxist dictatorship.

2279. **Cyber Rome**. Videocassette. Color. 39 min. Princeton, NJ: Films for the Humanities and Sciences, 1997. $149. 9 up

Virtual reality and 3-D computer graphics allow tours of Rome's monuments as they existed circa A.D. 200. Among the sites included and discussed are the Colosseum, Basilica Di Massenzio, Tabularium, Basilica Giulia, Curia, Tempio Di Vesta, the Tempio, and the Palatino.

2280. **Czechoslovakia: 1968**. Videocassette. Color. 15 min. Eugene, OR: New Dimension Media, 1991. $265. 7 up

This overview of Czechoslovakian history in the twentieth century ends with the Russian invasion of 1968. *Academy Award.*

D

2281. **D-Day**. Videocassette. Color and B&W. 52 min. Vision 7, distributor. New York: Central Park Media, 1997. $19.95. 9 up

Actual newsreel footage from the front describes the preparation and execution of the operation that many consider to have been the greatest military feat of all time.

2282. **D-Day and the Battle for France**. Videocassette. Color and B&W. 45 min. Bethesda, MD: Atlas Video, 1989. $19.95. (V for Victory). 7 up

This program presents the landing on the 6th of June in 1944, which allowed the Allies to eventually win France and the war.

2283. **D-Day Omaha Beach**. Videocassette. Color. 50 min. Bethesda, MD: Atlas Video, 1991. $99.95 set; $19.95 ea. (War Stories). 7 up

On-camera interviews with veterans make this series on World War II especially human. In this video, soldiers who sailed across the English Channel to land on the Normandy beaches recall their mission.

2284. **D-Day + 50 . . . Normandy, Vol. 1**. Videocassette. Color and B&W. 106 min. Shreveport, LA: Destination Images, 1994. $35. (World War II). 10 up

Archival black-and-white footage from D-Day and computer-generated maps combined with contemporary footage of the invasion area gives insight into the invasion. Towns and battle areas featured include St. Mère Église, Utah Beach, and Pointe du Hoc.

2285. **The Dark Ages**. Videocassette. Color. 30 min. WGBH Educational Foundation, distributor. Washington, DC: Annenberg/CPB, 1989. $650 set; $29.95 ea. (The Western Tradition, Program 17). 11 up

The professor presenting this topic projects his excitement for history as he provides insight into the people, politics, thoughts, and events that have shaped western society. Resources from the Metropolitan Museum of Art illustrate the invasion of peoples from Gaul and then from the North into Britain and Europe.

2286. **The Dark Ages: Europe after the Fall of Rome (410–1066 A.D.)**. Videocassette. Color. 29 min. Chariot Productions, distributor. Niles, IL: United Learning, 1995. $95. 7 up

The Dark Ages: Europe after the Fall of Rome (410–1066 AD) A time of political, social, economic, and religious upheaval, the Dark Ages were the result of the merger of classical Roman culture and its new Christian religion with that of the barbarian Germanic tribes.

2287. **Dark Passages**. Videocassette. Color. 60 min. Alexandria, VA: PBS Video, 1995. $69.95. 11 up

The documentary tells about the Atlantic slave trade focusing on Goree Island off the coast of Dakar, Senegal. On that island, millions of Africans stayed until they were transported to the New World.

2288. **Dateline: 1943 Europe**. Videocassette. Color. 22.40 min. ABC News/Weintraub Production, distributor. Deerfield, IL: Coronet/ MTI, 1989. $250. (The Eagle and the Bear). 9 up

This program traces the deterioration of relations between the United States and the Soviet Union as World War II came to an end. In addition to other information, it looks at the conferences at Tehran, Yalta, and Potsdam with the world leaders Joseph Stalin, Winston Churchill, and Franklin Roosevelt (Harry Truman at Potsdam) in attendance.

2289. **The Dawn of History**. Videocassette. Color. 30 min. WGBH Educational Foundation, distributor. Washington, DC: Annenberg/CPB, 1989. $650 set; $29.95 ea. (The Western Tradition, Program 1). 11 up

The professor presenting this topic projects his excitement for history as he provides insight into the people, politics, thoughts, and events that have shaped western society. Resources from the Metropolitan Museum of Art illustrate the time period leading up to the ancient Egyptians.

2290. **The Death of the Old Regime**. Videocassette. Color. 30 min. WGBH Educational Foundation, distributor. Washington, DC: Annenberg/CPB, 1989. $29.95. (The Western Tradition, Program 39). 11 up

The professor presenting this topic projects his excitement for history as he provides insight into the people, politics, thoughts, and events that have shaped western society. Resources from the Metropolitan Museum of Art illustrate the actions of the populace and the rulers who refused to listen to them.

2291. **The Decline of Rome**. Videocassette. Color. 30 min. WGBH Educational Foundation, distributor. Washington, DC: Annenberg/CPB, 1989. (The Western Tradition, Program 13). 11 up

The professor presenting this topic projects his excitement for history as he provides insight into the people, politics, thoughts, and events that have shaped western society. Resources from the Metropolitan Museum of Art illustrate the decline of Rome during the third century.

2292. **Defiance in the Townships**. Videocassette. Color. 31 min. Meridian Communications, distributor. Van Nuys, CA: Churchill Media, 1994. $99.95. ISBN 0-7932-3280-5. (The Last Days of Apartheid). 7 up

The first in a set of two videos (*The First Free Election* is the other) documents the race problems in South Africa from the arrival of Dutch settlers in 1652 until the establishment of apartheid in 1948. Interviews relate stories of suffering from separatism and mistreatment.

2293. **Details of Roman Life**. Videocassette. Color. 26.44 min. Thames, distributor. Princeton, NJ: Films for the Humanities and Sciences, 1991. $149. 7 up

Sculpture, cameos, silverware, portraiture, and coins from the British Museum help to explain details of Roman life, including religion, politics, historical figures, military campaigns, social events, and daily existence. The Roman art of engineering is shown by roads, cities, military encampments, and aqueducts.

2294. **Diamonds in the Snow**. Videocassette. Color. 59 min. New York: Cinema Guild, 1994. $350. 6 up

Mira Reym Binford was one of only twelve Jewish children to survive the Nazi occupation of the Polish town of Bendzin; she did so by pretending to be a Christian. A factory owner helped some Jews by hiring them to work for him. Binford returned to the town to interview relatives of the families who supported her.

2295. **Discovering Russia**. Videocassette. Color. 60 min. San Ramon, CA: IVN Communications, 1995. $24.99. ISBN 1-56345-284-7. (Video Visits). 7 up

The landscape of Russia from Moscow to Vladivostok shows its beauty and its variety. Ancient traditions remain and sometimes conflict with the rapid changes in Russian society. Information about arts, religion, history, and life in the country appears here.

2296. **Disgraced Monuments**. Videocassette. Color. 48 min. New York: Cinema Guild, 1996. $275. ISBN 0-7815-0620-4. 9 up

In the past one hundred years of Russian history, the party in power has either removed or erected symbolic monuments. Lenin ordered removal of the tsars and their generals while constructing monuments to revolutionary thinkers. Khrushchev removed many honoring the cult of Stalin. In the past few years since the end of the Communist regime, the current government and people have destroyed statues of Lenin and other leaders. The video traces these actions and their significance.

2297. **The Dissenter**. Videocassette. Color. 55 min. Medici Foundation, distributor. Irvindale CA: Barr Media, 1994. $810 series; $150 ea. (Renaissance: The Origins of the Modern World). 10 up

The research of Theodore Rabb, and interviews with experts and political figures, form the basis for this video, one of six in a series, that studies the lives and ideas of those who questioned the church. Those presented through dramatic reenactments are Jan Hus, John Wyclif, Argula Von Grumbach, Thomas Muntzer, and Martin Luther. These men were either put to death or excommunicated for their beliefs. *Golden Eagle, Council on Nontheatrical Events; Gold Apple, NEFVF.*

2298. **Dosvedanya Means Good-Bye**. Videocassette. Color. 30 min. Teaneck, NJ: Ergo Media, 1991. $34.95. 9 up

Tamara, a Soviet Jew, and her family requested exit visas from the Soviet Union in 1979, but she and her immediate family did not receive them until eight years later, in 1987. Then her parents were denied visas because her father was a scientist. In a country that did not want Jews but refused to let them leave, the situation was tenuous at best. The video gives insight to living in the former Soviet Union.

E

2299. **Early Christianity**. Videocassette. Color. 30 min. WGBH Educational Foundation, distributor. Washington, DC: Annenberg/CPB, 1989. $650 set; $29.95 ea. (The Western Tradition, Program 11). 11 up

The professor presenting this topic projects his excitement for history as he provides insight into the people, politics, thoughts, and events that have shaped western society. Resources from the Metropolitan Museum of Art illustrate the climate in the Roman Empire after the crucifixion of Jesus.

2300. **Early Italian Renaissance: Brunelleschi, Donatello, Masaccio**. Videocassette. Color. 27 min. New York: Academic and Entertainment Video, 1995. $29.95. ISBN 1-870512-25-4. 10 up

These three Renaissance artists—Brunelleschi (1337–1446), Donatello (1386?–1466), and Masaccio (1401–1428)—made critical breakthroughs in their respective media of architecture, sculpture, and painting. The video highlights them and examines their work.

2301. **Egypt: Gift of the Nile**. Videocassette. Color. 22 min. BBC, distributor. Deerfield, IL: Coronet/MTI, 1989. $250. 7 up

Costumed reenactments demonstrate farming and irrigation methods, artistic endeavors, and rituals during the annual flooding of the Nile in ancient Egypt. The video points out that the Aswan Dam, built in the 1970s, redirected the Nile flooding.

2302. **Egypt: The Nile River Kingdom**. Videocassette. Color. 20 min. Irwindale, CA: Barr Media, 1988. $75. 4 up

The video traces the history of Egypt from the time of the ancient pharaohs to today's modern cities.

2303. **The End Is the Beginning**. Videocassette. Color. 30 min. Ontario, Canada: TVOntario, 1990. $499 series; $99 ea. (Ancient Civilizations). 6 up

Part of a series examining the origins of civilizations, the video investigates the human needs for food, security, and creativity. This video looks at the reasons for the decline of civilizations and shows the cyclical movement of history, in which the ending of one is often the beginning of another civilization.

2304. **England's Historic Treasures**. 3 videocassettes. Color. 60 min. ea. Tadpole Lane Productions, distributor. Bethesda, MD: Acorn Media, 1997. $59.85 set; $19.95 ea. 6 up

The three videos in this series—*Treasures of the Trust*, *The Spirit of England*, and *A Celebration of Old Roses*—presents an overview of British history through its artifacts and ruins including King Arthur's castle, the former home of Winston Churchill, and a tribute to Old Roses.

2305. **Enigma of the Ruins**. Videocassette. Color. 50 min. Bethesda, MD: Acorn Media, 1993. $19.95. (Mysteries of Peru). 9 up

The Chimu culture built the city of Chan Chan and the religious center of Pakatnamu. Known for their textiles and pottery, the Chimu people were also able to raise and harvest crops with a system of irrigation that showed a high degree of technology. Researchers discuss the culture and its achievements, which seem to have been so far ahead of the time and the technology.

2306. **The Enlightened Despots**. Videocassette. Color. 30 min. WGBH Educational Foundation, distributor. Washington, DC: Annenberg/CPB, 1989. $29.95. (The Western Tradition, Program 33). 11 up

The professor presenting this topic projects his excitement for history as he provides insight into the people, politics, thoughts, and events that have shaped western society. Resources from the Metropolitan Museum of Art illustrate the reigns of persons such as the Holy Roman Emperor Joseph II, Catherine II of Russia, and Frederick II of Prussia in the eighteenth century.

2307. **The Enlightenment**. Videocassette. Color. 30 min. WGBH Educational Foundation, distributor. Washington, DC: Annenberg/CPB, 1989. $650 set; $29.95. (The Western Tradition, Program 34). 11 up

The professor presenting this topic projects his excitement for history as he provides insight into the people, politics, thoughts, and events that have shaped western society. Resources from the Metropolitan Museum of Art illustrate the various aspects of this time of reasoned thinking.

2308. **The Enlightenment and Society**. Videocassette. Color. 30 min. WGBH Educational Foundation, distributor. Washington, DC: Annenberg/CPB, 1989. $650 set; $29.95 ea. (The Western Tradition, Program 35). 11 up

The professor presenting this topic projects his excitement for history as he provides insight into the people, politics, thoughts, and events that have shaped western society. Resources from the Metropolitan Museum of Art illustrate the ways in which the Enlightenment affected the general population.

2309. **Ernesto Che Guevara—the Bolivian Diary**. Videocassette. Color. 94 min. New York: International Film Circuit, 1997. $195. 7 up

The video illustrates the diary that Che Guevara kept before the Bolivian army, with help from the CIA, executed him on October 9, 1967. He spent eleven months trying to start a revolution in Bolivia, which the diary details.

2310. **Estonia: A Story of Survival**. Videocassette. Color. 51 min. Washington, DC: Global View, 1990. $35. 9 up

Two segments in the video show the Estonian search for self after years of invasions and control. The first part, "Hitler and Stalin 1939," uses documentary footage impounded by the Soviets for forty years showing Estonia's experience during World War II; "Cogito Ergo Sum" records the reflections of a farmer who refused to accept the tenets of communism.

2311. **Europe and the Third World**. Videocassette. Color. 30 min. WGBH Educational Foundation, distributor. Washington, DC: Annenberg/CPB, 1989. $650 set; $29.95 ea. (The Western Tradition, Program 50). 11 up

The professor presenting this topic projects his excitement for history as he provides insight into the people, politics, thoughts, and events that have shaped western society. Resources from the Metropolitan Museum of Art illustrate the relationship of Europe to emerging nations in Africa and Asia.

2312. **Europe in the Middle Ages: The City of God**. Videocassette. Color. 52 min. Princeton, NJ: Films for the Humanities and Sciences, 1989. $249. 9 up

People returned to the church in the Middle Ages to find hope in the midst of civil chaos. The program looks at such figures as Augustine of Hippo (354–430) and his *City of God* and Jerome's (347–420?) translation of the Bible into Latin.

$$\boxed{\text{F}}$$

2313. **Facing Hate**. Videocassette. Color. 58 min. Princeton, NJ: Films for the Humanities and Sciences, 1997. $89.95. 9 up

Elie Wiesel, a survivor of Auschwitz, has become a Nobel Laureate and human rights advocate. In the video, he talks with Bill Moyers about his Holocaust experience and tries to identify the reason for Nazi hatred of Jews.

2314. **The Fall of Byzantium**. Videocassette. Color. 30 min. WGBH Educational Foundation, distributor. Washington, DC: Annenberg/CPB, 1989. $650 set; $29.95 ea. (The Western Tradition, Program 16). 11 up

The professor presenting this topic projects his excitement for history as he provides insight into the people, politics, thoughts, and events that have shaped western society. Resources from the Metropolitan Museum of Art illustrate the fall of Byzantium around A.D. 900.

2315. **The Fall of Byzantium, 1453**. Videocassette. Color. 30 min. Maryland Public Television, distributor. Washington, DC: Zenger Video, 1989. $395 series; $69.95 ea. (Timeline, Series I). 9 up

The program presents history as today's television news would relate the events. The narrator, Steve Bell, switches live to battlefield reporters, news analysts, and interviewers for the day's news. For the fall of Byzantium, the news comes live from 1453.

2316. **The Fall of Rome**. Videocassette. Color. 30 min. WGBH Educational Foundation, distributor. Washington, DC: Annenberg/CPB, 1989. (The Western Tradition, Program 14). 11 up

The professor presenting this topic projects his excitement for history as he provides insight into the people, politics, thoughts, and events that have shaped western society. Resources from the Metropolitan Museum of Art illustrate the fall of Rome, officially dated at A.D. 476.

2317. **The Fall of Soviet Communism (Part 4)**. Videocassette. Color. 32 min. Meridian Communications, distributor. Van Nuys, CA: Churchill Media, 1993. $250. ISBN 0-7932-3085-3. (The Torn Iron Curtain). 7 up

A combination of historical and archival footage and interviews with Soviet citizens help to tell the story of the fall of communism in Russia and the eventual breakup of the Soviet Union. Gorbachev's policies of *glasnost* (openness) and *perestroika* (economic reorganization) led to the independence of such republics as Lithuania. Boris Yeltsin's replacement of Gorbachev is part of the video.

2318. **Father's Return to Auschwitz**. Videocassette. Color. 20 min. Ivan Horsky Film, distributor. Evanston, IL: Wombat, 1990. $145. 9 up

The video describes Prague before and after the German invasion as it tells the story of Jaroslav Drabek, a member of the Czech Resistance, who went to Auschwitz in 1943. Some of the black-and-white film footage gives a graphic view of Auschwitz as it was when Drabek was there; color footage shows the current museum. Drabek tells the story as he returns with his son to Auschwitz.

2319. **Ferdinand and Isabella**. Videocassette. Color. 30 min. Schlessinger Video, distributor. Bala Cynwyd, PA: Library Video, 1994. $39.95. ISBN 1-57225-030-5. (Hispanic and Latin American Heritage). 7 up

Biographical information and an overview of the achievements of Ferdinand and Isabella, according to various experts, help to establish the contributions they made to Hispanic history during the fifteenth century.

2320. **The Feudal Order**. Videocassette. Color. 30 min. WGBH Educational Foundation, distributor. Washington, DC: Annenberg/CPB, 1989. $650 set; $29.95 ea. (The Western Tradition, Program 20). 11 up

The professor presenting this topic projects his excitement for history as he provides insight into the people, politics, thoughts, and events that have shaped western society. Resources from the Metropolitan Museum of Art illustrate the new world order of feudalism that evolved during the Middle Ages.

2321. **The Fight for Democracy**. Videocassette. Color. 60 min. Pacific Basin Institute, distributor. Washington, DC: Annenberg/CPB, 1992. $275 series; $29.95 ea. (Pacific Century). 11 up

This series looks at 150 years of the Pacific region's political and economic development, through maps, charts, archival footage, and interviews with journalists and historians. It examines each country's relationship with the United States. Here the changing role of women in Asia and the desire for greater political freedom and self-determination in the area comes to the front.

2322. **Fin de Siecle**. Videocassette. Color. 30 min. WGBH Educational Foundation, distributor. Washington, DC: Annenberg/CPB, 1989. $650 set; $29.95 ea. (The Western Tradition, Program 46). 11 up

The professor presenting this topic projects his excitement for history as he provides insight into the people, politics, thoughts, and events that have shaped western society. Resources from the Metropolitan Museum of Art illustrate the attitudes at the end of the nineteenth century.

2323. **The First Emperor of China**. Videocassette. Color. 42 min. New York: National Film Board of Canada, 1995. $195. 9 up

Developed for the Imax screen, this video shows ancient Chinese civilization and its achievements. It begins in 246 B.C. with the life of Qin Shihuang, son of a prostitute and a general, when China is at war. Qin gave China its name and led the longest-enduring nation-state in the history of the world. Documentary footage of his terra-cotta army of life-sized soldiers is included, as are battle recreations.

2324. **First Footsteps**. Videocassette. Color. 60 min. Falls Church, VA: Landmark Films, 1989. $295. (Man on the Rim: The Peopling of the Pacific). 9 up

The major concept examined in this first episode of eleven is the evolution of the two early Asian species, Java and Peking Man, who settled and explored the area. The narrator, a scientist, explains the archaeological and anthropological theories clearly and backs them with physical evidence.

2325. **The First World War and the Rise of Fascism**. Videocassette. Color. 30 min. WGBH Educational Foundation, distributor. Washington, DC: Annenberg/CPB, 1989. $650 set; $29.95 ea. (The Western Tradition, Program 47). 11 up

The professor presenting this topic projects his excitement for history as he provides insight into the people, politics, thoughts, and events that have shaped western society. Resources from the Metropolitan Museum of Art illustrate the horrors of World War I, 1914–1918, and the overturn of democracy in countries where fascism arose.

2326. **Forever Activists: Stories from the Veterans of the Abraham Lincoln Brigade**. Videocassette. Color. 60 min. Clarity Educational Productions, distributor. Waltham, MA: National Center for Jewish Film, 1992. $295. 9 up

In 1986, members of the Abraham Lincoln Brigade were interviewed at their 50-year reunion. They retraced their intentions and concerns that led them to fight in the Spanish Civil War beginning in 1936.

2327. **444 Days to Freedom: What Really Happened in Iran**. Videocassette. Color. 96 min. New York: V.I.E.W. Video, 1997. $19.98. 9 up

After the Shah left Iran and Khomeini came to power, Islamic students demanded that the United States return the Shah to Iran. A related problem is the hostages that zealots captured on November 4, 1979, and kept until January 20, 1981, even though the Shah died on July 27, 1980.

2328. **France: History and Culture**. Videocassette. Color. 22 min. Irwindale, CA: Barr Media, 1988. $100. (France). 7 up

This program traces French history from the time of the Roman Empire to the present.

2329. **French Gothic Architecture: The Cathedrals**. Videocassette. Color. 25 min. New York: Academic and Entertainment Video, 1995. $29.95. ISBN 1-870512-17-3. 10 up

The video examines the most important masterpieces in French Gothic architecture, beginning circa A.D. 1130 and extending for 400 years, by looking at its technical breakthroughs and its stunningly beautiful cathedrals.

2330. **The French Revolution**. Videocassette. Color. 30 min. WGBH Educational Foundation, distributor. Washington, DC: Annenberg/CPB, 1989. $29.95. (The Western Tradition, Program 40). 11 up

The professor presenting this topic projects his excitement for history as he provides insight into the people, politics, thoughts, and events that have shaped western society. Resources from the Metropolitan Museum of Art illustrate the civil disturbance in France that broke out on July 14, 1789, with the storming of the Bastille.

2331. **The French Revolution**. Videocassette. Color. 35 min. University of Warwick, distributor. Chicago: Encyclopaedia Britannica, 1990. $200. 7 up

The video gives a good overview of the events that began and then continued the French Revolution. Because even more sinister factors replaced previous ones in the name of the revolution, knowing what they were gives a better understanding of the progression.

2332. **From Bronze to Iron**. Videocassette. Color. 30 min. WGBH Educational Foundation, distributor. Washington, DC: Annenberg/CPB, 1989. $650 set; $29.95 ea. (The Western Tradition, Program 4). 11 up

The professor presenting this topic projects his excitement for history as he provides insight into the people, politics, thoughts, and events that have shaped western society. Resources from the Metropolitan Museum of Art illustrate the development of tools in society as people learned about the properties of metals.

2333. **From Mesopotamia to Iraq**. Videocassette. Color. 26 min. Falls Church, VA: Landmark Films, 1991. $250. 7 up

Ancient civilizations populated this area and used the natural resources of lime and oil as a way to advance their societies. The Babylonians, Assyrians, Byzantines, and Bedouins invaded and overran the area at different times through the centuries. Film footage from 1957 and a 1970s discovery of bricks on which the first known written words were found are included.

2334. **From the Barrel of a Gun**. Videocassette. Color. 60 min. Pacific Basin Institute, distributor. Washington, DC: Annenberg/CPB, 1992. $275 series; $29.95 ea. (Pacific Century). 11 up

This series looks at 150 years of the Pacific region's political and economic development, through maps, charts, archival footage, and interviews with journalists and historians. It examines each country's relationship with the United States. This segment looks at the Vietnamese revolutionary Ho Chi Minh and the Indonesian leader Sukarno.

2335. **From Vienna to Jerusalem: The Century of Teddy Kollek**. Videocassette. Color. 60 min. AVA Productions, distributor. Teaneck, NJ: Ergo Media, 1995. $39.95. 9 up

The mayor of Jerusalem from 1965 to 1993 was Teddy Kollek. This documentary traces his life and achievements.

2336. **The Future of the Pacific Basin**. Videocassette. Color. 60 min. Pacific Basin Institute, distributor. Washington, DC: Annenberg/CPB, 1992. $275 series; $29.95 ea. (Pacific Century). 11 up

This series looks at 150 years of the Pacific region's political and economic development, through maps, charts, archival footage, and interviews with journalists and historians. It examines each country's relationship with the United States. This episode looks at the current social problems of pollution, population growth, trade friction, and immigration.

$$\boxed{\text{G}}$$

2337. **Galileo: The Solar System**. Videocassette. Color. 24 min. Irwindale, CA: Barr Media, 1989. $50. 4-9

Galileo (1564-1642) was the first to use a telescope to study the stars, and his belief in Copernicus's theory that the earth revolved around the sun led the Inquisition leaders to punish him. The video features his discoveries and breakthroughs.

2338. **Genbaku Shi: Killed by the Atomic Bomb**. Videocassette. Color. 57 min. Gary DeWalt, 1993. $200. 7 up

Showing the long-term effect of World War II on the personal level, this documentary recounts the experiences of a member of one of the rescue teams who arrived after the truce between the United States and the Japanese. Vintage stills and narration mixed with interviews add to the video's effect.

2339. **Gerald of Wales**. Videocassette. Color. 24 min. Princeton, NJ: Films for the Humanities and Sciences, 1993. $149. 9 up

An animation of Gerald of Wales and his page as they search Wales for noblemen to go on the Crusades shows life during the Middle Ages. The page comments on religious beliefs, everyday habits, abbeys, monasteries, meals, hygiene, folklore, and the faults of church leaders, as well as the irony and ruthlessness of the Crusades themselves.

2340. **The German Way of Life**. Videocassette. Color. 25 min. Chatsworth, CA: Aims Media, 1990. $99.95. 5 up

Natural landforms, invading neighbors, and nationalism have formed the German psyche. The video looks at the role of the German public during the two world wars, the effects of the wars, and the current attempt to reunite.

2341. **Germany: From Partition to Reunification, 1945-1990**. Videocassette. Color. 22 min. Briarcliff Manor, NY: Benchmark Media, 1994. $395. (World Geography and History). 5-7

The video explains the reasons behind the separation of Germany into two countries following World War II. Explanations for the cold war, NATO, the Warsaw Pact, the Communist blockade of West Berlin in 1948, and the erection of the Berlin Wall clarify the difficulties that eventually led to the surprise fall of the Wall in 1989.

2342. **Germany: Past and Present**. Videocassette. Color. 16 min. Irwindale, CA: Barr Media, 1993. $325. 7 up

Germany as a country is younger than the United States, but its culture and language are much older. Otto von Bismarck established it as an empire around 125 years ago, but the individual areas were often in disagreement or at war with each other. This live-action program gives an overview of German history through its reunification in 1990.

2343. **Ghana**. Videocassette. Color and B&W. 20 min. Evanston, IL: Altschul, 1994. $305. 7 up

Archival black-and-white footage and modern color photography help to give the history, geography, and economics of Ghana, which has been occupied by the Dutch, Portuguese, and British since the fifteenth century. In 1957, Ghana became independent but soon depleted its money surplus.

2344. **Golda Meir**. Videocassette. Color. 24 min. Reuters Television, distributor. Morris Plains, NJ: Lucerne Media, 1997. $225. 7 up

Golda Meir (1898-1978) escaped from Russia with her parents and went to the United States before she became a leader in the state of Israel and its first female prime minister.

2345. **Granada, 1492**. Videocassette. Color. 30 min. Maryland Public Television, distributor. Washington, DC: Zenger Video, 1989. $395 series; $69.95 ea. (Timeline, Series I). 9 up

The program presents history as today's television news would relate the events. The narrator, Steve Bell, switches live to battlefield reporters, news analysts, and interviewers for the day's news. For Granada, the news comes live on January 6, 1492, four days after Queen Isabella and King Ferdinand of Castile expelled the Muslims.

2346. **Grave of the Fireflies**. Videocassette. Color. 88 min. New York: Central Park Media, 1993. $39.95. ISBN 1-56219-051-2. 8 up

This animation tells the story of a boy and his sister who fight for survival after a firebombing in Japan killed their mother during World War II. *1st Place, CICFF.*

2347. **The Great Wall of Iron**. 4 videocassettes. Color. 48 min. Falls Church, VA: Landmark Films, 1993. $225. 9 up

Four videos tell the story of the People's Liberation Army of China, from its creation by Mao in 1927 through the Tiananmen Square massacre in 1989. The titles, in order, are *The Blood Red Flag, The People's Army, Middle Ages with Missiles,* and *Better Expert Than Red.*

2348. **The Greek Thought**. Videocassette. Color. 30 min. WGBH Educational Foundation, distributor. Washington, DC: Annenberg/CPB, 1989. $650 set; $29.95 ea. (The Western Tradition, Program 6). 11 up

The professor presenting this topic projects his excitement for history as he provides insight into the people, politics, thoughts, and events that have shaped western society. Resources from the Metropolitan Museum of Art illustrate the role of the Greeks in philosophy, art, and theater as a basis for modern thought.

2349. **Greetings from Iraq**. Videocassette. Color. 28 min. Falls Church, VA: Landmark Media, 1997. $195. 10 up

Although not "history" to adults, the Persian Gulf War will seem ancient for some high school students. This video discusses the problems resulting for Iraqi families from bombings over Baghdad to the embargoes imposed on Iraq after the war.

2350. **Growing Up in Japan**. Videocassette. Color. 20 min. Evanston, IL: Journal, 1992. $275. 4-8

The video looks at the life of young people in Japan, from the extreme pressures of schooling to the dualization of western and eastern ways. By examining their religious roots in Shintoism and Buddhism and their values of politeness, respect, and recognition of beauty, the video helps to reveal modern Japanese culture. Part of the historical aspect is a journey to Hiroshima to see memorials and museums dedicated to the victims of the atomic bomb.

2351. **Guadalcanal and the Pacific Counterattack**. Videocassette. Color and B&W. 45 min. Bethesda, MD: Acorn Media, 1989. $19.95. (V for Victory). 7 up

The United States assaulted the Japanese Pacific Empire during War II. In this video, newsreel footage and stories from the home front show jungle warfare on Guadalcanal, the naval combat off the Solomon Islands, and the fight to control the Aleutian Islands.

2352. **Gulf War, Parts 1 and 2**. Videocassette. Color. 68 min. Independent Television News, distributor. New York: Central Park Media, 1995. $29.95. 10 up

The two videos feature battle footage, including General Norman Schwarzkopf taking command against Saddam Hussein, leader of Iraq.

H

2353. Haiti: *Kom Sa Ta Dweye*. Videocassette. Color. 26 min. Falls Church, VA: Landmark Media, 1995. $195. 9 up

This video gives the history of Haiti since the arrival of the Spanish in 1492. Haiti served as the center of the French slave trade, and was where slaves waited for shipment to other locations. Many escaped into the hills of Haiti, where they became known as Marrons and developed a variety of different languages and customs. The Haitians overthrew the European plantation owners in 1804 and became the second American nation to gain its independence. The country has continued to be unstable as it has tried to maintain democracy.

2354. Half the Sky: The Women of the Jiang Family. Videocassette. Color. 50 min. Global Graphics and TVE International, distributor. Oley, PA: Bullfrog Films, 1996. $250. ISBN 1-56029-658-5. 11 up

Four generations of women in the Jiang family reveal the cultural developments in China. An aunt bound her feet to get a husband. Advice to a daughter was not to question her husband's affairs, and a grandmother had to accept her husband's second wife and the demeaning reputation that she could only bear daughters. Since 1949, when Mao proclaimed women equal, changes have occurred that allow a granddaughter to work in a boutique.

2355. Heart of the Warrior. Videocassette. Color. 54 min. Oakland, CA: Video Project, 1991. $150. 9 up

This video brings together an unlikely pair in the persons of a United States Army paratrooper who fought in Vietnam and a former paratrooper in the Soviet Army who fought in Afghanistan. Both men lost a leg, and they find that their experiences of being wounded, facing unsympathetic people at home, and the teamwork required of soldiers are surprisingly similar. Photography of both war and peace complements the discussion.

2356. The Hellenistic Age. Videocassette. Color. 30 min. WGBH Educational Foundation, distributor. Washington, DC: Annenberg/CPB, 1989. $650 set; $29.95 ea. (The Western Tradition, Program 8). 11 up

The professor presenting this topic projects his excitement for history as he provides insight into the people, politics, thoughts, and events that have shaped western society. Resources from the Metropolitan Museum of Art illustrate the time of Pericles in Athens, which ended in the fourth century B.C.

2357. Hernán Cortés. Videocassette. Color. 30 min. Schlessinger Video, distributor. Bala Cynwyd, PA: Library Video, 1994. $39.95. ISBN 1-57225-029-1. (Hispanic and Latin American Heritage). 7-12

Biographical information and an overview of the achievements of Hernán Cortés (1485–1547), according to various experts, help to establish his part in Latin American history.

2358. Herzl. Videocassette. Color. 45 min. Israel Film Service, distributor. Clarksburg, NJ: Alden Films, 1997. $19.95. 7 up

Theodor Herzl (1860-1904) founded the political form of Zionism with the goal of establishing the state of Israel. He organized the First Zionist Congress in the late nineteenth century while growing up in Austria.

2359. Hildegard: Woman of Vision. Videocassette. Color. CTVC, distributor. Worcester, PA: Video Vision, 1995. $29.95. 7 up

Hildegard of Bingen was an abbess, visionary, naturalist, playwright, political moralist, and composer. The church put her on trial in 1148. *Worldfest-Houston Gold, Worldfest-Charleston Gold,* and *Christ Statuette.*

2360. The Hindenburg. 2 videocassettes. Color. 50 min. each. A & E Television Networks. New York: New Video Group, 1996. $29.95. 9 up

The video incorporates footage from the horrible explosion of the German Zeppelin in May 1937 when it was flying over New Jersey. It gives the history of the craft, invented by Ferdinand von Zeppelin in the early 1900s and discusses its relationship to Hitler's rise in Germany.

2361. Hiroshima Maiden. Videocassette. Color. 58 min. Arnold Shapiro, distributor. Chicago: Public Media Video, 1990. $29.95. (Wonderworks Family Movie). 5 up

In this professionally acted video, Miyeko, a Japanese girl badly scarred by the bombing of Hiroshima in 1945, comes to Connecticut to live with a family while she has plastic surgery. The son, Johnny, is fearful of her, and neighbors think she can cause radiation sickness in others. She and Johnny have to talk face to face before he can understand her needs and respond to the misconceptions of his friends.

2362. **The History of Orthodox Christianity**. Videocassette. Color. 90 min. Greek Orthodox Telecommunications, distributor. Worcester, PA: Vision Video, 1992. $79.95. ISBN 1-56364-095-3. 9 up

This video covers the founding of the church, the spread of Christianity, the rise of Constantinople, and Islamic and Communist conquests of the church. *Bronze Plaque, Columbus International Film & Video Festival.*

2363. **Hitler: The Final Chapter**. Videocassette. Color. 51 min. Cyril Jones, distributor. New York: Central Park Media, 1995. $29.95. 11 up

This documentary offers a look at the details of Hitler's last days in 1945, before he and Eva Braun committed suicide. Russian files now available indicate that authorities identified Hitler through dental records. The photographs, first-person accounts, and film are graphic.

2364. **Hitler's Assault on Europe**. Videocassette. B&W. 17 min. Institut fur Film und Bild. Chicago: Encyclopaedia Britannica, 1990. $270. 7 up

Original film footage and a map that changes to show Hitler's movements gives a clear overview of Hitler's advance through Europe in World War II. The important events here are the invasion of Poland, the Battle of Britain, the occupation of France, the evacuation of Dunkirk, and the invasions of Norway, Denmark, and Russia.

2365. **The Holocaust: A Teenager's Experience**. Videocassette. Color. 30 min. Niles, IL: United Learning, 1990. $95. 7 up

Although the material here is covered in two other videos, *The Holocaust as Seen Through the Eyes of a Survivor* and *Rails to Hell . . . and Back* (Aims, 1990), the narrator in this video is a Holocaust survivor, David Bergman. He tells of his experience of being deported to Auschwitz when he was twelve and living there until the Allied Forces freed him. The simple language does not detract from the power or gravity of the description.

2366. **The Holocaust as Seen Through the Eyes of a Survivor**. Videocassette. Color. 30 min. Remembrance Educational Media. Van Nuys, CA: Aims Media, 1990. $99.95. 7 up

David Bergman, a survivor of the Holocaust, talks about his experiences for fourteen months during World War II when he and his family were deported to Czechoslovakia. He was the only member of his family to survive. The program includes a question-and-answer sequence that will help viewers who lack prior knowledge of the Holocaust.

2367. **The Holocaust Wall Hangings**. Videocassette. Color. 23 min. New York: Carousel, 1997. $175. 7 up

An artist responsible for creating wall hangings about the Holocaust discusses the decisions necessary in such a work to keep it significant and appropriate.

2368. **How the Nazis Came to Power**. Videocassette. Color. 17 min. Pathe-Cinema/Hachette, distributor. Princeton, NJ: Films for the Humanities and Sciences, 1991. $99. (Archive of the 20th Century). 7 up

Excellent film footage shows Hitler, Himmler, Goering, and others as the Nazis began their rise to power during the 1930s. The film starts historically in 1918 and ends with the early days of the Jewish persecution; it covers such topics as inflation, the 1929 crash, and unemployment.

2369. **The Hungarian Uprising: 1956**. Videocassette. Color. 30 min. Visnews, distributor. Princeton, NJ: Films for the Humanities and Sciences, 1991. $149. 7 up

This video features the uprising of the Hungarians and the aftermath when their country had to resume its place in the Eastern Bloc. Eventually, Hungary's economic reforms led it to become the most westernized of the Eastern Bloc countries.

2370. **The Hunt for Pancho Villa**. Videocassette. Color. 56 min. History Consortium, distributor. Alexandria, VA: PBS Video, 1993. $69.95. 9 up

With black-and white-photographs as well as film footage, this video tells the story of Pancho Villa's unprovoked attack on Columbus, New Mexico, on March 9, 1916, during which he killed seventeen Americans. President Wilson sent John "Black Jack" Pershing to find Villa, but after eleven months, Pershing had not been able to penetrate the terrain or the troops. With both Mexican and American interpretations of the conflict, the video presents a balanced account.

I

2371. **The Iliad and the Trojan War**. 4 videocassettes. Color. 20 min. ea. Huntsville, TX: Educational Video Network, 1995. $189.95 series; $49.95 ea. 7 up

This animated introduction to the two classic stories also looks into the history of the ancient Greeks as Homer recorded it in his work.

2372. **The Illegals**. Videocassette. Color and B&W. 56 min. WZO, distributor. Teaneck, NJ: Ergo Media, 1997. $39.95. 7 up

After World War II, Holocaust survivors secretly tried to travel to Palestine through the Haganah's European underground, a movement known as the "Aliyah Bet."

2373. **Illuminated Lives: A Brief History of Women's Work in the Middle Ages**. Videocassette. Color. 6 min. New York: National Film Board of Canada, 1990. $75. 6 up

Animated drawings based on medieval illuminated manuscripts show the kinds of work in which women engaged during the Middle Ages.

2374. **Image Before My Eyes**. Videocassette. Color. 90 min. Yivo Institute for Jewish Research, distributor. Teaneck, NJ: Ergo Media, 1991. $59.95. 9 up

A four-part video presents Jewish life in Poland from 1914 until September 1, 1939, when the Germans invaded. "The Setting" shows life in the various areas of the country in the 1920s and early 1930s. "To the Stars" highlights education and the Yiddish theater in an examination of the cultural and community life. "Among the Organized" tells of several Jewish political groups. "Darkening Clouds" shows Europe in the 1930s, the increase of anti-Semitism in Poland, and Hitler's rise.

2375. **In the Blood of Man: The Sea of the Imagination**. Videocassette. Color. 26 min. Princeton, NJ: Films for the Humanities and Sciences, 1990. $149. (Blue Revolution). 9 up

The video looks at humankind's relationship to the sea during several historical periods. It covers Chinese, Japanese, South Pacific peoples, Arabians, Viking explorers, ancient Greeks, and Herman Melville's *Moby Dick*.

2376. **In the Land of the Inca**. Videocassette. Color. 23 min. Institut fur Film und Bild, distributor. Chicago: Encyclopaedia Britannica, 1990. $295. 7 up

The Inca Empire flourished from about A.D. 1200 until the mid-1500s, when Pizarro and the Spaniards captured and killed the Incan leader, Atahualpa. The video examines who the Incas were, their past, and how they created the largest empire in the Americas. Life today is much the same, and the video compares the two.

2377. **In the Reign of Twilight**. Videocassette. Color. 87 min. Primitive Features, distributor. Oley, PA: Bullfrog Films, 1997. $275. ISBN 1-56029-683-6. 10 up

The Inuit have long endured the harsh Arctic using primitive living methods, but the 1950s and the Cold War changed their lives. The DEW Line, an early warning system for Soviet attack, caused Canada to establish an education and welfare system for the people. This video shows the Inuit historically and currently by examining the culture and its changes.

2378. **Indonesia: The Jeweled Archipelago**. Videocassette. Color. 57 min. San Ramon, CA: IVN Communications, 1996. $24.95. ISBN 1-56345-382-7. (Video Visits). 7 up

Among the topics in this overview of Indonesia are geographical, cultural, and historical aspects of the nation, including its 1960s problems uner the late Sukarno. A look at daily life features a wedding ceremony, court dancing in the ancient terraced farms, Batak tribesmen and their music, and water buffalo races.

2379. **The Industrial Revolution**. 2 videocassettes. Color. 20 min. Huntsville, TX: Educational Video Network, 1995. $79.95 set; $49.95 ea. 7 up

During the late eighteenth century, mechanization of various processes shifted the center of work from the home to the factory. Many lost jobs to machines. The video looks at these and other changes that occurred during this period.

2380. **The Industrial Revolution**. Videocassette. Color. 30 min. WGBH Educational Foundation, distributor. Washington, DC: Annenberg/CPB, 1989. $650 set; $29.95 ea. (The Western Tradition, Program 41). 11 up

The professor presenting this topic projects his excitement for history as he provides insight into the people, politics, thoughts, and events that have shaped western society. Resources from the Metropolitan Museum of Art illustrate the change in technology that took jobs away from craftspeople and gave them to machines.

2381. **The Industrial World**. Videocassette. Color. 30 min. WGBH Educational Foundation, distributor. Washington, DC: Annenberg/CPB, 1989. $650 set; $29.95 ea. (The Western Tradition, Program 42). 11 up

The professor presenting this topic projects his excitement for history as he provides insight into the people, politics, thoughts, and events that have shaped western society. Resources from the Metropolitan Museum of Art illustrate how the Industrial Revolution changed the balance of work between the city and the countryside.

2382. **Inside Burma: Land of Fear**. Videocassette. Color. 52 min. Carlton UK, distributor. Oley, PA: Bullfrog Films, 1997. $250. 10 up

Aung San Suu Kyi, Nobel Peace Prize winner, discusses Burma's change from a rich to a poor country under a military dictatorship. She has been under house arrest for six years because of her support of the people and of democracy.

2383. **Inside Japan, Inc**. Videocassette. Color. 60 min. Pacific Basin Institute, distributor. Washington, DC: Annenberg/CPB, 1992. $275 series; $29.95 ea. (Pacific Century). 11 up

This series looks at 150 years of the Pacific region's political and economic development, through maps, charts, archival footage, and interviews with journalists and historians. It examines each country's relationship with the United States. This segment examines the political, historical, and cultural bases for Japan's postwar economic expansion.

2384. **Into the Deep Freeze**. Videocassette. Color. 60 min. Falls Church, VA: Landmark Films, 1989. $295. (Man on the Rim: The Peopling of the Pacific). 9 up

The major concept examined in this video (one of eleven episodes) is the adaptation of mankind to life in Siberia. Both the necessary physical adjustments and the use of local resources in this cold environment become clear. Also included is the migration of peoples from Siberia to North and South America across the land bridge that formed after the last Ice Age.

2385. **Introducing South America**. Videocassette. Color. 22 min. Huntsville, TX: Educational Video Network, 1995. $49.95. 7 up

The history, geography, cities, and people of South America, from the Caribbean to Tierra del Fuego, Amazon to the Andes, and in between, come alive.

2386. **Invasion**. Videocassette. Color. 28 min. Centra, distributor. Princeton, NJ: Films for the Humanities and Sciences, 1993. $89.95. (Before Columbus). 9 up

The white man invaded three tribes: Cuna of Panama, Cree of Canada, and Panara of Brazil. Interviews with tribal leaders tell of their first encounters with the conqueror and the results: land grabbing, greed, and disease. Therefore, the celebration of Columbus's arrival in the New World causes joy for some and intense sadness for others.

2387. **Iran/Iraq Afghanistan**. Videocassette. Color. 80 min. Independent Television News, distributor. New York: Central Park Media, 1995. $29.95. (Wars in Peace). 10 up

The program focuses on the wars that have wracked the Middle East in the latter half of the twentieth century. Newsreels and documentary footage show the technology and emotional and economic cost of these wars for the citizens of the countries involved.

2388. **Israel**. Videocassette. Color. 20 min. Irwindale, CA: Barr Media, 1994. $1,170 series; $395 ea. (Middle East). 4 up

Israel has distinct geographic regions from the coast of the Mediterranean to the Jordan River. The video visits Jerusalem and discusses the world's three largest religions, Judaism, Christianity, and Islam. The history of religious and ethnic tension underlies the explanation of Israel's world position.

2389. **The Italian Romanesque**. Videocassette. Color. 26 min. New York: Academic and Entertainment Video, 1995. $29.95. ISBN 1-870512-24-6. 10 up

The achievements of the Italian Romanesque style were myriad. This video examines the art and architecture associated with this style from the eleventh and twelfth centuries, including the cloister and the tower.

2390. **Iwo Jima, Okinawa and the Push on Japan**. Videocassette. Color and B&W. 45 min. Bethesda, MD: Acorn Media, 1989. $19.95. (V for Victory). 7 up

After bitter island fighting on Iwo Jima during World War II, soldiers raised the flag on Mount Suribachi. Newsreel footage and stories from home aid this program about the fighting in the Pacific, including the devastating fire raids on Toyko and the suicidal Japanese kamikazes dive-bombing into American ships.

J

2391. **Jane Austen and Her World**. 5 videocassettes. Color. 24 min. ea. Princeton, NJ: Films for the Humanities and Sciences, 1995. $425 series; $89.95 ea. 7 up

Jane Austen recorded the early-nineteenth-century world of the British middle class. This video, which tells of her life and times, includes dramatized readings from her literary works and her unpublished private writings.

2392. **Japan: Japan Today**. Videocassette. Color. 15 min. Signet Productions, distributor. Morris Plains, NJ: Lucerne Media, 1995. $195. (The Changing Face of Asia). 6 up

The third in a series, this video explores Japan as it is today, after World War II.

2393. **Japan: Nation Reborn**. Videocassette. Color. 15 min. Signet Productions, distributor. Morris Plains, NJ: Lucerne Media, 1995. $195. (The Changing Face of Asia). 6 up

The second in a series, this program looks at Japan when it opened to the West.

2394. **Japan: The Sacred Islands**. Videocassette. Color. 15 min. Signet Productions, distributor. Morris Plains, NJ: Lucerne Media, 1995. $195. (The Changing Face of Asia). 6 up

This program, first in a series, gives the early history of Japan.

2395. **Jerusalem: Gates to the City**. Videocassette. Color. 31 min. Smithsonian Folkways Recording, distributor. Ben Lomond, CA: Video Project, 1997. $59.95. 8 up

Some of the myriad stories of the historical Jerusalem and routines of the people living in contemporary Jerusalem reveal that the city is more than a collection of stones.

2396. **Jewish Communities of the Middle Ages**. Videocassette. Color. 30 min. Museum of the Jewish Diaspora, distributor. Teaneck, NJ: Ergo Media, 1995. $39.95. 7 up

Babylonia, Span, and Ashkenaz (Germany and France) were three different Jewish communities that flourished during the Middle Ages.

2397. **Johann Strauss**. Videocassette. Color. 26 min. Chicago: Clearvue/eav, 1997. $60. 7 up

Johann Strauss (1825-1899), known as the "Waltz King," lived in Vienna when the waltz craze hit the city, and he captialized on it. Footage of Vienna, paintings, and reenactments from Strauss's life emphasize the importance of his music.

2398. **John Locke**. Videocassette. Color. 52 min. Princeton, NJ: Films for the Humanities and Sciences, 1995. $149. 9 up

This video profiles the life of John Locke (1632–1704), an English philosopher who professed empiricism.

2399. **Jordan, the Desert Kingdom**. Videocassette. Color. 51 min. San Ramon, CA: IVN Communications, 1995. $24.99. (Video Visits). 7 up

Deserts and mountains form the landscape and background for the history of this country. The ancient ruins, Crusader castles, Hadrian's Arch, Byzantine mosaics, Petra, and other sites help to establish its continuity. The video looks at these as it presents interviews with the Bedouin and shows the sophistication of Amman.

2400. **Juan and Evita Peron**. Videocassette. Color. 30 min. Schlessinger Video, distributor. Bala Cynwyd, PA: Library Video, 1994. $39.95. ISBN 1-57225-032-1. (Hispanic and Latin American Heritage). 7 up

Biographical information and an overview of the achievements of Juan and Evita Peron, according to various experts, help to establish the contributions they made to Latin American history.

2401. **Judaism: The Religion of the People**. Videocassette. Color. Delphi Productions, distributor. Niles, IL: United Learning, 1994. $95. ISBN 1-56007-396-9. 7 up

On location in Israel, Egypt, and the United States, the video traces the history, development, and practice of Judaism.

$\boxed{\text{K}}$

2402. **Kanehsatake: 270 Years of Resistance**. Videocassette. Color. 120 min. National Film Board of Canada. Oley, PA: Bullfrog Films, 1994. $275. 10 up

The Mohawks and the Canadian army had an armed confrontation at the Mercier bridge in Quebec. *2nd Place, American Indian Film & Video Competition; Special Jury Award, San Francisco International Film Festival.*

2403. **Kontum Diary**. Videocassette. Color. 56 min. Oakland, CA: Video Project, 1995. $150. 9 up

After a battle during the Vietnam War, a nineteen-year-old American soldier found the diary of a North Vietnamese soldier. Later he had it translated, and what he found was poetry. The film chronicles the journey of the soldier, Paul Reed, as he returns to Vietnam with the diary and gives it to its owner. *Worldfest-Charleston Gold* and *New York Festivals*.

2404. **Korea/Vietnam**. Videocassette. Color. 80 min. Independent Television News, distributor. New York: Central Park Media, 1995. $29.95. (Wars in Peace). 10 up

The United States has been involved in two long wars since World War II. This program examines the role of the United States in those two wars through battle films, newsreels, and other documentary footage.

$\boxed{\text{L}}$

2405. **Lascaux Revisited: Exploring Cave Art**. Videocassette. Color. 35 min. French Ministry of Culture, distributor. Glenview, IL: Crystal, 1995. $29.99. 7 up

This video offers a tour of the cave wall paintings that artists created over 17,000 years ago. Special transition from lines on the walls to superimposed lines give a sense of what the lines represent. Because the actual caves have been closed to the public for almost forty years, this video is one of the best ways to see it.

2406. **The Last Seven Months of Anne Frank**. Videocassette. Color. 75 min. AVA Productions, distributor. Teaneck, NJ: Ergo Media, 1995. $49.95. 9 up

Surviving witnesses tell about the final days of Anne Frank. These were days about which she did not write in her diary.

2407. **The Late Middle Ages**. Videocassette. Color. 30 min. WGBH Educational Foundation, distributor. Washington, DC: Annenberg/CPB, 1989. $650 set; $29.95 ea. (The Western Tradition, Program 23). 11 up

The professor presenting this topic projects his excitement for history as he provides insight into the people, politics, thoughts, and events that have shaped western society. Resources from the Metropolitan Museum of Art illustrate this period of time from approximately A.D. 1000 until 1300.

2408. **Legacies**. Videocassette. Color. 30 min. Ontario, Canada: TVOntario, 1990. $499 series; $99 ea. (Ancient Civilizations). 6 up

Part of a series examining the origins of civilizations, the video investigates the human needs to search for food, to have security, and to be creative. This video looks at the debt owed to past civilizations, especially Rome. Architecture, law, government, language, drama, medicine, mathematics, and writing all come from the ancient world.

2409. **Legacy**. Videocassette. Color. 22 min. New York: Cinema Guild, 1994. $195. 9 up

The presentation questions the accepted Columbus myth by noting that the Tainos were not the unfriendly savages. Evidence from archaeological digs gives contrary views of the Columbus story.

2410. **Legacy of the Mound Builders**. Videocassette. Color. 17 min. Camera One, distributor. Eugene, OR: New Dimensions Media, 1995. $240. 5 up

The Mound Builders lived in North America and built an elaborate trade network that extended over half the continent more than 2,000 years ago. *Council on Nontheatrical Events, Golden Eagle*.

2411. **Lenin According to Lenin**. Videocassette. Color. 58 min. Pathe Cinema, distributor. Princeton, NJ: Films for the Humanities and Sciences, 1991. $159. 7-up

Lenin's own words tell the story of the Bolshevik rise to power.

2412. **Lenin and His Legacy**. Videocassette. Color. 30 min. Visnews, distributor. Princeton, NJ: Films for the Humanities and Sciences, 1990. $249. 7 up

This video recounts Lenin's (1870–1924) life and the legacy of communism that he left.

2413. **Lenin and Me, Parts 1 & 2**. Videocassette. Color. 30 min. each part. Derry, NH: Chip Taylor Communications, 1997. $99.99 each part. 9 up

The video examines the life of Lenin, a man whose hatreds made him responsible for the deaths of many Russians, through the eyes of a young Russian immigrant, Arthur Chidlovski. Chidlovski wants to know why his own parents and teachers revered this man. His search reveals twentieth-century Russian political history.

2414. **Life, Times and Wonders of Athens and Ancient Greece**. Videocassette. Color. 70 min. Chicago: Questar Video, 1995. $19.95. ISBN 1-56855-056-1. (Great Cities of the Ancient World). 7 up

Through a study of the twenty-five most significant structures and monuments from ancient Greece, this video looks at the contributions of the Greek civilization. Live video of contemporary sites morphs into computerized reconstructions of the sites, which are now in ruins. They include the Acropolis in the fifth century B.C., the Statue of Athena, the Parthenon, the Agora, the Theatre of Dionysus, Olympia, the Temple of Zeus, and Delphi's Temple of Apollo.

2415. **Life, Times and Wonders of the Pyramids and the Cities of the Pharoahs**. Videocassette. Color. 75 min. Chicago: Questar Video, 1995. $29.95. ISBN 1-56855-057-X. (Great Cities of the Ancient World). 7 up

To create the Egypt of 5,000 years ago, Egyptologists, historians, and computer and video artists have collaborated. Live video of contemporary sites morphs into computerized reconstructions of twenty-five structures, including the Temple of Luxor, the Temple of Ammon at Karnak, and the Temple of Ramses. The Egyptians were able to build magnificent structures using simple tools and great human effort.

2416. **The Lines**. Videocassette. Color. 50 min. Bethesda, MD: Acorn Media, 1993. $19.95. (Mysteries of Peru). 9 up

This video, one of two in the series, tries to explore both the mysteries and achievements of pre-Inca civilization. On the Peruvian desert floor, over 2,000 years ago, someone drew lines and large animal figures now called the Nazca Lines. One can only view them from the air. Interviews with research scientists lead to a discussion of the purpose of these mysterious creations.

2417. **Linnea in Monet's Garden**. Videocassette. Color. 30 min. New York: First Run/Icarus, 1994. $19.95. 5 up

This video helps viewers to understand Monet's work. Actual shots of Monet's garden today in differing lights, which are then blended into the oil painting, gives the sense of nature's importance to Monet and the other Impressionists. *Association for Library Service to Children Notable Film.*

2418. **A Little Tailor's Christmas Story**. Videocassette. Color. 14 min. Irwindale, CA: Barr Media, 1994. $290. 7-up

This dramatization, set in Germany in 1936, shows Mrs. Rubenstein threatening to tell everyone in town that the tailor Schiller has lost her family's clothes. As he searches, someone delivers his Nazi Secret Service card. He wields his newly found power over Mrs. Rubenstein.

2419. **Lodz Ghetto**. Videocassette. Color and B&W. 118 min. Jewish Heritage Project, distributor. Bethesda, MD: Acorn Media, 1994. $29.95. ISBN 1-56938-054-6. 9 up

The video begins with the German invasion of Poland in 1939 and tells the story, using documents, speeches, and diaries as sources, of the 200,000 Jews who went into the Lodz ghetto and of the 800 who survived until the Russian liberation in 1945. The difference between Lodz and other ghettos was that a large Jewish workforce produced uniforms and ammunition for the Germans in factories within the ghetto.

2420. **London: City of Majesty**. Videocassette. Color. 48 min. New York: V.I.E.W. Video, 1993. $39.98. ISBN 0-8030-1053-2. (Museum City Videos). 7 up

The video gives an overview of 2,000 years of London's history, from the Romans to the present, by looking at its buildings, statues, paintings, and literary works.

2421. **The Lonely Struggle: Marek Edelman, Last Hero of the Warsaw Ghetto Uprising**. Videocassette. Color. 60 min. AVA Productions, distributor. Teaneck, NJ: Ergo Media, 1995. $39.95. 9 up

The sole surviving member of the leadership in the Warsaw Ghetto Uprising, Dr. Edelman gives an account of the Jewish youngsters who encouraged a decimated ghetto population to fight against the Germans.

2422. **The Longest Hatred: The History of Anti-Semitism**. 2 videocassettes. Color. 2 hrs. WGBH Educational Foundation, distributor. Princeton, NJ: Films for the Humanities and Sciences, 1993. $159 set. 10 up

In three parts on two videocassettes, this program explores anti-Semitism from its first known beginning, through the Holocaust, to the situation today. The first part, "From the Cross to the Swastika," covers the Jews in Roman times and the historical basis for the association of Jews with money. The second, "Enemies of the Nation," looks at anti-Semitism today as a result of post–Cold-War nationalism. The third part, "Between Moses and Muhammed," details the Israeli-Arab conflicts, focusing on the Palestine situation.

2423. **Lost Childhood: The Boys of Birkenau**. Videocassette. Color. 48 min. Boys of Birkenau, distributor. Chicago, IL: SVE & Churchill Media, 1997. $79.95. 7 up

Men who survived the Holocaust together in the Auschwitz-Birkenau concentration camp meet on their 50th anniversary of escape, and while recalling their own trials and loss, plead for others not to forget what happened.

2424. **Lost City of the Aegean**. Videocassette. Color. 28 min. Princeton, NJ: Films for the Humanities and Sciences, 1994. $149. 7 up

Prepared for The Learning Channel's Archaeology series, this video looks at the excavations of the city of Akrotiri on the island of Thera in the Aegean and posits that this might have been the legendary Atlantis. The people of this Minoan colony lived on an island that produced the largest volcanic eruption in the last 20,000 years (1628 B.C.E.). The city's frescoes were preserved, as was the underground indoor plumbing; the inhabitants apparently had enough warning to escape.

2425. **Lost Tomb of the Sons of Ramses II**. Videocassette. Color. 15 min. Derry, NH: Chip Taylor Communications, 1993. $145. 7 up

Egyptologist Kent Weeks explains that he located the tomb of Ramses II's twelve sons, all of whom died before Ramses did, by using historical documents and modern scientific tools, along with common sense. This archaeological discovery, probably the most significant in the twentieth century, was made near Luxor (formerly Thebes) in Egypt.

2426. **Lost Treasures of Troy**. Videocassette. Color. 28 min. Princeton, NJ: Films for the Humanities and Sciences, 1994. $149. 7 up

When Heinrich Schliemann found the gold treasures of Troy at the end of the nineteenth century, he took them to Germany, and they disappeared after World War II. Only recently, they were found in the basement of the Pushkin Museum in Moscow. The video discusses the science of archaeology and the greed of warring nations.

2427. **The Lucky Ones: Allied Airmen and Buchenwald**. Videocassette. Color. 46 min. New York: National Film Board of Canada, 1994. $295. 9 up

In World War II, the Nazis captured 168 Allied airmen and held them at Buchenwald. They did not tell of the horrors they endured and witnessed until they had a reunion. As they walked around Buchenwald remembering, they decided to break the silence.

M

2428. **Machu Picchu Revealed**. Videocassette. Color. 20 min. Huntsville, TX: Educational Video Network, 1995. $49.95. 7 up

This program provides a brief overview of pre-Columbian civilizations in the Andes by locating the Incas in time and place (c. A.D. 1200–1525) and trying to explain the latest theories about the reasons for and the building of Machu Picchu.

2429. **Mandela: From Prison to President**. Videocassette. Color. 52 min. Princeton, NJ: Films for the Humanities and Sciences, 1995. $149. 7 up

Nelson Mandela spent twenty-seven years in a South African prison before he was freed and elected to the presidency.

2430. **Married with a Star**. Videocassette. Color. 33 min. AVA Productions, distributor. Teaneck, NJ: Ergo Media, 1995. $39.95. 7 up

A Dutch Jewish wedding occurred on May 25, 1942. The film of this wedding lay unnoticed for fifty years. The program looks at the wedding of this couple and many of their wedding guests who did not survive World War II.

2431. **Martin Frobisher's Gold Mine**. Videocassette. Color. 25.36 min. New York: National Film Board of Canada, 1996. $150. 7 up

Martin Frobisher took three trips across the Atlantic looking for a northern route to the East through modern-day Canada. The video, filmed on-site at his camp on Baffin Island, reveals his attempts and shows the progress.

2432. **Martin Luther: Beginning of the Reformation**. Videocassette. Color. 14.45 min. Chicago: Encyclopaedia Britannica, 1993. $99. ISBN 0-8347-9990-1. 6 up

Filmed on location in Germany, the program presents the main events in Martin Luther's life during the sixteenth century that led to his conflict with church doctrine. Pictures, letters, historical sketches, and shots of historical buildings and statues round out the information.

2433. **Martin Luther: Translating the Bible**. Videocassette. Color. 13.59 min. Chicago: Encyclopaedia Britannica, 1993. $99. ISBN 0-8347-9990-1. 6 up

After the Diet of Worms, Martin Luther took refuge in Wartburg, where he began to translate the Bible from Latin into German, the vernacular of the people. In the video, the second of two on Martin Luther, views of historical sketches, paintings, maps, and historical books, including Bibles, augment the production.

2434. **The Maya**. Videocassette. Color. 30 min. Schlessinger Video, distributor. Bala Cynwyd, PA: Library Video, 1993. $39.95. (Indians of North America). 4-10

This video tells the history and culture of the Maya, a civilization that reached its height around A.D. 300-900. It focuses on the unique history of the Maya, using photographs and film footage. It also discusses government, spiritual life, myths, and the role of women in that culture. The architecture and city planning, mathematics and calendar, and hieroglyphic writing system make the culture special.

2435. **The Mayans and Aztecs**. Videocassette. Color. 20 min. Chariot Productions, distributor. Niles, IL: United Learning, 1997. $99. 6-8

The video presents the history of the ancient civilizations of the Aztecs, who lived in Mexico before the Spanish explorers arrived, and Mayans who lived in the vicinity around 600.

2436. **Medieval Times: Life in the Middle Ages (A.D. 1000-1450)**. Videocassette. Color. 30 min. Niles, IL: United Learning, 1992. $136. 5 up

Historical reenactments and on-site filming at Penhow Castle in the British Isles help to illustrate life in the Middle Ages. It shows the lifestyles of the rich nobles, knights, soldiers, clergy, and serfs, and demonstrates how they interacted.

2437. **Medieval Women**. Videocassette. Color. 24 min. Chicago: International Film Bureau, 1989. $245. 6 up

This program shows the perception of women during the European Middle Ages and examines their daily lives.

2438. **Meiji: Asia's Response to the West**. Videocassette. Color. 60 min. Pacific Basin Institute, distributor. Washington, DC: Annenberg/CPB, 1992. $275 series; $29.95 ea. (Pacific Century). 11 up

This series looks at 150 years of the Pacific region's political and economic development, through maps, charts, archival footage, and interviews with journalists and historians. It examines each country's relationship with the United States. This video examines the political, social, and cultural changes that occurred in Japan when it was opened to the West following the arrival of Commodore Matthew Perry and his "black ships" of the United States Navy.

2439. **Memories of Childhood and War**. Videocassette. Color. 51 min. Washington, DC: Global View, 1990. $35. 9 up

The film chronicles Eastern Europe's history since World War I, using the story of Hungarian children orphaned by World War II to focus on the tragedy of the two world wars.

2440. **Mesopotamia**. Videocassette. Color. 30 min. WGBH Educational Foundation, distributor. Washington, DC: Annenberg/CPB, 1989. $650 set; $29.95 ea. (The Western Tradition, Program 3). 11 up

The professor presenting this topic projects his excitement for history as he provides insight into the people, politics, thoughts, and events that have shaped western society. Resources from the Metropolitan Museum of Art illustrate the ancient civilizations that have been rediscovered in the fertile crescent of Mesopotamia.

2441. **Mexico: The Heritage**. Videocassette. Color. 20 min. Evanston, IL: Altschul Group, 1993. $275. 4-8

One of three in a series, this video divides the history of Mexico into three time periods: pre-Columbian, Spanish colonial (lasting three centuries), and political independence, which began in 1917. Then it covers the attitudes and directions that Mexico has taken as a nation.

2442. **Mexico: The People of the Sun**. Videocassette. Color. 18 min. Briarcliff Manor, NY: Benchmark Media, 1995. $395. (World Geography and History). 5-7

The video shows how the cultures in Mexico have intermingled and how this has affected the way people live.

2443. **Mexico: Yesterday and Today**. Videocassette. Color. 19 min. Madison, WI: Knowledge Unlimited, 1993. $55. ISBN 1-55933-149-9. 7 up

In a thorough overview of major events in Mexican history, this video covers varied aspects of those events and the background for various troubles, usually cultural clashes. It simultaneously informs viewers about the geography, religion, politics, and native peoples.

2444. **The Middle Ages**. Videocassette. Color. 30 min. WGBH Educational Foundation, distributor. Washington, DC: Annenberg/CPB, 1989. $650 set; $29.95 ea. (The Western Tradition, Program 19). 11 up

The professor presenting this topic projects his excitement for history as he provides insight into the people, politics, thoughts, and events that have shaped western society. Resources from the Metropolitan Museum of Art illustrate the Middle Ages, which lasted generally from the fall of the Roman Empire in A.D. 476 until around 1000.

2445. **Middle Ages School Kit**. 4 videocassettes. Color. 29 min. ea. Alexandria, VA: PBS Video, 1989. $200. 5-10

David Macauley narrates these videos, which include animated productions of his books *Castle* and *Cathedral*. The live-action sequences show him visiting towers, spires, buttresses, roofs, and moats of castles in England and cathedrals in France. Extensive supportive material aids teachers.

2446. **Middle America: Mexico to Venezuela and the Caribbean Islands**. Videocassette. Color. 18 min. Briarcliff Manor, NY: Benchmark Media, 1995. $395. (World Geography and History). 5-7

The video demonstrates how physical geography affects the lives of people in Middle America, particularly as to how they make a living and the choices they have.

2447. **Middle East**. 2 videocassettes. Color. 60 min. ea. Falls Church, VA: Landmark Films, 1993. $495. 9 up

Two individual titles help to tell about the conflicts in the Middle East during the twentieth century. The videos are *1900–1956: From the End of the Ottoman Empire to the Suez Crisis* and *1956–1991: From the Suez Crisis to the Gulf War*.

2448. **Middle East: History and Culture**. Videocassette. Color. 20 min. Irwindale, CA: Barr Media, 1994. $1,170 series; $395 ea. (Middle East). 4 up

From the Sumerians (who invented cuneiform writing) to the present, the Middle East encompasses an extraordinary history. The modern civilizations, including the Egyptians, Jews, Muslims, Romans, Persians, and Greeks, have close ties to the past. Warring tensions have oppressed various parts of the region for centuries, from the Romans to the oil trade, but the inhabitants of the area have made some attempts toward peace.

2449. **Mirror, Mirror: Northern Ireland**. Videocassette. Color. 58 min. BBC Wales/Primedia, distributor. Princeton, NJ: Films for the Humanities and Sciences, 1994. $149. (Nationalism: Blood and Belonging). 7 up

The Loyalists of Northern Ireland are Protestant, anti-Catholic, anti-European, anti-Irish, and monarchist, belonging to the United Kingdom but apart because of clinging to tradition. Although not a history as such, this recounting of a conflict that has lasted for twenty-five years gives a sense of why Ireland remains divided.

2450. **The Modern Philosophers**. Videocassette. Color. 30 min. WGBH Educational Foundation, distributor. Washington, DC: Annenberg/CPB. 1989. $650 set; $29.95 ea. (The Western Tradition, Program 36). 11 up

The professor presenting this topic projects his excitement for history as he provides insight into the people, politics, thoughts, and events that have shaped western society. Resources from the Metropolitan Museum of Art illustrate the thought of the eighteenth century through such men as Voltaire, Jean-Jacques Rousseau, Montesquieu, Thomas Paine, Thomas Jefferson, and Benjamin Franklin.

2451. **The Mongol Empire, 1247**. Videocassette. Color. 30 min. Maryland Public Television, distributor. Washington, DC: Zenger Video, 1989. $395 series; $69.95 ea. (Timeline, Series I). 9 up

This program presents history as today's television news would relate the events. The narrator, Steve Bell, switches live to battlefield reporters, news analysts, and interviewers for the day's news. For the Mongol Empire, the news comes live in 1247, the year in which Buda was established to replace Pest, six years after the Mongols destroyed it.

2452. **The Moon Woman's Sisters: Highland Guatemala Maya Weaving**. Videocassette. Color. 40 min. Thousand Oaks, CA: Conejo, 1993. $40. 6 up

A brief introduction to four pre-Columbian Maya sites leads to a demonstration of the ancient art of back-strap weaving. While weaving, women share their daily lives. *Honorable Mention, Columbus International Film & Video Festival; 3rd Place, BVF.*

2453. **More than Rice**. Videocassette. Color. 51 min. New York: Carousel, 1997. $200. 9 up

The video looks at China's people and their past, present, and future from various perspectives.

2454. **Morocco: The Past and Present of** *Djemma El Fna*. Videocassette. Color. 18 min. New York: Filmakers Library, 1995. $175. 7 up

Arab and Berber cultures have met in Marrakech's main square for centuries. It has been a stop on the caravan trade route between the Sahara to the south and Spain to the north. The square's storytellers, musicians, dancers, acrobats, and snake charmers represent centuries of ritual and tradition. *Silver Award, Houston World Fest; Middle East Studies Association; Director's Choice, Atlanta Film & Video Festival.*

2455. **Mummies and the Wonders of Ancient Egypt**. 4 videocassettes. 50 min. ea. Color. A&E Television Networks, producer. New York: New Video Group, 1996. $59.95 series. ISBN 1-56501-773-0. 7 up

The four parts of this series are *Great Pyramids, The Sphinx, Hieroglyphs,* and *King Tut*. Historical reenactments along with historian and archaeologist interviews give insight into the culture, architecture, religion, and expectations of the Egyptian people.

2456. **Munch and Ensor: Fathers of Expressionism**. Videocassette. Color. 21 min. New York: Academic and Entertainment Video, 1995. $29.95. ISBN 1-879512-21-1. 10 up

The human actions of war and misery influenced these masters of Expressionism, the Norwegian Edward Munch (1863–1944), known for *The Scream* (1893), and the Belgian Baron James Ensor (1860–1949), known for works painted around 1900.

2457. **The Mystery of the Cave Paintings**. Videocassette. Color. 16.12 min. Morris Plains, NJ: Lucerne Media, 1996. $145. 3-8

This look at the French and Spanish caves where Ice Age artwork still exists reveals that a six-year-old found the cave in Spain and that teenagers found the Lescaux caves in France. Additionally, the computer graphics and examination of the way the paintings might have been done over 30,000 years ago will interest young viewers.

2458. **Mystery of the Maya**. Videocassette. Color. 25 min. Evanston, IL: Wombat, 1990. $145. (Tapestry of Civilization). 9 up

The Mayan civilization left behind examples of its advanced architecture, including the Mayan arch, the use of concrete, and sculpture and bas relief as decorations for buildings. Other important contributions included mathematics and astronomy. The Mayans did not borrow from other civilizations, and the mystery remains as to why they abandoned their cities while the civilization still flourished.

2459. **Mystery of the Maya**. Videocassette. Color. 38 min. New York: National Film Board of Canada, 1996. $195. 6-9

The Maya lived in Southeast Mexico and South America, and this video discusses their lives through dramatizations and photographs of their ruins. Among their achievements were a system of mathematics, writing, and astronomical discoveries.

2460. **The Mystery of the Pyramids**. Videocassette. Color. 23 min. Irwindale, CA: Barr Media, 1990. $295. 4-9

The video examines several different explanations for the building of the pyramids around 4,000 years ago. It also visits the Pyramid of Cheops, examines likely methods of construction, and discusses mysteries associated with the pyramids through the centuries.

2461. **The Mystic Lands Series: Australia: Dreamtime**. Videocassette. Color. 25 min. Duncan Group. Niles, IL: United Learning, 1997. $727.55 set; $79.95 ea. 9 up

The video looks at the aborigines in Australia and their concept of time and spiritual awareness.

2462. **The Mystic Lands Series: Bali: Island of a Thousand Temples**. Videocassette. Color. 25 min. Duncan Group. Niles, IL: United Learning, 1997. $727.55 set; $79.95 ea. 9 up

The religion behind Bali's temples shows the traditions of the people.

2463. **The Mystic Lands Series: Bhutan: Land of the Thunder Dragon**. Videocassette. Color. 25 min. Duncan Group. Niles, IL: United Learning, 1997. $727.55 set; $79.95 ea. 9 up

The people of Bhutan follow Buddhist beliefs, and this video examines their spiritual journeys.

2464. **The Mystic Lands Series: Burma: Triumph of the Spirit**. Videocassette. Color. 25 min. Duncan Group. Niles, IL: United Learning, 1997. $727.55 set; $79.95 ea. 9 up

Originally a Hindu country, Bali's religion is a mixture with an underlying belief in reincarnation.

2465. **The Mystic Lands Series: Egypt: Circle of Life**. Videocassette. Color. 25 min. Duncan Group. Niles, IL: United Learning, 1997. $727.55 set; $79.95 ea. 9 up

The video examines Egypt's religions through the centuries.

2466. **The Mystic Lands Series: Greece: Isle of Revelation**. Videocassette. Color. 25 min. Duncan Group. Niles, IL: United Learning, 1997. $727.55 set; $79.95 ea. 9 up

The pantheon of mythological gods and goddesses associated with the ancient Greeks had their places of worship scattered throughout the isles.

2467. **The Mystic Lands Series: Haiti: Dance of the Spirit**. Videocassette. Color. 25 min. Duncan Group. Niles, IL: United Learning, 1997. $727.55 set; $79.95 ea. 9 up

Many of Haiti's people follow Voodoo, a folk religion with a Christian god ruling African deities.

2468. **The Mystic Lands Series: Jerusalem: Mosaic of Faith**. Videocassette. Color. 25 min. Duncan Group. Niles, IL: United Learning, 1997. $727.55 set; $79.95 ea. 9 up

The city of Jerusalem is the center for three major world religions—Christianity, Judaism, and Islam.

2469. **The Mystic Lands Series: Maya: Messages in Stone**. Videocassette. Color. 25 min. Duncan Group. Niles, IL: United Learning, 1997. $727.55 set; $79.95 ea. 9 up

The Mayan ruins from 600 to 900 in South America reveal the ritual practices of the Mayan culture through extant hieroglyphs.

2470. **The Mystic Lands Series: Peru: Kingdom in the Clouds**. Videocassette. Color. 25 min. Duncan Group. Niles, IL: United Learning, 1997. $727.55 set; $79.95 ea. 9 up

The Incan culture in Peru existed before the Spanish conquerors arrived with its religion focusing on worship of the sun.

2471. **The Mystic Lands Series: Taj Mahal: Heaven on Earth**. Videocassette. Color. 25 min. Duncan Group. Niles, IL: United Learning, 1997. $727.55 set; $79.95 ea. 9 up

One of the most beautiful buildings in the world is the Taj Mahal, the mausoleum that the Mughal Shah Jahan began in 1632 for his wife. It includes a mosque on the grounds.

2472. **The Mystic Lands Series: Varanasi: City of Light**. Videocassette. Color. 25 min. Duncan Group. Niles, IL: United Learning, 1997. $727.55 set; $79.95 ea. 9 up

Varanasi, also called Benares, Banaras, or Kashi, is one of the Hindu's seven sacred cities.

2473. **Nagasaki Journey**. Videocassette. Color. 27 min. Independent Documentary, distributor. Oakland CA: Video Project, 1995. $79. 9 up

Trying to give a balanced approach, this video presents both the American and the Japanese perspective on the bombing of Nagasaki, through personal stories of two Japanese survivors and eyewitness accounts by an American Marine who occupied the city after the end of the war.

2474. **The National Monarchies**. Videocassette. Color. 30 min. WGBH Educational Foundation, distributor. Washington, DC: Annenberg/CPB, 1989. $650 set; $29.95 ea. (The Western Tradition, Program 24). 11 up

The professor presenting this topic projects his excitement for history as he provides insight into the people, politics, thoughts, and events that have shaped western society. Resources from the Metropolitan Museum of Art illustrate the monarchies that evolved out of the feudal system of government.

2475. **Nelson Mandela: The Man**. Videocassette. Color. 48 min. Henderson, NV: LDA Communications, 1995. $59.95. 7 up

By blending narration, news clips, and photographs, this video gives an informative view of Nelson Mandela's life and of his commitment to freeing black South Africans from apartheid. It shows how racism and injustice can almost destroy a nation.

2476. **Nelson Mandela and the Struggle to End Apartheid**. Videocassette. Color. 27 min. Chatsworth, CA: Aims Media, 1995. $275. 9 up

Film footage and interviews with Nelson Mandela and other leaders of the Youth League and the ANC trace the political events in South Africa from 1950 through Mandela's release from prison in 1990.

2477. **A New Public**. Videocassette. Color. 30 min. WGBH Educational Foundation, distributor. Washington, DC: Annenberg/CPB, 1989. $650 set; $29.95 ea. (The Western Tradition, Program 45). 11 up

The professor presenting this topic projects his excitement for history as he provides insight into the people, politics, thoughts, and events that have shaped western society. Resources from the Metropolitan Museum of Art illustrate the beliefs of the populace in the nineteenth century.

2478. **1914–1918: World War I**. Videocassette. B&W. 25 min. Washington, DC: National Geographic, 1992. $110. 8 up

This video uses historical footage from World War I in describing the causes of the war. Intermingled with diplomatic information is the action of battle and pictures of some of the graves of the more than 10 million soldiers who died in those battles.

2479. **1917: Revolution in Russia**. Videocassette. B&W. 28 min. Washington, DC: National Geographic, 1988. $110. 9 up

This video introduces Tsar Nicholas, along with Lenin (1870–1924), Kerensky (1881–1970), Trotsky (1879–1940), Stalin (1879–1953), and others, as they fought for control of Russia and then the Soviet Union.

2480. **1945–1989: The Cold War**. Videocassette. Color. 25 min. Washington, DC: National Geographic, 1991. $110. 8 up

Through newsreel footage, the history of the verbal conflict between the United States and the Soviet Union comes to life. The presentation of both obscure and well-known events helps viewers understand why this hostility occurred.

2481. **North Africa and the Global War**. Videocassette. Color and B&W. 45 min. Bethesda, MD: Acorn Media, 1989. $19.95. (V for Victory). 7 up

General Dwight Eisenhower led U.S. forces in Operation Torch in North Africa during World War II. This video relates occurrence in that area to the Allied campaign in Burma, the battle for the Atlantic Ocean, and the air assault on Fortress Europe. The presentation includes newsreel footage and stories from the home front.

2482. **November's Children: Revolution in Prague**. Videocassette. Color. 58 min. Four Oaks Foundation, distributor. Santa Monica, CA: Pyramid, 1992. $295. 9 up

Interviews with student leaders and Vaclav Havel put into perspective the amazing event of the freedom of Czechoslovakia from Communist rule in 1989, after forty years of subjugation. The film footage shows the history as it was made.

O

2483. **Ocean of Wisdom**. Videocassette. Color. 29 min. Alexandria, VA: PBS Video, 1990. $49.95. 9 up

The Chinese invasion of Tibet led to the exile of the Dalai Lama, Tenzin Gyatso, to India in 1959. He has continued to call for compassion and forgiveness as the Chinese killed over 87,000 Tibetans, so that they have become a minority in their own country. The Dalai Lama won the Nobel Peace Prize in 1989 for his work of creating new monasteries in India; meanwhile, the Chinese destroy them in Tibet, where they have ruined all but 53 of the 6,000 there.

2484. **The October 1917 Revolution and After**. Videocassette. B&W. 28 min. Visnews, distributor. Princeton, NJ: Films for the Humanities and Sciences, 1991. $149. 7 up

This video, using Russian and western newsreel footage and Soviet propaganda films, documents the events of the October Revolution, from the defeat of the czar's armies, through the famine in Russia, to the overthrow of Nicholas and the Communists' assumption of power.

2485. **On the Town**. Videocassette. Color. 30 min. Ontario, Canada: TVOntario, 1990. $499 series; $99 ea. (Ancient Civilizations). 6 up

Part of a series examining the origins of civilizations, the video investigates the human needs for food, security, and creativity. This video looks at the cultural high points of civilizations, including art, literature, architecture, engineering, and technology.

2486. **Operation: Dragoon**. Videocassette. Color and B&W. 30 min. On Deck Home Entertainment, distributor. Thousand Oaks, CA: Goldhil Home Media, 1997. $19.95. 7 up

As Allied forces invaded Normandy, "Operation Dragoon" was occurring on the Mediterranean coast of France. Although controversial, this invasion destroyed Hitler's 19th Army and captured over 100,000 German prisoners. Its soldiers move through the south of France and met the Allied forces from Normandy.

2487. **Other Voices, Other Songs: The Armenians**. Videocassette. Color. 28.45 min. New York: Filmakers Library, 1990. $195. 7 up

Although Armenians have many things to try to preserve from their culture (including rugs, costumes, embroidery, ceramics, and musical instruments), the emphasis in this video is on folk dancing. Interviews with elderly Armenians authenticate some of the dances, such as the wedding dance in which dancers join dyed little fingers in symbolism.

2488. **Other Voices, Other Songs: The Greeks**. Videocassette. Color. 28 min. Sapphire, distributor. New York: Filmakers Library, 1990. $195. 7 up

Focusing on Greek music, this video discusses the methods of making music, including goatskin bagpipes, clay drum, and lute. Music has always been a major part of Greek tradition, and there is concern as to whether this tradition can continue in the modern world.

2489. **The Ottoman Empire**. Videocassette. Color. 28 min. Polonius Films, distributor. Chicago: International Film Bureau, 1992. $295. 9 up

Photos and live-action footage present the architecture and art of the Ottoman Empire as this video defines the history and culture of Ottoman Turkey, which lasted about 500 years from approximately A.D. 1300. At the end of the video, a discussion posits how the current Middle Eastern states evolved from the empire.

2490. **Our Hiroshima**. Videocassette. Color. 43 min. Princeton, NJ: Films for the Humanities and Sciences, 1997. $129. 9 up

When the atomic bomb was dropped on Hiroshima, Setsuko Nakamuro Thurlow was thirteen. Most of her family was killed. Her account, coupled with archival footage, describes this tragic event.

P

2491. **Pablo Neruda**. Videocassette. Color. 30 min. Schlessinger Video, distributor. Bala Cynwyd, PA: Library Video, 1994. $39.95. ISBN 1-57225-031-3. (Hispanic and Latin American Heritage). 7 up

Biographical information and an overview of Pablo Neruda's achievements, according to various experts, help to establish the literary contribution he made for Latin Americans and to the rest of the world.

2492. **The Painted Princess**. Videocassette. Color. 16 min. New York: Carousel, 1995. $175. 7 up

In the seventeenth century, Spanish artist Velasquez (1599–1660) created a portrait of the Princess Margarita and her court. This video uses live-action video and animation to make his painting come alive.

2493. **Pancho Villa**. Videocassette. Color. 30 min. Schlessinger Video, distributor. Bala Cynwyd, PA: Library Video, 1994. $39.95. ISBN 1-57225-034-8. (Hispanic and Latin American Heritage). 7 up

Biographical information and an overview of Pancho Villa's achievements, according to various experts, help to establish the contributions he made to Latin American history.

2494. **Paradise Postponed**. Videocassette. Color. 60 min. Falls Church, VA: Landmark Films, 1989. $395. 9 up

Although emphasizing the role of Iran in the contemporary world before the Ayatollah Ruhollah Khomeini's death, this video also covers the history and roots of Islamic fundamentalism, the role of Iran in the Iran-Iraq war, and the use of terrorism to destabilize the Middle East and other areas. The timely information helps in understanding this culture.

2495. **Pearl Harbor to Midway**. Videocassette. Color and B&W. 45 min. Bethesda, MD: Acorn Media, 1989. $19.95. (V for Victory). 7 up

Selected newsreels of the actual World War II battle begin with Japan's surprise attack on Pearl Harbor, followed by the U.S. change from a peacetime to a wartime economy. Coverage of the Flying Tigers and Doolittle's air raid precedes the great naval battle off Midway Island.

2496. **The Personal File of Anna Akhmatova**. Videocassette. B&W. 63 min. Oakland, CA: Video Project, 1991. $150. 11 up

The biography of this Soviet poet gives a sense of the frustration of living in a Communist regime when one has no control over one's life. Akhmatova endured wars, separation, and imprisonment of her only son before she died in 1966.

2497. **Peru's Treasure Tombs**. Videocassette. Color. 11 min. Washington, DC: National Geographic, 1997. $49. 4-9

The Moche people lived in Peru 1200 years before the Incas. They created adobe brick pyramids, ceramics and pottery, and gold and turquoise jewelry. Looters have taken valuables from their tombs, but a few items have been recovered.

2498. **Pilgrimage of Remembrance: Jews in Poland Today**. Videocassette. Color. 48 min. Teaneck, NJ: Ergo Media, 1991. $49.95. 9 up

Before World War II, over 3.5 million Jews lived in Poland. After the war, only 350,000 survived there, and now the number hovers around 6,000. Contemporary scenes of Polish towns, integrated with original black-and-white film and photographs, tell the history of the Jews in Poland and what pilgrims to this country might find.

2499. **Pilgrims and Puritans: The Struggle for Religious Freedom in England (1517-1692)**. Videocassette. Color. 22 min. Chariot Productions, distributor. Niles, IL: United Learning, 1997. $99. 7 up

The impetus to settle the New World was a direct result of the religious persecution on the Pilgrims and Puritans in Europe.

2500. **Pirates: Passion and Plunder**. 2 videocassettes. 2 hrs. New York: Questar, 1995. $39.95. ISBN 1-56855-065-0. 7 up

Two cassettes cover the *Pirates of the Old World: 400 BC–AD 1575* and *Pirates of the New World: 1575-1810 AD*. In the Old World, subjects include Greek myths and pirates; the first identifiable pirate, Queen Teuta of Yugoslavia; Ramses II of Egypt's attempts to stop piracy; Julius Caesar; the Vikings; the Barbary Corsairs; the Barbarosa brothers; Sir Francis Drake; Sir Walter Raleigh; Sir Henry Morgan; Pierre LeGrand; and Lolonais. Part II presents Captain William Kidd, Bloody Morgan, Spanish galleons, Blackbeard (Edward Teach), Mary Read, Anne Bonny, Calico Jack Rackham, Black Bart (Bartholomew Roberts), and Nathaniel Gordon. Some pirates were robbers while governments licensed others to "steal" for them.

2501. **Poland: A Proud Heritage**. Videocassette. Color. 55 min. Chicago: Clearvue, 1989. $30. (Video Visits). 6 up

By looking at several sites in Poland and discussing why they are considered worthy of visits, this video teaches about Poland's history. The video shows Warsaw; Cracow's Wawel Hill, the ancient seat of Polish kings; the Tatra mountains; Gdansk, the birthplace of Solidarity; and Auschwitz, now a memorial of the Holocaust.

2502. **The Polish Experience**. Videocassette. Color. 51 min. Washington, DC: Global View, 1990. $35. 9 up

Segments include short documentaries on Polish history, the Solidarity labor movement, and the impact of four decades of Soviet domination. An animation of the citizens illustrates the difficulty of escaping history.

2503. **The Power of Conscience: The Danish Resistance and the Rescue of the Jews**. Videocassette. Color. 56 min. Santa Monica, CA: Direct Cinema, 1995. $95. 9 up

The Danish people covertly rescued about 7,000 Jews and took them to safety in Sweden after the Germans occupied Denmark. This program documents the Nazi occupation of Denmark and the Danish resistance.

2504. **The Prince**. Videocassette. Color. 55 min. Medici Foundation, distributor. Irvindale, CA: Barr Media, 1994. $810 series; $150. (Renaissance: The Origins of the Modern World). 10 up

The research of Theodore Rabb, and interviews with experts and political figures, form the basis for this video, one of six in a series, that looks at the world of Renaissance princes and the centralized governments that developed during this period. Among those discussed are Cosimo di Medici, Prince Philip of Spain, and Queen Elizabeth I of England. Holding power, bureaucracy in government, and centralized power as espoused by Machiavelli are also covered.

2505. **Psychology of Neo-Nazism: Another Journey by Train to Auschwitz**. Videocassette. Color. 52 min. Princeton, NJ: Films for the Humanities and Sciences, 1993. $149. 9 up

The video shows four neo-Nazis from Scotland, Austria, France, and Germany who travel to Berlin and then to Auschwitz. At Auschwitz, Kitty Hart, a Holocaust survivor, tries to talk to them about her experiences. They refuse to listen, but the video continues with her story of watching the march of people every day to the crematoriums to be gassed while she was imprisoned during World War II.

R

2506. **The Reformation**. Videocassette. Color. 30 min. WGBH Educational Foundation, distributor. Washington, DC: Annenberg/CPB, 1989. $650 set; $29.95 ea. (The Western Tradition, Program 27). 11 up

The professor presenting this topic projects his excitement for history as he provides insight into the people, politics, thoughts, and events that have shaped western society. Resources from the Metropolitan Museum of Art illustrate this period of history, which officially began on October 31, 1517, when Martin Luther nailed his *95 Theses* onto the door of a church in Wittenburg, Germany.

2507. **Reformation Overview**. 2 videocassettes. Color. 90 min. ea. Christian History Institute, distributor. Worcester, PA: Vision Video, 1995. $99.95. 9 up

The program profiles men who were important figures in the Reformation and defines their philosophies. Subjects include John Wycliffe, John Hus, Martin Luther, Huldreich Zwingli, John Calvin, the Anabaptists, and William Tyndale.

2508. **Reinventing Japan**. Videocassette. Color. 60 min. Pacific Basin Institute, distributor. Washington, DC: Annenberg/CPB, 1992. $275 series; $29.95 ea. (Pacific Century). 11 up

This series looks at 150 years of the Pacific region's political and economic development, through maps, charts, archival footage, and interviews with journalists and historians.. This video looks at the relationship between the United States and Japan after World War II, when one was the conqueror and the other the conquered.

2509. **The Renaissance and the Age of Discovery**. Videocassette. Color. 30 min. WGBH Educational Foundation, distributor. Washington, DC: Annenberg/CPB, 1989. $650 set; $29.95 ea. (The Western Tradition, Program 25). 11 up

The professor presenting this topic projects his excitement for history as he provides insight into the people, politics, thoughts, and events that have shaped western society. Resources from the Metropolitan Museum of Art illustrate the rebirth of interest in classical learning that occurred after Petrarch found the works of Livy, in the early fourteenth century.

2510. **The Renaissance and the New World**. Videocassette. Color. 30 min. WGBH Educational Foundation, distributor. Washington, DC: Annenberg/CPB, 1989. $650 set; $29.95 ea. (The Western Tradition, Program 26). 11 up

The professor presenting this topic projects his excitement for history as he provides insight into the people, politics, thoughts, and events that have shaped western society. Resources from the Metropolitan Museum of Art illustrate the interest in lands across the ocean that was heightened with Columbus's first voyage in 1492.

2511. **Rendezvous Canada, 1606**. Videocassette. Color. 30 min. New York: National Film Board of Canada, 1989. $350. 5-10

Film from two living history museums presents life in Canada around 1606, when the French arrived to settle near the Indians already there. The oldest son of a Huron chief and the French governor of Acadia relate experiences through actors who speak either French, Huron, or Micmac, and give a sense of life at that time.

2512. **Return of the Maya**. Videocassette. Color. 29 min. Oakland, CA: Video Project, 1993. $85. 9 up

While assisting in the excavation of elaborate Mayan ruins (Mayan ancestry has been traced to 1500 B.C.) in Mexico, Mayan refugees from Guatemala rediscover their heritage and identity.

2513. **Return to My Shtetl Delatyn**. Videocassette. Color. 60 min. AVA Productions, distributor. Teaneck, NJ: Ergo Media, 1995. $39.95. 9 up

The filmmaker and his daughter accompanied his father back to his Galacian (now Poland/Ukraine) shtetl sixty-one years after he left during the Holocaust.

2514. **The Reunification of Germany**. Videocassette. Color. 32 min. Meridian Communications, distributor. Van Nuys, CA: Churchill Media, 1992. $400 set; $250 ea. (The Torn Iron Curtain). 8 up

This video traces the transition of the two Germanies into one, using historical and current film footage as well as interviews with young people from both countries. The video covers the history of the expansion of communism after World War II until the fall of the Berlin Wall.

2515. **Revolution and the Romantics**. Videocassette. Color. 30 min. WGBH Educational Foundation, distributor. Washington, DC: Annenberg/CPB, 1989. $29.95 (The Western Tradition, Program 43). 11 up

The professor presenting this topic projects his excitement for history as he provides insight into the people, politics, thoughts, and events that have shaped western society. Resources from the Metropolitan Museum of Art illustrate the reaction to the Enlightenment and the Industrial Revolution, which manifested itself in emphasis on the individual and a return to nature.

2516. **The Revolution in Eastern Europe**. Videocassette. Color. 32 min. Meridian Communications, distributor. Van Nuys, CA: Churchill Media, 1992. $400 set; $250 ea. (The Torn Iron Curtain). 8 up

The reunification of Germany became possible, in part, because the desire for freedom swept through Eastern Europe in the late 1980s. In looking at the spread of communism after World War II and the aborted Hungarian and Czechoslovakian revolutions, the importance and power of the underground movements become clear.

2517. **Ripples of Change: Japanese Women's Search for Self**. Videocassette. Color. 57 min. New York: Women Make Movies, 1993. $295. 11 up

A young Japanese immigrant to New York, Nanako Kurihara, looks at the Japanese women's movement when she returns to Japan. It began in 1970, but supposedly many women did not embrace it because they already had charge of all aspects of family life, including finances. Other aspects of Japanese culture are also delineated in this program.

2518. **Rise and Fall of the Soviet Union**. Videocassette. Color. 25 min. Washington, DC: National Geographic, 1994. $110. 10 up

Tracing Soviet political history from the 1917 Revolution to the union's collapse in December 1991, this video uses film clips from each era and comments by an expert in Soviet studies. Lenin, Stalin, Khrushchev, Brezhnev, Andropov, Ghernenko, Gorbachev, and Yeltsin are the leaders featured.

2519. **The Rise of Greek Civilization**. Videocassette. Color. 30 min. WGBH Educational Foundation, distributor. Washington, DC: Annenberg/CPB, 1989. $650 set; $29.95 ea. (The Western Tradition, Program 5). 11 up

The professor presenting this topic projects his excitement for history as he provides insight into the people, politics, thoughts, and events that have shaped western society. Resources from the Metropolitan Museum of Art illustrate the forces that helped the Greeks rise to a preeminent position in the Mediterranean area.

2520. **The Rise of Rome**. Videocassette. Color. 30 min. WGBH Educational Foundation, distributor. Washington, DC: Annenberg/CPB, 1989. $650 set; $29.95 ea. (The Western Tradition, Program 9). 11 up

The professor presenting this topic projects his excitement for history as he provides insight into the people, politics, thoughts, and events that have shaped western society. Resources from the Metropolitan Museum of Art illustrate the military and organizational power of the leaders who helped Rome succeed.

2521. **The Rise of the Church**. Videocassette. Color. 30 min. WGBH Educational Foundation, distributor. Washington, DC: Annenberg/CPB, 1989. $650 set; $29.95 ea. (The Western Tradition, Program 12). 11 up

The professor presenting this topic projects his excitement for history as he provides insight into the people, politics, thoughts, and events that have shaped western society. Resources from the Metropolitan Museum of Art illustrate the power of the early Christian church, especially after Constantine declared Christianity the official religion in A.D. 312.

2522. **The Rise of the Middle Class**. Videocassette. Color. 30 min. WGBH Educational Foundation, distributor. Washington, DC: Annenberg/CPB, 1989. $650 set; $29.95 ea. (The Western Tradition, Program 28). 11 up

The professor presenting this topic projects his excitement for history as he provides insight into the people, politics, thoughts, and events that have shaped western society. Resources from the Metropolitan Museum of Art illustrate the development of an urban society that was neither poor nor extremely wealthy—but was needed to keep cities organized.

2523. **The Rise of the Trading Cities**. Videocassette. Color. 30 min. WGBH Educational Foundation, distributor. Washington, DC: Annenberg/CPB, 1989. $650 set; $29.95. (The Western Tradition, Program 30). 11 up

The professor presenting this topic projects his excitement for history as he provides insight into the people, politics, thoughts, and events that have shaped western society. Resources from the Metropolitan Museum of Art illustrate the evolution of cities in which trade developed throughout Europe, from the wool trade in England to the cloth trade in Italy.

2524. **Rising Above: Women of Vietnam**. Videocassette. Color. 50 min. Global Graphics with TVE International, distributor. Oley, PA: Bullfrog Films, 1996. $250. ISBN 1-56029-660-7. (A Woman's Place). 7 up

Women in Vietnam tell about their lives, their courage through the struggle of finding resources for their families during the thirty years of French occupation and then with the war in which the Americans fought. The women include former Vietcong guerrilla fighter Kim Lai; the late Mrs. Nguyen Thi Dinh, or "Auntie Ba," who was a general and deputy commander of Vietcong forces; and Mrs. Binh, a negotiator with Henry Kissinger at the Paris peace talks.

2525. **The Road to Wannsee: Eleven Million Sentenced to Death**. Videocassette. Color. 50 min. AVA Productions, distributor. Teaneck, NJ: Ergo Media, 1995. $39.95. 6 up

The program traces Hitler's rise to political power, his political aims, and his obsession with eliminating the Jews.

2526. **The Road to War: Japan**. Videocassette. Color. 50 min. BBC, distributor. Columbus, OH: Coronet/MTI, 1989. $250. (Road to War). 9 up

The viewer sees, through old newsreels, war footage, and interviews with Japanese historians, the Japanese point of view on why the Japanese decided to challenge the United States in World War II. They wanted more space and desired a Western style of life, in addition to other factors.

2527. **The Road to War in the Persian Gulf**. Videocassette. Color. 24 min. Chicago: American School Publishers, 1991. $89. 9 up

This video covers the Iran-Iraq War, Operation Desert Storm, and the insurrections in Iraq after the fighting had supposedly ended. Two scholars with divergent views give the history of Turkish control, Kuwait's lack of credibility, and Iraq's military buildup.

2528. **The Roman Arena**. Videocassette. Color. 50 min. Princeton, NJ: Films for the Humanities and Sciences, 1994. $149. 7 up

Firsthand Roman accounts and modern research tell the evolution of the Roman use of violence as mass entertainment. Computer reconstruction of Roman events from contemporary on-site footage shows a typical day at the gladiatorial games. The official show of political power in the games originated from a custom whereby families would gather at the grave of the deceased on a funeral day and watch two slaves fight to the death. Their spilled blood supposedly appeased the deceased's spirit.

2529. **The Roman Empire**. Videocassette. Color. 30 min. WGBH Educational Foundation, distributor. Washington, DC: Annenberg/CPB, 1989. $650 set; $29.95 ea. (The Western Tradition, Program 10). 11 up

The professor presenting this topic projects his excitement for history as he provides insight into the people, politics, thoughts, and events that have shaped western society. Resources from the Metropolitan Museum of Art illustrate the highlights and contributions of the Roman Empire.

2530. **Rome: Art and Architecture**. 2 videocassettes. Color. 35 min. New York: Academic and Entertainment Video, 1995. $29.95. ISBN 1-879512-22-X/-23-8. 10 up

This video leads viewers through the great sites of Rome in telling the history of its art and architecture.

2531. **Rome: The Eternal City**. Videocassette. Color. 45 min. LDJ Productions, distributor. New York: V.I.E.W. Video, 1994. $19.98. ISBN 0-8030-1054-0. (Museum City Videos). 7 up

This program explores the history of Rome through its architecture, art, and literature by looking at the details of the works. Contemporary film footage shows these icons as they are today.

2532. **Rome Revisited: The Renewal of Splendor**. Videocassette. Color. 45 min. Dundas, Ontario, Canada: Masterpieces in Video, 1995. $29.95. 9 up

The art and architecture of Rome and the Vatican are highlighted in this video. The historical background from 1515 to 1762 shows the works of Michelangelo, Bernini, and Bramante; Saint Peter's; the Farnese Palace; the Trevi fountain; and other sites. In 1585, Rome was reorganized, and the pattern imposed then still exists.

2533. **The Roots of African Civilization**. Videocassette. Color. 25 min. Madison, WI: Knowledge Unlimited, 1996. $59.95. ISBN 1-55933-205-0. 5 up

The civilization and history of ancient West Africa, as presented in this video, show the importance of the oral tradition, art objects, and the emergence of the slave trade in the pre-colonial era.

$$S$$

2534. **Safekeeping**. Videocassette. Color. 30 min. Ontario, Canada: TVOntario, 1990. $499 series; $99 ea. (Ancient Civilizations). 6 up

Part of a series examining the origins of civilizations, the video investigates the human needs for food, security, and creativity. This video looks at the evolution of government from Athens into Sparta and to Republican Rome.

2535. **Schindler: The Documentary**. Videocassette. Color. 78 min. Princeton, NJ: Films for the Humanities and Sciences, 1995. $149. 7 up

Interviews with Oskar Schindler's wife and many of the Jews he saved goes beyond the Hollywood film.

2536. **The Scientist**. Videocassette. Color. 55 min. Medici Foundation, distributor. Irwindale, CA: Barr Media, 1994. $810 series; $150 ea. (Renaissance: The Origins of the Modern World). 10 up

The research of Theodore Rabb, and interviews with experts and political figures, form the basis for this video, one of six in a series, that studies the lives and works of scientists in the Renaissance. It reviews their development and looks at the role of the scientist in society.

2537. **The Second World War**. 2 videocassettes. Color. 3 hrs. Repa Film, distributor. No-Bull, 1994. $89.95 set. 9 up

This unique view of World War II consists of film footage collected from combat photographers who represented the United States, Germany, Spain, Japan, England, Canada, the Soviet Union, and France. All of the main conflicts appear here with a balanced view of the action.

2538. **The Second World War**. Videocassette. Color. 30 min. WGBH Educational Foundation, distributor. Washington, DC: Annenberg/CPB, 1989. $650 set; $29.95 ea. (The Western Tradition, Program 48). 11 up

The professor presenting this topic projects his excitement for history as he provides insight into the people, politics, thoughts, and events that have shaped western society. Resources from the Metropolitan Museum of Art illustrate the prolongation of the war into a second world war and detail the hideous destruction of war.

2539. **Semana Santa in Seville**. Videocassette. Color. 52 min. Washington, DC: Yellow Cat, 1995. $29.95. 11 up

The five-century-old celebration of Holy Week in Seville is filled with a variety of rituals. The video shows these rituals and the images used in the parade through the city, along with interviews of the people. *Columbus International Film and Video Honorable Mention.*

2540. **Sentimental Imperialists**. Videocassette. Color. 60 min. Pacific Basin Institute, distributor. Washington, DC: Annenberg/CPB, 1992. $275 series; $29.95 ea. (Pacific Century). 11 up

This series looks at 150 years of the Pacific region's political and economic development, through maps, charts, archival footage, and interviews with journalists and historians. It examines each country's relationship with the United States.

2541. **Shtetl**. Videocassette. Color. 23 min. New York: Cinema Guild, 1997. $99.95. ISBN 0-7815-0627-1. 6 up

Folk artist Mayer Kirshenblatt bases his paintings on his childhood in a Polish *shtetl*.

2542. **Siberia: Land of the Future**. Videocassette. Color. 58 min. Falls Church, VA: Landmark Films, 1995. $195. 9 up

In 1913, the Norwegian explorer Fridtjof Nansen journeyed into Siberia, hoping to begin developing and using its natural resources. In 1917, however, the Russian Revolution canceled those plans. Siberia became the place of exile. In 1990, a film crew retraced Nansen's journey, and this video is one of the results. It shows the native people and their culture as well as the problems facing the area today.

2543. **Sight by Touch**. Videocassette. Color. 27 min. Conex, distributor. Falls Church, VA: Landmark Films, 1995. $195. 6 up

Louis Braille (1809?-1852) developed a system of notation for the blind. At first his method was rejected, but it proved to be an effective way for the blind to interact with the printed word.

2544. **Sigrid Undset—A Portrait**. Videocassette. Color. 52 min. Falls Church, VA: Landmark Films, 1997. $195. 10 up

Sigrid Undset (1882-1949) won the Nobel Prize for Literature in 1928 after writing her epic work on medieval Norway. Her religion was very important in her work, and she spoke against injustice, especially Hitler during World War II, while living in the United States. The video looks mainly at her childhood, with recollections of family members.

2545. **The Silk Road: A Heat Wave Called Turfan**. Videocassette. Color. 55 min. NHK, distributor. New York: Central Park Media, 1993. $29.95. 9 up

Because this series of documentaries was the first to be produced cooperatively between China Central Television and outsiders, it has attracted much attention. It has the merit of showing ancient works of art never before seen and taking viewers on a vicarious journey into areas never before filmed. Among the sites here, which Marco Polo and others must have seen as they traveled the Silk Road (the major trade route between Europe and China), are Thousand Buddha Caves, the Jiao-he Castle, and the ancient aqueduct system.

2546. **The Silk Road: A Thousand Kilometers Beyond the Yellow River**. Videocassette. Color. 55 min. NHK, distributor. New York: Central Park Media, 1990. $29.95. 7 up

Because this series of documentaries was the first to be produced cooperatively between China Central Television and outsiders, it has attracted much attention. It has the merit of showing ancient works of art never before seen and taking viewers on a vicarious journey into areas never before filmed. Among the sights here, which Marco Polo and others must have seen as they traveled the Silk Road (the major trade route between Europe and China), are goatskin rafts capable of carrying oxen across the Yellow River, the Giant Buddha at Bing-Li-si and the secret caves, the He-xi corridor between the Gobi Desert and the Qui-Lian Mountains, and the Niepan Buddha in Zhang-ye.

2547. **The Silk Road: Glories of Ancient Chang-An**. Videocassette. Color. 55 min. NHK, distributor. New York: Central Park Media, 1990. $29.95. 9 up

Because this series of documentaries was the first to be produced cooperatively between China Central Television and outsiders, it has attracted much attention. It has the merit of showing ancient works of art never before seen and taking viewers on a vicarious journey into areas never before filmed. Among the sights here, which Marco Polo and others must have seen as they traveled the Silk Road (the major trade route between Europe and China), are Xi-an, the starting point of the route; the Clay Army of Emperor Qin Huang Di; the underground murals of Princess Yong-tai's tombs; a Buddhist temple; and the Great Wall.

2548. **Simón Bolívar**. Videocassette. Color. 30 min. Schlessinger Video, distributor. Bala Cynwyd, PA: Library Video, 1994. $39.95. ISBN 1-57225-026-7. (Hispanic and Latin American Heritage). 7 up

Biographical information and an overview of Bolívar's achievements, according to various experts, help to establish the contributions he made to Latin American history.

2549. **Simon Wiesenthal: Freedom Is Not a Gift from Heaven**. Videocassette. Color. 60 min. AVA Productions, distributor. Teaneck, NJ: Ergo Media, 1995. $39.95. 9 up

The Nazi hunter, Simon Wiesenthal, talks about his life for the camera for the first time.

2550. **The Six-Day War/Yom Kippur**. Videocassette. Color. 80 min. Independent Television News, distributor. New York: Central Park Media, 1995. $29.95. 10 up

This account gives the facts and events that led to the Six-Day War in 1967 and the Yom Kippur War in 1973, using newsreels and other documentary footage.

2551. **Solidarity**. Videocassette. Color. 23 min. Princeton, NJ: Films for the Humanities and Sciences, 1990. $149. 7 up

Using historical and file film footage, this video documents the twenty-five years until 1980 when the Solidarity union became a reality under the leadership of Lech Walesa and the Polish government at the Gdansk Accords. The signing of the Accords did not solve all problems, and the video follows the progress of Solidarity through the 1980s, including Walesa's Nobel Peace Prize.

2552. **A Son of Africa**. Videocassette. Color. 28 min. Aimimage Productions, distributor. San Francisco, CA: California Newsreel, 1997. $49.95. 7 up

The video recreates the social and economic forces of the eighteenth-century slave trade with dramatic reconstructions, archival material, and discussions with scholars.

2553. **Sorrow: The Nazi Legacy**. Videocassette. Color. 33 min. Teaneck, NJ: Ergo Media, 1994. $39.95. 9 up

Six Swedish teenagers visit Auschwitz to find out about the Holocaust, and it becomes real to them when they meet a survivor whose baby was born and died at the camp. The Nazi archive clips are compellingly graphic. *Young Adult Library Services Association Selected Films and Videos; Honorable Mention, Columbus International Film & Video Festival.*

2554. **South Korea, Land of the Morning Calm**. Videocassette. Color. 60 min. San Ramon, CA: IVN Communications, 1996. $24.99. ISBN 1-56345-391-6. (Video Visits). 7 up

South Korean history shows that it is a country that has combined its technological advances with its traditions. The video emphasizes the culture by discussing its four keys of the flag, the rose of Shannon for its tenacity, the phonetic alphabet, and Korea's people.

2555. **The Soviet Union**. 2 videocassettes. Color. Las Vegas, NV: Library Distributors of America, 1992. $89.95 set. 7 up

These videos cover 700 years of Russian history, from the military conquests of Alexander Nevski in 1240 until the end of the Soviet Union in 1991. This segment covers the events from Nevski's heroism until the end of World War II, including Ivan the Terrible becoming czar in 1557; Boris Gudunov's establishment of a legal serf system in 1597; the reign of Peter the Great; Napoleon's 1812 invasion; the Crimean War (1854–1856); the Russo-Japanese War in 1904; World War I; the Russian Revolution; the rise and rule of Lenin; Stalin's purges; and World War II. Part II presents Stalin, Khrushchev, Brezhnev, Gorbachev, the fall of the Berlin Wall in 1989, and Yeltsin's election.

2556. **Spain: History and Culture**. Videocassette. Color. 21 min. Irwindale, CA: Barr Media. $100. (Spain.) 7 up

This program, part of a series on Spain, presents the major events and dates in Spanish history.

2557. **Speak It! From the Heart of Black Nova Scotia**. Videocassette. Color. 29 min. New York: National Film Board of Canada, distributor. New York: Filmakers Library, 1993. $295. 9 up

When black students in Canada wanted to know what happened to their history, they began researching 350 years of African-Canadian history to find it. They did, and they impart what they found in this video. *ALA Selected Films for Young Adults; Margaret Mead Film Festival; Melbourne International Film Festival; Sixth International Women's Film Festival, Creteil; Award Winner, Japan Prize International Educational Program Contest.*

2558. **Stalin**. 3 videocassettes. Color. 58 min. ea. WGBH, Boston and Thames Television, distributor. Chicago: Films Inc. Video, 1990. $299 series; $129 ea. 9 up

Included in these videos documenting the life of Stalin are interviews with relatives of Stalin, Lenin, Trotsky, and Bukharin. The three titles are *Revolutionary, Despot,* and *Generalissimo.*

2559. **Story of Islam: The Coming of the Prophet**. Videocassette. Color. 19 min. Polonius Films, distributor. Chicago: International Film Bureau, 1991. $250. 7 up

Beginning with a description of earlier religions, the video continues with Mohammed's life and a background of the various Islamic schisms that occurred after his death.

2560. **The Summer of Aviya**. Videocassette. Color. 96 min. Summer of Aviya Ltd., distributor. Teaneck, NJ: Ergo Media, 1997. $79.95. 9 up

Gila Almagor, a ten-year-old girl who is the daughter of a Holocaust survivor, lives in Israel in the first years of its independence.

2561. **The Surreal Eye: On the Threshold of Dreams**. Videocassette. Color. 23 min. New Canaan, CT: Double Diamond, 1996. $89. 7 up

The video looks at the evolution of surrealism including its subareas of antiart, dada, surrealism, and abstract impressionism. Among the artists covered are Arp, Dali, Ernst, Magritte, Matta, Miro, and Tanguy.

2562. **Survivors of the Holocaust**. Videocassette. Color. 70 min. Survivors of the Shoah Visual History Foundation, Turner Original Productions, and Turner Home Entertainment, distributors. Atlanta, GA: Turner Home Entertainment, 1996. $19.98. 8 up

The video traces the lives of Holocaust survivors from 1933 to the present. It is divided into three chronological segments: 1933, 1941–1945, and 1945. These people tell of their lives before Nazi occupation, life in the Warsaw ghetto, transports to the camps, what they and their families experienced, and life after the liberation with the Nuremberg trials, displaced person camps, and emigration. Archival film and photographs show both adults and children.

T

2563. **Tarawa and the Island War**. Videocassette. Color and B&W. 45 min. Bethesda, MD: Acorn Media, 1989. $19.95. (V for Victory). 7 up

Using newsreel footage and stories from the home front, this program on World War II presents the battles of Tarawa, Saipan, Guam, and Leyte Gulf in the Pacific area.

2564. **The Technological Revolution**. Videocassette. Color. 30 min. WGBH Educational Foundation, distributor. Washington, DC: Annenberg/CPB, 1989. $650 set; $29.95 ea. (The Western Tradition, Program 51). 11 up

The professor presenting this topic projects his excitement for history as he provides insight into the people, politics, thoughts, and events that have shaped western society. Resources from the Metropolitan Museum of Art illustrate the enormous changes in life that computers and television have created during the twentieth century.

2565. **Terrorism/Lebanon**. Videocassette. Color. 80 min. Independent Television News, distributor. New York: Central Park Media, 1995. $29.95. 10 up

Newsreels and other documentary footage show that terrorism usually punishes innocent victims with its evil intents. The Palestinian Liberation Organization (PLO) has been terrorizing Israel for years and thinks that Israel does likewise.

2566. **This Just In . . . Columbus Has Landed**. Videocassette. Color. 45 min. Creighton University & Mason Video, distributor. Englewood, CO: SelectVideo, 1991. $45. 6 up

Costuming, news footage, and good sound contribute to the authenticity of this video network news show. Interviews with people who knew Columbus include his brother, a friar, King Ferdinand, Queen Isabella, one of his ship captains, and others. Animation and maps trace Columbus's voyage.

2567. **Three English Cathedrals**. Videocassette. Color. 45 min. Santa Monica, CA: Direct Cinema, 1995. $95. 10 up

Three English cathedrals—Wells, Norwich, and Lincoln—give a sense of the Norman style of architecture of the eleventh and twelfth centuries.

2568. **Toward the Future**. Videocassette. Color. 30 min. WGBH Educational Foundation, distributor. Washington, DC: Annenberg/CPB, 1989. $650 set; $29.95 ea. (The Western Tradition, Program 52). 11 up

The professor presenting this topic projects his excitement for history as he provides insight into the people, politics, thoughts, and events that have shaped western society. Resources from the Metropolitan Museum of Art illustrate the concerns of the future in world relationships.

2569. **Trees Cry for Rain: A Sephardic Journey**. Videocassette. Color. 32 min. San Francisco: Bonnie Burt, 1989. $50. 7 up

The Sephardic Jews, expelled from Spain in 1492, emigrated to Turkey. Told by a Turkish Jew now living in the United States, this video reveals the attempt to keep the Ladino (Spanish-Judeo) language, the foods, and the music, while showing the differences between the Sephardic and Ashkenazi cultures.

2570. **Trinity and Beyond: The Atomic Bomb Movie**. Videocassette. Color and B&W. 90 min. Visual Concept Entertainment, distributor. Thousand Oaks, CA: Goldhil Home Media, 1997. $24.95. 7 up

William Shatner narrates a documentary with special effects that relates the history of the concept, production, and testing of the atomic and hydrogen bombs for possible use in World War II.

2571. **Trompe L'Oeil: Paintings That Fool the Eye**. Videocassette. Color. 23 min. New Canaan, CT: Double Diamond, 1996. $89. 7 up

Taking examples from the Romans, the Renaissance, and more recent time periods, the video covers the art that seems so three-dimensional that people want to touch it. Close-ups of the trompe l'oeil paintings show how much they can fool the viewer.

2572. **Trotsky**. Videocassette. Color. 58 min. Princeton, NJ: Films for the Humanities and Sciences, 1990. $159. 7 up

Nearly 1,500 previously unpublished photos and film clips tell the story of Trotsky's (1879–1940) role in the birth of the Soviet Union and his leadership before, during, and after the Revolution in 1917.

2573. **Tsiolkovski: The Space Age**. Videocassette. Color. 24 min. Irwindale, CA: Barr Media, 1989. $50. 4-9

This animation explains how Konstantin Tsiolkovski (1857-1935) conducted the crucial research that led him to the invention of the rocket in 1929.

2574. **Turkey: Between Europe and Asia**. Videocassette. Color. 19 min. Camera Q, distributor. Irwindale, CA: Barr Media, 1990. $90. 4-9

Byzantium, Constantinople, and Istanbul: The three names for one city through the centuries show that although the names have changed, the city has remained an important site in its location between Asia and Europe. The video presents the history, geography, religion, agriculture, economy, and culture of Turkey.

2575. **The 20's: From Illusion to Disillusion**. Videocassette. Color. 80 min. Princeton, NJ: Films for the Humanities and Sciences, 1991. $149. 9 up

During the 1920s, from the end of World War I through the stock market crash and worldwide depression in 1929, many events affected the political atmosphere of the world. Communism took control in Russia, Mussolini directed fascism in Italy, Germany and the Allies argued over reparations for World War I, Gandhi founded the Indian peace movement, and civil war occurred in China. People began to get electricity in their homes and the automobile went into mass production. Period films and newsreels relate this information.

2576. **The Two Coasts of China: Asia and the Challenge of the West**. Videocassette. Color. 60 min. Pacific Basin Institute, distributor. Washington, DC: Annenberg/CPB, 1992. $275 series; $29.95 ea. (Pacific Century). 11 up

This series looks at 150 years of the Pacific region's political and economic development, through maps, charts, archival footage, and interviews with journalists and historians. It examines each country's relationship with the United States. This video covers the collision of East and West in the early nineteenth century when western traders and colonizers in their gunboats wanted to "open" Asia.

2577. **Two Hundred Years of Mozart**. Videocassette. Color. 25 min. $60. Chicago: Clearvue/eav, 1997. 7 up

This video on Wolfgang Amadeus Mozart (1756-1791) begins with a rehearsal for *The Marriage of Figaro* and follows it through to its first performance. It then gives an overview of Mozart's early life and the last ten years during which his works gained fame. The aspects of Vienna that influenced Mozart's life become apparent, as well as Mozart's legacy since his death.

2578. **Ukraine: Kiev and Lvov**. Videocassette. Color. 25 min. Derry, NH: Chip Taylor Communications, 1992. $150. (Exploring the World). 6 up

Three brief segments give an overview of the Ukraine. The first relates the history and culture of Kiev, a fifth-century city with the Cathedral of St. Vladimir. The second segment presents the folk traditions of the area, featuring the folk dancing that was handed down by the Cossacks of the 1600s. The third part shows Lvov, the capital of West Ukraine, with its baroque architecture and collection of Ukrainian artifacts.

2579. **Unheard Voices**. Videocassette. Color. 16 min. Derry, NH: Chip Taylor Communications, 1991. $129.99. 9 up

During 10 years of civil war, El Salvador has had 8,000 of its population of 5 million disappear, 75,000 killed, and over 1 million displaced. The footage showing orphanages, hospitals, countryside, and cities was shot between 1986 and 1989.

2580. **Unknown Secrets: Art and the Rosenberg Era**. Videocassette. Color. 30 min. Turners Falls, MA: Green Mountain Post Films, 1990. $250. 9 up

The only Americans ever to be executed for espionage through a civil court decision were Ethel and Julius Rosenberg, who were electrocuted in Sing Sing in 1953. The video discusses this conviction and asks if they were convicted because they were guilty or because they were Jewish. Both literary and visual artists respond to this idea by commenting that people often rewrite history for convenience.

2581. **The U.S.A. vs. "Tokyo Rose."** Videocassette. Color and B&W. 48 min. New York: Cinema Guild, 1995. $295. 9 up

Iva Toguri was visiting relatives in Japan when World War II broke out. She had been born in the United States and spoke perfect English, but she had to stay in Japan. She began using her skills to broadcast messages to Allied troops intended to break their morale. After the war, she was prosecuted for treason. After her sentence was reduced, she served six years in prison; eventually, President Gerald Ford pardoned her.

2582. This number not used.

2583. **Vietnam: After the Fire**. 2 videocassettes (set). Color. 53 min. ea. New York: Cinema Guild, 1989. $395 set; $250 ea. 9 up

More bombs were dropped on Vietnam than on Europe during World War II. The program interviews Vietnamese who survived, albeit with physical and emotional scars, who seem to wonder why no one has helped them since the war's end.

2584. **The Vikings: Seafarers and Explorers**. Videocassette. Color. 15 min. Chicago: Encyclopaedia Britannica, 1993. $99. ISBN 0-8347-9992-8. 6-12

The video discusses the Vikings' culture, their expeditions into southern Europe and the West, and the communities they conquered. The four parts of the video are "Life," "Ship Building and Seafaring," "Voyages," and "Trade."

2585. **The Vikings, 1066**. Videocassette. Color. 30 min. Maryland Public Television, distributor. Washington, DC: Zenger Video, 1989. $395 series; $69.95 ea. (Timeline, Series I). 9 up

This program presents history as today's television news would relate the events. The narrator, Steve Bell, switches live to battlefield reporters, news analysts, and interviewers for the day's news. For the Vikings and William the Conqueror, the news comes live from 1066.

2586. **The Virgin and the Bull**. Videocassette. Color. 60 min. Chicago: Films, Inc. Video, 1992. $198. (Buried Mirror: Reflections on Spain and the New World). 9 up

Carlos Fuentes, the Mexican author, returns to Spain and examines the caves of Altamira, the bullring, and flamenco dancers in his quest to see if Mexico should celebrate Columbus's Columbus 500 years ago. He looks at the influences in Spain of invaders such as the Iberians, Romans, Arabs, and Visigoths. What he decides is that any celebration should include the Mexican culture, which, along with other groups, has helped to create Latin America.

2587. **The Visas That Saved Lives**. Videocassette. Color. 115 min. Kazumo, distributor. Teaneck, NJ: Ergo Media, 1995. $49.95. 9 up

In 1940, Chiune Sugihara, Japan's consul-general in Lithuania, sacrificed his own career to write the visas that saved the lives of 2,000 to 6,000 Jews who were trying to escape the Holocaust.

2588. **The Vistula**. Videocassette. Color. 45 min. Pathe Cinema, distributor. Princeton, NJ: Films for the Humanities and Sciences, 1992. $149. 7 up

The Vistula River has seen much brutality, from that of the Tatars in the thirteenth century through the inhumanity of the Nazis in the twentieth century. It runs by Cracow, home of Casimir the Great's university; Warsaw and its ghetto; Gdansk, the site of Walesa's leadership; and Auschwitz, site of horrors.

2589. **Voyage of Martin Frobisher: A Quest for Gold**. Videocassette. Color. 28 min. Princeton, NJ: Films for the Humanities and Sciences, 1993. $149. (Archeology). 9 up

More than 400 years ago, Martin Frobisher (1535?–1594) took two small ships from England to search for the Northwest Passage, a shortcut to China over the North American mainland. He returned to England carrying a black rock with what looked like gold on its surface. After extensive mining on Baffin Island, the explorers found that the rock was only hornblende. But the mission paved the way for Sir Walter Raleigh's voyage in 1584 and for future European colonization. It also gave the Inuits great treasures in what the miners left behind.

┌─────┐
│ W │
└─────┘

2590. **A Wall of Silence**. Videocassette. Color. 58 min. Netherlands TV, distributor. Clarksburg, NJ: Alden Films, 1995. $89.95. 7 up

In the Austrian border town of Rechnitz, fifty years ago, drunken Germans and Austrians shot more than 180 Jewish forced laborers and buried them in an unmarked grave. Many still refuse to acknowledge the event or to tell where the grave is located. Interviewees seem to be displeased with the questions.

2591. **War Years: Britain in World War Two, The Phoney War**. Videocassette. Color. 58 min. Princeton, NJ: Films for the Humanities and Sciences, 1990. $149. 9 up

Music of 1939 and 1940, along with film footage, gives a strong sense of the times during the war in England, which America said was "phoney" because no one was fighting visible battles. But the sandbagged buildings, gas masks, German radio broadcasts, blackouts, and evacuation of children from London give a different view. Additional information about the Munich Agreement, the blitzkrieg invasion of Poland, the British Expeditionary Force in Norway, the Atlantic sea war, the evacuation from Dunkirk, and the fall of France is also included.

2592. **The Warrior**. Videocassette. Color. 55 min. Medici Foundation, distributor. Irvindale CA: Barr Media, 1994. $810 series; $150 ea. (Renaissance: The Origins of the Modern World). 10 up

The research of Theodore Rabb, and interviews with experts and political figures, form the basis for this video, one of six in a series, that examines the changing concepts of the warrior and warfare as the knight's image became tarnished with the development of mechanized warfare.

2593. **The Wars of Religion**. Videocassette. Color. 30 min. WGBH Educational Foundation, distributor. Washington, DC: Annenberg/CPB, 1989. $29.95. (The Western Tradition, Program 29). 11 up

The professor presenting this topic projects his excitement for history as he provides insight into the people, politics, thoughts, and events that have shaped western society. Resources from the Metropolitan Museum of Art illustrate these wars, also called the Huguenot Wars, which lasted from 1562 until 1598 in France.

2594. **We Jive Like This**. Videocassette. Color. 52 min. Cinecontact/Kinoki Prods, distributor. New York: Filmakers Library, 1992. $445. 9 up

This video looks at the attempt in South Africa to create cultural centers for children who have had no exposure to any of the arts. This movement results from the Children's Uprising in 1976. Since that time, teachers, freelance choreographers, singers, and others have helped to open new avenues for the children.

2595. **We Must Never Forget: The Story of the Holocaust**. Videocassette. Color. 25 min. Madison, WI: Knowledge Unlimited, 1995. $55. 6 up

The video examines the historical context that allowed the Holocaust to occur, emphasizing anti-Semitic attitudes in Europe, the impact of World War I on Germany, and Hitler's rise to power. It includes interviews with survivors of the Warsaw ghetto and of Auschwitz. Film footage, political cartoons from the time, and color maps help show this period for what it was. *Council on Nontheatrical Events Golden Eagle*, *National Educational Media Silver Apple,* and *New York Festivals Finalist*.

2596. **Weizmann**. Videocassette. Color. 55 min. Israel Film Service, distributor. Clarksburg, NJ: Alden Films, 1997. $19.95. 7 up

Chaim Weizmann (1874-1952) was one of the Zionist Movement's main leaders and the first president of Israel.

2597. **Where *Is* Patagonia?** Videocassette. Color. 105 min. Hillsborough, CA: Ken Armstrong Productions, 1997. $34.95. 10 up

When Charles Darwin was twenty-three in 1833, he explored Patagonia and Tierra del Fuego for two years. His discoveries during the voyage of the HMS *Beagle* showed him new flora and fauna. The video presents some of the places that Darwin saw that influenced his publication of *On the Origin of Species*.

2598. **Where the Spirit Lives**. 4 videocassettes. Color. 27 min. ea. Evanston, IL: Beacon Films, 1991. $295. 7 up

This drama accurately relates the story of a young girl who was kidnapped from her Native American tribe by Canadian Indian agents in the 1930s and told that her family had died. She was sent to school and made to learn how to be white. Just as she is preparing to be adopted by a wealthy white woman, she finds that her family still lives. The Indian residential schools, which tried to take the culture away from young Indians, existed until 1988.

2599. **Who Built the Pyramids?** Videocassette. Color. 16 min. Washington, DC: National Geographic, 1997. $69. 4-9

In seventy years, men shaped six million limestone blocks into three pyramids, one of them forty stories high. Whether these men were slaves or skilled craftsmen is currently a debate, but the question remains as to what force kept these workmen on task; the methods they used are not too different from those used today.

2600. **William Blake**. Videocassette. Color. 52 min. Produced by LWTP. Princeton, NJ: Films for the Humanities and Sciences, 1996. $149. 11 up

William Blake (1757-1827) lived in London during the late Georgian period and saw the political and religious turmoil that permeated the atmosphere. He was a seer and visionary as well as a poet and artist. His unorthodox attitudes made many deem him mad, but contemporary study reveals his genius.

2601. **Windows to the World: China**. Videocassette. Color. 30 min. San Ramon, CA: IVN Communications, 1996. $69.95. ISBN 1-56345-308-8. 7 up

The video looks at China's geography, history, modern period, culture, and contemporary life as a basis for understanding its position in the ancient as well as the modern world.

2602. **Windows to the World: India**. Videocassette. Color. 30 min. Rand McNally and IVN, distributors. San Ramon, CA: IVN Communications, 1995. $69.99. 7 up

India's three distinct regional divisions are reflected in the cities of New Delhi, Calcutta, and Bombay. Among the religions in the country are Hinduism, Buddhism, Islam, and Sikhism, factions that continue to disagree. With each invasion of India has come new cultural ideas. In ancient times, the Aryans, Arabs, Turks, and six Mughal empires affected it. The Portuguese and British have ruled in more modern times. In the twentieth century, persons such as Jawaharlal Nehru, Indira and Rajiv Gandhi, and others have led the world's largest democracy.

2603. **Windows to the World: Japan**. Videocassette. Color. 32 min. Rand McNally and IVN, distributors. San Ramon, CA: IVN Communications, 1995. $69.99. 7 up

Ancient feudal clans warred until a powerful shogun emerged; such is the history of Japan before its modern era ended isolationism in the 1850s. This video looks at Japan's history and cultural traditions as the country measures its contemporary choices.

2604. **Windows to the World: Thailand**. Videocassette. Color. 30 min. Rand McNally and IVN, distributors. San Ramon, CA: IVN Communications, 1995. $69.99. 7 up

The video looks at the history, geography, economy, and culture of Thailand.

2605. **Windows to the World: Vietnam**. Videocassette. Color. 30 min. Rand McNally and IVN, distributors. San Ramon, CA: IVN Communications, 1995. $69.99. 7 up

The video looks at the history, geography, economy, and culture of Vietnam, especially the French colonialism leading to the war in Vietnam during the twentieth century.

2606. **Women's Stories of the Holocaust**. Videocassette. Color. 18 min. New York: Carousel, 1997. $100. 9 up

Three women who survived the Holocaust tell their stories.

2607. **Wonders of Man's Creation**. Videocassette. Color. 60 min. Reader's Digest and International Video Network, distributors. Pleasantville, NY: Reader's Digest, 1993. $25.95. (Great Wonders of the World). 9 up

This series uses live-action photography, archival documentary footage, and animation sequences to reveal some of the human creations that have become monuments of civilization. Featured are the Coliseum in Rome, Machu Picchu in Peru, the Great Wall of China, the Kremlin in Moscow, Versailles in France, the Statue of Liberty in New York, and Mount Rushmore and the Chief Crazy Horse Monument in South Dakota.

2608. **Wonders Sacred & Mysterious**. Videocassette. Color. 60 min. Reader's Digest and International Video Network, distributors. Pleasantville, NY: Reader's Digest, 1993. $25.95. (Great Wonders of the World). 9 up

This series uses live-action photography, archival documentary footage, and animation sequences to reveal important places in the world that have been foci for religions. The places are Stonehenge in England, the Great Pyramids in Egypt, the Hagia Sophia in Istanbul, Borobudur in Java, St. Peter's Basilica in Rome, and the Taj Mahal in India.

2609. **The World Reborn**. Videocassette. Color. 55 min. Medici Foundation, distributor. Irvindale, CA: Barr Media, 1994. $810 series; $150 ea. (Renaissance: The Origins of the Modern World). 10 up

The research of Theodore Rabb, and interviews with experts and political figures, form the basis of this video, one of six in a series, that traces the history and contributions of the Renaissance from the earliest pioneers (such as Petrarch and Jan Hus) through innovators such as Brunelleschi and Machiavelli, to the artistic, scientific, and political revolutions of the high Renaissance. At the end of the Renaissance, Europe finally realized that its world had forever changed.

2610. **World War I**. Videocassette. B&W. 25 min. Princeton, NJ: Films for the Humanities and Sciences, 1990. $149. (Modern History on Video). 9 up

Highlights of major battles on the Western Front, the Eastern Front, and the Dardanelles, and their major participants, appear through film footage. Technological innovations of the time, such as tanks, submarines, zeppelins, machine guns, barbed wire, and trench warfare, led to the Versailles Treaty and two new nations, Czechoslovakia and Yugoslavia.

2611. **World War II**. Videocassette. B&W. 30 min. Princeton, NJ: Films for the Humanities and Sciences, 1990. $149. 9 up

All of the highlights of World War II on both the Atlantic and Pacific fronts are telescoped in this video through newsreel footage, from the invasion of Poland in 1939 to the signing of the peace treaty with Japan in 1945.

2612. **Writers and Revolutionaries**. Videocassette. Color. 60 min. Pacific Basin Institute, distributor. Washington, DC: Annenberg/CPB, 1992. $275 series; $29.95 ea. (Pacific Century). 11 up

This series looks at 150 years of the Pacific region's political and economic development, through maps, charts, archival footage, and interviews with journalists and historians. It examines each country's relationship with the United States. In this video, the viewer meets the Chinese writer Lu Xun and the Japanese right-wing philosopher Kita Ikki, as part of a discussion of the role of intellectuals in revolutions and national political movements.

2613. **The Yidishe Gauchos**. Videocassette. Color. 28 min. New York: Filmakers Library, 1990. $295. 9 up

In Argentina, Moises Ville, the "Jerusalem of Argentina," boasted many synagogues, libraries, theaters, and businesses as a result of the Jewish Colonization Association's investment to buy land for Russian Jews fleeing the pogroms of the late nineteenth century (beginning in 1891). Each immigrant family got a homestead of 200 acres, cows, chickens, and a mortgage. They learned to farm the land from Jewish "gauchos" who had arrived earlier and learned the methods. After World War II, the Jewish energies were directed toward helping the state of Israel.

2614. **Ziveli: Medicine for the Heart**. Videocassette. Color. 51 min. El Cerrito, CA: Flower Films, 1988. $99.95. 7 up

Serbian-American communities began when the first immigrants arrived, over 100 years ago, during California's gold rush. Much of Serbian ethnic life is described in this video, including the rituals of the Eastern Orthodox Church and the love of music. *Silver Award, Chicago International Film Festival.*

2615. **Zwingli & Calvin**. Videocassette. Color. 28 min. Christian History Institute, distributor. Worcester, PA: Vision Video, 1995. $19.95. 7 up

These two men, Huldrych Zwingli (1484–1531) and John Calvin (1509–1564), were the leaders of the Swiss Reformation, centered in Zurich and Geneva. *Chris Awards Bronze Plaque.*

Author/Illustrator Index

Reference is to entry number.

Title Index

Reference is to entry number.

Subject Index

Reference is to entry number.

Abbeys, Benedictine; Fiction, 1515-32
Abenaki; Fiction, 542
Abominable Snowman. *See* Yeti
Aborigines, 1088; Fiction, 2019
Abraham Lincoln Brigade, 1049; Video, 2326
Absolutism; Video, 2182, 2190
Abu Bakr, 2076
Abu Simbel, 2072
Abubakari; Video, 2183
Abused children, 1138
Acting, Greek; Fiction, 1606
Adamson, George, 893
Adamson, Joy, 893
Aegean Cities; Video, 2424
Aegean Kingdoms, 1949
Afghanistan; Video, 2387
Africa, 478, 770, 947, 1312, 1927; Video, 2187, 2188, 2552
Africa, Central and Eastern; Video, 2186
Africa, Northeast. *See* Aksum; Egypt; *and* Kush
Africa, South, 866
Africa, Southern, 12
Africa, West, 48. *See also* Benin
Africa, West, Kingdoms, 996
African Civilization; Video, 2533
African Families; Fiction, 768
African National Congress, 866
Africans, Women, 285
Age of Reason. *See* Reason, Age of
Agnodice, 821
Ahmed, 876
Akhmatova, Anna 821; Video, 2496
Aksum, 12
Al Umm El Madayan, 91
Alaric, 2076
Alaska, Russian, 379
Albania; Video, 2194
Alchemy, 16
Alexander the Great, 66, 1853, 2036, 2076; Fiction, 1603, 1607; Video, 2196
Alexandria, 2072; Fiction, 236
Alhambra, 1112, 1768, 2070

Aliyah Bet; Video, 2372
Alonso, Alicia, 65
Alta California; Fiction, 484
Alvarez, Luis, 376
Amazon, 1371
Amazon Rain Forests, 502
Ambulance Drivers, 777
Amenhotep IV, 939
American Revolution, British View, 844
Americans, Native; CD-ROM, 2170
Ameru, 2015
Amin, Idi, 1217
Amnesty International, 2096
Amsterdam, 1121, 1748; Fiction, 1021
Amundsen, Roald 50, 1098
An-Yang, 1867
Anatolia, 47, 1928
Ancient Britain. *See* Britain, Prehistoric.
Ancient Egypt. *See* Egypt, Ancient
Ancient Greece. *See* Greece, Ancient
Ancient Japan. *See* Japan, Ancient
Ancient Rome. *See* Rome, Ancient
Ancient World, 1189. *See also* World, Ancient
Andalusia; Fiction, 1480
Anderson, Hans Christian, 1011
Angkor, 1768, 2077
Anglo Saxons, 759; CD-ROM, 2139
Anguissola, Sofonisba, 1008
Anning, Mary, 385
Anthropologists and Archaeologists, 690, 1703, 1865; Fiction, 1509-14, 1953. *See also* Archaeology, Underwater; Carnarvon, Herbert, Fifth Earl of; Carter, Howard; Champollion, Jean-François; Evans, Arthur; Goodall, Jane; Grotefend, Georg Fredrich; Kroeber, Alfred; Layard, Austen Henry; Leakey, Louis S. B.; Leakey,

Mary Nicol; Leakey, Richard; Mallowan, Max; Mouhot, Henri; Rassam, Hormuzd; Schliemann, Heinrich; Tutankhamen; Ventris, Michael; Wheeler, Robert Eric Mortimer; Woolley, Charles Leonard; *and* Yadin, Yigael
Anti-Semitism; Video, 2422
Antony, Marc, 980
Apartheid, 1215; Fiction, 729, 1683; Video, 2206, 2228
Apprentices; Fiction, 1091, 1226
Aquinas, Thomas, 939
Aquino, Corazon, 354, 802, 1316
Arab Heritage, 1281; Video, 2205
Arab-Israeli Conflict, 1660; Video, 2203
Arabs, 892; Video, 2204
Arafat, Yasir, 589, 1599
Arawak; Fiction, 663
Archaeology, Underwater, 1873
Archimedes, 861
Arctic Exploration, 140
Arctic Peoples, 1433
Arenas, Roman; Video, 2528
Argentina; Fiction, 1776; Video, 2613
Aristotle, 1447
Armenia 64, 1637
Armenian Refugees, 969; Fiction, 559
Armenians; Video, 2487
Arms and Armor, 744
Art, Medieval, 421
Arthur, King, 473, 522, 1426, 1858; Fiction, 419, 420
Artists, Men, 221, 445; Fiction, 1021; CD-ROM, 2156; Video, 2211. *See also* Bernini, Gian Lorenzo; Bruegel, Pieter; Brunelleschi, Filippo; Cézanne, Paul; Chagall, Marc; Corot, Jean-Baptiste-Camille; da Vinci, Leonardo; Dali, Salvador; David,

from **Libraries Unlimited**

LITERATURE CONNECTIONS TO AMERICAN HISTORY: Resources to Enhance and Entice
Lynda G. Adamson

If you found *Literature Connections to World History* useful, this book should be your next purchase. Hundreds of new titles are discussed, including historical fiction novels, biographies, history trade books, CD-ROMs, and videotapes. **Grades 7–12.**
xii, 624p. 7x10 paper ISBN 1-56308-503-8

AMERICAN HISTORY THROUGH EARTH SCIENCE
Craig A. Munsart

Classroom-ready activities allow students to apply the principles of earth science to events that have dictated America's past and present, from 30,000 years ago to today. An entire chapter is devoted to the topic of icebergs and contains activities relating to the sinking of the *Titanic*. **Grades 6–12.**
xxiv, 209p. 8½x11 paper ISBN 1-56308-182-2

CRIME SCENE INVESTIGATION
Barbara Harris, Kris L. Kohlmeier, and Robert D. Kiel

Get students involved in the drama of crime scene investigation through the excitement of examining clues, making a case, and bringing it to trial. Students have fun while building important problem-solving skills and developing knowledge in areas of language, science, history, and more. **Grades 5–12.**
xiii, 109p. 8½x11 paper ISBN 1-56308-637-9

MORE RIP-ROARING READS FOR RELUCTANT TEEN READERS
Bette D. Ammon and Gale W. Sherman

Find dozens of books that students won't want to put down. In this companion book to the ever-popular *Rip-Roaring Reads for Reluctant Teen Readers*, Ammon and Sherman describe 40 exciting, contemporary titles (20 for middle school, 20 for high school) written by outstanding authors. Special features make the matching process between students and books pain free and successful. **Grades 5–12.**
xii, 161p. 8½x11 paper ISBN 1-56308-571-2

For a FREE catalog or to place an order, please contact:

Libraries Unlimited, Inc.
Dept. B001 · P.O. Box 6633 · Englewood, CO 80155-6633
1-800-237-6124 · Fax: 303-220-8843 · E-mail: lu-books@lu.com